The Future of the Army Profession

Revised & Expanded · SECOND EDITION

Don M. Snider
project director

Lloyd J. Matthews
editor

with forewords by

Congressman Jim Marshall, Third District, Georgia

General (Retired) Frederick M. Franks, USA

 **Custom Publishing**

Boston Burr Ridge, IL Dubuque, IA Madison, WI New York San Francisco St. Louis
Bangkok Bogotá Caracas Lisbon London Madrid
Mexico City Milan New Delhi Seoul Singapore Sydney Taipei Toronto

The **McGraw·Hill** Companies

The Future of the Army Profession

The following chapters in the book are in the public domain: 1, 6, 7, 9, 10, 11, 15, 16, 18, 19, 20, 22, 23, 24, 26, 27, 28, and 33.

McGraw-Hill's Custom Publishing consists of products that are produced from camera-ready copy. Peer review, class testing, and accuracy are primarily the responsibility of the author(s).

4 5 6 7 8 9 0 DOC DOC 0 9

ISBN: 978-0-07-353609-5
MHID: 0-07-353609-1

Editor: Ann Jenson
Production Editor: Nina Meyer
Front Cover Photos: Night vision photo courtesy of U.S. Army; topographic map © Ryan McVay/Getty Images
Cover Design: Fairfax Hutter
Printer/Binder: R.R. Donnelley—Crawfordsville

Contents

List of Illustrations

List of Tables

Acknowledgments

My acknowledgments must begin with those who have had the greatest influence on this revised and enlarged second edition of *The Future of the Army Profession*—Lt. Gen. Howard Graves, Lt. Col. Gayle Watkins, and Col. (Ret.) Lloyd Matthews. Without General Graves, there would have been no Gayle at West Point, without Gayle there would have been no first edition, and without Lloyd neither edition would be as richly presented and useful to the Army as they are. Let me explain.

The roots of these research projects go back to the tenure of the late Lt. Gen. Howard Graves, the 54th Superintendent of the Military Academy, who decided to bring Gayle and me back to the Academy. He chose Gayle Watkins in 1991 to be a faculty member in the as-yet uncrystallized tactical officer graduate degree program. En route, Gayle completed a doctorate in sociology at Stanford University, refining her interest in the social organization of expert work, or what we know as professions. General Graves subsequently chose me in 1995 to be the Olin Professor of National Security Studies, a position I held for three years before joining the civilian faculty of the Academy. Thus I acknowledge my personal debt to a dear friend and professional colleague, Howard Graves—Army officer, intellectual, and leader whose tenure at the Academy will forever reflect his immense character and wisdom.

As we started the research project in 1998 leading to the 1st edition of *The Future of the Army Profession*, Gayle introduced me to the writings of Prof. Andrew Abbott, whom she subsequently invited to keynote the first research conference and persuaded to contribute a chapter to the first edition. In his prize-winning book *The System of Professions*, he established the methodological framework for both the first and second research projects with his descriptive and analytical schema on how all professions and would-be professions, including the Army and other military professions, struggle within an ecology of competitor professions for legitimacy in doing the expert work associated with their chosen jurisdiction. By design, hardly a chapter author in this edition, or for that matter in the first edition, fails to fit his or her chapter theme within the Abbott framework; it has become the only functional and realistic means for the next generation of Army officers to understand the dynamics of their profession's evolution within the larger context of all professional work and aspiration. Gayle also contributed, along with Randi Cohen, one of the seminal pieces of military field research which documented in 2000 what we all feared, namely, that mid-level Army officers did not view their Army membership as a professional calling and possessed no vital conception of the essential relationship between officership and the Army profession. The germ of all these ideas emerged from my early conversations with Gayle Watkins.

Lloyd Matthews has long possessed—as professor of English and Associate Dean at West Point, later as editor of the Army's premier journal *Parameters*, and still later as editor with his wife Phyllis of numerous books for the Army War College—the remarkable ability to imbue the tired prose of other scholars with lucidity, correctness, and verve, thereby remarkably enhancing the portability of the attendant ideas into classrooms across the nation and into Army school houses. Without his long experience in and published reflections on the Army profession, as well as his mastery of rhetoric and expression, our prospects for renewing the study and understanding of the Army as profession would have been sorely impaired. After editing two capacious anthologies with him, encompassing the work of some 67 contributors, I feel blessed by the singleness of mind and complementarity of purpose that so comfortably and naturally marked our partnership.

Certainly the next most influential individuals to be acknowledged are the chapter researchers and authors. Over the two editions, 29 uniformed and 38 civilian scholars have studied and reported on some aspect of the Army profession, and done so from the perspective of renewing its relevance, authenticity, and vitality. In most cases they are my close colleagues and friends drawn from the careers of public service and scholarship we have shared. To collaborate with them in professional camaraderie for the past six years has been a rich delight. In my judgment, the Army is deeply indebted to each of these scholars for having participated, after a 30-year lapse, in renewed study of the Army profession *as* profession. I am also pleased to acknowledge another source of intellectual and personal inspiration—Lt. Gen. (Retired) Walter Ulmer, one of the authors of the last similarly ambitious inquiry, the 1970 *Study on Army Professionalism* conducted when then Colonel Ulmer was a student at the Army War College.

I must also mention the support of Prof. Douglas Lovelace and the collegial group of scholars in the Strategic Studies Institute at the Army War College, Carlisle, PA. They graciously hosted me during my fall sabbatical in 2004, providing the needed opportunity for me to listen, reflect, write, and edit. In addition, the Commandant of the College, Maj. Gen. David Huntoon, penned the insightful introduction to this second edition, and fittingly so since much of the research reported here has been conducted by members of the War College faculty and designed for the development of their students.

I am also deeply indebted to those workers whose support made possible this anthology and the numerous conferences leading up to its publication. Primary among these are Maj. Beth Robbins, the executive secretary of the 2004 Senior Conference at West Point where the new chapters for this edition were vetted, and the conference organizer, Ms. Jo May. Their energy, skills, and attention to detail left me blissfully free to focus on the substance of the research presented. In addition, Maj. Len Lira has served for the past academic year as a very able executive assistant for this publication, working everything from the legal issues, with the assistance of Maj. Lisa Gossart and Ms. Janet Sloan from USMA's Staff Judge Advocate's office, to the design of the cover, to critiquing selected manuscripts.

Additionally, Mr. Greg Louks and USMA's Association of Graduates were pivotal in providing the public-to-private legal mechanism necessary to publish this book through the commercial publishing house McGraw-Hill. I also owe a great debt to the three foundations—the Smith Richardson Foundation, the Robert McCormick Tribune Foundation, and the Eisenhower Lecture Series—that provided the financial support needed for this expansive project. And certainly I must note the immense support I have received from the USMA Dean, Brig. Gen. Dan Kaufman, the Social Sciences Department Head, Col. Russell Howard, and the other leaders and members of the Department of Social Sciences, USMA, who provided the encouragement and atmosphere that proved, once again, that scholarly research could flourish alongside extraordinary classroom teaching.

I must also reaffirm my personal debt to the late Col. Kerry Pierce, USMA 1974, a fellow Army officer, Rhodes Scholar, SAMS graduate, Professional Engineer, and close personal friend whose intellectual and organizational skills, on behalf of the Superintendent, brought about the renewed study of officership at West Point in the late 1990s. Without the privilege of working with him in that effort, I would not have seen so clearly the nexus between the role of the Army officer in the 21st century and the future of the Army profession; nor would I have felt the urgency to undertake the original research project when we did, and then to pursue a second such project four years later.

Of course, others have paid a steep price because I chose to spend time doing a second research project and another book—my bride and Army wife, Caroline, our children, their spouses, and our grandchildren. For their unflagging love and gracious forbearance I am simply grateful.

Don M. Snider
West Point, New York
February 2005

Foreword

Frederick M. Franks, Jr.

Today as I write this foreword, the U.S. Army is doing its duty in the front lines of America's war against global terrorism—in Afghanistan, the Philippines, and numerous other (albeit less publicized) locations. The Army is also manning the ramparts of freedom around the globe—in the Balkans, the Sinai, Kuwait, and South Korea—as it has done so often during the 20th century, the first century in which its officers have held full professional standing. In all, over 173,000 soldiers are deployed outside the United States, to include 24,000 mobilized reservists. Soldiers and leaders of the Army profession are performing these duties in the highest traditions of service to our nation.

President George W. Bush paid tribute to this performance of duty on 28 January 2002 in his State of the Union address to the Congress and the American people:

> When I called our troops into action, I did so with complete confidence in their courage and skill. And tonight, thanks to them, we are winning the war on terror. The men and women of our armed forces have delivered a message now clear to every enemy of the United States: even 7,000 miles away, across oceans and continents, on mountaintops and in caves, you will not escape the justice of this nation. . . . Our war on terror is well begun, but it is only begun. . . . History has called America and our allies to action, and it is both our responsibility and our privilege to fight freedom's fight.

Yet, at the same time the Army profession is executing these duties to defend our freedoms, it is also in the midst of a vital transformation. Even as our military takes the fight to the terrorists in this war, there is also a concurrent need to think about changing our defenses in deeply fundamental ways. The Army Chief of Staff, Gen. Eric Shinseki, in the fall of 1999 disseminated a far-reaching *Vision for the U.S. Army* to transform it into a more strategically responsive and dominant force at every point on the spectrum of military operations. He sees the Army's duty today as not only to win decisively this current war but also to transform itself so as to win the next one. As Secretary of Defense Donald Rumsfeld recently told us, the transformation of the Army is a part of Defense Transformation, and "the war on terrorism is a transformational event."

Some early actions already indicate the clear path forward. Early in 2000, General Shinseki commissioned a series of studies of Army training and leader development. They began first with officers, then expanded to the noncommissioned officer study in 2001, and will finish in 2002 with warrant officers and civilians. These studies are demonstrating, once again, that at the very core of transforming the Army are, and must continue to be, its professionals. Vital to transforming the Army in this early decade of the 21st century is their dedication, commitment, and renewed focus on what it means to be an Army professional. General Shinseki confirmed as much in late November 2001:

> People are central to everything else we do in the Army. Institutions don't transform, people do. Platforms and organizations don't defend this nation, people do. And finally, units don't train, they don't stay ready, they don't grow and develop leadership; they don't sacrifice; and they don't take risks on behalf of the nation; people do.

The Army Chief of staff has confirmed from this series of studies that there is now an imbalance between what the Army profession says it is and what it is proving to be in actual practice. The studies reported, after extensive interviews with members of the profession, that Army culture is "out of balance"—the profession's doctrine and ethos, its beliefs, are not consistent with many current operational practices:

> The soldiers interviewed in the field transmitted their thoughts in clear text and with passion. They communicated the same passion and dedication for selfless service to the nation and the Army as any generation before them. Pride in the Army, service to the nation, camaraderie, and Army values continue to strongly influence the decisions of officers and their spouses to make the Army a career. However, they see Army practices as being out of balance with Army beliefs. . . . the Army's service ethic and concepts of officership are neither well-understood nor clearly defined. They are also not adequately reinforced throughout an officer's career.

Upon receipt of these conclusions and recommendations in early 2001, General Shinseki directed a series of actions to reform Army practices in training and leader development. For example, one specific action now being implemented will "define and teach an Army Service Ethic and Officership throughout OES (Officer Education System) from Officer Basic Course through the War College."

So, with the path to transformation becoming increasingly more clear, how are Army professionals to think about their profession in such times as these? That is what this very timely anthology is all about, filled as it is with the results of extensive research on the future of the Army profession, research conducted for the first time within a new framework of "competitive professions." Clearly, it is the duty of all professionals to reinterpret continually their profession and their individual roles within it, particularly as the external world and our nation's role in that world change so radically. Such continuous examination is a vital strength of our Army profession and marks the very core of its members' ability to best serve our nation.

My own involvement in the Army profession, like that of so many others, has been one of a lifelong calling. I knew I made the right decision in life a long time ago. In that choice I was influenced by the World War II generation in my own family and in my community as I grew up in Pennsylvania. I wanted to earn the right to lead such great Americans if it ever again became necessary to defend our freedoms. At West Point, I was influenced by many positive role models who inspired in me a desire to lead the kind of life they had led up to that point. I trusted what they had told me about the profession.

After graduation with the West Point Class of 1959, I took my place as a young Army officer among the professional officers and NCOs in the 11th Armored Cavalry Regiment along the Iron Curtain in Germany. They reinforced what I had learned and seen at West Point. And later, when my mandatory service was completed, I chose to continue to serve, to stay on, as did so many others through Vietnam and through the Army renaissance of the 1970s and early 1980s. I chose to stay because of the insights and inspiration I had earlier received from my professional associates and because of a "hot blue flame" of commitment lit in me at Valley Forge General Hospital in the early 1970s.

What a life it has been! It was not always easy and not always fair, as the old song goes, but given the opportunity to make those choices all over again, I would not do anything other than choose to be a soldier and a member of the profession of arms in the United States Army. It is a profession I have been privileged to be a part of almost my entire life from the young age of my cadet days in 1955 until I retired from active duty on 1 December 1994. I am forever grateful to our country and to the American people for entrusting me with high responsibilities and with the lives of their sons and daughters in two wars and countless other duties. And I am forever grateful to the splendid men and women soldiers with whom it has been my privilege to serve in peace and war and for the steadfast friends my wife and I have come to know and admire and respect over those years.

In May 1999 the Superintendent of the United States Military Academy invited me to become the "visiting scholar" in the newly formed Simon Center for the Professional Military Ethic (SCPME). It was an honor to be asked, and without hesitation I accepted those duties. In a sense it was an opportunity to continue that commitment made a generation ago to our Army profession and to the nation we serve. The vision for SCPME is not only to develop in each cadet a self-concept of what it means to be an officer in the United States Army prior to graduation, but also to reach out to the Army and foster continuing education within the profession itself. Fulfilling that mission is one reason I have prepared this foreword.

My own sensing is that there has not been any lessening of the desire of Army professionals for professionalism. Thus, it is both timely and relevant to the Army's transformation that this text be made available to current and future Army professionals, as they dedicate themselves to renewing, and indeed transforming, the very essence of the profession.

I am aware that many might interpret such a momentous initiative as a sign that something is drastically "wrong." Nothing could be further from reality. One of the great strengths of the U.S. Army has been, and is, its ability to learn, renewing its considerable strengths and transforming where necessary to continue its role in the vanguard of honorable and effective service to our nation. If anything is "wrong" now, it is that the prevailing rate of change and pace of operations has, until very recently, simply outstripped the opportunities for needed reflection and re-examination.

To help correct that, Professors Don Snider and Gayle Watkins have done our Army profession a splendid service by initiating this research project, drawing on the work of many military and civilian researchers, and then compiling this anthology. The ideas, analysis, and conclusions are far-reaching, just what are needed to provoke candid reflection and to build renewed consensus regarding a more effective and relevant, but transformed, Army profession. Even more important is the new framework they provide for analysis of the Army as one of several professions, and nonprofessions, competing for the same jurisdiction and legitimacy before the American people. This is the reality the Army now faces, and to which it must adapt.

I believe we are at the end of one period of professionalism begun in the U.S. Army late in the 19th century, and are now, in the first decade of the 21st century, beginning another period. We are examining how the Army profession should adapt itself to the new set of strategic realities that confront us today. As before, the challenge is to adapt but also to retain the many continuities of our profession we know are essential to success on the battlefield. We must continue, indeed strengthen, our values and ethos from the past, especially the moral requirement for expertise in land warfare, remaining always able to fight and win decisively in close quarters against enemies of every sort. We must also adapt the profession to the new strategic conditions for the use of force, more integrally combined with other elements of national power and necessitating new inter-relationships with civilian agencies of our government in this information age. Such adaptations will include evolving civil-military relationships and forms of joint warfare unforeseen at the time of the Goldwater-Nichols Act in 1986. This anthology will give readers issues galore to think about, and more.

I would not expect every professional who studies this text to agree with every idea here; I take exception with some of those ideas myself. Yet I do agree with many of them, and provide this foreword to make that point. This text offers an accessible and most useful place for individual professionals, and for the profession's strategic leaders, to join together in dialogue and mutual reflection. I recall that in 1962, British Gen. Sir John Hackett delivered a splendid series of lectures at Trinity College in Cambridge. For a time the U.S. Army reprinted these lectures in a Department of the Army pamphlet titled "The Profession of Arms." About the U.S. Army, Hackett noted: "The years between 1860 and the World War saw the emergence of a distinctive American professional military ethic, with the American officer regarding himself as a member of a learned profession whose students are students for life."

Hackett was an unusually insightful soldier-scholar. To follow that military ethic today, as we must, demands broad professional re-invigoration in the context of the ongoing transformations both at the Defense level and within the Army. I firmly believe that only through such a concerted, introspective process will the profession complete—as was done earlier in the 1970s and 1980s—the successful transformation that is needed to fight effectively the wars we'll confront in this new century.

As we were making our final preparations in VII Corps before attacking into Iraq in February 1991, I was visiting one of our divisions. As I was explaining our attack plan to a group of soldiers, one of them stopped me and said, "Don't worry, general, we trust you." I was humbled by that statement and vowed to do everything I could as corps commander to continue to earn that trust in battle. I also realized that in an instant that soldier had captured the essence of what we do as professionals: we gain and maintain our soldiers' trust by executing our duties to the highest levels of professionalism. We owe nothing less to our soldiers, to our nation, to ourselves, and to our profession.

Frederick M. Franks, Jr.
General, U.S. Army Ret.
West Point, N.Y.
February 2002

Foreword

Jim Marshall

In June 2004 I was invited to West Point to speak to a conference of scholars and military professionals who had gathered to debate the themes treated in the chapters that now appear in the present book. It was an immense privilege for me, as I hold great respect for the Army and those wonderful young soldiers and their families who serve within it.

Part of me wishes the Army profession had been my career. I grew up as an Army brat. My father and grandfather were schooled at West Point, served full careers in the Army Corps of Engineers, and retired as general officers. Throughout my childhood traipsing from one Army post to another, I seemed destined to follow in their footsteps. But that prospect ended at age 17 when my father asked me to promise him I would make a career of the Army if I received a nomination to West Point. Even now I recall my reply as we stood sheltered from an evening shower on the back porch of our ninth family home, this one in Mobile, Alabama: "Dad, I'm 17 years old and don't even know what I'm doing this Saturday night. How can I promise you what I'll do for the next 35 years?"

So in 1966 it was Princeton University for me instead of West Point. But my Army family heritage loomed large, and following the Tet Offensive in 1968, I left Princeton to enlist for service in Vietnam. Serving in Quang Ngai province as an Airborne-Ranger reconnaissance platoon sergeant was the capstone of my own brief Army career and, perhaps, of my entire life. Certainly it left me quite concerned about our national capacity for waging counterinsurgency warfare. Upon my separation, I returned to Princeton and spent time studying that subject as a University Scholar. Then I left the subject behind me for several decades during which I wore many hats, including a stint as a city mayor dealing with policing difficult neighborhoods. Now, years after Vietnam, I again find myself embroiled almost daily in Army matters as a member of the House Armed Services Committee, a position I sought because of the immense challenge jihadist followers of radical Islam now present on a global scale.

In my travels to Afghanistan and Iraq during the last two years, including a Christmas visit accompanying the Army's Chief of Staff, Gen. Peter Schoomaker, I saw an Army of exceptional professional competence, particularly at the tactical and operational levels of war. Small-unit leadership and cohesion in today's all-volunteer Army vastly exceeds that in the Army I served with in Vietnam and then studied as a University Scholar upon my return to Princeton. But I must add that *we, as a nation, are not well prepared to address the new jihadist threat*, particularly if it expands by crossing into other regions or deepens with the terrorists' acquisition of

Nuclear/Biological/Chemical weapons. Frankly, much of that lack of preparedness is plainly visible in how we are now fighting this war—with too little capability in our special operations forces, with little capacity for effective strategic communication campaigns, and with insufficient ability to establish security and assist rebuilding efforts. I say this in full knowledge that the major combat operations to topple Saddam Hussein and destroy his forces were extremely well executed by our heavy legacy forces.

For the foregoing reasons and because of my lifelong affair with the Army, I came eagerly to West Point to present my views as a Member of Congress to that gathering of soldiers and scholars who were studying the Army as a profession—a profession I had nearly chosen—even while it was fighting a war and undergoing an aggressive program of internal transformation. The Army's leadership at all levels must consider carefully how the jihadist threat can most effectively be countered by an Army that maintains, even through the welter of demands it now faces, the two essential characteristics of a true profession: a rapidly evolving body of expert knowledge that responds quickly to an adaptive enemy; and soldier-professionals trained with this knowledge to be the most competent, enduring warriors on the battlefield. All professions must do these two things—maintain a current body of expert knowledge and school their practitioners in its application—if they are to remain successful professions and attract those who want to serve America as members of a profession.

The quintessential feature of my own vocation of law, where in addition to practicing I have served as a Bar Association president, law professor, and legal scholar, is the freedom and ability of individual attorneys to adapt and respond to new issues and challenges on behalf of their clients. Bureaucratic management of the business aspect of the legal profession is common. But bureaucratic approaches to a law practice centered on resolving the individual legal problems of clients are completely ineffective. Each case, each client, is different, requiring that attorneys be free to adapt to the particular needs that clients present. Effective legal combat is a customized operation. Attorneys own the cases they prosecute.

The bureaucratic hierarchy of any good law firm defers entirely to the foregoing concept. My experiences and studies tell me the bureaucratic structure of the Army must similarly defer to the adaptive, customized analysis and actions of Army professionals at the forefront of the asymmetric battlefield. Stifling and frustrating though it can be, a by-the-book bureaucratic hierarchy is important to the effective husbandry of large, conventional forces. But that same hierarchy forms an Achilles heel when it comes to many of the challenges of asymmetric warfare, challenges that are best addressed by decentralized execution driven by local commanders given full sway to exercise discretion, seize the initiative, and tailor solutions as dictated by conditions at the tip of the spear.

What the Army must provide our joint commanders is the human expertise in land warfare needed to meet our current challenge from Islamic insurgents and radical jihadists. That expertise will not be developed in a timely manner and with sufficient quality by an Army operating as a governmental bureaucracy. I saw this happen in my own experience in Vietnam in the late 1960s. The chapters in this book, based on the Army's experiences in the Balkans, Afghanistan, Iraq, and elsewhere, constitute the best available current research on how the Army as a profession should adapt to the broad challenges of this period. When speaking within their special realms of training and experience on military matters, the professionals in the Army are the experts. As such they have tremendous influence, and I encourage them to use it. Some of the ideas in this book are controversial, but many are already in some stage of implementation. All are worthy of consideration by Army, Defense Department, and Congressional policy-makers.

The wonderful young Americans volunteering to serve in the Army today want to develop as professional warriors. Their aspirations coincide with our current national security needs. Clearly, their wishes, and hence our needs are best met if the Army's leaders, in cooperation with the Administration and Congress, make the extra effort to maintain, renew, and revitalize the Army as a profession.

Jim Marshall
Member, U.S. House of Representatives
Washington, DC
January 2005

Introduction

This second edition of *The Future of the Army* Profession is published at a critical time in the history of the profession of arms. We are an Army that serves a nation at war. We are engaged in two major campaigns—Operation Enduring Freedom in Afghanistan and Operation Iraqi Freedom in Iraq. We are moving resolutely to a joint and expeditionary mindset. And we are transforming our Army at the same time. We are doing all these things with the remarkable and selfless service of every member and component of our armed forces. This anthology addresses these new strategic challenges to the Army profession while at the same time attending to the profession's fundamental and defining features. It makes a compelling argument that we must adapt our profession, in all of its dimensions, to the realities of this new era even as it focuses on the broad spectrum of potential future conflicts, on our professional values, and on our traditional responsibilities.

The Army is rethinking many of its long-developed habits of mind and behavior, some of them representative of industrial-age warfare as practiced by Army professionals during the Cold War. That process of transformation has only just begun, and although it is taking place in the midst of a global war, it is moving forward with the energy essential for large-scale institutional change. And so it has been for many similar eras in the history of our service—synthesis wrought through the ceaseless march of change, adaptation, adjustment, innovation, and then more change. Our unique role as guarantors of the republic's security makes the rate of change more urgent because our success is predicated on the lives of our soldiers, upon whom rests the fate of our nation and the world.

In this turbulent period, the challenges for the strategic leaders of the Army profession are to see as accurately as possible through the volatility, uncertainty, complexity, and ambiguity of the contemporary operating environment, to visualize the broad outlines of the unfolding future, and to lead the profession in a manner that optimizes our nation's security. That leadership needs to be applied both in the Army's fighting formations and its developmental processes, and in those spheres of authority from which the Army will receive its future resources and missions. We must also keep the profession solidly connected to the American people through a historic social contract of our democracy under which we train and educate America's sons and daughters to be soldiers serving the nation by providing for its common defense. These are tough challenges for the Army's strategic leaders, placing an immense premium on their timely professional development and utilization.

The Army War College is an institution whose principal purpose is the development of those critical strategic leaders. Thus I take pride in introducing this text on the Army profession and in highlighting its contributions to the ongoing processes of transformation. We were honored to have Dr. Don Snider as a visiting professor in the College's Strategic Studies Institute for the past half year as he completed the text's compilation. His discussions with the students and faculty on the future of our Army added immensely to the intellectual environment of the Army War College, and his leadership of this groundbreaking effort speaks volumes about his own selfless professionalism.

This second edition, based upon privately-funded research, is the work of many hands, presenting multiple disciplinary perspectives on the military in general, and on the Army in particular. It provides a richness and diversity of thought that will help the Army's current and future strategic leaders in the successful execution of their unique missions, and in visualizing the institution's future as a vocational profession. This new edition also adds to and refines the major findings of the first edition (2002), which, after a 30-year hiatus, renewed formal study of the Army as a vocational profession rather than simply as a uniformed conglomerate or bureaucracy. By adopting a fundamentally new perspective of how American professions, including the Army, actually prepare and practice their expert work and behave within a dynamic system of professions, the 2002 edition offered new insights on the attitudes of junior professionals in the late 1990s, and shed light on the enlarged role of the Army's strategic leaders. It noted particularly that captains and majors, no matter how dedicated, cannot themselves convert the Army into a profession and preserve its status as a noble calling. Only its strategic leaders can undertake this task—by creating, adapting, refining, and prioritizing the profession's expert knowledge and then shaping the institution's personnel management systems to best develop and employ its professionals.

This second edition also extends the research within all four areas of the Army profession's expert knowledge, offering for the first time a basic mapping of such expertise, which provides fresh perspectives on when that knowledge should be internally maintained and adapted, and when the Army can afford to share it or relinquish primacy over it. It also extends the research to include Generation-Y soldiers and officers, those around whom the profession is now building its future. There is as well a careful examination of new demands on the profession's warrior ethic as entailed by the global war on terrorism. Finally, there are several new chapters on Army leaders and their development, covering the ranks from captain to general officer.

We owe a debt of gratitude to the many soldiers and scholars who have given generously of their time and talents to help our Army think carefully about its future as a profession, and about our own futures within it.

David H. Huntoon, Jr.
Major General, U.S. Army

I

The Study of Military Professions

1 The U.S. Army as Profession

Don M. Snider

Section I: Researching the Army as Profession

Introduction

This second edition of *The Future of the Army Profession* extends our research from the end of the Army's drawdown in the late 1990s through the initial years of combat operations in both Afghanistan and Iraq. What a difference those few years made!

As noted by the Army major quoted in the epigraph above, in the late 1990s it was very difficult for many young Army officers to see themselves as professionals, or to see the Army as a profession. With major loss of end-strength and tightened financial resources, it had been a hard decade for the Army; the catch phrase was "doing more with less," while supporting a remarkably increased rate of deployments to such places as Haiti, Bosnia, and Kosovo. These other-than-war missions brought sharply into question the Army's identity and its ability to prepare for what it still thought was core to its future, the conventional land battle. At home the economy was booming and young officers were leaving the Army at rates twice the historical norm. Studies by knowledgeable outsiders,[1] soon to be reinforced by the Army's own internal studies,[2] documented a stressed institution whose professional culture was in peril. "How the Army did things" had become increasingly bureaucratic, micromanaged, and then challenged and found wanting amid heightened distrust between the generations of the Army officer corps.[3]

This was the setting in the fall of 1999 when Dr. Gayle Watkins and I initiated at West Point the privately-funded research project that produced the first edition of this book, *The Future of the Army Profession*. We wrote then:

> As the Army continues to transform from a Cold War force to one appropriate for the 21st century, it must grapple with many issues. In this book, we propose that the most critical challenge the Army now faces in its planned transition is to reinforce the professional nature of the institution and to provide the opportunity for its soldiers to be members of a profession—the Army profession. The Army is neither a public-sector bureaucracy manned by civil servants nor is it a business with employees. It

How can I be a professional if there is no profession?
—AN ARMY MAJOR, 1999

Our core competencies remain: to train and equip Soldiers and grow leaders; and to provide relevant and ready landpower to the Combatant Commander and the joint team. . . . As the ultimate combination of sensor and shooter, the American Soldier is irrefutable proof that people are more important than hardware and quality more important then quantity.
—FORMER ACTING ARMY SECRETARY LES BROWNLEE
ARMY CHIEF OF STAFF GEN. PETER SCHOOMAKER

has been and must continue to be a profession, one in which military professionals serve with deep pride and immense personal satisfaction.[4]

The conviction remains that, for a number of reasons to be discussed later in this chapter, the Army must be a vocational profession—a calling—rather than just a big government bureaucracy, and it must be recognized as such by its client, the American people. However, as of this writing in the fall of 2004, just three years after our first study, the setting is starkly different. The economic bubble of the 1990s burst in scandal, recession, and entrepreneurial handwringing that are afflicting the economy to this day. America has been attacked on her homeland for the first time in generations and is now a nation at war, a "global war on terrorism" as it has become known. Financial resources for the war effort have flowed freely, with the Army budget now at heights entirely unforeseen just a few years ago.[5] In the initial phases of this global war, the Army's forces performed magnificently under great stress, quickly overcoming any conventional resistance that stood in their way.

But now, both in Afghanistan and Iraq, progress against tenacious insurgencies has slowed markedly. U.S. national elections this fall politicized the Iraq war like none since Vietnam, and once again in our history the travails of American ground forces almost precluded the reelection of a sitting American president.[6] Along the way the Army has found itself assuming a new identity and core focus as American and coalition forces assumed a constabulary role under joint command, supporting the new political regimes in both countries with limited use of military force, while seeking viable future governments rather than military victory.[7]

When the Army is viewed as a profession, however, even starker contrasts between the late 1990s and 2004 emerge. Specifically, with the third rotation of Army forces about to enter the Middle East theater, Army professionals have been practicing their expertise in numbers, intensity, and duration to a degree not experienced since the Vietnam War. Moreover, fully 40 percent of them now are reservists, members of the Army Reserve and National Guard. Unlike other professions such as law, accountancy, medicine, and theology, whose members practice their expertise daily, Army professionals—most fortunately, to be sure—do not often practice their expertise in combat. Many who retired from the Army circa year 2000 served in only one combat tour in a 20-year career, that being in the "hundred hour" ground war in Iraq in 1990-1991. But today, in sharp contrast to the late 1990s, Army professionals of all ranks are becoming deeply steeped in their professional practice, so much so that senior leaders must be concerned about professional development systems in which "the students at Leavenworth now know more than their faculty," and faithful Army families wonder how many more deployment separations they can endure.[8]

Thus the scope of the challenge facing the strategic leaders of the Army profession has changed in the course of just a few years: from *renewing the Army as a vocational profession*—to *capturing and maintaining the Army's renewed professionalism*. And this must be done while simultaneously transforming to "a campaign quality Army with joint and expeditionary capabilities."[9] While all of this frenetic activity is more applicable to the field Army and is creating more turbulence there than within the institutional side of the Army, transforming the profession remains a task of immense proportions, one that will likely take more than a decade to complete.

This was one of the principal reasons why I undertook in 2003-2004, along with other dedicated scholars and researchers, another privately-funded project to take a new look at the Army as profession. A second reason was the necessity to examine the influences of the ongoing defense transformation—were these influences, though primarily technological in nature, hindering (or, less likely, helping) the renewal of the Army as a quintessentially human institution and a vocational profession? Why was it that the human aspects of military transformations, so well researched in the historical literature, received so little attention in Defense and Army transformation plans?[10] Third, it was essential to look at the influences on the profession, particularly on its expert knowledge and jurisdictional competitions, which resulted from the Army's rapid acceptance and implementation of the Afghanistan/Iraq enterprise—the U. S. Army at war in the Middle East is now a joint and combined, expeditionary force with missions quite different from those of previous wars. Of special import to the profession's strategic leaders, this particular war, along with the global realignment of U.S. bases, will likely entail Army units deploying to combat one out of every three or four years, a pattern continuing well into the foreseeable future. It is likely to alter fundamentally how Army professionals are developed and employed. Finally, it was necessary to fill a research void left from the first study, that is, to look at how the Army is dealing with the infusion of Generation Y soldiers and officers (those born after 1981). They appear to have all the makings of another "greatest" generation, but as remarkable as they might be, the Army knows all too little about them. Thus, there is an extensive set of research reported in this second edition on issues cogent to them—Army officership, Army families, and how Generation Y soldiers can best be led.

In addition to such concerns within the Army profession, there is also the issue of whether influential external audiences view the Army as a profession. For example, as the number of veterans serving in Congress continues to decline in proportion to their representation in the American public,[11] new ways and avenues must be created to help such influential officials understand that the Army is much more than a government bureaucracy. In spite of the unprecedented information on Army combat operations from embedded news media in Iraq, there is still little public recognition of the Army as a profession.

For these compelling reasons, another remarkable group of military and civilian scholars assembled at West Point in the early spring of 2004 to tackle the research project following the same methodology used in the 2000 study. The research focus was on the influences of defense transformation and the anti-terrorist war on the profession's two internal jurisdictions. More specifically, the questions to be answered were threefold: (1) what are the influences on the Army's expert knowledge; (2) what are the influences on how the Army develops its professionals to practice this expertise; and (3) what are the implications for how the Army is deploying and employing its professionals, both now and in the future?

Individuals, or in several cases collaborating colleagues, undertook over a score of different inquiries concerning the evolving Army profession, with some capitalizing on research from the Army's operations in the Balkans, Afghanistan, and Iraq. Initial findings were vetted at a major conference at West Point in June 2004, then refined and finalized for this anthology.[12] Concurrently, I selected for revision and update a dozen or so of the chapters from the first edition, those bearing most significantly on the conclusions drawn about the state of the Army profession in 2000. Thus students and faculty who use this second edition can be assured that, with the exception of one chapter based on field research which could not be replicated, this 2005 edition represents a fresh look at the Army as profession in 2004 and early 2005.

In the present chapter, then, I shall preview for the reader what he or she can expect in the remainder of the anthology. First, I will review briefly the origins of the resurgent study of the Army as profession, tracing it from its emergence in the late 1990s to its culmination in the publication of the first edition in 2002. Without such context, readers will not understand why it is that the study of Army officership and the Army as profession cannot be well separated; that is, why the commissioned officer corps plays such a critical role in adapting military professions in times of transformations and war. Secondly, I will trace the theoretical framework for the common research methodology of both studies as set forth in Prof. Andrew Abbott's groundbreaking study titled *The System of Professions* (1988). His study provides the key to understanding vocational professions, which is the link between their abstract knowledge and its application (in situations which he calls jurisdictions). Also key in Professor Abbott's construct is understanding that such professions are, amidst a system of competing professions, always seeking to control more completely the expert work they do, thus enhancing their effectiveness and establishing legitimacy in the eyes of their clients for future expert work. Third, I will review briefly what we determined to be the state of the Army profession in 2000. I will then conclude the chapter with the findings of the second project, noting how the Army profession has evolved in the past four years and pointing to measures which, if adopted, will better ensure that America acquires a vibrant Army profession, with deeply committed and practiced professionals, to fight her land wars of the future.

For those readers who are familiar with the theory and language of the study of professions and not interested in how this study of the Army as profession was renewed, I suggest that you skip the remainder of Section I and proceed directly to Section II of this introductory chapter. Section II compares the state of the Army profession as revealed in our year 2000 research project with its state based on our 2004 research.

Renewal of Study of the Army as a Profession

Surprisingly, of all the research done both by the Army and for the Army, particularly in the decade of the post-Cold War drawdown, our initial research project in 2000 was the first in just over 30 years in which the Army had been studied *as a profession*. The last study, directed by then Army Chief of Staff Gen. William

Westmoreland during the waning stages of the Vietnam war, was completed at the Army War College in 1970. Thirty years later, it was no surprise to discover that many of the ideas offered at the beginning of that earlier period of re-professionalization,[13] marked by the end of the national conscription on 1 July 1973, were quite reflective of what we found was still applicable in 2000.

Neither had the Army showed a serious interest during the later decades of the Cold War in the subject of officership—the role, responsibilities, and identities of commissioned Army leaders. Such was not always the case. Early in the Cold War, Prof. Samuel Huntingon began his classic, *The Soldier and the State* (1957), with the following declaration: "The modern officer corps is a professional body and the modern military officer is a professional man. This is, perhaps, the most fundamental thesis of this book."[14]

Thus, at the beginning of the Cold War the connection between officership and the Army as profession had been made explicit, though historians have not yet agreed on the accuracy of Huntington's theorized causal relationships.[15] For decades Huntington's thesis, along with the writing of Walter Millis, Morris Janowitz, and other early theorists of civil-military relations, was central to Army officer development and leadership doctrines being taught widely throughout Army schools. But, by the mid 1990s, Huntington was no longer taught in core curricula at West Point nor in the Army's schools and had not been for a decade or so. Neither were future Army officers taught any course on civil-military relations as had been the norm earlier during the Cold War years.[16]

But West Point was not the only place within the Army that reflected the attenuation of the concepts of officership and the Army as a profession. For example, by the turn of the century the Army's leadership doctrine as set forth in FM 22-100, *Leadership* (August 1999), had relegated the subject of officers to an appendix. The increasingly egalitarian doctrine of that era basically held to the conception that "an Army leader is a leader," making no distinction between commissioned and not commissioned, between military and civilian. The doctrine also failed completely to recognize the Army as a profession, using throughout the manual the generic noun "organization" to describe the Army.

Clearly during this period, trendy but ephemeral organizational theories permeated the Army's approach to its formations and to its soldiers' development. The same was true of other capstone doctrinal manuals with the exception of FM 1, *The Army*. Customarily rewritten after the arrival of each succeeding Chief of Staff, these short and often history-laden statements contained several references to the Army as profession and its storied service to the nation. But this is one of the few places the concept of profession, however thinly, still survived in Army doctrine by the late 1990s. Little wonder, then, that by 2000 the Army had not been studied as a profession for three decades![17]

Fortunately, two separate but related debates were raging over post-Cold War American defense policy, each of which would strongly inform the framework we adopted to renew the study of the Army as profession and the role of Army officers within it.

Amid the Debate on Army Roles and Missions: The West Point Renewal of the Study of Officership

In the spring of 1997, the Superintendent of the U.S. Military Academy, Lt. Gen. Daniel Christman, requested a review of the capabilities required of the institution's graduates in the new post-Cold War security environment. The need for a thorough review reflected the intellectual ferment existing at the time across the Army. At the Academy, attrition of graduates after their mandatory five-year period of active service had risen significantly during the 1990s, while concurrently the use of Army forces in non-war-fighting roles in Haiti (1994), Rawanda (1995), and Bosnia (1996) had stirred up much larger concerns, both internal and external to the Army.[18] Essentially, this debate centered on future roles and missions for the Army—what types of core missions could Army leaders and soldiers expect in the future, and how should they be organized, trained, and equipped in accordance with that future? Were they "warriors" whose mission it was to fight and win the nation's wars as they had prepared to do for the past four decades on the plains of Central Europe, or were they now to be "peacemakers and peacekeepers" in the almost forgotten tradition of the Army's frontier days?

Included within the "warrior vs. peacekeeper" debate were issues of gays in the military, women in combat roles, gender-integrated training, casualty aversion, and force protection measures for peacemaking missions, all broached by the Clinton administration. In the minds of many senior Army leaders these issues tended to erode the essential warrior culture of both the Academy and the Army.[19] For most, this debate went right to the core of the institution, to its warrior ethic; and it ultimately led to the establishment at the Academy in 1998 of an interdisciplinary Center for the Study of the Professional Military Ethic.[20] Thus, for General Christman, the critical questions were, "How should Army officers think of themselves and the military missions they will undertake in the future; and how must the Academy adapt and best use its developmental capacities to produce this type of future leaders for the Army?"

Throughout the later decades of the Cold War, the Army's commissioning institutions had built their developmental programs around the goal of producing officers who thought of themselves and had developed themselves as "war-fighters" and "leaders of character." These two self-concepts had served the Army well as it re-professionalized after Vietnam and focused on its core mission of conventional land combat against the Warsaw Pact forces in Europe.

But a decade after the end of that conflict, with intense debate raging over the future core missions of the Army, the analysis that the Academy's faculty presented to General Christman argued that those two identities were now insufficient to guide the development of future Army leaders. Instead, they argued that two additional identities and associated developmental experiences were needed, specifically those of "servant to the nation" and "member of a profession." Accordingly, in 2000 Christman republished the Academy's foundational guidance, *Strategic Vision 2010*, enshrining for the next decade within the evolving developmental programs at West Point a renewed concept of officership marked by the new fourfold self-identity. Refined by the next Superintendent, Lt. Gen. William Lennox, and codified in the Cadet Leader Development System, the definition of Army officership—"the practice of being a commissioned officer imbued with a unique professional self-concept defined by the following four identities: Warrior, Member of Profession, Servant of Country, Leader of Character"[21]—now exercises influence well beyond West Point. Draft leadership doctrine, titled "The Army Officership Concept," has been provided to the Department of the Army, to the other services and the joint arena, and to the service academies of sister services.[22]

To understand the provenance of these two additional identities and the essential relationship between officership and the Army profession, we turn now to a second momentous debate.

The Army and the Debate over the Revolution in Military Affairs

The second far-reaching debate within the U.S. defense community in the late 1990s focused on whether American armed forces were undergoing a "revolution in military affairs."[23] It was, like the concurrent debate discussed above on the Army's own roles and missions, of immense importance to the Army as the major provider of land power for the world's ascendant military power. As we wrote in 2001 while composing the introductory chapter to the first edition:

> History shows that many armies do not adapt well in peacetime to changing environments such as the Army now faces; some do not adapt at all and no longer exist as deployable armies, witness most of those today in Western Europe. And even for those that are able to innovate and adapt in order to remain effective militarily and relevant to the societies they defend, the process is often long and difficult. Such processes take at least a decade or longer and often are not resolved when the next war starts, thus requiring the even more difficult process of wartime innovation and adaptation.

Little did we suspect that we were describing the unexpected and daunting situation the Army faces today in early 2005, only four years later—as it struggles to complete what began as a peacetime Revolution in Military Affairs (RMA), now known as "transformation," while fighting very tough counterinsurgency wars in Afghanistan and Iraq! As President Bush describes the challenge, "What's different today is our sense of urgency—the need to build this future force while fighting a present war. It's like overhauling an engine while you're going 80 miles an hour. Yet we have no other choice."[24]

The RMA debate recognized that modern armies reflect the national culture from which they are drawn and its state of technology, and that they have unique relationships with the civilian society and the nation they each defend. Thus, it is not surprising that there has been little consensus in the scholarly literature on just how these military transformations occur in peacetime—the specific causal relationships. In fact, there have been two rather distinct schools of thought that address the phenomenon, each with its own historical literature and each enjoying renewal and invigoration in the post-Cold War debates.

The most influential school of thought on military transformations—what might be termed the technological-agent school—is populated by futurists, technologists, policy scientists, and some historians.[25] This school tends to view change within military institutions in relation to the evolving conduct of warfare and how militaries fight—particularly to the influence of technology. Advocates hold that a historic revolution in military affairs started in the last years of the Cold War, as seen in the technological advances within the conventional arms race between the Warsaw Pact and NATO. Such claims subsequently gained momentum in 1991 as a result of the spectacularly destructive air campaign and remarkably successful, 100-hour ground campaign of the first Gulf War.[26] Their conclusion drawn from that war was that the high-tech American-led forces exemplified a new form of warfare which America should continue to exploit for its new superpower role in the world.[27]

The technological-agent school basically believes that the transition from the industrial age to the information age, at least among the great powers, is influencing warfare as much as it is other macro-social phenomena. Members hold that advances in precision weapons, surveillance satellites, robotics, and computer-based information processing have created a fundamental new way of warfare fought by a "system of systems"—with sensors networked to shooters and commanders at multiple levels enabled to suppress the fog of war by use of a common operating picture of the battle-space.[28] Within this school, some have focused primarily on how the Army should adapt to such a revolution.[29] Others, concerned with whether this new method of warfare would be applicable across the full spectrum of conflict facing the United States, have articulated more cautious views.[30] More recently, some have opined that the force transformation initiatives of the Bush administration are designed specifically to further such a RMA.[31]

The second school of thought—which for convenience I call the organizational-theory school—is populated by political scientists and organizational theorists. This school views armies as large, standing institutions, usually highly bureaucratic, whose changing behaviors in peacetime can be best understood in strategic context by the application of evolving theories of organizational behavior originally found in business, economics, and public administration literatures.[32] According to this school, the major determinants of an army's modernization decisions issue from its own intrinsic character and culture and its relationships with the external environment, particularly its structural relationship with other governmental institutions (executive and legislature) with authority over it.[33]

Of particular interest regarding this school is its emphasis on the culture of the military institution, the relationships between culture and strategic doctrines, and the influence organizational culture has in interpreting the external environments in which the Army is operating, both domestic and international. According to this school, one of the roles of strategic leaders, particularly commissioned military leaders, is to influence internal cultures in such a manner as to make profound change more acceptable and likely, such as abetting organizational learning and adaptation within the institution.[34]

When we began our first study in 1999, I was struck more by what defense analysts drawing on the literature did *not* recognize in these two schools of thought than by what they did. Certainly they did recognize the very influential role that technology played in peacetime military transformations and, as well, the strong transformational influences between large changes in an institution's external environment and its internal culture. But I was convinced, particularly after teaching much of the RMA literature in an elective course at West Point from 1995 through 1999, that *both* schools of thought deliberately gave weight to the role that human actors could play in military transformations, both as individual decision-makers and as members of coherent groups, such as an officer corps, whose influence on military culture is known to be immense.[35]

However, the defense policy debate raging inside the DC beltway largely ignored the human factor that both schools valued in common, focusing instead on the role of technology and the rapidly changing "military-technical" aspects of warfare. Unfortunately, as of this writing the human role is still largely under-appreciated and planned for by those within DoD designing transformation plans. Such plans are almost devoid of considerations of human resources and the necessity for what is becoming known as the "cognitive transformation" that must exist in the early stages of any successful RMA. Instead, they have too often tended to view human factors as little more than "cultural impediments" to change.[36]

Thus we knew when we started the first study in 1999 that we wanted to avoid the mistake we perceived defense analysts were making. We wanted to allow our analysis to focus on human actors, particularly military officer corps, in addition to the military-technical aspects of warfare and changing security environments. Further, from the debate over Army roles and missions it was apparent that to study the Army as profession we needed to approach it from at least two directions of analysis, that is, from both sides of the profession-client relationship (in the Army's case, the Army and the American people). As the debate on Army roles and missions showed—particularly during the Clinton administration—there were widely different points of view on many subjects on each side of that relationship. We wanted our researchers to capture those perspectives and their policy implications.

Thus, as we mapped our research method for the first study we drew from each debate in the separate dimensions of our analysis. Initially mapped into a four-by-three matrix (Figure 1-1), we divided the profession's expert knowledge into four coherent clusters (only the first of which, the military-technical, was being heavily debated in the RMA discussions) and then sought to research each of these clusters from the perspectives of the profession (Army leaders and individual professionals) and its client (civilian leaders representing the American public).

As Figure 1-1 makes clear (white vertical arrows), the fourfold identity of the Army officer corresponds one to one with the four clusters of expert knowledge that demark the Army among America's professions. First, the military-technical cluster is the expert knowledge of applying coercive, lethal force while employing Army units in actual combat or what Huntington much earlier called the "management of violence." Second, since Americans expect their armed forces to fight wars "rightly," adhering to both the moral and legal content of the nation's values and the profession's ethic, there is the moral-ethical cluster. Third, since war is a human endeavor and professions are quintessentially human institutions practicing their art with human minds and hands, there is the expert knowledge of human development. Such knowledge allows the Army to transform civilians into soldiers, to develop strategic

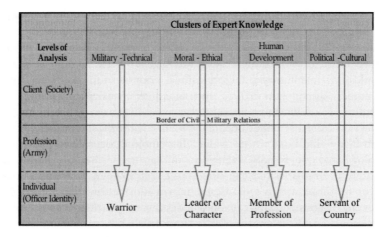

Figure 1-1. *The Army's Expert Knowledge and the Four Identities of the Army Officer.*

leaders over a life-long career, and to create cohesive units capable of withstanding the stresses of extended combat. Fourth, there is the political-cultural expert knowledge which allows Army leaders, particularly at the strategic level, to represent the profession within the political institutions of our government and, as well, in the multicultural coalitions and countries in which Army forces serve globally. Thus, the origin of the two additional officer identities, "member of profession" and "servant of country," which were recommended to General Christman by his faculty committee at West Point, came proximately from this knowledge mapping in our first effort to renew the study of the Army profession.[37]

The relationship between the Army officer and the Army profession is thus complete: officers, as individual professionals under the moral and legal mandates of their commission, embody the expert knowledge of the profession and apply it in their practices. They are personally called to, motivated by, and identify strongly with that expert knowledge and its trusted application on behalf of the profession's client, the American people. Their body of expert knowledge embraces four distinguishable clusters, albeit with different emphasis on each cluster as they advance through the ranks. We can conclude, therefore, that Army officership has little meaning in the absence of such concrete and deeply felt links between the expert knowledge of the Army profession and its service to the American people.

Stated another way in the language of the contestants of the RMA debate, individual officers as strategic leaders and as members of the nation's officer corps—those responsible for their institution's internal normative culture and therefore its adaptability—have a unique and irreplaceable role to play in the institution's efforts to transform in response to an RMA. They are not the sole players, but surely are vital ones. Gen. Eric Shinseki, then Army Chief of Staff, was right in 2001 when he said, "Institutions don't transform, people do."[38] Carrying General Shinseki's insight one step further, we connect with another wise observation: "Change how an officer corps thinks, and you will change how an army behaves."[39]

With this understanding of the relationship between officership and profession now established, I turn to the dual nature of the Army, as both profession and bureaucracy, and to the specific theory of modern professions used in the study efforts reflected in both the 2002 and 2005 editions of the present book.

The Army as Profession and Bureaucracy

As the second epigraph of this introductory chapter notes, the Army is a producing organization, the product of which according to the current Army Chief of Staff is "relevant and ready landpower [for] the Combatant Commander and the joint team."[40] Thus, as a producing organization the Army could be organized as a business, or a bureaucracy, or a profession, these three being the ideal types of producing organizations most commonly found in western capitalistic democracies.[41]

However, as has long been noted by those who have studied the Army deeply, the Army is most certainly not a business. The Army was established by the founding fathers to accomplish its operational missions, not to turn a profit. Unfortunately, this fact is too little recognized today by many outside the Army who frequently attempt to foist onto it business practices and management techniques. Rather, as a producing organization the Army has a dual nature—that of a hierarchical bureaucracy and that of a vocational profession. Huntington observed that "officership is a public bureaucratized profession. The legal right to practice the profession is limited to members of a carefully defined body. His commission is to the officer what his license is to the doctor."[42]

Thus the continuous challenge for the strategic leaders of the Army profession, at least since the latter years of the 19th century when the Army professionalized, has been to keep these two internal natures in proper proportion, with profession predominant over bureaucracy in all areas except those very few that are intrinsic to any large organization. The reasons for this are readily apparent in Table 1-1, which contrasts the ideal characteristics of a profession with those of a bureaucracy.

The right column of the table displays those characteristics of bureaucracy such as its work, which is the application of non-expert knowledge, embedded in organizational routine and process rather than in the employees themselves, to routine and repetitive situations.[43] The extreme of this repetitive sameness of routine, tantamount to an office assembly line, is epitomized by governmental bureaucracies— think of a state department of motor vehicles which issues drivers licenses and automobile registrations and license plates day in, day out, over the years!

In contrast, the coins of the professional realm are expertise and the knowledge underlying it. Far more so than other occupations and organizations, professions focus on generating expert knowledge and the ability of its members to apply that expertise to new situations. Medical professionals perfect medical techniques to apply to patients, lawyers apply legal expertise in trying cases, and the military develops new technologies, capabilities, and strategies to "provide for the common defense," most often in distant places and under difficult circumstances that cannot be foreseen in

Comparison	Profession	Bureaucracy
Knowledge	Expert, abstract; requires life-long learning	Nonexpert; quickly learned on the job
Practice	Knowledge applied with discretion to new situations by individual professional	Repetitive situations, work done by following SOPs, administrative rules, and procedures
Measure	Focus on effectiveness of applied practice	Focus on efficiency of resources used
Culture	Granted autonomy with self-policing ethic	Closely supervised; imposed governmental ethic
Investments	Priority investment in individual professionals	Priority investment in hardware/software, routines
Growth	Individuals develop coherent professional worldview	A worldview is irrelevant to the work
Motivation	Intrinsic, altruistic toward client; work is a calling	Extrinsic, egoism: work is a job for personal gain

Table 1-1. *A Comparison: Profession vs. Bureaucracy.*

detail. Such professional expertise is ultimately validated by the client (or professions would not survive), and forms the basis for the trust between the profession and the society served. Given such trust, professions are granted limited autonomy to establish and enforce their own professional ethics, the maintenance of which further enhances such trust. Furthermore, success in professional practice stems from effective and ethical application of the expertise—the patient is cured; the case is won; conflict is deterred or, if not, settled on terms favorable to the United States. Thus efficiency, while important, ranks behind effectiveness as a measure of success for professions.

And herein is the basis for the natural tensions within the Army's dual character. Predominantly, the Army is a profession focused on developing and adapting the four clusters of expert knowledge mentioned earlier. In other situations, generally in administrative, logistical, educational, and headquarters contexts, the Army is a hierarchical bureaucracy focused on apparatchik-type work familiar in any large organization in the western world today. In this world, the watchword is efficiency, "doing more with less." While this dual nature is unavoidable and healthy for the nation, it can be cause for considerable tensions, both for the individual professional and for the institution as a whole.

For example, by the late 1990s it was apparent to many that the Army had increasingly moved toward business and organizational concepts for decision-making within the institution's management systems, and away from the traditional panoply of military decision tools. Operations research, efficiency goals, outsourcing, civilianization, and monetary incentives dominated the institution's analyses and solutions. Efficiency had become a dominant goal, surpassing military effectiveness. The Army was losing competitions with other professions and organizations at the boundaries of its expertise. Moreover, it was resisting change because change threatened traditional roles, missions, and force structure, rather than viewing the Army as a profession and evaluating change in the context of how it affects the Army's future expertise and jurisdictions, and thus its professionalism.

Maintaining an appropriate balance between the Army's two natures is thus ever elusive; at any time, bureaucracy can come to predominate over profession. The result is an Army whose leaders, self-concepts, decisions, and organizational climate for soldiers reflect a high degree of bureaucracy and efficiency rather than military professionalism and effectiveness. In the bureaucratic mode, the self-concept of the Army's members is likely to be one of "employee," while in the mode of a calling their self-concept is one of "professional." The Army of Desert Storm in 1991 was a case of the latter. As our research in the 2000 study ultimately demonstrated, the Army at the end of the drawdown of the 1990s was all too much the former.

We argued in the first edition, and it remains a central thesis of this new edition, that the Army must remain foremost a profession. Skeptics, however, may still demand to know why it matters whether the Army is more like a bureaucracy or more like a profession. What difference does it make? The Army will still be here, doing its service to the nation, will it not? The short answer is: American society would lose two key benefits of military professionalism if bureaucracy came to predominate—(1) it would lose the development and adaptation of the expert knowledge undergirding effective land combat; and (2) potentially, it could see a weakening of discipline among soldiers within an institution capable of terrible destruction. Let me explain.

A principal reason for continued public support for the current worldwide war on terrorism, even with the massive stains of prisoner abuse at Abu Ghraib, is that the professionals in the most powerful Army in the world are considered to be experts at their art and unquestionably under the control of elected and appointed civilian officials. Professions excel where bureaucracies cannot—in the creation and adaptation of abstract expert knowledge and its application to new situations. Therefore, if America is to have the cutting edge of warrior soldiers, applied technology, and effective land combat forces for joint operations, the professional nature of its Army must predominate over its bureaucratic tendencies. There is simply no historical record of bureaucracies ever producing abstract, expert knowledge of such warfare. Other nations may be willing to renounce the leadership role in producing such military theory and perfecting its practice, but I do not believe America can, nor should, do so.

With regard to the second benefit of a professional force—maintenance of social control by nurturing a specific ethic within its members—a profession offers a better means of shaping human behavior in situations of chaotic violence, stress, and ambiguity than bureaucratic management can ever hope to achieve. In other words, within the culture of a profession is embedded an ethos that strongly informs the actions of the individual professionals, even in the direst of circumstances. A remarkable example appears in a letter that then Maj. Gen. George Patton wrote from North Africa in 1942 to West Point classmates in the states after his division had fared poorly against the Germans: "[Some] did not turn and run, because we were more afraid of our consciences than we were of the enemy."[44] Such social control within the Army profession—by inculcation of professional warrior ethics—

was under stress during the 1990s owing, among other reasons, to political guidance to deployed forces to avoid casualties at all costs, particularly in unpopular peacekeeping operations.[45] Such risk-averse behavior is natural and fitting for a bureaucracy; it is utterly pernicious for a military profession. In contrast, the subsequent restoration of the warrior ethic and the return of discretion to the Army officer corps to do its duty in combat as best fits the needs of mission accomplishment, always the first priority, has been absolutely vital to more recent Army successes.[46]

Thus it is of supreme importance to the nation how the Army's strategic leaders manage this difficult and constant tension between its professional and bureaucratic identities. Historically, militaries that do not resolve this tension in favor of their professional identity can experience the "death" of their professional character. As their bureaucratic nature comes to dominate, they cease to be a profession and become little more than an obedient military bureaucracy, treating their officers and soldiers as bureaucrats. One need only look to the current armies of the western European nations, with one or two exceptions, for examples of this phenomenon.

The Traditional Understanding of Military Professions

In seeking the most applicable theory on which to base our analysis about how professions (and therefore the Army) behave and change over time, we first turned to the traditional literature. Professions have long been identified as a unique means of organizing and controlling work, different from more common formal organizations and labor unions. Research into professions began as descriptive case studies, progressed through the identification of professions' differentiating characteristics, and, by mid-20th century, had modeled the professionalization process by which occupations were converted into professions.[47] As noted in Table 1-1, two important characteristics distinguishing professions from bureaucracies were the application of abstract expert knowledge and doing so to new situations. Other essential characteristics included organization of the occupation, extensive education of its members, service to society, and shared ethics.[48] Professionalization was seen as a threshold; an occupation's status as a profession, once achieved, was relatively static, but something that had to be maintained over time through its unique characteristics.

In addition to Huntington, classical writings on the military professions, including Alfred Vagts, Morris Janowitz, and Bengt Abrahamsson, drew on this more general study of professions.[49] Most important to them were those aspects of the institution that allowed the military to be identified as a profession. As succinctly summarized in the late 1970s by military historian Allan Millett, the attributes and character of the military occupation which induced society to give it "professional" status were as follows:

> The occupation was full-time and stable, serving society's continuing needs; it was regarded as a life-long calling by the practitioners, who identified themselves personally with their vocational sub-culture; it was organized to control performance standards and recruitment; it required formal, theoretical education; it had a service orientation in which loyalty to standards of competence and loyalty to clients' needs were paramount; [it] was granted a great deal of autonomy by the society it served,

presumably because the practitioners had proven their high ethical standards and trustworthiness; and, overall, the profession's work was the systemic exploitation of specialized knowledge applied to specialized problems.[50]

From this traditional conception of the military profession came the self-concept of the individual professional—partly inherited, partly self-developed. As Millet noted, Army professionals inherit the broadly defined characteristics of their career and the special institutional setting within which they find themselves. Certainly this was true of the WWII generation of officers and their protégés of the next generation. As explicated by Huntington and widely accepted by the post-WWII generations of American officers, subordination of the military to civilian authority could best be achieved by what Huntington termed "objective control": in return for limited autonomy in which to develop its expert knowledge and conduct its professional duties, the military's natural and self-interested role would be internally focused, self-policed, apolitical, and preoccupied with its expertise and moral responsibilities. In other words, objective civilian control depends on maximizing military professionalism, a major aspect of which is the apolitical ideal enforced by professional self-discipline.

The Vietnam War, however, began to shatter the illusions of a generation of Army officers concerning the traditional, apolitical role of the military professional in the predictable, always abiding Army profession. This process created an Army officer corps that was, contrary to Huntingtonian logic, both more professional *and* more political.[51] It is not at all surprising that this is the generation of officers who were party to the significant tensions in American civil-military relations during the Clinton years and the first George W. Bush administration,[52] tensions that were bound to surface as society turned, in a trend not without historical precedent, to more subjective forms of civilian control for that unique interwar period.[53]

It was, however, at the end of that unique interwar period that my colleagues and I were starting our first research project. And the evolution described above led us to believe that the traditional view of military professions (relatively static, perpetual) and military professionals (expert, autonomous, and apolitical) was no longer applicable. This is not to say that it had no explanatory power; certainly it did, particularly with its focus on expert work, the development of professionals, the moral obligations of the officer's commission, and the fiduciary relationship with the client as sustained by the application of effective services delivered with a self-policing ethic. But the traditional conception was incomplete in that it failed to address the dynamism that provides impetus for change with regard to professional work jurisdictions. Needing to address as well that vital aspect in our research methodology, we turned to a more modern theory of the social organization of expert work.

The Abbott Framework for a System of Competitive Professions

Before I discuss the model we chose to undergird our analysis, let me first place the Army as profession in context. There has long been a full literature on the profession of arms, and since WWII an equally rich one on the American branch of that global occupational grouping. Most of that latter literature holds that, because of the dictates of the Constitution, subsequent federal statutes, and tradition, the American branch of the profession of arms has evolved into three sub-professions, which I shall call war-fighting professions: army, maritime, and air-space.[54] These professions are generally (but not wholly) contained within the Departments of the Army, Navy, and Air Force, and are surrounded by the immense bureaucratic structures of the Department of Defense, the Congress, and the Executive. To be sure, there are many individuals in these governmental bureaucracies who consider themselves also to be professionals, but to what profession do they in point of fact currently belong? Who develops, adapts, and maintains the expert knowledge of their profession? Who certified their credentials to the client, and who exactly is their client? It is true that some scholars have been writing for several years about an emerging "national security profession."[55] But I believe it premature to describe such a nebulous entity as a profession in the same sense as America's military professions.

Rather, I believe that portions of these large bureaucratic entities are better understood, following the typology of Prof. Steve Brint, as "public-sector organizations of experts."[56] An example would be a policy office for strategic analysis within the Office of the Under Secretary of Defense for Policy, or comparable permanent sections of the Senate Armed Service Committee staff. DoD civilian experts, many of whom have extensive professional backgrounds, often from academia, no longer work within an integral professional grouping. The larger organization in which they work is a defense bureaucracy responsible, overall, for an annualized, routinized Federal budget process that extends from preparation in the executive branch to justification before the Congress to execution by the agencies of the executive branch, including the Army.

Returning to the three military professions, we find that although they may appear as static as the traditional theories hypothesized, modern professions, including the Army, also have a dynamic and occasionally indecorous side. They are continuously engaged in fierce competitions for control over the situations in which they apply their expertise.[57] As demonstrated conclusively by sociologist Andrew Abbott in his study *The System of Professions* (1988) such competitions—though often publicly deplored—are at once inevitable, necessary, and desirable. For just as a market economy more efficiently allocates production and distribution of goods, a dynamic system of professions, based on the clients' measures of effectiveness, more efficiently allocates work and jurisdictions among competing professional groups. In the language of bureaucracies, this competition is known within the Department of Defense as the traditional "roles and missions" debate. Today, however, at least for the moment, such competition is manifested formally in ongoing negotiations over the future of jointness and the effective integration of service capabilities under the combatant commanders.

In the private sector, as Abbott demonstrates so clearly, the same competitive dynamic is occurring among the medical professions as physicians and other medical professionals battle over the right to make patient-care decisions.[58] Within the medical profession itself, anesthetists vie with anesthesiologists over pain relief during surgery. Midwives vie with obstetricians over delivering babies. Internists vie with gastroenterologists over colonoscopies and esophagogastroscopies. Other professions, such as accountancy, face challenges as they seek to gain legitimacy in new fields, such as business consultancy, while retaining legitimacy in their traditional areas. Finally, the military profession itself is experiencing competition, much of it the result of our globalized information age as new vocations seeking to gain, via successful competition, legitimacy over expert work formerly performed by the uniformed services. One example is the International Information Systems Security Consortium, which is now, through its own exam-based certification processes, credentialing systems security professionals in several career fields.[59]

Abbott argues that an occupation's identification as a profession and its standing within society are outcomes of social competition within a system of professions for control over expert knowledge as applied to particular situations. Professional life in his theory has three characteristics.[60] First, professions should be seen for what they do, not just how they are organized to do it. In other words, the essence of a profession is its work, its legitimated claim to apply expert knowledge to a particular set of tasks which Abbott calls jurisdiction. Second, professions operate in an interdependent system—the "system of professions." He observed that they compete for the control of work, and that the jurisdictional boundaries among them are constantly disputed. Professions occupy a jurisdiction by filling a vacancy or fighting for legitimate control of it through a variety of channels—the legal system, public arena, and workplace. As a result, an adjustment by one profession inevitably sets off ripple effects that impact others. Third, many variables affect the content and control of work, including—and this is of relevance to our own research on the Army profession—technology, organizations, and culture. These three characteristics of a profession apply to the historical as well as the current competitions in which there has been Army involvement.

Arriving at these three characteristics as adduced in Abbott's construct ended our search for a theory in which to ground our research. We recalled that since the end of the Cold War, the Army had been embroiled in many such external competitions in a variety of settings, all having to do with the nature of the expert work to be done and whether the Army was the right institution to do it—e.g., counter-drug operations on the southern border, operations other than war in the Balkans, homeland security, and counter-terrorism prior to 11 September 2001. The Army's competitors within these jurisdictions ranged from other professions (the other military services and foreign armies) to other governmental agencies, private contractors, and nongovernmental organizations, both American and international.

Simultaneously, within its two internal jurisdictions (developing and adapting its abstract expert knowledge, and developing individual professionals to apply that knowledge discretionarily to new situations), the Army was "competing" with its own retirees and private corporations as it rapidly contracted out many functions during the "do-more-with-less" drawdown of the 1990s. Typical examples are the presentation of ROTC instruction and the writing of Army doctrine. In view of the direct relevance of Professor Abbott's work to our own research, we invited him to join us in our initial research project, and he graciously did so, providing the

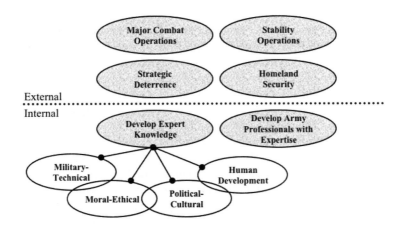

Figure 1-2. *Negotiated Jurisdictions of American Military Professions, 2004.*

keynote address at one conference and contributing to the first edition a very insightful chapter on the Army as profession.[61]

In conformity with his theory, Figure 1-2 presents a schematic diagram depicting the four external jurisdictions, mentioned in the previous paragraph, in which the Army profession currently competes. Also displayed are the two internal jurisdictions in which the Army as a profession develops and maintains its expert knowledge and develops Army professionals. It is this theoretical framework that provided a common structure and language for all of the researchers in both projects, those completed in 2000 and in 2004. Thus the reader will likely find at the beginning of most chapters in this anthology some discussion of the Abbott model and how it will be used in their authors' particular investigations.

Finally, in concluding this portion of the introductory discussion I must note that the selection of this model has not been without criticism. In this emerging age of strenuously enforced jointness, many in the Army, particularly at senior levels of leadership and within the retired ranks, are not familiar, nor comfortable, with discussing the idea that the Army, *like all professions*, is inherently "competitive." Nor are they normally familiar with the recent developments in the study of professions, particularly military ones, that postdate the writings of Huntington and Janowitz. Their acculturation into the profession and years of service lead them to believe, understandably, that the Army is purely a "servant" institution, accepting without question the work and jurisdictions assigned by its civilian masters, while eschewing "unseemly" competitive struggles with sister services over the corresponding roles and missions.

A second, and more cogent, criticism of the competition model, comes from those now deeply involved in transforming the Army, its doctrines, and its culture into what the current Chief of Staff, Gen. Peter Schoomaker, describes as "a campaign quality Army with joint and expeditionary capabilities," the core competencies of which are listed in the second epigraph to this chapter. The cogency of this criticism rests in the potential that some may view the Abbott framework adopted for our research and its results as reflected in the present anthology, as advocating a more "competitive" stance for the Army within the joint arena. In this view, the Abbott framework encourages a self-serving, uncooperative approach to the necessary and inevitable progression toward more effective integration of service capabilities.

In my opinion, however, such reservations are based on too narrow a conception of what Abbott's theory and the research-based arguments contained herein mean by "competition." What is meant, and stated in most cases, is "negotiated competition," a dialectic accurately reflective of how the Army, through its strategic leaders, dialogues within the joint community and the interagency to settle upon future Army missions and capabilities. Competitions do not have to be uncooperative and hostile; that is certainly not the construction employed by Abbott, nor by our chapter authors.

Ultimately, however, it is those who will assimilate the chapters of this anthology as they develop themselves and other Army professionals, who will decide whether this concern is valid. In the interim, I assert with confidence that the Abbott framework in chapter after chapter herein has made for a richness of insight and understanding regarding the Army as profession that would never have been possible in the theoretical and analytic void existing after the Army stopped troubling itself as to the meaning of profession. From that point, there simply was no central conception or language within which Army professionals could discuss the real state of their profession or their role within it.[62] And without such deep understanding, there would not now be the rapidly growing convictions among strategic leaders of the Army that theirs is indeed a profession and that they must lead it as a profession (not as business or bureaucracy) with a clear focus on its expert knowledge, the development of its professionals, and the state of its jurisdictional competitions, both internal and external.

Thus far in this chapter, I have established the context within which both research projects were conducted. I turn in Section II of this chapter to what we learned from these efforts.

Section II: The State of the Army Profession, 2000 and 2004

We documented nine conclusions from the 2000 research project, summarized below as a benchmark for the reader.[63] These nine conclusions were introduced with the following capsule condensation: *The Army profession is seriously compromised by excessive bureaucratization of major leadership and management systems and is so perceived by the individual members of the Army officer corps.*

Conclusion 1—*In 2000, the Army's bureaucratic nature outweighed and compromised its professional nature. This was true in practice, but, of greater importance,* *it was regarded as true in the minds of the officer corps. Officers did not share a common understanding of the Army profession, and many of them accepted the pervasiveness of bureaucratic norms and behavior as natural and appropriate. This was the core conclusion of the project, underlying everything that followed. Throughout its history the Army has had to balance its two natures: the Army is at once a government bureaucracy and a military profession. Although this dual nature has resulted in tension and stress for the Army, both aspects were necessary. However, if the Army is to provide the military capabilities expected of and needed by a 21st century military force, its professional nature must dominate. Our conclusion was that it did not; and in fact the ascendancy of the institution's bureaucratic nature had undermined professional identity and performance.*

Our research indicated that the officer corps shared basic Army values, but members did not have a shared understanding of the Army as a profession; they had little of a profession's common language, conceptions, or identity.[64] Many saw themselves as employees—as mere occupational timeservers—rather than professionals and members of a life-long calling. This inclination was further highlighted by their uncritical acceptance of bureaucratic norms and behavior, which had been reinforced internally by pervasive, bureaucratic Army management systems and externally by a decade of force- structure cuts and under-resourcing. Increasingly centralized management systems had shifted decision-making power upward while eroding the flexibility and authority of responsible professionals on the scene. The bureaucratizing effect of this movement had been compounded by a barren fiscal environment that pushed leaders toward efficiency measurements and "doing more with less." As a result, in 2000 the Army was more bureaucracy than profession— more preoccupied with efficiency than effectiveness—and was perceived as such by its members, including the officer corps.

To tip the balance back toward the preeminence of its professional nature, to restore the Army profession as a proud calling for experts in national defense, the Army's strategic leaders needed to cry halt to that trend, and then to initiate the process of regenerating a professional culture. In other words, the Army's strategic leaders were going to have to discover the time to get serious about professional renewal. In the broadest terms, they needed first to work to reverse the prevailing conceptions, that is, the leader attitudes, language, and behavior demonstrated throughout the Army, and then they needed to begin work to reform the Army's management systems. Key decisions had to be approached from the perspective of a profession first, rather than a government bureaucracy or a business venture. The most important of these key decisions was addressed in our next conclusion.

Conclusion 2—*The Army needed to redraw the map of its expert knowledge and then inform and reform its educational and developmental systems accordingly, resolving any debate over the appropriate expertise of America's Army.*

The fact that expert knowledge can be embodied in people for professional practice in new and unforeseen circumstances is the hallmark of professions. Professions establish their position in society by adapting, extending, developing, and refining their expert knowledge. Furthermore, professions negotiate with their client the issues of where and when this knowledge will be applied. The scope and boundaries of a profession's expertise, as well as those of related professions, make up the "map" of its expert knowledge. This map then provides a framework for professional education, development, and human resource management, as well as other institutional systems.

Since the end of the Cold War, the Army's external environment had changed dramatically. Adapting to these changes required significant shifts in the map of the profession's expert knowledge. Although the Army had debated these changes, it had not conclusively determined the new scope and boundaries; it had not redrawn the map of its expert knowledge. As a result, its organizational systems did not support the current map, and appeared even more maladapted for the future map. Although the Army was performing an increasing number of so-called "nontraditional" missions (a misnomer if there ever was one), its primary organizational systems—i.e., structuring, manning, equipping, training the force, and assessing its readiness—remained focused primarily on fighting conventional wars. This irresolution had resulted in professional education and development systems that were not clearly linked to the Army's evolving expert knowledge.

This fragile coupling between the Army education/developmental systems and current mission requirements had been further weakened by the Army's diminishing professional claim on the development of its members and doctrine. As contractors took on ever-greater roles—in professional education, ranging from Reserve Officer Training Corps instruction, to CGSC curriculum development, to general officer executive education; in analysis and writing of doctrine; in staff functions on the General Staff—the Army profession was abdicating its responsibility for performing these critical elements of its professional life. Unlike a business, for which the education and development of employees is typically a non-core function, the education and development of the members of the Army profession are its core, as are the creation and development of the doctrinal principles by which professional work will be undertaken.

Conclusion 3—*Since people are the Army's most important resource, understanding them should be an uppermost component of its expert knowledge, and Army management systems should be aligned to reflect that knowledge and its priority.*

Knowledge pertaining to people and human development is the foundation of Army expertise. Yet if resources are the measure, then in 2000 the Army's desire and ability to understand people fell well behind its desire to understand hardware and software. Technological research dominated funding, billets, and priorities while the human domains—behavioral science, social science, and physical development research programs—were under-funded and out of date. In the previous decade, the Army had slashed funding for research in the human disciplines of the social and behavioral sciences. Rather than pursuing cutting-edge knowledge in these areas, the Army based much of its "expert" knowledge of human behavior, specifically human behavior during war, on research done over 50 years ago. These earlier findings had not benefited from the increasingly sophisticated research methods and analytic tools that have produced over recent decades more reliable and compelling findings about such subjects as unit cohesion.

The Army had not well integrated extensive study of human behavior from such disciplines as psychology, sociology, and political science into the career-long professional education system. These disciplines have particular relevance to the Army's internal jurisdiction because decisions regarding personnel management are grounded in strategic leaders' understanding of people. Therefore, since the Army's understanding of human resources had fallen behind cutting-edge scientific knowledge, its management systems had not evolved in tandem with the scientific understanding of human behavior.

Conclusion 4—*The most important management concept needing alignment with the demands of the Army profession is career progression.*

The Army has historically reconciled its dual nature as both bureaucracy and profession through its system of career management, wherein a unique combination of centralized bureaucracy and individual development balanced the institution's conflicting natures. However, the evolution of Army personnel management practices over recent decades has shifted the balance away from individual development and toward a lock-step, centralized system that requires all officers to follow specific timelines and fill certain positions if they are to succeed. If they did not, most officers had no choice but to leave the Army. The result reduced variety in the careers of successful officers and a strong reluctance to pursue opportunities outside of the mainstream; officer development was tailored to neither the officer nor the Army, but to the promotion and assignment systems.

Sadly, this rigid system had evolved at an inopportune time for the Army; rather than needing officers with essentially identical career patterns, this was a time when the Army required educational, skill, and experiential diversity in its pool of members. To its credit, the Army moved slightly in this direction with the adoption of OPMS XXI, offering a limited degree of specialization. However, the rigidity of officer career timelines actually tightened under the new system. Unfortunately, officers themselves fought against the Army's specialization needs because the promotion, assignment, and educational systems did not in their view support it. Few promising officers were willing to risk their career (and with it their family's welfare) to pursue a career track outside the norm.

Officially, an Army career was still based on the traditional but increasingly obsolescent idea of a single occupational skill or identity characterizing individuals for a working lifetime. But though the system remained intact, the profession's younger members, like their peers across America, were seeking alternatives to the traditional concept of a 20- or 30-year career with a single company or institution. Unlike their predecessors, these young people saw jobs and positions as opportunities to gain the individual expertise and developmental experiences needed for personal growth and long-term upward mobility. Short employment contracts and increased inter-job movement pervaded the motives of the generations filling the Army's junior ranks. By and large they entered the Army neutral in their attitude toward a lifetime career. Far from winning them over to the idea of a long-term commitment, however, the dominance of the Army's bureaucratic nature in its personnel management systems was accomplishing the exact opposite. Young officers became cynical about "check-the-block" career management and tended to see the Army as just another transient job.

To accommodate this generational shift within the demands of a military profession, the Army needed to accept radical change in its concept of "career." The new conception needed to dilute the centralized authority of the "face-to-space" personnel management system, allowing senior officers in the field more flexibility to develop individually the professionals in their units, truly complementing the institutional and self-development components of the Army's professional development system. It should have encouraged officers to seek experiences outside of the Army organization and joint force structure, providing knowledge and expertise that comes from working closely with other government agencies, international organizations, educational institutions, and even businesses. It also required a review of, and perhaps consolidation within, the Army's commissioned and noncommissioned rank structures and progressions, a review that should have sought to identify the singular needs of the Army profession, those that are quite different from the other two military professions. Further, the Army's sole reliance on an internal labor market was no longer appropriate; the opportunity for lateral entries and exits with later returns needed to be created to enable the development of specialists to the degree needed by a 21st century Army. Lastly, this reformed system should have reversed the trend for higher-level defense bureaucracies to homogenize personnel policies across America's three military professions.

Conclusion 5—*Military character and the professional ethic were the foundation for the trust the American people place in their military and the foundation for the trust Army officers place in their profession.*

No matter how extensively the Army must transform nor how much of the profession must be redefined, we concluded that one foundation must remain unchanged: by the nature of the Army profession, only individuals of firm moral character could discharge adequately their professional obligations to the nation and to the soldiers they are called upon to lead—good officers, good professionals, are first of all men and women of good character.

The Army profession, because of its responsibility for wielding deadly force to defend the nation and the Constitution, had developed over two centuries an ethic that provided objective norms and standards for the behavior of the profession and its members. This ethic is cooperative and cohesive in spirit, selfless but meritocratic, and fundamentally anti-individualistic and anti-careerist. It required that members transcend the norms of the pack, particularly when under chaotic, stressful, and fearful situations such as combat.

Although the jurisdictions within which the Army was operating presented new and different challenges for the Army, the need for foundational professional ethics remained. This requirement stemmed both from the American people and from Army professionals themselves. One of the strongest findings in our research was the importance that Army officers correctly placed on the profession's ethics, particularly the duty concept and the moral courage of Army leaders. Their commitment to a culture of candor—clear truth-telling by all leaders at all levels at all times—was universally seen as an absolute requirement.

Conclusion 6—*The "trust gap" between junior and senior Army officers, the junior and senior members of the profession, had reached dangerously dysfunctional levels.*

This gap, which tears at the sinews of vertical cohesion in the chain of command, was both a cause and effect of the Army profession's inability to inspire and retain officers, company grade and field grade. In one sense, this conclusion was not new—the Army has long had, and likely always will have, some degree of disjunction between the outlooks of junior officers and those of their seniors.[65] This is the unavoidable result of perspectives informed by different levels of responsibility and years of experience within the profession.

However, the gap in 2000, documented by numerous investigations, had widened to a degree that threatened the Army's core functionality, as evidenced most prominently by the continued exodus of well-qualified officers into civilian life.[66] Perhaps more than civilian occupations, trust in the military goes to the heart of the profession's ethic and therefore to its effectiveness on the battlefield. Unless commanders establish a culture of trust within Army units, soldiers will not feel free to tell the truth, and without transparent honesty in interpersonal relations and official reporting systems, effectiveness suffers. This downward spiral induces micromanagement on the part of leaders, and risks adverse responses on the part of followers.

Conclusion 7—*The Army faced increasing jurisdictional competitions with new competitors. Thus its jurisdictional boundaries needed to be constantly negotiated and clarified by officers comfortable at the bargaining table and skilled in treating with professional colleagues on matters touching the profession's civil-military and political-military boundaries.*

The Army's competitors had multiplied well beyond the group comprising its traditional rivals—the maritime and air-space military professions. By 2000 the Army faced professional pressure from other professions, occupations, businesses, governmental agencies, nongovernmental agencies, and international organizations. One cause of this increased competition was the Army's expansion into arenas across the spectrum of conflict since the end of the Cold War—drug wars, border patrols, homeland defense, disaster assistance, and so on. While the Army had expanded its missions into new jurisdictions, other organizations had pursued work in the Army's traditional fields. There were private corporations providing logistical support during Army operations, while the U.S. Marines were executing inland expeditionary missions traditionally assigned to the Army.

This increased competition facing the Army was no different than that confronting other professions in the western world as they competed for legitimacy. If there is a difference, it is that the Army appeared unaware that it was in a long-term, in fact perpetual, struggle to defend its current jurisdictions and to determine other jurisdictions in which it should seek legitimacy. Throughout this jurisdictional battlefield, the Army was proceeding too often in an analytically superficial, haphazard, and expedient manner. The boundaries of the profession's jurisdiction were

unclear to those outside the profession, confusing them as to the optimum allocation of forces and responsibility for undertaking military operations. Even more disconcerting, the boundaries were unclear to members of the Army profession itself,
thus weakening their professional identity and commitment. This jurisdictional
ambiguity made it appropriate for the nation's civilian leadership to ask the Army
to undertake most any task, and it made it difficult for the Army to advise otherwise. Since effective advice-giving by the Army's strategic leaders increasingly necessitates expertise in negotiating at these critical political interfaces, the profession
needed a larger cohort of leaders at all levels well developed in the skills and norms
of such civil-military and political-military relations.

As a corollary to this conclusion, we noted that the boundaries *within* the Army
profession itself had also become unclear. As the Army outsourced more and more
inherently professional tasks to private corporations that employ retired military
members, it was implicitly if not explicitly acknowledging the continued professional affiliation of these former members. However, the nature of their affiliation
with the Army was unclear. Although often committed and loyal, these former professionals no longer had the same legal and fiduciary obligations to the nation and
the Army profession. Instead they had strong ties to for-profit commercial firms
with goals quite different from and often incongruent with the Army's. Thus it was
with some peril to its own legitimacy that the Army treated these retired professionals as an extension of itself but without imposing the bonds of professional
membership—certification, licensing, and legal obligation.

Conclusion 8—*Contrary to their preoccupations with technological transformation,
renewing the Army as a profession required strategic leaders to focus rather on (1) the
profession's expert knowledge, (2) the development of professionals (future and present), and (3) the Army's jurisdictional competitions.*

Owing to its unique characteristics as a profession, strategic leadership of the
Army differs from that of other types of organizations, such as a government
bureaucracy or a commercial business. Professions are built upon expert knowledge
and expertise, and the embodiment of that knowledge in future and existing professionals. Thus, leaders of a profession must focus on updating and redefining
expert knowledge through programs of research, investigation, and analysis. They
adapt the profession's capability to apply that expert knowledge to present and
future situations; and they concentrate the profession's efforts and resources on
imparting this expertise to its members, and inculcating in them a professional ethic.

Professions also engage in competition and negotiation for legitimate jurisdictions within which to apply their expertise. Therefore, the task of the profession's
strategic leaders is to identify its competitors, carefully analyze the competition,
renegotiate jurisdictions, and create and maintain professional legitimacy to ensure
that the profession can attract new members and compete successfully so as to
remain a viable profession. Since jurisdictions and legitimacy are strongly influenced
if not determined from outside the profession, these activities require strategic leaders with high degrees of familiarity with external constituencies such as the press,
the Executive, the Congress, international agencies, and the American people. Such

literacy appears best developed over many assignments and years of interaction with these constituents. Thus assignments outside the Army's traditional operator mold, perhaps in other government agencies or international organizations or even civilian corporations, are essential components of the career of a rising military leader. Yet, as we noted in Conclusion 4, the prevailing Army career pattern in 2000 discouraged sufficient numbers of officers from venturing out of the mainstream and into these less touted but strategically relevant billets.

Conclusion 9—*Though daunting, renewing the Army profession and redressing the balance between bureaucracy and profession were not impossible tasks; they had been done before and quite successfully so.*

As a profession, the Army had accomplished a similar revitalization in its recent past, roughly from 1972 to 1985. During that renewal, a handful of extraordinary strategic leaders redefined the profession's jurisdiction by focusing on the Soviet threat in the European theater. They reestablished the Army's identity as a profession that could "fight outnumbered and win." The ensuing war-fighting and training revolution produced a transformed Army profession of immense effectiveness, as exemplified in the first Gulf War. By 2000, the Army faced a more complex international environment, though with far less intellectual consensus among its leaders. Yet, the experience of the 1970s and 1980s indicated that the Army profession's renewal could, and must, be an essential element of the ongoing transformation.

The State of the Army Profession, 2004

When viewed as a profession, then, how much has the Army changed during the period from 2000 to 2004, or from the state described above to what is visible within the Army today? To provide insights into those changes is the purpose of this closing section of our introduction. I say "insights" to indicate the more limited nature of the conclusions that can be drawn from this second study, which focused only on the Army's internal jurisdictions and was executed over a shorter period. Recall that in the first project we were looking into both internal and external jurisdictions, drawing conclusions as to change in the Army over an extended period, from the end of the Cold War (and in some cases even earlier) to the end of the drawdown at the end of the century.

The last decade of the 20th century was one of massive change to which the Army profession had yet to adapt when the post-11 September 2001 demands were placed on the profession. The end of the Cold War, which coincided with the culmination of other shifts in the organization of Western post-industrial societies, had drastically altered the expectations of where, and more importantly how, their professions of arms would apply military expertise.[67] These expectations were only heightened for the U.S. Army, both in scope and in degree, by the initiation of the global war on terrorism.

Today, in the new strategic reality of protracted war, the Army is exceptionally well resourced financially and is being aggressively reshaped—in the current language, "transformed"— while simultaneously prosecuting the antiterrorist war at what appear to be unsustainable rates of repetitive deployments for both active and reserve components. The profession's current leadership believes that these circumstances provide an unprecedented "window of opportunity" for continued change,[68] and doubtless the researchers in this project would agree to a point. They would stipulate, however, that it is much too early to see with any certainty what the lasting effects on the *Army as profession* will be from this intensely war-focused (at least for the armed forces and their families) transformational period.

As has already been briefly noted, so far as the year 2000 **Conclusion 1** is concerned, the primary insight from the second project is self-evident and positive—the Army is a much more professional institution at its cutting edge today than in 2000, and the reason is that the units of the field Army are continuously at war and have been practicing their art daily since the tragic events of 11 September 2001. But whether that positive change spills over to the institutional side of the Army, where the real work of its internal jurisdictions is done, and whether any such change bubbles up the hierarchical structure beyond the battalions and brigades deployed to the Middle East region, is a question for a future research project.

Further, what we believe we should be observing within a profession during such a dynamic period as this is a huge expansion, followed by refinement and reprioritization, of the profession's knowledge base and in the methods of application of that expert knowledge. We would expect to see this pattern evident as the Army does its work in all of its external jurisdictions (see again Figure 1-2), but more so in the wartime jurisdictions of major combat and stability operations. Such dynamism within the profession's expert knowledge and current practice should then be generating changes throughout the Army's leadership and management systems—from organizational structure to applied technology, from measures of readiness to measures of effectiveness, from military training systems to professional military education systems, and from human development systems to the personnel systems that then utilize these professionals throughout their careers.

In the second research project, we did find that the knowledge base of the profession is rapidly expanding, primarily as a result of the necessity to be effective in the post-combat phases of the wars in Afghanistan and Iraq. Much of this expansion was into knowledge areas within which the Army formerly was reasonably expert, for example in counterinsurgency operations. But this expertise had been lost, along with that in several other fields, and was unavailable when its application was demanded by the Army's client. Further, there has not yet been time for that practice-driven expansion to be absorbed, processed, and refined within the institutional Army in any sufficiently substantive manner to drive essential changes in the institution's developmental and management systems. Thus, the 2000 **Conclusion 2** (urgent necessity to redraw the profession's map of expert knowledge) is perhaps even more valid today than originally.

Unless the size of the Army increases appreciably, the Army cannot continue—especially when the postwar flood of combat-driven resources inevitably slows to a trickle—to expect its junior leaders and lower-level units to be effective at such a wide range of tasks as they are now pursuing under the exigencies of war against a hyper-adaptive enemy. Being able to operate across "the full spectrum of operations" may be sound doctrine for the Army profession as a whole, but recent experience is showing quite clearly that it is misleading bureaucratic jargon when applied only to the lower echelons of the Army. They cannot do it all, all of the time. The current focus on leader "adaptability" at that level is overdue and much needed, but even adaptable leaders at the brigade level and below cannot make up for what the strategic leaders of the profession fail to do.

Assuming the global war eventually recedes, sharp delineations in missions and tasks will have to be renegotiated in the Army's external environment and then applied internally, some likely by role specialization among units, to enable the Army to successfully resize and reprioritize its expert knowledge, which should then rationalize its developmental systems (see Chapter 9 of the present anthology). To pose a single example, does the Army want to reclaim the jurisdiction of post-conflict governance and reconstruction tasks (in joint campaign language, Phase 4 operations) to ensure future unity of effort with its own security and stabilization operations? (See Chapters 11 and 15 of the present anthology.)

Simply stated, the boundaries of the Army profession, delineated by the content and relative priorities within its clusters of expert knowledge, are what the profession's strategic leaders use to decide what functions to contract out, which to contract in, how to negotiate new operational concepts and support arrangements within the joint community, etc. In other words, they are used, whether explicitly or not, to make most of the truly strategic decisions they make. But most of that critical readjustment of boundaries through a comprehensive mapping of what the expert knowledge of the Army profession should be in 2010, remains to be started.

The next two conclusions in the 2000 study had to do with human resources. **Conclusion 3** described how far behind current scholarship the Army profession really was in the field of human development, a surprising result given that the prosecution of war is a quintessentially human endeavor. **Conclusion 4** noted the need for radical restructuring of the Army officer career model. Within the human resources area, the second research project adds to our understanding of the identities now used to develop Army officers (see Chapter 6 of the present anthology) and offers insights into the motivations and obligations of future joint officers, perhaps even as part of their own military profession (see Chapters 7 and 10 of the present anthology).

There are also new insights into Y-Generation officers and soldiers from whom the Army of the 21st century is being built, and who are performing so admirably in the Middle East region today (see Chapter 22 of the present anthology). The primacy of spouses and children in their individual values, which influences the manner in which they seek to integrate work and family, holds potential problems for the Army, even after the pressure of repetitive deployments is relieved somewhat later in the antiterrorist war (see Chapters 21 and 24 of the present anthology). Moreover, they will be less responsive to the type of leadership techniques the Army is, unwisely, prone to borrow from American businesses (see Chapter 23 of the present anthology).

The issue of career is complex for both the active and reserve components, though in different ways. Without doubt, the Cold War D-day mobilization concept for calling reserve component professionals to active duty is now so severely ruptured by the repetitive deployments to Afghanistan and Iraq that a radical new approach will have to be conceived. (see Chapter 26 of the present anthology). There is simply no going back to the old model, even if the Congressionally mandated structures that defined and supported it for decades have not yet been dismantled. Certainly this is one of the truly urgent and strategic decisions yet to be made by the leaders of the Army profession and those above and outside the profession. For active-duty officers, the recent initiation of a serious review of OPMS 3 holds hope for more than incremental change in the career development and utilization of Army professionals. But however timely, it is clear that such change, if it is to be effective, will have to offer substantive, and in some cases radical, options for mid-level professionals—rapidly reversing the disastrous decline in advanced civil schooling; offering breaks in service after multiple deployments; extending active-duty careers to 35-40 years, thus ending the pernicious idea of "a second career"; etc. It is far too early to tell whether this hope will be fulfilled.

The 2000 **Conclusion 5** (individual moral character of Army professionals as the foundation of trust with the client) noted that a transformation which did not address the issues of trust, both between senior leaders and the officer/enlisted ranks and between the Army profession and the American people, was a hollow transformation indeed. In this context, the 2000 **Conclusion 7** also noted the increasingly undefined boundary of the profession, especially as occasioned by the use of retired officers in professional roles. It was suggested that their ambiguous professional status be clarified and resolved through appropriate certification, licensing, and legally imposed obligation. But rather than being clarified, in the ensuing four years the boundary has become even more blurred. Are private security firms and intelligence interrogators in Afghanistan and Iraq a part of the profession? Are they required to abide by the same professional ethics? Faced with such questions, the updated research project focused on the profession's moral and ethical expert knowledge in a more penetrating way than did the first, a wise choice given the devastating failures to apply the relevant Army expertise at Abu Ghraib and elsewhere in Iraq and Afghanistan.[69]

No profession can survive if it loses the trust of it client; and the Army now has much to do to restore its credibility as a self-policing institution. But beyond the unacceptable behavior of individual soldiers and the as-yet unaccounted-for failures in officer leadership lies a much more vexing issue—how to adapt the 20th century moral and legal foundations that were codified to "rightly" fight conventional wars between nation-states to the new reality of combating terrorism from nonstate sources (see Chapter 18 of the present anthology). This is an asymmetric form of warfare utterly without moral boundaries whose sheer brutality can erode adherence by Army professionals to their own warrior ethic. Thus, not only tactical adaptation but also moral inculcation must be at the forefront of the profession's approach to this issue.

Also to be discussed are the ethical aspects of the evolution toward joint warfare, a form which we have seen accelerated in the global antiterrorist war in which Army forces deploy and fight under joint command, execute increasingly joint concepts of operation, and are sustained by service logistics flowing through joint strategic distribution processes. In this environment what is the joint military ethic; where is it promulgated and codified? Or is it still the case that there are extant only individual service ethics, representing as they do the three war-fighting professions (see Chapter 19 of the present anthology)? And if this latter case is so, given their differences, to which service ethic does the joint community adhere? The converging movement toward defense transformation will continue, of course, but before we go too far in the inevitable homogenization of the cultures of the war-fighting professions, this void in joint military ethics must be addressed, particularly as America's land forces practice their art within the moral wasteland of antiterrorist war.

Finally, we came to understand from the 2000 project that captains and majors cannot themselves make officership into a profession—as with all professions, only the strategic leaders can address effectively the necessary balance between profession and bureaucracy by conforming bureaucratic management systems within professional molds (see 2000 **Conclusion 8**). Thus, the 2004 project intentionally focused more on the development and utilization of strategic leaders, both joint and Army (see Chapters 27 and 28 of the present anthology), even investigating the seldom-discussed role within the profession of general officers (see Chapter 25 of the present anthology).

Few things could be more difficult for most of the Army's strategic leaders, even with short background-expanding assignments outside the profession, than to pick up after two decades of intensive Army service the political-cultural expertise to lead effectively at the boundaries of the profession where strategic leaders do their work. Thus one researcher focused specifically on a set of norms to guide the personal and professional development of Army strategic leaders for service within the joint and interagency arenas (see chapter 30 of the present anthology). Overall the research showed that much has been accomplished in this area in just the past few years, even though the Army's doctrine for developing its strategic leaders has yet to be re-codified. True, the wartime demands to decentralize have mitigated the bureaucratic micromanagement observed as being so omnipresent during the first research project. But it is also the case that by learning from the vivid examples of successful civil-military relations in the Army's own past (see Chapter 33 of the present anthology) and by initiating innovative, focused efforts to increase their own awareness and capabilities, Army strategic leaders today are increasingly more adept and comfortable working at the civilian-military interface. Perhaps with even greater confidence than in the 2000 **Conclusion 9**, we can state today: *"Though daunting, renewing the Army profession and redressing the balance between bureaucracy and profession are not impossible tasks; they have been done before and quite successfully so."*

Conclusion

There are thousands of professionals in the Army today, those who go to work each day in war and at home station seeking little more than the opportunity to serve their country by improving their expertise and applying it to the tasks at hand. To us, these professionals include anyone who has made and is living a resolute commitment to a lifetime of ethical service in the Army profession—officer, noncommissioned officer, or Department of Army civilian. Many others aspire to such status, and will doubtless someday attain it.

But among these professionals one group must be singled out for special responsibility in this period of high demands and dynamic change. From the members of the Army officer corps, as the commissioned agents of the American people responsible for the continued stewardship of the profession and its soldiers in the global war on terrorism, more is expected legally and morally. *It is specifically for the professional education and development of these servants of the nation that this second edition has been prepared.*

We have no doubt that under their leadership, and that of the superb noncommissioned officers and civilians with whom they serve, the Army profession will negotiate this transition and the war on terrorists in the decade ahead with a record of remarkable effectiveness, emerging well prepared to continue the Army's service to the nation.

Notes

1. Walter F. Ulmer, Joseph J. Collins, and T. O. Jacobs, *American Military Culture in the Twenty-First Century: A Report of the CSIS National Security Program* (Washington, DC: Center for Strategic and International Studies, 2000).

2. *Army Training and Leader Development Panel Report (Officers): Final Report* (Ft. Leavenworth, KS: U.S. Army Combined Arms Center, 2001). For a detailed analysis of this internal Army research effort, see Don M. Snider and Gayle L. Watkins, proj. directors, Lloyd J. Matthews, ed., *The Future of the Army Profession* (Boston, MA: McGraw-Hill, 2002), chap. 22. Hereinafter referred to as FAP I.

3. See Joseph J. Collins and T.O. Jacobs, "Trust in the Profession of Arms," FAP I, chap. 3.

4. FAP I, 3.

5. The Army Budget for FY04 (TOA, current dollars) was $95.8b. The Army also received that year $40.6b in supplemental appropriations and adjustments for the global war on terrorism producing a total outlay of $136.4b. In FY97, close to the end of the drawdown, the Army budget was $63b, less than one-half of the FY04 amount. Data accessed 26 November 2004 from: http://www.asafm.army.mil.

6. I refer to the reelection of President Lincoln in 1864.

7. The classic definition of constabulary forces is as follows: "The military establishment becomes a constabulary force when it is continuously prepared to act, committed to the minimum use of force, and seeks viable international relations rather than victory because it has incorporated a protective military posture." See Morris Janowitz, *The Professional Soldier* (New York: The Free Press, 1960), 418.

8. Author's conversations with Lt. Gen. Scott Wallace, Commander, U. S. Army Combined Arms Command, Ft. Leavenworth, at West Point, NY, 3 June 2004.

9. This is the stated transformation goal of Army leadership, Acting Secretary Les Brownlee and Chief of Staff, Gen. Peter Schoomaker. See their article, "Serving a Nation at War," *Parameters* 34 (Summer 2004): 4-23.

10. The principal guidance for service transformation planning is practically devoid of any content on human resources. See Donald H. Rumsfeld, *Transformation Planning Guidance* (Washington, DC: Office of the Secretary of Defense, April 2003), accessed at: http://www.oft.osd.mil/library/library_files/document_129_Transformation_Planning_Guidance_April_2003_1.pdf.

11. See Otto Kreisher, "Fewer Military Vets Among Ranks of New Members of Congress," *San Diego Union*, 10 November 2004 accessed 11 November 2004 at: http://ebird.afis.osd.mil/ebfiles/e20041111336510.html.

12. Don M. Snider and Leonard Lira, "The Future of the Army Profession: Phase II—Senior Conference XLI," *Assembly* (September-October 2004): 52-54.

13. See *Study on Military Professionalism* (Carlisle Barracks, PA: U.S. Army War College, 1970). For the official history of this period, see Robert K. Griffith, *Today's Army Wants to Join You: The US Army's Transition from the Draft to an All-Volunteer Force* (Washington, DC: Center of Military History, 1995); and Anne W. Chapman, *The Army's Training Revolution, 1973-1990* (Ft. Monroe, VA: TRADOC, 1990). For a very readable current history of the same events, see James Kitfield, *Prodigal Soldiers* (New York: Simon and Schuster, 1995).

14. Samuel Huntington, *The Soldier and the State: The Theory of Civil-Military Relations* (Cambridge, MA: Belknap Press of Harvard University, 1957), 7. I am indebted to Prof. Richard Swain, USMA, for noting one earlier use of the term officership, found on pages 11-12 of the original version (1950) of *The Armed Forces Officer* (Washington, DC: Office of the Secretary of Defense, 1950): "These two qualities of mind and heart [goodwill, courage] are of the essence of sound officership."

15. Edward G. Coffman, "The Long Shadow of The Soldier and the State," *Journal of Military History* 55 (Spring 1991): 69-82.

16. This is the author's observation on returning to the Academy as a member of the civilian faculty in 1995. For writings contemporaneous with Huntington, see, e.g., Walter Millis, *Arms and Men* (1956; New Brunswick, NJ: Rutgers University Press, 1981); and Janowitz, *The Professional Soldier* (1960).

17. However, though not a formal study, Col. (Ret.) Lloyd J. Matthews published in 1994 a comprehensive case in behalf of the proposition that the military was indeed a bona fide profession, in fact a proud and honorable calling. See his article "Is the Military Profession Legitimate?" *Army* Magazine, January 1994, 14-23.

18. Recollections of this period have been sharpened by access to portions of General Christman's oral history, provided by Academy Historian, Dr. Stephen Grove; e-mail and telephonic communication with the author, 28 October 2004.

19. For a sense of the intensity of the debate over military culture, see the four articles published in *Orbis* 43 (Winter 1999), particularly Don M. Snider, "An Uninformed Debate on Military Culture," pp.11-26.

20. The first analysis published by this Center, in conjunction with the Strategic Studies Institute of the U.S. Army War College, focused exactly on these ethical issues. See Don Snider, John Nagl, and Tony Pfaff, *Army Professionalism, the Military Ethic, and Officership in the 21st Century* (Carlisle Barracks, PA: U.S. Army War College, Strategic Studies Institute, 1999).

21. See *The Cadet Leader Development System*, USMA Circular 1-101, published by the Office of the Superintendent, U.S. Military Academy, West Point, NY, June 2002.

22. These four identities of the commissioned officer will be quite visible in the new edition of the *Armed Forces Officer*, now being prepared by a tri-Academy committee, chaired by Prof. Richard Swain of West Point.

23. For the most recent analysis in depth of this continuing debate, one which sets it in correct political and strategic context, see Colin S. Gray, *Strategy for Chaos: Revolutions in Military Affairs and the Evidence of History* (London: Frank Cass Publishing, 2002).

24. President George W. Bush, at The Citadel, Charleston, SC, 11 December 2001, accessed at: http://www.whitehouse.gov/news/releases/2001/12/20011211-6.html.

25. I say "most influential" simply because much of what these authorities believe has been adopted by the Bush administration under the rubric "Defense Transformation." For the early literature of this school, see, Alvin Toffler and Heidi Toffler, *War and Anti-War: Survival at the Dawn of the 21st Century* (Boston, MA: Brown and Little, 1993); John Arquilla and David

Ronfelt, "Cyber War is Coming!" *Comparative Strategy* 12, no. 2 (1993): 141-165; Andrew F. Krepinevich, "Cavalry to Computers: The Pattern of Military Revolutions," *National Interest* (Fall 1994): 30-42; and Eliot A. Cohen, "A Revolution in Warfare," *Foreign Affairs* 75, no. 2 (March-April 1996): 37-54.

26. For the Army's version of that war, see Robert H. Scales, Jr., *Certain Victory* (Washington, DC: Office of the Chief of Staff, U.S. Army, 1993). For an alternative understanding of what, other than technology, made the Army so successful in the first Iraq War, see Stephen Biddle, "Victory Misunderstood: What the Gulf War Tells Us about the Future of Conflict," *International Security* 21 (Fall 1996): 139-79.

27. See Joseph S. Nye and William Owens, "America's Information Edge," *Foreign Affairs* 75, no. 2 (March-April 1996): 20-36.

28. For examples, see Adm. William Owens, *Lifting the Fog of War* (Baltimore, MD: Johns Hopkins University Press, 2001); Michael O'Hanlon, *Technological Change and the Future of Warfare* (Washington, DC: The Brookings Institution, 2000); Stuart J.D. Swartzstein, *The Information Revolution and National Security* (Washington, DC: Center for Strategic and International Studies, 1996); Stuart E. Johnson and Martin Libicki, *Dominant Battlespace Knowledge* (Washington, DC: National Defense University, Institute for National Strategic Studies, 1995).

29. See Robert Scales, *Future Warfare Anthology*, revised edition (Carlisle Barracks, PA; Army War College, Strategic Studies Institute, 2000); and *Yellow Smoke: The Future of Land Warfare for America's Military* (New York: Rowan and Littlefield, 2003); Douglas MacGregor, *Transformation Under Fire* (Westport, CT: Praeger Publishers, 2003) and *Breaking the Phalanx* (Westport, CT: Praeger Publishers, 1997; and Andrew Krepinevich, *Transforming the Legions: The Army and the Future of Land Warfare* (Washington, DC: Center for Strategic and Budgetary Assessments, 2004).

30. See Stephen Biddle, "Assessing Theories of Future Warfare, *Security Studies* 8, No. 1 (Autumn 1998): 1-74; and *Military Power: Explaining Victory and Defeat in Modern Battle* (Princeton, NJ: Princeton University Press, 2004); A. J. Bacevich, "Preserving the Well-Bred Horse, *National Interest* (Fall 1994): 43-49; and Williamson Murray and Allen R. Millett, eds., *Military Innovation in the Interwar Period* (Cambridge, England: Cambridge University Press, 1996).

31. For an overview of the Bush administration initiatives, see *Military Transformation: A Strategic Approach* (Washington, DC: Office of the Director, Force Transformation, Office of the Secretary of Defense, Fall 2003).

32. See Deborah D. Avant, *Political Institutions and Military Change* (Ithaca, NY: Cornell University Press, 1994); Elizabeth Kier, *Imagining War: French and British Military Doctrines between the Wars* (Princeton, NJ: University Press, 1999); Stephen Peter Rosen, *Innovation and the Modern Military: Winning the Next War* (Ithaca, NY: Cornell University Press, 1991); Theo Ferrell, "Figuring Out Fighting Organizations," *Journal of Strategic Studies* 19, no. 1 (March 1996): 122-135; Michael James Meese, "Defense Decision Making under Budget Stringency: Explaining Downsizing in the United States Army" (Ph.D. diss., Princeton University, May 2000); and Emily O. Goldman and Leslie C. Eliason, eds., *The Diffusion of Military Technology and Ideas* (Stanford, CA: Stanford University Press, 2003).

33. These are the fields of new institutionalism and principle-agent based theories of organizational behavior.

34. See Peter Senge, *The Fifth Discipline* (New York, NY: Doubleday, 1990); and Emily O. Goldman, "The U.S. Military in Uncertain Times: Organizations, Ambiguity, and Strategic Adjustment," *Journal of Strategic Studies* 20, no. 2 (June 1997): 41-74. A recent Army Chief of Staff, Gen. Gordon Sullivan, adopted such an approach to Army modernization during his tenure. See Gordon R. Sullivan and Michael V. Harper, *Hope is Not a Method* (New York: Random House, Times Business, 1996).

35. In particular, the human element is given its due in the theorizing of Stephen Peter Rosen (*Innovation and the Modern Military: Winning the Next War*) and in the very illuminating set

of historical case studies produced by Williamson Murray and Allen Millet for OSD Net Assessments and later published as *Military Innovation in the Interwar Period.*

36. See discussion between the Defense press corps and the Director of Force Transformation within the Office of the Secretary of Defense, Rear Adm. (Ret.) Arthur K. Cebrowski, 27 November 2001, accessed at http://www.defenselink.mil/news/ Nov2001/t11272001_t1127ceb.html.

37. I say "proximately" as Gayle Watkins and I first published this matrix with only three clusters of knowledge for the Army profession. We later re-divided the knowledge, adding the fourth cluster, human development, focusing on the profession's necessary capacity to constantly develop its own practitioners. See Don M. Snider and Gayle Watkins, "The Future of Army Professionalism: A Need for Renewal and Redefinition," *Parameters* 30 (Autumn 2000): 5-20.

38. General Shinseki is quoted from an Army White Paper in FAP I, p.3. For a journalistic view of his tenure as Army Chief of Staff, see Peter J. Boyer, "A Different War," *The New Yorker,* (1 July 2002): 54-67.

39. The observation is of uncertain authorship.

40. Brownlee and Schoomaker, 12.

41. See introduction and chap. 1 of Eliot Freidson, *Professionalism, The Third Logic* (Chicago, IL: University of Chicago Press, 2001).

42. Huntington, *Soldier and State*, 16.

43. For bureaucratic behavior within military institutions, see David C. Kozak and James M. Keagle, eds., *Bureaucratic Politics and National Security: Theory and Practice* (Boulder, CO: Lynne Reiner Publishers, 1988).

44. The quotation is from an unpublished manuscript, "The Inadvertent Demise of the Traditional Academy, 1945-1995," dated November 1995, by Prof. Roger H. Nye, Department of History, USMA.

45. See Snider, Nagl, and Pfaff, *Army Professionalism, the Military Ethic, and Officership in the 21st Century.*

46. At the same time, the return of such discretion highlights the responsibility of the Army officer corps to ensure that such discretion is not abused, that it leads only to the measured application of violence toward mission accomplishment. See chap.18 of this anthology.

47. See A. P. Carr-Saunders and P. A. Wilson, *The Professions* (Oxford, England: Oxford University Press, 1933) for initial case studies on professions. H.L. Wilensky, "The Professionalization of Everyone?" *American Journal of Sociology* 70 (1964), 137-58, presents the professionalization sequence for American professions. For more recent literature, see Eliot Freidson, *Professional Powers: A Study of the Institutionalization of Formal Knowledge* (Chicago, IL: University of Chicago Press, 1986).

48. Geoffery Millerson, *The Qualifying Associations* (London, England: Routledge, 1964).

49. The classics include: Alfred Vagts, *A History of Militarism* rev. ed. (New York: Free Press, 1959); Morris Janowitz, *The Professional Soldier*; Bengt Abrahamsson, *Military Professionalism and Political Power* (Beverly Hills, CA.: Sage Publishing, 1972).

50. Allan R. Millett, *Military Professionalism and Officership in America*, Mershon Center Briefing Paper Number Two (Columbus: Ohio State Univ., May 1977), 2.

51. For loss of political neutrality within American officer corps, see Oli R. Holsti, "A Widening Gap Between the US Military and Civilian Society? Some Evidence, 1976-1996," *International Security* 23 (Winter 1998/99): 8-28. See also commentary and reply by Joseph J. Collins and Oli Holsti, *International Security* 24 (Fall 1999): 199-207. For an overview of civil-military tensions at the time, see Deborah D. Avant, "Conflicting Indicators of Crisis in American Civil-Military Relations," *Armed Forces and Society* 24 (Spring 1998): 375-87. For the most recent and thorough treatment of these tensions prior to the attack on the United States on 11 November 2001, see Peter D. Feaver and Richard H. Kohn, *Soldiers and Citizens* (Cambridge, MA: The MIT Press, 2001).

52. For both sides of the debates over these civil-military tensions, as recorded at the time, see Richard Kohn, "Out of Control," *National Interest* 35 (Spring 1994): 3-17; Russell Weigley, "The American Military and the Principle of Civilian Control from McClellan to Powell," *Journal of Military History* 57 (October 1993): 27-58; and Deborah D. Avant, "Are the Reluctant Warriors Out of Control?" *Security Studies* 6 (Winter 1996/97): 51-90.

53. See Charles C. Moskos, "Toward a Post-Modern Military: The United States as Paradigm," in *The Post Modern Military*, ed. Charles C. Moskos, John Allen Williams, and David R. Segal (Oxford, England: Oxford Univ. Press, 2000), 14-31. I use "subjective forms of civilian control" in the Huntingtonian sense of maximizing civilian power. See Huntington, 80-83.

54. For one of the most insightful analyses of the real differences in these three war-fighting professions, see Carl Builder, *The Masks of War* (Santa Monica, CA: RAND Corporation, 1989). In chap. 10 of this anthology, Jeffrey Peterson and I make an argument that a new joint military profession, a fourth American military profession, should be emerging as the move toward "jointness" accelerates.

55. For one example, see chap. 11, David W. Tarr and Peter J. Roman, "Army and Joint Professionalism after Goldwater-Nichols: Seeking a Balance" in FAP I.

56. Steven Brint, *In an Age of Experts: The Changing Role of Professionals in Politics and in Public Life* (Princeton, NJ: Princeton University Press, 2001).

57. This discussion is drawn primarily from Andrew Abbott's *The System of Professions: An Essay on the Division of Expert Labor* (Chicago, IL: University of Chicago Press, 1988). Additional sources include Elliott Krause, *Death of the Guilds: Professions, States, and the Advance of Capitalism, 1930 to Present* (New Haven, CT: Yale University Press, 1996); Eliot Freidson, *Professionalism Reborn: Theory, Prophecy, and Policy* (Chicago, IL: University of Chicago Press, 1994).

58. See unpublished manuscript by Christopher R. Paparone, Ruth A. Anderson, and Reuben R. McDonald, Jr., "The United States Military: Where Professionalism Meets Complexity Science" (U.S. Army War College, May 2003); and Ruth A. Anderson and Reuben R. McDaniel, "Managing Health Care Organizations: Where Professionalism Meets Complexity Science," *Health Care Management Review* 25, no. 1 (2000): 83-92.

59. I am indebted to Arthur R. Friedman, CISSP, Technical Director, Office of Nuclear Command and Control, National Security Agency, Ft. Meade, MD., for this example. The International Information Systems Security Consortium, Inc. can be accessed at: https://www.isc2.org/cgi-bin/index.cgi.

60. Abbott, *System of Professions,* chaps. 2-4.

61. See Andrew Abbott, "The Army and the Theory of Professions," in FAP I.

62. I refer the reader again to chap. 5 of the present anthology.

63. For the original publication of the research results of the first project, see chap. 25, "Project Conclusions," in FAP I. The conclusions appearing in this section are direct quotations or close paraphrases of the originals.

64. Although we have data only for field and company grade officers, this finding is likely to pertain to those of higher ranks as well as to noncommissioned officers. These are both testable hypotheses that can be validated by future research.

65. See the Army War College's *Study on the Military Profession* (Carlisle Barracks, PA, June 1970).

66. See the applicable research as reported in FAP I: chap. 3 by Joseph J. Collins and T.O. Jacobs, "Trust in the Profession of Arms"; chap. 5 by Gayle L. Watkins and Randi Cohen, "In Their Own Words: Army Officers Discuss Their Profession"; and "Case No. 3: The 2000 Army Training and Leader Development Panel" by Joe LeBoeuf in chap. 22. Also, see *The Executive Summary of the Army Training and Leader Development Panel* [ATLDP], Department of the Army, April 2001.

67. See James Burk, ed., *The Adaptive Military: Armed Forces in a Turbulent World*, second edition (Somerset, NJ: Transaction Publishers, 1998).

68. See "A Game Plan for Advancing Army Objectives in FY05 and Beyond: Thinking Strategically," unpublished manuscript and briefing, Department of the Army, Pentagon, 1 November 2004.

69. There are already many substantive reports, both official and unofficial, for the reader interested in learning more about this immense stain on the Army profession's moral character. I suggest as a start point, *Final Report of the Independent Panel to Review DoD Detention Operations* (the so-called "Schlesinger Report"), accessible at: http://www.dod.gov/news/.

2 | Expertise, Jurisdiction, and Legitimacy of the Military Profession

James Burk

This chapter critically reviews the concept of the "professional soldier" as it applies to the American military from the end of the 19th century to the present.[1] There are many reasons why such a review is needed. First, the end of the Cold War closed a long period in which preparation to fight and win world wars was the primary mission of the military, thus defining the occupation of the professional soldier. It is natural to wonder whether (or how) the professional soldier's occupation has changed as a result of this historical event and of the proliferation of intrastate and terrorist conflicts that have followed in its wake. Second, the two classic and still influential studies of the professional military—Samuel Huntington's *The Soldier and the State* and Morris Janowitz's *The Professional Soldier*—were written over 40 years ago, in the shadow of the world wars and during the Cold War.[2] Neither is historically up to date, although that (in principle) is relatively easy to fix. The fundamental question about them is whether recent experience reveals flaws in the logic of their arguments or suggests that their influence on our thinking about the professional military should be qualified or limited. Third, since Huntington and Janowitz wrote, much new scholarly work has been done on the professions in general. This work has implications for contemporary studies of the military profession that have not yet been fully explored.

We should not pretend that a critical review of this issue is value-free or disinterested. To call an occupation a "profession" is usually to make a positive normative judgment about the work being done, and, since we think that professional work is a social good, whatever we call professional work also reveals something about what we believe is required for the well-being of society.[3] When we inquire about the state of the military profession, we do not want a simple description of what the military *does*; we want a description compared to particular standards that prescribe how military activities *ought* to be done if they are good. That comparison is essential. It lets us know whether the military is measuring up to (or falling short of) our normative expectations. As should be obvious, the quality of the comparison (and of the normative judgment reached) depends on the validity and currency of the prescriptive statements used to characterize professional work. Yet how do we know whether these statements are valid and current?

Our answer to that question depends largely on the theoretical position we take about what a profession is and how professions develop. We might hold that the concept of a profession is widely accepted, clear, and unchanging. If so, then the prescriptive statements are universal claims that define the essence of professional activity. Once they are stated, they are recognized as sufficiently authoritative to rely on and use without further question. The task of evaluating professional activity is limited to getting the description right and fairly comparing what is done with what ought to be done.

If we suppose, however, that the profession is a contested concept whose definition is historically opaque and changing, then the authority and universality of prescriptive standards is questionable and requires defense. This enormously complicates the task of evaluating professional activity because, in addition to description, we have to identify the normative standards appropriate to a particular period. Nevertheless, the most recent studies of professional development argue that this more complicated task is the one we face.[4] As the historian Samuel Haber tells us, statements defining professional activity are "social artifacts fashioned by public events and usage."[5] Their validity and currency are not given once for all time, but are socially constructed and reconstructed by the choices and chances affecting particular generations. In this case, substantive prescriptions about what the professions ought to be evolve historically, influencing and influenced by what the professions are.

Adopting the second position to guide this chapter, I argue that the military profession's role has expanded over the course of the last century, widening from the management of violence early in the century to encompass the management of defense following the Second World War and the management of peace after the Cold War. This role expansion has resulted largely from the changing nature of war, war being the object of professional expertise, and brought the military into closer contact and competition with other professions when it performs its tasks. No less important, when we examine historical fluctuations in the prescriptive factors that define what a profession ought to be and do, we find that changing public views of what constitutes legitimate expert knowledge pose a challenge to the military's claim to professional status. In short, compared to their counterparts early in 20th century, military professionals today must work harder to define and defend the domain within which they work and to overcome public skepticism about the value of their expertise.

My argument is developed in four parts. The first examines the idea of the professional in general. Here I propose a definition of the professions that depends on three prescriptive factors. These factors can be used to guide and characterize historical changes in professional activity. The second part considers how debates about military professionalism are connected to these prevailing ideas about the professions. Here I consider in particular (though not exclusively) the classic models of the military professional proposed by Huntington and Janowitz. I argue that neither model provides a wholly reliable guide for thinking about the military profession today. The third part tells how the military profession has changed over time. The description is not a simple narrative, but is organized around the three prescriptive factors identified in the first part that characterize professional activity. This analytic narrative tests the usefulness of these prescriptive factors for interpreting long-term trends in professional development. The fourth and last part draws out the practical implications of this study for creating and maintaining an effective military profession at the present time.

The Idea of a Profession

Social scientists and historians agree that a profession is a distinct kind of work, but disagree about what actually distinguishes it from other kinds of work. Eliot Freidson suggests that we should not become preoccupied with this disagreement, as if it were a matter that might someday be resolved. A resolution would be possible only if the idea of a profession were a "generic" concept, the one true meaning of which we might someday finally discover. In fact, Freidson argues, a profession is a "historic concept."[6] What it means changes with the particular period of history we examine. The standing of medicine, law, and the clergy as professions meant one thing in medieval Europe, another thing in 18th-century British society, and means something else again in present-day American society. The different meanings are telling. Beyond what they say about the progress of the division of labor, they connote something about the evaluative and often conflictual processes that make professions occupations of higher rather than lower social status. In short, disagreement about what a profession is stems partly from the historical development of occupational structures and partly from social conflicts about the allocation of occupational prestige.

Embracing this historical view of the idea of the professions does not excuse us from offering a definition of the profession. Some working definition is needed, if only to clarify what a historical approach to the study of professions should consider. In this chapter, I rely on the following definition: *A profession is a relatively "high status" occupation whose members apply abstract knowledge to solve problems in a particular field of endeavor.* The definition identifies three elements as critical to the idea of a profession: high status, which I will link to a notion of legitimacy; applied abstract knowledge, the source of expertise; and a field of endeavor or jurisdiction for problem-solving. These three elements are commonly, though not always or exclusively, referred to by sociologists writing on this subject.[7] It will be worthwhile briefly to consider what these elements mean and how they are interrelated.

The British sociologist, T. H. Marshall, identified the importance of high status to the professions in an early essay on the subject, first published in 1939.[8] The professions, he wrote, were "occupations suitable for a gentleman," which in Britain meant a person of high status. We should not suppose that he meant doing professional labor necessarily gave one high status. In 18th-century British society it was rather the other way around. An occupation qualified as a profession if it entailed work that a gentleman would do, that is, if it were compatible with "the good life." The source of prestige, on this account, was the high status of the person who performed the activity. As commerce was then a disreputable activity, work could not be professional if it entailed striving for money (although professionals had to make a lot of money to meet "the needs of a gentlemanly life"). By the 20th century, a profession's high status derived more from the work done than from the social standing of the worker. What counted were the effects of professional labor on the lives of the clients. "The idea of service," Marshall wrote, "became more important than the idea of freedom."[9] To ensure the quality of service, thus protecting their prosperity and respect, professionals organized into associations. Professional associations guaranteed the technical competence of their members by controlling their training and testing their ability; they imposed a code of ethics that put the needs of clients in first place and limited intra-professional competition by barring customary commercial practices (haggling over fees, advertising, etc.); and they protected the domain of professional practice from encroachment by nonmembers, not to preserve the revenue for association members, but in order (they said) to protect clients from unqualified encroachers.

According to Marshall, then, the contemporary professions enjoyed high status because they were "functional" occupations organized to meet important social needs. His was an idea widely shared in the mid-20th century.[10] By the 1970s, as sociologists became more skeptical of functional explanations, they began to locate the source of professional status in monopolies maintained by the operation of power, income, and education.[11] The main idea was that control over these resources could be used to secure and defend an advantaged place in the social structure. Without denying the relevance of these resources, Andrew Abbott has shown that, by themselves, they provide no satisfactory account of professional status.[12] Writing in 1981, he was prepared to revive a functionalist account, agreeing with Edward Shils that professionals possess esoteric knowledge that allows them to confront disorders—disease, crime, sin, war, etc.—and often to impose order on them or bring them to heel.[13]

By the late 1980s, however, Abbott had reformulated this idea to de-emphasize the functionalist assumption that professions met needs found naturally in society. He came to emphasize rather a constructionist account, arguing that an occupation's identification as a profession and its standing within society were outcomes of social competition within a system of professions for control over abstract knowledge applied within particular jurisdictions.[14] In keeping with this account, he defined professions quite loosely as "exclusive occupational groups applying somewhat abstract knowledge to particular cases."[15] In contrast with my own definition, his focuses on just two elements, professional expertise and jurisdiction, ignoring social status (though he seems to acknowledge the importance of legitimacy, he never incorporates it into his definitional construct).[16] I think that is a mistake because it wrongly assumes that an occupation's struggle for professional standing rests entirely on possessing and applying abstract knowledge.

It is certainly true that professionals apply abstract knowledge to solve social problems. All professionals have been instructed in and mastered a body of knowledge; their entry into professional practice is predicated on receiving some form of higher education. But the *form* abstract knowledge takes varies by profession and within professions over time. This variation in the form of knowledge is important because it affects the social standing of a profession among other professions and nonprofessional occupations. The historian Bruce Kimball has shown for example that in mid-18th century America, the highest-ranked profession was the clergy, but by the early 19th century the highest-ranked profession was the law, and by the early 20th century it was medicine. While each of these professions masters an abstract body of knowledge, the *form* of the knowledge of the highest-ranked professions has moved from the logic of theology to the logic of jurisprudence to the logic of natural science.[17] This historical succession indicates that the prestige of professions does not depend only on the mastery of knowledge. Professional prestige also depends on the legitimacy society accords to the form that knowledge takes.

It may be tempting to argue, as sociologists used to do, that the historical succession from theology through jurisprudence to science represents the growth and triumph of reason over superstition or at least over claims that cannot be tested empirically or verified. Talcott Parsons argued this way; although the professions originally descended from a "religious matrix," he contended they were now committed to the primacy of "cognitive rationality."[18] If we succumbed to Parsons's reasoning, we would say that professional expertise (i.e., the mastery of abstract knowledge) was proven by the ability actually to solve problems faced by individuals and society. With apologies to Christian Science, we would then say that medicine is ranked higher than the clergy among professions in the 20th century because the application of medical science to the problems of disease and public health is demonstrably more effective than the application, say, of prayer. Indeed, that was Parsons's view. By the 20th century, he said, occupational groups anchored in religious commitments were not professions; they only approximated professions.[19]

Nevertheless, this is a temptation we should avoid. It is true that professional standing requires control over a domain of social life—a jurisdiction—within which members of the profession try to solve particular problems by applying the special knowledge at their command. Because control over a jurisdiction is usually contested, as Abbott contends, professions are involved in competition to secure their place in society. They wage this competition by various means, from redefining the nature of the professional task to be performed to fostering legislation that bars competitors from practicing in the field. Still, the most important factor for gaining and maintaining control over a jurisdiction is demonstration that the professional activity succeeds, that it solves the problems it confronts.

Try as they might, however, professions do not perfectly control either the definition of problems to be solved or what counts as a solution. They cannot answer the question on their own. Consider the ascent of modern medicine among the professions. The rising social status of medicine rested in large part on its successful application of germ theory to the diagnosis and treatment of diseases. But the development of germ theory to approach the problem of disease reflected—it did not precede—the growing belief in society that science (not theology or jurisprudence) was *the* legitimate form of abstract knowledge, superior in practice to any other. In the future, should belief in the practical efficacy of scientific knowledge decline, as it has done over the last half-century, then professions whose abstract knowledge is scientific in form would lose status and legitimacy, even if they were demonstrably solving more problems than before.

In sum, my definition identifies three prescriptive factors that, when found together, mark an occupation as a profession. One is mastery of abstract knowledge, which occurs through a system of higher education. Another is control—almost always contested—over a jurisdiction within which expert knowledge is applied. Finally is the match between the form of professional knowledge and the prevailing cultural belief or bias about the legitimacy of that form compared to others, which is the source of professional status. We can refer to these three simply as expertise, jurisdiction, and legitimacy.

A final comment on my definition is warranted. Applying knowledge to solve social problems was thought by earlier students of the professions to entail a public service both to the client and to society. The idea of public service was an important element in their definition of the professions, because its demands supposedly overrode the dictates of the marketplace and self-interest. Relations with clients were based on the principle of trust (not caveat emptor), and professionals were expected to perform their duties even if that required an element of self-sacrifice.[20] Recent studies of the professions, however, have defined the professions more sparely as occupations based on expert knowledge, with the connection of service to the public welfare dropped by the wayside. As Steven Brint argues, the idea that professionals were "social trustees," applying knowledge to serve the public good gave way in the 1960s to the idea that professionals were knowledge "experts" hired to serve organizational authorities or market forces without much regard for the public good.[21] This change in ideas, he says, reflects a change in reality. It is at least an important shift in our understanding of the professions and one to which we will return.

The Profession of Military Service

Social science studies of the military as a profession begin in the mid-20th century, most notably with the work of Huntington and Janowitz. It is not difficult to say why military professionalism became an object of study at this time. The Cold War required that the United States maintain a large professional military during "peacetime." The country had never done this before. For a liberal political culture, traditionally ambivalent about war and standing armies, maintaining a large force in being posed questions about the quality of civil-military relations. Many thought that a high level of military professionalism was needed to ensure a technically competent military establishment and to ensure that the military establishment would act only to serve appropriate civilian authority. This thought was based on the idea that professionals were, to use Brint's term again, "social trustees" who were organized to serve the public good and not their own self-interest. But was this a reasonable idea? Was military service a profession, and if so what made military professionals effective?

The question of whether military service is a profession received different answers depending on who was asked for an answer and when. Scholars studying the professions in the first half of the 20th century did not usually include military service in their field of inquiry. In their seminal survey of the professions, published in 1933, A. M. Carr-Saunders and P. A. Wilson explicitly refused to count the Army as a profession. They were concerned with the professions only in relation to the ordinary business of life. "The Army is omitted," they wrote, "because the service which soldiers are trained to render is one which it is hoped they will never be called on to perform."[22] Unless the military's expertise is applied, it does not count. This is a novel and, some might say, utopian ground for exclusion that tells us more about social thought between the world wars than it does about the professions. Other scholars pointed out that military service was not professional because the military was controlled by the state; military officers lacked professional autonomy, which the scholars thought was a critical trait of the professions.[23] But the ideal of autonomy as a characteristic of the professions has lost influence as professional work is increasingly embedded within corporate and bureaucratic hierarchies. More typically, sociologists just ignored the military when they studied professions, failing to say why. It is likely that, for sociologists in this period, the prototype of a legitimate profession was science-based medicine; the military seemed unlikely to fit the mold. If the military was a profession, it was so only in the 18th-century sense that T. H. Marshall discussed. That is, it was a profession only because being a military officer was an occupation fit for the life of a gentleman. In the 20th century, this idea of the profession was no longer relevant.

The public held a more inclusive view of the professions, one that had room for the military. They did not count it among the higher-ranked professions. In 1955, Janowitz notes, the public placed the prestige of the military officer "below that of the physician, scientist, college professor, and minister"—and also below the public school teacher.[24] Still, they thought the military was a profession. Indeed, public consensus on this point, though unnoticed by social scientists studying the professions, was not recent but had already formed by World War I.[25] Early in the 20th century, it was plain that a cadre of professional military officers was necessary to train military forces in peacetime and to direct them during war.

What Huntington and Janowitz did was connect this public view of the professional military with then current social science theories about what a profession was. For them, it was largely rhetorical to ask whether military service was a profession. Neither had any doubt that it was. Huntington made a more explicit defense of the proposition than Janowitz, but both were engaged in a task of conceptual clarification, to place the military within the bounds of the professions. At the very beginning of *The Soldier and the State*, Huntington states: "The modern officer corps is a professional body and the modern military officer a professional man."[26] He then argued that expertise, responsibility (or service to society), and corporateness (or group unity) are the marks of a profession and that the military possesses all three of these, just as do the prototypical professions, medicine and law. In *The Professional Soldier*, Janowitz simply took for granted that the military was a profession. He too identified the officer corps as a professional group like medicine or law, marked by expert skill acquired over time, the rendering of a specialized service, and a sense of group identity, which entails a system of internal administration and a professional ethic.[27] In short, they agreed that the military was a profession and about what made it so.

Where they disagreed was in their answer to the second question, what made the military profession effective? Huntington believed that military professionals were effective under conditions of objective control; by objective control he meant that civilians would dictate the military security policy but leave the military free to determine what military operations would secure the policy objectives. There was, in essence, a swap of military loyalty to civilian authority in return for professional autonomy to control one's work. The alternative, he thought, was subjective control in which civilians would meddle in military affairs, trying to make the military more like society; the military would by necessity become politicized, with the result being a decline in military effectiveness. Janowitz, in contrast, believed that no clear line could be drawn between the military and civilian realms. He thought that effective civil-military relations in a liberal democracy required that the military identify with and be representative of the society it served. Isolation of the military from the larger society would reduce professional effectiveness. He also thought that the development of weapons of mass destruction fundamentally changed the nature of war in ways that required professional soldiers explicitly to consider the political consequences of military operations. Effective military professionals redefined their understanding of successful problem-solving. They downplayed their role as "heroic warriors" in pursuit of absolute military victory to emphasize their role as pragmatic managers of the minimum use of force needed to achieve political settlements and maintain viable international relations. Janowitz called a professional military that achieved this latter ideal a "constabulary" force. He contrasted a constabulary force with one that used violence to pursue "total victory" or "unconditional surrender."

Important as both these models are, neither stands without criticism today. Huntington argues that the military professional is to master the functional requirements of war, to organize and train the military to meet them, and to lead the military to fight when ordered by political authorities to do so. But the presumption that there is a clearly delineated military sphere defined by war-fighting that is independent of the social and political sphere is dubious at best, especially in an era when we possess weapons of mass destruction. There is no real distinction between the ends and means of war. What ends are possible to think about depend to a large extent on the means with which they are to be pursued. As a practical matter, this suggests that the distinction between the political sphere, where ends are decided on, and the military sphere, where means are deployed in pursuit of ends, is highly misleading. If so, then Huntington's theory of objective civilian control does not really tell us how military professionalism can be strengthened.

Also, Huntington's confidence in the value of military professionalism is uncritical. He ignores the possibility that professionals (like all social groups) may act in ways contrary to the interests of the larger group. But sociologists have identified a number of ways in which professionals may act in their own interest against the public good: cultivating an incapacity to grasp the insights from any perspective but one's own; treating the means of professional practice as if they were ends in themselves while forgetting the original purpose they were intended to fulfill; acting to protect the station and privileges of one's group—service or branch—above any other, simply because it is one's own; shirking those tasks one is assigned to undermine the assignment; or acting opportunistically to do what is required to advance one's career.[28] Taking these into account, we have to conclude that the degree of military professionalism varies for reasons other than the institution of objective or subjective control.

Janowitz's model is more helpful because it anticipates change in the character of the military profession, something Huntington fails to do. The change is driven by the need to adapt professional practice to the changing nature of war: that affects what counts as a solution to problems of military security. But he was perhaps naïve in expecting that the profession could alter its self-conception away from the heroic warrior to the pragmatic constabulary model without intensifying competition (from within the military and without) for control over its professional jurisdiction. And while he recognized that tensions existed among officers of differing specialties—e.g., whose work was oriented primarily to management, technology, or combat—he did not thoroughly explore the difficulties encountered between bureaucratic and professional cultures.

Even more objectionable, Janowitz failed to resolve the problems his theory poses for military professionalism. If the changing nature of war blurred the boundaries between the military and political spheres, as Janowitz said, then how was military professionalism to be reformed to ensure that its expertise was applied in the service of the state? The question is a serious one. Once boundaries were blurred, military officers were inevitably "politicized" as they prepared for their new roles to deliver strategic deterrence and fight limited wars. But a politicized military at least implicitly challenges civilian supremacy.[29] How was the challenge to be met? In *The Professional Soldier*, Janowitz's discussion of mechanisms of civilian control to ensure professional responsibility is extremely limited, being confined to control mechanisms that are easily worked around. The problem Janowitz faced was an old one in the theory of the professions, namely, how to ensure that professionals are acting in the best interests of society when those they serve lack the expertise to define the service they need, or even to know whether their needs have been adequately addressed. His answer was to strengthen the commitment of professional soldiers to the system of civilian control through programs of political education that would help them connect their professional training to national and transnational purposes.[30] But the thrust of this argument is circular: responsible military professionalism is made to depend on the strength of military professionalism.

When Huntington and Janowitz devised their pioneering models, they were both confident that strong military professionalism was essential to ensure the military security of American democracy. Their confidence rested in part on the logic of the functionalist theory of the professions that prevailed at mid-century and on which they both relied. According to that theory, professionals were thought to be social trustees, acting in a fiduciary capacity to ensure the public good. They possessed systematic knowledge acquired through a long period of training, and, as required by their occupational ethic, they applied it competently, objectively, and impartially to meet the needs of the client and improve public welfare.

A decade after Huntington and Janowitz's classic works appeared, sociologists abandoned this simple functional theory. In its place, they conceived a more conflict-oriented, class-based model that saw professions as group "projects" to obtain social mobility. According to this conflict approach, the professions did not necessarily serve social needs found in the natural order of things. They rather imposed their own definitions of needs on society and created self-serving means for meeting them.[31] It is mere speculation to wonder how Huntington or Janowitz might have concluded differently about the military profession had they written from the perspective of these later models. But the effects of these more cynical models of the professions were incorporated (though not explicitly) in the work of Charles Moskos and his associates.[32] Beginning in the late 1970s, Moskos argued that the military profession was moving away from its traditional institutional principles of social organization to embrace occupational or market-based principles of organization. It has proven difficult to trace development of the military profession along this single theoretical dimension. Over the years, those working on this model have multiplied the number of dimensions taken into account. Yet, despite refinements, in the end, there is consensus that a significant change has taken place. In recent years, the military profession has become more like Brint's "expert" profession simply doing its job for an organized authority and less like a "social trustee" profession rendering self-sacrificial service to the country.[33] A troubling symptom of this shift may be found in rules of engagement that give top priority to "force protection," even though these rules might result in higher levels of noncombatant deaths, as happened in the Kosovo War.

Still, we should not suppose that movement from "social trustee" to "expert" is absolute or irreversible. The war in Iraq, with its many casualties, suggests that the professional ideal of social trusteeship, expecting self-sacrifice, has survived and is not necessarily incompatible with the ideal of a professional expert. We will discuss this possibility further at the end of the chapter.

Trends in Military Professionalism

My approach to the study of change in the military profession is guided by our definition of the factors that mark an occupation as a profession: expertise, jurisdiction, and legitimacy. My hypothesis is that when we examine military professionalism from the late 19th century to the present, we see first a convergence of these three factors to strengthen military professionalism, and then an unraveling of these factors, especially in the last half-century, that subjects the military profession to strain. The reasons for this pattern of change are interrelated. As we shall see, they are not factors always within the power of the military profession to control.

To develop these ideas, I concentrate on three pivotal periods in the history of Army professionalism: the period between Reconstruction and World War I, when on most accounts the Army officer corps turned itself into a modern profession; the period just following World War II, when the Army faced a professional crisis centered largely on the problems of defining and defending its jurisdiction at a time when military roles and missions were hotly contested; and finally the period since the end of the Cold War, when the Army profession has been challenged by lost resources, increased deployments, and increased competition for control of its jurisdiction. The task is to identify the main themes that connect these three periods along the analytic dimensions of expertise, jurisdiction, and legitimacy.

Expertise

The period following Reconstruction was one in which the Army began seriously to cultivate the study of war as an applied science which officers must master if they were to be professional specialists in the management of violence. The emphasis on the *science* (not the art) of war, while not entirely new, was new in its scope. It underwrote the development of a new professional education system and the founding of professional associations and journals.[34] This movement within the Army had its parallels in the Navy and in the larger society. This was a period in which the "culture of professionalism"—a term used by Burton Bledstein—was widespread.[35] Many middle-class occupational groups were organizing themselves to stake a claim to professional status. The success of their claims often hinged on their being able to demonstrate expertise over an abstract body of knowledge that took the form of science. Here the themes of expertise and legitimacy are intertwined. By the late 19th century, science was believed to be *the* source of reliable knowledge about the world; claims to expertise were more readily recognized if they were obviously grounded in science. Even the ancient professions of theology and law were affected by this development—they began to recast the form of their specialized knowledge in a scientific mold.[36]

The scientific turn in the Army professional's claim to expertise was accepted without significant challenge until the end of World War II. Before then there was a close connection between the use of military force and military success or victory. If superior resources did not prevail, it was thought to be a failure to apply the science of war, not a challenge to the idea that greater military strength yields greater military security. But the development of weapons of mass destruction in the wake of the world wars made plain (sooner for some than for others) that sheer military might was no longer a guarantee of security if the use of that might was so destructive that its use was self-defeating. This shift in outlook spurred development of a new and broader science of national security and strategic studies, and the experts in this new science were not confined to those in the uniformed services.[37] Nevertheless, the Army professional did not abandon the claim to expertise in military science, but if anything pursued the claim with increasing vigor, extending its system of professional military education and augmenting it by dispatching officers to pursue graduate degrees in fields ancillary to or supportive of the military sciences. At the end of the 20th century, the Army's claim to expert knowledge in the management of violence, certified by science, was a foundation for its professional identity.[38] That is not to say, however, that the empirical challenge to that expertise posed by weapons of mass destruction had been successfully resolved.

Jurisdiction

A professional jurisdiction is defined by the boundaries of the domain within which expert knowledge is applied. It is sometimes an actual place, like a hospital, courtroom, or battlefield, and sometimes a slice or aspect of life. So, while an Army commander focuses on directing the course of battle, the chaplain is focused on the soldiers' souls and the medic on the soldiers' wounds. In broad strokes, the Army's jurisdiction narrowed over the late 19th century, as it shed domestic functions and focused on protecting the country's borders and fighting land wars abroad. Competitors who would ply their knowledge in this jurisdiction at the expense of the professional Army, notably volunteers and state militias, were effectively curbed early in the 20th century. State militias were upgraded, but subordinated to professional Army control by the Militia Act of 1903 and the National Defense Act of 1916. By World War I, well-meaning amateurs like Theodore Roosevelt were no longer allowed direct entry into the officer corps. The Army was following an old practice of the professions, protecting its jurisdiction by resort to the law. The Navy was a rival for resources, but not a competitor to fight land battles.

This neat arrangement was disturbed by the advancing technology of war over the course of the 20th century. The disturbance was severe at the end of World War II as evinced by the conflict over the creation of a "unified" Department of Defense and of an Air Force separated from the Army.[39] There was severe competition among the various services over what their roles and missions—their jurisdiction—should be. This contest arose because the technological development of war over the course of the 20th century had the effect of homogenizing the theater of war, undermining the clear connection of the three major services with a particular environment of warfare—land, sea, and air—and so creating an impetus for "joint" military operations. One could say that there is just one military profession, but the services resist this more abstract identity, in part because (as Kenneth Allard has shown) their dominant operating environments continue to support different kinds of expertise and modes of intra-professional cooperation, even to this day.[40] The interservice competition over jurisdiction has blown hot and cold ever since, and it has certainly not gone away.

However, the more important competition over the Army's professional jurisdiction has come from external sources. In effect, I argue that the jurisdictional claims of the military in general, including the Army, have expanded since the end of the world wars. We can reduce that to slogan form by saying the Army has moved from the management of war early in the century to the management of defense (a wider concern) during the Cold War to the management of peace (an even wider concern) since the end of the Cold War. With each broadening of the Army's jurisdictional claims, competition over the Army's jurisdiction has increased. As already suggested, the growth of national security studies after the world wars was propelled by the threat of weapons of mass destruction; war narrowly conceived could no longer be seen as a tool in the kit of foreign policy. The outbreak of general war had to be averted, and civilian scientists in relevant disciplines began to develop expertise outside the military profession to determine how this might be done. Within the Department of Defense, new techniques of rational planning were introduced to determine the most efficient use of scarce resources. This eroded claims of the Army and other service professionals that such judgments should not be based on the more general, quantitative language of cost-benefit analysis but rather on particular service expertise. Since the end of the Cold War, encroachment of civilian experts on the Army's jurisdiction increased in large part because military operations were no longer confined to actual war but had spread to include peacekeeping missions, broadly defined. Unlike actions in a theater of war, peacekeeping operations are not an endeavor of "sole practice" by the Army professional; they occur within what Abbott called a "multi-professional workplace."[41] Successful peacekeeping requires cooperative action among the Army, other national militaries allied in the effort, and a wide array of civilian service providers—none of whom may answer to a single authority.[42]

This new competition over the Army's jurisdiction could be limited if the boundaries of its jurisdiction were narrowed, as they were at the turn of the 20th century. But this approach, preferred by some, is unlikely given the changing nature of war, the object of the Army's professional expertise. As Janowitz argued long ago, it is the changing nature of war that is driving the expansion of the Army's definition of its professional jurisdiction, thus inviting the conflicts just observed.

Legitimacy

We have noted that the Army's claim to be a modern profession a century ago was bolstered by its ability to develop its expertise in the form of military science. This new science encompassed the study of battle, logistics, weapons development, and even the mobilization, assignment, and leadership of military personnel. Science at the time, enjoying a high point of its prestige, was considered the most reliable form of practical knowledge. It was not only the Army that advanced its claim to professional status by showing that its expertise was scientific. A new source of strain for the Army professional—as for many professionals—has been society's increasing skepticism of the legitimacy of expert knowledge based on science and the ideal of objectivity.

In 1962, Thomas Kuhn, a historian of science, famously cast doubt on naive claims that science provides objective and reliable knowledge with his analysis titled *The Structure of Scientific Revolutions*.[43] His argument, however, was only one of a number of studies to show that scientific knowledge often rested on hidden non-rational social factors. In any case the stock of scientific knowledge was always tentative and subject to revision. Sometimes the revisions required were disturbing, because the science once relied on was shown now to threaten human well-being. Rachel Carson documented the harmful unintended consequences of applying modern science to industry in her study, *Silent Spring*, which created a foundation for the ecology movement.[44] In the case of military science, even reliable knowledge was a threat to human welfare, symbolized powerfully by the threat of thermonuclear weapons and literally brought home to many whose milk contained strontium 90, a radioactive particle released in fallout from above-ground nuclear testing.

There are two important results of this increased skepticism about the legitimacy of science for the professions in general and for Army professionalism in particular. First, increased skepticism about science has encouraged nonexperts to question the exercise of professional authority more boldly than they had done in the past. Before World War II, students of the professions could write confidently, for example, of doctors giving orders that only foolhardy clients would ignore. By the end of the 20th century, resort to alternative medicine was more common, and medical doctors found it more difficult to silence competing claims from the practitioners, for example, of chiropractics, homeopathy, and acupuncture. More generally, professional pleas for deference had a hollow ring, resting, as they were accused of doing, on an ideological footing to secure the privileges associated with their practice. This is true for the military as well. A good illustration of the point can be found in debates over whether and how military technology and performance standards should be revised to accommodate greater integration of women.[45] Those skeptical of the wisdom of such integration regard the redesign, say, of airplane cockpits or basic training regimes as evidence that professionalism is on the decline, as expertise and technical competence are diluted for reasons of "political correctness." In contrast, those skeptical of professional expertise argue that the established standards are not universal, objective truths, but rest on social constructions of gender that can be modified without compromising military effectiveness.[46] Without a general belief in what constitutes a legitimate form of reliable knowledge, such debates are impossible to resolve except by the exercise of politics.

Second, when we lack common belief about what constitutes legitimate, truthful, and objective knowledge, it is difficult to sustain a professional ethic of service. Unquestioned trust between the professional and the client, which is needed to sustain the ethic, no longer exists. When professionals claim to be offering impartial, disinterested, even self-sacrificial service, their claims are not accepted at face value, but are examined cynically by clients and other interested observers who look for the self-interested "angle" in such claims, and find claims of self-interest more believable than claims of altruistic service. Uncertainty about "objective truth" also makes it more difficult for professionals to engage in self-sacrificing service with confidence that their self-sacrifice is justified, that the service is rendered in pursuit of what is unambiguously good. In the Army, such doubts began to emerge at the end of the Cold War, with doubts about the value of losing life when engaged in peacekeeping operations. Those doubts are less when fighting in the war against terror; but the war in Iraq has not been doubt free. It is not enough to assert that self-sacrificing service is central to professional practice.[47] The norm of self-sacrifice must be grounded in a general belief that the application of expert knowledge within a particular jurisdiction is legitimate. Otherwise the question—What is the dying for?—is difficult to answer.[48]

Implications for Military Professionalism

Professional practice is strong when the conditions of all three prescriptive factors are met, that is, when the application of expertise within a particular jurisdiction is uncontested and thought in general to be legitimate. Otherwise the quality of professional practice is cast into doubt. Applying this standard of evaluation to our historical analysis, it is clear that the military profession was strongest at the end of the 19th century through the end of World War II, but has weakened since then as a result of heightened jurisdictional competition and declining public confidence in science as a form of legitimate expertise.

Increased jurisdictional competition stems largely from the changing nature of war. The enormous destructive power of weapons of mass destruction has made clear the self-defeating character of unrestrained armed conflict; military security was no longer (if it ever really was) a simple function of military strength. The practical effect of this development, in the aftermath of World War II, did not diminish, but expanded the military's role. Still centrally concerned with the management of violence between armies at war, the military profession came also to manage defense, the aim of which was to avoid the outbreak of general war through a strategy of deterrence; and after the Cold War, the military began to manage the peace—not alone, but with others—with the aim of limiting armed conflict to the maximum extent and using the least force possible to promote a political settlement of differences, maintain respect for human rights, provide humanitarian relief, and combat terrorism. The difficulty here is that the military does not possess the same level of abstract knowledge about how to conduct peacekeeping missions (or how to deter global war) that it has for waging war. Even if it did, the military does not and cannot pretend to possess a monopoly of expert knowledge relevant for mission success in its expanded jurisdictions. To a greater extent than when fighting war, the management of defense and peace requires the military profession to cooperate and compete with other professions as it goes about its work.

To strengthen military professionalism under these circumstances, one might consider the obvious possibility of contracting out part of the military's jurisdiction. The Army could attempt to restrict its professional role by confining itself to problems of war, traditionally understood as conventional warfare between uniformed armies of nation-states and fought for the control of land—and forsake all other concerns. When threats stem less from the prospects of interstate war than from irregular religious and ethnic conflicts and attacks by terrorists, this possibility seems unrealistic. The need to prepare for general war cannot be ignored, but the Army could not justify a return to its world war jurisdiction while retaining its contemporary relevance.[49] Alternatively, one might deny the problem and emphasize the military's evident success in defending its expanded jurisdiction. The absence of a general war over the last half-century, the military could assert, demonstrates its professional competence in managing defense. Yet it is difficult to say with certainty whether or to what degree the absence of general war in this period resulted from the application of military expertise to the problem of deterrence. In fact, many wonder whether deterrence based on a nuclear standoff is a viable strategy. Consideration of an antimissile defense system suggests there are doubts about that even within the defense community.

A third approach considers how the Army professional can operate most effectively in its multi-professional workplace. Within the broad jurisdiction of the management of peace, mission success, say in Bosnia or Kosovo, cannot be achieved by relying on the expertise of the Army professional alone. Success requires the combined expertise of all the relevant professionals involved. The analogy is imperfect, but one can think for example about the combined expertise required in a hospital operating room before any complex surgery can succeed. It cannot be assumed, however, that professionals engaged in a peacekeeping arena or in the occupation of Iraq will wish to cooperate for a common goal. Even if they did, there is at the moment no well-established institutional authority with the expertise to identify, much less integrate, the various professional activities that are needed to maintain peace and substitute nonviolent for violent means of conflict resolution. Nevertheless, it is important that the various professional organizations cooperate, with each employing its particular expertise in a way that contributes to the overall objective of building peace in the region.

It is becoming clear with experience that the military's role in building peace is highly circumscribed. David Last, a major in the Canadian military, observes that while "military forces are effective at guaranteeing military security against organized military opposition . . . they are impotent in the face of bricks through windows or threatening telephone calls in the night."[50] He also notes that other agencies are needed to police, govern, provide relief, and move toward reconciliation if the conflict is to be resolved. He does not deny that military expertise is required in peacekeeping operations, especially to stop and prevent organized physical violence. But suppressing violence is only one step in the process, providing temporary relief.[51] Jurisdictional competition is limited and professionalism enhanced if the military's role within peacekeeping and humanitarian interventions is limited to fit its peculiar expertise. The same is true for other agencies involved. Achieving this outcome requires deliberate coordination across professional boundaries in which respect for the capacity of the others is acknowledged. There is no benefit in this setting if the military professional maintains a false sense of its own autonomy or attempts to usurp other agencies' roles.[52] Indeed, there may be horrible costs. The American military occupying Iraq, for instance, failed to heed warnings from human rights agencies about the mistreatment of protected persons in Iraq—mistreatment that the president later characterized as "abhorrent." That failure prolonged the abuse, inexcusable in itself. It also undermined Iraqi trust in the moral integrity of U.S. forces, complicating the task of a successful occupation.[53]

The public's declining confidence in science as a reliable form of practical knowledge is another troubling trend for military professionalism. This decline is a problem for all science-based professions, not just the military, because it makes it more difficult for all to establish the legitimacy of their authority. While science-based expertise continues to be used, and will be used far into the future, its use is no longer inevitably considered to be self-justifying. To shore up their authority, professions spend time building "sustainable partnerships" with those outside the profession whose expertise is other than their own and yet affects what they do.[54] That requires entering into a dialogue across professions and with the public (including the news media). The purpose is to increase the public's understanding of the reasons for a particular course of professional action and the profession's understanding of the reasons why that course of action might be resisted. There is no reason to expect that dialogue alone will lead to consensus. But without such a dialogue, it is hard to gain the public's trust on which professional legitimacy depends or to create the professional self-confidence required to embrace an ethic of self-sacrificing service.

This course, however advisable, also has a utopian ring to it. It seems to presume the persistence of the professions as "social trustees," committed to serving the public good. It seems to ignore the rise of "expert" professionals who serve only the interests of organizational authorities and market forces. But, as Brint has argued, the presumption of social trusteeship and blindness to the emergence of self-advancing experts are causes for concern; social supports needed for social trustee professionalism to thrive have eroded. This erosion has helped to elevate the authority of the market over moral elements in the life of the professions.[55] Brint's argument suggests that the new competitor to science as the form of objective and reliable practical knowledge is the market itself: what is true, objective, and useful knowledge is what sells in the marketplace; anything else is fancy. However crude that sounds when stated baldly, it is not far away from ordinary experience. We are used to people asking about the "bottom line" of our arguments and having them conclude that they "buy it" or not.[56] Making the market the new form by which the legitimacy of professional knowledge is judged does not unseat the science-based professions. But it poses a challenge to the customary pecking order of the professions, with those that can wrap their expertise in marketable form rising to the top (as economists and clinical psychologists have risen in the profession of social science). It also means that pressures will build within professions to formulate their expertise in the vocabulary of the marketplace. Such a change is what Moskos and others observed in the military profession beginning in the 1970s. The seeds of change were planted perhaps with Robert McNamara's introduction of cost-benefit analysis to evaluate the military budget and procurement programs in the early 1960s.

The triumph of the market cannot be ignored because it arises from and is part of society itself. Nevertheless, the triumph is not complete and so the choice is not between legitimating expertise based *either* on the market *or* on science *or* on more traditional moral grounds. Nor is it a matter of professionals abandoning their fiduciary responsibility to work for the public good, even when market gains might tempt them to do so—a lesson that the now-defunct accounting firm, Arthur Anderson, learned only after it abandoned its fiduciary duty and knowingly misrepresented the financial position of Enron, then a corporate giant.

The problem is to recognize when market legitimation is an appropriate basis for action and when it is not. In principle, this problem is not difficult to solve. Markets provide effective and legitimate diagnoses and prescriptions about the worth and allocation of social goods when there is real uncertainty about what goods to pursue at what cost. Historically, the rise of market-based legitimation in modern liberal democracies is connected with the growing heterogeneity of their populations and the diversity of their cultures. With the public committed to the principle of toleration as a foundation for society, there is reluctance to impose definitions of what is good or which goods are to be preferred over others. Instead, these definitions and valuations are established by free exchange whether in the marketplace of commerce or in the marketplace of ideas. Whenever the military profession confronts such uncertainty—as it may do for instance in decisions about the design of future weapon systems or in calculations about how much money soldiers should be paid—there is no reason why the profession should not employ the language of the market. Doing so is not completely foreign to military experience. The battlefield, after all, is full of uncertainty, and battles are decided by the exchange of fire. A great deal of military science is devoted to the end of gaining and sustaining the advantage in this deadly competition.

Many times of course it is not clear whether expertise rooted in the logic of the market or expertise rooted in some other moral or scientific logic should prevail. That is true for instance with respect to privatizing activities that once were handled within the military. Market efficiencies may justify privatizing some healthcare or finance functions or closing some bases. But other matters are more difficult to judge. For instance, Deborah Avant, in her chapter on privatizing military training in the present book, questions whether market efficiencies justify privatizing initial training of cadets who will become Army officers. The efficiencies are tempting to a downsized force that must stretch resources. Still, when the military relies on private contractors for instructors, it may subtly teach new entrants into the profession that, despite the rhetoric of self-sacrificing leadership, market logic trumps other considerations. As a result, young officers may leave the profession, abandoning command for the pursuit of economic opportunity.[57] Alternatively and worse, they may remain in the profession with a faulty understanding of what is required of them.

But when there is relative certainty about the goods to be sought or about comparative worth, then the language of the marketplace may be superfluous and the legitimacy of expert knowledge may rest on other grounds. The higher the degree of certainty, the more likely the public will regard such justifications as legitimate. Examples here include scientific questions about how to build thermonuclear weapons or to treat the psychological consequences for individuals subjected to prolonged stress in combat. Once the decision is made to do either, then scientific expertise is required. Professional diagnoses and prescriptions based on this knowledge should be defended against the logic of economic efficiency and "market tests." The same is true with respect to moral issues that the military professional must face. Relying on forms of discourse borrowed from the marketplace, one cannot explain or justify self-sacrifice for the public good that military (and other professional) service often requires. This was a lesson that Robert McNamara had yet to learn as he tried to monitor the "progress" and "efficiency" of the war in Vietnam by relying in part on body counts and ratios of enemy to American losses.[58]

In short, when possible, the military should wrap its expertise in the language of the market to enhance its professional legitimacy. But often that is counter-productive or not possible. Then, the military professional has no choice except to explain to itself and to the public why that language is inappropriate and why we might sometimes wish to act on alternative forms of knowledge to pursue a social good. This is especially important when military missions of war or peace put lives at risk, whether our lives or the lives of others. The military profession is not simply a market-based or scientific occupation. It is a soul-challenging pursuit. Neither the language of the market nor the language of science can comprehend, much less legitimate, what that means for members of the military or for those who recruit and deploy them. A moral vocabulary is needed.

Notes

1. Revision of a paper originally prepared for the Army Professionalism Project and read at the Senior Conference, held on 14-16 June 2001 at the United States Military Academy, West Point, New York. I am grateful for helpful comments on the original paper received from members of that project and for suggestions for revision received from members of the NEH Institute on War and Morality, hosted by Professor George Lucas and Dr. Albert Pierce of the United States Naval Academy, 1-25 June 2004.

2. Samuel P. Huntington, *The Soldier and the State* (Cambridge, MA: Harvard University Press, 1957); Morris Janowitz, *The Professional Soldier* (Glencoe, IL: Free Press, 1960).

3. I say usually because we sometimes use the adjective "professional" in a derisive way, as we do when we speak about "professional politicians" or "professional wrestlers." In these cases, we expect the word professional to denote a full-time occupation that is somehow dishonorable—the politician because politicians are often required to compromise on principles in order to rule and the wrestlers because we know that the outcome of the sporting events in which they compete is scripted. The use of the term professional in these cases is ironical; we use it to cast doubt on the integrity of the groups described and on their contribution to the well-being of society.

4. See, for example, Edward M. Coffman, "The Long Shadow of *The Soldier and the State*," *Journal of Military History* 55 (January 1991): 69-82; and Matthew Moten, *The Delafield Commission and the American Military Profession* (College Station: Texas A&M University Press, 2000), 6-15.

5. Samuel Haber, *The Quest for Authority and Honor in the American Professions, 1750-1900* (Chicago: University of Chicago Press, 1991), x.

6. Eliot Freidson, *Professionalism Reborn: Theory, Prophecy and Policy* (Chicago, IL: University of Chicago Press, 1994), 16. Freidson is not the only one to argue so. A brief but important summary of the historical development and changing meaning of the professions is found in Talcott Parsons, "Professions," *International Encyclopedia of the Social Sciences*, 12: 536-47. More comprehensive treatments can be found in Haber, *Quest for Authority*; and Bruce A. Kimball, *The "True Professional Ideal" in America* (Lanham, MD: Rowman & Littlefield, 1995).

7. For a review of definitions of the professions, see Geoffrey Millerson, *The Qualifying Associations: A Study in Professionalisation* (London: Routledge & Kegan Paul, 1964); and Freidson, *Professionalism Reborn*.

8. T. H. Marshall, "The Recent History of Professionalism in Relation to Social Structure and Social Policy," in *Class, Citizenship, & Social Development* (Chicago, IL: University of Chicago Press, 1977).

9. Ibid., 160.

10. So, for instance, Talcott Parsons argued that the professions were an "institutional framework in which many of our most important social functions are carried on." Talcott Parsons, "The Professions and Social Structure" in *Essays in Sociological Theory*, revised edition (New York: Free Press, 1954), 48.

11. See Eliot Freidson, *Professional Dominance* (New York: Atherton Press, 1970); Jeffrey Berlant, *Profession and Monopoly* (Berkeley and Los Angeles: University of California Press, 1975); and Magalí Sarfatti Larson, *The Rise of Professionalism* (Berkeley and Los Angeles: University of California Press, 1977).

12. Andrew Abbott, "Status and Status Strain in the Professions," *American Journal of Sociology* 86 (January 1981): 828-29.

13. Ibid., 829. See also Edward Shils, "Charisma, Order, and Status," in *Center and Periphery* (Chicago, IL: University of Chicago Press, 1975), 267-71.

14. Andrew Abbott, *The System of Professions* (Chicago, IL: University of Chicago Press, 1988).

15. Ibid., 8.

16. See ibid., 184-195. Abbott's discussion of legitimacy underscores his belief that legitimacy is peripheral—not central—to what constitutes the profession. He acknowledges that professional legitimacy rests on a fit between professional work and values in the larger culture. He notes that "changes in values can recast the *meaning* of a profession's legitimation arguments without any change occurring in the arguments themselves," as meaning changes when put in a different context (187, original italics). And he shows how changing values have affected the professions. Nevertheless, he contends that value shifts over the last two centuries have had "surprisingly small effects on the actual history of [professional] jurisdiction" (195)—a contention that ignores effects they may have had on the form of professional expertise.

17. Kimball, *The "True Professional Ideal" in America.*

18. Parsons, "Professions," 537-38.

19. Ibid., 539.

20. These ideas are expressed, for instance, in the writings of Marshall, Parsons, and Wilensky.

21. Steven Brint, *In an Age of Experts: The Changing Role of Professionals in Politics and Public Life* (Princeton, NJ: Princeton University Press, 1994).

22. A. M. Carr-Saunders and P. A. Wilson, *The Professions*, reprint ed. (London: Frank Cass, 1964).

23. See Arthur Larson, "Military Professionalism and Civil Control," *Journal of Political and Military Sociology* 2 (Spring 1972): 57-72; and Bernard J. Piecznski, "Problems in US Military Professionalism, 1945-1950" (Ph.D. diss., State University of New York at Buffalo, 1985), 34.

24. Janowitz, *Professional Soldier*, 4. More current occupational prestige scores, part of the General Social Survey, do not include military officers as an occupational category.

25. Allan R. Millett, *Military Professionalism and Officership in America* (Columbus, OH: Mershon Center, 1977).

26. Huntington, *Soldier and the State*, 7.

27. Janowitz, *Professional Soldier*, 5-7.

28. These professional pathologies that might affect military effectiveness are taken mainly from Larson, "Military Professionalism," 65-66. The idea that the military professional is an agent who might shirk his responsibilities comes from Peter Feaver, "Crisis as Shirking: An Agency Theory Explanation of the Souring of American Civil-Military Relations," *Armed Forces & Society* 24 (Spring 1998): 407-34.

29. Peter D. Feaver, "The Civil-Military Problematique: Huntington, Janowitz, and the Question of Civilian Control," *Armed Forces & Society* 23 (Winter 1996): 149-78.

30. Morris Janowitz, "Civic Consciousness and Military Performance," in *The Political Education of Soldiers*, ed. Morris Janowitz and Stephen D. Wesbrook (Beverly Hills, CA: Sage, 1983), 74-76.

31. Abbott, *The System of Professions*, 3-6.

32. See Charles C. Moskos and Frank R. Wood, eds., *The Military: More Than Just a Job?* (Washington, DC: Pergamon-Brassey's, 1988); and Charles C. Moskos, John Allen Williams, and David R. Segal, eds., *The Postmodern Military: Armed Forces After the Cold War* (New York: Oxford University Press, 2000).

33. This is a complicated matter. One should not think in terms of either/or categories, but of movements in one direction or another. Nor should we rule out the possibility that along some dimensions of military service the profession moves in one way while, along other dimensions, it moves another. For more on this contrast, see the references cited in note 32.

34. In 1877, Maj. Gen. John M. Schofield told an audience of Army officers: "It is the Science of War in the broadest sense, not simply the *Art* of War, that we are to study." Quoted in Carol Reardon, *Soldiers and Scholars: The US Army and the Uses of Military History* (Lawrence: University Press of Kansas, 1990), 9. For overviews of military professionalization in this period, see in addition to Reardon, for example, Huntington, *Soldier and the State*, 222-88;

Millett, *Military Professionalism*; Russell F. Weigley, *History of the United States Army* (New York: Macmillan, 1967), 313-54; and John M. Gates, "The 'New' Military Professionalism," *Armed Forces & Society* 11 (Spring 1985): 427-36. Historians have recently explored the seeds of American military professionalism in the first half of the 19th century. See, e.g., William B. Skelton, *An American Profession of Arms* (Lawrence: University Press of Kansas, 1992); Moten, passim; and, more briefly, Allan R. Millett and Peter Maslowski, *For the Common Defense* (New York: Free Press, 1984), 126-30.

35. Burton J. Bledstein, *The Culture of Professionalism* (New York: Norton, 1976).

36. Kimball, *The "True Professional Ideal" in America*.

37. For a broader discussion of these trends, see the chapters by Christopher Dandeker and James N. Rosenau in *The Adaptive Military*, ed. James Burk (New Brunswick, NJ: Transaction, 1998).

38. I am indebted to James S. Powell, a history graduate student at my university, for his content analysis of articles appearing in *Army* in 1980, 1990, and 2000. His analysis confirms the centrality of applied scientific expertise for professional identity within the Army.

39. "Piecznski, "Problems in US Military Professionalism"; Townsend Hoopes and Douglas Brinkley, *Driven Patriot: The Life and Times of James Forrestal* (New York: Knopf, 1992).

40. Kenneth C. Allard, *Command, Control, and the Common Defense* (New Haven, CT: Yale University Press, 1990).

41. Abbott, *System of Professions*, 69-79, 151, 153.

42. Increasingly, this is true in theaters of war as well. Think, for instance, of the complex chains of command and relations with civilian relief agencies which had to be coordinated while waging the Kosovo War. On this topic more generally, see Ian Wing, *Refocusing Concepts of Security: The Convergence of Military and Non-military Tasks* (Duntroon ACT: Land Warfare Studies Centre, 2000).

43. Thomas S. Kuhn, *The Structure of Scientific Revolutions* (Chicago, IL: University of Chicago Press, 1962).

44. Rachel Carson, *Silent Spring* (Boston, MA: Houghton Mifflin, 1962).

45. James Burk, "Three Views on Women in the Military," *Society* (May/June 2002): 70-77.

46. See, e.g., Rachel N. Weber, "Manufacturing Gender in Military Cockpit Design," in *The Social Shaping of Technology*, 2nd ed., ed. Donald MacKenzie and Judy Wajcman (Philadelphia, PA: Open University Press, 1999), 372-81.

47. For an interesting discussion of the doubts about the role of self-sacrificing service within the Army, see Don M. Snider, John A. Nagl, and Tony Pfaff, *Army Professionalism, the Military Ethic, and Officership in the 21st Century* (Carlisle Barracks, PA: U.S. Army War College, Strategic Studies Institute, 1999). Obviously the ethos of self-sacrifice has taken on greater salience with the casualties taken in the wars in Afghanistan and Iraq.

48. The issues raised here are multifaceted, and it is beyond the scope of this chapter to discuss them fully, much less to resolve them. Consider just one example. Without consensus about when and how the military profession should practice its expertise, its use is controversial. Given the principle of civilian control over the military, the proper object of the controversy is the civilian administration—often the president—not the military. Dissenters say, "We support the troops but not the war." But *if* the policy is wrong, so is the use of the military to pursue it. Here is a problem for the military profession: How ought the military profession to be used? Judgments about whether and how to use military force are ultimately moral. The military profession has a role to play in making that judgment, but it is not merely the role of technical or expert advisor. The expertise of the military professional must be grounded in a moral understanding of what justifies and is justified when using force. Sociological theories of the professions—and of the military profession in particular—have failed to consider the importance of morality for determining the legitimate use of professional expertise and the legitimate jurisdictions within which that expertise is applied. Theories emerging from other disciplines have not. See, for example, Shannon E. French, *The Code of the Warrior* (Lanham, MD:

Rowman & Littlefield, 2003) and Martin Cook, *The Moral Warrior: Ethics and Service in the US Military* (Albany: State University Press of New York, 2004).

49. This means that the slogan—the Army's purpose is to fight and win the nation's wars—is of little use in any serious discussion of military professionalism.

50. David Last, "Twisting Arms or Shaking Hands? How to Put Peacekeepers Out of Business" (paper presented at conference, Taking Stock of Civil Military Relations, sponsored by the Centre for European Security Studies [The Netherlands], the Centre for Security and Defence Studies [Canada], and the Geneva Centre for the Democratic Control of Armed Forces [Switzerland], held at The Hague, 9-11 May 2001), 4.

51. For a fuller discussion of these issues, see Thomas G. Weiss, *Military-Civilian Interactions: Intervening in Humanitarian Crises* (Lanham, MD: Rowman & Littlefield, 1999).

52. An official with the International Committee of the Red Cross (ICRC) observes that "it is somehow paradoxical that in several tragic situations over the past decade, when the need for military force to restore peace was critical . . . the military (implementing mandates assigned by their political masters) were more involved in activities of an essentially humanitarian nature. The most prominent example is the U.N. Protection Force in Bosnia (UNPROFOR)." Meinrad Studer, "The ICRC and Civil-Military Relations in Armed Conflict" (paper presented at conference, Taking Stock of Civil Military Relations), 5. See note 48 for complete citation.

53. The president's characterization is found in his "Global Message" released on 6 May 2004, which can be accessed at http://www.whitehouse.gov/news/releases/2004/05/20040506-1.html; Internet; accessed 14 July 2004. For information about the mistreatment, which was not confined to the prison at Abu Ghraib, and the warnings made long before the Abu Ghraib photographs were publicly published in the spring of 2004, see the *Report of the International Committee of the Red Cross (ICRC) on the Treatment by the Coalition Forces of Prisoners of War and Other Protected Persons by the Geneva Conventions in Iraq During Arrest, Internment and Interrogation*—February 2004 (http://download.repubblica.it/pdf/rapporto_crocerossa.pdf); Internet; accessed 14 July 2004.

54. The phrase is used in *The United Nations and Civil Society: The Role of NGOs*, Proceedings of the 30th United National Issues Conference (Muscatine, IA: The Stanley Foundation, 1999), 2, as quoted and discussed in Wing, *Refocusing Concepts of Security*, 99.

55. Brint, *In an Age of Experts*, 203-05.

56. On the importance of simple metaphors for the construction of practical knowledge, see George Lakoff and Mark Johnson, *Metaphors We Live By* (Chicago, IL: University of Chicago Press, 1980).

57. Thomas E. Ricks, "Younger Officers Quit Army at Fast Clip," *Washington Post*, 17 April 2000, A1 (available from Lexis-Nexis, academic edition; accessed 27 June 2001). For data on the rates of loss of officers from lieutenant through colonel, see the briefing by Lt. Gen. Timothy J. Maude, Deputy Chief of Staff for Personnel, U.S. Army, presented at the Commanders' Conference on 19 October 2000. Available from: http://www.defense-and-society.org/maude_com_conf/sld001.htm; Internet; accessed 20 August 2004.

58. Robert S. McNamara, *In Retrospect: The Tragedy and Lessons of Vietnam* (New York: Times Books, 1995), 48. In his own words: "I always pressed our commanders very hard for estimates of progress—or lack of it. The monitoring of progress—which I still consider a bedrock principle of good management [a market-based principle]—was very poorly handled in Vietnam. . . . Uncertain how to evaluate the results in a war without battle lines, the military tried to gauge its progress with quantitative measurements such as enemy casualties (which became infamous as body counts)."

3 | Anti-Intellectualism and the Army Profession[1]

Lloyd J. Matthews

In the epigraph here, taken from William Skelton's splendid 1992 study *An American Profession of Arms: The Army Officer Corps, 1784-1861*, we glimpse in finely wrought microcosm the current of anti-intellectualism that has coursed through American arms from its earliest beginnings to the present day. My purposes here are to trace the origins and manifestations of this anti-intellectual bias within the American military tradition; to demonstrate the existence and pernicious effects of such an attitude even in the celebrated age of information now upon us; and to suggest measures for ensuring that the intellectual potential of the officers'

Crossing the Plains on an expedition to Utah [in the 1850s], Major Charles A. May searched the wagons in an effort to reduce unnecessary baggage. When he reached the wagons of the light artillery battery, Captain Henry J. Hunt proudly pointed out the box containing the battery library. "Books," May exclaimed in astonishment. "You say books? Whoever heard of books being hauled over the plains? What in the hell are you going to do with them?" At that moment Captain Campbell of the Dragoons came up and asked permission to carry a barrel of whiskey. "Yes, anything in reason Captain, you can take along the whiskey, but damned if these books shall go."[2]

corps is capitalized on in optimal ways without impairing the warrior ethos of the profession.

Let us first glance at the historical antecedents of anti-intellectualism. Going back to medieval and even to classical times, a sharp distinction emerged between the so-called Active Man and Contemplative Man.[3] Though these two opposed types were fused for a time in Renaissance Man through an expansion of Baldesar Castiglione's notion of the ideal courtier (*The Book of the Courtier*, 1528), the dichotomy was unfortunately too much a part of early human typology to remain submerged much beyond the famous exemplar of Renaissance Man posed by the English soldier-poet-courtier Sir Philip Sidney (d. 1586).[4]

After Sidney and his circle of emulators passed from the scene, the Active Man and Contemplative Man reasserted themselves, with the seemingly natural tension between the two types generally manifesting itself within a soldierly context. The division has remained a prominent feature of the British, French, and American military traditions, with the Contemplative Man often the victim of condescension if not outright scorn by powerful men of deeds who molded the early value system of the profession of arms during a time when the only cerebral quality likely to be found useful was guile.

The theme of anti-intellectualism in Western arms is a staple of military studies, so frequently treated in fact that to do justice to the applicable literature in brief compass presents formidable problems in winnowing and summarizing. The prevailing attitude toward military service held by British officers during the 19th century and the interwar period of the 20th was marked by a deliberate spirit of amateurism that celebrated honor, physical courage, skill in field sports, and above all one's regiment, while deprecating professionalism, schooling, and such qualities as "keenness" and "cleverness" (i.e., intelligence).[5] Correlli Barnett summed it up well:

> Their traditions were against books and study and in favour of a hard gallop, a gallant fight, and a full jug. . . . The preference for character over intellect, for brawn over brain, has always taken the form of denigration of the staff college graduate and apotheosis of that splendid chap, the regimental officer.[6]

The British officer's calculated aversion to brains was noted by wartime Prime Minister Lloyd George (1916-1922), who caustically observed that the "military mind . . . regards thinking as a form of mutiny."[7] B. H. Liddell Hart put it only slightly less trenchantly: "The only thing harder than getting a new idea into the military mind is to get an old one out."[8] Closer to the present day, one commentator finds some abatement in the British military's traditional anti-intellectualism owing to the cognitive demands of a modern technology-based force, but warns nonetheless that "the legacy of the aristocratic or traditional [i.e. anti-intellectual] role model is far from dead."[9]

We need not pause long to examine the situation in France, since it paralleled the British experience in so many ways. One gains the impression, however, that anti-intellectualism among the French military never reached the depths of calculated dilettantism seen in the British.[10] Still, Paddy Griffith in his detailed study *Military Thought in the French Army, 1815-51* (1989) had to concede that "excessive intellectualism might be as much a qualification for premature retirement as illness, madness, or sloth."[11] Moreover, one notes the French predilection for stirring martial catchphrases which served as substitutes for penetrating tactical and strategic analysis, witness the celebrated cry of "Elan, Elan!" during the time of Louis XIII and later, and the clarion emphasis on an audacious offensive spirit toward the end of the 19th century: "L'audace, l'audace, toujours l'audace!"[12]

Finally, we should recall the pregnant words of Marshal Marie E. P. Maurice de MacMahon, who was later to lead the disastrous French "defense" at Sedan in 1870: "I eliminate from the promotion list any officer whose name I have read on the cover of a book."[13] It is an irony of ironies that during the German invasion of France in 1940, a full 70 years later, the fall of Sedan again figured so disastrously.[14] In discussing the French doctrinal preparation for defense against the anticipated invasion, Robert Doughty in *The Seeds of Disaster: The Development of French Army Doctrine, 1919-1939* (1985) states that "the army thus implicitly accepted doctrine as a substitute for thinking and an alternative to creative, imaginative actions. . . . Few soldiers questioned the verities uttered in lecture halls or published in field manuals or official journals."[15]

As we turn to anti-intellectualism in the American military, things really get interesting because the contemplative officer in this country receives a double whammy. For not only is he a citizen of a country itself notorious for its anti-intellectual tendencies, but he has come into a military establishment that in many respects has been more retrograde in its receptivity to ideas than the European militaries.[16] So far as American culture at large is concerned, one has only to examine Richard Hofstadter's unflinching book *Anti-intellectualism in American Life* (1963), particularly the two chapters titled "Anti-intellectualism in Our Time" and "On the Unpopularity of Intellect," to be forcefully reminded that respect for the speculative mind has never been this country's long suit. Hofstadter defines his subject as follows:

> The common strain that binds together the attitudes and ideas which I call anti-intellectual is a resentment and suspicion of the life of the mind and of those who are considered to represent it; and a disposition constantly to minimize the value of that life.[17]

I can promise that those who heretofore have taken pride in what they viewed as America's superior regard for intellectual standing will wince and squirm as they read of the habitual condescending put-downs of the egghead, highbrow, bookworm, absent-minded professor, woolly-minded intellectual, pointy head, recluse in the ivory tower, and all the other clever terms of opprobrium so frequently trotted out to stigmatize the scholar-thinker in American public discourse over the past 250 years.[18]

There are reasons for our anti-intellectual heritage, of course, revolving mainly around the rough-hewn and homespun life incident to establishing ourselves as pioneers on the shores of a savage continent and then advancing the frontier across a dangerous wilderness extending some 3,000 miles ("O beautiful for pilgrim feet whose stern impassioned stress, a thoroughfare for freedom beat across the wilderness!"). But our pioneer days are long past, and though we as a people have excelled in the scientific and engineering aspects of cognitive endeavor, we still can't quite let go of the notion that thinking for thinking's sake is just not macho.

As with the European militaries, the literature documenting anti-intellectualism among our own uniformed services is embarrassingly rich, copious, and conclusive.[19] Bernard Brodie, for example, pointed out in his influential book *War and Politics* (1973) that "soldiers have always cherished the image of themselves as men of action rather than as intellectuals, and they have not been very much given to writing analytical inquiries into their own art."[20] This is not to say that articulate uniformed thinkers have been entirely absent from the scene—witness the writings of Emory Upton, Alfred Thayer Mahan, Billy Mitchell, Maxwell Taylor, Dave Palmer, and, more recently, H. R. McMaster, Douglas Macgregor, and Ralph Peters—but it is to say that to the extent that such uniformed writers have succeeded they did so in spite of and not because of official encouragement.[21]

In 1890, U.S. Navy Captain Alfred Thayer Mahan published *The Influence of Sea Power Upon History, 1660-1783*, the most consequential book ever written by a serving officer with the arguable exception of Clausewitz's *On War*. For this feat, his endorsing officer, Rear Adm. Francis Ramsay, rewarded him on his fitness report with the following glowing encomium: "It is not the business of a Naval officer to write books."[22] It is precisely this sort of attitude on the part of the bosses of military intellectuals that has led such observers as H. G. Wells to claim that "the professional military mind is by necessity an inferior and unimaginative mind; no man of high intellectual quality would willingly imprison his gifts in such a calling."[23] More amusing than Captain Mahan's poor fitness report but no less tragic in its import is this lament from a Navy officer passed over for promotion: "I cannot understand why I wasn't selected: I've never run a ship aground; I've never insulted a senior officer; and I've never contributed [an article] to the Institute *Proceedings*."[24] Benjamin Foulois, Chief of the Army Air Corps in 1932, displayed a touchingly solicitous regard for the physical health of student pilots: "Addressing the 1932 graduating class at the Air Corps Tactical School at Maxwell Field in Montgomery, Alabama, General Foulois said that physical fitness took precedence over knowledge. He did not want his pilots imperiling their health with too much study. . . . The purpose of the school was 'not to put out bookworms.'"[25]

To further illustrate the tenor of the anti-intellectualism that has afflicted the Army over the years, often manifested in revolts by traditionalists against the "book learning" that progressives were attempting to incorporate into an upgraded Army education and training system, let us savor a few nuggets from Carol Reardon's *Soldiers and Scholars: The U.S. Army and the Uses of Military History, 1865-1920*, published in 1990. Col. George Anderson complained in 1898, even as the Spanish-American War descended upon the country, that "we are all too old to have wisdom crammed down our throats like food down the necks of Strasburg geese." Capt. James Chester, an indefatigable foe of professional education, asserted that "while a man may be educated into a *kriegsspieler* [i.e., wargamer], he cannot be educated into a commander of men any more than he can into a poet, or an artist, or a Christian." Lt. C. D. Parkhurst stoutly affirmed "that the system of theoretical instruction, education, evangelization, and reformation now so eagerly sought by some few among us, is not needed." As late as 1914, Army Chief of Staff Leonard Wood issued orders to the effect that "all military education must be severely practical; eliminate books as far as possible except for purposes of reference."[26] To Reardon's instances, we may add the amusing example of Gen. Andrew Jackson. Taxed for his poor orthography, he reportedly replied to the effect that he wouldn't have an officer in his command who couldn't figure out more than one way to spell a word.[27]

The common thread connecting the thought of all such traditionalists is that book learning was useless and that the only effective school of war was the battlefield itself. Today's U.S. Army officers, who take for granted what is probably the best military training and education system ever devised by man, will be hard put to appreciate the extraordinary difficulty faced by lonely occasional soldier-reformers— sometimes assisted by visionary civilian leaders like Secretary of War Elihu Root— during their jousts in the 19th and early 20th centuries with a grudging institution that saw expansion of officers' minds mainly in terms of on-the-job training.[28]

But what about the modern era? Haven't we wised up? To answer this question, we'll first have to be a little more specific with regard to terms. In its most basic sense, an intellectual is preoccupied with ideas and the play of the mind. This suggests a speculative mind, one given to reflection and efforts to see behind surface appearances. It suggests a mind that refuses imprisonment within conventional thinking or stale orthodoxy, but looks to see all sides of issues and insists upon discovering truth for itself rather than having truth prescribed. Moreover, it understands the complex, elusive, and provisional nature of "truth," intuitively grasping that things are rarely as simple as they seem. It suggests a mind that gives vent to the imagination, that is open to innovation, that seeks to be creative, that looks always for the best way to do things today rather than assuming that the well-worn path is preferable because it's where we've always trod before. The interests and curiosity of the intellectual are not compressed within the narrow confines of today's duty assignments, but rather range freely to all fields of disciplinary and cultural endeavor, not only for life's enrichment—though that is vitally important—but also to provide the broadest possible context in which to measure and examine professional concerns.

The intellectual thinks beyond the sound and fury of the daily grind, hearkening to George Santayana's caveat that if we "cannot remember the past we shall be condemned to repeat it," but embracing just as warmly Alvin Toffler's qualification that "if we no not change the future we shall be compelled to endure it—and that could be worse."[29] The intellectual is given to reading because, while personal experience is indeed an instructive mentor, it can never rival humanity's collective wisdom and experience as reflected in books. The intellectual takes it as an article of faith that just as the unexamined life is not worth living, so the unexamined profession is not worth following. Hence he regards the pursuit of truth as more important than the trappings of rank and station. So far as the military intellectual is concerned, he is wed to the belief that in war against a competitive foe, we shall have to out-think that foe if we are to be successful in out-fighting him.

That's what an intellectual ideally is. Now let's draw several important distinctions:

There are among the human race no pure intellectuals any more than there are pure men of action. There are no disembodied brains, divorced from human emotions, hormonal urges, and fleshly thoughts, engaged solely in disinterested play of the mind on the eternal verities. Instead, we are all arrayed on a spectrum, falling somewhere in the broad middle far from the impossible extremes of pure brain and pure instinct. We differ only in that some of us are perched a little more pronouncedly toward one end or the other. So when we speak of intellectuals or men of action, it is important to bear in mind that such distinctions are matters of degree, of mere tendencies, not absolutes.

Closely related to the prior distinction, uniformed intellectuals are not nerds or geeks. Morris Janowitz in his classic study *The Professional Soldier* (1960) makes a sharp distinction between what he calls the "military intellectual" and the "intellectual officer." By "military intellectual," he means the sniffy, pedantic, professorial officer who can't lead, can't manage, can't make decisions, and relates poorly to people, the type described by Brian Holden Reid in a wicked spoof as a "diminutive, blinking, bespectacled swot whose muscles compare with peas and who grows exhausted after lifting a knife and fork."[30] The "intellectual officer," by way of contrast, is the solid leader who brings the intellectual dimension to his job, accommodating it to the peculiar needs and demands of the profession: "He sees himself primarily as a soldier, and his intellectuality is part of his belief that he is a whole man."[31] There were doubtless significant numbers of "blinking swots" inducted into the officer corps during World War II and its lengthy aftermath, and perhaps a handful a year still wriggle through the sieve today. But thankfully they are very few, so that Janowitz's terminological distinction finds virtually no application in the contemporary U.S. officer corps.

Uniformed intellectuals today come from the same commissioning sources as the self-advertised warriors and men of action.[32] They engage in the same sports, meet the same physical and medical standards, choose the same branches, negotiate the same obstacle courses, qualify on the same gunnery ranges, pass the same PT tests, parachute from the same aircraft, stomp around in the same muddy boots, and shout "Ranger, Airborne, Hooah!" with the same lusty gusto. They receive the same professional acculturation, attend the same courses and schools, obtain the same degrees, receive the same early assignments, fight in the same wars, and win the same medals. The only external difference between the contemplative man and the active man in the officers' corps today is that the former may seek a doctorate, teaching tour, fellowship, attaché assignment, or other mind-expanding opportunities that the latter avoids like the plague because under the present career management system such excursions will time him or her out of transiting career wicket X, necessary if the officer is to remain competitive for brigade command and a possible star.

Interestingly, however, there is no evidence that the reputed active man fares any better than the reputed contemplative man as combat commander. It is astonishing to thumb through the biographies of the nation's military heroes and be reminded of the essentially intellectual nature of many of them. Always a distinct minority, they survived the stigma of intellectuality because of their transcendent skill as fighters during times of national peril, and because in personality and demeanor their intellectuality was masked by an undeniable spirit of take-charge self-confidence. Emory Upton, often referred to as "the Army's Mahan" and the most influential writer-reformer-soldier this country has yet produced, was a fierce, skillful, innovative leader in the Civil War, commanding a 12-regiment assault column at Spotsylvania and winning his first star for "gallant and distinguished services." He rose from second lieutenant in 1861 to brevet major general in only four years of action-packed combat service.[33]

Joshua Chamberlain, a professor of languages at Bowdoin College when the Civil War commenced, volunteered for service and eventually rose to command of the 20th Maine. During the war he was wounded six times, had 14 horses shot out from under him, became the Union hero at Little Round Top during Gettysburg, and was awarded the Medal of Honor. He returned to academic life in 1871 as president of Bowdoin, writing several books and major papers. Featured in Michael Sharra's *The Killer Angels* (1975), a novel about Gettysburg, and serving as exemplar in successive editions of Army Field Manual 22-100, *Military Leadership* (October 1983 and July 1990), Chamberlain is today virtually an icon of the quintessential combat leader.[34]

With the possible exception of Stonewall Jackson (himself, incidentally, a longtime professor at VMI prior to the Civil War), George Patton was the most pugnacious fighter-commander our nation ever produced. Yet, he was a true Renaissance Man: U.S. Olympian in the 1912 games in Stockholm, finishing fifth in the Pentathalon (riding, pistol shooting, swimming, running, swordsmanship), football player, polo player, boatsman, poetry lover, raconteur, writer, voracious reader, avid student of the military art and science, rare book collector, and letter writer. Roger Nye in his incisive study *The Patton Mind* (1993) here sums up:

> [Patton] has been celebrated as a highly energized and profane man of action—a doer rather than a thinker, many said. But he left behind the most complete record of exhaustive professional study of any World War II general—or any general in American history, for that matter. . . . Patton acquired and used a military library for almost daily study of his profession and [employed a] system of marginal notes and file cards to develop his thinking about tactics, strategy, leadership, and military organization. Those thoughts were expressed in a stream of lectures, staff papers, and journal articles, and also in diaries, poetry, and finally in a classic book, *War As I Knew It*.[35]

John Shirley "P" Wood was also of two natures. On one hand he was a football player, shrewd tactician, Distinguished Service Cross winner, and extraordinarily aggressive blitzkrieger who as commander of the 4th Armored Division spearheaded the reconquest of France by George Patton's Third Army, for which Liddell Hart bestowed upon him such honorifics as "the Rommel of the American armored forces" and "one of the most dynamic commanders of armor in World War II." On the other hand, Wood was a brilliantly precocious student (having entered the University of Arkansas as a sophomore at the age of 16 to study chemistry); a tireless tutor of less academically gifted cadets at West Point, earning the lifelong nickname P (for professor); a pioneer armor theorist; a devourer of books; a gifted linguist who read Charles de Gaulle on armor in the original French and Heinz Guderian in German; and a devotee of *Rosaceae*, or what we plainer folk call the rose family.[36]

Maxwell Taylor was similar to P Wood in having a divided sensibility. On one side, Taylor was a daring, dashing, athletic soldier, entering Italy behind German lines on a secret mission in 1943 and parachuting behind enemy lines into France on D-Day as commander of the 101st Airborne Division. But Taylor also had an intellectual and cultured side, spending 13 of the interwar years either as student or teacher, attaining fluency in several languages, writing two influential books, serving as president of the Lincoln Center for Performing Arts in New York, and performing the difficult role of U.S. Ambassador in Saigon during the Vietnam War.[37]

The list of those American officers who possessed an intellectual sensibility but who, when the chips were down, proved themselves as illustrious combat commanders, goes on and on.[38] Certainly their success validates Sir William Butler's apt admonition that the nation which "insists on drawing a broad line of demarcation between the fighting man and the thinking man is liable to find its fighting done by fools and its thinking by cowards."[39]

Not all writers and teachers are intellectuals, and not all intellectuals are writers and teachers. I have encountered intellectual instructors who couldn't teach worth a tinker's damn and intellectual writers who couldn't communicate their names. I have known non-intellectual teachers and writers with a marvelous capacity for getting recondite points across to the most obtuse student or reader. I have known Ph.D.s on the staffs and faculties of service schools who, despite their impressive scholarly credentials, remained at heart administrators and paper-shufflers, forever discovering excuses for their failure to sally forth into the arena of intellectual inquiry, speculative thought, or serious professional research. If the intellectual is to earn his keep, he must discover ways to put his ideas and capacity for penetrating reflection at the disposal of the institution. That means having what it takes to convey his ideas and the fruits of his reflections in the appropriate forums. An intellectual who can't or won't communicate is like a breeding bull that can't or won't service.

Not all defense intellectuals are in the military. In fact, I would go so far as to suggest that *most* of the bona fide defense intellectuals active in public discourse today are not in the military. The reasons have mainly to do with the services' refusal to encourage military professionals to become the chief expositors of their own craft and with the increasingly cross-disciplinary nature of security studies.[40] Setting aside uniformed officers, we can assign most defense intellectuals to the following categories, realizing that the categories are not mutually exclusive and that over time some individuals will fall into several of them:[41]

- *Retired Military Officers.* Some of our very best intellectual work is now performed by retireds. The late Harry Summers was a signal instance. The big advantages of retirees are their maturity, experience, and candor, but the fact that we single out their candor as a particular advantage is silent testimony to the enforced reticence of active-duty thinkers.
- *Journalists.* The large metropolitan dailies each have their specialists who handle most of the military reportage. These reporters, particularly those from the *New York Times* and *Washington Post*, often exercise considerable clout because it is they and their editors who shape the daily print news agenda and impart the spin on stories that together mold perceptions among national opinion-makers. Some branch out into books, which extends their influence further.[42]
- *Think Tankers.* Perhaps no intellectual centers for security affairs have proliferated in the last 30 years to the extent that the think tanks have. Think tanks, broadly construed here to include various defense advocacy organizations and certain academic niches, are a haven for unemployed refugees from the Federal government, for retired diplomats and military officers, and for civilian defense specialists who fail to receive tenure or a position on the faculties of civilian universities. They also often provide suitable sinecures for distinguished uniformed emeriti who in return for their names on the letterhead receive a plush office, a secretary, plenty of walking-around money, and a promise of few distractions. The tanks come in all ideological hues, and they thrive on grant money. Many of the tankers do valuable work. Now deceased Carl Builder, long-time denizen at RAND, produced the most insightful analyses of service cultures since Morris Janowitz, Samuel Huntington, and Charles Moskos.

- *Academics.* University faculty, principally in departments treating political science, history, sociology, diplomacy, and international relations, have long been vocal on various national and international security issues. More recently, with the emergence in the universities of accredited graduate degree programs devoted explicitly to military, defense, and security studies (Johns Hopkins' School of Advanced International Studies comes to mind), what once was a string quartet from the universities has now become a symphony orchestra. It is no longer unusual for civilian Ph.D.s from academe to challenge military officers even on their own narrow professional turf. They offer tough competition because in general they are better writers than military officers, more motivated to write, better educated, closer to research facilities, and blessed with more time to devote to intellectual inquiry. This is one reason why the services should nurture their own uniformed intellectuals—they need people who can contend with civilian academics on their own terms.
- *Contractors.* The outsourcing phenomenon has now become a dominant feature of the new century's downsized defense establishment.[43] We hire civilians to do what was formerly military assistance and advisory work; we watch benignly as commercial firms (e.g. Military Professional Resources, Inc.) serve as de facto general staffs for developing the militaries of second-world countries; we outsource to civilian contractors scores of essential functions once performed by the institutional Army, Navy, and Air Force. And a great deal of this outsourced work is intellectual in nature—preparing curricular materials and presenting instruction; writing doctrine; conducting studies and analyses; supporting war games and exercises. Most military exercises today would never get off the ground, much less fly, without their well-oiled complement of civilian contractors.

In thus hiring outsiders to do its thinking, the services risk selling their intellectual souls to the devil of deprofessionalization. The Army defends the practice on the ground that contractors are usually retired military personnel, the implication being that actives and retireds are interchangeable parts. But such is not the case. There is never perfect congruence between the thinking, interests, and outlook of a contractor, even one retired from the military, and the perspective of the active duty officer who lets the contract. The reason comes down to a matter of responsibility. The active duty officer has a solemn fiducial responsibility based on his oath of office and commission for the official tasks he undertakes. A contractor, however, even the most dedicated and conscientious one, has only a legal responsibility. One obligation flows entirely from duty, the other largely from money. There can be no true comparison. I say this with no malice whatever toward our huge tribe of military contractors, of which this author is a long-time member. But let's face it, retired personnel now serving as contractors no longer bring to the table precisely the same agenda they brought back in the glory days.

Drawing on its particular strengths but limited by its particular weaknesses, each of the five groups discussed above contributes usefully to the military marketplace of ideas, but it is a sixth group—the uniformed professionals themselves—who constitute the preeminent and uniquely essential voice. For they comprise the only group with currency, immersion, and expertise in today's operational problems, the only group composed of active, practicing members of the military profession, the only group with the credibility that goes with wearing the uniform now, the only group with the constitutionally mandated mission of defending our country. And it is upon this group that the profession must depend for intellectual sustenance and renewal.

As was convincingly demonstrated by Andrew Abbott in his prize-winning book *The System of Professions* (1988), a would-be profession, to have any legitimate pretense of qualifying as a profession, "must develop abstract, formal knowledge systems from their first origins."[44] Otherwise, there are no criteria to distinguish professional activity from such manual trades as carpentry, plumbing, and house painting. If the military hierarchy, under the banner "Only Warriors Need Apply Here!" systematically excludes from its hallowed higher ranks the one resource capable of conceiving and sustaining the profession's theoretical base and raison d'être, it risks nothing less than institutional suicide. Grizzled muddy-boots generals with rows of ribbons are received with exaggerated respect and exquisite forbearance during public occasions when pomp and ceremony are the order of the day. This is even true during ice-breaking opening statements before Senate and Congressional committees hearing testimony from DoD and departmental teams on service roles, missions, and resources. But when the pro forma bonhomie ends and the gloves come off, the day is carried not by those with the ribbons and crusty anecdotes but rather by those with the intellectual wherewithal to assemble a cogent case, deliver it with engaging precision and conviction, and defend it with nimble argument that bodies forth a complete command of the facts, issues, and stakes. Army partisans better hope that some very fertile green-suiter brains survive into the senior ranks to testify on Capitol Hill as to the enduring relevance of ground forces.

To be intellectual is not the same as to be intelligent. In fact, in the sense employed in this chapter, there is no intrinsic connection between having a bent for ideas and having a high IQ. There are engineers, for example, with impressive IQs who excel at applying borrowed knowledge toward solutions to practical problems in the workaday world, but who have no interest or aptitude for the intellectual, theoretical, and conceptual work that necessarily precedes practice. True, intellectuals who are creative at the highest levels of abstraction can be expected to have good intelligence, but such acuity is not what makes them intellectuals. After all, the intellectual Sir Isaac Newton, who first conceptualized the universal law of gravitation, who was one of the two men who independently invented calculus, and who became one of the greatest figures in the history of scientific speculation, had an IQ of only about 130, certainly sharp but not off the chart.[45]

If high intelligence alone represented sufficient mental endowment, then the U.S. officer corps would be in good shape. Owing to the necessity of professionalization during the American Civil War, with another wake-up call during the Spanish-American War followed by the steady march of military technologization thereafter, the U.S. military parted ways with the dumb-and-proud-of-it dilettantism of the British and gradually came to acknowledge the essentiality of education and training among officers, with respect for the trait of intelligence itself being a logical concomitant.[46] Today, though bookishness and intellectuality remain on the condemned list, high intelligence itself is a prized trait, and indeed tests conducted on Army brigadier generals during the Leadership Development Course at the Center for Creative Leadership in Greensboro, North Carolina, reveal an average IQ of about 124, which for technical reasons Center officials say is "almost certainly" an underestimate.[47] Yes, our general officers are a bright group and doubtless glad of it. To question the intelligence of any one of them would be construed as a deadly insult, almost as insulting as to call one an intellectual.

Advanced degrees do not necessarily an intellectual make. In a further evolution toward rendering intelligence respectable, possession of a master's degree has now become a de facto prerequisite for higher rank. To be on the safe side, virtually all serious operators manage to obtain this degree, in addition to the de rigueur baccalaureate. The degree field is irrelevant—just get the sheepskin. The services have been attentive to this impulse, and have cooperated by awarding master's degrees in strategic studies upon successful completion of the senior service college course and on a less inclusive basis at Leavenworth. Very probably, we shall soon see a de facto requirement for two master's degrees—one from a civilian institution and one from the military. The rage for advanced degrees has widened to embrace even the doctorate. Ph.D.s among the intellectually inclined are of course relatively common, but it is interesting to note that Ph.D.s among even the most inveterate operators are now cropping up on occasion.

Normally, we should rejoice at this proliferating thirst for higher education among our officer corps, but it does have a less noble side. Much of the impulse springs from career uncertainty—officers are hedging against the possibility of leaving the service at 30 years or earlier. This is perhaps understandable. But others are collecting advanced degrees as visible badges of professional merit, as obligatory or at least enhancing bases to be touched in their career progression. Advanced degrees for uniformed officers, particularly the Ph.D., should entail genuine disciplinary expertise, a capacity to perform serious study in the degree field, and a bent for reflecting deeply on disciplinary issues as they relate to the military profession. In short, advanced degrees should expand the recipients' intellectual capacities and hone them for professional utilization. Degree-collecting for other purposes may be understandable, but we should not mistake such degrees as sure evidence of intellectuality.

We now return to the question broached earlier concerning whether in the information-worshipping age of today, anti-intellectualism in our military has at last made its grudging exit. The answer, sadly, is no—overt manifestations of anti-intellectualism still come right out and slap us in the face. One of my favorite examples appeared in the *Colorado Springs Gazette Telegraph* a few years back:

> After a recent afternoon in the Pentagon's super-secret chamber called "the tank," Gen. Alfred M. Gray, the . . . commandant of the Marine Corps, complained about "too many intellectuals" at the top of the armed services. Naming no names, the 59-year-old Marine general said that what is needed is not intellectuals but "old-fashioned gunslingers" who like a good fight and don't spend their time with politicians.[48]

This sort of reflexive, unmeditated bashing of intellectuals fits perfectly into the traditional pattern of attitudes traced so exhaustively by Richard Hofstadter in his book *Anti-intellectualism in American Life*. Such bashing is unbecoming, just as it would be to slur any group of citizens on the basis of ignorant stereotyping. I say "ignorant" so far as the quotation above is concerned because the familiar sentiments expressed there again assume that an intellectual soldier can't fight and lead. As we saw at length earlier, nothing could be more wrong.

There are other examples of contemporary anti-intellectualism. Gen. H. Norman Schwarzkopf in his post-Gulf War autobiography *It Doesn't Take a Hero* (1992) casts in a condescending light the fact that his predecessor in brigade command "was an ex-White House fellow [and] a prolific contributor to military journals."[49] General Schwarzkopf will doubtless march into the history books as one of the ablest senior combat commanders this nation has ever produced—certainly he'll get my vote—and it is thus disappointing to read his assessment of a colleague that gives voice and weight to anti-intellectual considerations.

An irony here is that General Schwarzkopf, despite his public image as the quintessential muddy-boots soldier, is a man of no inconsiderable intellectual, philosophical, and cultural accomplishments himself. He is fluent in French and German. His musical tastes run from folk to opera. He is a member of the International Brotherhood of Magicians. He earned a master's degree in guided missile engineering at the University of Southern California and followed it with a teaching tour in the Department of Mechanics at West Point. While earning his degree at Southern Cal he moonlighted by teaching calculus and basic engineering at Northrop Institute and accounting at South Bay Women's College.[50] Classmates at West Point often referred to him as "Einstein."

To the extent that raw intelligence may facilitate intellectual accomplishment, General Schwarzkopf is prodigiously well equipped. His IQ as measured on the Stanford-Binet intelligence scale has been publicly reported in several sources as 170, which puts him well up into the genius category.[51] In fact, as shown in Catherine Morris Cox's pioneering study *The Early Mental Traits of Three Hundred Geniuses* (1926), not a single one of history's great military leaders for which data could be adduced possessed an IQ remotely rivaling that of General Schwarzkopf. Consider: Napoleon Bonaparte 135, Robert E. Lee 130, William Tecumseh Sherman 125, George Washington 125, Horatio Nelson 125, David Farragut 120, Hernán Cortés 115, Joachim Murat 115, Nicolas-Jean Soult 115, Ulysses S. Grant 110, Philip Sheridan 110, and Gebhard Blücher 110.[52] While attending the infantry officers' advanced course at Ft. Benning, then Captain Schwarzkopf won the George C. Marshall Award for Excellence in Military Writing.[53] Moreover, his autobiography *It Doesn't Take a Hero*, already mentioned, has taken its place as an important addition to the soldier's professional literature.

This tension between the active and contemplative selves that we observe in General Schwarzkopf is by no means uncommon. Dwight Eisenhower, also a crypto-intellectual, was as a young officer the victim of a crassly anti-intellectual assault by Maj. Gen. Charles Farnsworth, Chief of Infantry, after Ike had published an article on the promising future of tanks in the November 1920 issue of *Infantry*

Journal: "I was told that my ideas were not only wrong but dangerous and that henceforth I would keep them to myself. Particularly, I was not to publish anything incompatible with solid infantry doctrine. If I did, I would be hauled before a court-martial."[54] Yet, despite this searing lesson on the primitive smugness of the closed mind, we find Ike himself as president in 1954 pandering to the same type of anti-intellectual mentality that had victimized him 34 years before:

> We had so many wisecracking so-called intellectuals going around and showing how wrong everybody was who didn't happen to agree with them. By the way, [an intellectual is] a man who takes more words than are necessary to tell more than he knows.[55]

Over 30 years ago, Ward Just wrote, "There has never been a Clausewitz in the American Army because the writing of [*On War*] took time and serious thought. An Army officer has no time to think, and imaginative reflection is discouraged."[56] These words could as well have been written today. Col. Douglas Macgregor in 1997 managed to publish a seminal book called *Breaking the Phalanx: A New Design for Landpower in the 21st Century*, which presciently declared among other things that to escape the curse of irrelevance, the Army must reconfigure its gargantuan divisions into smaller, agile, rapidly deployable combat groups whose anti-armor capability would derive partially from inclusion of the armored gun system and light armored vehicles.[57] According to an article by Richard Newman in *U.S. News & World Report* (28 July 1997), Macgregor's ideas didn't sit well with much of the Army brass.[58] But today, seven years later, those same brass, prodded originally by civilians within Defense and the Department of the Army, are falling all over themselves in a mad rush to "transform" the Army into something suspiciously resembling the model sketched earlier by Douglas Macgregor, who remains a prophet without honor in his own time.

President George Bush during a speech to graduating Annapolis midshipmen on 25 May 2001, outlined his vision of a military that rewards imaginative thinking: the president sought "a renewed spirit of innovation in our officer corps" and decried the "old bureaucratic mind-set that frustrates the creativity and entrepreneurship that a 21st-century military will need."[59] Secretary of Defense Donald Rumsfeld, describing on 22 July 2001 the traits of an ideal JCS chairman, declared that the person must have "the ability to lead, intellectually as well as personally."[60] Were the admirals and generals listening? Very possibly they were, because on the same day that the president spoke the Army released a "brutally self-critical" study on Army officer training and leader development by a 37-member panel convened in June 2000 by Army Chief of Staff Eric Shinseki. Among the findings, Army officers suffer from stifling micromanagement—a fact long known and broadly acknowledged—and a promotion system driven by bureaucratic needs—also long known and broadly acknowledged.[61]

Let us therefore turn our focus more specifically on the Army's present promotion and personnel management system because it is here that we discover a form of anti-intellectualism more subtle than that discussed earlier, but no less virulent. This form manifests itself as an overpoweringly pro-muddy boots bias. Briefly stated, the present promotion and advancement system is rigged to favor those who have served the most time with troops. All other factors being equal, advancement to the highest grades goes to those with the most time in the field (with occasional detours to especially selected grooming slots in the Pentagon). This means that officers who spend significant time in mind-expanding positions developing their intellectual skills are pro forma noncompetitive for advancement to the higher rungs.

To put this reality in broader context, consider the more capacious assignment philosophy that governed the careers of the great combat commanders of an earlier day. From the summer of 1875 to the fall of 1876, Emory Upton was sent by the Army on an overseas tour—Japan, China, India, Russia, Europe—to study the world's major armies. In Stephen Ambrose's words, Upton "returned home filled with new ideas and a new purpose."[62]

Omar Bradley guarded copper mines in Montana during World War I, missing the war completely, and then spent most of the interwar years attending or teaching school.[63] Dwight Eisenhower missed World War I too. Like George Marshall, he became known as an outstanding staff officer, and also served such details as football coach at Ft. Benning and working for the American Battlefield Monuments Commission.[64] In addition to a steady diet of staff assignments, George Marshall served on a mapping expedition in Texas, held a command in the state of Washington devoted mainly to running Civilian Conservation Corps camps, and toured the Manchurian battlefields of the Russo-Japanese war in a quasi-official status.[65] Matthew Ridgway spent six years at West Point as a French and Spanish instructor, tactical officer, and faculty director of athletics.[66] James Van Fleet spent nearly 13 years in ROTC assignments, including two winning seasons as coach of the University of Florida football team, directed Civilian Conservation Corps camps, and served as a trainer of reserve component forces.[67] J. Lawton Collins prior to World War II served as an instructor at Leavenworth and on the faculty of the Army War College. Raymond Spruance, one of our finest World War II naval commanders, served two tours on the faculty of the Naval War College.[68] We've already noted that Maxwell Taylor spent 13 of the interwar years attending school or teaching it. Far from seeing their careers killed or stunted, each of these officers saw their minds and perspectives usefully broadened, and their careers prospered. Indeed, 31 of the 34 corps commanders who led the U.S. Army in its victories over Germany and Japan in the Second World War had served as instructors in various Army schools.[69]

But such assignment patterns as we observe above would be career-stoppers today. Theodore Crackel says that "if Clausewitz and Jomini had served in the American military, they would have been counseled to serve no more than a single three-year teaching assignment and to escape sooner if possible."[70] Similarly, former Chairman of the Joint Chiefs David Jones complained that "we've never sired a Clausewitz. In our system Clausewitz would probably make full colonel, retire at 20 years, and go to work for a think tank."[71] I was told recently by department professors at West Point that Pentagon assignment officers are discouraging many of the best and brightest from accepting West Point's graduate school-teaching tour package because they then won't have time to touch the remaining mandatory career bases. Ralph Peters weighs in with the observation that few of those "who won our wars would have made it in today's Army of nondescript careerists. Increasingly, our successful officers have identical career paths [and] interchangeable experiences and views of the world."[72] So whence comes this magical insight—belief in the superiority of promotion by checklist—that today's personnel handlers and promotion boards display that those of Marshall, Eisenhower, Bradley, Patton, Ridgway, Van Fleet, Collins, and Taylor's generation lacked?

Colonel Michael Cody in a study on selecting and developing the best leaders, conducted while he was a student at the U.S. Army War College in 1999-2000 and published by the Department of Command, Leadership, and Management, reaches the following disturbing conclusion:

> Had George C. Marshall begun his Army career in the late 20th century Army, it is arguable whether he would have survived long enough and risen high enough to develop into perhaps the greatest soldier-statesman who ever donned the uniform. Early on, he demonstrated transcendent skills as a staff officer, and it was essentially these skills that propelled him upward through the ranks to that point in 1939 when he became Army Chief of Staff, only 3 years after gaining his first star. But today's promotion and assignment system, with its inflexible insistence upon visits to each of several ceremoniously delineated stations of the cross as preconditions for further advancement, would have made it extremely difficult for Marshall to continue to progress in rank while cultivating the broad politico-military competencies that were to equip him uniquely to build America's World War II Army, organize the allied victory, and conceive the nation's successful early Cold War strategy.[73]

For today, as earlier noted, time with troops has become the ultimate measure of worthiness for promotion to the highest ranks. Many of today's generals are thus very good with troops, but, lacking a broader repertoire, they often find it difficult to adapt at the higher staff and ancillary positions. Retired Lt. Gen. Walter Ulmer, our most insightful thinker on contemporary military leadership, put it this way: "Research shows convincingly how strengths that served well to accomplish the tactical tasks of early managerial years can become dysfunctional when individuals move to the strategic level."[74]

General Ulmer is taking note of the fact that the Army's system for advancing officers is designed to reward those who extrapolate lower-level command skills rather than those who develop and demonstrate skills fitted to the new duties and responsibilities associated with higher rank. In Colonel Cody's words, "The embedded assumption is that if officers were paragons at lower levels, they will automatically be able to meet the demands of higher levels—no matter how different such demands might be from those encountered earlier."[75]

But such an assumption flies in the face of theory, experience, and common sense. Our World War II sergeants commissioned on the battlefield performed superbly as platoon and company commanders for the most part, but many later began to falter when faced with the more cerebral demands of staff work at battalion level. War is full of examples of brilliant tacticians who were dismal failures at the operational and strategic levels, and of peerless brigade and division commanders who blew it on assuming corps command. Witness Lee's problems with his corps and division commanders at Gettysburg.[76]

The reasons are clear: as the officer ascends from lower levels of command requiring direct modes of leadership to higher levels of command requiring successively greater applications of indirect leadership, or as he ascends from positions that are purely military in character to those with increasingly political, diplomatic, economic, cultural, and legal dimensions, the prerequisite skills, aptitudes, personality traits, and experience will change dramatically.[77] The object of the general officer promotion and assignment system should not be simply to select the fastest "gunslingers," to use General Gray's colorful term, but rather to achieve the appropriate aptitude mix among its general officer pool so as to be able to fit round-pegged generals in round holes, square-pegged generals in square holes, and fits-any-shape generals in those holes requiring a stalwart fighter capable of reflecting wisely and deeply on how he must adapt in order to win a particular war.

Indeed, a RAND study conducted in 1994 concluded that the pronounced "action bias" among the Army's top uniformed leaders, resulting in an impoverishment of essential skills in resource allocation, policy development, and programming, was seriously disadvantaging the Army in its competition for budgetary dollars with the other services, which expressly sought leaders with such relevant experience.[78] Ironically, for the overwhelming majority of our senior warriors, their most difficult and important wars will be fought not on the crimson fields of military battle, but rather within the genteel suites of bureaucratic strife.

In a detailed analysis of actual general officer positions conducted by John Masland and Laurence Radway in 1953, it was shown that only about a third of the 500 generals were serving with armies, corps, divisions, and brigade-level commands, that is, with operating units in the field (and this was during the Korean War). The remaining two-thirds were scattered among a mixed agglomeration of staff, administrative, technical, and training positions.[79] Since that time, the relatively small proportion of generals assigned to field duty has declined even further because, while force structure has been greatly reduced, the number of generals authorized has not been reduced correspondingly.

Moreover, the increased complexity of military missions today, along with increased reliance on information and advanced technology, has tended to place greater reliance on intellectual skills among senior leaders. Those intellectual skills now required among general officers in addition to field competence are reflected mainly under such duty categories as technical, policy, conceptual, doctrinal, educational, humanitarian, nation-building, peace-keeping, planning, futures, strategic, grand strategic, and political-military interface. For a general contending in these arenas, victory and defeat will have little to do with the mud on his feet, but everything to do with the ideas in his head. Marine Gen. Anthony Zinni, for example, recapitulated his duties in the early 1990s as follows:

> I have trained and established police forces, judiciary committees and judges, and prison systems; I have resettled refugees in massive numbers twice; I've negotiated with warlords, tribal leaders, and clan elders; I have distributed food, provided medical assistance, worried about well-baby care, and put in place obstetrical clinics; I've run refugee camps, and I've managed newspapers and run radio stations to counter misinformation attempts.[80]

Or consider the activities of Lt. Gen. Dave Petraeus, holder of a Ph.D. from Princeton, former instructor in the Department of Social Sciences at West Point, and commander of the fighting 101st Airborne Division (Air Assault) in the Iraq war:

> Listening to Petraeus tick off the accomplishments of his division—500 schools refurbished, nearly 20,000 security forces trained, foreign investment in hotels and shopping malls, telephones working, water flowing, lights on, cement and asphalt factories churning out their goods—is like listening to the mayor of a city that is struggling to make a comeback.[81]

It is now a commonplace to note that today's regional four-star commanders, preoccupied as they are with the highest matters of state, more nearly resemble proconsuls than military commanders: "[The regional CINC] has plainly become something more than a mere soldier. He straddles the worlds of politics, diplomacy, and military affairs, and moves easily among them."[82] Just being an "old-fashioned gunslinger" isn't enough.

Today, the Army has 330 general officers, enough to form a small battalion, but with only 10 or 11 division equivalents we don't need 330 general officer gunslingers. We can never find 330 gunslinger positions for them, meaning they'll often be slotted where they lack the intellectual horsepower to perform the duties required.[83] The Army will have to assign gunslingers to inappropriate positions because the intellectual officers with high potential for senior command will already have been eliminated under our formulaic promotion system, a system almost theological in its unwavering insistence that every single muddy-boots base be touched.[84]

The intellectual who aspires to apply his competency at high levels of responsibility thus faces an impossible dilemma: on one hand, if he hews to the muddy-boots straight and narrow he can never exercise his intellectual capacities and develop them to the fullest; on the other hand, if he accepts some intellectually developmental assignments along with as many of the familiar operational qualifiers as he can, he will likely be a non-select for battalion and brigade command, meaning he'll never receive a star. We shouldn't quarrel with this result on grounds of equity, though certainly that is important, but rather on purely pragmatic grounds: the Army shoots itself in the foot by effectively excluding intellectual officers from its highest rungs, thus depriving itself of those equipped to do the Army's intellectual heavy lifting.

Many operators also face a dilemma: to express their professional ambition, they feel constrained to suppress, disguise, or ignore their intellectual side. My beef isn't with ambitious operators—professional ambition can be a healthy, positive force—but rather with the *system* that forces many such officers to deny their intellectuality as the price of career success.[85] Military historian Richard Swain in a penetrating study of senior Army commanders during peace operations in Europe, 1994-2000, provides a telling example in Gen. Montgomery C. Meigs, who holds a Ph.D. in history from the University of Wisconsin, was a history instructor at West Point, served as the Distinguished Visiting Professor of World Peace at the LBJ School of Public Policy, University of Texas, is presently Professor of Government and Business Policy, Maxwell School, Syracuse University, and has published several intellectually venturesome articles over the past few years:

Meigs bears his [intellectual] gifts uneasily. He is embarrassed to be known as an intellectual. He has spent much of his career trying to overcome that reputation by long hours of hard work in the more practical side of his profession, more often as not in the field.[86]

Former Army Chief of Staff General Shinseki spent two years at Duke University earning his master's degree, followed by three years at West Point teaching literature and philosophy. It was a marvelously seminal intellectual and cultural experience for him, to which I'm sure he'd be the first to attest. But it is problematic in the extreme whether under the promotion and assignment system that General Shinseki inherited as Chief and still largely prevails today, similarly talented young captains can successfully risk a five-year detour from the anointed path.

This system is a perfect manifestation of what outsiders have long associated with the so-called "military mind," the tendency for the military to take a basically sound idea and then press it so literally and woodenly that it eventually arrives at an unwitting reductio ad absurdum. Lest one get the idea that such outsider sentiments are the dated remnants of a quaint bygone era of antimilitarism, listen to the words of Lt. Gen. Thomas Burnette, spoken when he was the Army's Deputy Chief of Staff for Operations in 1997: "The Army has an ingrained belief that if it's worth doing, it's worth overdoing."[87] With regard to the present promotion and assignment system, the Army has taken a laudable principle—getting officers off their duffs, out of their offices, and down with troops where they can master their branch skills and learn to operate in the field—and implemented it with such compulsive zeal that those officers now arriving at the top know nothing but the field.

An exaggeration? Yes, but there is no question that the present system has produced a lop-sided general officer corps infinitely more comfortable with practice than with reflecting on practice. As a result, this group has turned its thinking over to Pentagon civilians, discardable field grade staffers, contractors, and various outsiders. "We don't have to think," they are in effect saying, "we just run things." Whatever happened to the high premium formerly placed on officer assignment patterns that engender such professional qualifications as balance, roundedness, and versatility? We desperately need to alter our robotic assembly line for promotion and assignment. Its cookie-cutter uniformity and rigidity—lacking nuance, discretion, and latitude for genuine consideration of all the variable factors that coalesce in producing today's enlightened senior leader—continue to work against us.[88]

The virulent effects of the muddy-boots syndrome long afflicting the Army's senior leadership have now been documented in convincing detail in a landmark study project at West Point directed by Don Snider and Gayle Watkins. Based on investigations conducted by 39 uniformed and civilian experts on various aspects of organizing for land warfare, the results were reported in an anthology titled *The Future of the Army Profession* published in April 2002 by McGraw-Hill, the first edition of the present book.[89]

In a bare nutshell, this study concludes that despite recent Army successes on the battlefield, the Army profession is rapidly degrading because it is succumbing to bureaucratization and deprofessionalization, and because it is losing in the competitive sweepstakes for legitimacy and control of its core jurisdictions. Dr. James

Blackwell, of Science Applications International Corporation, for example, explains: "The Army claims primacy over the use of lethal force in land warfare. It is losing that claim in the current competition for jurisdiction over land warfare largely because its doctrine and doctrine process do not provide sufficient cognitive power in ongoing jurisdictional disputes with rival professions."

The problem is not a shortage of doctrine, Dr. Blackwell emphasizes, but rather the Army's inability to supply the theoretical underpinnings for future land warfare founded on a modern general theory of war that is persuasive to the nation's civilian leaders. In short, he says, "It is time for the institution to reestablish its intellectual curriculum vitae."[90] Over and over in reading this book, one encounters similar indications that the profession is in disarray because its alpha males are by and large such creatures of operating that they lack the time, interest, and capacity even to detect, much less reverse, the profession's declining intellectual fortunes.[91]

Snider and Watkins here add an apt commentary on whence might come the talent to generate the future military-technical expert knowledge essential for a thriving Army profession—but they are not optimistic:

> A very sobering theme centered on the questions of whether Army officers were cleaving into two types, perceived as either "thinkers" or "doers," and, if so, whether the professional future for each was equally bright. Since knowledge is the foundation of professions—expansion of that knowledge being fundamental to a profession's evolutionary success—it is essential to have valued members whose role is to create and develop expert knowledge *in addition to* those who apply professional expertise. If the Army is to flourish as a profession, both types of Army professionals need to be equally esteemed, and to have equally bright futures. Unfortunately, this is not the case today, nor without deep cultural change is it likely to be so in the future.[92]

Following immediately on the heels of the Snider-Watkins book was a shocking public testament to the growing impatience of political leaders with the "knuckle-dragging image" that so many of the nation's senior military leaders like to cultivate. In a front-page story in the *Washington Post* (11 April 2002) by Thomas Ricks titled "Bush Backs Overhaul of Military's Top Ranks," it was announced that Secretary of Defense Donald Rumsfeld would nominate Marine Gen. James Jones as the next Supreme Allied Commander in Europe in lieu of an expected Army general. According to Ricks, Rumsfeld was selecting a cohort of leaders

> who stand out among the current top brass as unconventional thinkers. . . . Picking Jones to be the top U.S. military officer in Europe may be a way for Rumsfeld to signal to the Army that he wants it to be more innovative. . . . Rumsfeld aides have privately expressed surprise at what they say is a lack of fresh thinking in the Army.[93]

There have been some positive notes in recent years, and we would be remiss in failing to acknowledge them. Among the last six commandants of the Army War College, for example, there have been a Rhodes Scholar, a published historian, a published military educator, and two Ph.D.s who have also published. Among the last five Superintendents at the U.S. Military Academy, there have been a Rhodes Scholar, a widely published historian, two Ph.D.s, and a J. D. At the Center for

Military History in Washington, DC, the practice seems to have taken hold of selecting Chiefs with Ph.D.s in history. Intellectuals, often tenured Ph.D.s, are also put to good use on the faculties of the War College, the Command and General Staff College, and the Military Academy. Yes, Army intellectuals have established a niche in the academic side of the house, but they remain remarkably under-represented in high-level command and policy positions.

It is true that a few transcendently talented and versatile officers in the last couple of years—by dint of zeal, perseverance, and artful balancing of assignments, plus a lot of luck—have managed to negotiate the operator's maze successfully while also doing justice to genuine intellectual development. They should be commended for their dedication and sacrifice. But the Army is foolish to make it so inordinately difficult for talented soldier-intellectuals to rise to important command and policy billets. As a general rule, military intellectuals tend to face mandatory retirement as lieutenant colonels or colonels, just as they are achieving full intellectual maturity.

During a productive conference on Army professionalism at West Point during the period 14-16 June 2001, retired Gen. William R. Richardson, a former Army Deputy Chief of Staff for Operations and Commanding General of Training and Doctrine Command, complained that there is an unhealthy bifurcation between "thinkers" and "doers" in the Army.[94] He was right, of course, and I was disappointed that his observation evoked little discussion in plenary session. There is indeed a separation of thinkers and doers, but the separation isn't simply between the two functions, it's also between the *ranks* associated with the two functions.

As we've seen, with few exceptions the thinkers—that is, the intellectuals—culminate their careers as field graders, while the doers, or operators, who run the Army, move on to monopolize the general officer ranks. This rank discrepancy between the two types has far-reaching adverse consequences, for it guarantees that the services' major doctrinal, theoretic, and philosophical decisions will be made by officers for whom the process of productive contemplation is alien. John Hillen, a veteran of the Gulf War, a writer of first-rate material on military professionalism and culture, and formerly a member of the bipartisan government National Security Study Group, commented as follows:

> The four-stars get to choose the next crop of four-stars, so they perpetuate themselves as a group. They're good fellows, they're fine fellows, they're heroic fellows, but I honestly think they'd be more comfortable with a copy of *Bass Fishing* magazine than with a book on military theory. . . . They're not bold thinkers, and they can't pretend to be.[95]

In my estimation, this is an overly harsh estimate, but it does capture an important kernel of truth: our seniors today are highly conventional operators, an operator being one who has single-mindedly pursued command or command-qualifying assignments to the exclusion of all others.[96] While they are superb at organizing and running things in the traditional mold, they are lamentably unequipped to conceptualize newly superior solutions themselves or even to recognize the arrival of a new idea whose time has come. In short, they are poor at achieving that delicate, ceaselessly dynamic balance between cycling out yesterday's tried and true, and welcoming in what will become today's and tomorrow's tried and true. For this task, we need the influential presence of minds at the highest grades who are comfortable in the cosmos of ideas. Of course, it's wrong to claim that a muddy-boots operator could never generate a momentous conceptual breakthrough, but to actually assign him responsibility for doing so would be like straining for plankton from the back of a whale: while it may be theoretically possible, it is certainly dangerous and inefficient, and one is entitled to suspect that precious little plankton would be harvested.

Nor are most senior operators good at eliciting big ideas from even the most talented staffs. A four-star operator milking a subject with a colonel intellectual can remain imperiously closed-minded, but a four-star operator consulting with a four-star intellectual will attend very carefully to what has been proposed. That is the nature of the beast. We need to propel more officers to the topmost rungs of rank who are truly capable of conceiving and defending an innovative approach. Even in the darkest hours of service anti-intellectualism, the Army always mustered the will to send three or four thinkers to the top—the Charles Bonesteels, Andrew Goodpasters, William Depuys, Maxwell Thurmans, John Galvins, and Gordon Sullivans—the latter of whom tirelessly urged that change is not a dirty word and that professional disagreement with one's superiors is not disrespect. General Shinseki, the Army Chief from 1999 to 2003, proceeded along a similar path. But the chances of that continuing to happen diminish steadily with each day's prolongation of the present system of professional advancement.

My complaint here isn't that our muddy boots operators necessarily lack intellectual potential. Many of them obviously do have such potential, but most have chosen to concentrate so narrowly on erecting their house of stars that they have neglected to build their mansion of the mind. Intellectual competence doesn't, like Athena from Zeus's brow, spring full-blown into being at the stroke of the oath-taking on commissioning day. Rather, like other competencies, its development requires time, practice, and focused effort. A distinguished Army four-star, now retired, once boasted(!) to me that he never read anything but the contents of his in-box. The Army culture that produced this sort of swaggering, know-nothing complacency simply has to give way to a tough insistence that our senior leaders be whole men and women, which is to say that they unapologetically and without career penalty give reasonable attention to developing their contemplative selves as well as the active.

Some have argued that Officer Personnel Management System XXI, now fairly well implemented in OPMS 3, will eventually accomplish the goal of moderating the Army's pro-operator bias. It may very well level the playing field somewhat between operators and specialists in promotions up to 0-6, but I see nothing in the new system that will weaken the operators' stranglehold on flag-level positions.[97]

Several of the Army's brightest and most articulate captains and majors of the early 1990s survived their outspoken forays into the world of contending ideas and are doing well in their careers as they climb toward their first star. Unfortunately, however, most have read the career tea leaves and have now clammed up. Their lately developed reticence recalls to mind Liddell Hart's observation concerning young British uniformed intellectuals:

Ambitious officers, when they came in sight of promotion to the generals' list, would decide that they would bottle up their thoughts and ideas as a safety precaution until they reached the top and could put these ideas into practice. Unfortunately, the usual result, after years of repression for the sake of their ambition, was that when the bottle was eventually uncorked the contents had evaporated.[98]

The Army is doubtless correct in insisting on the man of action as the predominant model for the combat commander—let there be no mistake about that. But it is dead wrong in assuming that uniformed intellectuals—simply because they have not negotiated every wicket in a general officer qualification course that could only have been devised by Genghis Khan's G3—cannot be men of action and hence are unqualified to command the higher line echelons. Moreover, the Army is on questionable ground in assuming that those who have been anointed by a zero-defects performance at each of the stations of the cross are thereby fit to serve in every general officer slot, even those for which they obviously lack the necessary intellectual qualifications. Rather than denigrating and marginalizing the uniformed intellectual, the Army should hearken to President Bush's call for a "renewed spirit of innovation in our officer corps." It should implement the necessary promotion and assignment adjustments to assure that the intellectual potential of the officers' corps is identified, cultivated, and exploited in optimal ways, which would include service at the highest echelons.

It is time finally to acknowledge that the active man and contemplative man do merge in many versatile people, and that the Army has as much need for the qualities of the latter as for the former. The intellectual man—and woman—have a vital role to play in all professional endeavor, not least military endeavor, and it is thus a fool's game to squander precious intellectual capital on the basis of a historical anti-highbrow shibboleth. The army that rejects seminal thinkers, thereby depriving itself of innovative ideas and the instruments for continuous intellectual self-renewal, will ultimately be an extraneous army, replaced by other services and entities which have come to realize that an invincible force and a thinking force are one and the same.

To bring to a close this excursion through the subtleties of Army anti-intellectualism and its corrosive effects on professional expertise and legitimacy, I here recapitulate the major lines of argument.

The Army's senior uniformed hierarchy systematically excludes from its ranks the one resource capable of conceiving and articulating the profession's theoretical base, thereby risking nothing less than institutional senility and irrelevance. Several foundational propositions support this thesis:

- Anti-intellectualism is deeply embedded in American military culture, with historical antecedents going back to our English forbearers and through them to classical and medieval times. Though anti-intellectualism has been endemic in the western military tradition (e.g., in England and France), it has been especially evident in American arms owing to the added factor of anti-intellectualism in American society itself.

- In American military culture today, anti-intellectualism is not directed against those with lofty IQs—indeed high intelligence is a prized trait; rather, it is directed against those who are seen to be preoccupied with ideas. It is directed against those seen to be thinkers instead of doers, against those seen to be contemplative and reflective instead of operators.

- Anti-intellectualism in American arms is manifested in at least two ways: (a) directly, through contemptuous or disparaging labeling and aloofness to new ideas and innovative approaches; and (b) indirectly, through an Army promotion system that effectively favors the operator by posing so many fixed operational prerequisites for advancement that the intellectual cannot compete without sacrificing his opportunities for intellectual development. A corollary to both (a) and (b) is the assumption that an intellectual cannot fight and cannot lead men in battle, either because he is effete or because he has failed to negotiate every qualifying career wicket. Military history, however, is well-populated by figures whose career patterns strayed far from the orthodox but who proved to be stalwart combat commander in war.

- Intellectuals tend to reach mandatory retirement in the grade of lieutenant colonel or colonel, just as they are reaching full intellectual maturity and potential. The Army thus siphons off for elimination the most fertile-minded of its officers, assuring that those who remain and rise to the top are the least capable of conceiving new solutions and adapting to necessary change.

- The Army's system for advancing officers is designed to reward those who extrapolate lower-level command skills rather than those who develop and demonstrate skills fitted to the new duties and responsibilities associated with higher rank. The underlying assumption is that if officers were paragons at lower levels, they will automatically be able to meet the demands of higher levels—no matter how different such demands might be from those encountered earlier.

- The reality, however, is that as an officer progresses from lieutenant platoon leader to 4-star general JCS chairman, the skill set required will gradually shift from tactical, hands-on, doer types of duties to diplomatic, grand strategic, thinker types of work. It is a breathtaking irony that under the Army's present promotion and assignment system, as officers rise in rank we begin to winnow out precisely that subgroup whose minds are best adapted to provide the brand of leadership required at the top-most rungs.

- The result has been a maladaptive Army senior officer corps. Like it or not, and without involving ourselves in personalities or in the pros and cons of various transformation particularities—Crusader, Commanche, Stryker, downsized brigades, etc.—the fact remains that over the last few years the Army's top leaders have been viewed as unresponsive by the civilian leadership. It has been a sad, humiliating experience to see the Army lose the expected billet of Supreme Allied Commander in Europe, to see the Army Chief of Staff lame-ducked over a year before his term's end, to see the Secretary of the Army unceremoniously kicked out the door, and to see some 50 active-duty Army generals and lieutenant generals passed over as the new Army Chief of Staff in favor of a retired officer—with all these snubs justified publicly on the grounds that the Defense Secretary was seeking "innovative thinkers."

- The Army is going to have to figure ways to operate successfully within the budgetary, end-strength, weaponry, and political parameters laid down by its civilian masters. That is the American way. It is the overriding reality and the bedrock axiom from which all discussion must begin. No matter how bleak prospects for military success may appear in the face of such irksome constraints, the Army must identify and elevate leaders with the imaginative and innovative capacity to devise a pathway to success. If the Army cannot find such leaders because those with the necessary cognitive prowess were long ago discarded, it faces distinctly unpalatable consequences: either our civilian leaders will shove their own solutions down the Army's throat, or, even worse, they will bypass the Army as a spent and irrelevant force and turn instead to competing professions promising the will, expertise, and fresh insights to get the job done.

- Thus if the Army is to survive as a respected, indispensable professional entity, it will have to bite the bullet of promotion and assignment reform. It will have to discard its bias against thinkers, and assure that they come to be represented at the highest ranks and in positions where the great decisions touching the Army's identity and future directions are made. A profession lives or dies by the vitality of its professional expertise. If that expertise withers in stasis because the thinkers, innovators, conceptualizers, theorists, intellectual renewers, and philosophers have been dropped by the wayside, the profession will have no one to blame but itself.

Notes

1. I wish to thank Col. Bill Lord (USA Ret.), Col. Leonard Fullenkamp (USA Ret.), and Col. Donald Boose (USA Ret.), all of the U.S. Army War College faculty, for vetting the original manuscript of this chapter and providing invaluable advice and assistance. Whether they agree with all the views expressed herein or not, they are each quintessential soldier-intellectuals. This chapter has been adapted from a two-piece series appearing in *ARMY* magazine in the July and August issues of 2002, under the title "The Uniformed Intellectual and His Place in American Arms." The author expresses his gratitude to *ARMY* for its kind permission to use the material.

2. Quoted in William B. Skelton, *An American Profession of Arms: The Army Officer Corps, 1784-1861* (Lawrence: Univ. Press of Kansas, 1992), 238. The excerpt has been slightly emended.

3. For a Boethius connection, see *De Consolatione Philosophiae*, tr. John Walton, E.E.T.S. o.s. 170 (London: Oxford Univ. Press, 1927), 17, n. 42; and Boethius, *The Consolation of Philosophy*, tr. Richard Green, The Library of Liberal Arts (New York: Bobbs-Merrill, 1962), 4, n. 1. For Chaucer of the medieval period, see *Boece* in *The Works of Geoffrey Chaucer*, 2nd edition, ed. F. N. Robinson (Boston, MA: Houghton Mifflin, 1957), ll. 27-32, p. 321, and n. Prose 1, 29ff., p. 798; also see *The Knight's Tale*, introductory explanatory note, p. 670; and *The Second Nun's Prologue*, n. 85ff., p. 757. In a work of prodigious scholarship and erudition, Ernst Robert Curtius (*European Literature and the Latin Middle Ages*, trans. Willard R. Trask [New York: Harper Torchbooks, 1963]), has traced the reappearance of classical intellectual themes (*topoi*) throughout Western literature. For such *topoi* as *armas y letras* and *sapientia et fortitudo*, see pp. 170-179.

4. See "From the Archives: Baldesar Castiglione and Renaissance Man," *Parameters* 11 (September 1981): inside rear cover; and "From the Archives: Sir Philip Sidney: Renaissance Soldier-Poet," *Parameters* 22 (Winter 1992-93): inside rear cover.

5. For the tradition of anti-intellectualism among the British officers' corps, consult Correlli Barnett, "The Education of Military Elites," *Journal of Contemporary History* 2 (July 1967): 15-35; John Baynes, *Morale: A Study of Men and Courage* (Cassell, 1967; repr. Garden City Park, NY: Avery, 1988), 109, 116, 119-120, 123-127; Norman F. Dixon, *On the Psychology of Military Incompetence* (New York: Basic Books, 1976), chap. 14; Stephen Brodsky, *Gentlemen of the Blade: A Social and Literary History of the British Army Since 1660* (New York: Greenwood, 1988), xiii-xiv, xviii-xxiv, 67-68, 164-168; Gwyn Harries-Jenkins, "The Education and Training of Military Elites," in *The Educating of Armies*, ed. Michael D. Stephens (New York: St. Martin's, 1989), chap. 1; John Winthrop Hackett, *The Profession of Arms* (London: Times Publishing Co., 1962), chap. 5; Jay Luvaas, *The Education of An Army British Military Thought, 1815-1940* (Chicago: Univ. of Chicago Press, 1964), 43, 244, 387, 428, and *passim*; Brian Holden Reid, *Studies in British Military Thought: Debates with Fuller and Liddell Hart* (Lincoln: Univ. of Nebraska Press, 1998), chap. 1; and Russell A. Hart, *Clash of Arms: How the Allies Won in Normandy* (Boulder, CO: Lynne Rienner, 2001), 35-26, 29, 38. See particularly Barnett, Brodsky, Luvaas, and Reid. For a brilliant fictional portrayal of British army anti-intellectualism (based on a thinly veiled caricature of Field Marshal Sir Douglas Haig), see C. S. Forester, *The General* (1936; Mt. Pleasant, SC: Nautical & Aviation Publishing Co., 1982), 24-25-164-165.

6. Barnett, 16, 18. Another apt characterization of British officers' aversion to serious study can be found in the following quotation of unknown authorship: "No one would attempt to make officers into bookworms, and any such attempt would certainly not succeed—you cannot do away with the idea that the fool of the family is good enough for the army." Quoted in unpublished, undated [May 2002] draft letter prepared by the Chief of Military History, Brig. Gen. John Sloan Brown, on the subject of Army budget cuts damaging to the infrastructure supporting the study of military history.

7. Quoted by Williamson Murray in "Thinking About Defeat," *Commentary*, July 1990, 62.

8. As quoted in Robert Debs Heinl, Jr., *Dictionary of Military and Naval Quotations* (Annapolis, MD: United States Naval Institute Press, 1966), 190.

9. Harries-Jenkins, 34.

10. Paddy Griffith, *Military Thought in the French Army, 1815-51* (Manchester, UK: Manchester Univ. Press, 1989). This book is presented as a corrective to the stock criticisms of the French army and the military thought that undergirded it in the wake of the Sedan debacle in 1870, but Griffith does have to concede the reality of anti-intellectualism. See, e.g., pp. 18, 69, 73, 91, 136-137. In his treatment of the education of military elites (see note 5), Correlli Barnett discusses the French experience along with the British, American, and German. For discussion of the adverse effects on the intellectual capacity of the Prussian officer corps resulting from the aristocratic landed gentry's depreciation of the value of formal education, see Trevor N. Dupuy, *A Genius for War: The German Army and General Staff, 1807-1945* (New York: Praeger, 1989), 27. The gentry, i.e., the Junkers, believed that education softened men, converting them to thinkers rather than doers.

11. Griffith, 91.

12. Hackett, 22; Luvaas, 232-233, 238; Robert Allan Doughty, *Seeds of Disaster: The Development of French Army Doctrine, 1919-1939* (Hamden, CT: Archon Books, 1985), 9.

13. Marie E. P. Maurice de MacMahon, as quoted in Paul-Marie de la Gorce, *The French Army: A Military-Political History*, tr. Kenneth Douglas (New York: George Braziller, 1963), 9.

14. Consult Robert Allan Doughty, *The Breaking Point: Sedan and the Fall of France, 1940* (Hamden, CT: Archon Books, 1990).

15. Doughty, *Seeds of Disaster*, 12; note also pp. ix, xi, 11.

16. Samuel J. Watson, "Knowledge, Interest, and the Limits of Military Professionalism: The Discourse on American Coastal Defence, 1815-1860," *War in History* 5 (Fall 1998): 284.

17. Richard Hofstadter, *Anti-intellectualism in American Life* (New York: Alfred A. Knopf, 1963), 7.

18. Hofstadter, 9-19.

19. Samuel P. Huntington, *The Soldier and the State: The Theory and Politics of Civil-Military Relations* (New York: Vintage Books, 1957), 256-57; Morris Janowitz, *The Professional Soldier: A Social and Political Portrait* (New York: The Free Press, 1960), 135, 430-35; Skelton, 238-39; Edward M. Coffman, *The Old Army: A Portrait of the American Army in Peacetime, 1784-1898* (New York: Oxford Univ. Press, 1986), 276; John W. Masland and Laurence I. Radway, *Soldiers and Scholars: Military Education and National Policy* (Princeton, NJ: Princeton Univ. Press, 1957), 44, 92, 440, 509; Carol Reardon, *Soldiers and Scholars: The U.S. Army and the Uses of Military History, 1865-1920* (Lawrence: Univ. Press of Kansas, 1990), 23-26, 45, 90-91, 110-111; T. R. Brereton, *Educating the U.S. Army: Arthur L. Wagner and Reform, 1875-1905* (Lincoln: Univ. of Nebraska Press, 2000), 121-122; Bernard Brodie, *War and Politics* (New York: Macmillan, 1973), 436, 479, 479-486, and *passim*; Ward Just, *Military Men* (New York: Alfred A. Knopf, 1970), 108-109, 120, 126-127, 137.

20. Brodie, p. 436. For a fuller exposition of this theme, see Lloyd J. Matthews, "Musket and Quill: Are They Compatible? *Military Review* 61 (January 1981): 2-10.

21. For a fuller discussion of professional expression by military officers and the services' attitude toward such expression, see my four articles titled "Censorship and Professional Writing in the Army Today," *ARMY* Magazine, November 1995, 11-17; "The Army Officer and the First Amendment," *ARMY* Magazine, January 1998, 25-34; "The Voorhees Court-Martial," *ARMY* Magazine, September 1998, 17-23; and "The Speech Rights of Air Professionals," *Airpower Journal*, Fall 1998, 19-30. With regard to Col. Douglas A. Macgregor's book on the need for reorganizing the Army's combat unit (*Breaking the Phalanx: A New Design for Landpower in the 21st Century* [Westport, CT: Praeger, 1997]), see Richard J. Newman, "Renegades Finish Last: A Colonel's Ideas Don't Sit Well with the Brass," *U.S. News & World Report*, 21 July 1997, 35. In the same vein, see Sean D. Naylor, "Shaking up the Status Quo," *Army Times*, 25 June 2001, 10. In his article "Two Armies" appearing in *Parameters* 19 (September 1989): 24-34, Daniel P. Bolger foreshadowed much of the conceptual underpinnings of *Breaking the Phalanx*.

22. Robert Seager II, *Alfred Thayer Mahan: The Man and His Letters*, Annapolis, MD: Naval Institute Press, 1977, 18-19; Robert Debs Heinl, Jr., *Dictionary of Military and Naval Quotations* (Annapolis, MD: United States Naval Institute, 1966), 236.

23. For the Wells quotation, see Heinl, p. 190. Cf. Lewis Mumford: "The army has usually been a refuge of third-rate minds, . . . [otherwise] civilization might easily have been annihilated long ago." Quoted in C. Robert Kemble, *The Image of the Army Officer in America* (Westport, CT: Greenwood Press, 1973), 180.

24. Quoted in Robert Greenhalgh Albion, *Makers of Naval Policy, 1798-1947* (Annapolis, MD: Naval Institute Press, 1980), 73. I am indebted to that splendid soldier-intellectual Col. Henry Gole, USA Ret., for calling my attention to this quotation.

25. "Air Corps Chief Addresses Class," *Montgomery Advertiser*, 12 June 1932, 1. I am indebted to Maj. Earl Tilford, USAF Ret., a soldier-scholar of the first water, for pointing out this quotation.

26. Reardon, 23, 26, 45, 91. In his mention of *kriegsspieler*, Chester was not referring to "wargamer" in the modern sense, but rather in all likelihood to those who played the board game Kriegsspiel, invented as an educational game for German military schools in the 18th century and imported to Leavenworth after the Civil War. See Sylvia Nasar, *A Beautiful Mind* (New York: Touchstone, 1998), 75-76; and Coffman, 276.

27. The source for this oft-repeated attribution is elusive. Maj. J. S. Parks, writing in the *Journal of the United States Infantry Association* in 1905, recorded it as follows: "I believe it was Gen. Jackson, mighty with the sword but rather weak in his orthography, who said he wouldn't give a continental for a man who couldn't spell a word in more than one way" (*ARMY* Magazine,

September 2001, 14). Robert P. Wettemann, Jr., recalls the quotation slightly differently: "Jackson is once reported to have said that 'it is a damned poor mind indeed that can't think of at least two ways of spelling any word'" (*West Point: Two Centuries and Beyond*, ed. Lance Betros [Abilene, TX: McWhiney Foundation Press, 2004], chap. 7, n. 21).

28. For a succinct survey of the reformers, see Huntington, 217-251 and *passim*; and Janowitz, 431-32. For a survey of U.S. military thought, see Russell F. Weigley, *Towards an American Army: Military Thought from Washington to Marshall* (Westport, CT: Greenwood Press, 1962). Despite the predominant anti-intellectual tendencies prevailing over the years, there have been localized intellectual renaissances from time to time. The doctrinal flowering in the Army following the Vietnam War provides a good example, as does the interwar period 1919-1945. For the latter, see Hart, *Clash of Arms*, 3, 8, 20-21.

29. For the George Santayana quotation, here slightly emended, see Heinl, p. 148; for Alvin Toffler, see "Introduction: Probing Tomorrow," in *The Futurists*, ed. Alvin Toffler (New York: Random House, 1972), 3.

30. Janowitz, 431; Reid, 2.

31. Janowitz, 431.

32. For an effective deflation of the self-advertisement of would-be warriors, see Lt. Gen. Richard G. Trefry, "Soldiers and Warriors; Warriors and Soldiers," in *The American Warrior*, eds. Chris Morris and Janet Morris (Stamford, CT: Longmeadow Press, 46-54.

33. Richard C. Brown, "General Emory Upton: The Army's Mahan," *Military Affairs* 17 (Fall 1953): 125-131; Stephen E. Ambrose, *Upton and the Army* (Baton Rouge: Louisiana State Univ. Press, 1964), 16-53 and *passim*.

34. Michael Shaara, *The Killer Angels* (New York: Ballantine, 1975), chap. 4; U.S. Army Field Manual 22-100, *Military Leadership* (October 1983), 4-16, 56-60; Willard M. Wallace, *Soul of the Lion: A Biography of Joshua L. Chamberlain* (New York: Thomas Nelson, 1960), chap. 10.

35. Roger H. Nye, *The Patton Mind* (Garden City Park, NY: Avery, 1993), x, 1-33.

36. Caleb Carr, "The American Rommel," *MHQ* 4 (Summer 1992): 76-85. See also Hanson Baldwin, *Tiger Jack* (Ft. Collins, CO: Old Army Press, 1979).

37. *The Oxford Companion to American Military History*, ed. John Whiteclay Chambers II (New York: Oxford Univ. Press, 1999), 713; David Halberstam, *The Best and the Brightest* (New York: Random House, 1969), 162-164 and *passim*.

38. Among the numerous other soldier-intellectuals worthy of brief mention are Col. Roger Hilsman, Jr. (U.S. Army Reserve) and Gen. Andrew Goodpaster. Hilsman fought as a member of Merrill's Marauders and detachments of the Office of Strategic Services in Burma in World War II, later earning a Ph.D. at Yale, becoming a professor of government at Columbia, serving as Assistant Secretary of State during the Vietnam War, and writing 12 books. General Goodpaster was awarded the Distinguished Service Cross, Silver Star, and two Purple Hearts for extraordinary heroism as commander of an engineer combat battalion in Italy in 1943-1944, and later earned a Ph.D. from Princeton. In subsequent years, he was commandant of the National War College, deputy U.S. commander in Vietnam, and superintendent of the U.S. Military Academy. See *Register of Graduates and Former Cadets* (West Point, NY: Association of Graduates, U.S. Military Aacademy, 2000), entries under graduation numbers 11336 and 13491.

39. William F. Butler, *Charles George Gordon* (London: Macmillan, 1907), 85.

40. See Just, 108, note; and Lloyd J. Matthews, Review of *Bernard Brodie and the Foundations of American Nuclear Strategy* by Barry H. Steiner, *ARMY* Magazine, December 1991, 52-53.

41. The following taxonomy of defense intellectuals was adapted from Reid, 3-4.

42. See, e.g., *Making the Corps* (New York: Scribner, 1997), by Thomas Ricks of the *Washington Post*.

43. Thomas K. Adams, "The New Mercenaries and the Privatization of Conflict," *Parameters* 29 (Summer 1999): 103-116; and John C. Deal and James H. Ward, "Second Thoughts on

Outsourcing for the Army," *ARMY* Magazine, May 2001, 49-54. For a counterpoint view, see the letters to the editor by J. Reid Everly and Holt Busbee, *ARMY* Magazine, July 2001, 3-5.

44. Andrew Abbott, *The System of Professions: An Essay on the Division of Expert Labor* (Chicago: Univ. of Chicago Press, 1988), 53.

45. Catherine Morris Cox, *The Early Mental Traits of Three Hundred Geniuses*, Vol. II of *Genetic Studies of Genius* (Stanford, CA: Stanford Univ. Press, 1926), Table 12A and p. 364.

46. For the lateness of the British to professionalize and upgrade the educational credentials of their officer corps as compared to other Western armies, see Barnett, 16-19; and Brodsky, 67-73 ff. See Just, 126, for the concise observation that the U.S. "Army is compulsively anti-intellectual as opposed to being anti-brains."

47. David Campbell, Address delivered at the American Psychological Association Convention, New York, NY, 30 August 1987 (p. 5 and Table 3, typescript). Other interesting observations: "The general officers' score is relatively lowest on the FLEXIBILITY scale, which says something about their willingness, or lack thereof, to consider new, innovative solutions to problems" (p. 8); "Not surprisingly, these people like action. . . . These men are not particularly attracted by the softer, finer activities of life" (p. 12).

48. Quoted by David Campbell, p. 18, from the 17 April 1987 issue of the *Colorado Springs Gazette Telegraph*.

49. H. Norman Schwarzkopf, written with Peter Petre, *It Doesn't Take a Hero* (New York: Bantam, 1992), 206. Maj. Wesley K. Clark, a fighting soldier high in both intelligence and intellectual capacity who would eventually gain four stars and lead the NATO forces during the war in Kosovo in 1999, felt the impress of Army anti-intellectualism in the early 1980s. See his book *Waging Modern War: Bosnia, Kosovo, and the Future of War* (New York: Public Affairs, 2001), 25.

50. Schwarzkopf, 42-43, 50, 96-101, 107. For Schwarzkopf's magicians affiliation, see Robert D. Parrish, *Schwarzkopf: An Insider's View of the Commander* (New York: Bantam, 1991), 3.

51. For the Einstein allusion, see "Biography" [Gen. H. Norman Schwarzkopf], Arts and Entertainment Channel, 22 May 1997. For the source of the 170 IQ allusions, see "Biography"; Parrish, 3; and Richard Pyle, *Schwarzkopf: The Man, the Mission, the Triumph* (New York: Signet, 1991), 8. Pyle says he took General Schwarzkopf's IQ of 170 from an "official biography."

52. Cox, Table 12A.

53. Schwarzkopf, 97.

54. Dwight D. Eisenhower, *At Ease: Stories I Tell My Friends* (Garden City, NY: Doubleday, 1967), 173.

55. As quoted in Hofstadter, 10.

56. Just, 108-109.

57. Macgregor, chap. 4. See also Peter J. Boyer, "A Different War: Is the Army Becoming Irrelevant?" *The New Yorker*, 1 July 2002, 58, 62, 63.

58. Richard J. Newman, "Renegades Finish Last." Another case roughly paralleling Douglas Macgregor's was that of Col. William L. Hauser. In 1973, then-Lieutenant Colonel Hauser, an up-and-coming officer of great promise and also a first-class intellectual, published the book *America's Army in Crisis: A Study in Civil-Military Relations* (Johns Hopkins University Press). In a frank but responsible manner, Colonel Hauser discussed the social problems rampant in the late-Vietnam War Army—drugs, discipline, morale—and offered some innovative solutions. His book was not well-received by those in the Army's upper echelons, and Hauser retired as a colonel in 1980. Ironically, the seriousness of the Army's ills of the period as rendered by Colonel Hauser has been broadly acknowledged by virtually all postwar commentators.

59. Mike Allen, "Bush Foresees More Open-Minded Military," *Washington Post*, 26 May 2001, A5; Roberto Suro, "Army Finds Itself Much at Fault," *Washington Post*, 26 May 2001, A6-A7.

In Vince Crawley and Rick Maze, "Congress Grows Impatient with Defense-plan Delay, *Army Times*, 4 June 2001, 8, President Bush is quoted as follows: "I'm committed to fostering a military culture where intelligent risk-taking and forward thinking are rewarded, not dreaded. And I'm committed to ensuring that visionary leaders who take risks are recognized and promoted."

60. Thom Shanker and Eric Schmitt, "Rumsfeld Set to Advise Bush on Picking Top Military Man," *New York Times*, 23 July 2001, A15.

61. Sean D. Naylor, "Study Blasts Army Culture," *Army Times*, 4 June 2001, 8; also, see Suro in n. 59 above. On over-control and micromanagement, see Lloyd J. Matthews, "The Overcontrolling Leader," *ARMY* Magazine, April 1996, 31-36; on the dysfunctional Army promotional and advancement system, see Michael H. Cody, "Selecting and Developing the Best Leaders," in *Building and Maintaining Healthy Organizations*, ed. Lloyd J. Matthews (Carlisle Barracks, PA: U.S. Army War College, Department of Command, Leadership, and Management, January 2001), chap. 5.

62. Ambrose, *Upton and the Army* 85-96.

63. Omar N. Bradley, *A General's Life* (New York: Simon and Schuster, 1983), 44-45; *The Oxford Companion to American Military History*, ed. John Whiteclay Chambers II (New York: Oxford Univ. Press, 1999), 90.

64. Ambrose, *Eisenhower*, Volume One: *Soldier, General of the Army, President-Elect, 1890-1952* (New York: Simon and Schuster, 1983), 65, 82, 125.

65. Forrest C. Pogue, *George C. Marshall: Education of a General, 1880-1939* (New York: Viking, 1963), 86-89, 124-125, 308-311.

66. Matthew B. Ridgway, *The Memoirs of Matthew B. Ridgway* (New York: Harper, 1956), 34.

67. Paul. F. Braim, *The Will to Win: The Life of General James A. Van Fleet* (Annapolis, MD: Naval Institute Press, 2001), passim.

68. Williamson Murray, "The Army's Advanced Strategic Art Program," *Parameters* 30 (Winter 2000-01): 32.

69. See excerpt from General Richardson's letter in note 93.

70. Theodore J. Crackel, "On the Making of Lieutenants and Colonels," *The Public Interest*, Summer 1984, 26.

71. "Retiring Chief Speaks Out on Military Council," *New York Times*, 25 February 1982, B14.

72. "Ralph Peters, "Wasting Talent the Army Way," *Army Times*, 16 March 1998, 35; also, see Peters' "Ruinous Generals Heroes Gone Astray," *Army Times*, 16 February 1998, 31.

73. Cody, 164-165; Pogue, 86-89, 124, 274ff.

74. Walter F. Ulmer, Jr., "Military Leadership into the 21st Century: Another 'Bridge Too Far'?" *Parameters* 28 (Spring 1998): 18.

75. Cody, 165.

76. *Oxford Companion to American Military History*, 297-299.

77. Cody, 163-164.

78. James Dewar et al., *Army Culture and Planning in a Time of Great Change* (Draft), DRR-758-A (Santa Monica, CA: RAND, July 1994), xvi, 52-53, 121-122. A final version of this preliminary study was never published. For the Army's failure to gain representation in important joint billets, see William J. Troy, "Is the Army Out of Step in the Joint Arena?" *ARMY* Magazine, December 1996, 7-8.

79. Masland and Radway, 515-16.

80. As quoted in Ricks, *Making the Corps*, 186.

81. Robert Hodierne, "Two Stars & Street Smarts," *Army Times*, 16 February 2004, 23.

82. Andrew J. Bacevich, "A Less Than Splendid Little War," *Wilson Quarterly* (Winter 2001), 93.

83. General Officer Management Office, Office of the Army Chief of Staff, *General Officer Roster*, 1 January 2001.

84. These inflexible career "wickets" are established in Department of the Army Pamphlet 600-3, *Commissioned Officer Development and Career Management* (Washington, DC: Headquarters Department of the Army, 1 October 1998). There is some hope that the Army may be finally waking up to the pernicious effects of promotion by checklist. See Jim Tice, "Command Decisions," *Army Times*, 21 June 2004, 24, 26. Regarding an updated version of DA Pamphlet 600-3 now being prepared, Tice reports the expectation "that officer career maps emerging . . . will be more general than the current guides. 'That will allow us to move away from being wedded to timelines, and having to hit very specific marks on the map,' [officer personnel chief Brig. Gen. Rhett Hernandez] said." Congress also appears to be aware of the problem. U.S. representatives Ike Skelton and Steve Israel, both members of the House Armed Services Committee, recently wrote: "The status of subject-matter experts—be they civil affairs officers skilled in building the institutions needed for a successful society or foreign-area officers with a deep understanding of the cultural and social forces at play in the region—must be elevated so that these experts are not shunted off into dead-end careers."

85. See Lloyd J. Matthews, "Is Ambition Unprofessional?" *ARMY* Magazine, July 1988, 28-37.

86. Richard M. Swain, *Neither War Nor Not War—Army Command in Europe During the Time of Peace Opertions: Tasks Confronting USAREUR Commanders, 1994-2000* (Carlisle Brracks, PA: U.S. Army War College, Strategic Studies Institute, May 2003), 197. Compare David Halberstam's reportage on Gen. Wesley Clark regarding the same dilemma: "Among the many distinctions that run through the army, one of the most important is that of pure warrior versus military intellectual. Warriors were greatly favored within the culture, while intellectuals were generally regarded with some degree of suspicion. . . . Clark was perceived by many as an army intellectual. But to those who knew him well he was also, in every sense, the complete warrior." David Halberstam, "Clinton and the Generals," *Vanity Fair*, September 2001, 236. For a sample of General Meigs's publications, see "Unorthodox Thoughts About Asymmetric Warfare," *Parameters* 33 (Summer 2003): 4-18; "Generalship: Qualities, Instincts, and Character," *Parameters* 31 (Summer 2001): 4-17; and "Operational Art in the New Century," *Parameters* 31 (Spring 2001): 4-14.

87. As quoted in USAWC Staff Action for the Commandant, subj.: Task for . . . Planning and Scheduling at the Army War College, 28 May 1998, p. 5.

88. In addition to a major attitude readjustment at the top, specific adjustments in the mechanics of selecting officers for the higher ranks can be made. For example, the Army Chief of Staff in his instructions to the Army's 1983 brigadier general promotion board directed that from four to six selections be made from among combat arms officers who had not commanded brigades. A similar principle, judiciously applied, should be observed in the selection process for all general officer grades. See Colonel Yasotay [pseudonym for John C. "Doc" Bahnsen], "Warriors: An Endangered Species," *Armed Forces Journal International*, September 1984, 119. I respectfully disagree with my friend Doc Bahnsen in this article, who argues against the 1983 BG selection process liberalization.

89. Don M. Snider and Gayle L. Watkins, project directors, Lloyd J. Matthews, ed., *The Future of the Army Profession* (Boston, MA: McGraw-Hill, 2002). Hereinafter referred to as FAP I. The present book represents the 2nd edition of FAP I.

90. James A. Blackwell, "Professionalism and Army Doctrine: A Losing Battle?" in FAP I, 101, 102, 117.

91. See, e.g., FAP I, chap. 11, p. 236; chap. 16, pp. 345-46, 348; chap. 17, p. 371; chap. 20, p. 427; chap. 22, pp. 489-90; chap. 25, pp. 532, 537, 538; Introduction to Sect. III, 193. See also Andrew J. Bacevich, "Not-So-Special Operation," *National Review,* 19 November 2001, 20.

92. FAP I, Introduction to Sect. II, 100. For other recent notices of the unhealthy division between operators and thinkers in our modern Army, see Michael P. Noonan and John Hillen, "The New Protracted Conflict: The Promise of Decisive Action," *Orbis* 46 (Spring 2002): 244 ("The Secretary of Defense and the civilian service secretaries must take measures to increase oversight of the service promotion processes to ensure that the proper mix of warfighters, innovators, and

soldier-diplomats are advanced through the system."); Eliot A. Cohen, "A Tale of Two Secretaries," *Foreign Affairs* 81 (May/June 2002): 45 ("One of the great military machines of the last two centuries, the German general staff, worked because it kept a tight link between its 'thinking' and its 'doing' elements. . . . A slavish or simple-minded imitation of the German formula would be ill-advised, but the example bears pondering."); and Kip P. Nygren, "Emerging Technologies and Exponential Change: Implications for Army Transformation," *Parameters* 32 (Summer 2002): 98 ("The professional military culture places great value on action and generally disdains process [the thinking and theorization upon which action is based]. Only comfortable with acting, we feel guilty if valuable time is given over to reflection. Rather, we are focused almost totally on the end result, the final product. If we are to progress successfully, the balance between product and process needs to shift in the future toward process . . . ."). See also Gen. William R. Richardson's letter, discussed in n. 94 below.

93. Thomas E. Ricks, "Bush Backs Overhaul of Military's Top Ranks," *Washington Post*, 11 April 2002, A1, A10, A11.

94. "The Future of the Army Profession," Senior Conference XXXVIII, sponsored by the Department of Social Sciences, U.S. Military Academy. Conference held at the Arden House, Harriman, NY, 14-16 June 2001. The book *The Future of the Army Profession*, cited above in n. 88, was an outgrowth of this conference. Gen. Richardson later expanded on his thoughts in a letter to Army Chief of Staff Eric Shinseki, with information copies to Gen. John Abrams, Commanding General, TRADOC; Lt. Gen. William J. Lennox, Jr., Superintendent, USMA; and Maj. Gen. Robert R. Ivany, Commandant, USAWC (letter dated 23 June 2001; copy provided to author by General Richardson). A pertinent excerpt is as follows: "The Army is bifurcated today into the 'doers' and the 'thinkers' or between the operating forces (doers) and the intellectual base of USMA, TRADOC, and the AWC (thinkers). . . . The bifurcation occurs in the minds of almost everyone, from the senior Army leadership to the personnel managers in the Army. This happens because the 'doers' are accorded Priority 1, while the 'thinkers' are at a much lower priority. Operational forces get the best cut of manpower and dollars, while the school system gets a much lower cut. It has been this way for years. Moreover, when the Army was faced with a drawdown, such as the one that took place after the Gulf War, the intellectual base of the Army took a disproportionate share of the manpower cuts. . . . What the leadership did not understand was that regardless of the size of the Army, it needed a robust base of thinking to develop its concepts and doctrine for the next war, determine what organizations it needed and the material systems to go in those organizations, and then how to train the Army. To maintain a viable institutional base required some very careful tailoring, not a salami slice of the Army schoolhouses. . . . Indeed, some of the schools, and even the Cadet Command, are having to hire retired personnel to do their work. This does not make for a professional Army. This bifurcation, which makes the intellectual base feel like they are second class citizens, reflects a failure of the Army to adopt the fundamental characteristics of Army professionalism. . . . What this says to me is that without a robust intellectual base to think about how to fight and then to expertly teach others how to fight, we really don't have a truly professional Army. . . . I have often made the observation that schools exist first and foremost for faculties and secondarily for students. Faculties have to perform the 'heavy lifting' for the Profession of Arms, namely, the thinking. The troop units then execute, using their acquired knowledge of the art and science of war, gained from the faculties. When faculty members go back to the field to serve as 'doers,' they have proven to be absolutely superb. To make this point even stronger, of the 34 corps commanders who led the American Army to victory in World War II, 31 had taught in the Army school system."

95. Quoted in Sean D. Naylor, "Holder Retires Sept. 1," *Army Times*, 18 August 1997, 14.

96. An operator is a member of the combat or combat support arms who, depending upon rank, single-mindedly seeks and obtains command, executive, and staff assignments to tactical and operational units in the field, i.e., platoon, company, battery, battalion, squadron, brigade, group, command, division, corps, etc., and supplementarily to prestigious positions on the Army or JCS staffs, or in the offices of the Secretary of Defense or Army. This pattern of

assignments is identified with the career track necessary for promotion to flag rank and command at the highest echelons. More broadly, an operator is one who occupies fast-track, narrowly operational, command-prerequisite positions in contradistinction to those who occupy peripheral or technical positions. Operators are thought to be those who actually run the field Army as opposed to those who merely administer or support it. An operator is also one who, regardless of the marginality of his position, possesses the temperament, predisposition, and aspirations of an operator.

97. Jim Tice, "Career Calculations," *Army Times*, 2 June 1997, 12-14; "Colonels Board a First," *Army Times*, 16 July 2001, 17; Jim Tice, "2,300 Field-Grade Officers Get Career Fields," *Army Times*, 23 July 2001, 20ff.

98. B. H. Liddell Hart, *Why Don't We Learn from History?* (New York: Hawthorn, 1971), 29.

4 Serving the American People: A Historical View of the Army Profession[1]

Leonard Wong and Douglas V. Johnson II

his chapter examines how the Army as a profession has served the American people over its lifetime, even as the very definition of a profession has evolved and matured and the people's demands regarding the Army have changed. We specifically analyze what "service to the American people" has entailed and how the boundaries of the profession have expanded or contracted over time. We take a systems approach to professions, using the work of sociologist Andrew Abbott.[3] A systems approach suggests that there is a universe of tasks or work performed by professions. The link between a profession and its work is called its jurisdiction. According to Abbott, to analyze a profession "is to analyze how this link is created in work, how it is anchored by formal and informal social structure, and how the interplay of jurisdictional links between professions determines the history of the individual professions themselves."[4] We take a historical look at the Army as a profession, examining the jurisdiction of the Army, its interaction with other professions, and its response to the demands of the American people as expressed through the Executive branch and the Congress.

> Whereas for most of our lives the default condition has been peace, now our default expectation must be conflict. This new strategic context is the logic for reshaping the Army.
>
> —GEN. PETER PETER J. SCHOOMAKER[2]

A systems approach to professions, as with many sociology-based methodologies, is concerned with conflict—in this case, conflict between professions. Viewing the Army in an ecology of professions implies that only the fittest will survive as competing professions jockey for jurisdiction. The armed services are unique in that while each is a profession, decision-makers not in the professions often dictate their jurisdictions. Thus, while uniformed soldiers comprise the Army profession, civilian appointees—often people with limited military backgrounds—can decide to shift the Army's jurisdictions to include new tasks or exclude old ones. Examples of past taskings include provision of environmental protection by creating artificial offshore reefs out of old tank hulls and of providing pre-school children's day care on Army posts. Other professions such as medicine, law, or engineering do not have members outside the profession making jurisdictional decisions. That the Army's jurisdictional boundaries may change not only due to competition from other professions but also because of civil control of the military becomes an important point when considering the authority of senior Army officers, who in fact may not be the final decision-makers determining the Army's jurisdiction.

Before we explore the historical development of the Army as a profession, it will be useful to review some of Abbott's key concepts. According to Abbott, professional work determines the vulnerability of professional tasks to competitor interference. Objective and subjective characteristics of the tasks determine the vulnerability of the tasks to poaching by other professions. This vulnerability is affected by how strong the link is between the profession and its tasks. Objective characteristics are empirical qualities that resist any redefinition of work. For example, in the treatment of alcoholism, an objective fact is that consumption of alcohol always produces central nervous system depression. Different professions may seek to include alcoholism treatment in their jurisdiction, but the effects of alcohol on the body is an objective fact that sets limits to how far professions will adjust their jurisdiction. Objective qualities can include technological, organizational, natural, and cultural characteristics.

Subjective qualities of tasks originate from the redefinition of the problem as bounded by objective properties. Thus, alcoholism, while maintaining its objective characteristics, could be redefined as a disease, mental disorder, or sin. A redefinition of the work may allow a different profession to include alcoholism in its jurisdiction. Subjective characteristics include diagnosis, treatment, and inference. *Diagnosis* takes information into the professional knowledge system by seeking the right professional category for a problem, but also removing the problem's extraneous qualities. For example, an architect would want to focus on design, not on costs. *Treatment* parallels diagnosis, but instead of taking information about the problem, treatment gives results. The more specialized a treatment, the more a profession can retain control of it. Laser eye surgeons, for example, enjoyed a protected jurisdiction for a period of time, but are now experiencing vulnerability as new technologies emerge. Finally, *inference* is undertaken when the connection between diagnosis and treatment is obscure. Inference is the application of professional knowledge to a particular problem. If the inference process is too routinized or too far-out, the profession can be degraded. Legal advice on the preparation of wills via the internet is an example of the former, while fortune-telling is an example of the latter.

Using Abbott's concepts and a systems approach to professions, we analyze the Army's history in five eras. We discuss the Army's tasks and jurisdiction applicable in each era and then examine the competition for jurisdiction using the objective and subjective characteristics of the tasks.

Period 1781-1901

Following the Revolutionary War, the task assigned to the Army was consistent with its size—80 men—55 of whom were detailed to secure military stores at West Point.[5] The day following the reduction of the standing Army to 80 men, Congress called for 700 militia to be mobilized to secure the frontier, opening the door to expansion of the force and the Army's new jurisdiction.[6] This expansion was not accompanied by an outpouring of enthusiasm for service on the remote frontier, and the Army experienced great difficulty in raising the 700 militia. Further, as the duties assigned this body offered little in the way of incentives, desertions and avoidance of service became common.

During the periods between the War of 1812 (really no more than the concluding act of the Revolutionary War), the Mexican War, the Civil War, and the Spanish-American War, most of the Army was involved in the business of doing whatever the nation, through the Executive and Congress, directed it to do. The initial tasks set before the Army were principally concerned with security of the frontier—protecting the treaty rights of the Indians from aggressive and unscrupulous settlers, and in turn protecting the legitimate settlers from Indian depredations.[7] But it was the Army that began the systematic exploration and development of the frontier region, later extending its work westward with the "march of civilization." Accompanying these tasks were those incident to sustaining life on a remote frontier—surveying, road building, local subsistence farming, peacemaking or peacekeeping, and some law enforcement.[8]

The southern frontier became the focus of attention during the 1830s with what was probably the most unpopular war before Vietnam—the Seminole Wars. This too was guerrilla war, whose critical phase lasted some six years (1835-1842) and came close to ruining the Army. The war was partly motivated by aggressive land-grabbing so transparent to the soldiers involved that there was considerable sympathy for the Seminoles combined with a great reluctance to serve in Florida's hot, inhospitable climate.[9] Officers used every imaginable device to avoid duty in Florida including ways we today would view as chargeable offenses.[10]

The Army's role in the life of the nation in these early years was essentially to fill in the gaps where no civilian institutions existed, or to perform the functions of existing institutions unwilling to operate in the less secure regions in which the Army tended to be stationed. Always at the forefront was the implicit if generalized requirement to "Fight and Win the Nation's Wars," but there was no special threat that required a force capable of doing more than suppressing an occasional outbreak of Indian violence. Essentially, the Army as a profession emerged to embrace any tasks levied by the American people that necessitated the deployment of trained, disciplined manpower under austere conditions on behalf of the nation. During the early part of this period, continuing hostilities with Great Britain gave substance to an external threat that put some pressure on the development of coastal fortifications, but even the aggressive behavior of the British along the Canadian border area was insufficient to induce a significant increase in the size of the Army.[11] Natural and cultural objective factors such as the absence of a threat due to a landmass bounded by oceans, the absence of a functioning fiscal system for the first decades of the republic, and the attendant shortage of entrepreneurs coupled with a relatively low population density all served to secure the jurisdictions of the Army from any serious competition.

Coast Artillery was the first branch to have a professional school, thus confirming the unique requirements of those charged with the land portion of coastal defense.[12] It was not so much that an authentic threat existed, but the memory of recent disasters such as the burning of Washington by the British forces in 1814 and the relative weakness of the Navy combined to cement this portion of the Army's jurisdiction into place until well into the missile age.[13]

From 1821 onward, West Point was looked to as an incubator of Army professionalism, going somewhat beyond a mere engineering school.[14] The influence of

West Point came from the simple fact that it was the only engineering school in the entire country before 1824, and its graduates were in high demand throughout the nation.[15] These engineers were the only portion of the Army in close continuing contact with the civil population. Their function, aside from the relatively minor involvement in coastal defense, was infrastructure development. Roads and canal systems had obvious dual-use merits. Beginning in 1833, military periodicals approximating professional journals began to appear, and in 1846 Lt. Henry Halleck published the first systematic study of military theory by an American seeking to establish "that principles of military art and science constitute a body of knowledge to be understood and mastered only through a professional education."[16] With the profession focusing on tasks demanding disciplined, trained personnel capable of being deployed to austere conditions, West Point implicitly brought nation-building within the purview of the military profession.

The remarkable combat performance of the Army during the Mexican War demonstrated military skills not normally associated with the Army of this period, and also provided a precursor to a new jurisdiction—post-conflict civil administration. Immediately following Winfield Scott's conquest of Mexico in 1846, a new civil administration was inaugurated in and around Mexico City that served as a model for years to come. Until its withdrawal from Mexico in 1848, the occupying forces of the U.S. Army provided the civil administration of the Mexican capital region.[17] That experience gave some impetus to the extension of Army jurisdictions that resumed following the Spanish-American War with the administration of Cuba, briefly of Puerto Rico, and the suppression of the Philippine Insurrection. This expertise was again exercised during the brief American occupation of the Rhineland following World War I, and returned full force with the occupations of Germany and Japan following World War II. Such capabilities were again called upon when the U.S. Army moved into Somalia, Bosnia, and Kosovo, and for a brief period following the liberation of Kuwait in 1991, and now in Iraq.

A unique feature of early Army life was that quartermaster operations were largely contracted out. For instance, the Mexican War offered the first instance in which the Quartermaster Department was solely responsible for clothing the Army.[18] As warfare became more sophisticated and the forces involved grew larger, the responsibilities and militarization of quartermaster operations increased. The debacle of quartermaster support during the Spanish-American War set expansionary measures in motion that increased further during World War I. By the time World War II became a reality for America, quartermaster operations had grown to rival major civilian industries. Interestingly, now in the early years of the 21st century, the Army is in the process of reversing that trend as the perceived need rapidly diminishes for the Army's control over its own supply and support system within the increasingly joint theater infrastructure. As long as Army manpower is in high demand for combat operations and the joint infrastructure can meet the Army's logistical demands in a timely fashion, the Army's jurisdictional claim over its own support structure will probably continue to diminish.[19]

From a system of professions viewpoint, the first era in the history of the Army saw the profession relatively unchallenged by other professions. The nation needed

a force capable of expanding its frontiers and developing the infrastructure necessary for growth. As a young nation, the United States had only the Army to turn to
for numerous functions. Fighting the nation's wars was the fundamental purpose of
its existence, but frontier protection and infrastructure-building dominated the early
years of the Army's existence.

Period 1902-1944

Events in 1902, highlighted by the end of the Philippine War, represented a sea
change in Army activities. Suddenly and without design, the United States found
itself a colonial power. While during Reconstruction the Army had administered the
former Confederate states in what were the darkest days of its existence, long-term
administration of conquered foreign territories was something entirely new, and it
changed the nature of the Army's professional tasks. The Army found itself administering distant possessions with largely unfamiliar cultures, and with a lack of political guidance that has in recent times become all too familiar. Although the regulars
and volunteers had sufficed to handle the Spanish-American War, it had been essential to call new volunteers to the colors to aid in suppressing the insurgency in the
Philippines. In this regard, the militia/reserve component of the Army regained a
reputation it had lost during the Revolutionary War in which its performance when
good, was very, very good; but, when it was bad, it was deadly.[20] Since that time,
the voice of the militia (after the 1903 Dick Act, the Army National Guard) has been
loud in proclaiming that it is the nation's strategic reserve (which it will be if ever
fully equipped and trained) and that it is the military's essential link to the American
people (which recent operations in Iraq and Afghanistan have demonstrated fully).
There, in an unusual twist in the jurisdictional reach of the Army profession, an
internal component emerged from the civilian population to assume regular duties
and to outnumber the regular members of the profession.

Repetitive soldier tours in foreign stations exposed the Army and the nation to
distant events formerly of little concern. It was as if a new nerve system had
sprouted and with it new sensitivities. U.S. Navy ships on distant stations could act
largely on the initiative of their individual captains until the arrival of telegraph
cables constrained their independence. The Army was dispatched after telegraph
connections had been established. The severing of telegraph cables from Cuba to
Spain in 1898 was one of the early instances of what we recognize as information
warfare today.[21] But telegraph lines ran to major cities only, not into the remote
Philippine, Cuban, Nicaraguan, or Puerto Rican countryside. Thus soldiers like Lt.
Conrad Babcock, U.S. Cavalry, found themselves acting as mayors of small
Philippine towns, responding to their captain or major, the Provincial Governors.
Like their Navy counterparts before them, their own good judgment, tempered by
training and personal discipline, was their guide with little else to rely on.[22]

During this period the evolution of the Army's system of courts-martial provides insights into the concurrent evolution of the Army profession's internal jurisdictions. The reforms of 1890 did away with physical punishments that today

would be considered torture.[23] Other reforms followed including the passage of the Uniform Code of Military Justice in 1950, which "extended civilian substantive and procedural legal principles to the armed forces."[24] The U.S. Supreme Court finally went the last mile in 1969, when Justice William O. Douglas in *O'Callahan* v. *Parker* dissolved the Army's jurisdiction over offenses committed by servicemen outside a military installation. This decision was not reversed until 1987, but the ebb and flow demonstrated here sharply defines just how dramatically the Army's internal jurisdiction can shift.[25]

In 1905, San Francisco was shaken and almost ruined by an earthquake. The Army quickly helped establish a functional infrastructure in and around the Bay City, received the citizens' thanks, and then went back to work policing the National Parks and trying out all sorts of new technologies. It was a period of intense technological experimentation, as basic research had matured to applications, permitting the production of numerous marketable devices (such as automobiles and aeroplanes). While Europeans concentrated on military equipment, the Americans stuck with peaceful applications. Caterpillar-treads, for example, allowed farm tractors to plow heavy soil. They were later recruited to provide cross-country mobility for armored gun platforms.

When Pancho Villa raided the southern Texas border in 1916, a "division" was formed to police the border and eventually to launch a suppression operation.[26] The greatest fear was that Mexican political disturbances would cross the border. Banditry and such disorders seemed to be synonymous.[27] Brig. Gen. John J. Pershing was accorded widespread public and political attention throughout his abortive counter-Villa campaign. His thoroughly apolitical conduct offered a refreshing contrast to past senior Army officer behavior. It set a widely noted example that continued to influence senior officer behavior well into the waning years of the century. In terms of jurisdiction, the Army served as the U.S. government's border police agent. Then, at Vera Cruz in 1914, it landed a military force that acted with a heavy hand to maintain American "rights."[28] But beyond those essentially military events and, of course, the imminent involvement in that greatest of military events in Europe, the Army gradually slipped into a quiet existence in the continental United States and the Philippine Islands.[29]

American participation in World War I exposed the problems attendant upon having an Army manned and equipped at a bare-bones level and focused on constabulary duties. Policing the Caribbean, the Philippines, and the Mexican border did not require large numbers of soldiers, and the national leadership's inability even to conceive of participation in a major European war had kept force structure on a level commensurate solely with immediate needs. While the war revealed for all to see the Army's insular thinking, at the same time it drove the Army to make broader jurisdictional claims including activities touching national industrial mobilization, hitherto the purview of civilians. The 1930 Industrial Mobilization Plan grew out of the war materiel manufacturing chaos of World War I.[30]

The sudden need to expand to a multimillion-man force was a surprise to the nation, but at least the Plattsburgh summer camp programs had kept the idea of leadership training and honorable service to the nation alive and relatively healthy.

Although initially created and administered by civilians, later assisted by Regular Army officers, the Plattsburgh program turned out to be the first in an expanding series of leadership training initiatives. Accompanying the upsurge in hostilities against the Mexicans, the Plattsburgh movement gained such increasing momentum that Congress stepped forward to pay for the 1916 camps rather than requiring the attendees to ante up. The Army thus found itself with the explicit task of leadership training under the guise of providing basic training to everyone interested enough to attend the camps, which was 16,000 in 1916.[31] Ironically, the ideas and initial execution of both leadership training and rifle marksmanship came from outside the Army.[32]

With the onset of the Depression a similar evolutionary change occurred in the Army's professional tasks. Over its vigorous objections, the Army was charged with operation of the Civilian Conservation Corps.[33] Whatever else the CCC accomplished in terms of conservation, it did build character and taught leadership, even if not overtly. Here the Army's strength in internal organization and personnel development was once again demonstrated and recognized by outsiders. Only later would the Army itself awaken to this strength, but it had gradually established a unique jurisdictional claim that was being alternately reinforced or challenged by developments in business practices. Alert progressive officers who admired the scientific management practices being developed by businessmen noted the new management practices with interest. But while civilian business management practices developed along scientific management lines, the civilian element never embraced leadership development to the extent the Army did.

During this era in the Army's professional history, imparting discipline, both internally to soldiers and externally to American society, became an Army jurisdictional claim. At first viewed by the freeborn men of a free land as the imposition of tyrannical rules of dubious value, military-style discipline gradually came to be seen as the panacea for salvaging damaged youth. The presence of regular troops has almost always been sufficient to quiet even the worst civil disturbances. The riots in the mining camps in the west, the Pullman strike of 1894, and more recently the racial integration of the University of Alabama in 1961 were all attended to by regulars who won the grudging admiration of those whose presence they were sent to control.[34] It has not been the case uniformly to be sure, but when civil law and order collapse, the appearance of the Regular Army is usually seen as a signal that such nonsense will no longer be tolerated and that evenhanded treatment will be accorded to all as order is restored. This continued projection of Army jurisdiction into civilian government conjures discomfiting specters of the man on a white horse and is thus closely regulated, but it remains a core function. Even into the 1990s, as the trait of self-discipline became more scarce in a broadly self-indulgent society, military discipline achieved new, if somewhat temporary, social value. As undisciplined youth got into trouble, many civil entities turned in desperation to the military for assistance in creating "Boot Camps" whose purpose was to inculcate the discipline society no longer provided.[35]

When the Army was founded, its resources for producing its own equipment, though slight, were very nearly adequate and remained so for most of its early history with the exception of the Civil War period. The Spanish-American War sent some signals that Army management practices were not up to the mark, and the arrival of World War I caught the nation and the Army still only partially prepared. The scale of weapon and munitions needs caught everyone by surprise and opened the door to such extensive Army involvement over the next several decades in the civilian industrial base that President Eisenhower was prompted in 1961 to caution against growth of the "military industrial complex."[36] The interaction between industry and the Army has recently matured to such an extent that General Electric claims to have benefited significantly from a series of strategic leadership seminars with Army officers at the U.S. Army War College.[37] The intermingling of industry and military has developed to the point that those relationships are tightly circumscribed by congressionally mandated rules of conduct to protect the government against irregularities stemming from too cozy a relationship.

The Second World War was as formative for the U.S. Army as it was for the nation. A global conflict required closer interaction among the services, civilian industry, government departments and agencies, and hitherto unimaginable alliance/coalition partners than ever before. The number and scale of the tasks that had to be performed stretched the capabilities of the entire nation. The U.S. Army was often the only organization with the resources, organization, and training structure to tackle the job. Despite the expansion of its activity into realms of action well beyond its normal jurisdiction, it was generally understood that these actions were wartime expedients and once global stability returned, the soldiers would revert quickly to their more familiar duties.

Thus the second era in the Army's professional history was marked by an expansion in several jurisdictions. The Army continued to develop infrastructure, but now technological advances enabled this to be done across the oceans. Administration of foreign lands reinforced the already well-established jurisdiction of frontier administration. Finally, as in earlier periods, war continued to be the central jurisdiction, but this too was taken to distant lands. Jurisdictional competition continued to be minimized, since the young nation had no other force to turn to for most of these needs.

Period 1945-1991

The world had changed mightily by the time World War II ended, and this affected the U.S. Army profoundly. No longer just a small constabulary force administering some Pacific or Caribbean island, the Army found itself essentially governing two major nations and operating dozens of smaller entities from Trieste to Saipan. Standing most of the Army down failed to reduce the burdens or the extent of dispersion. In some places the native citizens were able to reconstruct their societies and take charge of their own lives in relatively quick order. Italy did not require an occupation force although it might have been better for its economy had it had one. Soldiers acted in all kinds of civil capacities other than as warriors for the first few years after the war and returned to the combat role only after the "Iron Curtain" rang down in 1946. The Army thereupon began to resume its main focus on arms and war-fighting as the threat of "monolithic Communism" grew. The Berlin airlift and Korean conflict lent weight to the fears quietly developing.

With the advent of a nuclear standoff with the Soviet Union, America faced a major direct threat to its existence, and it reacted by the creating, for the first time in its history, large, permanently standing forces. What had emerged from the ashes of World War II was a new jurisdiction of forward presence, defending America and her allies with the strategy of containment. The traditional tasks of the profession had expanded enormously and were suddenly resident over the entire globe, not just in a few remote places. Further, the missions of preserving the world's peace and protecting our own vital national interests had expanded as well. The Army found itself doing something it had never seriously contemplated and for which, at the time, there was no substitute—serving as the world's policeman. The United Nations was too young and too weak to make any serious impact, and only the American armed forces had any capability to perform the role.

It is important to realize, however, that what became the Cold War was an aberration in American military history. This kind of war demanded a new description of the Army profession, at least in terms of the variety of duties in which one expected soldiers to be competent. The singular focus on a clear threat—even if its manifestations showed remarkable variety—drove a unique condition that persisted until The Wall came down in 1989. The Army profession, at least in the minds of its uniformed leaders, shifted its jurisdiction from infrastructure-building and administration to a clear combat capability to win the "First Battle." [38] Never before had that imperative existed with quite the same force; never before had it seemed to matter so much.

The backdrop to such jurisdictional considerations was the advent of nuclear weapons and intercontinental delivery systems. To some extent, and for one specific period, it looked as if the Army had become irrelevant. Quickly adapting to the nuclear situation, the Army attempted to recapture the jurisdiction lost to the Air Force's Strategic Air Command. The Davy Crockett, a nuclear "bazooka" to be employed at the infantry company level, was an abortive first step that eventually matured into the Atomic Annie 280mm cannon, the Army's first authentic field nuclear delivery system. From that point on experiments continued as the Army struggled to maintain its place on the nuclear battlefield. Although the struggle was never fully resolved, several generations of soldiers grew up in nuclear-capable artillery units and the associated planning staffs, knowing all the while that their efforts were next to suicidal and that the intercontinental ballistic missiles were the real insurance policy. The strategy of mutually assured destruction ultimately gave some credibility to battlefield nuclear weapons and the Army forces associated with them. Fortunately, the hope that such weapons would never have to be used, was realized.

Then came Vietnam and the frustration of another guerrilla war. Like the Seminole Wars, the goal was generally clear, but its legitimacy was not. Protecting Western Europe from the rapacious Soviet hordes was one thing, but protecting people who seemed to hate or were mostly indifferent to their own government cast the required sacrifices in a questionable light. Not everyone saw the war that way, but the frustrations inherent in counterinsurgency campaigns and the ambiguities at the strategic level—the failure to apply full power against known enemy refuges or lines of communication—brought serious questions into plain view. The result was catastrophic for the nation and only a little less so for the Army. The Seminole Wars could never have ended quite the same way as Vietnam, since the contested territory was homeland or land soon to be so. An intervening ocean made Vietnam very different. In its latter days, the Vietnam experience provided little assurance that the Army was "serving the American people" as it had done in the past.

Fortunately, however, the profoundly compromised Army that returned from the Vietnam conflict underwent a rapid transformation to focus on the "first battle" with the Soviets through what came to be known as the "training revolution," which inspired a new sense of purpose in an Army that once again found itself focused on the protection of mostly democratic Western civilization.[39] Whether such a revolution in an internal jurisdiction would even have been possible during Vietnam is questionable. But, by taking soldiers' jobs apart and analyzing them in minute detail, then assembling the details into trainable bits, the Army recovered its competence and its self-confidence—it knew what its jobs were and it knew whether it was proficient or not. From that time on until the late stages of the post-Cold War drawdown in the 1990s, the Army profession majored in training and was widely viewed as a model worthy of emulation by many segments of the civilian population as well as foreign militaries.[40] This renewal of an essential internal jurisdiction in many ways repeated that of leadership training and instilling discipline discussed in the section on the 1902-1944 era.

During the Cold War, the Army's jurisdictional claims continued to be largely uncontested. Three objective characteristics helped reduce the vulnerability of the jurisdiction. First, technological factors such as nuclear weapons and strategic delivery systems brought the prospect of war to the homeland itself. National survival became a tangible goal and the Army was ready to be a key element in its pursuit. Second, the aftermath of World War II combined with the immaturity of national governance structures in several former combat theaters left the Army performing civil administration in significant national territories of the world. Only the Army had the professional knowledge and ability to continue such administration in foreign lands. Third, the repercussions of the Vietnam War, along with memories of Desert One (the abortive embassy hostage rescue mission in Iran in 1980), changed the criterion for Army relevance from the general requirement to deploy trained, disciplined manpower under austere conditions to the more specific requirement to defend the nation's vital interests in situations where the political and military objectives are clear and there is a public commitment to victory.

Period 1992-2001

The late 1980s and early 1990s were marked by the confluence of several factors that impacted the Army profession. First, the tremendous successes in Operations Just Cause in Panama and Desert Shield/Storm in Southwest Asia reinforced the Army's emphasis on winning the first battle with overwhelming force after political and public support is gained. The focus on training, the realistic exercises at the Combat Training Centers, the reform of officer and noncommissioned officer personnel management systems, and the modernization of the Army succeeded in finally exorcizing from the profession the demons of Vietnam. While the battlefield successes buttressed the Army's war-fighting jurisdiction, the fall of the Berlin Wall eroded the nation's sense of urgency with regard to winning the next first battle. With the United States emerging from the Cold War as the world's only superpower, the Army found itself at the peak of its warrior preparation with no warriors to oppose.

As the nation rushed to cash its peace dividend, the Army underwent a 40 percent downsizing that, while much more compassionate in execution than the post-Vietnam drawdown, still had debilitating effects on the profession.[41] As competition within the officer ranks spiraled upward, morale began to plummet. Internally, the force struggled with its professional identity as the warrior ethos it had nurtured during the Cold War was questioned. Madeline Morris, a Duke law professor hired as a consultant by the Secretary of the Army, attacked the aggressive, "masculinist attitudes" of the military culture.[42] Much of the push to open the military to homosexuals and combat positions to women focused on the apparently diminishing role of war in informing the Army's identity.

With the absence of a clear threat to the nation, the meaning of "serving the American people" began to revert to the 19th century ideal of providing disciplined, trained manpower capable of deploying to a possibly dangerous environment. Soldiers found themselves once again patrolling the borders—this time in counter-drug operations. The Army deployed again to the national parks—this time to fight forest fires. Soldiers once again took postings to faraway lands—this time under the military-to-military engagement policy.[43] Support to civil authorities continued as in the past with troops assisting with the Olympics and the presidential inauguration. The nation, through Congress, recollected the Army's earlier role and deployed units to the horrendous scene of Hurricane Andrew in a domestic humanitarian effort. Then units were deployed to Haiti, Somalia, Rwanda, Bosnia, and Kosovo. In several ways these were a unique sort of employment with a general mission that could well have been stated as "Stop the killing." Haiti was actually more of an effort to install a government pledged to reestablish law and order, in the process bringing a halt to the long-standing practice of killing anyone who might threaten the regime. The other deployments were efforts arising indirectly out of the Nuremburg trials, implicitly giving the United Nations authority to intervene *within* a nation's borders to halt genocide.[44] Constabulary forces have been left behind in Kosovo with no end date in sight.

Resistance to the shift in jurisdiction was heard as some complained about the detrimental effects of peacekeeping or operations other than war on the Army and its core tasks of fighting conventional threats. Senior officers assured members of the profession that these missions were nothing new. Yet, while the missions were replays of history, something had changed. Collectively, Army members were still carrying the self-image of warriors, perhaps to a somewhat lesser degree among segments of the officer corps. Peacekeeping, humanitarian assistance, disaster relief, and civil support were all worthy missions, but the Army still retained an equal priority on winning the next first battle. The psychological strain of sustaining two major jurisdictions appeared to burden the force.[45] Furthermore, some of the peacekeeping missions quickly devolved to police activities with too little attention to the bald fact that military police of any description cannot cope with thugs who have tank and artillery arsenals. For these, heavily armed soldiers are required.

Additionally, deployments during this era, although paralleling those to the Philippines (1898-1902), Dominican Republic (1916-1924), and Cuba (1898-1902), were qualitatively different. In previous deployments, troops remained on duty as constabulary forces (to be completely accurate, only Cuba made it out of the tutelage stage in a timely manner). Their mission was to remain on station until the adversaries were subdued and legitimate civil government—preferably local—could be established. Deployments during the period 1992-2001 followed a similar pattern, but did not confront a clear-cut enemy. What is worse, although still having the establishment of the rule of law under local government as an ultimate aim, these deployments stalled in mid career, with only the military tasks accomplished. Hence, operations in Haiti, Somalia, Bosnia, and Kosovo began as if a clearly identifiable enemy existed, e.g., with the 10th Mountain Division launching an air assault, or the 1st Armored Division crossing the Sava River, but then evolved into noncombat actions in which political factors prevented the "bad guys" from being eliminated. The establishment of local government operating under the rule of law and order was not on the military mission list, and yet there was no civil agency—UN, allied, or coalition—with the capability of accomplishing that admittedly broad, multifaceted mission. Since establishing viable governments is usually an open-ended process, a date of withdrawal still remained uncertain. The broadening of the Army's jurisdiction to include deployments without a mandate to accomplish the implicit mission introduced feelings of unease among Army professionals.

This professional angst arose against a backdrop of intense jurisdictional competition. The world had seemingly become a much safer place in a macro sense. Consequently the potential for deployment to dangerous environments that helped secure the Army's jurisdictions had now lessened. With that change, the deployment of disciplined, trained manpower *other than the Army* became more feasible. Contractors, nongovernmental organizations, and other U.S. governmental entities all began to compete for expert work in the Army's jurisdictions once the environment was deemed secure. It became routine to see civilians working side by side with soldiers on deployments.

Despite America's predominance in military power, it has never wanted to be the world's only peacekeeper. Thus, troops from the North Atlantic Treaty Organization, often under the United Nations flag, competed for the peacekeeping jurisdiction during this period. The Russian race to the Pristina airport in Kosovo graphically illustrated the competition for the peacekeeping jurisdiction. Although the presence of U.S. peacekeepers tends to signal a more serious intent or perhaps more important value, it was interesting that the U.S. Army was getting involved in a jurisdiction traditionally held by countries as diverse as Fiji and Norway and was not particularly anxious to become more deeply engaged in it.

As the Army scrambled to find its professional identity in peacekeeping, while simultaneously not really being comfortable with that as a primary function, its warfighting jurisdiction was also being subjected to unprecedented competition. The Marines tried to establish themselves as the urban warfare experts—fighting the future "three block war."[46] That, of course, would leave the U.S. Army to deal with the remainder of the city. The Air Force repeatedly claimed that precision engagement makes land warfare moot since "it will be possible to find, fix, or track and target anything that moves on the surface of the earth."[47] Except, of course, individually armed people of uncertain identity and intent moving about within a local population. Meanwhile, failure to secure the Pentagon's approval for committing the Army's Task Force Hawk to the fight in Kosovo, along with memories of the 82nd Airborne Division potentially serving as no more than "speed bumps" before the advance of Saddam Hussein's armored divisions, gave the Army renewed impetus to transform itself into a more rapidly deployable multi-use force.

The jurisdiction for developing leadership and discipline within society also experienced some interesting developments during this period. The country still viewed the Army as a source of moral discipline, and the "Army of One" marketing campaign provoked serious debate about how that aspect of the profession was being manipulated to appeal to today's youth. Yet under the individualistic veneer of an "Army of One" lay the same discipline-conscious, team-oriented Army that has served the nation for centuries. A trend gaining particular momentum was the hiring of retired officers as school administrators to bring the needed leadership and vision to troubled school systems to include Seattle and Washington, DC.

Leadership development, however, began to show signs of a unique type of jurisdictional shifting with the introduction of contracted retirees. Quasi-military organizations, that is, service organizations manned almost entirely by retired military personnel, were already at work performing military-to-military functions, providing engineering assistance to remote, barely pacified or even hostile areas, and administering overt training to foreign militaries. The Army has always informally and formally welcomed the wisdom of retired officers. During this period, however, contracted Army alumni cemented their role as logisticians, ROTC professors of military science, and trainers of the Croatian, Macedonian, and Colombian armies.[48] The rationale for these contracts was often personnel shortages in the active force. Retired officers began to be heavily contracted as "senior mentors" to battle command training programs and other exercises as well as to battalion and brigade commanders themselves. The practical effect, however, of using contracted retirees was to blur the boundaries of the profession and to call into question its processes for certification of its own expertise.

11 September 2001 to the Present

Prior to 11 September 2001, the Army was busy attempting to establish itself as a relevant profession of the future. Peacekeeping seemed to be the major preoccupation of the Army while the Air Force and its precision strike capability appeared to be moving toward center stage in the jostling for jurisdiction. As far as American society was concerned, the Army was a necessary, but certainly not the most vital branch of service in the nation's defense. For example, in the May 2001 Gallup Poll asking Americans which of the branches they currently considered most important to national defense, the Air Force was declared to be the most important service by 42 percent of respondents while the Army trailed with only 18 percent.[49]

The events of 11 September 2001 and the ensuing operations in Afghanistan and Iraq changed the situation. The Army was back to war-fighting, and America realized that future warfare, at least in the near-term future, was going to be a land-centric endeavor. In contrast to previous polls, a May 2004 Gallup Poll showed that Americans viewed the Army, Marines, and Air Force as tied for the most important branch of service with about 23 per cent of respondents choosing each branch.[50] The Army, which had been nursing reservations concerning its role in the peacekeeping jurisdiction, was pulled by the global war on terrorism into new jurisdictions normally dominated by law enforcement professions such as the Federal Bureau of Investigation. With rulings by the Supreme Court on the detainees at Guantanamo Bay, and the cases of Hamdi and Padilla, it was firmly established that the United States was indeed engaged in a legally cognizable armed conflict with al Qaeda and the Taliban, to which the laws of war—as opposed to criminal laws—apply.[51] The shift from a criminal conception of terrorism to a military one greatly reinvigorated the professional identity of the Army in a remarkably short time.[52]

Initially, the Afghan campaign seemed to reinforce the promise of the precision approach to war, and a host of true believers sprang to their feet to proclaim the end of the need for an Army. Then reality returned. The destruction of the Afghan air force took two days, which was not surprising considering that none of its aging aircraft were flight-capable from the start. The battles around Shari-Kot made it appear that precision strikes could easily defeat entrenched enemy forces, but it was soon apparent that wars were not likely to be won by bombing obsolete aircraft and dropping 2,000 pound bombs on militias positioned on exposed hilltop positions. Soon it became evident that boots on the ground were needed to wage the war on terrorism.

As the United States attempted to rally allies to force regime change in Iraq, it became clear that not all other nations were so willing to move their militaries into the jurisdiction of preemptive military action. The jurisdictional competition with other militaries that seemed to be particularly intense in the peacekeeping environment of the Balkans was strikingly missing in Operations Enduring Freedom and Iraqi Freedom. With fewer allies contributing land forces, Enduring Freedom and Iraqi Freedom consolidated the Army's hold on its traditional jurisdiction that had begun to slip away in the face of a strategic environment offering no plausible opponent. On the other hand, the Marines abandoned their amphibious assault focus and, as they have done in all major conflicts, shifted to sustained operations on land, again sharing the jurisdiction over land warfare with the Army. The Army National Guard and Army Reserve were tapped to the point where, at the time of this writing, 40 percent of the reserves were deployed to Iraq, with nearly all of the force in the Balkans also being from the reserve component forces. [53]

While civilian contractors have always played a role in warfare, the number of civilian workers supporting Iraqi Freedom and Enduring Freedom grew enormously as security requirements beyond the capabilities of the numerically constrained forces expanded. Private military companies stepped in to fill the vacuum. The brutal lynching of four Blackwater employees, the alleged involvement of CACI and Titan[54] interrogators in the Abu Ghraib scandal, and the bizarre case of Jonathan K. Idema in Afghanistan raised public awareness and eyebrows at the extent contractors were involved in war.[55] In Iraq, private contractors employ 75,000 civilian workers with at least 20,000 performing roles that might once have been assigned to the military. Halliburton alone had more than 30,000 workers and subcontractors in the Middle East.[56] Questions of accountability, liability, and responsibility were legitimately raised and still remain to be resolved.

The use of contractors was also claimed to have been used to creatively extend the military's jurisdiction in politically sensitive venues of the war on terrorism. Because the stated U.S. policy was that no American troops could be inside Pakistan pursuing al Qaeda terrorists or training the Pakistani army, contracted former special operations forces were allegedly used to achieve the same ends through different means. Thus, when asked if there were any U.S. troops inside Pakistan, the Secretary of Defense could truthfully answer, "The U.S. Department of Defense people? I doubt it. Not that I know of."[57]

With the United Nations and many nongovernmental organizations shying away from operating in Afghanistan and Iraq due to the persistent instability and lack of security, the U.S. Army found itself conducting nation-building and humanitarian operations—in addition to fighting an insurgency. This had led to a surprising effect. In an interesting twist of jurisdictional maneuvering, the nongovernmental organization Médecins Sans Frontières (Doctors Without Borders) pulled out of Afghanistan, citing two reasons. First, the murder of five of its staff created questions about the security situation in Afghanistan. Second, this organization took issue with the use of military units to perform humanitarian and development tasks. From its perspective, humanitarian aid should be kept strictly separate from anything military; thus, when soldiers carrying weapons offer medical help or build a local clinic, the safety of neutral aid workers is jeopardized. Or, in the words of Médecins Sans Frontières, the "U.S.-backed coalition consistently sought to use humanitarian aid to build support for its military and political ambitions." Médecins is an internationally respected organization that does not shrink from danger or hardship. It failed to realize, however, that the current war is against Terrorists Without Borders. It is naïve for the organization to insist that today's terrorists somehow respect their neutral status just as it is naïve to expect the U.S. military to cede the entire humanitarian aid jurisdiction to nongovernmental agencies.[58]

Another nongovernmental organization, the International Committee of the Red Cross (ICRC), also showed signs of not adapting to this new nature of war. The ICRC, especially in regards to the detainees at Guantanamo Bay and Abu Ghraib, continually criticized the United States for not adhering to Geneva Convention Protocol 1—a controversial document that was long ago rejected by the United States because it would grant to terrorists and non-uniformed combatants prisoner of war status. The report of the Independent Panel (the so-called "Schlesinger report"), which investigated the Abu Ghraib scandal, noted that the ICRC had a vital role in serving as "an early warning indicator of possible abuse," but that "the ICRC, no less than the Defense Department, needs to adapt itself to the new realities of conflict, which are far different from the Western European environment from which the ICRC's interpretation of the Geneva Conventions was drawn."[59]

The 507th Maintenance Company debacle, in which several U.S. soldiers were killed, wounded, and/or captured (including a female soldier) after being ambushed south of Baghdad, became a catalyst for renewing the focus on the war-fighting expertise of the Army profession. The Army introduced the "The Soldier's Creed" and "A Warrior's Ethos," basic training incorporated more live-fire exercises, and the training centers began to include counterinsurgency scenarios, which are inherently messy but demand adaptive, imaginative leadership responses. In one sense the Army is experiencing déjà vu all over again as Afghanistan and Iraq present scenarios that somewhat remind it of the much earlier Philippine War and parts of the Vietnam War. In both, the Army task was to destroy or convert the insurgents in order that nation-building activities could proceed in relative security. In both cases, the Army was also the primary vehicle through which nation-building was pursued initially. In both cases there was no other institution capable of doing the job.

It would be disingenuous to insist that the Army profession stick to "Army" matters. The framers of the Constitution did not thus constrain the Army's roles or functions. The Army Chief of Staff was, until the relatively recent empowerment of the Chairman of the Joint Chiefs of Staff, the principal military advisor for ground operations to the Secretary of War and the President. General of the Armies George C. Marshall described that interface this way: "We probably devoted more time in our discussions, our intimate discussions of the American chiefs of staff, to such [political] matters as any other one subject. . . . I repeat again that we discussed these [diplomatic factors] more than anything else."[60] For senior leaders this is certainly the case. The Army is an instrument of national policy and must be capable of employment wheresoever and howsoever disciplined force is required in the pursuit of national security. If the nation requires that nation-building activities be pursued in furtherance of national security, and the security situation does not permit the use of commercial operators, the U.S. Army will be expected to handle it. Armies exist for security purposes beyond those provided by police forces. Where no threat beyond police capabilities exists, no army is required. In this world, such a condition apparently exists only in armiless Costa Rica.

The difference now with respect to the Army's jurisdictions is best captured by former Acting Secretary of the Army Les Brownlee and Army Chief of Staff Gen. Peter Schoomaker in *Parameters*: "This is not simply a fight against terror. . . . This is not simply a fight against al Qaeda. . . . This is not simply a fight to bring democracy to the Middle East. . . . This is a fight for the very ideas at the foundation of our society, the way of life those ideas enable, and the freedoms we enjoy."[61] While the global war on terrorism does not involve tank armies on the plains of central somewhere, it is clear that it transcends the capacities of even the most advanced police forces. It is a war that knows no boundaries, one in which the enemy respects no protected category of participant and no rules of war as established by international convention. No entity other than an army has the capacity to confront such an enemy. For the U.S. Army, this means that its jurisdictions will inevitably evolve in tandem with the evolving panoply of needs that require the application of disciplined force in "service to the American people."

Notes

1. The views and opinions expressed in this chapter are those of the authors and not necessarily those of the Department of the Army or any other U.S. government entity.
2. Les Brownlee and Peter J. Schoomaker, "Letter from the Army Leadership," *Parameters* 34, no. 2 (Summer 2004): 4.
3. Andrew Abbott, *The System of Professions: An Essay on the Division of Expert Labor* (Chicago, IL: University of Chicago Press, 1988).
4. Ibid., 20.
5. Russell F. Weigley, *Towards an American Army: Military Thought from Washington to Marshall* (New York: Columbia University Press, 1962), 81.
6. Allan R. Millett and Peter Maslowski, eds., *For The Common Defense: A Military History of the United States of America,* rev. and enl. (New York: The Free Press, 1984), 91.
7. Russell F. Weigley, *History of the United States Army* (New York: The Macmillan Company, 1967), 83; and Robert M. Utley, *Frontiersmen In Blue: The United States Army and the Indian, 1848-1865* (Lincoln: University of Nebraska Press, 1967), xii-xiii, 2, 4-5.
8. Utley, xii.
9. Weigley, *History of the United States Army,* 162.
10. Samuel J. Watson, "'Daily More Dissatisfied': Dissent Among U.S. Army Officers During the Second Seminole War" (Paper presented to Houston Area Southern Historians, Houston, TX, 20 September 1994).
11. Weigley, *History of the United States Army,* 98.
12. Ibid., 153.
13. Ibid., 163. The coastal defense gun forts were functionally replaced by bombers in the late 1930s and by North American Air Defense interceptor and NIKE air defenses in the 1950s and 1960s.
14. Weigley, *History of the United States Army,* 143.
15. Ibid., 164.
16. Ibid., 151.
17. Ibid., 188-89.
18. Ibid., 180.
19. The flip side of this reduction in direct control of the means of production of military supplies is the increase in the management of the development and procurement processes reflected in the Program Manager's program and now the Acquisition Corps. These developments have, in some measure, extended the Army's jurisdiction into areas previously ceded to civilianization of traditionally quartermaster functions. The argument seems to be that if the Army can no longer afford to control the metal-bending industries, it should at least have significant influence over how such industries execute Army contracts.
20. Weigley, *History of the United States Army,* 1-9.
21. G. J. A. O'Toole, *The Spanish War: An American Epic, 1898* (New York: W.W. Norton & Company, 1984), 205-209.

22. Draft manuscript titled "In the Beginning," Papers of Conrad Stanton Babcock, Jr., Hoover Institution for War and Peace, Stanford, CA, 108-227; also Edward M. Coffman, *The War to End All Wars: The American Military Experience in World War I* (New York: Oxford University Press, 1968), 18-19; and Allan R. Millett, *The General: Robert L. Bullard and Officership in the United States Army, 1881-1925*, Contributions in Military History Number 10 (Westport, CT: Greenwood Press, 1975), 168-83, 194-98.

23. Donna Marie Elean Thomas, "Army Reform in America: The Crucial Years, 1876-1881" (Ph.D. diss., University of Florida, 1980, MMI #8115686), 136-137.

24. Edward M. Coffman. *The Old Army: A Portrait of the American Army in Peacetime, 1784-1898.* (New York: Oxford University Press, 1986), 196-200; 375-76; 379.

25. O' Callahan v. Parker, 65 Supreme Court 1969; 395 US 258, 89 SCt. 1683, 23 L.Ed. 2d 29, (1969).

26. Millett and Maslowski, 337.

27. Coffman, *The War to End All* Wars, 13-14.

28. Weigley, *History of the United States Army*, 347.

29. Edward M. Coffman *The Regulars: The American Army, 1989-1941* (Cambridge, MA: The Belknap Press of the Harvard University Press), 2004.

30. Millett and Maslowski, 398-99.

31. Coffman, *The War to End All* Wars, 14-15.

32. Donald N. Bigelow, *William Conant Church: Army and Navy Journal* (New York: Columbia University Press, 1952), 184-86.

33. John W. Killegrew, "The Impact of the Great Depression on the Army, 1929-1936" (Ph.D. diss., Indiana University, 1960), xii, 1-22.

34. Jerry M. Cooper, "The Army's Search for a Mission, 1865-1890," in *Against All Enemies: Interpretations of American Military History from Colonial Times to the Present*, eds. Kenneth J. Hagan and William R. Roberts, Contributions in Military Studies Number 51 (Westport, CT: Greenwood Press, 1986), 189.

35. By 1997, 34 states had instituted boot camps. See for example Corey Kilgannon, "Changing Youth Attitudes About Police," *New York Times*, 13 August 2000, A7. Interestingly, however, the effectiveness of boot camps is being questioned, as participants are not becoming model citizens upon their return to society. See Jayson Blair, "Boot Camps: An Idea Whose Time Came and Went," *New York Times*, 2 January 2000, A4.

36. Dwight D. Eisenhower, "Farewell Radio and Television Address to the American People," 17 January 1961, in *The American Military: Readings in the History of the Military in American Society*, ed. Russell F. Weigley (Reading, MA: Addison-Wesley Publishing Company, Inc., 1969), 153.

37. "Why Welch Did an About-Face on GE's Strategy," *USA Today*, 28 March 2001, 2A.

38. Charles E. Heller and William A. Stofft. *America's First Battles, 1776-1965* (Lawrence: University of Kansas Press, 1986).

39. James Kitfield, *Prodigal Soldiers: How the Generation of Officers Born of Vietnam Revolutionized the American Style of War* (New York: Simon & Schuster, 1995).

40. See chap. 1 of the present anthology for a summary description of the Army profession at the end of the drawdown in the 1990s.

41. For a detailed discussion of the impacts of the 1990s drawdown on the Army profession, see Don M. Snider and Gayle L. Watkins, proj. directors, Lloyd J. Matthews, ed., *The Future of the Army Profession* (Boston, MA: McGraw-Hill, 2002), chap.25.

42. Madeline Morris, "By Force of Arms: Rape, War and Military Culture," *Duke Law Journal* 45 (1996): 651.

43. See for example the series by Dana Priest, "The Proconsuls: America's Soldier-Diplomats," *Washington Post*, 28-30 September 2000, discussing the role of the military in diplomacy.

44. William G. Eckhardt, "Nuremberg—Fifty Years: Accountability and Responsibility," *University of Missouri Kansas City Law Review* 65 (1996): 5-7.

45. See Volker C. Franke, "Warriors for Peace: The Next Generation of U.S. Military Leaders," *Armed Forces and Society* 24 (Fall 1997): 33, for a discussion of conflicting war-fighting and peacekeeping attitudes being developed in precommissioned officers.

46. See Joel Garreau, "Point Men for a Revolution: Can the Marines Survive a Shift from Platoons to Networks?" *Washington Post*, 6 March 1999, A1.

47. Air Force Competencies, U.S. Air Force Force Protection Battlelab, http://afsf.lackland.af.mil/Organization/AFFPB/org_affpb_precisionengagement%20.htm.

48. See David Adams and Paul de la Garza, "Contract's End Hints of Colombia Trouble," *St. Petersburg Times*, 13 May 2001, A1, for claims that contractors were not successful in Colombia.

49. Frank Newport, "Which Branch of the Armed Forces is Most Important?" *Gallup News Service*, 27 May 2004.

50. Ibid.

51. Hamdi, Yaser v. Rumsfeld, Donald, Defense Secy., 03-6696 Appealed From: 4th Circuit Court of Appeals (8 January 2003); Oral Argument: 28 April 2004; Opinion Issued: 8-1 for Hamdi (O'Connor-28 June 2004). On 28 June 2004, a day before the very end of the Court's 2003-04 term, the Court issued its opinion, along with opinions in the Padilla and Guantanamo cases. It held 8-1 for Hamdi, entitling him to a meaningful opportunity to contest the factual basis for his detention before a neutral decisionmaker. . . . The Court's split was somewhat misleading in that four justices constituted the plurality, in an opinion written by Justice Sandra Day O'Connor, concluding that Congress authorized the detention of combatants under such narrow circumstances (though they are still entitled to due process). In concurrence with the judgment that Hamdi is entitled to a hearing, Justice David Souter wrote for himself and Justice Ruth Bader Ginsburg that Hamdi's detention itself was unauthorized. . . . In noting the "difficult time in our Nation's history," Justice O'Connor also noted that the Government "has never provided any court with the full criteria that it uses in classifying individuals as [enemy combatants]." Nonetheless, the plurality concluded that Congress had authorized Hamdi's detention, through the Authorization for Use of Military Force (the AUMF) it passed one week after 11 Sept., that authorized the President to "use all necessary and appropriate force against those nations, organizations, or persons he determines planned, authorized, committed, or aided the terrorist attacks." . . . . In so holding, the plurality declined to resolve whether Article II of the Constitution provides such authority to the Commander in Chief in the absence of Congressional approval. . . . The majority also wrote specifically to state that Hamdi "unquestionably has the right to access to counsel in connection with the proceedings on remand," choosing not to address whether it was wrong for the Government to have denied him counsel in the first place.

52. See David B. Rivkin, Jr., and Lee A. Casey, "Bush's Good Day in Court," *Washington Post*, 4 August 2004, A19. For a more detailed discussion of the ethical and training issues now facing the Army profession as a result of the shift in policy from a criminal model to an enemy model, see chap. 22 by Tony Pfaff, in the present anthology.

53. Gregg Jaffe, "Caught Off Guard: As Ranks Dwindle In a Reserve Unit, Army's Woes Mount," *Wall Street Journal*, 4 August 2004, A1; Jonathan Eig, "Wives of Civilians Working in Iraq Forge Own Support System," *Wall Street Journal*, 3 August 2004, A1.

54. Blackwater, CACI, and Titan style themselves as a mixture of security and network companies. In reality at least a portion of their operations are what is currently termed "Private Military Companies" even though that is only a portion of what they engage in. There are dozens of PMCs according to a variety of sources. The following is extracted from the Blackwater homepage: "Blackwater USA comprises five companies; Blackwater Training Center, Blackwater Target Systems, Blackwater Security Consulting, Blackwater Canine, and Blackwater Air

(AWS). We have established a global presence and provide training and tactical solutions for the 21st century."

55. Nick Meo, "Afghan Court Jails US Bounty Hunter Who Claims to Have Tracked Down bin Laden," *The Independent* (London), 16 September 2004, Thursday, 28: Jonathan "Jack" Idema, a former Green Beret and a convicted fraudster, insisted that he had been working all along for Donald Rumsfeld, and had been in contact with the Pentagon and high-ranking Afghan officials throughout his vigilante career, exposed during the trial as part of the murky underside of the war on terror. Jonathan Idema had been caught with "terrorist suspects" hanging by their feet from the ceiling of a house in Kabul, including the senior cleric of one of the city's biggest mosques. Idema insisted the cleric had been implicated in plots foiled by his team, who called themselves Task Force Sabre Seven. With Kabul awash with armed men in and out of uniform, both NATO and the U.S.military were duped by Idema. NATO sent personnel on his raids and the U.S. military accepted a "terrorist suspect" from him. It remains unclear whether he was a fantasist or whether he really did have connections at the highest levels. Idema was sentenced to 10 years prison after being found guilty of torture, kidnapping, and entering the country illegally.

56. Rowan Scarborough, "Elite Veterans Prowl Pakistan," *Washington Times*, 9 August 2004, 1.

57. See Cheryl Benard, "Afghanistan Without Doctors," *Wall Street Journal*, 12 August 2004, 10.

58. See "A Rumsfeld Vindication," *Wall Street Journal*, 26 August 2004, 12.

59. James R. Schlesinger et al., *Final Report of the Independent Panel to Review DoD Detention Operations* (Arlington, VA: n.p. , August 2004), 92.

60. Larry I. Bland, *George C. Marshall: Interviews and Reminiscences for Forrest Pogue* (Lexington, VA: George C. Marshall Research Foundation, 1991), 415-16.

61. Brownlee and Schoomaker, 4.

II

Officership and the Army Profession

The first chapter in this anthology noted in some detail the relationships, both historical and vocational, between the Army officer corps and the Army profession within which officers serve. Particularly, the correspondence between officers' four shared identities—Warrior, Leader of Character, Servant of Country, and Member of Profession—and the four fields of expert knowledge of the Army profession was made explicit. The next three chapters then focused on the Army profession per se, leaving for later a discussion of the roles that officers play within the profession.

Thus it is our purpose here in Part II to address the Army officer corps, collectively and individually, in greater detail. Notably, Part II is entirely new to this revised edition of *The Future of the Army Profession*, having been included explicitly to help reverse the profoundly tragic situation as described in the first edition: "Officers do not share a common understanding of the Army profession, and many of them accept the pervasiveness of bureaucratic norms and behavior as natural and appropriate."[1] That reality was largely discovered during the field research done among Army officers during the period 2000-2001 by sociologists Gayle Watkins and Randi Cohen. That research effort is repeated here in its entirety (Chapter 5), as it remains one of the most insightful and analytically penetrating research projects of the contemporary period on mid-grade Army officers' understanding and perception of the Army profession and their relation to it.

Chapter 6, consisting of four mini-essays by myself, John Nagl and Paul Yingling, Tony Pfaff, and Suzanne Nielsen, respectively, consists of a statement of the professional practice of the Army officer followed by the informed views of mid-career officers who had the opportunity to deliberate on their generation's understanding of the four shared identities of Army officers. Originally published in *Military Review*, these views have been revised for this edition while the authors served in the expeditionary Army in Kuwait, Iraq, and Korea. This is easily one of the most teachable chapters in the anthology, as it will engage all readers who have experienced or reflected upon the various roles and challenges of Army officers.

Army officers do not, however, serve only in Army units or formations. Increasingly they serve in joint organizations of some type, working together with officers of other services and coalition partners. Are there elements of officer identity that cross these professional boundaries, enabling Army officers, with their own service identities, to work and cohere professionally with members of other military officer corps? This is the question addressed in Chapter 7 by Prof. Richard Swain. His thoughtful answer sheds badly needed light on the topic of a joint profession of arms flowing from common commitments and obligations as set forth in the officer oath of commission.

Part II ends with Chapter 8 by Col. George Forsythe and his colleagues on the development of individual identity, both a theoretical and empirical treatment of how Army officers mature and make sense of who they are in their professional worlds. Given that the Army's institutional identity has been changing at an accelerating pace since the end of the Cold War (that identity is currently framed as a "campaign quality Army with joint and expeditionary capabilities"), understanding how soldiers, and particularly officer leaders, develop over time becomes a critical piece of expert knowledge for those Army professionals charged with officer development. Unfortunately, the Army does not have a sanctioned model of human development. Thus the longitudinal research presented in this chapter, which reveals unsettling glimpses of the current disconnects between the products of the Army's officer development system and the demands of the positions to which they are assigned, clearly makes the case for generating such a model. Chapter 8 also describes critically needed ways of thinking anew about the fundamental differences among training, education, and development, and how each might best contribute to the ongoing transformation of the Army's officer corps.

Note

1. See Gayle L. Watkins and Don M. Snider, "Project Conclusions," in *The Future of the Army Profession*, project directors Don M. Snider and Gayle L. Watkins, ed. Lloyd J. Matthews (Boston, MA: McGraw-Hill, 2002), 537.

5 | In Their Own Words: Army Officers Discuss Their Profession

Gayle L. Watkins and Randi C. Cohen

In their article titled "The Future of Army Professionalism: A Need for Renewal and Redefinition," published in *Parameters* in 2000, Don Snider and Gayle Watkins posit that the U.S. Army is at risk of transitioning from a professional organization to a compliant bureaucracy, an organizational form that, while not an overt threat to the nation, will fail to provide the level of national defense demanded by the American people. Furthermore, they claim that this shift is deleterious for both the nation and the Army itself. By its nature, the professional mode has been and continues to be best able to address the Army's unique challenges because of its two key strengths: knowledge development and individual control.

The Army's first challenge is the development of military knowledge in advance of our adversaries. The coin of the professional realm is knowledge; professions are built on abstract knowledge and its application. This knowledge or expertise resides in professional members, rather than in organizational systems or technology; professions are positioned to create, expand, and develop knowledge. Military knowledge—doctrine, strategy, tactics, and technologies—is constantly evolving as adversaries seek advantage over one another. Many nations depend upon the advances made by others, preferring to be consumers of military knowledge rather than creators. However, the United States has wisely chosen to take a leadership role in the development of military knowledge. Therefore, although other nations' armies can become bureaucratized and still succeed, America's Army must maintain its professional status if it is to meet the country's expectations and needs in the 21st century. It must remain a professional institution capable of continued evolution and revolution in military affairs.

The second challenge the Army faces is controlling service members as they engage in the most lethal of social activities during security operations marked by chaos and complexity. This need to control behavior is established by the military's unique place among professions and organizations as the only American institution sanctioned to kill in the pursuit of national interests and objectives. Because of the potential threat inherent in this distinctive role, societal norms and laws govern how this professional task will be carried out. Not only do we expect our soldiers to fight with courage and skill but we also demand that they do so honorably, showing compassion for noncombatants and captured enemies, applying a sense of fair play even in combat, and always maintaining an awareness of the political requirements and repercussions of their actions.[1]

The environment in which the Army's professional tasks are undertaken further complicates the achievement of this degree of behavioral control. Much has been written about the uncertainty and chaos of military operations, both combat and noncombat. In fact, few organizational endeavors can match their inherent complexity, pace, risk, and uncertainty. Soldiers in these situations face the competing and often conflicting demands of self-preservation and honorable service.

Internalized values, traditions, trust, and member commitment provide the most powerful means of achieving a high degree of control over those engaged in this most lethal of societal services under arduous conditions that cannot be easily monitored. These control systems, known to organizational theorists as "clan control," are most often developed in small, horizontal organizations and professions.[2] With its members numbered in hundreds of thousands and its hierarchical structure, the Army is unable to develop the type of clan control present in small organizations across its depth and breadth. Instead, it is the internalized values and unwritten norms arising from the Army's professional nature that enable its members to fight honorably, to risk and even give their lives for the nation, and to support national and international conventions on the moral and ethical conduct of military operations.

Given that knowledge development and member control are critical to its success, sustaining the Army as a profession is paramount. We therefore set out to study the status of the profession, specifically from the perspective of some key professional members, the Army officer corps. To organize our efforts, we used the theoretical framework on professions presented by Andrew Abbott in his 1988 book, *The System of Professions*. Abbott's framework acknowledges professions as exclusive occupations embedded in a dynamic competitive system, vying for control over where and when their knowledge can be applied. Within this system, professions are organized around the abstract knowledge they develop, apply, and protect. Their workplace tasks consist of applying this knowledge under specific controls that enable the profession to gain and maintain social legitimacy. Battles for jurisdiction, resources, and legitimacy occur among professions and organizations through claims on abstract knowledge and the definitions and expansions of tasks.

This framework has been used recently to study other professions, embracing the development, expansion, and defense of their professional jurisdictions. Such groups have included physicians, nurses, lawyers, social workers, vision care providers, and funeral directors.[3] Researchers have also focused on professional expertise, particularly on how professions determine the tasks of their professional work, such as R.C. Cohen's study of financial planners (1997) and Y.M. Johnson's investigation of indirect tasks in social work (1999). Additionally, they have addressed the relation between expertise and professional education.[4] Following in the footsteps of these researchers, we applied Abbott's framework to the Army profession in order to understand how officers reflect the Army's professionalism in their thoughts about their work.

Methodology

Our chapter seeks to understand the Army profession from the perspective of a key segment of its membership, the officer corps. Since there have been no qualitative studies of the profession for the past 30 years, our work is neither longitudinal nor

comparative; we could not determine whether there has been a change in Army officer concepts of professionalism. However, we do provide a current and accurate
portrait, a rich and detailed description of how Army officers think about their profession's knowledge, tasks, control, and jurisdiction. This information will enable us
to make some recommendations to strengthen the profession.[5]

Data-Gathering

As we designed our research, we were well cognizant of problems confronted during
the last study of the Army profession, the U.S. Army War College's *Study on Military
Professionalism* (1970).[6] We were particularly concerned that officers would find it
difficult to express their feelings about their profession because of the intimate and
abstract nature of the topic. Earlier Army research had found that officers were either
reluctant or unable to discuss their profession from an individual perspective:

> Without exception, in group discussions or interviews, respondents, irrespective of
> grade level or experience, avoided coming to grips with the problem of definition.
> This finding coincides with the empirical research and theoretical studies of values.
> Values and value systems defy verbalization because they are abstract feelings and
> sentiments, and because they remain largely a personal matter.[7]

In addition to the intimate nature of the topic, the researchers found that its abstract
nature made it difficult for officers to discuss it:

> Values and value systems defy verbalization, not only because they represent ideo-
> logical *feelings*, but because they are general and not linked to specific objects. For
> example, it is exceedingly difficult to translate accurately a value such as "Duty"
> into operative guidelines for behavior.[8]

Furthermore, selection of the optimal data collection method was critical since
researchers have found that focus groups often impede accurate data collection: the
responses from one person often bias what another person says; an outspoken person
can dominate the discussion, thus preventing the ideas of others from being expressed;
and there may not be sufficient time to explore each participant's views in depth.[9]

To resolve these problems, we turned to recent advances in marketing research,
featuring methods that enable researchers to investigate concepts that people have
trouble verbalizing.[10] These techniques are designed to be consonant with how
humans think and communicate, thereby tapping into respondents' personally held
opinions and feelings. The methods use descriptive imagery—stories, pictures,
objects—to enable individuals to access their feelings indirectly by linking abstractions to more concrete images. Using such methods for data elicitation is best done
in individual interviews rather than in focus groups. Therefore, we designed a multiple-method interviewing technique that incorporated the following steps:

- We trained interviewers to ask unbiased and non-leading questions. While it
  may seem obvious that interviewers would ask neutral questions, it actually
  requires expertise to conduct interviews without assuming the meaning of
  words the respondents offer. Additionally, when Army officers interview, they
  need to take special care not to slip into their well-trained role of counselor.

- During the interviews, we focused on and leveraged the descriptive imagery that the respondents used. Stories, images, objects, metaphors, etc. enable individuals to better express their feelings and opinions. The interviewers therefore asked questions about the descriptive imagery to get in-depth responses.
- We also used laddering techniques common in marketing to connect concrete examples or attributes to more abstract values and consequences. By asking the respondents to explain why certain issues matter to them, we uncover important associations among ideas.

Sample

We selected six Army posts with deployable or deployed units, both in the United States and overseas, that would provide a well-rounded sample of branches and experiences. Since the environment heavily influences work identities, such as members' feelings about their profession, we selected officers who are in the field Army rather than in school or the Pentagon.[11] In this type of research, sample size does not need to reach that of statistical significance; rather, it need only be large enough to impart a consistent set of responses for any relevant subgroup. We asked the staff of each participating post to provide participants of certain ranks, but placed no restrictions in terms of gender, race, or career intentions. Our sample consisted of 80 company- and field-grade officers from combat arms, combat support, and combat service support branches who were presently serving in division or corps positions.[12] The distribution of ranks, branches, race, and gender is shown in Table 5-1. Additionally, in our sample, about twice as many officers indicated that they intended to stay in the Army as those indicating they were going to leave.

All interviewers were trained in the multiple-method interviewing technique. We used male and female, military and civilian interviewers to reduce potential bias in the interviewer-respondent interaction. The participants seemed comfortable with the interviewers and, in general, were quite engaged in the process. Many officers

		Number	Percentage
Rank	Lieutenant	18	22.50
	Captain	33	41.25
	Major	24	30.00
	Lieutenant Colonel	5	6.25
Race	White	74	92.50
	African-American	6	7.50
Branch	Combat Arms	32	40.00
	Combat Support	16	20.00
	Combat Service Support	32	40.00
Gender	Male	73	91.25
	Female	7	8.75

Table 5-1. *Distribution of Rank, Branch, Race, and Gender in Sample.*

expressed appreciation that someone was listening to their opinions, and that they had the opportunity during the interview to reflect on the "bigger issues." Some officers also became emotional during the interview, and we often had to stop the discussion before the officers were ready to end due to time constraints.

Interview

In preparation for the interviews, we provided all the participants with an assignment letter, asking the respondents to think in advance about what it means to be a professional officer so that they would be primed for the interview.[13] Additionally, we asked the participants to bring three items to the interview that symbolized their thoughts on the topic.[14] Such pictures or objects served as a springboard for discussion, facilitating access to deeper insights and feelings. For example, one officer brought a washer that signified technical expertise while another brought a green beret that symbolized his commitment to his team.

The one-on-one interviews lasted approximately 45 minutes each, were tape-recorded, and were transcribed into hard copy. All the interviewers began the discussion with the same introduction, emphasizing the confidentiality of the interview and requesting full and honest responses.

During the interview, the participants explained why they selected the items they brought with them and what those items and their associated ideas meant in terms of being a professional officer. The interviewer based follow-up questions on the words and ideas the participating officers offered, asking for definitions, feelings, and consequences associated with key ideas. As the final step in the interview, the interviewers asked the respondents to select someone (living or dead, real or fictional, military or civilian) who best epitomized to them what it means to be a professional officer.

Data Analysis

We followed widely accepted standards for the analysis of qualitative data, starting our inductive analysis by using a representative subset of transcripts to build a coding schema.[15] Multiple analysts looked at these same transcripts and developed a common list of variables that we then applied systematically to all of the transcripts. Using *Atlas.ti* software, we were able to link quotations to codes and then generate reports on these variables.[16] We iterated between the reports and hypotheses, developing themes and identifying issues.

We also approached the data in a deductive mode, looking for the answers to theory-driven questions. We specifically sought out information pertaining to professional knowledge, tasks, control, and jurisdictional issues. Additionally, we categorized the responses to the question about who best epitomizes what it means to be a professional, thereby gaining insight into the "ideal type" of the professional officer, which further clarified what matters in the profession.

The findings that we present in the results section emerged in multiple interviews. We took care in our analysis to weigh the frequency and intensity of responses. We generally indicate these using descriptive terms. Terms we use to describe the number of officers discussing a theme include: *most*, which indicates a substantial majority; *many*, which indicates a majority; *some*, which indicates a substantial minority; *several* and *few*. We also use very specific adjectives to indicate the respondents' level of intensity, ranging from *anguished* to *indifferent*.

Although this sample was not intended to be statistically significant, we were sensitive to potential patterns associated with the demographic profiles of the participants. Unless explicitly stated, we found no discernible differences by location, branch, rank, gender, race, or career intention.

Results

As noted in the methodology section, we used a two-pronged approach to analyze the data: a deductive assessment of the key components of a profession, including knowledge, task, control, and jurisdictional issues; and an inductive inquiry that, much like the data-gathering, enabled the officers' voices to emerge unfiltered.

Do Army Officers Consider the Army a Profession?

During these latter efforts, while letting the data speak for themselves, one dominant issue surfaced that was quite basic: officers do not necessarily consider themselves to be part of a profession. Although a majority of officers spoke positively about their work as a profession, a sizable minority revealed serious concerns. Some company-grade officers were surprised by the question we posed since thinking about the Army as a profession was not something they had considered previously. As one captain put it,

> I know very few Army officers that consider ourselves under the term "professional" in the same form that you consider lawyers and doctors. . . . I think professional— I've never heard that term used before. I've never heard senior officers use that . . . term.[17]

Expressing indifference, disappointment, or even sorrow, other officers referred to actions and policies of senior leaders and the institution as a whole that undermine the military as a profession. These officers' thoughts about the profession focused on its diminishment. For some officers, a profession requires a level of expertise or competence that is not currently present in the Army:

> People aren't confident in their unit's ability to do the wartime mission because people aren't technically competent. If the thing is a profession then it is a profession, I don't go to a doctor that doesn't know what he is doing 'cause the doctor works at the hospital XYZ then that must mean he is good. [If] the guy doesn't know anything, it doesn't make any sense. If the thing is a profession then the guy should be an expert in what he does. People [in the Army] aren't experts because they are way too heavily involved in the technical or the interpersonal but they don't have the right mix.

Finally, some of this group argued that the profession is being degraded by inducements to susceptible officers who stay for reasons other than the profession, such as educational benefits (italicized questions embedded in the quotations are those of the interviewer):

> I read in the *Army Times* where they are thinking of offering $100,000. . . . They are offering $100,000 bonuses to lieutenants if they sign something saying "Hey, I will spend twenty years in." *What does that mean in terms of what it means to be professional in the Army?* I think the Army is corrupting to what it means to be a professional. They have thrown the idealism of being a professional in the garbage to get numbers and the numbers they are getting are not the kind of numbers they need to sustain the profession.
>
> Officers have been given a choice of whether or not to consider it a profession. You can look at it as a stepping stone or something merely to pay back college or you can look back to its history. Like the anachronistic qualities of the pride or the glory and accomplishments and take that to embody a profession and then continue to live that and somewhat ignore the reality of what is going around you as far as how other people view it. And so well people are just using it to pay back college and they are not really leading soldiers and they are not really giving it their 100%. They are not really being an Army officer. They are being someone who wears the uniform and punches a clock.

What Does It Mean To Be A Professional Officer?

Beyond this initial, unexpected finding that a significant number of officers did not consider their vocation to be a profession, we further examined the officers' descriptions in terms of the professional characteristics outlined by Abbott: knowledge, tasks, control, and jurisdiction. Each of these attributes was developed by at least some of the respondents but the number varied widely. While offering their thoughts on the problems facing the Army, as well as on ways the profession could be strengthened, most of the officers articulated a strong sense of pride and satisfaction in their service.

Officers' discussions of their professional knowledge centered on the Army's unique abstract knowledge and expertise. They often distinguished the general expertise required of all officers from the specific expertise required by their branch or specialty. During these conversations, they also spoke of the importance of continuing education and self-study to their development as Army officers.

Abstract Knowledge

Some officers made the connection between the strength of the profession and the abstract knowledge associated with it. For example, one officer said that Gen. Omar Bradley epitomized the Army professional because of the way he used his intelligence to understand soldiering and accomplish the mission. Several of the interviewed officers emphasized the importance of lifetime study of military strategy and the warrior ethos when they brought in texts—some historical, others technical—as their objects. Others emphasized the uniqueness of their knowledge, such as the officer who described how a map his unit made while in Kosovo was representative of the unique knowledge held by the Army profession:

> Another part of it is kind of a unique item as opposed to another profession. A doctor as part of his profession doesn't make maps. Some other professions, it's not a unique artifact because obviously civil engineers and other types of people like that do it, but it is fairly specific to a profession to take a map and add control measures onto it, add land marks, TRPs, boundaries, whatever you have. And that kind of defines a more unique aspect of the military profession how you'd use something like that. . . .
>
> I would say that every profession has a fundamental base of actual knowledge that is different from everybody else. Engineers know about concrete, doctors know about anatomy, military officers are supposed to know about leadership, about capabilities of their equipment, about how to direct multiple elements, how to make a plan and communicate it to subordinates, and those are kind of the elements to acknowledge.

Expertise

For many of the participants, professional expertise is the hallmark of being an officer. The participants articulated two key aspects of this expertise: the general expertise of leadership and the more specific expertise of technical competence. The answer "leaders" dominated responses to the question, "Who best epitomizes what it means to be a professional officer?" Most officers cited individuals who set a standard for leadership, primarily past and present Army commanders, but also people such as Dr. Martin Luther King, Jr. Even when citing Army examples, admirable leadership qualities often had less to do with military prowess and more to do with personal accomplishment and bearing, e.g., Gen. Colin Powell. During the interviews, officers explicitly and implicitly discussed the importance of leadership expertise as part of the profession. Most felt that there was something unique to being a leader in the Army:

> If you looked up in the dictionary what a professional is it is pretty much a life's career, I would think. It's more than just a skill. It incorporates many skills. A lot of them cerebral if you have that power, and officership is a profession I think because it [includes] the task of leading soldiers into combat. A lot of people have lost sight of what our main job is. To lead soldiers into combat, uphold and defend the Constitution of the United States, and at the same time provide the tools, the equipment, the lifestyle for the Army soldiers.

Several officers, however, claimed that there was no special expertise to Army leadership, that it was no different from the basic management tasks undertaken by supervisors in other organizations, as this young officer describes:

> I thought about that, "Do I consider the Army to be a profession?" and I am not so sure I do or that I even care because I got a buddy that works for Sprint and he goes to a training class for four months which is [Officers Basic Course] for me. I majored in management but I could have majored in French or Chemistry and I go to my training class for four months and now I am an officer and he did the same thing. He sells whatever, long distance to businesses, and he majored in whatever he majored in and he goes to four months of training and then he sells long distance, so I don't know that the Army is any different than what he is doing. . . . What we

are doing is just general management training. I majored in management in college and I know more just from my undergraduate studies than I learned in actual Army training.

Many officers argued that being able to apply their expertise was essential to being a professional officer. They had acquired specific expertise through self-education and schooling, and that technical competence provided a sense of accomplishment and purpose, it pervaded their professional tasks and identity. They also admired, for example, the technical competence of golfer Tiger Woods. However, many of these officers felt that they were unable to act on their expertise because of Army management systems that limited their options. Responses to these limitations varied by rank. Company-grade officers were disturbed primarily by what they saw as hypocrisy:[18]

> So if I'm supposed to lock in my training calendar and that's the way it is, then how is it O.K. for me to receive an e-mail that tells me, "You will do this tomorrow?" Well, why didn't you, as the leader who's supposed to follow your own rules, plan this more than 24 hours in advance? What kind of example is that? So it's O.K. for you to tell me I can't do that to my soldiers, but you as a senior officer can now tell me that you're going to violate your own rule. I don't take kindly to that, and that happens quite frequently.

Other young officers expressed frustration with what they saw as a lack of trust in their abilities:

> When you're a staff member or whatever member of an organization you should be able to . . . work with your peers, work with other agencies. Go out and achieve things and make them happen and for me to go to the G4 or work within the DISCOM or do something, I shouldn't have to funnel it through and ask permission. Or I shouldn't have to provide information overload with a lot of details. I should be able to achieve it and work those missions, work those issues externally without being forced by the Commander to constantly provide updates and constantly provide reports. It's almost like a lack of trust.

This lack of trust is evident not only to the officers we interviewed but to others outside the Army, as related by this field-grade officer:

> And the Swedish officer on my staff group turned to me and said, "You know, they treat you like twelve-year-olds." So here's an officer also in the military profession but outside of our world looking at what we do and maybe not taking away what we hoped he would've taken away. I told him "Well, sir, in a certain respect you are right. We are being treated like twelve-year-olds."

It was the lieutenant colonels who expressed what could best be called anguish over their inability to apply their professional expertise with appropriate autonomy. The depth of these feelings was quite profound, sometimes overwhelming the officers, and quite apparent to the interviewers:

> What we've essentially done is we've replaced a fundamental belief in the professionalism of our officer corps and a notion that we will train our officers and equip our officers to apply their judgment in running their units. We've replaced that with a series of centralized programs and checklists, and it fundamentally undermines professionalism because it removes from us an individual responsibility that is

beyond that of a technician, that is in fact a calling . . . because in the Army you're asked to make decisions of life and death.

With cross-sectional data such as these in our study, we cannot know whether officers feel differently about this topic at different stages of their careers. However, it is worth noting that it is the captains who express uncertainty or disparagement regarding professional expertise issues compared with the profound anguish of the lieutenant colonels. One hypothesis is that having a sense of the uniqueness of expertise, a sense of being a professional and not a manager, develops with one's career. One officer described his personal recognition of this development in this way:

> You know you fill out the little form when you buy a new appliance and stuff and they always ask you what kind of job you have, and I tell you I check the professional block. When I was a platoon leader I think I always checked the middle management block and then one day it dawned on me, "You know I'm not really a middle manager." *Why aren't you a middle manager, why do you now check professional?* I don't know, it's just one of those things where I guess it's just the evolution as you grow a little older and you actually realize what you are doing and the impact that you have.

The Profession's Tasks

One element of being a professional officer that is truly unique involves the management, including the infliction, of violence. Some but not a majority of officers recognized that this expertise was central to the profession—a distinct feature they lay claim to on the ground of their associated knowledge.

> I mean a lot of people manage, and we manage money and we manage people. We manage equipment, maintenance fleets. As far as civilian-type managerial skills. But on the extreme end we manage violence or the applied use of violence and the graduations thereof. To me that is a very specialized skill that not everybody can do. My brother-in-law is a professional musician, and he actually supports himself and his family doing it, he's very good. And that's a skill I couldn't hope to replicate. On the other hand, doing what I do, he couldn't hope to replicate what I do either. So how we apply our managerial skills is one main difference. One application of that makes us different.

A number of officers linked this expertise to the importance of professional values and also to how the diminishment of the profession affects the specific application of violence.

> But ultimately we are a warrior profession. We are supposed to engage and kill other people so you have to rely on people having a certain level of self-reliance if you will. And if you are going to turn to your squad leader and say, "Go set up a position over there and defend it." You have got to depend on him and you've got to instill in him, "Here are your standards and you are held responsible for achieving those standards." And if we have a safety briefing to you majors every time we have a long weekend, we are kind of taking that responsibility away. We are kind of taking that responsibility from you as a professional to meet those standards of the profession.

Officers applauded frank discussions of the warrior facet of their profession. For example, one officer described how much he appreciated candor in a professional development session on "killing."

> This book *On Killing* was given by our commanding general to us in Special Forces when he took command. And the reason why I think that's an important part of professionalism is a lot of people when they talk about coming in the Army they advocate all the positive sides that those in civilian life would think is important. You're going to get these education benefits if you come in the Army. You're going to get these medical benefits if you come in the Army. If you stay for twenty years, you'll get these great financial benefits if you come in the Army. Very few people address up front what Special Forces soldiers have to do. And that is to kill other people, which is a very difficult thing to do. Which is the thesis of this book that a retired Army lieutenant colonel wrote and our commanding general not only got a copy of this book for all the leadership in all the Special Forces units. But he also had an [Officer Professional Development and Noncommissioned Officer Professional Development class] where this guy was the guest speaker and talked about that.

While the claim on abstract knowledge for the Army profession may lie with managing violence or even leadership, another fundamental task the officers consistently and emotionally discussed involved neither; there was a remarkable emphasis during the interviews about the work surrounding taking care of soldiers. A few officers clearly related the importance of taking care of soldiers to the accomplishment of their mission, as this officer did:

> If you're in a leadership position, serving soldiers is serving the nation. And I don't want to try to make it as coddling soldiers and serving soldiers is the same thing. But the idea that soldiers can look at that leader and know that that leader's perspective is to train them, to prepare them but also to—it's not for an evaluation report—it's for their ability to meet their mission and to save their lives but also to set them up for success whether it is in their civilian world if they're moving on or if it's family life. I'm mentoring them in different problems and taking extra time to know the soldiers instead of just being there to be in charge.

One field-grade officer describes the moment when he truly understood the relationship between the mission and taking care of soldiers as his unit prepared to parachute into a combat zone:

> It just instilled in me my duty and responsibility as a leader to prepare them because once I got them on the plane, the door opens and they exit the aircraft, I am no longer in control. So, before that I have to prepare them to do their job. As a leader I am responsible for getting down to that level and insuring that they are capable of doing that without me around, that that squad leader and that soldier can move out and do what is necessary.

Another related the breadth of his responsibility to his soldiers, regardless of time and place:

> I am always an officer. I am an officer on Sunday morning, I am an officer Saturday night. I am always accountable for the obligations and the responsibilities that I have assumed. If something comes up or I see a soldier downtown, I see something happening on post it is my responsibility to take any action that is necessary. The job

comes first. *And what does that have to do with calling?* Well, it is not like you work for IBM where you are done. You don't act like you have a total separate life. My life is integrated with my job. I think to some extent a civilian's life it too, but a civilian can leave, can just say, "I quit." He does not have to worry about what is happening to the soldier and his subordinates on the weekend. That is our responsibility.

However, for the majority of officers, their range of tasks extended far beyond accomplishing the mission or caring for soldiers in the field. A more accurate label for the tasks that the officers described as dominating their time and energy would be that of social work. The officers cited example after example of the work they do on behalf of their soldiers, including buying groceries for families or even more:

> I had an E7 that got a DUI. I went to the court with him. I went to all his meetings with the company commander. I stood there to look out for his best interests because if he's not being taken care of, then how can I expect him to do his job?

The Profession's Control Mechanisms

Discussions of control mechanisms, the means by which the profession controls its members' behavior, dominated many interviews. Although the Army also uses bureaucratic control systems (promotion, bonuses, etc.) like other organizations, its primary means of control is clan, based on internalized values, traditions, trust, and commitment. The officers clearly recognized the importance of these mechanisms when they discussed two categories of control: professional values and lifestyle.

Professional Values

Officers clearly understood the relative importance of values since they were the professional element most commonly identified by those we interviewed. The officers saw either the specific values or their Army application as unique. Some clearly recognized the importance of these values in gaining the confidence of the American public: "We are trusted by the public to perform a duty regardless of our personal feelings. When we are called on to do the job, and we report to do the job, we do it."

Officers often emphasized these values by identifying the profession as a calling. Sacrifice and patriotism were repeatedly mentioned as hallmarks of the Army that were rarely found in other jobs. A number of officers emphasized the extraordinary responsibility the Army is given when citizens allow their children to enlist. One officer described how values underlie the Army profession in this way:

> Well, basically I think what mainly sets apart being an Army officer as a profession is more in its ideals. And in the past, especially in the past being an officer was a calling and it was more of a, well, if you start off being an officer that unless something came up either physically or financially then you were going to make it a career. And a profession is something you begin that is a career not just a stepping stone.

The more prevalent professional value mentioned in the interviews was moral courage, often described as "doing the right thing." Examples of this ranged widely, from an officer speaking his mind even when he knew his boss did not want to hear it, to defending subordinates from unjust actions, to having the courage to tell a lieutenant he should not be in the Army.

Moral courage was frequently linked with communication skills, woven together in the officers' descriptive imagery. Some officers valued communication skills in isolation as "the ability to communicate effectively and clearly to a wide range of people," up and down the chain of command. But most often communication was tied to candor, a willingness to stand up for what was right regardless of whom the officer was speaking to. People who were seen to epitomize Army professionalism included those who were willing to tell the truth even when it was unpopular, or confront their superiors over important issues, or stand up for their subordinates. For example, one officer identified his former battalion commander as his exemplar of the profession because he had pulled their unit from a Grafenwoehr rotation when it was not properly prepared.

Although some officers mentioned the importance of "doing what's right even when no one is looking," most connected moral courage with being a role model for junior officers and soldiers:

> Because here you have folks that are coming in off the street and in many cases nobody has ever talked to them about the basic values that they should lead their life by. Their first examples of what it means to be a professional soldier, and naturally officers are soldiers but also professional officers, are consistent with what they've seen in basic training or what they've heard in basic training. And that becomes internalized to them and they understand that it's not just rhetoric and also they aspire to be like the best example of those core values, which in most cases should be the officers. We really are the standard-bearers of the values of the Army.

Officers also described physical courage as an important professional value. In these discussions, they often mentioned people they admired who were willing to risk their safety and lives for a cause they believe in. These exemplars of courage included historical figures such as King David, contemporary figures such as Lance Armstrong, the great cyclist, as well as people the officers had known personally who had risked themselves for others.

> There was a battery commander that I went to the desert with who put a vehicle in front of me and ran over a mine and . . . it didn't cause a lot of damage to the vehicle, but he was injured and . . . he didn't worry about himself. He ran over a mine and he knew that this had happened and he immediately got out of the vehicle and went around to the driver's side of the vehicle to see if his driver was all right without looking at himself, considering himself, so that was something that was admirable.

The concept of duty was another frequently mentioned professional value, often described as "getting the job done" without hesitation or comment regardless of what it takes to do it. Officers identified this quality through their objects and exemplars as a central facet of Army professionalism. One officer brought in a book and described its personal significance in this way:

> A Message to Garcia is a very short story that was published in a magazine in 1899, I believe. And it's the story of Lt. Andrew Rowan, who during the Spanish-American War, was told to take this message to Garcia. And he took the message and he got the message there. And it's talking about duty and accomplishing your duty and not

asking, "Well, where is he at?" "Where is he at?" the famous quote within the book. You know he didn't stop and say, "Where is he at? How do I get there? What's the message say? Why does he have to get the message? When does he have to get it?" It was just get the message to Garcia. And it's a very controversial kind of essay but it's something that I always think about. I don't always need to know where I'm going with that message or what's in the message. But I need to be confident that I'm taking the message for a good reason. *And how do you get that confidence?* By having confidence in the leader who gave me the message. And unfortunately I've had a lot of confidence in my leaders, good and bad, and that confidence is eroding, it really is. I'm starting to ask why I'm taking the message.

More than duty, commitment to the Army and the profession were often mentioned as important values. It was during these discussions on this topic that officers pointed out the inconsistencies they saw between the Army's recruiting programs and its base values.

And a profession is something you begin that is a career not just a stepping stone. And one of my thoughts that I find amusing . . . is that the Army nowadays attempts to bring people in [with mercenary appeals] . . . "To get paid for four years of college you only owe four years." So people are doing the four years of college and giving them the four years as good as they can, going all out and then saying "Okay, I am ready to go step on to my next point of life." Because the Army sold this bill of goods as "Hey, four years of college, four years of leadership experience, the civilian world is going to love you." And then so you go "Okay, I am going to go and see if the civilian world loves me" and the Army acts hurt.

Discussions of values differed across ranks. Young officers often described it as follows: "I do the right thing. I show up. I mean I am in the right place in the right uniform." More experienced officers however described duty as a more difficult task, e.g., giving up weekend family time for unexpected work requirements. One of these officers described this process of professional maturation in this way:

In my mind the only professionals, true professionals, you are going to have in the military are the masters. I kind of look at lieutenant colonel, colonel level as about where you get to that. Everything below that may be a journeyman at best, certainly at other levels in the enlisted . . . they are apprentices. . . . The apprentices and the journeymen are not the masters, and I think it's the Brigade Command level where the master is really. . . . That's where we truly understand the implication of our profession and then can implement that into policy whether it be on the battlefield or shaking the organization to face changes in the world. . . .

Not that everybody can't be imbued with the attributes of professionalism that we want them to. An apprentice by serving time is going to develop and strive to attain those attributes and professionalism and loyalty and duty and selfless service, personal integrity. So they are going to be growing those things that become part of their person. They now have a grasp and are living out the professional ethic but they aren't a professional yet because they just don't have the education and experience to be a master.

Lifestyle

Many officers pointed to the uniqueness of the Army lifestyle as evidence of their profession, particularly its all-encompassing nature. Although not always specifically mentioned, lifestyle elements were observable in the officers' indications of physical characteristics that set Army officers apart from the rest of society, from berets and Stetsons to physical standards. Others focused on the seamlessness between Army work and personal life—living on post, socializing with other officers, being "on duty" 24 hours a day, seven days a week, as this officer viewed it:

> It is unique because you are in your own society. When you . . . change jobs or you cease to be a doctor or you cease to be a lawyer, you don't "get out." When you leave the military, you "get out." That is a common phrase. "I am getting out." And it is its own society and I think that is what truly makes it a unique-type job because you are influencing the lives of soldiers and trying to develop them professionally in a job that has the utmost magnitude of importance which most of us have never experienced which is part of the problem. Because it is hard for us to imagine a mission that we have never done. I think that is what is most unique. You are in your own society of leading soldiers and this is all they have. They live on post. They eat and breathe Army. There are plenty of professions out there where people give as much time to their jobs, definitely so for the most part. But setting the example and never wavering, never letting soldiers see you get really flustered and frustrated, I think it is different. I don't know if it is more stressful or deeper than being a doctor or whatever.

The Profession's Jurisdictions

Prior to this study, we did not consider the family to be a competitor within any Army jurisdiction; however, we do today. The officers that we interviewed clearly identified their spouses and families as powerful agents who, although outside the control of the Army, affect critical career decisions and choices. This internal jurisdiction, the management of the Army's human resources, is an essential one for the Army.[19] Family members often seek to control their military spouses, sometimes to the point of forcing resignation or retirement. In the past, when relatively few wives held jobs outside the home, these families did not have much power in a jurisdictional conflict with the Army. They do now; the changing role and power of women in our society coupled with a new recognition of the importance of personal relationships with children have turned the tables on the Army. The needs of the Army no longer trump the needs of families.

Most officers, both single and married, repeatedly and consistently mentioned their family and (potential) spouse as being one of the most powerful forces bearing on their continuance in the profession. Many of the symbolic objects that the officers brought to the interviews reflected this substantial role of the family in the professional equation, for example, calendars demarcating time spent away from loved ones and photos of children. A large number of officers described the personal conflict they felt as they were pulled between the extraordinary demands of their profession and their own desire to be an active part of their families' lives. Numerous officers echoed the comment, "I never want to look back on my life and say that my career was more important than my family." One officer described his deployment to the Balkans this way:

> But the opposite side of the coin was that as much as it was professionally rewarding there was all this time flying by that I wasn't . . . and all these pictures my kids were

doing and sending me and part of their life that I was missing. Just at the same time that I was having more fun than I could have imagined applying myself in this professional regard, everything was on hold in Heidelberg. . . . [My wife] and the kids and, you know, kids losing teeth, kids finding out about sex for the first time, really it was explained to them in my absence and that's just when it came up, when they started asking those questions. And I mean that's just broken bones and school concerts and kind of all captured by these pictures. Just personal life happening without me. My family's life going on without me. So that's the sacrifice of being in this profession.

Many officers expressed greater frustration about this Army-family conflict when it arose from non-deployment-related requirements, ranging simply from the administrative demands of their jobs to post-deployment National Training Center rotation schedules. As one recently married officer said:

I've been married for 24 months and I've been gone for 14. So the time that I have with my family is crucial. But unfortunately I find myself getting there early and meeting other people's timelines that aren't there early until 1700, 1800; and as an average I never get home till 1930, 2000 back in garrison. So unfortunately I don't feel like I have much control over that at all. And it definitely, for my wife, it's really affected her desire for me to stay in the military. And she seriously wanted me to consider whether or not my kids are going to know me or know of me 20 years from now. And I do see a lot of, unfortunately, a lot of the senior leaders who I think are really good military officers who don't have very good families at all.

Some officers indicated their priorities had changed over their career, shifting from an Army focus to placing their families first. One officer described the effect of focusing too little on his wife when he was a young officer and how he has changed:

How does keeping your family first balance with your profession? I got to tell you I didn't know how to do it when I was younger and that is why I lost my first wife but now it works out really well. You make some calls. You make some decisions. I am not going to stay here and work on this report tonight. I'm going home to see my wife. I can work on the report tomorrow or I can . . . pass it off, give it to somebody else. You just realign your calls. . . . When we went to Saudi I was afraid of changing my outlook. *Changing your outlook from?* The Army first, family second. But it's been the best thing I've ever done simply because I feel now it is the right thing to do. If I'd have been that mature as a 2nd lieutenant, I probably wouldn't have lost my first wife.

The officers' interest in and devotion to the profession often reflected, or even hinged upon, spousal support. The involvement of their spouse in their professional decisions throughout their careers was significant. For example, a Medical Service Corps officer described his fiancée's role in his branch selection:

Oh the one other thing I was going to tell you about was the Ranger Challenge team. That was the third thing. *That dominated your life back then?* Yes, sir. My wife now was my girlfriend back then and she hated it. *She never saw you?* She hated it and like I got into the Army and told her, "I want to go Special Forces." I'm like "I've got to go Special Forces." I'm like Special Forces and Delta Force, seems to be like the last safe haven for warriors and people who don't get screwed with picking weeds out of the volley ball court anymore. But then she started talking to some of my buddies' wives who are in the Group and they are like "Oh, I've been single the five years he's been in the Group." And she's like "You are not going Special Forces." A good challenge for life? She is like "No, you will not. It will be even worse than the Ranger

Challenge Team." She hated it. We didn't have a social life. I mean here we are in college in the prime of our life and on the weekends I would just be like "Oh, if I was there at all." So yeah she wasn't too wide about it. *What does she think about it now?* She is honestly counting the days down until I get out.

Additional jurisdictional competition emerged as an issue during the officers' discussions about the various kinds of missions the Army is engaged in. While some officers noted that they did not care for the broadening range of missions being undertaken in recent years, most indicated that they did not mind or had even benefited personally and professionally. At one end of the continuum, officers were receptive to diverse missions being part of the profession:

> I'd say something like the military is a profession. We're professional soldiers. And what we do is, we're here to make sure that we're ready to fight our nation's wars, and we also do other things such as fight wild fires and do other public good, hurricane relief, things like that. It's all part—if we weren't professionals then we wouldn't be able to provide that service and we'd probably be challenged by some other country if we weren't professional in a military way.

At the other end of the continuum, they described fighting and winning wars as the sole focus of the profession:

> I think that has a definite impact on the hurting of the ideal of professionalism in the Army. You have Bosnia. I am a compassionate person. The whole Bosnian Serb and the Croats and the Muslim factions over there and all the genocide. Yes, on a personal level that affects me but if you look at what the Army is for, I feel that we have no business over there. . . . I mean it hurts when you join the Army to uphold and defend the Constitution of the United States and then you are sent for six months away from your family for a no-conflict because those people are smart. They are not going to do anything while we are over there. The day after we finally say "Oh, everything is okay" and leave, that is when they will re-begin the atrocities and everything like that. But they are not going to just do it while we're there and they haven't.

But most saw humanitarian missions, including peacekeeping, to be in line with what it means to be a professional officer:[20]

> This is a camel-riding crop. A nomad, camel herder, in Somalia made this for me. Every morning . . . I used to toss this guy a little water every now and then. . . . And you wouldn't see him the rest of the day. But I would see him every morning about daybreak and so one morning I threw him over a quart of water and he threw this stick to me. I think he carved it because it is pretty uniform. . . . I have heard people say that you know we are not the humanitarian Green Peace of the world. But I'll tell you, if you go on one of those missions and you see the people. And Somalia was an ugly thing. But anyway, when you see people like that and little kids starving, it was worth going over there to me and doing that and being part of that.

Conclusion

Our intention in this chapter was to examine the Army profession from the perspective of a key segment of its membership, the officer corps. We have sought to organize this investigation using Andrew Abbott's theory of professions, which emphasizes a system of professions in which each profession controls a unique body of abstract knowledge, conducts tasks based on that knowledge, exerts behavioral control over members, and jostles for jurisdiction with other occupational groups. We gathered data to speak to the profession using a proven methodology for tapping into the authentic thoughts and feelings of the Army profession's members.

The methodology as used in this research enabled us to acquire an in-depth and thoughtful view into the minds of Army officers. The approach allowed officers to dictate which issues got raised and define which issues were important regarding what it means to be a professional officer. Therefore, rather than responding to pre-set questions or other participants' opinions, officers were able to indicate their individual and genuine priorities. The analysis of these data illuminated consistencies across accounts that inform our understanding of Army officers and the study of professions in general.

Our analysis led us to six major conclusions: (1) the officer corps does not have a shared emphasis on or understanding of the Army's unique abstract knowledge, which is managing violence; (2) this lack arises from a failure to focus on the Army's unique abstract knowledge and an over-emphasis on another profession's abstract knowledge, that of social work; (3) the Army is bureaucratizing its professional expertise into checklists and forms, thereby reducing the expertise of its officers, frustrating them in their attempts to apply their knowledge and experience, and quite likely decreasing the effectiveness of professional decisions; (4) social or behavioral controls over officers' conduct are essential yet weaker than Army officers consider ideal; (5) most officers are open to broadening the Army's jurisdiction across the spectrum of conflict; and (6) the Army and officers' families are in competition over the officers' professional commitment: this remains an unresolved jurisdictional conflict. The foregoing conclusions can be aggregated into the following fundamental issue areas: the Army profession's knowledge and tasks; professional expertise; social or behavioral control; and the Army's jurisdictions. Let us discuss each in turn.

The Profession's Knowledge and Tasks

Key to understanding what it means to be a professional is the connection to and application of abstract knowledge. Although the respondents spoke to this issue in compelling ways indicating they felt strongly about the content of the Army's abstract knowledge and their professional responsibilities in its application, there was no agreement on the Army's *unique* abstract knowledge. Rather, officers focused heavily on a domain of abstract knowledge, taking care of people, that is dominated by another profession, namely social work. We found it striking that only a small number of officers focused their discussion on the Army profession's unique area of expertise, managing violence or killing, indicating it is not broadly viewed as the central, unique task of this profession.

Instead, most officers emphasized taking care of soldiers as the key element of their professional knowledge, either in terms of the amount of time they spent on the task and/or in terms of the priority it has in their minds. These data indicate that taking care of soldiers has become an end in and of itself for most officers, disconnected from the mission and unrelated to the profession's formal training in killing and managing violence. This disjunction leaves the Army's abstract knowledge base, managing violence, vulnerable to direct competition from other occupational groups and places the Army in direct competition with social work and other occupations over the subordinate knowledge regarding taking care of soldiers and families.

Our recommendations regarding the Army's professional knowledge emphasize making officers more aware of the Army's unique abstract knowledge through existing socialization mechanisms and educational programs. Specifically, senior leaders need to keep the unique task of managing violence central to officers at all levels and determine the emphasis officers should place on taking care of soldiers relative to other key professional tasks and activities. If managing violence is to rise in importance, then officers should be encouraged to talk about this knowledge in the context of what it means to be a profession through officer professional development programs, counseling sessions, and informal mentor opportunities. If taking care of soldiers is to be reduced in relative importance for officers, then senior leaders must determine who does it, under what circumstances, and to what extent. If, on the other hand, it is to be maintained or increased in emphasis, senior leaders should exploit it by formally incorporating it into the profession's expert knowledge and making the officer corps thoroughly aware of this change.

Professional Expertise

The details surrounding the application of a profession's abstract knowledge are as important as its content. Since professions differ from other occupational forms largely because they embed expertise in human beings rather than machines or organizational systems, ensuring that professionals are free to develop and then apply their professional expertise is essential for a profession's success. If instead it is organizational systems or machines that determine how, when, and where expertise is applied, then the occupation is not considered a profession and its members are not professionals. Furthermore, if the tasks truly are professional in nature, then the limitations of organizational systems and machines will result in less effective decision-making.

Our data indicate a clear encroachment of organizational management systems or bureaucracy into the domain of the professional. The issue of the application of professional expertise elicited the strongest emotional response from officers, indicating an understanding on their part of the importance of professional discretion. They felt thwarted by centralized organizational systems that kept them from exercising their core sense of being a professional, their expertise. As one officer stated:

> This is the way one soldier put it to me, the thing I don't like about the Army, he said, was the Army says if one guy steps on the nail we're going to give everybody in the Army a tetanus shot. And I thought there was a lot of insight in that statement, because instead of holding commanders responsible for the command climate they have, instead of court-martialing those who have failed, instead of removing them from those things, instead we set up a whole bunch of centralized programs to make

sure that no one will fail. And then it's really not for the purpose of making sure no one will fail. It's for the purpose of making sure that we look good in the end.

Moreover, these officers described the very outcome that arises from the bureaucratization of professional tasks—decreased effectiveness—when they worried that the lives of their soldiers and others would be risked because of their inability to exercise their expertise.

From our perspective, it is essential that the Army's senior leaders, through their own actions and organizational systems, establish trust in Army officers' ability to exercise the professional expertise appropriate to their rank. This will require that senior leaders scrutinize and vastly reduce the centralized systems and programs that hinder officers in these efforts. If Army professionals are to be able to act as professionals, the Army's organizational systems—operations, personnel management, training, research and development, etc.—must be conformed to support this.

Social (Behavioral) Control

In response to the discretion they are given by society, all professions enact some degree of behavioral control over their members to ensure that professional expertise is applied ethically. They use a variety of means to control their members' behavior including codes of ethics, espoused values, legal mechanisms, and regulated lifestyle. In an operational environment, the military professions enforce the Geneva Conventions and adherence to civilian control of the military, insist upon compliance with rules of engagement, indoctrinate members to protect innocent citizens, etc. These controls are essential for the military professions, which are executors of a society's violent power, its military machine designed to kill human beings and conduct wars. Not only is social control important for the military, but it is also one of the greatest challenges since it seeks to ensure ethical behavior from soldiers in times of chaos, uncertainty, danger, and fear. In fact, ethical behavior may conflict with a soldier's innate instinct for survival and self-defense. Therefore, to accomplish its mission, the Army must have very powerful and consistent social control mechanisms.

Our data indicate that Army officers clearly understand the importance of social control mechanisms in their profession. However, their interviews also indicated that they did not feel the Army's present mechanisms were adequate. Moral courage dominated the officers' discussions of values and their selection of professional exemplars. Bluntly, they desire candor. They want the freedom to speak and act without penalty, and they want honesty from their superiors, both immediate and the most senior. But many of them felt the Army's senior officers were not speaking candidly, either to the profession's members or to those important constituencies outside the profession.

Furthermore, unique Army lifestyle elements such as post housing, officers' clubs, and uniforms clearly mattered to officers in terms of their profession. These items serve both to publicly reinforce that the Army is a unique profession and to facilitate the sharing of values, thereby strengthening the profession.

Thus our recommendations focus on making senior leaders more cognizant of messages they are sending, directly and indirectly, to the profession's members. Modern news media, such as C-SPAN and the Internet, enable officers at all levels to see and hear the words of senior leaders in all venues, including testifying before Congress. Inconsistencies between what these officers experience in their daily work and the messages they hear from senior leaders weaken their confidence in the profession's values, especially moral courage. Recruiting commercials are one of the most critical means of communicating professional values *to the profession*, as well as to the American public and potential recruits. If the messages in these commercials contradict the profession's values (and the reasons are unexplained), then the profession's social control mechanism and status as a profession will be weakened.

Senior leaders should also consider establishing or reestablishing more lifestyle programs, such as officer and NCO clubs. When faced with lifestyle program decisions, these leaders must consider the impact on the profession.[21] Such programs are very important to officers, giving them access to each other so that they might share their values and serving as a touchstone, a public display of the profession's uniqueness.

The Army's Jurisdiction: Focus and Family Tension

Professions compete for control over jurisdictions where they are free to apply their abstract knowledge. Over the last decade, the Army has engaged in an extensive debate regarding the boundaries of its jurisdiction and the appropriateness of its involvement throughout the spectrum of violence. Some have argued that war is the only suitable jurisdiction for the Army; others have supported a broader jurisdiction that includes activities across the spectrum of conflict. From a professional perspective, the debate deals with changing the size and contours of the Army's jurisdiction—whether it should be narrowed, perhaps risking irrelevancy to the nation, whether it should be broadened, perhaps encroaching on other occupations, or whether it should be resized and reshaped into a configuration falling somewhere in between. Resolution of this debate should take place in negotiation between the profession's senior leaders and the nation's elected officials. However, the perspective of the profession's members should certainly be taken into account.

Our respondents indicated that most officers are comfortable undertaking a variety of missions involving potential or actual destruction, damage, injury, or death. The profession's key tasks—managing violence (be it from human or natural causes) and caring for others (be they soldiers or civilians)—enable them to apply their professional expertise to a range of missions. Therefore, for most officers humanitarian missions are consistent with the skills and knowledge developed within the profession and contribute to the values essential for professional control. From this perspective, the jurisdictional boundaries of the profession are in flux, with the members' sentiment being to expand them.

Finally, it is quite interesting that although the topic was the military profession, most officers at some point in their interviews broached their families, or lack thereof, as being integral to the discussion. What does it mean that so much control over the commitment of individual professionals resides outside of the organization? Clearly, the profession no longer dominates its members' commitment and their associated career decisions. In essence, there is a jurisdictional battle between the family and the profession.

In regard to jurisdiction, we recommend that the Army's senior leaders think strategically about the leadership of the profession, its jurisdiction, and its competitors. They must decide and then negotiate the profession's boundaries, cognizant that most officers believe humanitarian and peace-keeping missions are within the profession's domain. Furthermore, they must enable members of the profession to take care of their families, i.e., reduce workloads to give them time to do this, rather than establishing centralized programs that do it for them. It will also be important to find ways to directly involve spouses in career decisions and discussions since these are joint decisions with both partners essentially having veto power.

Future Research

As a rich mosaic of officers' views of what it means to be a professional Army officer circa 2000, this study provides a reliable starting point for research on the profession as experienced by individual officers. Future research could effectively build on this study in three main ways:

- Focus on understanding the tasks of the profession better. How much time, energy, and feeling do officers expend on given tasks? Are the tasks central to the abstract knowledge of the profession? For a time study of tasks, methodologies geared to structured self-reports or those employing ethnographic techniques would provide the most accurate data.
- Make the research longitudinal. Do officers' views of themselves as professionals change over time? In what ways? As changes in mission, the economy, and public support occur over time, it would be worthwhile to conduct the same type of study as reported here—two, five, or even ten years out. This longitudinal study of officers' views would, in effect, be a study of peacetime versus wartime/post-wartime understandings. It would be an invaluable investigation of the role of abstract knowledge in an evolving profession.
- The research could be broadened. It would be beneficial to compare the beliefs and feelings of U.S. Army officers to others in the military profession. Studying officers across services and internationally would help to discern which issues are fundamental to the profession and which are of particular relevance to the American Army.

Studying what the Army profession means to officers provides key insights into how to strengthen the profession in terms of its knowledge, tasks, control systems, and jurisdiction, as well as reinforcing the reality that the Army is indeed a profession. It is worth underscoring that these leverage points involve expanding the connection officers have to their profession, through underscoring its core abstract knowledge and emphasizing the relevance of certain tasks, rather than expending money on better technology or higher pay. The education of the profession in this sense requires foresight, vision, leadership, and diligence, not necessarily a larger budget.

Notes

1. Field Manual 100-5, *Operations* (Washington, DC: Headquarters, Department of the Army, 14 June 1993).
2. William G. Ouchi, "Markets, Bureaucracies, and Clans," *Administrative Science Quarterly* 25 (1980): 129-141; and "A Conceptual Framework for the Design of Organizational Control Mechanisms," *Management Science* 25 (1979): 833-48.
3. For physicians, see T.J. Hoff, "The Social Organization of Physician-managers in a Changing HMO," *Work and Occupations* 26 (1999): 324-51; nurses, see L.H. Aiken and D.M. Sloane, "Effects of Specialization and Client Differentiation on the Status of Nurses: The Case of Aids," *Journal of Health and Social Behavior* 38 (1997): 203-22; lawyers, see J.W. Stempel, "Theralaw and the Law-Business Paradigm Debate," *Psychology, Public Policy, and Law* 5 (1999): 849-908; social workers, see R. Fisher, "Speaking for the Contribution of History: Context and the Origins of the Social Welfare History Group," *Social Service Review* 73 (1999):191-217, M.S. Twui and R.K.H. Chan, "The Future of Social Work: A Revision and a Vision," *Indian Journal of Social Work* 60 (1999):87-98, B.S. Vourlekis, G. Edinburg, and R. Knee, "The Rise of Social Work in Public Mental Health through Aftercare of People with Serious Mental Illness," *Social Work* 43 (1998):567-75, and Andrew Abbott, "Boundaries of Social Work or Social Work of Boundaries?" *Social Service Review* 69 (1995):545-62; vision care providers, see F.F. Stevens et al., "The Division of Labour in Vision Care: Professional Competence in a System of Professions," *Sociology of Health and Illness* 22 (2000): 431-52; and funeral directors, see S.E. Cahill, "The Boundaries of Professionalization: The Case of North American Funeral Direction," *Symbolic Interaction* 22 (1999): 105-119.
4. For financial planners, see R.C. Cohen, "Who's Planning for Your Future? Jurisdictional Competition Among Organizations and Occupations in the Personal Financial Planning Industry" (unpublished diss., 1997); for tasks in social work, see Y.M. Johnson, "Indirect Work: Social Work's Uncelebrated Strength," *Social Work* 44 (1999):323-34; and on expertise and professional education, see Fisher, "Speaking for the Contribution of History," and D.M. Austin, "The Institutional Development of Social Work Education: The First 100 Years and Beyond," *Journal of Social Work Education* 33 (1997):599-612.
5. This study is purely qualitative in nature; our data arise solely from the words that officers used to express their feelings and thoughts about their profession. For readers more accustomed to quantitative research, our findings may appear vague and imprecise because they are not presented as percentages or numbers with significance levels. Instead, we will support our conclusions with statements such as "many officers" or "a few respondents." However, we want to assure our readers that these data have been rigorously collected and thoroughly analyzed using state-of-the-art qualitative software, in this case *Atlas ti*, and methods, such as those presented by Matthew B. Miles and A. Michael Huberman in *Qualitative Data Analysis: An Expanded Sourcebook* (Thousand Oaks, CA: Sage Publications, 1994). As a result, this study reflects the strengths of qualitative research—it provides a rich description of reality in today's Army officer corps and the meaning that officers make of their profession. This description provides an opportunity to draw conclusions and develop hypotheses unfettered by preconceived notions and expectations.
6. U.S. Army War College, *Study on Military Professionalism* (Carlisle Barracks, PA: U.S. Army War College, 1970).
7. Ibid.

8. Ibid.

9. D. Morgan, "Focus Groups," *Annual Review of Sociology* 22(1996): 129-152.

10. G. Zaltman, "Rethinking Market Research: Putting People Back In," *Journal of Marketing Research* (November 1997): 424-37.

11. B.E. Ashforth and F. Mael, "Social Identity Theory and Organization," *Academy of Management Review* 14 (1989): 20-39.

12. We focused this initial study on Active Component officers because of their traditional role in the leadership of the Army profession. However, the other elements of the Army profession— Reserve Components and noncommissioned officers—are also important and worthy of future study.

13. For detailed information concerning the interview protocol, including copies of the assignment letter, contact the authors.

14. If the participants did not bring in any items, the interviewers based the discussion on three issues the participant suggested regarding the profession.

15. Miles and Huberman, *Qualitative Data Analysis.*

16. T. Muhr, *Atlas.ti, version 4.1 for Windows 95 and Windows NT*, Scientific Software Development, Berlin.

17. This response and all those following are generally verbatim renderings of the respondents' oral remarks. In a few cases, responses have been emended to a very slight degree on behalf of clarity.

18. This finding is quite similar to those found in the *Army Training and Leadership Development Panel Report (Officers): Final Report* (Ft. Leavenworth, KS: Combined Arms Center, 2001).

19. See a more extensive discussion of internal jurisdictions in chap. 1.

20. For additional research on officer feelings about non-traditional missions, see Deborah Avant and James Lebovic, "U.S. Military Attitudes toward Post-Cold War Missions," *Armed Forces & Society* 27 (2000):37-56.

21. Many of these lifestyle programs now fall under the Army Well-Being Program. See Thomas A. Kolditz and Eric B. Schoomaker, "Three Case Studies on the Army's Internal Jurisdictions: Case Study No. 1—Army Well-Being," in *The Future of the Army Profession*, project directors Don M. Snider and Gayle L. Watkins, ed. Lloyd J. Matthews (Boston, MA: McGraw-Hill, 2002), 459-69, for more about this program.

6 | The Multiple Identities of the Professional Army Officer

Introduction: The Shared Identity and Professional Practice of Army Officers[1]

Don M. Snider

Given the more numerous Army expeditions of the past decade, all of us who are part of the Army family have lost comrades-in-arms, friends, even loved ones, someone we knew quite well and for whom we still mourn. Picture, if you will, one such young Army officer, one killed in action in recent conflict or who died in training for the missions at hand. The question I pose as you focus on that individual is: How are we to think of and remember the life, service, and sacrifice of this young Army officer?

In the words of Abraham Lincoln, did this young man or woman, who had lived so briefly, died so early, and left so much behind, "die in vain"? How are members of the Army profession, and the larger Army family, to make meaning of such tragedies and then of their own lives, which must go on? Really, who was he, or she; what was his or her life and sacrifice all about? To answer such questions in a compelling manner, Army officers must have a clear understanding of who they are, an understanding that goes far deeper than the work they do on a daily basis. This is not to say that they do not know who they are individually; certainly they do, for they each have many obvious identities in a single day—citizen, commander, trainer, counselor, spouse, parent, friend, etc. But it is to say, as research has recently shown, that their essential conception of their officerly identity varies widely from officer to officer. Even more troubling, the content of their self-identification as officers often does not approximate what the Army profession holds as the true meaning of *being* an officer under commission, with all that that shared professional identity entails.[2]

Simply stated, Army officers have been deprived of an immense store of inspiration and satisfaction because of their poorly conceived self-concepts as officers. In fairness, such lack of a commonly held self-identity was not the fault of the younger officers. In the previous decade or more—from the end of the Gulf War to the tragedy of 11 September 2001—now known as 9/11—the Army focused only slightly on the professional education and development of its junior officers, particularly on acculturating them to the meaning of and the requirement for professionalism. For the Army, it was a decade-long drawdown accompanied by more frequent operational deployments, doing more with less, only to be culminated by an attack on America requiring even more to be done with even more urgency.

The purpose of this chapter is to lay out for consideration by the Army officer corps an understanding of the self-identity required by all Army officers, junior or senior—a robust, inspirational identity drawn from renewed study of the Army profession.[3] Officership suggests a unique type of leadership, one that fulfills the "exceptional and unremitting"[4] responsibilities assumed when accepting the commission. Rightly understood, then, this inspiring self-concept has no meaning absent its context as derived from the responsibilities of the Army officer corps to lead the Army profession in service to its collective client, the American people. When understood and internalized deeply, such understanding can provide a resounding answer to this chapter's introductory question: "No, that young officer in my mind's eye most assuredly did not die in vain!" Thus from such understandings can be drawn the motivations necessary for a life of service to the republic and, with that life of service, an acceptance of the tragic sacrifices often required.

Of the four essays jointly comprising this chapter, the first summarizes the emergent understanding of the Army's dual status as a vocational profession as well as a hierarchical bureaucracy, and explains how the associated insights have led to a broader and more principled view of officership than had been held during the five-decade Cold War. Then the three essays authored by serving field grade officers will present perspectives on the various components of the Army officer's fully realized professional identity: the Officer as Warrior (Lt. Cols. John Nagl and Paul Yingling); the Officer as Leader of Character (Lt.Col. Tony Pfaff); and the Officer as Servant and Professional (Maj. Suzanne Nielsen).

What We Know about Professions

We know that human expertise and the relatively abstract knowledge underlying it are the coins of the professional realm. More so than other occupations and organizations, vocational professions focus on developing their expert knowledge in individual members in order for them to apply their specific expertise in a professional practice. Doctors perfect medical treatments, lawyers apply legal expertise to new cases, and military professionals develop and apply new technologies, organizations, and tactics to "provide for the common defense." In most cases, such professional expertise and practice are essential to the functioning of society but are beyond the capabilities of the average citizen, most often requiring so many years of study and preparation as to be considered a lifelong "calling" by the professional. This is the more traditional view of a profession as the "social trustee" of the body of expert knowledge on behalf of the society served.[5]

Further, we know that unlike other producing organizations, the success of such "trustee" professions is measured primarily by effectiveness—how well the professional practice succeeds—rather than by the organization's efficiency in producing the desired effect. Was the patient cured? Was justice rendered in the verdict? Was the battle won and the homeland defended? These are the predominant questions from the clients. Because of the difficulty and essentiality of their expert knowledge, and as well the moral obligations inherent in their professional practices, professions focus sharply on the development of their individual members and their expertise, especially new members. For all professions a significant part of such development is the inculcation of professional ethics and standards of practice (both individual and collective), for these spell out the norms of behavior that create and maintain the necessary trust between profession and client. If such trust is maintained, western societies generally grant to their professions a relative degree of autonomy to continue to set such standards, to cull from their ranks members who flout the standards, and to otherwise develop their future members professionally.

Professions also have a hidden, more self-serving side. Rather than being static producing organizations, they are engaged in spirited competitions for control over the arenas, or jurisdictions, in which they seek to apply their expertise.[6] An oft-noted current example of these competitions is occurring in the field of medicine, where physicians and HMOs battle over the right to make patient care decisions. Other professions face similar challenges as they seek to gain legitimacy in new fields while holding sway in their traditional jurisdictions.

The Army is embroiled in such competitions today in several jurisdictions. These are "negotiated" competitions in which the Army's senior leaders represent the profession before the nation's civilian leaders. Referring to Figure 1-2 in Chapter 1, these include, for example, the "Homeland Security" jurisdiction (e.g., counter-drug operations), where the Army has often sought, unsuccessfully, to opt out; and the Army's core jurisdiction of "Major Combat Operations," where the Army's competitors include the other two American military professions (air-space and maritime), foreign militaries, private companies/contractors (many run by former Army officers), and international organizations.[7] These rivalries are not trivial. Competitive failure by a profession, including the Army, may well result in its demise, much like a noncompetitive business.

We should note that the three American military professions are also government bureaucracies. Unlike professions, bureaucracies focus on routine applications of non-expert knowledge, usually through standing operating procedures, policies, and instructions rather than through the autonomous practice of employees in whose preparation much has been invested. Therefore, the Army is on the one hand a vocational profession focused on the development of the expert knowledge of land warfare and its application by human experts, and on the other hand a hierarchical bureaucracy focused on the application of routine knowledge through operating protocols, procedures, and check-sheets. The Army's current highly centralized approach to predeployment unit training "by template," which leaves little to the discretion of junior commanders, is an example of the bureaucratic model.[8]

This dual nature is unavoidable, though when the bureaucratic comes to predominate over the professional, as was arguably the case for the Army late in the 1990s (see Chapter 1), it is a cause of seriously debilitating tensions at both the individual and institutional levels.[9] Militaries that do not resolve this tension in favor of their professional nature can "die" in the professional sense. As their bureaucratic nature becomes predominant, they increasingly centralize control and squeeze professional practices into bureaucratic molds, begin treating their professionals as bureaucrats or mere occupational time-servers, and soon come to resemble a compliant military bureaucracy exhibiting little of the vibrant effectiveness of a vocational profession. One need only look at western European militaries in the post-Cold War era to find such phenomena.

Given this inherent tension within the Army, then, it is vital that all officers, junior and senior, develop the professional self-concept that can be drawn from a proper understanding of their role within the Army profession. Not only will such a self-concept provide a rich return in personal satisfaction from their life's work as it unfolds day by day, it will also contribute greatly to necessary unity and cohesion within the officer corps.

The Army Officer Corps' Expert Knowledge and Professional Practice

To introduce the needed self-identity, we must next consider briefly the profession's expert knowledge (which is discussed in much more detail in Chapter 9 of the present anthology). If the Army is to remain a strongly competitive profession, what should its expert knowledge be? What expertise does it provide that the American people require and want to be applied to situations of future need?

An infantry company commander, like other professionals, has developed in his mind an immense catalogue of expert knowledge—tactics, weapons capabilities, use of available fires, logistics, leadership and care of soldiers, how to work with other professionals (noncommissioned officers), the laws of land warfare, etc. When deployed in Afghanistan, Iraq, or elsewhere and given a specific operational mission, his "practice" is very similar to that of other professionals. He analyzes the situation (diagnosis), applies his expert knowledge to it (inference), and then develops a plan and leads in its execution (treatment).[10] The essence of the professional practice is no different if the stateside task is to employ a training facility, time, and other resources in training his unit to standards on certain operational tasks.

Beyond his expert knowledge, the officer's identity is also strongly influenced by the larger purposes of the Army in a deployment. Baldly stated, the basic tasks of the soldier are fourfold: to prepare to kill, to kill if ordered, to prepare to die, and to die if necessary.[11] The predominant reason that a society needs an Army or its soldiers is to be well schooled and effective in the arts of war-fighting as a democratic Army and to use that expertise when and where the society directs. And this fact points to the purpose of having commissioned officers within such an Army. Under commission from the executive of their government—and therefore acting as its moral agent—commissioned officers provide to American society and its youth who volunteer to be soldiers the overall direction and leadership of the armed forces. Army officers do this, for example, among their many other responsibilities, by exercising the legal responsibilities of command of each of the Army's units, at all echelons, everywhere, every day.

In his classic study, *The Soldier and the State*, Samuel Huntington referred to this expertise generally as the "management of violence"; others have used different formulations but to largely the same effect.[12] Recent theorists of the social organization of expert work, as well as military professionals themselves, have expanded on the officer's expertise in terms of tasks. Commissioned officers, particularly the profession's senior leaders, direct and lead the Army profession by performing three critical tasks:

- Bounding, prioritizing, and adapting the expert knowledge of the profession for current and future needs of the client;
- Developing such knowledge and expertise in the members of the profession for application by professionals to new situations (professional practice); and,
- Managing the jurisdictional competitions of the profession to ensure that the profession executes assigned tasks, remains legitimate, and survives over time to serve the client as needed (see Chapter 28 in the present anthology).

In the balance of this chapter, we shall focus on the expert knowledge of the profession—the foundation of the individual officer's expertise and professional practice—as noted in the first task above. More specifically, as in the case of the infantry company commander on deployment, we shall focus on *the professional practice of commissioned Army officers when viewed in the context of a profession in the daily exercise of their discretionary judgment while making decisions and taking actions that fulfill their moral and legal responsibilities under the commission.* And it is worth reemphasizing that they make these discretionary judgments on the basis of their accumulated expert knowledge many times a day.

Glancing back to the lower half of Figure 1-2 in Chapter 1, we can re-format the data into the form shown in the box below. It is in the internal jurisdictions of the Army profession and its four broad fields of expert knowledge that one finds the corresponding identities informing the unique self-concept needed for each Army officer. All professions have the same two internal jurisdictions: they all must develop their own expert knowledge, keep it current, and adapt it to the future; and they all must develop individual professionals to apply that knowledge. Thus, for the Army profession we have the following correspondences between an officer's sub-areas of professional expertise and his or her several professional identities.

Field of Army Expert Knowledge	Army Officer Identity
Military-technical	Warrior
Moral-ethical	Leader of Character
Political-cultural	Servant of the Nation
Human development	Member of a Profession

Clearly, not all Army officers blend these identities into their professional self-concept in the same manner or proportion. Infantry company commanders likely view themselves more as warriors than as members of a profession or as servants of the American nation. But the opposite is probably true of an Army major or lieutenant colonel assigned to the Army General Staff in the Pentagon, who is representing the needs of the Army amidst constant resource and jurisdictional battles with sister services and other professional competitors such as private contractors.

But the point is that all Army officers, regardless of branch or grade, should hold in some proportion all of these four identities, from the moment of commissioning forward. In this manner they share a common professional self-identity, a perspective on "who they are" that provides meaning and thus motivation to their daily lives. To know they are members of a unique profession—one separated from all other professions by the nature of its war-fighting expertise, by the high ethical ideals under which it is to be employed, and by the worthiness of their clients, the American people, and of the way of life that is then served—conveys indelibly the nobility of their "calling," a nobility magnified even further by the sacrifices that may be involved.

The self-denying character of one who chooses to serve his or her fellow Americans will not be lost on other Army officers as together they cohere within the profession, sharing their indispensable roles, leading themselves and their soldiers to higher levels of dedication, expertise, and service.

Living the Identity of the Army Officer— Walking the Talk with a "Principled" Life

One final subject remains. Two of the more disturbing conclusions of the Army's recent internal reviews of training and leader development programs found, first, that "the Army's service ethic and concepts of officership are neither well-understood nor clearly defined; and second, that Army culture is not "healthy" due to the existence of "a gap between beliefs and practices" that "is outside the band of tolerance."[13] Such findings are, on the one hand, troubling when one recalls the superb professionalism of the Army of the first Gulf War. On the other hand, they point out what is very well known but seldom acknowledged owing to the profession's often dysfunctional "can do" attitude—living the life of an officer day after day, deployment after deployment, is a very daunting task!

It is axiomatic, however, that one of the quickest and most effective ways to address the gap between beliefs and practices is for every officer to better "walk the talk" in each position of responsibility and authority in which he or she is currently serving. Change how the members of the Army officer corps conceive of themselves, each one, and thus how each is motivated to perform, and that will in turn change positively to some degree the climate and practices within every unit, command, and region of the world where Army forces are stationed.

Such a declaration should not be mistaken for the simplism that if all Army officers change their self-concepts and motivations, all will be well. But self-concepts are a source of individual motivation, and attitudes and motivation do influence behavior. And, I believe, such self-concepts can be even more effective if they are placed in the right professional context. Certainly if each Army officer better "walks the talk" daily, reflecting congruence between Army beliefs and personal practices, the problems noted within the profession's training and leader development systems would be quickly and forthrightly leveraged toward ultimate resolution.

To make that happen, all Army officers need now, as they have always needed, to live "principled" lives, which are the officer's visible but silent "walk of leadership." Soldiers never tire of observing their leaders! Whether deployed or stateside, whether on duty or off, whether with family or alone, officers should live a life that reflects the consistent set of time-tested principles that have proven best able to prompt decisions reflecting discretion and judgment and to enable self-control in all aspects of life. When the ideals set forth in the Army profession's ethic—the Army's Values, the Warrior ethos, the Ranger's Creed, the terms of the Commissioning Oath, the Declaration of Independence, the Preamble to the Constitution, etc.—are deeply internalized, they provide for consistent and professionally virtuous behavior in the daily lives of members of the Army officer corps. Consider the following such ideals:

- **Duty.** Professional officers always do their duty, subordinating their personal interests to the requirements of the professional function. They are prepared, if necessary, to lay down their own lives and the lives of their soldiers in the nation's interest. When assigned a mission or task, its successful execution is first priority, above all else, with officers accepting full responsibility for their actions and orders in accomplishing it—and accomplishing it in the right way. The officer's duty is not confined, however, to explicit orders or tasks; it extends to any circumstance involving allegiance to the commissioning oath.
- **Honor.** An officer's honor, derived through history from demonstrated courage in combat, is of paramount importance. It includes the virtues of integrity and honesty. Integrity is the personal honor of the individual officer, manifested in all roles. In peace, the officer's honor is reflected in consistent acts of moral courage. An officer's word is an officer's bond.
- **Loyalty.** Military officers serve in a public vocation, and their loyalty extends upward through the chain of command to the President as Commander in Chief and downward to all subordinates. Officers take care of their soldiers and their families. This loyalty is a central ingredient of the trust that binds together the military profession for its public servant role.
- **Service.** An officer's motivations are noble and deeply felt: a love for the technical and human aspects of providing the nation's security and an awareness of the moral obligation to use that expertise for the benefit of society. The officer has no legacy except for the quality of his or her years of faithful service.
- **Competence.** The serious obligations of officership—and the enormous consequences of professional failure—establish professional competence as a moral imperative. More than knowing one's job or having proficiency in the skills and abilities of the military art, professional competence in this sense includes attributes of cultural literacy, creativity, and confidence. Called to their profession and motivated by their pursuit of its expertise, officers are committed to a career of continuous study and learning.
- **Teamwork.** Officers model civility and respect for others. They understand that soldiers of a democracy value the worth and abilities of the individual, both at home and abroad. But because of the moral obligation accepted and the mortal means employed to carry out an officer's duty, the officer also emphasizes the importance of the group as against the individual. Success in war requires the subordination of the will of the individual to the task of the group. The military ethic is cooperative and cohesive in spirit, meritocratic, and fundamentally anti-individualistic and anti-careerist.

- **Subordination.** Officers strictly observe the principle that the military is subject to civilian authority and do not involve themselves or their subordinates in domestic politics or policy beyond the exercise of the basic rights of citizenship. Military officers render candid and forthright professional judgments and advice and eschew the public advocate's role.
- **Leadership.** Officers lead by example, always maintaining the personal attributes of spiritual, physical, and intellectual fitness that are demanded by their chosen profession and which will serve as exemplars for others.[14]

Thus one developmental goal of every commissioned officer should be to understand better the several identities of the Army officer and how they most appropriately are integrated in his or her own professional identity. That goal should include the moral development of personal character that enables a "principled" lifestyle, both professionally and personally. Shared across the officer corps, this identity will strongly inform the officer's professional practice—a life filled daily with discretionary professional judgments and actions and lived in a "principled" manner.

Returning to my answer to the introductory question, "No, the young Army officer I pictured surely did not die in vain." Nor, I suspect, did any such officer whom the reader may have thought about. My comrade was far more than a friend; we had endured together the horrors of war, its preparation, and its aftermath.[15] We knew we would never be paid our full worth as warriors of a democratic republic. But we also knew through the course of a career where to find and how to cherish those intrinsic remunerations that come from a life of service to others, rather than to self. The essays in this chapter have been prepared in the hope that they may in some modest fashion prompt the next generation of Army officers to do the same.

The Army Officer as Warrior[16]

John Nagl and Paul Yingling

The military officer must fill a number of roles, often simultaneously. He has responsibilities as a warrior, as the nation's multipurpose servant, as a member of the profession of arms, and as a leader of character. These four roles are interrelated almost to the point of inseparability, but examining each separately allows a better understanding of their inherent complexities.

> Battle is the ultimate to which the whole life's labor of an officer should be directed. He may live to the age of retirement without seeing a battle; still, he must always be getting ready for it as if he knew the hour of the day it is to break upon him. And then, whether it comes late or early, he must be willing to fight— he must fight.
>
> —Brig. Gen. C.F. Smith[17]

The central premise of this essay is that preparing for battle is a lifelong developmental process and a worthy life's work. While fighting America's wars is not the professional soldier's only task, it is the task that only the professional soldier can do. War-fighting's complex arrangement of activities includes generating, applying, and sustaining combat power from the fort to the port to the fighting position to achieve the aims of policy.

Developing the set of skills necessary to manage violence in the nation's service is a continuous developmental process that begins when an officer commences his or her pre-commissioning training and education and continues throughout a career. Professionalism is a combination of competence and devotion to service that grows over time, and that growth occurs differently in each individual. There is no rank or position or level of education that clearly delineates the professional from the mere jobholder. Furthermore, the relationship between professionals at differing stages of career development is symbiotic. The younger professional benefits from the older one's wisdom and dignity, while the older benefits from the younger one's idealism, adaptability, and energy.

Mastering the art and science of war-fighting encompasses every aspect of the human experience—physical, intellectual, and moral.[18] To understand fully the officer's responsibilities as a war-fighter, we must explore in detail each of these aspects.

The Physical Dimension

"The Army inspires soldiers to have the strength, the confidence, and the will to fight and win anywhere, anytime."[19] This excerpt from the Army Vision is as applicable to Gen. George Washington's crossing of the Delaware in 1776 as to Task Force Eagle's crossing of the Sava in 1995. War-fighting always has been and always will be a struggle, not only against hostile forces but also against hostile environments. The officer as warrior has a duty to prepare himself and his subordinates to cope with such physical rigors. This duty begins at the earliest stages of an officer's service.

After arriving at his first duty station, a second lieutenant is expected to set the standard for his platoon in physical toughness. Toughness, not mere fitness, is the standard by which soldiers measure leaders. That the lieutenant be in excellent physical condition is necessary, but not sufficient. More important is his willingness to share his soldiers' physical hardships. Sgt. Maj. John Stepanek, addressing a group of officer candidates, stated succinctly what they could expect from noncommissioned officers (NCOs):

> You can expect loyalty to your position, devotion to our cause, admiration for your honest effort, courage to match your courage, guts to match your guts, endurance to match your endurance, motivation to match your motivation, esprit to match your esprit, a desire for achievement to match your desire for achievement. . . . We won't mind the heat if you sweat with us. We won't mind the cold if you shiver with us. . . . And if the mission requires, we will storm the very gates of Hell, right behind you.[20]

The importance of leader presence in the worst possible conditions—in the mud and rain during training or at the point of maximum danger during combat—cannot be overestimated. When the officer endures such hardships alongside his soldiers, those hardships become the glue that binds the unit into a cohesive fighting force. If the officer uses his rank or position to exempt himself from such hardship, the effect is exactly the opposite. Those same hardships, endured only by lower-ranking members of a unit, become the acid that dissolves the unit into a group of sullen, angry individuals, each emulating his leader by looking first to his own safety and comfort.

As an officer grows in seniority, the obligation to endure hardships alongside his soldiers becomes ever more important. The sight of senior officers exposing themselves to the dangers of combat has an inspirational effect on soldiers that defies rational calculation. Great commanders are aware of this effect and make every effort to bring their leadership to bear at the decisive point in the same way they bring to bear firepower, maneuver, or information. Military theorist Carl von Clausewitz prescribed the commander's presence as an antidote to soldier's exhaustion:

> As each man's strength gives out, as it no longer responds to his will, the inertia of the whole comes to rest on the commander's will alone. The ardor of his spirit must rekindle the flame of purpose in others; his inward fire must revive their hopes.[21]

Gen. Matthew Ridgway, famous for his presence at the front, put the matter this way: "I held to the old-fashioned idea that it helped the spirits of the men to see the Old Man up there, in the snow and the sleet and the mud, sharing the same cold, miserable existence they had to endure."[22] Ridgway's ability to inspire his soldiers to face danger and hardship rested solely on his credibility. He did not order his soldiers into battle from a comfortable headquarters. He led them into battle and shared their dangers and hardships in the process.

The Intellectual Dimension

> The Nation that will insist on drawing a broad line of demarcation between the fighting man and the thinking man is liable to have its fighting done by fools and its thinking done by cowards.
> —SIR WILLIAM FRANCIS BUTLER[23]

Courage is a necessary attribute in every soldier, but courage alone can never be sufficient for an officer in the exercise of his duties as a warrior. A comprehensive knowledge of the theory and practice of warfare must govern his courage. Such knowledge enables him to win the nation's wars at an acceptable cost in blood and treasure. In the absence of such knowledge, warfare becomes (to use the Confederates' painfully accurate critique of the Union's suicidal tactics at Fredericksburg) "simply murder."

The officer as warrior is duty-bound to educate himself and his subordinates on the theory and practice of war. Such an education trains an officer not what to think but how to think. In this way, officers develop in themselves and in their subordinates what J.F.C. Fuller describes as "creative intelligence."[24] Applying creative intelligence allows officers to know when to adhere to time-honored rules and conventions and when to disregard them and attempt the unconventional. In such an education, theory and practice remain tightly linked, with each informing the other. The officer who studies theory at the expense of practice becomes guilty of what Fuller calls "military scholasticism." Such an officer is blind to the life-and-death struggle of combat, seeing his soldiers as so many pawns to be cleverly maneuvered and, ultimately, sacrificed. On the other hand, the officer who clings only to time-honored practice, uninformed by theory and blind to innovation, risks becoming a species of "Prince Eugene's mule." Frederick the Great remarked that this unfortunate animal, after having experienced some 40 campaigns, was still a mule.

The officer's duty to develop intellectually begins at the earliest stages of his service. Every officer basic course graduate is expected to demonstrate an elementary understanding of the theory and practice of small unit combat operations. The theoretical aspects of such operations are expressed in Army doctrine. Doctrine is essentially a distillation of theory on how best to employ combat power to ensure mission accomplishment. Even the most basic battle drill on reacting to contact is grounded in a theory on the relationship between fire and maneuver. The practical aspects of such operations include the technical knowledge required to employ available resources to accomplish assigned missions.

The new officer immediately puts this knowledge into practice on arriving at his first assignment. Commanders expect second lieutenants to accomplish missions by applying Army doctrine and resources to real-world problems. Noncommissioned officers, with their wealth of experience, help young officers put doctrine into practice. Every commander worth his salt advises the new lieutenant to "listen to your NCOs." However, that advice does not mean "do what your sergeants say." Rather, it means "understand what your sergeants know." As the young officer acquires more experience, his appreciation of the applications and limitations of doctrine grows as well.

As officers advance in seniority, their responsibilities increase and their education must keep pace. The lieutenant leads a platoon and conducts battle drills on a small objective. The lieutenant colonel commands a task force and employs combined arms tactics throughout an area of operations. The lieutenant general commands a joint task force and applies operational art to achieve the aims of national policy.

As an officer's challenges become more complex and differentiated from the conventional, doctrine recedes into the background, drawing into sharp relief the senior commander's creative intelligence—Robert E. Lee at Chancellorsville—or lack thereof—George A. Custer at Little Bighorn. Lee and Custer both violated the principle of mass by dividing their forces in the presence of a numerically superior enemy. Lee is rightly celebrated for his audacity, while Custer is rightly condemned for his stupidity. A commander's intellect might well mark the difference between success and failure, and the Army must continue to recognize and encourage its warriors' intellectual development so they know when to follow doctrine, when to violate it, and when to prefigure it themselves by their pioneering innovations on the battlefield.

Indeed, the ability to adapt and innovate in the face of changed circumstances may be the most important intellectual quality that the officer possesses. Because warfare is a life-and-death struggle not only for men but also for entire nations, it refuses to be constrained by rules, doctrines, or routines. The officer's mind must therefore be equally unconstrained so that his imagination can roam freely, anticipating and defeating the enemy's next move—before he makes it.

In assessing great generalship, Sun Tzu correctly observed that "to subdue the enemy without fighting is the acme of skill."[25] The logical corollary of this axiom is that to fight without subduing the enemy is the nadir of ineptitude. There are few sights as tragic as a general who is elevated to a position of high command and, not knowing what he should do, does what he knows. Generalship ignorant of societal and technological changes allowed the Prussians to pirouette into the jaws of death at Jena, and urged on the British lock-step march into the teeth of German machine guns at the Somme. In these and similar military debacles, the gaps in generals' imaginations were filled with the blood of their dying troops. Protracted wars of attrition, whether the currency squandered is blood or treasure or both, are the antithesis of professionalism. The officer as warrior is duty-bound to imagine and create the conditions for conflict termination at an acceptable price.

The Moral Dimension

> We are completely devoted; we are members of a priest-hood really, the sole purpose of which is to defend the Republic.
>
> —Gen. George C. Marshall[26]

While every aspect of war-fighting is demanding, only the moral aspect of war-fighting is paradoxical. To protect the state from the dangers of anarchy, the war-fighter must be fierce enough to kill the state's enemies, but to protect the state from the dangers of tyranny, he must be gentle enough to respect the freedoms of its citizens. Faced with this paradox, Socrates despaired of founding a republic that was both secure and just.

The American republic has proven Socrates wrong. Our country is, in President Abraham Lincoln's eternal words, "A nation conceived in liberty and dedicated to the proposition that all men are created equal."[27] This idea, our idea—the American Idea—which U.S. officers swear to defend against all enemies foreign and domestic is enshrined in the world's oldest living constitution, the U.S. Constitution.

An officer derives legal and moral authority to employ force from his subordination to America's ideals. Legally, the President and Congress confer the officer's authority in the form of a commission, which gives the officer broad authority to act within the law to protect the Constitution. Morally, the officer's authority is derived from his role as a servant of society. The officer who subordinates his personal safety and comfort to the security of society inspires soldiers to do likewise. America's Army of free citizens, inspired by examples of selfless service, has been and will remain the most potent military force on the planet. The graveyard of history is filled with petty tyrants and gangsters who underestimated the power of America's. arms and ideals.

The young officer learns early to wield his legal authority lightly and to assert his moral authority firmly. The unit held together by an officer who only threatens punishment will soon dissolve in the face of the enemy who credibly threatens death. However, the unit bound by a shared belief in what is true and right and just is actually made stronger in the crucible of combat. Sergeants teach young officers to speak to soldiers not by threatening punishment for doing wrong, but by explaining the necessity of doing right. In 1879, Maj. Gen. John Schofield admonished West Point cadets that "the discipline which makes the soldiers of a free country reliable in battle is not to be gained by harsh or tyrannical treatment."[28] A nation founded to affirm the dignity of every citizen can be defended only by affording that same dignity to every soldier.

As officers advance in seniority, the necessity of wielding arms in accordance with America's ideals becomes ever more important. In America's short history, the world has grown smaller and more dangerous, and the U.S. Army has necessarily grown larger and more powerful. So powerful a force can be an instrument of good or evil, depending on the character of those who command it. As a matter of duty, the officer must always be prepared to achieve the aims of policy through the application of violence. However, that violence must be applied in a manner consistent with America's laws and treaty obligations as well as our sense of decency. The officer must remember that he carries into battle not only America's arms, but also her honor.

Viewed in this light, incidents such as My Lai and Abu Ghraib are not merely moral debacles, but true military defeats. If a unit loses a piece of terrain that allows the enemy to reinforce his position or places friendly forces at risk, we rightly call such an action a defeat. When American forces forfeit the moral high ground, our enemies grow stronger while our friends around the world and fellow citizens at home become disheartened. When Army forces lose a piece of physical terrain, we counterattack immediately to set the record straight. When Army forces forfeit the moral high ground, this far more valuable real estate is not so quickly retaken.

Soldiers of every rank must never forget that the Army is raised by a free society to preserve the freedom of the American people and their allies. It must never be employed as an instrument of repression either abroad or at home. The singular challenge for the officer is to wield the enormous power of America's arms in such as way as to inspire awe and fear in our enemies while retaining the respect and affection of our citizens and allies.

The Changing Challenges of Leadership

The world has changed dramatically in only a few years, with profound implications for the military profession. It is not only the events of 11 September 2001 that have made officership more challenging: the end of the Cold War also forced us to rethink our responsibilities. The demise of the Soviet state and political system, which credibly threatened to destroy the United States,

> And through all this welter of change and development, your mission remains fixed, determined, inviolable. It is to win our wars.
>
> —GENERAL OF THE ARMY DOUGLAS MACARTHUR[29]

represented a sea-change in the international system, one creating corresponding changes in officers' responsibilities. We are guardians of our nation's place in the world order; when that order changes, so too must our understanding of our responsibilities change.

The Soviet Union's demise did not lessen the challenge of officership; on the contrary, when the threat to the nation is evident and symmetrical, the physical, moral, and especially the intellectual challenges of officership are comparatively simple to understand, if not always easy to achieve. Generations of Army officers came of age eating, sleeping, and breathing the tactics and organization of the Soviet forces east of the Elbe. Army leaders learned to fight in training centers that replicated, and almost certainly inflated, the capabilities of Soviet-like forces. However, when we can no longer be certain of our enemy's order of battle, or even who our enemy is likely to be, the officer's task becomes correspondingly more difficult.

At the beginning of the 21st century, America finds itself in a war unlike any it has previously fought. Our enemies are fueled by a toxic combination of the insurgent's anonymity, the fanatic's hatred, and the tyrant's ambition. In our struggle against this enemy, we are faced with a curious paradox. Each day, America's armed forces win every battle we fight against this enemy, only to find that tomorrow brings more battles, more violence, and more instability. This observation is not a criticism of our tactical forces, but rather an observation on the utter insufficiency of tactics. Faced with such an enemy, we are reminded that war and peace are profoundly political activities.

MacArthur is remembered in history as much for writing the Japanese constitution and establishing a peaceful and stable postwar Japanese nation as he is for his island-hopping campaign across the Pacific. The Army not only wins wars, it also maintains postwar peace almost everywhere it places its boots. In Germany, Bosnia, Kosovo, Korea, Japan, Afghanistan, Kuwait, and Iraq, U.S. Army officers serve the nation's interests by maintaining stability and acting as a check on potential aggressors. Peacekeeping goes hand in hand with war-fighting as a critical role of military officership, and it is likely to increase in importance in the post-Cold War world.

Saint Augustine reminds us that the only purpose for war is to create a better peace. As the officer applies his expertise in war-fighting, he must constantly keep that better peace in mind. The 21st-century officer must be able to transition rapidly across the spectrum of operations. To create a better peace, he must have the ability to lead troops in the conduct of offensive, defensive, and stability and support operations. These operations might occur simultaneously, and the transition from one to the other will often be made at the discretion of junior leaders. The commander who wins the war and loses the peace is no more professional than the physician who saves a patient's leg at the expense of his spinal cord.

The physical demands of peacekeeping do not differ appreciably from those of war-fighting. For the peacekeeper on his beat in Kosovo to remain alert and physically ready is just as essential as it is for the infantry squad leader in Iraq. However, the moral and intellectual requirements of officership are much more difficult in a world in which officers serve to deter and prevent conflict as much as to win it. Officers must understand and appreciate the languages and cultures of peoples and states that might or might not pose a threat to the nation. How well officers perform their duties may well be decisive in determining whether those actors become friend or foe.

On 11 September 2001, we learned again that military security in and of itself is insufficient. The most powerful military the world has ever seen was powerless against a cowardly attack on unarmed civilians. In his inaugural address, President John F. Kennedy issued "a call to bear the burden of a long twilight struggle, year in and year out, 'rejoicing in hope, patient in tribulation'—a struggle against the common enemies of man: tyranny, poverty, disease, and war itself."[30]

Today's Army officers must recognize the fundamental truth of Kennedy's call. Succeeding in the long twilight struggle that has been thrust on us demands all of the physical, moral, and intellectual energies we can muster in preparing for the responsibilities we must bear as warriors and as officers of the world's most vital and powerful Army.

The Officer as Leader of Character: Leadership, Character, and Ethical Decision-Making

> What the bad man cannot be is a good sailor, or soldier, or airman.
>
> —GEN. SIR JOHN WINTHROP HACKETT[31]

Tony Pfaff

In the fall of 2003, great controversy arose over whether to prosecute Lt. Col. Allen West, a 4th Infantry Division Battalion commander, who admitted to allowing his men to beat an Iraqi policemen they detained in order to obtain information about future attacks against his unit. When the beating failed to elicit the information, he threatened to kill the Iraqi and fired a pistol close to his head. This act of intimidation produced the information needed, and lives reportedly were saved.[32] Though the Iraqi was unharmed, beating and threatening a detainee are violations of international humanitarian law, which Colonel West had an obligation to uphold.[33] However, when the Army announced its decision to prosecute him, a loud chorus, including members of Congress, arose claiming that the prosecution was immoral and that Colonel West had done the *right* thing.[34]

Officership and Inspiration

Officership is about inspiring subordinates to do extraordinary things, but good officers do more than simply inspire. They know what acts to inspire and when to do so. They also set goals and convince people to spend time, effort, and other resources to achieve them. Doing these things well involves making practical as well as ethical decisions. Sometimes, situations will create a conflict between moral and professional imperatives that is not easy to resolve. When such a conflict arises, officers must attempt to balance the demands of morality with the demands of the profession, and to do so they must consider the consequences of their decisions and the rules and principles that govern the profession. These ethical considerations by themselves, however, do not provide an approach sufficient to answer all of the moral questions officers may confront, particularly in combat.

U.S. Army doctrine defines the traits of good officership within the framework of *Be, Know, Do*, which incorporates ethical as well as practical aspects.[35] We can therefore discuss an ethics of Being, an ethics of Knowing, and an ethics of Doing. This breakout explains in part why approaches based on consequences and rules are inadequate: they focus on the ethics of knowing and doing but exclude the ethics of being. Yet, being a certain kind of person is just as important to moral leadership as knowing consequences, rules, and principles and applying them in ways that serve the profession and the nation. This is because, as we observed from a somewhat different perspective, consequences and rules can come into conflict. When this happens ethical algorithms based on measuring consequences and applying rules will be insufficient to resolve the tension in a morally appropriate way. In such instances, it will be an officer's character that helps resolve conflicts in a consistent, coherent manner.[36]

Officership and Character

Colonel West had a choice, but one that pitted two important obligations against each other. He could permit the beating and the threats to coerce the detainee into cooperating, or he could decide not to and leave his men at risk. Unfortunately, this decision is not clear-cut. If he chooses the first option, he violates the law of war. If he chooses the second option, he will have directly contributed to his men's deaths. Deciding what to do is complicated; there is no clear way to choose one over the other. Preserving the lives of his men and accomplishing his mission are moral imperatives of considerable force. Yet, so is keeping the promise he made to uphold the Constitution, which includes abiding by the provisions of treaties to which the United States is party.[37] Resolving this problem will not depend on clever rationalizations or skillful manipulation of rules. Successfully resolving situations like this depend on the kind of person one is. To demonstrate this, it is necessary to examine why appealing to consequences—like accomplishing missions and preserving lives—and simple conformity to rules are inadequate to account for all moral considerations.

Military Necessity and the Laws of War

The ethics of consequences seeks to determine whether a particular action maximizes some nonmoral good, such as happiness or pleasure, or minimizes some nonmoral harm, such as misery or pain. While choosing any particular goal is not always in itself a moral choice, soldiers still have a prima facie moral obligation to accomplish their assigned missions. Therefore, when making moral decisions, officers weigh consequences in terms of whether a course of action maximizes their chance of victory or lessens it. Decisions thus arrived at are often justified or explained under the rubric "military necessity." Since maximizing victory includes minimizing the risks to soldiers so that they can continue the war effort, any course of action that directly contributes to mission accomplishment or that reduces risk to soldiers will be morally justifiable under an ethics of consequences. In fact, if military necessity were the only consideration, then such acts would be morally obligatory, regardless of what action is taken. If this were true, then officers would be free to disregard the laws of war as long as such was necessary to preserve the lives of their personnel. In fact, one would never have to consider the laws of war in the first place. In this context, Colonel West's actions were not just permitted, but *required*.

However, officers are obligated to take the laws of war seriously. By accepting a commission an officer promises to abide by treaties to which the United States is a party. Thus, regardless of how he feels personally about the law and morality of war, as a commissioned officer he has a moral obligation to uphold them.[38] In the case under consideration, military necessity comes into direct conflict with the moral obligation to abide by the law. Always deciding in favor of military necessity would thus undermine an officer's ability to make promises; however, promise-keeping is an essential part of maintaining one's integrity. Thus a policy that undermines an officer's integrity, when pursued as a general policy, corrupts the profession.

But to claim that even in the case of such conflict a good officer always abides by the rules would be too easy. Sometimes the answer to the question, "Should following the rules take precedence over the lives of soldiers?" will be "yes," but not always.[39] Making the correct distinction is one of the primary tasks of the professional Army officer, and the distinguishing mark of a leader of character.

Character, Leadership, and Ethical Decision-Making

There is a gap between the kinds of ethical questions officers confront and the kinds of answers that consequence- and rule-based approaches can give. When considerations of military necessity are insufficient and rules also fail, what officers do depends ultimately on the type of person they are. Thus, it is important to develop officers of character who understand what it means to be good officers—not just what it means to follow rules, perform duties, or reason well, although these are important to being ethical. If officers are to have the moral resources necessary to make ethically sound decisions, they need an approach to ethics that articulates what good character is, how it can be developed, and how it influences moral decision-making. Moral philosophers usually refer to the ethics of character as virtue ethics.

This approach to ethics seeks to determine systematically what kind of traits good people (or in this case, good officers) should possess, what it means to possess these traits, and how people can come to possess these traits. In this context, virtues are the traits of good character. An officer of character is more concerned with being the kind of person who does the right thing, at the right time, in the right way, and is not as concerned with the act itself. The ethics of character avoids most dilemmas because the focus is no longer on deciding between two unfortunate outcomes or two conflicting rules but on being a certain kind of person. Virtuous officers do not assign values to outcomes or preferences to duties. Virtuous officers have habituated dispositions that make them the kind of people who do the right thing, even in the complicated and dynamic environment of modern military operations.

The Virtues of Good Officership

In virtue ethics, the virtues are determined by understanding the purpose a person serves.[40] In nonmoral terms, knowing the purpose of a thing reveals whether it is functioning well or poorly. For example, if the purpose of pack animals such as mules is to bear burdens, their actions reveal which mules do better and which do worse. Further, we can tell what qualities a mule must possess, such as strength, surefootedness, and endurance, to do its task well. To the degree a mule possesses these traits, the better the mule is. A human being must also have certain characteristics to be a good human being. Aristotle claimed that the virtues of the excellent person include courage, temperance, liberality, proper pride, good temper, ready wit, modesty, and justice.[41] Plato listed prudence, courage, temperance, and justice.[42] Thomas Aquinas added faith, hope, and love.[43] Because what it means to function well for a human is much more complex than what it means to function well for a mule, defining "functioning well" is difficult. Part of the problem is that a complex combination of biology, environment, culture, and tradition determines what it means to function well. What this complex combination is and how its components relate to each other are not always well understood and are therefore subjects of much debate.

The function, environment, culture, and traditions of the military are well understood, however. The military's function is to defend the nation. This function is itself a moral imperative of the state. Officers have the additional functions of setting goals and inspiring others to achieve them to serve this purpose. Not only does this allow us to determine the virtues of the good military leader, it provides a way morally to justify them as well. This gives a clear framework for discussing the character of morally good leadership. Given these officerly functions, one can determine some of the virtues that are associated with officership, including selflessness, courage, prudence, caring, and integrity. If officers must establish goals and methods for defending the nation, they will need to be prudent and selfless.[44] The former is necessary to discern the proper ends, and the latter is necessary to mediate when proper ends conflict with self-interest. Officers require courage, caring, and integrity to inspire and direct others to achieve the goals they establish.

Having decided what the virtues of good officership are, we need to discuss what it means to act virtuously. Virtues are excellences of character, that is, they are fixed dispositions toward certain behaviors that result in good acts.[45] Aristotle viewed each virtue as the "golden mean," a mean between the two extremes (vices) of excess and deficiency in regard to certain human capacities. For example, with regard to feelings of fear, courage is the mean. A person can feel too much fear and be cowardly or feel too little fear and be foolhardy. A person who runs away in the face of danger, when the proper thing to do would be to stand his ground, is a coward. But the person who stands his ground because he does not comprehend the danger, is also not courageous.

The moderation criterion works the same way for other virtues as well. With regard to selflessness, one extreme is careerism, where officers are too concerned with personal advancement and fail to place the needs of the organization above their own. But officers can also be too selfless. Officers who never take care of personal interests might impede their ability to lead. For example, officers who deny themselves sleep, so as to demonstrate their commitment to the mission, quickly become incapable of making good decisions.[46] Neither is the mean an average. For instance, ten pounds of food might be too much, and two pounds might be too little, but this does not mean that the average of six pounds is the right amount. Instead, the mean is relative to our nature.

It is worth emphasizing that for Aristotle the mean is sought only because it is beneficial; the mean between two extremes enables the individual to live well. To discern what the mean is an officer must develop the ability to reason well, itself a virtue that Aristotle called prudence or practical wisdom. This virtue is necessary to resolve the tension between the feelings that emerge from natural appetites, concerns of self-interest, and the requirements of virtue.[47] The conflict between reason, feeling, and self-interest lies at the heart of the excellences or virtues. What drags us to extremes detrimental to our long-term happiness are passions and feelings, such as excessive (or defective) fear or excessive love of pleasure. Reason is required to control behavior, passions, and feelings. Excellences are applications of reason to behavior and emotion. These excellences can emerge with proper officer development.

Virtue ethics allows us to take into account consequences, rules, duties, and principles in a way that resolves the tension inherent among them. As in consequence-based ethical theories, we must be concerned with consequences of an action to determine its normative value. In virtue ethics, one must be sensitive to the conditions that frame moral choices. Acting on the principle of always telling the truth is good, but ignoring how that truth might affect others risks doing moral harm. A caring husband, for example, should bring to his overweight wife's attention matters negatively affecting her health. A vicious (or at least stupid) husband will simply announce that she is fat.

Determining how to embody a particular virtue requires an element of compassion. Failure to recognize this can result in disastrous consequences. Rule- or duty-based ethics evaluates actions in terms of how these actions correspond to certain rules or principles. In duty-based ethics, one has an obligation to perform certain duties conscientiously. In virtue ethics one must consciously and conscientiously cultivate a virtue—that is, one must habitually perform acts that reflect the relevant virtue if one is to say he or she possesses that virtue.[48] Psychologically, the habituation of virtue can take on the qualities of a duty. To develop integrity, for example, one must always tell the truth and always avoid lying.

Developing the Virtues of Good Character

A virtue ethics approach to officership can help resolve certain dilemmas that consequence- and rule-based theories cannot. Instead of focusing on doing good things, the virtuous person focuses on being good, and the doing good naturally follows. How one becomes good is by acquiring certain virtues or character traits that lead to doing virtuous things. However, rule-based approaches can play a key role. Virtues do not develop overnight. One cannot wake up one day and decide to be courageous, for example, and immediately be so. Being virtuous means knowing the right time, place, circumstance, and manner in which to be courageous. One acquires these traits by habituation.

According to Aristotle, whose writings greatly influenced modern virtue theory, one becomes virtuous only by performing virtuous actions until doing so becomes habitual. In other words, practice and experience are necessary. Aristotle makes this point by contrasting virtues with natural capacities:

> Of all the things that come to us by nature we first acquire the potentiality and later exhibit the activity (this is plain in the case of senses; for it was not by often seeing or often hearing that we got these senses, but on the contrary we had them before we used them, and did not come to have them by using them); but the virtues we get by

first exercising them, as also happens in the case of the arts as well. For the things we have to learn before we can do them, we learn by doing them, e.g., men become builders by building and lyre players by playing the lyre; so too we become just by doing just acts, temperate by doing temperate acts, brave by doing brave acts.[49]

Thus, just as one becomes a good musician only by practicing an instrument, one becomes a good officer only by practicing the profession. But how does one who has no experience in virtue development create such necessary experiences? When we try to describe a virtue, we tend to list the acts we must perform to embody the virtue. Listing these acts is just like listing rules and principles. This line of reasoning is, in fact, one of the major critiques of the virtue approach. When we consciously set out to put rules and principles into practice, we end up with what appears to be essentially a rule-based system. When this happens, we lose sight of the role of character.

To get a deeper understanding of what character is as well as how its virtues are best cultivated, consider the following example. To make his subordinates caring officers, a brigade commander established the rule that an officer's place is at the front of the mess line, but the officer is to eat last. When the commander found one lieutenant at the rear of the line, he immediately corrected the situation.[50] When the lieutenant subsequently stood at the head of a line, he was simply following the brigade commander's rule. If rules were the sole determinants of right and wrong, then the lieutenant was doing what was right.

This is good as far as it goes, but merely standing in a different spot will not make him a better lieutenant. If he knows why he is to stand at the front of the line, he will likely become a more caring person, for he should begin to notice anything that is not being done correctly. For example, the cooks might be giving out unusually small portions; the food might not be cooked as well as it should be; or the food might lack variety from day today. There is nothing in the rule that requires the lieutenant to do anything about these deficiencies. His only requirements are to stand at the head of the line and make sure everyone gets fed. But since he knows that the rule is designed to enable him to become a more caring person toward his soldiers, he is motivated to act to correct what he found wrong.

The foregoing might seem like a simple, inconsequential example, but the same dynamic works in many situations. At first, the junior officer is following rules; later, after doing it long enough within a properly critical and supportive environment, his attitude, and ultimately his beliefs, change to the degree that he is actually disposed to be caring. Once this happens, he is no longer simply following rules. He has actually developed the capacity to make them. What motivates him to adopt this attitude is an understanding that it is not enough to do good, it is just as important to be good. In fact, doing good flows from being good. Aristotle also points out that one cannot develop virtue by accident or by doing the right thing for the wrong reasons. The lieutenant in the example above might be motivated by self-interest because he knows the brigade commander will give him high marks for being so conscientious. This is why intent is important. One simply cannot become caring or wise or honest unless one is trying to become so. For an action to be truly virtuous, a person must be in the right state of mind, and have the right attitudes about his or her own development. He must know that his action is virtuous, and he must decide on it for the sake of his soldiers. He must act in a caring manner because being a caring leader is good, not because it will benefit his career.

The Role of Mentorship

If rules initially have a role in habituating virtue, it is critical for the person making the rules to possess that virtue. In this way, the rules are right-minded and constructive, becoming a pathway one can take to becoming a good officer. Aristotle likened the acquiring of virtues to playing an instrument, which requires a teacher and habitual practice. Unless one is a musical prodigy, he does not pick up a guitar and, by fooling around with it, play it well. He might, after a fashion, be able to make pleasant sounds with it, but without someone to provide instruction and example, developing true proficiency will be long and arduous, fraught with mistakes, and certainly inefficient. One might even pick up a book and memorize the principles of good guitar-playing. Those who have tried that method know that doing so might make them better to an extent, but to achieve true excellence it takes a good teacher.

For junior officers to become good officers, they must acquire the necessary virtues. Junior officers can learn from seeing how virtues are embodied by those who are effective at moral officership. Only then can they incorporate virtues into their own characters. Exercising a virtue involves a delicate balancing between general rules and an awareness of particulars. Awareness of the particular carries more weight, in the sense that a good rule is a summary of wise particular choices, not an exclusive choice itself. The rules of ethics, like rules of medicine, should be held open to modification in the light of new circumstances. The good officer must cultivate the ability to perceive, then correctly and accurately describe his situation and include in this perceptual grasp even those features of the situation that are not covered under the existing rule. The virtues provide a framework around which officers must engage in this process.

Lieutenant Colonel West: Resolving the Conflict

In resolving conflicts like that confronting Colonel West, we must understand that one cannot exercise one virtue, such as caring, by failing to exercise another virtue, such as integrity. In any particular situation, virtuous people act in such a way that they remain true to all of the relevant virtues. We could decide that it is better for West to save his men at the expense of fulfilling his duty to obey lawful orders, but we must then understand that he cannot be caring at the expense of his integrity. Somehow he must maintain or restore it. So to be fully virtuous, he must publicly take responsibility for his actions and the bad consequences those actions might have. To prevent or mitigate the bad consequences, he might report himself to his superiors or submit his resignation. This would send the message to all concerned that what he did might have been necessary, but it was not good. As discussed earlier, if he were obligated to consider only military necessity, he would rationally be able to conclude that beating and threatening the detainee was a morally obligated act (if he concluded that it maximized military necessity by limiting the risk to his men). Virtue ethics allows him to conclude that this might be the morally best course of action, but not that the results of the action are morally good. In fact, many of these considerations seemed very much to have influenced West's thinking, as he immediately turned himself in to his chain of command following the incident. In a subsequent interview on CNN he said:

> But I think that as a commander, I had, as I felt, a moral obligation to the—and responsibility to the safety and welfare of my soldiers. . . . I can't, you know, recommend that decision to be made. That's something that each and every person has to do within their own selves and within their own heart. . . . Well, I think that there's honor and integrity in things that you do and also I understand that there are two parts to the Army. The Army as an institution has to have good order and discipline, and that needed to be evaluated, as to whether or not I stepped outside the lines and allowed my commanding officers to make a decision as far as what should be done with me.[51]

In a separate interview on CNN, West's attorney, Lt. Col. (ret.) Neal Puckett, summed the issue up this way:

> A commander has many responsibilities. One of those is to follow rules and enforce rules himself. Another is to protect his men and women in combat. Those came into sharp contrast in this particular situation. Lieutenant Colonel West chose to err on the side of protecting his men, and assumed the risk that it would cause his career and has always been willing to stand up, accept responsibility for that, and whatever punishment the Army felt necessary.[52]

Virtue ethics is inherently anti-careerist. Military professionals must accept that they may be placed in difficult circumstances where lives will be at stake and the morally appropriate way to resolve conflicts in moral obligations may not be obvious. This risk should not preclude action, but one must be prepared to accept the moral, as well as legal, consequences. Failure to recognize such potential liability elevates one's career over the demands of the profession and the nation it serves.

Could West have been virtuous while leaving his men at risk? Only if there were a way to express the virtue of caring if he did so. So even if he had chosen to conform to the law, it likely would have been the honorable course to resign his position if it was the only way he could restore his integrity after having failed in the commitments he made to his men. What is left to ask is what kinds of things a good leader considers and how he weighs them. The things an officer should consider and how he should consider them depend on the virtues relevant to the situation. If he were simply following the rules, he would have to conclude that leaving his men at risk was the right thing to do, regardless of powerfully extenuating circumstances.

Offering a definitive virtuous solution is difficult because there really is none, at least not in the same sense that consequence- or rule-based systems offer. Such approaches attempt to determine what the right action is in a particular situation. They are intended to be formulas such that, when all of the relevant variables are put into the equation, the right answer pops out. They are not always up to the challenge, however. While virtue ethics does not offer a formula, it offers a way of developing officers and subordinates in a manner providing the best possibility for leaders to make ethical decisions in the moral crucible of the modern battlefield.

Conclusion: The Potential to Do Good or Evil

In the complex, dynamic, and dangerous environment of the modern battlefield there is great potential to do harm, even evil, and little time to apply rules or to calculate consequences to avoid doing evil. Even if there were time, such one-dimensional approaches to ethics are not always successful. Rules, duties, and principles can conflict. Sincere, well-intentioned compliance with them can sometimes lead to the most disastrous outcomes. But acting in such situations does not necessarily make someone a bad person. Actions might be evidence of the presence or the absence of virtue, but they are not in themselves virtuous. Acting virtuously might not spare one from the moral costs of leadership, but doing so provides a framework in which one can maintain one's integrity as well as the integrity of the profession.

This is why developing the virtues of good officership is so important for the military officer. In situations where any action can lead to a morally impermissible or harmful outcome, it will be officers of character who will be best able to resolve the conflict and maintain their own integrity and the integrity of the profession as well. Character is an essential part of an ethical framework for officership. When officers face the kind of situation that Lt. Col. Allen West faced, it is the character they have formed that will guide their actions. This does not mean that virtuous officers never consider consequences or rules to determine where their duties lie. The point is that the virtuous officer has developed the disposition to know how and when to do so in the best way possible.

The Army Officer as Servant and Professional

Suzanne Nielsen

Introduction

As men and women become officers in the U.S. Army, they take an oath to "support and defend the Constitution of the United States." However, despite this shared beginning, officers' views tend to diverge as to what it means to serve as commissioned leaders. As two researchers recently discovered when examining officers' views of themselves, Army officers do not have a shared conception of the nature of their special expertise or their role.[53] This essay will discuss two dimensions of officership: the officer as servant of the nation and the officer as professional. The underlying premise is that it would be useful for Army officers to share a common perspective and to think in similar terms about what it means to be a servant and a professional. In other words, there is institutional value in a shared professional identity.

The Officer as Servant of the Nation

In January 2000 while serving on the faculty at West Point, I had the opportunity to teach a military science class called "Perspectives on Officership" to second-year (sophomore) cadets. The course was organized around four perspectives on officership: the officer as warrior, the officer as leader of character, the officer as servant of the nation, and the officer as a member of a time-honored profession. During the block on the officer as servant, several cadets reacted quite negatively. To some of them, the prospect of becoming a "servant" upon graduation was uninspiring and even demeaning.

> Today's soldiers accept their responsibilities and perform every task and mission asked of them, just as veterans before them did.
>
> —GEN. PETER J. SCHOOMAKER[54]

So what does it mean for an Army officer to be a servant of the nation? Fundamentally, this perspective on officership is tied to the manner of appointment of officers and the oath officers take upon commissioning. Commissioned officers are appointed by the President with the advice and the consent of the Senate. Therefore, the authority of officers is derived from the executive authority of the President of the United States. However, as with many powers of the national government, the President and Congress share authority over military affairs. While the U.S. Constitution says that the President shall serve as the Commander in Chief, it also gives Congress the authority to declare war, to raise and support armies, to regulate the armed forces, and "to provide for organizing, arming, and disciplining the militia."[55] Being a servant of the nation as an Army officer thus means serving the American people as their interests and values are interpreted by the President and elected officials in Congress.

This latter point is important to remember. Army officers do serve the nation, but not based on directly expressed popular preferences. In America's representative system of government, it is the elected leaders and not Army officers who are responsible for deciding how the Army can best serve the American people. If the political leaders are wrong or make mistakes, they are accountable only to the other branches of government and ultimately to the citizenry. Therefore, being a servant of the nation requires that Army officers respect the democratic institutions of American society and have trust in the democratic process. One of the important contributors to this democratic process is a free and vital press. Although relations between the military and the news media in the United States have not always been harmonious, Army officers should appreciate that the press plays a vital role in preserving the open, democratic political process that officers swear to protect.

What, then, does being a servant of society not mean for an Army officer? As implied above, it does not mean that Army officers are responsible for interpreting the will of the American people or serving as policy entrepreneurs. Important policy choices, both foreign and domestic, are only partially determined by considerations of workability and almost always involve trade-offs in values. Take the example of health care policy. One relevant question might be whether a particular scheme will truly provide more and better care to those who need it. In other words, will it work? Technical experts should participate in answering this question. A second issue is whether it is of greater value to devote the resources to that plan than to some other worthwhile purpose. In other words, does the plan truly respond to the American people's interests, values, and priorities? This is a question for the nation's elected leaders.

Similar issues surround U.S. military interventions abroad. Important questions here relate to whether a particular use of military power will achieve its objectives, at what level of risk, and at what cost. In sorting through these issues, Army officers have a role to play. However, an equally important question is whether a particular use of military power reflects the American people's interests and values. Only the President and elected leaders in Congress have the responsibility and legitimate authority necessary to make this choice. As military theorist Carl von Clausewitz once said, political aims "are the business of the government alone."[56] It is the responsibility of military officers to preserve their status as apolitical and loyal junior partners of the nation's political leadership. Military leaders who fulfill their duties in this manner are best situated to serve as constructive contributors to the difficult decisions political leaders have to make.

Historically, the Army has been seen as a servant of society, fulfilling the country's needs at different stages of its development (see Chapter 4 of the present anthology). Carl Builder in the widely acclaimed book, *The Masks of War* (1989), examines the organizational personalities of the U.S. military services and their possible impact on U.S. defense policy-making. He describes the Army's view of its role as follows:

> Of all the military services, the Army is the most loyal servant and progeny of this nation, of its institutions and people. If the Army worships at an altar, the object worshiped is the country, and the means of worship are service.

He points out that when the Army writes about itself, the themes are "the depth of roots in the citizenry, its long and intimate history of service to the nation, and its utter devotion to country." In Builder's assessment, these themes represent deeply-held institutional beliefs about "who the Army thinks it is and what it believes in."[57]

However, Builder also saw a threat to this longstanding self-identity. In his view, "something happened to the Army in its passage through World War II" that diluted its self-concept of pliant, generalized servant of the nation. By 1989, some officers had come to see the Army in a narrower role as "defender of Europe," entailing a focus on high-intensity conflict. Others in the Army sought to return to the Army's traditional role as the nation's handyman.[58] Although Builder's depiction of an Army with a split personality was written during the last years of the Cold War, his insights resonate within the Army profession today. Assuredly there are still some officers who focus on high-intensity combat as the most appropriate mission for our contemporary Army.

This possibility of a restricted view as to the appropriate roles for the Army leads to some of the challenges officers face as servants of the nation. First, what if the Army's senior leaders view the missions the Army is given as inappropriate? If World War II showed some in the Army the kind of war it would prefer to fight, the Vietnam War showed military leaders the kind of war they wanted to avoid.[59] A speech given by Defense Secretary Caspar Weinberger in November 1984 that set out six criteria for the use of force became a touchstone in this debate.[60] Of those six, Weinberger's requirements that vital interests be at stake, that forces be committed wholeheartedly with the intent to win, that objectives be clear, and that public support be present before the commitment of forces were particularly attractive to many in uniform. The so-called Weinberger doctrine suggested to military leaders that force would be used only under conditions more favorable than those present during the Vietnam conflict.

In the 1990s, Chairman of the Joint Chiefs Gen. Colin Powell supplemented the Weinberger doctrine with his own views on the use of force. Although General Powell disavowed a rigid checklist, at least one observer argues that his view on the advantages of "overwhelming force" constituted a doctrine of its own, with an emphasis on "quick, decisive actions and prompt exits."[61]

A danger associated with simplistically embracing the Weinberger and Powell doctrines is that their premises potentially undermine the status of officers as servants of the nation. In effect, for military leaders to promulgate the doctrines amounts to asserting the desirability of establishing certain preconditions before arms are resorted to. Undoubtedly, senior military officers need to give political leaders assessments of feasibility, costs, and risks associated with planned military operations. Strategic leaders have an obligation to share with political leaders the benefit of their special expertise and experience. However, the ultimate decision to employ the armed services—regardless of interests, resources, missions, objectives, public support, whether first or last resort, etc.—belongs to political rather than military leaders. This perspective, of course, is perfectly in accordance with the Army's current capstone doctrinal manual, which highlights the Army's "Proud History of Full Spectrum Operations."[62]

A second potential challenge to the Army officer's identity as a servant of the nation arises when policy decisions act against the interests of the Army as an institution. Examples of such choices include budget reductions, the canceling of weapons programs, and changes in force structure. How should Army officers respond? As with the use of force, officers would be negligent if they did not provide their civilian leaders with their assessments of the costs and risks associated with such policy choices. In addition, officers at the most senior level face the challenge of remaining loyal to their executive branch superiors while also responding honestly to Congress' constitutionally-mandated right to exercise oversight. However, responses to Congress should be confined strictly to requested testimony and answering questions. Officers slip out of the role of servants of society and into some other capacity when they attempt to shape public opinion.[63]

Gen. Creighton W. Abrams, the Chief of Staff of the Army from 1972 to 1974, I would suggest, was one officer who set a remarkable example as a "servant of the nation." He was a key architect of major reforms in the Army that aided the institution's recovery from Vietnam, and ultimately helped to create the Army that was so successful in the Persian Gulf War. Those who knew him recall that loyalty, to both military and civilian superiors, was one of his essential attributes. In addition, he was known for avoiding the limelight. Perhaps the highest praise came from Lt.

Gen. Ralph Foster, who served as Abrams' Secretary of the General Staff. Foster said of Abrams, "He had a deep loyalty and I think you'll find if you talk to people that he didn't put the Army first. He put the Army first in his life because it was the thing that he had to do, but what he put first was the country."[64] It would be hard to find a better statement of what being a servant of the nation requires.

The Officer as a Professional

In addition to being a servant of the nation, an Army officer is also a member of a vocational profession. But what does this mean? Certainly the word "professional" has different meanings in different contexts.

> The duty of every leader is to be competent in the profession of arms.
>
> —FIELD MANUAL 3-0, *OPERATIONS*

When discussing athletes, for example, the term "professional" is contrasted with the term "amateur," meaning little more than that the athlete is paid for his or her performances. As a second use of the term, in the Army we may describe someone's behavior as "unprofessional." When we use the word (or rather, as here, its negative) in this normative sense, we are describing behavior that falls below generally accepted standards. In still another use, the term "professional" is associated with variations in social status. For example, one can contrast a profession with a *mere* craft or occupation. Given this connotation, claims made to professional status may be nothing more than claims to greater prestige.

None of these uses of the term really illuminate what it means to an individual Army officer to be a member of a profession. Fortunately, a recent project on the future of the Army profession has suggested a useful way of thinking about the issue.[65] The authors in the project took as a starting point a landmark work by sociologist Andrew Abbott titled *The System of Professions* (1988). Abbott defines professions as "exclusive occupational groups" that apply "somewhat abstract knowledge to particular cases." The tasks that professions perform are "human problems amenable to expert service."[66] Of course, the relatively exclusive group we are discussing in this chapter is the Army's officer corps; the human problem Army officers address with expert knowledge and expertise is the military dimension of the nation's security—particularly as it pertains to land-based warfare. Abbott's definition is useful because it helps to clarify just what it is about being an Army officer that makes one a professional while leaving behind much of the colloquial baggage that can be associated with that term.

Abbott's definition naturally leads to an exploration of the Army officer's special expertise. In his seminal study, *The Soldier and the State* (1957), Samuel Huntington adopts Harold Lasswell's phrase "the management of violence" to describe that special expertise, arguing that it sums up what professional military officers chiefly do. Huntington elaborates as follows: "The direction, operation, and control of a human organization whose primary function is the application of violence is the peculiar skill of the officer."[67] This is a useful starting point, but it could use further refinement.

In a recent effort to clarify the nature of the expert knowledge of the Army professional, Don Snider and Gayle Watkins argue that it resides in four different fields:

the military-technical, the moral-ethical, the political-cultural, and that of human development. At the individual level, military-technical knowledge encompasses what an individual officer needs to know to function in the service to effectively accomplish the military tasks assigned his or her unit; moral-ethical knowledge relates to the profession's ethic, which enables it to accomplish those military tasks "rightly" according to American values and the laws of land warfare; political-cultural knowledge relates to the larger environment in which Army officers serve, both domestically and in foreign countries; and knowledge of human development—understanding, motivating, and teaching people—is critical to a profession that relies so heavily on transforming American citizens into soldiers and growing leaders from among them with the maturity and decision-making skills necessary to lead in combat.[68]

Despite the usefulness of this four-part construct, several questions remain unanswered. Here I will give just two examples. First, is there a unique professional expertise required of the Army's commissioned officers that is distinct from that required of the Army's noncommissioned officers and civilians? It is easier to say with confidence that the answer is "yes" than it is to draw all of the boundary lines.[69] Second, what are the implications for the content of Army officers' expertise that stem from their increased specialization under the current officer personnel management system? In other words, what is the core expertise that remains common to all Army officer specialties, or even to all officers of America's armed forces? These are difficult issues that I trust the Army officer corps will wrestle to the ground and clarify as we transition to a "campaign quality Army."[70]

Even after the content of the particular expertise of Army officers is fully articulated, it should be recognized that for Army officers to remain effective the borders as well as the internal content of this expertise will have to change over time. They will require continuous adaptation to the changing needs of the nation served. It is possible to gain additional perspective on this issue by looking at the work of others who have thought deeply about ground combat, particularly Carl von Clausewitz, the Prussian general and theorist who wrote the classic work *On War* (1832). Much of what he says about military expertise is still relevant today.

One issue concerning which Clausewitz's insights are enduring is the relationship between politics and the use of force. Clausewitz famously recognized that war is a subordinate phenomenon whose rationale is always provided by political ends. Part of the particular expertise of Army officers is having an understanding of this relationship and an ability to support the achievement of political aims with military means. The Army has recognized this principle in its capstone doctrinal manual, stressing to strategic leaders the relationship between political ends and military means.[71] Even on this issue, however, the changing nature of warfare makes it useful to reconsider the level at which this understanding is important. In today's stability operations where small-unit actions can have strategic impact, even officers operating at the small-unit level need to appreciate the primacy of political aims over military expediency.

Another aspect of Clausewitz's continued relevance relates to the skills officers bring to bear in combat. While Clausewitz holds that the logic of resort to war comes from politics, he also argues that war has its own unique grammar.[72] The military officer must understand the grammar of war, to include the nature of military forces, tactics, and strategy, with a focus on the central task of combat.[73] Clausewitz also recognizes the special nature of the conditions under which officers apply their knowledge. Clausewitz portrays war as an environment ruled by physical exertion, uncertainty, and fear, in which friction and a determined enemy work to thwart success. According to Clausewitz, an expert operating in this realm must have both theoretical knowledge and experience, and these attributes must be underpinned by strong character.[74] In this portion of Clausewitz's argument, he reaffirms the importance of military-technical knowledge and the need to be able to bring it to bear under the most challenging conditions.

While Clausewitz's insights provide useful perspective, for the present age his conception of military expertise is incomplete in a number of ways. With respect to the four-part professional knowledge construct described above, Clausewitz focused too exclusively on the military-technical component and not adequately on that of human development. He discusses the importance of effective leadership to success in war, but emphasizes the leader's individual knowledge and technical skills rather than his ability to effectively interact with and motivate others. On the military-technical side, one could plausibly argue that Clausewitz's conception of expert knowledge is too static. For example, today's Army officer must be prepared to go to war with the Army's sister services as part of a joint team. This is an aspect of needed expertise Clausewitz does not address. These points illustrate that the special expertise of the Army officer will be dynamic, and that the profession will have to adapt along with changes in technology, society, national security strategy, and the international environment. Officers need to draw on operational experiences, the professional education system, and self-directed efforts to enhance their expertise and keep themselves up to date. It is not surprising, then, that Army professionals accept the concept of, and the responsibility for, life-long learning.

An important challenge to today's Army's officers is not only to know the "approved" doctrinal solution, but to understand why that solution does or does not make sense in a particular case and therefore the conditions under which it might have to change. As Col. Huba Wass de Czege wrote in 1984, "*The fundamental key to controlling and integrating change effectively is to raise the level of the knowledge and practice of the science and art of war in our Army.*"[75] The challenge implied in this remark is a call to Army officers to act as professional custodians of a particular and dynamic body of expert knowledge, and to take part in knowledge development and adaptation as well as knowledge application.

The conceptualization of professional knowledge developed by Snider and Watkins also usefully highlights the importance of its moral-ethical component. The U.S. Army is and must be values-based. At the level of the institution, the statement of the Army's values constitutes an important part of the total professional ethic. Values also operate at an individual level—officers bring to their service their own sets of personal values. The Army's professional ethic is strongest when two conditions are present: first, when the organizational culture prevalent in the Army actually reflects the Army's professed values; and second, when the values of the individual members and the values of the institution are compatible. When these two conditions are not present, the professional ethic is weakened.[76] Because of the importance of the Army's professional military ethic to effectiveness, the Army's officer corps must work hard to ensure continual adaptation and renewal.

The moral-ethical component of the Army officer's professional knowledge is critical for at least three reasons. First, armies can be dangerous to the societies they are created to serve. The Army officer's expertise must be accompanied by values such that his or her skills in ground combat will be put to use only in the service of legitimate authority as defined by the U.S. Constitution. Second, and this has been more obvious at some points in the nation's history than others, Army officers perform their service to the country by participating with the other armed services in its defense. Facility in this regard requires dedication, because failure is not an option. It also requires selflessness, because service members will be called upon to put their own lives at risk. The determinants of behavior when it matters most are found in the character of Army officers, and the resulting trust that soldiers place in them. This leads to the final point. The Army officer's expertise must be deeply steeped in the professional ethic because the Army's leaders (both commissioned and noncommissioned) are responsible for the lives and welfare of their soldiers. In all of these areas, the role of the officer as a servant of the nation and the officer as professional merge. Army officers apply their expert knowledge only when called upon to do so by legitimate authorities, in protection of the country's interests and values, and with a heavy sense of responsibility for the American sons and daughters under their command.

Because of the violence inherent in the military function, the values which are necessary in a military context cannot be expected to mirror the values of the society from which U.S. Army stems. For example, one aspect of the greatness of American society is the room it provides for individual expression, achievement, and growth. In contrast, while the individual is still valued in a military context, there must be greater emphasis on the capabilities of the group and the subordination of self in order for the military unit to be effective. It is up to the Army's officers to articulate these differences and justify them as necessary. It is also the responsibility of the Army's officer corps to serve as the custodian of the Army's professional ethic, and to police its own ranks accordingly.

In sum, the Army officer is a professional able to apply a body of expert knowledge about land warfare to particular situations. The necessary knowledge is gained through both theoretical study and practical experience, and grows over time. In addition, the officer's profession is intrinsically values-based, creating the necessary bond of trust between the professional and the nation served. The professional uses his or her expert knowledge to protect the values and interests of the American people, as ascertained by their political representatives. And in so doing, the officer accepts the immeasurable responsibility for the welfare of the soldiers under his or her command.

The Two Roles Considered Together

Having discussed each of the two roles separately, we now ask whether they can ever be incompatible. I would argue that although there can be tension between them, they should not be incompatible. As an example of such apparent tension, notice what happens when the military officer provides advice on the use of force (as a professional) to the properly constituted civilian authority (as a servant) and that advice is ignored. Though this situation may pose a serious moral dilemma for the individual officer, it actually reveals how the roles of servant and professional reinforce one another rather than how they conflict. The Army officer is a professional servant within a certain democratic context—his status as a servant of society and defender of the Constitution requires that civilian authorities have the final word. Any confusion of this principle would fatally erode the trust that must exist between political decision-makers and senior uniformed leaders if strategically sound policy is ever to be made. Even worse, confusion about the meaning of civilian control would cast into doubt the accountability and responsibility that properly rests with the political leader who makes the final decisions.

Conclusion

In the first paragraph of this essay, I mentioned that the officer's service begins when that officer takes the oath of commissioning. With the oath comes an obligation to be a servant to the nation, and to become an expert member of a challenging profession. Along with the two other identities of a professional Army officer—the officer as warrior and the officer as leader of character—these roles define what it means to serve as a commissioned officer in the Army. An officer corps that embraces the challenges of each of these identities, carefully integrated along the way in each career, will be able effectively and confidently to lead the Army through the 21st century.

Notes

1. The essays comprising this chapter were originally published in *Military Review* in 2003. They have been significantly revised by the authors for this anthology.
2. Gayle L. Watkins and Randi C. Cohen, "In Their Own Words: Army Officers Discuss Their Profession," in *The Future of the Army Profession*, project directors Don M. Snider and Gayle Watkins, ed. Lloyd J. Matthews (Boston, MA: McGraw-Hill, 2002), 77-100. Hereinafter referred to as FAP I.
3. A two-year, privately-funded study of the Army profession, executed by many of America's finest scholars both civilian and military, was completed in April 2002,and reported in FAP I.
4. S. L. A. Marshall wrote this description of an officer's responsibilities in the original version of *The Armed Forces Officer* (Washington, DC: Office of the Secretary of Defense, 1950), 2.
5. For a contrary view that such traditional professions no longer exist in America, see Steven Brint, *In an Age of Experts* (Princeton, NJ: Princeton University Press, 1994), particularly chap. 2.
6. The competitive nature of modern professions is described in Andrew Abbott, *The System of Professions* (Chicago, IL: University of Chicago Press, 1988).
7. For more on the Army's competitors, see Deborah Avant, "Privatizing Military Training: A Challenge to U.S. Army Professionalism," in FAP I, 179-196; and "America's Secret Armies," *US News and World Report*, 4 November 2002, 38-43.

8. Leonard Wong, *Stifled Innovation: Developing Tomorrow's Leaders Today* (Carlisle Barracks, PA: US Army War College, Strategic Studies Institute, April 2002.

9. Extensive support for this statement is contained in: "Project Conclusions," chap. 25 of FAP I.

10. For a detailed discussion of professional practice, see Abbott, chap. 2.

11. James Toner, *The Burden of Military Ethics* (Lexington, KY: University of Kentucky Press, 1995), 22-24.

12. For a comparison between earlier theorists of military professions (e.g., Huntington) and interpreters of the newer school of competitive, "turf-war" professions, see James Burk, "Expertise, Jurisdiction, and Legitimacy in Military Professions," in FAP I, 19-38.

13. See "The Army Training and Leader Development Panel Officer Study: Report to the Army," OS-8" Report accessed on-line at http://www.virtualarmory.com/youcannet/ycn6/resources/osm/Army_Officer_Study.pdf on 14 October 2002.

14. In this form, these principles were first published in *USMA Strategic Vision, 2010* (West Point, NY: Office of the Superintendent, 1999), 8. Some may wonder why I suggest a set of principles for commissioned officers to live by when the Army already has a set of Seven Values. The answer is straightforward: they are different constructs created for different developmental purposes for professional cohorts with different responsibilities. Of course Army officers must "value" what the institution values as, ideally, must all soldiers. But due to the moral responsibilities of their commission, their daily "walk" must in addition reflect principles not now addressed in the current version of what the Army values, e.g., the principles of subordination and the moral imperative of professional competence.

15. The difference between these two relationships—friend and comrade—has been often noted. For a recent discussion, see Chris Hedges, *War Is a Force That Gives Us Meaning* (New York, NY: Public Affairs Press, 2002): 115-117.

16. We would like to thank Col. (Ret.) Don Snider, Maj. Bill Innocenti, and 1st Lt. Mike Starz for their helpful comments on earlier versions of this chapter.

17. C.F. Smith, quoted in Bruce Catton, *This Hallowed Ground: The Story of the Union Side of the Civil War* (Garden City, NY: Doubleday and Co., 1956), 71-72.

18. Our division of the officer's responsibilities is borrowed from J.F.C. Fuller, *Generalship: Its Diseases and Their Cures*, (Harrisburg, PA: Stackpole Books, 1990), 61.

19. The Army Vision 2002, accessed on line at www.us.army.mil, 10 August 2002.

20. John Stepanek, "As a Senior NCO Sees It," *Army Digest*, August 1967, 5-6.

21. Carl von Clausewitz, *On War*, eds. Michael Howard and Peter Paret (New York: Alfred A. Knopf, 1993), 121.

22. Matthew Ridgway, quoted in U.S. Army FM 22-100, *Army Leadership* (Washington, DC: Department of the Army, 31 August 1999), 6-30.

23. William Francis Butler, *Charles George Gordon* (London: Macmillan, 1907), 85.

24. Fuller, 35.

25. Sun Tzu, *The Art of War*, trans. Samuel B. Griffin (London: Oxford University Press, 1963), 77.

26. George C. Marshall, quoted in Forrest C. Pogue, *George C. Marshall, Organizer of Victory, 1943-1945* (New York: Viking, 1973), 458-59.

27. Abraham Lincoln, "The Gettysburg Address," quoted in *Words That Make America Great*, ed. Jerome Agel (New York: Random House, 1997), 216.

28. Quoted in USMA, *Bugle Notes* (New York: USMA, 1984), 245.

29. Douglas MacArthur, Thayer Award Acceptance Speech, 12 May 1962, cited in *Bugle Notes*, 48.

30. John F. Kennedy, Inaugural Address, Washington, DC, 20 January 1961.

31. Gen. Sir John Winthrop Hackett, "Military Service in the Service of the State," *The Harmon Memorial Lectures in Military History*, U.S. Air Force Academy, CO, 1970, 1.

32. Dean Yates, "Emotional U.S. Officer Admits Wrongdoing in Iraq," *Reuters*, 19 November, 2003. http://news.myway.com/top/article/id/367598/top/11-19-2003::13:25/reuters.html.

33. Depending on the status one grants the detainee, an Iraqi policeman named Yahya Jhodri Hamoody, the Geneva Convention Relative to the Treatment of Prisoners of War, 12 August 1949 or the Geneva Convention Relative to the Protection of Civilian Persons in Time of War, 12 August 1949, would apply.

34. Numerous pundits and commentators argued that West should get rewarded for his actions. Notably, even some members of Congress joined the chorus as well. Tennessee Congressman John J. Duncan, Jr., claimed, "This is a man [referring to West] who has served honorably for almost 20 years in the United States Army. He should not be court-martialed. He should be given a medal for saving American lives." http://www.house.gov/duncan/2003/fs110703.htm.

35. FM 22-100, *Army Leadership* (Washington, DC: Department of the Army, 31 August 1999), 1-6.

36. For a discussion of the importance of consistency and coherence in ethical decision-making, see Donald M. Snider, John A. Nagl, and Charles A. Pfaff, *The Army Profession: Officership and Ethics in the 21st Century* (Carlisle, PA: U.S. Army War College, Strategic Studies Institute, 1999).

37. FM 27-10, *The Law of Land Warfare* (Washington, DC: Department of the Army, 1956, change 1, 15 July 1976), 6-7.

38. Military realists believe that in war there are no moral norms. Given the commitments officers make to honor the treaties to which the United States is a party as well as to the ideals the Constitution invokes, this view is incompatible with commissioned service.

39. For a more complete discussion of why rule- and duty-based ethics do not form complete ethical approaches, see Charles A. Pfaff, "Virtue Ethics and Leadership," unpublished presentation to the Joint Services Conference on Professional Ethics, available on-line at www.usafa.af.mil/jscope/JSCOPE98/PFAFF98.htm. See also Julius Moravcsik, "On What We Aim At and How We Live," in *The Greeks and the Good Life*, ed., David Depew (Fullerton, CA: California State University, 1980), 199.

40. Aristotle believed that a human being's function is to reason. Human beings who reason well will also live well because they are the best human beings they can be.

41. Aristotle, *Nicomachean Ethics*, trans., Terence Irwin (Cambridge, UK: Hackett Publishing Company), Book IV.

42. Plato, "Laws," trans., A.E. Taylor, 1.631d, 12.965d, and "Republic," trans., Paul Shorey, 4.427e, 433, in *Plato: The Collected Dialogues*, eds., Edith Hamilton and Huntington Cairns (Princeton, NJ: Princeton University Press, 1961).

43. Arthur F. Holmes, *Ethics: Approaching Moral Decisions* (Leicester, England: InterVarsity Press, n.d.), 119.

44. Distinguishing between what Plato and Aristotle referred to as practical wisdom (*phronesis*) and philosophical wisdom (*sophia*) is important. Practical wisdom expresses itself in the prudent conduct of one's public and private business. This virtue, also often called prudence, is distinguished from the theoretical wisdom of the philosopher. In the context of the discussion of leadership, Plato, in the "Laws," discussed what qualities a good legislator should possess and claims that a good legislator relies on prudence to determine what laws to enact. Since good laws achieve good ends, the good legislator must discern both the good end and the means to the good end. With regard to selflessness, my use of the term here is synonymous with the idea of public virtue. See Forrest McDonald, Novus Ordo Seclorum: *The Intellectual Origins of the Constitution* (Lawrence: University Press of Kansas, 1985), 71. See also James M. Stockdale, *Thoughts of a Philosophical Fighter Pilot* (Stanford, CA: Hoover Institution Press, 1995),75.

45. Louis Pojman, *Ethics: Discovering Right and Wrong* (Albany, NY: Wadsworth Publishing Co., 1999), 163.

46. Jonathan Shay, "Ethical Standing for Commander Self-Care: The Need for Sleep," *Parameters* 29 (Summer 1998): 93-105.

47. *Nicomachean Ethics*, Book II.

48. James Wallace, *Virtue and Vices* (Ithaca, NY: Cornell University Press, 1978), 90.

49. *Nicomachean Ethics*, Book II, 1103a27-1103b1.

50. Personal conversation with Brig. Gen. (Ret.) Ray Miller, Palo Alto, CA, 1 November 1996.

51. "American Morning: Military Career of Lt. Col. Allen West Coming to an End," Aired 23 December, 2003 - 08:15 ET; http://www.cnn.com/TRANSCRIPTS/0312/23/ltm.18.html.

52. "American Morning: Rules of War," Aired 11 December, 2003—08:35 ET; http://edition.cnn.com/TRANSCRIPTS/0312/11/ltm.05.html.

53. Gayle L. Watkins and Randi C. Cohen, "In Their Own Words: Army Officers Discuss Their Profession," in *The Future of the Army Profession*, Project Directors Don M. Snider and Gayle L. Watkins, ed. Lloyd J. Matthews (Boston, MA: McGraw-Hill, 2002), 94. Hereinafter referred to as FAP I.

54. Peter J. Schoomaker, "The Army: A Critical Member of the Joint Team Serving the Nation at War," *Army Magazine*, October 2003, 28.

55. *A More Perfect Union: The Creation of the United States Constitution* (Washington, DC: National Archives and Records Administration, 1986), 21.

56. Carl von Clausewitz, *On War*, trans. and eds. Michael Howard and Peter Paret (Princeton, NJ: Princeton University Press, 1976), 89.

57. Carl Builder, *The Masks of War* (Baltimore, MD: The Johns Hopkins University Press, 1989), 19-20.

58. Ibid., 38.

59. William J. Taylor, Jr., and David H. Petraeus, "The Legacy of Vietnam for the U.S. Military," in *Democracy, Strategy, and Vietnam*, eds. George K. Osborn et al. (Lexington, MA: Lexington Books, 1987), 250.

60. Caspar Weinberger, remarks to the National Press Club on 28 November 1984, *Defense 85* (January 1985): 10.

61. Charles A. Stevenson, "The Evolving Clinton Doctrine on the Use of Force," *Armed Forces and Society* 22, no. 4 (Summer 1996): 517.

62. Department of the Army, Field Manual 3-0, *Operations* (Washington, DC: Headquarters, Department of the Army, 14 June 2001), 1-3.

63. For a more extensive discussion of the norms that ought to guide the relationship between senior military officers and political leaders in a democracy see Marybeth Peterson Ulrich, "Infusing Civil-Military Relations Norms in the Officer Corps," in FAP I, 245-70.

64. Ralph Foster, Oral History Interview with Lt. Col. Tom Lightner and Lt. Col. Steve Glick, 1976, U.S. Army Military History Institute, Carlisle Barracks, PA, 40.

65. For findings from this project, see Gayle L. Watkins and Don M. Snider, "Project Conclusions," FAP I, 537-46.

66. Andrew Abbott, *The System of Professions: An Essay on the Division of Expert Labor* (Chicago, IL: University of Chicago Press, 1988), 8, 35.

67. Samuel P. Huntington, *The Soldier and the State* (Cambridge, MA: The Belknap Press of Harvard University Press, 1957), 11.

68. Don M. Snider and Gayle L. Watkins, "Introduction," in FAP I, 13-16.

69. Huntington, one of the few to address the subject directly, draws a sharp distinction between officers as professionals and enlisted soldiers as tradesmen. See *Soldier and State*, 17-18.

70. Les Brownlee and Peter J. Schoomaker, "Serving a Nation at War: A Campaign Quality Army with Joint and Expeditionary Capabilities," *Parameter* 34 (Summer 2004): 4-23.

71. FM 3-0 says that "commanders need to appreciate political ends and understand how the military conditions they achieve contribute to them." See p. 4-12.

72. Clausewitz, *On War*, 606.

73. Ibid., 95.

74. Ibid., 100, 141.

75. Huba Wass de Czege, "How to Change an Army," *Military Review* 64 (November 1984): 38. Emphasis is in original.

76. For a recent example of this difficulty, see *Army Training and Leader Development Panel Report (Officers) Final Report* (Ft. Leavenworth, KS: Combined Arms Center, 2001), OS-8. This report found that "Army culture is out of balance. There is friction between Army beliefs and practices." It also found that the Army's service ethic was not well-understood and not "adequately reinforced throughout an officer's career." Report accessed on-line at http://www. virtualarmory.com/youcannet/ycn6/ resources/osm/Army_Officer_Study.pdf on 14 October 2002.

7 Army Officership for the Joint Expeditionary Mindset

Richard Swain

T he broad topic of this anthology is transformation and the development of Army professionals. This chapter is intended to explore the implications of the Chief of Staff's concept of the "Joint Expeditionary Mindset" found in the 2004 Army Posture Statement and in the Chief's *The Way Ahead* pamphlet on development of 21st century Army officership.[1]

Thinking about the Chief's concept involves thinking about officership in the American profession of arms, then addressing Army officership in particular, and, finally, confronting the implications of the joint and expeditionary mindset for military officership in general and Army officership in particular. Let us first define some key terms and concepts to get our bearings: transformation, professionals, and the joint and expeditionary mindset.

Key Terms and Concepts

Transformation, according to Secretary of Defense Donald Rumsfeld, is "a process that shapes the changing nature of military competition through new combinations of concepts, capabilities, people, and organizations that exploit our nation's advantages and protect against our asymmetric vulnerabilities to sustain our strategic position, which helps underpin peace and stability in the world."[2] Its emphasis, in the first instance, is on exploiting information technologies as a means to enhance effectiveness and thus reduce the demands for uniformed manpower, particularly those deployed forward in the theater of war. Information technologies are expected to do this, on the one hand, by increasing effectiveness of friendly forces both in terms of enabling synchronization of action over wide distances and offering precision and lethality of attack; and, on the other hand, exposing the enemy to destruction whenever and wherever it is most productive for achievement of U.S. military objectives.

Professionals, as the term in used here, are workers pursuing a vocation involving the discretionary application of esoteric abstract knowledge to provide a valuable service to society. In exchange for effective application of this knowledge, practitioners are given wide autonomy in performance of their skills. Generally, the skill is one that requires long preparation and practice for mastery, and requires continuous updating and development of new knowledge and procedures as conditions change. The traditional professions have been medicine, law, and theology, vocations that have each varied widely in their own structure over time. As early as 1777, George Washington urged the maintenance of professional standards by his officers and men, and, by 1824, the military was listed as one of the learned professions in *Atlantic Magazine*, alongside divinity, medicine, and law.[3]

Since the 19th century, however, it has been characteristic of professionals that they organize themselves, or they are organized by governments, into identifiable self-conscious social groupings for the purpose of insuring acceptable standards of practice, ethical as well as technical; monopoly or shared control over work opportunities; training, socializing, and certifying new practitioners; and maintenance of professional discipline among all those permitted to practice—all in exchange for service on terms acceptable to society. Additionally, it was long apparent, even before the formation of modern professional bodies, that new knowledge is developed most effectively by the collective efforts of many practitioners and researchers, sharing their experiences and conclusions. Development of professional knowledge is fundamentally a collective activity.

Much of the wide sociological literature on professions is contradictory about the precise list of attributes that justifies the title of *profession* in this collective sense. This is hardly surprising in light of the wide variety in the content of professional activities involved in callings as diverse as medicine, law, and theology.[4] In the 1950s, Samuel Huntington and others applied the existing theory of professions to the armed forces, making the case that in most respects the services warranted the title.[5] It is arguable whether Huntington did any more than declare and justify the public status already accorded the military services in response to their development in the years following the Civil War and, more certainly, after the Spanish-American and World Wars.[6]

The traditional professions have undergone and continue to undergo dramatic structural changes, with the reflective sociology of professions following behind to record the changes. There is a tendency among theorists of professions to reduce the criteria for legitimating would-be professions to the most limited common notions. As early as the 1960s, Harold Wilensky, who drew the early period of macro-sociological speculation on the structural nature of professions to close in an essay titled "The Professionalization of Everyone?" argued for limitation of criteria to the twin notions of "autonomous expertise" and "the service ideal."[7] Andrew Abbott, whose seminal study *The System of Professions* (1988) provided the theoretical underpinnings for the first edition of the present anthology, described professions simply as "exclusive occupational groups applying somewhat abstract knowledge to particular cases."[8] The variation among theories according to their authors' focus and the radical changes in the structure of the foremost professions, particularly medicine, since the theory of professions became a salient sociological preoccupation a century ago, should warn of the danger of over adherence to what is largely a descriptive rather than normative theory of forms. What remains normative in the theory of professions is the requirement for effective and reliable performance; all other characteristics are judged according to their contribution or impediment to these outcomes. All in all, Huntington's notions of *expertise, responsibility*, and *corporateness* remain descriptive of collective professional practice within the one-sided contractual relationship between American military professionals and the people they serve.[9]

The term j*oint and expeditionary mindset* means simply a fixed philosophical resolve that the individual armed services' contributions to national defense will occur in an interservice context based on overseas deployment of forces with relatively circumscribed missions. This definition reflects two governing assumptions, one organizational and the other geographical. First, all military operations in the foreseeable future will involve members, units, and capabilities of multiple military departments committed together in a common enterprise under command of a uniformed national commander whose branch of service is essentially immaterial and not necessarily representative of the dominant service engaged. This concept implies that traditional service claims of sole jurisdiction over domains of action must be reexamined and perhaps revised. Second, most foreseeable military conflicts will involve strategic or operational deployment on short notice from the continental United States or bases overseas at strategic distance from the theater of operations, with the expectation that forces will fight a highly dispersed, three-dimensional battle on entry, under conditions of austere support.

Officership in the American Profession of Arms

American military officers are, first of all, creatures of law, called into being to perform a particular executive function of the government under the Constitution. How they carry out their task depends, in the first place, on how they perceive themselves *as officers. Officership* as used in this chapter is the practice of being a *commissioned* military leader. It is both what officers do and what they are.

American military forces are created by law under authority of the Constitution. The implementing legislation under that compact provides, in all services, for different categories of institutionally empowered leaders, among them, commissioned officers. In accordance with the provisions of Article VI of the Constitution, all commissioned military leaders of all services subscribe to the same oath as other officials of government, as prescribed in Title 5 U.S. Code. They pledge "to support and defend the Constitution . . . to bear true faith and allegiance to the same" and "to well and faithfully discharge the duties of the office" they are entering. In return, the President of the United States, acting as Commander-in-Chief and in a form essentially unchanged since the American Revolution, assigns them a commission addressed not to them particularly but "To all who shall see these presents. . . ." The President, after declaring "special trust and confidence in the patriotism, valor, fidelity, and abilities" of the subject, appoints him or her a commissioned officer in one of the armed forces of the United States.

The officer is charged to "carefully and diligently discharge the duties of the office to which appointed by doing and performing all manner of things thereunto belonging." Subordinate officers and "personnel of lesser rank" are bound to render the officer obedience. In turn, the officer is enjoined to obey orders of the President and other superior officers "acting in accordance with the laws of the United States of America . . . the commission to endure at the pleasure of the President under the provisions of Public Law."

Any understanding of officership must begin with these solemn obligations—the execution of a common moral undertaking in the oath and the instruction given in granting of the commission. Note that neither this oath nor commission mentions a profession or is dependent upon possession of a joint or expeditionary mindset. Those entailments come after and are contingent, while the individual responsibility of the oath and commission is ascendant.

Why do you have officers in the armed forces? You have commissioned officers to provide *reliable* and *purposeful* direction of other men and women in pursuit of some goal of government. All leaders presumably provide purposeful direction. Some leaders, particularly commissioned officers, are marked by the need for extraordinary reliability and authority—leaders who merit the "special trust and confidence" of those who appoint them. Those commissioned leaders, S. L. A. Marshall wrote, are distinguished by "exceptional and unremitting responsibility."[10] Only commissioned leaders command. Only they lead their profession at the highest level and serve as statutory advisors of the President and Secretary of Defense.

Officers are an elite within the armed forces, an elite possessed of conviction, courage, faithfulness, and capability. They are both leaders and magistrates, whose orders are endowed with force of law.[11] Penalties for disobedience of, or offenses against, commissioned officers acting in that capacity are much more severe than like offenses against other categories of leaders. Additionally, in the Uniform Code of Military Justice there are offenses reserved for officers alone—those against the public trust reposed in them, notably Articles 88 and 133. The Supreme Court has acknowledged the distinction as necessary for the proper functioning of the armed forces, finding:

> An army is not a deliberative body. It is the executive arm. Its law is that of obedience. No question can be left open as to the right of command in the officer, or the duty of obedience in the soldier.[12]

Institutional authority, while impressive, is not sufficient in itself to insure success in the battle zone where the least deviation from orders can cost a life. Officers must be able to inspire confidence, too, by the quality of their character and their competence in using the tools of combat.

Officers individually are *professionals* because they provide necessary specialized services to the society they serve. Collectively, they are *members of a profession* because the activity they engage in is a shared endeavor, requiring reciprocal recognition and respect among its practitioners, and because the government, which established the armed forces, deals with both officers and the services as a body, setting the terms of acceptable practice and bounding the autonomy within which officers are expected to work, so as to ensure their actions are always to society's benefit. The degree of autonomy granted to the profession collectively is, by necessity, considerable. Its extent in any particular endeavor is the measure of both the scope of the profession's recognized expertise, *their collective jurisdiction*, and society's trust in their collective reliability. Specific limits on even tactical practice are frequently set, of course, by promulgation of what are known as rules of engagement. These prescriptive principles place practical limits on the use of force to keep military actions within the bounds of policy and public tolerance.

As members of a profession, in the broad sense as leaders of the profession of arms, armed forces officers are expected to create and promulgate new knowledge about the practice of their trade; to recruit, socialize, and indoctrinate new members in accordance with the strictures of the law and the traditions and ethics of professional practice; to develop their membership individually, and to enforce standards of performance and character among their peers—again, all leading to effective service to society.

Each of the military services save one, the Coast Guard, is organized under Title 10, U.S. Code, with the attributes of a recognizable public service profession. The Coast Guard is organized under Title 14. Some mid and senior career officers of all the services also serve in joint staff assignments, as distinct from service department postings. Since 1986, officers designated as joint service officers have developed many of the instrumentalities of a separate vocation in schools, doctrine, and repetitive assignment patterns.[13] One of the principal benefits of transformation, and of the power of the distributed information technologies it seeks to exploit, is the promise of improving the capability to command and control multiservice operations at the joint level, which the 20-year-old Goldwater-Nichols law anticipated.

Army Officership

Armed forces officers are commissioned into the separate services, for each of which Congress has identified specific purposes in law. Each service has developed its own service culture and ethic based upon the common moral and ethical framework of the oath and commission as applied in their particular function. Joint service culture is not nearly as well developed or defined (see Chapter 10 of the present anthology).

Congress's purpose in creating an Army pursuant to Constitutional provision is not, some may be surprised to learn, only for it to engage in "prompt and sustained combat incident to operations on land." However, that is the focus Congress gave the Army, after stating as its purposes:

- Preserving the peace and security, and providing for the defense, of the United States, the Territories, Commonwealths, and possessions, and any areas occupied by the United States;
- Supporting the national policies;
- Implementing the national objectives; and
- Overcoming any nations responsible for aggressive acts that imperil the peace and security of the United States.[14]

In short, Congress intended the Army to be a versatile instrument of national policy. The better-known organizational and training guidance to the Army, defining its particular specialty as sustained land combat, comes later in the law to achieve these ends and is intended to set forth the means for attaining the stated purpose.

Each of the armed forces has its own raison d'être in Title 10 or Title 14. Distinctions in function and requirements for fighting in and from the different mediums of land, sea, and air-space, as much as history, divide the members of the profession of arms into identifiable subprofessions, differing in medium-based specialty even where they generally correspond in function. It requires many years to master the intricacies of each body of service expertise, much less the integration of it in a common joint endeavor.

In the mid-1990s, alarmed at the flood of young officers exiting the service, the Army convened the Army Training and Leader Development Panel. A factor contributing to officer disillusionment as found by the panel was that "the Army's service ethic and concepts of officership are neither well-understood nor clearly defined. They are also not adequately reinforced throughout an officer's career."[15] The Panel recommended that the Army develop a concept of officership and integrate it in leadership doctrine and officer education.[16]

In 2003, a group of general officers under the tripartite leadership of the heads of Combined Arms Command, Army Accessions Command, and the Superintendent, U. S. Military Academy, sought to define Army officership. They produced the following definition, the core of which is the four distinct identities that must characterize each officer: warrior, servant of the nation, member of a profession, and leader of character.

> Officership is the practice of being a commissioned Army leader, accountable to the President of the United States for the Army and its mission. *Officers swear an oath of loyalty and service to the Constitution.* Officers apply discretionary judgment and bear ultimate moral responsibility for their decisions. Their commission imposes total accountability and unlimited liability. Essential to officership is a unique, shared self-concept consisting of four identities—warrior, servant of the nation, member of a profession, and leader of character. Grounded in Army values, this shared self-concept inspires and shapes the officer and the Army Officer Corps.[17]

The first, *warrior*, involves a fierce determination to succeed in the face of adversity. This is bounded by a dedication to a life as a *servant to the nation*, at the cost of personal convenience and even life and limb; by the requirement to be a worthy *member of the profession*, remembering always that what is good for the nation is good for the service, not the other way around, and, finally, by the obligation to be a *leader of character*—a person dedicated always to doing what is right, no matter the personal cost. These four identities are derivative, not only of the function of the Army officer, which is to be a confident and competent leader of soldiers in land combat, but also of the virtues of the oath and commission: patriotism, valor, fidelity, and abilities. These four identities will remain the requirements of Army officers as they come to possess a joint and expeditionary mindset. What then will change?

Implications of the Joint and Expeditionary Mindset

According to the article "Serving a Nation at War: A Campaign Quality Army with Joint and Expeditionary Capabilities," written by former Acting Secretary of the

Army Les Brownlee and Chief of Staff Peter Schoomaker for the Army War College journal *Parameters,* expeditionary operations will be marked by the requirement for rapid deployment, austere operating environments, and the ability to fight on arrival throughout the battlespace, most often with limited information. To meet these expectations, the expeditionary mindset involves the confidence "that we are organized, trained, and equipped to go anywhere in the world, at any time, against any adversary, and accomplish the assigned mission."[18] This focus is combined with a view of multiservice operations marked by what is called *joint interdependence*, that is, the seamless combination of service capabilities "to maximize their total complementary and reinforcing effects, while minimizing their relative vulnerabilities."[19] The definition is qualified by the statement that "the prerequisites of a commitment to interdependence are broad understanding of the differing strengths and limitations of each service's capabilities, *clear agreement about how those capabilities will be integrated* in any given operational setting, and *absolute mutual trust that, once committed, they will be employed as agreed.* At the same time, the Army requires a similar commitment from its sister services" (emphasis added).[20]

It is the transformational capability for joint interdependence, as yet only an evolving Army concept, that begins to acknowledge a change in the historical salience in war of the individual branches of service. Heretofore, services pretty much fought their own wars, albeit with support from the others, each focused on the primary combat tasks in its particular domain. In World War II, the Navy provided transport to Europe for Army forces, swept the sea of submarines, and jointly conducted the great amphibious invasions. In the Pacific, naval units conducted fleet operations, interdicted Japanese trade routes, sent Marines ashore to secure air and sea bases, and provided General MacArthur interior lines for his island-hopping return to the Philippines. Strategic Air Forces under control of the Combined Chiefs of Staff conducted largely separate strategic air wars against Germany and Japan. At the same time air forces provided air support to the theater commanders in support of ground and fleet operations. Battle areas could be separated and bounded, and although Army units might fight under Navy or Marine operational command in the Pacific, they were assigned discrete tactical tasks and pretty much given resources to do them within a prescribed area and were expected to accomplish their mission with the tools provided. Special air units were collocated with or attached to Army headquarters to integrate air and ground attack of lucrative targets.

Today, the range of sea- and air-launched systems permits them to reach any point in the land area of operations, thus in the words of James Burk "homogenizing the theater of war."[21] Information resources and greater weapon ranges have in effect shrunk the size of the theater and the battlefield. The aim is no less than total complementary integration of capabilities, *joint interdependence*, enabled by effective interservice platform communications and a common information set. With true joint interdependence, operational distinctions between services in the theater will be no more apparent or inhibitive than those between Napoleon's cavalry, infantry, and artillery. Conceptually, a ground platoon leader at a critical point will be able to designate a target for a bomber he can't see, and it will destroy the target without fear of hitting the friendly position because the target display will indicate the location of every blue soldier or vehicle. At least that's the promise.

Joint interdependence appears logically to be predicated on the notion that other-service assets will be sufficiently numerous and versatile to compensate to an acceptable degree for service organic capabilities that require significant strategic lift and consequently are dispensed with. Secretary Brownlee and General Schoomaker state that "no concept of interdependence will suffice that does not enable the front-line Soldier or Marine." [22] The more likely standard, however, will be total force effectiveness per unit of strategic lift, perhaps at the cost of individual effectiveness and even lives at the tactical level. As Capt. Guy V. Henry, wounded on the Rosebud Creek in Montana, observed: "For this we are soldiers."[23]

In practical terms, this means ground elements will be structured at very low levels, taking cognizance of assets of other services reasonably available to accomplish assigned missions and dispensing with organic systems that may be more reliable and responsive but that require significant lift assets to accompany ground troops. Attempted with mixed success in Afghanistan, where infantry units deployed without their normal complement of field artillery and depended instead on air support to back up their organic mortars, the concept requires a clear understanding on all sides of the consequences of the presence or absence of particular other-service support for ground operations.[24] The experience in Afghanistan also demonstrated the need for integrated planning between services early on in the planning process.[25] To succeed in joint interdependence, Army officers' professional knowledge must penetrate to increasingly lower levels to include much more of the detail of sister service operations, not only in employment but in terms of what it takes for the source to deliver an effect. Transparency of the execution process will otherwise lead to misunderstanding and mutual frustration.

Secretary Brownlee and General Schoomaker acknowledge the increased need to educate soldiers and leaders:

> We can have "perfect" knowledge with very "imperfect" understanding. Appreciation of context transforms knowledge to understanding, and only education can make that context accessible to us. Only education informed by experience will encourage Soldiers and leaders to meet the irreducible uncertainties of war with confidence, and to act decisively even when events fail to conform to planning assumptions and expectations.[26]

The skills needed for a joint and expeditionary mindset are both procedural, which can come from repetitive training, and conceptual, which depends on consideration and manipulation of abstract ideas and principles, most often achieved in quality resident instruction. Much of the necessary tactical learning will be provided experientially by active campaigning, introducing joint effects into exercises at combat training centers, and conducting realistic, well-designed simulations. Armed forces officers will learn to work together by training and fighting together. They will become adaptable leaders by successfully confronting complex problems and solving them under pressure of time and circumstance.

Obviously, transformation alone can never guarantee a successful conclusion to the wars we choose to wage. Having disposed in short order of the Iraqi army, and the government that fielded it, with relatively minimal forces deployed, we have discovered that replacing a nation's government militarily comes with a heavy follow-up cost, especially in the third world where post-colonial memories, no less than religious fundamentalism, make western occupation an anathema. Of course many knew that to begin with, for example General Eric Shinseki, General Schoomaker's predecessor as Army Chief of Staff, and the Council on Foreign Relations.[27]

What we have learned is that transformation technologies, while very useful indeed—blue tracking systems, for example, still facilitate command and control and reaction to attack—don't have the same payoff against insurgents in Fiats or remote control roadside bombs as they do against armored battalions. Use of bombs from strategic bombers to dramatically change the coefficient of combat power in front of a pinned-down platoon may have associated political costs in security operations that negate their value. This is not to say that anyone has offered to give back his or her global positioning or blue tracking systems. It is simply another reminder that brute facts on the infinitely variable battlefield sometimes interfere with the promises of technology. Napoleon's cavalry didn't do much good in Spain either, once they turned to security operations against the Spanish guerrillas. So the first transformational lesson is that information technology may indeed increase unit effectiveness, but that does not mean it will guarantee adequacy of a small force to do a large force's job or rapidly solve other militarily complex political problems. Small and large are relative terms, not only to themselves, but to the magnitude and complexity of the task assigned.

It is important, then, to seek out what all this recent experience in the joint and expeditionary mindset means for the future requirements of Army officership. We have learned some pertinent lessons about future operations from the wars in Afghanistan and Iraq. First, we have seen that leadership, courage, competence, creative ability, and adaptability are still required of officers in the conduct of large and small unit operations, in supply convoys, and in platoon check points. Precision delivery has not obviated heroism in ground combat, nor does it seem likely to. Capt. Nathan Self, who led his Rangers in the attack at Takur Ghar in Afghanistan to recover a lost Navy Seal, was a warrior.[28] Lt. Col. Eric Schwartz and Col. Dave Perkins, whose armored raids into the enemy capital broke the Iraqi government, were warriors.[29] The soldiers and marines engaged in close combat in Iraq's cities during the fall of 2004 looked in vain for the precision systems that would have allowed them to become distant warriors fighting from outside of harm's way.

The example of the Army's 507th Maintenance Company, which found itself ambushed in the midst of inhospitable Iraqi citizens, has revised our understanding of the relative security of combat support units and changed the focus of the service ethic, as demonstrated by subsequent promulgation of The Soldier's Creed.[30] It has also changed the content and duration of basic training for all soldiers. The Army Basic Officers' Leaders Course, having been designed on the premise that officer development was best done in units, now scrambles to identify the essential combat skills every officer must learn in schools to bring to his first platoon of whatever arm. The joint and expeditionary mindset in wartime involves readiness to be in combat in hours, not days or weeks.

The battlefield proliferation of independent contractors, armed and unarmed, has complicated the soldier's task. After a hundred years militarizing the military support structure, we are moving back to the 18th century solution, when civilian teamsters moved Army supplies. Indeed, we are now even permitting civilian security contractors to fly armed helicopters in the area of operations. We have learned again that maintenance of active discipline in all forces is vital and requires continuous tending. Who would deny the effect on service self-respect and the strategic and, indeed, domestic political effects of the misconduct of a group of military police in the Abu Ghraib prison? Where were their officers? Not just generals and colonels but more particularly captains and lieutenants who knew right from wrong and were willing to stand up for right. What were they doing? Discipline begins with individual soldiers understanding their responsibility for everything that goes on within their sight and hearing.[31] Leaders of character would have understood that and ensured by their example and actions that the soldiers at fault were protected against the dehumanizing effects of war by clear articulation of standards and the continuous checking that keeps instructions alive. More clearly needs to be done to instill in some officers the nature of their professional obligations.

Conclusions

It is my view that military and Army officership, thus understood, will remain fundamentally unchanged by the nature of transformation and the military tasks implied by concepts such as the joint and expeditionary mindset. Professional status and the autonomy of practice that resides therein will continue to depend upon the officer corps' acceptance of responsibility for the effectiveness and reliability of their collective service. That will still require a lifetime of individual study and practice, willing subordination of self to a higher cause, and aggressive identification and removal of those who do not measure up ethically as well as functionally. New knowledge about the conduct of military operations on land still has to be created, integrated in joint and service doctrine and training, and implemented in the field. Creation of new knowledge will continue to be done best in institutional settings, just as the professional knowledge of physicians, gained largely from the collective experience of individual practices, is collated, validated, expanded, codified, and distributed by medical colleges and research institutes.

A joint and expeditionary mindset does imply a new acculturation for officers of all services. The Army Chief of Staff says that he is "a joint officer, who happens to be in the Army, who happens to be the Chief of Staff of the Army right now." That is a worthy mindset, essential if joint interdependence on the battlefield is to succeed. It implies recognition of the common purpose, ethics, morality, and kinship of all commissioned officers of all services. Perhaps it suggests that all future commissions should be as officers "in the Armed Forces of the United States," with assignment to a particular service rather than commissioning as an officer of the Army, Navy, Coast Guard, Air Force, or Marine Corps. This change would simply acknowledges what has long been true, namely, that the identity of all armed forces officers (and thus joint service officers) is already grounded in a common ethical core derived from their common oath and form of commission.

The acculturation of junior officers to recognize a common bond with officers of the other services will not materialize on its own. It will require active attention by leaders who, as senior authority figures, are responsible for the professionalization of their subordinates. It will require precommissioning sources to provide more instruction about the culture, strengths, and limitations of their own and sister services, so as to avoid misunderstanding and neglect through remediable ignorance. To manage joint interdependence requires a new way of thinking, a comprehensive view of the fitting together of the whole force, looking down from the top, rather than concentrating only on the requirements for one's own part, looking up from the bottom. It requires, ultimately, abandoning the view that one's service is a separate, totally autonomous profession, and viewing it instead as an integral part of a wider whole. The Army doesn't fight the nation's wars. The Navy doesn't fight the nation's wars, nor does the Air Force. The armed forces do.

Joint interdependence ultimately involves forgoing the acquisition, maintenance, or deployment of key organic capabilities, on the premise that another service's available capability will be adequate to do the job in a truly integrated operational whole. The discussion of joint interdependence formally presupposes among its prerequisites, "clear agreement about how . . . capabilities will be integrated in any given operational setting, and absolute mutual trust that, once committed, they will be employed as agreed."[32] This latter assurance is impossible to give, however, and certainly will lead to disillusionment if expected. Anticipated situations change. Commanders will inevitably allocate scarce resources based upon strategic and operational, as opposed to tactical priorities, and commanders of small units will find themselves forced to deal with the absence of key elements of combat power, required elsewhere for greater perceived payoff. Part of professional maturity will be the ability to judge and describe the difference in total combat capability, with or without availability of scarce high-payoff systems, and having the flexibility and determination to soldier on in their absence. Soldiers will pay the blood tax for the tool they don't possess, as they always have.

Continued regard for *the service ideal* is implicit in military service. Honoring the oath of service requires constant reinforcement and encouragement in units and educational assignments. The Army, within the wider profession of arms, appears to be reducing its asserted field of unique expert knowledge to matters of tactics, and engaging more fully with the other armed forces to define the necessary progression and expectations for joint interdependence in operations and education as well as training. This represents a significant institutional adjustment and it is likely to have lasting second and third order effects, particularly on the future concept of officership.

Notes

1. Department of the Army, *The United States Army 2004 Posture Statement; A statement on the Posture of the United States Army 2004 by The Honorable R. L. Brownlee and General Peter*

J. Schoomaker Presented to the Committees and Subcommittees of the United States Senate and the House of Representatives, Second Session, 108th Congress: 1. Chief of Staff, Army, The Way Ahead; Our Army At War...Relevant & Ready; Moving from the Current Force to the Future Force. Available on line at: http://www.army.mil/aps/04/index.html. Accessed on 16 September 2004. See also Les Brownlee and Peter J. Schoomaker, "Serving a Nation At War: A Campaign Quality Army with Joint and Expeditionary Capabilities," Parameters 34, no. 2 (Summer 2004): 4-23.

2. Department of Defense, Office of the Secretary of Defense, Transformation Planning Guidance (April 2003), 3.

3. George Washington, General Orders, Headquarters at the Gulph, 17 December 1777, in George Washington, Writings (New York: The Library of America, 1997), 280-81; "Lectures of Chancellor Kent," Atlantic Magazine 1 (May-October 1824): 148.

4. Terence C. Halliday, "Knowledge Mandates: Collective Influence by Scientific, Normative and Syncretic Professions," The British Journal of Sociology 36, no. 3 (September 1985).

5. Samuel P. Huntington, The Soldier and the State: The Theory and Politics of Civil-Military Relations (Cambridge, MA: Harvard University Press, 1957). See also Edward M. Coffman, "The Long Shadow of The Soldier and the State," The Journal of Military History 55, no. 1 (January, 1991): 69-82.

6. Mark R. Grandstaff, "Preserving the 'Habits and Usages of War': William Tecumseh Sherman, Professional Reform, and the U.S. Army Officer Corps, 1865-1881, Revisited," The Journal of Military History 62, no. 3 (July 1998): 521-45; Allan R. Millett, The General: Robert L. Bullard and Officership in the United States Army, 1881-1925 (Westport, CT: Greenwood Press, 1975). Millett provides an outstanding summary of the sociological literature of professions.

7. Harold L. Wilensky, "The Professionalization of Everyone?" American Journal of Sociology 70, no. 2 (September 1964): 137-158.

8. Andrew Abbott, The System of Profession: An Essay on the Division of Expert Labor (Chicago, IL: University of Chicago Press, 1988), 8

9. Huntington, The Soldier and the State, 8-18.

10. Department of Defense, The Armed Forces Officer (Washington, DC: United States Government Printing Office, 1950), 2. S. L. A. Marshall was the author.

11. Ibid., 143.

12. Parker, Warden et al., v. Levy, No. 73-206, 744. The quotation, used by Chief Justice Rehnquist for the Court majority, was originally found in In re Grimley, 137 U.S. 147, 153 (1890).

13. Refers to the four categories of professional knowledge set forth in Don M. Snider and Gayle L. Watkins, "Introduction," in The Future of the Army Profession, project directors Don M. Snider and Gayle L. Watkins, ed. Lloyd J. Matthews (New York: McGraw-Hill Primis, 2002), 8-9.

14. 10 U.S. Code, Section 3062.

15. Army Training and Leader Development Panel Study Report (Officers) (Ft. Leavenworth, KS: Combined Arms Center, 2001), OS-22.

16. ATLDP Panel Recommendations 1A2 and 1A3. Panel recommendations were consolidated and managed by the Army's Center for Army Leadership at the Army Command and General Staff College.

17. U.S. Military Academy, William E. Simon Center, The Army Concept of Officership (4 January 2004).

18. Serving a Nation At War, 10.

19. Ibid, 5–6.

20. Ibid, 6.

21. The phrase "Homogenizing the theater of war" is taken from James Burk, "Expertise, Jurisdiction, and Legitimacy of the Military Profession," The Future of the Army Profession, 29.

22. *Serving A Nation at War,* 11.

23. Quoted by John F. Finerty, *Warpath and Bivouac* (Chicago, IL: M. A. Donohue & Co, 1890), 130.

24. Robert H. McElroy, "Afghanistan Fire Support for Operation Anaconda; Interview with Major General Franklin L. Hagenbeck, Commanding General 10th Mountain Division and Coalition Joint Task Force Mountain in Afghanistan," *Field Artillery* (September-October 2002), 5-9.

25. Bruce Rolfsen, "General Defends Air Force in Anaconda," *Army Times,* 20 January 2003, 30.

26. *Serving a Nation at War,* 14.

27. Council on Foreign Relations, *Iraq: The Day After: Report of an Independent Task Force on Post-Conflict Iraq Sponsored by the Council on Foreign Relations,* Thomas R. Pickering and James R. Schlesinger, Co-chairs, Eric P. Schwartz, Project Director (New York: Council on Foreign Relations, 2003).

28. Bradley Graham, "Bravery and Breakdowns in a Ridgetop Battle: 7 Americans Died in Rescue Effort That Revealed Mistakes and Determination," *Washington Post,* 24 May 2002, A1.

29. David Zucchino, *Thunder Run: The Armored Strike to Capture Baghdad* (New York: Atlantic Monthly Press, 2004).

30. The Soldier's Creed, which begins "I am an American Soldier," was promulgated by General Schoomaker to define the warrior ethos at the heart of all Army members' core self-identity. Available at http://www.army.mil/thewayahead/creed.html. Accessed 17 October 2004.

31. *Serving a Nation At War,* 17.

32. Ibid., 11.

8 Professional Identity Development for 21st Century Army Officers[1]

*George B. Forsythe, Scott Snook,
Philip Lewis, and Paul T. Bartone*

Since the end of the Cold War, in a very fundamental way the U.S. Army has been under attack. Setting aside the Pentagon strike on 11 September 2001 and operations in support of the global war on terror, this onslaught has come not from terrorists, rogue states, or insurgents, and the target has not been our military formations in the field or along our nation's borders. Since 1989, what's been at risk has been our Army's professional center of gravity, its sense of self. One way to conceptualize this assault is to think of it as an "identity crisis," a social and psychological battle fought at both individual and institutional levels of analysis, with each dynamic reinforcing the other in a self-fueling vicious cycle. It is difficult to overemphasize the magnitude of the changes that have led to this crisis. The Berlin Wall came down; the Soviet Union collapsed; the Cold War ended; the global war on terror began. Gone was the relatively simple bipolar globe that had dominated our geopolitical landscape for almost 45 years. What would such monumental changes mean for the U.S. Army? What would this loss of the existing world order mean for a generation of Army officers whose extant professional identity was defined largely in opposition to an enemy now defeated? What would such global upheaval mean for how our Army thinks about itself? In the present chapter we provide a way of considering professional identity as part of the fundamental process by which we, as human beings, construct and periodically reconstruct a meaningful view of the world and our place in that world.

Identity, whether we are talking about the institutional identity of the Army or the professional identity of Army officers, does not occur in a vacuum. To a significant extent our identity as officers and as an institution is a reflection of how we are expected to function by the larger society of which we are a part. "Victory" in the Cold War resulted in significant change in both the quality and quantity of demands levied on the U.S. Army. With the Soviet Union gone, American society demanded more than simply trained and ready war-fighters. Over the past decade, our Army as an institution has been asked to execute a broad range of missions across the entire spectrum of operations. Such changes at the institutional level have required individual Army officers to adopt a wide variety of roles and operate in increasingly complex and ambiguous environments. Not surprisingly, such dramatic changes in the substance of what we do as an Army have sparked serious debate about fundamental issues of identity—who we are, what we're about, and, perhaps most fundamentally, *how* we make sense of what it means to be a military officer of the United States in the early 21st century.

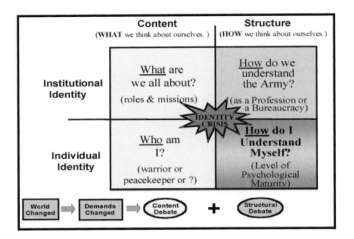

Figure 8-1. *Identity Matrix.*

Figure 8-1 illustrates the multidimensional nature of this struggle. We will argue that central to understanding the issue of identity and its development is the distinction between "content" and "structure." Identities at both institutional and individual levels of analysis consist of both content and structure. Consider for a moment the two types of individual identity depicted in the bottom row of Figure 8-1. In the left column is the content or "what" of our individual identities as Army officers. Content is the surface material—our behaviors, ideas, preferences, values, aspirations, and leadership style. The content of an officer's identity might include the seven Army values, or Duty-Honor-Country, or the principles of officership, or an amalgam of all of them.[2] Indeed, the debate within the profession about roles and missions, and the associated questions about an officer's identity—am I a warrior or more?—is fundamentally about the content of an officer's identity. How we answer this important "content" question will have significant implications for such issues as how we train and allocate our resources, and whether we, as individuals, choose to remain in the Army. This is the way we customarily think about professional identity. Our focus in the present chapter, however, is not primarily on this aspect of identity. Instead, we will focus mainly on the bottom right quadrant of Figure 8-1, the "structure" of individual identity. Focusing only on issues of identity content will lead to an incomplete understanding of professional identity issues and more importantly to a lack of understanding of the *process* of identity formation and transformation. What, then, are these other identity issues? What is the "structure" of identity and identity development?

The structure of identity refers to the way in which any particular identity, be it warrior or peacekeeper, or something else, is constructed. As Figure 8-1 suggests, it is the "how" of identity formation. For example, some officers will construct their understanding of the peacekeeper or nation-builder identity as a set of skills and behavioral roles that must be mastered to fulfill that identity. For these officers, if one has the requisite skills and can employ them effectively, then one is a peacekeeper. Other officers will construct these identities in a more complicated fashion. To them being a peacekeeper or a nation-builder may mean more than merely meeting a set of role expectations. These identities may also entail embodying a set of societal values about the proper place of a superpower in a unipolar world. For these officers, the fixed roles and narrow competencies of these identities are embedded in a broader context of societal values about the rights of ethnic minorities and the centrality of democratic social and political institutions to the creation of just societies. The "how" of the skills-roles identity entails enacting certain behaviors. The "how" of the contextual identity entails locating oneself within a broad set of societal views about the place of the military in a democratic, multiethnic society. We will argue that these contrasting perspectives on professional identity are not merely different in content. We will argue that the latter view requires and reflects a higher level of psychological maturity than the former. It entails a more sophisticated and psychologically mature way of structuring one's identity than does the former. Failure to appreciate the fact that identities vary by structure (level of maturity and sophistication) as well as by content will yield an incomplete understanding of our ongoing struggle with issues of professionalism in the Army.

Figure 8-1 maps how the content-structure distinction and the institutional-individual level of analysis interact to provide a more complete framework for our current debate. The most familiar arguments are found in column one. For the past 15 years, the Army has helped fight a war on drugs, drilled water wells in Africa, aided the victims of natural disasters around the globe, fought successful conventional conflicts in the Iraq and Afghanistan, battled warlords in Somalia, stemmed the tide of ethnic cleansing in the Balkans, and countered insurgents as part of the global war on terror. Such a significant shift in roles and missions was bound to have an impact on the Army's identity, its organization, its officers, and its profession. The resulting debate is about the content of our identity. What is the Army really about? Fighting wars, keeping peace, building nations, or something else?

Debate over these content issues at the institutional level has generated corresponding angst at the individual level. How should soldiers think of themselves? As warriors, peacekeepers, policemen, statesmen, or something else? Arriving on the heels of a relatively narrow professional self-concept adopted during the Cold War—that of warrior—this decade's increase in scope of institutional missions and individual roles has left the Army and its soldiers searching for a coherent new identity. Such uncertainty at the very heart of our profession can manifest itself in many dysfunctional ways. Alarming trends in recruitment, morale, readiness, leadership, and retention can all be viewed as symptoms of a deeper malaise, one rooted in fundamental questions about the very essence of who we are and what we do.

As emphasized above, however, identity is not only about content; there is an equally important structural dimension to our sense of self, both for the Army as an institution and for its members as individuals. While column one issues (Figure 8-1) have captured current headlines, we may find that column two holds greater promise for illuminating our current crisis and for generating new and better approaches to lasting change. While eventually we must resolve questions of content, perhaps a deeper understanding of *how* we think about ourselves and our experiences, the *structure* of our identities, will lead to more robust insights into these fundamental issues of self. We leave it to others to directly address issues of content; our work here is situated within the broader debate over *how* we think of ourselves, both collectively as an institution and individually as psychologically maturing adults.

In contrast to issues of identity content, issues of identity structure are universal. They pertain to all professional identities. The content of identities varies by profession. Questions like "What are we all about?" and "Who am I?" are boundary issues. Answers to such content questions are both vocation specific and time dependent; they serve to differentiate one profession from another. Structural issues, on the other hand, are more general; answers to these broader questions provide the framework within which issues of content are addressed. The two types of identity issues are related. Structure influences content; *how* we think about ourselves influences *what* we think about ourselves. In the example presented earlier, the peacekeeper who structured his identity in terms of roles will be limited to seeing himself in terms of specific peacekeeping behaviors. In contrast, the officer with a broader peacekeeper identity will construct his identity using shared, societal values and ideals. What each considers his professional identity to be will be the same (both embrace a peacekeeper identity). But it is important to note that the breadth and complexity of the two identities are very different. It is this structural component of identity that provides the lens through which we view ourselves, either collectively or as individuals. In this sense, structure constrains what level of content can be seen. Being clear about how an identity is structured will provide us with significant leverage in understanding all issues of identity, particularly in terms of how well we understand the issue of identity development.

At the institutional level, structural issues of identity (upper right quadrant of Figure 8-1) address questions of organization. How do we think of ourselves as an institution? What is the structure of our *collective* consciousness? Is it organized primarily as a large bureaucracy or as a time-honored profession? How we resolve such issues at the institutional level will not only shape how we collectively think about whether we should be war-fighters or peacekeepers, it will also frame individual-level issues of identity as well. Fundamental questions of individual member identity are colored by one's sense of being either a professional or a bureaucrat. Once again, however, we'll leave this question of structure at the institutional level to others. To repeat, our focus in this chapter is on the lower right-hand quadrant of Figure 8-1—the structure of individual identity.

Given that the lower right quadrant of Figure 8-1 describes the individual component of structural identity, we are taking a decidedly psychological approach. To understand officer development from this perspective, we have turned to the literature on adolescent and adult identity development for insights. Our work is grounded in the constructive-developmental theory of Harvard psychologist Robert Kegan.[3] We have found his approach provocative and illuminating because it allows us to focus on *how* officers understand themselves rather than on *what* they understand. In the remainder of this chapter we extend Kegan's general theory on adolescent and adult identity development to the specific context of officer development in the U.S. Army. We will not explicate Kegan's theory in detail; rather we extrapolate his work to the subject of the present volume—officer professionalism. We look first at the basic ideas of Kegan's theory as they apply to officer development. Next, we present the findings of our research within the officer corps. Our intent is to explain what we currently know about officer development. We conclude with a discussion of the implications of our work for re-professionalizing the officer corps.

Kegan's Theory of Identity Development

Robert Kegan is primarily interested in *how* people make sense of themselves and their world, what we have referred to above as the "structure" of identity. In Kegan's view, the level of sophistication of how one structures an understanding of oneself and one's experiences lies at the heart of self-concept or identity. Two key ideas underpin Kegan's view of identity. First, Kegan believes that we actively *construct* our understandings; we don't simply receive them from others. We build our understandings of ourselves from our experiences. It should be noted that two individuals may share a common experience but understand it (construct it) very differently. Second, Kegan believes that we progress through a finite series of universal and progressively more complex stages in *how* we construct our understanding. It is the foregoing two ideas in combination that make Kegan's approach to identity and identity development a powerful explanatory system. We shall extend these ideas to the officer corps, specifically to the proposition that *how* officers understand themselves and their experiences in the Army lies at the core of their professional identity—who they are as professionals. Note the use of the word "how" rather than "what" in the preceding sentences. Although the content of an officer's identity is important, we believe that how officers make meaning is more fundamental to understanding professional identity. In this regard, we offer an approach to this topic that differs from that of other authors in this anthology. Nevertheless, this approach should be recognizable to anyone who has ever heard the service school instructor's familiar refrain, "We are not trying to teach you what to think as much as we are teaching you how to think." Similarly, in terms familiar to Army officers, our approach offers a way of thinking about the BE in the Army's BE, KNOW, and DO framework for leader development.

Within Kegan's framework, development involves major qualitative shifts in how people construct their understanding of themselves and their world. Kegan's theory is about changes in meaning-making, where development involves progressively more complex ways of constructing this understanding—complex in terms of the breadth of perspective and the organization of internal and external experiences. From this perspective, as our understanding becomes more complex, it also becomes more encompassing—it's a broader worldview. We see more, we can step back and be objective about more things, we are more mature, and we are better able to deal with the psychological and interpersonal demands of life. Because we "see" more, we are able to establish deeper connections to others. Within this framework, officer development involves qualitative shifts in how officers make sense of themselves and their experiences. Each shift leads to a progressively broader perspective toward oneself as a professional and one's relationships to others within and outside the profession. These are precisely the sorts of changes advocated by the Army's literature on leader development—developing broad, encompassing, and abstract perspectives that enable leaders to deal with the mental and emotional challenges of operating in complex and ambiguous situations. The present analysis suggests that such changes will occur only if officers have reached a certain level of structural development.

Kegan explains the structure of the self-concept in terms of what he calls "subject-object relations." "Subject" refers to the psychological lens through which we construct meaning—the perspective from which we understand ourselves and our experiences. "Object," on the other hand, is that which can be can be understood psychologically; it is what we can be "objective" about. Subject-object relations, then, are an internal psychological process involving the interplay between *what* we can understand and *how* we understand it—between what we can take a perspective on ("object") and the perspective we bring to bear ("subject"). In general terms, therefore, development entails the shifting of subject to object, making it possible to take a perspective on and view more broadly our previous way of organizing our understanding of the world. In this manner, each step in development leads to an expanded worldview, which gradually becomes broader and more encompassing as we gain the ability to step back and "see" ourselves and our experiences in ways we couldn't before. We move from being embedded in a point of view to being able to step back and assess it. Table 8-1 shows Kegan's stages in terms of the subject-object distinction to illustrate this point.

Stage	Subject	Object	Features
0	Reflexes (sensing, moving)	None	Incorporation
1	Impulses, perceptions, feelings	Reflexes	Single perspective; can't take other's point of view
2	Needs, interests, wishes	Impulses, perceptions, feelings	Can take multiple perspectives, one at a time
3	Mutuality, shared meaning	Needs, interests, wishes	Takes multiple perspectives simultaneously
4	Self-authored system of values	Mutuality, shared meaning	Has own personal perspective on relationships and societal ideals
5	Universality	Self-authored system of values	Recognizes that own perspective on experience is a created convenience

Table 8-1. *Kegan's Developmental Stages.*[4]

Stages of Officer Identity Development

For purposes of understanding officer identity, we will focus on Kegan's post-child-hood stages, 2, 3, and 4, because it is these stages and their development that are most relevant to our understanding of officer identity and officer identity development. Stage 5, reserved for the rare and exceptional individuals among us, will not be treated. Although the ages at which the various stages emerge vary considerably, stage 2 begins to emerge at about age five for most children and is the typical stage of most early teenagers. There are, however, a significant number of successful adults who have not yet moved beyond this relatively early developmental stage.[5] Stage 3 thinking begins to emerge in adolescence for most individuals and, of the five stages, is the one most frequently occupied by American adults. Stage 4, when it develops at all, appears to be a feature of middle adulthood.

Kegan's Stage 2

As shown in Table 8-1, stage 2 individuals have moved their immediate impulses and embeddedness in a single perspective from subject to object. As a result, individuals who are functioning at stage 2 are able to play social roles, delay gratification, follow rules, develop and pursue enduring interests, construct a stable sense of self, and participate in close relationships based on social exchange and reciprocity. Unlike individuals at stage 1, these individuals are not impulsive; they possess the ability to postpone short-term indulgences in favor of long-term goals, and they have a sense of agency. Newly able to reflect upon their immediate desires, they can take responsibility for their actions. Stage 2 individuals' sense of who they are is tied up in their ability to effectively pursue their enduring interests, including enacting the behaviors associated with desired roles. As leaders, stage 2 individuals focus on following the rules and being responsive to the needs and interests of their subordinates and superiors. They believe that one usually has to "go along to get along." However, stage 2 officers tend to view others from the point of view of their own agendas (note that in Table 8-1 they are shown as being subject to their needs, interests, and wishes). Stage 2 individuals understand others in terms of how these others can help or hinder them in satisfying their own personal interests. As officers, they tend to view professional values and standards as rules to be complied with, and do so in order to accomplish something personally important to them or to avoid negative consequences. They are ultimately motivated by the desire to meet their own needs. While they may be concerned about what others will *do* to or for them, how others *feel* about them does not become a part of how they feel about themselves. There is no shared perspective, because a shared perspective is a structural achievement of stage 3. It is certainly true that in many cases the content of a stage 2 officer's agendas is professionally acceptable—getting more training or a more challenging job, for example. But because of structural limitations, the underlying motivation of a stage 2 individual is always to satisfy his or her personal needs. There is an absence of a shared reality—how others will be affected by what I do is often relevant, but it is not a part of my sense of my stage 2 self. Thus, interpersonal mutuality and a sense of corporateness are not possible for a stage 2 officer. In a fundamental way, any professional identity adopted by a stage 2 officer is always an individual identity. The identity of peacekeeper, for example, could be enacted as a set of desired role behaviors. But the stage 2 officer would lack the structural capacity to be identified with or have a sense of community with others who share that identity.

To illustrate, consider the following excerpt from a 20-year-old West Point cadet in his sophomore year who is describing what it means to him to be a leader. This cadet is describing why he feels more motivated when he has a leader who "puts out a hundred and ten percent." This excerpt, and the others that follow, are drawn from research we have been doing with West Point cadets and Army officers, research that we will describe in more detail later in the chapter.

> The leaders that I've had in the past, the ones that are really good, I perform well in there. If they are putting out a hundred and ten percent, and they are doing their best, you can visually see it; their uniform looks really cool. You know, if their shoes are really shined, you know, mine should get that good too. And if I see them putting a hundred and ten percent out for us, they're doing it for us—their own troops—and they really care about them, then I'm going to work that much harder for that person.

What sounds stage 2 about this is that the relationship between the cadet and his leader (platoon sergeant) is construed as a sort of quid pro quo exchange—he puts out for me, so I'll put out for him. This view can be accommodated by the stage 2 capacity to take two perspectives, the cadet's and the platoon sergeant's, one at a time. Still, it's possible that this cadet's orientation to the platoon sergeant's "caring" is more mature than a stage 2 perspective. The interviewer seeks to clarify this issue (interviewer's comments and questions are capitalized):

WHY IS IT IMPORTANT TO YOU THAT THEY CARE?

> I guess for me it's because of the tangible rewards of what will happen if somebody does really care about you. Maybe, like for instance, if they are putting a hundred and ten percent out, then you're going to put a hundred and ten percent out there. And then you are all going to feel better about everything else.

BECAUSE YOU THINK YOU'LL BE ABLE, YOURSELF, TO SUCCEED MORE?

> Yeah, yeah, definitely.

So we see that the interviewer's questions elicit the notion that the cadet will get more of his own needs met if he has a motivated leader (the "tangible rewards"). And presumably he "feels better about everything else" because he, individually, is being more successful. This is clearly a stage 2 perspective on leadership. Note that the interviewer got beyond the content of good leadership (putting out for your subordinates) to the underlying structure of how this cadet understands this particular leadership principle (balancing reciprocal needs and interests so you can get what you want).

Although stage 2 understandings are essential to effective performance as an officer, embeddedness in self-interest is both practically limiting and normatively anathema to officer professionalism. There is nothing wrong with having selfish interests. But military officers (and most other professionals) are expected to routinely subordinate self-interest to the greater good. In the terms of Kegan's theory (see Table 8-1), this is the shift from being "subject to" my needs and interests to having ("making object") needs and interests. It is this developmental shift that signals the emergence of stage 3.

Kegan's Stage 3

Stage 3 officers have developed the ability to hold multiple perspectives simultaneously, which enables them to regard themselves and others in terms of abstract, inner qualities and to be directly affected by what they think others think about them. Now that they can hold another's perspective simultaneously with their own perspective, that other perspective can be used to *co*-construct or make sense of the self. How others view them becomes a part of how they view themselves. This is a major psychological accomplishment. Unlike stage 2 individuals, those in stage 3 can be "team players," able to subordinate their self-interests to professional ideals.

We might think of the transition from stage 2 to stage 3 in terms of professional socialization—the shift from understanding the self in terms of individual interests to an understanding of self as a part of something larger than the self, as a member of a profession. It is important to note that this is a change of identity structure, not merely content. Because of this structural change, stage 3 officers have a much more sophisticated view of officer professionalism than those at stage 2. They are able to *internalize* the profession's expectations, and they strive to live by these expectations because of their shared bond with other professionals. They also are able to understand themselves in terms of abstract internal qualities such as honesty, duty, and responsibility. Stage 3 officers understand the seven Army values as more than simply rules to be followed; rather, they see these values as internalized qualities that the Army expects will characterize all soldiers.

To illustrate, consider the following excerpt found in an interview of a cadet scored at stage 3. Like the previous excerpt, the cadet is talking about good leadership. The content is similar, but the structure of his understanding is very different.

> I think the best cadet is the one who really understands that his real mission in life—in the Army—is being there for his troops. I mean he's got to have a commitment to the Army's goals overall.
>
> HOW DO YOU KNOW THAT'S THE RIGHT THING?
>
> I guess it's one of those gut feelings that you have. And I'm of the firm belief that if you don't want that, if you're here just for yourself, you know, get the heck out of here. And, you know, the Academy kind of makes you realize that taking care of your troops is the most important thing.
>
> SO YOU HAVE THAT RESPONSIBILITY. WHERE DOES THAT RESPONSIBILITY COME FROM?
>
> I think the responsibility as a leader to take care of your troops comes from the fact that you're the lieutenant. In addition to the fact that you're a human being. You know, as a human being you have a responsibility, I think, to take care of everybody else.

What makes this a stage 3 response is the cadet's embeddedness within other points of view (e.g., the Academy's) as the source of his own point of view. Those points of view include the Academy's expectations of an Army officer, the responsibilities of having a professional position ("you're the lieutenant"), and an idealistic societal view of the responsibilities of membership in the human race, all of which are part of this cadet's point of view. Missing is an embeddedness in his individual needs. Indeed, he critiques self-interest (self-interest being a stage 2 way of constructing the self) when he admonishes those who are "here just for yourself" to "get the heck out." Critique of a lower stage (i.e., of identification with a personal agenda) indicates the ability to take a broader perspective and signals a more advanced stage.

The transition to stage 3 is just the first step in the development of a professional identity. There are limitations to stage 3 capacities that lead to an incomplete understanding of what it means to be a professional. Because we are subject to shared meaning at stage 3, in many ways we are not psychologically distinct from our relationships. Others' feelings about us are a part of how we experience ourselves. As a result, we often expend far too much energy avoiding hurting others' feelings. And because we assume that others, like us, make our feelings about them a part of *their* identities, we tend to feel responsible for how others experience us. In the terms of Table 8-1, at stage 3 we are subject to mutuality. In a psychological sense, there is no independent "self" that we bring *to* our relationships, because there is no "self" apart from our relationships. We have a shared identity at stage 3 rather than a personal identity. With regard to professional identity, stage 3 professionals "are the profession"; they have fully "bought in" and take on all the expectations of the profession. As a result, stage 3 professionals are unable to reconcile the competing expectations that are a natural part of professional practice, because they have not yet "integrated" the expectations of the profession into an autonomous self system. Lacking such a system of self-authored values, the stage 3 professional has no basis for resolving competing expectations.

Kegan's Stage 4

Kegan asserts that psychological maturity—what he terms "psychological autonomy"—is not possible until stage 4 is achieved. Stage 4 officers are able to organize their stage 3 social and interpersonal identifications using individually constructed systems for organizing values and standards. At stage 4, one has developed the capacity to use self-authored principles and personal standards to reflect upon one's personal and professional experiences. At stage 4, officers' *shared* ideals and professional expectations shift from subject to object; stage 4 officers are capable of taking a perspective on their shared ideals and assessing them in terms of self-authored principles and standards. Officers with a stage 4 understanding of the profession now "own" the values of their profession; they have internalized these values in a fundamentally different way than have stage 3 officers. They can now take an entirely personal perspective on the profession's expectations, critique them, assess them, and organize them in more complex and sophisticated ways. And, importantly, stage 4 officers have developed a system of personal values and principles that permits them to reconcile professional and personal value conflicts.

The transition from stage 3 to stage 4 involves the transformation from being one's relationships to having relationships. For officers, the transformation involves a shift from being a member of a profession to being a professional. Stage 4 is concerned with psychological independence. Self-authored values and principles provide a perspective on one's relationships and socially defined identities. While both stage 3 and stage 4 officers can articulate broad values and ideals (content), only stage 4 officers can justify their values in terms of what they personally believe rather than appealing to a shared external standard. We believe that the transition from stage 3 to stage 4 is a critical transformation that must be made if officers are to *lead* and *shape* the profession as it faces the challenges of the new era. Such leadership requires officers who are not psychologically embedded in the profession, but who are professionals capable of stepping back and viewing the profession objectively. As we have said, this capability is characteristic of a stage 4 orientation toward the profession.

The following excerpt illustrates a self-authored stage 4 perspective. It comes from an interview with an officer at the Army War College (from research conducted by Philip Lewis and Owen Jacobs[6]). This individual is in his early 40s and has about 20 years of commissioned service. The officer is talking about an experience in which he felt his performance was particularly successful.

> I also feel to be successful you have to undergo hardships. You know, units and organizations, whether it's a staff organization—coming together not during good times, but overcoming bad times—inspections, field exercises, and stuff—that's where they come together. That's where you become successful. But my personal success is geared not by the jobs I have, by the ranks or medals I obtain, but by the accomplishments of the units and the people below me.

> WHAT'S THE MOST VALUABLE KIND OF INFORMATION THAT YOU GET FOR YOURSELF IN TERMS OF HOW YOU ARE DOING?

> It's my opinion, my assessment. I have never really doubted—even though OERs and awards from your superiors are nice pats on the back—probably my greatest satisfaction has always come from me just going out and watching somebody do something they could not do. Units who had problems before are now successful.

> SO IT'S YOUR OWN JUDGMENT ABOUT THESE THINGS?

> If I think that's the best we can do, then I feel good. That's my philosophy. There have been times where I thought we did a good job and my boss has not. But, once again, I felt good and at peace with myself.

This officer has a clear sense for how he evaluates his own success. It is a stage 4 understanding because it is based on an internal standard; it is not dependent on either tangible rewards (stage 2) or how others feel about or judge him (stage 3). What is most valuable about how this stage 4 officer constructs his understanding of his performance as a military officer is that he has his own internal compass for proceeding even when he is receiving ambiguous or conflicting signals from others.

In short, he can function as an independent decision-maker, one who shapes the environment in which he operates instead of merely reacting to it.

Transition between Stages

To this point in our discussion we have focused on Kegan's stages as if most individuals function at one of three adult stages. In fact, however, individuals spend a substantial part of their lives in transition between stages, as will be seen in the developmental data presented below. Committed as we are to the idea that it is desirable to attempt to facilitate psychological growth, it makes sense to try to understand the nature of developmental transitions. In general, individuals in transition demonstrate an ongoing involvement in both the conceptually simpler constructions of the earlier stage and the conceptually more complex constructions of the next stage. Consider the following excerpt from an interview with a West Point cadet:

> Like say you set a goal for, you know, I'm going to do a hundred push-ups. And you work real hard on it, and then one day you just get down—things are happening right—and you do a hundred. And you feel good about yourself, because you met the standard. And then you hand in your card and someone says, "Wow, a hundred push ups." Something like that, it boosts your confidence if you can do something. But I think it also boosts it a little bit if somebody would tell you that. "You did that well."
>
> TELL ME WHY IT SEEMS TO ADD TO THAT.
>
> I know it does add to it, but, ah, I'm not really sure why. . . . When people know that you can do something, well, then I think that's important.
>
> SO THERE'S SOMETHING ABOUT SOMEONE ELSE KNOWING YOU DID WELL THAT STRENGTHENS YOUR CONFIDENCE AT THIS POINT?
>
> And that's going back to it—if people have a good image of you then that boosts your confidence. You know, people will be more likely to put responsibility on your shoulders. People don't have to worry about you messing things up. And that is why, at times, I consider it a success. . . . But I think it's important to me to have a good image. And to have other people have a good image of you. And I think that, you know, that can only help in a whole bunch of different areas. I mean, it's hard to explain as to why I think a good image is important . . . . just don't think it's easy to explain.

From this excerpt and other portions of the interview, it is clear that this cadet was in the early part of a transition from Kegan's stage 2 to Kegan's stage 3. This is revealed in several ways. First, a whole new way of attaching meaning to the cadet's experience is beginning to emerge. It is so new that he is having difficulty explaining it to the interviewer. In addition, it appears that rather than merely determining his self-worth by meeting certain personal goals (the chief source of meaning at stage 2), he is attaining the ability to make another's image of him a part of his experience of himself (evidence of stage 3 simultaneous perspective-taking). So both a stage 2 and stage 3 source of identity are operating. It is early in the transition from stage 2 to stage 3, because the ultimate goal (and source of meaning) is his "getting things done," and the value of an internal sense of confidence, derived from how others see him, is that it helps him get things done.

A second example, illustrating early signs of the transition from stage 3 to stage 4, comes from an interview of an officer who is a student at the U.S. Army Command and General Staff College.[7] The officer is talking about how he has changed during his time at the Command and General Staff College and how he will present himself to his unit on taking up his next assignment.

> I can take a look at myself. What do I really stand for? Because when I leave here I don't want to be a product that is blown by the wind, you know, left and right. I want to enter an organization, introduce myself, interact, and then be known as, this is what _____ stands for. And I want to have a strong conviction that that's what's really important. And walk forward with that. And that they can count on that. That's where they hang their hat and say, okay, that's what he's all about. And to do that, I think again I've become more introspective.

In this excerpt, we see evidence of the beginning of the transition beyond stage 3, manifested in the officer's desire to have his own internal compass that guides his actions. He doesn't want to be blown about by external perceptions of who he is and what he should do. But his perspective is not yet a fully self-authoring (stage 4) perspective; it is still part of a shared experience—he wants to "be known as" an independent thinker. He is not yet centered in his *own* view of himself. We will have more to say about the types of experiences that promote developmental transitions at the end of the present chapter.

Research on Officer Identity Development

For the past decade, we have been involved in a research effort to understand Army officer development using Kegan's framework. Our goal has been to describe developmental shifts across an Army officer's career and to investigate the relationship between identity development and indicators of professional competence. In this chapter, we report our findings from a cross-sectional study of officer development from precommissioning through battalion command. Some of our data are taken from a much larger study of leadership development at the United States Military Academy, part of the Baseline Officer Longitudinal Data Set (BOLDS) Project. We have combined these longitudinal data with cross-sectional data gathered from majors and lieutenant colonels to produce an overall picture of officer identity development. One question we have addressed is whether there is evidence that cadets, who are just entering our profession, show lower levels of psychological maturity—narrower perspectives in Kegan's terms—than do mid-career and late career officers.

Research Participants

Cadet participants were randomly selected from the entire entering Class of 1998. Data from 38 cadets were collected during the first six weeks (Cadet Basic Training) of their first year (Time 1). Time 2 interviews were conducted with 31 of the original 38 participants during spring semester of the second year. Additionally, 24 new participants were randomly selected and interviewed for the first time, providing a total Time 2 sample of 55. During the senior year, 35 of those from the Time 2 group were reinterviewed (Time 3). Of these, 21 were part of the original Time 1 group, 34 had been interviewed at Time 2, and 20 were interviewed at all three points in time. Attrition was a function of a variety of factors, including resignation, involuntary separation, and refusal to participate. While these samples may appear small in size, they are actually quite large for this type of research—indeed, to our knowledge this is the largest longitudinal test of Kegan's theory, and it is the only one involving traditional college-age students in a professional school context. Officer participants represent convenient samples from two grade levels: majors and lieutenant colonels. Fourteen majors attending the U.S. Army Command and General Staff College in the Class of 1996,[8] and 28 officers attending the Industrial College of the Armed Forces and the Army War College in the Class of 1991, were interviewed.[9]

For all three groups of participants, developmental assessments involved semi-structured interviews using the method detailed by Lisa Lahey et al.[10] Following these procedures, trained interviewers prompted respondents to recall their own recent experiences in response to stimulus words printed on index cards. The stimulus words, reflecting emotion-laden themes, included *sad, success, torn, anxious and nervous*, and *important to me*. After thinking about their experiences and making notes on the cards, the respondents were invited to begin by describing one of the events that came to mind in response to a stimulus card. The interviewer then asked a series of follow-on questions to elicit the respondent's underlying perspective in seeking to understand the event. When the interviewer was able to elicit the respondent's underlying and most encompassing perspective, the interviewer invited the respondent to move on to describe an event elicited in response to another card. This second event was then explored to help the interviewer discover the most encompassing perspective the respondent was using to make sense of the event. An assessment interview normally lasted between 60 and 90 minutes during which three to four events were explored.

All interviews were audiotaped and transcribed into hard copy for scoring. Four psychologists trained in the Kegan interview and scoring procedures scored the cadet interviews at Time 1. Average inter-rater agreement across these 4 scorers ranged from 63 percent to 83 percent.[11] A single individual, a Kegan-trained expert with demonstrated expertise in administering and scoring constructive-developmental interviews, scored all the later (Time 2 and Time 3) cadet interviews, the CGSC interviews (majors), and the senior service college interviews (lieutenant colonels).

Cross-Sectional Data on Developmental Levels

Table 8-2 summarizes the developmental level scores for senior service college students, CGSC students, and USMA senior (Time 3) cadets. As can be seen, there is a general tendency for the senior service college students to have the highest developmental scores. Fully half of this sample of late-career officers were demonstrating full stage 4 levels. More than three-quarters of the rest were in the stage 3 to stage 4 transition, and none were scored below a full stage 3 level. The USMA seniors

Kegan Developmental Level Scores	USMA Seniors (N=32)	CGSC Students (N=13)	Senior Service College Students (N=28)
2	2 (6%)		
2-3 Transition	10 (31%)	4 (31%)	
3	14 (44%)	3 (23%)	3 (11%)
3-4 Transition	6 (19%)	1 (8%)	11 (40%)
4		5 (38%)	14 (50%)

Table 8-2. *Kegan Developmental Level Scores for Military Leaders at Three Different Career Points.*

showed the lowest developmental level scores. None were shown to be at Kegan's stage 4, and fully a third of this group had not yet reached stage 3. As expected, the mid-career CGSC officers were intermediate between the USMA cadets and the senior service college students in their developmental levels. Like the senior service college students, a substantial proportion (38 percent) of the CGSC officers had reached Kegan's stage 4. Interestingly, the same proportion of CGSC students scored in the stage 2 to stage 3 transition as did USMA seniors (31 percent in both groups).

In short, there was a much broader range of developmental level scores among the CGSC students than might be expected. It is not clear what to make of this finding. It should be acknowledged that the sample of CGSC students was quite small (N = 13), and it is not clear how this sample was selected. The CGSC interviewer was a CGSC student at the time of the interviews, and it appears that he recruited interviewees from those students he knew personally. If this is true, then the sample may not have been representative of the entire class of CGSC officers. In contrast, the senior service college students were nearly all of the students in three seminar groups. The senior service colleges (in this instance the U.S. Army War College and the Industrial College of the Armed Forces) attempt to assign students to seminar groups in a manner that insures that all the seminar groups are roughly comparable.

The other major difference between CGSC officers and senior service college officers is that the latter colleges are more selective. At the time the Kegan interviews were conducted, approximately 65 percent of the Army's majors were selected for the resident CGSC program, whereas only 10 percent to 12 percent of the Army's lieutenant colonels were selected for a resident senior service college program. In short, the senior service college students are a more highly selected sample than are CGSC students. It is possible, therefore, that the apparent increase in developmental levels between mid-career and late career suggested by these data is actually only a reflection of the selection effect. In other words, it is possible (perhaps even likely) that more of the officers who are already at Kegan's stage 4 when they are majors get promoted and sent to a senior service college than do majors who are at stage 3 or lower.

It is harder to argue that the differences between the senior cadet developmental level scores and the other two groups are a function of differential selection. None of the 32 USMA seniors who were interviewed had yet achieved Kegan's stage 4. Indeed, only two were well into the stage 3 to stage 4 transition. It seems likely, therefore, that the stage 3 to stage 4 developmental transition, if it is to take place

Kegan Developmental Level Scores	Freshmen (N=38)	Sophomores (N=52)	Seniors (N=32)
2	8 (21%)	12 (23%)	2 (6%)
2-3 Transition	24 (63%)	27 (52%)	10 (31%)
3	6 (16%)	10 (19%)	14 (44%)
3-4 Transition		3 (6%)	6 (19%)

Table 8-3. *Cross-Sectional Kegan Developmental Level Scores for USMA Class of 1998 as Freshmen, Sophomores, and Seniors.*

at all, is traversed only after officers have embarked on their Army careers. The other cross-sectional data bearing on the question of whether there are progressive changes in Kegan developmental levels are the USMA Class of 1998 interview data collected during the freshman, sophomore, and senior years (the senior year data were also presented above). Recall that not all cadets in the USMA sample were interviewed at all three time points. Indeed, a new sample of cadets was randomly selected and then added to the interview study during the sophomore year. These cadet data, therefore, can be considered cross-sectional; they are presented in Table 8-3. The longitudinal data for USMA cadets interviewed both sophomore and senior years are presented later in the present chapter.

In general, these cross-sectional cadet data are consistent with the proposition that Kegan interview scores reflect a progressive developmental process. The most striking finding shown in Table 8-3 is the dramatic increase in the percent of cadets scored as functioning at Kegan's stage 3 and above in the senior year. At the beginning of the freshman year only 16 percent were at stage 3. By the middle of the sophomore year this percentage had risen to 25 percent. By the senior year, these percentages had more than doubled to 62 percent. These data suggest that there is, for many cadets, significant developmental progress between the freshman and senior years.

Longitudinal Data on Developmental Levels

A more direct assessment of developmental change can be gained by inspecting the Kegan stage scores of those USMA cadets who were interviewed on two occasions. Data from the sophomore and senior years provide direct support for the proposition that for many West Point cadets the college years are a time of significant developmental change. Sixteen of the 28 subjects (57 percent) showed developmental progression. Only 2 subjects showed regression. Of the 10 subjects who showed no change from their sophomore to their senior years, half were already at stage 3 during their sophomore year, a stage beyond which many college students are not expected to move until somewhat later in adulthood, if at all. With the exception of the two instances of regression, which could be a function of the difficulty of obtaining a reliable developmental score, the longitudinal data suggest that Kegan developmental level scores are tapping a variable that shows progressive developmental change for many cadets during the college years.

Previous descriptions of the stage 2-to-3 transition have suggested that this developmental shift typically takes place during the preteen or early teen years.[12] However, these descriptions have not been based on actual data. The study we report here, the only one with a college-age cohort, suggests that this key transition takes place somewhat later, probably during the late teens and early 20s. We speculate that this finding also holds true for cadets in ROTC programs as well.

Implications for Officer Professional Identity Development

Preoccupied with their own needs and interests, those cadets who are still functioning at Kegan's stage 2 cannot be expected to have the broad, internalized understanding of and commitment to ethical codes and other professional standards that we ask in our officer development programs. Rather, stage 2 cadets will likely see ethical codes and professional standards solely as guides for behavior. They are likely to conform their actions to these guides in order to garner rewards and avoid negative consequences. Cadet development programs will not be successful in instilling desired values in these less mature cadets unless the broad educational environment in which they operate promotes identity development toward a shared perspective on officer professionalism (i.e., to Kegan's stage 3). Consequently, cadet development programs should be tailored with this in mind. Programs should encourage cadets to behave in ways that are consistent with the professional values while at the same time promoting development of a shared perspective for considering those values that is grounded in a sense of what it means to be a member of a profession. This is indeed what happens at the United States Military Academy, and, as our data suggest, many cadets appear to make progress toward a stage 3 understanding during their cadet years. Precommissioning programs at West Point appear to be successful in socializing cadets into the profession—cadets are "joining the profession" and becoming members of the officer corps. However, it is also clear that very few cadets at West Point are likely to have developed to the point where they are self-authoring professionals—stage 4—by the time they are commissioned.

Turning now to the cross-sectional findings for the officer samples, we see what appears to be progress from stage 3 to stage 4 between the end of precommissioning and mid career, at least for most officers. It seems highly likely that most lieutenants and captains function with at least a stage 3 perspective of themselves and their experiences.[13] Hence, they see themselves as members of the profession. From a stage 3 point of view, they understand themselves in terms of the expectations that the profession has of them, and these expectations are organized around qualities that characterize an officer. But the stage 3 officer is also subject to the expectations of others outside the profession—spouses, children, parents, and friends. Because stage 3 individuals internalize others' expectations, their primary developmental challenge comes about when the expectations of these different sources are in conflict—such as family and profession. We expect that stage 3 officers will experience considerable tension when trying to resolve these competing demands. Indeed, an inability to do so may be an important source of the recent retention problem with Army captains.

However, if properly managed these challenges can set the stage for the transition from stage 3 to stage 4. Our sample of majors showed considerable variability. A few are still completing the stage 2-to-3 transition. We were surprised to find evidence of stage 2 functioning—officers still subject to personal agendas—in this select group of officers. On the other hand, many officers in the sample of CGSC majors (38 percent) had completed the transition from stage 3 to stage 4, manifesting the internalization of personal value systems with which they should be able to resolve conflicting demands. An even larger proportion of our sample of senior service college lieutenant colonels (50 percent) had completed the transition from stage 3 to stage 4. The remaining officers are still in transition from Kegan's stage 3 to stage 4.

In the aggregate, these findings indicate a pattern of continued development toward a principle-centered, self-authored understanding of officer professionalism as one advances in rank. In the absence of complete longitudinal data, it is difficult to know for certain whether these findings actually represent development or whether they show the effects of selection of higher functioning officers across the career span. However, they are at least suggestive of developmental possibilities. Furthermore, the results suggest that experiences during the second decade of a career—roughly the period from the staff college to the senior service college—may encourage the transition from stage 3 to stage 4 perspectives.

To most Army officers, the term "officer professional development," or OPD, summons an image of dayroom classes, professional reading lists, and staff rides. Thus far, the Army's approach to professional development has primarily emphasized improving tactical and technical expertise by filling officers' professional kitbags with the latest knowledge and skills, the latest training and doctrine. While such an approach works well to keep officers "informed," it may be less effective in promoting professional identity development. If redefining and renewing the Army profession requires fundamentally changing officers' self-concepts, can we rely on our traditional training model to help us "*trans*form" the officer corps? Will officers who are simply better "*in*formed" be able to meet the increasingly complex demands of the 21st century?

The present chapter offers an alternative way to think about these questions and officer professional development, both as to what is being developed and how we might attempt to influence it. In terms of the Army's doctrinal BE, KNOW, DO leadership framework, the task of reprofessionalizing the Army is primarily one aimed at the BE component. Clearly, "developing" professional knowledge and skills is important to "being" a professional; but when we talk about "development" in this chapter, we are talking about influencing officers' self-concepts, their sense of who they are, their worldview, how they know what they know, their character, their identity.

To be successful in this new era, today's officers not only have to be better informed, they also have to be more mature psychologically. Increasingly, modern officers are required to make sense of unstructured tasks, exercise judgment under conditions of ambiguity and uncertainty, and do so with little or no direction from higher headquarters. Leading under such conditions, we argue, requires officers who are not only tactically and technically expert, but also those who operate from a broader perspective, who "see more of the world" —in short, those who are more psychologically mature adults. Developing enough officers equipped with such self-concepts or identities is an essential task if we are to succeed at redefining and renewing the Army as a profession. Our research has implications for how the Army approaches officer education, career management, and Army reprofessionalization itself. To tip the scales in favor of professionalization as opposed to bureaucratization, we will have to emphasize education (long-term, deep understanding) in addition to training (short-term, efficient performance) in overall officer development.

Many of the demands currently placed on officers throughout their careers require levels of psychological maturity beyond what they have achieved. Structural limitations imposed by each stage of adult development have significant implications for how officers make sense of their professional experiences. Knowing where officers are in their structural development should inform what we can reasonably expect from them, how we educate them, how we assign them, and ultimately how we approach their further development.

Recommendations

As a profession, we must come to grips with the fundamental differences between *training*, *education*, and *development*. Each intervention process has its place; each has its limitations. Redefining and renewing our profession are primarily an educational and developmental challenge. Our ingrained tendency will be to *train* our way out of this. But an approach based primarily on a traditional training paradigm will not achieve the types of outcomes we require to remain a vibrant profession. Our current organizational structure and culture do not support officer *development*; they support *training*. How do *education* and *development* relate to the Army's Training and Doctrine Command (TRADOC)?

We propose that the Army reorient TRADOC's mission to include *education* and *training* as subsets of the broader process of officer *development*. To the extent possible, the Army should focus on skill acquisition (training) in units and organize to educate and develop in the schoolhouse. As recommended in the *Army Training and Leader Development Panel Report (Officers)*, "Leaders should focus on *developing* the 'enduring competencies' of self-awareness and adaptability."[14] To develop these enduring competencies, we must acknowledge the limitations of training and better organize to support *education* and *development*.

If many officers are in over their heads from a psychological development perspective, then perhaps it's time to reconsider our entire approach to how we select, evaluate, promote, and assign officers within our profession. If the trend continues towards a more distributed battlefield, characterized by increased volatility, uncertainty, complexity, and ambiguity; toward smaller units having increasingly lethal weapons and mobility; toward command by officers who have to react faster to more significant challenges at lower and lower levels with greater and greater autonomy—then perhaps the British have it right. Perhaps we should consider 40-year-old company commanders.

We propose that promotions and assignments be based on a broader definition of officer development. Our post-Cold War Army requires officers who are more "psychologically mature" at more junior levels. We should reconsider our current approach to officer assignments, which is based primarily on the size of the unit, and instead align officers and positions based on the level of perspective-taking required by the position and the developmental level of the officer. We should consider, for example, assigning much more senior (psychologically mature) officers to much smaller units. The Army should also consider using complete 360-degree feedback and self-assessment mechanisms "with teeth" tied into officer evaluation reports for all officer operational assignments to better support the development of our two "enduring competencies"—self-awareness and adaptability.

The Army profession is currently facing significant boundary/jurisdictional issues—an identity crisis with both institutional and individual implications. This chapter adds an additional dimension to this debate—the psychological-structural dimension. Understanding officer development from this perspective raises several profound issues. First, it is very difficult to understand, let alone thoughtfully change, contexts in which you are psychologically embedded. Therefore, it may take officers with at least a stage 4 perspective (independent of the existing institution) to effectively resolve fundamental issues of professional identity. Second, one of the primary characteristics of a profession is its ability to "self-regulate." Our research suggests that perhaps it also takes someone with a stage 4 (self-authoring) perspective to truly "lead" a profession as opposed to merely being a "member of" a profession. Ultimately it is up to commissioned officers to redefine and renew the Army as a profession. Such a daunting task will require an officer corps made up not only of technically and tactically proficient bureaucrats, but also of psychologically mature professionals. We believe that understanding officer development from a psychological perspective will help us significantly in our quest to develop effective professional identities for 21st century Army officers.

Notes

1. An earlier version of this chapter appears in *The Future of the Army Profession*, proj. directors Don M. Snider and Gayle L. Watkins, ed. Lloyd J. Matthews (Boston: McGraw-Hill, 2002), 357-78. Research for this chapter was supported in part by the Army Research Institute for the Behavioral and Social Sciences. The views and opinions expressed in this chapter are those of the authors and are not necessarily those of the Department of the Army or any other U.S. government entity.

2. The 7 Army Values are: loyalty, duty, respect, selfless service, honor, integrity, and personal courage. The Principles of Officership as discussed in the United States Military Academy's Cadet Leader Development System are: duty, honor, loyalty, service to country, competence, teamwork, subordination, and leadership.

3. Robert Kegan, *The Evolving Self: Problem and Process in Human Development* (Cambridge, MA: Harvard University Press, 1982); Robert Kegan, *In Over Our Heads: The Mental Demands of Modern Life* (Cambridge, MA: Harvard University Press, 1994).

4. Derived from Kegan, *The Evolving Self*, 86.

5. Kegan, *In Over Our Heads*, 192-195.

6. Philip Lewis and T. O. Jacobs, "Individual Differences in Strategic Leadership Capacity: A Constructive/Developmental View," in *Strategic Leadership: A Multiorganizational-Level Perspective*, eds. R. L. Phillips and J. G. Hunt (Westport, CT: Quorum Books, 1992), 121-137.

7. We are indebted to Lt. Col. Patrick Sweeney for conducting interviews with officer students at the U. S. Army Command and General Staff College. The data from the interview sample were gathered by Colonel Sweeney while he was a student at the staff college in 1995-1996.

8. Interviews were conducted by Lt. Col. Patrick Sweeney.

9. Interviews were conducted by Dr. Philip Lewis as part of another study.

10. Lisa Lahey et al., *A Guide to the Subject Object Interview: Its Administration and Interpretation* (Cambridge, MA: Harvard University Graduate School of Education, Subject-Object Research Group, 1988).

11. Interview scores may represent a full stage (e.g., stage 2 or 3) or a transition between stages (somewhere between two stages).

12. Kegan, *The Evolving Self*, 167; Lahey et al., *Guide to the Subject-Object Interview*, 94-131.

13. Preliminary data from a sample of Army captains enrolled in a master's degree program in preparation for the role of West Point tactical officers for the Corps of Cadets suggest that the vast majority of these officers are functioning at stage 3.

14. *The Army Training and Leader Development Panel (Officers) Report* (Ft. Leavenworth, KS: Combined Arms Center, 2001), OS-3; available from http://www.army.mil/atld/report/pdf; Internet; accessed 16 August 2001.

III

The Expert Knowledge of the Army Profession

The social-trustee type of vocational profession provides a needed service to the society it serves, one that is based on the application of an expertise generally beyond the capabilities of citizens in that society. Unless that were the case, there would be no rationale for such professions; citizens could provide the services for themselves either individually or by forming markets and buying and selling services from each other. Thus, the underlying expert knowledge which undergirds the expertise of practice, developed over extensive years of study, reflection, and experience, is what sets professions apart from other producing organizations. In most cases professions come to hold a near monopoly over their expert knowledge, being careful to maintain and adapt it over time as needed to be able to serve their clients. And, while in this era of information-age economies many professions in Western countries are experiencing declining legitimacy due to the loss of control over their knowledge (e.g., one can download a draft will from the internet rather than hire a lawyer, etc.), that has not yet become the case with military professions.

Thus the critical core of the Army profession will remain its expert knowledge; and it will remain true, as has long been understood, that military professions cannot practice what they do not "know" within that core of abstract expert knowledge. One need look no further for the truth of this statement than to the U.S. Army in Iraq. With only a paucity of expert knowledge in the field of counterinsurgency, it is currently experiencing great difficulty in quelling an adaptive, resilient assortment of insurgents fighting to prevent the installation of a freely elected government.

Part III, then, is a set of four chapters that focus on different aspects of the expert knowledge of the Army profession. Central to these chapters, and indeed to all chapters that follow in the book, is the mapping of the Army's expert knowledge in Chapter 9 by Lt. Col. Richard Lacquement. To our knowledge this is the first attempt by anyone, Army professional or official agency, to disaggregate the four broad clusters of the Army profession's expert knowledge and correlate it with competing sources of expertise, with functional areas and specialty branches, and with jurisdictions. Of particular importance to the leaders of the Army profession is the attempt to ascertain the most appropriate source of each field of expert knowledge, i.e., whether it must be generated by uniformed professionals from within the Army or, alternatively, brought into the profession from other military professions or even from commercial sources. Over the past two years this mapping has been vetted before many audiences, both uniformed and civilian, before it reached the present form. As it is vetted further by those who study and teach from this text, we anticipate that this map will be refined, serving as an analytic tool for those responsible within the Army profession for keeping its expert knowledge current and for prioritizing its jurisdictional competitions.

In some form, the remaining chapters in Part III extend from the framework presented by Lacquement. In Chapter 10, Lt. Col. Jeffrey Peterson and I argue that it is in the Army profession's interest to recognize that a new field of joint expert knowledge has emerged, one lying beyond the expertise of America's warfighting professions, and it will best be maintained and adapted to the future by a new military profession—a joint profession. Establishing such a profession would stand in remarkable contrast to the inefficiencies of the present situation under the Goldwater-Nichols Act of 1986, wherein the war-fighting professions provide temporarily "borrowed" military manpower to staff the Joint Commands under which American forces now, and in the future, will fight. In Chapter 11, Nadia Schadlow and her colleagues argue that perhaps another category of expert knowledge needs to be added to the Army's map, the knowledge of post-conflict governance. Drawing both from Army history and from the current operational experiences in Afghanistan and Iraq, they make a compelling argument that, as the provider of durable land power for the nation's security, the Army profession should forcefully claim legitimacy over this expert knowledge and apply it within the jurisdictions of major combat operations and stability operations.

Extending the Army map in the direction of the provenance of its expert knowledge, Prof. Deborah Avant in Chapter 12 addresses one of the most disturbing conclusions from the first research project: the clearly recognized fact that the Army has been contracting out expert work at a dizzying pace since the drawdown of the 1990s, but doing so without a deliberated pattern or concern with the long-term effects. Professions that lose control over the production and adaptation of their expert knowledge are quickly headed for the status of nonprofessions. Avant's analysis will give pause to any Army professional who reads it and samples the research in this growing field.

Thus two themes emerge in Part III—jointness and outsourcing of expertise—trends that can have profound effects on the Army as profession, particularly as to the Army's claim on its professional knowledge, its professional practices, and the boundary distinguishing members of the profession from others. The researchers of these chapters, as well as many in the subsequent parts of this book, shared the concern that the Army has neither recognized the power of these influences nor critically and adequately thought through its responses.

9 Mapping Army Professional Expertise and Clarifying Jurisdictions of Practice

Richard Lacquement

Introduction

This quotation from FM 1, the Army's capstone manual, declares broad and compelling responsibilities for the Army. Aside from the priority for war-fighting, however, it provides an undifferentiated and almost limitless range of operations for which the Army must prepare. This is a noble aspiration reflecting the best can-do spirit of loyal service to the nation. But it is a problematic foundation obscuring significant limitations and trade-offs required to concentrate the Army's finite resources—personnel, material, and funds—on the most important requirements. Changes in the international security environment and in technology challenge leaders to redefine the Army's role for the future. Effective strategic leadership of the Army profession will be an essential component of successful transformation. To serve American society effectively, strategic leaders of the profession must redefine, prioritize, and delimit the declared expert knowledge of the profession; clarify the jurisdictions within which this knowledge applies; and then develop professionals who are experts in applying this knowledge.

> Our nonnegotiable contract with the American people is to fight and win the nation's wars. Every other task is subordinate to that commitment. To discharge our responsibilities to the Nation, we maintain several core competencies. These are the essential and enduring capabilities of our service. They encompass the full range of military operations across the spectrum of conflict, from sustained land dominance in wartime to supporting civil authorities during natural disasters and consequence management.
>
> —FIELD MANUAL 1, THE ARMY[1]

This chapter provides a framework for articulating more coherently the Army's professional expertise and jurisdictions. A centerpiece of this effort is a proposed knowledge map of the Army profession. This chapter also articulates an approach to the settlement of jurisdictional claims that should guide strategic leaders as they negotiate with the profession's clients—American society and America's elected leaders. It is also a framework for debate among *all* members of the profession. An important goal of this effort is to generate an exchange of ideas that leads to a renewed consensus on the Army's professional essence.

Statement of the Problem

The Army is at a crossroads. Its traditions, recent successes, and capabilities are praiseworthy, but its appropriate focus for the future is uncertain. "Full-Spectrum Dominance" makes for a great bumper sticker, but it is of limited practical utility as a doctrine for a profession. It glosses over too much. It lacks boundaries. It lacks priorities. Moreover, even though full-spectrum dominance may be an appropriate aspiration for the armed forces of the United States as a whole, it does little to clarify the unique and particularly valuable contributions the Army and its professional leaders should make to joint interdependence with other armed services and governmental agencies.[3]

The current era is one of broad missions and uncertain challenges. As the Cold War drew to a close, American performance in Operation Desert Storm benefited greatly from the long-time preparation for possible conventional warfare against the Soviets. The Desert Storm mission fit the Army's preferred concept of war and was well suited to the human expertise developed in the latter stages of the Cold War. In contrast, numerous peace operations such as those in Somalia, Haiti, Bosnia, and Kosovo were not well fitted to the training and organization of the Cold War-configured Army. Similarly, the Army has had impressive success in major combat operations in Afghanistan and Iraq; however, in both missions there have been difficulties in dealing with unconventional warfare and post-conflict stabilization. These difficulties are indicative of a persistent tension at the heart of the Army's understanding of its expert knowledge. The tension also affects how training, force structure, and other preparations condition the Army's performance when the institution is called upon by society.

> The Army needs to redraw the map of its expert knowledge and then inform and reform its educational and developmental systems accordingly, resolving any debate over the appropriate expertise of America's Army. . . .
>
> The Army faces increasing jurisdictional competitions with new competitors. Thus its jurisdictional boundaries must be constantly negotiated and clarified by officers comfortable at the bargaining table and skilled in dealing with professional colleagues on matters touching the profession's civil-military and political-military boundaries.[2]
>
> —Gayle Watkins and Don Snider

Intellectual Foundations

This chapter builds on two concepts. The first is the concept of the military profession provided in Samuel Huntington's classic study, *The Soldier and the State*.[4] Second is the concept of professional adaptation and adjustment as described by Andrew Abbott in *The System of Professions*.[5] Huntington provides a widely known and commonly understood definition of the military profession that I have adjusted slightly to provide an updated foundational meaning of the term *Army profession*. Abbott provides a framework for understanding how professions adapt and sustain themselves by negotiating and clarifying the content and control of their work relative to that of other professions.

In Huntington, a profession is "a peculiar type of functional group with highly specialized characteristics."[6] More specifically, to him a profession is defined by its expertise, responsibility, and corporateness.[7] With regard to the military officer,

Huntington states, "The direction, operation, and control of a human organization whose primary function is the application of violence is the peculiar skill of the officer."[8] The responsibility of a profession is to its client. "The military profession is monopolized by the state. The skill of the officer is the management of violence; his responsibility is the military security of his client, society."[9]

Thus, to Huntington the Army's professional core is found among its officers. They are required to master a body of abstract professional knowledge and understand the moral, ethical, political, and social contexts within which military work takes place. They must be experts, first and foremost, in the human dimensions—leadership, morale, and physical capacity—that underlie effective military operations to accomplish the objectives that society, through the government, assigns them.[10]

Refined to reflect this quintessentially human endeavor, the core expertise of American officers can be restated as follows: *The peculiar skill of the military officer is the development, operation, and leadership of a human organization—a profession—whose primary expertise is the application of coercive force on behalf of the American people; for the Army officer, such development, operation, and leadership occurs incidentally to sustaining America's dominance in land warfare.* In abbreviated form, I will refer to this core expertise as *leadership of Army soldiers in the organized application of coercive force.*

Huntington also suggests that the most appropriate means to attain effective military subordination is to maintain a clear division between the realms of civilian and military responsibility.[11] A common critique of Huntington is that this separation is easy to stipulate in theory but hard to realize in practice (see Chapter 2 in the present anthology). As Clausewitz implies, since war is merely an instrument of policy, it is difficult to separate the purely military from the purely political.[12] To validate the importance of military advice, there should be standards to help determine appropriate boundaries. Defining professional expertise and jurisdictions more distinctly will assist in establishing in a clearer manner these necessary standards for circumscribing the soldier's proper domain.

Andrew Abbott identifies another key property of professions. Professions compete with each other to determine legitimate realms within which to apply their expertise.[13] Abbott defines professions as "somewhat exclusive groups of individuals applying somewhat abstract knowledge to particular cases."[14] Professions provide social goods to address important problems. "The tasks of professions," Abbott tells us, "are human problems amenable to expert service."[15] The central phenomenon of professional life is thus "the link between a profession and its work, a link [called] jurisdiction."[16] A profession interacts with clients and other professions to clarify the jurisdictions within which it operates and the division of labor for work within jurisdictions. "Every profession aims for a heartland of work over which it has complete, legally-established control," Abbott concludes. However, *full* control is not always possible. There are five other possible settlements. Disputed jurisdictions may be settled by division of labor that can lead to *shared* jurisdiction over the same body of work or to *split* jurisdiction, a clear division of the same body of work. Other jurisdictional settlements occur when a profession maintains *advisory* control over certain aspects of work within a jurisdiction while letting other professions perform practical work; or, conversely, when a profession accepts a *subordinate* role such that another profession controls a jurisdiction but within which the first profession may still do practical work. Finally, professions may also divide jurisdictions according to the nature of the *client*.[17]

With so much as background, I shall now address the fundamental questions Army leaders must answer in order to redefine the Army profession:

- *What is the nature of the Army's expert knowledge? How should relevant expertise be prioritized?*
- *What are the jurisdictions within which this expertise may be legitimately applied? How should jurisdictions be prioritized? Which should be claimed and defended? Which should be avoided if possible? Which should be relinquished?*

These are recurring questions that leaders of the profession must constantly reexamine. The questions yield descriptive answers for the present and suggestive answers for the future. Strategic leaders of the Army profession must negotiate the answers with the civilian leaders who act as agents for American society, producing yet another important civil-military interface.

Ultimately, civilian leaders decide the Army's jurisdictions. But, Army strategic leaders must represent the profession in the negotiations that occur in this decision-making process. Civilian leaders' decisions become part of the process that requires strategic leaders of the profession to reevaluate and modify conceptions of expert knowledge and jurisdiction.

This chapter is focused explicitly on the Army profession as consisting of the commissioned officer corps.[18] This is not meant to slight warrant officers, noncommissioned officers, or junior enlisted soldiers. These highly skilled workers are the experts in the numerous necessary tasks that allow the Army to succeed; their tremendous skills are undoubtedly central to Army success. But the nature of their responsibilities is fundamentally different from that of the Army's commissioned officers. The diagnoses, inferences, and treatments of societal problems for which such skills are appropriately applied are the responsibilities of the commissioned officers who are guardians of the profession's and the institution's essence.[19]

The framework provided is also applicable to officers of all components of the total Army (active, U.S. Army Reserve, and Army National Guard). With respect to the National Guard, the dynamic of jurisdictional definition and negotiation is complicated by the dual allegiance to national and state leaders. For Army National Guard leaders, the negotiation may be more nuanced, but the principles and logic are the same.[20]

Defining the Map of the Army's Expert Knowledge

Professions succeed or fail to the degree that they provide expertise that clients need. Most professions operate in market, consumer-driven environments. The Army profession, even though encompassed within a government-monopolized bureaucracy, is hardly immune to somewhat similar market-driven forces; however, American society is the sole client of the Army. The Army's legitimacy and effectiveness are measured entirely in relation to meeting American society's demands for defense and security.

The suggested knowledge map of the Army profession represents an effort to portray what is unique about the Army and its expertise. It also suggests how such expertise is related to society. There are four broad categories of expertise required by the Army:

> Our unique contribution to national security is prompt, sustained land dominance across the range of military operations and spectrum of conflict. The Army provides the land force dominance essential to shaping the international security environment.[21]
>
> —FM 1, THE ARMY

- *Military-Technical*. This is the Army's core expertise, that is, "how the profession prepares for and conducts land operations combining Army soldiers with organizations, doctrine, and technology."[23] This skill requires mastery of applying violent means to accomplish policy ends.

> To provide dominant land power, the Army balances its core competencies and capabilities to train and equip Soldiers and grow leaders and provide relevant and ready land power capability to the combatant commander and the joint team.[22]
>
> —ARMY TRANSFORMATION ROADMAP, 2003

- *Human Development*. This skill is the vital leadership component, that is, "the Army's management of its human resources" and "creating, developing, and maintaining expert knowledge, and embedding that knowledge in members of the profession."[24] This expertise includes how to maximize the effectiveness of the Army's people. It also includes professional development and understanding academic fields relevant to Army training and education.
- *Moral-Ethical*. Here, the expertise concerns the moral nature of professional duties—both to members of the institution and to society. According to Don Snider and Gayle Watkins, "The nature of the profession is such that only moral soldiers can discharge their professional duties, and the Army's strategic leaders are morally obligated to the client to maintain a profession of both competence and character."[25] This obligation includes an understanding of how to apply coercive force ethically and the ethics that govern the appropriate relationship of military professionals to society itself.
- *Political-Cultural*. To cite Snider and Watkins again, "The Army profession serves its collective client, the American people, through interactions with the citizenry's elected and appointed leaders and the nation's other government agencies."[26] Army leaders require expertise to manage interaction between the Army and the broader defense community (public, industry, government). Such expertise includes the critical task of representing the profession to society and advising society on the use of the profession's expertise.[27] This expertise also includes cultural awareness and sensitivity fundamental to the governance of local populations in combat zones and in constabulary missions.

Relevant aspects of expertise include where the expertise is applied, where it should be acquired, and how it is applied.

Where applied? If practitioners in an area of expertise must be readily available within combat zones, there are good reasons for the Army to commission the practitioners in order to acquire such expertise within the organization. In these cases, the expectation of operating in a violent environment is a key consideration (e.g., medics, chaplains, drivers, pilots).[28] If the expertise doesn't ever need to be applied in a combat zone, there may be no need for the practitioners to be Army members.

Where acquired? Who controls the life cycle of expertise development and educational advancement? For Army-prime expertise, the Army should be responsible for the entire life cycle of expertise development and application. For expertise created elsewhere in society, but with specialized Army applications, the Army is responsible for developing the capacity for Army-specific aspects. For expertise with general applications in society, the Army should leave training and development to others, but must impose quality control in the recruitment and hiring process.

How applied? Is there a particular ethical or moral element peculiar to Army application of specific expert knowledge? Is there need for ethical control of such expertise that is lacking in society? A good example would be the use of information technology as a form of warfare (to hurt, kill, or disable civilians through effects on societal infrastructure or other public goods).

Table 9-1, portraying schematically a map of the Army profession's expert knowledge, provides an institutional perspective on the relevant elements. Fields of expert knowledge are identified by their applicability to the Army's core expertise: the leadership of Army soldiers in organized application of coercive force. This is the heartland of the Army's abstract expert knowledge to which all other expertise relates. Reading down the five columns—Ia, Ib, II, III, and IV—we find skills and functions that assist in classifying and prioritizing areas of relevant expertise:

Ia. Army Primacy: Here, the Army has prime, if not unique, expertise. The ability to succeed in sustained land warfare is the indisputable core responsibility of the Army. The Army cannot delegate this responsibility. The expertise shown here differs from that of other military services by its identification with *sustained* land warfare.

Ib. Army and Other Services Share Unique Expertise: These are elements of expertise shared by the Army and at least one other military service. They relate the unique expertise of the Army to that of the other American military services (as in joint operations) and American military allies (as in combined operations) as applied on behalf of American society.

II. Army Adapts Civilian Professional Expertise: These elements of expert knowledge have counterparts within the broader society; however, within the Army profession, the application of this expertise requires an important and unique adaptation. For example, medicine is a body of expert knowledge required by society as a whole. The Army has a requirement for adapting this expertise to the demands of Army operations—especially combat. The adaptation requires additional training or schooling.

	Expertise Applicability and Priority	Ia. Army Primacy Ib.	Ib. Army and Other Services Share Unique Expertise	II. Army Adapts Civilian Professional Expertise	III. Army May Adapt Civilian Professional Expertise or Hire Civilian Professionals	IV. Army Hires Civilian Professionals
	Character of Expertise	Core	Core	Core Support	Acquired	Borrowed
	How Acquired	Army Exclusive	Military Exclusive	Army and Society	Contract in from society	Contract out to society
	Developmental Responsibility	Army	Military	Society with Army Component	Society with Army Quality Control	Society
	Certification	Army	Military	Army	Army and Society	Society
Military-Technical Expert Knowledge	Leadership of Human Organizations in Application of Coercive Force	X (sustained land warfare)	X (general warfare)			
	Land Combat	X				
	Land Combat Support	X				
	Joint Operations		X			
	Combined Operations		X			
	Admin/ Logistics			X		
	Engineering/Science			X		
	Info Technology			X		
Human Development Expert Knowledge	Leadership	X				
	Human Behavior			X		
	Physical Fitness			X		
	Education			X		
	Combat Medicine			X		
	Family Medicine				X	
	Social Work				X	
Moral-Ethical Expert Knowledge	Military Ethics	X	X			
	Character Development	X	X			
	Legal			X		
	Solider Spirituality			X		
Political-Cultural Expert Knowledge	Advice on Behalf of and Representation of the Profession	X	X			
	Military Governance	X				
	Political Negotiation			X		
	Diplomacy (attaché)		X	X		
	Resource Acquisition & Management				X	X
Other	Basic Research					X

Table 9-1. *Map of the Army Profession's Expert Knowledge.*

III. Army May Adapt Civilian Professional Expertise or Hire Civilian Professionals: These are elements of expert knowledge for which society and military applications are the same. For example, resource acquisition and management expertise is the same for the Army as it is for most civilian businesses. The key distinction is that the Army has frequently recurring needs for this expertise and of the individuals who can apply it for Army missions. When extensive familiarity with the Army's operations, norms, and values is important to the appropriate exercise of such expertise on the Army's behalf, individual experts in these areas may be developed among members of the profession. To the degree that such familiarity is less crucial, experts can be hired directly from civilian society to apply the expertise on behalf of the Army. The exercise of expertise in these areas often involves a combination of Army professionals and civilian experts. The Army professionals in these areas provide the valuable capacity to lead, conduct liaison, and conform an area of general expertise to Army purposes. Civilian experts in these areas are hired by the Army on contract, e.g., as Title 10 appointees. Whether individuals with such expertise are drawn from the uniformed ranks of the Army or are given formal appointments within the uniformed Army should be driven by considerations of necessary ethical and legal controls required either in the application of the expertise or by the need for the work to take place in a combat zone.

IV. Army Hires Civilian Professionals: The last column reflects areas of expertise in society that may be borrowed and applied by non-Army professionals as needs arise and without the more demanding social and ethical controls created by integrating such practitioners directly into the Army. If such expertise is available to be borrowed, there is no need to integrate it internally. Such functions or work can be contracted out.

Defining the Expert Knowledge of Individual Professionals

The previous section provided a framework for understanding the areas of expert knowledge required by the Army at the institutional level. The combination of numerous professionals with diverse paths of development and integration provide the aggregate pool of expertise to serve the profession. The next step is to suggest a map of the expertise of individual Army professionals.

Future challenges will place high demands on new officers.

> The art and science of leadership continues to be our stock in trade, with leader development the lifeblood of the profession. The Army supports Joint Transformation by developing innovative and adaptive leaders comfortable operating in joint, interagency, and multinational environments.[29]
>
> —ARMY TRANSFORMATION ROADMAP, 2003

Officers of the 21st century must be flexible, principled, and self-learning. These officers will be challenged to lead American soldiers and make complex decisions in complicated environments with little or no time. They will be part Harvard professor, part professional athlete, part ambassador, and all disciplined war-fighter. It will take each one of these attributes to be successful on the 21st century battlefield.[30]

This set of requirements is a tall order for the individual officer. The Army as a profession needs the expertise of professors, athletes, ambassadors, and war-fighters. The degree to which each professional must possess all this expertise is an important consideration. This section suggests a framework for understanding the appropriate relationship of the profession's general requirements with the manner in which individuals develop expertise to meet the profession's specific demands. It suggests a framework for professional expertise appropriate to both generalists and specialists. It notes that all members of the profession cannot be masters of every area of expert knowledge required by the Army as an institution. It recognizes that soldiers and their leaders must be "warriors first, specialists second" and thus focuses on the Army's core expertise in land warfare.[31]

The Army seeks to create generalists *familiar* with many or all of the major aspects of the profession's expertise and the appropriate use of such expertise in mutually complementary combination. These generalists are the core from which we obtain the strategic leaders of the profession.

> The ambiguous nature of the operational environment requires Army leaders who are self-aware and adaptive. Self-aware leaders understand their operational environment, can assess their own capabilities, determine their own strengths and weaknesses, and actively learn to overcome their weaknesses. Adaptive leaders must first be self-aware—then have the additional ability to recognize change in their operating environment, identify those changes, and learn how to adapt to succeed in their new environment.[32]

Complementing generalists are the specialists who *master* areas of knowledge that support the Army's success in its core expertise. Specialists serve the profession through high-level expertise in a particular field.

The schools and assignment process must be designed to nurture these traits over time so that it creates the foundation of professional expertise at higher levels. Familiarity with the higher-level concepts among junior members of the profession also ensures that they understand the context of decisions and guidance. The demand for education (how to think) as opposed to training (what to think or do) increases as officers rise in rank and experience. Mastery of specific skills and tasks should give way to the acquisition of broader theoretical and conceptual skills. Education is a means to greater flexibility, versatility, psychological maturity, and mental agility. Emphasis on education is also responsive to the higher levels of uncertainty and greater opportunities for choice and judgment that accompany promotion and commensurately weightier professional responsibilities.

Precommissioning must address all elements of the Army's expertise and jurisdiction as candidly as possible with rising officers. The commissioning sources for the Army are the United States Military Academy (USMA), the Reserve Officers' Training Corps (ROTC), and Officer Candidate School (OCS). All officers should have the same foundations of professional ethics, understanding of officership, and the intellectual seasoning provided by a broad but balanced technical-scientific and humanities education. Core military programs and supporting academic programs are designed to work in tandem. The academic program provides a broad context for expertise appropriate to the Army profession. The core military program reinforces these elements with Army or military-specific academic courses, practical experience, and rigorous training. Success in this comprehensive agenda permits the profession to certify that its new members have an acceptable foundation for a career of principled service to the nation. The functional imperatives of the profession require that its commissioned leaders have the mental agility to recognize problems and then draw on a rich body of knowledge to formulate appropriate diagnoses and treatments.

Officer preparation should be standardized to the maximum extent feasible across all commissioning sources. Large portions of the military program are already standardized.[33] Less consistent are the academic requirements to support Army professional expertise. A bachelor's degree is considered generally sufficient to meet professional academic qualification from ROTC programs. For OCS, a bachelor's degree is not required before commissioning, but must be attained before attending the Captain's Career Course.[34] For ROTC and OCS, the specific components of the academic program are largely at the individual's discretion.[35] Precommissioning academic requirements should be better standardized to meet Army professional needs. Table 9-2 provides a recommended map of Army precommissioning expertise to support this effort.

Area	Military-Technical		Human Development	
Program	Core Military	Supporting Academic	Core Military	Supporting Academic
Examples	Basic Training (weapons, common tasks) Field Training Small Unit Operations	Science (physics, chemistry) Math Engineering Information Technology	Leadership Physical Fitness Human Motivation	Psychology Physiology Sociology

Area	Ethical-Moral		Political-Cultural	
Program	Core Military	Supporting Academic	Core Military	Supporting Academic
Examples	Law of War Just war Professional Ethics Army Values Officership UCMJ	Philosophy English Law (constitutional & criminal) Religions	Military History Civil-military Relations	U.S. History American Politics International Relations Economics Language Anthropology

Table 9-2. *Precommissioning Map of Army Professional Expertise.*[36]

The body of relevant knowledge requisite for the Army's ability to function effectively has increased dramatically over time. Masters of particular fields require specialization and long-term experience. Over the course of an officer's career, the opportunities and requirements for exercising professional judgment in diagnosing increasingly difficult problems and deriving imaginative, innovative solutions will increase. There are strong reasons to emphasize military-technical training to execute well-known and specific tasks at early stages in an officer's career. However, the emphasis on education and familiarization with the wider context of operations to include political-cultural factors and moral-ethical considerations must be increased. Moreover, the execution of expert leadership in the application of coercive force must also be accompanied by increased emphasis on the education and development of rising professionals—a demanding and crucial additional leadership challenge both for immediate mission success and long-term health of the profession.

Table 9-3, illustrating numbered functional areas and specialty branches currently identified by the Army as they relate to the categories of Army expertise, depicts several important concepts. It is important to note that all Army professionals enter the

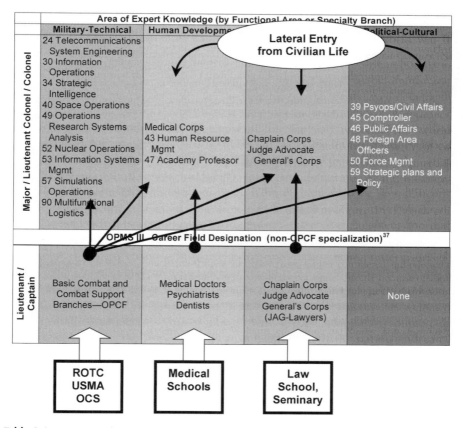

Table 9-3. *Army Professional Specialization.*

profession through ROTC, USMA or OCS. That is the area representing commissioning sources for the operational force (combat and combat support). Ultimately, the operational force will provide the aptly named general officers who will lead the profession. Medical, legal, and religious experts are acquired from their appropriate professional education systems. Additional orientation or training occurs to integrate these non-Army professionals into the institution. The arrows with their origins in the basic combat and combat support branches box represent the OPMS III mid-career specialization options for officers who have a strong professional foundation in the operational force.

Table 9-3 reflects the concept that there are specialty experts in the civilian world who can serve the Army's needs while working in any of several employment statuses. Specialties that are not unique to the Army lend themselves to lateral entry. Examples include civilian professors within the Army education system, public affairs experts, comptrollers, and systems analysts. The argument for including Army professionals with significant combat and combat support experience in these specialties rests heavily on the degree to which such experience is necessary to integrate the particular knowledge into the Army's requirements.

Map of Professional Expertise: Practical Implications and Applications

The priority expertise of the Army profession is leadership—the human dimension. The Army depends most importantly on its people and their ability to apply their skills in a potentially violent environment to serve American society. The abstract knowledge of leadership, particularly for combat, must dominate the Army's professional essence. Knowledge of technology, military doctrine, human development, professional ethics, and political-cultural context all support the quintessential focus on the leadership of human organizations to achieve appropriate military effects. The focus of the Army profession on the leadership of soldiers in the organized application of coercive force suggests potential new approaches to the structure and composition of the officer corps. They include:

- **Elimination of Combat Service Support Branches for Officer Accession.** These branches—finance, adjutant general, quartermaster, transportation, and ordnance—have no peculiar or unique skill related to leadership of Army soldiers in the organized application of coercive force. Instead, these skills can be provided through functional area specialization and civilian contracts at higher level. Within tactical units, combat service support task execution should be allocated to warrant officers and NCOs. Service support elements should be integrated into existing combat and combat support units where the commissioned officers provide the most important professional skill—leadership. Command and staff assignments should be allocated to combat and combat support officers. The practical result is the elimination of the five traditional combat service support branches for officer accession.
- **Realignment of Precommissioning System.** Precommissioning programs should better distinguish between officer candidates for operational force basic branches

and candidates for special branches (medical, legal, chaplain, etc).[38] Operational force officers should have roughly the same educational foundations. These should include common core military programs and common core academic requirements. Eligibility requirements for accession to combat and combat support branches should include Army-*certified* completion of the military core program and a baccalaureate degree that includes Army-specified elements. Additionally, Army-sponsored programs (USMA, OCS, and ROTC scholarships) should require accession to basic branches (combat and combat support arms). Transfer to special branches (medical, legal, religious) should be permitted only after an initial service obligations in basic branches have been met.[39]

- **Career Management and Education.** Army leaders must ensure that professional values—not bureaucratic imperatives—drive the military education and assignment system. The two key elements of this structure are the Army's professional military education system and the closely related assignment patterns that shape individual professionals.

Senior military leaders are not laterally appointed from other sectors of society. They must enter at the lower ranks of the profession and advance within the boundaries of the profession's assignment, education, and promotion system. It is through this process of professional development that the services establish and reinforce concepts of professionalism to meet the diverse and shifting challenges of an uncertain era.

The Army requires a professional development system that produces individuals who can also adapt to uncertain future challenges as well as individuals trained to meet current and short-run challenges. Such a system must place less emphasis on narrow technical skills that are perishable and greater emphasis on qualities of enduring value (physical, spiritual, and ethical). The system must seek to develop individuals with the capacity to learn and grow professionally throughout a lifetime of service to the nation. In an era of rapidly changing technology, mastery of particular weapons and equipment may provide only fleeting benefit. More important is the intellectual agility to deal with the dynamics of change and to readily adapt new capabilities to enduring requirements and old capabilities to new requirements.

Defining the Army's Professional Jurisdictions

The System of Professions

The Army operates in jurisdictions ultimately legitimized by the demands of society as voiced by its civilian leaders. In a literal sense, the Army is simply a loyal servant of society and does what it is asked to do. Superficially accurate and normatively supportable, this narrow formulation overlooks the profession's important responsibility to participate in clarifying appropriate jurisdictions in negotiation with its client's leaders. The Army's professional expertise and capabilities are finite. True, the Army is also capable of performing tasks unrelated to its core expertise, but doing so must be measured against the consequent impact on its ability to effectively perform duties for which it is uniquely designed and for which it is society's sole executor. Army leaders must be able to reconcile the jurisdictions within which the profession operates with the expertise and capacity it possesses. Though civilian leaders have the final decision, Army leaders should nonetheless be clear about the nature of the Army's appropriate role in specific jurisdictions.

Expertise is developed for application within particular jurisdictions. If jurisdictions are no longer relevant to a client's needs, a profession with expertise in that area may no longer be useful. Similarly, if more effective performance of critical work can be found elsewhere, client support for a profession may decline. A decline might be measured in terms of reduced resources such as money, people, or equipment. Such reductions may in turn lead to constriction of the profession's autonomy or possibly even elimination of the profession.

The uncertainties and challenges of the present era provide an impetus for professional innovation and adaptation. Other military services, other government agencies, and private organizations vie, along with the Army, to address American society's security concerns. Many responsibilities traditionally associated with the Army have been challenged and claimed by others. Moreover, laudable Army service in missions that have little to do with the use of coercive force blur public understanding of the Army's core roles, thus making it easier to challenge those core roles. Strategic leaders must recognize this dynamic context as they define the Army's appropriate roles.

With claims for battlespace dominance that blur distinctions of air, sea, and land domains, the other military services challenge the Army's role of dominating land combat. Even regarding land warfare, the rapid-reaction, expeditionary use of the Marine Corps challenges central claims of the Army's relevance and importance. Contracting civilians to train Army officers (within the ROTC program) and to train foreign armies represent further encroachments on jurisdictions previously accorded to the Army. In a variety of military operations other than war, Army efforts overlap with international governmental organizations, nongovernmental organizations, and private contractors. There is no doubt that the Army works as part of a team to serve society's goals; however, to provide "complementary and reinforcing"[40] capabilities requires awareness and clarification of the specific contributions the Army makes to interdependent joint, interagency, and combined operations.

At the center of the Army's map of expert knowledge are the development, operation, and leadership of a human organization whose primary expertise is the application of coercive force on behalf of the American people incident to dominance in land warfare. The jurisdictions within which this expertise applies are *major combat operations (war), stability operations, strategic deterrence*, and *homeland security*. Table 9-4 lays out these jurisdictions and associated military tasks to analyze appropriate Army jurisdictional negotiation claims. The four major jurisdictions are drawn from the 2004 *National Military Strategy* and the November 2003 *Joint Operations Concepts*.[41] Doctrinally, the subordinate tasks are taken from Army Field Manual 3-0, *Operations*, and the *Joint Operating Concepts* working documents.[42] The table does not provide a comprehensive list all subordinate tasks, but rather those most closely related to Army expertise.

Jurisdictions	Army Negotiation Claims	
Army Tasks	**Expert Knowledge (internal)**	**Expert Work/ Priority (high, medium, low)**
Major Combat Operations		
OFFENSIVE *LAND* OPERATIONS "Aim at destroying or defeating an enemy."[44]	FULL	HIGH
Defeat/destroy the enemy decisively	FULL	HIGH
Disrupt enemy defenses/coherence	FULL	HIGH
Secure or seize terrain	FULL	HIGH
Deny enemy resources	FULL	HIGH
Fix the enemy	FULL	HIGH
Gain information	FULL	HIGH
DEFENSIVE *LAND* OPERATIONS	FULL	HIGH
Defeat enemy attacks	FULL	HIGH
Defend terrain (including homeland)	FULL	HIGH
Develop conditions favorable for resuming offense	FULL	HIGH
Stability Operations "Promote and protect U.S. national interests."[45]		
Peace Operations (peacekeeping, peace enforcement, support of diplomatic efforts)	FULL	HIGH
Foreign Internal Defense (includes counterinsurgency combat)	FULL	HIGH
Security assistance	SHARED	MEDIUM
Support to insurgencies	FULL	HIGH
Combating terrorism	SHARED	HIGH
Noncombatant evacuation	SHARED	HIGH
Humanitarian and civic assistance	SUBORDINATE	LOW
Relief operations (foreign)	SUBORDINATE	LOW
Arms control	SUBORDINATE	LOW
Strategic Deterrence (Deter adversaries; assure allies)		
Global situational awareness (intelligence)	SHARED	HIGH
Presence and deterrence	SHARED	HIGH
Peacetime military engagement (mil-to-mil contacts—exercises, training, education, visits)	SHARED	HIGH
Rapid response and preclusion	SHARED	HIGH
Deterrence information operations	SHARED	HIGH
Show of force	SHARED	HIGH
Homeland Security		
Defeat threats in forward regions	SHARED	HIGH
Defeat land threats to the homeland	FULL	HIGH
Relief operations (domestic)	SUBORDINATE	LOW
Support to domestic consequence management	ADVISORY	MEDIUM
Support to counter drug operations	SUBORDINATE	LOW
Support to civil law enforcement	SUBORDINATE	LOW
Community Assistance/Emergency preparedness	SUBORDINATE	LOW

Table 9-4. *Jurisdictions and Army Expertise.*

A jurisdiction is the link between a profession's abstract knowledge (expertise) and its work. The Army achieves agreement about the content and relative control over areas of practical work (jurisdictions) in negotiation with its civilian masters who represent society's interests. Table 9-4 identifies the major jurisdictions of joint practice and some of the related professional tasks (defined in terms of the work requiring abstract expert knowledge performed for society). Associated with these jurisdictions and major tasks are two aspects of recommended negotiation claims for the Army profession. The first column, labeled "Expert Knowledge (internal)," recommends the negotiation claims the Army should pursue relative to the control and content of the expertise for internal professional development (see Table 9-1). The second column, labeled "Expert Work/Priority (high, medium, low)" recommends the priority of Army negotiation claims for areas of practical work to support joint interdependence and interaction with relevant civilian professions.

Jurisdictional settlement claims are also closely related to a profession's priorities. Using the claims described earlier, the most important settlement claim is for full and complete control of work. This claim entails the highest obligations and responsibilities of a profession to its clients. Next in priority are jurisdictions shared with other professions. The other two forms of settlement addressed here (advisory and subordinate) reflect lower-priority jurisdictions.[43]

The basic reason to have an Army is to support national security, and, in particular, to defend against armed forces—irregular, uniformed, foreign, or domestic—that threaten the security of the nation and it citizens. But the Army's utility and value have also been understood in a much broader context: "Essentially, the Army as a profession emerged to embrace any tasks levied by the American people that necessitated the deployment of trained, disciplined, manpower under austere conditions on behalf of the nation."[46] This broader conception of the Army's utility beyond war accounts for the extensive involvement of the Army in nation-building tasks at home and abroad. Examples are exploration of the continent (Lewis and Clark), development of vast civil engineering works, and occupation and pacification of North American territories (entailing conflicts primarily with Native Americans) as well as occupation and administration of territories abroad (such as Mexico, Cuba, the Philippines, Germany, and Japan).

The most important jurisdiction of the military professions is major combat operations or war. Major combat operations are led, if not monopolized, by the military services. Leadership of people in the organized use of coercive force on behalf of the state is the special expertise of military professionals. The increasingly intertwined effects of military operations on land, in the air, at sea, in space, and, according to many, in cyberspace preclude clear distinctions between the domains of combat within which the military services specialize. The overlap and interplay of capabilities optimized for air, sea, and land operations permit application in the physical domains of other services, albeit it with varied degrees of efficiency. This situation makes healthy interservice competition possible. Such competition is a valuable mechanism for identifying, debating, and deciding issues with respect to societal goals.

The Army profession provides complementary and reinforcing capabilities to the maritime profession (Navy and Marines) and the aerospace profession (Air

Force) regarding a variety of national objectives best achievable by the use of coercive force. The Army is rarely sufficient and often not even necessary to address particular challenges. The Army and other military services offer a menu of capabilities from the U.S. government can choose. The perception of a particular profession's utility is a function of the manner in which problems are defined, diagnosed, and suggested for treatment.

For example, in a conventional war, it is not necessarily clear in advance what strategy will prove most effective in compelling an enemy to conform to our will. Will naval blockade be sufficient? Will air power alone be sufficient? Will it be necessary to seize and hold portions of territory? Typically, all means that can affordably contribute to success will be applied. The issue is to determine the most effective combination. Sometimes, effective diplomacy (the expertise of Foreign Service professionals) can obviate any military action. If there are several apparently effective combinations and permutations, assessment of relative risk and cost-effectiveness will influence choices.

The manner in which various professions define the issue will be important. For war and preparation for war, there is unlikely to be one correct answer.

> Military science is not normally so exact as to rule out all but one school of thought on the question of how battles are to be fought and wars won. As a result, military planners frequently find themselves uncertain or divided regarding the kinds of preparations necessary to support the foreign policy purposes of the nation. There is, moreover, the additional complication that some purposes might alternatively be met through nonmilitary means, that is, through economic or diplomatic arrangements, or through the allocation of American resources to advance the military power of other nations.[47]

Each American military service differs in its dominant concept of war and the best means to carry it out.[48] Candidly, these service-specific diagnoses and suggested treatments are usually grounded in organizational self-interest. This does not mean, however, that the professionals advancing such arguments are unpatriotic or unreasonable. They are all trying to achieve success for society. The services and their strategic leaders are responsible for articulating the appropriate ways that service capabilities best serve societal needs. This competition is a healthy one that identifies alternatives for national leaders. The services sustain or create capabilities through a variety of methods. The government does not have infinite resources and must therefore constantly evaluate trade-offs both across and within a variety of jurisdictions. There is nothing self-evident or exclusive about the claims the Army advances concerning appropriate national strategy and appropriate resource allocation. In negotiations, strategic leaders of the Army profession must clearly articulate the relevance of the Army's expertise to appropriate jurisdictions. These negotiations will not hamper joint interdependence—they will enhance it. Such negotiations will help clarify Army capabilities to reinforce those of the other military and civilian assets in serving society's interests.

Society aspires to attain policy goals in the most effective manner at the least possible cost. The lack of objective criteria to determine the relative value of one course of action or combination of means versus another simply suggests that there is value to the advice of various professions' leaders to clarify the relevance and application of their profession's expertise.

For stability operations, strategic deterrence operations, and homeland security, the unique tasks for which the military is well suited are those that require the use or possible use of coercive force. With regard to peacekeeping missions, military-to-military contacts, peace enforcement, humanitarian assistance, and other non-war-fighting missions, there is a strong case for the employment of the readily available and robust capabilities of the Army to undertake missions that other agencies of the U.S. government or private organizations are unable to accomplish. For some missions, such as humanitarian assistance and disaster relief, the issue is not whether Army capabilities are unique, but rather the speed with which the Army can respond and its ability to undertake such tasks in an austere, remote, or unsecure environment. In these situations, the premium Army capacity is rapid response, assuming the necessary transportation is available. The capacity to support such missions is an inherent part of the Army's war-fighting ability. The Army is prepared for the exigencies of war, to include loss of parts of the organization in combat. Hence, military units are capable of rapidly providing infrastructure and support mechanisms. Professionally, however, these are not unique Army jurisdictions. The Army can apply its skills while remaining subordinate to civilian governmental and nongovernmental experts in these jurisdictions. These other experts should assume long-term responsibility for such tasks as soon as possible.

Defining Appropriate Jurisdictions: Practical Implications and Applications

The jurisdictions for which the Army should have full responsibility are those relevant to leadership of Army soldiers in the organized application of coercive force. In particular, this includes all aspects of sustained land warfare (major combat operations) as well as peacekeeping, peace enforcement, foreign internal defense, support to insurgencies, and military-to-military contacts with other land forces. These are all missions where the potential for using coercive force—if not its actual use—is present. The Army must develop the relevant expertise for these jurisdictions and accord the tasks entailed the highest priority.

All other jurisdictional claims should be secondary. Among those that are shared with other military professions, the interdependence and overlap of expert knowledge require close coordination between the Army, the other services, and in some cases allied armed forces. In jurisdictions with high or medium priority, the Army should actively seek to maintain a prominent if not lead role in the practical work.

Tasks for which Army expert knowledge is advisory or subordinate are of lowest relative importance. Although being supportive when directed, the Army should not seek important roles in the practical work involved. The common element of these lower-priority tasks is that other entities besides the Army can perform them. Professionally, the Army does not possess unique expertise in these areas. Other professions possess the expertise to lead or manage operations. The Army may possess expertise or capabilities that can be applied, but only at the cost of neglecting higher-priority tasks.

Note that the relative priority of a *professional* jurisdiction is an important distinction. There are certainly many tasks that Army units or Army individuals will be well-suited to perform in secondary jurisdictions that entail minimal if any opportunity costs for the individuals or units involved. A more appropriate way to conceptualize this would be to note that Army capabilities may be lent for application in jurisdictions outside the Army profession if not required for higher-priority work. Professionally, the Army's role is advisory or subordinate within these jurisdictions, and strategic leaders of the Army profession should thus seek to avoid accepting full responsibility for them. Army leaders should, however, maintain the expertise to manage effective liaison with those individuals or professions that do control or lead these jurisdictions (political-cultural expertise).

Strategic leaders of the profession must be active in negotiations to clarify and sustain control of primary jurisdictions. For secondary jurisdictions, strategic leaders should negotiate vigorously to limit Army work.[49] The Army's strategic leaders must actively advise civilian leaders on how to define and clarify service jurisdictions. Army leaders cannot afford to be passive and merely accept civilian preferences. A "can-do" attitude is a laudable trait when tasks are clear or decisions are already made. It does not require silence in shaping decisions. At the other extreme, it is also unacceptable for military leaders to insist on controlling the definition of jurisdictions. Strategic leaders must draw on their experience and their vision for the profession to advise and negotiate with civilian leaders.

Ultimately, military leaders are bound by civilian leaders' decisions about the Army's jurisdictions. On one hand, Army leaders as the stewards of the profession must make certain that members are aware of the tasks society may require. Continued emphasis on the "fight and win the nation's wars" mantra must be imbedded in a larger context of protean service to the nation on behalf of national security objectives. War is only one, albeit the most important, professional jurisdiction. On the other hand, strategic leaders of the Army must advise civilian leaders on appropriate definition of the Army's jurisdictions and the prospective costs of shifting jurisdictions capriciously. This balancing is necessary to help maintain a consistent core identity for the members of the profession and to sustain the reliability of the institution's performance. The strategic leaders of the Army profession play a critical role negotiating a resolution to the tension between the profession's vision of what it is and society's vision of what it ought to be.

Recommendations for Further Study

Additional study is necessary to refine the map I offer here for the profession's expert knowledge and the expert knowledge of individual professionals. Additional work is also needed to create the professional development pathways for individuals. The principles that led me to suggest boundaries for the Army's expert knowledge may lead some readers to different conclusions. Ultimately, specific decisions needed to operationalize this approach are the responsibility of the profession's strategic leaders.

Further, this framework can serve as a useful point of departure for examining sub-elements of the Army profession. Additional study and application by leaders of the current Army branches and functional areas would be useful to define the expert knowledge of branches and the jurisdictions within which they should appropriately operate. The focus of this chapter is at the institutional level of the Army. More precise definition will help us to better see how these principles apply to the specialties that comprise the profession. The future of the infantry profession, armor profession, field artillery profession, and other areas of Army expert knowledge would be useful adjuncts to the areas treated here.

Although this chapter contains broad implications for other members of the organization (warrant officers, noncommissioned officers, junior enlisted soldiers, and civilians), it does not provide detailed analysis or recommendations for the transformation of these members' roles. This is another fruitful area for additional study. Key to such an analysis would be an inquiry into the manner in which warrant officer and noncommissioned officer specialization might incorporate former tasks and expertise of commissioned officers that no longer require the application of abstract professional knowledge. It may also be appropriate to civilianize such tasks.

Conclusion

Army leaders must nurture a strong, healthy relationship between the Army and the society it serves. To do this effectively, they must think strategically about the future of the profession. Strategic leaders need a clear understanding of the nature of the Army's expertise and the jurisdictions within which it can be usefully applied. Strategic leaders of the profession must base their jurisdictional negotiations with society's civilian leaders on the firmest possible foundation, that is, one derived from what Clausewitz called "the grammar of war."[50] Military advice not derived from professional expertise compromises the legitimacy of advice in other contexts. As stated by Suzanne Nielsen,

> Positions based on either an overly narrow or an overly broad conception of the military's professional expertise could ultimately have negative consequences. The input of military officers could come to be seen either as irrelevant to the needs of the policy-maker, or as having dubious professional credibility.[51]

Strategic leaders imperil the Army institution if they lose sight of the professional foundations of their role and allow themselves to be drawn into policy and other debates that exceed their professional expertise and professional experience. There is a fine line between Clausewitz's wise counsel for officers to be sensitive to the political context within which they operate and actually attempting to determine policy goals. The framework presented here can help draw that line more clearly.

The security challenges of the future will be even more complex, demanding, and uncertain than they are proving to be today. The territory may be difficult to negotiate, but there are many sound guidelines available to map a successful course. The Army needs strategic leadership to map out the required expert knowledge for specific professional jurisdictions and to develop the individual professionals to apply this professional expertise appropriately. The Army's strategic leaders must also negotiate with the civilian leaders representing society the boundaries and priorities of the profession's jurisdictions and expertise. These efforts will more resolutely set the Army on a successful axis of advance to meet the nation's future security challenges.

Notes

1. Department of the Army, FM 1, *The Army,* 14 June 2001, 32.
2. Gayle L. Watkins and Don. M. Snider, "Project Conclusions," in *The Future of the Army Profession,* project directors Don M. Snider and Gayle L. Watkins, ed. Lloyd J. Matthews (Boston MA: McGraw-Hill, 2002), 538, 543. Hereinafter referred to as FAP I.
3. For a description of joint interdependence, see Les Brownlee and Gen. Peter Schoomaker, "A Campaign Quality Army with Joint and Expeditionary Capabilities," *Parameters* 34, no. 2 (Summer 2004): 5-23; and Brownlee and Schoomaker, *United States Army Transformation Roadmap 2003,* 1 November 2003, 1-7.
4. Samuel P. Huntington, *The Soldier and the State* (Cambridge, MA: Harvard University Press, 1957).
5. Andrew Abbott, *The System of Professions: An Essay on the Division of Expert Labor* (Chicago, IL: University of Chicago Press, 1988).
6. Huntington, *The Soldier and the State,* 7.
7. Ibid., 8.
8. Ibid., 11.
9. Ibid., 14-15.
10. This is significantly different from our expectations of warrant officers, noncommissioned officers, and junior enlisted soldiers. In Huntington's formulation, the difference between officers and other members of the force is that officers must be experts in the management of violence whereas the other members of the organization must be expert in the application of violent means. Huntington, *The Soldier and the State,* 11.
11. Ibid., 83.
12. Carl von Clausewitz, *On War* (Princeton NJ: Princeton University Press, 1976), 87.
13. Huntington, *The Soldier and the State,* 33.
14. Abbott, *The System of Professions,* 318.
15. Ibid., 35.
16. Ibid., 20.
17. These settlement claims are described on pages 69-79 of Abbott's book. With respect to split jurisdictional claims, the differentiation of one profession's jurisdiction from that of another is captured by the description or redefinition of the task. For example, with respect to land warfare, the Army and maritime professions have treated coasts and littoral regions as special arenas or workplaces of land warfare that split that jurisdiction between the Marine Corps and the Army. With the increasing range of Navy and Marine operations inland "from the sea" and the extensive participation of Marines in sustained land warfare in Afghanistan (a land-locked country, no less) and Iraq, this distinction between the concept of littoral regions seems to serve little value. Regarding settlement claims with respect to clients, Abbott notes that this particular claim is fundamentally different from the others and has more to do with organization of the workplace where professional expertise is applied. With one dominant client—American society—this claim has less relevance to armed forces; however, there are some examples, such as the state role

of National Guard forces and the domestic responsibilities of the U.S. Army Corps of Engineers, where the workplace, in this case the application of Army expertise in the domestic environment, could be seen as a jurisdictional settlement based on client differentiation.

18. In this chapter, "commissioned officers" refers to officers in the rank of 2nd lieutenant and above and does not include warrant officers.

19. Huntington, *The Soldier and the State*, 8, 17-18.

20. There is one major difference between the active federal force and federal reserves compared to the National Guard. In terms of the Abbott framework, it provides a division of jurisdiction—in particular homeland security—by client. In this case, the distinction is between state and federal government clients.

21. FM 1,*The Army,* 21.

22. Brownlee and Schoomaker, *Army Transformation Roadmap 2003*, ix.

23. Snider and Watkins, *The Future of the Army Profession*, 101.

24. Ibid., 355, 438.

25. Ibid., 291.

26. Ibid., 197.

27. Huntington, *The Soldier and the State*, 72.

28. Commissioning entails creation of a significant legal status that enhances accountability of the individual and extends institutional legal protections and benefits to the individual and his or her family.

29. Brownlee and Schoomaker, *Army Transformation Roadmap 2003*, 8-2.

30. William J. Lennox, Jr., "The Supe's Letter: A Soldier of the 21st Century," *Assembly* 60, no. 4 (March/April 2002): 8.

31. Brownlee and Schoomaker, "A Campaign Quality Army with Joint and Expeditionary Capabilities," 17.

32. FM 1, *The Army,* 12.

33. For a detailed list of the common core tasks for the Officer Education System at the precommissioning and company grade levels, see http://cgsc.leavenworth.army.mil/cal/LETDD/COMMON1.htm.

34. Attendance occurs after approximately three years of commissioned service. DA Pamphlet 600-3, *Commissioned Officer Development and Career Management*, 1 October 1998, para. 4-16b, 19.

35. The Army regulation does require that ROTC scholarship candidates have an approved major. However, the list of approved majors is extremely comprehensive and appears to suggest very little restriction on academic programs. The only specific requirement listed in the regulation is for one semester of language.

36. The academic and military components represented on this table are largely parallel to the current core curriculum and military program at the U.S. Military Academy. See USMA 2001-2002 Catalog, "It's Still About Leadership."

37. Operations Career Field (OPCF)

38. The special branches are the Judge Advocate General's Corps (legal), Chaplain Corps (religious), and Medical Corps. Medical Corps includes the following six sub-elements: Medical Corps, Dental Corps, Veterinary Corps, Army Medical Specialists, Army Nurse Corps, and Medical Service Corps. DA Pamphlet 600-3, para 8-2c, 31.

39. Current service obligations are as follows. Military Academy graduates are obligated for eight years of service, five of which, at a minimum, must be served on active duty. ROTC scholarship recipients incur an eight-year service obligation of which four must be on active duty and the remaining four to six years in the reserves or National Guard (ROTC information from U.S. Army Cadet Command Headquarters, available from http://www.rotc.monroe.army.mil/

scholarships/green/obligation.asp, Internet, accessed 30 May 2002.) OCS commissioned officers have a three-year active duty service obligation. Data from Department of the Army, *Army Regulation* 350-100, *Officer Active Duty Service Obligations,* 4 May 2001, 5.

40. Brownlee and Schoomaker, "A Campaign Quality Army with Joint and Expeditionary Capabilities," 10.

41. Joint Chiefs of Staff, "Joint Operations Concepts," November 2003, http://www.dtic.mil/jointvision/secdef_approved_jopsc.doc, accessed 6 July 2004.

42. The four major jurisdictions are referenced in the National Military Strategy (2004) as well as in separate draft publications posted to the Joint Doctrine web site (http://www.dtic.mil/jointvision/). The Joint Operating Concepts are Major Combat Operations (http://www.dtic.mil/jointvision/draftmco_joc.doc, version 1.07, 24 March 2004, accessed 6 July 2004); Stability Operations (http://www.dtic.mil/jointvision/draftstab_joc.doc, version 1.03, 5 March 2004, accessed 6 July 2004); Strategic Deterrence (http://www.dtic.mil/jointvision/draftstrat_joc.doc, February 2004, accessed 6 July 2004); and Homeland Security (http://www.dtic.mil/jointvision/drafthls_joc.doc, February 2004, accessed 6 July 2004). For subordinate Army tasks, see also Department of the Army, FM 3-0, *Operations,* June 2001.

43. As noted earlier in the chapter, there are two other settlement claims identified by Abbott that do have some specialized application for the Army. Split jurisdictional claims and differentiation of settlement claims by client are also possible. Abbott, *The System of Professions,* 71-72.

44. FM 3-0, *Operations,* 1-15

45. Ibid.

46. Leonard Wong and Douglas V. Johnson II, "Serving the American People: A Historical View of the Army Profession," in FAP I, 62.

47. Warner R. Schilling, "The Politics of National Defense: Fiscal 1950," in *Strategy, Politics and Defense Budgets,* (New York: Columbia University Press, 1962), 13.

48. For an excellent treatment of these differences, see Carl H. Builder, *The Masks of War: American Military Styles in Strategy and Analysis* (Baltimore, MD: Johns Hopkins University Press, 1989): especially chap. 5, 57-66.

49. If nonetheless directed to accept secondary jurisdictions (a distinct possibility for a profession defined by loyal service to society), professional leaders should seek appropriate ways to hand off the jurisdiction. If there is no acceptable way to relinquish such a jurisdiction, strategic leaders must explore adaptations to the profession that may involve segmenting off a portion of the profession to handle the new jurisdiction while shielding the rest of the profession (e.g., the creation of specific constabulary forces for peacekeeping in benign environments). A historical example of this may have been those portions of the Army Corps of Engineers responsible for domestic duties such as river/flood management.

50. Clausewitz, *On War,* 605.

51. Suzanne Nielsen, "Rules of the Game? The Weinberger Doctrine and the American Use of Force," in FAP I, 219.

10 Opportunity for the Army: Defense Transformation and a New Joint Military Profession[1]

Don M. Snider and Jeffrey Peterson

Introduction

This chapter reviews the evolution toward jointness since the Goldwater-Nichols Act in 1986,[3] relates that progress to the newer initiative of defense transformation, and derives a need for a new joint military profession. What has been meant by the ubiquitous term "jointness," however, is not agreed; it is not listed in Joint Pub 1-02, *Department of Defense Dictionary of Military and Associated Terms*. Thus for this analysis we will simply use the term to mean the effective integration of the combat capabilities of the uniformed services, America's war-fighting professions. The evolution of this "effective integration," as well as the mindset among military officers who facilitate it, has progressed very unevenly since 1986. There have been clear evolutionary successes in some areas and consistent lack of progress in others.

> But an Army at war must change the way it changes. In peacetime, armies change slowly and deliberately. . . . Today, that measured approach to change will not suffice. . . . No longer satisfied merely to deconflict the activities of the several services, we seek joint interdependence. . . . The air-, sea-, or land-power debates are over. Our collective future is irrefutably joint. To meet the challenges of expeditionary operations, the Army can and must embrace the capabilities of its sister services right down to the tactical level.
>
> —FORMER ACTING ARMY SECRETARY LES BROWNLEE
> ARMY CHIEF OF STAFF GEN. PETER J. SCHOOMAKER[2]

Evolutionary success in attaining jointness has been manifested perhaps most clearly in the execution of joint warfare—America now fights wars almost solely under joint commands. Most recently and vividly this was seen in the integration of combat effects in Afghanistan and Iraq. In addition, there have been other less visible successes in the global war on terrorism. There have also been less pronounced but consistent steps towards jointness made in peacetime—the steady evolution in joint doctrine and exercises, to name only one.

But it is also the case that jointness has failed to evolve in other areas in which it was anticipated and intended in the mid-1980s by the framers of Goldwater-Nichols. There are still very few standing joint forces ready for joint deployment and employment.[4] Rather, joint forces are, by and large, still assembled ad hoc at the time of deployment. Further, there has only been glacial movement toward joint force training and experimentation and the determination of force requirements based on combatant commanders' war plans.[5] In other words, while recent decades have shown remarkable improvement in developing war-fighting concepts and in planning for and executing joint warfare, they have not shown the same progress, if any at all, in creating truly ready joint forces in peacetime nor in rationalizing the services' future capabilities on joint war-fighting needs.

Why is this? Why successful evolution in some areas and evolutionary failure in others? It is certainly not because those personnel assigned to command and staff positions within the Joint Staff, the combatant commands, and DoD agencies are not solid military professionals deeply steeped in the doctrines and war-fighting expertise of their respective services. Nor are those who have cycled through joint assignments people of bad intent. There are today a few officers truly joint in mind-set and practice, i.e., those who have entered the joint arena and then stayed or returned for repetitive joint assignments, notwithstanding the bureaucratic pressures to serve elsewhere. And in them we glimpse the real model for the future.

We will suggest in this chapter that the very uneven evolution toward jointness is symptomatic of a deep systemic problem—simply stated, it is that there has been no evolution toward a joint military profession. Instead, such evolution has been constrained by the intent and language of the original Goldwater-Nichols Act: "To establish policies, procedures, and practices for the effective management of officers of the Army, Navy, Air Force, and Marine Corps on active duty who are particularly educated, trained in, and oriented toward joint matters."[6] Clearly, the intent of the act is that joint-qualified officers will remain identified with their original services. Thus, at no point has the joint community evolved beyond a collection of "borrowed military manpower" as determined by bureaucratic selection and assignment procedures, serving their roughly 2.6-year average tour as a joint specialty officer mindful that such a "diversion" is needed to earn credit for advancement within their own service professions.

Other than growing in size and bureaucratization, this system for management of officers assigned to joint duty has evolved little since the initial implementation in the early years after 1986. Such a "management" approach, hoping as it does to establish "jointness" by the cultural interpenetration gained from brief educational and joint duty assignments, will, we believe, accomplish no more in the future than it has in the past 18 years.

And, clearly, what this approach has not developed is "joint professionals" in the sense that they are: (1) deeply schooled in a unique and necessary body of expert knowledge and its practice, and (2) collective members of an esteemed vocation who are "called" with deep moral conviction to adapt and practice that expert knowledge in service to the nation.

Further, the lack of a joint profession is now critically damaging to the intended defense transformation. In the words of the Secretary of Defense, "The [defense transformation] outcome we must achieve [is]: innately joint, network-centric, distributed forces capable of rapid decision superiority and massed effects across the battle space." We shall argue that such transformation is, and will continue to be, completely contingent on resolving this systemic personnel issue that precludes the emergence of a joint profession.

Rightly understood, military transformation is less about emerging technologies, hardware, and software and more about the mindset of military and civilian professionals, including the vision and commitment they carry into their future professional service in behalf of the American people. The exploding contemporary literature on how militaries change, much of it financed by DoD itself, has made this point with resounding clarity: *Military institutions do not transform, people do; and in so doing they transform the institution.*[7]

Ironically, this fact is not acknowledged by DoD; witness the recently published Transformation Planning Guidance (April 2003), which scarcely mentions the human aspects of military transformation. It does note the need to create "a culture that supports transformation founded on leaders who are innately joint and comfortable with change." Unfortunately, however, it does not recognize that culture as a professional culture. Other than directing a review of joint education, there is no transformation guidance whatsoever for the human development of military and civilian professionals within the joint community.[8]

We argue that what is needed for the future is a fundamentally different approach for developing the human dimension of jointness—an approach that recognizes and fosters the professional character of the existing war-fighting professions while establishing the additional profession needed specifically for modern joint warfare. In capsule, we need a new joint profession serving under the JCS Chairman, the combatant commanders, and joint agencies.

Proposal for a Joint Military Profession

If Secretary of Defense Donald Rumsfeld approached defense transformation seeking to increase the expertise and the professional character of the joint community, he would view the community as a joint profession rather than a bureaucracy of borrowed personnel and would accordingly design policies to bring such a community into being. He would do so by seeking from Congress passage of legislation in the mold of Goldwater-Nichols to:

- *Create a new joint profession with full authority over its own internal jurisdictions for: (1) creation and adaptation of the profession's expert knowledge, and (2) development and utilization of joint professionals.* All professions, if they survive over time, maintain these two types of internal jurisdictions, including America's current war-fighting professions: army, maritime, and air-space.[9] Such legislation would also have to address for these three war-fighting professions the intractable problems that have been created by the currently inflexible assignment demands of "joint officer management" under Goldwater-Nichols and its amendments.

- *Create a Joint Doctrine and Education Command within the new profession for the creation and adaptation of the new profession's expert knowledge.* The challenge here is bounding and prioritizing the new profession's expert knowledge, reconciling it with the knowledge maps of the current war-fighting professions, and developing professional institutions to ensure its continued adaptation and use in professional development. Fortunately, many such institutions already exist, at least in name, but they remain ill-focused on the expert knowledge of the new profession.

- *Create a Joint Personnel Command with authority to manage the careers of all members of the joint profession, including selection, evaluation, assignment, promotion, and professional development.* Once accepted into the new profession, members would stay until retirement, except for short, periodic returns to their original war-fighting professions to be updated in service capabilities.

The new profession would be a lateral entry profession with military officers entering as majors and Department civilians entering at rank/expertise equivalents. Ultimately the profession would encompass the roughly 9,000 billets of the current Joint Duty Assignment List (JDAL), though it should be established initially below that level and expand as members mature in expertise and rank. Once the profession is filled, its members would serve, as today, within all of the joint command structures and defense agencies.

The two new joint commands proposed above would be responsible for the members' professional development and career management through the rank of brigadier general. All positions within the joint community from major general to general, and civilian equivalents, would remain nominative and competitive for civilians and general officers from all professions within DoD, including the new joint profession. Thus, the influence and expert knowledge of the war-fighting professions would continue to be felt largely as they are today, through the careful selection of those professionals seeking to serve in the new profession (at the point of lateral entry), and by the selection of those strategic leaders who serve at the top three ranks within the new profession.

We shall now consider in greater detail the rationale for such a "Goldwater-Nichols II" legislative request. What follows are five separate, but quite interrelated reasons, along with supporting argument, for establishing a new joint profession.

First, there has been a demonstrated inability of the bureaucratic management procedures established under Goldwater-Nichols I to meet Secretary Donald Rumsfeld's stated requirement for "innately joint" officers. To understand this proposition, we must revisit briefly the original idea of creating "jointness" through congressionally mandated policies for "joint officer management" (Title IV of the Act). The principal congressional findings held that the quality of officer personnel assigned to the joint arena was inadequate; the best officers stayed in their services, there was little incentive to go joint, and service practices and priorities, if continued without alteration, would never address this issue. Thus with the intent of enhancing the quality, stability, and experience of officers in joint assignments, which would in turn improve the performance and effectiveness of joint organizations, Congress created a detailed system of joint officer management, including assignment policies, promotion objectives, and educational and experience requirements. Keys to supporting the spirit and intent of Title IV were to be the sharing of quality officers with the joint community and not disadvantaging officers with such joint experience when they returned to their service.

Title IV has turned out to be one of the most contentious aspects of the Goldwater Nichols Act simply because it has never produced the results anticipated by the Congress. Consequently, there have been numerous studies and reports over the years by an array of agencies and institutions recommending tweaks either to the legislation or to its manner of implementation by the services and the joint community. One of the most thorough of those reviews was completed in 1996 when experts from RAND undertook a detailed review of both the supply and demand sides of this personnel issue.[10] Reading through their three reports, as well as many others, we are struck by the degree to which Admiral William Crowe was absolutely right in his concern expressed as the legislation was being created: "The detailed legislation that mandated every aspect of the 'Joint Corps' from the selection process and the number of billets to promotion requirements was . . . a serious mistake that threatened a horrendous case of Congressional micromanagement."[11]

Currently, many management problems remain unsolved even after 18 years of implementation, studies, analysis, and legislative changes. Morale problems remain within the joint community because only a limited number of positions may be designated on the JDAL; these are unevenly allocated across the community, thus slighting the joint agencies. Many of the highest-quality officers still do not experience joint duty until they are flag-selected; too many officers arrive at their first joint duty assignment without having completed the requisite educational requirements; and the services have not created (nor does it appear that they will) sufficient numbers of joint specialty officers with the right skills to fill the designated "critical" billets (which as a result have been recently reduced from the original 1,000 to 800). Finally, very few officers ever return to joint duty, leaving an insufficient number to continue enriching the expertise of the joint officer community.

Thus, it is no overstatement to say that the "average" service officer now reluctantly spends from six months to a year acquiring joint professional military education to qualify for two plus years service as "borrowed military manpower" in a JDAL-designated position upon completion of which he or she then exits the joint community, never to return.

In sum, the intent as envisioned by Title IV of the Act has never been met, nor can anyone point to the time in the future when it will be met nor to the mechanisms that will make it happen. Though well-intentioned, the framers of the Act failed to grasp that socialization and professionalization, while related, are not coextensive—socialization is only a small part of professionalism. While seeking to professionalize the role of the joint officer, they actually created a set of highly bureaucratic personnel management routines that can at best produce an officer only mildly socialized to joint affairs. James Locher, one of the most involved and astute participants in this long history, recently concluded: "Congress had hoped that DoD, after several years of implementing Title IV, would develop a better approach to joint officer management. That has not occurred."[12]

Second, there is now a recognized and necessary field of expert knowledge at the nexus of the technical and the operational—the joint command and control (C2) of operational forces as it supports and facilitates the planning and conduct of modern joint and combined warfare through all phases of its activity. Military officers no longer question whether America's armed forces will fight under joint command;

that has been resolved, as noted earlier, with the steady nudging of provisions of the Goldwater-Nichols Act.[13] Thus, in recent years war planning at the operational level, both deliberate and contingent, has become and will remain within the joint domain. In fact, one can plausibly argue that the same is true at the strategic level, since the two have become so indistinguishable in recent operations in the Balkans, Afghanistan, and Iraq.

Neither is it questioned that emerging joint command structures are creating common architectures for the integration of communications, intelligence, and command and control functions to knit together the effects of assigned forces and supporting agencies. Thus, the new expert knowledge, drawing from both the technical and operational, is essentially a newer form of traditional command and control, the directional functions in both planning and execution that allow joint commanders the decisional superiority (faster, better informed) to provide mutually reinforcing integration of service capabilities and effects. But these functions are now accomplished simultaneously at multiple levels of joint command, from headquarters distributed over vast regions, networked together with assigned elements of the war-fighting professions by creation of common operational awareness of the battlefields enabled by the emerging architectures.

Moreover, these structures allow joint commanders to fight under operational concepts that are themselves increasingly joint in origin and which require for successful execution capabilities drawn not only from the war-fighting professions but also from sources outside of DoD. Two vivid recent examples of such integration occurred in Joint Exercise Millennium Challenge '02, conducted by U.S. Joint Forces Command, and the conduct of the joint war-fighting phases of the war in Iraq. It appears that this new expertise, fetchingly known in the jargon as "joint C4ISR," is evolving largely outside the current maps of expert knowledge of the war-fighting professions.[14] This should not be surprising, and in fact is most desirable. Of course, the maps of expert knowledge will always overlap to some degree, as is necessary for the redundancy necessary for success in high-risk ventures such as war. But in the main the current evolution is progressing outside the traditional knowledge domains of the established military professions.[15]

Logically, this new expertise in integrating the effects of the war-fighting professions, that is, in blending military means with the other coercive means of power, should have been laid out and agreed upon before the C2 architectures were established. Such knowledge and expertise have to be considered "logically prior" to that of the war-fighting professions and supporting agencies. Without such knowledge and expertise manifested in the forms of the C4ISR architectures, joint operational concepts, and adaptable warplans, how can the war-fighting professions and supporting agencies possibly know how to plan for their own individual capabilities for the future?

This has been one of the most pronounced problems in the overall evolution towards jointness since 1986—the services have resisted for years the development of operational concepts and capabilities that were at variance with their parochial interests.[16] But DoD is now at a critical point—a critical mass of new expert knowledge and architecture/structure for its application has evolved. It is now clear that future wars will be fought and the better peace gained under these new concepts, procedures, and architectures.[17] Thus the time is right to establish permanent cadres of professionals—the joint profession—to become the dedicated stewards of that developing knowledge and expertise. In turn, it will fall to this group to develop the future corps who will apply it in the years and decades ahead.

Third, far better than other types of organizations, military professions uniquely create the expert knowledge and human expertise to fight modern warfare jointly and thus develop, in Secretary Rumsfeld's words, professionals who are "innately joint."[18] The changing nature of modern warfare has been caused by America's singular role in the post-Cold War world, by the tragic events of 11 September 2001, and by major advances in technology.[19] This new character of war has brought with it the addition of new fields of expert knowledge for military professionals and new forms of expertise to be practiced by them on behalf of their client, the American people. However, by their very character, bureaucracies do not create expert knowledge (mares don't foal lions!), nor do they invest in their "employees" in ways that create, sustain, and adapt human expertise. Bureaucracies focus on the "efficiency" of repetitive, routine operations using non-expert knowledge applied through a variety of means of which humans are only one, and quite often not the most important one. Professions focus rather on "effectiveness" in nonroutine applications of expert knowledge (every patient has a different chemistry, every legal case its own facts, and every conflict its unique forces, history, and causes) by humans extensively skilled through schooling and experience. They apply their expertise through a variety of means, perhaps the most important of which is the exercise of discretionary judgments.[20] More so than bureaucracies, professions also have a fiduciary obligation to their client, and thus are often characterized by their professional ethos.

Given this understanding, it follows that the new expert knowledge inherent in, and necessary for, the conduct of modern joint warfare and the "better peace" that must follow it will best be developed and adapted to changing needs by a dedicated corps of individuals, military and civilian, each "called" to the organization by its unique service to society and then remaining there for the reminder of their active service. These experts would serve within a career environment that fosters their development and practice, individually and collectively, thereby enhancing the institution's service to society. Such a pursuit in life is, in fact, a vocational profession, not a bureaucracy inhabited by an assemblage of ever-changing personnel without portfolio.

Fourth, modern public-sector professions do not emerge miraculously; within DoD they will need to be established and legitimized by overt political actions such as the recommended Goldwater-Nichols II type of legislation. This reason is quite straightforward. Entry into the competition among occupational groups as it occurs in the private sector is quite different from that occurring in the public sector, and particularly within the Department of Defense. In the private sector, occupational groups can "go after" professional work whenever they believe their form of work potentially meets the needs of the client. As an "alternative medicine," acupuncturists initially took this aggressive approach with regard to pain management. Eventually, their expert knowledge came to be included within that of the professional medical community. While some jurisdictions are regulated by associational, educational, or licensing barriers (e.g., medicine, law, and engineering), there are still generally fewer barriers to entry in the private sector.

In the public sector, however, the government holds much more client power. In essence, the government determines in advance what occupational groups may compete. And while the trend in recent decades has been for the U.S. government to open the competitions for selected areas of work to participation by more and more groups—a process known as outsourcing—it has not pursued that course for provision of the nation's critical war-fighting capabilities. Military institutions are still established by law. Thus, the only way in which a new joint military profession will emerge is for it to be founded by Congress in the statutes that govern the Department of Defense.

Fifth, and finally, establishing a joint profession is a win-win policy with immense benefits to both the Army as a war-fighting profession and to the new joint military profession—deeper expertise and improved effectiveness in both. We believe that a separately managed joint profession will reduce the current tensions for Army field grade officers caused by the requirement to "fit it all in before brigade command," including joint schooling and a joint assignment. At the same time, owing to a much slower rotation of Army officers into and out of joint billets, it will allow deeper professional expertise in the Army and in the joint community, thus enabling more effective joint operations in support of defense transformation. These benefits are attainable and increasingly important as the demand for joint and combined ground warfare expertise continues to increase. Here is why.

The first benefit of a new joint profession impacts the individual professionals within each profession, Army and joint. As the new joint profession is created and joint billets are filled permanently, there will be a significant reduction in the number of service officers required each year to fill JDAL billets.[21] This will significantly reduce field grade assignment turbulence caused by the tension between bureaucratic career management requirements, on one hand, and the need for professional development in their own career management field, on the other. For individual professionals, this issue is one of career identify and focus, closely related as it is to the sense of "calling" that professionals have for their work and service. As Andrew Abbott has noted:

> The idea of career—that is the idea of a single occupational skill or identity characterizing individuals for their entire working lives—is probably the most central single constituent of the idea of profession as it emerged in the nineteenth century . . . and more importantly for the present case is the fact that the development of formally patterned careers is the Army's chief mechanism for reconciling the demands of its dual nature as an organization [bureaucracy] and a profession.[22]

In other words, Army officers tolerate over the long term the bureaucratic aspects of service life in order to be fulfilled by the professional aspects. A prime example is their acceptance of orders to a joint assignment (interrupting their own branch development) because the joint billet offers the opportunity for professional development and service within a critical theater recently brought to a wartime posture.

But there is a tipping point where the bureaucratic demands of a career pattern can be perceived to outweigh the professional satisfactions. Such occurred to Army junior officers in the late 1990s, inciting a major exodus of captains. "Reduced career satisfaction" was usually the first or second reason adduced in the many empirical studies attempting to analyze the reasons for the exodus and why the "stayers" remained. Insofar as they could be isolated, contributing factors to career dissatisfaction, and ultimately to career decisions, included time away from family due to the high optempo, micromanagement within the systems of the field Army (the "Power Point" Army), and rigid, inflexible assignment systems that *left little room for individual choice in professional development*.[23] This last factor, which becomes even more important in the early field grade years (major) when the officer is assuming more responsibility for his or her own professional development, is clearly exacerbated by the addition of a three-year joint duty assignment. There simply is not enough time for majors to "fit it all in," and neither do they feel they have any real choices, any real control, over what is finally fitted in.

Recent research has shown that a majority of Army field grade officers have accepted the necessity for "radical change in their approach to warfare," implying that they must gain new expert knowledge and expertise just to stay current in their Army career management field or branch.[24] But it also shows they are keenly aware of the very limited time available to fulfill their responsibilities as professionals to develop this new expertise, both in terms of general leadership abilities and the technical competencies of their specific field or branch.[25] Thus career, and therefore personal, satisfaction for these professionals is in increasing jeopardy as Army majors are forced to choose between a joint assignment desirable for future promotion competitiveness, and an Army operational position immediately needed in preparation for the next deployment and subsequent competitiveness within the core of their chosen profession.

A new joint profession will help resolve this conflict. In both the Army and in the new joint profession, officers can spend more time developing without penalty. They will no longer need waivers to minimize joint time so they can "get back to troops." Likewise, joint professionals who have chosen that new profession can maintain satisfaction and promotion potential by working consecutively in joint assignments. In both cases the quality of career satisfaction and thus of personal contentment is advanced.

It should be clear by now that the second win-win benefit is the opportunity for richer professional expertise in both professions. Longer time spent uninterrupted in one profession naturally produces higher proficiency and with it greater pride and acceptance. With a new joint profession, there will be less assignment churning as fewer officers go back and forth between service and joint assignments. Joint professionals will spend the majority of their career in joint positions while Army professionals devote more service time to operational and developmental positions. Each profession collectively expands their expertise as officers spend more time serving in their respective professional assignments.

Additionally, there is an important benefit falling outside the operational forces. There will be an opportunity for better-qualified officers to serve in professional education systems where they can train future professionals and serve as stewards of the profession's expert knowledge. Today, the Army's professional schoolhouses and doctrinal centers are practically devoid of branch-qualified operational officers and ex-battalion and brigade commanders teaching and codifying doctrine for the Army's future professionals. Why is this so? It is largely because the Army sends over 1,000 professionals each year to fill JDAL-designated positions. Of these 1,000 officers, 20-24 percent are the Army's most deeply committed and developed field grade officers, those who have chosen to remain in the operational career field of each combat, combat support, and combat service support branch. As the branches allocate their remaining officers, particularly in a period of very high optempo, the field Army takes priority, of necessity. Thus, the institutional Army, the schoolhouses, doctrinal centers, and training centers, suffer most of the shortfall.

Unfortunately, the cost to the profession is not limited to the educational institutions of Army. The Army's Training and Doctrine Command (TRADOC), the single institution responsible for all doctrinal development, training development, and professional education, is now able to do far less than in the past when it was the engine for the profession's revitalization during the post-Vietnam period. In recent years, TRADOC has turned to contracted civilian firms to do what Army professionals had formerly done. Perhaps the most telling example is its recently let contract for development of the professional education curriculum for Army majors at Ft. Leavenworth! In essence, the Army as profession has had to dilute its control over its critical internal jurisdictions, those where its expertise is developed and adapted.

Prior to the Goldwater-Nichols Act in 1986, the received wisdom for junior Army officers from their branch leaders was to spend their career either "leading troops in the field army, studying as a student in a branch schoolhouse, or teaching there the future officers of the branch." Allowing for some obvious parochial bias, this schema nonetheless quite accurately conveyed one of the central tenets of any successful profession's culture, military or otherwise—aspiring professionals must be deeply involved over their career in supporting the profession's critical internal jurisdictions, those activities in which it develops and adapts its expert knowledge and in which it conveys that knowledge to future professionals, preparing them for their individual and collective practices. Establishing a joint profession will provide opportunities for the Army to regain control of its own internal professional jurisdictions and professional education system.

Establishing a joint profession will also improve joint effectiveness in support of defense transformation. Because joint professionals will laterally enter from the war-fighting professions, each service is permanently integrated and represented in the development of joint doctrine and the planning and execution of joint operations. The additional officers that will rotate between joint and service assignments will have an even deeper and more current service expertise. This combination of permanent integration of each service's perspective and deeper expertise within each profession will, we believe, result in more effective joint operations.

Lastly, another benefit realized with a joint profession is an equitable distribution of readiness across all unified commands. If joint professionals are managed by their own Personnel Command, they can be more equitably distributed to ensure that adequate expertise is permanently available to all unified commands—an important dimension of the *global* war on terror. Additionally, the equitable distribution of joint expertise will eventually elevate joint culture to a level of importance equal to that of service cultures, providing an opportunity to reduce interservice rivalry and enhance the development of officers who have completely internalized joint spirit, values, and habits of mind.

It is important to note that a feasible structure already exists for managing a new joint profession. The Army's current officer career management model, Officers Professional Management System (OPMS 3), is an established structure that can be applied to management of joint professionals. The Army officer career model offers two lateral entry points into the joint profession as shown in the career model diagram in Figure 10-1. The first entry point occurs at 10 years of service when the officer chooses a career field designation. Army officers could select the joint profession in the same manner they now choose other career fields under OPMS 3, opting to serve as a joint professional for the remainder of their career. Of course, they would have to be accepted and certified by the new Joint Personnel Command. An officer who is selected to become a joint professional brings 10-12 years of service experience and 8-10 years additional longevity for the joint profession. Further, since joint professionals will not be serving directly on the battlefield, it is conceivable that the

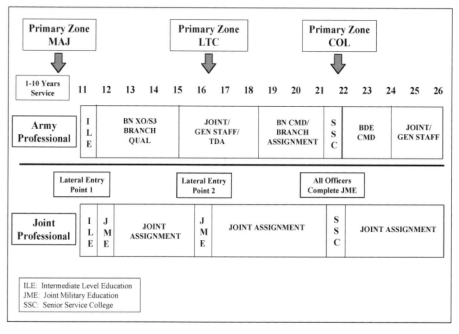

Figure 10-1. *Joint Profession Timeline.*

implementing legislation could increase their careers to 35 years. There is a second opportunity, around year 16, for lateral entry by branch-qualified Army majors who are not selected for command or who desire joint service for the rest of their career. Remaining Army professionals would continue service under the current career management model, but with the reduction in urgency for a joint assignment.

Summing Up: A Better Approach to Jointness and Defense Transformation

The argument we have made here is that "jointness"—both in mindset and in practice—will best be realized in the future, and the desired defense transformation best pursued, if a new joint military profession is created. For this to happen, amendments to the Goldwater-Nichols legislation are necessary. Though military institutions are both profession and bureaucracy, the evolution of expert knowledge and human expertise flows primarily from individual motivations and means of social control—a relationship of trust—found within successful, competitive professions. Thus the challenge for the Secretary of Defense is to ensure that his policies are, in every decision and at every level, reflective of the military institution's professional character rather than its bureaucratic character.

The most urgent and apt place to gain this assurance is directly within DoD itself—through a new joint profession. What is *not* needed at this critical moment, contrary to what some have suggested, is to push jointness "lower" into the force structure and knowledge maps of the war-fighting professions. That approach would only confuse and dilute the necessary but very different fields of expert knowledge and exacerbate further the problem of junior field grade officers who don't have time to "fit it all in." Rather, as has been argued here, the better approach is to "deepen" jointness specifically where a long period of trial-and-error evolution has finally created a new field of expert knowledge and thus the need for a new military profession to practice it. Now is the time, by the rapid establishment of a new joint profession, to institutionalize that corps of professionals who will be responsible to the nation for the successful conduct of modern joint and combined warfare.

Notes

1. An earlier version of this argument was published as "Jointness, Defense Transformation, and the Necessity for a New Joint Warfare Profession," *Parameters* 34 (Autumn 2003): 17-30.

2. Les Brownlee and Peter J. Schoomaker, "Serving a Nation at War: A Campaign Quality Army with Joint and Expeditionary Capabilities," *Parameters* 33 (Summer 2004): 5-23.

3. For an excellent short overview of the evolution, see James R. Locher, "Has it worked? The Goldwater Nichols Reorganization Act," *Naval War College Review* 54 (Autumn 2001): 95-105.

4. The obvious exception to this generalization is the special operations forces under the unified Special Operations Command.

5. Douglas A. MacGregor, "The Joint Force: A Decade, No Progress," *Joint Force Quarterly* (Winter 2000-2001): 18-23.

6. Congress, House, Committee of Conference on Report (H.R. 99-824), *Conference Report on H.R. 3622*, 99th Congress, 2d Session, 12 September 1986, Title IV, Section 401, chap. 38, Section 661(a).

7. The best place to start in this immense literature remains Stephen Peter Rosen, *Innovation and the Modern Military: Winning the Next War* (Ithaca, NY: Cornell University Press, 1991). Perhaps the best place to end is with Colin S. Gray, *Strategy for Chaos: Revolutions in Military Affairs and the Evidence of History* (London: Frank Cass Publishers, 2002).

8. Donald H. Rumsfeld, *Transformation Planning Guidance* (Washington, DC: Office of the Secretary of Defense, April 2003), 21.

9. For a description of the services as military professions, their fields of expert knowledge, and their competitive jurisdictions, see chap. 1 of this anthology.

10. James F. Shank, Harry J. Thie, and Margaret C. Harrell, "Identifying and Supporting Joint Duty Assignments, Executive Summary"; "How Many Can Be Joint: Supporting Joint Duty Assignments"; and "Who Is Joint? Reevaluating the Joint Duty List," RAND, National Security Research Division, 1996.

11. William J. Crowe, Jr., *The Line of Fire: From Washington to the Gulf, the Politics and Battles of the New Military* (New York: Simon and Schuster, 1993), 158.

12. James R. Locher, "Taking Stock of Goldwater-Nichols," *Joint Force Quarterly* (Autumn 1996): 15.

13. If there was any lingering doubt among Army officers, it was dispelled when Gen. Peter Schoomaker became CSA; see the epigraph to the present chapter.

14. For an approach to mapping the expert knowledge of the military professions, see Richard Lacquement, *Army Professional Expertise and Jurisdictions* (Carlisle, PA: Strategic Studies Institute, Army War College, November 2003). The acronym C4ISR stands for Command, Control, Communications, Computers, Intelligence, Surveillance, and Reconnaissance.

15. For further discussion of the joint C4ISR architectures and their impacts on the Army profession's jurisdictions, see chap. 13 of this anthology by Elizabeth Stanley and G. F. Deimel.

16. For one such argument, see MacGregor, 18-23. For a more recent, biting comment, see the autobiography of Gen. Tommy Franks, *American Soldier* (New York: Regan Books, 2004), 274, where he describes the service chiefs' critique of his Afghan War Plan at a 20 September 2001 Pentagon meeting as "parochial bull****."

17. For a more complete discussion of the new Joint Operational Concepts and their relationship to the Army profession's expert knowledge, see chap. 9 of this anthology by Richard Lacquement.

18. For greater detail on the critical differences between professions and bureaucracies and the inherent tensions within the current war-fighting professions, which have characteristics of both, see Chap. 1 of this anthology.

19. For a brief introduction to post-Cold War war, see chap. 1 of Wesley K. Clark, *Waging Modern War* (New York: Public Affairs Press, 2001), 1-28.

20. Don M. Snider, "Officership: The Professional Practice," *Military Review* (January-February 2003): 3-8.

21. The Army's share of the JDAL in 2004 is just over 3,000 officers. The average assignment length is 2.6 years, meaning that each year roughly 1,100 officers rotate out of JDAL positions and must be replaced by other Army professionals. How much this rotation is reduced will be determined by the initial size of the new joint profession, which would be determined by new legislation.

22. Andrew Abbott, "The Army and the Theory of Professions," in *The Future of the Army Profession*, proj. directors Don M. Snider and Gayle L. Watkins, ed. Lloyd J. Matthews (Boston, MA: McGraw-Hill, 2002), 523-36.

23. Michael Matthews and John R. Hyatt, "Factors Affecting the Career Decisions of Army Captains," Research Report 1760 (Washington, DC: U.S. Army Research Institute for the Behavioral and Social Sciences, June 2000).

24. See chap. 8 of Thomas G. Mahnken and James R. FitzSimonds, *The Limits of Transformation: Officer Attitudes Toward the Revolution in Military Affairs* (Newport, RI: U.S. Naval War College, 2002).

25. Gayle L. Watkins and Randi Cohen, "In their Own Words: Army Officers Discuss Their Profession," chap. 5 of the present anthology.

11 | A Return to the Army's Roots: Governance, Stabilization, and Reconstruction

Nadia Schadlow, Charles Barry, and Richard Lacquement

Introduction

On 9 April 2003, a jubilant crowd toppled the statue of Saddam Hussein in central Baghdad. Within hours of the liberation of Baghdad, amid spreading disorder and growing expectations, debate began over the "postwar" phase of Operation Iraqi Freedom. Therein also began many of the problems that beset the United States in Iraq. On 1 May 2003, President Bush announced to sailors on the USS Abraham Lincoln that "major combat operations in Iraq" had ended, sending a signal that the toughest part of the war was over. Although major combat operations had ended, the deaths of American service members and the war for the future of Iraq have continued.

President Bush's remarks on the aircraft carrier reflected a misconception common in American history—held by Americans in and out of uniform and of every political stripe—that overlooks the distinction between strategic victory (defined as the achievement of policy objectives) and battlefield or combat success.[1] Until stable security, governance, and basic services are established in areas where U.S. armed forces have assumed control in the course of battle, the war is incomplete and the durable achievement of political objectives is unlikely. In short, the war is not yet won. The U.S. armed forces, most often the Army, have been the critical link between battlefield victory and the establishment of political and economic stability. But until very recently the Army has shown little enthusiasm for such missions and has not accepted associated jurisdictions as critical for the development and application of its own expert knowledge. Professionally, the Army should be eager to claim critical aspects of stability operations as part of its war-fighting and war-winning jurisdictions in a way that does reach the level of expert knowledge. The cultural challenge for the Army now is to re-embrace vigorously critical stability operations, particularly those associated with governance, economic stabilization, and reconstruction, as integral, inevitable parts of war itself.[2] All Army forces—not merely the civil affairs or special operations communities—will, to some degree, be involved in stability operations essential to the achievement of strategic victory. Combat and efforts to establish a stable local order are not separate phases of war as is often implied by the current distinction between Phase III operations (major combat operations) and Phase IV (post-conflict operations). They are interrelated components of war. Unless the Army is successful in both components, wars will not be won.[3]

This chapter focuses on the Army's primary role in stability operations, arguing that governance, economic stabilization, and reconstruction of basic infrastructure are integral tasks of war-fighting and war-winning within a critical jurisdiction of the profession. The chapter provides a conceptual framework for stability operations buttressed by historical evidence of the Army as central actor in such operations.

There are two principal products of this discussion. The first is a coherent conceptual underpinning for accepting stability operations as integral to war-fighting and war-winning. This rationale is grounded in Army history as well as in the ecology of vocational professions elaborated by Professor Andrew Abbott. This higher-order conceptual thesis focuses on *how to think* about critical stability operations. It also yields urgent questions for the Army profession's strategic leaders.

Our second objective is to show how application of such expert knowledge will help the Army prepare for operations in transformed U.S. armed forces that are committed to joint operations. For example, acceptance of key stability operations as intrinsic to war will allow for more realistic joint net assessments and more informed decision-making about national security policy and strategy. It will also facilitate clearer mission analysis, stronger command and control, smoother transition operations, more rapid achievement of strategic success, and, hence, speedier disengagement for all U.S. forces. The sooner these tasks are accepted as intrinsic to the mission of war-fighting, particularly by the Army, the more likely that military planning and execution will be suitably shaped by all the policy considerations that rightfully govern outcomes in war. Additionally, efforts by military planners to plan, organize, and train for these tasks *prior* to combat operations should highlight related areas that require policy guidance from civilian leaders.

Conceptual Underpinnings—
The Abbott Theory of Professions

Andrew Abbott's theory of professions argues that professions are bound to jurisdictions defined by sets of tasks over which the profession establishes control and promulgates expert knowledge.[4] Expert knowledge is theoretical knowledge, that is, knowledge of practices in the abstract. It is independent of situational factors yet applicable to them as expert practice when the two bodies of knowledge—abstraction and situation—are combined. Abstract knowledge or *abstractions* about professional practices describe how we should *think expertly* about the task under consideration.

Abbott's theory indicates that professions compete with other producers of expert (abstract) knowledge to meet client demands and achieve control over the application of that knowledge in jurisdictions of practice. Army strategic leaders represent the profession in negotiating jurisdictional claims with the civilian leaders that represent American society. Army negotiating claims emerge primarily with respect to four external jurisdictions of military work: major combat operations, stability operations, strategic deterrence, and homeland security.[5]

Abbott's theory asserts that a profession engages competitively within jurisdictions. Thus, where pockets of expert knowledge are considered to reside is always under scrutiny. In the jurisdiction of medicine, for example, over many decades nurses and others, through research, publication, and professional associations, have gained acceptance as the source of expert abstract knowledge complementing or supplanting doctors (the dominant medical professionals) on some aspects of medical care. In the case of stability operations incident to war, high-level expertise on the part of the Army, recognized and accepted by other practitioners and participants in the field, would be the logical extension of being the primary actor in such operations. However, were the Army not to nurture its stability operations expertise, other groups having expert knowledge within the jurisdiction could move in to fill the void and would be regarded increasingly as the source of expert knowledge on how stability operations should be implemented. The Army is "competing" (in the sense of Abbott's theory) with other actors on how stability operations should be done (i.e., as to whose knowledge is most expert), and who should do the work or apply the expertise (Army professionals or others). Such competitors include international organizations, nongovernmental and private voluntary organizations, civilian government agencies, foreign police and militaries, and elite policy institutions, such as the U.S. Institute of Peace and the National Defense University.

Of course, not all players compete directly to determine core Army practices involved in stability operations. Yet, to the extent that outside expert know-how is accorded legitimacy by planners, decision-makers, and the public in lieu of Army expert methods *in areas of the jurisdiction that are mainly the business of Army professionals*, the Army's implementation may be modified in ways counter to its best judgment or even in ways beyond its control. If the Army cedes, as Abbott says, the "creation and adaptation and application of abstract expert knowledge to new situations," it runs the risk of becoming just a bureaucratic implementer of its operations, instead of a professional expert that can influence the conceptual development of its operations.[6] Charged with the control of deadly force by society, military leaders must be experts in any operation that requires the effective employment of its organized capacity for applying coercive force to achieve societal objectives. Within the American joint military establishment, the emergence of joint professional expertise in this area might facilitate shared jurisdiction of stability operations by the Army and joint professions. While bureaucratic management of stability operations is well established at the joint level, the development of commensurate joint professional expertise is unclear. Recognizing that the Army is the institution of the American armed forces most often charged with execution of stability operations, strategic leaders of the Army profession should take the lead in defining the appropriate expertise and jurisdictions for such operations. Although Army leaders can and should take into account the knowledge of other experts, we will argue here that the Army itself has to possess its own expertise over this jurisdiction.

Abbott tells us further that the strength or weakness of a profession's link to the tasks within its jurisdictional competition determines the profession's vulnerability to ceding its jurisdictional claim to a professional competitor.[7] To the extent a profession weakens its emphasis in an area within its external jurisdiction, it risks shrinking its influence over that jurisdiction. A competition for recognition and legitimacy as the source of expert knowledge also exists in the public arena, where expert knowledge is sought, as well as inside the profession among its own members. Therefore, of primary concern for the Army, and the focus of this chapter, is the nature of the Army's jurisdictional claim over stability operations.

The Army's Jurisdictional Claim for Wartime Stability Operations

When Army professionals talk about their profession, the expertise they claim with the greatest fervor is that of "fighting and winning the nation's wars."[8] That profound, straightforward commitment—what the Army goes on to say is a "non-negotiable contract with the American people"—homes in on the Army's central role in ensuring the nation's security; it is where the Army directs its resources and intellectual energies. The validity of this focus is unquestionable, and, given the stakes, there can be no other. But what falls within the jurisdiction of war-fighting and, in particular, war-winning? The conduct of combat operations is central. The art and science of war concentrate on destruction of the enemy force and the conquering of territory. Once these tasks are accomplished, it is expected that the hard part is over. Peace is reestablished, and, with far less effort and resources presumably, civil control will soon end the Army's role. To the extent that instability in the post-conflict environment postpones the Army's disengagement, the Army dutifully and resolutely turns its energies to stability operations. Yet, there has been an underlying reluctance in the Army to embrace stability missions in full, to accept them as truly central to a professional army's core area of expertise. Rather, there is an eagerness to be done with them and return to a focus on combat operations.

Recent history suggests that, for a number of reasons mainly having to do with informational technologies and the growing global awareness of political and social injustices, modern warfare is now much more complicated. In a similar manner, the successful transition to a just and durable peace has become more arduous. Destruction of the enemy force often sweeps away any semblance of governance, leaving an expeditionary Army to fill the roles of temporary government, emergency service provider, and stop-gap law enforcer until a new civil order *commensurate with the political objectives of the war* can be put in place and undertake permanent nation building strategies.

Following battlefield victory, the U.S. armed forces—the Army in particular—are typically the only readily available institutions capable of controlling territory and people. The armed forces are capable of dispersing throughout a country and are trained to operate under a well-established chain of command. As an inherent part of their organization and capabilities, American armed forces are very effective self-governing entities. The Army is adept at moving, fighting, and meeting the basic needs of its members (to include food, shelter, fuel, medical support, communications, transport, and so on) under the direction of a clear, hierarchical governing structure (the chain of command). Moreover, the Army as a whole has some organic units (e.g., civil affairs, public affairs, psyops, military police, and even civilian political advisors) that lend themselves directly to civil governance (more on this later). Thus, with some adaptation, a combat unit's organizational structure and its associated individual skill sets can be extended to governance of the local civilian population within a unit's area of operations.

Conceptually and practically, however, it is impossible to draw a line between the end of major combat operations and reestablishment of the social and political order essential to the accomplishment of policy objectives. Combat operations and stability operations have consistently overlapped for long periods before and after the declaration of an end to major combat operations.

It is also important for Army professionals to distinguish between stability operations (such as those related to basic governance, economic stabilization, and the maintenance or reconstruction of basic infrastructure) that are core elements of all wars, and activities such as peace operations and peacekeeping that may occur independently of war. This is not merely an issue of semantics. The two are strategically different types of operations, although they may share similar types of tasks. Humanitarian assistance and peacekeeping operations often reflect political decisions to use the military in non-war situations. Some of these situations may be more dangerous than others, but the political rationale for intervening in peacetime operations is different from the rationale for committing the United States to war. Moreover, when Army professionals label political and economic reconstruction as a postwar problem, they discount the fact that central to strategic victory in all wars fought by the United States has been the creation or reestablishment of a favorable local political order. Another way to think about this is that American leaders may or may not choose on occasion to commit U.S. armed forces to stability operations in peacetime. In conjunction with war, however, the armed forces will always face the inevitable requirements to perform stability operations.

Historical Overview

The Army's first experience with stability operations was in securing and building the United States itself. From the earliest days of its existence, the Army played an active role in supporting settlement and rudimentary governance in the growing republic. During the country's western expansion, the Army operated at the fringes of established government and control. It was a central participant in instituting and protecting basic governing functions in often hostile environments.

During the Civil War, Army units not only fought the Confederates, but also were responsible for governing the territories of the southern states as they were reclaimed for the Union.[9] Following the Civil War, the Army played a substantial (and often controversial) role in the occupation and reconstruction of the South. The Army was also at the center of the country's continued westward expansion. The role of a multifunctional Army in overlapping combat, governance, and stabilization efforts was a hallmark of this era.

The Army's familiarity with handling routine governance and other stabilization tasks carried over to the long postwar governance of territories acquired during the Spanish-American War of 1898. In Cuba, Puerto Rico, and the Philippines, the Army played an active role in stabilization, governance, and reconstruction in the midst of and following combat. In the Philippines from 1899 to 1902, military-led nation-building and governance took place while the Army continued to fight an extensive insurgency. Military leaders often had dual responsibilities—to fight elements of Emilio Aguinaldo's forces while performing duties as military governors of local territory and populations.[10] The Army remained extensively involved in the Philippines for the next four decades. The Army was actively engaged in stability operations, to include fighting against Moro insurgents, as well as creating and training Philippine armed forces in anticipation of national independence.[11] Similarly, after World War II, several military leaders served as military governors of Germany, Japan, Korea, and Italy.[12] Gen. Dwight Eisenhower, for example, exercised supreme command over allied military forces and also assumed responsibilities as the military governor of portions of Germany as it was conquered.[13] Gen. Douglas MacArthur assumed similar duties for those territories liberated from Japanese rule in the Pacific during active combat operations. After Japan's surrender, MacArthur assumed the position of military governor of that vanquished foe.[14]

Historically, the Army often *sought* control over governance operations due to commanders' perceptions of military necessity and the desire to preserve unity of command. Army commanders recognized that operational control over all activities in the theater was critical for maintaining stability and for protecting U.S. forces during the course of the war. During World War II competition between the Army and civilian postwar planners arose less because of the Army's desire to lead governance operations than because of the Army's determination to rise above the confusion of civilian planning and preserve unity of command. Frustrating coordination problems had arisen in North Africa in the summer of 1942, and General Eisenhower was determined to avoid a situation in which civilian and military authority over the same territory existed. This was not just a matter of controlling turf or building bureaucratic empires. Military commanders have realized that the security of their command and the territory within which it operates is dramatically affected by the quality of life among the local inhabitants. In short, the establishment of basic governance and order enhanced security for all concerned.

A significant institutional legacy of Vietnam is the present structural segregation of elements most likely to engage in governance and other stability operations. These elements were placed outside the Army's mainstream combat structure, exemplified most clearly by the placement of civil affairs units within Special Operations Forces. The separation was further reinforced by placing these capabilities mainly in the reserves. The institutional inclination toward specialization and separation after Vietnam ignored one of the broader lessons of the Vietnam War—the requirement to treat pacification (Gen. William Westmoreland's "other war") and "big unit" conventional war as inseparable elements of one seamless strategic effort.

An important contemporary problem is that the American approach to war has changed. Sizable forces required in earlier campaigns (such as World War II in both

Europe and the Pacific) performed constabulary duties as populated areas were captured.[15] Over time the whole territory was controlled with small garrisons that provided public security and addressed threats to it, such as insurrections, before they could gain momentum. Using military resources these forces also reconstituted basic civil institutions and services as part of establishing the peace and security desired by locals and needed for winning strategically.

During the major combat phase in Afghanistan and Iraq, however, the United States armed forces took advantage of new concepts and technologies to field fast moving and highly capable forces *in minimum numbers* to achieve victory. This is a counterforce strategy that does not emphasize territorial control. In both Afghanistan and Iraq, forces quickly toppled political leaders and, with them, the governmental authority that was responsible for security and basic services for the population. Early battlefield victory deposed the enemy leadership but did not destroy its forces, leaving the potential for an insurgency to emerge. Most importantly, in capturing population centers, the smaller number of forces employed greatly limited the ability to garrison outlying towns and cities and thereby prevent power vacuums following the sudden removal of authority. That is, the tactic restricted our ability to create legitimate institutions that could provide law enforcement, basic civic services, and utilities.

With so much as context, in the sections that follow we will analyze the professional challenges of stability operations and suggest ways for the Army profession to more effectively address them. The sections explore challenges of stability operations with respect to doctrine; organization; training, leadership, and education; material; and personnel.[16] Each section begins with questions to frame considerations for effective stability operations. Subsequent paragraphs explore preliminary answers and recommendations for improving stability operation performance. However, underlying any effort to implement the improvements suggested here will have to be a fundamental revamping by the Army of its own professional culture.

Stability operations mainly have been and will remain the business of the Army. The Army must thus work to regain the intellectual high ground in that endeavor. The Army is at risk of becoming the primary bureaucratic actor in a field defined and directed by outside experts if it continues to grudgingly regard stability operations as being on the periphery of its professional jurisdiction but threatening to usurp intellectual capital and resources hitherto devoted to war-fighting.

Reversing the post-Vietnam and post-Somalia resistance to stability operations is more of a cultural and intellectual challenge than simply an organizational one. The sentiment "we don't do windows" all too often captures the profession's attitude toward these "fringe" operations. Contrarily, we believe that stability operations belong *within* the core expert knowledge and practicing expertise of the Army professional as much as war-fighting because they are essential to, and part of, winning the war strategically.

Doctrine

Sound doctrine on stability operations capabilities should lay out the dimensions of the Army's strategic interests. A key question already suggested is: How should doctrine address distinctions between stability operations in war and similar tasks that are pursued in peacetime? What principles apply? How and when should interagency participation be integrated? If available, how should allied forces, peacekeepers, or international police units be integrated? Based on emerging experience and expertise, how should lessons and best practices be incorporated?

Governance and reconstruction must be explored to find the logical doctrinal boundaries for the Army. Governance and reconstruction using military capabilities alone should be temporary expedients driven by the imperatives of war. Governance of a local population is a requirement for the occupying military forces under the laws of land warfare.[17] As armed forces assume control of territory, they assume control of the people and responsibilities for basic governance. Key questions that doctrine should address with respect to governance are: How do land forces prevent the breakdown of order and the emergence of chaos during and in the immediate aftermath of combat operations? What governance and basic services must be put in place by the Army and in what priority? What organizations within the battlespace should have a mission for stability operations, particularly when combat operations are still ongoing? What are the essential stability operational tasks of the Army that are inherent to war-fighting? What kinds of Army forces are needed for stability operations? What command and control structure is optimum? What are the appropriate circumstances and methods for transition from military to civilian authority?

Reconstruction efforts should seek to relieve the worst disruptions in services and to reestablish vital infrastructure related to food, fuel, health, transportation, and electricity generation. How much initial reconstruction should the Army undertake? Where does civilian contracting or other support fit? What sharing of this domain is best for mission effectiveness?

A body of doctrine already exists to help guide Army and joint force efforts to better integrate stability operations; however, there is substantial room for improvement.[18] Army doctrine (such as FM 3-0, *Operations*) and emerging joint concepts represent important steps forward in legitimating the need for concurrent execution of stability operations within war.[19] Army and joint doctrine should be streamlined to reflect seamless integration of combat and stability operations.[20]

Political objectives are rarely if ever attained through fighting alone. Major combat operations must be accomplished with a strong appreciation for the political objectives for which the war has been undertaken. In this regard, all parties to the war effort—civilian as well as military—should re-read their Clausewitz. The continued engagement of the United States in both Afghanistan and Iraq illustrates this reality. Defeating the Taliban and al Qaeda requires more than simply military measures. Defeating armed formations and displacing them from particular geographic areas do little to dry up sources of enemy support or eliminate all the potential areas in which they can operate. In both countries, a major part of the effort to eliminate the base of support and tolerance for American enemies is the creation of a stable, functioning society that will eschew support for violence.

To the degree that military operations in combat are "merely the continuation of policy by other means,"[21] it is worth considering another aspect of this well-worn Clausewitzian axiom: *with the cessation of major combat operations, politics con-*

tinues by means other than war. So far as successful combat operations against armed opponents are concerned, it behooves leaders to consider the relevance of perseverance, legitimacy, and restraint in a long-term strategic context as well as tactical and operational contexts. In this regard, although Clausewitz also cautions that "in war the result is never final,"[22] it is worth considering the manner in which the positive outcomes of fighting can be made more enduring.

The Army should think beyond its own tasks and extend its abstract knowledge to consider how the overall stability operations mission ought to be done. Naturally, joint and multinational perspectives will inform Army knowledge. In the creation of Army doctrine and the shaping of joint doctrine, much of what is done during stability operations will involve increasing interaction with civil agencies from other parts of the U.S. government, local government officials, and numerous international, private, and nongovernmental organizations. The Army, as the biggest and most capable force in the earliest stages, needs to carefully consider its interface with these stakeholders and how to optimize their collective effect and resource uses.

The strategic framework that underpins expert knowledge of stability operations is unique in many of its tenets.[23] Thinking about such operations in their broader strategic context yields many important considerations that should inform doctrine. In recent American operations, the distinction between so-called "Phase III" (major combat operations) and "Phase IV" (post-conflict stability operations) has been sharply drawn. The tendency to see these phases as sequential and separate has been problematic to say the least. As operations in Afghanistan and Iraq have clearly demonstrated, Phase III and Phase IV occur concurrently and overlap for long periods, even when either combat or stability operations are clearly primary. Moreover, with the acceleration of combat operations occasioned by recent transformation efforts (characterized by the ability to swiftly defeat enemy military formations and the governing parties they support), the need to address many of the tasks associated with Phase IV has also shifted into Phase III operations. Unity of effort within coherent war-winning and peace-winning strategies must be well understood by all strategic and operational commanders. The same commanders and staffs that plan for major combat operations must, at an appropriate organizational level, be responsible for execution of post-conflict operations. Indeed, planning for combat should carefully consider the conditions to be set for successful stabilization and reconstruction. Doctrine should reflect this basic tenet of war-fighting.

Doctrine for intelligence and information operations is also critical to enabling effective stability operations. Doctrine for intelligence must emphasize regional, ethnic, religious, cultural, and political characteristics and actors. Doctrine for information operations should prescribe adherence to a compelling and consistent strategic message, the early introduction of indigenous capabilities, both governmental and commercial, and the achievement of demonstrable early success in reconstruction.

A long-standing challenge is the timing and coordination of the transition from military to civilian authority. Establishing means to facilitate this transition can draw on many historical examples to provide patterns related to the transition from military control to civilian. Series of mutually reinforcing events often occur to facilitate the shift: creation of a provisional government; reestablishment of general public security (not security from remnants of enemy forces alone but from vigilantism, reprisals, and lawlessness); holding of local elections and national elections; adoption of a new constitution; reestablishment of schools; and re-creation of indigenous security forces.

From the well-known Clausewitzian axiom that wars are fought for political aims, we know that unless the identified political goals are achieved, the war is not won.[24] Achieving such political goals takes place not in the air or at sea, but on land. For that reason, the Army as the dominant practitioner of land warfare should have professional jurisdiction as well as the requisite expert knowledge to execute initial post-conflict missions. To accomplish these successfully, Army doctrine must be improved to recognize and more coherently confront the challenges of stability operations in war.

Organization

Force structure issues are always among the most daunting within resource allocation because they are far more permanent and costly than the majority of choices strategic leaders have to make. How should the Army organize for stability operations? Are specialized units appropriate? Are they required? What are the limits to multi-tasking existing organizations to perform stability operations, combat operations, and other tasks? At what organizational level should combat and post-conflict missions be planned and executed by different organizations, and where should responsibility be combined? Should the same command executing the combat operations initiate stabilization operations? Can the Army count on soldiers fresh from combat—or still engaging in mop-up or counterinsurgency combat operations—to fill the public security gap in a foreign culture until civilian police can be organized and put in place? With the Army already engaged in multiple stability operations around the globe, is the reservoir of stability operations capabilities sufficient for force rotation? How should other capability providers (for example, units from the other services, allied forces, international organizations, and NGOs) factor into the analysis? What is the expected active/reserve component profile and how do anticipated readiness conditions within each component inform the solution?[25] How does the organizational framework influence second or third order considerations for recruitment of personnel and equipment investment?

Within organizational issues, some of the most influential aspects derive from command arrangements. A critical assumption to be challenged is that the combat commander can do it all. Can he be successful in combat and in post-combat when the endeavors overlap for a considerable period of time? What is the optimal command arrangement for planning and overseeing stability operations in their earliest stages? What are the headquarters' competencies for stability operations and what is the right headquarters design to carry them out? Would separate commands for concurrent combat operations and stability operations violate unity of command? And even if the answer is yes, is that an acceptable cost if it relieves the combat commander of conducting two types of operations simultaneously—major combat and crucial post-conflict stabilization?[26]

As mentioned earlier, there are parts of the Army's existing force structure that are well suited for stability operations; however, they are structured as part of units optimized to support combat operations rather than stability operations. Examples of such elements include civil affairs, military police, medical, legal, and engineer units. There should be greater integration of the specialized capabilities and tasks associated with stability operations as components of the overall structure of combat forces. Recent problems in execution suggest the need for better organization from the top to bottom, not just of Army forces, but of all forces in the joint war-fight. Success will require improvements from the national military command structure (Department of Defense and Joint Staff) all the way down to tactical units (particularly those of the Army and Marine Corps). Stability operations capabilities and forces must be organized as joint capabilities that are ready, deployable, modular, and properly sized.[27]

Certain recent studies recommend the assembly or creation of forces customized specifically for stability operations and military operations other than war, including how military units might be organized to better undertake such missions.[28] One proposal includes the creation of two stability and reconstruction units of approximately division size (one in the active force and one in the reserves).[29] It also explores detailed proposals for the types of units—some already existing, some to be created—that would comprise these specialized units. A related effort is the recent proposal by Senators Richard Lugar and Joseph Biden to create a pool of reserves from other government agencies, especially the State Department, readily available for call-up in the event of an emergency.[30] Robert Perito proposes the creation of separate U.S. constabulary forces tailored to better execute fundamental law enforcement functions on an expeditionary basis.[31] Perito focuses on the creation of civilian capacity, especially for police tasks, to better address the gap between military capabilities and the need for civilian police in post-conflict societies.

Regardless of specific organizational structures, we believe it is important to avoid drawing too strong a line between war-fighting forces and units created to support better execution of stability operations. Indeed, the creation or integration of the new capabilities must not relieve combat commanders of responsibility for the overarching stability operations. The command structure itself should reinforce the integration of war-fighting and stability operations, particularly among members of the chain of command. Commanders and their primary staffs must be closely engaged in the realization of key stabilization, governance, and reconstruction objectives. Units adapted for governance operations should not become the repository for tasks that war-fighting commanders prefer to divest.

Solutions to how to design a particular functional force are often found over time by means of experimentation. Exercises, provisional commands, and ad hoc task forces are tried, and subject matter experts study the trade-offs among the best organizational options. Drawing on the analysis of its competitors, the Army can leap ahead in this area by testing one or more of the proposed solutions against current methods. Synthesis and further refinement would be required to reach a validated result. Ultimately, investing in such an engagement with other stakeholders would assert the Army's interest and expertise at least in the sub-areas of the stability operations jurisdiction covering its own operations.

In the past, ad hoc arrangements tended to prevail, as the Army began to oversee and implement political and economic reconstruction tasks in a theater of war. Army commanders on the ground faced the challenge of how to adapt the chain of command to deal more effectively with tasks that differed from combat. World War II illustrated the challenges of operations focused mainly on enemy combat forces and the need to establish territorially oriented military governance. Even after the German surrender, it was difficult to meet shifting demands for manpower and the need for continuity in territorially focused governance.[32]

Because they were commanding a much smaller force that was still engaged in combat in many areas, commanders in Iraq had a difficult initial transition from war-fighting to stabilization.[33] Subsequently, combat unit commanders did a better job at stability operations because they turned to them in earnest even as they engaged in major counterinsurgency operations. In those regions U.S. forces could cover, civil affairs teams, civilian agencies, and other forces with skills critical for stabilization and reconstruction were integrated, and staffs better understood the unique challenges of stability operations. This adjustment took time, however, because these disparate forces were not used to working together and were not able rapidly to bring all their capabilities to bear.[34] During that time the stability operations task grew to critical dimensions as the insurgency grew. Some of the initiative lost in the early days and months has been recovered, but a price has been paid in loss of support at home and from the Iraqi people.[35] The need for the Army profession to create solutions is obvious.

Training, Leadership, and Education

What adaptations are required in the training and leader development systems to better prepare the Army profession for stability operations? Do precommissioning programs and basic training provide adequate foundations to socialize new soldiers to the realities of stability operations as well as war-fighting? Does the military education system address throughout a leader's career the demands of stability operations? Are the Army's combat training centers providing realistic scenarios for stability operations?

Stability operations clearly do complicate, often in dramatic ways, combat planning and execution. To the degree that standard tactics, techniques, and procedures for stability operations can be developed and rehearsed, the training system will doubtless be a critical aspect of this process; however, one of the fundamental aspects of stability operations is the great variety of possible situations that arise. Different cultures, habits, and degrees of acquiescence to a foreign military presence exponentially complicate the challenges of stability operations. Quite frequently, when there is talk of "strategic" corporals and lieutenants, it is with regard to these ambiguous situations in stability operations, particularly those on the blurred boundary between peace and war that require the most exquisite judgment and sensibilities. There is evidence from Iraq that our junior leaders have learned tremendously valuable lessons from their experience about how to adapt and innovate to deal with the ambiguous situations that often arise in stability operations.[36] A crucial task for the profession will be to reinforce the systems that have contributed to this success and to improve training, leadership, and education systems based on input from soldiers schooled and tested in combat and stability operations. One of the best ways to prepare for the uncertain and the unexpected is to condition the minds of our soldiers with the habits of thought that will allow them to exercise sound judgment. This conditioning requires the use of training to prepare for identifiable challenges and requires rigorous education to create the intellectual capacity to adapt to unforeseeable scenarios. These are quintessential professional obligations.

Our central argument has been that the Army must re-embrace stability operations as part of its core professional expertise and jurisdictions. Absolutely essential to the realization of this requirement is the adoption of a training and leader development paradigm that inculcates the principles governing effective stability operations. The professional education system plays a critical role in both reflecting and shaping this professional culture.

Acceptance of the conceptual approach we suggest has a myriad of cascading implications. Appropriate venues to focus on improved education and training are the command and staff colleges, the senior service colleges, and the combat training centers. Whatever structures are employed, improved education and realistic training should emphasize the interactive and complementary aspects of combat and stability operations. Combat units must train and exercise to understand the culturally ambiguous and in many ways more demanding tasks related to stability operations. This includes understanding of the complexities of civilians on the battlefield as well as rudimentary aspects of nation-building that take place concurrently with combat. Better preparation of existing units should include governance tasks as part of Mission Essential Task Lists (METL) for all units that might operate in foreign countries during or after combat. Competence in these tasks must be part of individual and collective training. Reinforcement and evaluation of these tasks should be integrated into the programs at the combat training centers.

One aspect of stability operations that must be injected thoroughly into the Army's professional development systems is the importance of understanding the politico-cultural environment that characterizes the area of operations. Identifying, valuing, nurturing, and employing broader cultural knowledge and language skills within the officer corps will also enrich the abstract knowledge related to stability operations, especially knowledge of regional cultures and languages, their sociology, history, civil governance, and public administration. Experience in stability operations and with international organizations should be valued as additional institutional expertise and promoted as a way to deepen the Army's commitment to reclaiming the stability operations jurisdiction. Finally, development of expert knowledge in interpersonal skills and negotiations would serve the Army well in the field of stability operations.[37]

Material

What are the material demands for stability operations? What are the sources available to meet the most pressing basic needs of populations within the zone of conflict? What can Army units provide to assist with stability operations from among resources provided for unit sustainment? What are the local assets likely to be available to assist? How do vulnerabilities and challenges of Army units in stability operations differ from combat-focused capabilities they possess? Are material or technological solutions available to mitigate the risks to stability operations forces that must exercise greater restraint and discrimination in the midst of potentially hostile local settings? Can critical material needs be prepositioned for ready availability in likely theaters of operation? Should the Army plan to deploy additional support units, for example, transport or medical, solely to provide for civilian needs in post-conflict stabilization?

An important difference between stability operations and rapid combat operations is the stand-off range with which the armed forces are able to operate. The current trends in high technology developments for combat operations are to identify, engage, and destroy adversaries well beyond the ranges at which those adversaries can engage American forces. Protection for friendly forces is enhanced by distance. In contrast, however, stability operations bring the armed forces into close proximity with local populations. That proximity permits adversaries with very low-technology weapons to mask their activities within the population and get within range where their weapons and tactics can exploit remaining American vulnerabilities. As insurgencies throughout history have often demonstrated, the stronger military force does not always win. In fact, by relying too heavily on superior military force, the side that began with the greatest military power has often been goaded into actions that only alienate local populations and undermine popular support and local allegiance that are often crucial political objectives in war. Therefore, high technology weaponry, while still valuable, has important limits.[38] No doubt, when the use of force is required, the ability to apply violence with great precision and discrimination is crucial. But the current emphasis on precision kinetic munitions delivered from stand-off ranges, no matter how discriminant, still has a high propensity to inflict collateral casualties among innocent bystanders and damage nearby property, thus counteracting efforts to build local support.

A host of advanced technologies are applicable to stability operations. Investment in technologies is important because of the urgency of understanding and maintaining control over a complex, chaotic, and unfamiliar area of operations.[39] Available technologies will need to be scrutinized and demonstrations conducted to identify best capabilities. But more to the point, the laboratories for experimentation should include current stability operations missions around the globe.

Many technologies used by combat forces are also essential for stability operations forces, including weapons, night-vision devices, personnel protection, individual Blue Force tracking, global positioning systems, unmanned aerial vehicles, and tough, damage-resistant computing technologies/hardware. Other key technology areas to explore for stability operations include security, infrastructure protection, and human relations. Security technologies focus on communications architectures (including analog-digital interface); networked analysis; and decision support tools adapted for counterterrorism, biometric identification, and nonlethal weapons. Infrastructure technologies should include civil infrastructure simulations for critical node mapping, electrical power generation, water purification, and emergency medical systems. Finally, at least two human relations technologies are of keen interest in stability operations. One is emerging mobile real-time language translators. The second is the promise of elite leadership modeling systems capable of modeling community leaders' influence and relative areas of authority and administrative control.

Personnel

Do Army personnel systems provide adequate flexibility and fidelity for identification and assignment of personnel and units to meet the demands of stability operations? Is the right mix of individual specialties available to the Army? Are sufficient personnel for immediate deployment available in the active forces? Are high demand stability operations specialists such as civil affairs and military police available in the reserve components in sufficient numbers, readily deployable and sustainable over multiple deployments? Does the personnel system adequately track information on relevant stability operations skills among reserve members with other relevant civilian specialties (for example, an infantryman with police, construction, or local government experience)?

As many have noted, stability operations draw more heavily on certain personnel specialties (such as civil affairs, medical, and legal personnel) than the Army's combat-oriented force structure has been able to sustain. As the organizational aspects we've addressed have already made clear, the global war on terrorism creates demands for particular specialties that far exceed the supply, particularly among the active duty forces. The combat-focused structure of the active forces has placed an unsustainable burden on activation of reserves to perform many critical stabilization tasks. Although there is often a good match between the skills reservists perform in peacetime and what they are called upon to do in stabilization operations, there is an imbalance in the number of deployments that many of these specialists have been required to undertake. Moreover, it is an imbalance that invites the question of the long-term retention of these critical personnel as well as whether the basic concept of reserve service and structures the Army has today are valid, or even relevant to the future.[40]

Another way to maintain within Army forces personnel in specialties more commonly found in civil society is to employ periodic assignment of active duty officers to positions in civil society that provide skill and experience for stability operations. During peacetime or in between deployment, certain active duty personnel could be assigned as fellows in civil government organizations, businesses, and the academic community in line with their expected responsibilities in military stability operations.

Future headquarters and staff organizations, in most cases joint, should include appropriate restructuring for stability operations so as to be able to provide expertise on political, cultural, legal, financial, economic, and even religious matters for Army commanders down the chain of command. Not every military officer or soldier can be expected to be a regional expert in a particular theater. But theirs is the job of execution, of flexibility in figuring out how to get a job done, of resourcefulness and adaptability. These qualities have always been core strengths of the American solider. While the military will be held accountable for getting the job done—organizing new police forces, reopening schools, etc.—those who provide the essential expertise must be readily available and be held accountable as well. The appropriate way to capitalize on these areas of traditional civilian professional expertise would benefit from further joint stability operations experimentation, including interagency and perhaps multinational participants. Important areas for additional research and exploration of more effective mechanisms for governance in the wake of war or other major conflicts should include improvements to the federal interagency processes, the creation of a rapidly deployable civilian capacity to augment that of the military in such operations, and the overhaul of the legislative processes to supervise and support such operations.[41]

Conclusion: A Return to the Army's Roots

Critical stability operations, such as governance, economic stabilization, and reconstruction, are not a deviation from war-fighting. They are not lesser-included missions. They are not the sole domain of civilian agencies or specialized units. They are not band-aids but rather part of a full triage of a deeply wounded social order. Stability operations are an integral, intrinsic part of war itself. They are a core task of any army, and particularly so for America's expeditionary Army.

In every war in which the Army has fought it had to face stability challenges. There have been many times in American history when our armed forces had to pursue complex political objectives and meet strenuous responsibilities to local populations in the midst of persistent violence or the threat of violence.

> The object in war is to attain a better peace—even if only from your own point of view. Hence it is essential to conduct war with constant regard to the peace you desire. This is the truth underlying Clausewitz's definition of "war as a continuation of policy by other means"—the prolongation of that policy through the war into the subsequent peace must always be borne in mind. A state which expends its strength to the point of exhaustion bankrupts its own policy, and future. If you concentrate exclusively on victory, with no thought of the after-effect, you may be too exhausted to profit by the peace, while it is almost certain that the peace will be a bad one, containing the germs of another war.[42]
>
> —B.H. Liddell Hart

Army professionals must acknowledge and internalize the simple but important truth that when the fighting is over their job is only half complete. In wars for regime change, in particular, the end of major combat operations is just the beginning of a difficult period of upheaval, turmoil, and risk. It is in this critical transition period from one form of rule to another that the Army's role is especially central and critical. The stages immediately after major combat operations help set the tone and trajectory for recovery and stabilization. If American armed forces are perceived as only weakly committed to governance and other critical stabilization tasks, they may severely impair the mission's chances of success. The Army can jeopardize the achievement of stable local conditions by shaky control, incoherent plans, and the absence of resources for effective implementation.

Recognition by both political and military leaders of the fundamental relationship between policy and war will lead to the adoption of more sensible command arrangements that will give the Army a better chance of getting the job done as quickly and painlessly as possible. The belief that outside organizations—the State Department, the NGO community, international organizations, etc.—can enter the scene immediately and assume control fails to recognize an immutable characteristic of war: that political reconstruction and instability go hand in hand. A clear chain of command and a clear understanding of the inextricable relationship between the restoration of order and security are required.

Since political considerations and effects are integral to a successful war effort, civilian and military leaders must include them at all levels of planning: tactical, operational, and strategic. It is well understood that major policy decisions about the goals of military operations and the treatment of local populations figure prominently in how targeted groups calculate stakes and consider resistance.[43] Many ostensibly small tactical decisions are also important and can have troubling consequences with strategic implications.

The re-conceptualization of war we recommend is more than just a matter of semantics or idle academic hair-splitting. Forthrightly confronted, better crafted and resourced stability operations will permit a safer and more timely drawdown of American and other foreign armed forces in the wake of combat. Recognizing certain stability operations as intrinsic to war improves prospects for safer, faster, and more durable strategic victory.

Of all the armed forces, the Army has the biggest stake in stability operations, and its expert knowledge and ownership of governing theory should follow from this reality. Thus the Army would be well served, as we have argued in this chapter, by a strong, permanent investment in creative thought about stability operations. Only in that way can the Army profession attain legitimacy among those staking claims to this jurisdiction. If others prevail without the benefit of the Army's best thinking, the result will be an Army undertaking long-term operations in the field based primarily, or even solely, on the expert knowledge and applied expertise of others far less vested in either the task or the outcome. As the profession of arms that conducts land warfare, the Army has to regard these operations as a core competency and ensure that its leaders are the nation's reservoir of expertise in these endeavors. In stability operations as in combat, American forces must be unsurpassed in the world.

Notes

1. For a more detailed description of this general tendency to equate battle with war in American history, see Antulio J. Echevarria II, *Toward an American Way of War* (Carlisle Barracks, PA: US Army War College, Strategic Studies Institute, 2004).

2. Governance operations are those political and economic tasks necessary, as combat winds down, to establish relative political stability so that an eventual transition to a permanent political authority can take place. See also Nadia Schadlow, "War and the Art of Governance," *Parameters* 33 (Autumn 2003): 85-94.

3. See Conrad Crane, "Peacekeeping, Nation-Building, and Stabilization," in *Winning the War by Winning the Peace: Strategy for Conflict and Post-Conflict in the 21st Century*, ed. Lloyd

J. Matthews (Carlisle Barracks, PA: U.S. Army War College, Strategic Studies Institute, 2004), 27-29.

4. Andrew Abbott, *The System of Professions: An Essay on the Division of Expert Labor* (Chicago, IL: Chicago University Press, 1988).

5. The four major jurisdictions are referenced in the *National Military Strategy, 2004* as well as in separate draft publications posted to the Joint Doctrine web site (http://www.dtic.mil/jointvision/). The Joint operating concepts are Major Combat Operations (http://www.dtic.mil/jointvision/draftmco_joc.doc, version 1.07, 24 March 2004, accessed 6 July 2004); Stability Operations (http://www.dtic.mil/jointvision/draftstab_joc.doc, version 1.03, 5 March 2004, accessed 6 July 2004); Strategic Deterrence (http://www.dtic.mil/jointvision/draftstrat_joc.doc, February 2004, accessed 6 July 2004); and Homeland Security (http://www.dtic.mil/jointvision/drafthls_joc.doc, February 2004, accessed 6 July 2004). See also chap. 1 of the present volume for an overview of internal and external jurisdictions based on Andrew Abbott's theory.

6. Don M. Snider and Gayle L. Watkins, "Introduction," in *The Future of the Army Profession*, project directors Don. M. Snider and Gayle L. Watkins, ed. Lloyd J. Matthews (Boston MA: McGraw-Hill, 2002), 11. Snider and Watkins make the insightful distinction between a profession that has the legitimacy to determine through its own acknowledged expertise how to go about its practice, and a bureaucracy that merely practices as others have prescribed. In the jurisdiction of stability operations, the Army is at risk of being reduced to a bureaucracy as its internal expertise has lagged that of competitors. In the "workplace" arena of stability practitioners, the Army has gained the reputation of being a reluctant practitioner, impatient to be done and longing to return to what it regards as the nobler and worthy practice of winning wars. This is a narrow, incomplete perspective of the complex challenge of winning wars.

7. Abbott, *The System of Professions*, chap. 2.

8. Department of the Army, U.S. Army Field Manual 3.0, *Operations* (2001), 1-2.

9. For example, Nashville, Tennessee, was the first of the southern state capitals to fall to Union forces in early 1862. Until the end of the war, Union officers served as military governors in Tennessee and other parts of the Confederacy as they came under Union control.

10. Brian Linn, *The Philippines War, 1899-1902* (Lawrence, KS: University of Kansas Press, 2000).

11. The U.S. program to establish Philippine independence was interrupted by World War II and the Japanese invasion of the Philippines. American and Philippine forces fought together in the failed effort to defeat the initial Japanese invasion and remained active in guerrilla warfare and other resistance activities until allied forces were able to return to the Philippines. After World War II, the United States completed the process of effecting Philippine independence.

12. John W. Dower, *Embracing Defeat: Japan in the Wake of World War II* (New York: WW. Norton & Company, 1999); John Gimbel, *The American Occupation of Germany: Politics and the Military, 1945-49* (Stanford, CA: Stanford University Press, 1968); and Harry L. Coles and Albert K Weinberg, *U. S. Army in World War II: Civil Affairs: Soldiers Become Governors* (Washington, DC: Government Printing Office, 1986).

13. Gen. Lucius Clay was later appointed military governor of the American zone of occupation at Eisenhower's request.

14. Note that General Clay in Germany was not subordinate to local American civilian representatives until several years after the war; John J. McCloy became the civilian administrator in Germany in 1949. In Japan, MacArthur ruled the country until a new Japanese government was elected.

15. James Dobbins, et al., *America's Role in Nation-Building From Germany to Iraq* (Santa Monica, CA: RAND, 2003), 9-11, 32-34.

16. These sections are titled to reflect the current joint doctrine framework captured by the acronym DOTLMPF—doctrine, organization, training, leadership and education, material, personnel, and facilities. This chapter addresses all the elements except facilities.

17. Department of the Army, FM 27-10, *The Law of Land Warfare* (Washington, DC: 1956).

18. Prominent sources of doctrine include, Joint Publication 3-07, *Joint Doctrine for Military Operations Other than War*, 16 June 1995; JP 3-07.3, *Joint Tactics, Techniques, and Procedures for Peace Operations*, 12 February 1999; JP 3-57, *Joint Doctrine for Civil-Military Operations*, 8 February 2001; JP 3-08, *Interagency Coordination During Joint Operations*, Volumes I and II, 9 October 1996; and *Joint Commander's Handbook for Peace Operations*. Valuable U.S. Army doctrinal manuals include Field Manual 3-0, *Operations*, June 2001; FM 100-23, *Peace Operations*, February 1995; FM 41-10, *Civil Affairs Operations*, 2000; FM 3-05.401, *Civil Affairs Tactics, Techniques, and Procedures*, September 2003; and FM 3-07, *Stability and Support Operations*, February 2002. There is also the tantalizing resurrection of the Marine Corps' *Small Wars Manual* of 1940 as an example of thoughtful consideration of complex military operations that include a substantial component of military participation in stability and governance tasks. U.S. Marine Corps, *Small Wars Manual* (Washington, DC: Government Printing Office, 1940. Reprinted by Sunflower University Press, Manhattan, KS, with introduction by Ronald Schaffer).

19. FM 3-0, *Operations*, 1-14 to 1-17. The Joint operating concepts are detailed in note 5.

20. As an example, current Army and Joint doctrine differ on the identification of principles of war and principles of military operations other than war. Separate principles of perseverance, legitimacy, and restraint in joint doctrine for military operations other than war (joint Publication 3-07, *Joint Doctrine for Military Operations Other than War*, 16 June 1995, II-1) are subsumed as part of the supporting description of the objective principle of war in Army doctrine (FM 3-0, *Operations*, 4-12). The Army definition of objective differs from the Joint doctrine definition in Joint Publication 3-0, *Doctrine for Joint Operations*, 10 September 2001, Appendix A.

21. Carl von Clausewitz, *On War*, ed. Michael Howard and Peter Paret, trans. Bernard Brodie (Princeton NJ: Princeton University Press, 1976), 87.

22. Ibid., 80.

23. Douglas A. MacGregor, "New Strategic Concepts," in *Transforming for Stabilization and Reconstruction Operations*, ed. Hans Binnendijk and Stuart E. Johnson (Washington, DC: National Defense University Press, 2004). This anthology was sponsored by the Office of the Secretary of Defense, Office of Force Transformation.

24. Clausewitz, *On War*, 605-610.

25. Richard L. Kugler, "Scenarios for Force Sizing" in Binnendijk and Johnson.

26. Charles Barry and Stuart E. Johnson, "Organizing for Stabilization and Reconstruction," in Binnendijk and Johnson.

27. The idea that stability operations capabilities should be joint is a key principle of the Binnendijk and Johnson study. Although the Army is the likely anchor service for a joint capability, especially when rotational considerations are a factor, the resources of the other services—and allies—are crucial and must be a part of the concept from the beginning. The resources of all services in civil affairs, medical, engineers, and military police are not small. See Appendices to "Rebalancing the Active/Reserve Mix," in Binnendijk and Johnson, 81-86.

28. See, e.g., the chapters in Binnendijk and Johnson, cited in n. 23 above.

29. Ibid. See especially chap. 4 (primary author, Charles Barry).

30. Proposed Stabilization and Reconstruction Civilian Management Act of 2004.

31. Robert Perito, *Where Is the Lone Ranger When You Need Him?* (Washington, DC: United States Institute of Peace, 2004).

32. The most common command adaptations developed during World War II were "territorial" command arrangements that often replaced "tactical organizations" after major combat operations wound down. The World War II experiences informally codified these two types of operational organizations for military government. In the territorial organization, the civil affairs/military government chain of command was separate from combat units, and their leaders below the theater level. Civil affairs teams would report to the military governor or to the

theater commander. Several arguments existed for organizing military government along territorial lines. These included placing fewer burdens on a military staff focused on tactical combat considerations and allowing for more efficient control of civil affairs and military government units. A territorial organization also took into account the particular political and geographical needs of the occupied country. Furthermore, civil affairs teams were assigned to towns and cities on a long-term basis, thereby creating greater continuity of policy.

33. This is one of the themes in the PBS *Frontline* broadcast, "The Invasion of Iraq," Internet, http://www.pbs.org/wgbh/pages/frontline/shows/invasion/ aired February 2004. See particularly the transcripts of interviews with former Secretary of the Army Thomas White (http://www.pbs.org/wgbh/pages/frontline/shows/invasion/interviews/white.html) and V Corps Commander Lt. Gen. William Wallace (http://www.pbs.org/wgbh/pages/frontline/shows/invasion/interviews/wallace.html).

34. See interview with former Coalition Forces Land Component Commander (CFLCC), Lt. Gen. David McKiernan, in Ron Martz, "Power Vacuum Hurt in Iraq, General Says," *Atlanta Journal Constitution*, 14 October 2004, 3B.

35. White interview, *Frontline*, 31 January 2004. With respect to Iraq, a useful source of data about the costs, evidence of progress, and public opinion (to include American and Iraqi polling data) is the Brookings Institution's Iraq Index, Internet, http://www.brookings.edu/iraqindex, Also, as this chapter is being finalized, coalition forces are reentering the Sunni towns of Samarra, Ramadi, and others north and west of Baghdad.

36. Leonard Wong, *Developing Adaptive Leaders: The Crucible Experience of Operation Iraqi Freedom* (Carlisle Barracks, PA: U.S. Army War College, Strategic Studies Institute, 2004).

37. Leigh C. Caraher, "Broadening Military Culture," in Binnendijk and Johnson.

38. For an excellent study of the limitations of high technology in the campaign in Afghanistan, see Stephen Biddle, *Afghanistan and the Future of Warfare: Implications for Army and Defense Policy* (Carlisle Barracks, PA: U.S. Army War College, Strategic Studies Institute, 2002).

39. Joseph J. Eash, III, and Elihu Zimet, "Supporting Technologies," in Binnendijk and Johnson.

40. See chap. 26 of this anthology by Dallas Owens for a detailed examination of the unsustainable pressures on current Reserve Component structures.

41. Clark A. Murdock, lead investigator, *Beyond Goldwater-Nichols: Defense Reform for a New Strategic Era* (Washington, DC: Center for Strategic and International Studies, 2004).

42. B.H. Liddell Hart, *Strategy* (New York: Frederick A. Praeger, 1954), 366.

43. For example, after major combat operations in Iraq, the decisions to disband Iraqi military and security forces and the extensive de-Baathification program have received considerable attention as potential sources of Iraqi discontent and violence after the coalition assumed control of the country.

12 | Losing Control of the Profession through Outsourcing?[1]

Deborah Avant

S ince the privatization revolution of the Reagan years, outsourcing has become a central part of the way the U.S. military does business. Some argue that private contractors are cheaper, others that using contractors gives the government more flexibility, and still others that privatization allows the military to focus on its core missions. Though the validity of these justifications varies widely, privatization and outsourcing have expanded unabated.[2] Consider this: during the first Gulf War, U.S. forces employed one civilian contractor in Iraq for every 50 military personnel; at the start of Operation Iraqi Freedom, that figure was about one in 10, and as the insurgency developed in the war's aftermath the number rose even further.[3] Contractors now do much more than building and maintaining camps, preparing food, and doing laundry for troops. They support M-1 tanks and Apache helicopters on the battlefield; they provide the military with security and crime prevention services; and they even interrogate military prisoners (a fact widely noted in the wake of the Abu Ghraib prison scandal in Iraq). Contractors have also become integral to military training efforts. They train American forces, Army ROTC units, and foreign militaries.[4]

Privatization efforts in the Army give us insight into what the Army sees as its core professional activities and thus reveal the future direction of the profession. A glance at these efforts suggests that the Army is quite representative of American society, reflecting the prominent mindset that looks positively at the marketing of previously public goods. The Army's decisions, however, also reflect an increasing divorce between the Army and key tasks in the development of the Army profession as well as important new security undertakings. This divorce invites serious unintended consequences. The privatization of training, perhaps the activity most central to the future of the profession, provides a particularly important example. The Army's ready delegation of training missions to the private sector so that it can focus on executing tasks most closely associated with ground warfare erodes the Army's influence on the future shape of its profession and cedes important security tasks to the private sector.[5]

Professionalism and the U.S. Army

Andrew Abbott argued in 1988 that the key variable in the development of a profession is the relationship between the profession and its work, or jurisdiction.[6] Professionalization inevitably entails the pursuit of jurisdiction in competition with rival professions. Army professionalism, though, could be imagined in different ways, with each implying competition with different rivals. The Army could be thought of as an organization (e.g., the U.S. Army) or as a generic professional grouping (e.g., all soldiers), and these in turn imply different competitors (e.g., the U.S. Marines, armies in other states, or other institutions that exercise force on land such as police). Analysis could focus on the jurisdictional battles between services within an individual country or could be undertaken internationally to see how all armies protect (or extend) their jurisdictions vis-à-vis competitors. A variety of contextual factors—the state of technology, the state of organizational development, the surrounding politics, the power basis of society—affect the success of the jurisdictional claims a profession like an army makes. In the last 150 years, most armies—and most military forces—have generally been public forces created by political entities. As a profession in a formally subservient position to government, armies pursue their jurisdiction by interpreting objective, external information through their professional lenses based on established knowledge systems. In the midst of changes to any of these contextual factors, army professionals may find themselves fending off challenges to their jurisdiction.

The U.S. Army, in particular, has constituted its tasks by balancing the norms and standards of the profession with the political goals of its masters. If it leans too far in the direction of Army norms and standards to the detriment of civilian goals, it risks retaining control of a jurisdiction decreasingly in demand. The profession might then die because there would be no one to employ and pay those who practice it. If it leans too far in the direction of the political goals of its masters, it may lose its ability to pursue its jurisdiction at all, and thus its professional status. The profession is best placed to maintain this balance if it plays an active negotiatory role in interpreting changes in its context and insuring that the Army's response is within the bounds of professional norms and practices.

Changes in the Army's operational context in the late 20th and early 21st centuries (that is, new global realities and new political goals) have challenged the Army to reconstitute itself. As we have noted, in its reconstitution the Army has given up some tasks to contractors. The Army's privatization choices demonstrate that the organization thinks of its core tasks as being those closest to what has traditionally been its core: the execution of ground warfare. Its ready use of contractors for tasks that are crucial to both the development of the profession in the future and to the success of new missions (such as stabilization), however, has generated competition between the Army and private security companies over who will shape the development of future professionals and has degraded the Army's ability to undertake successful missions on its own.

The Impetus to Private Training

The Cold War's end was bound to affect the Army and its jurisdictional claims. While peer threats evaporated and U.S. forces were downsized, ethnic conflict, humanitarian emergencies, and, particularly, the war on terrorism caused the number of operations involving the U.S. military to rise. In scrambling to meet more and different requirements with fewer personnel in the face of a competitive labor market, policy-makers (and military leaders) increasingly turned to private contractors to carry out a variety of tasks—including private training.

The general inclination toward privatization and outsourcing of government functions in the United States encouraged this response. [7] Belief that the private sector could more efficiently deliver many public services led to a prominent privatization movement in many Western countries, and the Defense Department was not immune to the effect of this movement.[8] Throughout the 1970s and 1980s, U.S. military services launched several initiatives to transfer education and training of recruit and enlisted forces to private, or at least nonmilitary, entities.[9] The Commission on Roles and Missions of the Armed Forces chartered in 1994 looked specifically into privatization as a way to improve defense logistics.[10] In 1996, a DoD report, "Improving the Combat Edge through Outsourcing," focused on several additional areas for which privatization looked promising, including education and training. Later that year, the Congressional Research Service set out a framework for discussing further privatization of DoD functions.[11]

Widespread interest in privatization and outsourcing in the United States also led to a growing private capacity for providing military-type services. In some cases new private security companies were established—for instance a group of retired U.S. Army officers formed Military Professional Resources, Inc. (MPRI) in 1987 to capitalize on what they saw as an increasing demand. In other cases, recognized defense contractors deepened or widened their capacity to provide military services—both Science Applications International Corporation (SAIC) and Booz Allen moved into operational contracts. As services proved lucrative, established defense conglomerates have bought out profitable service companies—L-3 Communications acquired MPRI, Northrup-Grumman acquired Vinnell, and CSC bought DynCorp. These companies have continued to enlarge their reliance on retired military and police personnel to staff contracts. The military downsizing that accompanied the end of the Cold War (about 30 percent across the board) insured an adequate supply of skilled personnel, at least in the short run. As time has passed, companies have continued to look to those leaving the U.S. military for a steady supply of personnel. Moreover, they have also begun to recruit abroad and from nonmilitary backgrounds.

Part of the Army's justification for privatization has been to insure that, in the midst of downsizing, it can preserve core roles by relinquishing non-core missions. In some cases, the tasks privatized do make sense—why have scarce military personnel producing paychecks if you can contract out that job to a specialized firm? In other cases, such as conducting training, the logic is less obvious—training, it would seem, is a key task in translating general political wishes into professional responses through the development of the wanted specialized professional knowledge. Nonetheless, the Army has proceeded with privatizing a variety of training missions for U.S. troops. At the same time, the Army has also outsourced the training of foreign troops to private contractors. Furthermore, security companies that provide training services have also begun to sell them directly to foreign governments.[12]

The privatization of these tasks promises to affect the Army's professional jurisdiction in several different ways. Outsourcing the educating and training of U.S. forces represented a loosening of the Army's control of the profession itself. Because educating and training its own members are critical tasks for fostering professional identity and for maintaining the profession's internal control system, outsourcing this mechanism will likely lead to less professional coherence. Furthermore, by outsourcing the training of its own forces, the Army may be limiting its ability to define and retain its jurisdiction. Few in the Army have looked at the privatization of training in a critical or skeptical way. Indeed, the Army's senior leaders have been so distracted by the pressures of ongoing wars that they have failed to summon the time and interest to attend to or even think about their solemn, never-ending responsibility to serve as stewards of the Army profession as profession. Training is no longer considered a core task (the core tasks being those closest to the execution of ground warfare). As it feels itself being asked to do more and more with fewer bodies, the Army is not resisting the competition with contractors, but happily ceding these training tasks. In light of Andrew Abbott's compelling model of professional development and demise, the Army should reconsider this perspective.

The privatization of foreign military training poses a different set of issues. First, the political importance of the Army is tied to its role (or jurisdiction) in U.S. defense. Training foreign armies came to play a significant role in the defense strategy of the United States in the 1990s— according to the Office of the President's 1999 statement "A National Security Strategy for a New Century," training was a prime component of the administration's engagement strategy. Foreign military training was said to further U.S. contacts with other countries, to aid in the spread of democracy and good civil-military relations, and to express specific U.S. strategic concerns over such issues as counter-narcotics and counterterrorism. U.S. Special Forces accordingly trained with over 100 countries annually in the 1990s. This strategic concern has intensified in the wake of the 11 September 2001 terrorist attacks and the global war on terrorism, as the United States has stepped up foreign military training efforts in Indonesia, the Philippines, Africa, and many parts of the Middle East and former Soviet Union—areas that Thomas Barnett calls the "non-integrating gap."[13]

However, if training foreign militaries is a more and more important part of national defense and private companies are providing more of that training, it follows that the Army's jurisdiction in national defense is declining. Consider that the goals of foreign military training are to further U.S. contact with foreign militaries, to model "good" civil-military relations, and to counter terrorist activities. Privatizing these missions leads the foreign militaries to increased contact with private contractors rather than with U.S. military officers, negates the traditional model of civil-military relations, and transfers the counterterrorist role to private contractors.

Though these tasks are less critical to the Army as a profession than the professional training of its own members, there is a relationship between training foreign armies and the development of abstract professional knowledge for armies as a whole. Having commercial companies that sell military training opens the way for a new process by which military knowledge is shared and spreads. Companies like

MPRI, Cubic, SAIC, and DynCorp offer military knowledge outside the structure of the Army. Their position outside the U.S. government may give them a vantage point from which to offer variants of knowledge that compete with the Army's line. Or they may simply sell knowledge derived from the U.S. Army in a way that the Army has little influence on (for example, unclassified field manuals, including those that are dated, in the public domain). Either way, privatization changes the process by which military professional knowledge and norms spread, reducing the Army's unique claim—as an institution—to develop abstract knowledge about the Army profession and enabling others with different bases of expertise a legitimate position from which to offer knowledge.

Outsourcing Internal Training

The Army outsources a number of its own education and training programs. MPRI alone has staffed ROTC detachments, writes U.S. Army doctrine, coordinates Training and Doctrine Command's (TRADOC) efforts in joint and combined arms training, and assesses TRADOC's battle command and awareness division.[14] Perhaps most controversial among these examples is privatization within the ROTC program. At this date, Communication Technologies, Inc. (COMTek) provides retired officers and NCOs to staff Army ROTC programs. Though such outsourcing of education and training is not inconsistent with DoD guidelines, which state that education and training are commercial activities that could be (but not necessarily should be) outsourced, the Army as we noted earlier may be giving away its capacity to control the profession internally by having private contractors perform these tasks.[15]

In the Army ROTC program, future officers are shaped through their educational careers at civilian universities. In a typical ROTC program, there were formerly five authorized officers (though typically the positions were staffed at only four), three training noncommissioned officers (NCOs), and one general schedule (GS) civilian. Among the officers, one lieutenant colonel served as the professor of military science and commander of the battalion, while one major (often an active Guard or Reserve officer) and two captains served as assistant professors of military science. Two of the NCOs were responsible for organizing and conducting training while one handled supply and logistics.[16] A plan designed by the RAND Arroyo Center and published in 1999 proposed that two of the assistant professors of military science and two NCOs—one trainer and the one responsible for logistics and supply—be contracted out. Though this was expected to have uncertain cost impacts (in fact, some assumptions resulted in increased cost), it would reduce the strain on Army personnel.[17] The Army began experimenting with this plan in 1997-98, outsourcing portions of ROTC staffs: first to MPRI, which by 2001 was providing ROTC staff at 220 colleges across the country, and then to COMTek, which provided staff at more than 260 colleges in 2004.[18] The majority of positions that have been contracted out are assistant professors of military science, trainers, and logistics specialists.

There are clear standards that retired officers who serve as assistant professors of military science or enlisted instructors must meet. They must have been retired no more than two years, wear a uniform during performance of their duties, meet height and weight standards, pass the Army Physical Fitness Test, and participate in ROTC advanced and basic camps during the summer.[19] The personnel fielded by MPRI and COMTek have met these standards.

Given the importance of the military personnel that staff these programs as role models for future officers, however, some question the wisdom of having for-profit companies staff the programs with retired officers. Questions do not arise over the quality of the retired officers, but over whether the normative framework the program is supposed to instill in future officers may be compromised by the use of a commercial company to perform this function—particularly for a profession whose defining tenet is self-sacrifice. Many have noted the "deprofessionalization" of the military in recent years—charting the trend whereby military service has come to be seen by many of those serving as just a job or a means to achieve side benefits (like education, travel, technical skills, etc.).[20] Outsourcing ROTC training means turning over the education and modeling of professional behavior to profit-seeking firms.[21] This practice may further promote the deprofessionalization of the Army. Indeed, there are signs already that soldiers frustrated with what they see as a bureaucratized personnel system in the Army are thinking about taking advantage of opportunities in the private sector sooner than they might have otherwise because they believe they can do their job better or make more money with fewer hassles outside the Army than in.[22]

Much more research is required to determine the impact of outsourcing ROTC training and evaluate its relative benefit. This research should obviously focus on whether the program saves money and meets standards. It should also, however, evaluate deeper issues regarding the Army's success in instilling its standards of professionalism by using contractors to train officers. Can a contractor who is a profit-seeker impart and model the same standards of service as an active duty officer or NCO? If not, what does this portend for the future of the Army profession?

Private Training of Foreign Militaries

Private training for foreign militaries happens in two different ways—through U.S. government outsourcing to private security companies and through foreign government contracting directly with private security companies. Though related, these activities pose different dilemmas to Army professionalism.[23] Let us discuss each in turn.

U.S. Outsourcing of Foreign Military Training

Outsourcing foreign military training affects the role the Army plays in U.S. defense. Foreign military training is a component of U.S. defense policy and clearly falls within the realm of potential Army jurisdiction, considering that the Army's role in training is important for what the Army should look like in the future. Some have argued that, given the post-Cold War downsizing, the Army should shed responsibility for non-core tasks such as training. To the degree it sheds these tasks, it is better able to focus on its core mission to fight and win the nation's wars. Others argue that if the Army sheds responsibility for missions that are close to the core of U.S. grand strategy, it marginalizes its importance. Questions over the proper long-term shape of the Army's jurisdiction underlie the debate over what a core mission is and therefore what is most (and least) properly outsourced.

There are three ways in which privatizing foreign military training will weaken the Army's capacity for participating in future training activities. First, by providing stop-gap solutions, private training options reduce the incentive for the Army to change its structure to better meet the new, enlarged training demands it faces. Indeed, as several involved in training the Iraqi army have noted, it was no surprise that the United States would have to train this military after the war.[24] Why, then, did it not have troops available to do the training? Partly, it was because the Army knew that it could turn to the private sector to do this job.

Second, when the U.S. government pours money for training into commercial companies rather than into its national forces, it encourages development of private rather than public expertise. Also, given that private expertise is drawn directly from U.S. forces, buying from private providers undermines the long-term supply of the expertise in general. Companies like MPRI, SAIC, Vinnell, and others have an impressive list of personnel with varied language and experience portfolios because these individuals were trained in and by the U.S. Army. Every contract that private security companies win for training, however, takes away from developing comparable internal training experience in the Army itself.

Third, hiring private companies to train foreign militaries signals to the members of the Army that training is not an important task. There has been ambivalence within the Army (and the other services) as to whether some new missions are really military jobs. When the Army decides to privatize missions, it signals that they are considered to lie further from the core and are therefore less important for the Army's mission (and less important for soldiers' careers). Privatizing training makes it more likely that the Army as an organization will take training less seriously.

Some History of Military Training

U.S. training for foreign militaries is accomplished through the International Military Education and Training (IMET) program. Created by Congress in 1976, IMET was designed to strengthen mutual understanding between the United States and its friends and allies and to facilitate these countries' ability to insure their own security. The IMET legislation separated military training from the Military Assistance Program (MAP) and set up funding to help countries unable to afford purchasing U.S. military training. The general program to sell U.S. training to personnel from other countries operates under the Foreign Military Sales (FMS) Act. Basically, the IMET program provides scholarships for students to enter professional military education (PME) programs in the United States or subsidizes countries that cannot afford the entire program. Those that can afford it send students to the PME courses under FMS at their own expense.

IMET was amended in 1978 to increase the participating countries' awareness of human rights. In 1991, an amendment titled Expanded IMET (E-IMET) focused on defense resource management, respect for and grasp of democracy and civilian rule, military justice in a democracy, and human rights. Additional legislation made possible civilian and nongovernmental organization participation in the program.[25] General foreign military training under the umbrella of IMET and FMS takes place either on U.S. soil at one of the PME facilities or in short-term on-the-job-training, orientation tours, or instruction by a Mobile Training Team (MTT) outside U.S. territory.

The burgeoning of democratizing states in the post-Cold War era led to an increased demand for professional military education from the United States. The United States has managed (in many eyes) to balance operational competence with firm civilian control under democratic principles. As political and military officials struggled with these issues in many democratizing countries, they wanted to expose their promising personnel to the education and political practices of the U.S. system. Many countries were also interested in U.S. operational insight into combat, peacekeeping, and humanitarian operations. Finally, there was a sense among many participant countries that such education qualifies them for inclusion in a larger global professional security community. As it was put by one Australian officer, "I don't think we seek 'expertise'—its more education, exposure, and breadth of understanding. Nonetheless, the management skills discussed . . . and the intellectual exposure . . . *must* make students *much* better [officers]."[26]

The U.S. training missions have not gone without criticism. For instance, the Western Hemisphere Institute for Security Cooperation (formerly School of the Americas), once located in Panama but now at Fort Benning, Georgia, was condemned as the "School of Assassins and Dictators" by those who alleged adverse effects of U.S. training on democracy and human rights.[27] Furthermore, it has not always been clear that military education equates to U.S. influence. Proponents of foreign military training point out obvious benefits of IMET such as access to foreign personnel and subjective ties—those that participate in U.S. professional military education develop lasting ties with their colleagues. Though this debate is not settled, IMET, E-IMET, and foreign military education for both civilian and military personnel became a cornerstone of U.S. foreign policy in the 1990s. It is received wisdom in the Pentagon and elsewhere (though wisdom needing validation through empirical research) that "low-visibility defense instruction has exceptional value in promoting both democracy and military cooperation."[28]

Despite the received wisdom about the value of military engagement, however, there have been questions within the Army about how central this mission should be. Some who believe in the centrality of this mission to American security are clearly behind it. Others are behind these missions because they come with funds. Many others, however, suggest that in an era of more tasks and less people something has to go—and that training foreign armies is a good thing to cede to contractors. This is an example of an internally contested jurisdiction where the Army has not yet decided whether to embrace these missions or not.

Private Military Training in Africa

The former African Crisis Response Initiative (ACRI), now African Contingency Operations Training Assistance, or ACOTA, grew out of the same ideas that are prevalent in IMET, FMS, and JCET. The idea was to reward democratizing countries, enhance the capacity of their militaries, and encourage military professionalization. In both programs, however, private companies have come to play a substantial role. ACRI began as a program run with U.S. troops which later privatized some of the training. Conceived to work with international partners and African nations to enhance African peacekeeping and humanitarian relief capacity, ACRI was launched in 1966 by former Secretary of State Warren Christopher. The United States offered training and equipment particularly to those African nations dedicated to democracy and civilian rule that would like to improve their peacekeeping abilities. The United States intended to use ACRI to coordinate its African peacekeeping initiatives with the Organization of African Unity (OAU) and other interested parties (Britain, France, etc.). And this has worked. In December 1997, representatives from these countries, interested donors, and troop contributors met at the United Nations Department of Peacekeeping Operations in New York for the first peacekeeping support group meeting ever. Initial plans called for a five-year program run out of the State Department whereby U.S. Special Operations Forces from Central Command and European Command would provide equipment and training to 10,000-12,000 African soldiers before 2002.[29] In FY2004, ACRI was succeeded by the ACOTA program. It includes training for offensive military operations, including light infantry tactics and small-unit tactics, to enhance the ability of African troops to conduct peacekeeping operations in hostile environments; under ACOTA, African troops are also being provided with military weaponry, including rifles, machine guns, and mortars. The United States has completed training for battalions from Senegal, Uganda, Malawi, Mali, Ghana, Benin, Cote d'Ivoire, and Kenya.

As the ACRI program developed, however, Special Forces personnel were stretched thin. New battalions needed to be trained, and those already trained needed to be kept current. Thus the State Department began to look for help. Both MPRI and Logicon won contracts to support ACRI. The program continues to be run through the State Department, though many of the personnel in the former ACRI office are also contractors—employees of USATREX.[30] As ACRI transformed into ACOTA, MPRI continued to provide battalion and brigade task force-level command and staff training in cooperation with some U.S. troops.[31]

Private support was sought due to a shortage in personnel. There was no dissatisfaction with the job that U.S. Army personnel were doing, and there was no clear choice on the part of the Army to discard these jobs. The Army simply did not have enough personnel to staff the programs. This reality is common to many military outsourcing decisions. Partly due to beliefs about the peace dividend that was not fully realized and partly due to a preference among the military for core missions, the U.S. military has been downsized despite an increase in operational tempo. Pragmatic policy implementers have scrambled to come up with solutions that satisfy the U.S. desire to maintain an international presence and influence in many unstable parts of the world without unduly stretching a smaller military. Private companies have seen this coming and organized themselves to take advantage of a new kind of government demand. Using private companies to staff these programs provided a flexible solution that did not require increasing the size of U.S. military forces.

Most people overseeing these programs have expressed strong support for MPRI's and Logicon's services in ACRI and ACOTA. Many of the personnel involved are former U.S. armed forces personnel. They have been indoctrinated into a system of public service and know the standards of appropriateness expected from military professionals. On the other hand, these firms are clearly different from the Army. In offering military advice to foreign countries, they are providing a voice separate from that of the Army. They operate for profit, and the profit motive underlies their search for contracts and is bound to influence their decisions about appropriate behavior in borderline situations.

Small steps taken to get around personnel shortages can have long-term and unanticipated effects. In this instance, the decision to privatize may end up further reducing the capacity of the Army to perform these kinds of tasks. More and more U.S. training for foreign militaries in unstable parts of the world may be left to private hands. This may mean more expensive training. It may also mean training that is not always successful. Regardless, it is training that the Army has relatively less control over. And yet, as the recent experience in Iraq demonstrated, private failures can have significant impacts on the Army's future. Thus several questions arise about the implications of this jurisdictional shift both for the Army as a profession and for civil-military relations:

- Is it cost-efficient to pay to train personnel in the U.S. armed forces who take their retirement only to sell their service back for profit?
- Is it wise for foreign policy goals if more and more of the U.S. presence abroad is private?
- Do we want to give up our Army's capacity for conducting foreign military training?
- Might there be a connection between foreign military training and expert military knowledge in general? Once the Army cedes its unique role in generating expert knowledge (by privatizing foreign military training), will it be able to compete effectively with contractors?

U.S. Firms Contracting Directly with Foreign Militaries

Contracts for military training between private U.S. firms and foreign governments have also been on the rise. MPRI's contracts with the Croatian and Bosnian governments received a lot of press in the 1990s, but there are many others. Hungary has contracted with Cubic for help in reorganizing to meet the standards for entering NATO. MPRI also worked with Columbia, Equatorial Guinea, and Nigeria (though some of its funding for the contract with the Nigerian government comes from the United States).

These contracts are regulated within the International Transfer of Arms Regulations (ITAR), which are monitored by the Department of State's Office of Defense Trade Controls. Before a license is granted, the appropriate regional office, political-military bureau, country desk officer, and others (such as the Bureau of Democracy, Human rights, and Labor) all have input. In the event that a country with no State Department restrictions wants to buy nonlethal training (such as leadership training or instruction in appropriate civil-military relations), the license is not controversial. At the other extreme, for a country on the State Department Embargo Chart, a license would not be issued.

For in-between cases, where a country is making the headlines for one reason or another or has some informal policy holds against it, a variety of offices make their case and the Assistant Secretary makes a final decision. For instance, the African Regional Office rejected MPRI's application for a license with Equatorial Guinea the first time around. Upon appeal, consideration of the nature of the activity (evaluating the need for a Coast Guard and restructuring the defense department so as to professionalize the military) and the amount of U.S. investments in the country ($3 billion by U.S. oil companies) led the regional office to change its mind. It concluded that improvement of security for U.S. citizens and their investments was worth the risk.[32] At that point, however, the Bureau of Democracy, Human Rights, and Labor held the contract up over human rights concerns. MPRI appealed to the Assistant Secretary for Human Rights and lobbied in Congress. In the end, MPRI received the license and has carried out its initial assessment in Equatorial Guinea.[33]

Once a license is issued, there is no formal oversight process required by ITAR. In its day-to-day work, of course, the State Department monitors the behavior of other countries. If a country licensed to receive military advice and training commits egregious transgressions, the State Department can freeze the contract (just as it can freeze weapon transfers). In some cases, as with the Train and Equip program in Bosnia, significant oversight structures are put in place. In others, there are no reporting or oversight mechanisms aside from routine monitoring by embassy staff. Finally, only contracts of more than $50 million in defense services require congressional notification before they begin.

MPRI's work with Croatia provides an enlightening example. As mentioned above, MPRI was founded in 1987 by retired U.S. generals.[34] It boasts a database of over 10,000 potential employees, all having significant experience in the U.S. armed forces, and has managed to bring in over $12 million in annual revenue.[35] The company began by contracting with the U.S. government to train (and provide other support for) the U.S. armed forces and has gradually moved overseas. Part of what makes MPRI advice so sought-after is that this is the same advice that is sold to the U.S. armed forces.[36] MPRI's endeavors in the Balkans have received much attention. The Train and Equip program in the Bosnian Federation was a cornerstone of the Dayton Accords. Because of its relationship to the Dayton Accords, however, the contract with the Bosnian government is very specific to that conflict and therefore is probably not the most useful to generalize from. The company's work with Croatia is more typical; thus that contract will be the illustrative focus here.

The genesis of MPRI's contact with the Croatian government is disputed. Some have argued that the United States sent the Croatians to MPRI. MPRI claims instead that the Croatians were motivated by a presentation MPRI made to states eager to get into NATO. For whatever reason, the Croatian Defense Minister Gojko Susak sent a letter in March 1994 requesting permission from the Pentagon to negotiate with MPRI to obtain training in civil-military relations, programs, and budget.[37]

Croatia and MPRI signed a contract in September 1994 and the State Department licensed the project in December. MPRI then teamed its experts with English-speaking Croatians to set up courses in budgeting, leadership development, military ethics, and relations with civilian society. According to a Pentagon official, MPRI personnel were briefed for days by defense officials before they went to Croatia and were closely monitored once they were there (MPRI officials claim to have no contact with the Pentagon).[38]

Many find to be noteworthy the coincidence between MPRI's presence and the turn-around in the Croatian army's performance and tactics. Shortly after MRPI started working with the Croatian army, the Croats began to experience success in their quest to regain their territory (Serb forces were occupying about 30 percent of Croatian territory when MPRI arrived). In May 1995, the Croats retook the areas to the southwest of Zagreb, then recaptured parts of western Slovenia, and finally, in August 1995, the Croatian forces launched Operation Storm to retake the Krajina region.[39] The offensive in Krajina looked (to observers in the region) like a textbook NATO operation, leading to endless speculation about whether MPRI was instrumental in Croatia's operational success.[40] According to Roger Cohen, "The lightning five-pronged offensive, integrating air power, artillery, and rapid infantry movements, and relying on energetic maneuvers to unhinge Serbian command and control networks, bore many hallmarks of U.S. Army doctrine."[41]

According to MPRI spokesman Lt. Gen. (ret.) Harry Soyster in 1995, the instruction "has no correlation to anything happening on the battlefield today."[42] He explained that MPRI had far too much to lose to violate the terms of its license by advising the Croats on battlefield strategy, weapons, or tactics.[43] Of course, this assumes that MPRI would have lost its license. More likely is the speculation that if MPRI did violate its license, it was with the knowledge of officials in the Pentagon and elsewhere.[44] As Juan Zarate argues, MPRI's training (even as it was touted as a long-term venture) *was meant* to have a positive effect on the Croatian military—otherwise, why would they have landed the job?[45]

As it was, the Croatian successes changed events on the ground such that strategic bombing by NATO was able to push the Serbs over the edge and to the negotiating table—the results of which were the Dayton Accords (and another contract for MRPI). By licensing MPRI, the United States retained its neutral status while influencing events on the ground.[46] MPRI continues to operate in Croatia. It works through the Democracy Transition Assistance Program (DTAP), the democracy transition long-range management plan (LRMP), the Croatian Army Readiness Training System (CARTS), and the NATO-sponsored Partnership for Peace (PfP) program.[47] The U.S. government now pays the bill for MPRI's work in Croatia.

Much of the controversy over MPRI's work with Croatia had to do with its impact on the relative power of different institutions in the U.S. government over U.S. policy. It has implications, though, for Army professionalism as well. Having private companies responsible for transmitting Army professionalism induces the Army (and the U.S. government) to relinquish its monopoly on the spread of knowledge about an army's proper behavior. Though it may be the case that MPRI works closely with the U.S. Army, to the degree that those who work for MPRI develop a slightly different perspective, this perspective potentially competes with the Army's. Furthermore, though MPRI hires retired Army officers precisely because they are imbued with the normative and professional standards of the Army, as Andrew Abbott points out these standards are most clearly and practically put forward during work. While MPRI is doing work, it is also potentially influencing these standards—and doing so from a different perspective. Just as in the case of private foreign military training with U.S. dollars, MPRI's work is undermining the Army's claim to unique expert knowledge.

This is not to suggest that private foreign military training is undermining military or Army professionalism generally. Indeed, some would argue that private companies operating in Africa and other parts of the world are doing more to spread professional norms—about the proper role for army personnel, about the proper role for police, about proper civil-military relations, etc.— than professional militaries are. To the degree that private companies are spreading these norms, however, it is increasingly general military professionalism rather than U.S. Army professionalism. The increasing capacity of the private sector to offer military advice to foreign countries may thus be putting at risk the U.S. Army's leadership position in establishing jurisdiction for the system of army professions.

Private Professionals?

One of the hallmarks of private military and security services in the 1990s was their claim to professionalism. This claim was based on the extensive training and education their personnel possessed as well as the fact that most companies claimed to operate within national and international rules and norms. They claimed to be neither rogue companies nor mercenaries, but rather professional providers of military and security services. Can retired Army officers working as private military contractors be considered Army professionals? What about persons working for contractors without prior military training, as is increasingly the case in Iraq? If retired personnel are considered professional, how does their professional status relate to that of active duty personnel? How is private security expertise certified to the client? Does it make sense to distinguish between private security contractors with military experience and those without? How will organizational interest and professional jurisdiction change as a result of this process? If the Army is entering a competition with potentially professional contractors for training missions, it should think about these questions as well as about the larger implications for recruitment, retention, and morale within the service.

An argument to exclude retired officers from working in the private sector in their professional status would most likely be based on the public nature of military service in the last 150 years. That is a difficult argument to sustain, though, simply because the public nature of military service is frequently tied to the notion of a citizen army rather than a professional army.[48] In some sense, outsourcing military services could be thought of as just another step in the continuing move away from a citizen army. Rather than assuming ipso facto that private companies are not professional, it may be more useful to think about the ramifications of different types of professionals competing for jurisdiction.

Thinking about it this way requires us to distinguish between the organizational interest of the Army and the professional jurisdiction of armed service. The Army may be competing with different entities such as private contractors for the rights to jurisdiction. The fact of this competition alone may change the process of establishing jurisdiction. Perhaps professional officers working in a variety of capacities—in private firms, in public organizations, in international organizations—are all struggling to define the profession of armed service. How this bodes for the Army may or may not matter for how it bodes for the profession of armed service. Indeed, Abbott speaks of the contrast between professions that are highly structured and thus need to mobilize themselves against attack, on the one hand, and those that are loosely organized and therefore more flexible and competitive, on the other. If the Army remains committed to its traditional core jurisdiction, it may be less adaptive for use in the world. Perhaps the proliferation of private military companies (as well as innovations by other national militaries) will maintain the relevance of the military in general vis-à-vis other competitors in the use of violence for political means.[49]

Contested Jurisdictions and Individual Choices

How will individual members of the military (and potential members) respond to contractors competing for professional status in the world of armed service? As the recent experience in Iraq demonstrates, this is an issue involving far more than training. In many instances, private security personnel, acting ostensibly as security guards or bodyguards, have found themselves participating in activities that are hard to distinguish from defensive ground warfare. The surge of private security personnel into Iraq casts worries about privatization's impact on Army professionalism in bold relief—having extended beyond logistics and even training to the very nature of what is unique about members of the armed forces.

Anecdotal evidence—both from the 1990s missions and from the more recent experiences in Afghanistan and Iraq—suggests a mix of reactions. During the initial deployment of U.S. soldiers to Bosnia, the efforts of private firms received much attention. Newspapers routinely quoted soldiers as saying they could not wait to retire and then go to work for Brown and Root or MPRI where the real money was. Similar sentiments have been voiced in Afghanistan and Iraq. One could argue that contracting opportunities could be recruitment plugs because they render military experience more easily transferable to the private market. Also, individual soldiers report satisfaction with particular training opportunities provided by private contractors. Some have expressed relief that the private sector had the capacity to send forces quickly to the field in Iraq.[50]

Many accounts, though, are less optimistic. First, though contracting opportunities may be recruitment plugs, they may also hurt retention. As private security activity in Iraq skyrocketed—and with it reports of huge private sector salaries—

U.S. Special Forces suffered a greater than average separation rate, leading some to speculate that private security companies were recruiting soldiers away from their uniformed service. The Army should consider the market impact on the potential for greater turnover in key specializations.

Furthermore, many members of the U.S. military are not pleased to be competing with contractors. Contractors frequently receive greater financial rewards and exercise greater freedom while they are at it. Contractors get regular days off, get paid overtime, and can always quit. Soldiers do not have those luxuries. Anecdotes suggest that military personnel are often frustrated when they are doing the same jobs as contractors for less pay and with fewer benefits. Moreover, Army personnel report that if a contractor can be hired to do a job, soldiers generally view the job as less important. The very fact that the Army focuses on non-core tasks for privatization suggests that the task is marginalized or does not measure up. Members of the Army take pride in conducting missions that only soldiers can do. Missions that are contracted out become inherently less respected and valued among the members of the service.

Adding to the perception of inequities are differences in the legal rights and responsibilities of soldiers and contractors. Members of the U.S. military are subject to strict codes of conduct, a robust chain of command, and a separate judicial system. The legal responsibilities of contractors are less clear. This was apparent in Bosnia when civilian contractors maintaining U.S. military aircraft or deployed as civilian police were implicated in sex-trading schemes. They were never prosecuted, only fired. The contrast between soldiers and contractors was most striking, though, in the treatment of those implicated in the abuses at Abu Ghraib prison in Iraq— civilian contractors had not even been charged by the time reservist MPs were tried and convicted.[51]

Less remarked upon is the difference between the rights of soldiers and contractors, which can work to the contractors' detriment: they may be less likely to be accorded prisoner of war (POW) status. The U.S. military has worried for some time that its contractors may not be granted POW status by the enemy if captured. However, when three contractors working for California Microwave Systems were shot down flying over territory controlled by anti-government FARC insurgents in Colombia, the insurgents were happy to grant them POW status—it was the U.S. government that designated them as "kidnappees."[52] Contractors may also be less likely to receive backup in the event of a firefight. When employees working for Hart Group were attacked in Iraq, Coalition support was not forthcoming and one employee bled to death on the top of a building.[53]

It is increasingly clear that when soldiers and contractors work side by side doing the same jobs, the potential for frustration on both sides mounts. When they work side by side in a combat zone the consequences of unequal treatment are more extreme—as are the frustrations. If more and more jobs are contracted out, issues of equity between military and civilians are bound to arise. Settling jurisdictional issues will be important for both the future of Army professionalism and for the success of U.S. policy.

Conclusion

Relying on private contractors for training has undoubtedly provided flexibility for the Army in meeting the many demands of the last 15 years. It appears that the Army leaders have made these decisions, however, in the manner of managers of an oversubscribed bureaucracy, often failing to consider how their decisions would impinge on the Army as a profession in the longer term. Army leaders need to think about how much they value training Army professionals, the interaction between internal and foreign training missions, the multifaceted impacts of ceding expertise to the private sector, and the impact of competing with contractors on the individual professionals within the service.

In the end, decisions about what to privatize should depend on how the Army views its future, and how civilians view the Army's future. The Army would do best to attune its vision with that of the civilian leadership and the demands of the world so as to avoid clinging to its traditional professional jurisdiction at the cost of its relevance. If the Army sheds its capacity for training missions at the same time that training missions become a greater part of U.S. grand strategy, it may be left with a tradition but lack a constituency. Of course, the Army is part of the society and economic system in which it operates. Resisting the tides of privatization could turn out to be useless and counterproductive. Thinking clearly about its future and the implications of different strategies for privatization, however, may help the Army manage these changes more effectively. Though the ultimate decisions are (and should be) civilian decisions, the professions' strategic leaders will have considerable influence on them and would be wise to deliberate fully on professional costs and benefits in both the wider context and the longer term.

Notes

1. The author wishes to thank the John D. and Catherine T. MacArthur Foundation for its generous support of the research for this chapter.

2. For general overviews of this trend, see Thomas K. Adams, "The New Mercenaries and the Privatization of Conflict," *Parameters* 29 (summer 1999): 103-116; Eugene Smith, "The New Condottieri and U.S. Policy: The Privatization of Conflict and Its Implications," *Parameters* 32 (winter 2002-03): 104-119; Peter Singer, *Corporate Warriors: The Rise of the Privatized Military Industry* (Ithaca, NY: Cornell University Press, 2003). For an analysis of its impact on the control of force, see Deborah Avant, *The Market for Force: The Consequences of Privatizing Security* (Cambridge, England: Cambridge University Press, 2005).

3. Steven J. Zamparelli, "What Have We Signed Up For?" *Air Force Journal of Logistics* (December 1999), 10; Kathryn McIntire Peters, "Civilians at War," *Government Executive* (July 1996); P.W. Singer, "War, Profits, and the Vacuum of Law," *Columbia Journal of International Law* 42 (2004); Kenneth Bredemeier, "Thousands of Private Contractors Support U.S. Forces in Persian Gulf," *Washington Post*, 3 March 2003, E01.

4. http://www.mpri.com/subchannels/nat_ROTC.html.

5. Training is only one manifestation of this focus. In the high-technology area, as well, the private sector looms large. During the March 1997 Task Force XXI Army War-Fighting Exercise,

1,200 contractors from 48 vendors participated in the field with the EXFOR. See Mark Hanna, "Task force XXI: The Army's Digital Experiment," *Strategic Studies* 119 (July 1997).

6. Andrew Abbott, *The System of Professions: An Essay on the Division of Expert Labor* (Chicago, IL: University of Chicago Press, 1988).

7. Harvey Feigenbaum, Jeffrey Henig, and Chris Hamnett, *Shrinking the State:The Political Underpinnings of Privatization* (New York: Cambridge University Press, 1998).

8. Feigenbaum et al., *Shrinking the State.*

9. Most of these programs were in concert with established institutions, community colleges, technical institutes, or proprietary schools. A 1991 RAND report commissioned by DoD (in concert with the GAO) found little firm evidence on which to base a conclusion about the cost savings associated with these programs or their relative benefits. See Lawrence Hanser, Joyce Davidson, and Cathleen Stasz, *Who Should Train? Substituting Civilian Provided Training for Military Training* (Santa Monica, CA: RAND, 1991).

10. Loren Thompson, "Privatization of Defense Support Functions: A Public Sector Case Study" (presentation to Kennedy School of Government, Cambridge, MA, 28 April 1995).

11. Gary Pagliano, "Privatizing DoD Functions Through Outsourcing: A Framework for Discussions," *CRS Report*, 6 August 1996. As of this time, DoD had already outsourced 25 percent of base commercial activities, 28 percent of depot maintenance, 10 percent of finance and accounting, 70 percent of army aviation training, 45 percent of surplus property disposal, 33 percent of parts distribution, and portions of other functions.

12. This is a disputed claim. Many argue that U.S. contractors that have sold military training in places like Croatia are actually acting at the behest of the American government, albeit informally. See Ken Silverstein, *Private Warriors* (New York: Verso, 2000), 145.

13. Thomas Barnett, *The Pentagon's New Map: War and Peace in the Twenty-first Century* (New York: G. P. Putnam's Sons, 2004).

14. http://www.mpri.com/site/nat_jointdocdev.html,assessed, May 2004.

15. http://www.acq.osd.mil/inst/icim/icim/newpriv/newpriv.htm. Cites Appendix 2, Office of Manpower and Budget Circular No. A-76, Revised Supplemental handbook, "Performance of Commercial Activities," March 1996.

16. Charles A. Goldman et al., *Staffing Army ROTC at Colleges and Universities: Alternatives for Reducing the Use of Active-Duty Soldiers* (Santa Monica, CA: RAND, 1999), 7-8.

17. Ibid., p. 12.

18. http://www.mpri.com/subchannels/nat_ROTC.html, accessed March 2001; http://www.comtechnologies.com/, accessed May 2004.

19. Ibid.

20. See Charles Moskos and Frank Woods, eds., *The Military: More than Just a Job?* (McLean, VA: Pergamon-Brassey's, 1988).

21. Interestingly, in designing the plan for the Army, the Arroyo Center considered and rejected the possibility of having ROTC programs hire retired military personnel directly because of administrative hurdles. Hiring former military members as civilians would subject the Army to limited civilian personnel ceilings, the requirements of which would negate any cost savings from the outsourcing effort. See Goldman et al., *Staffing Army ROTC*, 3. For a review and critique of the military personnel system, see Cindy Williams, ed., *Filling the Ranks: Transforming the US Military Personnel System* (Boston: MIT Press, 2004).

22. Interviews with serving soldiers May 2002, September 2003, July 2004.

23. They are also regulated by different laws and overseen by a different process. The first category represents a classic form of outsourcing. The contracts operate according to Federal Acquisition Regulation (FAR) and additional rules unique to the Defense Department as outlined in the DoD FAR Supplement (DFARS). Contracts with other countries are not really outsourcing at

all under U.S. law, but a category of military export. The State Department must approve such contracts under the International Traffic in Arms Regulations (ITAR).

24. Interview with Col. T.X. Hammes, USMC, July 2004; interview with Col. Paul Hughes, US Army, July 2004.

25. John A. Cope "International Military Education and Training: An Assessment," *McNair Paper* 44 (Washington, DC: Institute for National Strategic Studies, National Defense University, October 1995), 5-6.

26. Ibid., 15. There is some tension among foreign participants in the U.S. education and training programs. Some, including Central Europe, the former Soviet states, and Africa, are quite interested in the restructuring efforts promoted by E-IMET focusing on civil-military relations, enhancement of democratization, human rights, etc. Other long-standing IMET customers would prefer greater attention to traditional military and operational missions and expanded opportunities for officers as opposed to civilians. See Cope, "International Military Education," 17.

27. In July 1999 the House voted to eliminate funds for training foreign officers at the facility. See John Lancaster, "House Kills Training Funds for School of the Americas," *Washington Post*, 31 July 1999.

28. Cope, "International Military Education," 41; "U.S. Training of Foreign Military and Police Forces: the Human Rights Implications and Issues for Consideration by AI," Interim Report prepared by Lora Lumpe, March 2000.

29. The sum of $15 million was allocated the first year, and $20 million each for the next two years.

30. The program was funded through 2001. Scott E. Brower and Anna Simons offer support for the program but argue that it must develop a command and control system to ultimately succeed. Part of MPRI's contract is to develop just such a system. See Scott E. Brower and Anna Simons, "The ACRI Command and Control Challenge," *Parameters* 30 (Winter 2000-2001).

31. http://www.mpri.com/subchannels/int_africa.html accessed May 2004.

32. Interview with State Department official in African Regional Affairs Office.

33. Interview with Lt. Gen. (Ret.) Harry E. Soyster, 1 December 1998.

34. Gen. Frederick Kroesen (Chairman of the Board), Maj. Gen. Vernon Lewis, Jr. (President, CEO), Gen. Robert Kingston, Gen. Robert Sennewald, and Lt. Gen. Richard West.

35. Jakkie Cillers and Ian Douglas, "The Military as Business: Military Professional Resources, Incorporated," in *Peace, Profit or Plunder? The Privatisation of Security in War-Torn African Societies*, eds. Jakkie Cillers and Peggy Mason (South Africa: Institute for Security Studies, 1999); Mark Thompson, "Generals For Hire," *Time*, 15 January 1996, 34-36; Juan Carlos Zarate, "The Emergence of a New Dog of War: Private International Security Companies, International Law, and the New World Disorder," *Stanford Journal of International Law* 34 (1998): 75-162.

36. Interview with Lt. Gen. (Ret.) Harry E. Soyster, 1 December 1998.

37. Bradley Graham, "US Firm Exports Military Expertise: Role in Training Croatian Army Brings Publicity and Suspicions," *Washington Post*, 11 August 1995, A1.

38. Interview with Pentagon official, October 1997.

39. Zarate, "The Emergence of a New Dog of War," 106-107.

40. Robert Fox, "Fresh War Clouds Threaten Ceasefire: Secret US Military Advice Helps Cocky Croats Push toward Eastern Slovenia," *Sunday Telegraph*, 15 October 1995, 26.

41. Roger Cohen, "U.S. Cooling Ties to Croatia After Winking at Its Buildup," *New York Times*, 28 October 1995, 1.

42. Ibid.

43. Ibid.

44. Cohen, "U.S. Cooling Ties." Cohen reports that senior State Department officials admitted that Croatia became our de facto ally—that arms flowed in despite the embargo and top retired American generals were allowed to advise the Croatian Army.

45. Zarate, "The Emergence of a New Dog of War," 108.

46. An assessment of the costs and benefits of the policy is complicated by the Croatian human rights abuses in the Krajina region in the wake of Operation Storm. It was, up until Kosovo, the largest incident of ethnic cleansing since the end of the Cold War. It is estimated that Croatian forces uprooted between 150,000 and 170,000 Serbs from their homes. Cohen, "US Cooling Ties"; Mark Danner, "Endgame in Kosovo," *New York Review of Books*, 6 (May 1999), 8.

47. http://www.mpri.com/subchannels/int_europe.html accessed May 2004.

48. Eliot Cohen, *Citizens and Soldiers: The Dilemmas of Military Service* (Ithaca, NY: Cornell University Press, 1985); Martin Van Creveld, *The Transformation of War* (New York: Free Press, 1991).

49. Though it would be unwise to stretch the analogy too far, the age of feudalism was also accompanied by restrictions on the use of feudal knights. In England, for instance, feudal obligations to do war service was 40 days per year and did not extend overseas. This led kings as early as Edward I (1274-1307) to contract for service with willing warriors. See Fritz Redlich, *The German Military Enterpriser and his Workforce*, vol. I (Wiesbaden: Franz Steiner Verlag GMBH, 1964), 22.

50. Interviews with Army personnel back from Iraq, December 2003, May 2004, June 2004.

51. Renae Merle, "Contractor Investigated by Justice," *Washington Post*, 22 May 2004.

52. Vanessa Arrington, "Videotape Shows Columbia Captives Alive," *Associated Press*, 28 August 2003; "60 Minutes II," CBS television transcript, 8 October 2003; John McQuaid, "US Hostages in Columbia Mark One Year," *New Orleans Times Picayune*, 13 February 2004.

53. Jamie Wilson, "Private Security firms call for more firepower in combat zone," *The Guardian*, 17 April 2004.

IV

The Army's Military-Technical Expertise

Each of the final four parts of this book (IV through VII) focuses on one of the four broad clusters of the Army profession's expert knowledge as introduced in the opening chapter. Some of the individual chapters are the result of research conducted for both the 2002 and 2005 editions, while others were added to the 2005 edition based on what we learned in the first effort. Just as the discussions about the mapping of the Army profession's expert knowledge in Part III could present only an overview, we do not presume that these four sections are at all complete in their treatment of the Army's expert knowledge. They have been selected, however, to provide needed insights into those specific areas of expert knowledge that we believe are most relevant to the ongoing transformation of the Army and to its current status as a vocational profession. As such they raise serious questions for consideration by all members of the Army profession.

Here in Part IV, we begin with four chapters about the Army's military-technical knowledge—how the profession prepares for and conducts land operations under joint and coalition commanders by combining Army soldiers with organizations, doctrines, and a certain state of technology embedded in their equipment. Several themes have arisen from the vetting of these chapters, which I offer here both for introductory synthesis and for reflection while reading and studying.

First, while the authors initially focused on the Army's expert knowledge, they were quickly and logically led toward analyses of jurisdictions and the Army's ability to compete within them, whether through prior negotiations among military and civilian leaders or more directly within the battlespace. Since, for the purposes of this book, the Army's expert knowledge should be viewed only relative to jurisdictional competitions rather than in absolute terms, the essential question becomes: "Within a particular jurisdiction, e.g., major combat operations or stability operations, is the Army's expert knowledge more applicable than that of its professional competitors?" rather than "Can the Army effectively win wars in its jurisdictions with its present state of knowledge and expertise?" Logically, we must ask and resolve the first question before taking up the second.

If recent operations in the Balkans, Afghanistan, and Iraq have demonstrated anything, it is that other agencies and organizations are competing for legitimacy within the Army's traditional jurisdictions, and that in some cases the Army does not have the best expert knowledge. Thus if the Army chooses to remain legitimate within these arenas (and it may not; it cannot be expert at all things!), it must both establish and defend the superiority of Army expertise for the evolving tasks within these jurisdictions. In this regard, Chapters 13 and 14 focus more on Army capabilities for major combat operations, while the research reported in Chapters 15 and 16 is focused more on the jurisdiction of stability operations under joint and combined commands.

Second, a very sobering theme from both Parts III and IV, glancing back to Chapter 3 in Part I, centers on the question of whether the Army is cleaving into organizations in which the professionals within them are perceived as either "thinkers" or "doers" and, if so, whether the professional future for each is equally bright. Since knowledge is the foundation of professions and the expansion and currency of that knowledge is fundamental to a profession's evolutionary viability, it is essential for all professions to value those members whose role is to create and develop expert knowledge as well as those who apply professional expertise. If the Army is to flourish as a profession, both types of Army professionals need to be equally esteemed, and to have equally bright futures. Unfortunately, our research casts doubt on whether this is the case today, and whether, without deep cultural change, is it likely to be so in the future.

Both of these themes—maintaining preeminent expert knowledge within desired jurisdictions and maintaining a cadre of professionals who produce that preeminent expert knowledge—reinforce the necessity for the profession's strategic leaders to capture and maintain the renewed professionalism evident in an Army redeploying to and from Iraq/Afghanistan, while at the same time raising the institution's esteem for and utilization of the intellectual base resident in the institutional side. Both are essential for the Army's future effectiveness, relevance, and vitality.

13

The Digital Battlefield: Transformation Efforts and The Army's Future Professional Jurisdictions

Elizabeth A. Stanley and G. F. Deimel

F ive years have passed since the Army first announced its intention to transform its force structure and composition to capitalize upon the ongoing Revolution in Military Affairs (RMA). Since that time, the plan remains to create a "Future Force" capable of full spectrum dominance—from major combat operations through stability operations, strategic deterrence, and homeland defense operations. Encompassing the entire Army, the Future Force will combine heavy force lethality, survivability, and sustainability with near-light force deployability. The Army plans to achieve these capabilities largely through dominant battlefield awareness.[2]

While recent events have focused a great deal of attention on interim developments in the transformation process—the fielding and employment of the first Stryker Brigade Combat Team, the announcement of force modularization efforts, and daily developments in the ongoing operations in Iraq and Afghanistan all dominate the mainstream media—the central and long-term goal of Army transformation remains progression toward the Future Force. And while it draws less attention, digital networking is an essential thread of continuity, if not the central element, in this process. It composes the core of the Future Force's Command, Control, Communications, Computers, Intelligence, Surveillance, and Reconnaissance (C4ISR) capability, promising to "link people and systems—vertically and horizontally . . . to increase situational understanding."[3] It will thus provide all participants in a theater a common operating picture while minimizing the fog of war and increasing lethality, survivability, and operating tempo within the digital force.[4]

In this chapter, we outline the Army's efforts to create a fully networked force in light of its evolving professional jurisdiction. The Army's methods for adopting new information technologies and the consequences of these efforts, intended and otherwise, speak to its future professional jurisdictions. *We argue that information technologies from the contemporary RMA are both an objective and subjective*

> The revolutions in information technologies (IT) and knowledge-based systems hold almost unimagined promise for the army that grasps them. IT will be a breakthrough in warfighting. . . . Discriminating sensors providing information on enemy and friendly forces will link to computers that display relevant information in real time in digestible bites. Using IT more than explosive weapons, forces will maneuver against and defeat their enemies more quickly and with less risk. Targeting the enemy's fighting forces and, more decisively, his command and control facilities will provide an unprecedented ability to defeat him.
>
> —STEVE MAINS[1]

force for jurisdictional change and that some changes may possess unintended con-sequences for the profession of arms. While the Army has displayed the foresight to capitalize on technological opportunities to enhance its conventional war-fighting capability, it may not recognize or want to address the wider threats that such change could bring to its traditional core jurisdictions. Our exploration of some of these threats has significant implications for how the Army should renegotiate its jurisdictional claims—and thus redefine its professional expertise.

The chapter contains four sections and a conclusion. The first section reviews the theoretical considerations at the foundation of our analysis, defining the military "system of professions" and the RMA technologies affecting this system. The following three sections examine the implications of Army digitization in light of three concentric visions of the professional system: the inside of the Army profession itself, the wider professional system of traditional warfare, and the broad context formed by the national security arena.

RMA Technologies and Professional Jurisdictions

In his widely acclaimed study *The System of Professions: An Essay on the Division of Expert Labor* (1988), Andrew Abbott argues that an occupation's status as a profession and its standing within society are outcomes of social competition within a system of professions for control over expert knowledge as applied to particular jurisdictions. He describes professions as "exclusive occupational groups applying somewhat abstract knowledge to particular cases."[5] Professional life has three characteristics.[6] First, professions should be seen for what they do, not just how they are organized to do it. In other words, the essence of a profession is its work—its legitimated claim to apply expert knowledge to a particular set of tasks, which Abbott calls jurisdiction. Second, professions operate in an interdependent system—the "system of professions." Professions compete for the control of work, and the jurisdictional boundaries among them are constantly disputed. Professions occupy a jurisdiction by filling a vacancy or fighting for legitimate control of it through a variety of channels—the legal system, public arena, and workplace. As a result, a move by one profession inevitably affects others. Third, many variables affect the content and control of work, including technology, organizations, culture, etc. Perhaps the most important of these is technology.

From a jurisdictional perspective, technology is a double-edged sword. On the one hand, technological change can create new jurisdictional opportunities by (1) causing existing professional competitors to disappear; (2) creating new tasks; or (3) providing a new way to perform existing tasks. On the other hand, technological change can destroy jurisdictional opportunities by (1) introducing new professional competitors; (2) allowing existing competitors to take over existing tasks; or (3) driving existing tasks into obsolescence. Moreover, although technology can create new jurisdictional opportunities, rapid jurisdictional expansion is very difficult because there is a qualitative challenge to institutionalizing new work. As a result, even jurisdictional opportunities can lead to an invasion by outsiders seeking to claim legitimacy over those new tasks. The dramatic expansion in recent years of the number and role of civilian con-tractors in the maintenance support of digitally integrated Army units is perhaps the most prevalent example of this.

The Army's preferred professional jurisdiction is fighting and winning the nation's wars, but the technological innovations of the current RMA may change this jurisdiction.[7] Therefore, one must understand the principal concepts of the cur-rent RMA to fully grasp their capacity for introducing change within the system of professions.

The contemporary RMA is generally postulated as being the result of linking precision weaponry to knowledge in a manner that will radically enhance military capabilities in future warfare. The emerging picture of the future battlefield centers on an integrated system of battlefield assets—a reconnaissance-strike complex—that promises continuous, real-time, sensor-to-shooter links between all targets and all available weapons in the battle space. Technological innovations of the contempo-rary RMA fall into three categories: (1) intelligence, surveillance, and reconnaissance; (2) advanced command, control, communications, computers, and intelligence; and (3) precision strike weapons. Applications of these three technologies together form a "system of systems."[8] Through these new technologies, using conventional weaponry, the RMA's advocates promise rapid, decisive victory, very low casualties and collateral damage, and strategic results.

Scholars generally concur that RMA technologies provide three major improve-ments in operational capability: precision strikes, increased velocity, and informa-tion dominance. Precision strikes not only allow the military to conduct operations at a significant distance from the enemy—what Michael Mazarr calls "disengage-ment"[9]—but also have the potential to reduce the number of casualties and collat-eral damage associated with combat operations.[10] Second, increased velocity will create preemptive warfare "between cohesive, fast-moving friendly forces and unready, disrupted enemy forces."[11] RMA information technologies will increase velocity by enhancing leaders' battlespace awareness and command and control capabilities, thus eliminating irrelevant and counterproductive movement.

Third, and perhaps most importantly, information dominance promises to erode or destroy the enemy's means of collecting, processing, storing, and dissemi-nating information.[12] The Army has defined information dominance as "the degree of information superiority that allows the possessor to use information systems and capabilities to achieve an operational advantage in a conflict or to control the sit-uation in operations short of war, while denying those capabilities to the enemy."[13] Military theorists believe that information dominance is comprised of three effects. First, it will enhance situational awareness by providing accurate, complete, real-time information about friendly and enemy forces and the surrounding environ-ment, thus answering those questions that have plagued soldiers in battle from time immemorial: "Where am I? Where are my buddies? Where is the enemy?"[14] Second, as a result of situational awareness, it will dissipate the fog of war so that all soldiers, at all levels, will share a common view of the battlespace at all times—the common operating picture.[15] Retired Adm. William Owens calls this common view "dominant battlespace knowledge," explaining that "this kind of knowledge constitutes an insight into the future, for it enables us to understand how the enemy commander sees his own battlefield options, and therefore increases the accuracy of predicting what he will try to do."[16] Third, armed with this information, U.S. forces can operate within an enemy's decision and action cycles,[17] thus enmeshing the "adversary in a world of uncertainty, doubt, mistrust, confusion, disorder, fear, panic, chaos. . . . And/or fold [him] back inside himself so that he cannot cope with events/efforts as they unfold"[18]—achieving a state of operational existence currently termed "decision superiority."[19]

Of these three potential improvements at the operational level of warfare—precision strike, increased velocity, and information dominance—this chapter will concentrate on the third. Fundamentally, information dominance requires that a military organization have both the technology and the doctrine for managing and processing information to empower commanders with fused, real-time knowledge of the battlefield. This is the ultimate goal of Army efforts toward digital integration.

The Army has attempted to incorporate contemporary RMA technologies into its war-fighting capability since the 1970s. From Sigma Star in 1978 to today's Army Battle Command System, the Army has tried to minimize the fog of war and leverage new information technologies to improve the way it fights.[20] Initially, Army digital integration efforts primarily concentrated on heavy, or mechanized, forces. Starting in 1994, the Army launched a series of exercises—called Advanced Warfighting Experiments (AWE)—to evolve the digitization concept. The Army's strategy uses a bottom-up approach that experiments echelon by echelon with several experimental systems simultaneously. By early 1996, experimental equipment was fielded by the 1st Brigade, 4th Infantry Division (Mechanized) at Ft. Hood; that unit became the core of a brigade combat team designated the Experimental Force (EXFOR).[21] EXFOR experimented with 72 different initiatives—operational concepts and equipment prototypes—during its milestone, two-week AWE in March 1997 at the National Training Center, Ft. Irwin.[22] Following the EXFOR AWE, the Army conducted an AWE at Ft. Hood based on a division-level simulation in November 1997.[23]

Most of the equipment initiatives tested in these and subsequent AWEs are components of the Army Battle Command System (ABCS), which integrates the command and control systems found at each echelon—from dismounted soldier or individual weapons platform up to the ground force commander at the theater or joint task force level. In its present configuration, ABCS has three major levels. First, at the highest level, the Army Global Command and Control System (GCCS-A) operates at the division, corps, and theater levels, overlapping with the DoD's own GCCS. GCCS-A provides the communications underpinning for force tracking, host nation and civil affairs support, theater air defense, psychological operations, C2, logistics, and medical support. Created from existing Army-wide communications systems, GCCS-A was first fielded to Army units in Hawaii and South Korea in September 2000.[24]

Second, the upper level of the Tactical Internet (formerly known as the Army Tactical Command and Control System, or ATCCS) operates in the middle command echelons, from corps to brigade. This level is organized into five battlefield functional areas: maneuver, field artillery, intelligence and electronic warfare, combat service support, and air defense.[25] Third, the lower level of the Tactical Internet uses the Force XXI Battle Command Brigade and Below (FBCB2) system to provide situational awareness and command and control to the lowest tactical echelons— from the brigade down to dismounted soldiers and individual weapons platforms. The FBCB2 system is comprised of (1) a computer that can display a variety of information, including a common picture of the battlefield overlaid with icons of friendly and enemy forces; (2) software that automatically integrates global positioning system (GPS) data, military intelligence data, combat identification data, and platform data (such as fuel and ammunition status); and (3) interfaces with communications systems.[26] Battlefield data are communicated to and from users of FBCB2 through the Tactical Internet, a radio network comprising a positional navigation and reporting capability[27] and a voice- and digital-converting radio.[28] For dismounted soldiers, these components were mounted into a man-portable system called Land Warrior.[29]

While much of the development to date has been Army-centric, the Army will operate digitally in a much more joint and global context in the decades to come. In recent years, DoD has made great efforts to provide joint controlling concepts to guide the development of the various services' transformation plans.[30] These joint concepts promise a global information grid that provides joint connectivity within a "horizontally and vertically integrated network" extending from the ground into space.[31] The Army's Future Force will operate within this grid providing "relevant and ready land power capability to the combatant commander and the joint team."[32] Presently the Future Combat System (FCS) is the "cornerstone" of technological development of the Future Force which will enable the Army to function in a networked context across the full spectrum of operations.[33] As planned, the FCS is suite of 18 manned and unmanned systems which are, by definition, digitally integrated through the Joint Tactical Radio System and the Warfighter Information Network-Tactical.[34]

In sum, the Army has been trying since 1994—in a very determined and structured way—to digitally integrate its heavy forces for major conventional combat. The Army has made less progress with lighter forces except for the new Stryker brigades which are addressed below. While the digitization process has not necessarily been a smooth one, these new technologies do promise "increased lethality, survivability, and operating tempo." Yet, as discussed earlier, new technologies— like those embodied in the Army's battlefield digitization effort—have the potential to change professional jurisdictions in a manner detrimental to the Army's interests. The remainder of the chapter explores such potentially undesirable effects which future technological adaptation may produce.

Implications of Digitization within the Army Profession Itself

The Army draws its mission mandate from the National Security Strategy, the National Defense Strategy, and the National Military Strategy. These documents (2004) define the national military objectives as (1) protecting the United State against external attacks and aggression; (2) preventing conflict and surprise attack;

and (3) prevailing against adversaries. As such, the "armed forces' foremost task is to fight and win wars."[35] Given this guidance, the Army currently envisions its professional jurisdiction as providing "[the] necessary forces and capabilities to the Combatant Commanders in support of the National Security and Defense Strategies." From this mission, the Army abstracts two "core competencies": (1) to train and equip soldiers and grow leaders; and (2) to provide relevant and ready land power capability to the combatant commanders as part of the joint team.[36] As digital integration efforts continue, the adaptation of new technologies will impact these competencies, with subsequent effects on the Army as a profession, both internally and in relation to other professions in the wider national security system.

There are five significant ways that digital integration may change the Army profession. First, the real-time sensor-to-shooter architecture may eliminate the need for some command echelons by "flattening" combat organizations. Second, the basis for learning and professional development appears to be changing as simulations become a more important—perhaps even the principal—means for training soldiers. Third, there is potential for degraded decision-making ability among tactical leaders. Fourth, digital integration could facilitate top-down command centralization—a concept currently anathema to a generation of leaders that professes to disdain overcontrol and micromanagement. And finally, information saturation could change the Army's organizational methods for decision-making and, consequently, its perspective on professional knowledge. We will address these five effects in turn.

Eliminating Echelons

Battlefield awareness resulting from digital integration will create synergies that facilitate a reduction in organizational structure. As in the business community, the real-time information link among various echelons and between sensors and shooters may make it possible to flatten the Army's hierarchy by eliminating some command echelons.[37] Moreover, because information technology enhances the ability to reallocate combined arms assets quickly and more flexibly, operations may no longer require all capabilities at every echelon. Simultaneously, the link between sensors and shooters may blur the traditional distinction between operations and intelligence.

Because of these synergies, most proponents of streamlining Army organizational structure—including Douglas Macgregor and John Brinkerhoff—have argued that the division is too large and cumbersome to fit the needs of the digital battlefield. Instead, in their view the Army should adopt a brigade-sized combat group as its basic combined arms organization, and scale back or eliminate the divisional echelon.[38] This trend is already present in the Army's modularization initiative as evinced by the movement to brigade-sized Units of Action (UAs) and a proposed joint floating headquarters at the higher tactical level dubbed the Unit of Employment (UEx).[39] While a full discussion of eliminating command echelons is beyond the scope of this chapter, it is important to note some risks associated with flattening the hierarchy. First, eliminating command echelons implies that the span of control for senior leaders necessarily increases, thus reducing their ability to supervise their subordinates. Possessing the informational wherewithal to dispense with echelons does not in itself give the higher commanders the additional time and opportunity required to interact personally with additional subordinate commands. While technological development may streamline processes and facilitate interaction in some instances, leaders will be hard-pressed to find a substitute for individually tailored professional interactions with subordinates, particularly mentor relationships.

Simulations

In previous eras, learning and professional development were products of real-world experience. Today much learning and development now occurs though simulations. The Army conceives training with simulations as a toolbox with three different tools: (1) live simulation, in which soldiers use assigned equipment with some form of simulator for weapons systems; (2) virtual simulation, in which soldiers and crews in simulators replicating combat vehicles "fight" as if they were in the field; and (3) constructive simulation, in which large-scale computer simulations replicate units at or above the battalion level.[40] While the Army has undoubtedly gained a great deal of real-world experience in stability operations and counterinsurgency in Iraq and Afghanistan, circumstances will probably necessitate continued use of simulation exercises in preparation for major combat operations.

Simulations create a number of training efficiencies. First, and most obviously, they can be cheaper and safer than training in the field. Without burning fuel, firing live ammunition, or imposing wear and tear on equipment, crews and units can learn skills necessary to fit their actions into a broader combat context. Second, they create training synergies by allowing units to train together over a network or via remote conferencing. For example, during the AWE in November 1997, digital simulation tools allowed the 4th Infantry Division at Ft. Hood to compete against the Army's World Class Opposing Force at Ft. Leavenworth.[41] Third, simulations can be used for soldiers to complete online components of a professional development course before attending it and thus reduce the time they are away from home station. Finally, simulations can help soldiers prepare for fielding new equipment in a more efficient manner.

But virtual and constructive simulations can also have adverse professional consequences. First, prior to the rise of computerized simulation training, professional learning was largely a product of direct real-world experiences. Real-world experiences favored a professional development system that valued seniority; the more senior the soldier, the more experiences he or she had. Mentors were prized because they passed on tricks of the trade and provided institutional memory.[42] Learning through simulation can forfeit the advantages of seniority and experience, in a sense leveling the learning base among junior and senior officers.

Second, training with simulations ignores both Murphy's Law and the human dimension of decision-making. Senior exercise controllers can develop proficiency in the training unit by stopping and starting the simulation process at will, perhaps correcting some mistakes while allowing others to go unaddressed. Simulation exercises can assume away vehicles breaking down or getting mired in the mud, support elements arriving late, personnel becoming disoriented and lost, and all the other manifestations of Clausewitzian friction. Moreover, during simulation, soldiers get more rest and suffer less stress than they do training in the field. Simulations also disregard subordinate input or low morale. As Robert Bateman argues, even with increased digital integration there are two constants on the battlefield that will not change: fear and leadership.[43] Yet simulations-based training very rarely takes these into account.

Finally, most Army simulations are still founded on attrition-warfare models. Attrition models are part of the "old" way of waging war, as will be discussed further below. Although simulations create training efficiencies, these efficiencies are meaningless if the training portrays a battlefield environment that no longer exists. For example, as Robert Leonhard argues, these simulations "cannot, in their current state, simulate perpetual unreadiness or vulnerability to dislocation,"[44] both key issues for future warfare.

Degraded Decision-Making Ability

Digital integration could ultimately result in degraded capacity for decision-making among tactical leaders. If digital networking functions as promised, soldiers may come to depend on the icons presented on their computer screens. Those icons may come to be taken as the "true" battlefield, and thus the lifeline by which leaders make decisions and soldiers fight. Yet the digital picture will never fully lift the fog of war. One informed observer argues that the "best truth" we can expect from the digital picture is "80/80/50"—80 percent accuracy for friendly forces, 80 percent accuracy for the environment, and 50 percent accuracy for the enemy.[45] The majority of leaders today have experience in analog, pre-digital units and thus can operate in a non-digital environment. This may not be the case in two decades, however. What would happen if future leaders assumed a perfect common operating picture when it was not or if they had to operate in its absence?

There are three ways that digitization could degrade tactical decision-making. First, and most obviously, over-reliance on the computer screen could degrade traditional warfare skills. Basic skills like navigating and calling for fire could atrophy as the digital equipment automates navigation and target acquisition processes.[46] In a more general statement of this argument, Donn Parker tells us that today's information technologies create "noledge," which is "information that we do not know and that we may never know by study or experience."[47] For example, "noledge" would include the fire control formulas that are used to compute artillery fire sequences. The end user enters the relevant positional data into the computer, but never sees— and possibly never even learns or remembers—the formulas used to plot trajectories or loads. This is fine until the "noledge" disappears or becomes unavailable as a result of human programming error, enemy hacking, or computer malfunction.

Second, the digital technology could create indecisive leaders who become overwhelmed by data they have not been trained to assimilate. On the one hand, soldiers could become so dependent upon their screens that they lose the ability to infer information from real-world environmental clues. Soldiers will need to compare conflicting inputs from the electronic sensors that created the digital picture with inputs from their own eyes and ears. When conflicting data arrive, soldiers may be unable to work out the cognitive dissonance between the screen "reality" and the sensory reality around them. The greater the dissonance, the slower and less confident soldiers may be in distinguishing reality from misrepresentation. One company commander in the 3rd Infantry Division during Operation Iraqi Freedom explained that he primarily used his FBCB2 system to verify his position within the friendly picture but relied intrinsically on his eyes and ears for situational awareness with regard to his unit. The officer's background in this instance was not in digitally integrated formations, and his unit had received only a partial issue of FBCB2, lacking a complete suite of applications.[48] However, reconciling sensory reality with the digital picture may become more difficult as the Army's leaders are increasingly immersed in formations with expanding digital capability.

On the other hand, having a digital picture may obscure awareness of other key inputs to decision-making, especially inputs that cannot be measured with electronic sensors in the digital system. In certain situations, like stability operations, other inputs such as political and environmental conditions could be more important than the data provided by the screen. Lester Grau argues that the most effective software tools for stability operations in Iraq, Afghanistan, and others like them would be those used by police departments for handling gang-related crime.[49] Grau also emphasizes the centrality of human intelligence and the degree of footwork required for collecting data. Gathering such data will be time and manpower intensive, and coding it risks divesting it of critical intangible characteristics, which are impossible to quantify or portray graphically.

Finally, inherent to reliance on a digital common operating picture is the risk of losing it. Jamming and hacking could have disastrous consequences for tactical leaders who have come to rely on digital technology to fight. Yet as more units rely on such technology, the more likely it will become a target for enemy disruption.[50] Currently a Russian-made GPS jamming device with an effective range of 150 miles can be purchased for $35,000 a copy.[51] Or worse, what would happen if the enemy entered the network and manipulated the digital picture? Tim Rosenberg argues that the best technique is often not to steal or destroy information, but to corrupt it because people generally defer to computer-generated information over human observation.[52] Furthermore, two other factors previously discussed—cognitive dissonance and atrophied skills (such as navigation and calling for fire)—reinforce such adverse effects.

Without overstating the threat, computer viruses, equipment failures, faulty software, enemy intrusion, casual hackers, data theft, and overloaded communications circuits all raise the possibility of having degraded digital capabilities. While the advanced warfighting experiments have simulated some disruption of friendly networks, most jamming and hacking has been innocuous so as not to interfere with new equipment testing.[53] As the Army's digitization effort continues, enemy information warfare simulation should be stepped up, so that leaders can practice making decisions in a degraded information environment.[54]

Top-Down Command Centralization

The Army's nine tenets of battle command include initiative, agility, depth, integration, versatility, flexibility, judgment, intuition, and empathy[55]—values embodied in what German military thinkers called *Auftragstaktik*, or tactics based on mission orders. In this method of command, only the outline and minimum goals of an effort are established in advance; the rest is left to subordinate leaders. *Executing mission orders requires a mindset and value system that support independent thinking, decisive action, and risk-taking.* Many theorists claim that mission orders are the key to successful maneuver-based operations in the fog of war. In other words, as the fog of war thickens, commanders at the lower echelons are better positioned to make decisions.

The digital battlefield could potentially disrupt such highly valued decentralization. Digitization increases the risk of top-down command, or what Martin van Creveld calls "command by direction."[56] As Thomas Czerwinski points out, the Army's digitization effort does indeed embody the first of van Creveld's "iron rules" for improving command performance—increase information processing capabilities and thus strengthen the "central directing organ." Czerwinski's analysis suggests, however, that the interventionist capabilities of command by direction, as made possible by the Army's digitization effort, risk being self-defeating.[57] The question becomes one of efficiency (from command by direction) versus effectiveness (from decentralized command).

Digital technologies adopted by the Army can encourage top-down centralization in two ways. First, although in theory everyone has the same digital picture of the battlefield at the same time, lower echelons cannot see the whole battlefield as well as higher echelons. This has been the rather prosaic result of the size of the computer screens in tanks, Bradley fighting vehicles, and Land Warrior headgear sets. Computer screens in individual weapon platforms are much smaller than those in command vehicles and thus can show only a small portion of the battlefield at a time. Moreover, even if they wanted to scroll around and discern the bigger picture, soldiers in these platforms (and dismounted soldiers) have less time for interfacing with their digital screens than commanders and staff officers.[58] Consequently, higher echelon commanders have a better picture of the total digital battlefield than their subordinates and may choose to intervene to capitalize on the opportunities that such digital information provides. With increased digital integration, a perception may develop that the command post is the best place from which to command, thus tying the commander to his or her C2 vehicle. Jim Dunivan argues that Army leaders flirted with centralized command once before with the use of C2 helicopters during Vietnam. The "results were erosion of trust between subordinates and leaders, and a weakening of the chain of command" as well as "a tragic decline in junior officers' and noncommissioned officers' willingness to initiate action without orders."[59]

The second effect flows from the first: with a supposedly better picture of the battlefield, commanders risk micromanaging their subordinates, discouraging independent thought and initiative, while training them to follow detailed orders. Army Col. Rick Lynch, who commanded the EXFOR from 1997 to 1999, warns future leaders:

In a setting where abundant amounts of information are available, leaders of the U.S. Army must be empowering and decentralized. As a commander of a digital brigade combat team, I had visibility on the location of each and every vehicle in the 1BCT. For example, I could focus on the actions of D32—the wingman tank of the 3rd platoon, Delta Company, 3-66 Armor. . . . But I chose not to do that. I set the filters on my digital equipment to show me company level icons. . . . However, there are individuals who, given the opportunity to micromanage their units, will do so. This will have a disastrous effect on subordinate leadership.[60]

The digital battlefield thus risks creating an overly-centralized organization, where the commander remains in his C2 vehicle watching the screen, merely moving his subordinates about the battlefield. The question then becomes: how does such an organization grow officers to direct the battle via the digital picture, if these same officers spend their whole junior careers responding to chess moves by the incumbent digital warrior chief?

There is a tension between the abstract knowledge of the higher echelon commander—embodied in the digital common operating picture—and the particular knowledge of the lower echelon commander. Professions have confronted this tension forever, and for good reason: professions need both types of knowledge—abstract and particular—for proper diagnoses and treatment. Top-down command centralization, enabled by digital integration, risks missing the proper professional balance. What seems most *efficient* from the perspective of fighting the battle may not be what is most *effective* from the perspective of those fighting the tactical engagements, nor from the perspective of building a profession.

Information Saturation

While over-centralization of battle command is one potential by-product of digital integration, a second and countervailing effect could be that of information saturation. As leaders come to rely on the common operating picture, their screens may display data, not processed information. A commander who bypasses the staff that was supposed to filter and analyze the data will now have to undertake the task himself. This effort actually increases the commander's cognitive workload, because he or she must perform both analytical and decision-making tasks.[61]

A system that produces mountains of unassimilated data could be as overwhelming as an enemy force. Maj. Geoff Norman, a participant in the Army's Project Warrior Program, served as an observer-controller during multiple digital exercises at the National Training Center. He relates that leaders of digitally networked units were very careful to avoid "data saturation"—a situation in which the leader, submerged in raw intelligence, struggles to synthesize it into useful knowledge.[62] In their training, they found that networked digital systems could easily overwhelm them with data yet failed to provide the necessary intelligence for decision-making. Such problems are evident in all units. During one division-level simulation exercise in 2002, a division commander told his personnel staff that an artillery strike on the artillery's headquarters area that occurs in the middle of a battle killing X number of personnel was not nearly as significant as the fact that the strike had killed the majority of his experienced radar signal analysts—a critical group of soldiers often in short supply within the division. He needed them to analyze the data and provide him with critical knowledge.[63] On a digitally integrated battlefield, the variety and volume of information will increase exponentially, and such problems, left unresolved, may only grow worse.

Ultimately leaders within the Army may come to rely on "decision enablers." Indeed, the current literature points to technology-assisted decision-making. The transformation roadmap addresses "decision aides" as one enabler to help translate "information superiority" into "decision superiority."[64] Such aids might consist of software tools that facilitated information management by sorting and collating data to determine such things as event correlation and conduct predictive analysis. However, the use of such tools has two adverse ramifications. First, as discussed previously, not all data are appropriate for numerical or graphical expression; shochorning it into digital format thus risks stripping it of important intangible dimensions. To process such data digitally compounds a potential data-set bias that existed even before the operator coded it. Such a compounded bias could degrade decision-making and compromise effectiveness at the operational and tactical levels. Second, decision-making tools represent a more advanced degree of "noledge." While the inability to comprehend the ballistic solution for a tank or artillery projectile is one level of ignorance, lack of familiarity with limitations of software models and data management devices is a problem on an altogether different plane.

In sum, we find five possible ways digital integration may alter the Army profession— elimination of echelons, thereby flattening organizations; increased emphasis on skills harvested through simulations; atrophy of traditional warfare skills; increased centralization of command; and creation of a data-saturated environment. All of these developments pose potentially damaging side-effects on the profession of arms. More importantly, they will not act independently upon the profession but will work in synergy, reinforcing one another with non-linear effects. These forces will likely be present in varying degrees, producing uneven effects inside the command hierarchy. Furthermore, the Army has stated that its battle command systems are the bridge between the current force and the Future Force.[65] If digital integration is to be the thread of operational continuity across the next two decades, such effects may be experienced not as a radical cultural shift but as gradual changes over time. It may thus be difficult to identify the undesired professional by-products. Members of the profession should therefore maintain a heightened sensitivity to such change. Evaluations of systems, organizations, and doctrine should not only assess quantifiable objectives, but should seek to understand how those objectives are achieved and what ripple effects result.

Implications of Digitization within the Wider Professional System of Traditional Warfare

This section addresses change in the Army's professional jurisdiction within the system of professions that participate in traditional conflict—what is currently termed major combat operations. There are three ways that digital integration could affect the wider system of traditional warfare. First, digital networking will add a new player to the professional system—civilian contractors. Second, the development of new joint operating concepts and transformational plans implies that digital integration is not exclusively an Army jurisdiction, but that the Army's developments are actually nested in a greater transformation taking place. At the same time, the Army may struggle to achieve interoperability both internally and across its spectrum of allies. Finally, the ongoing development of new operational concepts indicates that some traditional jurisdictional tasks are in danger of being poached while the Army struggles to meet professional obligations within others.

Reliance on Civilian Contractors

Even under the best conditions, information technology is sensitive and complex; difficulties increase enormously during tactical employment in a field environment. The equipment comprising the digital battlefield includes computers, radios, satellite terminals, switches, and software—all of it potentially faulty, weak, or insecure. This added complexity and fragility—requiring a special process of diagnosis and treatment—introduces a new kind of battlefield professional: the civilian contractor.

Information technology has created new jurisdictional tasks that the Army cannot itself fulfill, thus civilian contractors are becoming indispensable on the digital battlefield.[66] The digital Army relies on contractors to train and equip units and maintain systems. For example, building the Tactical Internet required integrating the efforts of 48 different contractor vendors. During the Task Force XXI AWE in March 1997, 1,200 contractors from these 48 vendors were in the field at the NTC with the EXFOR, providing advice, maintenance, and technical support.[67] Such support requirements are projected to increase as the number of digital systems fielded to Army units rises.

At least two issues warrant consideration within this trend of ever-greater civilian involvement. First, civilianizing military functions raises the issues of whether we will need civilians in times of crisis and whether we can guarantee reliable support .[68] For example, one company commander from the 3rd Infantry Division explained that his task force received a limited issue of FBCB2 under the Rapid Fielding Initiative prior to the invasion of Iraq. During major combat operations, the division had one contractor and a very limited ability to perform basic maintenance on the systems, amounting to little more than removing the hard drive to install operational graphics. He estimated that approximately 50 percent of the systems had ceased to function within the first two months of conflict.[69] While one must be careful not to draw too many conclusions from such a limited test, such indications certainly raise questions regarding the reliability of equipment and the maintenance system. The increasingly clouded issue of combatant/noncombatant distinction that is critical to the law of armed conflict becomes a second important issue rising from the first. Operating high-tech systems moves civilian contractors from traditional support functions to what are arguably hostile activities, increasing the risk they will become characterized as "unlawful combatants" under international law.[70] To prevent such characterization, some authorities suggest establishing a new type of part-time military, lacking "much of the military regimen" in the way of dress and physical fitness standards.[71] Although an adjunct military structure might create the necessary legal framework to compel civilians to remain on the job during crisis, it would not fully replicate the professional ethics, unit cohesion, and training of the Army profession.

Digitization and Joint Interdependence

In a future conventional conflict, the Army will fight as part of a joint or coalition force. Operations Desert Storm, Enduring Freedom, and Iraqi Freedom bear witness to the truth of these propositions. Digital integration and increased joint interoperability open the Army to change in its jurisdictional tasks on the one hand, and strain its ability to provide collaborative C2 structures on the other. What are the ramifications of digital integration for the Army in the context of this increasingly interdependent system of professions?

First, the prospect of joint integration through a network of systems poses new possibilities not only for the Army, but for its sister services. Such thorough connectivity means services must develop common protocols, operating procedures, and technical standards. Currently, two systems, the Joint Tactical Radio System and Warfighter Internet-Tactical (WIN-T), form the command and control backbone of the Army's FCS, serving as the Army's tactical "plug" to the future Global Information Grid.[72] Thus the Army will be one service relying on a very complex global structure under civilian and/or joint management. Furthermore, interoperability among the armed services will require not just adhering to the same technical standards, it will require common doctrine and procedures in network management. By definition, common protocols and standards mean that network-centric combat is not a U.S. Army-exclusive jurisdiction. And while resulting synergies promise to increase military capability dramatically, the Army will not be the sole proprietor of the digital battlefield. If all services have claim to operations intertwined in the joint domain, does this not create a conduit for them to usurp what may traditionally be exclusively Army jurisdictions? For example, Army generals have served as the combatant commanders in all the conflicts previously cited; however, might a more integrated joint force be commanded by flag officers from its sister services who have different perspectives on the employment of the joint force?

Second, the execution of coalition operations could become much more difficult because communications must be standardized across the battlefield. Digitally integrated forces must be able to accommodate least-common-denominator communication systems—what the Army calls analog (non-digital) systems. Nora Bensahel points out that coalition partners' capabilities can run the gamut: from those that have incorporated information-based technology to others who fight on horseback, like the Northern Alliance forces in Afghanistan. Furthermore, political sensitivities sometimes require that coalition partners have an entire national chain of command parallel to that of the joint/coalition force.[73] Her prediction is that Army transformation will only exacerbate this problem, resulting in increased requirements for liaison teams and complications that arise from sharing sensitive information. For example, the 2nd U.S. Infantry Division (currently an analog unit) serves as the headquarters for a combined force of American and Korean artillery units. Such a mission requires multiple cells of liaison teams within the division and artillery brigades' headquarters for coordinating operations with Korean artillery elements across an Army sector. The coalition forces attain this level of interoperability by leveraging a 50-year alliance between the two armies with extremely similar operational doctrines, and with augmentees from the Korean Army who live with American units permanently.[74] As Army capabilities expand and coalitions fracture and reform, will the U.S Army have both the trust and capacity to provide such specialized skills and technology to facilitate inter-operability with ever-changing partners?

However, the question of digital and analog interoperability is much broader than merely communication among units. Because of the vast differences in command and control capabilities, digital and analog units cannot seamlessly integrate and respond to orders in an equivalent manner. A digital commander can see the battlefield and thus decides where and how to attack the enemy from a position of advantage before the enemy discovers his unit. In contrast, an analog unit must still go forth and find the enemy physically. This has profound importance for how the forces are employed in battle.

Furthermore, although the Army aggressively seeks a baseline level of digitization throughout the current force based upon the present Army Battle Command System,[75] there may be significant problems with the digital integration of reserve units. These units face training challenges that active units do not—they train at lower echelons, less frequently, and for shorter periods of time. These training disadvantages become a critical issue because digital skills are very perishable.[76] As a result, the National Guard and Army Reserve may not be effective in networked warfare.

Recognizing these differences, David Fautua has argued against assigning *any* digitization-dependent role to the Guard and Reserve. Because of the inherent speed that digitization creates, a digitized force will be designed to conduct "burst operations" as opposed to sustained campaigns.[77] Yet burst operations may not allow for mobilization, in which case the contribution of reserve forces would be less. Fautua argues that the Army Reserve and National Guard should develop competencies in "shaping" and peace operations missions, because these missions play to their strengths: small-unit cohesion, a comparative inclination toward expeditionary-type missions, and fewer manpower-intensive training requirements.[78] Current Army literature echoes this sentiment to some degree. The Transformation Roadmap calls for a restructuring and reshaping of assets between the active and reserve component, whereby the active force will "typically respond in the first 15 days of an operation," while reserves will "provide strategic depth to reinforce the warfight and support and stability operations (SASO), as well as lead our efforts to protect the homeland."[79]

Exploiting the Digital Advantage: Future Concepts

The Army has attempted to incorporate new technologies into operational concepts for nearly a decade. It has achieved a great deal of success with precision fires, but struggled to leverage information technologies to facilitate changes in maneuver warfare. This imbalance threatens the Army's relevance in major combat operations in general. The Army may thus find its jurisdiction over fire support usurped on the one hand and its jurisdictional claim to maneuver warfare unfulfilled on the other. This section will explore the ramifications of future concepts with regard to the system of traditional warfare.

The Army's initial experimentation with networked fire support achieved significant success. During the AWEs, digitized spot reports reached the fire support battalion in five minutes, as opposed to nine minutes under conventional communications means, and needed repeating only 4 percent of the time, whereas one-third of conventional messages needed repeating. The conclusion was that digitized spot reports save time and can rapidly synchronize direct and indirect fires:[80]

> As a result, both experiments revealed an enormous increase in the logistical demand for more ammunition. Suddenly able to perceive, track, and identify literally thousands of targets, Experimental Force commanders reclined in their natural tendency toward [maneuver] caution and long-range fires. Information Age warfare degenerated into a turkey shoot. . . . Army officials pushed beyond rational limitations on available ammunition and allowed Experimental Forces the freedom to blast the enemy into nonexistence at extreme ranges to their hearts' content. Realistic limitations on transportation, ammunition, and the ability to fire into inhabited areas were tacitly ignored. The simulated enemy enthusiastically and obediently cooperated with the cyber-carnage, stupidly charging into terrain that was easy to target, unit after unit, never learning and never adapting to fires like a real enemy would.[81]

As James Blackwell observes in the present anthology (see Chapter 14), the Army's RMA doctrine seems to be acquiescing in the notion that the best way to destroy the enemy is through long-range precision fires—fires throughout the depth of the battlefield. Thus, one of the key results of Army digitization has been to increase the power and role of long-range fires.

While still in its infancy, it seems that the Army has begun to leverage information technologies to facilitate maneuver as well. The reconnaissance, surveillance, targeting, and acquisition squadron (RSTA) within the Stryker Brigade Combat Team (SBCT) reflects a shift in organization structure with the intent to capitalize upon these new technologies. The reconnaissance squadron, traditionally a division-level asset, is now organic to the SBCT (which has the one squadron and three Stryker infantry battalions). At the same time, the squadron has been equipped with a robust suite of C4I systems to facilitate parallel planning with the brigade headquarters. Thus equipped the squadron is responsible for "reconnaissance pull—providing information (and possibly conducting shaping operations) on threat forces to allow the SBCT elements to maneuver out of contact and gain positional advantage."[82] The Army's current modularization initiative will eventually restructure brigade combat teams to give each of them a reconnaissance squadron with two battalions, thus dedicating one third of the maneuver force to reconnaissance and surveillance by 2008. While current authorizations in these units are still provisional, it certainly appears that the Army is attempting to leverage C4ISR capabilities across the entire force to facilitate a new method of maneuver.

Within the system of professions, two issues arise. First, land power through fire-supported maneuver, not precision strike, is arguably the Army's core jurisdictional task. However, the Army has used its digital capability to expand its jurisdiction deeper into the battlefield, to take deep fire missions away from the Air Force and the Navy. Yet, it may prove more operationally efficient for those services to provide such long-range fires. Given the U.S. proclivity to use military force in the most restrained and surgical manner possible, the continued attractiveness of air power alone bodes poorly for the Army. Second, in an attempt to balance firepower with maneuver on the digital battlefield, the Army has created the RSTA squadron to capitalize on new technologies and facilitate "maneuver out of contact" in the short term.[83] In the long term, the Army is developing the Future Combat System with this specific doctrinal concept in mind. However, recent studies indicate that system development relies on several immature technologies that in turn depend upon an unproven C2 backbone.[84] Should the system not meet expectations, the Army may find its fire support capability irrelevant and its capacity for maneuver inadequate.

In sum, digital integration has given rise to a new professional within the military system of professions—the civilian contractor. At the same time it promises to integrate the Army into the joint community from "space to the mud." These two developments have opened to poaching Army professional tasks once within the Army's jurisdictions, and at the same time have placed greater emphasis on the Army's need to bridge the capabilities of the Future Force with reserve and coalition forces. Furthermore, the operational concepts currently at the heart of the Future Force's core jurisdiction, maneuver warfare, remain in their infancy with years of testing and development ahead.

Implications of Digitization within the Broadest Professional System of National Security

Thus far, we have examined the Army's digital transformation efforts through the Army's preferred lens. The Army's methods for digital integration express its perspective of its professional jurisdiction, and to date Army efforts have focused on the high end of the conflict spectrum, using technology to facilitate operational concepts that fall under the auspices of major combat operations (MCO).[85] Yet the professional system of national security encompasses much more than MCO; indeed both joint and Army documents advocate "full spectrum dominance." This section explores the Army's digital integration efforts within this wider professional system, arguing that the Army may ultimately leave itself inadequately prepared for future national security requirements.

The Wider Conflict Spectrum

The Army's digitization efforts are not a new way for the Army to do business, but rather a new way of doing existing business better. Its current concept of the future digital battlefield envisions improved ability to conduct fire-supported maneuver as the basis of its operational art. Indeed the Army's Transformation Roadmap acknowledges MCO as a primary driver in transformation, declaring the ability to conduct major combat operations the cornerstone of national power: "Major Combat Operations are the ultimate military coin of the realm for a global power." "The ability to conduct MCO," it continues, "underscores the credibility of the Joint Force across the full spectrum of operations, fundamentally influencing the success of other operations."[86] As the current struggle in Iraq indicates, however, successful conduct of MCO does not imply the successful execution of stability operations.[87]

Over the last decade, nontraditional adversaries and asymmetric forms of conflict challenge assumptions underpinning the DoD and Army visions of the future battlefield. For example, the National Intelligence Council forecasts that, through 2015, the most common threats to stability around the world will be internal conflicts, transnational terrorism, and weapons of mass destruction.[88] The 11 September 2001 terrorist attacks on the Pentagon and World Trade Center, which gave birth to the current mantra—Global War on Terrorism—lend weight to this prediction. Potential future adversaries will acknowledge U.S. military superiority in major combat operations and simply avoid such conflict, seeking instead to exploit vulnerabilities elsewhere:

> This perception among present and potential adversaries will continue to generate the pursuit of asymmetric capabilities against U.S. forces and interests abroad as well as the territory of the United States. U.S. opponents—state and such non-state actors as drug lords, terrorists, and foreign insurgents—will not want to engage the U.S. military on its terms. They will choose instead political and military strategies designed to dissuade the United States from using force, or, if the United States does use force, to exhaust American will, circumvent or minimize U.S. strengths, and exploit perceived U.S. weaknesses. Asymmetric challenges can arise across the spectrum of conflict that will confront U.S. forces in a theater of operations or on U.S. soil.[89]

Furthermore, dominance of precision fires may force enemy combatants into complex terrain such as we have observed in the mountains of Afghanistan and neighborhoods of Baghdad, Najaf, and Fallujah in Iraq. Such a strategy increases the inherent risk of higher casualties and collateral damage, degrades U.S. military advantages, and creates an intensive ground force manpower requirement.[90] Recent experiences in Iraq validate this argument. Capt. Dave Hibner explained that on the march to Baghdad, two massed armor formations attempted to confront his task force, but the Joint Strategic Targeting and Reconnaissance System (JSTARS) identified them within 30 minutes of initial movement and every single vehicle was destroyed by air support: "We forced them [Iraqi combatants] into the cities because they realized any other way of trying to fight us was futile." He further observed that "what really hurt the Iraqis was poor but organized defenses because it made identification [i.e. distinguishing enemy from noncombatant] and destruction of the enemy easier."[91] By compelling American forces to operate in a physically and politically restricted environment, adversaries can limit U.S. technological advantages. Lt. Col. Jim Rainey described a 15-day urban battle in the town of Najaf fighting "through a 100,000 [inhabitant] urban area, 2 1/2 kilometers by 3 kilometers, against a pretty committed enemy" to surround an enemy strongpoint.[92] Given that half the world's population today lives in urban areas—and by 2025 that figure is expected to reach 85 percent—future scenarios similar to these are hardly unlikely.[93]

While transformation efforts have attempted to address the full spectrum of operations to some degree, the application of digital technology to stability operations remains questionable. For example, Land Warrior, the prototype system designed to integrate the individual soldier into the tactical internet, weighed more than 90 pounds, in addition to the food, ammunition, and other gear that a dismounted infantryman carries.[94] One could never reasonably employ such a system in combat; as Daniel Bolger says: "Imagine carrying another guy on your back forever and you get the idea. You cannot fight like that no matter how much physical training you do."[95] The goal for the next model is a "fightable" weight of 50 pounds, still a significant load for a dismounted soldier to bear in a tactical engagement. Furthermore project outcomes remain questionable as development costs rise, footnoted by one review panel as a generally "neglected variable."[96] Another factor to consider is that digitally integrating dismounted soldiers may have counterproductive effects. For example, sniper weapons have been developed to focus on the frequencies transmitted by the Land Warrior system, potentially making the sniper's job easier—the sniper would not have to see a body but merely shoot at the source of an electromagnetic transmission at a particular frequency.[97]

However, more significant than the integration of digital hardware and software is the assumption that the Army's digital battle command system will be equally suitable across the entire spectrum of operations. As the Army Transformation Roadmap states, "battle command capabilities required for MCO [major combat operations] are applicable to SO [stability operations], and, as with MCO, battle command is the transformational underpinning for success in future stability operations." At the same time, the Army acknowledges that "the C2, communications, and ISR challenges of SO may be more complex than those encountered in MCO, requiring unique mixes of sensor and communications suites, HUMINT, CI, and special attention to information fusion enablers for urban environments."[98] The problem with such a system is not just questionable software capabilities but also unreliable system inputs. To illustrate, Maj. Odie Sheffield related his experience hiring translators for his unit in Baghdad. The unit parked a truck with a loudspeaker in the downtown area and broadcasted in English the message, "If you understand this, come see me." One Iraqi eventually responded and returned with over 50 English speakers the next day.[99] In the future, information garnered through such individuals would pass from an observer/informant through the translator—perhaps of questionable credibility—to a U.S. Soldier who either passes it along or enters it into the digital data stream. The ability of any device to capture intangible facets of various pieces of intelligence and correct human error would be astounding. Furthermore processing such a "data byte" with others compounds such problems, reinforcing the issues of data-set bias and advanced levels of "noledge."

The Army's digital integration efforts appear to focus on missions at the high end of the conflict spectrum, and their applicability to operations other than major combat operations seems questionable. In this approach, the Army may be expressing its preferred view of its professional jurisdiction—conventional warfare in open terrain. Yet if the Army does not focus on military operations in other parts of the conflict spectrum, it may find itself irrelevant in one sense and incapable in the other. Recent events indicate that policy-makers inside DoD may be very concerned about the direction of the department's transformation; the Secretary of Defense is currently reviewing concept proposals that place less emphasis on platforms and more on personnel and intelligence.[100]

The Media Threat to Information Dominance

As discussed previously, the Future Force's promised capability enhancements depend largely on information superiority. However, challenges to joint and Army information superiority will take forms other than enemy actions and counteractions. The news media are exploiting information technology as well, and the consequent developments in reporting practices could affect security. In the last decade, civilian technologies have made a substantial qualitative advance, and the military's ability to secure the information environment during conflict has eroded significantly.

Like the U.S. military, the news media drew lessons from the first Gulf War. During the Operations Desert Shield/Desert Storm, journalists had to take their stories to Allied Forward Transmission Units (FTUs), which had satellite links with London and Washington. In the opinion of many journalists, military dispatchers delayed physical transport of stories to the FTUs and reviewed all stories before they were released for transmission.[101] After the war, journalists vowed never again to be prisoner to such military "censorship" and have capitalized on technology to become as independent from the military as possible.

A decade ago, mobile uplinks required a flatbed truck and came with a crew of five journalists. Today, a two-person journalist team can go to war with a digital camera, a wideband cellular phone to uplink to a satellite, and a laptop computer to coordinate the transmission. The equipment fits into two cases and weighs about 100 pounds. "Live from the battlefield" will no longer be primitive or cumbersome—it will be routine.[102] For example, a Thrane & Thrane satellite phone, which can be set up anywhere in 30 seconds and retails for about $3,000, allows "voice and data transmission from any place on the planet outside the Polar zones."[103] Advent Communications offers an International Mobile Satellite (INMARSAT) system that is small enough to be handled by one person.[104] Indeed, Lara Logan, a reporter for a British morning news program on assignment in Afghanistan, used a similar INMARSAT system to broadcast live from the frontlines in Afghanistan.[105] And Aerobureau of McLean, Virginia, can already deploy a self-sustaining flying newsroom. The aircraft is equipped not only with multiple video, audio, and data communications links, but also gyro-stabilized cameras, side- and forward-looking radars, and its own pair of camera-equipped remotely piloted vehicles.[106]

With the rise of such technology, reporters can move anywhere in the world and provide live coverage with a minimal support footprint, transmitting digital video footage at their discretion. In one report, Lara Logan sent a video transmission of U.S. carpet bombing prior to the Pentagon's admission of such activity. In another, she describes listening to Taliban transmissions on a Northern Alliance radio system.[107] Real-time public revelations of such transmissions could potentially compromise various aspects of military operations. Stephen Jukes describes a similar instance:

> Ismael Khan, a Northern Alliance commander in Afghanistan, was weighing his military options in a fight with the Taliban outside the city of Herat when his satellite phone rang. The voice on the other end was that of Reuters reporter Andrew Marshall, who, within minutes, had relayed around the world news that the city was under siege.[108]

And, while most news media cannot own a high-resolution satellite themselves, they can purchase satellite products on the open market, thus presenting a threat of a different dimension. Imagery from these satellites is not prohibitively expensive. For example, SpaceImaging, Inc. offers "news pix" for about $500 each, and it will re-task satellite coverage for about $3,000.[109] Most new commercial companies have focused their efforts on supplying relatively high-resolution imagery (objects five meters across or even less) of visible and infrared data.[110] Since five-meter resolution is enough to identify buildings and large weapons accurately, these satellites create a profoundly intrusive capability for prying news organizations and other paying customers—including potential adversaries.[111] Moreover, advanced software, along with a cadre of expert ex-military consultants, will enable them to fuse the raw inputs into usable, real-time or near real-time reportage. In other words, the news media will become the "poor man's intelligence service."

The most recent military response to potentially damaging battlefield reportage has been the embedding of reporters with units prior to and during operations in Afghanistan and Iraq. While many senior military officials viewed this program as a success, the results evoked much discussion in media circles. In order to rely less on military support, journalists have increasingly come to advocate a more professional approach to combat reporting, to include acquiring a more thorough knowledge of the battlefield on the part of correspondents. Peter Copeland states that "the press should do a better job of training people for the next conflict and reduce its dependency on the military."[112] Mark Mazzetti argues that reporters need improved "situational awareness" to better analyze developments within military campaigns. While not intrinsically harmful, developing such analytical acumen enhances prospects for the reporter to become an inadvertent intelligence source. At the same time, many reporters also advocate the presence of "unilaterals" or "freelancers" on the battlefield. [113] These are independent reporters who often go where the sanctioned journalists of the new media conglomerates cannot. There is some speculation that large media organizations actually encourage freelancing by creating a market for footage requiring risks that their own reporters are not allowed to take.[114] Regardless, the market for an increasing number of highly skilled, well-equipped freelance journalists appears to exist, potentially threatening military information dominance.

In short, the Army's goal of seeking information dominance on the future battlefield is profoundly unrealistic. The proliferation of inexpensive compact global communications equipment, affordable satellite imagery products, and professionally savvy combat journalists translate into increasingly mobile, independent, penetrating reporters who can report from every corner of the battlefield. Charles Dunlap rightly states that modern militaries must "focus on developing doctrine and strategies for operating in an environment of information transparency or information parity."[115] At a minimum, the Army needs to recognize that there will be non-traditional professions competing for information on the future battlefield, and it must be ready to operate in an environment lacking the information dominance it has heretofore assumed it would have.

Strategic Information Warfare

Finally, the term "information warfare" (IW) is increasingly used to encompass a broader set of information-age warfare concepts. These emerging concepts are directly tied to the prospect that the ongoing evolution of cyberspace—the global information infrastructure—will create new opportunities and vulnerabilities. In this sense, information warfare is much broader than electronic warfare or anti-C2 network warfare. Instead, in future conflicts, battlefield C4I vulnerabilities may be less lucrative targets than vulnerabilities within national infrastructure.[116] The essential U.S infrastructures—those "whose incapacity or destruction would have a debilitating impact on our defense or economic security"—include systems like the public telephone network, securities and commodities exchanges, water-supply systems, utility networks, air transportation, highways, and the Internet.[117]

Today, strategic IW remains largely theoretical. However, the 11 September 2001 attacks on the World Trade Center and the Pentagon, which temporarily crippled air travel and financial markets, could be characterized as anti-infrastructure warfare. Furthermore, the electrical grid blackout in September 2003 that left the northeastern United States without power simply illustrates the effects an IW "cyberstrike" might hope to achieve. If such concepts reach fruition, state and non-state actors with the capacity will probably attempt them because of their potentially high level of effectiveness married with low risks and entry costs. When it becomes possible to wage war with a handful of computers, a new group of organizations will compete for this professional jurisdiction—military services, government agencies, security divisions of transnational corporations, and private security firms. The Army must stay abreast of these emerging forms of warfare—and of the competitors that such warfare will bring into the professional system of national security.

In summary, the Army's choice to employ digital networks to achieve conventional ends tacitly expresses its perspective of its expert knowledge and professional jurisdiction. These efforts have focused on the high end of the conflict spectrum—major combat operations. Yet the professional system of national security encompasses much more than conventional warfare. Evolving asymmetric threats and operations in Iraq and Afghanistan suggest that conventional warfare, while the "cornerstone" of military credibility, may not be the most prevalent operational demand. Moreover, concept developers and senior military leaders should question assumptions regarding information dominance. The findings in this section indicate that the Army may be unprepared for the future, and by consciously or unconsciously ignoring nontraditional operations, the Army risks being caught unaware and disregarded.

Conclusion

How the Army has chosen to adopt new information technologies says much about its future professional jurisdiction. As the forgoing analysis has shown, information technologies from the contemporary RMA are both a subjective and an objective force for jurisdictional change. This chapter has examined the implications of Army digitization in light of three concentric visions of the professional system—within the Army profession itself, within the wider professional system of traditional warfare, and within the widest professional system of national security. The analysis has suggested that although the Army has been capitalizing on technological opportunities to enhance its conventional war-fighting capability, it seems unwilling or unable to address the wider threats that such technological change could bring to its traditional jurisdiction.

Digital integration has the potential to generate a number of undesirable trends within the profession itself. Each of these impulses may be felt in varying degrees at different echelons within the command hierarchy. While adopting a pessimistic view of change would be detrimental to the long-term health of the profession, a healthy skepticism of the information technology "miracle" and its alleged benefits for the profession is advisable. Furthermore a reliance on battle command capabilities (products of digitally networked systems) as the bridge between the current force and Future Force will make it difficult to identify gradual, undesirable shifts in professional competence and culture that occur unevenly across the profession over a significant period. Thus in development and experimentation Army leaders must be sensitive to the potential outcomes and ask questions that address not only ends—victory and peace—but the means by which they were achieved. In a sense they must rethink the definition of failure.

In the professional system of traditional warfare, the introduction and expansion of digital networks into the joint realm has exposed the Army to jurisdictional poaching by contractors and sister services. Furthermore, two of the Army's core conceptual methods for capitalizing on digital networks—precision fires and maneuver out of contact—may be unbundled, leaving the Army less able to compete in its traditional jurisdiction of major combat operations. Networked precision fires are subject to jurisdictional usurpation, as joint assets may increasingly deliver them throughout the battlefield. And maneuver out of contact remains in its infancy with no clear indications for long-term success.

Furthermore, at the national security level, the assumption of information dominance that underlies DoD joint operating concepts remains questionable, especially in regard to ground forces that may have the most to lose in the realm of information competition. Additionally, the increase of nontraditional threats and potential for future conflict in complex terrain indicate that the Army's focus on major combat operations may leave it less prepared to meet national security requirements for urban operations that demand less conventional and more nonstandard capabilities.

This chapter does not argue that transformation is to be resisted; on the contrary, transformation is like the rising sun—it's going to happen and can both blister and pleasure. Whether its influences are malign or benign will be largely determined by the recipient. Thus, there are good reasons for the Army to pause and evaluate its current position in relation to other services, its current operations, and future projections. Of course, uncertainty will abound; it is impossible to identify and extrapolate the effects of every influence in the process. Not only the direction, but the pace of transformation is in question. Perhaps it is best, then, to heed the advice of Michael O'Hanlon when discussing the 2001 Quadrennial Defense Review:

> RMA proponents are certainly right to believe that a successful military must always be changing. But the post-World War II U.S. military has already taken that adage to heart. The status quo in defense circles does not mean standing still. It means taking a balanced approach to modernization that has served the country remarkably well for decades. Indeed, it brought about the very technologies displayed in *Desert Storm* that have given rise to the belief that an RMA may be under way. It is not clear that we need to accelerate the pace of innovation now.[118]

Notes

1. Steve J. Mains, "Adapting Doctrine to Knowledge-Based Warfare," *Military Review* 77 (March-April 1997), available from http://www-cgsc.army.mil/milrev/english.marapr97/mains.html; Internet; accessed 6 March 2001.

2. Briefing by Chris Lamb, Acting Deputy Assistant Secretary of Defense for Requirements, Plans, and Counterproliferation Policy, 14 December 2000 at Georgetown University.

3. Gen. Peter J. Schoomaker, *2003 United States Army Transformation Roadmap*, chap. 1, p. 7, available at http://www.army.mil/2003TransformationRoadmap/; Internet; accessed 27 September 2004.

4. Donald H. Rumsfeld, *Joint Operations Concepts, November 2003*, 15, available at http://www.dtic.mil/jointvision/secdef_approved_jopsc.doc; Internet; accessed 27 September 2004. DoD currently believes that future battle command systems built around new information technologies will help to minimize the fog of war. Clausewitz explained this conceptual fog: "War is the realm of uncertainty; three quarters of the factors on which action in war are based are wrapped in a fog of greater or lesser uncertainty." See Carl von Clausewitz, *On War*, ed. and trans. Michael Howard and Peter Paret (Princeton, NJ: Princeton University Press, 1976), 101. The Army has experimented heavily with information technology-enabled tactical battle command systems since 1994. The hypothesis the Army tested during its digital experiments was as follows: "If information age battle command capabilities and connectivity exist across all battle operating systems and functions, then enhancements in lethality, survivability, and tempo will be achieved." See Ron Gregory, "Army XXI: Issues Associated with Development

of Doctrine and TTP [Tactics, Techniques, and Procedures] for the Digitized Force," available at http://www-tradoc.army.mil/jadd/adxxi2/sld001.html; Internet; accessed 20 October 2000.

5. Andrew Abbott, *The System of Professions: An Essay on the Division of Expert Labor* (Chicago, IL: University of Chicago Press, 1988), 8.

6. Abbott, chaps. 2-4.

7. For a good introduction to the contemporary RMA debate, see Andrew Krepinevich, "From Cavalry to Computer," *The National Interest*, no. 37 (Fall 1994): 30-43; and Eliot A. Cohen, "The Revolution in Military Affairs," *Foreign Affairs* 75 (March-April 1996): 20-36.

8. William A. Owens, *Lifting the Fog of War* (New York: Farrar, Strauss, Cirouk, 2000), 118. See also Owens, "The Emerging US System-of-Systems," Institute for National Strategic Studies, *Strategic Forum*, no. 63 (February 1996); and Joseph Nye, Jr., and William A. Owens, "America's Information Edge," *Foreign Affairs* 75 (March/April 1996).

9. Michael Mazarr, *The Revolution in Military Affairs: A Framework for Defense Planning* (Carlisle Barracks, PA: U.S. Army War College, Strategic Studies Institute, 10 June 1994), 16-21.

10. Steven Metz and James Kievit, *Strategy and the Revolution in Military Affairs: From Theory to Policy* (Carlisle Barracks, PA: U.S. Army War College, Strategic Studies Institute, 10 June 1994), 5.

11. Robert R. Leonhard, "A Culture of Velocity," in *Digital War: A View from the Front Lines*, ed. Robert L. Bateman (San Francisco, CA: Presidio Press, 1999), 146.

12. Alvin and Heidi Toffler, *War and Anti-War: Survival at the Dawn of the 21st Century* (Boston, MA: Little, Brown and Company, 1993), 65-79.

13. "The 2001 Trained and Ready Division," draft document, 13, available at http://www-cgsc.army.mil/dao/fa30/New%20Information/DIGITAL%20TRAINING.html; Internet; accessed 16 March 2001.

14. "Digitization 101," available at http://www.armyexperiment.net/aepublic/digit_101/digi.html; Internet; accessed 16 March 2001. TRADOC Pamphlet 525-5 (Fort Monroe, VA: Headquarters U.S. Army Training and Doctrine Command, 1 August 1994) defines situational awareness as "the ability to have accurate and real-time information of friendly, enemy, neutral, and noncombatant locations; a common, relevant picture of the battlefield scaled to specific level of interest and special needs."

15. "Force XXI Operations," TRADOC Pamphlet 525-5, chap. 3.

16. Owens, *Lifting the Fog of War*, 117-18.

17. This is based on the widely-quoted concept of Air Force Col. John Boyd's observation-orientation-decision-action (OODA) loop. The Army specifically addresses this concept in its discussion of information and decision superiority (chap. 1) and operating within the enemy's decision cycle at every level (chap. 2) in *2003 United States Army Transformation Roadmap*. These capabilities are directly credited to the networked characteristics of the future force.

18. Edward Mann, "Desert Storm: The First Information War?" *Airpower Journal* (Winter 1994): 6-7.

19. Current operational concepts, both joint and Army, outline decision superiority as an essential element of future combat, and define it as a product of information superiority. While definitions of information superiority vary between agencies, the concepts are generally consistent with that offered in this chapter. Furthermore, all texts consider information superiority a direct benefit of digitally networked systems. For more discussion of information superiority and decision dominance, see *Joint Operations Concepts* (November 2003), 16, and *2003 United States Army Transformation Roadmap*, chaps. 1 and 2.

20. For a more detailed history of Army attempts to automate C2 systems, see Elizabeth A. Stanley, *Evolutionary Technology in the Current Revolution in Military Affairs: The Army Tactical Command and Control System* (Carlisle Barracks, PA: U.S. Army War College, Strategic Studies Institute, 25 March 1998).

21. Mark Hanna, "Task Force XXI: The Army's Digital Experiment," *Strategic Studies*, no. 119 (July 1997).

22. Mark Thompson, "Wired for War," *Time*, 31 March 1997, 72-73.

23. Elke Hutto, "Reaping the Battlefield Digitization Harvest," *International Defense Review Special Report*, Quarterly Report No. 2 (1 June 1998): 3.

24. Frank Tiboni, "Global Command System Speeds Planning," *Defense News*, 25 September 2000, 4.

25. Each battlefield functional area has a different automated system in ATCCS. They include the Maneuver Control System (MCS), the Advanced Field Artillery Tactical Data System (AFATDS), the All-Source Analysis System (ASAS), the Combat Service Support Control System (CSSCS), and the Air and Missile Defense Work Station (AMDWS, formerly known as FADC2I). For more information about ATCCS, see Stanley, *Evolutionary Technology*, or "The ABCS Primer," available at http://www.armyexperiment.net/aepublic/abcs/default.html; Internet; accessed 24 January 2001.

26. On weapons that already have an embedded computer, like the M1A1 Abrams tank and the Bradley infantry fighting vehicle, FBCB2 software is added to the existing computer system. For more information on FBCB2 see "Battlefield Automation: Acquisition Issues Facing the Army Battle Command, Brigade and Below Program," Report No. NSIAD-98-140 (Washington, DC: U.S. Government Accounting Office, 30 June 1998).

27. Today, this capability is embodied in the Enhanced Position Location and Reporting System (EPLRS), which constantly transmits an update of the soldier's or weapon platform's current location.

28. Most systems still have a Single Channel Ground and Airborne Radio System (SINCGARS) radio, although there has also been experimentation with newer radios capable of moving the large amounts of data that digital forces require. These other systems include the Near-term Digital Radio (NDTR), the Joint Combat Information Terminal (JCIT), and the Joint Tactical Radio System (JTRS). See Steve T. Wall, "Multifunctional Communication on the Battlefield," *Army Logistician* (July-August 2000), available at http://www.amlc.army.mil/alog/JulAug00/MS507.html; Internet; accessed 24 January 2001; David C. Isby, "US Army Considers Alternatives to JTRS," *Jane's Defence Upgrades* 3, no. 3 (9 January 1999): 3; "Improved Radio Eases Digitization Traffic," *International Defense Digest* 31, no. 10 (1 October 1998): 5; and Bruce D. Nordwall, "Software Radios Give Army Helo C2 Systems," *Aviation Week and Space Technology* 151, no. 11 (13 September 1999): 85.

29. Barbara Jezior, "The Land Warrior," in *AY97 Compendium Army After Next Project*, ed. Douglas V. Johnson, II (Carlisle Barracks, PA: U.S. Army War College, Strategic Studies Institute, 6 April 1998); "Army's Restructured Land Warrior Program Needs More Oversight," Report No. NSIAD-00-28 (Washington, DC: U.S. Government Accounting Office, 15 December 1999).

30. In the past decade the body of literature on DoD transformation has matured from a collection of theories and disparate concepts to a more formalized plan providing top-down guidance for Joint Operational Concept (JOC) development, integration, experimentation, and evaluation. For a more thorough understanding of the collection of JOCs under development, see the Future Concepts library website at http://www.dtic.mil/jointvision/index.html; Internet; accessed 27 September 2004.

31. For a discussion of the Global Information Grid's capabilities see Gen. Richard. B Meyers, *National Military Strategy of the United States of America, 2004: A Strategy for Today; A Vision for Tomorrow*, 22; at http://www.oft.osd.mil/library/library_files/document_377_National%20Military%20Strategy%2013%20May%2004.pdf; Internet, accessed 27 September 2004; and Gen. Peter J. Schoomaker, *2003 United States Army Transformation Roadmap*, chaps. 2, 3, and 8.

32. Gen. Peter J. Schoomaker, *2003 United States Army Transformation Roadmap*, chap. 1, p. 1.

33. Ibid., p. xiv.

34. "The Army's Future Combat System's Features, Risks, and Alternatives: Testimony before the Subcommittee on Tactical Air and Land Forces, Committee on Armed Services, House of representatives," GOA 04-635T Defense Acquisitions (Washington, DC: U.S. Government Accounting Office, 1 April 2004).

35. Gen. Richard B. Meyers, *National Military Strategy of the United States of America, 2004: A Strategy for Today; A Vision for Tomorrow.*

36. Gen. Peter J. Schoomaker, *The Way Ahead: Our Army at War . . . Relevant & Ready Moving from the Current Force to the Future Force . . . Now!*, at http://www.army.mil/references/; Internet, accessed 7 October 2004.

37. Michael Evans, "Fabrizio's Choice: Organizational Change and the Revolution in Military Affairs Debate," *National Security Studies Quarterly* 7, no. 1 (Winter 2001): 15; Francis Fukuyama and Abram N. Shulsky, "Military Organization in the Information Age: Lessons from the World of Business," in *Strategic Appraisal: The Changing Rules of Informational Warfare*, eds. Zalmay M. Khalilzad and John P. White (Santa Monica, CA: RAND, 1999), 327-60.

38. Douglas A. Macgregor, *Breaking the Phalanx: A New Design for Landpower in the 21st Century* (Westport, CT: Praeger, 1997); John R. Brinkerhoff, "The Brigade-Based New Army," *Parameters* 27 (Autumn 1997): 60-72. See also David Fastabend, "An Appraisal of 'The Brigade-Based New Army,'" *Parameters* 27 (Autumn 1997): 73-81. For a history of the Army divisional structure, see Richard W. Kedzior, *Evolution and Endurance: The US Army Division in the Twentieth Century* (Santa Monica, CA: RAND, 2000).

39. The Unit of Employment, UEx (higher tactical), and Unit of Employment, UEy (operational land), reflect a flattening into two echelons of what used to be three: Division, Corps, and Army. Furthermore, both echelons will have the capacity to serve as joint task force headquarters with minimal augmentation. Discussion found in "Building Army Capabilities," *HQDA, DCS G3 Media Roundtable*, 17 February 2004, at http://www.sftt.org/PPT/article03022004a.ppt; Internet, accessed 16 October 2004.

40. National Simulation Center, *Training with Simulations* (Fort Leavenworth, KS: Combined Arms Center, November 1996), 34-35.

41. Leonhard, 135.

42. Paul T. Harig, "The Digital General: Reflections on Leadership in the Post-Information Age," *Parameters* 26 (Autumn 1996): 133-40.

43. Bateman, "Introduction," in *Digital War*, 2.

44. Leonhard, 150.

45. Daniel P. Bolger, "The Electric Pawn: Prospects for Light Forces on the Digital Battlefield," in *Digital War*, 118.

46. Ralf Zimmerman makes a similar point in his column, "In a technology-filled battlefield, let's not forget the basics of combat," *Army Times*, 7 May 2001, 62.

47. Donn B. Parker, *Fighting Computer Crime: A New Framework for Protecting Information* (New York: J. Wiley, 1998).

48. Interview with Capt. Carter Price, Commander of C Company, 2-69 Armor, 30 September 2004.

49. Lester W. Grau, "Something Old, Something New: Guerillas, Terrorists, and Intelligence Analysis," *Military Review* (July-August 2004): 42-49.

50. Robert H. Scales, Jr., "Adaptive Enemies: Achieving Victory by Avoiding Defeat," *Joint Forces Quarterly* no. 23 (Autumn/Winter 99-00): 7-14.

51. T. Trent Gegax, "Wired for Battle," *Newsweek*, 3 March 2003.

52. Interview with Tim Rosenberg, CEO of Whitewolf Security Consulting Co. and instructor on information warfare at George Washington University, 1 October 2004.

53. For example, when the Land Information Warfare Activity (LIWA) provided hackers for the DAWE, the hackers would leave "calling cards" reading "You've been hacked" so that operators would know when they had been invaded. These were used to avoid running the risk of interfer-

ing with the ongoing AWE. Hackers did not try to manipulate the friendly systems or use the information they obtained through the hacking to help the enemy forces. See Hutto, 3.

54. GAO made a similar point in its recent study, "Battlefield Automation: Opportunities to Improve the Army's Information Protection Effort," Letter Report No. NSIAD-99-166 (Washington, DC: U.S. Government Accounting Office, August 11, 1999).

55. Department of the Army, *Battle Command, Draft 2.1* (Fort Leavenworth, KS: Battle Command Battle Lab, April 1994).

56. Martin van Creveld, *Command in War* (Cambridge, MA: Harvard University Press, 1985).

57. Thomas J. Czerwinski, "Command and Control at the Crossroads," *Parameters* 26 (Autumn 1996): 121-32.

58. Hanna, 3.

59. Jim Dunivan, "Surrendering the Initiative? C2 on the Digitized Battlefield," *Military Review* (September-October 2003): 2-10.

60. Rick Lynch, "Commanding a Digital Brigade Combat Team," Special Edition, No. 01-21 (Fort Leavenworth, KS: Center for Army Lessons Learned, TRADOC, December 2001), 5.

61. Lawrence G. Shattuck, "A Proposal for Designing Cognitive Aids for Commanders for the 21st Century," in *Future Leadership, Old Issues, New Methods*, ed. Douglas V. Johnson, II (Carlisle Barracks, PA: U.S. Army War College, Strategic Studies Institute, June 2000), 104.

62. Interview with Maj. Geoff Norman, 23 September 2004.

63. The coauthor served on a division staff in a non-digital unit from August 2002 to July 2003. The cited exchange occurred during an exercise in August 2002.

64. Gen. Peter J. Schoomaker, *2003 United States Army Transformation Roadmap*, chap. 3, p. 5.

65. Ibid., chap. 2, p. 1.

66. Katherine McIntire Peters, "Civilians at War," *Government Executive*, July 1996, 23; David Silverberg, "Crossing Computing's Cultural Chasm," *Armed Forces Journal International*, February 1997, 38-39; Bryan Bender, "Defense Contractors Quickly Becoming Surrogate Warriors," *Defense Daily*, 28 March 1997, 490.

67. Hanna, 4.

68. Charles J. Dunlap, "Organizational Change and the New Technologies of War," available at http://www.usafa.af.mil/jscope/JSCOPE98/Dunlap98.html; Internet; accessed 30 March 2001.

69. Interview with Capt. Carter Price, Commander of C Company, 2-69 Armor, 30 September 2004. Captain Price explained that the task force received about 12 systems under the RFI with a limited appliqué suite of digital tools. This method of fielding has been referred to as the "Leader Distribution" option and will be the backbone of the future fielding initiative for standardizing command and control systems in the current force, termed the "Good Enough" strategy. The objective of the Good Enough strategy is to create a baseline battle command capability that will serve as the bridge between current and future forces. See Gen. Peter J. Schoomaker, *2003 United States Army Transformation Roadmap*, chap. 8, p. 7

70. An unlawful combatant is an individual who is not authorized to take a direct part in hostilities but does. The term is frequently used also to refer to otherwise privileged combatants or noncombatants in the armed forces who use their protected status as a shield to engage in hostilities. Unlawful combatants are a proper object of attack while engaging as combatants, and if captured they may be tried and punished. See Dunlap, "Organizational Change."

71. Stephen Bryer, "New Era of Warfare Demands Technology Reserve Force," *Defense News*, 17-23 March 1997, 27; Brig. Gen. Bruce M. Lawlor, ARNG, "Information Corps," *Armed Forces Journal International*, January 1998, 26-28.

72. "U.S. Army Selects General Dynamics-Lockheed Martin Team for Combined WIN-T Approach," General Dynamics Corporation News Release, 11 March 2004, available at http://www.generaldynamics.com/news/press_releases/2004/NewsReleaseTuesday,%20Septem ber%2014,2004-2.htm; Internet, accessed 27 September 2004.

73. Nora Bensahel, "Preparing for Coalition Operations," in *The US Army and the New National Security Strategy*, ed. Lynn E Davis and Jeremy Shapiro (Arlington, VA: RAND, 2003) 112-117.

74. The coauthor had the opportunity to plan and participate in several exercises with the 2nd Infantry Division and its ROK counterparts while serving in various positions as a member of the division staff. During this time, several senior officers commented on the unique relationship shared by the two armies (down to sharing the same operational graphic symbols) that made such interoperability conceivable.

75. See discussion in endnote 72.

76. For more information about the challenges of digital training for National Guard units, see Mike Pryor, "Digitization, Simulations, and the Future of the Army National Guard," in *Digital War*, 81-112.

77. Steven Metz, "Which Army After Next? The Strategic Implications of Alternative Futures," *Parameters* 27 (Autumn 1997): 15-26.

78. David T. Fautua, "Transforming the Reserve Components," *Military Review* 80 (September/ October 2000): 57-67.

79. Gen. Peter J. Schoomaker, *2003 United States Army Transformation Roadmap*, chap. 1, p. 11-12.

80. John A. Antal, "The End of Maneuver," in *Digital War*, 161.

81. Leonhard, 137.

82. Michael C. Kasales and Matthew E. Gray, "Leveraging Technology: The Stryker Brigade Combat Team," *Armor Magazine* (January-February, 2003): 7-13.

83. The concept of "maneuver out of contact" and the formations developed to facilitate such maneuver remain largely untested. See "Army Transformation: Implications for the Future," *Statement of Colonel Douglas Macgregor, PhD, USA (ret.), Testifying before the House Armed Services Committee on July 15, 2004 in 2118 of the Rayburn Office Building*, at http://www. house.gov/hasc/openingstatementsandpressreleases/108thcongress/04-07-15Macgregor.pdf; Internet, accessed 16 October 2004.

84. "The Army's Future Combat System's Features, Risks, and Alternatives: Testimony before the Subcommittee on Tactical Air and Land Forces, Committee on Armed Services, House of representatives," GOA 04-635T Defense Acquisitions (Washington, DC: U.S. Government Accounting Office, 1 April 2004), 10.

85. The Army states that major combat operations include "all actions associated with immediate preconflict shaping, force projection, campaign execution, and conflict termination, including transitions to and from stability operations." Gen. Peter J. Schoomaker, *2003 United States Army Transformation Roadmap*, chap. 3, p. 1.

86. Ibid.

87. The Army outlines its general objectives during stability operations as "restoring or establishing order, providing humanitarian assistance, establishing new governance, restoring essential services, and assisting in economic reconstruction." These operations include a range of missions: "peace enforcement, peacekeeping, counter-insurgency, and foreign internal defense." Gen. Peter J. Schoomaker, *2003 United States Army Transformation Roadmap*, chap. 4, p. 1.

88. National Intelligence Council, *Global Trends 2015*, available at http://www.cia.gov/cia /publications/globaltrends2015/index.html; Internet; accessed 26 March 2001.

89. "Reacting to US Military Superiority," *Global Trends 2015*.

90. James Kitfield, "War in the Urban Jungles," *Air Force Magazine* 81, no. 12 (December 1998); Jennifer Morrison Taw and Bruce Hoffman, *The Urbanization of Insurgency: The Potential Challenge to US Army Operations* (Santa Monica, CA: RAND, 1994); Daryl G. Press, *Urban Warfare: Options, Problems, and the Future*, Conference Summary, January 1999, available at http://web.mit.edu/ssp/Publication/urbanwarfare/urbanwarfare.html; Internet; accessed 30 March 2001.

91. Interview with Capt. Dave Hibner, Commander of C Company, 10th Engineer Battalion, assigned to Task Force 1-64 Armor—the lead task force in the invasion of Baghdad during Operation Iraqi Freedom, 30 September 2004.

92. Matthew Cox, "2-7 Cav: 15 Days in the Fight," *Army Times*, 13 September 2004, 28-29.

93. DoD officials believe that urban operations may require nine times the ground forces of operations on open terrain. For more information about the Army and Marine efforts to prepare for urban conflict, see U.S. GAO, "Military Capabilities: Focused Attention Needed to Prepare U.S. Forces for Combat in Urban Areas," Report No. NSIAD-00-63NI (Washington, DC: U.S. Government Accounting Office, February 2000).

94. See GAO, "Battlefield Automation: Army's Restructured Land Warrior Program Needs More Oversight." See also Maj. Gen. (Ret.) John R. Greenway, "The Soldier Is the System," *Military Information Technology Online*, March 2001, available at http://www.mit-kmi.com/features/5_3_Art3.html; Internet; accessed 24 April 2001.

95. Bolger, 123.

96. "The Army Science Board FY 2001 Summer Study, Final Report: The Objective Force Soldier/Soldier Team," *Vol. II Science and Technology Challenges*, November 2001, available at https://webportal.saalt.army.mil/sard-asb/ASBDownloads/OFS-ST.htm; Internet; accessed 7 October 2004. See sections on "Weight" and "Affordability."

97. Interview with Tim Rosenberg, CEO, White Wolf Consulting, an information security consulting firm, 18 March 2001.

98. Gen. Peter J. Schoomaker, *2003 United States Army Transformation Roadmap*, chap. 4, p. 3-4.

99. Taken from a presentation by Maj. Odie Sheffield to the Army Science Board in Arlington, VA, 30 September 2003.

100. Thomas E. Ricks, "Shift From Traditional War Seen at Pentagon," *Washington Post*, 3 September 2004, A01.

101. Philip Taylor, *War and the Media: Propaganda and Persuasion in the Gulf War,* 2nd edition (New York: Manchester University Press, 1998), 56.

102. For more information about the new media capabilities, see Steven Livingston, "Remote Sensing Technology and the News Media," in *Commercial Observation Satellites: At the Leading Edge of Global Transparency*, eds. John Baker, Kevin O'Connell, and Ray Williamson (Santa Monica, CA: Rand Corporation and the American Society for Photogrammetry and Remote Sensing, 2000); Steven Livingston, "Transparency and the News Media," in *Power and Conflict in the Age of Transparency*, eds. Bernard Finel and Kristin Lord (New York: St. Martin's Press, 2000); Barrie Dunsmore, "Live from the Battlefield," in *Politics and the Press: The News Media and Their Influences*, ed. Pippa Norris (Boulder, CO: Lynne Rienner, 1997), 237-73; and Ed Offley, "The Military-Media Relationship in the Digital Age," in *Digital War*, 257-91.

103. Nicholas Kristof, "Have Adapter, Will Travel—A Foreign Correspondent Reflects on the Technotricks of Life on, and off, the Road," *New York Times*, 24 September 1998.

104. Livingston, "Transparency and the News Media," 275.

105. "Report from the Frontline via INMARSAT," INMARSAT Website, available at www.inmarsat.com/news_story.cfm?id=76; Internet; accessed 8 March 2002.

106. Charles J. Dunlap, "21st Century Land Warfare: Four Dangerous Myths," *Parameters* 27 (Autumn 1997): 27-37.

107. "Report from the Frontline via INMARSAT."

108. Ed Braman, "To What End? War Reporting in the Television Age," *RUSI Journal* (December 2003): 26-30.

109. See http://www.spaceimaging.com/aboutus/corpFAQ.htmlpricing; Internet; accessed 14 May 2001.

110. Derek D. Smith, "A Double-Edged Sword: Controlling the Proliferation of Dual-Use Satellite Systems," *National Security Studies Quarterly* 7, no. 2 (Spring 2001): 31-68; Ann M. Florini

and Yahya Dehqanzada, "Commercial Satellite Imagery Comes of Age," *Issues in Space and Technology* 16, no. 1 (Fall 1999): 45-52; John C. Baker and Ray A. Williamson, "The Implications of Emerging Satellite Technologies for Global Transparency and International Security," in *Power and Conflict in the Age of Transparency*, 221-55; Vipin Gupta, "New Satellite Images for Sale," *International Security* 20, no. 2 (Summer 1995): 94-125; and George J. Tahu, John C. Baker, and Kevin M. O'Connell, "Expanding Global Access to Civilian and Commercial Remote Sensing Data: Implications and Policy Issues," *Space Policy* 4 (August 1998): 179-88.

111. Bruce D. Berkowitz and Allan E. Goodman, *Best Truth: Intelligence in the Information Age* (New Haven, CT: Yale University Press, 2000), 53.

112. Jack Shafer, "Embeds and Unilaterals," *The Press Box*, 1 May 2003, available at http://slate.msn.com/toolbar.aspx; Internet, accessed 2 May 2003.

113. Jack Shafer, "Embeds and Unilaterals"; and Ed Braman, "To What End? War Reporting in the Television Age."

114. Steven Jukes, "Real-time Responsibility: Journalism's Challenges in an Instantaneous Age," in *Harvard International Review* 24, no. 2, available at http://www.hir.harvard.edu/articles/index.html; Internet, accessed 17 October 2003.

115. Dunlap, "21st Century Land Warfare," 31.

116. Roger C. Molander, Andrew S. Riddile, and Peter A. Wilson, "Strategic Information Warfare: A New Face of War," *Parameters* 26 (Autumn 1996): 81-92.

117. Roger C. Molander, Peter A. Wilson, and Robert H. Anderson, "US Strategic Vulnerabilities: Threats Against Society," in *Strategic Appraisal*, 257. For more information about the essential U.S. infrastructures, see the recent study by the President's Commission on Critical Infrastructure Protection (PCCIP), *Critical Foundations: Protecting America's Infrastructures* (Washington, DC: GPO, 1997).

118. Michael O'Hanlon, "Transforming U.S. Forces," in *Quadrennial Defense Review2001: Strategy-Driven Choices for America's Security*, ed. Michele A. Flournoy (Washington, DC: National Defense University, 2001), 312.

14 | Professionalism and Army Doctrine: A Losing Battle?

James A. Blackwell

Army doctrine, and the Army's doctrinal process, have served the war-fighter well. "Doctrine," according to *Webster's Third International Dictionary*, "is the body of principles in any branch of knowledge." For the Army it is the way the Army fights.[1] Presently, 634 publications define Army doctrine authoritatively.[2] The Army's doctrine development process is maintained systematically by the U.S. Army Training and Doctrine Command (TRADOC), with doctrine centers at Fort Monroe, Virginia, and at each of the relevant schoolhouses.[3] There are over 100 soldiers and 47 Department of the Army civilians assigned as full-time doctrine developers and writers throughout the Army, and they are working on the largest doctrinal publication list the Army has ever developed.[4] The workload is such that other soldiers provide doctrine writing support in a matrix management process, and contractors are frequently hired to supplement the work force.

The Army's methodology for doctrinal review and revision is more rigorous than ever before. As Army units conduct training exercises at the Combat Training Centers (CTCs), Observer-Controller teams assess not only unit training proficiency in doctrinal aspects of operations, they also conduct periodic reviews of the adequacy of doctrine as demonstrated by those units. The CTCs prepare assessments of Army doctrine every 18 months or so and make recommendations for doctrinal changes needed.[5] This includes thorough review of doctrine for non-warfighting operations.

The Army's doctrine process also involves a serious attempt to link the lessons learned of recent combat experience to its written doctrine products. The Army contributed the majority of the expertise and structure to Joint Forces Command's Lessons Learned projects for Operations Enduring Freedom and Iraqi Freedom. The lessons documents were directly linked to rapid doctrinal change and a completely re-vamped and accelerated program for implementing the Future Force and its associated capabilities.

In 2001 TRADOC completed a thoroughgoing revision of its doctrine development process and now has a Five-Year Doctrine Literature Master Plan and a new implementing regulation. In 2004 TRADOC totally restructured this approach to the doctrine process, embedding it in a broader change-management methodology guided by a new three-star Deputy Commanding General and a more robust organization. The TRADOC Futures Center is designed to "manage rapid change in our Army, an Army at war."[6]

Thus, the Army's doctrine and doctrine process have never served the war-fighter better. They do an outstanding job of teaching soldiers *how to fight*. But professional doctrine must do more than that. It must also educate soldiers *on how to think about how to fight*. In this, Army doctrine falls short.

When soldiers think of themselves as members of a *profession*, they tend to think of themselves in terms of the classic organizational approach to professionalism. Typified in Samuel Huntington's book *The Soldier and the State* (1957), Army professionals focus on organizational patterns—the idea that there is a common process of development that cuts across such otherwise disparate callings as medicine, law, accounting, the ministry, and the military. A profession, in this view, is an organized body of experts who apply esoteric knowledge to particular cases. They have elaborate systems of instruction and training, together with entry examinations and other formal prerequisites, and they normally possess and enforce a code of ethics or behavior.[7] The focus of understanding the nature of a particular profession is, in this view, the structure of the organization and how closely a specific group comes to reaching the ideal.

Sociologist Andrew Abbott, however, says that there is more to it than that. He maintains that a profession is an occupational group that controls the acquisition and application of various types of knowledge. His theory goes beyond the identification of the ideal type to suggest that the defining quality of a profession is how well it succeeds in the competition for dominance over expert knowledge and its application: "Jurisdictional boundaries are perpetually in dispute, both in local practice and in national claims. It is the history of jurisdictional disputes that is the real, determining history of the professions."[8]

In Abbott's scheme, regardless of how well or poorly a group fits the ideal model of a profession, an organization must have firm control over its knowledge base in order to compete successfully with all the other organizations that contend for the same jurisdiction. He calls that knowledge base the profession's *abstraction*, that is, how it thinks about what it does. He argues that professions are in a constant state of struggle for jurisdiction over that knowledge base, a state that he calls *the ecology of professions*.

It is in this sense that we should consider whether the Army's doctrine is serving the Army well as a fundamental element of its institutional professionalism. If Abbott's theory is right in the distinctions he chooses to emphasize—and there is every indication that he is—then Army doctrine must be more than "the concise expression of how Army forces contribute to unified action in campaigns, major operations, battles, and engagements."[9] In the context of the ecology of professions, doctrine is an occupational group's codification of the abstractions it employs to control the acquisition and applications of the various kinds of knowledge over which it asserts jurisdiction.[10] The Army claims primacy over the use of lethal force in land warfare.[11] However, I will argue that it is losing that claim in the current competition for jurisdiction over land warfare largely because its doctrine and doctrine process do not provide sufficient cognitive power in ongoing jurisdictional disputes with rival professions.

In the general system of professions, abstraction is an essential function that any profession must master if it is to survive in the struggle over occupational control.[12] It provides the basis for a profession's inferences—its link between diagnosis and treatment. Only a knowledge system governed by abstraction can redefine problems and tasks to defend them from interlopers and seize new problem areas as treatable by the profession's expertise. It provides a profession with the strongest form of control over its jurisdiction by controlling its knowledge domain. A profession challenged by objective change in technology must have a system of abstraction to survive. Some professions employ abstraction as a polemical strategy or tactic in the professional ecology itself, though the Army's institutional value structure tends to shun such rhetorical stratagems. For example, in the early 1990s a consensus emerged among military analysts that a Revolution in Military Affairs (RMA) was emerging. The Air Force, Navy, and Marine Corps argued that their then-current plans, programs, and budgets in fact already embodied that revolution. They made their case in glossy vu-graph presentations such as "Global Reach, Global Power," "From the Sea," and "Operational Maneuver from the Sea." The Army, in contrast, treated the notion of a Revolution in Military Affairs as a hypothesis. It never argued that its existing programs *were* the RMA, as did its sister services; instead it made the case that the RMA was a concept yet to be demonstrated. The Army did not link its then-current plans, programs, and budgets to the RMA, but rather embarked on a series of conceptual exploratory inquiries, including "Louisiana Maneuvers," "Advanced Warfighting Experiments," "Force XXI," and "The Army After Next." The Army did not engage the other services at the RMA level of abstraction until nearly a decade later, after it had made major changes in several of its principal programs (for example the complete restructuring of the Future Combat System Program and the design of the Objective Force). Only then, in October 2000, did Army Chief of Staff Gen. Eric Shinseki publicly denominate the Army's abstraction under the "Transformation" label.

An effective system of abstraction must be strong enough to compete, although this does not require reaching some absolute standard of abstraction across all professions. At a minimum the system of abstraction should provide rational consistency to the system of inferences and clarify the definitions of the boundaries of the profession as well as their rationale. The body of doctrine must legitimize the work of the profession by clarifying its foundations and tracing them to major cultural values and geo-strategic realities. It should of course provide for research and instruction among the members of the profession. But it must also provide for the generation of new diagnoses, treatments, and inference methods (to use Abbott's medical analogy.)

It is against this measure of effectiveness that Army doctrine needs to be evaluated in order to judge the role of doctrine in Army professionalism. The effectiveness of Army doctrine as a pedagogical instrument is indisputedly best-in-class. The object of this chapter, however, is to reach a judgment on how well Army doctrine serves the profession in the competition for jurisdiction.

The outcomes of jurisdictional competition form six types:[13]

- Full and final jurisdiction, one profession winning at the expense of all others;
- Subordination of one profession to another;
- Split jurisdiction into two interdependent parts;

- Shared jurisdiction without a division of labor;
- A losing profession is allowed an advisory role vis-à-vis the winning one; or
- Division of jurisdiction by client type.

To the extent that the Army is able to assert full and final jurisdiction as technology and organizations change, it maintains and even enhances its position in the ecology of professions. But if the Army increasingly subordinates, splits, shares, advises, or divides jurisdictions, its claims to legitimacy and monopoly over the use of lethal force in land combat erodes. Doctrine, as the systematic codification of the Army's abstraction about its occupational authority and control, is the essential measure of effectiveness on how the Army is competing in this milieu.

The Army finds itself today in three elemental professional competitions (see Table 14-1). Each competition forces the Army to adapt professionally as the nature of its core competence changes, and as other professions or entities challenge the Army's traditional occupational exclusivity. The first of these is technological in nature, brought on by the emergence of the Revolution in Military Affairs.[14] The RMA represents a dramatic change in the nature of warfare, resulting from a complex interaction among new operational concepts, innovative organizational designs, and emerging technological capabilities. The currently emerging RMA consists of new warfare areas in Long-Range Precision Strike, Information Warfare, Dominating Maneuver, and Space Operations. The Army terms its engagement in the RMA as *Army Transformation.*

The second set of competitions that Army doctrine must engage in is the evolving joint character of military operations. The Goldwater-Nichols Act of 1986 created a fundamental shift in the nature of the professional competitions for jurisdiction, among other changes, by legally and institutionally legitimizing the contribution of joint functions, organizations, and people to U.S. war-fighting. That the Army has found it necessary to engage in this competition was dramatically revealed in a survey of Army general officers conducted by TRADOC in 1998.[16] Respondents uniformly concluded that TRADOC, rather than publish a revision of Army Field Manual 100-5, *Operations,* should instead defer that revision and

Competitions	Competitors
Revolution in Military Affairs	Other Services
	Office of the Secretary of Defense
	Joint Forces Command
Jointness	Joint Staff
	Combatant Commanders
Nonwar	Federal Agencies
	Multinationals
	Nongovernmental Organizations

Table 14-1. *The Army's Competitions for Occupational Jurisdiction.*[15]

immediately begin to align Army doctrinal publications, including their numbers, titles, and content, with the growing body of joint doctrinal publications.

The third area of engagement is in non-war-fighting competencies. While the Army has always had a role in such operations, the decade of the 1990s followed by the post-combat insurgencies in Afghanistan and Iraq has clearly heightened the role of the Army in them.

Army doctrine provides an objective indicator of how effectively the Army is able to assert its claims of jurisdiction in these competitions among rival professions. Trends in Army doctrinal change can be observed at the institutional level in official documents, both in terms of the titles and in the content of key writings. The impact of doctrinal change can also be observed at the individual level, although in a more subjective manner, by means of a survey of published professional writings and in the results of recent surveys of soldiers. In both approaches, the doctrinal writings themselves can be evaluated as to the emergent settlements of the three current jurisdictional competitions.

Levels of Analysis

In this chapter, I examine Army doctrine at the institutional level through two methodologies. First, the Army reveals its professional cognitive map over time by way of its Index of Doctrinal Publications. The titles of the manuals themselves and the subject areas into which they are classified change as the Army's definition of its occupational jurisdiction changes. It is a straightforward process to identify the deletions and additions as a quantitative measure of change in Army doctrinal coverage, then to subjectively classify the implications of those changes along the dimensions of the three jurisdictional competitions. In this analysis I have examined the index in decennial increments from 1940 to 2000.

The second measure of Army abstractional adaptation lies in the content of the doctrinal statements contained in successive editions of Field Manual 100-5, *Operations*.[17] This is the "heartland of work over which [the Army] has complete, legally established control, legitimated by the authority of its knowledge."[18] The published versions of FM 100-5 over time form a data set from which a content analysis can reveal trends in terms of the three jurisdictional competitions. In this chapter I have limited the content analysis to the 1982, 1986, and 1993 editions of FM 100-5 and the June 2001 edition of FM 3-0, *Operations*. At the individual level of analysis, two data sources provide some insight into the effectiveness of Army doctrine in the ecology of professions. First, in 1998-99 the Center for Strategic and International Studies, as part of a larger study on military culture, commissioned the Center for Creative Leadership in Greensboro, North Carolina, to conduct a survey of attitudes among military professionals on a number of cultural issues, some of which relate to the jurisdictional competitions considered in this analysis. Second, there is a robust professional Army literature available, primarily in the publications *Parameters* and *Military Review*, which, though journals of ideas as opposed to outlets for prescribed policy, nonetheless reveal which way the doctrinal winds are blowing.

Institutional Level: The Army's Cognitive Map

In 1940, before the outbreak of World War II, the Army had perhaps 45 identifiable field manuals.[19] Numbering was inconsistent, with separate publications variously identified by title, volume, and chapter as well as by number. This system was the culminating point of the Army's doctrinal transformation that began after World War I. That early transformation resolved ongoing jurisdictional disputes within the Army among its infantry, cavalry, and field artillery branches (infantry emerged dominant at that time), producing the first comprehensive codification of the Army's jurisdictional abstraction in the Field Service Regulations of 1923, the progenitor of FM 100-5.[20] During and after World War II the Army's doctrinal system became more systematized.

Eric Heginbotham has attributed the effectiveness of the U.S. Army in executing combined arms warfare, compared to the British experience, in large part to doctrinal processes just before and during World War II. He argues that doctrine became a common language for all American Army officers to employ in discussions about employment of combined arms, thus becoming the base upon which improvements were made and guidelines for operations were created. Doctrine was the mechanism for producing rapid adaptation within a dense network of channels among Army professionals for communication within the force.[21]

This networking among Army professionals produced, by 1945, the first consistently codified cognitive map of the Army's abstraction of its occupational domain. For example, FM 21-6, *List of Field Publications for Training* (March 1945), was the first to apply integrated regular groupings of subject matter and to assign consistent numerical designations for Army field manuals. The robustness and rigor of the Army's doctrinal process continued to grow throughout the post-World War II period.[22] The broad changes that have occurred are observable in the indexes that report the titles and subject matter covered by the Army's field manuals.[23]

The 1950s emphasized traditional combined arms as tactical nuclear weapons doctrine emerged. Manuals of the 1960s reflected the epitome of tactical nuclear weapons doctrine, especially with the emergence of Army missile systems. The 1970s manuals were characterized by a resurgence of combined arms warfare as applied to conventional war-fighting in Europe and by a growth in coverage of subjects required for fighting in Vietnam. The dominant changes in the 1980s manuals reflected the training revolution that occurred within the Army beginning in the late 1970s. Books on individual occupational specialties, covered earlier (and since) in technical or training manuals, were elevated to field manual status in the 1980s. By the 1990s this emphasis began to change, with the training revolution being gradually displaced by the operational revolution characterized by AirLand Battle doctrine and the Persian Gulf War. The latest index of Army doctrinal publications (2000) reveals particularly a growth in coverage of logistics matters and jointness of Army operations.

There are some interesting continuities demonstrated in the Army's cognitive map (Table 14-2). Some weapons are apparently timeless, with the M2 caliber 50

Old Series Number	Subject Area	1945	1970	2000	New Series Number	New Subject Area
1	Aviation	15	8	15	3-04/3-xx	Aviation
2	Cavalry	6	0	0		
3	Chemical Warfare	8	2	14	3-11/3-xx	Chemical (NBC)
4	Coastal Artillery	59	0	0		
5	Engineer	16	18	40	3-34/3-xx/4-04	Engineer
6	Field Artillery	24	129	19	3-09/3-xx	Field Artillery
7	Infantry	9	3	13	3-21/3-xx	Infantry
8	Medical	7	6	26	4-02/4-xx	Medical
9	Ordnance	6	4	6	4-xx	Ordnance
10	Quartermaster	3	5	86	4-xx	Quartermaster
11	Signal	6	16	9	6-x/6-xx	Signal
12	Adjutant General	1	2	2	1-x/1-xx	Adjutant General
14	Finance	0	0	1	1-06	Finance
16	Chaplain	0	3	1	1-05	Chaplain
17	Armor	26	7	9	3-20/3-xx	Armor
18	Tank Destroyer	9	0	0	3-xx	Management Information Systems
19	Military Police	2	11	9	3-19/3-xx	Military Police
20	Miscellaneous	1	10	3	3-xx/7-xx	General
21	Individual Soldier	19	20	14	3-xx	Individual Soldier
22	Infantry Drill	1	3	4	3-xx/7-xx	Leadership, Courtesy, and Drill
23	Basic Weapons	21	31	15	3-xx/7-xx	Weapons
24	Communications Procedures	14	7	12	6-xx	Communication Techniques
25	Transportation	4	0	5	7-x/7-xx	General Management
26	Interior Guard Duty	1	0	0	7-xx	Organizational Effectiveness
27	Military Law	3	2	4	1-04/1.xx	Judge Advocate/Military Law
28	Welfare, Recreation and Morale	2	0	0		
29	Combat Service Support	0	15	0	7-xx	Composite Units and Activities
30	Military Intelligence	13	17	0	2-x/2-xx/3-xx	Military Intelligence
31	Special Operations	7	29	9	3-05/3-xx	Special Forces
32	NOT USED				7-xx	Security
33	Psychological Operations	7	29	9	3-53	Psychological Operations
34	Intelligence	0	0	20	2-xx/3-xx	Combat Electronic Warfare and Intelligence
35	Women's Army Corps	1	1	0		
36	NOT USED				3-xx/4-xx	Environmental Operations
38	Logistics	0	19	2	4-xx	Logistics Management
39	NOT USED				3-xx/7-xx	Special Weapons Operations
40	NOT USED				3-14	Space
41	Civil Affairs	0	2	1	3-57	Civil Affairs
42	Quartermaster	0	0	2	4-xx	Supply
43	NOT USED				4-xx	Maintenance
44	Anti-Aircraft/Air Defense	10	30	10	3-01/3-xx	Air Defense Artillery
45	Censorship	0	2	0		
46	Public Affairs Operations	0	0	1	3-61	Public Information
50	NOT USED				7-xx	Common Items of Nonexpendable Material
51	NOT USED				3-xx.x	Army
52	NOT USED				3-xx.x	Corps
54	Higher Echelons	0	8	2	4-xx	Logistics Organizations and Operations
55	Transportation	6	17	17	4-01/4-xx	Transportation
57	Airmobile/Pathfinder	0	3	2	3-xx	Airborne
60	Amphibious	1	1	0	3-xx	Explosive Ordnance Disposal Procedures
61	Divisions	0	2	0	3-xx.x	Division
63	Combat Service Support	0	0	9	4-x/4-xx	Combat Service Support
67	NOT USED				3-xx	Airmobile
70	Mountain and Winter	2	0	0	7-xx	Research, Development, and Acquisition
71	Division Operations	0	0	7	3-xx.x	Combined Arms
72	Jungle	0	1	0		
74	NOT USED				7-xx	Military Missions
75	NOT USED				7-xx	Military Advisory Groups
77	NOT USED				3-xx	Separate Light Infantry
90	Operations	0	0	17	3-xx/3-xx.x	Combat Operations
97	NOT USED				7-xx	Division (Training)
100	Operations	4	5	37	3-x/3-xx.x	General Operational Doctrine
101	Staff	4	9	3	5-x/5-xx	Planning/Staff Officers
105	Umpire	2	3	0	3-xx	Maneuver Control
145	NOT USED				7-xx	Reserve Officers' Training Corps
300	NOT USED				7-xx	TOE Consolidate Change Tables
J-Series	Joint	0	0	25		

Table 14-2. *The Army's Cognitive Map.*[24]

machine gun serving as a familiar example in FM 23-65. Some subjects change name and number but have stayed around since the earliest recorded times; the 1940 index lists FM 25-5, *Animal Transport*, while the 2000 index shows FM 31-27, *Pack Animals in Support of Army Special Forces Operations*. This database also reveals some insight into the effectiveness of the Army's system of abstraction in its current jurisdictional competitions.

While there are no immediately observable references in the latest index to the Revolution in Military Affairs, there is an implicit gradual movement in subject matter coverage in the direction of the dramatically new ways of waging warfare contained in RMA concepts. There is now a separate manual devoted exclusively to information warfare, FM 100-6. Likewise, the Army recognizes the importance of another emerging new RMA warfare area in the publication of FM 100-18, *Space Support to Army Operations*, although, if we can believe the hoopla surrounding the RMA, space operations will themselves become a new warfare area. The precision strike warfare area of the RMA is covered, implicitly, in the Army's doctrinal coverage of new fire support and communications techniques, revealed in such new manuals as FM 6-20-10, *Tactics, Techniques, and Procedures for the Targeting Process*; FM 6-24.8, *TADIL-J, Introduction to Tactical Digital Information Link J and Quick Reference Guide*; FM 11-55, *Mobile Subscriber Equipment (MSE) Operations*; FM 24-7, *Tactical Local Area Network Management*; and FM 34-25-1, *Joint Surveillance Target Attack Radar System (JSTARS)*.

Notably absent from this review is any new title covering abstractions relating to dominating maneuver in the RMA. Content analysis of the specific coverage in FM 100-5 sheds some light on this topic, but for the moment the assessment of the Army's cognitive map indicates only grudging acknowledgment that some fundamental changes attributable to an emergent RMA may be in motion in the Army's occupational jurisdiction. That acknowledgment is more a recognition of the impact of new technologies and systems than an exploration of new operational concepts.

The Army is conducting such an exploration of the potential for an RMA in its Army Transformation process. As a result of a decade of work, beginning with the Louisiana Maneuvers Task Force, progressing through a series of Army War-Fighting Experiments, and continuing through the promulgation of Army Digitization Doctrine, the Army has addressed some of the issues associated with the RMA, especially those concerning battle command. [25] The Army has also developed and fielded its Interim Brigade Combat Teams that will eventually become part of the Future Force, a design that focuses on architectures associated with the Future Combat System. [26] The most dramatically observable change in the Army's cognitive map is the emergence of joint doctrine. An entirely new meta-subject-area has been created in the renumbering of certain Army publications from field manuals to joint publications. This move is as radical a departure as the creation in 1923 of the Field Service Regulations that unified the Army's infantry, cavalry, and field artillery schools of warfare into a single integrated body of abstractions.

The Army's cognitive map also shows insight into how the Army has responded to jurisdictional challenge in non-war-fighting areas. The data indicate that the Army's adaptation to the 1990s requirements to conduct stability and support operations has been to reinvent what had been its traditional approach to such operations before the birth of AirLand Battle doctrine.

While they were not on the street in time for operations in the early 1990s in Haiti, Somalia, and the Balkans, the Army has quickly produced new doctrinal publications such as FM 100-23, *Peace Operations,* and FM 100-23-HA, *Multiservice Procedures for Humanitarian Assistance Operations,* both of which were promulgated in late 1994. It also published FM 7-98, *Operations in Low-Intensity Conflict* (1992); FM 90-29, *Noncombatant Evacuation Operations* (1994); and FM 100-19, *Domestic Support Operations* (1993). More significantly, the Army relied on a number of its older doctrinal publications, trying to make some of them more relevant to these challenges of the 1990s. Falling into this category are FM 100-20, *Military Operations in Low Intensity Conflict* (1990); FM 19-15, *Civil Disturbances* (1985), born of the Army's role in domestic operations of the 1960s; and FM 90-8, *Counterguerrilla Operations,* FM 31-23, *Stability Operations,* and FM 31-20, *Doctrine for Special Forces,* each of the three from the Vietnam era.

The Army's cognitive map of its abstraction of occupational jurisdiction is revealing. It implies an evolutionary approach to incorporating the advances of the RMA into the heartland of its core competence for full and final jurisdiction over land warfare. It reveals an attempt to share in jurisdiction over joint operations. And it seems to be establishing a preference to serve in an advisory role in the non-war jurisdiction in its approach to stability and support operations.

The Bible of Army Core Competence: FM 3-0

The Army's foundational document for claiming jurisdiction is Field Manual 3-0, *Operations* (2001). Whereas it is the Index of Publications that identifies the cognitive *structure* of the Army's occupational domain, it is this manual that defines for society the Army's cognitive *content* in such a way as to legitimize its claim to exclusivity over land warfare. The document has served that function at least since the 1982 version of FM 100-5 that was published in response to widespread external criticism of the 1976 version of the manual. Editions since 1982 have served as the Army's codification of its adaptation to jurisdictional competition as new tasks emerge. It has provided for the elaboration of Army knowledge at several layers of abstraction by means of amalgamation (absorbing new jurisdictions and groups) and division (creating new jurisdictions and groups to occupy them). Other manuals provide details of diagnosis and treatment of Army problems—this is what the Army means by its frequent colloquial reference to "how to fight." FM 100-5 provides the ordering of abstractions for inference.[27] It claims to supply enduring principles that can be applied to almost any problem that confronts military professionals.

The absence of significant change articulated across the 1982, 1986, 1993, and 2001 versions of *Operations*[28] in the Army's basic approach to offensive and defensive operations will surprise many observers of the Army's doctrinal evolution. Every one of these manuals states at the beginning of the section dealing with the offense, "The offense is the decisive form of war," although important modifiers and explanatory statements vary somewhat across the versions. The characteristics of the offense itself are almost unvarying (see Tables 14-3 and 14-4).

1982	1986	1993	2001 (FM 3-0)
Concentration	Surprise	Concentration	Surprise
Surprise	Concentration	Surprise	Concentration
Speed	Speed	Tempo	Tempo
Flexibility	Flexibility		
Audacity	Audacity	Audacity	Audacity

Table 14-3. *Comparative Characteristics of the Offense within the FM 100-5 Series.*

The forms and types of maneuver for the offense are identical in all four editions.

Forms of Maneuver	Types of Offenses
Envelopment	Movement to Contact
Turning Movement	Attack (Hasty or Deliberate)
Infiltration	Exploitation
Penetration	Pursuit
Frontal Attack	

Table 14-4. *Forms and Types of Offensive Maneuver.*

There is no mention of jointness in these discussions of offense, nor is there any discussion of non-war-fighting operations. The 2001 version of Student Text 3-0 (the authoritative text used at the U.S. Army Command and General Staff College while FM 100-5 was under revision) does include a brief discussion of RMA-related issues in an appended one-page section on technology, suggesting that intelligence, surveillance, and reconnaissance technological advances may allow commanders to lead from the front, avoid the movement-to-contact, increase the tempo of the offense, and create more options during the conduct of offensive operations.

FM 3-0 does reveal some fundamental change in the abstraction of the defense. Each version of the manual begins with the statement that the purpose of the defense is to defeat an enemy attack until the friendly force can go over to the offense. There has been more change in description of the basic characteristics of the defense, in contrast to the consistency in the discussion of the offense. In particular, in the 1983 and 1986 versions, the emphasis in the defense is on detailed planning to allow the concentration of forces in adaptation to enemy actions as the defensive battle progresses. The 1993 version replaces the focus on detailed planning with greater adaptability in battle command. It refers to massing effects rather than forces, and agility in execution rather than detailed branches and sequels.

The forms of the defense also change by the time FM 3-0 is published in 2001. The 1982 version of FM 100-5 articulates the basic forms of the defense, while the 1986 edition instead creates a conceptual framework within which those forms take place (Deep Battle Area, Security Area, Main Battle Area, Rear, Reserve). The 2001 version of FM 3-0 radically departs from that framework, moving to a higher level of abstraction with the introduction of Decisive Operations, Shaping Operations—including Information Operations—and Sustaining Operations in Depth. It asserts that defensive operations will be nonlinear and noncontiguous.

In the domain of defense operations, there is greater evidence than in the offense that the Army is attempting to incorporate RMA concepts into its basic doctrine, but as with its coverage of the offense, this treatment of the RMA is implicit, not confronted head-on. Similarly, there is no content on jointness in the discussion of the defense, nor is there any treatment of non-war-fighting operations.

Clearly, if the Army believes it faces jurisdictional competition in the emergent concepts of the RMA, jointness, and non-war-fighting operations, it does not consider the challenges to its traditional knowledge domain to be serious enough to cause it to adapt or revise its core offense and defense concepts. To the extent that the FM 100-5 series recognizes an emerging RMA, the Army appears to be asserting that this development will not result in any fundamental change in the Army's full and final jurisdictions.

The doctrinal embodiment of Army professional abstraction changes dramatically once the analytic focus shifts away from the heartland material involving the offense and defense. One set of such changes observable in the cognitive map is the growing role of logistics concepts in Army operations. This change has more to do with the changing nature of the Army's internal approach to conducting operations than with forming a response to jurisdictional competitions. Nevertheless, the impact of changing logistics requirements on Army doctrine is significant. FM 3-0 (2001) devotes 21 pages to logistics concepts, the previous manuals only half or less than that. The resulting modifications are related to changing policy and strategy trends as the Army shifts from a forward-based posture to one of force-projection.

More relevant to this analysis, the manuals reveal a growing concern with non-war-fighting operations. Except for a veiled reference to the Vietnam War era, the 1982 edition of FM 100-5 barely mentions that Army forces may again be called upon to conduct unconventional warfare operations. The 1986 version introduces the concepts of low-intensity conflict in addressing such operations as foreign internal defense, counterinsurgency, peacetime contingency operations, peacekeeping operations, and anti-terrorism. The 1993 manual devotes an entire chapter, for the first time in the FM 100-5 series, to such activities as "Operations Other Than War." That chapter provides greater specificity in the definitions of the types of non-war-fighting operations the Army must be prepared to conduct, but, in a revealing argument, it maintains that such operations are subsumed within standard Army operational doctrine.[29]

FM 3-0 (2001) renames these operations as "Stability and Support Operations," or SASO (actually a throwback to 1960s terminology), and devotes two chapters to the abstractions Army professionals need to apply. The types of operations included in SASO are expanded to include security assistance, support to insurgencies, support to counterdrug operations, arms control, show of force, and civil and domestic support operations. FM 3-0 maintains the argument, although in more sophisticated form,[30] that such operations are not the Army's primary business of war-fighting, but that Army forces are very good at them as lesser included capabilities.

The various editions of FM 100-5 leading up to FM 3-0 are quite explicit in their treatment of the issues related to the increasing jointness of the Army's professional jurisdiction. The 1982, 1986, and 1993 versions of FM 100-5 maintain that there are two chains of command in joint operations, one for operations and a separate one for administration. The operational chain of command is usually joint, the administrative chain is nearly always service-specific. This bifurcation disappears in FM 3-0, which states that there is a single chain of command from the National Command Authority through the Joint Force Commander to forces provided by the services. *This represents a fundamental shift in the Army approach to conceptualizing jointness.*

It is significant that FM 3-0 makes this statement not in the context of core Army defensive and offensive operations, nor in its discussion of battle command. Rather, it makes this point about such a fundamental change in Army concepts in the context of a discussion on a higher level of abstraction about the levels of war—tactical, operational, and strategic. This point was made again in a briefing posted to TRADOC's Doctrine Developer's Course web site. On slide number three of the briefing titled "Army Doctrine Hierarchy and Numbering Update," there is an interesting audio voice file that plays as the slide builds. In the panel of the slide discussing how the existing doctrine numbering system needs to be revised to be compatible with the joint system, the narrator asserts that joint doctrine will become an extension of Army doctrine.

One way to interpret these statements about the relationship between Army and joint doctrine is as an attempt by the Army to share jurisdiction with emerging and competing joint organizations over land combat. By casting the jurisdictional conflict in terms of abstractions that the Army traditionally has mastered—the levels of war—the Army seems to be attempting to exert greater control or influence over the terms of the jurisdictional division emerging. By asserting that joint doctrine is really nothing more than a logical outgrowth of Army doctrine, the Army may be trying to establish the basis for later arguments. In doing so, it may be that the Army recognizes it will inevitably lose some control over land combat and hopes to retain greater residual jurisdictional control by participating in the defining of terms relevant to sharing jurisdiction. In other words, rather than risk permanent loss through mutually exclusive claims of subordination or splitting jurisdiction, claims that the Army perhaps fears it would lose, it may be attempting to lay out a broader claim for shared jurisdiction with joint institutions. If it can win this claim for shared jurisdiction, the Army will at least salvage the opportunity to make a future argument for jurisdiction.

In sum, the institutional evidence seems to indicate that the Army is attempting to adopt an amalgamation strategy in its current jurisdictional competitions over the RMA, increasing jointness, and the reemergence of non-war-fighting operations. The doctrinal evidence, especially as to the Army's core competence embodied in FM 3-0, suggests that the Army believes it can exert full and final jurisdiction over new warfare areas in the emerging RMA insofar as they continue to involve land combat. The Army's cognitive map, as well as FM 3-0, clearly reveals the Army's search for accommodation in the jurisdictional competition with joint organizations. And the available institutional evidence implies that the Army does not believe that emerging requirements for non-war-fighting operations represent a competition that it wants necessarily to win. Rather, the Army seems to be pursuing a strategy of making itself available in an advisory capacity for such operations.

The Individual Level of Analysis

At the individual level of analysis, the role of Army doctrine in the ecology of professions is more subjective than it is at the institutional level. While there are some interesting data available at the individual level, it is problematic to extrapolate from the responses of a population sample to behaviors and concepts of the Army as a whole. Nevertheless, it is useful to examine the role of Army doctrine at this level for additional insight into the trends observed at the institutional level.

Two data sets provide insights for this analysis. The first set of data comes from the investigation by the Center for Strategic and International Studies (CSIS) titled *American Military Culture in the Twenty-First Century* (2000).[31] Second, a review of Army professional journal articles focused on the three jurisdictional competitions provides some insight into the nature of the debate over professional jurisdiction.

Of the 99 questions in the Ulmer-Campbell Military Climate/Culture Survey (MCCS) conducted for the CSIS project, and the 88 questions in the companion Staff Survey, some related to the three competitions of interest in this analysis. Two MCCS questions related to the RMA:

> **No. 45** (No. 30 in the MCCS Staff Survey). Our organization can adjust to new technologies and changing doctrine.

> **No. 56.** Our leaders consider the future, exploring new doctrine, tactics, equipment, and procedures.

Both sets of respondents provided a highly positive response that their organization adjusts to new technologies and changing doctrine. Staff respondents were more positive (mean score of 4.92 on the survey 6-point scale, compared to 4.21 on the broader survey), but in both sets the response was in the top 20 most favorable responses on the survey. This indicates a willingness among soldiers to adapt to the RMA. But there is a significant difference in perception between staffs and the broader population about the willingness of Army leaders to adapt to such change. The broader population, when asked to narrow their response to the willingness of the leaders to adjust to the RMA, rated their leaders at 3.84, a substantially lower score than the leaders gave themselves on the same question. In other words, Army leaders think they are adapting to the RMA, but soldiers do not think their leaders are changing fast enough. This finding lends support to the institutional data suggesting that the Army is not adapting its doctrine with regard to the RMA fast enough to compete in this area of professional jurisdiction.

Several MCCS questions also dealt with the issue of jointness:

No. 23 (No. 29 on the Staff Survey). I have confidence in the other American military services that we might work within joint operations.

No. 53 (No. 36 on the Staff Survey). This unit would work smoothly with units from other military services.

No. 92 (No. 66 on the Staff Survey). Emphasis on joint education, doctrine, and training has contributed to the effectiveness of my service.

No. 81 (Staff Survey Only). My future value to my service would be enhanced by my completing a tour on a joint or combined staff.

On both surveys, confidence in other military services ranked very positively. For the total active Army this question received the 11th highest positive ranking, with a mean score of 4.35 out of 6, and on the Staff Survey it was the third highest positive score (5.45). Both surveys rated the question of working smoothly with units from other services positively (3.95 on the total active Army survey, 4.83 on the Staff Survey) as well as the question of the value of joint education, training, and doctrine (3.81 on the total survey, 4.22 on the Staff Survey). While these data do not shed any new light on the institutional question of the Army's attempt to negotiate a shared jurisdiction over land combat, it does indicate that service members would be supportive of such an outcome.

Three questions covered issues related to the Army's jurisdictional adaptation to non-war-fighting operations:

No. 28 (Staff Survey No. 18) Members of this unit believe it is appropriate for us to be involved in a variety of operations—from "humanitarian" to combat.

No. 43 (Staff Survey No. 28) The essential mission of America's armed forces is to be prepared to win in combat.

No. 90 (Staff Survey No. 78) My service has the flexibility and resources to handle "peacekeeping" and other noncombat missions without significantly degrading its wartime readiness.

These three questions can usefully be considered together. The responses to question No. 43 (Army mean = 5.08, Staff mean = 4.50) were more generally positive than those for questions No. 28 (Army mean = 3.63, Staff mean = 4.50) and No. 90 (Army mean = 3.77, Staff mean = 3.50). But there is a substantial difference in the perceptions of the total active Army respondents as compaed with those of the Staff respondents. Staff respondents seem to hold the view that the Army can simultaneously be prepared to win in combat and still be involved in a variety of operations from "humanitarian" to combat. The overall lower positive scores in this area tend to support the Army's institutional approach of seeking an advisory role in this jurisdictional competition.

The Army's professional literature contains additional insight into the individual level of analysis of Army approaches to its jurisdictional competitions. On the subject of the RMA, the Army's professional dialogue was lively for five years from about 1993 until about 1998.[32] The subject has now virtually disappeared from the pages of *Parameters* and *Military Review*. Interestingly, just before his retirement in 2001, Army War College Commandant, Maj. Gen. Robert Scales, published a provocative, though largely unnoticed, article on the RMA in which he argued that the U.S. Army, far from dominating its battlefield opponents through mastery of the RMA, is in fact increasingly more vulnerable to counter-RMA approaches presently under study in the military forces of several foreign countries.[33] If the Army's institutional strategy in this jurisdictional competition is one of presumed dominance, then the absence of a continuing dialogue in the professional literature is indicative that Army professionals have bought in to the presumption.

Very few articles relate to issues of the jointness in the ecology of professions. Gen. Robert Riscassi argued persuasively in a 1993 article that the underlying abstractions of then-current Army doctrine formed the conceptual basis for emerging joint doctrine and should form the basis for the development of doctrine for combined operations as well.[34] David Keithly and Stephen Ferris made a similarly veiled case for employing Army abstractions concerning command and control as the underlying principles for sharing jurisdiction with joint organizations in joint operations, especially in a multinational context.[35] The general officer doctrine survey undertaken by TRADOC in 1998 seemed to settle the issue as far as the Army's senior officers were concerned. Those senior Army leaders expressed belief that in seeking to work out a system of shared jurisdiction, the Army would gain a competitive advantage in the struggle for jurisdiction at the abstract level.[36]

In the third area of jursidictional competition there is no lack of professional dialogue. It seems that one of the hottest topics among Army writers has been the concepts and issues associated with the non-war-fighting operations characteristic of the 1990s.[37] All seem to support the idea that such operations are a legitimate mission area for the Army. None disagree with the notion surfaced in the institutional assessment and the other individual data sets that the successful conduct of non-war-fighting operations, while requiring increasingly complex skills, can be accomplished exemplarily by Army units and soldiers well-schooled in combat operations.

Settlements in the Professional Competitions

The evidence supports the conclusions that in the three basic competitions the Army is presently engaged in, it is seeking a settlement giving it full and final jurisdiction over the RMA, it seeks to share jurisdiction over joint operations, and it is content to serve in an advisory role in non-war-fighting operations (see Table 14-5). Given these apparent settlement strategies, then, how will the Army fare in the ensuing competition for jurisdiction? I believe the prospects are troubling for the Army as a profession because pursuit of these strategies may lead to an erosion of the Army's ability to maintain legitimacy successfully with regard to its asserted and traditionally secured jurisdiction over land combat.

Competitions	Possible outcomes of jurisdictional competition					
	Full & Final	Subordination	Split	Shared	Advisory	Divided
RMA	X					
JOINTNESS				X		
NONWAR					X	

Note: The Xs indicate which outcomes the Army is seeking in the three competitions for jurisdiction over land warfare.

Table 14-5. *Outcomes Sought by the Army in the Competition for Jurisdiction.*

In the RMA domain, the Army is largely losing the intellectual battle over the definition of this emerging future of combat. It is losing this battle at the abstract level. While Army war-fighting concepts are steeped in the tradition of AirLand Battle, Air Force concepts are exploring innovative new areas such as Global Precision Strike and Effects-Based Operations.[38] Although the Army plan for the Interim Brigade Concept Team and the Future Combat System-oriented Objective Force may well rival such Air Force concepts at an abstract level, the Army has chosen to develop its RMA concepts entirely in-house, avoiding intellectual engagement with non-Army analysts. The Army will never achieve full and final jurisdiction over land combat during the RMA so long as it refuses to participate in public give-and-take over the meaning of the RMA. Based on my own observations of the joint concept development process, the Army no longer exerts its former leadership over the Dominant Maneuver component of Joint Vision 2020, having acquiesced in an understanding of the RMA dominated by the proponents of Precision Strike and Information Warfare. The Army is not institutionally equipped to win this debate in the abstract since the Army's imperative is control of territory, people, and things.

The Army is engaged in a risky approach to the competition over jointness. The Riscassi argument for grafting joint and combined doctrine onto 1993 Army doctrine has worked but it is almost too clever. The particular sharing arrangement that the Army prefers may not turn out to be the one the Army achieves. Rather than defining the abstraction upon which the doctrinal-sharing arrangement will be based, the Army may find itself reacting to alternative concepts proposed by other competitors for professional jurisdiction.

Competing operational models are already emerging from joint sources, such as the Effects Based Operations (EBO) concept developed by the Joint Futures Lab of Joint Forces Command. The Army has not been enthusiastic towards this concept, which fails to provide for an Army role that comes anywhere close to the war-fighting concept articulated in FM 3-0. But the Army cannot win such an intellectual fight by avoiding getting into the ring with the Joint Staff as it has avoided doing in the EBO exercises to date. In 2001 the Joint Staff conducted three studies in support of a joint war-fighting capabilities analysis (JWCA), including studies on precision engagement, dominant maneuver, and command and control. In response, the Army employed an outdated briefing package on its approach to the Quadrennial Defense Review that did not come close to addressing the issues raised in the joint staff studies. Doctrinal competition, to include its theoretical underpinnings, may also include not only the other services and joint organizations, but, perhaps even more likely, such influential players as members of the Office of the Secretary of Defense (OSD). It would not be the first time a Secretary of Defense has mastered the services as a result of superior intellectual powers of abstraction.

The Army improved its performance in this competition for jurisdiction during the 2003-2004 Transformation Strategic Assessment, when it demonstrated to OSD that it was adapting rapidly to the lessons of Operations Enduring Freedom and Iraqi Freedom. But its programmatic leadership may be eclipsed by its lack of moral leadership in its handling of the Abu Ghraib detainee abuse scandal of 2004. Although the Army rightly concluded that the sensationalized actions of a few soldiers in late October 2003 were not part of a systemic pattern of abuse, the Army refused to acknowledge that its doctrinal failures constituted a direct contribution to other, more widespread incidents of prisoner abuse.[39]

Even in the seemingly less risky domain of Stability and Support Operations (SASO), the Army's approach to jurisdictional competition carries not-so-hidden dangers for its claims to exclusive jurisdiction over the use of lethal force in land combat. Andrew Abbott argues that advisory jurisdiction is "the bellwether of interprofessional conflict. Where there is advice today, there was conflict yesterday or will be conflict tomorrow."[40] In my view, the Army's strategy of settling for an advisory role in non-war-fighting-operations is indicative of conflict both before and yet to come. In the professional conflict leading up to the mid-1990s, the Army attempted to avoid taking on SASO as much as it could. It largely viewed such operations as incompatible with the hugely successful combat organization it had revolutionized after Vietnam and that had secured the dramatic victory in the first Persian Gulf War. As it became clear that the nation intended to call on its Army increasingly for SASO operations, however, the Army accepted this enlargement of its preferred jurisdiction by adopting its Cold War approach to them—they would be a lesser included set of capabilities to be offered in support of other organizations who would have the lead. In the case of domestic operations, the Army would support some other designated lead federal agency. In the case of overseas operations, the Army held that other nations with more direct interests would take the lead.

While the Army has largely succeeded in this approach, at the abstract level the Army has made itself vulnerable to a multitude of rival claims for such advisory support in the future. Typical of such arguments is Mary Caldor's call for the Army to lead the way in a new global era of employing armed forces strictly for humanitarian interventions.[41] The Army cannot afford to brush off such arguments as so much drivel from the liberal left. They are intellectually powerful arguments, reinforced by the Army's own jurisdictional strategy. The Army needs transcendently seminal minds of its own to respond, thinkers cut from the same mold as Canadian Brigadier Lewis MacKenzie, who has argued brilliantly in this area.[42] And those thinkers need to generate abstractions that articulate the Army's claims to legitimate monopoly over the use of lethal land force in global conflict.

The Army and the nation's civilian leadership were caught painfully off-guard by the emergence of the post-major conflict insurgency in Iraq in 2003. As casualties mounted in August and September, the Army searched its cognitive map in vain for applicable concepts. This was not a Vietnam-like insurgency, it was more like T.E. Lawrence's "guerilla warfare"[43] writ in a larger context of globally networked terrorist cells. Although Central Command Commander Gen. John Abizaid had declared publicly in July that the war in Iraq had become an "insurgency," a term previously avoided, Army leaders were too slow in conceptualizing and implementing an effective response, one that could avoid the surge in casualties arriving in the late summer and early fall of 2003 and again in the spring of 2004. The slowness to adapt can be attributed in part to the lack of a general theory of war sufficiently encompassing to provide a ready counter to the insurgents' inevitable effort to find an asymmetric reply to American conventional power.

Toward a General Theory of War

So how might the Army go about establishing a firmer intellectual foundation for its abstraction concerning its professional jurisdiction? As argued earlier, the Army does not need more doctrine. It has more doctrinal publications now than it ever has had before and even more are on the way. Nor does the Army need a new approach to the development of doctrine. The interaction of TRADOC with the schoolhouses, the Combat Training Centers, and units in the field is working better than it ever has. These components of the Army doctrinal machine are not broken, so they need not be fixed.

What the Army needs is a higher level of abstraction to provide it with stronger influence over its jurisdiction by means of greater control over the associated knowledge domain. The Army must seize the intellectual high ground in the current doctrinal competition. It needs to develop a general theory of war. Although the Army as an institution generally disdains theory-building and theorists,[44] it is time for the institution to reestablish its intellectual curriculum vitae. Today is an ideal time for such a development since there has been so little new thought at the theoretical level during the post-Cold War era. Even Cold War military theory was dominated by early nuclear-era theorists such as Bernard Brodie, Albert Wohlstetter, and Andrew Marshall.[45] Yet the Army's theory of war remains steeped in the 19th-century concepts of Jomini and Clausewitz. It is time to shed the principles of war and develop new knowledge for the new era of warfare. This is not to say that the classic principles of war are irrelevant, any more than it is to say that in the era of quantum mechanics the laws of physics articulated by Isaac Newton no longer apply. It is not that the old laws have zero explanatory power—it is that those Newtonian laws are largely irrelevant to the most interesting problems of modern physics. Likewise, simply stating, for example, that the Somalia operation in 1993 failed because it violated the principles of mission and unity of command is not helpful in approaching similar operations in the future.

If the Army is to win the intellectual battle of abstraction upon which its future occupational jurisdiction depends, it must begin now to elevate the level of its debate. Presently such discussions receive official recognition only in a very limited circle that includes the Army War College's Strategic Studies Institute, Leavenworth's School of Advanced Military Studies, and TRADOC's office of the Deputy Chief of Staff for Doctrine (DCSDOC). The Army needs to broaden its approach by undertaking development of a general theory of war for the 21st century.

Such an undertaking would require at least three basic components. First, the Army should create a core institution for theory-building. The Army War College and the Command and General Staff College already make important contributions to the development of the "How to Fight" process at the strategic and operational levels. The TRADOC DCSDOC integrates these processes across the Army. Many of the people who accomplish these tasks for the Army are eminently capable of developing theory and implicitly do so in the course of their work. But these organizations have no mandate to generate theory and certainly do not have the time to do so. The Army needs a separate new organization dedicated to this function.

Two existing institutions could house such an organization. The U.S. Military Academy could be effective in this role. USMA now has the kind of interdisciplinary faculty possessed by institutions of higher learning, research, and theory-building in other successfully competing professions (e.g., medicine, engineering, law). Alternatively, the Army has a considerable investment in the RAND Corporation's Arroyo Center, a federally-funded research and development center that could provide similarly broad access to scholars with a well-established—and well resourced—bureaucratic organizational infrastructure already in place.

Wherever the theory-building function is housed, the organization would need to be empowered to reach within the existing Army research enterprises as well as out to other institutions. The theory center could be a funding source for Army graduate students pursuing advanced degrees and dissertations, command and staff college theses, and advanced military studies focusing on the theory of war. It could also commission outside scholarship and hold conferences to debate and discuss research. The organization should also collect intellectual intelligence about the jurisdictional competitions confronting the contemporary Army. It should address such research questions as these: What are the dimensions and boundaries of the current competitions at the abstract level? Who is competing for what jurisdiction? For what purpose? The center should examine relevant theoretical developments in foreign countries. Most importantly the center would serve to stimulate innovative thinking across the Army by identifying good theorists and encouraging them to think out loud through both personal communications and professional forums.

The second necessary component is the promotion of theory-building across the profession. This will require a cultural shift among Army professionals to recognize the intrinsic value to the profession of those who choose primarily to pursue intellectual abstraction as a career goal over "muddy boots." Many medical and legal professionals who teach or conduct pure research do not concentrate on being practitioners because that is not where their interests primarily lie. They are creating the necessary inferential framework for future adaptations in diagnosis and treatment that will be required in the competition among professions. There is no reason why some of the Army's senior theory-building professionals could not likewise be set apart from its practitioners.

The third component is for the Army to open its professional dialogue at the abstract level to outside contribution and review, and to do so enthusiastically and in good faith. It should welcome rival claims by proponents of ideas from other services, the joint community, and even the Office of the Secretary of Defense. It must overcome the natural bureaucratic tendency to view every new idea as a potential threat to Army plans, programs, and budgets. Rather it should look positively on the opportunity to demonstrate the superiority of Army doctrinal concepts at the intellectual level.

However, as the Army allows outsiders to enter the game, it must carefully clarify the rules, focusing initially on those issues touching the Army's claims to legitimacy. This suggests that the debate should focus not on the peripheral issues of future battle in the RMA, jointness, or stability and support operations, but rather on the macro issues of an emerging theory of war for this century. Thus the Army should set the agenda of abstractions by challenging traditional notions of offense and defense in war with innovative contributions of its own in these Army heartland core competencies. Here, the Army's newly formed Futures Center at TRADOC shows promise. If it is able to achieve its vision to "be the Army's leader in integration and development of future capabilities, bringing together all Army, as well as joint and other agencies, to manage rapid change,"[46] the Center may be able to leverage Army contributions to war at the theoretical level into the broader competition for jurisdiction.

There have been some attempts at theory-building that could serve as a launching point for a new Army approach. These approaches have largely been derived from general systems theory[47] and have thus far fallen short of providing the kind of generalized theory needed for successful jurisdictional competition. More recent attempts at thinking about a new theory of war have pursued certain biological metaphors such as complex adaptive behavior and complexity sciences.[48]

Success in creating a process for building a new theory of war would go a long way toward enabling the Army to escape the negative outcome I believe it otherwise faces in the present professional competition for jurisdiction.

Notes

1. Field Manual 100-5 is one source of the Army's definition of *doctrine*. The 1982 and 1986 versions of this manual discuss, almost exclusively, the war-fighting aspects of doctrine in its definition of the term. The 1993 edition expands its scope to include operations other than war and its domain to include how to think about war-fighting as well as how to fight. In the October 2000 version of Command and General Staff College Student Text 3-0, a surrogate for the new (June 2001) edition of Field Manual 3-0, *Operations*, which replaced the 1993 version of FM 100-5, the notion of doctrine is adjusted to connote greater jointness. Training and Doctrine Command Regulation 25-36 *Coordinating Draft*, http://www-tradoc.,monroe.army.mil/dcsdoc/; Internet, accessed on 24 May 2001, also offers a view of the nature of doctrine, "which consists of principles and [tactics, techniques, and procedures], and defines, in terms of existing capabilities, how the Army intends to conduct operations across the full range of military operations. It is the fundamental principles by which military forces . . . guide their actions in support of national objectives. These principles reflect the Army's collective

wisdom regarding past, present, and future operations. It is the body of thought on how the military fights in the present to near term with current force structure and material. They focus on *how to think* about operations, not *what to think*."

2. Current manuals in force and under development are listed in a database at http://doctrine. army.mil. Authoritative complete text of Army doctrinal publications is available at the Reimer Digital Library, "Field Manuals," and "Joint Chiefs of Staff Publications," http:// 155.217.58.58/cgi-bin/atdl.dll?type=ANY&school=ANY; Internet; accessed 20 October 2000.

3. Headquarters, U.S. Army Training and Doctrine Command, "Joint/Army Doctrine Directorate," http://www-tradoc.monroe.army.mil/dcsdoc/jadd_roster.html/; Internet; accessed on 30 January 2001.

4. Brig. Gen. Stanley E. Green, Deputy Chief of Staff, Doctrine, Headquarters, U.S. Army Training and Doctrine Command, "Doctrine Study 00/01 Study Advisory Group," 27 September 1999, 11.

5. See, for example, U.S. Army Combined Arms Center, Center for Army Lessons Learned, "National Training Center Trends Analysis 4QFY94-2QFY96 NO.97," at http://call.army.mil/ call/ctc_bull/97-3anly/ta1.htm; and http://call.army.mil/call/ctc_bull/llcmtc96/c2.htm; Internet; accessed 2 February 2001.

6. http://www.monroe.army.mil/futurescenter/festraplan.htm, accessed, 1 August 2004.

7. Samuel P. Huntington, *The Soldier and the State* (New York: Vintage Books, 1957); Andrew Abbott, *The System of Professions: An Essay on the Division of Expert Labor* (Chicago, IL: Chicago University Press, 1988) 4.

8. Abbot, 2.

9. U.S. Army Command and General Staff College Student Text 3-0, *Operations* (Fort Leavenworth, KS: U.S. Army Command General Staff College: 1 October 2000), 1-14.

10. My own exegesis of Abbott, 2,4.

11. The Army makes this case in its capstone manual, FM 1-0. It is excerpted in Student Text 3-0 as "Army Forces are the decisive component of land warfare."

12. Abbot, 98-108.

13. Ibid., 69-79.

14. Jeffrey McKitrick et al., "The Revolution in Military Affairs," in *Battlefield of the Future*, eds. Barry R. Schneider and Lawrence E. Grinter, Air War College Studies in National Security No. 3 (Maxwell Air Force Base, AL: Air University Press, 1995).

15. The Army's view of the division of doctrinal turf is summarized in a table accompanying a briefing on the relationship between Army and joint doctrine. The table lists the numbers of joint doctrinal publications by proponent: Army 26, Navy 5, Air Force 14, USMC 5, USCG 3, CinCTRANS 8, CinCSPACE 1, CinCSOC 7, CinCSTRAT 1, CinCJFC 7, J1 2, J2 7, J3 7, J4 7, J5 1, J6 2, J7 10, PA 1, SP 1.

16. Lt. Col. Mike Goodwin, "Update: Army Doctrine XXI," slide 7 of 12 , http://www-tradoc. army.mil/jadd/adxxi/; Internet; accessed 20 October 2000. Nota bene: this site is no longer accessible to the public. I will provide hard copy to any researcher who desires to examine this document. Aggregate results of the survey are contained in the briefing "Doctrine Study 00/01 Study Advisory Group" cited in n.4.

17. During this study, FM 100-5 was in the process of revision and was released after the completion of the research. Its number was changed to FM 3-0 as part of a complete revision of the Army Manual numbering system. As a surrogate for FM 3-0, I used USACGSC Student Text 3-0.

18. Abbott, 71.

19. U.S. War Department, FM 21-6, *Basic Field Manual List of Training Publications*, 16 March 1940.

20. William O. Odom, *After the Trenches: The Transformation of U.S. Army Doctrine, 1918-1939* (College Station, TX: Texas A&M University Press, 1999).

21. Eric Heginbotham, *The British and American Armies in World War II: Explaining Variations in Organizational Learning Patterns,* Defense and Arms Control Studies Working Paper, Defense and Arms Control Studies Program (Cambridge, MA: MIT Center for International Studies, February 1996). Timothy Lupfer has argued that a similar robustness gave the German Army a relative tactical advantage over the Allies during World War I: Timothy T. Lupfer, *The Dynamics of Doctrine: The Changes in German Tactical Doctrine During the First World War,* Leavenworth Papers No. 4 (Fort Leavenworth, KS: U.S. Army Command and General Staff College, July 1981).

22. Robert A. Doughty, *The Evolution of U.S. Army Tactical Doctrine, 1946-76,* Leavenworth Papers No.1 (Fort Leavenworth, KS: U.S. Army Command and General Staff College, Combat Studies Institute, August 1979); *Sixty Years of Reorganizing for Combat: A Historical Trend Analysis,* Combat Studies Institute Report No. 14 (Fort Leavenworth KS: U.S. Army Command and General Staff College, January 2000); John L. Romjue, *Prepare the Army for War: A Historical Overview of the Army Training and Doctrine Command 1973-1993* (Fort Monroe, VA: U. S. Army Training and Doctrine Command, 1993); John L. Romjue, *American Army Doctrine for the Post-Cold War* (Fort Monroe, VA: U.S. Army Training and Doctrine Command, 1996).

23. I have compiled a cross-referenced longitudinal database index of all Army FMs sampled from the following publications: War Department Field Manual 21-6, *List of Field Publications for Training,* March 1945; Department of the Army Field Manual 21-6, *List and Index of Department of the Army Publications,* 10 April 1948; Department of the Army Pamphlet 310-3, *Military Publications Index of Training Publications,* 14 March 1960; DA PAM 310-3, *Military Publications Index of Training Publications,* 1 October 1954; DA PAM 310-3, *Military Publications Index of Doctrinal,Training and Organizational Publications,* 31 August 1970; DA PAM 310-3, *Military Publications Index of Doctrinal, Training and Organizational Publications,* 1 January 1982; DA PAM 25-30, *Military Publications Index of Doctrinal Training and Organizational Publications,* 30 September 1990.

24. The Coordinating Draft of TRADOC Regulation 25-6 provides a table cross-referencing Functional Categories, Numbers Series, and Title for Doctrinal Publications between the old and new numbering systems. Among the new categories appearing for the first time in this table are: Management Information Systems, Organizational Effectiveness, Environmental Operations, and Research Development and Acquisition.

25. As of this writing, the Army has not granted public access to its ongoing development of doctrine for the digitized force. Before it became password-protected the following was available: Lt. Col. Ron Gregory, "Army XXI Issues Associated with Development of Doctrine and TTP for the Digitized Force"; Internet; http://www-tradoc.army.mil/jadd/adxxi2/; accessed 20 October 2000.

26. Col. Michael Mehaffey, "Vanguard of the Objective Force," *Military Review* 80 (September-October 2000); Col. Kent E. Ervin and Lt. Col. David A. Decker, "Adaptive Leaders and the Interim Brigade Combat Team," *Military Review* 80 (September-October 2000). Although the Army does not allow public access to its doctrine development websites for the Interim and Objective Forces, it is possible to obtain recent versions of briefings on those subjects provided to Doctrine Developer's Course at the TRADOC and Combined Arms Center doctrine websites: "The Foundations of Army Transformation," "The Interim Force: Organizations and Capabilities," 30 January 2001, and "L07 Doctrine Development," Doctrine Developer's Course 13 February 2001.

27. Abbott, 48-52.

28. Again I am using Student Text 3-0 as a surrogate for the 2001 edition of *Operations,* which has been renumbered as FM 3-0.

29. See Thomas L. McNaugher, "The Army and Operations Other than War: Expanding Professional Jurisdiction," in *The Future of the Army Profession,* proj. directors Don M. Snider and Gayle L. Watkins, ed. Lloyd J. Matthews (Boston, MA: McGraw-Hill, 2002), 155-178, for a fuller treatment of this argument.

30. Student Text 3-0, 9-1.

31. Joseph J. Collins, Project Director, *American Military Culture in the Twenty-First Century: A Report of the CSIS International Security Program* (Washington, DC: Center for Strategic and International Studies, February 2000).

32. Maj. Steven J. Mains, "Adapting Doctrine to Knowledge-Based Warfare," *Military Review* 77 (March-April 1997); David Jablonsky, "U.S. Military Doctrine and the Revolution in Military Affairs," *Parameters* 24 (Autumn 1994); Maj. Jon J. Peterson, "Changing How We Change," *Military Review* 78 (May-June 1998); Ryan Henry and C. Edward Peartree, "Military Theory and Information Warfare," *Parameters* 28 (Autumn 1998); Antulio J. Echevarria II, "Tomorrow's Army: The Challenge of Nonlinear Change," *Parameters* 28 (Autumn 1998); Steven Metz, "The Next Twist of the RMA," *Parameters* 30 (Autumn 2000).

33. Maj. Gen. Robert H. Scales, Jr., "Adaptive Enemies: Achieving Victory by Avoiding Defeat," *Joint Forces Quarterly* (Fall 1999).

34. Gen. Robert W. Riscassi, "Doctrine for Joint Operations in a Combined Environment: A Necessity," *Military Review* 73 (June 1993). This article also appeared in the first edition of *Joint Force Quarterly* (Summer 1993). General Riscassi retired in July 1993.

35. David M. Keithly and Stephen P. Ferris, "*Auftragstaktik*, or Directive Control, in Joint and Combined Operations," *Parameters* 29 (Autumn 1999).

36. See note 4.

37. Maj. John Robert Evans, "*Task Force 1-22 Infantry From Homestead to Port-Au-Prince*" (Master's thesis, U.S. Army Command and General Staff College, 2000); Mark Edmond Clark, "US Army Doctrinal Influence on the War in Bosnia," *Military Review* 79 (November-December 1999); Maj. Mark A. Tolmachoff, "Is Army Aviation Doctrine Adequate for Military Operations Other Than War?" (Master's thesis, U.S. Army Command and General Staff College, 2000); Lt. Col. Daniel Ward, "Assessing Force Protection Risk," *Military Review* 77 (November-December 1997); Lt. Col. Walter E. Kretchik, "Force Protection Disparities," *Military Review* 77 (July-August 1997); Thomas Knight Adams, "Military Doctrine and the Organizational Culture of the United States Army," (Ph.D. diss., Syracuse University, 1990); Robert Bunker, "Failed-State Operational Environment Concepts," *Military Review* 77 (September-October 1997); Brig. Gen. Stanley F. Cherrie, "Task Force Eagle," *Military Review* 77 (July-August 1997); Col. Benjamin C. Freakley et al., "Training for Peace Support Operations," *Military Review* 78 (July-August 1998); Lt. Col. Wray R. Johnson, "Warriors Without a War," *Military Review* 79 (December-February 1999); David Fastabend, "The Categorization of Conflict," *Parameters* 27 (Summer 1997); Col. Andrei Demurenko and Alexander Nikitin, "Concepts in International Peacekeeping," *Military Review* 77 (May-June 1997); Lawrence A. Yates, "Military Stability and Support Operations: Analogies, Patterns and Recurring Themes," *Military Review* 77 (July-August 1997); Col. Charles H. Swannack, Jr., and Lt. Col. David R. Gray, "Peace Enforcement Operations," *Military Review* 78 (November-December 1997); Capt. Gregory R. Sarafin, "UN Observer Mission in Georgia," *Military Review* 77 (November-December 1997); Lt. Col. John Otte, "UN Concept for Peacekeeping Training," *Military Review* 78 (July-August 1998); Maj. Charles J. McLaughlin, "US-Russian Cooperation in IFOR: Partners for Peace," *Military Review* 78 (July-August 1997); Lt. Col. Douglas Scalard, "People of Whom We Know Nothing: When Doctrine Isn't Enough," *Military Review* 77 (July-August 1997); Maj. Gen. Robert H. Scales, Jr., "From Korea to Kosovo: How America's Army Has Learned to Fight Limited Wars in the Precision Age," *Armed Forces Journal International* (December 1999).

38. On Effects-Based Operations (EBO), see the briefing by Dr. Maris McCrabb, "Effects-Based Operations: Examples & Operational Requirements," 14 June 2000, available on-line from the Air Force Research Laboratory, Wright-Patterson Air Force Base. The USAF is now conducting a three-year-long Advanced Concept Technology Demonstration to experiment with technology concepts associated with EBO.

39. Department of the Army, The Inspector General, *Detainee Operations Inspection*, 21 July 2004. See p. ii for the basic conclusion. See also pp. 31-32 and 47-50 for the inconsistent discussion of the significant role of doctrine in contributing to the abuses.

40. Abbott, 76.

41. Dr. Mary Caldor, "New Wars in the Global Era" (keynote address at Tel Aviv University/IDF/AUSA Symposium on Martial Ecologies, March 2000); Internet; www.martialecologies.com; accessed 30 May 2001.

42. Lewis MacKenzie, "A Crucial Job, But Not One for a Superpower," *Washington Post*, 14 January 2001, B3.

43. T. E. Lawrence, "Science of Guerilla Warfare," in *Encyclopaedia Britannica*, 14th edition, 1929.

44. In contrast to today, there were at least two periods in the post-World War II Army in which theory-building was valued and had a direct impact on Army professionalism. One was the development of AirLand Battle under Gen. Donn Starry, the other was the development of the 1993 FM 100-5 under Gen. Frederick M. Franks, Jr.

45. Edward Mead Earle, ed., *Makers of Modern Strategy: Military Thought from Machiavelli to Hitler* (Princeton, NJ: Princeton University Press: 1943, 1971).

46. See TRADOC Futures Center website address in n. 6.

47. Majors E.A. Bryla, M.S. Lancaster, and W.C. Rennagel, *Contending Concepts, Tactics & Operational Art*, Vols. 243 (Newport, RI: U.S. Naval War College, Center for Advanced Research, June 1979); Robert H. Scales, Jr., *Firepower in Limited War* (Washington, DC: National Defense University Press, 1990); Shimon Naveh, *In Pursuit of Military Excellence: The Evolution of Operational Theory* (London: Frank Cass, 1997); Zvi Lanir, *SRT and Military Innovation* (Tel Aviv, Israel: Praxis Ltd , March 1999); Maj. John W. Taylor, "A Method for Developing Doctrine," *Military Review* 59 (March 1979); not to mention the voluminous Soviet literature on the systems approach to a general theory of war, although it is steeped in ideological considerations that even at the time most Soviet theorists did not really believe.

48. *SWARM Marine Infantry Combat Model (C-SWARM)—Beta Version User's Manual,* Office of the Secretary of Defense (Net Assessment) in support of the Marine Corps Combat Development Command, 20 October 1998; Dr. Michael L. Brown, *Thinking Biologically: The Impact of Complexity Sciences on the Future of Warfare,* Report of a Workshop Conducted for the Office of Net Assessment, 18 February 1997; Michael Brown and Andrew May, *Defeat Mechanisms: Military Organizations as Complex Adaptive Nonlinear Systems,* Report Prepared for the Office of Net Assessment, 10 March 2000.

15 New Requirements for Army Expert Knowledge: Afghanistan and Iraq

Michael J. Meese and
Sean M. Morgan[1]

The wars in Iraq and Afghanistan reflect a persistent and troubling problem for the American Army—it has not been able to provide post-conflict stability sufficient for strategic success in the type of wars it seems destined to face in the coming decades. Although the American Army is without question the most powerful fighting force on the globe, ironically it is hard-pressed to accomplish its mission in Iraq and Afghanistan. Others have addressed several of the reasons that contribute to the Army's difficulty, including the challenges of facing an insurgency, an adversary consisting primarily of nonstate actors and terrorists, and planning problems associated with the postwar phase of Operation Iraqi Freedom.[2] This chapter accepts those explanations as factors contributing to the Army's challenges, but then focuses on the Army itself to evaluate its intrinsic ability to conduct stabilization operations in the absence of such complicating extrinsic factors.

Merely directing the Army to develop a new capability would lead to a laundry-list of lessons to learn and tasks to do. However, such an approach would not suffice because it would overlook the fundamental concept that the Army is not just a public service organization, it is also a profession. If, as has been argued elsewhere in this anthology, Army members do truly comprise a profession, then the relevant discussion concerning the challenge of stabilization and security operations must be cast in the context of how professions change—the relationships between their evolving expert knowledge and the changing jurisdictions in which they do their work.[3] As sociologist Andrew Abbott has explained, "Change in professions can . . . best be analyzed by specifying forces that affect the content and control of work and by investigating how disturbances in that content and control propagate through the system of professions and jurisdictions."[4] Understanding the need, process, and imperative for change has been particularly difficult for military professions. As Don Snider and Gayle Watkins noted, "History shows that many armies do not adapt well in peacetime to changing environments; some do not adapt at all and no longer exist as armies. And, even for those that are able to innovate and adapt in order to remain effective militarily and relevant to the societies they defend, the process is often long and difficult."[5] Today, as the Army faces the challenges of both peacetime operating procedures in Washington and fighting the global war on terrorism abroad, it is essential to understand the way that a profession's work changes in response to new requirements.

The purpose of this chapter is to examine the requirement for the Army to address the problems of providing stability and good governance in "sovereignty-challenged" regions. We use the term "sovereignty-challenged" regions because of its broad applicability. Regardless of whether those areas are created because of a postwar regime change (Iraq), the absence of a coherent central authority (Somalia), or the inability of a state government effectively to exert sovereignty (parts of southern Colombia), the relevant fact for U.S. national security is that inadequately governed spaces create opportunities for terrorist action, sanctuary, and support. It is therefore likely that the Army will continue to be called upon to provide stability to such areas.[6] In this chapter, we address questions concerning the specific nature of changes required for the Army to develop the necessary expertise to assume the new task of providing stability in inadequately governed areas. We explain the capabilities required to facilitate stability and identify which of those capabilities are within the Army's current expertise and which are new responsibilities that the Army must prepare for. We conclude by discussing a practical example of adaptation by the 173rd Infantry Brigade (Airborne) as it conducted stability operations in Kirkuk, Iraq, in 2003.

As we researched new requirements for stability and governance in Afghanistan and Iraq, we found that officers can be prisoners of their own experiences; thus, we want the reader to be aware of our personal biographies. Colonel Meese was commissioned in 1981, and, like others of his generation, had his fundamental developmental experiences in the Army profession during the 1980s buildup for the Cold War when peacekeeping operations were considered "lesser included cases" which should not distract from the Army's main purpose. His specialized expertise—and the mission of his artillery battery in Germany—was to confront a Soviet attack in Central Europe. When the Cold War ended and his generation of officers viewed the challenges of peacekeeping operations, the Army coined the term "Operations Other Than War" to emphasize that these operations were distinctly subordinate to "real war," which should be the primary, if not sole, focus of the Army. A deployment to Sarajevo in Bosnia from January to July of 2002 and to Mosul, Iraq, during the period June-August 2003 caused Meese to recognize new requirements for military professionals. Major Morgan, on the other hand, was commissioned in 1992 and, like other officers of his generation, has primarily known only "operations other than war," or what the Marine Corps would call "small wars."[7] His operational experiences in the Army profession were in preparation for and deployment of his infantry company with the 1st Cavalry Division to Bosnia in 1998-99. He also deployed to Kirkuk, Iraq, from May to August 2003. He has lived small wars throughout his military career and endeavors to acquaint others with the importance of these conflicts. As academic researchers, we attempt to approach these matters with dispassionate objectivity, but our career experiences—like those of the other officers witnessing and contributing to the change of the profession—necessarily influence our thinking and reflect, in part, the difficulty of change in the Army profession.

What Capabilities Are Missing?

The U.S. military is without question highly capable of achieving its objectives during major combat operations, or in what military planners somewhat misleadingly refer to as "decisive operations" (also sometimes labeled Phase III operations).

However, it is often not until the aftermath of high-intensity conflict that the true political objectives of armed conflict are achieved. Military planners often use the term "Stability and Support Operations" (SASO), or Phase IV operations, to identify these activities. In his classic treatise *On War,* Carl von Clausewitz identifies the importance of the political objective in warfare. He writes:

> No one starts a war—or rather, no one in his senses ought to do so—without first being clear in his mind what he intends to achieve by that war and how he intends to conduct it. The former is its political purpose; the latter its operational objective. This is the governing principle which will set its course, prescribe the scale of means and effort which is required, and make its influence felt throughout down to the smallest operational detail.[8]

The political objectives in both Afghanistan and Iraq were not merely the defeat of military powers. They also included the establishment of stability and good governance in inadequately governed areas. These operational objectives supported the strategic goal of eliminating the conditions that foster the growth of terrorist organizations.

In World War II, for example, military operations did not end with the change of regimes. The military occupation of Japan and Germany was necessary to create conditions suitable for long-term peace between former adversaries. As articulated in the Potsdam Declaration of 1945 on the eve of Japan's defeat in World War II:

> There must be eliminated for all time the authority and influence of those who have deceived and misled the people of Japan into embarking on world conquest, for we insist that a new order of peace, security, and justice will be impossible until irresponsible militarism is driven from the world.[9]

Substituting the words "Iraq" or "Afghanistan" for "Japan," "regional" for "world," and "terrorism" for "militarism" suggests a suitable end state for Phase IV of contemporary conflicts. There are clearly specific governance capabilities required for Phase IV operations, all of which the military needs to be aware of, and in some of which the military will need to take the lead.

The activities for postwar stabilization are identified in Figure 15-1, each component of which will be described briefly in turn.

Foundation

The base of the diagram is the foundation upon which all other aspects of the local society are built. These include the basic social and cultural structure, as well as the fundamental components of economic growth—people, capital, resources, and geography. Notably, the foundation is an integral part of the nation and can be modified only over long periods of time. It needs to be considered as one of the "givens" by policy-makers because to alter culture, social structure, or physical geography is unfeasible within a one-to-three year period. Only through sustained intervention, such as the seven-to-ten-year formal occupations of Germany on Japan, can an external force begin to modify such fundamental aspects of a nation. Moreover, labor, capital, and resources have frequently been disrupted or destroyed

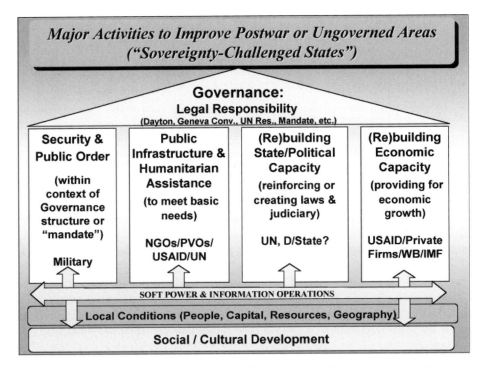

Figure 15-1. *Categories of Effort Commonly Undertaken by Various Entities in Post-Conflict Scenarios.*

during conflict. Merely replenishing what has been lost in war to provide an adequate foundation upon which to build constitutes a large, and initially critical, part of providing stability in any poorly governed area.

The military must recognize that there are intractable cultural, social, and other local conditions that dominate the foundation of the ungoverned region. In Iraq, for example, this means understanding that the social/political system was simultaneously authoritarian and tribal. Iraqis place a premium on being listened to, but are very willing to accept centralized decrees from many sources, including government officials, local leaders, or tribal elders. Society functions informally, and formal government leaders enhance their effectiveness by listening to and considering the informal input of respected societal leaders. Similarly, the Iraqi economic system was highly planned and subsidized by a huge government bureaucracy that endeavored to control nearly everything. The combination of the command economy and authoritarian political system systematically stripped initiative from most Iraqi citizens so that, while they have the technical ability to accomplish important tasks, they frequently are reluctant to empower themselves to take action. These social, political, and cultural phenomena have obvious implications for the way the military deals with Iraq. Cultural understanding is an absolute prerequisite for Army leaders.

While it would be ideal for every Army officer to have a broad understanding of every conceivable culture in which he or she might be deployed, that would be nearly impossible to achieve. However, officers must appreciate the importance of cultural distinctions, and that the study of other cultures, even if not directly applicable to the region in which the officer eventually deploys, is an appropriate first step.[10]

Superstructure

In Figure 15-1, the roof on top of the activities is a governing structure that must both function effectively and be perceived to be legitimate by the nation's citizens. It represents some form of sovereign power to which citizens subordinate themselves. This does not mean that the best-suited style of governance is necessarily a Jeffersonian democracy modeled according to the structure set forth in the U.S. Constitution. In an immediate postwar environment, it could be a structure defined by terms of a peace treaty (e.g., Dayton Accords for Bosnia), a U.N. resolution (Kosovo), or, in the absence of any formal agreement, international law codified in the Geneva Convention.[11] As the fundamental pillars of society develop, sovereignty can shift from legal frameworks imposed by international or occupying powers to popularly supported structures, which provide governance with less external support and greater internal legitimacy. For such governance to be supported, however, four major pillars of activities must be developed. They will be discussed from left to right on the diagram: (1) security and public order, (2) public infrastructure, (3) rebuilding political capability, and (4) rebuilding economic capability.

Before discussing the four pillars, however, we should note that the requirement for military expertise will be based partly on the legal details of governance, which will be the primary purview of operational law and international law specialists who accompany deploying forces. More importantly, all Army officers need to understand the overall structure of the applicable governance, its foundation in society, and its supporting pillars.

Security and Public Order Capabilities

The Army will need to expand and sharpen its low-intensity conflict capabilities. An adequate level of security is an absolute prerequisite for all other aspects of development. As the organization primarily responsible for establishing security, especially in the immediate aftermath of high-intensity land combat, the Army must take the lead in this endeavor.

During the 1990s, many military analysts argued that participation in stabilization and support operations would degrade the military's ability to conduct high-intensity combat. While this argument had some merit, it overlooked the fact that peace support operations in Haiti, Bosnia, and Kosovo were important preparatory experiences for Army leaders at all levels. These operations taught through experience the types of expert knowledge that would be needed in both combat and in postwar stability operations in Afghanistan and Iraq.

It is critical that conventional training (such as battle drills) not be sacrificed; soldiers may have to escalate to higher-intensity combat skills at a moment's notice. However, the adaptation of war-fighting skills to a more ambiguous security environment will require soldiers to be just as decisive, but far more discriminating, in their use of violence.[12] In stabilization operations, the center of gravity is not the enemy forces. It is the attitude and actions of the local citizenry whose support is essential to long-term strategic success.

Fortunately, just as the requirement for carefully graduated responses has become more necessary, technology, tactics, and doctrine have changed to enable much more precise engagements in both high- and low-intensity combat. The military mission requires, and the local population recognizes, that those who violently attack coalition forces must be killed or captured. However, it is essential that military force be applied in as precise and focused a way as possible.

For example, beginning in the summer of 2003, some units in Iraq conducted operations known as "cordon and knock" or "raid and aid" missions. When local citizens provided intelligence indicating that enemy fighters were in an area, military forces would surround the area, "knock" on house doors and provide the occupants an opportunity to surrender, seize them by force if necessary—with the force concentrated only on the enemy—and then return the next day with funds and humanitarian assistance to repair any damages and improve the neighborhood. These operations disrupted the enemy, engendered support among the population, and frequently led to additional intelligence.

As an even more effective step, Army leaders must develop their ability to work in conjunction with indigenous security forces. At low levels, military forces should patrol with local police forces, introduce concepts of community policing, and train special response (SWAT) teams and riot control formations. At higher levels, integration of some intelligence, planning, and operational activities should occur as well. While Army leaders are often familiar with conducting such tasks with other nations' armed forces, working with a local security force poses significant challenges.[13] However, developing such indigenous capacity is critical to success.

Additionally, since at least the implementation of the Dayton Accords in Bosnia, the military has assumed the mission to disarm, demobilize, and reintegrate combatant armed forces, paramilitary forces, and militias.[14] For the Army this was an unfamiliar mission, lying outside the traditional war-fighting jurisdiction. However, it was an essential mission, both as a force protection measure for allied forces themselves and as a means to enhance local stability. In central Iraq in the summer of 2003, lack of success in this final part of the operation (the reintegration of combatants into society) fueled much of the ongoing insurgency. Because of failure to address this issue, tens of thousands of former Iraqi security and military personnel had no sustainable means of feeding their families, no clear positive vision of their future, and ultimately came to doubt the legitimacy of the interim government established for just these purposes. Many quickly became frustrated and served as a ripe recruiting base for those who opposed Coalition forces.

The Army must also intensify development of expertise to facilitate situational awareness by exploiting intelligence capabilities at the lowest possible levels. In high-intensity combat, the best situational awareness arguably accrues at higher levels where all of the input from multiple systems can be integrated to provide senior commanders with a comprehensive view of the battlefield. In stability operations, however, the best view is usually at much lower levels where soldiers are in contact with the local citizenry and get a firsthand sense of what is really happening on the street. Army leaders have used the phrase, "Every soldier is an intelligence collector and every officer is an intelligence officer," to emphasize the importance of local situational awareness.[15] The impressions and assessments of soldiers are not as neatly packaged as the impressive technical displays from high technology intelligence platforms; nevertheless, Army officers must integrate human intelligence effectively with all other intelligence assets to provide effective situational awareness in stabilization operations. Specifically, fundamental low-intensity intelligence techniques, such as link and pattern analysis, must become routine at all levels, from the company on up.[16]

Public Infrastructure and Humanitarian Assistance Capabilities

Response to the immediate collapse of emergency services in post-conflict situations is a common occurrence that military forces often handle well.[17] At the end of Operation Desert Storm in 1991, when Saddam Hussein attacked the Kurds in northern Iraq, the United States carried out Operation Provide Comfort in compliance with U.N. Security Council Resolution 668 to provide humanitarian assistance to the Kurdish rebels. In this circumstance, humanitarian aid was provided in conjunction with a military operation; hence, the only real option was for the military to provide immediate humanitarian assistance.[18] Although this case may have been the most prominent one in the mind of the war planners for Iraq, it is not the most likely case.

In most cases where the United States is attempting to stabilize ungoverned areas, a modicum of stability exists such that professional aid organizations, which have the specific expertise in assistance and the administration of public infrastructure, can meet the needs. The U.S. Agency for International Development (USAID) has established a robust capability to assess needs and then to provide either direct support or, in most cases, to contract for third party organizations to provide support. The Army may not need to develop additional military expertise to deal with humanitarian assistance missions. Instead, Army officers should focus on expanding their political-cultural expertise to be competent in understanding and coordinating, even synchronizing, the efforts of USAID, nongovernmental organizations (NGOs), international organizations (IOs), private volunteer organizations (PVOs), and other humanitarian assistance agencies. By virtue of its efforts in providing a robust security pillar, the military will normally have the most sophisticated communications, intelligence, and transportation network, which can facilitate operations by humanitarian assistance agencies. The expertise required is a capability to work across the boundaries of organizational cultures—between the military and other governmental and private organizations—to ensure unity of effort in providing humanitarian assistance.

In the area of public infrastructure, such as communications, electricity, roads, and hospitals, the role of military forces is different. Army units have organic expertise in these areas, which is required for expeditionary combat campaigns. When a 15,000-soldier unit deploys, for example, they are supported by a robust team of telecommunications experts to provide computers, phones, and radio networks; medical experts to provide hospital support; engineering experts to build roads, buildings, and runways; power experts to secure electrical power. The peak military requirement for most of these services is during high-intensity combat (Phase III operations). However, once an Army division is established in an area of operations, the combat-related requirements for these support forces decline as the division's internal infrastructure is established. The specialized engineer, medical, and communications units that possess these capabilities can then either redeploy to other areas, or the excess infrastructure expertise can be applied to assisting local public facilities.

For example, in northern Iraq in 2003, after establishing the signal network for the military units, the 501st Signal Battalion rebuilt the telecommunications network for the civilian population in the five northern provinces of Iraq. Through a combination of about $100,000 in funds, 300 kilometers of fiber-optic cable donated by Bell South, and 212 donated computers, the 501st Signal Battalion was able to provide national and international telephone access to northern Iraq for the first time in history.[19] This was not an inherently military task, nor was it one in which the military needed to develop expertise beyond that which it required to support its expeditionary combat responsibilities. However, because the expertise is available in excess of military requirements, it is appropriate for commanders to use that capability to contribute to the overall mission.[20]

(Re)Building State/Political Capacity

Before World War II, the chief political goals at the end of conflict encompassed limited objectives, such as changes in territorial boundaries, indemnities and reparations, or restrictions on a perpetually antagonistic adversary's armed forces. Correspondingly, Article 43 of the Hague Rules on Land Warfare, created in 1899, provided limited powers to occupation forces, specifically that:

> The authority of the legitimate power having passed into the hand of the occupant, the latter shall take all measures to restore and ensure, so far as possible, public order and safety, while respecting unless absolutely prevented, the laws in force in the country.[21]

However, with the advent of "total war" the political objective changed. As reflected in the chief post-WWII planning document issued by the U.S. government, the goal in postwar Japan was to change the political culture: "To foster the conditions which will give the greatest possible assurances that Japan will never again be a menace to the peace and security of the world."[22] Specifically, the method by which long-term peace was to be established in Japan reflected the major precepts of democratic liberalism:

> The Japanese Government shall remove all obstacles to the revival and strengthening of democratic tendencies among the Japanese people. Freedom of speech, of religion, and of thought, as well as respect for the fundamental human rights shall be established.[23]

The Army does not currently have the capability to accomplish these tasks. Establishing a sustainable and more just peace requires that the political culture of a nation-state be changed so that it is an inhospitable environment for those entities seeking to oppose effective, accountable government and freedom.[24] Accomplishing this goal serves as the strategic objective for the use of military force, particularly when such force is used to establish stability and good governance.

However, the political culture of a country cannot be altered through force alone. Instead, occupation forces must allow latitude for representative political groups and supporting institutions to grow. For example, when occupation forces in postwar Japan learned about the activities of communist subversives, they did not respond with raids or military operations. Instead, they allowed for political dissent through legitimate means (such as newspapers) as long as such activity did not condone violence. When violence was instigated by subversive communist elements, indigenous (Japanese) law enforcement agencies dealt with it. On occasion, occupation forces lent support to these organizations. However, nonviolent channels of political dissent were promoted as a means to foster a democratically inspired political culture.

Changing political culture, or any form of culture, is difficult at best, and takes time. Working within the existing political culture and influencing public perceptions can most readily achieve the desired changes. The Army currently recognizes the need for this activity and now includes it as part of its core doctrine under the catch-all moniker "information operations." Specifically, this perception management effort falls under the sub-category of "offensive information operations," which is slightly less vague than the parent concept.[25] Nonetheless, further expansion of the Army's expert knowledge in this field remains badly needed, recognizing that the effort to create it has just started.

(Re)Building Economic Capacity

There are two chief aims of postwar economic development. Initially, the society must have the means to sustain itself. Immediately after the cessation of major hostilities, this may not be possible. Foreign humanitarian assistance may prove essential to the survival of elements of the population. If sufficient quantities of basic necessities are not available, little progress in any other dimension is possible. People will resort to whatever means necessary to ensure their own survival and that of their families, so security-related reforms would be nearly impossible to conduct. Political reform will be even more difficult under such circumstances.

As the country stabilizes, Army forces must be prepared to facilitate further economic development. The purpose of economic growth at this stage is to reinforce the success of democratic political reform. Unless people realize, as a result of the regime change, tangible improvements in their material well-being, support for continued change will diminish. Usually most of such improvements will be funded by international donor governments as "reconstruction" or "development" assistance. This type of assistance overlaps with humanitarian assistance in many aspects, but is generally implemented at a much slower pace.

Specific capabilities needed during this period will likely include a mix of public and private activities. Such public-sector related activities might include (in conjunction with local officials) the management of state-owned enterprises and payroll management for government employees and pensioners. Private sector activities will likely include reform of the banking sector to foster domestic capital accumulation and lending, solicitation of foreign investment capital, and the identification of key industries with long-term growth and employment potential.

The military has three roles in support of such indigenous economic development. First, the military must contribute meaningfully to the previous pillars—providing security, supporting public infrastructure, and building state political capacity that includes the rule of law. Success in these efforts increases confidence that firms can expect to reap positive returns from investments. Such expectations are, of course, essential preconditions to economic development. Second, as in the case of humanitarian assistance, the military "works the borders" of its political-cultural expertise to facilitate understanding, coordination, and support of public organizations and private firms that step up to facilitate economic growth and development. Some military leaders themselves may need to have or acquire specific economic or business expertise to work relationships with local economic actors. In any event, while there is not a specific military requirement for detailed economic expertise, all Army leaders should have a general background in basic economics. Finally, notwithstanding some unusual exceptions, recent experience indicates that the Army profession should also develop the expertise to disburse seed capital for private firms, particularly until such time as local banking institutions are viable.

Third, one of the most under-appreciated aspects of post-conflict economic development is the importance and impact of the spending done by the military itself. Just as the government is the largest single purchaser in most nations, U.S. military expenditures in support of their own operations frequently provide a huge and significant economic boost to the economies in which they are operating. In Bosnia, for example, when U.S. forces were first deployed in 1996, they generated an estimated $1.5 billion of additional economic activity each year—which was more than 10 percent of the prewar national economic output. U.S. stability operations provide a de facto "Marshall Plan" through the creation of local economic activity in war-devastated regions through the rebuilding of infrastructure to support U.S. and coalition military forces.

In Iraq, this trend continued. In the four northern provinces, which were under the control of the 101st Airborne Division (Air Assault), the U.S. military employed over 15,000 Iraqi citizens in a variety of jobs. These included 11,559 in security forces for military, government, border, and other sites; 2,184 general laborers; 386 interpreters; and 368 workers in cafes, barber shops, and other enterprises.[26] These figures do not include thousands of other workers who were indirect hires in support of projects to rebuild Iraqi infrastructure, that is, those hired by contractors and those employed because of the ripple effects from economic activity that this initial employment generated. An Iraqi Veterans Employment Office was established to facilitate the vetting and hiring of former Iraqi soldiers for many of these jobs. These jobs provided some social dignity to former soldiers, which gave them a greater tendency to support rather than oppose the Coalition forces, especially if the source of their livelihood was a Coalition job.

While there is no specific expertise required to contribute to economic development beyond contracting skills (which the Army already has), commanders need to recognize that the manner in which military units spend funds can have a significant impact on the economy, and that they should use those expenditures as a tool to facilitate stabilization. The Commanding General of Central Command, Gen. John Abazaid, made this point when he testified before Congress: "You are absolutely correct that ammunition is money, and money is ammunition."[27] In stabilization operations commanders need to think of the expenditures of funds in support of their soldiers as ammunition, which they can use to promote the operation's success.

Summary and Application

Given the forgoing discussion of the need for new expert knowledge and soldier expertise, it is useful to identify the extent to which these relate to the Army's current knowledge and expertise. Figure 15-2 depicts the new expertise which the Army needs to adopt arrayed around the boundaries of the Army's current expertise. Each of the four major sections of the chart identifies the particular expertise of specific

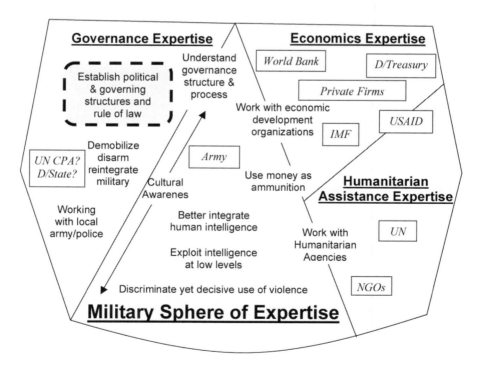

Figure 15-2. *Map of Expertise Needed for Successful Stability Operations.*

professions or organizations, with the military sphere of expertise in the center. The new skills required are generally arrayed hierarchically, with those skills employed at the small-unit level (such as the discriminate use of violence or exploiting intelligence) near the bottom and those skills employed at higher levels of command (such as understanding governance) at the top. Cultural awareness is applicable at all levels as the arrows indicate. Representative organizations already holding such expertise are indicated in italics in the boxes within each section.

It is important to note that a "dotted line" should surround the entire schematic to reflect the military's *responsibility* in the period immediately following combat operations before security is established and other organizations are available. Current Army doctrine states that:

> Prompt Army assistance to civil authorities is often a decisive element in . . . crisis resolution. Army forces continue sustained support until civil authorities no longer require military assistance.[28]

This does not mean that the military necessarily has exclusive expertise in these areas; but it does have the responsibility until organizations with specific expertise begin to arrive and take hold.

The diagram is helpful in identifying how the new skills required for stabilization in ungoverned spaces relate to the military profession today. Just as the Cold War and changing technology spawned a particular set of skills for the Army during that era, those skills that are fully within the wedge of military expertise in Figure 15-2 are those we believe need to be developed within the existing Army systems of knowledge (doctrine) and soldier expertise. These include better integrating human intelligence, exploiting intelligence at the lowest level, and more discriminate use of violence. Those skills shown on the border of the wedge, such as working with humanitarian or economic development organizations, using money as ammunition, and understanding governance, require Army officers to comprehend the other professional jurisdictions, to be adept at negotiating the jurisdictional boundaries and, on occasion, to operate within the other jurisdictions when the security situation precludes the presence of more specialized organizations. Finally, two cross-jurisdictional tasks are identified as new missions outside the Army's traditional jurisdiction, but which now need to be incorporated: (1) demobilizing, disarming, and reintegrating local military forces; and (2) integration of Army efforts with those of local security and police forces. These two have now become core tasks for the land component forces in the worldwide war against terrorism. The Army should therefore accept that its own professional jurisdiction should be expanded to embrace them along with the necessary doctrines and expertise.

The task of establishing political and governing structures and rule of law is highlighted in Figure 15-2 because of the current absence of any U.S. organization with expertise in this area. In Operation Iraqi Freedom, the Coalition Provisional Authority (CPA) was given this mission, but it was an ad hoc organization, lacking individuals who had preparation or expertise in postwar governance.[29] We believe the Army should negotiate expansion of its core jurisdiction to include the development of expertise in governance, which would include developing democratic political processes and (re)establishing the rule of law. The U.S. Marine Corps conducted these types of operations throughout the late 19th and early 20th centuries, particularly in Latin America. The Marines met with mixed results, often due to lack of doctrine and expert knowledge.[30] When, in World War II, the Marines changed their core competence from small wars to amphibious, forced-entry operations, the tasks associated with small wars were largely transferred to the Army.[31] The U.S. Army also has experience in similar endeavors, but mostly in the post-conflict era of major campaigns—in the western United States in the 19th century, in Cuba and the Philippines after the Spanish-American War, and in Japan and Germany after World War II. However, the Army's subsequent disagreeable experiences in Vietnam and more recently in Haiti and Somalia soured the institution's mindset toward such undertakings. Thus, in Afghanistan and Iraq the Army avoided conducting such tasks at the national level, although some visionary commanders successfully provided interim governance structures at the city and provincial levels.

One such example is the 173rd Infantry Brigade (Airborne), which successfully reorganized and adapted its existing structure to the new work requirements of stabilization operations in Iraq in March of 2003. After its parachute assault in northern Iraq opened the second front, the Brigade quickly joined forces with Special Operations Forces and Kurdish Peshmerga to liberate several key cities in northern Iraq. After the rapid collapse of Ba'athist forces, the Brigade quickly transitioned to

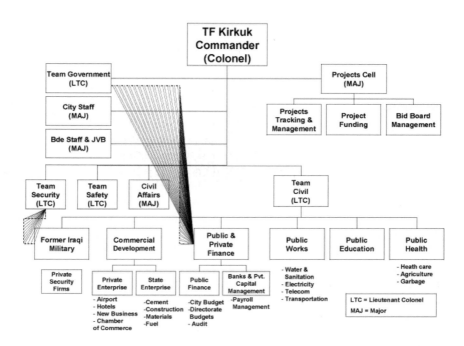

Figure 15-3. *Task Organization of the 173rd Airborne Brigade in Iraq for Political, Economic, and Societal Development Operations.*

stabilization (Phase IV) operations. Realizing that long-term stability in the region, particularly in the city of Kirkuk, would occur only after the successful transfer of authority to legitimate indigenous civilian control, the Brigade commander quickly set to the task. Instead of relying solely on the 54 personnel of its attached civil affairs company to build governance within Kirkuk, the Brigade made one of its maneuver battalions wholly responsible for political and economic development (Team Civil, in Figure 15-3).

This Battalion worked closely with the Brigade's Civil Affairs teams and quickly laid the groundwork necessary for rapid political and economic development within the region. Unfortunately, lack of support from the Coalition Provisional Authority mired subsequent efforts; but had both the financial and political resources been provided, the Brigade's structural adaptation would have prepared it for rapid and far-reaching success.

The Army has made some more permanent structural adjustments by adding a small cell of organic Civil Affairs personnel to the staff of the new Units of Action (UA).[32] Having this small team permanently assigned is clearly preferable to the previous lack of any organic Civil Affairs personnel at that level. Yet, this measure may also constitute a trap for future unit commanders. Having such a small number of personnel responsible for the myriad tasks required for Phase IV operations will likely overwhelm the team's capabilities. This team, we believe, should instead serve as the catalyst for planning at the UA level, while operational execution should then occur through the UA's subordinate maneuver elements. These new tasks of governance must be warmly embraced as new areas of specialized expertise by the UA—and the Army as a whole—not merely relegated to staff section personnel and forgotten.[33]

Conclusion

The ability of American and coalition forces to provide stability in sovereignty-challenged areas has become a common requirement during the global war on terrorism. As the single profession with the broad mission to "win our nation's land wars," the Army will continue to be called upon to provide such stability as a necessary follow-on to combat operations, thus ensuring establishment of the "more just" peace that overall strategic success requires. Stabilization operations in both Afghanistan and Iraq have identified new expertise that the military in general and the Army in particular need to develop. As we have demonstrated, some of these functions are clearly within the traditional purview of the Army. Others require new understandings of related functions for which expert knowledge and expertise must be developed or acquired by the Army. The examples of the 173rd Infantry Brigade (Airborne) and other units in Iraq demonstrate that Army units have the agility and versatility to adapt to the new requirements. But that is not the same thing as the Army profession embracing, within the context of evolving joint operations, the task of providing effective, post-conflict governance. We believe the Army needs to do just that—in the creation of its expert knowledge, in the development of its future leaders, and in the training of its operational units. A start has been made, as emerging doctrine confirms.[34] But the task is remains far from being completed.

Notes

1. Col. Michael Meese is the Professor and Deputy Head of the Department of Social Sciences at West Point. Maj. Sean Morgan recently completed his assignment as an Assistant Professor of Economics at West Point and is currently a student at the Command and General Staff Officer. They greatly appreciate the input, review, and comments from Lt. Col. Roland de Marcellus and other participants in the June 2004 Senior Conference at West Point.

2. For insurgencies, see John A. Nagl, *Counterinsurgency Lessons from Malaya and Vietnam: Learning to Eat Soup with a Knife* (Praeger, 2002). For terrorism and nonstate actors, see Russell D. Howard and Reid L. Sawyer, *Terrorism and Counterterrorism: Understanding the New Security Environment, Readings and Interpretations,* Revised and Updated (Boston, MA: McGraw-Hill, 2004). For the challenges of postwar planning see James Fallows, "Blind into Baghdad," *The Atlantic Monthly* (January/February 2004). For a recent insightful analysis of nation-building, see James Traub, "Making Sense of the Mission," *The New York Times Magazine,* 11 April 2004.

3. A jurisdiction is a "a domain of social life." It is essentially a societal need. Professions compete, often by negotiation, to provide the service which fills this need. See Don M. Snider and Gayle L. Watkins, "Introduction," in *The Future of the Army Profession,* project directors Don M. Snider and Gayle L. Watkins, ed. Lloyd J. Matthews, (Boston, MA: McGraw-Hill, 2002), 19.

4. Andrew Abbott, *The System of Professions: An Essay on the Division of Expert Labor* (Chicago, IL: University of Chicago Press, 1988), 112.

5. Snider and Watkins, "Introduction," 3.

6. This does not imply that regime change and deployment of a large conventional force are necessarily the preferred strategy for the global war on terrorism; however, some of the skills required in Iraq and Afghanistan will likely be necessary in future cases of inadequately governed areas.

7. The classic reference manual originally published in 1940 has been reprinted as *Marine Corps Small Wars Manual, United States Marine Corps, 1940* (Manhattan, KS: Sunflower Press, 1996).

8. Carl von Clausewitz, *On War,* Michael Howard and Peter Paret, eds. and trans. (Princeton, NJ: Princeton University Press, 1976), 579.

9. Article 6 of the Potsdam Declaration, August 1945, accessed at http://www.isop.ucla.edu/eas/documents/ potsdam.htm.

10. For example, at West Point, most members of the class of 2007 now have a requirement for one additional "culture" elective (foreign language, regional politics, geography, or history courses). Further, Academy and Army leaders are endeavoring to give as many cadets as possible an immersion experience in a foreign culture prior to their commissioning.

11. See *Geneva Convention (IV) Relative to the Protection of Civilian Persons in time of War* (6 U.S.T. 3516, signed on 12 August 1949 at Geneva) in W. Michael Reisman and Chris T. Antoniou, *The Laws of War: A Comprehensive Collection of Primary Documents of International Laws Governing Armed Conflict* (New York: Vintage, 1994), 233-83.

12. For a discussion of the ethical implications inherent in this new need for a more discriminate use of force, see chap. 18 of the present anthology.

13. One of the key distinctions is that local police forces are likely to be penetrated by the enemy; units must thus be particularly cognizant of operational security procedures.

14. The mission of military restructuring and peace support was given to the military forces, which were designated as the Implementing Force (IFOR), in Annex 1A, "Agreement on the Military Aspects of the Peace Settlement," *Dayton Peace Accords*. The military has continued with the mission of demobilization, disarmament, and reintegration of armed forces in Kosovo, Afghanistan, and Iraq.

15. Among other places, a senior flag officer used the phrase as he explained the importance of intelligence to effective operations in Iraq in a National War College lecture in April 2004.

16. Link and pattern analysis is one of the techniques of describing how individuals in a particular area are related with each other through business, family, social, government, and other relationships. It helps military leaders track who is working with whom so that they can direct intelligence assets to develop a more complete picture and take action to promote or disrupt specific associations, if necessary.

17. Field Manual 3-0, *Operations* (Washington, DC: Department of the Army, 14 June 2001), 1-7.

18. The Commander of the Task Force in northern Iraq was then Maj. Gen. Jay Garner, who concentrated on the humanitarian assistance mission during Operation Provide Comfort. Much later, in 2002, he was appointed as Director, Office of Reconstruction and Humanitarian Affairs (ORHA), which was designated to direct Phase 4 of Operation Iraqi Freedom.

19. "U.S., Iraqi Leaders Gather For Telecom Summit," CJTF-7 Release 031215c, accessed at http://www.cjtf7.com/media-information/december2003/031215c.htm, 1 June 2004.

20. Several cautions are in order in the use of excess military expertise. First, although military individuals may be experts in their field, they are probably not development experts, so it is essential that they do not create systems that are unsustainable when they leave. In the signal battalion example, this pitfall was avoided as they fully integrated their efforts with existing Iraqi telecommunications companies and private firms that continued what they started.

21. See *Hague Convention (IV) Respecting the Laws and Customs of War on Land, Annex to the Convention* (1 Bevans 631, signed on 18 October 1907 at The Hague) in W. Michael Reisman and Chris T. Antoniou, *The Laws of War: A Comprehensive Collection of Primary Documents of International Laws Governing Armed Conflict* (New York: Vintage, 1994), 232.

22. Joint Chiefs of Staff, Basic Directive for Post-Surrender Military Government in Japan Proper (JCS 1380/15), 3 November 1945, para. 3a.

23. Article 10 Potsdam Declaration, Aug 1945, available at http://www.isop.ucla.edu/eas/documents/potsdam.htm.

24. Political culture in this context means, "A pattern of basic assumptions–invented, discovered, or developed by a given group as it learns to cope with its problems of external adaptation and internal integration–that has worked well enough to be considered valid and, therefore, to be taught to new members as the correct way to perceive, think, and feel in relation to those problems." Edgar Schein, *Organizational Culture and Leadership* (San Francisco, CA: Jossey-Bass, 1998).

25. See FM 3-13, *Information Operations* (Washington, DC: Department of the Army, 28 November 2003), especially pp. 2-1 to 2-6; and Glenn A. Tolle, "Shaping the Information Environment," *Military Review 82* (May-June 2002):47-49.

26. Data on employment is from "AO North Briefing," 101st Airborne Division (Air Assault), 3 February 2004.

27. Gen. John Abizaid, quoted in U.S. Congress, Senate, Armed Services Committee, "U.S. Senator John W. Warner (R-VA) Holds Hearing on the FY 2005 Central Command And European Command Budget Requests," 4 March 2004, Federal Document Clearing House.

28. Field Manual 3-0, *Operations* (Washington, DC: Department of the Army, 14 June 2001), 1-7.

29. L. Elaine Halchin, The Coalition Provisional Authority (CPA): Origin, Characteristics, and Institutional Authorities, RL32370 (Washington, DC: Congressional Research Service, 29 April 2004).

30. This point is reflected in the opening chapter of the *USMC Small Wars Manual*, 1940.

31. Earl F. Ziemke, *The U.S. Army in the Occupation of Germany, 1944-1946* (Washington, DC: Center of Military History, 1990); and James Dobbins et al., *America's Role in Nation-Building: From Germany to Iraq* (Washington, DC: RAND, 2003), ch. 1.

32. Headquarters, Department of the Army, G-3, Media Roundtable, "Building Army Capability," 17 February 2004.

33. The Army used a more robust model with U.S. military forces serving in Japan in 1945 with considerable success. See James Dobbins et al., chap. 3. In the initial phase of that occupation, some of the troops were organized into "military government" teams distributed across Japan's eight regions and 46 prefectures. Each local team had functional sections dealing with such areas as government, economics, information and education, and public health that were parallel to the structure of the local government. Decisions were made in Tokyo and sent to governors and mayors for implementation. It was the job of the local military government teams to observe and report back to headquarters on how well their decrees were being implemented at the local level. These teams were later renamed Civil Affairs teams.

34. Field Manual-Interim 3-07.22, *Counterinsurgency Operations* (Washington, DC: Department of the Army, August 2004).

16 Transforming the Army's Way of Battle: Revising Our Abstract Knowledge

Antulio J. Echevarria II

Contrary to various claims that a new American way of war has arrived, the United States does not yet have a way of war. What it has is a way of battle.[1] The phrase "way of war" conveys a holistic view of conflict, one that extends from pre-war condition-setting to the final accomplishment of national strategic objectives. By contrast, the phrase "way of battle" suggests a tactical focus, one that centers on defeating an adversary on the field of combat. We are not speaking here of the distinction that characterizes the traditional dichotomy between war and operations other than war. The core issue is *not* how, or whether, the American military should balance war-fighting and operations other than war. Rather, it is whether we want the term "*war*-fighting," long in vogue among military professionals, to mean the actual prosecution of a war from beginning to end or merely the brutal mechanics of close-quarters' combat.

The issue is a salient one. Americans clearly need a way of war rather than a way of battle. This is especially true given the socio-cultural complexity of waging a war of ideas as part of the global war on terror, and the attendant need to rebuild failed states both politically and economically.[2] Otherwise, the world's greatest military power may eventually find itself in the unenviable position of having the capability to win battles anywhere on the globe without necessarily being able to achieve its principal strategic ends in any of them.

To be sure, moving fruitfully toward a way of war will require the entire joint community as well as key members of the interagency process to re-conceptualize warfare itself, that is, to view war more holistically and not as a compartmented and discrete activity focused primarily on achieving military victory. That notwithstanding, the U.S. Army, though only one member of the joint team, has a central role to play in transforming the way Americans think about war. The Army contributes considerable expertise and wherewithal to the prosecution of conflict on land, an indispensable ingredient of warfare as it was practiced in the past and likely will be for the foreseeable future.[3] We can expect that the people and places that one must control to ensure victory will continue to reside on land. Moreover, the Army has the responsibility—perhaps even the obligation—by virtue of its status as the senior military profession to help the joint community develop a more holistic view of conflict. To perform this role effectively, however, the Army must first reevaluate its own views and assumptions about warfare. It must, in the terminology of sociologist Andrew Abbott, update its abstract knowledge—or theory and doctrine—so that they better reflect a vision of war commensurate with the realities of conflict in the 21st century.[4] In short, the Army must transform its piece of the American way of battle into a legitimate way of war, just as the other services must transform theirs.

Clearly, the overall transformation of America's way of battle will remain incomplete until the other members of the joint team contribute to it in whatever ways they deem appropriate. The Army profession should, therefore, welcome input from the other services. The purpose of this chapter is to assist the Army in thinking about the knowledge-aspects of its own transformation and to help it make similar contributions to the overall joint effort.[5] By accepting its responsibility as a profession to adapt its knowledge to changing circumstances, the Army enhances the overall effectiveness of the joint team. While it may be true that the whole is greater than the sum of its parts, the quality of the individual parts does matter.

The American Way of War: Historical Perspectives

Serious inquiry into the American approach to waging war began with the publication of the late Russell Weigley's classic, *The American Way of War* (1973).[6] Examining how war was thought about and practiced by key American military and political figures from the 1770s to the 1970s, Weigley concluded that, except in the early days of the nation's existence, the American way of war generally centered on achieving a crushing military victory over an opponent.[7] U.S. military men and political leaders typically saw the destruction of an adversary's armed might—whether through a strategy of attrition or one of annihilation—and the occupation of his capital as marking the *end* of war and the beginning of a *postwar* settlement. The American concept of war rarely extended beyond the winning of battles and campaigns to the gritty work of turning military victory into strategic success. Consequently, the American approach to war—to take the liberty of rephrasing Weigley's argument—was more a way of *battle* than an actual way of war.

More recently, historian Max Boot examined the American approach to warfare from a different perspective. Whereas Weigley analyzed the American involvement in major wars, Boot in *Savage Wars of Peace* (2002) examined U.S. participation in history's so-called small wars, such as the Boxer Rebellion, the Philippine Insurrection, and contemporary interventions in Bosnia, Kosovo, and Somalia—conflicts that rarely involved vital national interests.[8] American military forces participated in many more of these smaller conflicts than they did major wars.[9] Nonetheless, with the U.S. Marine Corps' *Small Wars Manual* representing the exception that proves the rule, Boot's *Savage Wars of Peace* tells the story of a military unwilling to see its raison d'etre as anything but defeating major opponents in a more or less conventional clash of arms.[10] Thus, Boot's argument both complements and updates Weigley's.

Taken together, the historical perspectives of Weigley and Boot reveal that, in martial endeavors large and small, the U.S. military and its civilian leadership have typically seen war as consisting almost exclusively of battles or campaigns aimed at the destruction of an opponent's armed might.[11] They tended to assume that wars ended when combat operations ended. War thus equated to battle, and battle was not so much an extension of diplomacy as an admission that diplomacy had failed. The "aftermath" of war, the untidy process of arriving at a settlement, including the expensive and time-consuming management of political and economic reconstruction, was not considered part of war, even though it was during such post-conflict activities that victories on the battlefield were ultimately translated (or not) into strategic successes.[12] Thus, the focus of war was on defeating an enemy rather than on achieving a particular strategic-political end state.

A New American Way of War?

While Boot clearly complements Weigley's thesis, his arguments go much further—from mere historical interpretation to overt advocacy. In an article published in *Foreign Affairs* in 2003, for example, Boot established himself as one of the leading advocates of a so-called new style of American warfare.[13] This purportedly new approach was characterized by an emphasis on "precision firepower, special forces, psychological operations, and jointness" and the concomitant qualities of "speed, maneuver, flexibility, and surprise"—as opposed to the alleged traditional dependence on overwhelming force, mass, and concentration.[14] Boot claimed, moreover, that the new American way of war would make it possible for the United States to wage the "savage wars of peace" more effectively *and* more efficiently, thereby enabling it to enlarge its "empire of liberty"—by which he meant the "family of democratic, capitalist nations" that benefit from America's largesse. In his view, the United States was morally obligated to expand its "empire of liberty" because its huge military and economic might gave it the power to do so.[15]

The characteristics that Boot described bear a conspicuous resemblance to the qualities of "speed, jointness, knowledge, and precision" that underpin the model of the new American way of war currently championed by the Office of Force Transformation (OFT) and the Office of the Secretary of Defense (OSD).[16] This model reflects a crude blend of terminology extracted from complexity theory and airpower theory, particularly John Warden's concept of launching a series of precise, parallel strikes at an adversary's so-called centers of gravity to inflict so-called strategic paralysis.[17] The origins of the concept stemmed from the initial spate of ideas that emerged after Operation Desert Storm, and gained considerable momentum through the 1990s. These ideas highlighted an air-centric approach that appeared to promise quick results with minimal cost in friendly casualties and collateral damage. Defense analyst Eliot Cohen pointed out that the potency of contemporary American air power gave the American way of war a certain "mystique" that U.S. diplomacy would do well to cultivate, though he cautioned that air power was hardly a silver bullet.[18] However, his warning did little to curb the enthusiasm of airpower zealots, such as one-time historian at the Smithsonian Institute, Richard Hallion, who claimed that the results of Desert Storm proved that U.S. air power had literally—and almost single-handedly—revolutionized warfare.[19] Indeed, according to some briefings circulating in the Pentagon at the time, air power was not only America's asymmetric advantage, it was the future of warfare. Thus, for a time, the new American way of war seemed to involve only one service.

Shortly after the end of the conflict in Kosovo, Cohen summed up the salient impressions circulating among defense intellectuals about the new American way of war. With views similar to those of Weigley and Boot, Cohen saw the traditional U.S. approach to war as characterized by a certain aggressiveness or desire to take the fight to the enemy, by the quest for a decisive battle, by an explicit dislike of diplomatic interference, and by a low tolerance for anything but clear political objectives. In contrast, the new style of warfare reflected a decided aversion to casualties, typified by a greater preference for precision bombing and greater standoff, and seemed willing to step away from the restrictive Powell doctrine and to participate more in coalitions, even those created only to address humanitarian concerns.[20] The reduced risk of U.S. casualties, in turn, made wars for less-than-vital interests more palatable. Cohen also expressed concern, however, that this new way of war increased military authority at the expense of civilian control by permitting the combatant commander, in the Kosovo case Gen. Wesley Clark, to become the focal point for strategic decision-making.[21]

Critics quickly responded that, in its most important aspects, this new style of war was already passé—operating in a world where its premises were "no longer valid."[22] In light of the thousands of lives lost on 11 September 2001 (9/11) during the terrorist attack on the World Trade Center and the Pentagon, Americans seemed willing to return to an aggressive style of warfare and to bear whatever costs were necessary, even in terms of significant U.S. casualties. Indeed, the U.S. military's campaigns in Afghanistan and Iraq were to prove that the capability for waging the close fight, even if based more on precision than mass, remained indispensable for achieving favorable combat outcomes.[23] Those campaigns also demonstrated that civilian control over the military was alive and well when a strong civilian personality, like Defense Secretary Donald Rumsfeld, has the helm.

The major differences between the new American way of war as understood by defense intellectuals and that conceived by OSD lay in the latter's emphasis on the characteristics of jointness and knowledge superiority, which defense intellectuals regarded as little more than rhetorical excess. They preferred to see the new U.S. way of war in terms of how it played itself out within the context of modern conflict, while OSD tended to project a list of desired (some would say ideal) capabilities into the future. This is not to say that OSD's model was entirely divorced from current events, for it later morphed to accommodate the Bush administration's emerging doctrine of strategic preemption.[24] The OSD model now acknowledges, for example, that future military operations overall will have to "shift from being reactive (i.e., retaliatory and punitive) to largely preventative."[25]

A New Way of Battle

The principal similarity in the views of defense intellectuals and OSD resides in the lack of emphasis on the end game, specifically, on the need for systematic thinking about the processes and capabilities needed to translate military victories into strategic successes. As retired Marine Gen. Anthony Zinni remarked, the U.S. military is becoming more efficient at "killing and breaking," but that only wins battles, not wars.[26] While OSD's model acknowledges the importance of "interagency constabulary forces," it does so *not* with the intent to achieve a better result in the end game, but with the goal of freeing up "elite forces" for further combat operations.[27] Consequently, the new American way of war seems headed for the same trap that snared the traditional one as portrayed by Weigley and Boot, that is—it appears geared to fight wars as if they were battles and thus confuses the winning of campaigns or small-scale actions with the winning of wars.

If the history of strategic thinking is any guide, however, this trajectory is not necessarily inevitable. After reaping the fruits of its so-called golden decade (1955 to 1966) and after years of self-examination in the wake of Vietnam, U.S. strategic thought generally came to acknowledge that, in the long run, the winning of battles counts for much less than the accomplishment of one's strategic objectives.[28] Col. Harry Summers' account of his April 1975 conversation in Hanoi with a North Vietnamese colonel has been cited often—and with good reason—to illustrate the point that winning battles does not suffice for winning wars. When Summers confronted his counterpart with the fact that the North Vietnamese Army had never defeated U.S. forces on the field of battle, the NVA colonel replied, "That may be so, but it is also irrelevant."[29] Summers' account, of course, maintains that American soldiers did their job, but U.S. political leadership failed to do its. Almost in spite of itself, however, the account also reinforces the point that accomplishing one's strategic objectives serves as the ultimate measure of success in war.

The tendency of military professionals, and Army officers in particular, to think tactically rather than strategically is both symptom and cause of a long-standing bifurcation in American strategic thinking: military professionals concentrated on winning battles and campaigns, while policy-makers focused on the diplomatic struggles that precede and follow the actual fighting. This bifurcation was partly a matter of preference and partly a by-product of the American tradition of subordinating military command to civilian authority—arguably, a vital interest of the United States. Preference and precaution have thus created two separate spheres of responsibility, one for combat and one for diplomacy. Robert Osgood, a prominent political scientist of the 1950s and 1960s, once labeled these two spheres rather appropriately as "power and policy," with the former belonging to the military and the latter to the political leadership.[30]

The Army as a Profession

As noted earlier, as a profession the Army has a major responsibility for transforming the nation's way of battle. For purposes of this chapter, a profession is defined as a "relatively 'high status' occupation whose members apply abstract knowledge to solve problems in a particular field of endeavor."[31] The Army's "high status" comes from civil society's perception that the Army's abstract knowledge, or expertise, is legitimate, that is, it accords with prevailing cultural values and appears to solve problems related to its field of endeavor.[32] This accord is especially important. For example, recent events reaffirm that American civil society does not condone the abuse of prisoners of war, even if that abuse yields useful information. Therefore, while brutal methods might prove effective in solving military problems, civil society would not likely grant the Army the high status of a profession if it employed them.

Sociologist Andrew Abbott recently refined his definition of a profession by demonstrating that professions control not only the application of abstract knowledge to their fields of endeavor—or jurisdictions—they control the acquisition of that knowledge as well.[33] Abbott maintains that, over the long run, the most successful professions are those that manage to retain positive control over their bases of knowledge, revising them as necessary to keep them relevant in the face of change. The quality—i.e., the pertinence and efficacy—of the abstract knowledge, and the control over it, in turn, enable a profession to compete more effectively against other professions or occupations vying for a role in that particular jurisdiction. Put differently, in Abbott's system of professions, knowledge (and the conscious protection of it) is power. His premise is that professions not only serve society, they compete for the right to do so.

Doctrine: The Army's Abstract Knowledge

Abbott's model provides useful insights regarding the function and importance of the Army's abstract knowledge. That knowledge is primarily contained in the Army's doctrine, a hierarchy of linked documents that lay out principles and guidelines, as well as tactics, techniques, and procedures.[34] The most important of the doctrinal documents, especially for the purposes of this chapter, is Field Manual 3-0, *Operations*, which sets forth the Army's "keystone" or essential doctrine for full-spectrum operations.[35] It also serves as a "capstone" document, providing overarching doctrinal direction for other Army manuals.[36] Thus, FM 3-0 is considered the Army's "principal tool for professional education in the art and the science of war."[37] If Army doctrine had a center of gravity, FM 3-0 would be it.

FM 3-0 corresponds in function and significance to Joint Publication 3-0, *Joint Operations*, which does everything for the joint team that FM 3-0 does for the Army. Both documents are currently undergoing a synchronized revision that will more closely align joint and Army doctrine. As presently scheduled, the revision of JP 3-0 will be completed toward the end of December 2005, with FM 3-0 following shortly thereafter.[38] FM 3-0 will borrow some structure and content from JP 3-0, and vice versa. Currently, the changes approved for the first draft of JP 3-0 include: (1) reorganizing the document according to principles applicable to the conduct of joint "Campaigns and Major Operations" across the range of military operations; (2) describing the linkages between strategic aims, principles of war, and operational art and design; (3) incorporating offensive, defensive, and stability operations as categories in the discussion of the fundamentals of joint operations; (4) incorporating effects-based language as an approach within campaign planning; and (5) changing the categories of war and military operations other than war to major combat operations, small-scale contingencies, and security cooperation.[39] Thus, as the discussion below will make clear, FM 3-0 has already influenced the revision of JP 3-0. Accordingly, the Army must have a clear understanding of the strengths and weaknesses of its abstract knowledge—especially regarding the issues on which it will yield and those to which it will hold fast—so that it can participate effectively in the ongoing revision of two of the U.S. military's keystone documents. FM 3-0 is therefore a pertinent and timely focal point for discussing revisions of the Army's abstract knowledge; moreover, thoughts concerning FM 3-0 could well influence the further development of JP 3-0.

When FM 3-0 appeared in June 2001, it incorporated combat operations and military operations other than war (MOOTW) as part of the same spectrum of operations as the 1993 edition had done, but it treated both types in more detail, investing them with equal importance.[40] Its categories of operations—offensive, defensive, stability, and support—were broad enough to encompass virtually all land or land-based missions, to include most homeland security missions identified—or, more accurately, re-identified—after 9/11. These categories are currently undergoing review as part of the revision of FM 3-0.

However, FM 3-0 fell short in one critical respect—it failed to provide a holistic perspective of war, that is, it failed to distinguish war from battle. In fact, FM 3-0 never defined the term "war" at all, though it used the terms "war" and "conflict" as if they meant different things.[41] Instead, FM 3-0 sent a contradictory message. On one hand, it correctly stated that "military operations influence, and are influenced by, political direction and the integrated use of other instruments of power," and that success in these operations necessitates "commanders with a clear sense of strategic policy goals and objectives."[42] On the other hand, it contradicted those statements by declaring that "the military objective in war is rapid, decisive victory," and that it is the National Command Authority (NCA) who determines "how that victory contributes to the overall policy objectives."[43] In other words, even though military commanders must have a clear sense of the strategic goal, they are nonetheless to have only one military objective—rapid, decisive victory—whether or not such a victory facilitates or impedes the accomplishment of the strategic objective. Thus, rather than encouraging commanders to think and plan strategically, FM 3-0 reinforces the traditional bifurcation in American strategic thinking by taking the position that the NCA determines "how" such victories contribute to policy objectives. Military commanders acknowledge the need for political influence, but concern themselves only with defeating the enemy.

Put differently, FM 3-0 fails to convey the sense that military victory should not be pursued as an end in itself. Hence, the document does not do as much as it might to reduce the many difficulties that accompany the accomplishment of strategic goals. For example, in Operation Iraqi Freedom, the information campaign convinced the bulk of the Iraqi army to abandon its vehicles and fighting positions and "go home" rather than offer resistance. On this score, it was a brilliant tactical coup. However, its result actually hindered the accomplishment of the overall strategic objective of installing a stable and responsible Iraqi government, since many

Iraqi soldiers took their personal weapons home with them, thereby compounding the security problems that Coalition forces encountered in the stability phase of the conflict.

In fact, the assumption that winning battles equates to winning wars underpins much of FM 3-0. For example, the manual equates achieving tactical success—defeating one's opponent—as the center of gravity in the accomplishment of strategic objectives. Once the former is achieved, the latter inevitably follows. However, FM 3-0 fails to mention that the center of gravity might lie—*not* in an opponent's physical or psychological capacity to fight (i.e., wage a successful campaign or battle)—but rather in the successful political and economic reconstruction of the vanquished state, as in Iraq.[44] Unfortunately, the Army (and joint) definition of center of gravity—"those characteristics, capabilities, or locations from which a military force derives its freedom of action, physical strength, or will to fight"—is a "capabilities-based" one, revealing a decidedly battle-oriented focus because it aims solely to eliminate or reduce an opponent's physical and psychological capacity to fight at the expense of other actions critical to accomplishing the political objectives.[45]

In another example, FM 3-0 emphasizes the importance of tactical and operational-level experience, but fails to acknowledge the value of strategic-level experience.[46] Clearly, operational commanders would benefit from having had experience at the level at which strategy and policy interface. Such experience, though perhaps more difficult to come by due to the limited number of such positions available compared to the size of the officer pool, would surely help commanders develop the instincts, intuition, and broader knowledge-base necessary to anticipate strategic requirements and tailor tactical actions so that they better support desired strategic outcomes.

Such disconnects between strategic and tactical aims reveal, among other things, that the Army's abstract knowledge lacks an overarching conceptual framework that both defines war as something different from mere battle, and describes its essential anatomy, the typical parts or phases through which it progresses. The declared purpose of the operational level of war is to link tactical actions to strategic objectives, and vice versa.[47] An operational framework would help accomplish that by describing how commanders use the forces at their disposal to advance from one phase to the next. To be sure, FM 3-0 identifies three phases of conflict—"sustained land combat, war termination, and post-war stability."[48] However, it overlooks a fourth, preconflict condition-setting. Moreover, it fails to use this framework to provide a consistent context for describing the categories of military operations and how they contribute to the prosecution of a war, from start to finish. The use of phasing, though artificial in some respects, has already become common practice in war planning. Thus, the Army faces a perennial problem: its implicit or *tacit* expert knowledge, which officers gain in the field, in the schoolhouse, and (hopefully) at the level of strategic-political interface, is (once again) well ahead of its explicit expert knowledge, which is recorded in doctrine.

Unfortunately, such major publications as Joint Publication 1-0, *Joint Warfare of the Armed Forces of the United States*, which should provide such doctrinal direction for FM 3-0 and JP 3-0, do not.[49] JP 1-0 is the "capstone" joint doctrine publication that provides guidelines for the U.S. military in joint, multinational, and interagency activities at all levels and across the range of military operations. In short, capstone doctrine provides the integrative guidance for keystone documents such as JP 3-0 and FM 3-0. However, JP 1-0 does not provide a framework for understanding how to prosecute a war. Much like FM 3-0 or JP 3-0, it declares merely that "the fundamental purpose of the Armed Forces is to win the Nation's wars," but it does not define "war" nor what is meant by the term "win."[50]

Improving the Army's Explicit Abstract Knowledge

While others have argued that revising the Army's abstract knowledge requires the development of a general theory of war appropriate for the 21st century, they have not proposed the particular revisions that address the concern of this chapter.[51] After all, Clausewitz's general theory of war, though either oversimplified or endowed with unnecessary complexities by its critics, has nevertheless stood the test of time. Instead of a new general theory of war, what is really necessary is a new Joint Pub 1-0 that provides a framework for the Army's FM 3-0 and the joint team's JP 3-0. This framework should be similar to the one illustrated in Figure 16-1, which breaks the prosecution of war down into its major parts.

One can debate the number of phases depicted here, or their labels. To be sure, phases tend to overlap, with activities assigned to one sometimes spilling over into or running concurrently with those in another. During Operation Iraqi Freedom, for example, some cities and towns in Iraq were already experiencing Phase IV (Security and Stability) activities before others had seen Phase III (Decisive Operations). In some cases, certain locales might move directly from Phase I (Deterrence and Engagement) to Phase IV. Nor do all wars necessarily start at Phase I, though history shows that even wars of aggression—such as Iraq's invasion of Kuwait in

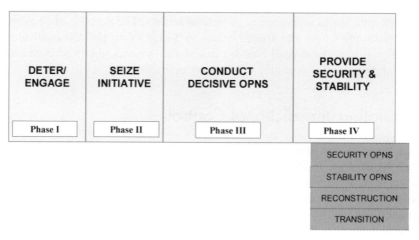

Figure 16-1. *Proposed Joint Pub 1-0 Framework for Phasing the Prosecution of War.*

1990—involved some measure of Phase I deterrence or engagement on the part of the aggressor to discourage or preclude participation by the target country's friends and allies. Perhaps surprisingly, the prosecution of unconventional wars, such as the United States' global war on terror, essentially accords with this general framework.

The critical point, however, is that prosecuting a war from start to finish requires a logical, though not necessarily rigid, sequence of events. Decisive battle itself (Phase III) is only one part of that sequence. The purpose of Phase III is not necessarily to crush an opponent militarily—though it might be in certain circumstances—but rather to help the NCA move the state of the conflict to Phase IV. To be sure, crushing one's opponent in battle is sometimes a sure step to moving into stability and support operations. Yet, it avails little if it is seen as an end in itself. FM 3-0 and JP 3-0 should explain this vital distinction, describing how the various military operations defined in Army and joint doctrine actually contribute to prosecuting a war by moving the conflict from phase to phase.[52] Such a discussion would put military operations into a larger, more purposeful context, enabling the operational level of war to tie strategic objectives more closely to tactical actions. Similarly, it would help officers think of "war-fighting" as prosecution of the whole war, rather than merely the part given over to combat. FM 3-0 and JP 3-0 do not completely overlook the wider perspective of war, but they lack a unifying framework capable of pulling it all together. The best way to address shortcomings in the Army's abstract knowledge, therefore, is to provide a compelling treatment of the strategic prosecution of war as supported by a fully fleshed-out operational framework.

Given such a framework in a revised JP 1-0 (and revised JP 3-0), the Army would then bring itself into conformance by incorporating a similar framework in FM 3-0, and by modifying its doctrinal emphasis on the tactical aspects of warfare in its operational-level manuals. It should, for example, revise such declarations as "the military objective in war is rapid, decisive victory," which give rise to the sorts of contradictions noted in this critique. It should also revisit certain important concepts like center of gravity, which are vaguely defined and generally conceived of only in a tactical or operational sense. The purpose of FM 3-0 is not to justify tactical concepts, but to link strategy to tactical actions. The purpose of decisive operations is simply to get the United States to Phase IV in the most advantageous posture possible. The revised FM 3-0 would then provide the needed overarching doctrinal direction for changing other Army manuals.

Negotiating Jurisdictional Control

As the Army begins to apply its revised abstract knowledge—for prosecuting wars rather than merely fighting battles—it might seem, however unintentionally, to be challenging the traditional relationship between "power and diplomacy." Its professional advice may frequently cross over into the realm of diplomacy, a realm traditionally reserved for the nation's political leadership, and thus be perceived as encroaching upon civilian authority. This is all the more so because the Army's preferred role of fighting battles rather than wars actually helped to preserve civilian control—it tended to curb Army professionals from assuming a dominant role in political decision-making and restricted their purview to combat. Some political scientists and historians maintain, perhaps with justification, that the standard for civilian authority should be as absolute as possible in order to prevent its gradual erosion over time.[53] This includes the right for civilians to be "wrong"—which is to say they should get what they ask for, even if it is not what they really want.[54] Preserving civilian control, according to this view, is indeed tantamount to a vital national interest. By extension, accepting military failures is preferable to incurring a—perhaps irreversible—loss of civilian authority. The traditional argument that the military will not act in ways that threaten civilian authority because to do so would be to act contrary to its code as a profession is not universally accepted.[55]

The joint team and the Army should therefore make it clear that they expect to remain in what—in social-science parlance—amounts to a "subordinate-advisory" jurisdictional relationship with civilian authority. Abbott makes the case that jurisdictional resolutions usually assume any of six forms of which 2. and 5. are most salient for our purposes here:[56]

1. Full jurisdiction—with one profession winning at the expense of the others.
2. Subordination—one or more professions become subordinate to another profession or occupation.
3. Split jurisdiction—two interdependent partners.
4. Shared jurisdiction—with no division of labor.
5. Advisory—a profession is relegated to an advisory role.
6. Division by client type—with professions serving different social groups.

Accordingly, the joint team and the Army will have to demonstrate to the public and to the nation's political leadership that merging the realms of power and diplomacy would not result in a loss of civilian control, because any share of the diplomatic jurisdiction gained by the Army and joint team would be confined strictly to rendering advice to their civilian superiors in the negotiation.

The Way Ahead

To transform its way of battle into a way of war, the Army must revise its abstract knowledge as embodied in doctrine so that it reflects an understanding of war as well as combat. It must do this, first, by assisting the joint team in developing an operational framework that conveys a sense of how operations contribute to the prosecution of war and to the accomplishment of desired political outcomes; it must then assist the joint team in incorporating that framework into JP 1-0, JP 3-0, and FM 3-0. Second, in the application of its revised abstract knowledge, the Army must demonstrate that its role remains one of subordinate-advisor. The tradition of civilian control over the military must be preserved even at the expense of additional friction and inefficiency in the conduct of war.

Beyond these measures, there are others that warrant mention despite lying somewhat outside the limited scope of this chapter. For instance, as Abbot points out, the Army as a profession must consciously treat its doctrine not as a mere collection of manuals, but as a corpus of expert knowledge, a corpus that reflects and supports the Army's status as a profession. It should therefore examine ways to update its abstract knowledge so that it keeps pace with practical knowledge as developed in the field. The development of the Army's abstract knowledge should remain firmly in the hands of certified professionals. Admittedly, the Army also needs the collective wisdom of its retired officers, especially its "gray-beards." The Army should reexamine its relationship with appropriate retired experts to find a means of allowing them to remain certified.

However, even a complete revision of the Army's abstract knowledge and the systems that produce it will not suffice to transform the Army's and the nation's way of battle into a way of war. The Army should take additional measures, such as reexamining the levels at which its officers are introduced to strategic-level thinking. Specifically, it should study whether it is necessary to increase the amount of strategic-level training that occurs in the officer basic and advanced courses and at the staff college. In the same vein, the Army should consider whether to increase the percentage of its officers who receive professional education at a senior-service college, or equivalent. Such an education, whether in residence or by correspondence, broadens the professional perspectives of officers, and helps them understand the complex processes behind the formulation of policy and strategy. For instance, the recently uncovered abuse of Iraqi prisoners of war at Abu Ghraib was not merely a violation of the provisions of the Uniform Code of Military Justice, it had profound strategic ramifications that ran counter to the nation's interests in the Middle East. A better understanding among officers and soldiers of the interrelationship between strategy and tactics may not itself deter such acts, but it would heighten sensitivity to potential political fallout and it would contribute to their deterrence by adding additional moral weight to the legal force of military law. The point of broadening the baseline of strategic thinking in the Army would be to emphasize that if actions at lower levels run counter to the nation's strategic aims, they undermine the entire war effort, not just the work of one's unit.

Yet, a full transformation of the nation's way of battle must go beyond the Army, even beyond the joint team. It would require that America's political leaders become more familiar with war's ever-evolving grammar, that is, the operational art. Just as Army professionals must begin to think more strategically, diplomats and policy-makers must learn to think more operationally. To keep a conflict on course and to preserve civilian control, those who dictate the aims of war must aggressively and continually question and challenge war's grammar, even to the extent of intervening in technical matters. To be sure, those who determine the aims of war must develop a better appreciation for what the grammar can and cannot accomplish. However, while those diplomats and policy-makers may be well-educated and expert within their various governmental fields, collectively they are not a profession. Consequently, the burden for reforming the American way of battle will fall primarily to the U.S. military, the joint team. As the senior member of the joint team and as an established profession, the Army should embrace this challenge.

Notes

1. The argument that America has a way of battle rather than a way of war is developed in more detail in Antulio J. Echevarria II, *Toward an American Way of War* (Carlisle Barracks, PA: U.S. Army War College, Strategic Studies Institute, 2004). Portions of that argument are replicated here in order to build a case for transforming the Army's way of battle.

2. Evidence suggests that such challenges will probably become more frequent over the next few decades, partly as a by-product of the global war on terror, but also because the number of crises requiring military interventions appears on the rise. It is worth noting, for example, that the United States averaged one intervention every ten years during the Cold War, compared to one intervention every two years since 1990. Hans Binnendijk and Stuart Johnson, eds., *Transforming for Stabilization and Reconstruction Operations* (Washington, DC: National Defense University, 12 November 2003), 11. Similarly, nearly 80 percent of the peace operations conducted by the United Nations from its establishment in the late-1940s occurred after the end of the Cold War. James Dobbins et al., *America's Role in Nation Building: From Germany to Iraq* (Santa Monica, CA: RAND, 2003), xiv.

3. For example, the Army has defined itself as the "decisive component of land warfare in joint and multinational operations." FM 3-0, *Operations* (Washington, DC: Department of the Army, June 2001), 1-2.

4. Andrew Abbott, *The System of Professions: An Essay in the Division of Expert Labor* (Chicago: Chicago University Press, 1988).

5. Some of the knowledge-aspects of the Army's transformation are detailed in "The U.S. Army Transformation Roadmap," 1 November 2003. However, none addresses transforming the Army's way of battle into a way of war. http://www.army.mil/2003TransformationRoadmap.

6. Russell F. Weigley, *The American Way of War: A History of U.S. Military Strategy and Policy* (Bloomington, IN: Indiana University Press, 1973).

7. Weigley, *American Way of War*, 475. It is worth mentioning that Weigley's description of the American approach to warfare is marred by shortcomings in at least two respects: in the errors he makes in military terminology; and in his tendency to oversimplify the complexities of American military thinking, though generalizations are to be expected in a work that spans the better part of two centuries. With regard to terminology, he incorrectly defines the strategies of annihilation and of attrition, describing the former as seeking the complete "overthrow of the enemy's military power" and the latter as pursuing lesser objectives by means of an "indirect approach," which he mistakenly says is characterized primarily by the gradual erosion or exhaustion of an opponent's forces. For more detail on the shortcomings of Weigley's argument, see Echevarria, *Toward an American Way of War*, 4-5. See also Brian M. Linn, "*The American Way of War* Revisited," *The Journal of Military History* 66, no. 2 (April 2002): 501-30; Linn suggests that if there is an American way of war per se, it lies in a utilitarian blend of operational considerations, national strategy, and military theory as it is understood historically. Weigley more or less conceded Linn's points in Russell F. Weigley, "Response to Brian McAllister Linn," *Journal of Military History* 66, no. 2 (April 2002): 531-33.

8. Max Boot, *Savage Wars of Peace: Small Wars and the Rise of American Power* (New York: Basic Books, 2002).

9. Between 1800 and 1934, for example, U.S. Marines made 180 landings on foreign shores, more than one per year. During roughly the same period, the U.S. Army deployed numerous small contingents in actions virtually all over the globe. Likewise, the U.S. Navy, though small, was involved in many actions at sea over the same time-span that, both directly and indirectly, assisted the British Royal Navy in keeping the oceans open for commerce. Boot, *Savage Wars*, xv-xvi. Boot goes beyond historical analysis, however, to advocating the establishment of a military capable of fighting the "Imperial wars of peace." He thus opens himself up to the criticism that he produced a "potted history" designed merely to advance his own neo-conservative

views. Benjamin Schwartz, "The Post-Powell Doctrine: Two conservative analysts argue that the American military has become too cautious about waging war," *New York Times Book Review*, 21 July 2002, 11-12.

10. United States Marine Corps, *Small Wars Manual* (Washington, DC: U.S. Government Printing Office, 1940; 1990); Boot, *Small Wars*, 283-85.

11. One notable exception was Abraham Lincoln; see the discussion in Eliot Cohen, *Supreme Command: Soldiers, Statesmen, and Leadership in Wartime* (New York: Free Press, 2002).

12. The term is aptly used in Frederick W. Kagan, "War and Aftermath," *Policy Review* 120 (August-September 2003): 3-27.

13. Max Boot, "The New American Way of War," *Foreign Affairs* 82, no. 4 (July/August 2003): 41-58.

14. Ibid., 42.

15. Boot, *Savage Wars*, 352. For his description of the American empire, see Max Boot, "Everything You Think You Know About the American Way of War Is Wrong," *Foreign Policy Research Institute*, 12 September 2002, 5. http://www.fpri.org/enotes/americawar.20020912.boot.americanwayofwar.html.

16. Summary of Lessons Learned, Prepared Testimony by Secretary of Defense Donald H. Rumsfeld and Gen. Tommy R. Franks, presented to the Senate Armed Services Committee, 9 July 2003. See also the remarks by Vice President Dick Cheney, "A New American Way of War," to the Heritage Foundation, 1 May 2003, which ascribes many of the same characteristics to a new style of American warfare.

17. Adm. (Ret.) Arthur K. Cebrowski, Director of OFT, in fact, recently used terms—such as "lock out" and "self-synchronization"—drawn from complexity theory along with Wardenesque terms like "precision effects" to describe several of the characteristics of OFT's version of the new American way of war. Arthur Cebrowski, Speech to the Heritage Foundation, delivered 13 May 2003, reprinted in *Transformation Trends*, 27 May 2003. For Warden's views on airpower, see John A. Warden III, *The Air Campaign: Planning for Combat* (Washington, DC: NDU, 1988); David R. Mets, *The Air Campaign: John Warden and the Classical Airpower Theorists* (Maxwell AFB, AL: Air University Press, 1988); Daniel Gouré and Christopher M. Szara, eds., *Air and Space Power in the New Millennium* (Washington, DC: CSIS, 1997); Phillip Meilinger, ed., *The Paths of Heaven: The Evolution of Airpower Theory* (Maxwell AFB, AL: Air University Press, 1997).

18. Eliot A. Cohen, "The Mystique of U.S. Air Power," *Foreign Affairs* 73, no. 1 (Jan/Feb 1994): 109-124.

19. Richard P. Hallion, *Storm Over Iraq: Air Power and the Gulf War* (Washington, DC: Smithsonian Press, 1992); and Richard P. Hallion, "Airpower and the Changing Nature of Warfare," *Joint Force Quarterly* (Autumn/Winter 1997-98): 39-46; Daniel T. Kuehl, "Thunder and Storm: Strategic Air Operations in the Gulf War," in *The Eagle in the Desert: Looking Back on U.S. Involvement in the Persian Gulf War*, eds. William Head and Earl H. Tilford, Jr. (Westport, CT: Praeger, 1996); John F. Jones, "Giulio Douhet Vindicated: Desert Storm 1991," *Naval War College Review* 45 (Autumn 1992): 97-101; Phillip S. Meilinger, "Giulio Douhet and Modern War," *Comparative Strategy* 12 (July-September 1993): 321-38.

20. The Powell doctrine emerged in 1991-92, as a modification of the Weinberger doctrine developed by Defense Secretary Casper Weinberger in 1984. Briefly stated, it holds that wars should be fought only for vital national interests and must have clear political objectives and popular support. It further emphasizes that the military should be allowed to use decisive force and that the political leadership must have a sound exit strategy for bringing the troops home. The Weinberger doctrine consisted of six points: (1) commitment of U.S. forces to combat should only be done to protect vital interests; (2) the U.S. should enter such conflicts with the clear intention of winning; (3) commitment of U.S. forces to combat overseas demands clearly defined military and political objectives; (4) the commitment of U.S. forces must be continu-

ally reassessed and adjusted based on the changing conditions of the conflict; (5) commitment of U.S. forces is contingent on the support of the American public; and (6) commitment of U.S. forces to combat should occur only as a last resort. Casper Weinberger, Speech delivered at the National Press Club, on 28 November 1984, reprinted in *Defense* (January 1985): 1-11. Powell discusses the timing and rationale behind his doctrine in Colin Powell with Joseph E. Persico, *My American Journey: An Autobiography* (New York: Random House, 1995), 20-21.

21. Eliot A. Cohen, "Kosovo and the New American Way of War," in *War Over Kosovo: Politics and Strategy in a Global Age*, eds. Andrew J. Bacevich and Eliot A. Cohen (New York: Columbia University Press, 2001), 38-62. Studies by industry think tanks also reflect similar views with regard to trends in coalition partnering and precision-standoff capabilities. See Christopher J. Bowie, Robert Haffa Jr., and Robert E. Mullins, *Future War: What Trends in America's Post-Cold War Military Conflicts Tell Us about Early 21st Century Warfare* (Washington, DC: Northrup Grumman Analysis Center, 2003).

22. Stephen Biddle, "The New Way of War?" *Foreign Affairs* 81, no. 3 (May/June 2002): 138-144. Official views within the military also highlighted the importance of ground troops. See The Kosovo After Action Reviews of the Secretary of Defense, the Chairman of the joint Chiefs of Staff, and "A View from the Top," brief by Adm. James O. Ellis, Commander, U.S. Naval Forces, Europe; Commander, Allied Forces Southern Europe; and Commander, Joint Task Force NOBLE ANVIL. In the same regard, Adm. Bill Owens, *Lifting the Fog of War* (New York: Farrar, Straus, & Giroux, 2000), 181-83, stated that expectations that precision bombing alone could bring about the defeat of Milosevic were "*absolutely wrong,*" resulting in a 78-day campaign that severely tested the NATO alliance.

23. Robert A. Pape, "The True Worth of Air Power," *Foreign Affairs* 83, no. 2 (March/April 2004): 116-130; Frederick W. Kagan, "War and Aftermath," *Policy Review* 120 (August-September 2003): 3-27; Stephen Biddle, "Afghanistan and the Future of Warfare," *Foreign Affairs* 82, no. 2 (March/April 2003): 31-46; and Biddle's statement before the House Armed Services Committee, "Operation Iraqi Freedom: Outside Perspectives," dated 21 October 2003.

24. The advantages and disadvantages of the Bush doctrine are evaluated in Larry Korb and Michael Kraig, "Winning the Peace in the 21st Century," A Task Force Report of the Strategies for US National Security Program, The Stanley Foundation, October 2003. See also Christopher S. Owens, "Unlikely Partners: Preemption and the American Way of War," in *Essays 2003*, Washington, DC: National Defense University, 2003, 1-16.

25. Arthur K. Cebrowski and Thomas P.M. Barnett, "The American Way of War," *Transformation Trends*, 13 January 2003, 3.

26. Anthony Zinni, "How Do We Overhaul the Nation's Defense to Win the Next War?" Special transcript of a presentation delivered at the U.S. Naval Institute, 4 September 2003.

27. Cebrowski and Barnett, "American Way of War," 3.

28. Colin Gray, *Defining and Achieving Decisive Victory* (Carlisle Barracks, PA: U.S. Army War College, Strategic Studies Institute, 2002), 2. This is one of several works to refer to the period of about 1955-1966 as the golden decade of American strategic thinking. See also Weigley, *American Way of War*, 474-75.

29. Harry G. Summers, Jr., *On Strategy: A Critical Analysis of the Vietnam War* (Novato, CA: Presidio, 1995), 1.

30. Robert E. Osgood, *Limited War: The Challenge to American Strategy* (Chicago, IL: University of Chicago Press, 1957), 22. See also Robert E. Osgood, *Limited War Revisited* (Boulder, CO: Westview Press, 1979).

31. This definition is borrowed from James Burk, chap. 2, titled, "Expertise, Jurisdiction, and Legitimacy of the Military Profession," in the present volume, which in turn draws from, but improves upon, Andrew Abbott's "constructionist" definition which holds that a profession's identity and status are the outcomes of social competition over control of abstract knowledge as that knowledge applies to a certain field of endeavor.

32. Many social scientists consider such knowledge to represent the hallmark of a profession. The doctrine developed by the Army constitutes the body of knowledge—the expertise—that underpins its claim to professional status. The client (in this case society) validates the knowledge and expertise of a profession (in this case the Army) and entrusts it to practice. This trust, in turn, permits the profession to carry out the services that it claims it has the special knowledge to perform. See, for example, Don M. Snider and Gayle L. Watkins, "Introduction," in *The Future of the Army Profession*, project directors Don M. Snider and Gayle L. Watkins, ed. Lloyd J. Matthews (Boston, MA: McGraw-Hill, 2002), 3-18.

33. Abbott, *System of Professions*, 2-4; and Andrew Abbott, "The Army and the Theory of Professions," in *Future of the Army Profession*, 523-36.

34. One can make the case that the Army's abstract knowledge also resides, at least in part, in its concepts and theories that have official sanction and which reflect how the Army envisions the conduct of war in the future. However, limitations of space preclude examining the Army's many theories and concept papers. In general, comments concerning FM 3-0 also apply to the Army's concepts. For example, the focus for the Army's Future Force—consisting of Units of Action (UA) and Units of Engagement (UE)—is clearly tactical in nature. The Future Force is designed to conduct operations in the following areas: operational maneuver from strategic distances, entry and shaping operations, and decisive operations. All of these missions essentially focus on winning battles. Army Concept Branch, Concept Development Division, Concepts Development & Experimentation Directorate, "Army Concepts Summaries," Ft. Monroe, VA, TRADOC Futures Center, 1 March 2004, 2-3.

35. FM 3-0, vii.

36. Capstones and keystones are of course different things, serving different purposes. A capstone is the top stone or "crown" of a wall or spire; a keystone is the final stone in the top of an arch which, if removed, causes the arch to collapse. For the Joint team and the Army, a document like FM 3-0 can serve as a capstone for one level of doctrine (e.g., operational art) and a keystone for documents like FM 1-0, *The Army*, that address a higher level of doctrine. Unfortunately, the use of these metaphors tends to cause confusion. For example, the foreword to FM 3-0 states that the manual is the Army's "capstone document for operations," while the purpose statement indicates that FM 3-0 is the Army's "keystone doctrine for full spectrum operations." If the U.S. military continues to use these metaphors, it will need to be more consistent in their application.

37. FM 3-0, vii.

38. The milestones for the revision of JP 3-0 are: First Draft, 31 August 2004; Second Draft, 14 February 2005; Final Coordination, 15 July 2005; Approval, 15 December 2005. Program Directive, dated 25 March 2004, Subject: Revision of JP 3-0.

39. Executive Summary of Joint Program Directive Working Group, dated 27 March 2004.

40. The 1993 edition rolled all MOOTW into one chapter; consequently, they appeared as an afterthought. FM 3-0, *Operations* (Washington: DC: Department of the Army, 1993), chap. 13.

41. The 1993 version of FM 3-0 does not define war either, but distinguishes between limited war and general war, 2-3.

42. FM 3-0, 1-10.

43. FM 3-0, 1-10.

44. Antulio J. Echevarria II, "Clausewitz's Center of Gravity: It's *Not* What We Thought," *Naval War College Review* 56, no. 1 (Winter 2003): 71-78, discusses the problems with the center of gravity concept.

45. FM 3-0 *Operations*, 5-7; see also Joint Pub 3-0, *Doctrine for Joint Operations* (Washington, DC: Department of Defense, 1 February 1995), GL-4.

46. Ibid., 2-5.

47. Ibid., 2-2, 2-3.

48. Ibid., 1-11.

49. Joint Pub 1-0, *Joint Warfare of the Armed Forces of the United States* (Washington, DC: Department of Defense, 14 November 2000).

50. JP 1-0, v.

51. See, e.g., James A. Blackwell's chapter titled "Professionalism and Army Doctrine: A Losing Battle?" in the present volume. His preoccupation is not with Army doctrine's effectiveness in linking battles to wars or tactics to strategy, but rather with the possible loss of legitimacy for the Army's core jurisdictions from lack of a general theory of war that validates such legitimacy.

52. This framework is also absent from doctrinal documents that lay out principles for planning. See Joint Publication 5-0, *Doctrine for Planning Joint Operations* (Washington, DC: Department of Defense, 13 April 1995).

53. Richard H. Kohn, "The Erosion of Civilian Control of the Military in the United States Today," *Naval War College Review* 45, no. 3 (Summer 2002): 9-60. See also Eliot A. Cohen, "Kosovo and the New American Way of War," in *War Over Kosovo: Politics and Strategy in a Global Age*, eds. Andrew J. Bacevich and Eliot A. Cohen (New York: Columbia University, 2001), 38-62; and Eliot A. Cohen, "The Unequal Dialogue: The Theory and Reality of Civil-Military Relations and the Use of Force," in *Soldiers and Civilians: The Civil-Military Gap and American National Security*, eds. Peter D. Feaver and Richard H. Kohn (Cambridge, MA: MIT Press, 2001), 429-58.

54. Peter D. Feaver, "The Civil-Military Problematique: Huntington, Janowitz, and the Question of Civilian Control," *Armed Forces & Society* 23 (1996), 154.

55. This argument was advanced originally by Samuel Huntington, *Soldier and the State*; see Feaver's critique in "Civil-Military Problematique," 153-55.

56. Abbott, *System of Professions*, 69-79.

V

The Army Profession
and the Army Ethos

B y page count, this is the smallest Part of the book, perhaps suggesting that the
profession's moral and ethical expert knowledge is of lesser importance than
the other fields of expert knowledge. Little could possibly be further from the
truth! Professions stand or fall based on the trust they engender and maintain with
their client. Most unfortunately, because of the soiled legacy of soldier behavior at
Abu Ghraib and other episodes of detainee abuse documented thus far in the global
war on terror, the Army profession will be years recovering the trust lost with large
segments of American society. Thus Part V, though brief, continues and amplifies the
very cogent themes already developed in Part I (The Study of Military Professions)
and Part II (Officership and the Army Profession). Part V should be studied,
reflected upon, and taught as an extension of, and in conjunction with, those earlier
Parts. It is simply impossible to separate the profession's ethos, i.e., its content and
necessary adaptation, from the institution and officer corps responsible for its perpetuation and dissemination throughout the profession, especially as manifested on
the battlefield.

The Army's moral and ethical knowledge and its application in practice are the
subject of intense discussion, particularly among Army leaders at all levels. The traditional Huntingtonian view of military professions, still the dominant view within the
Army, focuses sharply on the institution's ethos and the responsibility of soldiers to
adapt it and to police it. Lt. Col. John Mattox here tackles this very subject, presenting in Chapter 17 a straightforward derivation of the moral obligations of Army officers. In Chapter 19, Col. Richard Hooker investigates the effects on the Army ethic if
transformation entails changing the Army from one devoted to close land combat to
one that views war as essentially a targeting process at stand-off ranges. In between,
Lt. Col. Tony Pfaff presents one of the most insightful analyses available on the currently unresolved ethical tensions existing for Army soldiers and their leaders in the

war on terror (Chapter 18). That is the tension created by the simultaneous presence of both combatants and criminals among the innocents on the battlefield. For each category there exist, under the laws of land warfare, different rules for the use of force. Pfaff argues cogently that Army transformation, to be at all coherent and complete, must address the needed adaptation of ethics and legal rules to the complex terrorist-ridden battlefields of the future. Too often, he notes, the Army's use of force in such situations turns out to be politically self-defeating; thus the adaptation of such ethics is imperative.

The theme which emerges clearly from these chapters is the critical role the Army's professional ethic plays at all levels in the current war, where many on the opposing side adhere to no moral strictures at all. How can the Army profession continue effectively to inculcate a moral ethic in its soldiers, one that controls their behavior in the face of the savagery of today's combat? The authors in this Part propose a return to first principles; the nature of the profession is such that only moral soldiers can discharge their professional duties, and the Army's strategic leaders are morally obligated to the client to maintain a profession of both competence and character. America's soldiers must have, and indeed deserve, moral leaders. Leaders and commanders lacking in character are not fit for command. But how do we succeed in developing moral soldiers and moral leaders? Morality cannot be taught via rote rules, clever acronyms, long laundry lists of ideal traits, or other such bureaucratic approaches. Thus the research clearly shows that an essential component of the Army's transformation must be the renewal of moral development for Army professionals at all levels, including reestablishment of the absolutely essential culture of candor and truth-telling. Such a culture will at last conform Army management systems as well as individual behavior to the profession's essential character.

17 The Moral Foundations of Army Officership[1]

John Mark Mattox

Introduction

Ever since the end of the Cold War, the U.S. Army has found itself in a period of profound transition. For all the enormous challenges the Cold War presented, it was, in its own peculiar way, a time of remarkable stability: The United States knew which nations it considered to be adversaries, and it knew which nations viewed the United States as an adversary. Moreover, its adversaries were nations.

With the demise of the Warsaw Pact, all of that changed, and an Army equipped to defeat the world's other superpower found itself "all dressed up with no place to go." While the success of the Persian Gulf War postponed the necessity to decide immediately the new shape that the Army of the future should take, the reprieve thus attained was brief indeed. As the euphoria of victory passed, the question of how to transform the Cold War Army into something yet unspecified was as unavoidable as the problem of how to transform it was intractable. Predictably, the process proceeded in a somewhat willy-nilly fashion.

A recent study by respected historians Donald and Frederick Kagan summarized the effects of United States defense policy in the 1990s as follows: "Beginning in 1994, reports began to surface that the readiness of the armed forces to fight a war on short notice was eroding—training could not be paid for, equipment was breaking down, overworked people were burning out and leaving the services. The House and Senate armed forces committees began taking testimony and uncovered many problems. By 1998 it was widely recognized that the readiness of the armed forces had eroded seriously."[2] In geopolitical terms, these historians concluded that "the international situation has already begun to slip from our control. The [1991 Gulf War] coalition has shattered; NATO and the United States risk drifting apart. Challengers to the status quo proliferate, along with weapons of mass destruction and the means to deliver them."[3] Moreover, they concluded that the remedial actions were far from adequate:

> The military deficit is probably already too great for any 'reasonable' politician to contemplate, and it will only get worse. Not only have readiness and 'quality of life' issues (which affect recruiting and retention of qualified people) suffered badly, but the experiences of even the past few years show that the armed forces are too small. Worse than that, since at least 1995, the Department of Defense has been forced to reprogram money earmarked for modernization toward readiness and

current operations. The systems that America will need to fight the major war of 2010 or 2020 are not now in place and are being developed too slowly or not at all. America is not ready now to face a major challenge, and current plans, even in light of current proposals to increase the defense budget, will not make it ready to face a major challenger in the future.[4]

The civilian masters of armies throughout the Western world—not alone the United States—seem to have found themselves largely at a loss as to what to do with their sizable standing armies, and ambivalence on this question has served to reveal a latent ambivalence on related questions. For example, they have wondered what their armies' proper jurisdiction should be, what place their armies should occupy in their societies, and what kind of moral standards should be expected of the members of those armies. Evidence of this general air of uncertainty typically has manifested itself in three ways:

1. Drastic defense budget reductions based on the assumption that armies of Cold War proportions are no longer needed;
2. Assignment to those armies of missions well outside the scope of the labor traditionally reserved for armies alone; and
3. Formulation of foreign policies that seek full economic engagement with the world—an engagement totally dependent on international tranquillity—without accounting adequately for the self-serving agendas of power-hungry despots ready to expand their influence as soon as they realize that they will be unopposed militarily.

Some preliminary responses to these manifestations have taken shape as a result of the terrorist attacks against the United States on 11 September 2001. A "new kind of war" appears destined to occupy the attention of the United States and its allies for the foreseeable future.[5] As new threats are identified, the general strategy that underpins the global war on terrorism will continue to evolve in response to the threats. Indeed, strategies may be required to change much faster in the future than they have in the past, and that means that tactics may be required to change, in comparison to earlier eras, at lightning speed.

However, while it is true that questions of tactics and even of strategy come and go, there are larger concerns that rightly demand the ongoing attention of reflective U.S. Army officers. These include concerns for the long-term welfare of the nation and its Army, both on and off the battlefield. Such reflection is healthy and productive for leaders committed to the proposition that the institution entrusted to their care by the nation must survive the test of time. Moreover, the act of questioning what the Army's role should be and how it should set out to accomplish the tasks that lie ahead is certain to produce, as it already measurably has, a desire on the part of its leadership to transform the Army as necessary to ensure that it is relevant to the times. As the 1999 Fletcher Conference observed, "The Army has proclaimed that 'Everything is on the Table' as it pursues transformation."[6] Indeed, *everything should* be on the table if the Army is to gain an honest assessment of its current status and make the changes necessary to maintain its "nonnegotiable contract with the American people to fight and win our Nation's wars"[7] in a rapidly changing world.

However, the fact that the Army has placed everything on the table as it undergoes its transformation does not mean, and cannot mean, that everything necessarily must change. Reflective Army leaders certainly realize this as they confront questions of the kind that the leaders of any enduring profession must answer:

- What does it mean to belong to a profession? That is to say, what obligations does membership in the profession entail?
- Are there any "fixed points," i.e., professional commitments that never change, or does everything that it means to be a member of the profession hinge ultimately on factors external to the institution (in the case of armies, for example, the international situation or the perceived threat, or perhaps on less glamorous notions such as supply and demand, budget cycles, and the like)?
- What enduring moral obligations are entailed by membership in the profession? In the case of the U.S. Army, the question becomes, "What is the nature of the moral bond of obligation—if, indeed, such a bond actually exists or should exist—between the U.S. Army officer corps and the nation it serves and the soldiers it leads?"

This chapter will argue that, no matter how extensively the Army must change, adapt, or transform in order to be prepared to meet the uncertain challenges of the future, the answers to the moral-philosophical dimension of these questions *must not* change. Furthermore, the Army officer corps must feel safe in the assurance that the answers *will not* change.[8] Not only must the answers to these questions remain unchanging in the face of the institution's grand transformation, but the answers given to these questions all must point to the following conclusion: *By the nature of the profession of arms, only officers of firm moral character can discharge adequately their professional obligations to the nation and to the subordinates they are called to lead.*

While it is gratifying that some (hopefully most) Army officers may find this claim to be self-evident and thus not one requiring a rigorously argued defense, it is at the same time true that potent cultural forces are at work that could have the effect of forcing a radical reinterpretation of the nature of the officer corps' bond of moral obligation. With this in mind, let us examine the philosophical grounds for moral obligation within the officer corps.

The Grounds of Moral Obligation

The officer corps' moral bond of obligation to the nation and to the Army's soldiers ultimately derives from two sources: (1) the essential and distinguishing characteristics of the profession of arms, and (2) the obligations freely incurred through the oath of office by which officers bind themselves to the Constitution. These will be considered in turn.

The Place of the Profession of Arms among the Professions

A well-established corpus of literature exists on the subject of what constitutes a profession and which human labors properly can be called professions.[9] In this context, the question periodically arises as to whether, properly speaking, the "profession of arms" may, in fact, be considered a profession. However, in order to answer that question, there first must be some agreement as to the nature of professions in general. For the purposes of this chapter, it is not necessary to establish the status of every human endeavor that aspires to be labeled a profession. It merely is necessary to demonstrate that the profession of arms falls completely within that set of human endeavors that may be labeled "the set of all professions" (see Figure 17-1). Given the premise that any human endeavor that falls completely within **B**, the set of all professions, is itself a profession, then it follows that any human endeavor that falls completely within a subset of **B** is likewise a profession. In this case, the subset of **B**

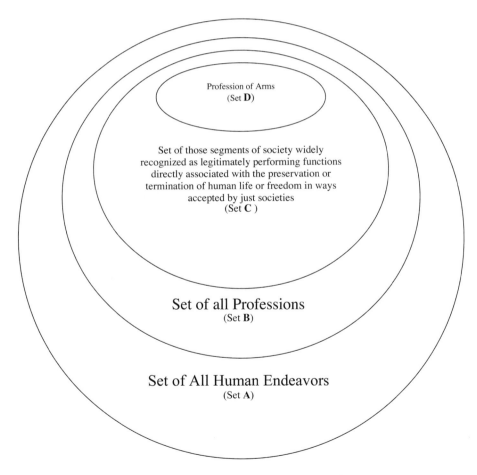

Figure 17-1. *Sets Enclosing the Profession of Arms.*

at issue is **C**, the set of those segments of society that are recognized widely (if not universally) as legitimately performing functions directly associated with the preservation or termination of human life or freedom in ways accepted by just societies. The qualifying phrase "in ways accepted by just societies" must be added to exclude organizations like the Mafia that engage in the termination of human life but do so illicitly. (For example, the Mafia might claim that, within the context of Mafia subculture, the terminating of human life is legal and otherwise socially acceptable. To this we may reply, without any harm to the argument, that the killing of Jews may have been legal and otherwise socially acceptable in the context of Nazi culture, but that any reasonable, morally sensitive person might be expected to conclude that the Mafia, the Nazi Party, and other organizations like them can be excluded from **C** because of their inherently evil nature.)

This argument embraces the premise that all members of **C** are themselves professions. In this connection, it is worth noting that at least some of the confusion over what counts as a profession exists for semantic reasons rather than logical ones. This is so because of the unfortunate practice in popular culture to elevate the social status of almost any human endeavor by labeling it "professional." Thus, one commonly hears of "professional" hair stylists, "professional" air conditioner installers, and even "professional" golfers and bodybuilders, by which is meant that these pursuits are undertaken on a more or less full-time basis as a source of income.

The confusion could be avoided altogether by applying to these pursuits the traditional vocational titles of "apprentice," "journeyman," and "master" that have been used by tradesmen over the centuries. For example, one can readily imagine an apprentice hair stylist, a journeyman plumber, or even a master golfer or bodybuilder. However, to apply in common, nontechnical discourse the term "profession" to a pursuit that has little or nothing to do with the central questions of human existence does a double disservice. First, it artificially elevates the status of some pursuits whose existence is not truly fundamental to a well-ordered society. (Many societies have functioned without hair stylists, plumbers, and golfers, but few if any have functioned without some form of medical care, legal order, military protection, etc.). Second, it obscures the crucial point that some professions exist in the first place because society has recognized them as essential for the promotion of the public good.

Accordingly, within **C** one finds, among others, the medical profession and the legal profession because both are recognized as having the responsibility to adjudicate issues involving the preservation or termination of life or freedom. However, since **D**, the "profession" of arms, also has as its principal function the preservation or termination of human life or freedom in ways accepted by just societies, one may conclude that **D** is a subset of **C** and therefore also a subset of **B**. Accordingly, the human endeavor generally denominated the "profession of arms" is, in fact, a profession.

Notice that the logical claim is not that all professions (i.e., the members of **B**) are members of **C**, nor is it necessary for them to be. In fact, it probably is not the case that all entities that properly can be called "professions" have as their central function the preservation or termination of human life or freedom. There may be many human endeavors that do not have the central identifying characteristic of **C** but that may be called professions on other grounds. However, it seems reasonable that those segments of society that generally are regarded as having a legitimate claim over matters of life and death, of bondage and freedom, appropriately may be called professions. Accordingly, this argument does not purport to establish the identity of all members of **B**, but merely to establish that among its members one necessarily finds **D**, the profession of arms.

In a way that is particularly important in light of the aims of the present chapter, it should be noted that regardless of what other sets **D** may intersect or be a subset of, **D** definitely is a member of **C**. This is significant because, as even minimal reflection will reveal, the professions that belong to **C** have moral obligations, i.e., obligations derived from the fact that the principal functions of these professions affect the happiness, well-being, flourishing, and, potentially, the life or death of human beings. Indeed, nothing could be more central to the moral enterprise than those matters most directly affecting human existence. Hence, by virtue of its membership in **C**, it must be concluded that **D** is not only a bona fide profession, but also a profession with moral obligations. Thus can be established the claim that Army officers have moral obligations that derive, in part at least, from the fact that they are members of a profession entrusted by society with making decisions that concern the preservation or termination of human life. This is not to say that the profession of arms has only moral obligations, nor is it logically necessary to insist that such is the case. It merely is necessary to establish that, among the professional obligations that Army officers have, some of those obligations are properly denominated moral ones.

The Place of the Profession of Arms in Society

Since ancient times, the Western intellectual tradition has held that the highest quality of human life could best be realized within the context of the state—the highest form of society. This view was common among the greatest philosophers of ancient Greece and Rome. For example, Cicero regarded the preservation of the state as essential to the moral and physical well-being of the human race. Should this highest form of society cease to exist, man simply would become unable to flourish to the degree otherwise possible, or perhaps not at all. Hence, by Cicero's account, the death of any man is less to be lamented than the extinction of the state.[10] In Augustine's paraphrase of Cicero, "Death often rescues individual men from pain, instead of being a disaster to them; but the death of a whole community is always a disaster."[11] Thus, in order to ensure the preservation of this highest form of society, it would seem that, as long as the present bellicose state of human affairs remains, armies will be a sine qua non for any stable state. Similarly, Plato, writing in the *Republic*, pointedly argues that even the ideal state must be prepared to secure itself by having "a special class of guardians"[12] exclusively charged with conducting the "business of fighting"[13] (an enterprise which, one might note with interest, he regards as both an "art and a profession"[14]).

Even Augustine, who takes a radically different view of the state than that found in Plato or Cicero, argues that armies are understandable, if not essential, features of the best of states. The "earthly city," as he refers to human society, never can become an ideal state; that eventuality is reserved for the "city of God" that cannot have its complete realization among fallible human beings. Nevertheless, the earthly city properly has an army to preserve order within, to defend it from without, and by Augustine's account, even to serve as an instrument of divine justice. If nothing else, the army properly exists to enable the righteous citizens of the earthly city to cope with their imperfect circumstances until such time as they can partake of perfect justice in the city of God. Whether or not one embraces Augustine's transcendental view (a view which underwrote much of the social and political thought in the West for over a thousand years between Augustine and the Peace of Westphalia), it is nonetheless interesting that even Augustine's worldview includes a privileged place for the profession of arms.

It may be conceded that one of the important perspectival differences between the ancient and modern world concerns the primacy of the state versus the primacy of the individual: Nevertheless, it is also true that prominent thinkers from the modern era have maintained recognition of the state as an indispensable social institution. No place is this idea plainer than in the writings of the English philosopher Thomas Hobbes (d. 1679). For Hobbes, all human beings live in constant fear of death because of the unremitting forces of the "state of nature," where all humans find themselves as combatants in "the war of all against all": "During the time when men live without a common Power to keep them all in awe they are in that condition called Warre; and such a warre, as is of every man against every other man."[15] According to Hobbes, human beings find refuge from this chaotic world only as they bind together in societies in which they submit their agency to the will of a sovereign (be that one person, such as a monarch, or an assembly of persons, such as in a republic). In exchange for the promise to obey the sovereign, the sovereign "guarantees" (to the extent that it is humanly possible) the security of the members of society by protecting them from the encroaching forces of the state of nature. The sovereign accomplishes this by raising an army. Without such a mechanism to guarantee the security of the state, life is bound to become, in the famous words of Hobbes, "solitary, poore, nasty, brutish, and short."[16]

Armies and Moral Obligation

If the Hobbesean argument is extrapolated one step further, a particularly striking conclusion arises: Since, according to Hobbes, ethical notions such as right and justice cannot exist except within the protected confines of the state,[17] and the state cannot maintain its existence without the guarantee of safety afforded it by an army, the army becomes for Hobbes not only the guarantor of the state's existence but also the guarantor of morality (or at least the guarantor of the potential for the existence of morality). It may, in fact, be unnecessary to insist upon this latter point. Nevertheless, it is worth noting that in social contractarian moral philosophy of the kind advocated by Hobbes, one can argue that the sovereign is able to "guarantee" the security of the state (i.e., a place where morality can exist—for it cannot exist in the chaotic Hobbesean state of nature) only because the sovereign has at his disposal an army. At the very least, and in a similar vein, we can fairly conclude that, to the extent that an army serves as the guarantor of the state's safety, and to the extent that the preservation of the state represents a moral good, the army has a moral obligation to do all within its power to ensure the preservation of the state.

One can arrive at the same conclusion by any number of other avenues. For example, the Kantian moral philosopher might argue that if, as the ancients held, an orderly society is necessary to human flourishing (in which, among other things, the society's members enjoy maximum liberty to discharge their moral obligations), there exists a moral duty to defend such a society's existence. Those officers appointed to lead the state's army, then, might properly be said to have a moral duty to ensure, to the best of their abilities, the preservation of the state from outside danger. On this premise, the state has an army both as a matter of practical necessity and as a matter of moral imperative, and the officers who lead the army are morally obligated to lead it well.

Still another school, the utilitarian moral philosophers, might argue that the interests of the greatest number of society's members are best served when a segment of society devotes itself to the defense of the whole. If this be the case, then the utilitarian could likewise conclude that the army exists as a matter of moral imperative, and that its officers are morally bound by utilitarian principle to lead it well.

In sum, whether one elects to embrace Hobbesean principles, or whether one applies Kantian, utilitarian, or similar tests, all permit the conclusion that armies—and therefore most certainly the officers who lead them—are bound by moral obligation to the societies whose defense is their responsibility.

The Constitution as a Source of Professional Moral Obligation

The idea of a "constitution" exists inseparably from the idea of a nation-state. The idea is one that far transcends the sum total of the meanings of the words contained in a written document, for indeed a constitution need not be written (as in the case of the English constitution). Broadly speaking, each state has a "constitution" in that it exhibits some kind of broadly sanctioned political structure. According to Herbert Spiro, "Aristotle used the Greek word for 'constitution' (*politeia*) in several different senses. The simplest and most neutral of these was 'the arrangement of the offices in a *polis* (state). In this purely descriptive sense of the word, every state has a constitution, no matter how badly or erratically governed it may be."[18]

In the generally accepted sense of the word today, a "constitutional" state is one in which the institution of government is bound, in some meaningful way, by *contract* with at least some of those it governs.[19] Of all the constitutions in history, none illustrates this idea of "contract" better than the Constitution of the United States. (Inasmuch as the idea of "constitution" transcends the written document itself, one can properly speak of the U.S. Constitution as including not only the governmental structure outlined therein, but also the ideals associated with representative and limited democratic government. It also includes the ideals enshrined in allied documents like the Declaration of Independence and the Bill of Rights, as well as laws made under the authority of the Constitution.)

Given the philosophical, theological, and experiential soil from which sprang the Constitution of the United States, it seems clear that the ultimate aim of the social contract it codifies is not merely law and order, or even merely the preservation of liberty, but rather the promotion of human flourishing—protecting all that is virtuous, lovely, of good report, or praiseworthy,[20] while at the same time serving as a hedge against any malicious influence subversive of that aim. In short, it has the highest of human goods as its aim[21]—an aim that it shares with the moral enterprise.

Against this background, the officer's oath of office assumes a much deeper moral significance than otherwise might be supposed. Properly understood, the oath taken by Army officers to "support and defend the Constitution of the United States against all enemies foreign and domestic" comprehends not only the governmental structure itself but also all the *ideals* of government and the way of life (including the protection of all those beliefs and practices—morality—that make human flourishing possible) implicit in them. Furthermore, the oath requires that the gravity of the obligations it entails be acknowledged "without mental reservation or purpose of evasion." It binds the officer not merely to "do his or her job," but to "well and faithfully discharge the duties of the office." It concludes with an invocation of divine assistance in fulfilling the duties of this public trust. If any doubt lingers as to whether the profession of arms is indeed a profession, let us note that no baker or butcher or hair stylist or golfer in *any* society—as important as these undertakings might be—is ever required to incur such a weighty set of obligations!

It is equally important to note that Army officers do not swear allegiance to any particular person or even to all of the people of the United States in the aggregate. Rather, they swear allegiance to the *ideals* embodied in the Constitution. Hence, the obligation of Army officers to defend the Constitution is a *direct* obligation, whereas the obligation to defend the American people is a *derivative* obligation. It derives from the common allegiance to the Constitution acknowledged both by the American people and by the officers of their Army.

The Army Officer as Moral Exemplar

Of course, the claim, however well established, that the Army has a moral obligation to defend society does not, in and of itself, imply that the Army's officers themselves have an obligation to be moral persons. However, this logical consideration does not fully account for the complexity of the issue. Logic deals only in what is possible; but when the realities of human nature are superimposed upon the demands of logic, one must be willing to include in his or her calculation the timeless truth that "as a man thinketh in his heart so is he."[22] This chapter takes as axiomatic that men and women such as Army officers, faced with tasks that require the most exacting capacity for moral reasoning, can best accomplish those tasks if they are themselves morally well-founded persons.

If the Army's officers are themselves bereft of sensitivity for what is moral—a sensitivity which, as Aristotle would tell us, is cultivated by practice and dulled through disuse—then they are no better than the amoral forces of the state of nature. As a practical matter, "if the Army merely replicates the state of nature, as in societies run by warlords, it ceases to be useful to society."[23] Beelzebub cannot cast out Beelzebub, a house divided against itself cannot stand,[24] and the state of nature cannot defend against the state of nature. Hence, the defenders against the state of nature must themselves be of a different—and one might argue better—nature: one that not only recognizes the demands of morality but also one that consistently makes choices that reflect that recognition.

As a result of Army officers' solemn Constitutional obligation to ensure the defense of principle, it is altogether reasonable to expect them to embody the moral virtues enshrined in the Army's own rendition of soldierly values: loyalty to the ideals embodied in the Constitution (as evidenced, among other things, by their strict personal obedience to the laws established under the authority of the Constitution— "the supreme law of the land"[25]), an unwavering commitment to the performance of duty, a spirit of selfless service, and both moral and physical courage.

Even if moral obligations were not inherent in the professional status of Army officers, the oath they take is sufficient to establish de facto that Army officers are themselves bound to live in accordance with a definite and clearly discernible set of moral obligations. More to the point, they are bound to embody certain specific moral virtues. This is so because, without these virtues, officers would be unable to fulfil their derivative obligations to the American people. If officers fail to defend the Constitution through unwillingness to perform their duty without regard for the personal risks involved, or through unwillingness to face those risks courageously, selflessly, or even sacrificially, then the American people could not be guaranteed that Army officers will do all in their power to defend the people's safety and way of life.

Hence, if soldiers—and thus all the more the officers who lead them—historically occupy a position of unique and recognized status in society (i.e., as instruments appointed by the state to preserve or terminate human life), it seems altogether reasonable to expect that they should be men and women of character who can be counted upon to conduct their task with due sobriety and moral awareness.

The Army Officer as a Moral Exemplar in War

The claim that Army officers have moral obligations in time of war is well established in the history of the profession of arms. For example, according to Augustine, army officers are to be persons of such honor and integrity that they can be counted upon to deal justly even with their enemies. Augustine urged Boniface, a Roman general, that "when faith is pledged, it is to be kept even with the enemy against whom the war is waged."[26]

Likewise, it has long been understood that, inasmuch as Army officers are entrusted by the state with the power to preserve or terminate lives, they must be individuals of character who are committed to the properly constrained use of that power, both in its legal and moral dimensions. Moreover, officers were not to be bound merely by the external constraint of law, but even more so by the internal constraint of conscience. Augustine urges that officers be guided during war by the desire to achieve a just and lasting peace and not by a lust for blood or a desire to harm: "Even in waging war, cherish the spirit of a peacemaker, that, by conquering those whom you attack, you may lead them back to the advantages of peace."[27] To another officer he writes, "Let necessity, therefore, and not your will, slay the enemy who fights against you."[28] Thus, he urges that the taking of lives in war ought to be minimized to the greatest extent possible. Says Augustine, "For he whose aim is to kill is not careful how he wounds, but he whose aim it is to cure is cautious with his lancet; for the one seeks to destroy what is sound, the other that which is decaying. . . . In all . . . cases, what is important to attend to but this: who were on the side of truth, and who were on the side of iniquity; who acted from a desire to injure, and who from a desire to correct what was amiss?"[29] Augustine unambiguously advocates that a spirit of mercy and forbearance be displayed toward all those who fall into the power of their enemies: "As violence is used towards him who rebels and resists, so mercy is due to the vanquished or the captive, especially in the case in which future troubling of the peace is not to be feared."[30] In the light, then, of such demanding moral imperatives as these, it follows that only men and women of the deepest compassion, clearest sense of justice, and highest integrity would be both able *and willing* in time of war to distinguish between justified and unjustified applications of violence.

The just war tradition has long acknowledged the possibility that the cause for which the state summons its military to war may be less than perfectly just (probably a morally generous description of at least one side of every war that ever has been fought). On the one hand, therefore, Army officers must be men and women of integrity who, confronted with dark realities, still are willing to do their professional duty, unpleasant though that duty may be, as honorably as they can.

Of equal importance, Army officers are not, and indeed cannot be, automatons. They are moral agents who must recognize their responsibility (1) never to issue an immoral order, and (2) to refuse an order—or even a suggestion—to undertake military operations inconsistent with the ideals they are sworn to defend. Moreover, when an informed judgment leads them to the conviction that an order is morally wrong, they also must possess the maturity to recognize, and the fortitude to accept, the personal consequences of refusal.

The Army Officer as a Moral Exemplar in Peace

That Army officers have fundamental moral obligations in time of peace as well as in war is also well established. For example, according to Plato, those chosen to defend the state "are not to be savage animals, preying on those beneath them, but even if stronger than their fellow-citizens, they will be their friendly allies, and so it is necessary to ensure that they should have the right education and mode of life. . . . [G]old and silver they should neither handle nor touch. And this will be their salvation and the salvation of the State."[31] More recently, the Joint Chiefs of Staff have declared: "Our military service is based on values—those standards that the American military experience has proven to be the bedrock of combat success. These values are common to all the Services and represent the essence of our professionalism."[32]

Unfortunately, there are those in influential positions both in and out of uniform whose conduct suggests a less-than-enthusiastic endorsement of this ideal. For example, one at the highest political level recently made the appalling claim that what a public official does in private is not a public concern and, therefore, is no one else's business.[33] Thus, there doubtless are those in contemporary society who would shy away from the claim that Army officers have an obligation, by virtue of their privileged position in society, to be moral exemplars not only in war, but also in the conduct of their private, peacetime lives. One version of the argument takes the following form:

Premise 1. In a democratic republic such as the United States, those who occupy positions of public trust are expected to act in the public interests.

Premise 2. If such a person functions successfully in that public trust (i.e., "does his or her job"), that person deserves approbation for his or her service, and no other demands can be made on him or her with respect to matters of moral character.

Premise 3. Person X, who holds a public trust, has functioned successfully (as defined above) in his or her office, but has failed miserably in terms of living a virtuous private life.

Conclusion. Therefore, person X deserves the approbation of the American people for a job well done, regardless of how deep the moral flaws evident in person X's private life may be.

The position of this chapter is that the foregoing argument is unsound by reason of the falsity of Premise 2. This and similar arguments hold a seductive appeal for many members of a liberal democratic society. Nevertheless, such arguments are as pernicious as they are seductive. This is particularly so as applied to Army officers. As has already been established, Army officers belong not only to a profession but also to that significant subset of professions whose primary function pertains to the preserving or terminating of human life (recall Fig. 17-1, Set C). The professional status conferred by society upon members of this subgroup makes of them the moral demand not only that they *know* how to perform their professional tasks but also that they *be* persons of high moral quality and that they maintain the highest moral standards at all times.

The same is true for other professions in Set C. For example, the physician cannot rightly claim moral license to use cocaine in the privacy of his or her "off-duty time" and then come to the hospital to perform brain surgery. The judge cannot rightly associate with criminals and accept bribes from them during his or her "off-duty time" and then expect to enjoy the public's confidence that he or she will deal justice to those same criminals facing racketeering charges in court. Likewise, because Army officers are charged to preserve or terminate life in the most untidy of circumstances, they cannot afford to act cavalierly, flippantly, or immorally in their private lives and then credibly claim they will act properly in the far more morally demanding exigencies of their official lives. Thus, the Army in its continuing transformation must take as its inalterable stance that, even in so-called "postmodern" liberal democracy, the Army still will hold itself firmly committed to its traditional ideals of military virtue.

Some may argue that idealized thinking of this kind is fine for ideal societies, but that since American society is itself demonstrably less than ideal, any such talk is out of place in the real world. However, those who argue in this way altogether miss the point because they fail to understand the essential meaning of "America." America is special *not* because it is the realization of any social ideal; it never has been ideal, and perhaps it never will be. America is special because it *aspires* to be ideal; it has always so aspired. America's early pioneers—the Pilgrims, the Founding Fathers, and others—conceived of themselves as men and women with a divine mission. The life they built in the New World was to constitute an ideal—"a city on a hill."[34] As poet Stephen Vincent Benét reflects,

> They were founding Zion, not the United States
> —And the seed is sown, and it grows in the deep earth,
> And from it comes what the sower never dreamed.[35]

Indeed, as long as the current state of human nature prevails, the realization of the perfect society must remain beyond our grasp. Nevertheless, societies, like individuals, that strive for the ideal are bound to come closer to realizing it than those that do not.[36] Likewise, it seems reasonable that any approach to the ideal in the present world would include a professional military led by officers who cling tenaciously to the highest moral standards.

Some may argue that an Army that espouses—or even claims to espouse—moral virtues that are "higher" than those of contemporary society at large cannot but be "out of step." They may claim that such an Army is certain to adopt a sanctimonious, "holier than thou" attitude about the way it regards the society it is sworn to defend. "How could such an Army," they would ask, "truly possess the motivation necessary to fight the wars of a society it regards as its moral inferior?" Again, however, such questioning misses the point. The Army never has itself been an ideal organization; it is composed of men and women taken from American society and possessing the same foibles as Americans not in uniform. The taking of the oath of Army officership does not automatically transform, as it were, a "sinner" into a "saint." The point is that by the nature of the demands of professional Army officership, those who would serve the state as Army officers must commit to *strive to transform themselves* into men and women who can live up to and preserve the high ideals of the profession of arms. Officers are not expected to be perfect, but they are expected to endeavor, in the words of the West Point prayer, "to live above the common level of life."[37]

The suggestion that the nation does not want to be defended by men and women who hold themselves to a higher moral standard than that found in society at large is pure nonsense. No reasonable person who considers the matter would prefer that those charged by the state with the responsibility to make decisions relative to the preservation or termination of human life be men or women of deficient moral character. On the contrary, such a reasonable person would desire that those who undertake these and similar tasks be among the most virtuous persons that the society can produce. Even the most morally depraved person suffering from a terrible disease would rather be operated upon—all other things being equal—by a medical professional of high moral character who could be counted upon to act in the patient's best interest than by a member of the profession who, although as technically qualified, was a moral derelict. Surely a helpless widow who had lost her life's saving through the actions of an unscrupulous swindler would want the lawyer she engages to be one she could depend on to act vigorously to protect her interests and to right the wrongs done to her—not to compound them for selfish purposes. Likewise, any society that entrusts its war-making powers to military professionals would want, and indeed expect, those professionals to apply judiciously and honorably the powers entrusted to them. (Else, why would a nation full of admittedly less-than-morally-ideal citizens find itself enraged and appalled by the actions of decidedly less-than-morally-ideal Army officers at My Lai?[38]) Even in times of peace, those same citizens can be expected to hold those who lead their Army to standards of moral conduct above and beyond what they might find themselves willing to tolerate in society at large. (Else, why the national outrage at the apparent turning of a blind eye to sexual abuses by those in positions of authority at Aberdeen Proving Grounds? [39])

In short, there is no warrant whatsoever for the claim that the ancient wisdom which for millennia has served as the touchstone for professional military conduct in peace and war has suddenly become irrelevant. Thus, while it may be true that professions in jurisdictional competition that do not adapt are destined to die, it is not clear that the profession of arms can meaningfully exist in a democratic society apart from its foundational moral commitments.

Professions exist because, among other reasons, they lay proper claim to special expertise within the purview of their jurisdiction. Thus, when persons outside the profession of arms foist upon the profession a perspective or a practice that is foreign to and resisted by traditional military culture, there is reason to wonder whether those persons (even if they happen to be politically astute) actually possess the wisdom necessary to justify having their way. It is fully conceded that policy-making authority rests ultimately with civilians outside (and authoritatively above) the profession. Surely, no reflective Army officer questions this arrangement that has served the republic well for over two centuries. By the same token, there is great danger in implementing in the Army politically motivated policies against the considered opinion of the uniformed professionals who have devoted their lives to rendering effective military service to the nation. It is incumbent upon the senior members of the officer corps to articulate this reality to the Army's political masters.

In sum, thus far this chapter has sought to establish the following claims with respect to Army officers and moral obligation:

- Service as an Army officer is indeed a profession—the profession of arms;
- The profession of arms has moral obligations to society;
- Constitutional government imposes both explicit and implicit obligations on those who live under the order that government is designed to ensure;
- Army officers incur a direct moral obligation by binding themselves to defend the Constitution and a derivative moral obligation to defend the people of the United States; and
- Army officers thus have a solemn obligation to serve as exemplars of morally well-founded conduct in peace and in war, in public and in private.

With these claims in mind, we now can consider, in moral terms, the kind of professional officer corps that will best enable America's Army to accomplish effectively its aim of winning the nation's wars during the new century.

A Morally Well-Founded Officer Corps

The value of any philosophical reflection for policy-makers is conditioned upon the degree to which philosophical promptings are capable of practical implementation. In the critique that follows, we shall examine three matters of particular moral import that, if not dealt with, may effectively erode the bond of moral obligation between the officer corps and the nation, and between the officer corps and the soldiers it leads. These issues merit serious consideration by thoughtful persons who have an interest in the Army's long-term well-being.

The Army as a Business

Since the end of the Cold War, much has been done to make the Army a more efficient organization (that is, efficient in the commercial sense of generating greater output at less cost). While the attainment of efficiencies is, in principle, a good thing, care must continually be taken to ensure that the Army does not, in the name of efficiency, become a less effective organization in terms of its raison d'être—its ability to fight and win the nation's wars.

Logic does not dictate any necessary relationship between efficiency and effectiveness. Take, for example, the case of a company under contract with the Army that produces replacement parts for attack helicopters. Since the raison d'être for parts manufacturing companies—like all companies in a capitalist society—is to make a profit, the goal the company probably will strive for is to produce the best helicopter parts (hence, maximum effectiveness) at the least possible cost (hence, maximum efficiency). Both concepts are important, because both help the company to achieve its ultimate aim of making money. Efficiency ensures the minimum expenditure of resources on the front end of the company's investment, while effectiveness ensures that those who buy the company's product will return to buy the product again, thus ensuring continued revenue. Again, however, this end state is merely an ideal, not a logical necessity. For example, if the company undertakes to develop, say, a new kind of replacement part for helicopters, one of four possible cases, or outcomes, will obtain:

1. The part will be cheaper to produce (more efficient) and more reliable (more effective); or
2. It will be cheaper to produce (more efficient) but less reliable (less effective); or
3. It will be more expensive to produce (less efficient) but more reliable (more effective); or
4. It will be more expensive to produce (less efficient) and less reliable (less effective).

In Case 1, the project manager overseeing the production of the part gets a promotion. In Cases 2 and 3, the project manager may manage simply to keep his or her job. In Case 4, the project manager gets fired (as the CEO simultaneously departs the firm via golden parachute)! In any event, an increase or decrease in efficiency does not necessarily imply an increase or decrease in effectiveness; the two variables are logically independent.

While this independence is fairly easy to recognize in the world of business, it may be somewhat more difficult to see when the notions of efficiency and effectiveness are applied to an organization like the Army that does not exist to generate profits. An Army that is given fewer resources with which to operate will not necessarily be more effective at its task of winning the nation's wars. On the contrary, a well-resourced Army is likely to be more effective, even if more expensive.

Since businesses have as their ultimate aim the generation of profits, businesses—even those that supply the Army—may from time to time find it prudent to sacrifice effectiveness in order to maximize efficiency. However, no such luxury accrues to the Army; the Army can never afford to sacrifice effectiveness in the name of efficiency. To do so means that the Army is willing to risk being unable to accomplish its most basic and critical function of defending the nation. Hence those who insist that greater efficiency will necessarily result in a more effective Army ignore the realities of logic. What is worse, they push the Army to a crossroads not unlike the one at which Alice finds herself in Wonderland when she encounters the Cheshire Cat. Alice asks the Cat:

> "Would you tell me, please, which way I ought to go from here?"
> "That depends a good deal on where you want to get to," said the Cat.
> "I don't much care where—" said Alice.
> "Then it doesn't matter which way you go," said the Cat.
> "—so long as I get somewhere," Alice added as an explanation.
> "Oh, you're sure to do that," said the Cat, "if you only walk long enough."[40]

So it is when the crucial distinction between efficiency and effectiveness is lost. Pursuing the path to efficiency does not necessarily ensure arrival at the aim of effectiveness; it merely ensures arrival somewhere. If the Army chooses to understand efficiency as the necessary precursor to effectiveness, or worse, if it chooses to become more efficient at the expense of becoming more effective, the whole nature of the institution's moral commitments will require revision. This is so because the business world is, by nature, mercenary in character: Businesses exist to make a profit, investors buy stock in companies to realize a return on their investment, and employees work for businesses in order to receive a salary; rarely, if ever, is the principal motivation that underwrites these actions based on ideals that have nothing to do with money. The claim here is not that there is anything wrong with the profit motives of businessmen per se, but only that such thinking is inappropriate in many military settings. In practical terms, whenever the claim is made that a policy or program will increase efficiency, the Army's leadership must ask the claimant to demonstrate how the increase in efficiency will produce a commensurate increase in the overall effectiveness of the institution or at least not decrease effectiveness. In fact, it may well be that a justification of this kind should accompany all program proposals that require strategic-level approval.

The Military-Industrial Complex

In a separate but related vein, the Army's longtime effort to realize additional efficiencies has resulted in its becoming directly dependent to an unprecedented degree on the commercial services of companies and personnel working under contract, but not necessarily under an oath of allegiance to support and defend the Constitution. Both in garrison and on the battlefield, hosts of jobs that traditionally were performed as military duties by men and women in uniform are now performed by civilian men and women working by their side. These contracted personnel may be neither armed nor trained in the use of arms nor equipped with the other special skills that result from formal military training. Consequently, President Dwight D. Eisenhower's 1961 observation seems to be more applicable now than ever: "Our military organization today bears little relation to that known by any of my predecessors in peacetime, or indeed by the fighting men of World War II or Korea."[41]

As incredible as it may seem to readers in the early years of the 21st century, prior to World War II, the United States had no armaments industry in the modern sense: "American makers of plowshares could, with time and as required, make swords as well," but no permanent industry existed merely to make arms.[42] However, the Cold War imperative not only to "raise" but to "maintain" a standing Army[43] meant that the nation could "no longer risk emergency improvisation of national defense,"[44] and instead found itself "compelled to create a permanent armaments industry of vast proportions."[45] Today, the Army relies upon the military-industrial complex to provide far more than just arms; it provides goods and services of every description, to include security services, battlefield delivery of replacement parts, front-line fuel transport, and the maintenance of an ever-expanding computer and telecommunications network.

In principle, the decision to outsource certain functions that arguably do not require the soldier's special training may make good economic sense. Moreover, it must be assumed, in all fairness, that the men and women who are hired under contract to perform these functions are competent, dedicated, faithful individuals in the same proportion as the soldiers with whom they serve side by side. Indeed, many are themselves former servicemen and women. By the same token, it likewise must be recognized by officers entrusted with the obligation to defend the nation and to care for the soldiers put in their charge that service under civilian contract is not the same thing as service under an oath of allegiance to the Constitution. Contractors are not subject to the Uniform Code of Military Justice. Moreover, their legal status under international agreements such as the Geneva Convention is recognized as increasingly problematic as their numbers increase on the battlefield. Thus, significant issues concerning their moral status within the framework of the just war tradition demand careful evaluation and thoughtful resolution.

Although logic does not dictate dire consequences from this oath-bound soldier and contract-bound civilian service dichotomy, Army officers alert to the lessons of human history should be cognizant of the "grave implications" of having loyalties ultimately divide along economic lines.[46] Try as one may to avoid the perils of divided loyalties, the time-tested dictum continues to ring loud and clear: "No man can serve two masters."[47] Neither the ultimate aims nor the immediate priorities of the commercial company that must realize a profit or fail are the same as those of the Army that must win a war at any morally justifiable cost. For the Army officer, these latter aims and priorities must ever take precedence over the former. Those who lead the Army must always be vigilant—as a matter of moral imperative—to ensure that such contractual arrangements as the Army concludes with entities not bound by oath to support the Constitution truly serve the ends for which the Army exists.

Risk Aversion

Central to the traditional Army ethic is the idea that Army officers are the defenders of the defenseless; officers use the power and the authority of their office not to defend themselves, but rather to defend from injustice those who cannot defend themselves. The profession of arms is truly to be a selfless undertaking in which risk to self is understood to be the price of the privilege of being entrusted with the life-taking and life-preserving power of the state.

This point figures into Hobbesean social contract theory. According to Hobbes, the sovereign is able to "guarantee" the security of all members of society except those in the sovereign's army, for they must be sacrificed if necessary in order to preserve all else. Hence, if Hobbes conceives morality to mean anything at all, he must conceive that the sovereign's army is morally bound to protect society, if necessary at the cost of the complete sacrifice of its members' lives and welfare.

However, one need not adopt Hobbes' concept of morality in order to conclude, with Hobbes, that to suppose that society can be defended without personal risk to those in the army is patently absurd. An army exists to assume risks on behalf of those who rightly lay claim to the army's protection. It exists as a corps of trained professionals who are better equipped to perform the task of defense than any layman would be. Risks to the army are not to be mitigated by never putting it in harm's way, for in harm's way is the place where the army, better than any other organization, is suited to be. Risks to the army are mitigated through the thorough training and proper equipping of officers and soldiers; and, indeed, they require thorough training and proper equipping. As Plato asks: "[A]re we to believe that a man who takes in hand a shield or any other instrument of war springs up on that very day a competent combatant in heavy armor or in any other form of warfare—though no other tool will make a man be an artist or an athlete by his taking it in hand, nor will it be of any service to those who have neither acquired the science of it nor sufficiently practiced themselves in its use?"[48]

Risk assessment as it is currently practiced in contingency operations merits thorough review. The standard applied in training that the death or serious injury of a soldier is unconscionable cannot be conceived as transferring directly to contingency operations. Soldiers must be trained to assume that the environment into which they are being sent is hostile and that they are there to act and not to be acted upon. If a task regarded as vital to the national interests requires Americans to go to a place with instructions to "hunker down" and neither get hurt nor allow anyone in their charge to get hurt, the task so described arguably does not belong to the Army. Indeed, the idea that the Army will go anytime, anywhere, for any reason with the expectation that no one will get hurt is a romantic notion that requires thorough reassessment.

While it is understood that the ultimate decision on how to use the Army is one reserved for the highest political level, the Army leadership must articulate this concern vigorously and repeatedly to the Army's controlling but non-professional masters so that the institution's position relative to risk assessment is well understood: If the Army's political masters wish to reduce the risk of death or injury to America's sons and daughters in uniform, the answer is not to avoid sending them to places where they legitimately should be sent or to discipline their officers because someone in the officers' charge gets wounded or killed in the line of duty. Rather, the way to reduce risk is to provide the Army with adequate funding and other resources so that its officers can adequately train and equip the soldiers placed in their care and thus prepare them to the greatest possible degree to encounter and overcome risks successfully.

Conclusion

Undoubtedly, there are certain things about the Army that require continual evaluation with an eye toward taking such course corrections as are necessary. As pertaining to those things of moral import that are subject to continual evaluation, the Army's tasks are clear:

- It must examine itself for moral shortcomings, with special attention to those shortcomings that are of its own making or sufferance. This is an urgent and continuous need because, while the Army cannot cure many of society's ills, it can act to remedy its own shortcomings, and then hold itself accountable to fulfil its moral obligations.
- It must communicate its moral commitments in ways that will appeal to the moral sensitivities of reasonable men and women in a liberal democratic society who may not embrace for themselves the same moral imperatives as does the officer corps. In this regard, even if the American people were either to expect or to require less in terms of moral commitment from its Army officer corps, the officer corps can neither expect nor allow less of itself.

Although the officer corps does and should seek to refine its understanding of its own profession and to adapt to the exigencies of the new century, it does not need a new set of moral commitments. It simply must face up squarely to the moral commitments it already has. The good news is that the task of living in a way that acknowledges the institution's deeply rooted moral commitments is accomplishable by good men and women who are willing to put service before self. Virtue can be taught; people can be transformed tomorrow into something better than they are today. Moreover, some of the most morally committed men and women to be found anywhere in the world are among the ranks of the U.S. Army—its officers, non-commissioned officers, and soldiers.

However, as the Army continues to transform—and the world's security demands suggest that it will have to do so for the foreseeable future—its professional officer corps must take great care to distinguish those things that may or must change from those that must not. Whatever transformation the Army and its officer corps undergo, that transformation must not assume that the work of the officer corps can be divorced from moral considerations—considerations grounded in history and in tradition, as well as in the nature of professions and constitutional government.

Notes

1. The views and opinions expressed in this chapter are those of the author and are not necessarily those of the Department of the Army or any other U.S. government entity.

2. Donald Kagan and Frederick W. Kagan, *While America Sleeps* (New York: St. Martin's Press, 2000), 432.

3. Ibid., 434.

4. Ibid., 433.

5. Donald H. Rumsfeld, "A New Kind of War" (speech as published by *the New York Times*, 27 September 2001); available from http://www.defenselink.mil/speeches/2001/s20010927-secdef.html; Internet; accessed 4 June 2004.

6. 1999 Fletcher Conference—Findings and Recommendations; available from http://www.army.mil/cmh-pg/documents/fletcher/fletcher-99/F99-F&R.html; Internet; accessed 20 November 2000.

7. "On the Army Transformation," Congressional Testimony delivered by Gen. Eric K. Shinseki, Chief of Staff, United States Army, before the Airland Subcommittee on Armed Services, United States Senate, Second Session, 106th Congress, 8 March 2000.

8. Naturally, it is hoped that claims of the kind advanced here would find appropriate application to the Army as a whole, the Army's sister services, and, in principle at least, the services of many of America's allies. However, in keeping with the purpose of the present anthology on Army professionalism, the arguments that follow will be tailored to apply directly to the U.S. Army Officer Corps.

9. Of particular note in the context of the larger study on the Army profession of which this chapter is a part, an important representative of this corpus of literature on professions is the work of Andrew Abbott titled *The System of Professions: An Essay on the Division of Expert Labor* (Chicago, IL: University of Chicago Press, 1988).

10. As Cicero argues, "But private citizens often escape those punishments which even the most stupid can feel—poverty, exile, imprisonment, and stripes—by taking refuge in a swift death. But in the case of a State, death itself is a punishment, though it seems to offer individuals an escape from punishment; for a State ought to be so firmly founded that it will live forever." Hence, Cicero argues, "There is some similarity, if we may compare small things with great, between the overthrow, destruction, and extinction of a State, and the decay and dissolution of the whole universe" (Marcus Tullius Cicero, *De Re Publica* 3.23, in *De Re Publica* and *De Legibus*, trans. C. W. Keyes [Cambridge, MA: Harvard University Press, 1928], 211-13).

11. Augustine, *City of God*, 22.6, trans. Henry Bettenson (London: Penguin Books, 1984), 1032.

12. Frederick Copleston, *A History of Philosophy* (New York: Bantam Doubleday Dell Publishing Group, Inc., 1985), 1:226.

13. Plato, *The Republic* 2, 374 b, in *The Collected Dialogues*, ed. Edith Hamilton and Huntington Cairns (Princeton, NJ: Princeton University Press, 1961), 620.

14. Ibid.

15. Thomas Hobbes, *Leviathan* (London: Penguin Books, 1985), 185.

16. Ibid., 186.

17. Ibid., 188.

18. *Encyclopaedia Britannica*, 15th ed., s. v. "Constitution and Constitutional Government," by Herbert John Spiro.

19. Col. Alexander P. Shine, USA Ret., personal correspondence with the author, 11 March 2001.

20. Philippians 4:8. In this era when, at times, the profane is embraced uncritically and the sacred viewed with suspicion, the reader is invited to consider that recognition of the truths embodied in this citation (and others that follow below) from sacred writ does not require the dogmatic acceptance of any particular system of religious belief.

21. Shine, 11 March 2001.

22. Proverbs 23:7.

23. Shine, 11 March 2001.

24. Luke 11:17, 18. The secular application of these words is evident from the fact that they serve as the inspiration for Abraham Lincoln's famous "House Divided" speech. See Abraham Lincoln, "A House Divided Against Itself Cannot Stand" (speech accepting the Republican nomination for the U.S. Senate from Illinois, June 1858); available from http://www.nationalcenter.org/HouseDivided.html; Internet; accessed 4 June 2004.

25. U.S. Constitution, art. 6.

26. Augustine, *Letters* 189.6, trans. J.G. Cunningham, in *The Nicene and Post-Nicene Fathers*, ed. Philip Schaff, First Series (Grand Rapids, MI: Eerdmans Publishing Company, 1956), 1:554.

27. Ibid.

28. Ibid.

29. Augustine, *Letters* 93.8, 1:385.

30. Augustine, *Letters* 189.6.

31. Copleston 1:228; Plato, *The Republic* 3.417 a 5-6.

32. Joint Publication 1, *Joint Warfare of the US Armed Forces* (Washington, DC: U. S. Department of Defense, 11 November 1991), 7.

33. William Jefferson Clinton, nationally televised address, 17 August 1998; available from http://www.cnn.com/ALLPOLITICS/1998/08/17/speech/transcript.html; Internet; accessed 13 March 2001.

34. Matthew 5:14.

35. Stephen Vincent Benét, "Pilgrims' Passage."

36. Shine, 11 March 2001.

37. Ibid.

38. For a brief summary of issues surrounding the My Lai Massacre, see "The American Experience—Vietnam Online—In the Trenches—My Lai Massacre"; available from http://www.pbs.org/wgbh/amex/vietnam/trenches/mylai.html; Internet; accessed 4 June 2004.

39. See, for example, Philip Shenon, "Army's Leadership Blamed in Report on Sexual Abuses," *New York Times*, 12 September 1997, Late Edition-Final, Section A, Page 1, Column 6.

40. Lewis Carroll, *Alice's Adventures in Wonderland* (Cambridge, MA: Candlewick Press, 1999), 103, 104.

41. Dwight D. Eisenhower, "Farewell Radio and Television Address to the American People," 17 January 1961; available from http://eisenhower.archives.gov/farewell.htm; Internet; accessed 5 June 2004.

42. Ibid.

43. The distinction here is significant. Note that the Constitution authorizes Congress to "*raise and support Armies*" with the proviso that "no Appropriation of Money to that use shall be

for a longer Term than two years." In contrast, the Constitution authorizes Congress to "provide and *maintain* a Navy" without any specified budgetary constraint. See U. S. Constitution, art 1, sec 8, italics added.

44. Eisenhower, 1961.
45. Ibid.
46. Ibid.
47. Matthew 6:24.
48. Plato, *The Republic* 2.374c, d.

18 | Military Ethics in Complex Contingencies[1]

Tony Pfaff

Prologue

Soldiers searching for insurgents knocked on an apartment door where they were told loyalists of Saddam Hussein were hiding. They yelled out in English and Arabic, "U.S. Army, open the door!" After a few minutes they heard a shot come from the apartment. In the confusion it was not clear whether it was aimed at them or not. The patrol leader, with little time to react if he was to prevent the enemy from escaping or the injury or death of his men, decided to act. He ordered one of the soldiers to break the door down and another to throw in a percussion grenade. After the dust cleared, they found they had killed a teenage girl and her father, who fired the shot because he thought criminals were at the door.[2]

It is not the purpose of this chapter to second-guess hard decisions made by military professionals in the heat of battle. However, situations like the one described above make the warrior ethic, by which soldiers make and judge such decisions, seem inadequate. Given the ethics of the military profession, arguably these soldiers did nothing wrong. Civilian deaths in war are legally and morally permissible. But what troubles some about this example is that the family in question had survived the major combat operations and was going about the business of reconstructing their lives in post-Saddam Iraq. While all death in war is tragic, *deaths of noncombatants after a war is apparently over seem especially so* because they undermine the ideal of a just and stable Iraq for which soldiers are ostensibly fighting.

Introduction

Situations like the one described above are indicative that the increasing range of missions the Army is called upon to accomplish is stressing the warrior ethic and complicating its application in real-world environments. The warrior ethic evolved in the context of a Westphalian worldview where states have rights and can redress certain violations of those rights with military force. In this context, threats to those rights were other states and the military forces they employed. But today there is a mismatch between worldview and threat that is eroding the professional military ethic. This mismatch can have moral as well as practical implications. Shortly after the United States began conducting military operations in Afghanistan, an article appeared in the *Los Angeles Times* claiming that the military's overwhelming concern for avoiding noncombatant casualties, driven largely by a desire to avoid domestic and international criticism, hampered its ability to accomplish its mission of finding Osama Bin Laden and ending the war quickly. Ironically, the article pointed out, such concerns lengthened the war and led to more noncombatant deaths.[3]

What complicates matters is that the military is confronting not only a wider range of threats, but, with the emergence of fourth-generation warfare, different kinds of threats as well. Over the last decade, the military has been called upon to keep the peace in Bosnia, confront terrorism in Afghanistan, and fight a war in Iraq as well as rebuild it. To do so it has had to conduct a range of operations in an environment where the overuse of force can undermine the domestic political will to continue the mission and its underuse can jeopardize mission accomplishment. This dilemma is most acutely felt in Operation Iraqi Freedom where Coalition forces, originally organized for war-fighting, are conducting a variety of operations, including counterinsurgency, peacekeeping, and nation-building. Further they are confronting diverse enemies with varying ideologies, goals, and capabilities that make operations in Iraq a complex hybrid category not easily described by our traditional military lexicon—including words such as war, peacekeeping, peacemaking, insurgency, or counter-terrorism. Yet domestic and international criticism over continued civilian deaths and detainee abuse threatens to undermine support for a continued U.S. presence.

Ethically speaking, these operational distinctions can be important. While the warrior ethic treats mission accomplishment as a moral imperative, it also recognizes the moral and legal limitations that shape our judgment regarding the application of military force. These constraints call on members of the military to always strive to use the least force necessary, whether fighting wars or keeping peace. However what is necessary in war can be excessive in peace, and failure to recognize this distinction can have dire consequences. *When transforming the military profession, one must address not only its structure and organization, but its ethics as well. To resolve the confusion and prevent ethically—and politically—self-defeating applications of force, we will need to extend the warrior ethic to account for the increasing range and changing nature of the threat.*

The most salient difference between the use of force in peace (the criminal model) and war (the enemy model) is the allowance each makes for civilian casualties. In the enemy model, soldiers may legally and morally act in such a way that noncombatants may be harmed or even killed. Under the criminal model, where soldiers are acting in the capacity of "police," they may not. In the former, combatants have greater permission to put noncombatants at risk, while in the latter the protection soldiers owe civilians is nearly absolute.[4] This difference, when applied in the environment of complex contingencies, provides a significant challenge for the military professional. In both models, the obligations owed noncombatants and bystanders depend on the kind of threat soldiers are facing and thus the role they are playing. However, the nature of the threat is not always clear, and this has led to confusion and, in some cases, tragedy as soldiers faithfully apply in conditions of peace an ethic better suited for war, and in conditions of war one better suited for peace.

To illustrate the point and hopefully resolve some of the moral confusion, I shall discuss first how the potential conflict between apparent restrictions of the "police" ethic and the perceived obligations of the "warrior" ethic create and produce moral confusion. This requires a discussion of the sources of the professional military ethic as well as the civic peace that members of the military forces acting as police are obligated to protect, i.e., the distinct permissions, prohibitions, and obligations that are binding when doing so. The result, as glanced at above, gives us two models of the ethics of force—"criminal" and "enemy" models—for which we can articulate distinct "police" and "warrior" ethics that define the ethical environment in which members of the military find themselves along with the requisite moral obligations and permissions. Such concerns entail an examination of the threats faced by the state and how they have evolved in an age of fourth-generation warfare. The chapter concludes by showing how this complex problem can be recognized and resolved by modifying and extending the *jus in bello* requirements of proportionality and discrimination to account for the demands of both models and resolve a good part of the underlying moral confusion.

The Professional Military Ethic

The professional military ethic, which I will treat as synonymous with the warrior ethic, derives its substance primarily from three sources: (1) functional imperatives of the profession; (2) national values, beliefs, and norms; and (3) international laws and treaties (see Figure 18-1). While these sources normally complement each other, they can also be a source of ethical tension. The functional imperative obligates military professionals "to put the mission first, refuse to accept defeat, [and] never quit."[5] This essentially utilitarian imperative, captured in the notion of "military necessity," obligates military professionals to maximize the good by undertaking missions that will most likely lead to victory and do everything in their power to accomplish them.[6] The other components, national values and beliefs as well as international law and treaties,

Figure 18-1. *Sources of the Professional Military Ethic.*

which philosopher Michael Walzer refers to collectively as the "war convention," are largely constraints based on obligation and duty without regard for consequences.[7] These constraints give substance to what it means for military professionals to execute their duties ethically. Since utilitarian ethics seeks to maximize some good—in this case victory—while duty-based ethics seeks to uphold a principle regardless of the consequences, it is not hard to see how conflicts can arise. But we cannot simply resolve the conflict by prioritizing one over the other. Values, beliefs, and law can restrict the means by which military professionals fulfill the obligations of the functional imperative; however, violating them can undermine the domestic and international political will necessary to sustain the fight. According to a 12 May 2004 Pew Research Center survey, "News of the abuse of Iraqi prisoners by American military personnel, coupled with continued unrest and violence throughout the country, have combined to send public assessments about the war to their lowest levels yet. Just 46 percent believe the war is going well, the first time that less than a majority of Americans have felt that things in Iraq were going at least "fairly well.""[8]

The Increasing Range of Threat: Criminals and Enemies

The war convention includes the range of articulated norms, customs, professional codes, legal precepts, religious and philosophical principles, and reciprocal arrangements that aim to prevent war, and, failing that, to limit the misery caused by war. These constraints require soldiers to subordinate the use of force to the aim of establishing or preserving a just and stable peace.[9] This convention is more than a set of rules; rather, it is a framework providing the range of reasons we can use to tell when wars are just, and what actions are just when fighting them.

According to the war convention, war is permissible when the political sovereignty and territorial integrity of a state are violated.[10] These define an "act of aggression" warranting a military response. [11] It is beyond the scope of this chapter to give a complete account of why this is the case, but, in brief, the state has a moral obligation to preserve civic peace,[12] which is necessary if citizens are to enjoy the rights to life and liberty specified in the Declaration of Independence and which the Constitution requires members of the U.S. military to defend. For the state to do this, it must exercise political sovereignty over the territories in which its citizens reside. *This principle is important, since it allows us to distinguish enemies from criminals: enemies are capable of violating a state's rights; criminals are capable of violating only an individual's rights.*

In the face of an enemy, military forces must restore the stable peace that existed before hostilities began, one demanding defeat of the enemy. In the face of crime, law enforcement professionals aim at maintaining a state of civic peace that allows citizens to go about their lives without fear of crime.[13] This stability does not need to be free of conflict, but it will be generally characterized by a willingness on the part of parties in conflict to resolve their difference nonviolently. Thus, at the end of a war, not only must warring states be able to coexist peacefully, but the citizens within each state must be able to do so as well. This requires just and stable political and judicial systems. In the case of Iraq, the restoration of civic peace is a necessary condition for establishing a stable peace and thus is a necessary though not sufficient condition for the war to have served a moral purpose.

Establishing political stability is dependent on the restoration of civic peace, which is the kind of peace necessary to attain and secure fundamental human goods, including security and distributive justice.[14] According to political philosopher Mortimer Adler, civic peace is possible only in the context of community. A necessary feature of a community is a government capable of administering a process by which conflicts are resolved nonviolently. For this to be possible, members of the community must cede some sovereignty to the community. This then gives us a set of conditions that must be present if we are to say a state of peace holds:

- The enemy is defeated or transformed into a threat not capable of violating political sovereignty or territorial integrity;
- Institutions necessary for law enforcement must be functioning, including police, courts, and prisons;[15] and
- These institutions must be credible, that is, people must be willing to rely on them to resolve disputes.

When these conditions hold, the criminal model will apply. When they do not, the enemy model will be more appropriate. This is because the civic peace a society enjoys is fundamentally different from the state of peace that can exist between states. Independent states, says Adler, have not ceded sovereignty, and are thus always in a state of potential war. This does not bar states from entering into arrangements in which nonviolent conflict resolution is preferable. It means simply that when a state's rights to political sovereignty and territorial integrity are violated, the state may take matters into its own hands; however, when an individual's rights to life and liberty are violated, he must rely on the state to restore them.

The following example serves to illustrate the importance of this distinction. During a joint Marine-police operation conducted during the 1992 Los Angeles riots, Marines and police both responded to a domestic disturbance. As the police were ready to forcibly enter the room where the disturbance was occurring, they yelled to the Marines, "Cover me!" The Marines promptly fired approximately 200 rounds through the door. Fortunately, no one was injured.[16]

This example is instructive because it shows that even while working together there is a different understanding between police and members of the military as to how much force is minimally *necessary*. Even though they had been shot at, the police did not feel they or others were in immediate danger. In their view, it would be better to develop the situation and ascertain whether there were nonviolent ways to resolve the issue. However, as far as the Marines were concerned, it would be morally appropriate to respond with any degree of force that eliminated the threat even if it put civilians at some risk. The different reactions were due to the way each perceived the threat, and the way each was trained to deal with it. To the police, if the threat is a criminal they must apprehend in order to minimize the disruption to the peace that crime represents. Since the use of violence represents a further disruption of the peace, police are always looking to use the *least force possible*. But Marines and soldiers are trained to defeat enemies, who must be killed if there is to be peace. They are always looking to use the *most force permissible*. In complex contingencies, however, it is not always clear what kind of threat soldiers and Marines are facing.

In Bosnia, rather than defending against threats to American territorial integrity and political sovereignty, the U.S. military prevented rival militias from violating the life and liberty of Bosnian citizens. In Afghanistan, the U.S. military opposes tribal leaders and international terrorists who hope to drive Coalition forces from the country and restore a radical fundamentalist regime to power. In Iraq, the U.S. military is not only fighting remnants of the former regime, but also multiple groups of Islamic extremists as well as Iraqi and Arab nationalists. While each of these enemy groups has a different and sometimes competing vision of Iraq's future, they do all have a common goal: drive the Coalition from Iraq and prevent a Coalition-sponsored government from asserting control.[17] Though not capable of defeating Coalition troops force-on-force, some of these groups are organized, resourced, and capable of sustained guerrilla operations, which could make a continued Coalition presence untenable or ineffective. Given their aim, it is these groups that threaten not only the sovereignty of the emerging Iraqi government, but to the extent their operations will create a permissive environment for international terrorists, they threaten the United States and other nations as well.

To make matters more complex, in both Iraq and Afghanistan many attacks do not come from political or ideological enemies, but rather from family and tribal-based groups seeking to obtain power or avenge a perceived wrong such as the death or detention of a member.[18] Other attacks come from criminal elements that oppose Coalition forces only when they interfere with their activities. Rather than being a threat to the sovereignty of the emerging government, they are a threat to individual Coalition troops and Iraqis.

This diversity of threats, coupled with the moral imperative to accomplish missions,[19] dramatically complicates ethical decision-making. In fact, a Human Rights Watch report issued in October 2003 argued that Coalition forces in many cases needed to conduct themselves more like law enforcement officials, but lacked the capability and training.[20] The truth of such an observation is not intuitively obvious, however, at least not from a soldier's point of view. Combatants are permitted to conduct operations in which noncombatants will be harmed; however, at some point it is reasonable to ask, "Do civilians have a right to expect the kind of protection U.S. citizens would receive if the same kinds of operations were conducted in the United States?"

The Changing Threat: Fourth-Generation Warfare and Complex Contingencies

For it to be permissible to harm noncombatants the acts that threaten the peace will have to be more than mere crimes, they will have to be "acts of war." This is an important point because it suggests that while the current response to some terrorists and insurgents may be justifiable, that may not always be the case. Some are more like criminals, and to pursue them as enemies risks doing more moral harm than good.

In the context of the global war on terror, the military has confronted conventional military threats, insurgencies, common criminals, and international terrorists. While alone these threats are not new, having to confront them often in the same battle-space has greatly complicated military operations. In Iraq and Afghanistan the U.S. military, after defeating organized military forces, is fighting crime, keeping peace, and confronting increasingly well organized and resourced insurgencies. Further, rather than a single insurgency with a unified goal, these insurgencies are motivated by a variety of ideologies and interests. Some represent remnants of the Ba'ath and Taliban regimes, but others are linked to the larger international Islamic terrorist threat. In some cases, insurgents represent only local interests. Additionally, the military must continue to confront terrorism worldwide to prevent future attacks on the homeland. The challenges this complex threat environment implies are immense.

America has confronted armies, insurgents, and terrorists before, but globalization has made the United States and other nations vulnerable in new ways. More powerful weapons, better global communication systems, and increased opportunities to divert non-weapon technologies to destructive ends have dramatically increased the ability of small groups to achieve their goals, regardless of their political support. The ability to leverage these developments to wage war makes the threat enemies can represent *asymmetric* to their size or power base. By waging this kind of asymmetric warfare, insurgents and terrorists can do more than simply instill fear in the civilian population. They can also directly attack and destroy the institutions that serve to administer and defend the United States, or any state for that matter. Terrorists' well-documented attempts to obtain weapons of mass destruction only underscore this point.

Further, these asymmetric means are available not only to well organized and resourced international terrorist groups. They are available locally as well. U.S. soldiers and their Coalition partners have defeated the armored divisions of the Republican Guard, but are still fired on by forces using antitank weapons and surface-to-air-missiles. Complex contingencies require soldiers to be simultaneously capable of conducting traditional peacekeeping tasks such as separating belligerents, one moment, and the next moment fighting force-on-force engagements normally associated with war-fighting. For this reason, it is difficult to describe many aspects of the global war on terrorism in current doctrinal terms such counterinsurgency, peacekeeping, nation-building, or even war.

What particularly complicates matters is the ability of anti-Coalition forces to conduct fourth-generation, or asymmetric, warfare, which joint doctrine defines as attempts to circumvent or undermine an opponent's strength while exploiting his weaknesses using methods that he either cannot or will not use.[21] This does not mean simply that smaller forces can defeat larger ones by exploiting unexpected weaknesses. It means small forces can violate the political sovereignty and territorial integrity of a state without the support of another state.[22] Thus, the ability of an opponent to wage fourth-generation warfare suggests that some threats, though they resemble those posed by criminal organizations, may be more appropriately regarded as emanating from enemies.

	War	Peace	Complex Contingencies
Threat	Enemies: threaten states' political sovereignty and territorial integrity	Criminals: threaten individuals' lives and liberty	Enemies and criminals coexist
Obligations	Defend nation while observing restrictions of war convention; may not intentionally harm noncombatant	Must maintain peace; must use the least force possible to protect life and liberty; must not harm bystanders	Must not harm bystanders, but must preserve political sovereignty and territorial integrity
Permissions	Use the most force permissible to establish peace given the war convention; may unintentionally harm noncombatants	May detain suspected criminals; may use armed force against violent criminals who represent continued threat	May harm noncombatants only to prevent violation of political sovereignty and territorial integrity

Table 18-1. *Obligations, Permissions, and Threats.*

Before 11 September 2001, when terrorists attacked critical military, financial, and governmental institutions in the United States, the power to wage war on a state rested solely in the hands of other states. Now it can also rest in the hands of a few dozen highly motivated people with cell phones and access to the Internet. *This means that far from simply terrorizing individual civilians, certain insurgent and terrorist organizations have now come to represent a new category of threat from non-state actors that is characterized by an ability and willingness to violate the political sovereignty and territorial integrity of sovereign nations in order to achieve their political ends.* Their capabilities distinguish them from mere criminals, but their methods do not. In the context of Iraq and Afghanistan, it means the enemy may not only possess the capability to prevent the restoration of sovereignty, they may also take advantage of the chaos they create to threaten the sovereignty of other nations.[23]

In view of these developments, the criminal and war models are inadequate to fully account for the moral obligations, permissions, and prohibitions that accrue to law enforcement officials and members of the military vis-à-vis innocents and noncombatants in the conduct of complex contingencies. They are inadequate, as summarized in Table 18-1, because the threats they are designed to respond to are not the kind of threats represented by the insurgents, terrorists, and criminals currently confronting the United States in the global war on terror.

Restraining the Use of Force: Noncombatant Immunity and Necessity

If the goal of military force is to establish or maintain a just peace, it must be applied in a just manner. However, as noted earlier, moral restrictions on force can impede the military's ability to fulfill its operational obligations. It is a nearly universally accepted moral principle that it is wrong to intentionally harm innocent people, but combatants must sometimes attack enemy military targets located close to where noncombatants live. So in upholding the state's obligation to protect its citizens from harm, military professionals must sometimes risk violating the prohibition against harming innocents to do so. Police too sometimes must put bystanders' lives at risk when they pursue criminals. The application of these principles is further complicated by the fact that combatants may intentionally kill enemy soldiers—most of whom are not guilty of any act of aggression.

International law simplifies some of this complexity by prohibiting combatants from intentionally killing citizens of enemy states who are not directly involved in the fighting, regardless of their innocence or guilt.[24] They are immune from harm because they are not immediate threats to the ability of military forces to prosecute the war. Because they do not represent an immediate threat, their deaths are not necessary in order to achieve the goals of the war. Thus in the context of fighting wars, the law and morality of war typically distinguish between noncombatants and combatants as opposed to the innocent and guilty or civilians and soldiers. This is because many combatants are innocent of any act of aggression and some civilians are guilty of it. This is also because some combatants, such as those who have surrendered or are wounded and not capable of fighting, no longer represent a threat and are thus immune from harm. Likewise, some civilians, e.g., munitions workers, because they are engaged in an activity that is logically inseparable from war-fighting when they are performing munitions work, are subject to harm.[25]

Since police do not typically fight wars, it may seem odd to discuss noncombatant immunity in this context; but because they also deal with threats to the peace, analogous notions apply. For police, only those civilians who have somehow demonstrated themselves to be a violent threat may be killed. And even then, police must make reasonable attempts to apprehend them first.[26] Thus, in the context of the pursuit of criminals we can make a distinction between (1) innocent civilians, who are not a violent threat and are not subject to harm, and (2) suspects, who may have committed a crime, but who must be given the opportunity to surrender first. With regard to this latter category, police may use deadly force only after they have offered the suspect a chance to surrender and then only to prevent someone suspected of a violent crime from fleeing or committing a violent crime. Typically, police do not use deadly force against nonviolent criminals.

Noncombatant Immunity and the Limits of Risk

Noncombatant immunity, as well as immunity for its law-enforcement analogue, bystanders, obligates soldiers and police to take additional risks in order to fulfill their respective functions. For the soldier, it most often means establishing peace between the society he serves and other societies; for the police officer, it most often means detaining, and under certain circumstances killing, someone who represents an immediate threat to the peace the society currently enjoys.[27] Inasmuch as this action often involves the use of deadly force, it sometimes puts bystanders at risk as well. Police functions, however, limit whom they may put at risk and the kinds of risks they may take.

This is not to say that police are prohibited from taking some risks that *might* place civilian lives in danger. For example, police are permitted to engage in high-speed chases though such pursuits can result in accidents in which innocent bystanders are killed. But police are not permitted to engage in such pursuits, or any other activity, if they *know* civilians *will* be killed or seriously injured.[28] *This means that police should seek to use the least force possible, and never in such a way that an innocent is harmed, as this would represent a breach of the peace their purpose is to serve.*

The risks soldiers may subject noncombatants to are also limited, but in a qualitatively different way. The deadly force that circumstances sometimes force soldiers to employ is justified by the fact that their role is to defend innocents against aggression, thus fulfilling in part the moral obligation states have to protect their citizens. But if the defense of innocents is a moral imperative, then the intentional taking of innocent life must be morally prohibited. Thus while soldiers have the positive duty to protect their own civilians, they also have the negative moral duty not to intentionally harm civilians of other nations.

However, to effectively protect their own civilians, soldiers must seek to minimize risk. This is not simply prudential self-interest, but is necessary if they are to sustain the manpower and equipment for operations to end the war. Generally, when engaging enemy forces, the more long-range and indirect fire soldiers can place on an objective the less resistance they experience in taking it. For example, soldiers attempting to assault an urban area can greatly reduce their risk by using artillery and close air support to reduce to rubble buildings the enemy would use for cover. In densely populated areas, however, this tactic is almost certainly going to result in deaths of civilians.

While such heavy stand-off fires reduces the risk to the combatants, they are often less discriminating and increase risk to noncombatants. However, by virtue of their soldierly moral duty, combatants obligate themselves to accept risks that noncombatants do not, regardless of the noncombatant's nationality.[29] Of course, this obligation is limited to some degree by the sometimes competing obligation to accomplish missions that are necessary for combatants to protect the citizens of their state. If there were no such limits, then the ability of combatants to accomplish their missions would be untenably undermined, as it would be possible for the enemy to use civilians as shields and render it impossible to prosecute the war in a moral fashion.[30] Lack of such a limitation would render the positive duty to defend innocent life illogical and morally self-defeating. Thus, combatants are not obligated to take so much risk that the mission will fail, nor are they obligated to take so much risk that it is certain their unit will not be able to continue the war effort. [31]

Since the amount of obligated risk is limited, it is permissible for combatants to engage in courses of action in which they may unintentionally, but knowingly, harm civilians. But this permission also has its limits. Judgments about what constitutes the kinds of risk that may lead to mission failure are notoriously difficult to make. Thus if our ethical obligations ended at balancing risk to soldiers with risk to noncombatants, the potential for abuse would fatally undermine the entire concept of noncombatant immunity since even well-meaning soldiers would be hard-pressed to come up with reasons to take the safety of noncombatants into account. Recall the logic of the soldiers in this chapter's prologue, who chose to employ a weapon (percussion grenade) that could not discriminate between combatants and noncombatants given the manner and conditions in which the soldiers employed it. This moral calculus underscores the need for professionals who have the education and experience required to maintain the profession's integrity by balancing mission accomplishment with moral and legal restrictions. So while it makes sense to limit duty-based constraints on military necessity in this manner, we also have to recognize that these constraints are in potential conflict with other moral constraints and must be interpreted in the context of particular situations.

Essential to understanding just conduct in war, or *jus in bello,* are the concepts of *proportionality* and *discrimination.* As noted above, combatants may engage the enemy knowing, though not intending, that harm to noncombatants and their property will occur. However, just because this harm is unintended, it does not follow that it is not subject to moral limits.[32] Proportionality means that the good achieved is commensurate with the harm done. Second, as our discussion of noncombatant immunity demonstrated, combatants must discriminate among targets and avoid killing noncombatants or destroying infrastructure that is necessary for the survival of civilians.[33] But though combatants should not harm noncombatants, it is a brutal reality of war that they do, no matter how careful and measured their use of force may be. Thus combatants must also discriminate among effects and not regard the inevitability of noncombatant harm a loophole to be exploited. *In the enemy model, this means that soldiers may minimize risk using the most force permissible, given the restrictions of proportionality and discrimination.*

The relationship between obligations regarding the use of force and the acceptance of risk can be displayed schematically, as in Figure 18-2. In this figure the black line illustrates the inverse force vs. risk relationship that exists for military personnel. The more force they use, roughly speaking, the less risk to themselves. The solid portion of the black line depicts the full range of permissible uses of force for the criminal model as well as the partial range of the enemy model. When so much force is used that bystanders would knowingly be harmed (marked by the white star) then increased use of force is no longer permissible under the criminal model, though it might be under the enemy model, as represented by the dashed line. When so much force is used that it violates *jus in bello* constraints of proportionality and discrimination (marked by the black stars), then increased use of force would be impermissible under either the criminal or the enemy model, as represented by the dotted line.

The white line illustrates the direct relationship between the use of force by military personnel and increased risk to noncombatants. The solid represents acceptable risk in peace and war, the dashed line acceptable risk in war, and the dotted line risk that is never acceptable. The arrows left of the intersection of the two lines (marked by the white star) indicate that in peace one should always use the least force possible. The arrows to the right of the intersection indicate that in war one is permitted to increase force only up to that point where *jus in bello* strictures come into play.

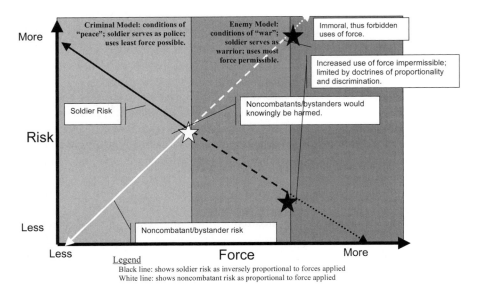

Figure 18-2. *Relationship among Obligations, Force, and Risk.*

Doctrines of Proportionality and Discrimination in Complex Environments

As noted earlier, proportionality and discrimination require combatants not only to minimize the deaths of noncombatants, but also to make positive commitments to (1) preserve noncombatant lives by not exploiting the harm combatants do; and (2) assume additional risk to minimize that harm in the first place. However, application of these provisions in complex contingencies is unclear, thus generating a great deal of discussion and confusion as soldiers attempt to apply an ethic that evolved to deal with traditional military enemies in environments where the status of the principals is problematic.

According to a Human Rights Watch Report, more than 20 civilians were killed in Baghdad between 1 May and 30 September 2003, well after major combat operations ended, under "questionable" circumstances:

> The individual cases of civilian deaths documented in this report reveal a pattern by U.S. forces of over-aggressive tactics, indiscriminate shooting in residential areas, and a quick reliance on lethal force. In some cases, U.S. forces faced a real threat, which gave them the right to respond with force. But that response was sometimes disproportionate to the threat or inadequately targeted, thereby harming civilians or putting them at risk.[34]

While some of this criticism may be justified, what the HRW report fails to take into account is that much of what it criticizes is not prohibited by the war convention. But in applying an ethic developed for war in environments other than war, members of the military risk undermining what peace they may have established as well as the moral purpose the major combat operations served. While the transition from war to peace has always been a complicated process, it is much more so for complex contingencies. Simply defeating Saddam's conventional forces did not end the fight, obviously, and the escalated participation of Islamic terrorists suggests that to lose now would jeopardize far more than restoration of the political sovereignty and territorial integrity of Iraq. Should Iraq or Afghanistan become a haven for international Islamic terrorists, then the political sovereignty and territorial integrity of the United States is ultimately at risk as well.

The Human Rights Watch report argued that the problem Coalition forces have is "attitudinal." However, it is not the case that Coalition forces are unconcerned about noncombatant deaths, for they routinely take actions to prevent them. The problem is better described as doctrinal, related to lack of clarity in the profession's expert knowledge and its practicing expertise. Proportionality and discrimination, even though they constrain military necessity, do not proscribe harm to civilians absolutely. What is needed, then, is to modify our understanding of these restraints in a way that incorporates the ethical restrictions of the criminal model and provides a flexible, yet comprehensive moral framework for the application of military force.

Application of the Doctrine of Proportionality in Complex Contingencies

On 10 July 2003, Coalition forces shot and killed a man who was allegedly brandishing a gun in front of a police station. The first shot incapacitated him, the second killed him. In a separate incident, recorded for the TV Frontline episode, "Truth, War, and Consequences," U.S. soldiers in Baghdad, while exchanging fire with gunmen in a building, are shown killing a bystander.[35] Given that the soldiers were engaged in a legitimate operation, nothing about proportionality requires that Coalition forces have acted differently.[36] Yet these actions further isolated the Iraqi populace from Coalition forces, whom they began to see as a threat. Domestically, when citizens see the police forces as a threat, breakdown of civil order is not far away, as evidenced in the 1992 LA riots mentioned earlier.

With regard to the examples above, the principle of proportionality was upheld in terms of civilian lives and property destroyed when weighed against enemy killed or captured, or operations impeded. However, what is not measured is the cost to the fragile peace the major combat operations achieved. The law and morality of war do not speak to that concern. However, if only on political and strategic grounds, if one accepts that the conditions of peace hold (even a fragile one), then the criminal model will be the most appropriate to apply. Thus once the man brandishing the gun in the first example above was incapacitated sufficiently to detain him, the appropriate response was to arrest, not kill him.

However, simply telling soldiers to behave more like police—which is appropriate in most peace-keeping situations—ignores the complex environment of the global war on terror. By hiding among civilians, insurgents can escape harm and thus continue their own operations since even with precision weapons some noncombatants would be harmed. Such security dilemmas pose problems in the context of fourth generation warfare, for if they are resolved in ways that enable the enemy to survive, they begin to bring into question our success in accomplishing the war's purpose.

Therefore, one must not fall into the trap of calculating proportionality strictly in terms of noncombatant lives lost versus enemy lives taken. To the extent that enemy activity itself represents a threat to the restoration of sovereignty, permissions associated with inflicting noncombatant casualties are going to be more liberal. In this case what fundamentally matters is how much closer any particular operation will bring us to eliminating the threat. If certain key insurgent leaders are the essential to the insurgents' ability to conduct operations, then military leaders need to consider this when determining how best to pursue them. In this kind of warfare, the number of civilian lives lost and property destroyed needs to be measured against how much harm the targeted insurgent could do if he is allowed to escape. But this does not mean that the enabling permissions will be unlimited. If the insurgent target in question is relatively inconsequential, then proportionality requires U.S. forces to forgo engaging him at the cost of noncombatant lives and property. Thus, in the environment of complex contingencies, proportionality should be adapted as follows:

> The harm to noncombatants and their property must be proportional to the desired military objective and measured against the threat to political sovereignty and territorial integrity; however, when the establishment of a stable peace is no longer at risk, the harm must be measured against the threat to individual life and liberty.

The undesirability of noncombatant deaths also suggests that military forces need to develop nonlethal means of dealing with the insurgent threat. Not only should military forces be trained in law enforcement techniques, they should also have available nonlethal weapons and passive control means in order to lower the cost to lives and property of conducting counterinsurgent operations.

Application of the Doctrine of Discrimination in Complex Contingencies

As noted earlier, it is morally self-defeating to intentionally kill noncombatants. For this reason, combatants must discriminate between enemy combatants who represent a threat and noncombatants who do not. Thus while the military may engage in courses of action in which noncombatants may be killed, they cannot intend those deaths to occur. However, in complex contingencies, not only can it be difficult to distinguish combatant from noncombatant, it is also difficult to distinguish whether harm to noncombatants will be permissible. Two levels of discrimination are thus necessary: (1) deciding between targets, and (2) determining an acceptable risk to noncombatants and bystanders. If the threat is an enemy combatant then some harm will be permissible as long as it is also proportional. If the threat is a criminal, then some *risk* of harm will be acceptable as long as it too is proportional. In the former, soldiers may foresee, but not intend, the harm. In the latter, they may foresee, but not intend, the risk.

The following example serves to illustrate the importance of this distinction. On 7 August 2003, U.S. soldiers in Baghdad fired on two cars they believed were trying to run a checkpoint. They killed the driver of the first car and the driver and three passengers in the second car. The driver of the first car was reportedly a student out visiting friends, while the driver of the second car was a father and the three passengers were his children. According to the report, streetlights were out and the checkpoint was difficult to see. Survivors claimed not to realize they were near a checkpoint before being fired upon. In the case of the second car, it is not clear there was a warning.[37]

In the examples above, the deaths of noncombatants were certainly unintended—the soldiers manning the checkpoints were simply dealing with a threatening situation in accordance with their rules of engagement. Given the nature of combat at the time, there was no way, in principle, for the soldiers to tell whether the individuals in the cars were civilians or Saddam's fedayeen. But if one accepts that conditions of peace hold, then noncombatant deaths must not only be unintended, *they may not knowingly be permitted*. Soldiers must therefore take extra precautions to ensure that risks to civilians are minimized, for example, by marking checkpoints (in this case), ensuring that warnings are heard, and training soldiers so that they are capable of employing alternate nonviolent means to stop suspected insurgents and criminals.

Thus in complex contingencies, the *jus in bello* provision of discrimination should be modified to read: combatants under the war model must discriminate between enemy combatants and noncombatants and not intend, though they may foresee, harm to the latter. When the establishment of peace is no longer at risk, *foreseen harms to noncombatants must be prohibited*. This has broad implications for training, organization, and employment of armed forces that need to be addressed before the conduct of operations commence. Failure to do so could itself represent an ethical failing. It is not morally sufficient to place soldiers in harm's way without the indoctrination they need to conduct themselves ethically.

In addition to discerning whether it is permissible to engage a particular target, soldiers must also discern whether it is permissible to risk harm to civilians when doing so. During operations in Bosnia in early 1996, U.S. troops on patrol were fired on by what turned out to be a lone, disgruntled Bosnian. Though they did not know this at the time, the soldiers chose not to return fire, which could have harmed noncombatants. Because they held their fire, neighbors apprehended the gunman and turned him over to authorities; but in the aftermath, the soldiers were both criticized and praised for the decision they made. Some argued that by failing to send a clear and decisive signal to all the factions that NATO forces would impose peace, even at a cost to civilian lives if necessary, the soldiers had sent a clear signal that it was now "open season on IFOR."[38]

In Iraq, beginning in November 2003, the United States bombed and bulldozed houses and other buildings suspected of harboring anti-Coalition forces. The purpose, according to a *Time Magazine* report, was to send a message to the local population and intimidate those who have made the area notoriously permissive to the insurgents."[39] According to a separate press article, U.S. forces dropped 500-pound bombs outside the Sunni stronghold of Tikrit as a warning to its residents not to support insurgents who had, hours earlier, shot down a Black Hawk helicopter killing six soldiers. While it succeeded in scaring residents, it "only confirmed for many that the United States is their enemy."[40]

While it is certainly permissible for soldiers to fire on a gunman shooting at them or to destroy facilities used by insurgents, even if they are not using them at the time, placing civilians in harm's way to "send messages" to intimidate the populace would violate soldiers' obligations to discriminate in terms of targets as well as harms. However, it is important to note that when insurgents use populated areas as cover for their operations, they put civilians at risk and thus bear at least some responsibility for any harm. Further, to the extent civilians consent to insurgent operations, even if they are not active participants, they too bear some responsibility for this risk. This does not diminish the responsibility members of the military to avoid doing harm to noncombatants and bystanders, much less intending to do it. However, it does beg the question as to what permissions the military has, especially if the war model applies.[41] If the insurgents are capable of conducting war, then targeting their facilities is permissible, even if it intimidates the local populace. However, if the conditions of peace hold, then such tactics will more likely threaten life and liberty and disrupt the peace rather than maintain it. In this case, such tactics should be prohibited. Under the war model, targeting the enemy and enemy facilities is permissible, regardless of whether it intimidates the population. Under the criminal model, targeting criminals and their facilities is permissible unless it intimidates the local population, which presumably has a right to the civic peace such intimidation violates.

Policy Implications: Adapting the Warrior Ethos

Several policy implications follow from the above discussion. First, military professionals, just war theorists, diplomats, and international lawyers, as well as others who rely on the various provisions of the war convention to form policy and law, need to take into account in their deliberations the nature of the threat (criminal or enemy) when determining permissions and obligations with regard to noncombatants and bystanders. Second, Army tactical and operational doctrine needs to be modified so as to acknowledge and describe the difference between criminal activity and enemy threats, and then to develop morally acceptable tactics, techniques, and procedures to handle each. Third, in complex contingencies, the language of operations orders and rules of engagement must reflect the ethical demands of the environment. This would mean finding language that specifies whether a particular operation, or parts of an operation, permit noncombatant or bystander casualties.

Fourth, the Army should experiment with developing forces that can function within the moral limits of both the enemy and criminal models. It should consider developing and educating new forces that are trained in law enforcement procedures and provide them with nonlethal weapons so that they have a wider range of options for applying the least force possible. This experiment may include reconsidering whether certain weapons and ammunition currently not permitted for soldiers' use such as CS gas and dumdum bullets should be permitted. Though they can have undesired effects, they also give soldiers a wider range of options for applying the least force possible. Last, the Army should increasingly integrate doctrinal development and training with civilian government and nongovernment organizations to broaden the range of nonviolent options available. Many current programs and exercises do include civilian organizations in a limited way to make soldiers aware of their presence on the battlefield. But that is now insufficient; these organizations can contribute operationally to conditions that reduce threats, strengthen the sense of civil peace a community feels, and offer a variety of nonmilitary means of increasing security for soldiers and civilians. Increased integration would take two forms: (1) jointly developing courses of instruction for both civilian and military leaders at professional education centers such as staff and senior service colleges; and (2) integrating civilian organizations' activities into Army doctrinal development and training center exercises. The more complete the integration, the better able the Army will be to elevate soldiers from merely having an awareness of moral concerns to having the ability and determination to incorporate them completely in the decision-making process.

Conclusion

U.S. operations over the last decade provide scores of instances in which our troops restrained the use of force in order to preserve civilian lives, even when the law and morality of war did not require it. This author does not question the commitment of the military as an institution to upholding the principle of noncombatant immunity. However, what is lacking is an updated ethical framework that accounts for how to apply the principle in the wide variety of environments members of the military find themselves—often within the scope of a single operation. Such a framework is necessary if we are to have consistency in the face of this complexity.

What also precipitates from this discussion is that some ambiguity will always exist; it will not always be clear what threat soldiers are facing. Ambiguity means it will be up to military professionals to rely on their experience and judgment to discern which approach, criminal or enemy, is appropriate to apply. The critical need is thus underscored for a professional development approach that does justice to the demands of both models. Further, while the discussion of proportionality and discrimination was meant to suggest the kinds of obligations, permissions, and prohibitions that exist regarding the use of military force in complex contingencies, it is by no means complete. The restoration of civic peace is not a job for the military alone, and more work needs to be done to build a comprehensive approach that draws on the professional resources and experience of civilian institutions involved in creating the conditions for civic peace.

Some may argue that placing legal and moral constraints on fighting a deadly enemy will needlessly and irresponsibly restrain soldiers from pursuing courses of action that allow them to effectively protect themselves, as well as the civilians they are sworn to defend. But it is also true that prosecuting war in a way that violates our own values risks undermining the national political will necessary to see the war through to a successful end. Coalition forces should pursue an aggressive policy engaging insurgents and terrorists wherever and whenever they find them. But they must also must recognize when violations of an individual's right to life and liberty is not permissible and restrain the use of force accordingly.

Military necessity—through enlightened policies and procedures—must be constrained and interpreted in different ways, depending on the situation in which it is applied. In some cases it means using the most force permissible, given the restrictions of proportionality and discrimination. In others, it means using the least force possible and never in such a way that civilians are knowingly put at risk. Furthermore, even if in particular situations conformity to moral obligations leads to restraint and perhaps missed operational opportunities, it may be better to pay this modest price than to lose the far greater long-term benefit that maintaining the moral high ground would have brought.

Notes

1. I am grateful for the help of my colleagues Dr. P. J. Ivanhoe, Maj. Joe Rank, Mr. Charley Metcalf, Ms. Lorelei Kelly, Dr. Jean-Marie Arrilligo, Ms. Traci Canterbury, Ms. Laura Worley, and my wife Julia in writing this paper.

2. Adapted from "Hearts and Minds: Post-war Civilian Deaths in Baghdad Caused by U.S. Forces," *Human Rights Watch* 15, no. 9 (October 2003): 26-29.

3. William Arkin, "Fear of Civilian Deaths May Have Undermined Effort," *Los Angeles Times*, 16 January 2002.

4. Tony Pfaff, *Peacekeeping and the Just War Tradition* (Carlisle, PA: Strategic Studies Institute, U.S. Army War College, 2000).

5. See http://www-tradoc.army.mil/pao/web_specials/warriorthos/. See also USMA Circular 1-101, *Cadet Leader Development System* (West Point, NY: United States Military Academy, June 2002), 9.

6. Utilitarian ethics seeks to maximize some good while minimizing some evil. In the context of military operations, victory in a just war presumably maximizes the good. Since such a victory maximizes the good, members of the military have an obligation to conduct operations that will lead to that victory and conduct them in such a way that will maximize the chances of victory.

7. Duty-based ethics is sometimes referred to as deontic ethics. Deontic ethics seeks to describe those principles that must be followed regardless of the consequences.

8. Pew Research Center News Release, "Iraq Prison Scandal Hits Home, But Most Reject Pullout," 12 May 2004. http://www.pewtrusts.com/pdf/pew_research_iraq_prison_051204.pdf see also :http://www.pollingreport.com/iraq.htm.

9. Michael Walzer, *Just and Unjust Wars* (New York: Basic Books, 1992), 44.

10. Ibid.

11. Ibid., chap. 4. There are a number of "aggressive acts" that fall short of warranting war such as raising tariffs, breaking a treaty, harassing one's citizens abroad, etc. For the purpose of this chapter, "acts of aggression" will exclusively refer to acts that violate political sovereignty and territorial integrity.

12. States are obligated to maintain peace and protect citizens from harm. This obligation arises from the belief that all persons have a right to life and liberty. While it is beyond the scope of this chapter to argue this point, it does posit that if persons have such rights, then someone has an obligation to guarantee them. In this case, this obligation falls to the state.

13. Walzer, 21. What justifies the use of force in both contexts is to correct or prevent an injustice. It is presumed the state of affairs that leads to injustice is unstable. Thus if force only returns affairs to their original state it has served no moral purpose.

14. Mortimer Adler, *How to Think About War and Peace* (New York: Fordham University Press, 1995), 59-70.

15. Ibid., 65-66.

16. James D. Delk, *Fires & Furies: The LA Riot* (Palm Springs, CA: ETC Publications, 1995). Quoted in Christopher M. Schnaubelt, "Lessons in Command and Control from the Los Angeles Riots," *Parameters* 27 (Summer 1997): 1.

17. Dana Priest, "U.S. Struggling to Identify Enemy," *Washington Post*, 7 September 2003.

18. Michael Hirsh, "Blood and Honor," *Newsweek*, 2 February 2004. http://msnbc.msn.com/id/4052404

19. If the state has a moral obligation to protect its citizens, then members of the military have a prima facie moral obligation to attempt to fulfill all orders not morally prohibited to serve that end.

20. "Hearts and Minds," 7-9.

21. Roger Barnett, *Asymmetrical Warfare* (Washington, DC: Brassey's Inc, 2003), 15. The definition here is a modified version of the one found in Joint Publication 1.0.

22. A stark example of this, of course, is 11 September 2001, when terrorists used modern communications and civilian aircraft to coordinate and conduct a direct attack against the political, military, and economic institutions that are indispensable to the United States' exercise of its political sovereignty and preservation of its territorial integrity. It is this ability to threaten political sovereignty and territorial integrity that makes the current war on terror *qualitatively* different from earlier ones. Political scientist Charles Hill describes the U.S. response as the "first war on terrorism." Prior to the 11 September attack, the terrorists simply were not capable of waging war, only of committing crimes.

23. Tony Pfaff, "Noncombatant Immunity and the War on Terror" (unpublished presentation at the Joint Services Conference on Professional Ethics, Washington, DC, January 2003). http://www.usafa.af.mil/jscope/JSCOPE03/Pfaff03.html.

24. *1923 Hague Rules of Aerial Warfare*, Article 22, 1949 Geneva Convention IV, Article 3.

25. Walzer, 138-175.

26. John Kleinig, *The Ethics of Policing* (Cambridge, England: Cambridge University Press, 1996), chap. 1.

27. Pfaff, 17-18.

28. Kleinig, 118-122. See also Pfaff, 13-20.

29. James M. Dubik, "Human Rights, Command Responsibility, and Walzer's Just War Theory," *Philosophy and Public Affairs* 11, no. 4 (1982): 355.

30. This has been, in fact, a feature of the Taliban strategy against the United States. By placing military equipment and other military targets in the vicinity of civilian populations they hoped to compromise U.S. attacks by turning public opinion against them.

31. Paul Christopher, *The Ethics of War and Peace: An Introduction to Legal and Moral Issues*, 2nd ed. (Trenton, NJ: Prentice Hall, 1999), 93.

32. Richard Norman, *Ethics, Killing and War* (Cambridge, England: Cambridge University Press, 1995), 84.

33. Walzer points out that destroying infrastructure, such as that related to the production of food and potable water, may also lead to civilian deaths and thus must be avoided. Michael Walzer, *Arguing About War* (New Haven, CT: Yale University Press, 2004), 94-98.

34. "Hearts and Minds," 4.

35. Frontline: "Truth, War, and Consequences," produced by Martin Smith. http://www.pbs.org/wgbh/pages/frontline/shows/truth/etc/anger.html.

36. "Hearts and Minds," 26-29.

37. Ibid.18-23.

38. David Fastabend, "The Categorization of Conflict," *Parameters* 27 (Summer 1997): 75. http://carlisle-www.army.mil/usawc/Parameters/97summer/fastaben.htm.

39. Hamza Hendawi, "Military in Iraq Deepens US Resentment," Associated Press, 8 November 2003. Tony Karon, "Shock and Awe II," *Time*, 3 November 2003.

40. Ibid.

41. Theodore Koontz, "Noncombatant Immunity in Michael Walzer's *Just and Unjust Wars*," *Ethics and International Affairs* 2 (1997): 79-80.

19 The Impact of Transformation on the Army Professional Ethic

R. D. Hooker, Jr.

W hat are the implications of force transformation for the Army's professional ethic? Although the question is extraordinarily important, the answer is unclear, for reasons that resist easy or facile analysis. To date, force transformation—for all the news media attention it has received and all the packaging and marketing surrounding it—is still little more than "power point" deep. While the Army understands fairly specifically what it is trying to do in the transformation arena, the larger, longer-term picture outside the Army profession remains less well understood.[1] Potentially, it suggests a more peripheral and secondary role for landpower than at any time in our history. If so, the effect on the Army professional ethic will be far-reaching and profound.

> Our overall goal is to encourage a series of transformations that in combination can produce a revolutionary increase in our military capability and redefine how war is fought.
>
> —DEPUTY SECRETARY OF DEFENSE
> PAUL WOLFOWITZ, 2002

This concern stems from the relationships that have existed historically between the Army's professional ethic and its functional focus on land combat. On the one hand, the primary emphasis on land combat and the direct fire battle has been a defining influence on the profession's ethic, and thus on how the Army trains its soldiers, develops it officers, and organizes its forces to win the land battle.[2] On the other hand, as the ethic is accepted and adapted by the professionals serving within the Army, it informs their individual intentions and collective actions over time, and through these shapes the successes (and failures) of Army forces in combat—in turn re-informing the profession's ethic. Thus, as we transform we must remain conscious of the important role of the Army's ethic as both a wellspring of values and an engine of victory on future battlefields. An Army that comes to view its professional ethic, consciously or not, as anachronistic is an Army in danger of losing its soul.

The Army as Profession

In what sense is the Army a profession? We ought not (perhaps) view the question uncritically. Do the medical and legal professions look on the military as a true profession? Very possibly they do not.[3] Yet while military service in general may not satisfy the particular and exacting standards which define professional status, military officership does, especially beyond the chrysalis stage of the junior officer.

As "traditional" interpreters have argued, the Army exercises a unique professional jurisdiction through its functional imperative: to fight and win the nation's wars on land.[4] No other institution provides this service.[5] There are physical and social barriers to entrance by the physically or mentally unfit. There is a professional qualification component that requires both academic and technical qualification in the form of a university degree and branch training and certification. (Later in their careers, Army officers will attend year-long staff and senior service colleges and in most cases earn a civilian graduate degree.) There is a complete professional lexicon for position and precedence which excludes nonmembers and classifies the professional officer by rank and branch. There is a rigorous weeding-out process ensuring that most officers will not survive to retirement; various levels of required service and increasingly advanced education and training are demanded if the officer is to progress, remain in good standing, and, indeed, remain in uniform at all.

Army officers and their counterparts in other services perform a function that benefits society as a whole and is not fundamentally focused on self-gratification or remuneration. The military professional occupies a special position in society and possesses unique expertise; no one else can do what he or she does. Perhaps most importantly, there is a moral/ethical component which transcends all others, incorporating a strict code of conduct. The officer must be honorable, with all that implies.

If the Army officer meets the objective standards for professional status, what obligations are imposed by virtue of membership in the officer corps? The officer is expected to put the needs and interests of the profession ahead of personal desires for advancement or compensation. To guard against abuse of the officer's authority, the professional ethic demands personal integrity of a high standard—far higher than that required in the larger society. In the basic branches, the combat and combat support communities most likely to engage in ground combat, the office must possess broad knowledge, both general and specific, of Army and joint systems, including their capabilities and doctrine. Even junior commanders must know the essentials of Army operations, logistics, intelligence, administration, and the planning process. Constant study and evaluation ensure that the officer masters increasingly demanding responsibilities that accompany promotion to higher grades.

By any measure, the professional ethic is a stern one. Even a single instance of professional incompetence, lack of integrity, or unwillingness to face danger or hardship can be career-destroying. The officer is expected to model the standards which define military service, especially on the battlefield, where the price exacted by the professional ethic can extend to death in action, the so-called "unlimited liability clause." All this was as true 50 years ago as it is today. Yet, as many have argued, military professionalism has been in decline for at least that long.[6] Practice and theory have clearly diverged. What has changed?

The short answer is, almost everything. The values, mores and attitudes of the larger society have altered dramatically in the last half century. The Army has integrated, reorganized, downsized, and reequipped itself at least twice over. It has fought in Southeast and Central Asia, Latin America, Africa, and the Middle East, in jungle, desert, mountain, and urban environments. It has transitioned from a conscript to a volunteer force, opened 97 percent of its specialties to women, and performed dozens of peacekeeping, humanitarian assistance, and stability operations in addition to its combat missions. Today, more than half of the force is married, with junior officers marrying more often than formerly. Their spouses often work and have careers and professions of their own, which often do not mesh well with military lifestyles and demands. Many Army families live off post in civilian neighborhoods, where life takes on a much more non-military flavor.

The officer ethic of selfless service to the nation has consequently been weakened in practice as the traditional, more insular patterns of Army life have changed. Officer skills and attributes are much in demand in the private sector. High standards of personal conduct are increasingly questioned in an affluent society that extends the boundaries of personal freedom and expression more than ever before. Such factors as access to graduate education and the civilian job skills it imparts, much freer flow of information via the internet, an exacting and pressure-filled Army work environment, and the requirement to move frequently and to deploy overseas for extended periods encourage officers to explore their many options and look outside the profession. While the military as an institution is highly valued by society, the officer occupies only a middling place on the social and economic scale, well below the doctor, lawyer, engineer, and even the successful business person. Increasingly, the military employs marketplace incentives to attract and retain officer talent, to the detriment of the ethic of selfless service that is the foundation of our value system.[7]

For these reasons it thus seems clear that other demands and values compete strongly with the Army professional ethic. Nevertheless it persists as an organizing construct and as a set of enduring values. As Tennyson put it, "though much is taken, much abides." How well the officer corps protects, nurtures, and transmits its professional ethic to succeeding generations of officers will have much to do with the quality of our national security in the years to come. Indeed it may be the most important factor of all.

Deconstructing Force Transformation

To explore the question of how transformation will affect the military professional ethic, we must first attempt to understand transformation itself. What is it, and where is it taking us?

The Department of Defense Office of Force Transformation defines it somewhat ambiguously as "a process that shapes the changing nature of military competition . . . first and foremost, transformation is a continuing process. It does not have an end state."[8] In general terms, defense transformation seeks to exploit the power of the microchip to control information. Variously linked to "network-centric" or "effects-based" warfare, it focuses on the use of precision-guided munitions employed at standoff ranges—all networked to the same information grid—to defeat opponents in major theater war and in lesser contingencies.[9]

This approach emphasizes the use of high technology on future battlefields. The thrust of this approach is the exploitation of America's edge in high technology to achieve rapid victory with smaller ground forces and fewer casualties.[10] In this construct, networked, digitized intelligence and information systems can give a precise and shared picture of the battlefield to commanders for immediate targeting and engagement. Increasingly, transformation proponents assert that new technology and new organizations will combine to eliminate the fog and friction of war, giving commanders "pervasive" and "persistent" intelligence and, in theory, even the ability to predict the decisions and intent of enemy commanders.[11]

Force transformation has its roots in the "Revolution in Military Affairs" (RMA) debates of the 1990s and gained a new level of interest and intensity after the 2000 presidential election. RMA thinking was heavily influenced by business innovations and practices which exploited new information technologies to achieve business efficiencies.[12] In many places, business strategies and jargon have been grafted wholesale into transformation documents, suggesting that armed conflict and the marketplace are somehow, if not equivalent, then certainly analogous.[13] The intent was to apply business practices and emerging technologies to transform the armed forces from an "industrial" to an "information" orientation characterized by greater efficiency.

Today, transformation is focused on the notion of the networked information grid. Intellectually, transformation envisions an interconnected sensor grid able to pass information and intelligence instantaneously to firing platforms. In theory, this grid will provide full situational awareness to commanders, who can then select and attack the most critical and vulnerable target sets for maximum effect. Information superiority, enabled by systems that can "seamlessly" relay data from sensors to shooters, thus translates into faster decision cycles; forestalls enemy reactions; creates more friendly options; and minimizes risks.[14]

The Army's Role in Force Transformation

Although Army roles and missions are not specifically discounted in the literature, the transformation effort is not neutral on the question of where the Army fits into the overall vision for future warfare. Programatically, air, space, command and control, naval, and missile systems predominate over land systems by a very wide margin.[15] As recently as the 2000 Quadrennial Defense Review, the Department of Defense pushed hard to downsize the active Army from 10 to 8 divisions.[16] Even the unprecedented demands of stability operations in Iraq and Afghanistan and enormous Congressional pressure have resulted in only a modest and temporary end strength increase of 30,000 spaces. By any measure, the focus for transformation is on precision- strike delivered from standoff ranges by air and naval platforms. Army forces play at best only a supporting and much less integral part in this vision of future war. In fact, in most transformation briefings and presentations the Army is not mentioned at all.

Of particular interest to Army officers is the common assumption of transformation advocates that precision-strike and seamless information flow will largely reduce land warfare to a simple targeting process.[17] Heavy emphasis on "jointness" at the expense of the unique distinctions which define and delimit air, land, and naval warfare increasingly blurs these fundamental differences, especially at the operational and tactical levels. Instead of improving the interface between the services during combat operations, force transformation literature speaks generically about "effects- based operations" and "network-centric warfare," as though aerospace, land, and naval warfare and the different capabilities resident in the services are entirely fungible, instead of complementary and mutually supporting.[18] Largely absent as well are references to the levels of war or to the importance of service core competencies.[19] That is because transformation, in its current form, largely discounts them.

The Sources of Army Professionalism

These issues are relevant to the Army professional ethic because they speak to the role of the Army in future war. The Army's corporate values and perception of itself and its role are derived from the ground combat mission.[20] The primacy of the group over the individual, the importance of individual and collective discipline, the role of leadership, the emphasis on combined arms to achieve synergistic effects on the battlefield, the unavoidable necessity for close combat, and *the absolute requirement to seize and control the land and the populations and resources found there* permeate and influence virtually everything the Army is and does. At a more basic level, the Army professional ethic exists to enable soldiers and small units to overcome the instinct for self-preservation—the fear of death—in order to accomplish the ground force mission. The Army's most sacred values—embraced in the cherished motto "Duty Honor Country"—at bottom are about shared sacrifice to achieve a common goal in service to the nation at the risk of one's life. Put another way, the Army ethos is rooted in close combat.[21]

Similarly, the institutional core values of the Army officer corps are grounded in command of soldiers in combat. While some officers serve in specialties which have civilian counterparts, such as Army lawyers, doctors, logisticians, personnel officers, and so on, most serve in combat and combat support specialties directly relevant to the land battle. When assigned to units, all serve as unit leaders and commanders, or as staff officers where they directly support commanders and prepare for command themselves. Command of troops in combat is the defining role of the Army officer, as command at sea is for the naval officer. Were that to change, the Army profession as we know it today would be altered fundamentally and dramatically.

Clearly, command of troops in combat presupposes that the Army retains primacy in military operations conducted on land. But if transformation advocates are correct, that will likely change. Today, one finds few references in transformation literature to the "land battle" or "ground campaigns." Of course, ground forces have traditionally relied on joint fires delivered by air and, when possible, naval platforms. But the Army has always dominated the effort to seize and control the land, while its sister services concentrated on strategic bombing and sea control.[22]

All that is changing fast. In current transformation literature, the arena for warfare is described not in terms of air, land, and sea but simply as a homogenous, undifferentiated whole. This development is cast in bold relief when one considers that, while the Army can do almost nothing to win command of the air or command of the sea, the other services have refocused almost entirely on operations in the land domain. That is, their principal contribution is now found in attacking targets on the land.[23] With no opposing navies or air forces left to fight, the land battle has become the only game in town. It is now generally referred to not as the land battle or the land campaign, but rather as the "joint warfight." The consequences for the Army professional ethic can well be imagined.

If the Army's core mission changes as a result of force transformation, its view of itself as a profession will evolve as well. In a military structured and indoctrinated to fight from a distance and to view warfare as essentially a targeting process, many of the imperatives and operating routines that shape the Army's culture would change. An Army conditioned to fight at long range, to move in only after major resistance has ended, and to conduct security and stability operations in the aftermath of massive aerial campaigns, would prize and value different skills, choose its leaders based on different criteria, articulate its values and norms differently, and view itself in an entirely changed way. Put simply, leading soldiers in harm's way will no longer define the Army officer's role or contribution to the nation.

In this construct, the principal focus for ground forces in major combat operations ("MCO" in current parlance) would be target engagements at long range (most likely employing multiple launch rocket systems, indirect fire variants of the Future Combat System (FCS), rotary wing aircraft using long range fire-and-forget weapons, and perhaps armed unmanned aerial vehicles or UAVs), controlled from highly instrumented and networked command posts well to the rear. Tactical maneuver units, while presumably still in the force, would perform less demanding security and stability operations and not routinely engage in high-intensity direct fire engagements. (The main battle tank's eventual replacement by the lightly armored FCS supports this thesis.)

One example of this trend can be seen in the field of information operations, or IO. Although gaining information on the enemy, denying it to him, and shaping his perceptions through deception and psychological operations have always been vitally important, this process has assumed almost a life of its own. Where previously the operations officer coordinated the various activities needed to achieve these ends, today there is an entire IO community, with separate career fields, staff sections, and doctrine. Different communities—PSYOPS, signal, and military intelligence in particular—have fought hard to gain primacy and proponency in the IO field. The Army has worked strenuously to create separate IO career fields that would promote internally, and to move information operations out from under the operations staff at higher echelons and make it coequal with other staff activities under the general direction of the chief of staff. Although reviews of the effectiveness of formal information operations staffs in Iraq and Afghanistan are mixed at best, this process continues in full force. Many officers now see their future not as troop leaders in combat and combat support units, but as information managers, intelligence analysts, or targeting specialists in staff settings.[24]

This trend could be replicated in other Army branch communities related to precision-strike functions (such as computer attack and defense, targeting, UAV operations, or battle damage assessment). For example, the decline of Army tubed artillery and short-range air defense communities has elevated rocket and missile systems—which engage at vastly greater distances—to primacy in these branches.[25] Should standoff precision-strike become the focus of effort in the conduct of major combat operations on land, the Army's traditional claim to unique expertise in the planning and conduct of major ground operations would materially weaken, since most precision-strike systems are found in other services. This will alter the Army's institutional ethos and the professional orientation of the officer corps, and degrade the Army's unique contribution to national defense.

The Enduring Relevance of Landpower

Preserving the Army professional ethic *is not, of course, a reason to slow force transformation at the expense of enhanced national security.* As the current Army Chief of Staff has said, "nothing is sacred except our values." If ground warfare becomes less relevant to success on the battlefield, the Army must change. However, there is little to support the implicit theme that landpower will markedly decline in importance as our technology improves. On the contrary, there is great danger that we may contrive a military establishment that is lop-sided—that is, too heavily weighted towards some capabilities at the expense of others. The requirement for powerful, sustainable landpower will not go away. If we are not careful, we may blunt America's ground forces so much that they will be unable to meet the enduring need to seize and control the land in future conflicts.[26]

However, this trend toward deemphasizing land warfare is already well underway. Through the 1990s the Army struggled to remain focused on war-fighting as its primary core function. During the tumultuous drawdown, as it cycled through Bosnia, Kosovo, and the Sinai (punctuated by other missions in Somalia, Rwanda, Haiti, Liberia, and elsewhere), the Army found its tactical units distracted from higher-level, combined arms training for major combat operations. Although the Army performed well in Afghanistan and Iraq against spotty opposition, in both cases major combat operations soon gave way to extended stability and security operations (or SASO). Today the Army is fully absorbed in these missions. When not actually deployed, the maneuver brigades and divisions of the Army are focused on preparing to return to these environments, where the primary operational focus is on small-unit actions, not high-intensity major combat operations.[27]

At the same time, the Department of Defense Office of Force Transformation has linked the need for transformation directly to the events of 11 September 2001 and the ongoing global war on terrorism.[28] While asserting a need to transform to a capabilities-based force and not a threat-based one, DoD clearly appreciates the budget and policy power and momentum generated by the threat of international terrorism and thus seeks to link transformation to this "strategic imperative." Operationally, the Army's role in the global war on terrorism does not center on major combat operations.[29] Rather, the Army provides Special Operations Forces, as well as certain key enablers (such as intelligence and logistic support). By far the bulk of the Army's forward-deployed combat forces are dedicated to stability operations, not direct action against known terrorist locations or assets. Should the war on international terrorism become a primary operational focus for the transforming force, it is likely that the Army's traditional focus on large-scale, sustained land warfare—the wellspring of its professional ethic—will erode.

The Army has always performed whatever tasks the nation assigned, many of which were ancillary to war-fighting. But the Army's senior leadership understands full well that sustained land combat is the most demanding and high-stakes mission for the forces it provides to the combatant commanders. But Army divisions do not really train for MCO today and have not for several years. Now, and for at least the near future, the Army will organize, train, and equip for its currently assigned real world missions. And those do not encompass large-scale, combined arms ground combat—the Army's traditional functional imperative. The business of the Army today is dangerous and demanding. But it is constabulary in nature, the business of an occupation force in hostile lands. If this holds true over time, the officer corps may come to view itself and its contribution to the common defense in a different light.

The current trend towards outsourcing functions not defined as "core business" may also dilute the perception of Army officers as subject matter experts in land warfare, challenging the unique expertise that in part defines the officer's professional status. A key part of defense transformation, outsourcing is already pervasive in the doctrine-writing, acquisition, force management, and logistics fields. As technology enhances "reach back" capabilities, civilians will more and more replace planners, intelligence analysts, targeteers, communicators, military lawyers, and other military specialists.[30] In an Army where many functions are increasingly performed by civilians and contractors and where close combat and direct fire engagements are deemed less important and relevant, professional values and attributes built on the foundations of unique military expertise and leadership of troops in combat will diminish.

All this is not to suggest that the sky is falling. The Army is an enduring and adaptive institution that has bounced back from adversity many times. Nevertheless, there is cause for concern. The foregoing discussion suggests that force transformation, as currently articulated, could potentially alter the Army's professional ethic in important ways. The fundamental issue is whether or not the Army's traditional role as the primary agent in sustained land combat will be replaced by new technologies, systems, and organizations. If so, the character of officership may assume a more occupational flavor as officer skills become more vocational and as land warfare becomes optimized for network-centric or effects-based operations. The traditional emphasis on command of combat and combat support formations directly involved in the land battle, placing a premium on "warrior" attributes with its demands for physical fitness, strong decisive character, charismatic leadership under stress, and a generalist background in combined arms operations, will give way to a more specialist officer at home with high technology, managerial leadership styles, office settings, and complex command post operations.[31]

Conclusion

The powerful momentum of transformation notwithstanding, there are compelling reasons to conclude that a competent national defense must include the ability to seize and control territory. As Adm. Isaac Kidd famously opined, "Someone must take the land and say 'this belongs to me.'" While improved information-sharing and precision weaponry will increase our competitive advantage exponentially against future opponents, the requirement for balanced, capable ground forces able to take and hold ground will endure. There is real danger in constructing a military establishment that assumes otherwise. To ensure we remain capable of performing our indispensable function, we can rely with confidence on an Army professional ethic which has served the nation so well for so long.

Notes

1. "After four years, however, translating this very general description of future war into detailed and specific systems and operating concepts—into concrete capabilities placed into the hands of war-fighters—has not progressed far. Exactly how, for example, a satellite image of a high value target or a signal intercept picked up by national technical means would be relayed to one tactical unit among hundreds for realtime engagement remains to be seen. To date, no joint C4ISR system that can interface securely and digitally across all services and commands is in sight. Exactly how specific, individual systems might fit into a larger, over-arching transformation framework remains sketchy. To be useful to the war-fighter, transformation must progress beyond broad rhetorical generalities to grapple with the specific realities of future war." See the author's "Proud Legions: Getting Transformation Right," with H.R. McMaster and David Gray, forthcoming in *Joint Force Quarterly*.

2. The term "direct fire battle" subsumes those communities and systems that directly support direct fire engagements, such as field artillery and short-range air defense.

3. The standard which seems to matter most is one of academic qualification above the undergraduate level. Although most senior field grade and general officers in the Army possess civilian graduate degrees, as well as staff college and war college diplomas, the medical, legal, and engineering fields do not ascribe the same level of demanding rigor to Army professional qualification processes as they do to their own fields.

4. For "standard" interpretations of the Army as a profession, see Samuel Huntington, *The Soldier and the State* (Cambridge, MA: Harvard Univ. Press, 1957), and Morris Janowitz, *The Professional Soldier* (Glencoe, NY: Free Press, 1960).

5. While it is true that the Air Force, Marines, and even Navy play important roles, wars fought on the land still require an Army to seize and control terrain and the populations who live there. This will not change as technology advances.

6. See Charles Moskos, *The Military—More than Just a Job?* (New York, NY: Brassey's, 1988).

7. The impact of this phenomenon on retention of service academy graduates has been severe. They now attrit at higher levels than OCS and ROTC officers, a striking change.

8. See "Military Transformation: A Strategic Approach," Department of Defense Office of Force Transformation, 2003, 8.

9. See Eliot Cohen, "A Revolution in Warfare," *Foreign Affairs* (March/April 1996), 37-54.

10. "Post military-revolution ground forces will likely be dramatically smaller." See "The Emerging RMA," *Center for Strategic and Budgetary Assessments*, 16 February 2000, 2.

11. "The emerging system . . . promises the capacity to use military force without the same risks as before—it suggests we will dissipate the fog of war." Adm. (Ret) William Owens, cited in Colin Gray, "Why Strategy is Difficult," *Joint Force Quarterly* (Summer 1999), 9.

12. Frederick W. Kagan, "The Art of War," *The New Criterion*. 22, no. 3 (November 2003), 5.

13. Most of the implementing concepts discussed in transformation literature—such as corporate strategies for innovation, focusing on core missions, the importance of incremental improvements and adaptations, and so on—are lifted directly from the commercial business sector.

14. "No capability is more important than situational knowledge shared among all elements of the joint force." Gen. Jim McCarthy (USAF Ret), *Transformation Study for the Secretary of Defense*, 12 June 2001, 5.

15. The Army share of the DoD Research and Development budget is 15%. *Inside the Army*, 1 March 2004, 1.

16. "Post military-revolution ground forces will likely be dramatically smaller." See "The Emerging RMA," 2.

17. Frederick W. Kagan, "War and Aftermath," *Policy Review* (August 2003), 22.

18. While systems found in the Army and other services may be similar, they are almost never interchangeable. The most obvious case is found in the debate over artillery and close air support. Artillery's ability to provide immediate, close, continuous all-weather support of ground troops, to include illumination and smoke, is not replicated by close air support or even army aviation.

19. The current draft of Joint Forces Command's "Major Combat Operations Joint Operating Concept" avoids any mention of specific service roles or competencies altogether.

20. See the author's "Soldiers of the State," *Parameters* 33 (Winter 2003-2004).

21. "Close combat" as used here means direct fire engagements supported by close artillery and rotary wing aviation fires.

22. Gaining air supremacy, though often mistaken for the Air Force's core function, is an enabler that permits the application of airpower to achieve strategic ends—usually the destruction of "strategic" targets far behind the contending ground forces.

23. This thinking has progressed to the point where the Air Force now contends that the Joint Force Land Component Commander (JFLCC) is not necessarily the "supported" commander within the Joint AOR, and that the Joint Force Air Component Commander (JFACC) should not exist below the level of the Regional Combatant Commander. In other words, Air Force assets can and perhaps should be the focus of the joint fight supported by the other services. See the author's "Joint Campaigning in 2010," *Joint Force Quarterly* (Fall 1999).

24. This process is already well advanced. In 2001, for example, the promotion rate for Acquisition Corps officers to full colonel was 70%, but only 43% for infantry officers.

25. Beginning in 2004 the Army will convert 40 reserve component tubed artillery battalions and elements of three active component corps tubed artillery brigades to military police, civil affairs, and other types of units better suited to stability operations. Army Stinger and Avenger SHORAD (short-range air defense) units are being converted to infantry to provide manpower for the Army's modularized brigades. Since the Gulf War there have been calls for MLRS and Patriot systems to be controlled by the JFACC, who doubles as the Joint Airspace Manager and by joint doctrine controls the deep fight beyond the Fire Support Coordination Line (FSCL).

26. Of interest is the fact that in the current counterinsurgency operations in Iraq, commanders have issued urgent appeals for more tanks and better armored tactical vehicles.

27. As one example, the 1st Battalion, 77th Armor deployed to Iraq in the spring of 2004 as a provisional infantry unit. Its tanks were left behind in Germany. Steve Liewer, "1st Battalion 77th Armor Aims to Transform into Infantry Unit," *European Stars and Stripes*, 29 February 2004.

28. See "Military Transformation: A Strategic Approach," 12.

29. In the effort to unseat the Taliban and destroy the Al Qaeda presence in Afghanistan in 2002, the Army conducted brigade-level ground operations, but 31 or the Army's 33 maneuver brigades were not involved, and only one maneuver brigade-equivalent was employed .

30. "Reach back" refers to the ability to pull intelligence and information forward from secure locations outside the theater of operations.

31. In the late 1990s the Army embarked on a fundamentally different approach to officer professional management called "OPMS 21" (now referred to as "OPMS 3"). The intent was to offer equal promotion opportunities to officers with specialty, non-troop leading qualifications. Today approximately one third of the field grade officer population migrates out of the "command track" as they reach promotion to major. They will be promoted to lieutenant colonel and full colonel at the same rate as those who remain in combat and combat support branches, but will never serve in troop units again.

VI

The Premier Expertise—
Human/Leader Development

As we all know, neither tanks nor helicopters nor rifles kill enemy combatants; American soldiers kill enemy combatants. War is always, and only, a human endeavor the goal of which is to destroy our enemies' will to continue the conflict. Thus military professions are quintessentially human organizations, with their art practiced at the point of the spear and all along its supporting shaft by human professionals. It is not an overstatement, therefore, to call the knowledge of developing and leading soldiers the premier knowledge of the Army profession, and more particularly so as the Army transforms for a new era of warfare. It will be so as long as the Army remains a profession.

All professions do the same two tasks within their own internal jurisdictions: they develop and maintain their expert knowledge and they imbue individual professionals with the expertise to put that knowledge into practice in new and different situations. Only by being effective in these critical internal jurisdictions can the Army be effective in its external jurisdictions of major combat operations, stability operations, and homeland defense.

In this Part of the book, researchers address from several perspectives these critical internal jurisdictions of the Army, in particular the subject of leadership. For example, in Chapter 20 Professors Jacobs and Sanders provide one of the first unclassified views into the extraordinarily successful leader development techniques and practices used by the Army's Special Operations Forces. They make specific recommendations for the remainder of the Army growing out of their close study over the years of those forces, recommendations that should receive careful and urgent consideration as the Army transforms its officer personnel systems.

There are also in this Part of the book two chapters specifically commissioned to address separate leadership issues little discussed within the Army in the past decade or so: the spiritual needs of soldiers in combat and their leaders' responsibility to provide for those needs (Chapter 21 by Chaplains John Brinsfield and Peter Baktis); and the development and utilization of Army general officers (Chapter 25 by Dr. Margaret Harrell and colleagues). The results presented in both of these chapters are straightforward, seriously challenging current Army doctrine and practices. Doubtless they will appear contrary to much of the conventional wisdom among Army professionals, but the Army can transform successfully only when prevailing orthodoxies are thoroughly challenged.

Other chapters here address leadership issues that carried over from the first research project in 2000 or that have arisen specifically from the Army's current operations in Afghanistan and Iraq. In Chapter 22, Dr. Leonard Wong presents the results of field research in Iraq documenting for the first time since the beginning of the all-volunteer force that current American soldiers, many now from Generation Y, are motivated to fight not only by their comradeship with other soldiers, but also importantly by their understanding and support of the mission of liberating oppressed peoples. Away from the battlefield on the home front, research into soldier values as elicited from personnel of one of the Army's new Stryker Brigades and as reported in Chapter 24 by Maj. Todd Woodruff and Col. Thomas Kolditz, documents the number one priority Generation Y soldiers and officers accord to their families, quite in contrast to the generations before them. In Chapters 23 and 27, researchers address current controversies over Army leadership doctrine and techniques, i.e., the "McDonaldization" (super-efficient bureaucratization) of the Army, and the Army's infatuation with laundry lists of traits as a means of teaching leadership. In Chapter 26 Dr. Dallas Owens presents a new sociological analysis of the differences between professions in the active Army and the Army Reserve. Given the declining state of the Army Reserve, which still is operating under personnel policies designed for WWII, those charged with its redesign to better support Army transformation would do well to study this analysis.

Lastly, Dr. Wong and I offer in Chapter 28 a new view on Army strategic leaders, one that emphasizes why and how strategic leaders of professions—particularly the military professions—must differ from strategic leaders of other producing organizations such as businesses. If the first research project demonstrated anything at all, it was that captains, majors, and noncommissioned officers could not themselves convert the Army into a profession. They can be individually very fine professionals, but that is insufficient. Only the strategic leaders of the Army can transform it into a profession since only they can reshape the bureaucratic management systems of the Army to support it as a profession. This is particularly true of the Army's most centralized and bureaucratic management systems, those for personnel development and utilization and those for training.

Research presented here indicates that many new developmental ideas need to be incorporated now into the ongoing transformational initiatives. In so doing, however, the Army must be careful to maintain firm control over the work done in its internal jurisdictions. Strategic leaders of the Army profession must remember that the Army can never be more successful in its external jurisdictions than it is in developing its expert knowledge and its own professionals who put that knowledge into practice.

20 | Principles for Building the Profession: The SOF Experience

T. O. Jacobs and Michael G. Sanders

In their introduction to the first edition of *The Future of the Army Profession* (2002), Don Snider and Gayle Watkins come to the conclusion that professions are mainly people, as opposed to technologies or organizational structures. Military transformation thus must be concerned with transforming people and not things. Many might argue that transformation must also concern itself with things, and some might argue that professions must also—haven't the "professions" profited hugely in what they can accomplish by virtue of the technologies developed during the last half of the last century?

> The Army is neither a public-sector bureaucracy manned by civil servants nor is it a business with employees. It has been and must continue to be a profession, one in which military professionals serve with deep pride and immense personal satisfaction.
>
> —DON SNIDER AND GAYLE WATKINS[1]

But Snider and Watkins argue convincingly that *people* are primary in any profession, and we will make a similar argument, grounded on the assertion that the essence of professionalism is the discretionary exercise of initiative in decision-making that depends on specialized and in-depth expertise typically not shared by the client system served.[2] The exercise of initiative is discretionary in the sense that *the professional decides what to do and how to do it*, by virtue of mastery of professional expertise. This expertise establishes the professional in a privileged position of trust and authority, from which spring requirements for ethical conduct and service. Because the professional's expertise typically exceeds that of the client, the potential for exploitation is great. For this reason, professionals typically form associations which are capable of generating and enforcing ethical standards and norms of conduct to govern the provision of services to the client. In many of the industrialized nations, these associations enforce professional norms and standards by (1) requiring anyone who wishes to practice the profession to belong to the association and subscribe to its values, and (2) influencing governmental authorities to "license" members of the profession who wish to engage in the delivery of services to the client. However, the "license to practice" in almost all cases is conditional on standards set by the association (or by select professionals within the association), and revocation of the "license to practice" is typically based on a failure to conform to the values and ethical standards of the profession in some way. *That is, professions are self-forming, self-regulating, and self-initiating in the provision of expert services to a client which the profession is ethically constrained not to exploit in its own self-interest.*

The development of specialized expertise and the consequent necessity for an independent set of values, norms, ethics and self-policing oversight of a group of practicing experts thus marks a profession. In that sense, the U.S. military is a profession,

441

whether or not all individual members recognize that and/or act as professionals. The distinguishing aspect of the military profession is the expertise required to master and visit deadly force upon an enemy. This expertise confers enormous power, which can be misused. The risk that it could be turned against civilian government was the basis for the concern by the founding fathers that civilian control of the military be an established principle. This concern is today reflected in the value systems of the armed forces of the United States, reinforcing the allegiance of the forces to the nation—the collective client. This, among many other indicators, exemplifies the professional nature of these forces.

However, Don Snider and Gayle Watkins think that professionalism in the Army is at risk because of a "natural tension" generated by its dual nature. It is not only a "calling," but also "a huge hierarchical bureaucracy, only one of many within the U.S. government."[3] The tension manifests itself in contrasting pulls between a concern for effectiveness and the creation of expertise, on the one hand, and bureaucracy and efficiency—doing more with less, a result of the endless competition among departments for resources—on the other hand.

Snider and Watkins contend that declining professionalism in the military can be attributed to bureaucratization of the armed forces. The present authors agree. At the heart of bureaucracy's underlying philosophy is the objective of reducing the dependence of the organization on any single individual or the expertise of any single individual. As the great industrial empires unfolded at the beginning of the 20th century, the thrust of mass production was to simplify the work each individual performed, so that the intrinsic value of any one person was held to a minimum with the result that the cost of replacement also was held to a minimum. Bureaucracy's tools include formalization (extensive specification of written procedures for how processes are to be performed), differentiation and specialization of roles (more finely defined separation of different "jobs," with tasks, conditions, and standards for their performance, aimed at reducing the instrumental value of individual expertise), and centralization of critical processes (personnel management, promotions, career path specification). To the extent that these functions can be carried out, the role of the individual in the organization becomes less critical, and the organization itself operates more efficiently. By its very nature, bureaucracy is antithetical to professionalism.

Table 20-1 illustrates the conflicting pulls exercised by bureaucratic and professional organizations. The essence of bureaucracy is efficient pursuit of self-interest. While individual members are expected to subordinate themselves to the needs of the organization, the organization itself is typically engaged in pursuit of its own purposes, in most cases in competition with other actors in a "system of systems" sense. By contrast, the essence of profession is effective (because of the special expertise requirement) satisfaction of client needs. Individual members are expected to subordinate themselves *to the ethical demands of the profession* while acting as independent agents when seeking to solve client problems or satisfy client needs. A bureaucracy is an industrial-age organization; a profession is an information-age organization in which members are knowledge workers, having gained depth in uniquely valuable specialized expertise.[4] Members of a bureaucracy are production workers; members of a profession are problem-solvers.

	Bureaucracy	**Profession**
Values	Internally generated and rules based, vetted against pragmatic externalities	Internally defined, vetted against internal criteria of morality and justice
Orientation	Efficient operation in defined areas, which may include service to an external client	Service to an external client
Ethic	Competitive advantage within the law, in a basically competitive and essentially amoral world	Beneficial service to client system; exploitation prohibited and punished by organs internal to the profession
Culture	Anchored in subsystems and operating procedures, validated by consensus about what works well	Anchored in values and a professional ethic that mandates normative behavior
Membership	Willingness to conform to expectations and ability to add value to the organization	Willingness to conform to the ethical mandates and ability to acquire needed expertise to a level mandated by the profession

Table 20-1. *Bureaucratic and Professional Contrasts.*

The contrast between industrial and information-age concepts is nowhere more clearly drawn than in a study by J. P. Womack et al., who conducted an analysis of assembly line operations in Japanese factories in comparison with automobile assembly line operations in most of the rest of the world.[5] One of the most telling differences is the amount of training given new production workers by Japanese and North American manufacturers at the time of the analysis. Japanese workers received an average of 380.3 hours, while North American workers received an average of 46.4.[6] North American assembly line workers could do only one job; Japanese workers could do several. Where this difference paid off was in the quality of the product—a measure of service to the client. At GM, for example, only the foreman could stop the line, so if a car came down the line with an assembly error, the worker at the next station could do only one of two things—allow the vehicle to pass down the line minus the part he was supposed to install, or install his part and thus cover up the error by the previous worker. In either case, the vehicle could not pass muster at the end of the line and would have to be transferred to a separate rework area where a crew of skilled mechanics disassembled the vehicle, corrected the error, and reassembled the vehicle—an extraordinarily costly process.

At Toyota, by contrast, each worker was empowered to stop the line, and was expected to do so, when an incorrectly assembled vehicle appeared at his/her work station. That worker was expected to correct the error, and then do his/her own operation, before sending the vehicle on down the line. This was possible because that worker had been trained on several different jobs and could do them all. With this broader skill, he/she could diagnose the error and then take the initiative to make it right. The vehicle was thus highly likely to arrive at the end of the line in condition to pass the quality control checks and be certified as ready for shipment.

The rework area at Toyota was small in comparison with the rework area at all the other companies examined, as were their rework costs.

The relevance for the military of this diversion into the private sector is not Toyota's invention of a more effective assembly line; rather, it is Toyota's transformation of a factory's culture and basic philosophy of operation. At the time Womack et al. did their analysis, the GM assembly line worker was just that. The factory was bureaucratized with a high degree of formalization, centralization of initiative and decision-making, and emphasis on codified procedure as spelled out in its contract with the union. *In contrast, the Toyota employee was actually a knowledge worker in the true sense of the word, expected to problem-solve and take initiative on his/her own.* At the organizational level, this meant that Toyota could produce a higher-quality product at a lower cost, and their increasing dominance of the American automobile market is a result.

Of even greater importance, evidence suggests that this difference is attributable to culture and management, and not to any difference in the quality of American and Japanese workers. The NUMMI factory in California is a joint venture of GM and Toyota, with Japanese management and the Toyota system. At the time the Womack book was written, the factory produced Toyota Corollas and a small Chevrolet. These two automobiles were of equal quality, as indicated by frequency of repair records, and the Corolla was equal in quality to the same car produced in Japan by Japanese workers. *The difference was culture and professionalism.* While Toyota's assembly line workers are not professionals in the sense described by Snider and Watkins, they are "professionals" in comparison with assembly line workers in virtually all other organizations in the industrial world. This is a powerful transformation. It has produced enormous competitive advantage for Toyota, and is likely to do so for any other company that replicates the Toyota system.

This suggests that the "professional" described by Snider and Watkins is the product of a culture that fosters the development of expertise and internalization of values and mandates regarding service to a client. It also suggests that military transformation similarly must be cultural at its roots, in contrast to many current descriptions of the key elements of military transformation. Since culture is about people rather than about things, it must address the people side of the equation rather than the equipment side. Obviously, equipment is essential; however, transformation is fundamentally about people, and military transformation into an information-age mind-set is not about electrons. It is about how members of the organization are inducted, socialized, acculturated, enabled to become expert, and empowered to act. When bureaucratization interferes with these processes, professionalism suffers.

A strong case can be made that the U.S. Army has become more bureaucratic over the past half century, largely in response to external demands that made efficiency an essential objective. However, not all the Army has become more bureaucratic. We contend that the U.S. Special Operations Forces (SOF) are distinctly less so, and may perhaps provide insights into how conventional military organizations can retain strong elements of professionalism.[7] The balance of this chapter will therefore be devoted to key features of SOF units, particularly Army Special Mission

Units, and an analysis of how their professional features were enabled by early decisions that shielded against bureaucratization. *The central thesis is that processes inherent in bureaucratization establish an organizational culture that diminishes both the drive and opportunity for professional development. Professionalism can exist only when individual excellence counts and the opportunity exists to exercise decision-making initiative based on unique expertise.*

SOF—Some History and Culture-Shaping

It is entirely fitting that SOF had its origin in concepts of unconventional warfare. In order to understand current SOF professionalism fully, it is useful to review these origins and their legacy for the current force. The Army Special Operations Command commands the Army Special Forces (SF), the Army Rangers, Task Force 160, and some Army Special Mission Units (SMUs). American unconventional operations date to World War II in the Office of Strategic Services (OSS) of World War II.[8] The OSS had two broad missions. One was intelligence collection, but the second and more important for present purposes was recruiting and training partisan forces to harass occupying Axis forces through sabotage and interdiction, and to disrupt their rear when friendly conventional forces became capable of offensive operations. This modus operandi established a tradition that has continued to the present—independent forces working flexibly under conditions of great complexity, danger, and uncertainty, exercising innovative and sometimes entrepreneurial leadership.

However, the actual and spiritual forebear of an Army SMU was the British Special Air Service (SAS), which conducted operations in Malaya. The Malayan insurgency was initiated on 16 June 1948 by Chinese guerrillas, who in simultaneous attacks executed two British planters and then harangued their work forces on the need to struggle against imperialism. The "Malayan Emergency" was declared the next day. The insurgency plan was classical. The first phase was to be a terror campaign; the second was to be creation of areas firmly under guerrilla control. The third was to be a general uprising led by the Malayan People's Anti-British Army (MPABA). MPABA combatants were supported by a large number of Chinese squatters in the rural areas, an aftermath of Japanese occupation.

Despite intensive efforts to suppress the MPABA, the war intensified, and by 1951 insurgents were killing an estimated seven civilian or security personnel per day.[9] In response, the "Briggs Plan" was developed that would constitute a new approach to counterinsurgency operations. It envisaged resettling the Chinese squatters in fortified villages so as to remove the insurgent infrastructure, together with direct efforts to break the MPABA organization. To accomplish the latter, a British ex-Special Forces officer, Mike Calvert, formed the Malayan Scouts (SAS), which in 1951 became the Regular 22 SAS Regiment.[10] The SAS conducted long-range patrol operations in the sanctuary areas, determining the location of main guerrilla forces which could then be engaged by conventional forces. SAS elements also operated in northern Malaya, where most of the country's aboriginal minority were located. The plan there was to build a string of fortified encampments into which the aboriginals would be enticed by free food and medical care, thereby further removing guerrilla infrastructure. However, this worked primarily because the SAS and other units such as the Gurkhas and the Royal Marine Commandos were able to pursue guerrillas who had engaged in terrorist events deep into their sanctuaries. These elements were highly successful because they had the capacity to operate under the most challenging of conditions, deep in denied areas.

The insurgency was not totally quelled until 1987 after the remnants of the Malayan Races Liberation Army, which had fled to Thailand, finally surrendered and were resettled. They had essentially been driven out of Malaya by the ability of SAS to pursue guerrilla groups wherever they went, thereby denying them safe haven anywhere. Terry White notes that

> lessons were learnt from this rather special and restricted insurgency war. Specialised military units capable of operating for long periods in the jungle, working with indigenous people, were well suited for such "low-intensity" wars, fought mainly between infantry and guerrillas, but as demanding as any conflict on the battlefield and requiring "a whole new kind of strategy, a wholly different kind of force."[11]

The connection between the SAS and Army Special Operations Forces stems largely from the assignment of Maj. Charlie Beckwith, a Special Forces officer, to the SAS as an exchange officer in June 1962. While his tour with the SAS was foreshortened by leptospirosis, an acute infectious disease contracted in the Malayan jungle, he had sufficient time with the Regiment to understand what it was all about, and to appreciate the remarkable effectiveness of the Regiment's performance. He also had sufficient time to understand that SAS was different from the conventional Army and also from conventional Special Forces.

Creating the Special Mission Unit

After returning to duty following his bout with leptospirosis, Beckwith prepared a white paper describing the 22 SAS and its capabilities. He proposed that the U.S. military create a similar capability. Unfortunately, this paper was written just as American involvement in the Vietnam war was deepening, and the paper's thesis fell on deaf ears. However, shortly after Beckwith was given command of the Special Forces School in 1974, Brig. Gen. Robert Kingston was given command of the JFK Special Warfare Center and School at Ft. Bragg, North Carolina. Kingston had been responsible for Beckwith's selection to serve an exchange tour with the SAS, and had himself served an exchange tour with a British parachute regiment. He now surprised Beckwith by requesting that he write another paper describing the SAS which Kingston could take to Lt. Gen. E. C. "Shy" Meyer, then the Army Deputy Chief for Operations in the Pentagon. Meyer, while the Deputy Chief of Staff for Operations in Europe in 1973-74, had become convinced of the need for the Army to have a counterterrorist capability, particularly in view of the terrorist attack against Jewish athletes during the 1972 Olympics in Munich. Beckwith describes in detail the numerous obstacles that stood in the way of establishing the Army Special Mission Unit.[12] He gives full credit to Meyer for recognizing the need, orchestrating the delicate political processes involved in the effort, and protecting the fledgling unit until it could fly on its own.

As the SMU progressed from concept to reality, Beckwith was able to negotiate several critical conditions:

- Personnel were to be selected by the newly-born SMU itself, not unilaterally assigned. They were to be volunteer NCOs (or promotable company-grade officers). They could be reassigned from the unit for violation of norms, values, or rules, or for injudicious behavior.
- Members were to be stabilized in the unit for as long as they performed effectively and wanted to remain. A member who failed to perform or who wanted out could be immediately reassigned. On the other hand, a member who performed at the level of excellence expected could elect to remain in the unit on an indefinite basis. Conventional reassignment practices would not apply.
- It was accepted that the SMU would be top-heavy in enlisted rank.
- The conventional Army training establishment, the U.S. Army Training and Doctrine Command, would not prescribe the training content or standards. Rather, both training and performance standards were to be patterned closely after those of other experienced counterterrorist organizations, particularly the 22 SAS, and were designed to develop counterterror professional soldiers with both the will and the capability to execute highly demanding counterterror operations.[13]

At first glance, this short list of conditions seems hardly sufficient to foster the level of excellence that has in fact resulted. Indeed, over the two years following its activation orders, the command and control relationships of the SMU with senior echelons changed several times in ways that almost certainly enhanced its capacity to develop elite professionals.[14] However, the key factors over the three decades or so of its life span seem to stem from the small set of special circumstances above. In the remainder of this chapter, we will attempt to draw some of the linkages and derive some principles that seem exportable to the more conventional Army.

The Information-Age Professional Soldier

A strong convergence exists among (1) the Snider-Watkins definition of a professional, (2) the concept of the special operator, and (3) the concept of the information-age knowledge worker. As previously noted, there is a tension between industrial-age and information-age operational concepts. Toyota's transformation of the factory culture was essentially the transformation of the factory from a purely industrial-age organization to one more closely reflecting information-age understandings. The SMU, while unquestionably military in nature, also much more closely mirrors information-age understanding than does the conventional Army. Finally, the very concept of professional is more reflective of information-age understanding than of industrial age work conventions.

The point, and its relevance to Army transformation, is that *professionals are not mass-produced, and organizations of professionals are not conventional.* Henry

Mintzberg describes five major organizational forms, to include *adhocracy*. Organizations exist for a purpose, and the form that an organization takes should match the intended purpose. Adhocracy is especially suited to the purpose of "sophisticated innovation," for which none of the other forms is.[15] He offers the following adhocracy design parameters:

> Highly organic structure, with little formalization of behavior; high horizontal job specialization, based on formal training; a tendency to group the specialists in functional units for housekeeping purposes but to deploy them in small market-based project teams to do their work; a reliance on the liaison devices to encourage mutual adjustment—the key coordinating mechanism—within and between these teams; and selective decentralization to and within these teams.

In other words, these are teams of professionals in some domain, who have the authority to coordinate with one another in deciding how to proceed, and who have discretion to make decisions as experts in these domains. The key point is that the organization and its processes have a great deal to do with whether it can "grow" professionals.

Beckwith's vision for the new unit was strongly shaped by his experience while serving with the 22 SAS. The conventional U.S. Army personnel management system, with its addiction to a system of individual replacements, its insistence on individual assignment equity at the expense of unit excellence, and its apparent unconcern with the inevitable erosion of collective skills, could not be applied to the new unit.[16] In addition, the unit had to be able to focus on missions at the strategic level, and consequently required direct access to national-level intelligence. If it was to be capable of rapid response (literally within hours) to terrorist events, it had to have direct lines of communication and command and control from the National Command Authority. Finally, if members were to develop extraordinarily high levels of expertise in their business, they had to train more extensively and intensively than conventional units. This required both release from typical garrison duties and funds to procure specialized weapons and the massive amounts of training ammunition the SMU operators expended during its organizing phase.[17] As Beckwith describes it, these conditions were not all set at the beginning. The requisite freedom from local control, for example, was gained only over time. However, once gained, these key conditions enabled leaders to set the essential policy and operating structure that produced the growth of the unit to what it is today. We shall discuss each of these essential conditions in turn under the following rubrics: selection of members, personnel management, training, leadership, and leader development.

Selection of Members

Then, as now, the unit recruited volunteers from a wide range of sources in the Army. The SAS philosophy was to recruit from a wide range of professional disciplines, and SMU philosophy was patterned directly after the 22 SAS model. The 22 SAS had a rigorous selection process that tested all candidates for their capacity to deal with uncertainty and to maintain focus under conditions of great pressure and fatigue. Both physical and psychological stamina were essential if a candidate were to succeed. For officers, there was an additional selection process that tested psychological stamina, and capacity for self-mastery and logical thought while under great psychological stress. Beckwith used essentially the same selection process for his new unit. However, the SMU also developed an extensive psychological screening process modeled more in the light of American psychological practice than that of the British.[18] Again, the objective was to find soldiers who were emotionally mature and likely to be stable under stress.

Personnel Management

One of the most important contributions Beckwith made was his insistence that a soldier who passed the initial selection hurdle and the subsequent operator training would then be a member of the unit as long as (1) the soldier wanted, and (2) the soldier performed well. This is a remarkably important consideration if one is to develop truly professional expertise and operational teams with authentic professional-level collective skills. Initial members of the new unit were drawn from the Special Forces—not surprising considering Beckwith's own Special Forces background. To some extent following SF practice, special operations teams, troops, and squadrons were to be stabilized so as to develop to a high level of excellence the collective skills essential in special operations missions. Stabilization also made possible the development of highly effective family support mechanisms for deployed soldiers' families. In short, performance excellence became the criterion by which unit members and teams were assessed, and the only basis on which unit membership could be maintained. This practice allows the growth of excellence in collective skills well beyond that typically attainable in a conventional unit faced with the high levels of personnel turbulence forced onto the Army by the current system.[19] It also permits cross-training (an area of SF emphasis), which creates unit robustness and resilience. And, finally, it permits the development and handing-down of unique traditions and cultural continuities that support high levels of performance under conditions of high stress. The point is not so much that this is an elite unit, though it is, but rather that any unit can become *more elite* if its circumstances are set so that unit excellence is the sine qua non, unit members are allowed to stay together in order to develop and maintain that excellence, and *the tradition of excellence becomes embedded in the culture not only of the organization as a whole, but also of the individual elements*.

Training

Training in the SMU always has been demanding, with little tolerance for repeated poor performance. To some extent, training is of course facilitated by adequate resourcing for training.[20] However, it is facilitated to a much greater extent by greater freedom to decide what and how to train, the level of expertise demanded, and the time to do needed training. In the conventional Army, the intrusion of higher-level demands for noncombat-related training or other activities is endemic. The Blue Ribbon Panel on Training and Leadership Development found this to be a huge impediment to the ability of company commanders to assess and remedy training deficiencies. Their training schedule "white space" at the time of the Blue Ribbon Panel was virtually nil. In the SMU, resources, stabilization, and protection from some non-mission-oriented requirements have allowed development of performance excellence rarely found elsewhere. Of great interest, similar observations were made by on-the-ground observers of U.S. forces during Operation Desert Storm, undoubtedly the result of the stabilization these units experienced, and the extended time between deployment and employment which permitted extensive unit training. The point is that these conditions foster unit excellence, and all units would get better if these conditions were manifest.

According to Beckwith, General Meyer also directed the SMU to develop a set of tasks, conditions, and standards, which would not only serve as a basis for performance evaluation but would also institutionalize performance expectations after Beckwith's command tour ended.[21] After successfully completing the selection phase, both noncommissioned and commissioned officers enter operator training and are held to the same standards. Then, and now, inability to master the specialized skills required of operators in the conduct of counterterror operations results in reassignment. In essence, the SMU has had the freedom to establish its own training objectives, tasks, conditions, and standards, and then to be evaluated as a unit through their use. This freedom clearly corresponds to one of the attributes of a profession.

The expectation of perfection in execution is carried forward in large part by the rigor with which after-action reviews (AARs) are conducted. Teams take the responsibility for AARs on themselves, conducting them behind closed doors. These AARs are brutally frank and are productive of high performance. They are typically conducted by the NCOs (even if officers are present), with an emphasis on how improvements can be made. NCO "ownership" of this process suggests a culture strikingly like that in Toyota factories in which workers have a great deal of latitude to stop the production line and make corrections—essentially acting much like knowledge workers. (Granting decision discretion to knowledge workers is an essential step in the evolution toward knowledge-based organizations, and thus the transition from industrial age to information age.) The AAR process also reinforces interdependencies, thereby increasing both team robustness and team agility in the sense that each member knows better what each other member is likely to do in a future situation, and is therefore able to "read" what is happening more quickly. The fact that NCOs conduct the AAR is recognition that they hold professional status, and that this status is conferred by expertise and not rank.

Leadership

An especially perplexing aspect of the SMU, for those accustomed to the conventional Army, is the question of who leads and what discipline is all about. Beckwith experienced this perplexity in his first days with the 22 SAS when he was given command of Three Troop, A Squadron. Upon walking into Three Troop barracks, he found the long room "a mess." Equipment was strewn—to his view—in a disorderly manner, reminding him more of a football locker room than a barracks. Two members of the Troop were brewing tea in the middle of the floor. The following excerpts from his book show a chain of encounters that began to transform his mindset:

> I said, "What we need to do is get this area mopped down, the equipment cleaned, straightened, and stored, and the tea brewed outside." Two troopers, Scott and Larson, spoke up at once. "No, sir. That's not what we want to do. Otherwise, we might as well go back to our regular regiments. One of the reasons we volunteered for the SAS was so we wouldn't have to worry about the unimportant things."[22]

> I couldn't make heads or tails of this situation. The officers were so professional, so well read, so articulate, so experienced. Why were they serving with this organization of non-regimented and apparently poorly disciplined troops?[23]

> I'd been in camp about ten days when I was told a sketch map exercise would be conducted. . . . Peter Walter told me I'd accompany Sergeant Major Ross, who would design and formulate the exercise. Life was full of surprises. In the American military system officers usually ran everything. But this was Britain.[24]

> Little by little, I began to see the picture. The squadron was not playing games. They were deadly serious. They'd had a lot of experience, going back to World War II, whereas our own Army Special Forces hadn't actually been established until 1954. The Brits had made lots of mistakes, but they'd learned from them.[25]

> I hadn't "earned" my green beret. I'd just been handed it. I got assigned to Special Forces and put the hat on. Now I knew that wasn't right. Men ought to earn the right to wear a distinctive badge. . . . in the SAS I realized the importance of a system that permits an individual to earn the right to wear a particular hat.[26]

Obviously, the point here is not that indiscipline and disorderliness are essential attributes of profession. Rather, it is that these soldiers were recognized by their service as professionals and were judged by how well they performed in their professional roles, not by surface appearance.[27] The 22 SAS, as is the case with the SMU, does far more training than the average conventional unit, which means that a member's performance is constantly under surveillance. In the SMU, this is not punitive; rather, it is laced with the zest of challenge: Can it be done better? This climate is thus one of a constant quest for better ways to operate, new technologies that would make possible the previously impossible, and new ideas that will enable future capabilities. Beckwith's account of the 22 SAS suggests the same climate existed there. We will return subsequently to a deeper exploration of unit climate and culture. For now, it is enough to note that the intense focus on training and realistic mission practice makes very visible a member's level of expertise and performance effectiveness on what counts in the profession. Of much greater importance, leadership within both of these units could then be and is based to a substantial extent on *demonstrated ability to lead,* whether commissioned or not.[28]

This last statement is certain to send a cold shudder down the spine of every conventionally-minded officer, regardless of service. However, as we continue transitioning into the information age and working to develop a transformed joint force, the force must become far more like an information-age organization than it currently is. These organizations are differentiated from industrial-age organizations primarily by their investment in their members to create knowledge workers, and by their structure/processes, which are designed to take advantage of the added capability knowledge workers have gained. In an information-age organization, knowledge workers are empowered to make decisions and initiate action within their expertise domains. When decisions are made closer to the point at which sufficient information and perspective can be brought together to make good decisions, the organization becomes more agile. As the ability to make good decisions becomes more widely shared within the organization, it becomes more robust. These are qualities of information-age organizations. They are also qualities of an organization of professionals. In essence, both individual performance and collective performance become a concern for all members, and individual members become accountable to all members for maintaining the standards and the ethics of the profession. In this sense, leadership is *distributed* within an organization of professionals, because all are mandated to be accountable for both individual and collective outcomes. Within the SMU, leadership is distributed based largely on expertise—the ability to influence outcomes.

Leadership in an information-age organization is marked by important characteristics that facilitate member ownership of outcomes:

- "Share" problem-working with those who are impacted by the problem and must be involved in solution implementation.
- Share control of the process as others become "owners." Help others to be "owners."
- Strongly facilitate and reward information-sharing and collaboration on problem-solving.
- With regard to well-understood overarching objectives, monitor outcomes rather than details, facilitate rather than control.
- Build a positive climate that values the contribution (initiative) of the individual member, and produces a client-centered culture.[29]

The key question in transformation is how far in this direction a conventionally disciplined force can go, and how fast it can get there. For this particular SMU, the key elements were in place within the first two years of its activation. However, it did not become fully mature as an organization of self-policing professionals for nearly a decade.

Leader Development

Those who pass the SMU selection process have a level of socio-emotional maturity and self-discipline that is well above average. In addition, they typically will already have several years of service and will have demonstrated the capacity for leadership prior to applying for selection. However, leadership in the special operations community is much more demanding than in the conventional Army, and the SMU focuses strongly on leader development.

A key function which must be served by all leaders is making sense out of situations which demand that effective action be taken. The ability to make sense of a pattern of events is mediated in part by the prior construction of mental models that allow attribution of meaning to what is going on. Mental models are created, in turn, by reflection on experience. When a leader has a mental model that fits the current circumstance, understanding of the situation comes almost as a flash of insight.[30] Everyone develops these mental models at least to some extent; however, some tend to develop more complex models—essential for understanding more complex issues or situations. The requirement that special operators—at all ranks—have complex understanding is underscored by the global nature of terrorism and the potential strategic impact of operator decisions and actions. The tendency to develop complex models is enhanced by a natural tendency to reflect and proactively inquire beyond immediate events. Selection tends to identify candidates with this tendency. Beyond that, unit experience is intended strongly to exploit this tendency, to enable individual operators and teams of operators to deal with progressively more complex challenges.

The manner in which AARs are conducted is an example. Most conventional Army units conduct AARs at the conclusion of exercises or rotations to a major training center. For example, observer/controllers at the National Training Center conduct extensive critiques of unit performance at the end of a rotation. Admittedly, units profit from this critique. However, they almost certainly do not profit to the extent they could if they followed the original model, as does the SMU. In this unit, AARs are conducted by NCOs and are ruthlessly frank. If officers are present, and they may be, they are expected to participate and to be as accountable for their actions as much as are other operators. In an AAR, the individual member speculates not only about what he did that did not work, but also about what he might try next time instead. If synchronization in movement and action was lacking, for example, members exchange information on what constitutes a cue and what the timing needs to be—to include who was lacking and why. This openness to examination of individual and collective performance not only emphasizes individual accountability for performance, but also reinforces collective accountability for individual performance. This search for "better ways" was embedded in the unit's culture from the beginning.[31]

There is a dynamic here that interfaces with the culture of the organization. Frank debate and criticism in AARs, actually a culturally mandated process, are strongly encouraged. However, this process produces superior performance without challenging self-efficacy, and so it feeds positively into the cultural norm of open discussion/debate about a wide range of issues. The dynamic thus is that the unit becomes more capable of discovering what it doesn't know and isn't doing well. On the leader development side, this dynamic teaches that reflection is extraordinarily important and effective in achieving better future performance, at both unit and individual levels. For leaders, the self-reflective environment also enhances development of the mental models essential for dealing with future complexity, and which are an essential part of expertise characterizing the professional. Since mental model-making is future-oriented, goal-sensitive, and performance-enhancing, there is an embedded cultural element in the SMU that pushes members to value these orientations—all relevant to a professional calling in the sense that they push the unit constantly to strive to develop new knowledge and new technology in this professional domain.

One final element of leader development in the SMU is worth noting. From the preceding discussion, it should be clear that an enormous amount of time is spent by the SMU on training, in both individual and collective skills. However, there is more to leader development than just the *amount* of training. From the very beginning, there was insistence on individual performance excellence, measured against demanding standards. However, for exercises designed to build collective skills, there was a consistent effort to make every situation contain a surprise or, preferably, multiple surprises. It became expected that leaders would ask subordinates to set up training missions that include surprises for the leader. The expectation for quality individual performance on individual skills never declined, and neither did the expectation for quality collective execution. However, it was always in the face of something unexpected. Leaders were thus trained in virtually all exercises to recognize anomalies, to think through them in real time under high time pressure, and thus to deal with the sudden onset of the unexpected and uncertain. This has, over the years, built a much higher level of flexibility and capacity for problem-solving into the leadership of the unit.[32] These, of course, are essential marks of professionalism.

Summary of Key Practices

Membership in the unit is an earned privilege, retained only by virtue of continued demonstrated performance. Selection is demanding and rigorous. However, "demanding and rigorous" are relative to the capacities of individuals seeking entry, and the mission performance requirements of the unit they are seeking to enter. Selection for the SMU is a demanding event, and the members are, in the impression of the present authors, truly outstanding soldiers and human beings. They are "quiet professionals" in every sense of the word, and, for the uninitiated, stand out to a large extent by *not standing out*. Two aspects of the selection process are worth particular mention, if only to demonstrate their applicability to non-special mission units.

- Selection is physically demanding, but not irrationally so. The intent is to determine whether candidates can retain their situational awareness and mental grasp even though deeply fatigued. We described this earlier as self-mastery. It relates clearly to future mission performance requirements, when it may be necessary for a unit member to continue to be self-reliant even when pushed near his physical limits.[33]
- Selection is values-sensitive. A part of the selection process is an examination of the candidate's understanding of legal and moral imperatives associated with the profession of arms as expressed by membership in this unit. This examination also addresses past behavior that shows commitment to a lifestyle reflecting these values. The overarching philosophy behind selection is that all unit members must be committed to these values and principles as a condition of entry into the unit and of continued membership in the unit. In conventional units, members may also be removed for moral/ethical transgressions. However, in the SMU the additional requirement is continued desire to live according to the values and principles held central by the unit. These values and principles are actively supported by all members, in part because they have been internal-

ized, and in part because this active commitment is supported by the leadership of the unit at all levels.

In essence, selection based on future performance requirements acts as a significant event that helps to make membership meaningful and valuable. A similar process, Special Forces Assessment and Selection (SFAS), which appropriately has a somewhat different focus, has been exported to the Special Forces. The Marines view their individual entry training as a kind of rite of passage. Most professions have them. It would seem useful to consider how this principle might be extended to conventional units. While this would be useless with the Army's current turbulence, plans are now in place to enhance stabilization in units throughout the force.

While there can be no question that the selection process identifies soldiers of greater maturity and ability to focus on what is important, that is not the whole story. Excellence is almost certainly an equal function of the climate and culture of the unit, which has been made possible by the special conditions under which the unit operates.

Perhaps the most important of these is assignment stabilization. As previously described, Beckwith, with support from General Meyer, was able to assure that soldiers accepted into the SMU would be separately managed, thus permitting retention of a member for many years. Unit teams are also stabilized for much longer periods than is customary in conventional Army units. Stabilization has a massive positive impact on the level to which collective skills can be raised, and on the resistance of collective skills to deterioration over time. It also has great positive impact on team unity and expectations for individual and team performance. If the team members know they are going to be together for a period of several years, the motivation to "invest" in one another, and to "invest" in team excellence is simply greater. Teamwork can develop, in which one member really can compensate for inability of another to perform.[34] This, of course, is at the heart of team robustness. The issue is twofold. One is trust that each will handle his own responsibility. However, in addition there is sensitivity to what *should* be happening but is not— that is, "seeing" what is not there—which is very hard to do when under stress. However, it is essential for team survival and mission success.

Unit and team stabilization also enhance mutual commitment. This is the "investment" notion just mentioned. Stabilization encourages the establishment of deep roots. Research in Korea found that the best fighters were soldiers who were drafted, who were married, and who had held responsible jobs before they were drafted. In other words, soldiers who had a history of assuming and living up to responsibility in earlier venues also assumed and lived up to responsibility in combat. Stabilization that allows a soldier to establish and maintain a satisfying family life also permits that soldier to understand responsibility and to mature in his ability to act responsibly in any number of spheres. Longevity of assignment and unit stabilization also promote mutual commitment in the performance of missions, as well as unit identity. This is one of the great drivers of unit excellence. A natural extension of the sense of mutual commitment is "heroic" behavior under stress. A prime example is the unquestioning decision by two operators to be inserted to rescue crew members of a grounded helicopter in Mogadishu. These crew members would not have characterized the operators' behavior as heroic, though an observer certainly would label it as such. The difference in perspectives comes from the member's certainty that he has "back-up" based on deep mutual commitment among all team members. Brave acts do of course require great courage, but they are aided by the assurance that one is not acting alone in the face of danger. All successful combat units will have bred this sense of mutual commitment among its members.[35]

Stabilization does one additional thing: it makes the growth of excellence an aspect of unit culture. Most SOF leaders spend major portions of their careers in assignments related to special operations, which permits them not only to learn from their own training and experience, but also to be taught by wise seniors who have walked the same path. This has particular significance in the sense that traditions about excellence arise from stories from and about seniors who are deeply respected for what they have accomplished. So traditions of excellence are passed along by stories of what others have done, and themselves become a source of the drive to achieve. The expectation is that performance is eventually going to be perfect. The performing element will train to a point of extreme overlearning on the purely mechanical aspects of performance, but at the same time will be expected to remain flexible/adaptive with regard to the unexpected. This creates the constructive tension possible only in teams/units that have a long time to train and remain together.

As is the case with most of the rest of the Army, the strength of the SMU lies in its NCOs. However, NCOs play a much more significant role in the unit than anywhere else in the Army. Commissioned officers come and go, though at a slower pace than in the conventional Army. They go to schools and accept assignments outside the unit in conformity with officer personnel management requirements, in order to develop the capabilities required for later high command and staff assignment. By contrast, with rare exceptions, NCOs stay. Some can and do remain at the operator level for very long periods, while others move up. Key chain of command assignments are based on talent, proficiencies, and values. The SMU has an NCO "slating" process that determines which NCOs will move into leadership positions and which ones will not.[36] These decisions are made by NCOs in the slating process, which they run. NCO rank does not necessarily determine who will have a formal leadership role. This is vastly different from how the conventional Army operates. The slating process thus results in a separation of leadership role and pay grade, which has been suggested more than once in the past 30 years as a way to compensate those with scarce but highly valued skills, but who may not be the best leaders. In this case, it is a recognition that a high level of operational skills should earn respect and compensation even if not accompanied by a high level of leadership ability.

In a related vein, the unit minimizes turbulence within a team when an existing team leader moves out because of promotion. Someone from within the team will probably move up to take his place, and a new graduate of operator training will be brought in at the bottom. In other words, the integrity of the team is preserved by internal practice and custom.[37] The slating process operates to maintain internal stability, which in turn operates to sustain collective skills. It also maintains team robustness, in the sense that valuable and hard-to-acquire "team knowledge" and institutional memory are not lost; it is relatively easy to break in a new operator training course graduate. It would be much harder to break in a new team leader. The process also promotes stronger buy-in to the values embraced by the organization. The NCOs who do the slating are more likely to have in-depth knowledge of the other NCOs than are either officers or a centralized assignments command. In the SMU, the NCO slating process is an indication of the professionalism of the NCOs who make up the practicing core of the unit. Yet another indication of the extent to which they are recognized as professionals is that NCO special operators evaluate both noncommissioned and commissioned officer candidates during both selection and operator training.

One anecdote illustrates the power of the values orientation of unit members and their internalization of these values. It has been unit policy since its activation that a member who has an accidental weapon discharge is immediately removed from the unit. There is no other punishment, and there is no reclama. The member is simply reassigned. In one documented incident, a unit member while alone experienced an accidental discharge of his weapon. No one witnessed it; no damage was done, and only the member was aware that it had happened. This member reported himself, and accepted the inevitable immediate reassignment. A year later, he was allowed to reapply and was reassigned to the unit.[38]

While performance standards are high and the press for perfection in execution is relentless, training has both an immediate and a future focus. The immediate focus is on the mechanical perfection required for precise execution of a specific mission. The future focus is on developing situational sensing and problem-solving skills that gain strength and mature over the course of many exercises. The objective is in fact to use ordinary training to enhance thinking skills in addition to action skills. (That also fits into the cultural expectation for individual self-reliance and adaptability.) Training structured in this way produces desirable outcomes at several different levels. First, it teaches leaders—both commissioned and noncommissioned—to be thinkers under pressure, and it also conditions operators to react calmly to the unexpected. It teaches both to resort to problem-solving as a first response to uncertainty. Uncertainty is a little like fear in its capacity to disrupt cognitive performance. If fear has been experienced once, then it is a less disruptive factor the second time around. In the same way, when leaders have been accustomed to the need for problem-solving in training, they become better able to recognize and solve unanticipated problems in operational conditions. Because leaders tend to remain in the organization for extended periods of time, the inclination toward problem-solving and the capacity to deal effectively with uncertainty become embedded in the culture.[39]

One final aspect of the SMU culture is of particular importance. While several indirect references have already been made to the notion of "ownership," this is a useful point at which to make the importance of this construct explicit. In the sense used here, ownership is a sense of "my job, my unit." This sense is found in many places in the conventional Army; it is not unique to the SMU. However, in the SMU there are additional overtones of "our jobs, our unit." The importance of this overtone cannot be overestimated. When the sense of "my job, my unit" is not tempered by "*our* job . . . ," leaders often over-generalize the reach of their own particular roles. At the extreme, a leader who has over-generalized his role assumes expertise in areas where it does not exist, does not defer to those who have greater knowledge or wisdom, and fares poorly in developing the wisdom, initiative, and problem-solving ability of subordinate leaders. Tempering by "our" facilitates sharing of roles, particularly leadership roles, and promotes a sense of ownership far down into the ranks of operators, along with the accountability and commitment outcomes already described.

This notion of shared ownership and shared leadership is threatening to conventional thinkers in a bureaucracy, but not in an association of professionals.[40] Commissioned officers in the SMU have indispensable roles, but they are not expected to be "the best" in all roles, particularly those requiring operator action skills. A professional will abstain from deciding an issue on which he has insufficient expertise, because the overriding professional concern is to serve the client; similarly, a core value in the unit is that performance must count more than individual power. A more senior member will defer to a more junior member with clearly greater expertise, especially when the stakes are high..

The value system is a product of professionalism, and in turn promotes professionalism. In addition, because of the stability in the unit, levels of expertise are understood, and sources of expertise are known. This reality facilitates the seeking of expertise when expertise is needed. It also motivates the member to build expertise, because he knows he will be in the unit long enough to build the required level of expertise himself. Time is not going to run out. Thus, noncommissioned officers also have leadership roles in the presence of commissioned officers, as do operators who are not in formal leadership roles. The question then arises as to who are the professionals? In the SMU, it is clear that, at a minimum, all who have attained "operator" status are. It is also clear that there are degrees of professionalism, based on the level of excellence an operator has attained over time.

Principles Generalizable to the Conventional Army

We have already mentioned changes in Ranger Regiment psychological screening and training. The most important changes were in mission training, which became more SOF-like in that problem-solving and a capacity to deal with complex and unexpected events was made an objective of training, replacing a more conventional form. In addition, a psychological program was initiated to increase assignment to the Ranger Regiment of members who were more flexible and thus more effective situational problem-solvers.

Also, some of the selection procedures pioneered in the SMU were adapted to Special Forces selection. Our subjective estimate is that the selection process in the SMU succeeds, among other things, in identifying individuals with generally higher socio-emotional maturity, which is important for high reliability under stress. If J. F. Dunnigan's data on SFAS and subsequent SF Qualification ("Q") Course success rates are accurate, our hypothesis would be that the SFAS also succeeds in identifying individuals with higher socio-emotional maturity, and that this has made a difference in the SF "Q" course success rate.[41] It logically should also improve leader development.

The central question is how much of what works in the SMU can be exported to the conventional Army. Our sense is that a great deal of exportability is in fact possible, and that transformation of the Army into an information-age force makes export essential.[42] Following are the areas showing the greatest promise for emulation by the conventional Army:

- **Stabilization.** In our view, the primary factor permitting emergence of professional excellence in the SMU is stabilization of unit membership. This permits socialization, in-depth acquisition of expertise by leaders and other operational personnel, and the development of a clearly articulated and well-understood set of cultural mandates about performance and accountability for mission success. These same benefits could be attained at least to some extent by conventional Army units through increased unit member stabilization, a process now being implemented.[43]
- **Selection and Training.** We would argue that these are of second priority, in that they would not attain their potential impact unless unit membership is stabilized. With stabilization, selection and training seem to produce a mature unit member who has a much greater-than-average capacity to perform under conditions of high stress and uncertainty. While understanding that the same actual practices might not be applicable in the conventional Army, we would contend that the concepts inspiring these practices are. A demanding qualifying experience clearly related to ultimate performance requirements, one that stimulates respect and admiration for the member who has succeeded in something difficult, is the beginning of "ownership." Training that produces in-depth expertise and quality judgment is at the heart of any profession.
- **Shared Initiative to Lead.** This principle is stated thusly because the essential element is mutual respect for expert knowledge and ability in the execution of a role. This, in turn, is at the heart of role-sharing, which is central to a professional, information-age organization. Application of this concept in the conventional Army will require a degree of culture change, but probably less than imagined by some, given the fundamental egalitarian nature of American culture.
- **Shared Ownership.** This also is possible only with stabilization. It is aided by training and leader development practices in the unit, which tend to produce a higher level of professionalism than is found in most conventional Army units.[44] It is expressed as "our" unit, and reflected in both mutual commitment and the willingness to defer to the judgment of others with greater expertise. Shared ownership also is an information-age concept that can and should be exported to combat arms units.[45]

Conclusion

In this chapter, we have described some of the history of an Army Special Mission Unit, and some of its attributes and practices. It was created for unique purposes and was given unique privileges in order to serve those purposes. Clearly, the conventional Army cannot imitate all of its practices. However, much of what works within the SMU is fundamental to leadership in general, and to information-age leadership in particular. While this assertion will be discounted by some, our response is that if Toyota can do it, then the U.S. Army can do it. An information-age culture, with its associated practices and mandates, cannot be built quickly. Taiichi Ohno is said to have spent two decades developing the Toyota system, and to have thought it necessary for a manager to spend a decade in the system in order to understand it fully so as to be able to duplicate it.[46] Purposeful cultural change is neither easy nor fast. However, we would contend that it is essential if we are to preserve our ability to enjoy the fruits of freedom and to share that freedom with the rest of the community of nations.[47]

Notes

1. Don M. Snider and Gayle L. Watkins, "Introduction," in *The Future of the Army Profession*, proj. directors Don M. Snider and Gayle L. Watkins, ed. Lloyd J. Matthews (Boston, MA: McGraw-Hill, 2002), 3.

2. Ibid., 5-6.

3. Ibid., 8.

4. A knowledge worker is someone who exercises initiative in applying understanding of a body of expert knowledge to the solution of a range of non-routine problems. Peter Drucker, "The Age of Social Transformation," *The Atlantic Monthly* 274 (November 1994): 53-80.

5. J. P. Womack, D. T. Jones, and D. Roos, *The Machine that Changed the World: The Story of Lean Production* (New York: Harper Perennial, 1991).

6. Ibid., 92.

7. While all the services contribute members to SOF, the authors are writing primarily from their understanding of Army Special Operations Forces. Though we believe our observations would hold in the SOF of other services, no empirical claim can be made to that effect.

8. This statement should not be construed as disregard of "unconventional-like" warriors throughout much of America's recorded history. See L. Q. Zedric and M. F. Dilley, *Elite Warriors: 300 Years of America's Best Fighting Troops* (Ventura, CA: Pathfinder, 1996).

9. T. White, *Swords of Lightning: Special Forces and the Changing Face of Warfare* (London, Brassey's, 1992), 121.

10. Ibid., 122.

11. Ibid., 124.

12. Charles A. Beckwith and D. Knox, *Delta Force* (New York: Harcourt, Brace, Jovanovich, 1983).

13. Two of the German snipers assigned to take out Black September terrorists at the Munich airport had failed to fire, with the result that Israeli Olympic athletes were murdered (Beckwith, 131). Both the will and the capability to take out a terrorist are nonnegotiable for a professional special operator. This is, of course, one reason for the enormous emphasis on character in the selection of U.S. Special Operators. As with any profession, the possession of such lethal capability must be anchored in an unassailable ethical and moral foundation.

14. The term "elite" is in itself paradoxical. Almost by definition, a "professional" is elite in some way. Yet the conventional Army is anti-elite in its operating value system; the SMU for years stringently avoided in every way possible being seen as "elite." Yet, information-age professionals must be elite; anti-elitism is almost by its very nature industrial-age thinking.

15. The references to H. Mintzberg's discussion of organizational forms are taken from his book *The Structuring of Organizations: A Synthesis of the Research* (Englewood Cliffs, NJ: Prentice-Hall, 1979), 432-33. His view of the innovative organization is especially instructive: "To innovate means to break away from established patterns. So the innovative organization cannot rely on any form of standardization for coordination. In other words, it must avoid all the trappings of bureaucratic structure" (pp. 432-433).

16. In fairness, MILPERCEN historically went to great lengths to accommodate SMU needs, as has its successor.

17. Perhaps understandably, the freedom and resources enjoyed by the SMU in its early days created a great deal of jealousy and charges of unfair favoritism from critics.

18. Because the unit was aided initially by a CIA psychologist, it seems likely that these procedures also reflected Agency practice; however, this has not been and cannot be verified.

19. It should be noted that at the time of this writing, the current CSA, Gen. Peter Schoomaker, has taken a number of initiatives to cause the conventional personnel management system to operate more like that of SOF in general.

20. For example, Beckwith states (p. 144) that operator training involved shooting three to four hours a day, five days a week. This was criticized for unfairness in resource availability during the formative months and years of the unit's existence, perhaps a reason for the sensitivity of the unit's leadership to avoid the appearance of elitism.

21. This set of tasks, conditions, and standards went into what Beckwith called the "Black Book," which later also served as a guide to the unit's final accreditation evaluation in 1979 at Fort Stewart (p. 179).

22. Ibid., 13-14.

23. Ibid., 14.

24. Ibid., 15.

25. Ibid.,18.

26. Ibid., 18.

27. In the current SMU, the conventional Army's orderliness and good appearance remains; the critical point is that it is not the most important thing, just as is the case with the conventional Army during actual combat operations. For example, long hair, moustaches, and beards are "issue items" when they facilitate mission performance.

28. This comment explicitly differentiates command and leadership. Command is the legal authority to issue orders; it is conferred by commission and is associated with rank. Leadership is the persuasive "capacity" to define direction and purpose, and to energize others to achieve them. Leadership is based in large part on respect for perceived expertise (expert or referent power), a crucial element of a profession.

29. T. O. Jacobs, *Strategic Leadership: The Competitive Edge* (Student Text) (Washington, DC: Industrial College of the Armed Forces, 2004), 3.

30. G. Klein, *Intuition at Work* (New York: Currency Books, 2003), 39-42.

31. For example, Beckwith notes that the SMU had a "think tank" session once a week (p. 171).

32. This difference was dramatically shown in Mogadishu. Ranger elements had been trained in a much more stereotyped manner, and thus, though valiant in the extreme, were at a loss in coping with the chaos of the ambush sprung by Somalian irregulars in October 1993. Ranger unit training has since been modified, based on SMU principles, to enhance the capacity of leaders to cope with uncertainty and chaos.

33. In the mid-1980s, TRADOC became concerned that the SMU was accepting too few candidates, and wanted standards changed. The U.S. Army Research Institute was asked to evaluate the selection process and standards. The USARI conclusion was that the process and standards were appropriate in view of operator performance requirements. This, of course, is the longer-term objective, as contrasted with the shorter-term objective of simply filling a TDA more rapidly For the SMU, passing selection had deeper meaning.

34. Robustness in the form of cross-training has been an element of Special Forces training for a long time. However, robustness in the SMU extends beyond cross-training to awareness that a given team role is not being performed, and the capacity to assume it. It is a higher degree of capability and redundancy, and thus robustness.

35. Its lack was probably one factor responsible for the much higher casualty rate of unit replacements in World War II, when contrasted with other unit members who had already experienced at least one engagement.

36. J. Galland and M.G. Sanders, *Small Group Leadership for Elite Units* (Army Research Institute, 1998), 4.

37. This stands in contrast to findings on unit turbulence in the late 1980s, which found one NCO PCS typically generated an average of about one and a half additional position changes within infantry units as other NCOs were moved around. The logic appeared to be a concern that a fire team leader, for example, might not be able to be sufficiently "distant" from squad members if moved up to be squad leader. If that is in fact the logic, it is distinctly industrial-age as opposed to information-age thinking.

38. Of course, his ability to return to the unit appeals to our sense of justice. However, the incident as a whole illustrates that ethical standards are nonnegotiable, and that an organization of professionals will voluntarily subscribe to them.

39. It should be noted that these principles are not acting in an all-or-nothing manner. A key additional principle is that a small change in emphasis which acts consistently over time can make a major change in a system. Thus, "tendencies" can act over a period of years to produce stable characteristics in unit culture and professionalism.

40. The very term "association" when applied to a hierarchical military organization is likely to strike fear in the heart of a bureaucrat. After all, isn't hierarchy the source of power? The point is that in a profession, hierarchy is never the sole source of power, and may not even be the primary source. Knowledge, expertise, and the capacity to act in the service of the client—in this case, the American people—are are primary.

41. J. F. Dunnigan, *The Perfect Soldier: Special Operations, Commandos, and the Future of U.S. Warfare* (New York: Citadel Press), 269.

42. In this discussion two points should be kept in mind. First, "export" does not mean all-or-nothing. Some of the unique attributes of the SMU that cannot be duplicated can be imitated to a degree, probably with intermediate outcomes. Second, not all conventional Army units need to be the same. The ones most needful of change are those which will, by virtue of their missions, be required to have higher levels of professional expertise and initiative.

43. The CSA has initiated policy changes that will result in a greater degree of stabilization in units. If retained for the long haul, they will almost certainly produce units that are more combat-effective.

44. As of this writing, all officers commanding operational troops have themselves succeeded in selection and operator training. It might be argued that this is a critical factor in their capacity to defer to the situational leadership of a more capable but lower-ranking member, and in their observed openness to suggestions for improvement in unit operations. We would offer in addition that this is an essential element of effective information-age leadership which can and should become culturally embedded in combat arms unit leadership. See R. A. Heifitz, *Leadership Without Easy Answers* (Cambridge, MA: Harvard Univ. Press, 1994).

45. The NCO slating process is an example of a process reflecting and strengthening "ownership." It contrasts with the centralized system of senior NCO promotions in the conventional Army. The argument of centralized promotion advocates, that this produces a more uniform quality in the NCO ranks, is powerful. However, the obvious beneficial effects of the SMU practice are also powerful. The present writers profess no prescience in this matter, but suggest that enlisted personnel management system experts should be able to devise a system that might preserve the benefits of both practices.

46. J. P. Womack et al., 62.

47. Of course, culture change is progressive; it is going on all the time. The only question is whether it will be grudgingly responsive to external pressures, or insightfully proactive in shaping the organization for the future, and perhaps thereby shaping the future as well.

21

The Human, Spiritual, and Ethical Dimensions of Leadership in Preparation for Combat[1]

John W. Brinsfield and Peter A. Baktis

I n the quest to reexamine and possibly redefine the Army profession, the key roles, skills, and knowledge required of military leaders are indispensable elements for analysis. No profession can compete with competent outsiders without defining itself, its special expertise requirements, and its solutions to the problems of transformation in perceived influence, power allocation, internal organization, and organization of knowledge to support its special claims to jurisdiction.[3]

> If I learned nothing else from the war, it taught me the falseness of the belief that wealth, material resources, and industrial genius are the real sources of a nation's military power. These are but the stage setting . . . national strength lies only in the hearts and spirits of men.
>
> —S.L.A. Marshall[2]

The historical mission and jurisdiction of the joint military services are to win the nation's wars. Traditionally, all other missions were secondary to this national security responsibility. Yet at the beginning of the 21st century, our conception of America's security umbrella has been broadened to include domestic police, fire, and drug enforcement activities as well as international humanitarian and peacekeeping missions—to the detriment, some would say, of the Army's main war-fighting role. In fact, the system of professions within which the Army competes is crowded with American government entities such as the other military services, the State Department, Border Patrol, Drug Enforcement Administration, Federal Bureau of Investigation, Central Intelligence Agency, Federal Emergency Management Agency, and a growing cadre of commercial contractors performing battlefield tasks. The nation's formerly well-integrated system of professions addressing security has mushroomed "without a commensurate expansion in the legal, cultural, or workplace mechanisms that legitimate each profession's jurisdiction."[4] Mission creep and the post-11 September 2001 ethos, combined with an erosion of the professional military culture by the commercialization of traditional military roles, have challenged the Army's understanding of its role in the nation's defense.

Moreover, in the quest to establish its professional boundaries, the Army has had to rely on a civilian leadership often having little or no experience in the military for its mission definition and resources, all the while competing with the lure of college and the job market for the hearts, minds, and purses of the recruits who may become its future leaders.[5] These challenges, among many others, seem to require a redefinition of the components of military professionalism and leadership for the future.

Soldiers are the Army's heart, life force, and strength no matter what their mission may be. They determine the Army's effectiveness, success, or possible failure. They must respond to the unique demands of the profession of arms: total commitment, unlimited liability, possible lengthy separations from family, community, and civilian primary support systems; and total loyalty to a values-based and service-based organization. In time of war, they may be asked to sacrifice themselves for the nation and for one another as guardians of the republic.

The new warrior ethos that assigns many of the skills and responsibilities traditionally reserved for officers to enlisted soldiers challenges traditional roles and definitions in the profession of arms. Likewise, the advent of new technological tools of war threatens to ignore the human dimension. Any internal analysis and definition of the profession of arms must include, therefore, an inquiry into the soldier's human, spiritual, and ethical needs, lest, to paraphrase the words of one Civil War general, they be asked for more than they could possibly be expected to give.[6]

As part of such an effort, this chapter seeks to analyze the human and spiritual needs of soldiers as part of the special knowledge required by Army leaders to motivate, train, and command their personnel and their units in peace and war. It also suggests some considerations for preparing soldiers psychologically, spiritually, and ethically for future combat operations.

The working hypothesis is that all soldiers have human needs and most have spiritual needs broadly defined, and that converting these needs into strengths of will and character is an important part of combat leadership—and thus of Army professionalism itself. The chapter is composed of three major parts: (1) definition and discussion of human and spiritual needs, including an analysis of the theory of needs as applied to soldiers; (2) description of some of the past efforts to capitalize on human and spiritual needs so as to achieve confidence, cohesion, and courage; and (3) consideration of proposed combat training approaches as related to the human dimension of soldiers serving in the Army. Because certain aspects of human nature cannot be directly observed but must be inferred from observed behavior, the data for analysis rely on multidisciplinary sources which include the humanities as well as the social sciences.

Assumptions

Since the subject matter of this analysis deals with the needs of the soldier, a review of sources relating to the individual will be useful before we move to the level of the organization or profession. Much of the research data involve individual responses from soldiers in small units rather than Army-wide studies. In taking this approach, we may assume, first, that military leaders do and will recognize their dual obligations to complete their missions successfully and take effective measures to ensure the health and welfare of as many personnel as possible within their commands. This is an ancient canon of the military art, as explained by Sun Tzu in *The Art of War* in the early part of the fourth century B.C.:

> And therefore the general who in advancing does not seek personal fame but whose only purpose is to protect the people and promote the best interests of his sovereign,

is the precious jewel of the state. Because such a general regards his men as his own sons they will march with him into the deepest valleys. He treats them as his own beloved sons, and they will die with him. If he cherishes his men is this way, he will gain their utmost strength. Therefore the Military Code says: "The general must be the first in the toils and fatigues of the army."[7]

There are, of course, many other authoritative utterances regarding the commander's duty to care for soldiers, but few of such established antiquity. Field Manual 22-100, *Army Leadership: Be, Know, Do*, perhaps the most authoritative contemporary guidance, states simply, "Accomplish the mission *and* take care of your soldiers."[8]

Our second assumption is that a holistic knowledge of the human and spiritual needs of soldiers, yet to be defined, will be of value to the military leader in providing support and resources for meeting these needs, thereby strengthening the capacity of the fighting force to complete its missions successfully. In war, soldiers' comfort, insofar as comfort is possible, affects morale and thus combat effectiveness.[9] The Creed of the Noncommissioned Officer embraces this concept in its brief declaration that "all soldiers are entitled to outstanding leadership; I will provide that leadership. I know my soldiers, and I will always place their needs above my own."[10] Further, the new Soldier's Creed implicitly suggests that it is not solely the responsibility of officers and noncommissioned officers to be self-aware and adaptable, but rather that all soldiers will exemplify those traits. Gen. Creighton Abrams, former Army Chief of Staff, goes to the heart of the matter:

> The Army is not made up of people; the Army is people. They have needs and interests and desires. They have spirit and will, strengths, and abilities. They are the heart of our preparedness and this preparedness—as a nation and as an Army—depends upon the spirit of our soldiers. It is the spirit which gives the Army life. Without it we cannot succeed.[11]

If leadership means gaining the willing obedience of subordinates who understand and believe in the mission's purpose, who value their team and their place in it, who trust their leaders and have the will to see the mission through, then leaders must understand two key elements: leadership itself as well as the people they lead.[12]

Religion, Spirituality, and Human and Spiritual Needs

Toward the end of his classic study of the psychology of soldiers, *The Anatomy of Courage* (1967), Lord Charles Moran turned to the subject of religion and spiritual power:

> I have said nothing of religion, though at no time has it been far from my thoughts. General Paget asked me once to talk to officers commanding divisions and corps and armies in the Home Forces. When I had done, they broke up and came to me, one or two at a time, questioning. Often that night I was asked about the importance of religion. Speaking as if they did not know how to put it, they separately told me how faith had come into the lives of many of their men. Is it so strange? Is it not natural that they are fumbling for another way of living, less material, less sterile, than that which has brought them to this pass? What are they seeking?[13]

Lord Moran's questions are well posed, for the separate disciplines of psychology and religion often look to separate sources of authority, separate methodologies, and different language to describe human behavior. Nevertheless, many psychologists, sociologists, anthropologists, and physicians recognize the phenomenology of religion as abstracted from any claims concerning its essence. In other words, religion may be studied and respected as an element of culture without subscription to its content. W.I. Thomas, one of the leading sociologists of the past century, explained that "if a culture believes something to be real, we must respect that belief in dealing with that culture."[14] Recently the profession of arms has developed a growing interest in the pervasiveness of religious authority in traditional cultures and the necessity of understanding religion as a motivating force in many world communities.

Many soldiers in the American Army culture identify with a specific religious faith—some 299,958 or 64 percent of active duty soldiers in April 2001—but many are also reluctant to define too closely what they mean by religion, faith, and especially spirituality.[15] Even though spiritual strength is mentioned in many Army publications, e.g., the 1999 edition of the U.S. Army Training and Doctrine Command's *TLS Strategy: Change, Readiness, and the Human Dimension of Training, Leader Development and Soldiers,* as well as the 2001 edition of the Department of the Army's Well-Being Campaign Plan, there are comparatively few published definitions.[16]

Part of the reason why soldiers are reluctant to discuss religion openly is their perception that religion is a very personal subject. Two generations ago Prof. Morris Janowitz found "a tendency among leaders in a political democracy, and especially among the military, to resent being questioned about their religious background."[17] A strong adherence to a particular religious point of view can be perceived as politically divisive and detrimental to unit cohesion. More commonly, religious language itself is not well understood, for the same terms may have different meanings in different faith groups. Military leaders like to have a clear idea of what they are saying and supporting, as do most people.

At the same time, many educational institutions, including the U. S. Military Academy, have recognized a spiritual domain in their philosophies of comprehensive education. The Cadet Leader Development System, a strategy for total commissioned leader development at West Point, links the spiritual domain to a common quest for meaning in life:

> This [spiritual] domain explicitly recognizes that character is rooted in the very essence of who we are as individuals, and discerning "who we are" is a lifelong search for meaning. Cadet years are a time of yearning, a time to be hungry for personal meaning and to engage in a search for ultimate meaning in life. Formally recognizing this fundamental aspect of human development is not unique to West Point; educators have long held that individual moral search is an inherent, even vital, component of any robust undergraduate education. In other words, cadets' search for meaning is natural, it will occur, whether or not we explicitly recognize and support it as an institution or not.[18]

For some, the quest for meaning will lead to questions of religion. For others, meaning is found through spirituality, a broader and possibly less distinct category than institutional religion. Is there a useful lexicon for such terms as religion, spirituality, identity, ultimate meaning, and self-actualization in individual development?

Dr. Jeff Levin, Senior Research Fellow at the National Institute for Healthcare Research and a scholar of the relationship between religious faith and health, tackles the problem of defining religion and spirituality as follows:

> Historically, "religion" has denoted three things: particular churches or organized religious institutions; a scholarly field of study; and the domain of life that deals with things of the spirit and matters of "ultimate concern." To talk of practicing religion or being religious refers to behaviors, attitudes, beliefs, experiences, and so on, that involve this domain of life. This is so whether one takes part in organized activities of an established religious institution or one has an inner life of the spirit apart from organized religions.
>
> "Spirituality," as the term traditionally has been used, refers to a state of being that is acquired through religious devotion, piety, and observance. Attaining spirituality—union or connection with God or the divine—is the ultimate goal of religion, and is a state not everyone reaches. According to this usage, spirituality is a subset of a larger phenomenon, religion, and by definition is sought through religious participation.[19]

Dr. Levin goes on to observe, however, that in the last 30 years the word "spirituality" has taken on a wider meaning. New Age authors and some news media have limited "religion" to those behaviors and beliefs that occur in the context of organized religious institutions. All other religious expression, particularly private meditation and secular transcendent experiences including feelings of awe in the presence of nature and oneness with it, are now encompassed by the term "spirituality." This wider definition reverses the relationship between religion and spirituality to make the former now the subset of the latter.[20]

Many scholars of world religions agree that Levin's wider definition of spirituality seems to fit the beliefs of many faith groups, even those with non-theistic views. Although the majority of the world's religions do claim to be the vehicles for a personal experience with God, Allah, Brahman, or one of the other of the world's named deities, there are others for whom spirituality is a non-theistic pilgrimage to individual enlightenment, wisdom, and transcendence. For example, in Zen or Ch'an Buddhism, "the highest truth or first principle is inexpressible," that is, the divine is so remote from human perception as to make its essence indescribable, thereby rendering an organized, doctrinal religion impossible; however, a mind-expanding, experiential awakening called "satori" is still available through meditation, mentoring by masters, and self-discipline.[21] In the Shinto religion of Japan, the perception of "kami" may be simply the reverence one has for the awesome power and beauty of nature even though gifts are frequently left at Shinto shrines for the spirits that inhabit such places.[22] The spiritual goal of reaching Nirvana is found in both theistic Hinduism and non-theistic Theravada Buddhism. The Falun Gong meditation which began in China in 1992 consists of spiritual exercises to promote health, cure illnesses, and allow the practitioner to absorb energy from the universe in order to ascend to a higher plane of human existence, but there are no named deities.[23]

Thus, to summarize the period since the 1970s, the context of religious institutions and spiritual practices in America has become enormously more diverse. Although in 1998 approximately 90 percent of the American people professed to be religious and 63 percent (169 million) identified themselves as affiliated with a *specific* religious group, the number of separate religious denominations has grown in a 60-year span from about 45 in 1940 to more than 2,000 at present.[24] This proliferation of religious and spiritual options suggests that Levin and others are correct to identify spirituality with the individual quest for greater insight, enlightenment, wisdom, meaning, and experience with the numinous or divine. Religion does refer in most current literature to the institutionalization of symbols, rites, practices, education, and other elements necessary to transmit the specifics of religious culture to the next generation.

However, there is no evidence that the world's major religions are in decline. Indeed, as Samuel Huntington has argued, there is a worldwide revival of interest in traditional faiths, including Christianity in Russia, Buddhism in Japan, and Islam in Central Asia, faiths which offer meaning, stability, identity, assurance, and fixed points of reference in the face of the "clash of civilizations and the remaking of world order."[25] Moreover, in a recent poll taken by Blum and Weprin Associates of New York, which surveyed adults across America, 59 percent of those polled said that they were *both* religious and spiritual. Only 20 percent identified themselves as "only spiritual," and still fewer (9 percent) viewed religion in a negative way.[26] Nevertheless, with the phenomenal growth of communication technologies and availability of knowledge at the individual level, the spiritual quest by future generations may depend on some traditional religious institutions but will certainly be directed toward meeting broader individual needs. In a current study conducted from 29 November to 7 December 2003 regarding Operation Iraqi Freedom, Dr. Charles Moskos found that 26 percent of his study group of 500 soldiers stated that being deployed had a positive effect on their religious feelings.[27]

Theory of Human Needs Applied to Soldiers

The psychological study of soldiers is a relatively new academic endeavor. In the preface to his book, *The Anatomy of Courage*, Lord Moran, who had served as a medical officer in France and Flanders during World War I, explained that "there was no book in the English language on the psychology of the soldier before 1945."[28] *The Anatomy of Courage* was designed to fill that gap. It was an attempt to answer questions about what was happening in men's minds during combat and how they overcame fear. Since 1967, when Moran's book was published, there have been numerous studies on military psychology, military psychiatry, and combat motivation.[29] It was from an analysis of motivation and behavioral theory that the theory of needs as applied to soldiers found its most eloquent proponents.

The nature of the relationship between motivation and human behavior has been a subject of philosophical and psychological interest for centuries. There are multiple modern formulations which seek to explain motivation in general, including hedonistic, cognitive, drive reduction, and needs theories, to mention a few.[30] For more than 40 years, a theory popular in U.S. Army literature was Dr. Abraham Maslow's concept of *self-actualization* as the driving force of human personality, as set forth in his 1954 book *Motivation and Personality*.[31] Dr. Maslow was associated with the humanistic movement in psychology which emphasized the person and his or her psychological growth.[32] Maslow described self-actualization as the need "to become more and more what one is, to become everything that one is capable of becoming," or, in other words, to be all one can be.[33]

According to Maslow's self-actualization theory, the components of identity arise from two sources: the individual's unique potential and the different ways the individual copes with impediments placed in the way. Maslow placed human needs in three categories: (1) basic needs arranged in a hierarchy which included physical necessities, safety and security, and love and social belongingness, (2) esteem or recognition needs; and (3) metaneeds, which include spiritual qualities such as order, unity, goodness, and spirituality itself.[34] Basic needs are deficiency needs, necessary for functional survival, and must be fulfilled before a person can turn attention to the metaneeds. Esteem or recognition and metaneeds are growth needs; if properly satisfied, a person will grow into a completely developed human being—physically, emotionally, and spiritually—and have the potential to become a self-actualized person.[35]

Maslow recognized a spiritual component in the human personality, but argued that it was a natural component which sought meaning in a cause outside oneself and bigger than oneself, something impersonal, not merely self-centered.[36] Moreover, the spiritual need impelled persons toward vocations, callings, and missions which they described with passionate, selfless, and profound feelings.[37]

Maslow believed that such metaneeds are universal, but that usually only self-actualized people attempted to meet them.

> This is to say, that the most highly developed persons we know are metamotivated to a much higher degree, and are basic-need-motivated to a lesser degree than average or diminished people are. The full description of human nature must then include all intrinsic values. These intrinsic values are instinctoid in nature, i.e., they are needed to avoid illness and to achieve fullest humanness or growth. The highest values, the spiritual life, the highest aspirations of mankind are therefore proper subjects for scientific study and research.[38]

Finally, Maslow argued that the spiritual aspirations of the human personality are a natural phenomenon, not a theological construct nor limited to the domain of religious institutions. In his book *Religions, Values, and Peak-Experiences* (1970), Maslow explained, "I want to demonstrate that spiritual values have naturalistic meaning, that they are not the exclusive possession of organized churches, that they do not need supernatural concepts to validate them, that they are well within the jurisdiction of a suitably enlarged science, and that, therefore, they are the general responsibility of all mankind."[39]

The Army leadership adopted Maslow's theory of basic and metaneeds enthusiastically after 1970. This was because, in part, it correlated well with observable behavior among soldiers and because it was in consonance with the compelling analogies that if missions have requirements and weapons have a basic load, then soldiers must have human requirements and basic needs. In a collection of Bill Mauldin's World War II cartoons titled *Up Front*, G.I. Willie in his torn and dirty fatigues tells a medic, " Just gimme a coupla aspirin, I already got a Purple Heart."[40] Willie's basic needs, in Maslow's terms, clearly claimed priority over his esteem or recognition needs.

The October 1983 edition of Field Manual 22-100, *Military Leadership*, a standard text for thousands of the Army's present leaders, incorporated Maslow's hierarchy of basic physical, safety, and social needs almost verbatim.[41] The manual's authors explained, "As a leader, you must understand these needs because they are powerful forces in motivating soldiers. To understand and motivate people and to develop a cohesive, disciplined, well-trained unit, you must understand human nature."[42]

However, there were three divergencies from Maslow's theory in the 1983 leadership manual. First, rather than discuss the need for esteem or recognition, which is the fourth need in Maslow's hierarchy, the leadership manual addressed "Higher Needs," i.e., the need for religion, the need for increased competence, and the need to serve a worthwhile cause. With regard to the need for religion, the manual's writers explained that historically,

> many people not normally religious become so in time of war. The danger and chaos of war give rise to the human need to believe that a greater spiritual being is guiding one's fate for the best, regardless of whether one lives or dies. In this sense it helps soldiers to believe that they are fighting for a cause that is moral and right in the eyes of their religion. This is an important source of motivation for soldiers all over the world.[43]

Although the authors may have reflected their own beliefs accurately, Maslow argued that spiritual needs are universal, not dependent upon crises in war except perhaps as one of many catalysts for revealing such needs and not *always* leading to faith in a greater spiritual power so much as to a greater potential state of individual spirituality.

In more recent years, the Army has modified its language in describing the needs of soldiers and their families. Part of this change was due to advances in medical and behavioral research, notably by the Army Research Institute for the Behavioral and Social Sciences and by the Academy of Health Sciences at Ft. Sam Houston, Texas, among others. Nevertheless, human needs as embodied in the soldier are still represented in roughly the same hierarchy Maslow propounded. The Army Well-Being Strategic Plan of 2001, produced by the Office of the Deputy Chief of Staff for Personnel, defined Army well-being as "the personal—physical, material, mental, and spiritual—state of soldiers [Active, Reserve, Guard, retirees, veterans], civilians, and their families that contributes to their preparedness to perform the Army's mission."[44] The spiritual state (of well-being), according to the Army Well-Being Plan, "centers on a person's religious/philosophical needs and may provide powerful support for values, morals, strength of character, and endurance in difficult and dangerous circumstances."[45]

In summary, contemporary psychologists have challenged Maslow's hierarchy of needs, which they describe as "one size fits all," instead pointing to a more complex model to explain motivation and behavior. Steven Reiss, a psychologist at Ohio

State University, has identified at least 15 fundamental motivational desires in human beings, including honor, morality, and order. Reiss does not present "spirituality" as a category of human motivation and desire, but he does say that further categories are open to scientific study.[46]

Likewise, but from a different perspective, research in the relationship between spirituality and healing has increased dramatically in the past ten years. The National Institute for Healthcare Research in Rockville, Maryland, has accumulated more than 200 studies from researchers at such prestigious institutions as Harvard, Duke, Yale, Michigan, the University of California at Berkeley, Rutgers, and the University of Texas at Galveston showing that religious beliefs and practices benefit health and rates of recovery from illness in many patients.[47] According to one study by Dr. Andrew Newberg, published in 2001 under the title *Why God Won't Go Away*, research on the human brain suggests that a particular area of the brain is activated by prayer and meditation, at least among the subjects involved in the research. This led some interpreters to claim that "the human brain is wired for God."[48]

Yet none of the studies discovered to date claims that *all* people are either spiritual or religious. Levin and Maslow agreed, after 60 years of study between them, that while everyone has a range of needs, not everyone reaches an awareness of either innate or acquired spiritual needs even though Maslow believed that all human beings are potentially motivated by metaneeds to some degree.[49]

What can be demonstrated, and what may be of most import for the Army leadership and Army professionalism, is that the American culture from which the military services draw support puts a high premium on spirituality, organized religion, religious freedom, and the Constitutional right to the free exercise of religion, a right which both Congress and the Federal courts have applied to military as well as to civilian communities. The *Journal of Family Psychology* reported in 1999 that in America,

> many individuals report that religion and spirituality are integral parts of their lives. As many as 95% of American adults express a belief in God, 84% believe God can be reached through prayer, and 86% state religion is important or very important to them. Surveys also suggest religion may play a significant role in many marriages. Religiousness, as reflected by church affiliation or attendance, emerged as a correlate of higher marital satisfaction in early, classic studies on marital adjustment. More recently, greater religiousness has been tied to higher marital satisfaction and adjustment in large, nationally representative samples.[50]

The rate of attendance at religious services at least once a month among a national random sample of 1,000 families, as reported by the *Journal of Family Psychology,* was 37 percent, with 25 percent of the same sample reporting attendance at religious services weekly or more than once a week.[51]

Among Army soldiers in 2001 the rate of identification with one of the seven larger religious faith groups in the Army—Protestant, Catholic, Orthodox, Jewish, Muslim, Buddhist, or Hindu—was 64 percent, one percentage point higher than the national average.[52] Although chapel attendance figures for soldiers and family members of all faiths in the Army worldwide were not available, the U.S. Army Forces Command reported 10,563 field and chapel worship services were conducted in FY

2000 for active duty soldiers.[53] In addition, FORSCOM documented among chapel-supported functions 821 weddings, 611 funerals, 334 memorial services, 2,644 family skill/enhancement classes, and 1,304 separate suicide prevention classes which reached a total population of 89,979 soldiers, retirees, and family members. In a volunteer Army with 65 percent of its active force soldiers of all ranks married and with 52,000 physically handicapped members included in the families, these services were indispensable to soldier welfare and readiness.[54]

Since church attendance by the retiree population has not been separately tabulated, the estimated church attendance figures for active duty soldiers and family members cannot be accurately determined. However, of 12,561 waiting spouses during lengthy separations due to deployments, 30.6 percent (3,844) reported use of worship programs and services provided by Army chaplains.[55]

Although all relevant inputs have not been considered (e.g., religious activities in the Reserve components), it seems reasonable to conclude that the active duty Army population is a microcosm of American society and culture. The majority of citizens and soldiers profess to be religious. Moreover, many more people have an interest in spirituality and religion than attend religious services, at least on a regular basis. During periods of prolonged stress to both individuals and families as exemplified by deployment to a combat zone, most soldiers and spouses indicate that religion is an important support for their pre-deployment readiness, their morale, the well-being of their deploying units, the durability of their marriages, and the welfare of families back home.[56]

Leveraging the Human Dimension to Build Soldier Confidence, Cohesion, and Courage

On 15 June 1941, Gen. George C. Marshall addressed the faculty and students of Trinity College in Hartford, Connecticut, a college linked to the Episcopal Church, on the subject of morale in modern war:

> You must speak to the soul in order to electrify the man.
> —NAPOLEON BONAPARTE[57]

> I know that this association with you here this morning is good for my soul. If I were back in my office I would not have referred to my soul. Instead I should have used the word "morale" and said that this occasion increased my "morale"—in other words was of spiritual benefit to me. One of the most interesting and important phenomena of the last war was the emergence of that French word from comparative obscurity to widespread usage in all the armies of the world. Today as we strive to create a great new defensive force, we are investing the word "morale" with deeper and wider meaning. Underlying all the effort back of this essentially material and industrial effort is the realization that the primary instrument of warfare is the fighting man. We think of food in terms of morale—of clothing, of shelter, of medical care, of amusement and recreation in terms of morale. We want all of these to be available in such quantity and quality that they will be sustaining factors when it comes to a consideration of the soldier's spirit. The soldier's heart, the soldier's spirit, the soldier's soul are everything. Unless the soldier's soul sustains him, he cannot be relied on and will fail himself and his commander and his country in the end.[58]

General Marshall gave a good deal of his personal attention to supporting the soldier's morale, moral behavior, and spiritual strength, authorizing more than 550 cantonment chapels and 9,111 chaplains—one for every 1,200 soldiers—to the Army and Army Air Corps.[59]

However, General Marshall recognized that the soldier's morale—or spirit—included much more and demanded much more than religious support alone. Morale is a disciplined state of mind which embraces confidence in the self and confidence in the unit. It encompasses courage, zeal, loyalty, hope, and at times grim determination to endure to the end.[60] Morale, élan, esprit de corps, the will to fight, and the will to win are the human dimension's most important intangible assets. Strong morale is an emotional bonding of purpose, common values, good leadership, shared hardship, and mutual respect.[61] Of all of the factors which produce strong morale in a unit—of whatever size—leadership by example and unit cohesion are frequently mentioned first.[62] Lord Moran's experiences with unit cohesion in the British regiments during World War I led him to conclude that "there was only one religion in the regular army, the regiment; it seemed to draw out of them the best that was in them."[63] Such morale, such fighting spirit, coupled with faith in their leaders, have been important factors in the survival and ultimate victory of soldiers throughout military history.

The morale of the soldier and the esprit de corps of the unit, however, may have a short shelf life in extended combat. Like courage, morale is an expendable commodity and needs replenishment and support to withstand prolonged combat stress. John Keegan reflected on the experiences of British and American doctors during World War II in his book *The Face of Battle*. Of all British battle casualties during the active phase of the Battle of France in 1940, "ten to fifteen percent were psychiatric, ten to twenty percent during the first ten days of the Normandy battle and twenty percent during the two latter months, seven to ten percent in the Middle East in the middle of 1942, and eleven percent in the first two months of the Italian campaign."[64] The official American report on combat exhaustion during the same period stated:

> There is no such thing as "getting used to combat." Each moment of combat imposes a strain so great that men will break down in direct relation to the intensity and duration of their exposure [thus] psychiatric casualties are as inevitable as gunshot and shrapnel wounds in warfare. Most men were ineffective after 180 or even 140 days. The general consensus was that a man reached his peak of effectiveness in the first 90 days of combat, that after that his efficiency began to fall off, and that he became steadily less valuable thereafter until he was completely useless. The number of men on duty after 200 to 240 days of combat was small and their value to their units negligible.[65]

Not only individuals but also whole units became ineffective as a result of fatigue, stress, high casualties, poor leadership, and a loss of hope. In the Tunisian campaign of 1942, veteran American combat troops joined newer recruits in "going to ground," "burning out," and breaking down. One 1944 report pointed out that in the North African theater nearly all men in rifle battalions not otherwise disabled ultimately became psychiatric casualties even though some of them made it as far as

Cassino and Anzio.[66] Other examples of whole units becoming combat ineffective may be gleaned from the experience of some German units on the Eastern Front, American units during the Korean War, and Iraqi units during the Gulf War.[67]

What types of support did soldiers find helpful in enduring and coping with the stresses of combat for as long as they did? John Keegan identifies four critical elements in British armies: (1) moral purpose—believing in the "rightness" of the war; (2) unit cohesion—formed in hard training, sports competitions, and rewards for being the "best"; (3) selfless leadership from first-line officers; and (4) spiritual or religious fortification before battle.[68]

William Manchester, who experienced intense fighting in the spring of 1945 as an enlisted Marine on Okinawa during World War II, wrote of his survival in his book *Goodbye Darkness*:

> You had to know that your whole generation was in this together, that no strings were being pulled for anybody. You also needed nationalism, the absolute conviction that the United States was the envy of all other nations. Today the ascent of Sugar Loaf [on Okinawa] takes a few minutes. In 1945 it took ten days and cost 7,547 Marine casualties. And beneath my feet, where mud had been deeply veined with human blood, the healing mantle of turf [I murmured a prayer: *God] take away this murdering hate and give us thine own eternal love.* And then, in one of those great thundering jolts in which a man's real motives are revealed to him, I understood why I jumped hospital and, in violation of orders, returned to the front and almost certain death. It was an act of love. Those men on the line were my family, my home. They were closer to me than I can say, closer than any friends had been or ever would be. They had never let me down, and I couldn't do it to them. I had to be with them, rather than let them die and me live in the knowledge that I might have saved them. Men, I now know, do not fight for flag or country, for the Marine Corps or glory or any other abstraction. They fight for one another.[69]

If morale is the human dimension's most important tangible asset, cohesion must be the most important single asset for a unit. Cohesion consists psychologically of recognition, stability, and safety.[70] Yet the coping strategies Keegan and Manchester identified, which included maintaining cohesion, did not exist as separate elements. For Manchester, combat was a spiritual exercise, a willingness to sacrifice for a greater cause (moral purpose) but mostly for his fellow Marines (brotherhood). Moral purpose, selflessness, courage, and spiritual strength as prescribed by Keegan and Manchester all contributed holistically to unit cohesion and survivability.

American surveys of other World War II combat survivors tended to center on similar coping mechanisms and their relative order of importance for survival of the individual. Although the methodologies involved in these surveys may be questioned, the general conclusions that spiritual strength and "not letting others down" were two of the most important motivations underlying endurance, seem to be validated by other observers, not the least of whom were senior officers.

In November 1945, the Research Branch in the Information and Education Division of the War Department queried a representative group of enlisted men who had returned from combat zones about their experiences in the U.S. Army during World War II.[71] There were few aspects of their experience that elicited positive responses. Most of the soldiers said they were "fed up" with the Army. When asked how they coped in combat, however, many responded that loyalty to one another and prayers for strength were important supports.[72]

In a survey of 1,433 enlisted infantrymen taken in Italy in April of 1945, 84 percent of the privates and 88 percent of the noncommissioned officers said that prayer helped them more "when the going got tough" than unit cohesion, the cause they were fighting for, thoughts of finishing the job to get home again, or thoughts of hatred for the enemy.[73] Among company grade infantry officers questioned in the European and Pacific theaters in the spring of 1944, approximately 60 percent said that prayer helped them significantly in tough circumstances.[74] Thus, in both Italy and in the Pacific, at different times, prayer as an aid to combat adjustment generally ranked higher among enlisted men than did the other personal coping mechanisms listed in the questionnaires. While officers reported being helped primarily by the desire not to let others down, even with them prayer ranked second.[75]

Among very senior officers who expressed religious faith, prayer seemed to be important to remind themselves and their soldiers of their dependence upon a Higher Power, to help senior leaders make decisions calmly, and to help them bear the burdens of their immense responsibilities. Lt. Gen. George Patton recognized the power of spiritual petition when he circulated 250,000 copies of a weather prayer, one for every soldier in the Third Army, during his efforts to relieve Bastogne in December of 1944.[76] President Dwight Eisenhower, in recalling his prayerful decision to launch the Normandy invasion in 1944, reflected that "prayer gives you the courage to make the decisions you must make in a crisis and then the confidence to leave the result to a Higher Power."[77] General of the Army Douglas MacArthur told the cadets at West Point in his "Duty, Honor, Country" address of May 1962:

> The soldier, above all other men, is required to practice the greatest act of religious training—sacrifice. In battle, and, in the face of danger and death, he discloses those divine attributes which his Maker gave when He created man in His own image. No physical courage and no greater strength can take the place of the divine help which alone can sustain him.[78]

In the World War II surveys of combat veterans, prayer was not of itself a sufficient indicator of religious faith; it may have been adopted as an instrument of psychological self-defense. There were no data that could prove a relationship specifically between prayer in battle and formal religion. However, the experience of combat did seem to have an effect on spiritual attitudes, for 79 percent of combat veterans surveyed in both theaters believed that their Army experience had increased their faith in God.[79] As Lt. Gen. A.A. Vandegrift, Commandant of the United States Marine Corps, reflected on his experiences at Guadalcanal:

> The percentage of men who devoted much time to religion might not make a very impressive showing. The average marine, or soldier, or sailor, is not demonstrative about his religion, any more than he is about his patriotism. But I do sincerely believe one thing: every man on Guadalcanal came to sense a Power above himself. There was a reality there greater than any human force. It is literally true—there are no atheists in foxholes—religion is precious under fire.[80]

Thus, from the commander's point of view, the soldier's spirit, his or her morale, is not exactly coterminous with the soldier's personal views on, or experience with, religion. The fighting spirit of the soldier may be motivated by any emotion, idea, or complex of ideas that will inspire the soldier to accomplish the mission. These compelling drives may include personal confidence, competence, and pride in self, faith in leaders, unit bonding and cohesion, a belief in the moral necessity and rightness of the cause, a consonance between personal values and national purpose, and a belief that others are depending upon the soldier for success. As the reality of danger increases, however, and as casualties pile up, religion seems to provide many soldiers a strong buttress for the spirit and will to endure.

Historically, therefore, religious support for the soldier's spirit has been an important source of strength for many in coping with difficult and dangerous situations, especially over prolonged periods of time. Religious services before battle and the presence of chaplains in the lines, at aid stations, and even in POW camps have helped thousands of soldiers face the uncertainties of war. For example, during Operation Desert Shield, from August through December 1990, 18,474 soldiers from the XVIII Airborne Corps attended voluntary religious services. The U.S. Army Central Command sponsored 7,946 religious meetings with an attendance of 341,344 soldiers. Maj. Gen. Barry McCaffrey remarked that "we had the most religious Army since the Army of Northern Virginia during the Civil War."[81] Moskos in his study on Operation Iraqi Freedom found that 33 percent of active component and more than 50 percent of reserve component soldiers attended a religious service conducted by a chaplain.[82]

At midnight on 17 January 1991, Gen. H. Norman Schwarzkopf held a staff meeting with 30 generals and colonels in his war room in Riyadh to read his announcement of the beginning of combat operations. In his message General Schwarzkopf reminded his staff of their purpose, their just cause, and his total confidence in them. He then asked his chaplain to offer a prayer. The chaplain reflected later that even though it was not discussed as such, the prayer for a quick and decisive victory with few casualties had a unifying, cohesive effect on the staff as they set about the business of war.[83]

In the discussion of spiritual fitness for soldiers in the Army's Health Promotion Program, the term is defined as "the development of those personal qualities needed to sustain a person in times of stress, hardship, and tragedy."[84] No matter how pluralistic the sources for spiritual fitness may be, in the estimation of many senior leaders the ability of the soldier to draw on his or her own spiritual or philosophical resources in times of stress is an undeniable component of readiness. Gen. Gordon Sullivan, former Chief of Staff of the Army, noted a relationship between courage and the spiritual fitness of soldiers in Field Manual 100-1, *The Army*, published in December 1991:

> Courage is the ability to overcome fear and carry on with the mission. Courage makes it possible for soldiers to fight and win. Courage, however, transcends the physical dimension. Moral and spiritual courage are equally important. There is an aspect of courage which comes from a deep spiritual faith which, when prevalent in an Army unit, can result in uncommon toughness and tenacity in combat.[85]

Gen. John Hendrix, a veteran of Operation Desert Storm and former Commanding General of U.S. Army Forces Command, stated at a Memorial Day Prayer Breakfast at Ft. McPherson, Georgia, on 22 May 2001:

> Spirituality is an individual matter. We must not cross the line between church and state. But in general spiritual fitness is important to any organization. Spiritual fitness helps shape and mold our character. Spiritual fitness provides each of us with the personal qualities which enable us to withstand difficulties and hardship. When properly exercised, spiritual fitness enhances individual pride in our unit.[86]

Gen. George C. Marshall's comments on the subject to Army chaplains in 1944 in Washington, DC, reinforce the message: "True, physical weapons are indispensable, but in the final analysis it is the human spirit, the spiritual balance, the religious fervor, that wins the victory. It is not enough to fight. . . . It is the spirit which we bring to the fight that decides the issue. The soldier's heart, the soldier's spirit, the soldier's soul, are everything."[87]

Training Considerations: Preparing Soldiers for Future Combat

Two essential ingredients for success in combat—that is, for creating high morale, unit cohesion, bonding among soldiers, increased personal courage, spiritual strength, and determination to succeed— are inspirational leadership and tough, realistic training.[88] The Army Training and Leader Development Panel (Officer) study states that the Combat Training Centers must "recapitalize, modernize, staff, and resource to provide multiechelon, combined arms operational and leader development experience in all types of environments, across the full spectrum of conflict."[89] Therefore we shall glance briefly at the characteristics of the contemporary operating environment and the leadership skills soldiers must possess to prevail. Then, as part of the human dimension, we shall turn to a generalized description of the millennial generation, those Americans born in 1982 and after, from whose ranks the Army will recruit its future force. Finally, we will examine two incidents that occurred during Operation Iraqi Freedom and their implications for training in the Army.

Battlefield Visualization and Soldier Skills

Army literature on battlefields of the future is complex and copious. For several years at the U.S. Army War College and the U.S. Army Command and Staff College, among other institutions, numerous subject-matter experts prepared briefings, training models, and articles on the Army After Next, on the digitized battlefield, and on Army transformation into a true 21st-century fighting force. The purpose of these efforts was to prepare the military for future wars and to tailor the reduced forces available to meet changing, possibly asymmetric, threats with a multi-dimensional national military strategy. A former deputy commander, U.S. Army Training and Doctrine Command, visualizes the future battlefield as follows:

> Battlespace—the use of the entire battlefield and the space around it to apply combat power to overwhelm the enemy—includes not only the physical volume of breadth, depth, and height, but also the operational dimensions of time, tempo, depth, and synchronization. Commanders must integrate other service, nation, and agency assets with their own to apply their effects toward a common purpose. The digitized battle staff—a deputy commander and three planning and operations teams—is one concept to help the commander handle the current battle, the future battle, and sequels to the future battle with an information exchange system that produces virtual collocation between staff and external elements. Emerging technology includes interactive graphics, enemy and friendly force tracking, scalable map displays, three-dimensional terrain visualization, course-of-action analysis, and video-teleconferencing capabilities among other assets.[90]

At the operational and tactical levels, this means that soldiers will have to be proficient not only with their weapon systems, but also with emerging technologies which would function in all shades of weather, terrain, and illumination. Moreover, dispersal of units, to prevent detection by an enemy with over-the-horizon targeting capabilities, will produce a force with mobile combat power and logistical support as opposed to the iron mountains of stockpiled equipment familiar on Vietnam-era firebases or on forward-deployed Desert Storm logistical bases.

The specific geography for future engagements is, of course, speculative. In the 20th century American soldiers have fought in foreign areas on snow-bound tundra and sandy beaches, and in forests, mountains, deserts, jungles, and urban areas. For the future, all of these settings must be considered along with the special problems of homeland defense amidst one's own citizens.

Responding to current after-action reviews of Operation Enduring Freedom and Iraqi Freedom, as well at as the post-11 September ethos, the Department of Defense and the Army in particular have reevaluated their doctrine, organization, training, materiel, leadership and education, and personnel facilities with a view toward accelerating the transformation to a new Army. This transformation is rooted in an understanding that the contemporary operational environment is not static and predictable, but in fact fluid, unpredictable, nonlinear, and asymmetrical. We are an Army at war, and the very culture must change. As Brig. Gen. David A. Fastabend wrote in *Army Magazine,* "We must be prepared to question everything. Development of a culture of innovation will not be advanced by panels or studies. Cultural change begins with behavior and the leaders who shape it. We have the mindset and culture that will sustain the Army as ready and relevant, now and into the future."[91]

What, then, are the special skills soldiers of the future must possess? In the U.S. Army Training and Doctrine Command's strategy for dealing with change, readiness, and the human dimension, some of these qualities are described:

> First, the leveraging of the human dimension is all about leading change with quality people, grounded on Army values, and inspired by an American warrior ethos. Adaptive leadership remains an essential aspect. Quality people will need to have the character and interpersonal skills to rapidly integrate individuals and groups of individuals into tailored organizations. They will need to adapt quickly to new situations, and form cohesive teams, and demonstrate competence and confidence operating in complex and ambiguous environments.[92]

In short, the Army will need not just soldiers but soldier-leaders who are committed to the professional ethic, who are talented in small-group facilitation, who are flexible and mentally agile, and who can integrate technological and interpersonal skills in the midst of uncertain and possibly chaotic combat conditions. The metacompentencies of self-awareness and adaptability are being channeled so as to change the Army culture into what has been coined a "Culture of Innovation." As Gen. Kevin Byrnes wrote, "We need to create a culture of thinkers and innovators who look at a challenge and input a set of ways of doing it, not just apply band-aids and bailing wire to fix old ways of doing business. If something needs to be changed and it makes sense to me, let's figure out the best way to do it."[93]

Gen. George Casey in his opening statement to the Readiness Subcommittee of the House Armed Services Committee stated that "the Army's training programs have also been, and will continue to be, the cultural drivers for the future. Leaders will not learn what to think, but instead how to think—jointly, strategically, and within the context of an expeditionary mindset."[94] This is a major paradigm shift in the transformation of how and what the Army will train. It influences not only the officer education system but also basic combat training and all NCO Schools. In consonance with the lessons learned from Afghanistan and Iraq, every soldier must know how to make decisions independently where necessary to accomplish the mission.

Concerning the human dimension, John Miller and Kurt Reitinger have observed:

> Command of soldiers is, first and foremost, a human endeavor requiring the commander to be a decision-maker and leader. As is the case today, these competent commanders will establish their moral authority by tough, demanding training to standard and by the caring, holistic preparation of their subordinate leaders, soldiers, and units for mission operations. The significance of the bonds of trust and confidence between the leader and the led will grow as the potential for decentralized execution over larger battlespace increases.[95]

Clearly, then, with the current rate of deployments and missions, the Army's recruiting and leadership challenges are daunting. We no longer have the leisure to complete complex and lengthy training before units find themselves engaged in combat operations. In the long history of the Army, however, this has often been the case.

The Millennials: What Soldiers for the Future?

Drawing upon approximately 210 national surveys, interviews, and studies of American young people, Neil Howe and William Strauss have described a group they call the Millennials. These are American young people born in 1982 or later; in other words, they were 18 or younger in the year 2000. Some of the characteristics of these young people will be of interest to Army recruiters.

First, they are a large group of approximately 76 million, with 90 percent native-born and about 10 percent who immigrated to the United States.[96] By the year 2002 they will outnumber the surviving Baby Boomers. They are the most diverse group ethnically in American history, with 36 percent nonwhite or Latinos in the 1999 youth population.[97] At least one Millennial in five has one immigrant parent, making the Millennials potentially the largest second-generation immigrant group in U.S. history. As the authors point out, their presence will contribute to the irreversible diversification of America.[98]

In terms of religious identity, approximately 20 million are Roman Catholic, which helps account for the growth of the Roman Catholic constituency in the United States from 26.6 percent of the U.S. Christian population in 1958 (30.6 million) to 38.3 percent in 1998 (61.2 million). That is an increase of 30 million American Roman Catholics in 40 years, making the Roman Catholic Church in America four times the size of the Southern Baptist Convention, the largest Protestant denomination.[99]

For many Millennials there is no separation of church and state in their primary education. Two million attend Catholic elementary schools and another two million attend Catholic high schools. Nine in ten private schools in the United States in 2000 had at least a nominal religious affiliation, many with their own mandatory chapel programs. Within the public schools there were no prayer clubs or circles in 1990; now, with the 1995 Federal court ruling that students had a right to organized prayer gatherings as long as they were not official school programs, there are more than 10,000 of them.[100]

Among the Millennials who are over 14, some 65 percent plan on attending college, while 55 percent go to church regularly as opposed to 45 percent of Americans as a whole.[101] The ones in high school are bright. They have scored well in science and reading as compared with students from other industrialized countries.[102]

These figures appear even more impressive in light of the report that one-fourth to one-third of all Millennials lives in single-parent families. More than half of these single parents are living with partners to whom they are not married.[103] It may not be surprising, then, that about 48 percent of Millennials have been sexually active as teenagers.[104] The *Chronicle of Higher Education* has reported that in order to meet the psychological needs of many of these families, there has occurred an increase in "the spiritual dimensions" of social work. Edward Canda, a professor of social work at the University of Kansas, noted that "in a crisis or occasion of grief and loss, there is often a shaking of the foundation of one's sense of meaning, who one is, what life is about, and what reality is about. We cannot escape these questions. It would be malpractice to avoid them."[105]

Significantly, the war in Kosovo is the only U.S. military action that most Millennials remember. The oldest young people in this sample were only eight to nine years old during the first Gulf War. The events surrounding the subsequent Oklahoma City Federal Building bombing and the Columbine school shootings made greater impressions.[106]

Other sources, outside the studies surveyed by Howe and Strauss, paint a somewhat different picture. The State School Superintendent's Office for the state of Georgia reported on 5 May 2001 that of the 116,000 high school freshmen who were enrolled in 1997, only 72,000 graduated in June of 2000. This reflected a high school dropout rate of 38 percent.[107] Moreover, 47 percent of Georgia's high school seniors who graduated in the class of 1999 were unable to keep their scholarships as college sophomores because they could not maintain a B average.[108] Finally,

United Way reported on 13 May 2001 that there were 230,000 troubled children under some form of care in the state of Georgia—all Millennials under the age of 18. If one assumes that Georgia, with half of its eight million people living in Atlanta, is not too different from many other states, one suspects that the rosy reports by Howe and Strauss were based on the most privileged of the Millennials.

One trait that has not been questioned, however, is the growing interest among older young adults in discovering their own interests, vocations, and, in some cases, spiritual insights. Many college students and young business people want to be part of an organization or movement which transcends the ordinary. The Campus Crusade for Christ, for example, has experienced an amazing growth in the past five years among college students looking for meaning in their lives. Campus Crusade has 1,000 college chapters—including one at Harvard—comprising a total of roughly 40,000 students. Donations to Campus Crusade, as reported by the *Chronicle of Higher Education*, exceeded $450 million in the year 2000. "They're bombarded and blasted with all kinds of atheistic teaching from the classroom and they need help," according to William Bright, the lay founder of the movement.[109]

In his recent book, *Capturing the Heart of Leadership*, Prof. Gilbert Fairholm of Hampden-Sydney College describes a similar kind of restlessness among young workers:

> Whether we like it or not, work is becoming or has become a prime source of values in our society and our personal lives. American workers are uncomfortable, uncommitted, and adrift. They are searching for new organizational patterns and new paradigms. Integrating the many components of one's work and personal life into a comprehensive system for managing the workplace defines the holistic or spiritual approach. It provides the platform for leadership that recognizes this spiritual element in people and in all of their behavior.[110]

Fairholm argues that young people expect leadership to be a relationship, not just a skill or personal attribute. Leaders are leaders only so far as they develop relationships with their followers, relationships that help all concerned to achieve their spiritual as well as economic and social fulfillment.[111] This concept is not far from the Army's definition of the transformational leadership style and may be a constructive bridge in thinking about what "leadership" might mean to the next generation of American soldiers.[112]

Implications for Combat Training

Two events that occurred during Operation Iraqi Freedom have important implications for training in combat.[114] They underscore the belief that the meta-competencies of self-awareness and adaptability should be fully integrated not only with the warrior ethos, but also at all levels of leadership training. After two days of heavy combat operations on the

> War, the most dramatically physical of all human works, does indeed become the vehicle for the most spiritual of achievements. And the morale springing from such philosophy may be counted on to win the wars.
>
> —WILLIAM E. HOCKING[113]

outskirts of Najaf, the Division Commander of the 101st, Maj. Gen. David Petraeus, told his staff, "It is time to stop dipping around the edges and jump in the pool. Tomorrow the 2-327th Battalion and its sister units will push deeper into the city and possibly determine once and for all who owns it."[115] On 3 April 2003 the soldiers of the 2-237 Infantry moved into the city, the home of one of Iraq's leading holy men, the Grand Ayatollah Ali Hussein Sistani, in order to gain his crucial support for their mission in Najaf. Turning the corner, a group of men blocked their way shouting in Arabic, "God is Great." The crowd grew into the hundreds, many of whom mistakenly thought the Americans were trying to capture the Grand Ayatollah and attack the Imam Ali Mosque, a holy site revered by Shiite Muslims around the world.[116] Someone in the crowd lobbed a rock at the troops, then another. Lt. Col. Christopher Hughes, the battalion commander, was hit on the head, chest, and the rim of his sunglasses with rocks.

Hughes subscribed to the philosophy of Sun Tzu: "A great commander is one who does not wield a weapon." It followed that the best way to defuse the impending confrontation was to demonstrate peaceful intent. Hughes ordered his troops to "Take a knee and point your weapons to the ground, smile, and show no hostilities." Some of the Iraqis then backed off and sat down, which enabled Hughes to look for the troublemakers in the crowd. He identified eight. Wanting it to be clear who started the shooting if it erupted, he told his soldiers, "We're going to withdraw out of this situation and let them defuse it themselves."

Hughes had trained his troops previously in understanding cultural differences and in the meaning and value of restraint. With his own rifle pointed toward the ground, he bowed to the crowd and turned away. Hughes and his infantry marched back to their compound in silence. When tempers had calmed, the Grand Ayatollah Sistani issued a fatwa (decree) calling on the people of Najaf to welcome Hughes's soldiers.

The second event occurred on 20 August 2003 when Lt. Col. Allen B. West, commander of the 2nd Battalion, 20th Field Artillery Regiment, 4th Infantry Division, took a prisoner out of the detention center near the Taji air base and threatened to kill him. The prisoner was an Iraqi policeman who, according to informants, was involved in the 16 August attack against American troops at Saba al Boor near Tikrit. West commented in an email interview with the *Washington Times* that he had "asked for soldiers to accompany him and told them we had to gather information and that it could get ugly." Some soldiers had already assaulted the prisoner. After other interrogation techniques failed to secure the prisoner's cooperation, West brandished his pistol. "I did use my 9 mm weapon to threaten him and fired it twice. Once I fired it into the weapons clearing barrel outside the facility alone, and the next time I did it with his head close to the barrel. I fired away from him. I stood between the pistol and his person. I admit that what I did was not right, but it was done with the concern of the safety of my soldiers and myself."[117] After the shots were fired, the Iraqi policeman provided the information West wanted on a planned ambush near Saba. The Army, however, subsequently charged West with criminal assault for improper coercion of a prisoner.

Both commanders had the well being of their soldiers as a paramount concern. However, their actions were different. Hughes stated in his interview that but for the psychological operations and civil affairs personnel, the chaplain, and the translators who taught me the cultural and religious implications, I would not have been as successful."[118] Facing a different but no less difficult problem, West was equally successful, but his coercive methods ended his career.[119]

In war and in combat the metacompentencies of self-awareness and adaptability are critical. The Army Training and Leadership Development Panel study defines these metacompentencies in the following manner: "Self-awareness is the ability to understand how to assess abilities, know strengths and weaknesses in the operational environment, and learn how to correct those weaknesses. Adaptability is the ability to recognize changes to the environment [and] assess that environment to determine what is new and what must be learned to be effective, all to standard and with feedback."[120] It is important to note there is no warrant for doing anything illegal, or morally or ethically unsound, in either FM 22-100 or in the ATLDP study.

During the preparation for Operation Iraqi Freedom there were many chaplains involved in both the ethical and spiritual training of units. Twenty of the Army's training centers had chaplain instructors who were charged explicitly not to preach in the classroom, but to discuss professional values, ethics, and leadership. In field units, chaplains focused on "spiritual fitness training, or battle proofing," a command program to address, among other topics, the full spectrum of moral concerns involving the profession of arms, the conduct of war, and personal spiritual care. Chaplains were their commanders' staff officers of choice to be responsible for conducting these programs.

Spiritual fitness training by chaplains is part of unit preparation for deployment to combat zones. The chaplains could answer questions about morals and morale, they had connections to family support systems back home, they enjoyed legal confidentiality so that soldiers could report to them suspected violations of the law of war without fear of recrimination, and they could address the soldier's personal spiritual needs and ethical questions. Although not all chaplains were fully trained in the ethics of war, they helped religious soldiers find the bridge between their spiritual and professional values in a way no other staff officer could be expected to do.

The question that must be asked regarding our innovative Army is how to develop leaders who know how to think, who have internalized the Army values and the warrior ethos, and who are flexible, adaptive, confident, competent and self-aware. This task is an ambitious one, for it requires leaders who can control their emotions and can analyze situations on the fly in order to make the right decision at the right time.

The focal shift in the Army's leadership development, given all the complexities of the post-11 September environment, continue to be a challenge. The implication of confronting enemies whose numbers include stateless terrorists conducting preemptive strikes and covert operations may tempt leaders, and therefore their subordinates, to disregard the Law of Land Warfare and the Geneva Conventions as outdated and irrelevant. A philosophy of ends justifying means can become the pretext for employing cruel and unusual interrogation techniques, not to mention questionable strategic operations and plans. However, if soldiers truly embrace and live the current Army Values and the Warrior Ethos, they will be fully equipped with the moral and the ethical wherewithal to eschew committing bestial acts of war. Leaders of all ranks must remember that their actions reflect not only upon them, but also upon the nation they have sworn to defend. The American people are eager to praise principled leaders, but will not tolerate military actions that violate their own values. The challenge we face in the Army is to find the means to help soldiers make the right moral and ethical decisions in the presence of their enemies even when they are isolated from fellow soldiers.

Conclusion

The purpose of this chapter has been to examine the literature available on the human and spiritual needs of soldiers and how they may be trained for combat in the 21st century. The working hypothesis, that all soldiers have human needs and most have spiritual needs broadly defined, seems to be supported from a wide variety of sources in a number of fields. As Carl von Clausewitz tellingly observed in his treatise *On War* : "All effects in the sphere of mind and spirit have been proven by experience: they recur constantly and must receive their due as objective factors. What value would any theory of war have that ignored them."[121] There also seems to be no question as to whether the Army profession should continue to try to address these needs in the future as part of its leadership doctrine. Indeed, the unique aspects of the profession of arms in requiring the total commitment and unlimited liability of soldiers often deployed in difficult and dangerous situations would seem to mandate such care and concern. Moreover, the Constitution, Congress, and the American people expect and demand it.

A corollary question is to what extent the profession of arms should try to meet the spiritual needs of a military population becoming ever more ethnically, morally, and religiously diverse. At the present time, the Army seems to have struck an appropriate balance between facilitating the free exercise of religion and in protecting the freedom of individual conscience for soldiers and their family members. Most religious services and ceremonies are voluntary. The Army Chaplain Corps, in implementing commanders' religious support programs, currently represents more than 140 different denominations and faith groups in its own ranks. There is no prospect that the Army will institutionalize a single religion, nor should it. There is a concern, however, as a shortage of young ordained clergy grows in both the Roman Catholic and Protestant communities nationally, that there will be a corresponding shortage of chaplains for the Army. Part of a solution could lie in the way the Millennial generation chooses to respond to its own spiritual challenges in the 21st century.

The preparation of soldiers for future combat seems to involve more knowledge, more technological skill, and perhaps more maturity on the part of junior leaders than has been the case in the past. Yet the basic principles involved in building relationships, unit cohesion, confidence, and courage have not changed very much over the years and will likely not change markedly in the near future.

There are valid, practical considerations for commanders, staff officers, senior noncommissioned officers, chaplains, surgeons, psychiatrists, and other leaders in preparing soldiers for combat. Some of the more important of these, based on historical experience and analysis, may be summed up as follows:

- Soldiers need to have time to get their personal affairs in order. This may include time for family and legal preparation, as well as physical, mental, and spiritual.
- Soldiers and family members need to have the most accurate and current information possible on what they may expect. The importance, necessity, and moral justification of the mission are essential elements of information for the soldiers, their families, and communities if the unqualified support of all affected parties is to be forthcoming.
- Soldiers must be briefed on the cultures they will encounter in the area of operations and be thoroughly familiar with Army values, the Rules of Engagement, the Law of Land Warfare, and the Geneva Conventions.
- Commanders and other leaders need to spend some personal time with soldiers in their primary units to reinforce relationships, cohesion, confidence, and courage. Soldiers must know the commander's intent and their specific jobs to include how they fit into the total effort of the unit.
- Soldiers must be challenged by tough, realistic training and have confidence in their leaders, training, equipment, battle plans, teamwork, and ultimate chance for success. They must know and trust one another.
- Rituals before deployment and before battle based on unit history, esprit de corps, and spiritual preparation are important. These should include voluntary opportunities for religious sacraments, services, or meditation.
- Soldiers need to know that their commanders, senior NCOs, chaplains, and other key personnel are present at every stage during combat operations. The soldiers' morale is strengthened if the total team is demonstrably present and involved.[122]

One caveat: To paraphrase William Hocking, war is not a thing which can be seen; it must be thought.[123] No one has ever seen war in all of its dimensions—physical, moral, and spiritual—because each participant sees the event from his or her own narrow, partial perspective. In the distant future, war and the professional skills needed to survive and prevail may be very different with the advent of robotics, information warfare, and even space technologies. Therefore the combat training strategies developed for the first decades of the 21st century may not be immutable, but they will certainly be important for their insights and wisdom in the evolution of future training doctrine and for appreciating the human dimension in Army professionalism.

Notes

1. The views and opinions expressed in this chapter are those of the authors and are not necessarily those of the Department of the Army or any other U.S. government entity. For assistance in researching and writing this chapter, the authors are indebted to Chaplain (Colonel) Richard Kuhlbars, Director of Combat Developments, U.S. Army Chaplain Center and School, and to Chaplain (Colonel) James Daniels, Office of the Chief of Chaplains, Washington, DC.
2. S. L. A. Marshall, *Men Against Fire: The Problem of Battle Command in Future War* (New York: William Morrow Co., 1947), 208, 211.

3. Andrew Abbott, *The System of Professions: An Essay on the Division of Expert Labor* (Chicago, IL: University of Chicago Press, 1988).

4. Don M. Snider and Gale L. Watkins, "The Future of Army Professionalism: A Need for Renewal and Redefinition," *Parameters* 30, no. 3 (Autumn 2000): 17.

5. Richard A. Gabriel, *To Serve with Honor: A Treatise on Military Ethics and the Way of the Soldier* (Westport, CT: Greenwood Press, 1982), 5-6. Gabriel outlines many of the same handicaps during the Army's shift to the All-Volunteer Force 30 years ago.

6. Attributed to Gen. Robert E. Lee by Douglas S. Freeman as cited in Ken Burns, "The Civil War," PBS video production, 1990, part V.

7. *Sun Tzu: The Art of War,* trans. Samuel B. Griffith (London: Oxford University Press, 1963), 128.

8. FM 22-100, *Army Leadership: Be, Know, Do* (Washington, DC: Headquarters, Department of the Army, 31 August 1999), 3-3.

9. Ibid., 3-4.

10. Ibid., 3-1.

11. Ibid.

12. Ibid., 3-1 and 3-2.

13. Lord Charles Moran, *The Anatomy of Courage* (Boston, MA: Houghton Mifflin, 1967), 202.

14. Interview in Atlanta, Georgia, with James Eric Pierce, former Associate Professor of the Sociology of Religion at Pfeiffer College, on 6 April 2001.

15. Data furnished by Chaplain Michael T. Bradfield, DA Office of the Chief of Chaplains, Washington, DC, 25 April 2001. This is actually a low figure because the 64% of active duty soldiers who profess a specific faith does not count those who belong to faith groups other than the seven largest by population, i.e., Protestant, Catholic, Orthodox, Jewish, Muslim, Buddhist, and Hindu.

16. Task Force TLS, *Training, Leader Development and Soldiers Strategy* (Ft. Leavenworth, KS: U.S. Army Command and General Staff College, 1 October 1999), 75 and slides 14, 17; Lt. Col. Steven W. Shively, Project Officer, DA-ODCSPER, Directorate of Human Resources, *Draft Army Well-Being Campaign Plan,* 5 January 2001, 2.

17. Morris Janowitz, *The Professional Soldier* (New York: The Free Press, 1960), 97.

18. United States Military Academy, Office of Policy, Planning, and Analysis, "Cadet Leader Development System," Draft, July 2001, chap. 3, 3.

19. Jeff Levin, *God, Faith, and Health* (New York: John Wiley, 2001), 9-10. Emphasis supplied.

20. Ibid., 10; also see David F. Swenson and Walter Lowrie, trans., *Soren Kierkegaard: Concluding Unscientific Postscript* (Princeton, NJ: Princeton University Press, 1968), 495, for Kierkegaard's condemnation of " faithless religiousness."

21. Robert D. Baird and Alfred Bloom, *Indian and Far Eastern Religious Traditions* (New York: Harper and Row, 1971), 214; and Huston Smith, *The Religions of Man* (New York: Harper and Row, 1958), 149.

22. Geoffrey Parrinder, *World Religions: From Ancient History to the Present* (New York: Facts on File Publications, 1985), 355.

23. Saeed Ahmed, "Falun Gong: Peace of Mind," *Atlanta Journal Constitution*, 19 May 2001, B-1.

24. John W. Wright, ed., *New York Times Almanac 2000* (New York: The Penguin Group, 1999), 414; Levin, 20; and Ron Feinberg, "Amen Corner," *Atlanta Journal Constitution*, 5 May 2001, B-1. This 63% may also be a low figure. The World Christian Encyclopedia published in 2001 reported 192 million Christians in the United States, 32 million more than *The New York Times Almanac* reported in 1998. The difference may be in counting numbers reported by independent congregational churches as opposed to counting only figures from major denominations. See Ron Feinberg, "Report: Christianity Still Largest Religion," *Atlanta Journal Constitution*, 20 January 2001, B-1.

25. Samuel P. Huntingdon, *The Clash of Civilizations and the Remaking of World Order* (New York: Simon and Schuster, 1996), 95-97.

26. A survey of 502 adults from across the country with a 4.5% margin of error as reported in *Atlanta Journal Constitution*, 12 May 2001, B-1.

27. Charles Moskos and Laura Miller, *December 2003 Sociological Survey on Operation Iraqi Freedom Results, April 2004*, c-moskos@northwestern.edu, 5.

28. Lord Moran, ix. Lord Moran must not have been as familiar with American sources as with British ones, for Yale University Press published William E. Hocking's *Morale and Its Enemies* in 1918.

29. See, e.g., V.V. Shelyag et al., eds., *Military Psychology: A Soviet View* (Washington, DC: Government Printing Office, 1972) ; Richard A. Gabriel, *Military Psychiatry: A Comparative Perspective* (New York: Greenwood Press, 1986); and Anthony Kellett, *Combat Motivation: The Behavior of Soldiers in Battle* (London: Kluwer-Nijhoff Publishing Co., 1982).

30. Robert W. Swezey, Andrew L. Meltzer, and Eduardo Salas, " Some Issues Involved in Motivating Teams," in *Motivation: Theory and Research,* eds. Harold F. O'Neil, Jr., and Michael Drillings (Hillsdale, NJ: Erlbaum Associates, 1994), 141; and Josh R. Gerow, *Psychology: An Introduction* (New York: Longman Publishers, 1997), 360.

31. Gardner Lindzey et al., *Psychology* (New York: Worth Publishers, 1978), 481.

32. Gerow, 360.

33. Lindzey, 481.

34. Ibid.

35. Ibid.

36. Abraham H. Maslow, "A Theory of Metamotivation," in *The Healthy Personality, eds.* Hung-Min Chiang and Abraham H. Maslow (New York: D. Van Nostrand Co., 1969), 29.

37. Ibid.

38. Ibid., 35.

39. Abraham H. Maslow, *Religions, Values, and Peak-Experiences* (New York: Penguin Books, 1970), 4.

40. Bill Mauldin, *Up Front* (New York: W.W. Norton, 2000), 133.

41. FM 22-100, *Military Leadership* (Washington, DC: Headquarters, Department of the Army, 1983), 144-145.

42. Ibid., 135, 144.

43. Ibid., 145.

44. Shively, 2.

45. Ibid., 4.

46. Interview with Chaplain (Major) Daniel Wackerhagen, U.S. Army Chaplain Center and School, Ft. Jackson, SC, 15 May 2001; Steven Reiss, "Toward a Comprehensive Assessment of Fundamental Motivation," *Journal of Psychological Assessment* 10, no.2 (June 1998): 97-106.

47. Interview with Dr. Thomas R. Smith, Executive Director for the National Institute for Healthcare Research, Rockville, MD, 4 May 2001; see also Levin, 3-6; and Phyllis McIntosh, "Faith is Powerful Medicine," *Reader's Digest*, October 1999, 151-155.

48. Quoted from a discussion with Col. Eric B. Schoomaker, M.D., former FORSCOM Surgeon and currently Commander of the 30th Medical Brigade in Germany, 11 May 2001. Also, see Dean H. Hamer, *The God Gene: How Faith Is Hardwired into Our Genes* (Garden City, NY: Doubleday, 2004).

49. Levin, 9; Maslow, *The Healthy Personality*, 35.

50. Annette Mahoney et al., "Marriage and the Spiritual Realm: The Role of Proximal and Distal Religious Constructs in Marital Functioning," *Journal of Family Psychology* 13, no.3 (1999): 321.

51. Ibid., 325.

52. Bradfield.

53. Chaplain (Colonel) Donald Taylor, FORSCOM Command Chaplain, Memorandum for Record, Analysis of FORSCOM Installation Activity Reports for FY 00, Office of the FORSCOM Chaplain, Ft. McPherson, GA, 2 March 2001.

54. Discussion with Dr. Bruce Bell, Army Research Institute, 11 May 2001, who kindly furnished a number of studies used in this paper.

55. U.S. Army Community and Family Support Center, *1995 Survey of Army Families III* (Alexandria, VA: Army Personnel Survey Office, 1995) 5, question 27.

56. James A. Martin et al., eds., *The Military Family: A Practice Guide for Human Service Providers* (Alexandria, VA: The Army Research Institute, 2000), 143,159.

57. FM 22-100, *Army Leadership: Be, Know, Do*, 19.

58. H.A. DeWeerd, ed., *Selected Speeches and Statements of General of the Army George C. Marshall* (Washington, DC: The Infantry Journal, 1945), 121-122.

59. Ibid., 93.

60. Ibid., 123.

61. John Keegan, *The Face of Battle* (New York: Penguin Books, 1976), 274; FM 22-100, *Army Leadership, Be, Know, Do*, 3-3.

62. *Sun Tzu: The Art of War*, 128.

63. Lord Moran, 184.

64. Keegan, 335.

65. Ibid., 335-36.

66. Gabriel , 39.

67. John W. Brinsfield, *Encouraging Faith, Supporting Soldiers: A History of the United States Army Chaplain Corps, 1975-1995* (Washington, DC: Headquarters, Department of the Army, Office of the Chief of Chaplains, 1997), part two, 155-156; Russell F. Weigley, *History of the United States Army* (New York: Macmillan Publishing Co., 1967) 519-20.

68. Keegan, 279, 280, 333.

69. William Manchester, *Goodbye Darkness: A Memoir of the Pacific War* (Boston, MA: Little, Brown, 1980), 391, 393.

70. Jonathan Shay, "Trust: Touchstone for a Practical Military Ethos," in *Spirit, Blood, and Treasure: The American Cost of Battle in the 21st Century*, ed. Donald Vandergriff (Novato, CA: Presidio Press, 2001), E-1-2.

71. Samuel A. Stouffer et al., *The American Soldier: Combat and Its Aftermath* (Princeton, NJ: Princeton University Press, 1949), 611-13.

72. Ibid.

73. Ibid., 177.

74. Ibid., 173.

75. Kellett, 194.

76. John W. Brinsfield, "Army Values and Ethics: A Search for Consistency and Relevance," *Parameters* 28, no. 3 (Autumn 1998): 79-82.

77. Ibid.

78. Ibid.

79. Kellett, 195.

80. Ellwood C. Nance, *Faith of Our Fighters* (St. Louis, MO: Bethany Press, 1944), 242.

81. John W. Brinsfield, *Encouraging Faith*, part two, 91.

82. Charles Moskos and Laura Miller, 5.

83. Ibid., 123; interview with Chaplain (Colonel) David P. Peterson, Ft. McPherson, GA, 22 May 2001. Approximately an hour after General Schwarzkopf's staff meeting concluded, President George Bush, Vice President Quayle, General Powell, Secretary Cheney, and most of the President's cabinet attended a prayer service at Ft. Meyer, VA, for the same purpose. The service was also attended by the three Chiefs of Chaplains and by Dr. Billy Graham, the guest speaker. Ibid., 125.

84. Department of the Army Pamphlet 600-63-12, *Fit to Win: Spiritual Fitness* (Washington, DC: U.S. Government Printing Office, 1987), 1.

85. As cited in Brinsfield, "Army Values and Ethics: A Search for Consistency and Relevance," 82.

86. Gen. John W. Hendrix, Personal Notes, Memorial Day Prayer Breakfast Welcoming Address, Ft. McPherson, GA, 22 May 2001, 1.

87. Nance, 190-191. Chaplain Nance, a faculty member at the U.S. Army Chaplain School at Harvard University in 1944, recorded many of Gen. George C. Marshall's comments on the soldier's spirit and the type of chaplains he wanted in the Army. Nance's work was later quoted by Daniel B. Jorgensen, an Air Force chaplain, in *The Service of Chaplains to Army Air Units, 1917-1946* (Washington, DC: Office of the Chief of Air Force Chaplains, 1961), 277; and by Robert L. Gushwa, an Army chaplain, in *The Best and Worst of Times: The United States Army Chaplaincy, 1920-1945* (Washington, DC: Office of the Chief of Chaplains, 1977), 186. Evidently Chaplain (Maj. Gen.) William Arnold in Information Bulletins sent to Army chaplains worldwide as early as August 1941 also regularly quoted General Marshall. See Daniel B. Jorgensen, 146, 299.

88. FM 22-100, *Army Leadership: Be, Know, Do*, 20, para. 3-82. Inspirational leadership is intended to combine transformational and transactional leadership styles as indicated in FM 22-100.

89. The Army Training and Leader Development Panel (Officer) Study Report to The Army, OS-61.

90. Lt. Gen. John E. Miller and Maj. Kurt C. Reitinger, "Force XXI Battle Command," *Military Review* 75, no. 4 (July-August 1995): 6-9.

91. Brig. Gen. David A Fastabend and Robert H. Simpson, "The Imperative for a Culture of Innovation in the U.S. Army: Adapt or Die,"*Army* Magazine, February 2004, Introduction by Gen. Peter J. Schoomaker, 14.

92. Task Force TLS, 16.

93. Gen. Kevin P Byrnes, TRADOC News Service interview, 3 June 2003.

94. Opening Statement (As prepared by) Gen. George W. Casey, Jr., Before Readiness Subcommittee of House Armed services Committee, Washington, DC, 11 March 2004.

95. Miller and Reitinger, 9.

96. Neil Howe and William Strauss, *Millennials Rising: The Next Great Generation* (New York: Vintage Books, 2000), 14.

97. Ibid., 15.

98. Ibid., 16.

99. Wright, 418; Winthrop S. Hudson, *Religion in America* (New York: Charles Scribner's Sons, 1965), 354.

100. Howe and Strauss, 149, 234.

101. Ibid., 164, 234.

102. Ibid., 144, 164.

103. Chris Roberts, "Number of Single-parent Families Increases 42%," *The State* [Columbia, SC], 23 May 2001, A-1, A-12.

104. Howe and Strauss, 197.

105. D.W. Miller, "Programs in Social Work Embrace the Teaching of Spirituality," *Chronicle of Higher Education*, 18 May 2001, A-12.

106. Howe and Strauss, 19.

107. Reported by Channel 3 Television News, Atlanta, GA, 5 May 2001.

108. *Atlanta Journal Constitution*, 13 May 2001.

109. Beth McMurtrie, "Crusading for Christ, Amid Keg Parties and Secularism," *Chronicle of Higher Education,* 18 May 2001, A42.

110. Gilbert W. Fairholm, *Capturing the Heart of Leadership:Spirituality and Community in the New American Workplace* (Westport, CT: Praeger Publishers, 1997), 24-25.

111. Ibid., 1.

112. FM 22-100, *Army Leadership: Be, Know, Do*, 19, para. 3-77.

113. William Ernest Hocking, *Morale and Its Enemies* (New Haven, CT: Yale University Press, 1918), 200.

114. During the time of this writing the Abu Ghraib Prison incident is unfolding which may make this a good case study for future leadership studies.

115. This story is based on a personal interview given by Lt. Col. Christopher Hughes to CH (Maj.) Peter Baktis during the summer of 2003 as a member of the OIF Study Group.

116. As the burial site of Ali, son-in-law of the Prophet Muhammad.

117. Rowan Scarborough, "Army files charge in combat tactic," *Washington Times*, 29 October 2003.

118. Baktis, OIF interview.

119. *Washington Times*, 13 December 2003, reported that Maj. Gen. Raymond Odierno fined Lt. Col. West $5,000 in lieu of a court-martial. West returned to Ft. Hood, Texas, to await retirement orders.

120. The ATLDP (Officer) Study Report to the Army, p. 0S-3.

121. As cited in Maj. Michael D. Slotnick, "Spiritual Leadership: How Does the Spirit Move You?" Defense Technical Information Center Technical Report AD-A258 523 (Alexandria, VA: DTIC, 1992), 4.

122. A summary of findings from previous references including the U.S. Army Community and Family Support Center, the Army Research Institute, Lord Charles Moran, William E. Hocking, and John Keegan. For advice to chaplains see Chaplain Milton Haney's "The Duties of a Chaplain" as cited in John W. Brinsfield, "In the Pulpit and in the Trenches," *Civil War Times Illustrated*, September/October 1992, 72-73; and FM 16-1, *Religious Support Doctrine: The Chaplain and the Chaplain Assistant* (Washington, DC: Headquarters, Department of the Army, November 1989), 5-2.

123. Hocking, 49.

22 | Why Professionals Fight: Combat Motivation in the Iraq War[1]

Leonard Wong

Introduction

This chapter seeks to answer the question—Why do soldiers fight? It begins with a historical overview of the combat motivation literature, examining studies from World War II, Korea, and Vietnam. The focus then shifts to the recent Iraq War, analyzing the results of interviews with Iraqi army prisoners of war, U.S.

Four brave men who do not know each other will not dare to attack a lion. Four less brave, but knowing each other well, sure of their reliability and consequently of mutual aid, will attack resolutely.

—ARDANT DU PICQ, 1870[2]

combat troops, and embedded news media representatives. The various perspectives combine to show the critical importance of unit cohesion in combat motivation but also highlight how today's soldiers are different from U.S. soldiers of the past.

Why Do Soldiers Fight?

During the early stages of World War II as the Army ranks swelled with freshly drafted soldiers, there was a growing concern about the motivations of America's conscripted force. As Kansas newspaper editor William Allen White noted, soldiers of a draft army "haven't the slightest enthusiasm for this war or this cause. They aren't grouchy, they are not mutinous, they just don't give a tinker's dam."[3] After noting the ineffectiveness of canned motivational lectures read to bored troops, Chief of Staff of the Army Gen. George C. Marshall brought in movie producer Frank Capra and told him to make a movie that would "explain to our boys in the Army *why* we are fighting, and the *principles* for which we are fighting."[4] Critics claimed that there were more important things to do, but Marshall insisted on men motivated and knowledgeable about the democratic cause. The seven-part film series *Why We Fight* resulted and became widely used during World War II.[5] The riveting film series emphasized that the war was not "just a war *against* Axis villainy, but *for* liberty, equality, and security."[6]

After World War II, a series of studies emerged that examined the motivation of soldiers during combat—to determine why a "tired, cold, muddy rifleman goes forward with the bitter dryness of fear in his mouth into the mortar bursts and machine-gun fire of a determined enemy."[7] Was it for ideological reasons, as suggested by the *Why We Fight* series?

In the widely acclaimed work, *The American Soldier*, Samuel Stouffer and his colleagues documented the attitudes of World War II combat infantrymen. When soldiers were asked what kept them going during the war, the most common response was getting the war over so that they could go home. The second most common response and the primary combat motivation, however, referred to the strong group ties that developed during combat.[8] When asked about sources of support during combat, responses concerning loyalty to one's buddies and the notion "that you couldn't let the other men down" were second only to the number of combat soldiers who said they were helped by prayer.[9] Contrary to the *Why We Fight* films, Stouffer's study argued that ideology, patriotism, and fighting for the cause were not major factors in combat motivation for WWII soldiers. Cohesion, or the emotional bonds between soldiers, appeared to be the primary factor in combat motivation.

Historian S.L.A. Marshall reemphasized the importance of the bonds between soldiers in his classic 1947 study of World War II infantrymen *Men Against Fire*. He noted, "I hold it to be one of the simplest truths of war that the thing which enables an infantry soldier to keep going with his weapons is the near presence or the presumed presence of a comrade. . . . He is sustained by his fellows primarily and by his weapons secondarily."[10] As for fighting for a cause, Marshall wrote, "Men do not fight for a cause but because they do not want to let their comrades down."[11]

In another landmark study on combat motivation, Edward Shils and Morris Janowitz interviewed *Wehrmacht* prisoners in an attempt to determine why some continued to fight so determinedly despite the overwhelmingly obvious evidence that Germany would lose the war. Contrary to the belief that good soldiers were those who clearly understood the political and moral implications of what was at stake, Shils and Janowitz concluded that the behavior and attitudes of infantrymen who fought to the end derived, instead, from the interpersonal relationships within the primary group (although they did note an allegiance to Hitler as a secondary motivation.) From their research, they concluded that:

> When the individual's immediate group, and its supporting formations, met his basic organic needs, offered him affection and esteem from both officers and comrades, supplied him with a sense of power and adequately regulated his relations with authority, the element of self-concern in battle, which would lead to disruption of the effective functioning of his primary group, was minimized.[12]

The consensus on unit cohesion as the primary source of combat motivation continued into the Korean War. Sociologist Roger Little observed a rifle company in combat for several months and found that the bonded relationships between men in combat—what he called "buddy relations"—were critical to basic survival.[13] To Little, buddy relations could refer to a specific soldier or the entire unit. After interviewing soldiers during the Vietnam War, noted military sociologist Charles Moskos concluded that combat primary group ties serve an important role in unit effectiveness. Interestingly, however, Moskos argued that the close bonds with other soldiers may be a result of self-interested concern for personal safety rather than an altruistic concern for fellow soldiers.[14] Regardless, Moskos validated the critical role of cohesion in combat performance.

Despite the wide acceptance of the importance of interpersonal relationships among soldiers in combat,[15] complicating undercurrents began to emerge in the later stages of the Vietnam War. In their controversial book, *Crisis in Command*, Richard Gabriel and Paul Savage claimed that the individual replacement system in Vietnam and the lack of professionalism in the officer corps led to the dissolution of primary group cohesion in the Army. While their conclusions about the causes of the decline of cohesion can be questioned, they did draw attention to a potentially deleterious effect of cohesion—fragging. They pointed out that cohesion between soldiers without the proper norms can work against organizational goals as in the nearly 800 alleged cases of attacks against authority figures by enlisted men in Vietnam.[16]

Cohesion in the military has also been addressed by several recent critical studies. These studies go beyond the issue of potentially detrimental effects of cohesion; instead they actually challenge the correlation of performance with unit cohesion as traditionally construed. Interestingly, the essential preoccupation of many of these studies is not cohesion per se, but the current Department of Defense policy on homosexual conduct. The current policy assumes that "the presence in the armed forces of persons who demonstrate a propensity or intent to engage in homosexual acts would create an unacceptable risk to the high standards of morale, good order and discipline, and *unit cohesion* that are the essence of military capability."[17] Any demonstration that unit cohesion is *not* critical to military capability would tend to refute the validity of DoD policy. To this end, researchers such as Elizabeth Kier examined the cohesion literature and concluded that "fifty years of research in several disciplines has failed to uncover persuasive evidence . . . that there is a causal relationship leading from primary group cohesion to military effectiveness."[18]

In a 1993 RAND report, Robert MacCoun argued that there are actually two types of cohesion. According to MacCoun, *social* cohesion refers to the quality of the bonds of friendship and emotional closeness among unit members—the type of cohesion referred to by the post-WWII studies. *Task* cohesion, on the other hand, refers to the commitment among unit members to accomplish a job requiring the collective efforts of the unit. MacCoun argued that it is task cohesion that is correlated with unit performance, not social cohesion. Social cohesion, according to MacCoun, has little positive relationship to performance, and can even degrade unit accomplishment (e.g., through rate busting, groupthink, or fragging).[19] MacCoun's arguments are echoed by David Segal and Meyer Kestnbaum, who state that "there is no clear causal link that can be demonstrated using rigorous methods between social cohesion and high levels of military performance."[20]

Despite this emerging debate about cohesion in the academic realm, it is tempting to assume that it has little relevance in the Army policy arena. Three factors suggest otherwise. First, the homosexual conduct policy is based firmly on the conviction that unit cohesion is essential to military capability. Determining the role of cohesion in combat motivation is obviously relevant to that policy debate. Second, the Army is pushing ahead with force stabilization initiatives resting on the premise that "full-spectrum forces must be highly cohesive teams whose shared experiences and intensive training enable them to perform better in combat."[21]

Under a unit manning personnel system, soldiers will arrive and train together through a standard 36-month tour. If cohesion is truly unimportant to unit performance as recent critics suggest, then the Army is putting an abundance of resources into a radical change that may produce only a modicum of results.

Third, discussions at the DoD level have been exploring the difference between task and social cohesion and which has the biggest impact on the military. In contrast with proponents of the traditionalist view, some maintain that the services already do a good job of getting people who "don't like one another" to work well together, so that social cohesion may be unnecessary. Given that the academic debate concerning cohesion has moved into the policy arena, an exploration of cohesion—specifically *social* cohesion—and the broader topic of combat motivation is warranted.

Methodology

This chapter analyzes motivation and cohesion in combat. The backdrop for analysis was Operation Iraqi Freedom with major combat operations occurring roughly from 20 March 2003 to 1 May 2003. To examine the concepts of combat motivation and cohesion, views were solicited from three distinct samples that experienced combat during Iraqi Freedom.

The first sample consisted of Iraqi regular army soldiers. The combat motivation of Iraqi soldiers was analyzed through interviews with enemy prisoners of war (EPWs) held at Camp Bucca at Umm Qasr, Iraq.[22] Nearly all of the EPWs questioned were lower-grade enlisted soldiers; two officers, a lieutenant colonel and a lieutenant, were also interviewed. Only two soldiers, both sergeants, claimed membership in a Republican Guard or Special Republican Guard unit. In this sample, then, views are probably representative of rank and file soldiers, rather than elite units or senior leaders. Over 30 interviews were conducted, recorded, translated, and transcribed using a structured interview format.[23]

To gain a U.S. military perspective, researchers met with troops assigned to the maneuver units of the three U.S. divisions conducting the majority of combat operations—the 3rd Infantry Division, the 101st Airborne Division (Air Assault), and the 1st Marine Division.[24] Interviews were conducted at unit locations in the vicinity of Baghdad and Al Hillah prior to the official cessation of major combat operations. Interviews with over 40 soldiers were conducted, recorded, and transcribed.[25] It should be noted that the same structured interview format was used with both Iraqi EPWs and U.S. troops—thus providing a good comparison and contrast of issues across both armies.

The third sample used to analyze cohesion and motivation in combat consisted of embedded news media representatives. Over a dozen members of the media who were embedded in U.S. Army ground units were interviewed in person or telephonically, or responded to an email questionnaire. This media sample provides a valuable perspective on cohesion and combat that augments the views given by U.S. military members.

Motivated by Coercion

In 1949, Stouffer asked combat veterans the following question: "Generally, in your combat experience, what was most important to you in making you want to keep going and do as well as you could?" The same question concerning combat motivation was asked of the Iraqi EPWs. They were expected to respond that they were motivated to fight for each other (as earlier research had shown with the *Wehrmacht*), or that they were simply defending their homeland.[26]

Instead, the near universal response was that the Iraqi soldiers were motivated by coercion. Even with the powerful Coalition forces to their front, they were more fearful of the dreaded Baath Party to their rear. Their behavior was driven by fear of retribution and punishment by the Baath Party or the special paramilitary group "Fedayeen Saddam"[27] if they were found shirking from combat. Iraqi soldiers related stories of being jailed or beaten by Baath Party representatives if they were suspected of leaving their units. Several showed scars from previous desertion attempts. One soldier related how he still felt guilty that his mother was jailed in response to his AWOL status several years before.

When Iraqi soldiers described the desertion of comrades, they noted the universal practice of retaining their small arms rather than burying their weapons in the sand as U.S. psychological warfare leaflets had urged. Deserters remained armed to protect themselves against the Fedayeen Saddam death squads they expected to find in Iraqi rear areas. The decision to desert with arms is one not taken lightly because it increased the likelihood of being killed by U.S. or British forces, particularly by reconnaissance units common to the most forward elements. Armed desertion, then, represented clear evidence of the fear of retribution experienced by those who wished neither to fight nor to surrender.

Surprisingly, the retribution Iraqi soldiers feared was not administered by officers serving in Iraqi units. Most of the enlisted soldiers saw their officers as distant, but usually not as a threat. Iraqi officer training was described by a captured graduate of the Baghdad Military Academy as "on the Sandhurst model," suggesting a sharp separation between the ranks of officers and enlisted similar to the British custom. Iraqi officers were often politically appointed and not regarded as tactically competent by their men. Such circumstances led to little mutual respect between officers and the enlisted soldiers, but the strained relationship was far from intimidating to the enlisteds. Several prisoners reported that if their officers had tried to force them to fight, they would have simply killed them and deserted anyway. No prisoner ever described an attempt by officers to compel resistance against Coalition forces.

Surrender decisions, in the sample interviewed, were usually made at very low levels, often among small groups of soldiers, and were not attributed to the capitulation of a higher headquarters. Surrender was sometimes catalyzed by artillery shelling or air attack—though none of the soldiers interviewed had to withstand lengthy bombardment. Officers permitted surrender, sometimes along with their own desertion, sometimes by benign neglect. One officer replied, when questioned about why he had not forced his men to fight, "As a man before Allah, that would have been the wrong thing to do." Although he understood that his mission was to defend along the edge of an oil field, he had no map, no plan, and no communication with his higher headquarters. The ability of the Iraqi small unit leadership to elicit loyalty and compliance up and down the command chain was almost completely lacking, unquestionably contributing to the disintegration of Iraqi army units in the face of advancing Coalition forces.

As far as cohesion being a factor in combat motivation is concerned, questioning revealed that if Iraqi army soldiers had emotional ties to other soldiers, they were almost always with soldiers from their own tribe or region. Squads and platoons had little or no cohesion. Iraq's approximately 150 major tribes are comprised of more than 2,000 smaller clans with a wide range of religions and ethnic groups. Soldiers spoke of units fragmented by tribal or regional differences. In addition, units were at such reduced strength that manning issues may have exacerbated the effects of fragmentation. No Iraqi soldier reported a unit strength greater than 40 percent. One of the two officers in the sample, a platoon leader, described his unit as composed of only nine men of more than 48 authorized.

Many soldiers reported the frequent practice of asking (even bribing) their officers for permission to go home to their families for ten or so days out of every month. As Shils and Janowitz in the WWII study of German prisoners found, surrender decisions are greatly facilitated when primary groups are disrupted. The surrendering Iraqi soldiers showed little or no concern about letting their comrades down since their allegiances to their fellow soldiers in the unit were already strained or never fully cultivated. One armored personnel carrier driver related how, despite the fact that one of his friends was both his vehicle commander and his immediate supervisor, his surrender decision was easily made at home where he was physically and emotionally separated from his unit.

Interviews uncovered no evidence of higher order loyalties such as commitment to national service or the Arabic obligation to demonstrate steadfastness (*Sumoud*) among the Iraqi soldiers interviewed. In response to questions about why they were in the Army, or what would cause them to try their hardest in battle, the soldiers never invoked Iraqi nationalism or the need to repel Americans as an invading army.[28] The Iraqi army appeared to be a poorly trained, poorly led, and disparate group of conscripts who were more concerned with self-preservation and family ties than defending their country. This army provided a good case study of what happens to military units when social cohesion and leadership are absent.

Motivated in Behalf of Others

When U.S. troops were interviewed shortly after their experience in combat (for most, it was three weeks of continuous enemy contact), one of the first questions posed addressed their reasons for entering the military in the first place. The responses were what most recruiters already know—to get money for college, to gain experience before looking for a job, to follow in the footsteps of a family member who had been in the military, or just to find some adventure before settling down. Although one or two mentioned that they were motivated to enlist because of the events of 11 September 2001, most did not cite patriotism or ideology as their enlistment rationale.

As the interview progressed, soldiers were asked the same question posed to WWII combat soldiers by Stouffer and also to the Iraqi EPWs in this study—"Generally, in your combat experience, what was most important to you in making you want to keep going and do as well as you could?" For WWII soldiers, besides finishing the job so they could go home, the most common response was solidarity with one's comrades. For Iraqi army soldiers, it was coercion. For U.S. soldiers in the Iraq War, responses also dealt with going home, but importantly the most frequent reason given for combat motivation was "fighting for my buddies." Soldiers answered with comments such as: "In combat, just the fact that if I give up, I am not helping my buddies. That is number one"; or "Me and my loader were talking about it and in combat the only thing that we really worry about is you and your crew." The soldiers were talking about social cohesion—the emotional bonds between soldiers.

Social cohesion appears to serve two roles in combat motivation. First, because of the close ties to other soldiers, it places a burden of responsibility on each soldier to achieve group success and protect the unit from harm. Soldiers feel that although their individual contribution to the group may be small, it is still a critical part of unit success and therefore important. As one soldier put it, "I am the lowest ranking private on the Bradley [fighting vehicle] so I am trying to kind of prove something in a way that I could do things. I did not want to let anyone down."

This desire to contribute to the unit mission comes not from a commitment to the mission per se, but from a social compact with the members of the primary group. One Bradley Commander (BC) spoke of the infantrymen in the back of his vehicle and the responsibility he felt for them:

> You have two guys in the back who are not seeing what is going on, and they are putting all their trust into the gunner and the BC. Whatever objects or obstacles, or tanks or vehicles are in front of you, you are taking them out, because they don't know what is going on. They are just like in a dark room. They can't do nothing. Having that trust . . . I guess that is one thing that kept me going.

Another soldier simply stated, "I know that as far as myself, sir, I take my squad mates' lives more important than my own." Still another soldier described the intense burden he felt for his fellow soldiers, "That person means more to you than anybody. You will die if he dies. That is why I think that we protect each other in any situation. I know that if he dies and it was my fault, it would be worse than death to me."

The second role of social cohesion is to provide the confidence and assurance that someone soldiers could trust was "watching their back." This is not simply trusting in the competence, training, or commitment to the mission of another soldier, but trusting in someone they regarded as closer than a friend who was motivated to look out for their welfare. In the words of one infantryman, "You have got to trust them more than your mother, your father, or girlfriend, or your wife, or anybody. It becomes almost like your guardian angel."

The presence of comrades imparts a reassuring belief that all will be well. As one soldier stated, "It is just like a big family. Nothing can come to you without going through them first. It is kind of comforting." One soldier noted, "If he holds my back, then I will hold his, and nothing is going to go wrong." Another added, "If you are going to war, you want to be able to trust the person who is beside you. If you are his friend, you know he is not going to let you down. . . . He is going to do his best to make sure that you don't die."

Once soldiers are convinced that their own personal safety will be assured by others, they feel empowered to do their job without worry. One soldier attempted to describe how the close relationship he had with another soldier provided the psychological cushion to drive his vehicle without concern:

> I knew Taylor would personally look out for me. . . . It was stupid little things like, "Dude, you look like you need a hug." He would come over and give me a big old bear hug. He knew that I looked out for him and vice versa. . . . Knowing that there is somebody watching when I didn't have the opportunity to watch myself when I am driving—Taylor watched everywhere. When I am driving down the road, I have to watch in front of me knowing where I am driving and knowing that I am not going to drive over anything. I don't know what is behind me. I don't know what is to my side. I trusted Taylor was going to keep an eye on everything. He always did. Obviously, he did. We are still here. Thank God.

It should be noted that soldiers understood that totally entrusting their personal safety to others could be viewed as irrational. One young soldier commented on his parents' reaction— "My whole family thinks that I am a nut. They think, 'How can you put your life in someone's hands like that? . . . You are still going to be shot.'" Despite the occasional skepticism of outsiders, soldiers greatly valued being free of the distracting concerns of personal safety.

Of course, anyone who has been around soldiers for any period of time recognizes that there is always a level of petty bickering and quarreling occurring between soldiers—especially in austere conditions. Social cohesion in combat, however, manages to overcome trifling disputes. A soldier put it this way,

> I think that when we are here and we are living and seeing each other every single day going on six months, there is a lot of [stuff] that you just get irritated with and don't want to be around one another. But in the same sense, I think that everybody learned that no matter how [ticked] off we were at one another and how bad we were fighting, when the artillery started raining down and [stuff] started hitting the fan,—it was like the [stuff] never happened. Everybody just did what we had to do. It was just looking out for one another. We weren't fighting for anybody else but ourselves. We weren't fighting for some higher-up who is somebody; we were just fighting for each other.

The bonds of trust between soldiers take weeks and months to develop. Soldiers related how shared experiences prior to combat helped develop those bonds. One soldier here describes how the weeks of training prior to deployment helped build relationships between soldiers:

> Going out and constantly training together, NTC rotations. . . . We are together every day for the majority of the day, five days a week. You are going to start know-

ing what ticks people off, what makes them happy, what you need to do to work with them. Eventually a bond is going to form.

Once deployed, soldiers spent more time together training. As one soldier noted, "We have worked a lot together. We did a lot of field training together, so it is like we are brothers. Suffered through it all together."

But cohesion is not developed just in training. In the long, often mundane periods of time spent neither in training or actual combat, the bonds between soldiers are often nurtured. One infantryman spoke of cultivating relationships while pulling security:

> I knew we were going to end up spending some time together, but I never knew that we would be sleeping nose to nose, waking each other up to stand guard over the hole. . . . You are waking somebody up to help keep you awake and they will get up and talk to you for however long it takes.

Interestingly, much of the social cohesion in units is developed simply because there is nothing else to do except talk. As one soldier observed, "In a fighting hole with somebody for so many hours, you get to know them real good because there is nothing else to talk about. You become real good friends." Another pointed out:

> You are sitting in the dirt, scanning back and forth, [and] the only person you got to talk to for me is him, which is on my left right here, about 18 inches away, sitting shoulder to shoulder. After about a month or so in the dirt like that together, you start talking about family. You start talking about everything . . . family, friends, what is going on, and your life in general pretty much, what is not right at home. Everything.

While some soldiers referred to the relationships between soldiers as "friendships," most tried to convey the depth of the relationships by using the analogy of the family. One soldier insightfully noted,

> You are away from your family and everybody—I don't care who you are, even if you are in the States and you are not in the military—you are going to look for something to attach yourself to. In the military, especially when you come out to the field, you have no family. Everyone here becomes your family. With my wife, for the first couple years of being with her, I had to learn to live with her—her routine in the morning and how my routine fits in with that, who uses the bathroom first and what have you. It is the same thing with a bunch of Joe's walking around. You learn everybody's personality—who is grumpy in the morning, who is grumpy at night, and who is grumpy when they miss chow and let them up in front of you. It is pretty much the same deal.

Another soldier echoed the family analogy in this manner:

> We eat, drink, [go to the bathroom]—everything—together. I think that it should be like that . . . I really consider these guys my own family, because we fight together, we have fun together. . . . We are to the point where we even call the squad leader "Dad."

Despite the academic debate that questions social cohesion and its beneficial effects on performance, social cohesion in fact remains a key component of combat motivation in U.S. soldiers. Social cohesion is what motivates soldiers not only to perform their job, but also to accept responsibility for the interests of other soldiers.

At the same time, social cohesion relieves each soldier of the constant concern for personal safety as other members of the unit take on that responsibility.

Reporting the War

To provide still another perspective on social cohesion in combat units, views were solicited from members of the embedded news media. They present a valuable point of view for two reasons. First, they could describe small-unit dynamics in combat from an observer viewpoint, helping to validate the findings resulting from soldier interviews. Second, embedded media representatives could relate their own experiences concerning the development of bonds with soldiers in their assigned units. It was expected that most of the embedded media would avoid becoming too emotionally connected with soldiers so as to maintain their objective, dispassionate journalist role. Prior to the war, critics of the embedding process warned that the embedded media could "end up 'in bed' with their military protectors" if bonds did form.[29] As CBS anchor Dan Rather cautioned early in the war, "There's a pretty fine line between being embedded and being entombed."[30]

Embedded reporters were asked if their intentions initially were to establish close bonds with the soldiers and then to describe the actual outcome as far as establishing such bonds was concerned. Surprisingly, the overwhelming majority of the journalists interviewed did not attempt to prevent any bonds from forming. One journalist commented, "I knew they would form, I just didn't know how strong they would be."[31] For the embedded reporters, cohesion provided the assurance that their personal safety would not be imperiled. One media person noted, "We were going to war. It was potentially dangerous. I needed to get to know people to figure out who to trust if things got ugly." Another stated, "My intention all along was to form as close a bond as possible, since my main objective was to come home safe, second to telling the story."

Nearly all of the embedded media personnel declared that close emotional bonds did form, although the bonds were not instantaneous. Similar to the experience of soldiers, time spent together provided an opportunity for relationships to develop. As one embed stated, "It's impossible to spend that much time living and working with people round-the-clock and not develop both a rapport and an affection." In the words of another journalist,

> I felt at first the soldiers were very suspicious and leery of me. But as the days went by and I faced the threats they faced and I went through the hardships without complaint, and I helped wherever I could, and I tried to do good deeds for them whenever possible, they came around and actually ended up feeling quite a bit of affection for me. I certainly did for them.

Another reporter related how he became close to his "minder":

> At the battery level, I rode with this young lieutenant who was "in charge" of media relations through the initial race across Iraq in the opening few days of the war. We faced snipers and an enemy artillery attack together and I think that helped form a bond. When we finally made camp out in the desert and stayed there for a week or

so, he and I often chatted for hours on end (there not being much else to do most of the time).

To many of the embeds, the relationships that formed were surprisingly profound. One reporter stated, "I don't really have many close male friends back here at home. So I didn't expect much in the way of close emotional relationships. I was pleasantly surprised that I made some very close friendships with some of these guys." Another journalist reflected upon the experience this way:

> I am still in contact with the wives, who pass on messages from their husbands. We also learned after we returned home that the two cots [I and my photographer] used . . . were still in place and no one else was allowed to sleep there, either out of respect for us or because they think we might be back. Either way, I thought it was a nice tribute and demonstrates in some small degree the respect they have for us and the friendships we developed while telling the story of Charlie Co.'s war.

Perhaps surprisingly, once a level of personal trust was established through emotional bonds with the soldiers, the embedded media felt as if they could accomplish their job better. With their personal safety assured through the trust gained by closer personal relationships, they could fully concentrate on reporting the war. One embedded journalist contrasted his experience in the 1991 Gulf War with that of the Iraq War. In the Gulf War, he felt like an outsider and "a spy." In the Iraq War, he was able to deliver a better product—reporting the war uninterrupted by a lack of trust. "War is a barrier by itself," he commented, "so you don't need another barrier with a lack of trust." Another reporter noted, "I became so familiar with them that I became part of the team. I was serving my nation as well, in a different way, just like the soldiers."

As far as becoming too close to the unit and losing objectivity were concerned, the embedded media saw that the trust that comes with cohesion works both ways. They could trust the soldiers, but the soldiers could also trust the media to report fairly. After a serious incident occurred in one unit, a reporter commented on how the relationship he had formed with the brigade commander helped him to report on the incident:

> What was really helpful was that by then, he and I had already got to know each other. I liked him and trusted him. When he said he was concerned about releasing certain information, he would give me a reason, and the reason made sense. That is not generally the case even in civilian life when dealing with officials in a crisis.

Another reporter, after experiencing the combat intensity of purposely driving into ambush after ambush on a "Thunder Run" into Baghdad, described how the bonds he had formed helped him overcome his reluctance to go again:

> The company first sergeant, in whose APC I rode, asked me if I wanted to stay behind that day because he knew it was going to be bad. But I felt that if I opted out of that, it would be abandoning those guys. I felt I had to be there to tell their story of the day they went into Baghdad to stay. So, despite a great deal of concern, I went with them.

The perspectives of the embedded media are important because it was a group that could choose its approach to establishing relationships. While the bonds the embeds described were often qualitatively different from the intense, almost familial relationships described by soldiers, the presence of soldiers with whom relationships had been established gave the embedded media a reassurance of their personal safety and an empowerment to do their job.

Motivated by the Cause

The conventional wisdom established by post-WWII studies of the American soldier is that soldiers fight for each other. This generalization was and continues to be reinforced in American society through media ranging from Bill Mauldin's *Willie and Joe* cartoons to movies such as *Blackhawk Down* and *Band of Brothers*. Indeed, the findings of this chapter provide still more support for the proposition that social cohesion serves as an important element of combat motivation for U.S. soldiers.

However, it would be a mistake to neglect other sources of combat motivation. The possibility that soldiers may be motivated in combat by ideology—e.g., fighting for the cause—has been a frequent theme. But past researchers have almost always concluded that ideological conviction is not a prime source of combat motivation for American soldiers. For example, Civil War researcher Bell Wiley, who studied both the Confederate and Union armies, concluded concerning Confederate soldiers that "it is doubtful whether many of them either understood or cared about the Constitutional issues at stake."[32] With regard to the Union soldiers, he wrote, "One searches most letters and diaries in vain for soldiers' comment on why they were in the war or for what they were fighting. . . . American soldiers of the 1860s appear to have been about as little concerned with ideological issues as were those of the 1940s."[33]

The soldiers in the 1940s were of course the subjects of Stouffer's *American Soldier* study. In that multivolume work, he noted that "officers and enlisted men alike attached little importance to idealistic motives—patriotism and concern about war aims."[34] He added that except for expressions of flagrant disloyalty, the strongest taboo for World War II combat soldiers was "any talk of a flag-waving variety."[35]

Surprisingly however, in interviews for the present chapter, many soldiers *did* respond that they were motivated by ideological notions. Ending Saddam's oppression and bringing freedom to Iraq were common themes in describing their combat motivation. In the words of one soldier, "Liberating those people. Liberating Iraq. Seeing them free. They were repressed for, I don't know how many years, 30 something years. Just knowing that they are free now. Knowing that is awesome to me." Another soldier noted,

> There were good times when we [saw] the people. . . . How we liberated them. That lifted up our morale. Seeing the little children. Smiling faces. Seeing a woman and man who were just smiling and cheering "Good! Good! Good! Freedom Good!" . . . That lifted us up and kept us going. We knew we were doing a positive thing.

One embed wrote, "By far the most powerful motivation for many soldiers here is the belief that they will improve life for the Iraqi people."[36] Another commented that soldiers did fight out of a sense of camaraderie and duty, but there was an "icing of patriotism that guides their decision to go down this path."

Three points are important here. First, this combat motivation centered on bringing freedom and democracy to Iraq. It was not nationalism or even a national security issue. Rather it was an idealistically unselfish outcome addressing the people of Iraq. True, much of the official rationale for the war was much more complex, as in the following DoD public affairs photo caption insert: "Operation Iraqi Freedom is the multinational coalition effort to liberate the Iraqi people, eliminate Iraq's weapons of mass destruction, and end the regime of Saddam Hussein."[37] But in practice, soldiers focused on the more altruistic liberation aspects of the war aims.

Second, it is important to note the timing of this response. Many soldiers described how this particular combat motivation was revealed to them as combat progressed. The cumulative images of Iraqi citizens, especially the children, helped crystallize the realization of liberation as a motive. As one soldier related,

> After everything settled down we actually got to see some of the people we liberated and we got to talk to them. I think that was the most rewarding part of it. Getting to do presence patrol and seeing all the little kids coming out and waving, everybody honking their horns, everybody being happy because we came over here and we kicked some ass.

Another infantryman noted,

> We were down for a while because we were in cities—all we did was get shot at and we didn't see no civilians until like now. . . . I didn't see it at first, and then I saw the people coming back who are happy, it was like, "Thank You!" That really was the turning point. Now I know what I am doing.

It appears that today's soldiers are motivated in actual combat by fighting for their buddies, but once the outcomes of the major combat phase become apparent, the motivation shifts to more ideological themes. Additionally, these soldiers were interviewed just a few days after major combat operations, but before units transitioned to the peace enforcement role. It is possible that as soldiers experience a protracted deployment conducting counterinsurgency operations, their attitudes may shift again.

Third, while it is no longer taboo to talk in ideological terms about their loftier values—especially after 11 September 2001, soldiers still find it difficult to express this moral dimension of their combat motivation. It was not uncommon for soldiers to tell of the difficulty of describing morally charged values. Comments such as, "You just have to be there and see it for yourself" or "You can't really explain it" were frequent. As one tongue-tied infantryman put it,

> It may be a cornball answer, but believe me, I'm not into all that, but just actually seeing some of them waving and shooting thumbs up. They are like, "We love you America!" . . . I am not like a very emotional person, but the kids come up to you, they give you a hug. One lady came up to one of our soldiers and tried to give him the baby so that the baby could give him a kiss. It was like, "Whoa!!" It was a heartfelt moment there for me.

Despite the results of previous studies and the conventional wisdom that American soldiers are not motivated by ideological sentiments, many soldiers in this study did report being motivated by the ideals of freedom, liberation, and democracy. Why would today's U.S. soldiers be more apt to speak of being motivated by idealistic aims? Two possible reasons emerge.

First, U.S. soldiers throughout history may have had ideological motives, but did not realize it. In his study of American enlisted men, Moskos argued that while cohesion is often the primary combat motivation, there must be supplementary factors (other than training and equipment) to explain why cohesion alone does not determine battle performance. He posited that cohesion will "maintain the soldier in his combat role only when he has an underlying commitment to the worth of the larger social system for which he is fighting."[38] He called this commitment a *latent ideology* that supports cohesion as a combat motivator. According to Moskos, soldiers may not acknowledge or even know about this latent ideology, but it nevertheless exists. Thus, while today's soldiers still feel awkward speaking of ideological motivations, they seem to be relatively less inhibited about articulating such feelings compared to soldiers of the past.

Civil War historian James McPherson proposed another possibility concerning why soldiers sometimes fight for ideology. McPherson argued that ideology did serve as a combat motivation during the Civil War. He proposed that three situational characteristics were present during the Civil War that helped ideology emerge as a combat motivation for both sides of that war. First, he noted that the Confederate and Union armies were the most literate armies in history to that time. Over 80 percent of the Confederate soldiers and over 90 percent of the Union soldiers were literate. Second, most of the soldiers were volunteers as opposed to being draftees or conscripts. They were not forced to take up arms. Finally, McPherson noted that Civil War soldiers came from the world's most politicized and democratic society.[39] Soldiers voted, read newspapers, and participated in discussions concerning national issues. The interaction of these three factors produced soldiers who were able, inclined, and encouraged to debate ideological notions. Troops who are educated, are comfortable discussing ideological topics, and are volunteers seem more likely to fight for a cause. Following this line, McPherson argued that Confederate soldiers fought "for liberty and independence from what they regarded as a tyrannical government," while Union soldiers fought "to preserve the nation created by the founders from dismemberment and destruction."[40]

Interestingly, the same three situational characteristics that McPherson stipulated for the Civil War exist today. Contemporary soldiers are well educated. The average new soldier in 2002 had 12.1 years of formal education, implying that today's average new soldier has had some college experience. Today's soldiers are also older and more mature than what we might expect. In 2002, the average new soldier was 21.1 years old.

Today's soldiers are also in touch with the pressing issues of the day. Through the Internet, Fox News, and CNN, they learn the world situation, the key players, and the essence of the policy debates. In June 2003, the *New York Times* quoted an infantryman of the 3rd Infantry Division as saying, "You call Donald Rumsfeld and tell him our sorry asses are ready to go home."[41] It was surprising not only to hear such a direct message being conveyed publicly, but also that a Private First Class would even know who the Secretary of Defense was.

One embedded journalist commented on the underestimated sophistication of today's soldiers: "Soldiers I encountered were trained, ethical, thoughtful, and intelligent. It was not unusual to talk to a Private or PFC and be absolutely astounded at how well he could talk about why they were [fighting in Iraq]." Today's soldiers are attuned to values and ideological principles. Since the day they took their enlistment oaths, they have been conditioned by ideology. New soldiers are socialized to be comfortable talking about value-laden ideas ranging from the seven Army values to the Soldier's Creed.[42]

Finally, today's soldiers are volunteers. They were not coerced into service and they did not approach the military as the employer of last resort. They come from a generation that trusts the military institution. In 1975, a Harris Poll reported that only 20 percent of people ages 18 to 29 said they had a great deal of confidence in those who ran the military.[43] A recent poll by the Harvard Institute of Politics, however, found that 70 percent of college undergraduates trust the military to do the right thing either all or most of the time.[44] Today's soldiers understand that they are professionals in a values-based institution. They trust each other, their leaders, and the Army, and they understand the moral implications of war.

The Army has matured steadily from its status as a conscript army, and then a fledgling all-volunteer army, to what is now a truly professional army. Professional soldiers still fight for each other, but they also accept the higher responsibility that they have been entrusted to shoulder. Evidence of this transition is found even in the families of today's soldiers. When reporters interviewed wives about their husbands' delayed return from Iraq, one sergeant's wife responded, "As military spouses, we know our husbands have responsibilities. They are professionals doing their jobs." Another spouse added, "I wonder how [complaining] must sound to someone who's lost someone."[45] Still another spouse noted, "I could have married anyone else who would have been at work 9 to 5. [But the job my husband] does is an amazingly honorable one."[46]

Conclusion

Shortly after the latest Iraq War, a Col. Abdul-Zahra of the former Iraqi army commented that "the U.S. Army is certainly the best in the world. But it's not because of the fighting men, but because of their equipment."[47] Colonel Abdul-Zahra missed the point. The Iraq War showed that while the U.S. Army certainly has the best equipment and training, there is a human dimension that is often overlooked. As military historian Victor Davis Hanson observed shortly after the end of major combat operations in Iraq,

> The lethality of the military is not just organizational or a dividend of high-technology. Moral and group cohesion explain more still. The general critique of the 1990s was that we had raised a generation with peroxide hair and tongue rings, general illiterates who lounged at malls, occasionally muttering "like" and "you know"

in Sean Penn or Valley Girl cadences. But somehow the military has married the familiarity and dynamism of crass popular culture to 19th-century notions of heroism, self-sacrifice, patriotism, and audacity.[48]

The soldiers interviewed for this chapter sometimes came across as crude, vulgar, and cynical, yet that impression was leavened by a surprisingly natural acceptance of the institution's values. The U.S. Army is the best in the world because, in addition to possessing the best equipment, its soldiers also have an unmatched level of mutual trust. They trust each other because of the close interpersonal bonds. They trust their leaders because their leaders have competently trained their units. And they trust the Army. They trust the Army because, since the end of the draft, the Army has had to win them over rather than conscripting them. Unable any longer to compel service by force of law, the all-volunteer Army saw that it must "transform itself into an institution that people would respect and trust. Bonds forged by trust replaced bonds forged by fear of punishment."[49] Because our soldiers trust the Army as an institution, they now look to the Army to point the moral direction for war. As this chapter has shown, soldiers still fight for each other. In a professional army, however, soldiers are also sophisticated enough to grasp the moral and ideological reasons for fighting.

In sum, then, social cohesion, or the strong emotional bonds between soldiers, continues to be a critical factor in combat motivation. One of the main purposes of assignment stabilization is to increase unit cohesion. While critics may decry the potential adverse effects on officer assignment diversity or the increased personnel management complexities, questioning the need for social cohesion is nonsensical in the face of generations of battlefield experience. Likewise, attempting to dissect cohesion into social or task cohesion and then measuring correlations with performance is best left to the antiseptic experiments of academia. For those whose real agenda is to overturn the DoD homosexual conduct policy, it would be prudent to build their argument on grounds other than questioning the linkage between social cohesion and combat performance.

The Iraq War confirms what every combat soldier already knows—cohesion places a shared responsibility for the success of the unit on each individual while giving each soldier the confidence that someone else is watching over them. Spending large amounts of time together, usually in austere conditions, develops this trusting relationship. The Iraqi and American armies provide an interesting contrast in cohesion. In the former, the absence of cohesion made the desertion or surrender decisions easy. In the latter, the presence of social cohesion was a primary source of combat motivation.

The transition from a struggling all-volunteer army to a truly professional force has not been easy. Early problems in the "hollow" Army included declining enlistment rates, low-quality recruits, high attrition, and plummeting morale.[50] Seven years into the experiment, Richard Nixon, who introduced the all-volunteer Army, wrote, "The volunteer army has failed to provide enough personnel of the caliber we need for our highly sophisticated armaments."[51] The Army rebounded in the 1980s with "Be All You Can Be" and a recruiting overhaul, but the 1990s witnessed a dismantling of much of what had been accomplished through a demoralizing downsizing. The survivors picked up the pieces, however, and overcame another recruiting crisis in the late 1990s. Today, the "Army of One" is the culmination of 30 years of movement toward a professional Army. It is a high-tech, highly trained, and highly *professional* force.

The bonds of trust between soldiers, their leaders, and the Army as an institution, however, are not invulnerable. Horror film director John Carpenter was once asked what he thought scared people the most. His answer: "Uncertainty."[52] Uncertainty can unravel the trust that provides the underpinnings for the professional Army. Uncertainty can be imposed on the Army through open-ended deployments. Soldiers will salute and deploy to distant parts of the world when ordered, but when their redeployment date is uncertain, trust of the institution is strained. Much like the society they represent, today's soldiers view wars in terms of weeks, not months. A CBS poll early in the war, for example, showed 62 percent of Americans believing that the war would be "quick and successful."[53] While today's wars may be prosecuted quickly, the ensuing peace operations may continue indefinitely. As a result, the U.S. Army is now stretched over 120 countries. Because of the consequent lack of a sufficient rotational base, the ability to redeploy soldiers home after an operation has diminished significantly. After observing the current situation, Brookings Institution defense analyst Michael O'Hanlon noted, "It would be the supreme irony, and a national tragedy, if after winning two wars in two years, the U.S. Army were broken and defeated while trying to keep the peace."[54]

Postwar Update

The original research for this chapter was conducted in April and May of 2003. During that period, polls showed that 76 percent of the American public believed that it was worth going to war in Iraq. One year later, the polls showed an evenly divided public, with 50 percent saying that it was worth going to war in Iraq, and 47 percent saying it was not.[55] Operation Iraqi Freedom's switch from a surprisingly quick, high-intensity war to an extended period of nation-building and counterinsurgency operations raises questions concerning the findings detailed in this chapter. Is cohesion still a component of combat motivation in an environment of counterinsurgency? Is fighting for the cause likely to diminish as a factor in combat motivation as public support for a protracted war decreases?

In March 2004, I made a return trip to Iraq to examine these questions as well as other research issues. This closing section of the chapter examines some of the findings resulting from interviews conducted in locations throughout Iraq with over 50 junior officers from the 1st Armored Division, 1st Cavalry Division, 2nd Infantry Division, and the 82nd Airborne Division. The interviews, which were recorded for transcription, followed a standardized protocol. It should be noted that, unlike the original interviews that focused on enlisted combat troops, the follow-on study focused on combat arms lieutenants and captains. This perspective is unique in that these junior officers were at the edge of the primary social group. They were not totally included in the social circle of their combat troops, yet they spent nearly all their time with them while leading them. Unlike the embedded news media personnel who also spent long periods of time with combat soldiers, the junior leaders interviewed had responsibility for accomplishing the mission in addition to taking care of their troops.

The follow-on research showed that social cohesion remains a key combat motivator in an environment characterized by counterinsurgency operations and nation-building. As in high-intensity war, cohesion in an insurgency provides the social compact calling for soldiers to watch out for each other. One lieutenant noted:

> The brotherhood that we have between the platoon—the fact that we felt close—made everything work so well. It just fell into place. There were no questions asked. We were just protecting each other. We are just a tight-knit platoon. . . . There is a brotherhood, and they are all taking care of each other and we feel very close, including myself.

Another lieutenant commented on taking over his new platoon: "One day they are complete strangers, next I am the platoon leader and living with them 24 hours a day. They really become your new family. You get that much more of a bond."

These emerging bonds sometimes surprised the junior officers since they saw how the concern for other soldiers could transform low performers into key players. As one lieutenant observed:

> You have your guys who in the rear are a nuisance, but out here, you love them. Where they were irresponsible, drinking, and doing stupid stuff in the rear, out here they are pulling guard, they are waking up other people, they are taking care of each other like you never thought they would. Never.

Because junior officers are part of the chain of command, their experience with cohesion is slightly different from that of squad, section, or crew members. Cohesion entails a social compact between followers and leaders that allows leadership to be based on trust—not fiat. One officer noted how the relationship with his squad leaders had changed and how it impacted unit effectiveness:

> Now they are like brothers. By doing that, you bring them into a family and they are still respectful. There is still no fraternization; they still call me by my rank. They still call me "sir" and I still call them "sergeant," but there is a brotherhood that forms that you can't replace. . . . It is better to have that respect as opposed to a fear. They have that respect and it is almost like they don't want to let you down as opposed to fearing you.

Cohesion enhances combat performance because trust replaces fear. From the leader's perspective, cohesion motivates the leader because of his strengthened concern for the soldiers. One lieutenant, reflecting on the bonds he had formed with his soldiers, bluntly stated:

> These are my boys. This is my platoon. No one messes with it. . . . If we are out there and we are in a fight, we are going to win it; and if it is something back here with some administrative thing or whatever, we will do what we have to do. But other than that, my boys are my boys.

Probably the most salient indicator of the importance of cohesion emerged when junior officers were asked what their biggest fear was. The overwhelming majority of junior officers responded with deep feelings that the thing they feared most was losing one of their soldiers. Many of these leaders added that the potential agony of losing a soldier would be greatly compounded if it were due to the leader's negligence. In other words, subordinates have entrusted their lives with their officers, and the officers feared ever breaking that trust.

The role of ideology in an environment characterized by fighting an insurgency and nation-building differed slightly from the role of ideology as emerging from the original research. The slow, hard process of rebuilding a long-abused nation had replaced the euphoria of freeing the Iraqis. Establishing democracy remained the motivating cause, but now the soldiers on the ground were the ones who had to make it happen. Lofty goals of freedom and liberation shifted to an ideological program for *eventual* democracy in Iraq. The junior officers interviewed knew that progress would be made toward a democratic Iraq, but they also had a realistic appreciation that achieving a totally free and stable Iraq would be a task extending beyond the term of their own deployment. One lieutenant noted:

> We have all the answers for everything—or so we seem to think we do—and we don't. . . . The thing is, like we had all these wonderful ideas how to set up [an] interim government and do the smaller councils down the line—district and neighborhood councils—and establish a secure stable government. All the brain power in the world doesn't solve problems when they don't sit down and think about what these people on a very basic level are like. Not accounting for their religious differences and their basic human needs right off the bat, just throws everything askew to begin with.

Nevertheless, this same lieutenant noted that despite the seemingly slow pace of nation-building, he remained supportive of the moral direction of the war: "I am optimistic that I think there are enough good-hearted people and intelligent people who will eventually float to the top and this place will get itself back on its feet." Thus, ideology as a motivational factor shifted from abstract *liberation* to the more concrete *progress* toward a stable democracy. Because total democracy in Iraq was not attainable during their watch, junior officers reported being motivated by observable progress towards democracy and stability. One lieutenant recounted how a small gesture reinforced his motivation:

> It is getting close to summer, what are these kids going to do when they get out of school? . . . We thought a good idea would be to fix up these soccer fields. Believe it or not, I think that was one of the best things that we did initially. The families, the kids—they all loved us for it. They are like, "Hey, you are out here helping us out!"

Here, a captain reflects upon his motivation in postwar Iraq:

> For the first time in my army career—seven years—I have seen the look of gratitude on someone's face when we got rid of an oppressor. I have seen people that were hungry—get fed. I have seen people who had no schools to go to—have a school to go to. For me, that is it.

A lieutenant talked about being motivated even by small evidences of progress:

> The majority of the population really appreciates you being there. You see them smile. You see kids thank you. When you go to areas outside of [a hostile neighborhood,]

they are extremely happy to see you. They invite you for tea and you see the smile. They are very excited. They are anticipating what is going to come out of this and they see that you are the start. You are sort of the flame that is igniting this fire. Eventually one day, hopefully, things will get better. They see you as a starting block. That is what makes it rewarding.

Because these postwar Iraq interviews focused on junior officers, it may be possible that their ideological combat motivation differs from that of enlisted combat troops. News media reports, however, reflected a similar way of thinking in the enlisted ranks. For example, an embedded reporter with a Marine battalion battling militants in Fallujah commented as follows: "To a man, the troops believed they had been sent to Fallujah to help free its people."[56]

Interestingly, many officers spoke of ideological inspiration in terms of defending the nation from future terrorist attacks—perhaps because many of the officers interviewed had fought against foreign fighters in Iraq. One lieutenant observed, "I know I have a much better understanding of why our nation is at war now. . . . I don't want to get into it, but I am surprisingly very motivated to continue the war on terrorism." Another commented:

> The fact that there haven't been any terrorist attacks on U.S. soil is very satisfying. They know we are here. They know now that if they try anything, we will be up in their face. It is like if some country tries to come out and attack the U.S. again and we link it to that country, they know our policy now, we will go to your country.

One junior officer stated simply, "There is no doubt in my mind that our presence here is making the U.S. safer from an attack within our borders back home. It makes it worth it."

Although there are frequent charges that the messy postwar counterinsurgency campaign in Iraq was avoidable, is undesirable, and is unwinnable,[57] the results of the follow-on study reinforce the conclusion that social cohesion remains an integral part of combat effectiveness. Soldiers still fight for each other and their leaders. The follow-on study also demonstrates that in postwar Iraq, the motive for fighting (and nation-building) has shifted from the short-lived jubilation of liberation to the resolute determination of establishing a stable and democratic Iraq. The lightning quick Iraqi War validated the war-fighting effectiveness of a cohesive but transformed professional U.S. Army. The years of military involvement in a postwar Iraq that lie ahead will doubtless validate as well the nation-building effectiveness of a cohesive U.S. Army fully transformed.

Notes

1. This chapter is an updated and revised version of *Why They Fight: Combat Motivation in the Iraq War* (Carlisle Barracks, PA: Strategic Studies Institute, 2003) that I coauthored with Thomas A. Kolditz, Raymond A. Millen, and Terrence M. Potter. I am indebted to them for their assistance and friendship in this research. The points of view in this chapter are mine and not necessarily those of my colleagues. Moreover, the views expressed herein are not necessarily those of the U.S. Army War College, the Department of the Army, or the Department of Defense.

2. Ardant du Picq, *Battle Studies: Ancient and Modern* (Harrisburg, PA: Military Service Publishing, 1947), 110.

3. *Why We Fight*, http://history.acusd.edu/gen/filmnotes/whywefight.html, accessed on 17 September 2004.

4. Frank Capra, *The Name Above the Title: An Autobiography* (New York: De Capo Press, 1997), 327.

5. Thomas Doherty, *Projections of War: Hollywood, American Culture, and World War II* (New York: Columbia University Press, 1993), 70.

6. Ibid., 73.

7. Samuel A. Stouffer et al., *The American Soldier: Combat and Its Aftermath,* vol. 2 (Princeton, NJ: Princeton University Press, 1949), 107.

8. Ibid., 110.

9. Ibid., 136.

10. S. L. A. Marshall, *Men Against Fire* (New York: William Morrow and Company, 1947), 42-43.

11. Ibid.,161.

12. Edward A. Shils and Morris Janowitz, "Cohesion and Disintegration in the Wehrmacht in World War II," *Public Opinion Quarterly* 12 (Summer 1948): 281.

13. Roger W. Little, "Buddy Relations and Combat Performance," in *The New Military: Changing Patterns of Organization*, ed. Morris Janowitz (New York: Russell Sage Foundation, 1964), 221.

14. Charles C. Moskos, Jr., *The American Enlisted Man: The Rank and File in Today's Military* (New York: Russell Sage Foundation, 1970), 146.

15. Other works confirming the important role of cohesion in combat include Nora Kinzer Stewart, *Mates and Muchachos: Unit Cohesion in the Falklands/Malvinas War* (New York: Brassey's, 1991); William D. Henderson, *Why the Vietcong Fought: A Study of Motivation and Control in a Modern Army in Combat* (Westport, CT: Greenwood Press, 1979); and Reuven Gal, *A Portrait of an Israeli Soldier* (Westport, CT: Greenwood Press, 1986).

16. Richard A. Gabriel and Paul L. Savage, *Crisis in Command: Mismanagement in the Army* (New York: Hill and Wang, 1978), 43. The fragging data are from the period 1969-1972.

17. U.S. Code, Title 10, Subtitle A, Part II, Chapter 37, Section 654, (a) (15). Emphasis added.

18. Elizabeth Kier, "Homosexuals in the U.S. Military: Open Integration and Combat Effectiveness," *International Security* 23, no. 2 (Fall 1998): 18.

19. Robert J. MacCoun, "What is Known about Unit Cohesion and Military Performance," in *Sexual Orientation and U.S. Military Personnel Policy: Options and Assessment*, study group directors Bernard D. Rostker and Scott A. Harris (Santa Monica, CA: National Defense Research Institute, MR-323-OSD, 1993), 298.

20. David R. Segal and Meyer Kestnbaum, "Professional Closure in the Military Labor Market: A Critique of Pure Cohesion," in *The Future of the Army Profession*, project directors Don M. Snider and Gayle L. Watkins, ed. Lloyd J. Matthews (New York: McGraw-Hill Primus, 2002), 453. Interestingly, two decades earlier, Segal coauthored a chapter stating that "research on U.S. forces after World War II has repeatedly shown the impact of affective primary group ties and cohesion on effectiveness." See David R. Segal and Joseph H. Lengermann, "Combat Effectiveness," in *Combat Effectiveness: Cohesion, Stress, and the Volunteer Army,* ed. Sam C. Sarkesian (Beverly Hills: Sage, 1980), 182.

21. Task Force Stabilization, https://www.stabilization.army.mil/Overview_items/mission_statement.htm, accessed 17 September 2004.

22. The Iraqi soldiers required special consideration due to their status as captured combatants. Both the Geneva Conventions and specific guidance from DoD (Department of Defense Directive 3216.2, *Protection of Human Subjects and Adherence to Ethical Standards in DoD-Supported Research* [Washington, DC: Office of the Secretary of Defense, 25 March 2002]) protect enemy prisoners from exposure to the idly curious and from use as human subjects in

behavioral research. Questions were therefore restricted to issues involving individual and unit military effectiveness, following the advice and consent of staff judge advocates in Iraq, Kuwait, and CONUS. Although camp rules dictated that prisoners remain under military guard at all times, the interview setting was made as comfortable as possible. A U.S. military intelligence officer oversaw the collection of information from EPWs.

23. Col. Terrence Potter, an Arabic professor at the U.S. Military Academy, conducted all the interviews.

24. While 16 U.S. Marines were interviewed, the majority of the U.S. sample consisted of U.S. Army soldiers. There were no noticeable differences in demographics or attitudes between the Marine and Army infantrymen interviewed.

25. Subsequent quotations from soldiers are taken directly from the transcribed interviews.

26. Perhaps the Iraqis would have been expected to fight because that is what soldiers do when their country is attacked. *Sumoud* (as in the *al-Sumoud* missile) means "withstanding" or "steadfastness" in Arabic; soldiers might have been expected to respond that they fought just to resist the invaders.

27. The paramilitary Fedayeen Saddam (Saddam's "Men of Sacrifice") was founded by Saddam Hussein's son Uday in 1995.

28. Such questions are sensitive in a prison setting and responses may have been influenced by a desire to say what was felt would please the captors. It should be noted that during the interviews, significant numbers of prisoners were being released from the camp—as many as 350 per day during the final two days of interviews. Under such circumstances, prisoners may be less likely to express defiant or nationalistic attitudes to military interviewers. On the other hand, knowing that freedom was imminent may have encouraged them to speak more freely. On "Sumoud," see the preceding note.

29. Howard Kurtz, "After Invading Kuwait, Reporters Need Boot Camp," *Washington Post,* 10 March 2003, C1.

30. Justin Ewers, "Is the New News Good News?" *U.S. News & World Report,* 7 April 2003, 48.

31. All embedded news media personnel interviewed for this study were assigned to Army ground units. One could expect different responses from Air Force or Navy embedded media as well as from journalists embedded with higher headquarters. Unless otherwise noted, quotations from embedded media are taken from phone, email, or personal interviews.

32. Bell Irwin Wiley, T*he Life of Johnny Reb: The Common Soldier of the Confederacy* (Indianapolis, IN: Wiley, 1943), 309.

33. Bell Irwin Wiley, *The Life of Billy Yank: The Common Soldier of the Union* (Indianapolis, IN: Wiley, 1952), 39-40.

34. Stouffer, 111.

35. Stouffer, 150.

36. Ann Scott Tyson, "Oceans Away, US Troops Crave Approval at Home," *Christian Science Monitor,* 8 April 2003, 1.

37. Photo caption insert on all Operation Iraqi Freedom imagery, Joint Combat Camera Center, a division of the American Forces Information Service (AFIS), a field activity of the Assistant Secretary of Defense (Public Affairs).

38. Moskos, 147.

39. James M. McPherson, *What They Fought For: 1861-1865* (Baton Rouge: Louisiana State University Press, 1994), 4. See also Earl J. Hess, *The Union Soldier in Battle: Enduring the Ordeal of Combat* (Lawrence: University Press of Kansas, 1997), 97-102, for a discussion of the role of "The Cause" in the combat motivation of Union soldiers.

40. McPherson, 7.

41. Steven Lee Myers, "Anxious and Weary of War, G.I.'s Face a New Iraq Mission," *New York Times,* 15 June 2003, A1.

42. The seven Army values are Loyalty, Duty, Respect, Selfless Service, Honor, Integrity, and Personal Courage. These values are on posters, wallet cards, and even tags to accompany each soldier's identification tags (dog tags). A copy of the Soldier's Creed is issued to soldiers along with their Soldier's Manual on the first day of basic training. It contains statements such as, "I am doing my share to keep alive the principles of freedom for which my country stands."

43. Harris Poll, *Harris Confidence Index*, 22 January 2003.

44. Institute of Politics, Harvard University, *A National Survey Of College Undergraduates* (Cambridge, MA: Harvard University, 2002), 2.

45. Jack Kelley, Gary Strauss, and Martin Kasindorf, "Troops, Families Await War's Real End," *USA Today*, 12 June 2003, A1.

46. Gregg Zoroya, "Spouses, Kids Endure Own Agonies of War," *USA Today*, 11 July 2003, 9A.

47. Charles J. Hanley, "Iraqis Find Price of Battle Too High," *York Sunday News*, 1 June 2003, A3.

48. Victor Davis Hanson, "Anatomy of the Three-Week War," *National Review Online*, 17 April 2003, http://www. nationalreview.com/hanson/hanson041703.asp.

49. Richard A. Posner, "An Army of the Willing," *New Republic*, 19 May 2003, 27.

50. See Mark J. Eitelberg, "The All-Volunteer Force After Twenty Years," in *Professional on the Front Line: Two Decades of the All-Volunteer Force,* ed. J. Eric Fredland et al. (Washington, DC: Brassey's, 1996), 66-98.

51. Richard M. Nixon, *The Real War* (New York: Warner Books,1980), 201.

52. Mark Seal, "What Scares the Scary People?" *American Way*, 15 October 1993, 71.

53. CBS News Poll, *Americans See Longer War*, 25 March 2003, http://www.cbsnews.com/stories/2003/03/25 /opinion/polls/main545991.shtml.

54. Michael O'Hanlon, "Breaking The Army," *Washington Post*, 3 July 2003, 23.

55. Gallup News Service, *War Support Drops; Bush, Kerry in Dead Heat,* 9 April 2004, http://www.gallup.com/poll/ content/login.aspx?ci=11260.

56. Pamela Constable, "Letter From Fallujah: Amid An Unseen Enemy, The Welcome Dog Of War," *Washington Post,* 27 April 2004, C1.

57. James Fallows, "Blind Into Baghdad," *Atlantic Monthly*, January/February 2004, 52-74; Bob Herbert, "No End In Sight," *New York Times*, 2 April 2004, A19; John Harwood, "Former General Sees 'Staying the Course' in Iraq as Untenable,' *Wall Street Journal*, 28 April 2004, 4. The general referred to is Lt. Gen. William E. Odom, U.S. Army, Ret.

23 | McDonaldization in the U.S. Army: A Threat to the Profession[1]

Remi Hajjar and Morten G. Ender

cDonaldization leaves no institution in society unscathed. McDonaldization is "the process by which the principles of the fast-food restaurant are coming to dominate more and more sectors of American society as well as the rest of the world."[2] The "McDonaldization thesis," according to its major proponent, George Ritzer, has had both deep and wide penetration.[3] The thesis is applicable to many areas of social life including theme parks, chain stores, the criminal justice system, the church, the family, sex trade industries, and the university (McUniversity), among others.[4]

Given the infusion of McDonaldization into so many parts of American culture and society, we wondered to what extent it applied to the U.S. Army. In this chapter we aim to establish the deleterious effects of McDonaldized practices in the Army by showing how this process can stifle creativity, reduce leadership effectiveness, and degrade professional performance. In other words, McDonaldized systems can cause the Army to act like a huge, antiquated, and questionably relevant bureaucracy rather than a dynamic, salient, vibrant profession for the society it serves. We begin by introducing the dimensions of McDonaldization—efficiency, calculability, predictability, control, and the irrationality of hyper-rationality—for the reader unfamiliar with the thesis. This introduction to the theory includes representative examples of the McDonalds method in practice. Next, we review the literature of the McDonaldization of other institutions and professions including medicine, religion, education, and the news media. Third, we cite findings from several studies to illuminate McDonaldization's impact on the Army profession at the end of the force drawdown in the late 1990s. Finally, we offer some reflections intended to help military professionals avoid McDonaldized practices.

McWhat? What is McDonaldization?

Those unfamiliar with the idea of McDonaldization may be tempted to dismiss it offhand, thinking it applies only to McDonalds—or "Mickey Dees," as it is often referred to in the popular vernacular—and fast-food restaurants. On the contrary, Ritzer's McDonaldization thesis is a powerful new theoretical heuristic, with relevance to myriad aspects of modern society; social scientists have illustrated its relevance by applying it throughout the American economy and culture. Ritzer's book has sold thousands of copies and is taught in colleges and universities around the world. It is translated into 15 languages and is slowly inching forward to become the biggest all-time seller among sociology books.

The McDonaldization theory originated from Max Weber's concerns over hyper-rationality in modern society. Weber spent much time developing theories of bureaucracies, including their merits and pitfalls, as well as their relationship to modern society. Ultimately, Weber concluded that bureaucracies possess a dark side—he called them iron cages of rationality—that proved problematic and deeply troubling:

> A bureaucracy can be a dehumanizing place in which to work and by which to be serviced. Rationalized settings [included] places in which the self was placed in confinement, its emotions controlled, and its spirit subdued. They are settings in which people cannot always behave as human beings—where people are dehumanized. In Weber's view, bureaucracies are cages in the sense that people are trapped in them, their basic humanity denied. Weber feared most that bureaucracies would grow more and more rational and that rational principles would come to dominate an accelerating number of sectors of society. He anticipated a society of people locked into a series of rational structures, who could move only from one rational system to another—from rationalized educational systems to rationalized workplaces, from rationalized recreational settings to rationalized homes.[5]

Ritzer rendered Weber's thesis relevant to modernity by creating his McDonaldization thesis. He constructed the theory by performing an examination in depth of the institutional processes that are most evident in McDonalds. The relevance and applicability of the thesis seem limitless in modern society; indeed, the reach of McDonaldization extends beyond American borders—it is a globally emergent trend. Many even view it as a symbol of western hegemonic expansionism. The widespread and growing popularity of McDonaldization results from the allure of its four main applications within modern society: efficiency, calculability, predictability, and control. It is to these that we now turn.

Efficiency: *Quick is Better*

Efficiency in the McDonaldization process refers to the most economical method of getting from point A to point B.[6] In McDonalds this means quicker service to customers, streamlined cooking and serving operations, and faster training of employees. McDonalds has perfected efficiency with the ubiquitous drive-through window. Other examples of efficiency include serving foods that require no utensils such as the hamburger, french fries, and the hot apple pie, and persuading customers to act as their own busboys. Examples of more efficient food services in other venues include TV dinners, cooking with the microwave oven, and vending machines.

Efficiency spills over into other areas of social life as well. Grocery stores now encourage customers to do their own scanning and purchasing of groceries, which eliminates the need for a checkout clerk. Easy Pass allows us to speed through tollbooths on American highways, which saves time and removes the need for toll booth attendants. Even drug dealing has been influenced by the trend: impatient customers can purchase drugs from their cars as they drive through neighborhoods—drug dealers with a friendly curbside manner meet them at their car window. One McDonalds franchise was recently busted after teenage employees were caught selling crack cocaine at the drive-through window.

On the surface, maximizing efficiency seems attractive and practical. It provides the optimum answer to the utilitarian question: how can I save time, money, and resources? But the deeper and often unasked question remains: "What are the social costs of being too efficient?" We shall return to this question later.

Calculability: *Bigger and More Are Better*

Calculability refers to "an emphasis on the quantitative aspects of products (portion size, cost) and services offered (the time it takes to get the product)."[7] In the world of McDonalds, quantity is emphasized over quality. This begins with the language on the Golden Arches—"Over 6 Billion Served." Note that this globally recognized sign refers to the amount sold—not the quality of the product. Likewise, the size of McDonalds products has grown considerably beyond that of the regular offerings. Now there are "Quarter Pounders," "Big Macs," "Super-sized fries," etc. At the same time, some costs have remained quite low: McDonalds offers some one dollar meals—more food for less money.

The concept of calculability or quantification has permeated society. In the criminal justice system, we now have more people in larger prisons than ever before, we have more "cops on the street," and criminals must calculate how many strikes they have against them, with three strikes yielding nonnegotiable longer sentences. A student's college possibilities are often directly related to his or her high school grade point average (GPA) and standardized test scores (e.g., ACT, SAT). Likewise, one's class ranking can determine what types of jobs one finds within reach, since employers use college GPA and class standing as quantifiable predictors of success.

Predictability: *Same Ole, Same Ole*

Predictability, or uniformity, refers to the "assurance that products and services will be the same over time and in all locales."[8] For McDonalds, this means that Quarter Pounders with cheese, whether ordered in Roanoke, Rangoon, or Riyadh, will all taste the same. Predictability means consistency; or at least minimal variation, thus enabling customers to know what they are getting. The authors of this chapter, for example, are writing part of it while sitting in a McDonalds in Munich, Germany, and the fries are as delicious (and artery-clogging) as in New York.

Myriad other food establishments have now come to offer a similar element of predictability. Pizza Hut, Burger King, Popeyes, Kentucky Fried Chicken, White Castle, and Taco Bell are a handful of examples where the customer knows exactly what to expect in the product. Even Baskin Robbins ice cream remains constant, with the invariable 31 flavors to choose from.

Other areas of our culture are predictable as well. Many actors are typecast—Sean Penn the punk, Jack Nicholson the aging playboy. Comedians have predictable humor—the late Rodney Dangerfield "never got no respect." Numerous commercial enterprises are predictable—motels, book stores, coffee shops, and hardware stories—where the sameness and lack of originality are excruciating.

Likewise, spatial arrangements within institutions become all too similar. Malls, churches, military bases, schools, and large chain stores such as Wal-Mart are all of similar design within their function type. Experience with one large and successful chain store prepares the customer for any other.

Control: *Do the Customer's Thinking*

Finally, Ritzer refers to control. In the McDonaldization process this refers to the tendency in McDonaldized systems to exert *control* over people, usually through the use of nonhuman technologies.[9] For the worker, this means that a process of "deskilling" is continually taking place, whereby human skills are being taken away from workers and built into nonhuman technologies, thereby permitting the use of increasingly unskilled labor. For example, cash registers have pictures rather than numbers—it is not necessary to be able to read in order to work the counter at McDonalds. Likewise, McDonalds attempts to control its customers. Rather than allowing customers to order specific items, McDonalds has come to control individual choices (based on their own in-house research). Individual products such as burger, fries, and drink, are now marketed in clusters with individual numbers. Employees routinely encourage customers to order by number rather than by specific names of items. For example, a "one" is a Big Mac value meal. Similarly, other fast-food chains now market by clusters; Kentucky Fried Chicken, for example, has "comes with" items. Bookstores offer discount cards to encourage repeat customers—indirectly controlling where they'll make their next purchase and what they may read.

Control is evident in educational institutions. Control includes the length of the scheduled class period—university and high school classes consume 55 or 120 minutes regardless of the time dictated naturally by content. Clocks, bells, calendars, syllabi, and lesson plans all control the student, the teacher, and the school, where any disruption of the system undermines the McDonaldized educational assembly line process as a McStudent moves from one McTeacher to the next McTeacher from frosh to senior year as they are cranked through the diploma mills that characterize contemporary American education.

Elsewhere, one of the more powerful features of control is the emerging use of nonhuman technology to replace or adapt humans. An example is found even in the flesh trade. As Kathryn Hausbeck and Barbara Brents note, women modify their bodies with "fat cut off here, implants added there, scars removed, makeup permanently added. Women's performing bodies become cyborg-like machines, carefully crafted for a particular look, with interchangeable parts."[10] In the future, we may see perfectly controlled, flesh-like, robotic, McDonaldized bodies performing a striptease and catering to a highly specialized sexual fetish market.

The Problem with McDonaldization:
The Irrationality of Rationality

In addition to the four main applications defining the essence of McDonaldization in practice, Ritzer discusses a fifth aspect highlighting some of the potential dangers of this process. He calls it "the irrationality of rationality," which reveals the dark side of McDonaldization. Despite the advantages (e.g., significant profits, speedy service, etc.) of McDonaldization as a rational (e.g., efficient, controlling, predictable, and calculable) system, it produces some irrational consequences. First, dehumanization occurs in extremely rational systems: "Another way of saying this is that [hyper-] rational systems serve to deny human reason; rational systems are often unreasonable."[11] Employees and customers are so directed and regulated that "people cannot always behave as human beings," which often results in the failure of organizational members to live up to their human potential.[12] Overly controlling, synchronized, and hyper-rational systems stifle innovation, creativity, spontaneity, morale, a sense of autonomy and efficacy, and ultimately marginalize and alienate the people trapped in them. This is the dehumanization caused by irrational rationality.

A second flaw in hyper-rationality is that it can become self-defeating, forfeiting the very advantages it was designed to cultivate. Ritzer describes this interesting paradox as follows:

> In addition to dehumanization, bureaucracies have other irrationalities. Instead of remaining efficient, bureaucracies can become increasingly inefficient because of tangles of red tape and other pathologies. The emphasis on quantification often leads to large amounts of poor-quality work. Bureaucracies often become unpredictable as employees grow unclear about what they are supposed to do and clients do not get the services they expect. Because of these and other inadequacies, bureaucracies begin to lose control over those who work within and are served by them. Anger at the nonhuman technologies that replace them often leads employees to undercut or sabotage the operation of these technologies. All in all, what were designed as highly rational operations often end up quite irrational.[13]

Thus, in a complete reversal of its original aim, a McDonaldized or highly rational system will often produce outcomes that directly oppose efficiency, predictability, control, and calculability.

The more that McDonaldization comes to characterize a particular organization or social institution, the more those entities tend to behave like pure bureaucracies. In these McDonaldized settings, otherwise rational systems are pushed to the point of reductio and absurdum, unreasonably frustrating innovative human impulses and ideas. McDonaldization inhibits the professional's ability to act autonomously and inspire others to do likewise, thus reducing effectiveness. More importantly for professions, McDonaldization dilutes a profession's essence and core (i.e., expert knowledge practiced in relatively autonomous and discretionary settings by human experts) by creating rigidly over-controlling, bureaucratic management systems and procedures.

McDonaldization: Transcending Time, Space, Social Institutions, and Professions

A number of scholars have identified, defined, and applied characteristics of McDonaldization to a host of diverse institutional contexts. Sociologist Andrew Abbott stresses that change is an inevitable feature not only of the Army profession but indeed of all professions in the larger society.[14] Those professions that embraced McDonaldization as a means of confronting change may have hindered their own progress and even jeopardized their own survival. In this section we review findings of other studies in organizational contexts that illustrate the McDonaldization thesis.

Some argue that the tendency toward McDonaldization is not peculiar to the contemporary American scene. Louis Cain, for example, contends that the main features of McDonaldization predate the post-industrial period.[15] Using the early meat-packing industry as an illustration, he shows that elements of the McDonaldization system were present a century ago. Others, however, have found the thesis most applicable in post-industrial, cross-cultural contexts, including global consumer culture in East Asia, Europe, and Israel.[16]

McDonaldization has shown robust explanatory power in the analysis of Korean mega-churches.[17] With the great expansion of Christianity in Korea, churches and their leaders have come to control members through technological devices such as radio and television when they aren't in church, and they influence followers to purchase specified products in predictable, controlled consumption patterns. While the increase in the number of worshipers is positive for the church, the church may well lose credibility given its McDonaldized treatment of adherents. John Drane found similar evidence of the McDonaldization of U.S. and United Kingdom churches through efficiency (e.g., "10- step spiritual growth programs"); calculability (e.g., "filling the building instead of filling people with the spirit"); predictability (e.g., identical beliefs among followers); and control (e.g., members' consumption patterns controlled by the bookstores or markets attached directly to churches).[18]

The leisure and news media industries are also subject to McDonaldization. Disneyland may be the quintessential McDonaldized entertainment institution—where staffs are forced to exhibit and engage in constant emotive labor.[19] Indeed, some even argue that—in a rebellion against the sterility of McDonaldization—that de-McDonaldization is now occurring in American leisure settings where leaders and managers are attempting to recapture the enchantment of the past.[20] However, the attempt to de-McDonaldize may simply be cheap faux antique, with just enough artificial resonances of the "past" to generate a momentary touch of nostalgia and thus loosen the customer's purse.

The management of educational institutions is also becoming increasingly McDonaldized. In Hong Kong, critics see an "economic rationalism" emerging in higher education, characterized by financial constraints, an expansion of responsibilities for faculty and staff, and greater internal scrutiny.[21] Thus, managerialism (the adoption of mechanisms and principles from the private sector) has been imposed to achieve tidier administration, or control, within the institution and among its members. A similar process is happening in Scotland, where the schools are now characterized by distance learning (efficiency); set grading scales for assessment (calculability); nationalized university level education (predictability); and a move toward more public accountability and control of faculty, all of which hampers faculty autonomy, inventiveness, and motivation.[22] Similarly, professional librarians have been confronted with the prospect of McDonaldization, and are collectively seeking alternatives to avoid it.[23]

McDonaldization of the Medical Profession

McDonaldization also impacts the medical profession. In Germany, researchers fear the impact of rationalization on drug treatment policies, where competition is used to foster efficiency; health insurance calculations override individual care; and the standardization of treatment compartmentalizes patients and reduces the autonomy and creativity of doctors.[24] The likelihood of niche legalization of illicit drugs (such as marijuana for medical use) represents an effort of the medical profession and patient advocacy groups to stifle the McDonaldizing tendencies by seizing control of the situation and making a folk medicine a legal commodity.

The preparation of physicians in medical schools has increasingly become rationalized.[25] The professionals who teach and develop new practitioners are themselves distracted by close scrutiny (efficiency), thereby increasing the burden on students to learn by themselves; this results in more uniform requirements for accreditation and specified syllabuses (predictability); it also increases the quantification of assessment outcomes (calculability) and increases the reliance on technology in the classroom (control). Ritzer and David Walczak stress that "McDoctors" are the result of such increased formal rationality and represent a move away from substantive rationality.[26] The result is greater external control of the medical profession by others on the periphery or outside of the profession—patients, medical delivery systems, politicians and appointees who set national policy, insurance companies, medical staff, and administrators. The pernicious influence of McDonaldization can even be seen on the military profession, and we now turn specifically to its effects on the U.S. Army.

McDonaldization of the Army Profession

Several contemporary studies, including the 2002 edition of the present anthology, *Army Training and Leader Development Panel Report (Officer)* (2001), and *American Military Culture In the Twenty-First Century* (2000), have examined from various perspectives the state of the Army profession at the end of the drawdown of the 1990s.[27] We have meshed these rich data sources with our own research and insights to illustrate the penetration of McDonaldization within the Army profession at the turn of the century. We believe that McDonaldization severely threatens the Army as a profession by causing it to act more like a bureaucracy than a profession.

These studies all point out that during the 1990s the Army failed to take adequate cognizance that people are its most valuable resource, a signal manifestation of McDonaldization. Although many Army leaders at lower levels certainly made great efforts to treat people as their principal professional asset, many large-scale Army management systems, particularly those for human resources, failed to do so. And without serious reform they will continue to do so. A major conclusion from *The Future of the Army Profession* (2002) richly illustrates this point:

> Technological research dominates funding, billets, and priorities while the human domains—behavioral science, social science, and physical development research programs are under-funded and out of date. In the last decade, the Army has slashed funding for research in the human disciplines of the social and behavioral sciences. The Army bases much of its expert knowledge of human behavior, specifically human behavior during war, on research done over fifty years ago. [Consequently] many of the Army's recent personnel policies have derived from business practices, which are more appropriate for profit-driven firms with employees. The Army's retention problems and high levels of dissatisfaction are evidence that its management systems, such as soldier acquisition, evaluations, assignments, career development, housing, and community development, are not meeting the needs of the profession, its members, and their families.[28]

The Army's obsession with researching and integrating new technology, while failing to incorporate contemporary research and expert knowledge associated with understanding people, illustrates McDonaldization. McDonaldized systems increasingly incorporate new technologies that tend to replace humans, and also more pervasively control those humans who are not replaced. Instead of creating personnel management systems that apply contemporary expert knowledge of the science of human development, which would better serve the interests of both the profession and its client, the Army uses highly centralized, industrial-age management systems which, ironically, utilize the latest, most efficient Microsoft software programs and computers with ever-increasing memory capabilities. Let us glance briefly at three aspects of such McDonaldization: the Army's career development model, its personnel evaluation system, and its training management system.

The degree to which a McDonaldized career management system plagues the Army is described in the following synopsis:

> Army personnel management practices over recent decades have shifted the balance away from individual development and toward a lock-step, centralized system that requires all officers to follow specific timelines and fill certain positions if they are to succeed [and survive via promotion and consequent retention]. The result is reduced variety in the careers of successful officers and a strong reluctance to pursue opportunities outside of the mainstream. Sadly, this rigid system has evolved at . . . a time when the Army needs educational, skill, and experiential diversity in its pool of members. [Furthermore] young officers become cynical about "check-the-block" career management and tend to see the Army as just another transient job.[29]

Career progression in the Army is thus predictable, controlled (i.e., each rank has crucial, well-known, "branch qualifying" jobs as a prerequisite for promotion), and calculable (i.e., a specified minimum amount of time is required in each job for it to count toward promotion).

This McDonaldized system produces significant problems for the Army, the lack of a diverse pool of members being one result. One telling example of how lack of experiential diversity impairs the professional performance can be observed in many strategic Army leaders, who need crucial politico-military skills, knowledge, and abilities to most effectively lead at the interface of the professional and political realms, but who lack these essential skills because many of them have never ventured into positions outside the mainstream Army.[30] Thus, these strategic leaders often fail. With their zealous "can-do" attitude, they tend to accept over-tasking and under-resourcing, which contribute even more to the downward spiral of professionalism within a McDonaldized Army.

For junior officers the effects are different. By the end of the drawdown, according to research, junior officers felt slighted and frustrated by the limited number and short duration of developmental assignments. For example, combat arms officers received only a limited time as platoon leaders, often little more than a year. As one report concluded, "Personnel management requirements drive individual operational assignments at the expense of quality developmental experiences."[31] This practice—which on the surface may seem like an efficient method to allocate assets in the officer pool—leads to several problems, particularly for junior officers just getting started in their careers. Being responsible for the lives of the soldiers they command, they want developmental opportunities to enhance their effectiveness and leadership abilities. Being robbed of developmental experiences, many junior officers tend to feel they are less capable leaders.

The Army's McDonaldized personnel management system thus contributed to ineffectiveness, to individual frustration, and ultimately to lower officer retention rates (witness the exodus of captains in the late 1990s). It also contributed to a long-standing division within the Army officer corps, that is, the "trust gap" between senior and junior officers, which to some extent can normally be explained by generational differences. But during the late 1990s the gap widened to a yawning gulf, which contributed to hemorrhage-scale losses in the junior officer corps.[32] These losses were traceable to a diminished "culture of trust," which "induces micromanagement on the part of leaders and risk-averse responses on the part of followers."[33] An Army that focuses too little energy and resources on exploiting contemporary expert scientific knowledge on what makes human beings tick should not be surprised when significant people problems emerge within the profession.

The Army evaluation system is related to career management and progression, and it also possesses features of McDonaldization. The primary instrument the Army uses to assess and promote its officer corps is the Officer Evaluation Report (OER). The OER attempts to quantify (i.e., to make calculable) officer performance, and it also forces raters to stratify a pool of officers into ability and potential categories. But should the message of the OER be expressed through statistics and quantifiable feats, or through holistic, qualitative narration and description of accomplishments? Are leadership performance and potential quantifiable? As for limiting the number of officers that can receive the best ratings (e.g., the above-center-of-mass/center-of-mass dichotomy), this system seems to be an improvement over the former highly inflated system, yet difficulties remain. For example, the very first officer whose rating is reflected in a given senior rater's profile can receive no better than a center-of-mass report, which unfairly penalizes the officer whose performance merits a higher mark. The rater comments on the OER are highly predictable and well known; the websites of the Army personnel commands abound with verbatim comments that raters must use if they wish to get subordinate officers promoted (implying that the absence of such wording will prevent other officers from getting promoted). Given the existence and use of these boiler-plate code words and phrases modify or limit performance block evaluations, how far have we truly moved from inflatable numbers? Do selection boards ever really get to know or understand the performances or potential of the officers they consider? These McDonaldized parts of the OER (and the noncommissioned officer version) detract from the overall effectiveness of the evaluation system, which impacts the profession at large.

The Army's training management systems also evince the effects of McDonaldization, diminishing the profession's effectiveness. While this development has been documented in the aforementioned ATLDP report, it is most clearly seen in the findings of a highly critical study subsequently published by the Army War College demonstrating how current training management systems stifled innovation and development among junior officers.[34] As summarized by Snider and Watkins, this leads to:

> Officers learning skills in the schoolhouse they are not using in their deployments, and failing to learn skills in the schoolhouse that are critically necessary for them to succeed in present deployment missions. Unit training by template in just-in-time preparation for deployments, which is highly centralized in organization and design, has filled this void, but at an immense price in loss of junior leader initiative and satisfaction.[35]

This "just-in-time" and "highly centralized" training by template illustrates several aspects of McDonaldization. The centralized training clearly entails excessive control, while the element of last-minute training leads to an over-focus on efficiency measurements and calculability, given that units feel compelled to complete many tasks in the least amount of time possible so they can check it off the list. The templated pre-deployment training also entailed predictability since units must follow exactly the headquarters' script. But are the tasks checked off well correlated with what officers will encounter when deployed? Clearly the research shows that at least through the major phase of Operation Iraqi Freedom, there had been too little training time allotted to develop the culturally-aware, innovative thinking needed among small-unit leaders for success in that theater.

Concerning supervision at the Department of the Army level, it was found that "top-down training directives and strategies . . . lead to a perception that micromanagement is pervasive."[36] "Increasingly centralized management systems have shifted decision-making upward while eroding the flexibility and authority of responsible professionals on the scene."[37] Additionally, "absent enlightened [local] leadership, military organizations under stress often tend to develop a dysfunctional zero-defects rigidity that stifles effectiveness."[38]

These findings illustrate several elements of McDonaldization, including predictability and control. Insofar as officers give and receive strict guidance on how to accomplish a given mission, operations become more predictable, "less risky," and unimaginative, exactly the opposite of what are needed to counter an insurgency focused asymmetrically on Army weaknesses. Clearly, irrationality sets in when such micromanagement and over-control by officers rob their subordinates of opportunities to improvise new approaches to best accomplish the mission. The widespread reports of micromanagement suggest that excessive control exists today in the training management systems of the Army. Micromanaged officers (and warrant officers, noncommissioned officers, and capable soldiers) are unable to fulfill their human potential, unable to bring to bear their full creative prowess in behalf of the profession, and unable to develop themselves by acting independently and feeling the impact of their efforts. Such insidious effects of McDonaldization ultimately induce them to act more like bureaucrats, managers, technicians, and officeholders, and less like visionaries, creators, motivators, and leaders within a profession.

McDonaldized Army Practices in Operation Iraqi Freedom

A preliminary assessment of data from an ongoing study of Army soldiers and units deployed in Operation Iraqi Freedom provides additional evidence of micromanagement, an excessive operational tempo, and some measure of tactical rigidity in mission performance, all of which hamper the profession's effectiveness in a combat theater.[39] One theme that has emerged from the preliminary analysis is that many soldiers in the theater believe they are micromanaged there just as they were in the predeployment training environment. The following quotations from interviewed soldiers are illustrative:

> "They try to tell us how to do our jobs as well as define what we have to do. Even though we know ways that work more effectively."

> "Certain tasks that I have been given have been spelled out for me. Some of these tasks I was told exactly how to do it, no change [in] thinking was allowed."

> "They should let the soldiers put in their opinions cause we are the ones carrying out the missions."

> "Creativity is 'ceremonially' encouraged, but whenever anyone—especially lower enlisted—exhibit some, it is stomped out by the control freaks above them."

> "Sometimes I get the feeling that the commanders are not allowed to command their batteries, make decisions without prior approval from higher."

Despite such comments, other soldiers felt their leadership encouraged and acted on innovative insights from below. Consider these statements from two soldiers and a company commander:

> "Officers and NCOs in my unit (battery) work very well together. Good ideas come to the table."

> "For the most part, if anyone has an idea that is different from the one already underway, it is weighed and if thought a more direct approach or a better way, it is followed through."

> "I talk daily to my Bn CO and share my thoughts and ideas. He always passes them up or gives the green light. I talk to my [platoon leaders] and NCOs daily and go on patrol with them. Many times they come up with ideas that I give the green light on."

On the whole, however, this preliminary analysis of data had more compelling evidence of excessive control or micromanagement than the contrary. Given that soldiers with a greater sense of autonomy would likely feel a stronger connection with the mission, this micromanagement might, in some cases, decrease overall combat effectiveness through the loss of innovation, creativity, and motivation.

A second concern that has emerged from the Iraqi Freedom data is a strong collective sense of being over-tasked, as statements from several different soldiers suggested:

> "We task ourselves to death."

> "My unit is over-tasked. We get no days off due to too many missions and lack of people."

> "My unit is much overtaxed and the personnel are working too hard and being pushed too hard."

> "I have worked 18-20 hours per day for six months with 5 days off."

> "The battery is over-tasked. The soldiers are pushed to the limits. We tell [Jr. NCOs] to get them time off, but we give them another mission at the same time to add to a plate that's running over. Attitudes are beginning to flair up. Soldiers are burned out and we still have six to ten months to go."

> "The Bn commander complains but almost always volunteers."

> "My platoon sergeant is trying to make himself look good by saying yes to everything even [if] it puts a strain on the number of soldiers it takes to perform 24 hour Ops."

> "My S-4 shop is overtasked because my major takes on too many tasks that do not concern us."

Not a single interviewee said he or she was under-tasked, and only a few stated they were adequately (i.e., not excessively) tasked. Some soldiers re-framed the issue as a lack of manpower, which hindered their unit's ability to complete its many tasks. But the preponderance of responses reflected in this preliminary analysis suggest soldiers in Iraqi Freedom definitely feel over-tasked, which, as we have seen, contributes to McDonaldized practices. When units are faced with an excessive number of tasks, they tend to focus simply on finishing things rather than excelling on things. When such a state of mind takes hold, professional performance is obviously degraded.

With regard to predictability, the survey sought to discover whether soldiers felt their units' movement patterns and tactical procedures could be anticipated by the enemy based on repetitive patterns. If so, the enemy would find it far easier to devise effective counters. The data were generally mixed on this topic, with some soldiers feeling that Army forces seemed too predictable, while others felt their units deliberately varied movements and other activities to complicate the enemy's ability to plan successful attacks. The following quotations from several soldiers illustrate the mixed data for predictability:

> "We take the same routes six times a day with only a 15-minute variance during patrols."

> "The only thing I can see that is predictable is the routes we drive on in Baghdad. There are only a few roads that will handle our equipment. So it's easy for the enemy to put [remotely detonated bombs] on all of them."

"Our company is not predictable at all. Routes and times are never the same."

"We are very predictable—we drive the same roads day after day for months. We enter/exit through two gates—the enemy (if they are watching) knows when we enter/leave our sector."

"The entire army is predictable in certain areas, shift changes, guard mounts, chow times, etc."

"I think our unit is good about not being predictable and becoming an easy target."

"Sometimes repetitive patterns [are used]. We are observable to the enemy everyday and we might be predictable. We do the same counter measures every time until something goes wrong then we change them."

When units do not vary their patterns and activities, they make themselves more vulnerable to enemy attacks. Although the data were not unanimous, this preliminary analysis suggests overall that the majority of soldiers feel their units' impending behavior is too easy for the enemy to divine. Perhaps the combination of over-tasking and micromanagement steals the opportunity for some units and soldiers to invent effective ways to reduce transparency. Such a reduction could potentially increase force security and decrease the number of successful enemy attacks. Thus, so far as this preliminary analysis of Iraqi Freedom data is concerned, the element of predictability is a disconcerting measure of how far McDonaldization has penetrated our deployed force, thereby decreasing its ability to accomplish its mission.

Preventing McDonaldization in the Army Profession: Avoid McLeadership!

This chapter has explained the meaning of McDonaldization and its relevance to many parts of modern society. It particularly highlighted how McDonaldization impinges on and threatens the Army profession. The main areas of concern in the Army itself include an over-focus on new technology coupled with a failure to capitalize on contemporary expert knowledge in the social and behavioral sciences. Such expert knowledge could enhance understanding of people and of management systems that oftentimes unreasonably generate people problems. Such professional dysfunctions as McDonaldized career evaluation and progression systems and excessive micromanagement all add to the troubles of an over-tasked and under-resourced Army profession. This preliminary analysis of data collected in Iraqi Freedom confirms the existence of situations where the specter of McDonaldization seemed to hinder mission performance and professional effectiveness. Our fear is that if McDonaldization persists or becomes more widespread, the Army will devolve to a classic governmental bureaucracy pure and simple, void of a professional core.

How can the Army counter McDonaldization so as to retain its professional essence? Strategic leaders must begin by renewing the profession's focus on empowering and inspiring its members, as opposed to allowing the perpetuation of McDonaldized systems and practices that tend to control, alienate, and dehumanize people. This revitalization starts by altering the conditions that breed McDonaldization: the Army needs an adequate number of members, sufficient resourcing, and a realistic number of missions and tasks in order to perform exemplarily across the board. In addition to making such adjustments, strategic leaders need to reestablish the profession's focus on the human dimension, first by capitalizing on contemporary research and expert knowledge of people. Renewed investment in the sciences that generate this expert knowledge, including psychology, social psychology, sociology, political science, and other disciplines, will provide the profession with fresh and useful insights for revamping its McDonaldized systems and practices as highlighted in this analysis. These actions must occur if the Army

1. **Efficiency**. Do I sacrifice human potential by being too efficient?
   - Do I take the necessary time to develop followers?
   - Do I fight for followers to get them enough time in key developmental leadership positions?
   - Despite the fact that empowerment of followers may not be the most efficient way to accomplish organizational mandates in the short term, do I stick to the long-term view, confident that empowerment will ultimately build solid members who keep our profession vibrant and effective?

2. **Predictability**. Is my leadership style sufficiently consistent?
   - Do I adjust to each unique situation with appropriate leader actions, or do I tend to use the same set of actions regardless of the situation? Do I adapt well to new, different circumstances?
   - Do my followers understand the moral compass of the unit? Am I a consistent moral exemplar for followers to emulate, which influences their behavior regardless of my presence?

3. **Calculability**. Am I sacrificing the quality of my unit's mission performance for quantity? Is my unit doing too much? Do I do too much?
   - Do I over-emphasize quantity at the cost of quality?
   - Is my unit over-tasked? Is it trying to do too much? Do I contribute to or detract from this potential problem, a problem that may lead to further McDonaldization in my unit?
   - Am I seeking to expand my domain rather than enhance effectiveness with the unit's present missions (breadth over depth)?

4. **Control**. Is my style too controlling; am I de-skilling my unit's people?
   - Do I micromanage? If so, how can my followers creatively contribute to the profession and unit if I steal their opportunities and freedom to conceive innovative, useful ideas?

Figure 23-1. *Strategic Leaders' Quiz on the Four Dimensions of McDonaldization.*

wishes to preserve its professional core and avoid the dangerous movement towards bureaucratization.

To reverse the misguided trend toward McDonaldization in the Army, we offer some preliminary intervention strategies in the form of reflective questions (see Figure 23-1) for the leaders of the Army profession. These questions are relevant to leaders at all three levels of the Army—strategic, operational, and tactical. They aim to help the professional stewards of the Army avoid acting as bureaucratic McLeaders. McLeadership is an unimaginative, risk-averse, dehumanizing, and ultimately counterproductive style of leadership; it squanders the opportunity to truly lead a profession. McLeaders are hyper-efficient "bean-counters," but they fail to inspire and develop their subordinates." Professionals wanting to lead should ask themselves the hard questions—and arrive at the appropriate answers—if they are to avoid the trap of drive-through Mcleadership, creating McFollowers while wasting human potential and jeopardizing the professional core of the Army.

Notes

1. The authors wish to thank members of the Department of Behavioral Sciences and Leadership and others who participated in the 2003-2004 Global Leadership Conference at West Point in September 2003 for their helpful comments on previous versions of the this chapter. They also wish to thank the editors of this book whose helpful comments enhanced this chapter. The views of the authors are their own and do not purport to reflect the position of the U.S. Military Academy, the Department of the Army, or the Department of Defense. A previous version of this chapter was presented at the Eastern Sociological Society Meetings, New York City, NY, 1 March 2004.

2. George Ritzer, *The McDonaldization of Society,* New Century Edition (Thousand Oaks, CA: Pine Forge Press, 2000).

3. Ritzer, "Preface," in *McDonaldization: The Reader,* ed. George Ritzer (Thousand Oaks, CA: Pine Forge Press, 2002), x.

4. Ibid., passim..

5. Max Weber, *Economy and Society* (Totowa, NJ: Bedminster, 1921; rpt. 1968), as quoted by George Ritzer, ed., *The McDonaldization of Society,* 24-25.

6. Ibid., 12.

7. Ibid.

8. Ibid., 13.

9. Ritzer, *McDonaldization: The Reader,* 3.

10. Kathryn Hausbeck and Barbara G. Brents, "McDonaldization of the Sex Industries? The Business of Sex," in *McDonaldization: The Reader.*

11. Ritzer, *McDonaldization: The Reader,* 20.

12. Ibid., 21-22; also, George Ritzer, *The McDonaldization of Society,* 25.

13. Ritzer, *The McDonaldization of Society,* 25.

14. Andrew Abbott, "The Army and the Theory of Professions," in *The Future of the Army Profession,* project directors Don M. Snider and Gayle L. Watkins, ed. Lloyd J. Matthews (Boston, MA: McGraw-Hill, 2002), 523-36 (hereinafter referred to as FAP I).

15. Louis Cain, "From Big Shoulders to Big Macs," *American Behavioral Scientist* 47, no. 2 (2003):168-87.

16. See the chapters by Malcolm Waters, James L. Watson, and David Morse in *McDonaldization: The Reader*; also Eva Illouz and John Nicholas, "Global Habitus, Local Stratification, and Symbolic Struggles Over Identity," *American Behavioral Scientist* 47, no. 2 (2003): 201-30.

17. Hong Yong-Gi and Young-Gi Hong, "Encounter with Modernity: The 'McDonaldization' and 'Charismatization' of Korean Mega Churches," *International Review of Mission* 92 (2003): 239-56.

18. John Drane, "The Church and the Iron Cage," *McDonaldization: The Reader,* 151-161.

19. Alan Bryman, "McDonalds as a Disneyized Institution," *American Behavioral Scientist* 47, no. 2 (2003):154-168.

20. George Ritzer and Todd Stillman, "The Postmodern Ballpark as a Leisure Setting: Enchantment and Simulated De-McDonaldization," *Leisure Studies* 23 (2001):99-113.

21. K.H. Mok, "The Cost of Managerialism: The Implications for the 'McDonaldization' of Higher Education in Hong Kong," *Journal of Higher Education Policy & Management* 21, no.1 (1999):117-128.

22. David Hartley, "The 'McDonaldization' of Higher Education: Food for Thought?" *Oxford Review of Education* 21, no.4 (1995): 409-23.

23. Brian Quinn, "The McDonaldization of Academic Libraries," *College & Research Libraries* 61, no. 3 (2000):248-61.

24. Uwe E. Kemmesies, "What Do Hamburgers and Drug Care Have in Common: Some Unorthodox Remarks on the McDonaldization and Rationality of Drug Care," *Journal of Drug Issues* 32, no.2 (2003): 689-709.

25. Kevin M.G. Taylor and Geoffrey Harding, "Teaching, Learning, and Research in McSchools of Pharmacy," *Pharmacy Education* 2, no.2 (2002):43-49.

26. George Ritzer and David Walczak, "Rationalization and the Deprofessionalization of Physicians," *Social Forces* 67, no.1 (1988):1-22.

27. FAP I; *Army Training and Leader Development Panel Report (Officers): Final Report* (Ft. Leavenworth, KS: Combined Arms Center, 2001) (Hereinafter cited as ATLDP); Walter F. Ulmer, Jr., Joseph J. Collins, and T.O. Jacobs, *Report: American Military Culture in the Twenty-First Century: A Report of the CSIS International Security Program* (Washington, DC: CSIS, 2000) (Hereinafter cited as American Military Culture Report).

28. Watkins and Snider, FAP I, 540.

29. Ibid., 541.

30. Ibid., 543-45.

31. ATLDP, OS-2.

32. Watkins and Snider, FAP I, 543.

33. Ibid.

34. Leonard Wong et al., *Stifled Innovation: Developing Tomorrow's Leaders Today* (Carlisle Barracks, PA: U.S. Army War College, Strategic Studies Institute, April 2002).

35. Watkins and Snider, FAP I, 539.

36. ATLDP, OS-2.

37. Watkins and Snider, FAP I, 538.

38. American Military Culture Report, xxi.

39. Data comes from an ongoing study by Dr. Morten Ender, who spent June and July 2004 in Iraq during Operation Iraqi Freedom. He distributed surveys to portions of a division during this study, but the present preliminary assessment uses only data from part of the surveys. Some open-ended questions on the survey aimed to determine whether, and to what extent, soldiers perceived or experienced the different variables of McDonaldization during their Iraqi Freedom deployment.

24 The Need to Develop Expert Knowledge of the Military Family

Todd D. Woodruff and Thomas A. Kolditz

According to his wife Aerin, Specialist Tom Davila is a great soldier and a great husband, who is looking forward to being a great father. Specialist Davila has been in the Army four years and married for the last two. The Davilas were expecting to have their first child while he was in Afghanistan, about midway through a 10-month deployment. Specialist Davila's platoon sergeant knew the unit would be deployed, and recognized how important it was for the husband in the meantime to be an active partner in the pregnancy and to be there for his wife. He suggested that Specialist Davila make the doctor's appointments, listen to his unborn son's heartbeat, and care for his wife during her worst periods of morning sickness. Specialist Davila had not asked for this time off, but the platoon sergeant, having made it a point to know the times of Aerin's appointments and when she was not feeling well, took the initiative in telling the soldier to take time off.

This level of support continued even after Specialist Davila deployed to Afghanistan. He was given ample opportunities to call and email, and when his wife went into labor, he was immediately sent to the tactical operations center. While Aerin delivered their child, Specialist Davila was on the phone coaching her, as the family readiness group leader held the phone to Aerin's ear in a delivery room a half world away. Aerin and Specialist Davila were only one of six families in this infantry company to have babies while the unit was deployed. Each time, the company commander ensured that the soldier was sent to the tactical operation center and participated in the delivery by phone. Aerin cannot stop talking about how supportive her husband's leaders and the family readiness group have been, or about the depth and importance of the new relationships she has developed with the other spouses. It is no coincidence that Specialist Davila just reenlisted, or that the company to which Specialist Davila belongs has the highest retention rate in the brigade.

The case of Specialist and Aerin Davila is not an isolated one. In the first nongovernmental survey of military spouses since 11 September 2001, sponsored jointly by the Kaiser Family Foundation, the *Washington Post*, and Harvard University, it was found that 62 percent of spouses rate the Army's support as excellent or good, with only 14 percent opining that support was less than adequate.[1] This is good news for the Army, suggesting that the broad network of Army agencies and family readiness groups providing support to spouses is working well. Institutional support, however, is only part of the equation.

Rather, it is the frontline leaders who will have the greatest effect on the day-to-day lives of soldiers and families, a point illustrated by the actions of Specialist Davila's chain of command. In that case, the unit leaders had applied expert knowledge in

531

understanding the needs of the unit's families and providing the individualized support that each required. They effectively lengthen the organizational boundary, sending the message that families are part of the total team. This strongly expressed concern brought about a trusting relationship among the unit leadership, their soldiers, and the soldiers' families. Ultimately, it resulted in increased retention and satisfaction, and likely increased organizational commitment.

Unfortunately, not all Army leaders have developed adequate expert knowledge to care for families, and the retention picture for the Army overall has shown signs of possible problems. The Kaiser-*Post*-Harvard survey found that 76 percent of polled spouses believe the Army will face retention problems; a survey of soldiers by Charles Moskos and Laura Miller found that their service in the Middle East has made almost half of them less likely to reenlist; and the Office of Economic and Manpower Analysis is projecting retention shortfalls.[2]

This chapter argues that: (1) Army leaders must effectively expand the organizational umbrella, bringing military families more fully under its protective folds because they have significant influence on the performance of the organization; (2) leaders must develop the expert knowledge necessary to care for families, accommodate their needs, and understand how they can improve their soldiers' and their families' satisfaction with military life; and (3) if Army leaders fail to do these things, soldiers with families will be more likely to experience military-family conflict, and in the long term resolve the conflict in favor of the family and at the expense of the Army. The chapter will conclude with recommendations based on a synthesis of recent relevant data and existing military family literature.

The Greedy Institutions

By any measure, the Army overflows with families. Over 50 percent of the Army's membership are married, over 60 percent are either married or have dependent children, and family members outnumber soldiers by a ratio of three to two.[3] In the typical Army platoon one third of the junior enlisted soldiers and over half of the noncommissioned officers will have families.[4] This means that most soldiers live at the intersection of the military and family institutions. Each exercises powerful social control and places great demands on the soldier beyond those of most other institutions by requiring a significant degree of loyalty, participation, and commitment.[5] Both the family and military institutions are often considered forms of "greedy" institutions, which are characterized by their demand for exclusive, undivided loyalty and their attempts to prevent, weaken, or eliminate their members' ties to other organizations through largely non-physical, symbolic boundaries.[6]

Together, military and family obligations can exceed the service member's ability to adequately meet expectations; they can create conflict between the demands of both, and ultimately force the service member to choose. The interface of the family and military institutions has practical importance for numerous reasons. For the U.S. military, families can impact performance, absenteeism, retention, commitment, and job satisfaction. For the family, the military may affect marital and family satisfaction, harmony, cohesion, stability, developmental outcomes for children, and individual well-being.[7] The U.S. military's current operations in Iraq and Afghanistan have resulted in heightened risk to the soldier and significantly increased frequency and duration of family separations, all of which will likely have profound effect on interface issues.

American families vary by structure (e.g., marital status, number of adults, number and age of children), social organization (division of labor), norms and expectations for individual roles and behaviors, mutuality of support (i.e., financial and emotional), and level of commitment and cohesion.[8] In general, societal trends in the United States are creating changes in most if not all of these family characteristics, with the result that military families are becoming increasingly greedy in the sense of heightened emotional needs and expectations.[9] For most families, members are expected to be emotionally committed, display affection, identify with the family, and perform diffuse role obligations.[10] The variation in family characteristics is responsible for making the family greedier for some members and families. Typically, women and single parents have the strongest perceptions of family greediness, though a shift towards more egalitarian family roles and increased participation of women in the workforce is now increasing the sense of family greediness as experienced by men. Greediness also varies according to the family's life stage, with newly married couples and those with very young children or adolescents experiencing the greatest family demands. Single parents and parents with more children or with children having exceptional needs are also likely to experience increased family demands.[11]

Greedy characteristics of the military vis-à-vis soldiers and their families include risk of injury or death, separation of the soldier from the family, geographic mobility, overseas living, and normative pressures on family members to do volunteer work and to behave.[12] These characteristics result in a cascade of other difficulties that include: unpredictable short- and long-term schedules, financial management problems, housing concerns, obstacles to spousal employment, increased need for childcare, lessened support from and access to extended families and long-term friends, increased tensions between spouses, the absence of the soldier from critical family events, and disruptions in friendships and education for children and the spouse.[13]

The military and the family have always placed great responsibility on soldiers, but changes in both institutions are affecting the nature and scope of this responsibility.[14] Like their civilian family counterparts, military families have become less willing to tolerate the demands of work (the military) at the expense of the family.[15] These and other changes, such as the increased number of dual-service couples, dual-income households, single parents, and women in the military ranks, reflect larger societal trends with serious implications for the military and soldiers with families.[16] Changes in the military itself are also placing greater demands on families. On one hand, the military is implementing a wide range of family-friendly policies and programs, attempting to improve family quality of life and mitigate the hardships of being a military family;[17] yet the operational demands of the war on terrorism in Iraq and Afghanistan, as well as the broader post-Cold War trend towards increased deployments, has resulted in greater risk, longer and more frequent separations, and other hardships for military families. It is not uncommon today for soldiers, having just spent several months in Afghanistan, to find themselves deployed to Iraq after a few months home. Moreover, after returning home from a year in Iraq, many learn they are scheduled to return the following year. With this heightened level of demand, it would not be surprising to find that soldiers feel they cannot adequately serve the best interests of both the family and the military. The resulting competition between the military and the family for the soldier's limited time, energy, and personal resources puts these two societal institutions on a collision course.[18] The Army, its frontline leaders, the family, and the soldier all play critical parts in determining whether and to what degree the conflict occurs and how it is resolved.

Military-Family Conflict and Family Support

The military's ability to obligate behavior and time spent in performance of the military role typically means the conflicts are likely to be resolved in favor of the military in the short term, but the military's ascendancy has the potential to create profound conflict with the family, and may result in the military losing soldiers in the long term.[19] As James Martin and Dennis Orthner stress, "When the employer is also the governor, it is not uncommon to have conflict concerning the boundary between work and private life."[20] The military's ability to enforce demands for greater involvement can clearly lead to work-family imbalance. In the case of the military, there is both the power of negative sanctions and significant social control in the form of duty, patriotism, allegiance, unit cohesion, and friendships acting to create imbalance in favor of the military. However, the family is not without its own power to obligate behavior through powerful social control. The demands of the spouse or the illness of a child can also be "greedy," acting as strong forces to compel behavior. Cumulatively, then, the greediness of both the Army and the family can result in significant conflict.

The payoff of successfully reducing military-family conflict can be significant, resulting in decreased absenteeism and increased performance, commitment, retention, and job satisfaction. Families may experience increased marital and family satisfaction, cohesion, and stability; lessened child developmental problems and family conflict; and improved individual well-being.[21] The good news is that both family-friendly policies and leader support are effective in minimizing this conflict.[22]

Supportive, family-friendly policies, procedures, and programs, such as family support groups and affordable childcare and housing, have reduced military-family conflict. In general, much of the literature suggests that the current services and programs are effective when utilized.[23] This conclusion is supported by the recent Kaiser-*Post*-Harvard research that found almost two-thirds of spouses rate the Army's support as excellent or good.[24] The development of mutually supportive relationships between the spouses of deployed soldiers is also critical. Those who are best coping with the current environment cite the solidarity and friendships they have developed with other spouses as being critical. "We have become a sorority of separation," said one Army spouse, whose husband is in the 3rd Armored Cavalry Regiment.[25]

However, as noted earlier, it is the frontline leaders who, because they have the most frequent, intimate, and authoritative contact with soldiers and their families, are perhaps the most efficacious. This is where our Army leaders' expertise regarding the military family must be most energetically applied. Junior leaders, who make most of the routine decisions that impact families, are also the group least likely to have any family experience of their own or to understand how to care for or minister to the needs of military families. Many of our young lieutenants (and to a lesser extent young noncommissioned officers), owing to a lack of family experience[26] and limited indoctrination on military family issues, are ill-prepared to promote the well-being of their soldiers and their families. Adequate expertise is important because, other things being equal, leaders who are effective in caring for soldiers and families are more successful in general, as reflected in having units with higher morale, readiness, and retention.[27]

If the military is to reduce military-family conflict, frontline leaders must have the expert knowledge and the boundary spanning skills to (1) demonstrate supportiveness in behalf of families, and (2) increase families' satisfaction with the military.[28] Cumulatively, the evidence strongly suggests the chain of action is composed of the following relations:

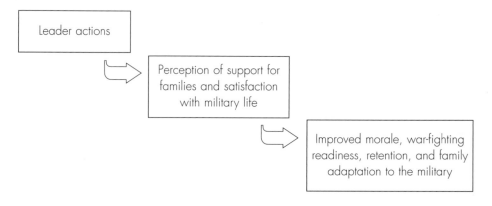

Leader Support

Leader support for families and family satisfaction with Army life go hand in hand, with the spouses' level of satisfaction being positively related to both their perception of the military's support for families and their improved adaptation to military life.[29] In fact, families impact on unit readiness the least, and in some ways may improve readiness, when the family perceives it has the support of the Army and unit leaders. The importance of leader support for families and soldiers with respect to enhancing a unit's readiness cannot be overemphasized.[30] The Army Family Research Program found the single greatest family-related factor contributing to unit and individual readiness was the level of perceived support provided by unit leaders to their soldiers and their families.[31] Reports by RAND and also by Mady Segal and Jessie Harris echoed these arguments, finding a correlation between perceptions of positive leadership and readiness.[32] Retention is similarly impacted, with the perception that unit leaders care about families having a direct positive effect on soldiers' and their spouses' commitment to continued service.[33]

Increased Satisfaction with Military Life

The ability of unit leaders to improve family satisfaction with military life also reduces military-family conflict and enhances readiness.[34] Leaders have enormous control over the day-to-day lives of soldiers and their families, and thus play a critical role in determining the satisfaction soldiers and families have with military life. The level of satisfaction impacts in turn on readiness, retention, and motivation. Stephen Burke argues that "there is a positive relationship between families who are satisfied with the military way of life and their readiness level."[35] Army Research Institute reports on the impact of family factors on individual and unit readiness make the same argument, noting that soldier and spouse satisfaction levels significantly impact motivation and both individual and unit readiness.[36] Retention is affected in a similar way. Families who are not satisfied with military life are likely to leave the service, degrading readiness by leaving positions at least temporarily unfilled, increasing personnel turnover, and requiring increased recruitment, training, and retention of replacements.[37] The spouse's satisfaction and perceptions are critical in this equation.[38] Spousal satisfaction is highly influential in both the soldier's job satisfaction and retention decisions.[39] Throughout the entire body of evidence, one thing is clear: leaders make a difference and are critical in the prevention and reduction of military-family conflict.

The Role of Soldier and Family Identity

The relative salience (i.e., prominence or conspicuousness) of the soldier's family and military identity may also play an important role in determining whether military-family conflict occurs and how such conflict is resolved. The relative salience of one's competing identities determines how they will be prioritized in the course of life. That is, identities are ordered in a hierarchy of salience based on the likelihood they will be invoked in an actual situation or form the basis for action.[40] Sheldon Stryker offers a number of testable identity theory hypotheses that would have application to military-family conflict:[41]

- The higher an identity in the salience hierarchy, the more likely role performance will live up to expectations for that identity.
- The higher an identity in the salience hierarchy, the more likely one will seek opportunities to act out that identity.
- The higher the salience, the more likely role performance will reflect institutionalized values and norms.

These hypotheses, which Stryker finds valid, argue that most salient identities are closely tied to actual behavior.[42] For Stryker and his colleague William Serpe, identity salience answers the question, "Why is one behavior selected rather than another when both are options?"[43] For example, why does one soldier take his or her kids to the park during free time while another soldier chooses to catch up on work? According to these researchers, the choice is a function of the relative salience of the father and soldier identities.[44] Research supports the notion that "people prefer to engage in behaviors that provide outcomes consistent with the salient aspects of their identities through their choice of lines of action."[45] The linkage of salient identities with behavior indicates that the development of highly salient identities is extremely important to both families and the military. Sharon Lobel argues that a person's identification with a group creates loyalty to the group (despite any negative traits), conformity to group norms, and support of the group's values and practices.[46] Career identity salience has also been found to have a direct and positive effect on work effort, with individuals having salient career identities willing to expend more effort at work and receiving higher merit rewards than those with salient family identities.

There are differences in how men and women balance work and family identities. William and Denise Bielby found that married women working outside the home still gave precedence to the family identity. Women achieved work-family equilibrium not by accommodation, compromise, and balance, but instead by giving precedence to the family identity at the expense of the work identity. The work-family interface was very different for married men. Men were able to maintain strong or weak identity salience for one role regardless of the salience of the other. For men, there was no trade-off or zero-sum relationship because they could maintain high levels of commitment and identity salience for both roles simultaneously.[47] This finding has serious implications for understanding work-family conflict, because it suggests that the conflict may differ greatly based on gender, with women more likely than men to experience conflict from occupying both work and family roles.

Identity theory also enlarges the issue of military-family conflict beyond the zero-sum competition for the soldier's time, energy, and commitment. Lobel argues that conflict between multiple identities occurs when the distinct values and behaviors required of each identity can be enacted only in situations that are separated by time and place.[48] To achieve a balance of work-family identities, a person can either keep the conflicting identities physically and psychologically separated or apply consistent personal values/behavior across both identities.[49] In a military context, this means that if the military and family institution can achieve compatible values and required behavior, military-conflict should be reduced or prevented. When roles require conflicting values and behavior, they require time, place, or psychological separation, a condition that is unlikely given that both the family and the military often exist in a single environment. In this case, the roles are competing for the scare personal resources of the individual. For this reason, it is important for the Army to develop a relatively strong soldier identity in its members, thereby increasing the likelihood the soldier will behave in a manner consistent with the desires of the Army. It is also apparent that the Army should try to align its behavioral expectations with those identities that are typically more salient than the soldier role. To this end, data on soldier or family identity salience has been collected and analyzed.

Data and Methodology

Data on soldier and family identity salience were collected in 2002 from a 193-man sample drawn from two active-duty, all-male infantry battalions at Fort Lewis, Washington. Both battalions were in the final stages of transformation to Stryker units, having been undergoing challenging training and receiving the Army's best and newest equipment. The sample, though containing soldiers with various occupational specialties, is largely composed of infantrymen and includes enlisted soldiers in the grades E1 to E7. The absence of women is a result of our having access to two combat units without women rather than a decision to exclude them. The sample is racially diverse (though it under-represents Blacks relative to the Army enlisted population because Blacks tend to enlist in support specialties), and varies in educational and family background (though none had graduate degrees).[50] *Only soldiers that are married or have children are included in this sample.* Though not random, the sample seems to be representative of the entire battalion populations. These data were collected using written surveys from soldiers primarily while they were at work and in uniform. Soldier and family identities were measured by asking the soldiers to "*describe who you are, meaning how you define or identify yourself. Think of it as if you were meeting someone for the first time, and they know nothing about you.*" Soldiers provided the description by selecting three roles from a list and/or writing in the roles (up to three) and ranking them one, two, or three. Both soldier and family roles were included in the listed identities. Analysis of the data was accomplished by comparing soldier and family identity means, cross-tabulating, and deciding what this data suggest based on Stryker's hypothesized relationships. Identities were coded as "soldier identity" if they listed any military occupation (for example, infantryman), their rank, any officer, noncommissioned officer, or soldier status, or warrior. The general role of worker or provider was not considered to be a soldier identity and was coded as a separate identity. Identities were coded as "family identity" if they were expressed as family, father, mother, spouse, husband, or wife.

Soldier and Family Identity Findings

Table 24-1 shows family and soldier identity salience among the 193-man sample, all of whom are married or have children. Over 75 percent of the sample list their family identity as most salient, while 93.8 percent selected family as one of their three most salient identities. In comparison, only 11.4 percent of these soldiers with families see their soldier identity as most salient, and only 57.5 percent select it as one their top three most salient identities. The family identity is highly concentrated in the top two most salient identities held (92.2 percent). This tendency is reversed for soldier identity salience, with 76.2 percent listing soldier identity third or not

Family Identity			Soldier Identity		
	Frequency	Percent		Frequency	Percent
Family identity selected 1	146	75.6	Soldier identity selected 1	22	11.4
Family identity selected 2	32	16.6	Soldier identity selected 2nd	24	12.4
Family identity selected 3	3	1.6	Soldier identity selected 3rd	65	33.7
Family identity not selected	12	6.2	Soldier identity not selected	82	42.5
Total	193	100.0	Total	193	100.0

Table 24-1. *Family and Soldier Identity Salience among Soldiers Who Are Married or Have Children.*

selecting it at all. Progressively smaller percentages of the group select the soldier identity as their third, second, and first most salient identity, respectively.[51]

A cross-tabulation of the data demonstrates that soldiers who select their family identity as most salient also tend to select soldier identity salience low (3rd) or not at all. Specifically, almost 66 percent of the soldiers selected their family identity as most salient and their soldier identity third or not at all.

Further cross-tabulation and correlation suggest that having a salient family identity typically decreases soldier identity salience as shown by a statistical correlation of –.294. The minus indicates that as one variable falls the other tends to rise and visa versa, while the decimal fraction indicates the degree of correlation on a scale ranging from zero, i.e., complete randomness, to one, i.e., perfect (inverse) correlation. The mean identity scores are just as telling. The soldiers had an average mean family identity salience score of 2.62 (range of 0 to 3), with three reflecting the highest possible family identity salience. The mean for soldier identity salience among these soldiers was only 0.93 on the same scale.[52] NOTE: Statistically inclined readers will find a full technical encapsulation of family and soldier identity saliences, including correlation and mean scores, in Table 24-2 located in endnote 52.

Analysis for Policy

The data shown above strongly suggest that the family is the most salient identity for the large majority of soldiers with families. That family identity is highly salient should not be surprising, however, since an earlier study by Denise Bielby found that 50 percent of employed men and 73 percent of employed women rated their families higher in personal importance than work.[53] The relatively low soldier identity salience should be surprising, given the degree of socialization most soldiers experience and the amount of time soldiers spend with their units. It should be noted, however, that Denise Bielby also found that lower-middle class men report primary satisfaction from family over work to a greater degree than upper-middle class men.[54] This last finding is important because it suggests that the data from the Stryker battalions (limited to input from E7 and below) may not be as pronounced for officers and the senior enlisted ranks who were not included in the analysis.

What are the implications of the dramatic differences in the mean scores of family and soldier identity salience for soldiers with families? While this chapter does not measure soldier behavior, it may be significant in predicting soldier behavior. On the basis of Sheldon Stryker's hypotheses introduced earlier and of the family identity as being the most salient identity, it becomes likely that:

- Because the family identity is higher in the salience hierarchy, soldiers with families are more likely, when they have the freedom to choose, to behave consistent with expectations attached to family identity rather than soldier identity.
- Because the family identity is higher in the salience hierarchy, soldiers with families are more likely to perceive a given situation as an opportunity to perform in terms of that family identity (versus the soldier identity), and are more likely to seek out opportunities to perform in terms of that family identity (versus the soldier identity).
- Because the family identity is higher in the salience hierarchy, the behavior of soldiers with families will be more likely to reflect institutionalized values and norms of the family rather than those of the military.

Findings by Sharon Lobel and Lynda St. Clair indicate that soldier identity salience should have a direct and positive effect on work effort, with individuals having more salient soldier identities willing to expend more effort in that role than those with more salient family identities.[55] Much of this discussion would imply that enlisted soldiers with immediate families would be less effective soldiers, though most military leaders and soldiers with families would argue that this is not the case. One explanation that may account for this inconsistency is offered by William and Denise Bielby, who found that men were able to maintain strong or weak identity salience for one role regardless of the salience of the other. For men, there was no trade-off or zero-sum relationship because they could maintain high levels of commitment and identity salience for both roles simultaneously.[56] This is similar to Chris Bourg and Mady Segal's argument that soldiers have such abundant personal resources that they can maintain commitment and roles in both the military and family institutions.[57] In this case, for example, the soldier devoting effort and time to work may view this behavior as consistent with the family and soldier identities. After all, the soldier supports his family by his work as a soldier, and if he fails in that work role his family could suffer. The key here is that the behavior is consistent with both roles, a point we shall address in greater detail below.

A second possibility discussed earlier was that the military obligates behavior through powerful negative sanctions and social control such as duty, patriotism, and allegiance. This pressure likely serves as a counterweight against the power of the far higher family identity salience, at least partially balancing the military-family relationship. However, the ability of the military to obligate behavior as against the greater salience of the family role makes it more likely that soldiers construe any military-family conflict as having been caused by the military rather than the family. We would also argue that there are times when the military cannot obligate behavior. At these times, for example when a soldier is deciding whether or not to reenlist or leave the military, the soldier has the freedom to act as identity theory would predict. Because the family identity seems to be so much more salient, *the Army must create a situation where the behavior they desire is consistent with the behavior desired by the family. The individual must be able to believe that being a soldier and a father/mother/spouse are not only compatible but are advantageous to the family.* This argument is consistent with Lobel's argument that when two roles are invoked concurrently, conflict does not necessarily occur if the roles are compatible.[58] This is also consistent with the evidence that leader support of families and leader actions to improve satisfaction with Army life reduce Army-family conflict and increase soldier/family commitment to the Army.[59]

There is some evidence, however, that the frenetic pace of current operations (2001-2005) and the resulting deployments may be creating a situation wherein soldiers believe they cannot behave in a way consistent with both the needs and expectations of their families and those of the Army. Specifically, the frequency and duration of family separations may be creating military-family conflict that, given the higher level of family identity salience, may result in soldiers choosing to leave the Army as they decide the needs of their family take precedence over their soldier role in the frequent-deployment or high-risk environment. This conclusion is supported by several recent studies. In a survey of more than 1,000 Army spouses living on or near the ten most deployment-stricken Army posts, about 76 percent said that they believed "the Army is likely to encounter retention problems as soldiers and their families tire of the post-9/11 pace and leave the service."[60] Two other studies, though not limited in their scope to soldiers with immediate family, raise additional concern. Charles Moskos and Laura Miller surveyed 389 deployed soldiers in December 2003, finding that, for almost half, the deployment made them less likely to reenlist. This result contrasts with only 6 percent who said the deployment made them more likely to reenlist.[61] The Office of Economic and Manpower Analysis found that once deployments exceed seven months, soldiers are less likely to reenlist, and that accordingly it expects a recruiting shortfall in 2004 and 2005 assuming other factors remain unchanged.[62]

The Development of Expert Knowledge and Leader Actions

The U.S. military is and will remain an extremely demanding institution. Because it must also recruit and retain an all-volunteer force, many of whom are married and thus have powerful family identities, it is clear that the military must take the lead in reducing or preventing military-family conflict. One vital method for reducing military-family conflict is the development of leaders with the expertise to understand and engage military families.

We are currently in an environment where Specialist Davila is on his second combat deployment in the last 24 months. Not long after he gets back, he will experience training-related family separations as he prepares to go to Afghanistan or Iraq for the third time in as many years. We must develop leaders who, given this extraordinarily stressful environment, can: (1) create the perception and fact that they are supportive of families; (2) actually improve families' satisfaction with Army life; and (3) create a situation within their units wherein the norms, values, and behaviors of the family and the Army are compatible. These are certainly no easy tasks. There is no cookie-cutter solution. It takes mature, knowledgeable, and caring leaders. It also requires a deliberate institutional effort to develop in our frontline leaders an expert knowledge of military families and the skills necessary to put this knowledge into practice.

Leaders must be educated in how to care. But caring is not enough; leaders must understand the needs and concerns of families and how they as leaders can help. Yet, our junior officers are currently exposed to very little and sometimes no pre- or post-commissioning training on military families. Our junior NCOs are often no better prepared. Given the limited exposure of junior leaders to military family indoctrination, commanders and senior NCOs should seek to develop this competence in the leaders they coach and mentor. Leaders should be held accountable for the level of support provided to families, and the plan and support for families should be nested at all levels of leadership so that each unit is working together and augmenting the support provided by higher and subordinate commands.

Each family requires individualized attention, but there are critical overarching skills and knowledge that should be developed in our leaders that contribute to improved readiness, retention, and family adaptation throughout the military.[63]

The Profession's Expert Knowledge of Military Families

Based on our research, we suggest that the Army's frontline leaders must master a prescribed body of expert knowledge on families. Specifically, our leaders must know:

- *How and why leader decisions affect military families, recognizing that even routine decisions can have large consequences for families. (Example: keeping soldiers later than scheduled and beyond the installation daycare hours.)*
- *How their decisions and behavior are perceived by the unit families and how to create the perception (and fact) of caring, accommodating leadership.*
- *How to identify and help high-risk families (very young junior enlisted families, new parents, families new to the Army, single parents, families with special needs or conditions).*
- *The socioeconomic issues facing the enlisted families of varying family types and situations (on/off post housing, single vs. double income).*
- *The demands of various demographic factors (single parents, dual military, dual career, large families, etc.).*
- *Readiness cost-benefit analysis. Recognize when extra time spent training may actually degrade readiness (commitment, retention, and motivation) if it results in excessive or unnecessary separation from families.*

- *How information is disseminated to families (e.g., rumors, newsletters, phone trees, through the spouse) and how this impacts on accuracy and the tone of the message.*
- *The various support agencies and other forms of assistance that are available to families and how to encourage their use.*
- *The demands and nature of child-rearing and the limitations of childcare facilities.*
- *How to develop informal spousal support networks in the unit.*
- *How to create the perception and fact that they care for those they lead.*
- *How to increase the satisfaction of families with military life.*

Leader Actions and Practices

Assuming that what we have outlined in the previous section accurately represents the needed knowledge for the Army professionals, we suggest that such expert knowledge should be put into practice in optimum ways, many of which are just good, commonsense techniques of leadership. Specifically, we believe that frontline leaders should employ the following practices and techniques:

- *Train subordinate leaders in family support/care, model these practices in your own leadership, and evaluate partly on the basis of the success in meeting soldier/family needs.*
- *Allow families as much control over their family situation as possible. Allow time off for family emergencies and non-emergency family activities. Provide a sense of freedom to soldiers and control over personal time by avoiding callbacks. Provide the most predictable short- and long-term schedule possible, make sure spouses have a schedule that indicates time off, days deployed, late nights, and key events. Do not waste soldiers' time, and compensate soldiers with time off after they return from deployment or routine training that occurs over a weekend.*
- *Communicate with spouses, provide avenues for spouses to communicate with unit leaders, and act as an advocate and information source for families. (Spouses may be reluctant to approach unit leaders. Leaders should make a point of introducing themselves and getting to know their soldiers' families. Do not count on soldiers to bring home information to their spouses!)*
- *Listen to families' problems; show real interest in the well-being of families. Treat soldiers and families with respect.*
- *Provide unit activities that include families, inform soldiers/spouses about family programs in the unit and elsewhere and what they provide. Unit social events provide a great opportunity to: meet the families of your soldiers, pass information such as schedules and phone rosters directly, and, most importantly, provide an opportunity for spouses to meet and interact. It is clear from research on adaptation and the reports of spouses dealing with deployments to Iraq and Afghanistan that the informal network of support and friendship is incredibly important.[64]*

- *Have or support an effective family readiness group that encourages communication, volunteers, and avoids hierarchy. Provide family support programs in the unit and facilitate/encourage use of family programs. (A lieutenant or platoon-level noncommissioned officer should know all the spouses in his or her unit and seek out opportunities to interact and communicate with them.)*
- *Minimize family separation when possible and when it does not degrade training.*
- *Take steps to reduce the stress of family separation with predeployment information, quality rear detachment plans and commanders, and updated information.*
- *Consider families to be part of your organization and not some distraction to buffer your unit from.*
- *Seek to identify new ways to increase spousal satisfaction with military life. To do this, you must know your unit's families and their issues and concerns.*
- *Encourage/promote soldier financial responsibility; encourage families to use on-post housing when available. (Soldiers living on-post will typically have fewer financial challenges and a greater network of support from other military families. This results in fewer problems and increased ability to cope with problems.)*
- *Provide quality sponsorship to new soldiers and allow new soldiers time to get families settled. Try to have a sponsor that has a similar family situation (if the incoming soldier has a spouse and kids the sponsor should have a spouse and kids). When a spouse is involved, try to arrange a sponsor whose own spouse is willing to sponsor the incoming spouse.*
- *Target at-risk families for help (young families, single parents, and families new to the military). This high-risk group requires special attention.*

Future Research

There are numerous areas within the profession's expert knowledge as related to family and retention issues that require future research. The use of identity salience in the analysis of military-family conflict appears to be quite promising, but is under-explored. The empirical testing of the identity salience-behavior link should be one of the Army research community's first priorities. This chapter has demonstrated the relative salience of the soldier and family identities, but it is unclear exactly how their salience influences soldier behavior or how soldier behavior would change as the salience of these identities changed. The conflicts in Afghanistan and Iraq are certain to have made new demands on soldiers and families and changed the salience of existing demands. It is important that the military ascertain these changes and take measures to mitigate any increased military-family conflict.

There are, of course, some resources that remain restricted for the soldier. The soldier/family member has only so much time and may not be able to satisfy the demands of both the military and the family simultaneously. With the current level of demands (risk and family separation) placed on the Army (both active duty and reserves), we must inquire whether there is a threshold for risk and repeated, long-term family separations beyond which the family and the military roles are simply incompatible? As soldiers deploy for their second or third time to Afghanistan or Iraq, facing the prospect of more to come, it is unclear whether any level of leader support or family adaptation will be sufficient to maintain families' satisfaction with military life.

Conclusion

The Army is likely to remain a force with families, and the demands of the Army and the family are likely to continue to be significant. Because of this inevitable reality, the Army must maintain an environment where the soldier and the family believe a person can be a great father/mother/husband/wife AND a great soldier. The Army has done well in developing family-friendly policies and creating agencies and groups to provide family support, but as a professional force, we cannot outsource our human issues. It is our leaders who will make the greatest difference in the lives of Army families. It is their decisions, behaviors, knowledge, skills, and abilities that will most impact our families' day-to-day lives. Therefore, the development of expert knowledge about military families and the ability to span effectively the organization-family boundary has become critical. Yet it remains a largely unaddressed aspect of professional expertise, with few of our frontline leaders receiving education on the military family and some lacking family experience of their own.

If our leadership is going to maintain an environment in which soldiers believe they can serve both their family and the Army well, that leadership must first recognize that families are uniquely a part of the Army and have significant influence on the performance of their organizations. They must also recognize that, as leaders, they have considerable influence on the quality of the lives of the unit's families. They must develop the expert knowledge necessary to create both the perception and reality of caring for families and understand how they can improve satisfaction with military life on the part of soldiers' families as well as the soldiers themselves. Lastly, leaders must understand that if they fail to do these things, soldiers with families will be more likely to feel that having a family and being a soldier are incompatible. In the long term, soldiers who come to have such feelings will likely resolve the conflict in favor of the family. On the other hand, by more fully developing this critical area of the profession's expertise, the Army is very capable of having many more success stories like those of Specialist Tom Davila and his wife Aerin.

Notes

1. Thomas E. Ricks, "Army Spouses Expect Reenlistment Problems," *Washington Post,* 28 March 2004, 9. These findings were based on a poll conducted by the *Washington Post*, Henry J. Kaiser Family Foundation, and Harvard University, plus dozens of supplemental interviews. The poll was the first nongovernmental survey of military spouses since the terrorist attacks 11 September 2001. The survey included more than 1,000 spouses living on or near the ten most deployed-from Army posts.

2. Ibid. Charles Moskos and Laura Miller, *December 2003 Sociological Survey on Operation Iraqi Freedom,* April 2004 (This is a report of 389 soldiers serving in Iraq, Kuwait, and Qatar). Casey Wardynski et al., "Analysis of the Stress on the Army" (presentation, West Point, NY, Office of Economic and Manpower Analysis, 5 February 2004).

3. Deputy Assistant Secretary of Defense Military for Community and Family Policy, "Profile of the Military Community: 2000 Demographics Report" (Washington, DC: Office of the Deputy Assistant Secretary of Defense for Community and Family Policy, 2000).

4. Ibid.

5. Mady Wechsler Segal, "The Military and the Family as Greedy Institutions," *Armed Forces and Society* 13 (1986): 9-38.

6. Lewis A. Coser, *Greedy Institutions: Patterns of Undivided Commitment* (New York: The Free Press, 1974); Segal (1986).

7. Patricia Voydanoff, "Linkages between the Work-Family Interface and Work, Family, and Individual Outcomes," *Journal of Family Issues* 23 (2002): 138-164.

8. Ibid.

9. Segal (1986).

10. Segal (1986); Mady Wechsler Segal, "The Nature of Work and Family Linkages: A Theoretical Perspective," in *The Organizational Family*, ed. Gary L. Bowen and Dennis K. Orthner (Westport, CT: Praeger, 1989); and Jay Stanley, Mady Wechsler Segal, and Charlotte Jeanne Laughton, "Grass Roots Family Action and Military Policy Responses," *Marriage and Family Review* 15 (1990): 207-23.

11. Segal (1986); Segal (1989); and Stanley, Segal, and Laughton (1990).

12. Ibid.

13. David S. Wolpert et al., "The Special Case of the Young Enlisted Family," in *The Military Family: A Practical Guide for Human Service Providers*, eds. James A. Martin, Leora N. Rosen, and Linette R. Sparacino (Westport, CT: Praeger, 2000), 43-53 ; Segal (1986); Segal (1989); and Stanley, Segal, and Laughton (1990).

14. Segal (1989).

15. Stanley, Segal, and Laughton (1990).

16. Ibid.

17. Ibid.

18. Ibid.

19. Jeffrey H. Greenhaus and Nicholas J. Beutell, "Sources of Conflict between Work and Family Roles," *Academy of Management Review* 10 (1985): 76-88.

20. James A. Martin and Dennis K. Orthner, "The 'Company Town' in Transition: Rebuilding Military Communities," in *The Organizational Family*, eds. Gary L. Bowen and Dennis K. Orthner (Westport, CT: Praeger, 1989), 163-77.

21. Voydanoff (2002).

22. Chris Bourg and Mady Wechsler Segal, "The Impact of Family Supportive Policies and Practices on Organizational Commitment to the Army," *Armed Forces & Society* 25 (1999): 633-52.

23. Mady Wechsler Segal and Jessie J. Harris, *What We Know About Army Families*, Special Report 21 (Alexandria, VA: Army Research Institute for Behavioral and Social Sciences, 1993). It is important to identify ways to better inform families about the programs and supports that are available to help them and develop tried and true methods to maximize their use.

24. Ricks.

25. Ibid., 3.

26. The demographics of age, marital status, and lack of children makes this group the least likely to have family experiences of their own. Also, their socioeconomic status may differ significantly from that of their soldiers.

27. Segal and Harris (1993).

28. Ibid.

29. Ibid.

30. Ibid., 57.

31. Robert Sadacca, Rodney A. McCloy, and Ani S. DiFazio, *Preliminary Analysis of the Impact of Army and Family Factors on Unit Readiness*, Human Resources Research Organization Report (Alexandria, VA: U.S. Army Research Institute for the Behavioral and Social Sciences, 1992); and Robert Sadacca, Cathy A. Stawarski, and Ani S. DiFazio, *Preliminary Analysis of the Impact of Army and Family Factors on Individual Readiness*, Human Resources Research Organization Report (Alexandria, VA: U.S. Army Research Institute for the Behavioral and Social Sciences, 1991).

32. Audrey M. Burnam et al., *Army Families and Soldier Readiness*. Unclassified Report 3884-A (Santa Monica, CA: The RAND Corporation, Arroyo Center, 1992); and Segal and Harris (1993).

33. David R. Segal and Mady Wechsler Segal, "Changes in the American Armed Forces: Implications for Military Families," in *Pathways to the Future: A Review of Military Family Research*, ed. Peggy McClure (Scranton, PA: Military Family Institute, Marywood University, 1999), 1-10.

34. Joe F. Pittman and Dennis K. Orthner, "Gender Differences in the Prediction of Job Commitment" in *Work and Family: Theory, Research, and Applications*, ed. F. Goldsmith (Newbury Park, CA: Sage, 1989), 227-47. Orthner and Pittman confirm the importance of family satisfaction and leader/organizational support in creating a military-family fit, finding that among Air Force personnel military-family fit was a product of satisfaction, the perception of organizational responsiveness to families, spousal support for the airman's career, and the quality of the military as a child-rearing environment.

35. Stephen C. Burke, "Family Readiness," in *Pathways to the Future: A Review of Military Family Research*, ed. Peggy McClure (Scranton, PA: Military Family Institute, Marywood University, 1999), 209-31.

36. Sadacca, McCloy, and DiFazio (1992); and Sadacca, Stawarski, and DiFazio (1991).

37. Segal and Segal (1999).

38. Joe F. Pittman, "Work/Family Fit as a Mediator of Work Factors on Marital Tension: Evidence from the Interface of Greedy Institutions," *Human Relations* 47 (1994): 183-209. Pittman found that soldiers' perceptions of military-family fit were predicted not only by their own attitudes about work time and job satisfaction, but also by their wives' opinion of military-family fit.

39. Segal and Harris (1993).

40. Michael A. Hogg, Deborah J. Terry, and Katherine M. White, "A Tale of Two Theories: A Critical Comparison of Identity Theory with Social Identity Theory," *Social Psychology Quarterly* 58 (1995): 257; Sheldon Stryker, "Symbolic Interactionism: Themes and Variations," in *Social Psychology Sociological Perspectives*, eds. Morris Rosenberg and Ralph H. Turner (New Brunswick, NJ: Transaction Publishers, 1992), 24-25; and Sheldon Stryker and Richard T. Serpe, "Identity Salience and Psychological Centrality: Equivalent, Overlapping, or Complementary Concepts?" *Social Psychology Quarterly* 57 (1994): 17.

41. Stryker, 24.

42. Hogg, Terry, and White, 257.

43. Stryker and Serpe, 18.

44. Richard T. Serpe, "Stability and Change in Self: A Structural Symbolic Interactionist Explanation," *Social Psychology Quarterly* 50 (1987): 44-55; Stryker, 24-25; and Stryker and Serpe, 18-19.

45. Mark R. Leary, David S. Wheeler, and T. Brant Jenkins, "Aspects of Identity and Behavioral Preference: Studies of Occupational and Recreational Choice," *Social Psychology Quarterly* 49 (1986): 11-18.

46. Sharon A. Lobel, "Allocation of Investment in Work and Family Roles: Alternative Theories and Implications for Research" *The Academy of Management Journal* 16 (1991): 510.

47. William T. Bielby and Denise D. Bielby, "Family Ties: Balancing Commitments to Work and Family in Dual Earner Households," *American Sociological Review* 54 (1989): 776-89). For

both men and women, hours devoted to child care and household chores was positively related to family identity salience. It is also interesting that when married men had family responsibilities of a typical working wife, they formed a family identity very similar to that of working women. This could mean that increased parity in the work place and household roles should lead to higher family identity salience for men and higher work identity salience for women.

48. Ibid., 511. Denise D. Bielby argues in an article titled "Commitment to Work and Family," *Annual Review of Sociology* 18 (1992): 281-302, that the work-family intersection has unnecessarily been treated as a social problem and seen as mutually constraining. Bielby and Bielby argue that in addition to the zero-sum or scarcity model, that the multiplicity model may be appropriate to the work-family interface, with individuals being able to form strong commitment and maintain participation in numerous and diverse roles. This is similar to the Bourg and Segal argument that soldiers have abundant personal resources with which to maintain commitment and roles in both the military and family institutions.

49. Lobel.

50. Charles Moskos and John Sibley Butler, *All That We Can Be: Black Leadership and Racial Integration the Army Way* (New York: Basic Books, 1996), 39.

51. An alternate question was also used to measure identity salience and produced similar results.

52. The table below provides further statistical particulars regarding the relation of family and soldier identity salience:

	Mean	N	Std. Deviation	Std. Error Mean
Soldier Identity	.9275	193	1.00256	.07217
Family Identity	2.6166	193	.80243	.05776
Soldier Identity-Family Identity Correlation = -.294				

Mean Family and Soldier Identity Differences						t	df	Sig. (2-tailed)
Mean	Std. Deviation	Std. Error Mean	95% Confidence Interval of the Difference					
			Lower	Upper				
−1.6891	1.45657	.10485	−1.8959	−1.4823		−16.110	192	.000

Table 24-2. *Family and Soldier Identity Salience: Mean and Correlation Scores.*

53. Bielby. While the personal importance of one domain is not quite the same as identity salience, they are related through commitment. Further, placing greater personal importance on a role should contribute to its salience.

54. Ibid.

55. Sharon A. Lobel and Lynda St. Clair, "Effects of Family Responsibilities, Gender, and Career Identity Salience on Performance Outcomes," *The Academy of Management Journal* 35 (1992): 1057-69.

56. Bielby and Bielby.

57. Bourg and Segal, 634.

58. Lobel.

59. Bourg and Segal, 644-47.

60. Ricks.

61. Moskos and Miller.

62. Wardynski, et al.

63. Segal and Harris.

64. Ricks.

25 Developing and Using Army General Officers[1]

Margaret C. Harrell, Harry J. Thie, Peter Schirmer, and Kevin Brancato

Transformation requires a change in how one should view the Army profession.[2] Understanding and determining the best development and utilization of the Army's strategic leadership, which heads that profession, is thus a vital component to this changed mindset. There are external pressures for change: Secretary of Defense Donald Rumsfeld has expressed concern that general and flag officer assignments are too short, that the length of service after promotion is too brief, and that careers don't last long enough.[3] Those critical of rapid job turnover cite reduced organizational effectiveness, diluted individual accountability among the leadership, limited career satisfaction of senior officers, and eroded confidence of junior and mid-level officers who see their profession's leaders moving so quickly through organizations that the leaders gain no more than a superficial familiarity.

However, the Army has long been concerned about maintaining promotion flow, as the profession lacks reward or compensation mechanisms that are not linked to promotion. Is the Army correct to focus its concern on promotion opportunities for all officers, even if the profession's strategic leaders are under-utilized? The apparent shortcomings of the current system suggest that Secretary Rumsfeld's concerns merit consideration in any discussion of the best utilization of general officers.

What, then, are the appropriate practices for assigning and developing general officers and for utilizing the Army's most senior strategic leaders? If current practices are changed to give effect to the new ideas, what would the effects be? This chapter answers these questions. It does so by first developing an empirical picture of how the current system manages Army general officers, reviewing the literature about the private sector to determine how private organizations manage their senior executives, and modeling different ways of managing the most senior military officers. The modeling goal is to identify utilization approaches that address the concerns described above.

We then consider whether there are applicable lessons that can be drawn from private sector executive management to increase the contribution of the Army's general officers. That is, we explore the likely effects on the Army of developing and using general officers based upon the private sector theoretical frameworks. We also consider whether the concerns of the Secretary of Defense, as well as the internal concerns regarding promotion, are addressed with this application. Finally, we discuss briefly the comments of current military leaders regarding their profession and their likely responses to such changes.

Rapid Movement of Army Strategic Leaders

An initial data assessment of the promotion patterns and career tenures of general officers confirms that the Army's general officers retire relatively early,[4] and they are able to do so by moving relatively rapidly through both assignments and ranks. Army generals spend approximately three years as brigadier general (O-7), two to two and a half years as major general (O-8), and approximately two and a half years as lieutenant general (O-9). The three years at O-7 typically split between two one- or two-year assignments, and then most officers will fill one or two positions at each subsequent paygrade. Officers who continue to be promoted are more likely to have only one assignment at O-8 and O-9 on their way to general (O-10). Thus the result is an assignment pattern by which retiring Army O-10s typically have had six assignments as a flag-level officer before retiring with approximately 35 years of service.

Lessons from the Private Sector

Cumulative Learning Through Work Experience

Work experience accumulates through a series of assignments that ideally prepare a person for increasingly demanding and complex jobs. An organization, therefore, might define a professional career as "a sequence of work roles that are related to each other in a rational way so that some of the knowledge and experience acquired in one role is used in the next."[5] This definition assumes a logic to the job sequence so that it creates an executive skill set valuable to the organization.

The knowledge and experience gained through the typical job sequence follow a predictable pattern: Early assignments generally build specific functional skills, general and often tacit organizational knowledge, and idiosyncratic personal insights. Later assignments tend to have more complex and ambiguous responsibilities that require application of functional, organizational, and personal knowledge gained in earlier assignments. Thus, as reported by Morgan McCall and his associates in their study, *The Lessons of Experience: How Successful Executives Develop on the Job,* private sector executives state that their early assignments tended to have core elements that were fairly simple, providing only a few basic managerial challenges.[6] Their early assignments also provided a high degree of organizational and personal learning. As they moved to higher organizational levels, they found their technical and functional skills less helpful because of greater ambiguities in their responsibilities, because they were assigned to different functional units, and because they were assigned to more conceptual and strategic positions. In these higher-level positions, executives learned to gather and synthesize information and to make decisions that involved some guesswork. They also had exposure to corporate culture, attitudes toward risk, and the broader context within which decisions are made. The authors of the study conclude that such assignments bring about a mental transition from thinking tactically to thinking strategically.

These identifiable patterns suggest that accumulated experience is not serendipitous. On the contrary, corporations actively manage the careers of their high-potential employees. A study of executive career management examined 33 large U.S. corporations, with each reporting that it had some sort of program for identifying and developing future corporate leaders. Job rotation is by far the most common and most important developmental tool in high-potential employees' careers, and assignments typically last two to three years; assignments for other employees are longer, meaning job rotation is less common.[7] This distinction corroborates other research not specifically focused on high-potential employees, which found that job rotations are more common among employees who are performing well.[8]

Taking the basic concept of cumulative experience a step farther, Robert Morrison and Roger Hock argue that as a person moves from job to job, his capacity and authority to influence his position gradually increase.[9] They draw their conclusion based on studies of various occupations, including Navy surface warfare officers, who progress from division officer to department head to executive officer to commanding officer. Along the way, an officer's responsibilities become more complex and less prescribed; eventually, the Navy depends heavily on the officer's good judgment and accumulated professional expertise to command a ship. By that time, a commanding officer can draw upon the knowledge, experience, organizational understanding, and personal growth he has nurtured over a 20-year career. The pattern is similar to that of the corporate executives who found that later assignments had more ambiguous responsibilities and required more guesswork, making personal judgment and experience more important. To put it simply, early in a career the job shapes the person, but later in a career the person shapes the job.

Based upon these observations, Morrison and Hock posit a career development model in which a sequence of assignments prepares a person for a "target position."[10] We propose a taxonomy of "developing jobs" and "using jobs," in which the former confer knowledge, skills, and personal growth that are put to use in the latter. Almost all jobs have some "using" aspect in the sense that organizations want to put to use the incumbent's existing knowledge, skills, and abilities; the key distinction, therefore, is the extent to which the job prepares a person for a higher-level position. By this definition, many using jobs logically occur at the end of one's career, regardless of how high the person has advanced in an organization. For those who have risen to the senior levels of management, their using jobs are critical to the success of the organization and demand a high degree of accountability and stability—the most obvious example of such a using job in the private sector is the CEO. In using jobs such as these, executives shape not just the job but often the entire organization.

To refine our framework with developing jobs and using jobs as the basic building blocks of a full career, we suggest that careers might have multiple sequences of developing assignments and using assignments. Consider infantry officers. For the vast majority, their careers will end at or before the rank of colonel. A small number will become general officers, setting an even smaller number on the course to become combatant commanders, Chiefs of Staff, or even Chairmen of the Joint Chiefs of Staff. These represent an entirely different type of using job, where an officer's judgment, experience, knowledge, and personal characteristics could conceivably affect not just the Army profession but also the entire military or even the nation itself. Before reaching one of these positions, general officers go through another round of formal schooling, probably serve as division commanders, and may have special assignments to NATO, the Joint Staff, or other key Army positions in the Pentagon. These are important jobs that require high levels of knowledge, experience, and so forth, but they are nonetheless part of a developmental process that teaches strategic thinking, prudent risk-taking, knowledge of the international political environment, and other qualities needed in strategic leaders. This is not unlike the developmental process of their private sector counterparts in higher levels of corporate management.

The Developing and Using Distinction Applied to a Career

The developing job/using job distinction provides a framework for analyzing when learning and action (i.e., performing) take place within a career or within an assignment. Research has found that executives follow predictable patterns in the timing of learning and decision-making in a new job. Based on longitudinal studies of high-level executives in large corporate units, John Gabarro identified five stages of learning and action that executives move through after entering a new position:

- *Taking Hold*—Orientation and evaluative learning and corrective action that lasts three to six months.
- *Immersion*—Relatively little change but more reflective and penetrating learning; this stage could require nearly a year following the Taking Hold stage.
- *Reshaping*—Major change during which the new manager acts on the deeper understanding gained in the preceding stage; lasts about six months.
- *Consolidation*—Earlier changes are consolidated; lasts four to eight months.
- *Refinement*—Fine-tuning and relatively little major additional learning.[11]

After entering a new managerial position, executives need between two and a half to three years to progress through these stages, beyond which they are no longer considered new to their position and enjoy substantial influence and knowledge.

Combining the developing job/using job concept with the stages of learning and action, we conclude that not only the sequence but also the duration of assignments affects an executive's usefulness in a position. In order for executives to exert their influence in using jobs, they must remain in those positions long enough to learn the new role, to take meaningful action, and to be held accountable for their actions. But organizations must balance effectiveness and accountability with other goals, such as executive development, promotion opportunity, promotion selectivity, and job satisfaction. If high developmental value is ascribed to certain jobs, organizations may choose to sacrifice some effectiveness and accountability, which could lead to shorter assignments. Recall that high-potential executives change jobs faster than their peers, typically every two to three years until they reach the later stages of their careers. On the other hand, corporations evidently make accountability and stability a high priority in critical using jobs, where an executive could serve many years if performance is good. CEOs average more than eight years on the job, with almost 70 percent serving to age 60 or older.[12] Thus corporations, desiring to capitalize on their CEOs' hard-earned influence and knowledge, routinely allow them to serve many years.

The Developing and Using Framework Applied to General Officers

The subsequent analysis and modeling of general officer careers is based on the developing job/using job career framework and demonstrates how these competing interests might be balanced. We assume that freshly minted O-7s are entering a new developmental phase, albeit at a relatively high level, that will prepare some of them to become O-10s, the most senior leaders in the profession. As such, they can have enormous influence on their service and on national military strategy by serving in the ultimate using jobs.

Current General Officer Development in the Developing Job/Using Job Framework

Individual experience and organizational practices in the military and in the private sector indicate that the developing job/using job framework provides a useful career model. However, developing jobs and using jobs probably cannot be defined in anything other than very general terms, because they depend on the type of organization and the skills it values in its executives. Furthermore, most jobs do not fit neatly into one category or the other. Regional vice presidents or division commanders, for example, are in jobs important to their organizations but also in positions that lead to CEO or CSA. Ultimately, developing jobs and using jobs are those that an organization or a profession determines them to be. About the best indicator that we, as outside observers, have of the nature of a job is its timing: We can be reasonably certain that CEOs and O-10s are in using jobs and that junior analysts and O-1s are in developing jobs, but it gets tougher to discern the status of those in the middle.

These issues arose as we attempted to identify developing jobs and using jobs for general and flag officers. It is far beyond the scope of our research for us to make value judgments about the desirability of specific skills and experiences in senior military leaders or to discern which jobs best confer them. However, we did want to get a picture of how the services develop and use general and flag officers, so we applied a few commonsense rules to categorize positions. Once we identified developing jobs and using jobs empirically, we looked at how they compare across the services and at how they are managed in light of what we know from the corporate world. We present our findings, as they pertain to the Army profession, in this chapter.

A Shorthand Method for Identifying Developing Jobs and Using Jobs

For this analysis, we address only Army officers in occupations that have historically led to O-10. This category is usually confined to armor, infantry, and field artillery officers.[13] Given this subset of officers, we included in our analysis all assignments officers in these specialties had as general officers, which included some assignments to technical, support, and in a few instances even positions held by other professions, such as medical.

We examined the assignment history of O-10s from these selected line communities in order to see how they were developed after promotion to O-7. (The assumption was that they had entered a second, high-level developmental stage upon becoming general officers.) To this information we applied our commonsense rules. The underlying logic is that the timing and frequency of jobs provide a reasonable indication of whether they are developing or using. Thus we assumed that all O-7 jobs are developing jobs and all O-10 jobs are using jobs. As for the jobs in the middle—those at O-8 and O-9—we assumed that those appearing frequently on O-10 resumes are developing jobs. These rules were designed to be conservative in identifying using jobs, because all general officers are eligible for promotion or a new assignment. In theory, of course, anything short of Chairman of the Joint Chiefs of Staff could be a developing job.

Before we provide the details of how we separated O-8 and O-9 positions into developing and using jobs, an important caveat is in order: This is a descriptive, not a prescriptive analysis. We believe it is useful to identify developing jobs and using jobs at these grades because they shed more light on how the careers of strategic leaders are managed, and because we use that information in our modeling efforts. But if at any time the Army chose to identify developing jobs and using jobs, it might follow a course different from historical precedent. In short, we are not recommending which jobs should be identified as developing jobs, nor are we recommending a process by which the Army should identify developing jobs.

For each assignment, we know the officer's unit and job title (when officers are dual-hatted they have multiple units, multiple job titles, or both). Using this information, we grouped positions into 11 broad job categories based on the type of unit an officer was assigned to and the duties associated with the job title, as shown in Table 25-1. With only 11 categories and 711 unique combinations of Army units and job titles in our database, most of the groupings are rather large, so that it would have been possible to sort positions into additional categories. However, as the num-

Organization Type	Position Type
Operational	Command
Operational	Deputy Command
Operational	Staff
Training and Education Center	All
International or Multi-organizational	All
Joint	Command
Joint	Staff
Headquarters	Command
Headquarters	Staff
Professional (e.g., Medical, Legal)	Command
Professional	Staff

Note: Some of the categories, e.g., Professional Command and Professional Staff, do not generally apply to line officers and their peer groups from the other branches. These categories were included as a framework appropriate to other kinds of officers. Still, there were some assignments that fell into these categories.

Table 25-1. *Categories of General Officer Positions.*

ber of categories increases, the distinctions between them become less clear, and even with only 11 categories there is occasional ambiguity in how a position is classified.

We next found how often each job category appears on officers' resumes. If less than 10 percent of O-10s had a particular category of job while they were O-9s, that category is considered "low-frequency" for the grade of O-9. Likewise, if less than 10 percent of O-9s had a particular category of job while they were O-8s, that category is considered "low-frequency" for the grade of O-8. The 10 percent cut-off could have been set higher or lower, which obviously would have resulted in either fewer or more categories being counted as "low-frequency."[14] All categories that surpassed the 10 percent threshold are considered "high-frequency" for the grades O-8 or O-9.[15]

All jobs that fell into the low-frequency category (appearing in fewer than 10 percent of officers' resumes) were counted as using jobs and were set aside. We returned to the jobs in the high-frequency category and identified individual jobs in each category that are rarely, if ever, filled by an officer who will subsequently be promoted. These, too, are using jobs because they typically appear at the end of an officer's career. Again, we established some rules for identifying career end-points. Specifically, if no officer who has held a particular position since 1990 (to include officers assigned in the late 1980s and were still there in January 1990) has subsequently been promoted, that job is considered a career end-point and therefore a using job.

To summarize our methodology, it could be thought of as a pair of filters that separate using jobs from developing jobs at the grades of O-8 and O-9. The first filter is applied to job categories, and sorts them into high-frequency and low-frequency categories. The second filter is applied to individual jobs within the high-frequency categories to identify career end-points. Positions that are in low-frequency categories or that are career end-points we count as using jobs; those that are in the high-frequency categories and are not career end-points we count as developing jobs. We applied these filters separately for O-8 and O-9 jobs. Once we had our lists of developing jobs and using jobs, we counted the number of such jobs each month since January 1990 in order to determine the percentage of using and developing jobs. From this process, we determine that 60 percent of Army O-8 jobs appear to be developing jobs. This includes positions such as division command. The other 40 percent of Army O-8 jobs are either within low-frequency job categories or are career end-points. Likewise, 45 percent of Army O-9 positions emerge as developing jobs, to include corps command and the senior military assistant to the Secretary of Defense. The complementary 55 percent of O-9 positions are using jobs.

The Current Length of Developing Job and Using Assignments in the Army

We have asserted the linkages between job type (developing or using) and assignment duration, with using assignments requiring substantial time for individuals to reach a point of effectiveness, accountability, and deep influence and knowledge, but with developing assignments requiring only about two years for a person to acquire new skills and knowledge. Now that we have identified developing and using jobs for Army general officers, the natural question is whether the job type is currently correlated with job duration.

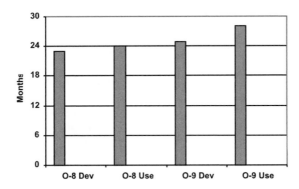

Source: General and Flag Officer Database, Directorate for Information Operations and Reports, Washington Headquarters Services.

Figure 25-1. *Median Assignment Length in O-8 and O-9 Developing and Using Assignments since 1990.*

Figure 25-1 presents the median duration, in months, of developing and using assignments at the grades of O-8 and O-9 since 1990. It indicates that O-8 developing and using assignments average 23 and 24 months, respectively, while O-9 developing and using assignments average 25 and 28 months. O-9 assignments are slightly longer than O-8 assignments, and using assignments are slightly longer than developing assignments, but the differences are small. We conclude that there is currently little connection between job type and job duration at the grades of O-8 and O-9. Thus we assert that while professional leaders are assigned to both developing and using positions, the tenures for these assignments do not vary. Nor are they long enough for leader effectiveness if private sector norms are applied.

Thus far we have sought to ascertain whether the strengths of civilian, private sector executive development could be applied to general officer career paths by managing the tenure of developing assignments differently from using assignments. The intent was to stabilize some individuals and organizations by getting the maximum use from the most senior general officers as well as those individuals not likely to be promoted further. The concern frequently cited within the Army (and other services), as well as by Congress, is that such stabilization would clog or cause stagnation in the system, precluding other officers from rising to the top in their profession. The system proposed below maximizes the utilization of senior leaders by increasing the stabilization in the system without unduly clogging promotion opportunities for other officers.

Proposing a New System for Assigning General Officers

The basis of the policy alternatives examined in this analysis was a variation in job tenure between developing and using assignments; we deliberately set the developing assignments at shorter durations than the using assignments. Two-year developing assignments are similar in length to many current general officer assignments.

Maintaining two-year developing assignments will continue to allow sufficient numbers of officers to gain developing experiences and be evaluated in them.[16] These assignments emphasize the development of officers for subsequent, higher-level responsibility and enable the Army and DoD to judge their potential for such positions. The downside of having shorter developmental assignments is reduced stability and reduced accountability. In contrast, longer using assignments maximize stability and accountability in certain organizations, without compromising developing opportunities for officers. Such assignments would also clarify an officer's expectations and permit him the opportunity to have more significant effect on an organization at the height of his career.

This analysis was conducted using two independent quantitative models. The primary model is of the steady-state system dynamics type designed on the basis of stocks and flows, wherein the officers "flow" through stocks of developing and using positions. The pivotal inputs for this model include the mix of developing and using jobs at each grade, the length of each kind of assignment, and the number of each kind of assignment officers receive at each pay grade. The outputs, which are calculated separately for officers in developing assignments and using assignments, include:

- Number promoted (throughput)
- Promotion probability to each grade
- Probability of an O-7 reaching O-10
- Number of officers developed who are not promoted
- Average time in service overall
- Average time in each grade for those promoted
- Average time in each grade for those retiring
- Average time in position

A second, more detailed model validated the findings of the primary model. This entity-based model was designed to permit an understanding of the particular assignments an individual receives, and of the effects upon others of fast-tracking certain individuals through the system. This model was also developed within the context of this research effort, but with different software and modeling techniques.

Our analysis included multiple steps:

1. Identify developing and using positions, by grade
2. Set goals for time in position (e.g., 2 years in developing assignments)
3. Set goals for number and timing of positions (e.g., 2 using assignments for each O-10)
4. Assess feasibility of system
5. Assess soft "cost" of changes (i.e., any change in promotion probability) and hard costs of change (monetary)
6. Revise, from Step 2, as necessary.

This iterative modeling process evaluated 14 different cases. Some cases were judged to be infeasible. For example, if all O-7s serve two complete developing assignments (for a total of four years) the result can be insufficient numbers of promotions to O-8. In this instance, either O-8 jobs go unfilled, or officers are promoted to O-8 before completing two developing assignments.

The management paradigm that emerged from the multiple alternatives as being best at balancing all concerns is one in which using assignments are four years long, and developing assignments are two years long. Officers in the grades of O-7 and O-8 on the development track will serve in one or two developing jobs in each of those two grades.[17] Thus officers promoted to O-9 will have served in a total of three developing jobs during their O-7 and O-8 tenures. Officers may retire or be separated after any of these developing jobs. Those O-9s likely to be promoted to O-10 will serve in a single developing job, and those who are not promoted to O-10 will retire at the conclusion of the developing assignment. Officers who serve in using jobs at O-8 will have a single four-year assignment before retirement at that grade. Officers likely to retire from the grade of O-9 will serve in two using positions at that grade. All O-10s will serve in two using positions. The results of this analysis are discussed below in several different contexts. We judged this system as best because it satisfied the established outcome criteria of maximizing stability and accountability in some positions without sacrificing considerable promotion opportunity.

Modeled Outcomes of the New Utilization Paradigm

Despite the concern expressed by the Army and some in Congress that slowing the system to increase accountability and stability in organizations would clog the system and substantially reduce promotion opportunities, this is not the case, certainly not for O-7s and O-8s. Figure 25-2 indicates that the annual number of officers promoted to O-7 increases, as compared with the status quo.[18] This is a result of some officers spending less time at the grade of O-7. However, O-7 assignments are longer, so even with less individual time in grade, organizations benefit from greater stability in O-7 positions. The number of officers promoted to O-8 is equal to that of the status quo. The number of officers promoted annually to O-9 and O-10 each decrease by one, because of the much longer tenure that some O-9s and all O-10s will spend in grade before retirement.

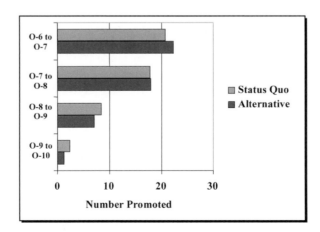

Figure 25-2. *General Officer Promotions—Status Quo Compared to Alternative.*

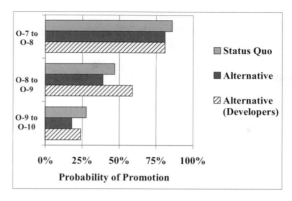

Figure 25-3. *Promotion Probability—Status Quo Compared to Alternative.*

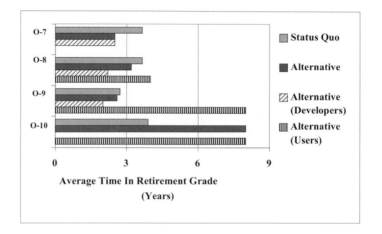

Figure 25-4. *Time in Retirement Grade—Status Quo Compared to Alternative.*

Figure 25-3 shows the likelihood of promotion for officers in the modeled alternative compared with current practice.[19] A promotion probability is indicated for the overall population of officers in the alternative system and also for those officers serving in developing jobs, as compared with the status quo. The probability of promotion from O-7 to O-8 is slightly lower for Army officers in the alternative compared with the status quo. Promotion to O-8 is the same for those in developing jobs and the total population because all O-7 jobs are developing positions. Promotion probability from O-8 to O-9 decreases for the Army as a whole compared with the status quo, but developers are promoted to O-9 at a rate higher than the total population in both the alternative system and the status quo. The likelihood of promotion to O-10 is less than that seen in current practice for both the total population and developers.

Figure 25-4 displays the average time senior officers spend in their retirement grade. For example, under the proposed management paradigm officers retiring from grade O-7 average approximately two and a half years in grade. This average results from the retirements of officers who have one two-year assignment and those who have two two-year assignments. While two and a half years are less than the average O-7 time in grade for current retirees, the alternative is based on assignments longer than those of the current system, in which officers typically fill, on average, two 18-month assignments.

Average time in retirement grade for O-8s in the alternative is slightly shorter. However, the data are for officers serving in developing positions in the modeled alternative as well as officers serving in four-year using positions.[20] Thus, the average time in grade for the modeled alternative tends not to reflect accurately the dual-track system having some O-8s and O-9s who serve two years in grade and having others who serve four years (in the case of O-8s) or eight years (in the case of O-9s). Because all O-10 assignments are in using positions, all modeled officers promoted to O-10 will serve two using assignments, for a total of eight years time in grade, which is considerably longer than the past average of three years time in grade for O-10s.

Figure 25-5 shows the average career length at retirement. The total career length is determined by adding our modeled time as a general officer to the average commission time preceding promotion to O-7.[21] While modeled O-7s who are not promoted to O-8 serve slightly less time in the service than do currently retiring O-7s, officers at the other grades typically have similar (in the case of developers) or longer (in the case of users) military careers in the modeled alternative than in current practice. The longer careers are especially notable among O-9s in using jobs, and O-10s, who are all serving in using jobs.

Figure 25-6 compares average time in job for general officers in the status quo with that in the modeled alternative paradigm. For the alternative, average time is always 24 months for developers and 48 months for users. The mix of developing and using jobs at each grade determines the alternative average time in job.

For Army O-7s, the alternative provides seven months more time in job than the status quo. At O-8, the time in job for the alternative averages approximately

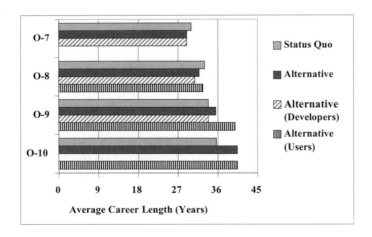

Figure 25-5. *Army Career Length at Retirement—Status Quo Compared to Alternative.*

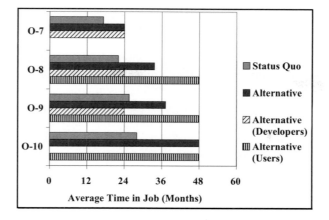

Figure 25-6. *Average Time in Job—Status Quo Compared to Alternative.*

one year longer than the status quo. Because O-9s serving in using jobs in the alternative stay much longer than in the status quo, the average time in job at O-9 is longer in the alternative than in the status quo, even though some developers will serve slightly less time in job than they do in the status quo. By far the largest increase in job tenure occurs at O-10: the alternative provides the Army with 20 more months of utilization from each general officer in each job.

In summary, the Army will experience a greater number of officers promoted to O-7 annually, an equal number to O-8, and one fewer annual promotion to O-9. About half as many rise to O-10, as the length of time that O-10s serve before retirement nearly doubles. Average career length will increase for O-9s and O-10s. Career length will decrease for O-7s and O-8s, but these officers will remain in positions longer than they do in the status quo. In fact, average time in job increases for all grades, and thus organizations will benefit from the stability of leadership tenures longer than those witnessed today. Moreover, individuals will have clearer expectations about their future and, at the apex of their careers, an opportunity to have a more significant organizational and professional impact.

Caveats and Concerns

During the course of our research, several concerns were raised about repercussions from the proposed changes:

- *Retention.* While we heard concerns that officers would not be willing to serve longer time in service and in longer assignments, our interviews with serving and retired general and flag officers suggest that retention will continue to be an individual issue; there will be voluntary leavers and unexpected retirements, but retention of sufficient numbers of general and flag officers should not be a problem. Analytically, we can also assert that, if officers do not behave as predicted, the system may not achieve all the increases in stability and accountability expected, but in no case will the system look worse than today's.

- *Flexibility*. We agree with assertions that the system must remain flexible and that an improved system should not be overly rule-bound; performance and common sense are important. Officers in developing positions may serve longer than two years, and officers in O-8 and O-9 using jobs may get promoted.

- *Performance*. Just as 15 percent of CEOs are derailed for performance-related reasons, the Army should anticipate some performance issues, particularly in cases where officers are promoted into positions beyond their depth or for which they are otherwise unsuited.[22] If unsatisfactory performance is evident during a four-year using assignment, then the situation will need to be confronted and will not be as simple as the graceful exits permitted from the current system of shorter assignments.

- *Compensation*. Many of the senior officers we interviewed mentioned existing shortcomings of the compensation system. Such shortcomings will become even more evident if officers serve longer careers. There should not be penalties for longer service.

Conclusions

With the exception of some O-10 jobs (e.g., service chief, Chairman of the JCS) the current senior officer assignment and promotion system generally does not determine assignment tenure based either on the inherent qualities of different positions or on the way these jobs are used to develop officers. Some assignments should be longer than others. By making the distinction between developing and using positions, the length of some assignments can be extended—which mitigates the Secretary of Defense's concerns—without blocking the promotion of officers—which is a concern of the military services. These longer assignments can coexist with equal or better number of promotions and promotion probability, although some decreased time in grade at O-7 results. Thus, it is possible to extend assignments for the most-senior officers and for some selected O-8 and O-9 positions without limiting the developmental opportunities for fast-trackers destined for further promotion.

Our analysis suggests the value of a revised system based on the paradigm described above. Such a revised system can increase individual accountability and contribution to organizations as well as overall organizational stability. Enhanced organizational performance would result. These benefits come from maximizing the contribution of members of the Army profession who have attained strategic leadership positions, rather than discarding them soon after they have reached the apex of capability to contribute. Time in job is managed, and career tenure and time in grade at retirement become second-order outcomes. Moreover, such a system clarifies expectations for officers in it.

Currently, officer management is generally thought of in terms of "managed flow," and its language is that of fluid dynamics.[23] The central question is: Where do officers go next and how fast? While more attention is paid to the career development of general officers, including consideration of which positions will best pre-pare officers for senior leadership assignments and which individuals are the best candidates for current and future opportunities, the officer management system overall has been focused on rapid movement, as our data show. The metrics are time spent in grade, time spent in service, promotion timing, and promotion probability. The development rule is that all flow on a fixed schedule, with a few exceptions in which the Secretary and the service chief believe more time is needed to develop skills and have the desired organizational impact.

The private sector uses comparable processes in terms of frequent movement of high-potential executives to positions of higher responsibility as a means to test and develop them and for the organization to learn about their capabilities for higher posi-tions. However, the private sector slows the movement of individuals at the apex of their careers, even if they have not reached the highest levels of the organization or of their professions. Further, because the ends of this process are to find the best people for such terminal positions as CEO, service in these positions is longer and continues until performance expectations are not met, or an individual leaves voluntarily, or a company age-based retirement point is reached. This is a "managed use" system. With managed use, the central question is: "Where do they come from and how good are they for higher-level positions?" The metrics are performance, the "quality" of past experience, and the quantity of it.[24] One does not necessarily become broad by the accumulation of specialties, but rather by seeing the business as a whole. Retention is governed by performance; in development, some move and some do not.

While the Army does consider metrics of the type discussed above, the major emphasis is on movement. There are consequences for the Army if such a managed use system were more fully adopted. First, departures would be more episodic than routine. Upon selection of a long-serving executive, those who are competitive but not selected would be expected to leave for other opportunities. Departures cluster around successions, rather than routinely at fixed times. Second, performance departures would be more visible because they would occur with much less service than expected. As one senior officer stated, the system would be less graceful. However, if the private sector experience is any guide, longer tenure in terminal positions would be correlated with greater organizational performance.

If the pattern of developing and using changes for the Army general officers, how will the career paths of other Army officers, particularly the field grades, change? Longer time in job for some or all positions at the top has ripple effects that need to be understood. This question is germane especially for the Army that appears to be moving in this direction. For example, longer time in job without changing the number of jobs would limit access to those jobs for some who now get them. Longer assignments also limit the number of different assignments officers can experience during their career, potentially making it more difficult to satisfy career development requirements. Longer time in service overall might accommo-date the longer time in job to some extent but would reduce promotion opportunity. Extending the promotion zones to maintain promotion opportunity could mitigate the promotion effects of longer time in job or service. Increasing variability around the promotion point, with some officers getting promoted earlier and some officers getting promoted later (to a much greater extent that the Army already does), can also mitigate the effects. Creating alternative career paths based on different definitions of success are also a possibility. These and other options are currently being analyzed in order to understand how to balance the various concerns discussed earlier within a less constrained officer promotion and assignment system.

We conclude that management changes described above could be implemented largely without additional legislation. Present Title 10 authority for 40-year careers for O-10s; 38-year careers for O-9s; and retirement at age 62 (along with the current waiver authority in law) generally is sufficient. However, a change in law could simplify the management of general officers while providing needed flexibility. For example, it should be made possible to extend the assignments of service chiefs, the JCS chairman, and the other officers with fixed terms, without invoking condition of war or national emergency, as required under existing law. Allowing officers to retire with less than three years time in grade would allow them to leave as sound management demanded.[25] Furthermore, as the normal (i.e., Social Security-eligible) retirement age in the United States gradually rises to age 67, there appears to be no reason why the military retirement age should not increase as well. (The current age of 62 in law dates from the 1860s; the intervening 150 years have seen great strides in health, vigor, and longevity.)

Although this system could mostly be implemented within current legislative management constraints, DoD should consider requesting compensation changes. Such changes could include uncapping pay at senior levels, continuing the accumulation of retirement benefits to 100 percent at 40 years of service, and basing retirement pay on uncapped figures. Additionally, because some officers who serve in the shorter developing assignments will not be promoted, they will require time-in-grade waivers at retirement. High-3 retirement will be an issue for these officers in future years because it bases retirement pay on the highest three years of basic pay, and they will not have spent three years in their last grade.

Finally, a changed system will require some flexibility. For example, nonperformers must be susceptible to early termination; otherwise, longer assignments might entail keeping them on for an unconscionable period.

Recommendations

We consider the input from the interviews with serving and retired generals and flag officers in our recommendations, but the recommendations are largely drawn from the analysis. The Army and the Department of Defense should:

- Rationalize career paths.
- Identify positions at each grade as either developing or using jobs. This process should allow job responsibilities and the developmental experiences desired for members of the profession to form the basis of the position designation.
- Set goals for time in jobs and for the number and timing of jobs an individual officer fills. Using assignments should be longer than developing assignments. Ideally,

developing assignments for line officers would be a minimum of two years and using assignments a minimum of four years. Our research suggests that officers promoted to O-9 should complete three developing assignments while in the grades of O-7 and O-8, that officers retiring from O-8 should complete one four-year using assignment, and that officers retiring from the grades of O-9 or O-10 should complete two four-year using assignments in their retirement grade.

- Pursue changes in compensation.
- Maintain a flexible system in order to deal with individual performance shortcomings and other exceptions.

Notes

1. This chapter summarizes RAND research addressing changes to general and flag officer management in all four military services, published in Margaret C. Harrell, Harry J. Thie, Peter Schirmer, and Kevin Brancato, *Aligning the Stars: Improvements to General and Flag Officer Management*, MR-1712-OSD (Santa Monica, CA: RAND, 2004).

2. William L. Lennox, Jr., "Introduction," in *The Future of the Army Profession*, project directors, Don M. Snider and Gayle L. Watkins, ed. Lloyd J. Matthews (Boston, MA: McGraw-Hill, 2002), xv-xvi.

3. Army general officers include those in pay grades O-7 (brigadier general), O-8 (major general), O-9 (lieutenant general), and O-10 (general). By law there are about 900 general and flag officers in the four military services, of which approximately 50 percent are O-7s, 35 percent O-8s, and 15 percent O-9s and O-10s.

4. Army O-10s serve, on average, 3.9 years as O-10s, and 83 percent of them retire before age 60; whereas, CEOs serve, on average, 8.4 years, and 69 percent of them stay past age 60. (Charles J. Hadlock, Scott Lee, and Robert Parrino, "Chief Executive Officer Careers in Regulated Environments: Evidence from Electric and Gas Utilities," *Journal of Law and Economics 45* (October 2002): 535-63; and Chuck Lucier, Eric Spiegel, and Rob Schuyt, "Why CEOs Fall: The Causes and Consequences of Turnover at the Top," *Strategy & Business* (Third Quarter, 2002).

5. Robert F. Morrison and Roger R. Hock, "Career Building: Learning from Cumulative Work Experience," in *Career Development in Organizations* (Indianapolis, IN: Jossey-Bass, 1986) 237.

6. Morgan W. McCall, Jr., Michael M. Lombardo, and Ann M. Morrison, *The Lessons of Experience: How Successful Executives Develop on the Job* (New York: The Free Press, 1989).

7. C. Brooklyn Derr, Candace Jones, and Edmund L. Toomey, "Managing High-Potential Employees: Current Practices in Thirty-three U.S. Corporations," *Human Resource Management* 27 (Fall 1989): 275.

8. Michael A. Campion, Lisa Cheraskin, and Michael J. Stevens, "Career-Related Antecedents and Outcomes of Job Rotation," *Academy of Management Journal* 37 (December 1994): 1535.

9. Morrison and Hock, 240.

10. Ibid., 241.

11. John J. Gabarro, *The Dynamics of Taking Charge* (Boston, MA: Harvard Business School Press, 1987).

12. Based on a study of CEO turnover between 1971 and 1994. Tenure and age at retirement of CEOs in 15 industry groups were compared to those of CEOs in regulated industries using *Forbes* executive compensation surveys, S&P's COMPUSTAT database, and succession announcements reported in the *Wall Street Journal*. The data we report are for CEOs in the 15 industry groups; data for CEOs in regulated industries are not much different. Charles J. Hadlock, Scott Lee, and Robert Parrino, 535-63.

13. We recognize that "general" officers are no longer considered to be part of a particular branch, so this is really a description of their background as company and field grade officers. There were approximately 2,500 officers and 1,150 positions (many no longer in existence) included in our original analysis of all four military services, reflecting over two decades of data. All further references to the line are to this more narrowly defined group of officers.

14. We recognize that 10 percent may not seem to be a particularly high cut-off, but there are 11 job categories, and officers have only one or two assignments in the grades of O-8 and O-9. If the categories were of equal size, we would expect to see each one on only about 10 to 20 percent of officer resumes.

15. "High-frequency" is more convenient terminology, but it really just means "not low-frequency."

16. This permits service flexibility and selectivity of officers for promotion. Since developing experiences entail a sacrifice of performance, the astute organization will try to minimize developing experiences, subject to the constraint that they provide just enough developing experiences to meet their long-term needs.

17. That is, some officers will serve in one developing job as an O-7 and then complete two such assignments as an O-8. Other officers will serve in two developing positions as an O-7 and then one as an O-8.

18. This is the annual number for the three branches cited earlier (Infantry, Armor, and Artillery) and not the number for all Army promotions to O-7.

19. Promotion probability is defined as the number promoted from a grade divided by the number promoted to that grade. We calculated the status quo and alternatives on that basis. This is different from promotion opportunity, which uses the total number in a promotion zone as the denominator.

20. Officers not promoted to O-9 or O-10 after serving in a two-year developing assignment would retire with two years in grade.

21. In general, most services (with the exception of the Marine Corps) promote to O-7 soonest those officers who will eventually be promoted to O-10.

22. Charles J. Hadlock, Scott Lee, and Robert Parrino, 535-63.

23. See, for example, Part III: Officer Flow Data, in the *Defense Manpower Requirements Report*, USD (P&R), May 2000. This part provides Flow Management Plans for each of the military services for the commissioned officer grades of O-1 to O-10. The health of the officer management system is demonstrated by flows, that is, the promotions "in" and "out" over a five-year period in response to retirements and other losses.

24. "Achieving generalization by accumulating specialties is not sufficient for obtaining the broad view of the organization necessary for high-level management effectiveness." John Boon, RAND, unpublished research. See also Peter Drucker, *The Practice of Management* (New York: Harper and Row Publishers, 1954).

25. At the time of this writing, Congress was considering several of these proposals as part of the National Defense Authorization Act for FY2004.

26 From Reserve to Full Partner: Transforming Reserve Professionals[1]

Dallas D. Owens

Two Army chiefs of staff have now carried the banner for Army transformation. The focus has changed from fielding the "objective" force to reorganizing for a "future" force. Even as transformation's leadership and goals have changed, it remains primarily focused on the combat arms and the active component (AC). Other portions of the Army, whether AC combat support or service support branches or reserve component (RC)—which includes both Army National Guard (ARNG) and U.S. Army Reserve (USAR)—are expected to adapt to meet the needs of changing AC combat formations. And adapt they will, just as they have in past periods of rapid change. But one portion of the Army, the RC, is faced with the additional, simultaneous burden of a transformation designed to change the very nature of reserve military service.

> What was once a "force in reserve" has become a full partner across the spectrum of operations to satisfy the demands and needs of our country and our Army around the world.
>
> —LT. GEN. JAMES R. HELMLY
> CHIEF, ARMY RESERVE, 2003[2]

Current Army transformation is essentially structural and will result in a variety of organizational changes, including equipment and doctrine. These changes will certainly have an impact on the RC, but they are the kind of change that the current reserve leadership and many of its soldiers have dealt with in the course of their service.[3] With less training time and fewer resources, the RC adjusts more slowly than its AC counterparts, but has always changed sufficiently to meet new military requirements.

In October 2003 the Department of Defense (DoD) announced that simply "rebalancing" the force structure between the AC and RC would meet military manpower requirements for the global war on terrorism.[4] Only three months later, however, DoD determined that world conditions offered a "window of opportunity to transform and change our Guard and Reserve forever."[5] In January 2004 DoD released the detailed plan to transform the RC; DoD continued to call the plan "rebalancing," but proposed far more sweeping changes, designed to alter the philosophical and legal underpinning of reserve service.[6] Concurrently, the ARNG and USAR made public their support for portions of the DoD plan by announcing their own initiatives. The Army Reserve named its undertaking the Federal Reserve Restructuring Initiative,[7] while the Army National Guard simply used the term "transformation plan."[8]

Transformation has many aims, but at bottom it is intended to increase the force's effectiveness for conducting future operations. The individual soldier's importance is often noted, but success is generally measured in terms of the force's collective capabilities. When "soldiers" are used as the unit of analysis, recruitment and retention rates are the predominant measures of impact, often used as indexes for career satisfaction and other individual variables. An equally valuable measure, and the theme of other chapters in this book, is the impact of transformation on the Army profession (collectively) and on the nature of individual participation in that profession.

The goal of this chapter is to extend research about defense transformation and its impact on the Army profession to the members of the RC. First, I shall define transformation as experienced by the RC. Second, I will examine the characteristics of AC soldiers as members of the Army profession to determine the extent to which they are also shared by RC soldiers. Demonstrating shared profession-defining characteristics should serve as the basis for claims to common professional membership. Third, at the individual level of analysis, I will examine the likely impacts of transformation on those centrally defining characteristics to determine impacts on RC professionals. Finally, mitigating measures will be proposed to avoid or lessen the negative impacts of defense transformation as identified by the previous analysis.

Soldiers are members of the RC in one of several categories, each with unique requirements for peacetime participation in the Army and legal stipulations for federal mobilization. The analysis here, however, is restricted to the membership category with the most members, i.e., drilling reservists, consisting of those unit members who constitute the majority of the Selected Reserve. Within the two reserve components these reservists are called "M-day" (mobilization-day) soldiers in the ARNG and "TPU" (troop-program unit) soldiers in the USAR. These two categories are of great concern to the AC since they comprise the majority of the reserve forces used during times of foreign deployment or domestic emergency. Accordingly, they are the first priority for transformation. Full-time reservists, or Active Guard Reserve (AGR), are excluded from this analysis because they comprise only a small percentage of the force and resemble the AC in their form of service. The Individual Ready Reserve (IRR) and Retired Reserve are large categories, but they are also excluded because their service contribution during emergences is relatively small, mobilization requirements for them are more restrictive, and current transformation policies focus on them less significantly.[9]

Transformation: What Will Change for Reservists

Reservists are affected by two different aspects of transformation: structural, i.e., organizational change; and changes to the nature of reserve service. Today, in the early stages of the Army's structural transformation, long-term effects on the RC are largely speculative. For the AC, the most apparent early results are the Stryker brigades, originally intended to be an interim change until objective force equipment and structure could be developed toward the end of the decade. Gen. Peter Schoomaker, the current Army Chief of Staff, revised this intent, resulting in a "Modularity Execution Order for the 3rd Infantry Division (Mechanized),"[10] with similar orders soon following for other combat arms formations. But it is unclear how deeply or how soon AC modularity will affect RC organizations.[11] Current plans as of this writing (January 2005) call for the ARNG to field one Stryker brigade and some number of modular combat arms brigades, a process eventually to embrace the entire National Guard force. The RC units affiliated with the 3rd Infantry Division (3ID) will, however, "continue to source the 3ID," meaning they will require some change to meet 3ID support requirements.[12]

Ultimately, the ARNG's echelons and its formations will reflect the AC modular and rotational realignment, affecting most of its combat arms and associated lower-echelon support forces. However, the USAR, with an emphasis on logistics functions, will also require reorganization to support rotational and lower-echelon AC formations. Evan a rotational AC expeditionary force sized well below foreseeable levels of employment, which is the current case, requires a complementary RC force. To complement the AC effectively, the RC must be capable of providing a matching force that can sustain some acceptable constant rate of mobilization for expeditionary deployment and supporting missions. But the RC historically has not served such a role. Moreover, it is not currently designed to do so effectively, and there are Title 10 impediments to achieving the necessary degree of training flexibility.[13]

Transformation of the RC is thus designed to create a force capable of sustaining its new expeditionary role, as envisioned by DoD, for an indefinite period. The DoD vision is a RC force that is flexible, competent, quickly accessible, and capable of sustaining moderate levels of mobilization. Projected levels of mobilization, primarily ARNG and USAR forces, are 100,000 to 150,000 for the next three to five years, possibly falling later to about 30,000 to 40,000, the level prevailing on 11 September 2001 when the terrorists launched their attack on the United States.[14] Methods proposed for achieving such a force include: (1) enhancing early responsiveness by increasing the number of units that are more often used (at the expense of lesser-used formations), increasing modularity, and increasing accessibility and flexibility; (2) resolving stressed career fields by shifting forces from lower- to higher-use specialties and from heavier to lighter combat forces; and (3) employing innovative management practices to create a "continuum of service," an RC rotational overseas presence, reach-back initiatives, and mobilization process improvements.

The first two methods are traditional techniques for reforming RC organizations and, though expensive and requiring years to implement, are relatively benign for the Army profession. The third method, however, will require changes to current laws and actual revision through updating of the purpose of the RC.[15] The first and second methods have impact on organization, but the third greatly affects the lives and careers of individual reservists and has the potential to alter the very nature of the reserve components of the Army profession.

Of course, some of the changes in the purpose of the RC are merely the formalization of the de facto situation. For instance, a sustained RC mobilization has existed for over a decade, but as Table 26-1 indicates, the number mobilized increased significantly during that period.

In the early 1990s, the average number mobilized at any point in time was about 15,000; it rose to 35,000 in the late 1990s, and jumped to over 100,000 after September of 2001, where it has remained. Before Operation Desert Shield/Storm in 1990-1991, reservists assumed that they existed more for deterrence than fighting

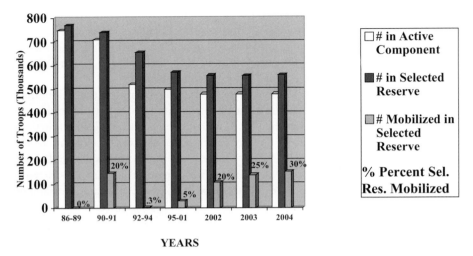

Table 26-1. *Profile of Selected Reserve (ARNG/USAR) Mobilization.*

wars, while accepting that they might have to fight the "big one." Following Desert Shield/Storm, however, it became clear that their "unwritten contract" had changed. Having to fight the dreaded big war with the entire RC was now much less likely, but much more of the RC would be required to support frequent non-big-war operations.

Today, at the beginning of 2005, expectations are that at any point in time much of the RC will be deployed to fight in the global war on terror. The most optimistic prospect is that the numbers required for such a constant mobilization will be reduced from the 100,000+ to a manageable and more predictable rotational level. Clearly, expectations of RC have changed from "if" to "when" and "how often" and "how long" their service will be required.

RC Soldiers and the Army Profession

A profession may be defined in its simplest form as an occupation that is based on theoretical and practical knowledge and training.[16] Others would further restrict the concept to "relatively high status occupations whose members apply abstract knowledge."[17] RC soldiers certainly share an occupation with AC soldiers (a type of work), albeit usually on a part-time basis. But it is less clear how the AC and RC soldiers share in the Army profession The Army profession, like all complex organizations, is stratified across multiple dimensions, with power and prestige being two of the more important. The analysis of internal relationships between the profession's sub-groups should reveal much about their relative ability to affect their profession and their susceptibility to internal and external influences such as the current transformation of the Army profession.[18] Thus the degree to which Army RC soldiers are members of the Army profession can best be evaluated in terms of four concepts that are central to defining that profession: jurisdiction, legitimacy, expertise, and career.

Jurisdiction and Legitimacy

A jurisdiction is a "domain within which expert knowledge is applied . . . it is sometimes an actual place . . . and sometimes a slice or aspect of life."[19] The Army's jurisdictions are primarily an aspect of life (fighting wars), but occasionally tied to a place (homeland security). The three Army components (Active, Reserve, and National Guard) combine efforts when negotiating with other institutions for control of jurisdictions. When such negotiated competitions are settled favorably for the Army, all components win.[20] But RC members are not necessarily equal partners either in the negotiations or as benefactors when the Army wins. The predecessor organizations to today's RC ceased to be competitors within the Army's jurisdictional competitions when the RC was subordinated under federal authority in the early 20th century.[21] That subordination is in part responsible for the RC's disproportionate relegation to functions needed in non-war-fighting jurisdictions such as stability operations and homeland security, where the Army shares the expert work with other competitors.[22]

In such situations, the components' prestige rises and falls together, but is not equal. Most clients view the RC as having less "sustained" expertise for performing most of the Army's core and some core support functions, but view them as sufficiently competent to warrant legitimacy as AC partners.[23] Put another way, with less training time and money, the RC, as units if not as individuals, is not expected to sustain readiness or to manifest professional attributes to the degree expected of the AC.

Thus, relative component prestige within the Army is linked to the RC's subordination and is important in the internal debate over which jurisdictions it should pursue. The consequences of this unequal internal debate are that the more powerful component, the AC, negotiates for and garners those "core" jurisdictions and associated tasks in behalf of which it is the exclusive repository of expert knowledge, and it defines as less "core" those jurisdictions it must share. Hence, the units capable of conducting war have become more concentrated in the AC. This differential concentration of high-prestige expert knowledge is both a product of differential power and prestige and a perpetuator of the condition ensuring the AC-RC jurisdictional partnership remains unequal.

Professional Expertise

The RC contains all categories of Army expertise, but not equally across both of its components. The ARNG is heavily invested in the Army's core expertise of warfighting while the USAR is more associated with core support and acquired (i.e., non-specifically military) expertise.[24] Although the RC shares core expertise with the active forces, the AC tightly controls certification, RC readiness is uneven, RC leadership is clearly subordinate, and RC size is in decline. Examples: the ARNG must have its combat units certified "ready" by the AC prior to deployment; readiness across RC combat brigades varies greatly; RC leadership is not found above brigade command for combat formations (and is usually much lower), and the ARNG is currently shifting structure away from combat arms.

The certification and readiness issues have been addressed in recent years. The certification process now has more RC input, thanks largely to the Army Forces Commands' Training Support XXI program.[25] This program created integrated (AC and RC) training support brigades and divisions. The program was clearly having positive impacts on RC training by the late 1990s, several years after its creation through the enactment of the 1993 National Defense Authorization Act. A survey of RC officers attending the concluding two-week residency phase of the Army War College Distance Education class of 2004, most of whom had experienced mobilization, was much more positive about RC input into the certification process than anecdotal evidence of previous years would have predicted.[26] With regard to the history of uneven readiness among RC combat brigades, the issue is being addressed in the current transformation. The designation of selected brigades as "higher priority" has been removed, and transformation guidelines give assurances that all transformed brigades will be resourced equally, though there may be fewer of them.

However, the issue of differential leadership positions remains especially salient. Only since 2001 have two RC Army members consistently held the rank of lieutenant general.[27] The Army's organizational elite is clearly composed of AC generals. Good reasons for this arrangement may abound, but the results remain clear—the RC leadership has little power to affect Army policy.

Both the ARNG and the USAR, particularly the latter, have extensive core support and non-specifically military expertise, which are more often the shared developmental responsibility of the Army and society. This shared character, even with specific Army application, places such expertise on the fringe of the profession. For example, logistics support such as land surface transportation is very similar in either a civilian or military setting. The trucks may be different, as might be the cargo, but the linking of cargo to wheels at origin and delivering it to some destination involve similar management techniques and technologies. The Army is responding with an increasing tendency to contract some of that work to civilians, thus placing military transportation personnel and assets in competition with those civilians. Civilian firms now move most military cargo outside of combat settings. Even within "hazardous duty" areas, such as Afghanistan, nearly all of the fuel and dry cargo, except ammunition, is transported by civilian firms, either U.S. or host nation.[28] Similar transport patterns have evolved in Iraq, much of it paid for by a $327 million "theater transportation" contract between DoD and Halliburton subsidiaries.[29]

Thus, the RC does share professional expertise with its AC counterparts, but as we have seen they are short of being equal partners. The RC's expertise is more heavily in fringe core support (low-prestige) areas or, when in high-prestige (core) areas, they are subjected to a number of constraints on their application of the expertise. There are certainly reasonable explanations for these constraints, such as lack of resources, but that only partially removes inter-component friction.

RC Careers

In a manner similar to that of the AC, RC members may choose to participate in a formally patterned military career. However, the RC "part-time" career does not fit Andrew Abbott's description of a career as a "single occupational skill or identity characterizing individuals for their entire working lives," and thereby misses "probably the most central single constituent of the idea of profession."[30]

Both AC and RC soldiers, like all people, have competing and prioritized identities, but unlike the AC, most RC soldiers have competing work identities. And, of the competing work identities, the Army work is often the one with less economic value. Many RC members have careers or professions that are not only economically essential for them, but may also have been acquired only through previous large personal investments in education, training, and commitment. Traditional duty requirements for reservists, typically some number of weekends and two weeks during the summer, were designed to avoid incompatibility with most civilian jobs or careers, thus allowing individuals an opportunity to pursue both Army and civilian work. Individual reservists, however, especially those in leadership positions, have historically encountered conflicting work demands, even during times when the RC was not being mobilized.[31] As demands from the Army have increased in recent years, work conflicts have increased proportionally for many RC members. Those conflicts have not been evenly distributed across the RC force, since all members have not been mobilized and RC soldiers' civilian work situations vary greatly. In fact, civilian work situations for RC soldiers vary as greatly as they do for the general population; some are retired from civilian jobs, unemployed, or students while others are CEOs of major corporations, members of Congress, and all variations of white- and blue-collar workers.

Unlike the characteristics of professions discussed above, participation in careers is, by design, not similar for AC and RC soldiers. Even without proposed transformational changes, RC members are at a decided career disadvantage compared to their AC peers. To the extent that transformational changes make competitions between civilian jobs and military service more difficult to balance, the RC members' ability to have a career in the Army profession is further reduced. Transformation's impact on the Army is obviously intended to produce positive changes, and there will no doubt be many. However, change is seldom entirely positive or negative and is most likely to be positive for those aspects of an organization that it targets for improvement—but the Army *as a profession* was not that target. Though unintended, the profession will be affected, as will its RC subset.

The Impact of Structural Transformation on RC Professionals

The preceding comparison of RC and AC soldiers across the four characteristics that define the Army profession supports the position that RC soldiers' membership in the profession is similar to that of the AC except for career pattern. But RC soldiers' membership is likely to be in less prestigious roles, outside of core expertise, and less internally legitimate. Their more marginal, tenuous, and vulnerable status places the RC at risk to both internally and externally imposed disruptive forces, such as the two types of transformation-induced change discussed earlier—change in structure and change in the nature of reserve service itself.

It does not appear that structural changes required of the RC will strike at the heart of its constituent soldiers' professional characteristics; rather, it will have minor impacts. For example, the proposed changes in organization, equipment, and doctrine further relegate the RC to expertise of lower priority and often in competition with that of civilian contractors. The USAR is acquiescent to these changes because of its selected core competencies; the ARNG, fighting to retain its combat role, is less enthusiastic. Thus, the results from implementing proposed structural changes would be to further decrease RC soldiers' prestige and solidify the AC's dominant leadership role in the profession.

To counter the potential loss in prestige, the USAR has proposed measures to increase self-certification as part of its Federal Reserve Restructuring Initiative. The ARNG attempted similar measures with its "home-station mobilization" proposal in 1998. The ARNG efforts produced only minor by-exception changes to the process, and it remains to be seen whether the USAR proposal will fare better in repairing a process that has been described as "lethargic, slow, cumbersome, and weighted with redundancies and multiple stops."[32]

An argument of some appeal is that the increased frequency of expeditionary deployments by RC soldiers will entail greater AC and RC convergency, thereby mitigating differences in prestige through the de facto removal of the distinctions discussed earlier. Statements to the effect that "I could not tell who was AC and who was RC" are more frequently heard in today's Army. Such anecdotal attaboys may be complimentary to individuals or small groups of soldiers, but are far from universal and not yet sufficient to illustrate significant gains in the RC's overall stature.

The current high demand for and dependence on the RC are not purely a function of the AC's desperate short-handedness. Based on recent contributions, the demand is in part the result of confidence that the RC can perform. Increased confidence and willingness to call on the RC are indicators of the AC's acceptance of RC peers into the profession. Yet, many of the presentations by senior Army leaders at the U.S. Army War College indicate that acceptance remains qualified, with support varying by category of reservist and type of unit. The AC's leadership is not unanimous in its preferences, but it also is clearly not unified in its enthusiasm for embracing RC members as equal participants in the profession.

The Impact of Transformation on the Nature of RC Service

Like structural changes, impacts on the nature of reserve service are neither all positive nor all negative. Impacts on individuals are largely a function of their particular civilian occupational status, and thus are highly variable. Emphasis here will be on the negatives, not because they predominate, but rather because identifying them is a necessary prelude to the possibility of avoidance or mitigation.

These impacts on reservists are of two types—increased time requirements and new patterns of those requirements. Excessive time requirements, especially for mid-level and senior leaders, have long been an issue creating Army-civilian occupational conflicts. Charles Moskos said in 1990, that those conflicts were responsible for increasingly populating the reserves with "career NCOs and officers . . . from a narrow band of civilian backgrounds" that excluded successful business executives and professionals.[33]

For the past few decades the pattern of time requirements was designed to decrease the likelihood of such Army-civilian occupational conflicts. In other words, the times traditionally designated for reserve service—weekends and short periods in the summer—were selected to minimize conflicts with civilian job demands for most workers. Proposals for a rotational expeditionary force capable of supporting constant high levels of mobilization, however, will require a radical change in that pattern. The most obvious change, using optimistic scenarios, is the likelihood of repetitive long-term (one year or more) mobilizations in cycles of five or six years. The less obvious change is the additional time necessitated by post-mobilization reconstitution and intensified pre-mobilization train-up periods.

Increases in service requirements will have consequences that are both real and, perhaps more importantly, perceived. The actual increased time demands will require career conflict resolution by many more soldiers; the Army has developed legal and support mechanisms to assist them. But the formalization of a rotational RC, with well-publicized plans for long-term continuous mobilization, makes clear to reservists what their future holds and sharpens perceptions for the longer-term change. Prior generations of reservists safely assumed that national policy and legal constraints made it very unlikely that they would ever be mobilized. Even during the late 1990s, only a small percentage of the RC were mobilized and those were often confined to specific career fields or volunteers. Now, however, transformation to a rotational RC will remove the illusion that mobilization will be infrequent and for the few.

What is most important, individuals are affected negatively by the increased demands of deployments when that increase diminishes their ability to resolve conflicts among their competing work identities. Individuals from nearly any occupation experience some level of increased conflict when their absence is not explicitly part of the condition of their employment. That conflict increases when absences are longer, more frequent, more unpredictable, or perceived as less legitimate. Further, both research and anecdotal evidence confirm that RC members in leadership positions are expected and often required to spend significant amounts of unpaid time to fulfill their duties.[34] The new demands of a deployable RC are likely to increase the likelihood that occupational tensions will be resolved in favor of the "full-time," economically ascendant occupation. Potentially, the results could well be a younger, less experienced, and less expert RC force.

To achieve heightened focus and emphasis in light of this leadership challenge, the Chief of the Army Reserve declared 2004 "The Year of the Army Reserve Leader" and created a Directorate of Leadership Development to redesign the Army Reserve's leadership program.[35]

Identifying RC Professionals Most Affected

As explained above, negative impacts occur when the reservist can no longer balance Army requirements with civilian work requirements. Balance can be made difficult by frequent short requirements or by periodic long requirements, depending on the civilian occupation or profession. Legal protections prohibit employers from discriminating against employees who are mobilized or ordered to annual training; it encourages employer support for short-term demands. However, legal issues are not the primary consideration for most RC soldiers; the individual dilemma faced by soldiers is with competing occupations where their client base, career progression, or some other aspect of their occupation is damaged by short-term demands or long absences.

One approach to understanding the conflicts created by soldiers holding dual professional memberships is to categorize civilian professions by common characteristics and then analyze the compatibility of those characteristics with the increased demands for reserve service. Edgar Borgotta and Rhonda Montgomery have generated such categories. Though the category names are not always intuitively meaningful or universally accepted, the resulting groupings of professions have heuristic value for examining negative impacts of transformation.[36] In this categorization, members of "high prestige" professions are the most obviously affected by such changes in the nature of reserve service; they would experience adverse client-based effects that are relatively easy to predict. This category of professional includes doctors, lawyers, and clergy.[37] Short-term reserve activations are difficult for these professionals to reconcile, but periodic long absences are simply disastrous to their professional practice. The success of their practice depends on professional-client service continuity; if professionals are not available to their clients and service needs are frequent, competitors will take over their work.

Members of the "newer" professions, which include dentists, engineers, accountants, and architects, encounter a similar set of work conflicts, though more of them work in larger organizations that can provide client continuity. Since these professions are less established, to be successful their members must be conscientious in meeting occupational gates, building relevant experience, and demonstrating skill requirements. Their ability to meet these requirements and sustain a client base is negatively affected to some degree by short-term competing demands and certainly by periodic long absences.

The third category of adversely affected professionals consists of the emergent professions (e.g., pharmacists and chiropractors) and the "semi-professions" (i.e., nurses, public school teachers, social workers, and librarians).[38] This third category might also include police officers, firefighters, and various other public officials. Some of these individuals also have clients, but competition for clients is seldom the source of their occupational conflict. Rather, they are faced with day-to-day issues created by changing schedules, after-hours work, work-team commitments, periodic training requirements, loyalty to their community-based constituents, and a host of other requirements expected from such demanding occupations. Short-term reserve demands are an irritant and stress to already busy schedules. Long-term demands can stress their place of employment, particularly when it is a small organization, and create hardships for fellow employees. Either of these consequences can cause guilt or employment insecurities, even though the law prevents blatantly negative consequences.

Though DoD and the Army "have long recognized the need to collect and report [reservists'] civilian occupation information . . . the track record of comprehensively collecting and reporting current and accurate information remains spotty at best."[39] Given this caveat, Table 26-2 shows the number of RC officers and enlisted soldiers serving in military occupations that match the Borgotta and Montgomery classification of civilian professions.

Of the three professional categories treated in Table 26-2, the first two are the most likely to be civilian professions that match RC members' Army occupational skills, and they are also the most likely to be negatively affected by changes to the nature of reserve service transformation. As the numbers demonstrate, however, the third category is the source of far more RC soldiers than the other two combined. Many in this category hold RC skills that are in high demand, such as military police. Some also depend on their civilian occupations for experience that is directly transferable to their reserve skills; others, such as nurses, usually depend on non-Army training, development, and certification and are likely to be civilian professional nurses.

Category	Professions	RC Officers*	RC Enlisted*
1. High prestige professions	Doctors Lawyers Clergy	2,448 2,410 1,068 *Total:* 5,926	1,625 Legal Assistants 1,230 Chaplain Assistants *Total:* 2,855
2. Newer Professions	Dentists Engineers Accountants Architects	830 1,044 651 0 *Total:* 2,525	1,300 Dental Assistants 5,000 Engineers*** 495 Accountants *Total:* 6,800
3.a. Emergent Professions	Pharmacists Chiropractors	0 0	373 Pharmacy specialists
3.b. Semi-professions	Nurses School Teachers Social Workers** Librarians Police Officers Firefighters Public Officials	6,442 0 2,855** 0 2,385 0 1,972 *Total:* 13,654	28,000 Medical Care, Biomedical Services, and Allied Health Care Specialists. Over 10,000 in Law Enforcement and Firefighting. 4,000 in Civil Affairs. *Total:* 42,000

*SelRes members, taken from Official Guard and Reserve Manpower Strengths and Statistics (FY2003 Summary) and converted using DoD Occupational Conversion Manual 1312.1-M.
**Includes all behavioral scientists.
***Mapping, surveying, and drafting specialists and construction engineers.

Table 26-2. *Military Job Overlap with Civilian Professions.*

Though relatively small, the first group consists mostly of officers who are the most difficult to replace because their skills require long periods of non-military training and require development and certification by non-Army organizations. Doctors especially are likely to perform the same duties in either a military or civilians setting; they are likely to be more committed to their medical "master" profession than to the practice venue.

All three categories of professions have large numbers of enlisted support personnel, but the higher-prestige and newer professions rely more on civilian education and certification for their officers than for their supporting enlisted soldiers. With the exception of nurses and to some degree public officials (civil affairs), the Army certifies its own within the third category. Civilian experience is valued for police officers and firefighters, but is not a prerequisite for becoming either an officer or enlisted soldier in military police and firefighting units. The number of reserve military police who are civilian police is unknown, but nearly 50 percent of the personnel in the first reserve military police brigades to deploy to Iraq were civilian police officers and firefighters. That percentage is likely to be less for the new military police units being created from less-often-used units such as artillery,[40] but police officers and firefighters are a frequent source of personnel for other types of units.[41]

Decreasing the Negative Impacts

Any attempt to avoid, correct, or mitigate the negative impacts of defense transformation should not be allowed to threaten its primary goals, since that would be self-defeating. The RC is currently a de facto full but unequal partner with the AC; transformation to a rotational RC merely formalizes that arrangement and attempts to make it more effective. It also removes any chance for RC soldiers, except for the most irrational, to deny the immediacy and seriousness of their RC service requirements. Recent trends towards increased requirements for RC forces will not be reversed without huge increases in the size of the AC or significant reductions in the number or magnitude of military operations. Neither of these courses appears likely in the next few years.

It is unknown how long and at what level RC "full partnership" will be needed in the open-ended war on terrorism. The assumptions about how many RC soldiers are required, and for how long, determine how completely the concept of service as a reservist must change. Returning to Table 26-1, the rate of mobilization during the 7-year period prior to the terrorist attacks of 11 September 2001 averaged about 5 percent of the RC. This rate could be supported indefinitely without fundamental changes in the nature of reserve service. Efficiencies, re-balancing, and rotational policies for a portion of the force would still be needed, but not changes to the fundamental concept of service. But if the post-2003 spike to over 30 percent of the force is to be sustained for several years, fundamental changes in the concept of service are imperative. Nothing short of legislative mandates to the Army Reserve and National Guard—changing purpose, size, structure, and service obligations—can effectively meet such demands.

Moving to the individual level of analysis, and assuming this worst-case of sustained high levels of full partnering for many years, how can we lessen the negative impacts of transformation for the individuals in the most affected portions of the RC profession? Changes in roles and missions are never a win/win outcome for all service members. No matter what is done to decrease impacts, some service members will simply be unable to accommodate changes and will be lost to the RC. The goal is to reduce such loss or somehow replace those who cannot be retained. In other words, the strategies for decreasing impacts on the Army and RC can have the goal of retaining expertise by reducing or accommodating the impact, or, failing that, relinquishing uniformed expertise by resorting to non-specifically military sources. The former is most desirable from the perspective of the profession and many of its members; the latter may damage the profession, but retains the Army's access to expertise that is necessary for performing its most highly valued jurisdictions.

Reducing Negative Impacts: Retaining Expertise

Negative impacts on groups can be reduced either by modifying the source of impact or by changing some aspect of the group. Modifying the source is less disruptive and more desirable for reducing the impacts of reserve service transformation, but must be done without diminishing the desirable effects of transformation. Omitting doctors, lawyers, and dentists from the rotational base would reduce impacts on those professionals most likely to be negatively affected (see Table 26-2). Their service contracts could be designed to restrict duration, frequency, or type of service for any mobilization short of what is now called full mobilization—the outright defense of the homeland. Without such exceptional measures, the services of this small but valuable group will almost certainly be lost to the RC. Such service contract adjustments are an extension of DoD's proposed "continuum of service," a subset of "innovative management practices"[42]

Another method for reducing impacts on the force is to change the group's internal Army affiliation. If the RC cannot sustain the expertise, perhaps the AC can. With effective incentives, the AC could expand their medical, legal, and dental corps and retain the expertise within the Army. This would not, however, benefit individuals who are current members of the RC profession, unless they joined the AC. An alternative would be to share functions with other military services by creating Joint Corps for the desired fields of expertise.

Neither of these methods would be particularly successful for reducing impacts on the emergent professions or "semi-professions." RC soldiers from these professions are needed in current operations for their civilian expertise (police and firefighters) or civilian-certified skills (nurses and public officials). Even when individuals from this personnel pool are not used by the RC for their civilian skills, they are an important source for RC leaders and hence are the heart of the RC profession. Current rebalancing proposals increase the number of AC soldiers in military police and civil affairs, removing some early deployment demands on their RC counterparts but not reducing the need for large RC numbers for stability and reconstruction operations. Most replacement military police and firefighters, many from artillery ARNG units, are less likely to bring civilian police and firefighting experience into their reserve jobs. Additionally, if Moskos' predictions of 1990 are correct, these replacements will come from an increasingly "narrow band of civilian backgrounds" that demand less achievement and leadership skills.[43]

Better screening and placement procedures for individuals entering RC service will somewhat decrease losses in expertise. More effort must be given to ensure matching of civilian to military skills and identification of potential leaders. With a diminishing pool of specialized skills and leadership ability, the RC cannot afford lost opportunities to identify and develop valuable expertise that is also sought by the Army's competitors for jurisdictions. Any further expertise lost to the Army lessens its chances of favorable settlement in those competitions.

Reducing Negative Impacts: Relinquishing Expertise

A final method for managing negative transformational impacts is to concede some expertise to competitors, but only in ways that retain the Army's access to that essential expertise. This method is most practical for that portion of the higher-prestige and newer professions that are most at risk to transformational changes—doctors, lawyers, dentists, and perhaps clergy. The importance of expertise provided by these professionals makes it essential to concede functions only to others who can guarantee Army access. When fighting a war the Army needs relatively large numbers of these professionals to serve in dangerous situations. Current methods for supplying that number vary by expertise, but generally call for a mix of RC and AC in the theater of operation, with other RC replacing those deployed AC members at AC peacetime facilities. Replacing the RC requirement might best be achieved by relying on a combination of other governmental agencies and contractors for in-theater support and contract personnel for replacing deployed AC soldiers in the United States, Europe, or other stable locations. This proposal is merely an expansion of the current practice of contracting medical doctors, physician assistants, nurse practitioners, and nurses to complement existing staff in most Army facilities. Similarly, in mobilization plans the Veterans Administration is the existing backup agency for casualty overflows in the United States. The DoD/VA agreements might be expanded to provide additional U.S. or theater support at much lower thresholds.

This method of reducing transformational impacts, at a minimum, narrows Army application of generally applied expertise and removes the RC from participating in its application. Some do not lament such a loss; for instance, Richard Lacquement is not alone in his characterization of these "expert knowledge" areas as not being "military-technical" and therefore, though needed internally, not at the core of the profession.[44] However, in relinquishing expertise to external sources, we must always be concerned for its availability when needed.

As is usually the case with solutions to difficult problems, the best strategy for reducing negative transformational impacts is to apply several methods, each responding to some aspect of the problem. Of the methods discussed, priority of application should be given to strategies that retain expertise first in the RC and then in the remainder of the Army. If these measures are not enough to guarantee that the Army will have sufficient expertise, then expertise should be gained through share agreements with the other services. If this option is still insufficient, then external sources should be sought, first from other governmental agencies and then from contracting. Discrete and sequenced application of the methods is not practical, but the sequence illustrates that some methods are preferable over others to ensure Army needs are met while caring to the extent possible for members of the Army profession.

Notes

1. The views and opinions expressed in this chapter are those of the author and are not necessarily those of the Department of the Army or any other U.S. government entity.
2. Lt. Gen. James R. Helmly, Chief, Army Reserve, "A Streamlined Army Reserve," opinion editorial in the *Washington Post*, 22 September 2003.
3. The "off-site" of 1993 resulted in major force structure changes in the Army Reserve and Army National Guard. The resulting shift of combat arms to the Army National Guard and Combat Service Support to the Army Reserve took several years to complete, required billions of dollars for equipment and retraining, and required many units to change flags and locations. The colonels and generals of today's RC experienced the turmoil produced by those changes.
4. Thomas F. Hall, Assistant Secretary of Defense for Reserve Affairs, "Sometimes Rebalancing Is Just Rebalancing," *Officer*, October 2003, 14-16.
5. Doug Sample, "DoD to Transform Reserve And Guard by Rebalancing Mission," American Forces Press Service, 28 January 2004.
6. Office of the Deputy Assistant Secretary of Defense for Reserve Affairs, *Rebalancing Forces: Easing the Stress on the Guard and Reserve* (Washington, DC, 15 January 2004).
7. James R. Helmly, "At War and Transforming," *Officer*, December 2003, 38-41.
8. Lt. Gen. H. Steven Blum, Chief, National Guard Bureau, "On Point," *Officer*, December 2003, 53-55.
9. For a complete description of the personnel categories within the USAR and ARNG, see "Manpower, Personnel, and Force Structure," in *Reserve Component Programs*, published by the Reserve Forces Policy Board, Office of the Secretary of Defense (Washington, DC, 2001), chap. 3. The relatively less significant focus on the IRR seems to be changing, however, as the manpower crunch in Iraq and Afghanistan becomes more acute. See Jane McHugh, "Nearing a Breaking Point," *Army Times*, 17 January 2005, 8.
10. Headquarters, Department of the Army, *Modularity Execution Order for 3rd Infantry Division (Mechanized)* (Washington, DC, 26 February 2004).
11. U.S. General Accounting Office, *Reserve Forces: Observations on Recent National Guard Use in Overseas and Homeland Missions and Future Challenges* (Washington, DC, April, 2004), 21.
12. Headquarters, Department of the Army, *Modularity Execution Order*, 13.
13. Office of the Deputy Assistant Secretary of Defense for Reserve Affairs, *Rebalancing Forces*, 19. The "fiscal year 2005 Omnibus Legislative Program" is a proposal by OSD to significantly amend Title 10, US Code, to eliminate reservists' barriers to participation "beyond the traditional 39-day training requirement." These proposed changes would support OSD's concept of a continuum of service and new approaches to mobilization training.
14. Ibid., 9.
15. Ibid., 17, 20.
16. Allan G. Johnson, *The Blackwell Dictionary of Sociology* (Malden, MA: Blackwell Publishers Inc., 2000), 242. It is beyond the scope of this chapter to address debates about the nature of

professions or whether the Army or military should be considered a profession. Even if the Army is rejected as constituting a profession and is only considered an occupation, the principle holds true that transformation will have an impact on individuals in that occupation. The value of analyzing impacts on a "profession" is that consequences go beyond affecting behaviors of individuals whose only affiliation is that they just happen to do the same type of work. Rather, the consequences are for members of an organization responsible for perpetuating knowledge about how to best perform national defense functions.

17. James Burk, "Expertise, Jurisdiction, and Legitimacy of the Military Profession," in *The Future of the Army Profession*, project directors Don Snider and Gayle Watkins, ed. Lloyd J. Matthews (Boston, MA: McGraw-Hill, 2002), 21. Hereinafter referred to as FAP I.

18. An example of literature examining one type of stratification within professions (by gender) is summarized by Edgar Borgatta and Rhonda Montgomery, eds., *Encyclopedia of Sociology* (New York: Macmillan Reference USA, 2000), 2262-2263.

19. Burk, 29.

20. Andrew Abbott, *The System of Professions* (Chicago, IL: The University of Chicago Press, 1988). For elaboration on jurisdictional claims and settlements, see pp. 59-85.

21. Burk, 29.

22. See Richard Lacquement, "Transformation of the Army Profession: Mapping Army Professional Expertise and Clarifying Jurisdictions of Practice," chap. 9, Table 9-4, in the present anthology.

23. Ibid., passim.

24. Ibid., Table 9-1. Lacquement provides a "map" of expert knowledge that characterizes expertise and its relation to forms of expert knowledge.

25. U.S. Army Forces Command, FORSCOM Regulation 350-4, *Training, Army Relationships* (Washington, DC: Department of the Army, 20 July 2000).

26. Dallas D. Owens, informal unpublished survey of 42 attendees (25 USAR, 16 ARNG, 1 AC) at a noontime lecture, U.S. Army War College, 15 July 2004. Of the 42 lieutenant colonels and colonels, 28 had been mobilized and 35 were TPU or M-day soldiers.

27. The two lieutenant generals are the Chief, Army Reserve, and Director, Army National Guard. Before 2001, these two positions were authorized as major generals. The Director, National Guard Bureau, is currently an Army lieutenant general, but that position alternates between the Army and the Air Force.

28. James J. McDonell and J. Ronald Novack, "Logistics Challenges in Support of Operation Enduring Freedom," *Army Logistician* (September-October 2004), 9-13.

29. Seth Borenstein, "Trucks made to drive without cargo in dangerous areas of Iraq," Knight Ridder Newspapers, 21 May 2004.

30. Andrew Abbott, "The Army and the Theory of Professions," in FAP I, 531.

31. Charles C. Moskos, *The Sociology of Army Reserves: Final Report*, Army Research Institute Research Note 90-88 (Alexandria, VA: U.S. Army Research Institute for the Behavioral and Social Sciences, July 1990), 6-7. In this report, written 14 years ago, Moskos noted that "because of the double [career] bind, a continuation of present trends [of increased time demands] could mean that future NCOs and officers in the reserve will likely come from a narrower band of civilian backgrounds than in the recent past."

32. Gina Cavallaro, "Reserve Chief Determined to Make Mobilization Better," *Army Times*, 21 July 2003, 20.

33. Charles C. Moskos, *The Sociology of Army Reserves: An Organizational Assessment*, Army Research Institute Research Note 90-86 (Alexandria, VA: U.S. Army Research Institute for the Behavioral and Social Sciences, July 1990), 11.

34. Amy S. McBurnie, "Transformation and the Development of Army Reserve Professionals" (paper presented at the Senior Conference XLI, West Point, NY, 3-4 June 2004). McBurnie's

observations were nearly unanimously confirmed by comments from the informal survey cited in note 26. Some battalion commanders even contended that their duties commonly required nearly 40 hours per week, particularly when their units were preparing for mobilization.

35. Ibid.

36. Borgatta and Montgomery, 2259-2260. These editors provide a classification scheme for those occupations laying claim to being a profession. The list is neither exhaustive nor accepted by all who study professions, but serves to make some important distinctions among occupational groups and to organize comments about the impact of transformation. In place of Borgatta and Montgomery's term for Category 3.a. ("Marginal Professions") as appearing in Table 26-2, I have substituted the term "Emergent Professions."

37. Ibid.

38. Ibid.

39. U.S. General Accounting Office, *Reserve Component Civilian Occupation Information Final Report* (Washington, DC, December 2002), iv.

40. Dave Moniz, "General Tells of National Guard's Transformation," *USA Today,* 13 November 2003.

41. Thomas Hargrove, "Conflict with Iraq: Iraq contingent leans heavily on military reservists," *Naples Daily News,* 21 March 2003.

42. Office of the Deputy Assistant Secretary of Defense for Reserve Affairs, *Rebalancing Forces,* 17-18.

43. Moskos, *The Sociology of Army Reserves: Final Report,* 7.

44. Lacquement, Table 9-1.

27 | Leadership Development: Beyond Traits and Competencies

George Reed, Craig Bullis, Ruth Collins, and Christopher Paparone

One of the hardest things for successful professions to do is question the assumptions on which their success is founded. The U.S. military has reached its preeminence on the battlefield, in part due to a highly systematic approach to training and leadership development.[1] Much of the program planning and curriculum in our system of professional military training and education was developed through a systems analysis approach, best illustrated in the Army's use of detailed tasks, conditions, and standards. Systematic training models drive the design, resourcing, execution, and assessment phases of a variety of schools and courses in a multitude of settings and specialties. It is second nature for many in the military to abdicate to these technically rational processes, not only for training in basic soldier skills, but for professional military education as well. Unfortunately, such familiar preferences of our leaders combine with a planning culture that can result in approaches to leader development more applicable to the industrial age than to the current and future information age.

> Strategic leaders, more than direct or organizational leaders, draw on their conceptual skills to comprehend national, national security, and theater strategies, operate in the strategic and theater contexts, and improve their vast, complex organizations. The variety and scope of the concerns demand the application of more sophisticated concepts.
>
> —FM 22-100, ARMY LEADERSHIP

One ongoing debate within the military relates to a Joint Competencies Leader Development Framework proposed by the Experimentation Directorate of the Joint Forces Command (JFCOM) in early 2004.[2] The initiative is a commendable effort to enhance joint education with a view toward improving joint operations. When JFCOM first developed the proposal, a number of service entities were already in the process of devising leader competency lists, including the Air Force, Army Research Institute, and the Army's Command and General Staff College. Contractors at Fort Leavenworth were also instrumental in developing a "competency map" that guided the redesign of Army intermediate level education. Unsurprisingly, competency mapping also appeared promising to JFCOM. Competency-based program planning is attractive to a military community that holds concrete rational processes in high esteem.

Reviewing the JFCOM proposal caused us to step back and review educational strategies for developing leaders, particularly strategic leaders who chart and guide the course of their military professions. Senior service colleges are charged with educating the nation's future strategic leaders and preparing them to lead into the 21st century. The joint competencies initiative is an important one because it represents an effort to think seriously about elements of abstract knowledge that are characteristic of

585

war-fighting professions and to ensure that such knowledge is passed to practicing members via an admittedly eclectic system of schools and courses. This is no small task. The results of the proposal have implications for every school in the professional military education system involved in leadership development. At stake in this initiative is the process by which the joint community identifies areas for inclusion in the curriculum of our service and joint schools and then holds them accountable through the program for joint education accreditation.

After a critical analysis of list-based approaches such as competency mapping, we shall argue in this chapter that they represent a control-oriented approach to leadership development that is ill-suited for the education of future senior leaders. When carried to the extent of detailed point-by-point connections between course content on one hand and metrics on the other, competency mapping becomes an over-engineered approach to leadership development and education that is more bureaucratic than professional. In so arguing, we briefly consider the uniqueness of strategic leadership within professions, the nature of abstract knowledge and leadership of military professions, and the propriety of outsourcing the educational components of leadership development. Finally, we suggest an alternative approach that is more adaptive to our rapidly changing geo-strategic environment and better suited to develop the stewards of military professions.

Competency Mapping

Competency mapping can take on a variety of forms, but it is generally described as a formal, top-down effort to identify, list, label, track, and measure competency descriptors. The competencies might also be called knowledge areas, skills, attributes, attitudes, components, tasks, or traits. Once listed and numbered, they are usually broken down into sub-competencies or components, which are also numbered, so they can be associated with a broader competency area or a cluster of competencies. The "mapping" aspect comes into play when the competency areas are then linked to or correlated with training and educational objectives and events of some kind, and then ultimately to leadership behaviors. Competency mapping models thus appear very comprehensive (or at least impressive in their voluminous nature) due to the multiple linkages of competencies themselves. They might be displayed in elaborate hierarchical diagrams, multiple fold-outs, or some other illustrative scheme designed by the administrators of the process. With their elaborate tracking and mapping mechanisms, the models promise horizontal and vertical integration in developing leadership competencies throughout organizational levels and educational institutions.

Once mapped, metrics can then be developed purporting to measure the relative success of an individual in a particular competency with an eye to predicting associated leadership behaviors. The goal is to identify gaps in an individual's leader development progress so they can be recorded, monitored, and remediated. One can imagine the allure of an elaborate computer-based model of competency mapping that provides an instructor, superior, mentor, or individual the opportunity to "push a button" and see the educational opportunities available to improve any particular competency.

Competency mapping appears adaptive because administrators can periodically revise the list of competencies and educational experiences that complement them.

The goal of competency mapping is to develop a blueprint, map, or matrix of desired skills, knowledge, attributes, and attitudes at various levels of an organization. The map is typically used to channel recruiting, hiring, and training decisions. Competency mapping has gained a following in the human resources community and spawned a cottage industry of business consultants and vendors who profess expertise in its application. It is often advertised as a means to save time and resources in the hiring of new personnel and to document occupational training needs of employees.

Echoes of Trait Theories

At the heart of list-based approaches like competency mapping is the assumption that certain attributes such as motives, values, and skills can be identified and instilled in apprentice leaders through training and education so as to produce effectively-led organizations. While billed as an information age concept, the lineage of competency mapping actually lies in trait theories of leadership that recall industrial-age concepts derived from Taylorism and Fordism. Frederick Taylor, the early 20th-century father of "scientific management," used time and motion studies of work to construct the standardized tasks. Henry Ford capitalized on Taylor's theories, creating a workforce trained and organized around the standardization of worker tasks on the assembly line. Indeed, trait theory is one of the earliest frameworks for leadership study. As education scholars Joe Donaldson and Paul Edelson explain:

> Trait theory was developed in the first part of the twentieth century and took a psychological approach to specifying the personality traits of effective leaders. Although research has shown no relationship between individual traits and effectiveness, this approach still finds modern expression.[3]

The well-known leadership authority Gary Yukl likewise observed:

> Early leadership theories attributed managerial success to extraordinary abilities such as tireless energy, penetrating intuition, uncanny foresight, and irresistible persuasive powers. Hundreds of studies were conducted during the 1930s and 1940s to discover these elusive qualities, but this massive research effort failed to find any traits that would guarantee leadership success. One reason for the failure was a lack of attention to intervening variables in the causal chain that could explain how traits could affect a delayed outcome such as group performance or leader advancement.[4]

Nor, Yukl notes, have later studies effectively advanced notions of trait theory. The trait approach has largely been supplanted by more sophisticated frameworks; yet, recent applications of leader competency mapping is proof positive that the approach endures despite its dubious foundation in educational theory. Peter Northouse, author of *Leadership: Theory and Practice* (2004), noted a resurgence in comprehensive skills-based models of leadership characterized by a map for developing effective leadership in organizations.[5] He suggested that the identification of specific skills which can be enhanced by training has an intuitive appeal: "When leadership is framed as a set of skills, it [seems to become] a process that people can study and practice to become better at their jobs."[6] Moreover, the trait approach provides a ready hook on which training and educational institutions can hang their curriculums. It also results in an expansive list of desired skills. Northouse's criticism of this approach includes the observation that the skills model of leadership has weak predictive value: "It does not explain specifically how variations in social judgment skills and problem-solving affect performance."[7] He also suggests that although the skills-based approach claims not to be a "trait" model, it often includes individual attributes that look awfully much like traits.

When attempting to influence the large and dispersed system of professional military training and education institutions, there is a powerful tendency to seek solutions that are definitive, prescriptive, and quantitative. Such solutions seek integration and promise measurement of performance in the best tradition of systems analysis. It is therefore not surprising that the military's proposed approach to leadership includes competency mapping. It reveals a penchant for an unambiguous list that is both definable and measurable. It suggests that the paradigm of technical rationality, with its emphasis on logical reasoning, science, and empirical method, is applicable. It seeks prediction, standards, and control in a realm of training and education that, by its nature, must remain unruly, subjective, and heuristic.

Abstract Knowledge—Professional Theories and Applications

At the heart of any profession is a body of abstract knowledge and expertise that its members are expected to apply within its granted jurisdiction. Don Snider defines the art of professional practice as the repetitive exercise of professional judgment.[8] Those who learn and employ that knowledge in unique contexts are rightly described as professionals. However, abstract professional knowledge can be frustratingly hard to pin down. It extends beyond discrete tasks to include the synthesis of experience and intuition. It involves elements of art as well as science in both analysis and implementation.

Industrial-age organizations seek routine and habit achieved through standardized procedures. Complex tasks are broken into simpler steps that are assigned to organizational positions to ensure that employees, much like parts in a machine, are both interchangeable and easily replaced. Bureaucratic hierarchies tend to value quantifiable assessment of specific aspects of complex managerial tasks. There is merit to this type of approach when the external environment is predictable and unambiguous.

The abstract knowledge and comprehensive tasks required of strategic leaders defy such an industrial-age approach, however. At the strategic level, tasks are not easily defined, isolated, or standardized, nor can they be easily "measured" by anything but subjective, qualitative evaluation. While we recognize that leaders at all levels have responsibility for effective direct and organizational level leadership, the challenges of leadership at the strategic level differ significantly from those at lower organizational levels.[9] At the strategic level, leaders should have a long-term perspective, generally positioning the organization for success 10, 20, or more years into the future. Leaders at this level develop policy and strategic plans, considering implications of both the internal and external environments. Strategic leaders must broaden their focus so as to embrace multiple external constituencies with their often competing interests. They must identify, acquire, and employ scarce resources so that the organization moves towards the accomplishment of its vision. Strategic leaders need frameworks to help develop their abilities to scan for both threats and opportunities in the environment. Similarly, they need to develop a capacity to recognize and appreciate the independence and reciprocal influence relationships between the organization and the environment.[10]

Given this context, transferring abstract knowledge in the training, development, and education of strategic leaders poses unique challenges. The complexity of the strategic leader's environment, combined with the responsibility to deal with elaborate organizational systems and to lead the profession, necessitates a developmental approach that resists dissection into specific tasks. Likewise, the professional military education system involves more than delivering content. Good teaching is an art form in its own right, one that transcends application of explicit scientific practice and enters the realm of new thinking and approaches. This is why a good teacher can overcome a poor curriculum, while a great curriculum will never substitute for a poor teacher. Joe Kincheloe summarized this perspective well:

> Educational experts from the systems analyst school seek to impose research-based techniques on teachers in the place of the knowledge of teaching derived from experience, apprenticeship, and study of educational purpose. Such context-stripped research-based knowledge cannot substitute for professional knowledge.[11]

The Mapping Approach to Leadership Education: A Critique

We should be very circumspect regarding our ability to identify an adequate, much less complete, list of competencies applicable to leadership in a rapidly changing operational environment. As the competencies are linked to skills, then to behaviors, and then to intermediate, enabling, and terminal learning objectives in the training and education base, they could actually drive us to a place we do not want to be. The more we try to describe and prescribe a list of defined, specific competencies, the more we are led away from the agile, adaptive, self-aware leader we want to produce. The paradox is that *more* would actually be *less*. The danger of prescriptive lists is that they create the impression that success can be assured by mastering specific competencies. We believe that Leonard Wong and his colleagues are correct when they say:

> In the military's zeal to address all aspects of systems level leadership, the lists of strategic leader competencies are actually *too* comprehensive. At the individual level, it is difficult to assess one's leadership ability when the lists suggest that a strategic leader must be, know, and do just about everything. At the institutional level, the lack of parsimony makes it difficult to focus an institution's attention and resources on leader development when such a broad array of competencies is advocated.[12]

Even the originator of the skills-based approach, noted social psychologist Robert Katz, limited his list to three broad personal skills: technical, human, and conceptual.[13] A military study in the early 1990s developed a model of leadership comprised of only five components: competencies, individual attributes, leadership outcomes, career experiences, and environmental influences.[14] Northouse notes that problem-solving, social judgment, and knowledge are at the heart of the skills model of leadership.[15] Such broad and ill-defined categories are not satisfying to bureaucracies seeking to achieve certainty and predictability through standardization and routinization. Yet, high-performing professions thrive within ambiguity because it allows for human creativity and adaptation. Faculty members in the system of professional military education charged with collecting and passing abstract knowledge of the profession welcome such ambiguity as an opportunity for innovation and improvisation.

Another concern with list-based approaches like competency mapping relates to a known deficiency of trait listing. Is there any positive attribute that should be left off the list? What positive attributes should leaders not have? Will not the list change as the times change? Of course we want military leaders to have all the virtues of the Boy Scout: be trustworthy, loyal, helpful, and the rest. We also want them to be compassionate in some situations and dealers of death and destruction in others. We want leaders to be decisive, yet prudent. We want them to be doers, but also thinkers. Such ambiguities and paradoxes are rarely resolved in trait lists. Nobel laureate Herbert Simon defined proverbs as those statements of principle having an equally plausible and acceptable contradictory principle absent a guide to indicate which one is proper to apply in a given situation.[16] Proverbs almost always occur in mutually contradictory pairs, and thus their selective use is ideal for action that has already taken place. Yes, you should "*look before you leap,*" but it is also true that "he who hesitates is lost." Left unstated is the contextual information that helps discriminate when it is appropriate to hesitate and when one should leap. Proverbs are not a basis on which to base human leadership development.

In fact, an overly detailed list-based approach could result in professional military education that is contrary to what is actually needed. It could restrict what is taught solely to what's on the list. It could become self-perpetuating, exempt from the continuous review that a profession's expert knowledge must be subject to and therefore detached from what is needed by those practicing in the field. Further, such lists suggest skills that can be mastered once and for all, a concept anathema to the humanist ideal of lifelong learning. This form of competency mapping encourages normative stratification between levels of professional military education rather than the desired integration. R. L. Shaw and Dennis Perkins provide a relevant observation:

> The ideals of worker empowerment, reflection, process, and collaboration often conflict with organizational norms of authoritarian management, [producing a] bias towards activity and measurable performance, and competitive "competency traps."[17]

A competency trap "reflects the ways in which improving capabilities with one rule, technology, strategy, or practice interferes with changing that rule, technology, strategy or practice to another that is potentially superior."[18] Defense institutions will eventually make improvements to the Joint Forces Command list, but it would be unfortunate if those improvements were limited to the scope and methods of competency mapping. Improvements to the competency list will themselves appear to signal a series of "successes," thereby reinforcing the list's use and reducing incentives to search for a better way to develop leaders. Hence, leadership development will be caught in a competency trap created by its own restricted learning processes. In reality, the adaptation really needed is ignored because the existing paradigm has been institutionalized to the point of being culturally imbedded.[19] It ossifies into something sacred and inviolable on no other grounds than "that's the way it's always been done."

Avoiding competency traps can be achieved by adopting principles associated with organizational learning and professional reflexivity. Competency traps can be explained as *single-loop learning*, wherein the leaders and the organization observe the consequences of action (e.g., experimenting with a leadership competency map) and then asking for feedback to gain knowledge as to its effectiveness (e.g., whether it helped in developing leaders). The organization then adjusts subsequent action to avoid similar mistakes (or deviations from what an ideal list or map should accomplish) in the future. According to organization behaviorist Chris Argyris of Harvard University, single-loop learning appears to solve problems, but ignores the issue as to why the overall solution was sought in the first place (e.g., what problem were we trying to solve when we decided that leadership competency maps would solve it?).[20] From this perspective, competency mapping seems to be a ready-made solution that gives false clarity to the otherwise complex and often ambiguous nature of leadership.

Double-loop learning, on the other hand, requires a higher-order form of awareness and reflection. It bypasses the single feedback loop of the top-down approach. Double-loop learning requires a multiple-lens strategy that facilitates "knowledge of several different perspectives and forces the organization to clarify differences in assumptions across frameworks, rather than implicitly assuming a given set."[21] Similarly, viewing leader development from a variety of perspectives would help the continuously transforming military sustain a double-loop learning posture that is always ready for more significant adaptation than a single perspective would allow.[22]

The act of leadership is also an exercise of moral reasoning, which does not lend itself to competency mapping. In their book *Unmasking Administrative Evil,* Guy Adams and Danny Balfour caution against elevating the scientific-analytical mindset above all other forms of rationality. While the rise of "technical rationality led inexorably to specialized, expert knowledge, the very life blood of the professional," it also "spawned unintended consequences in the areas of morals and ethics as the science-based technical rationality undermined normative judgments and relegated ethical considerations to afterthoughts."[23]

Ronald Heifetz has developed a definition of leadership that takes values into account. He maintains that we should look at leadership as more than a means to organizational effectiveness. Effectiveness means reaching viable decisions that implement the goals of the organization. According to Heifetz, however, "This definition has the benefit of being generally applicable, but it provides no real guide to determine the nature or formation of those goals."[24] Heifetz goes on to say that values such as "liberty, equality, human welfare, justice, and community" are inculcated in good leaders.[25] Certainly the military professions affirm the necessity for infusion of these values into their leaders and through these leaders into the organization itself. We question whether this can be achieved through competency mapping.

Recently, Anna Simons of the Naval Postgraduate School briefed the results of a DoD study titled "The Military Officer of 2030."[26] Those conducting the study wisely determined that outside of a short list of universal beneficial leadership traits (e.g., responsible leaders of good character), we simply do not know the specifics of the kind of leader we will need in 30 years. It is unwise to attempt to predict the specific traits that will be required, and even if we had the temerity to lock onto such a list, we could do the nation great harm if we were wrong. According to the study group, the correct organizational response under such uncertain conditions is to build in as much variation in skills and attributes as tolerable. The idea behind this approach is that with a broad range of variability you will likely have some leaders in the inventory with the skills needed at any critical point in time, thus giving the organization a population with which to adjust. If the conclusion of the study group is correct, then competency mapping would appear to be a roadblock to achieving the necessary flexibility and versatility the professional pool requires.

Additional Concerns

Also at stake in the JFCOM and other current competency mapping proposals is the issue of who drives this leader development process, a process we believe is key to the future of military professions. We must ask whether it is wise to outsource the development of a list of competencies that then drives the curriculum of professional military schools. Civilian vendors under contract to JFCOM developed the proposed joint leader competency list, and contractors were also instrumental in developing the competency map used for intermediate level education at Fort Leavenworth. It is appropriate to question just how much we should rely on individuals outside the profession working for profit-based corporations to chart and transfer the military's professional knowledge.

The human development of professionals is a critical field of expert knowledge in its own right. The extent to which the military professions are apparently willing to voluntarily hand over this core function to those outside of the profession is alarming. It is difficult to imagine other professions such as law and medicine permitting nonprofessionals to have such influence over the primary mechanism of transmitting professional knowledge. To a healthy profession, human development and maintenance of its body of abstract knowledge are not ancillary functions. On the contrary, as sociologist Andrew Abbott demonstrates beyond dispute in his prize-winning study *The System of Professions*, development of an abstract body of expert knowledge by the professionals themselves is the sine qua non, the defining quintessence, of professional identity.[27]

We have noticed among Army War College students, who eventually comprise the cadre of senior Army leaders, a predominant personality type. These students have a penchant for details, specifics, early closure, and structure.[28] Moreover, within the Army profession at large there is a clear preference for objective, concrete, and pragmatic solutions.[29] We should not be surprised then that leadership competency mapping, essentially an engineering approach, appeals to many in this community. It is highly rational and neat. One can easily trace up and down the matrix from competencies to skills and behaviors and back again. Therein lies the problem; it is too neat.

Fundamentally, still-developing professionals must recognize that their existing frames of reference are inadequate to deal with challenges at higher levels. Change (development) occurs when the leaders' existing frames are modified so that they consider new information or reorganize existing information and "come to understand the world in fundamentally different ways than [they] did using less advanced frames of reference."[30] Developmental systems, especially at the strategic level (but certainly at all levels) should be structured so that they support the "psychological maturity and independence" that results when leaders develop their own personal perspective of leadership.[31]

We must also remember that most of our professional military education process is oriented on adult learners. Education scholar Raymond Noe observed that a great deal of contemporary educational theory and practice is oriented to children and youth where the instructor makes decisions about learning content and the students are passive receptors with few experiences to contribute.[32] Adults have a need to be self-directed, are best motivated when they understand the need for such learning, and prefer a work-related and problem-solving orientation.[33] With limited time for education in our system of schools and courses, we should ensure that extensive top-down competency lists do not fill the curriculum to the extent that they drive out self-direction, reflection, and other heuristic learning opportunities.

As suggested earlier, leadership and leader development are both art and science. Leadership scholar Bernard Bass here cautions against focusing solely on quantitative approaches in leadership research and makes an important observation about the nature of leadership in general:

> Often, qualitative research can deal better with the art and craft of leadership than can the more objective quantitative analysis. There is much in leadership that is difficult or impossible to put into a test tube. Nevertheless, there is much regularity in this art that can be made understandable by detecting and describing the patterns that appear.[34]

We are concerned that competency mapping is a pseudo-science with close similarities to the test tube approach that Bass counsels against.

Even though well-defined competency maps initially seem innovative, we risk the inevitable "new idea lifecycle" problem that occurs when the list becomes institutionalized by the bureaucracy.[35] While the map could be updated periodically with fresh interpretations of events and feedback on current leadership and organizational shortcomings, we expect the inevitable emergence of an institutionalized process that could inhibit necessary changes. That is, we fear the competency mapping process will take on a life of its own, at the expense of opportunities lost for truly improving joint military education.

What we really need from joint military education are leaders adept at learning almost anything very fast, or are skilled at recognizing patterns and converting abstract knowledge to theory and action appropriate for a given situation. Leaders should be values champions for organizations and must be attuned to issues of climate and culture. We also need leaders who can communicate effectively to a wide range of audiences. They need to inspire soldiers as well as address the American public and the international community through the unblinking eye of the television camera. We must focus on *how* to think, not *what* to think, but these "fuzzy" concepts too often do not sell well within the military culture.

An Alternative Collaborative Leadership Development Framework

Our view of leadership as senior service college professors is changing as our vision of military professions change. In the words of a colleague, when you attempt to lead yesterday's military, you are fighting yesterday's wars.[36] We are concerned that detailed leader competency maps comprised of extensive databases and matrices rely on traditional notions of leadership appropriate for industrial-age bureaucratic hierarchies. They thus fail to capture emerging leadership concepts suitable to a future military viewed as a complex adaptive or networked system. We recognize that leadership in complex adaptive systems relies on relationship-building over role-defining, loose coupling over standardization, learning over knowing, self-synchronization over command and control, and emergent thinking over planning based on estimates.[37]

As with most goals in complex systems, there are multiple ways of achieving them. Some aspects of the systems analysis approach to education are useful. There is nothing inherently harmful in developing competency lists provided they are kept general in nature. We are concerned, however, that the approach lacks the complex contextual and relational elements that combine to determine leadership effectiveness or failure, particularly at the strategic level.

There are alternatives to the top-down, control-oriented, list-based approach, e.g., perspectives that emphasize the more humanist themes in use by the organization, the underlying cultural values and beliefs in operation, and the relationship between symbolism and action. Those holding these perspectives are less concerned with identifying specific leadership variables leading to effectiveness and efficiency. Recognizing that all social science measurement is fallible, if not actually suspect, we advocate the use of a double-loop learning approach and the application of multiple perspectives to leadership study and curriculum development.

The effort currently being invested in detailed competency lists and maps should be diverted to the following specific initiatives: (1) improving the means by which we assess the needs of the emerging joint warfare profession, viz., the means by which we can quickly identify joint war-fighting competencies requiring improvement;[38] (2) conveying information gained from that assessment to those responsible for joint training and education; (3) facilitating a network through which the myriad institutions involved in professional military education can collaborate, exchange information, and share professional expertise; and (4) revising leadership development frameworks to include multiple perspectives.

We caution against compiling an exhaustive (and exhausting) list of dubious traits and skills of the ideal joint leader and then mandating it to the system of professional military education. Instead, we argue that the professions should take careful stock of our current state against the backdrop of the contemporary operational environment. By examining the current state in light of near-term needs, we can determine the gap between the existing and desired system. The desire to narrow the gap can then drive the system of professional military education.

We are confident that the institutions comprising the system of professional military education are capable of engaging in double-loop learning that addresses emerging needs. The process can be speeded by a vibrant network that encompasses the various schools and courses in the system. Speaking for our own institution, the U.S. Army War College, we note that it conducts a variety of surveys of stakeholders and graduates, and reviews numerous reports and studies as part of the curriculum development process. However, there is no comprehensive means to identify joint leadership development requisites that extend across institutional boundaries. There is no shortage of good ideas about where the Army War College should focus its efforts, but it is not always clear that those ideas relate to the real needs across the joint field. An alternative curriculum development approach that would accomplish this for the joint community can be modeled as in Figure 27-1.

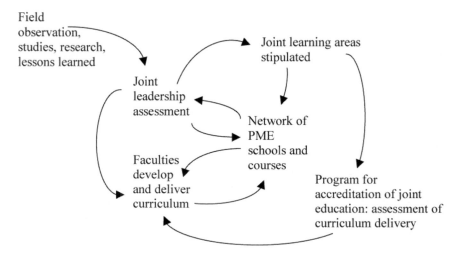

Figure 27-1. *Proposed Adaptive Model of Curriculum Development for Joint Professional Military Education.*

We should not underestimate the scope of an endeavor that would result in creation and dissemination of the joint leadership assessment. What we suggest is a comprehensive assessment of the state of joint leadership using the best tools and minds available for the effort. Such collaborative assessments are expensive and manpower intensive, so much so that they are not repeated on a frequent basis. In order to remain relevant to a rapidly changing environment, we recommend that the assessment be conducted on an essentially continuous basis. Optimally, the assessment would coincide with the annual curriculum development processes of the institutions engaged in joint professional military education.

Joint war-fighting leadership assessments would provide a substantive basis for continual reframing of professional military education. As an example, if it were determined that officers of a particular service have difficulty reacting to unplanned events and developing creative solutions, then curricular emphasis could be redirected from operational planning to adaptability and creativity. If senior leaders are perceived to lack news media skills, then additional public speaking and media opportunities could be arranged in the appropriate schools and courses. Such modifications need not necessitate wholesale institutional change, and they need not await the revision of a competencies list. Changes conducted uninterruptedly based on continual internal feedback mechanisms can result in radical transformative shifts over time. This process encourages action at the lowest level to adjust to emerging needs. Such an active and continual process makes a competency list outdated if not superfluous upon publication.

An organizational learning process of continual examination and change is preferable to a prescribed list of tasks that takes months and years to develop. Under the existing process that relies on an entity known as the Military Education Coordinating Council, it can literally take years to change the joint learning areas mandated in Joint Chiefs of Staff Instruction 1800.01, *Officer Professional Military Education Policy*.[39] We note that the current list of joint learning areas fails to adequately address the subject of leadership. The process for accreditation of joint education conducted at the various schools involved includes an on-site review conducted every five years. Despite the long timelines involved in this process, we do not recommend its abolishment. Instead we suggest that it be supplemented with a timely joint leader assessment that the faculties can then use as a basis for lesson planning.

We further recommend establishment of an inter-professional network so those involved in professional military education and leadership studies can collaborate, exchange information, and share professional expertise. This could be accomplished through symposiums, conferences, communities of practice, faculty exchange programs, and faculty development initiatives. When these events and resources are targeted to address areas for leadership improvement, then the responsiveness of the educational system will dramatically increase. Imagine giving students at one senior service college the opportunity to enroll in electives taught at another, or broadcasting an address by the Secretary of Defense held at one college to the others. Outside of some notable service-sponsored initiatives such as the annual Teaching Grand Strategy Conference,[40] there are few mechanisms for sharing pedagogical techniques and resources among faculty members. There are significant advantages to a networked approach to leadership education. Our proposal establishes an agile and flexible system of professional military education that can adapt to emerging needs and facilitate exchanges of ideas through dialogue.

Conclusion

Strategic leaders bear the burden, as well as enjoying the privilege and honor, of maintaining the professional identity of the organization—they are the "stewards of the profession." Effectively imbuing these leaders with a passion not only for accomplishing short-term organizational objectives but also for nurturing and developing the profession itself is critical for progress in service to America's security.

In dealing with the complexity of the responsibilities for strategic leaders, we believe that a framework for development should focus not on *what* to think (inherent in industrial-age perspectives), but on *how* to think. In other words, we find it tempting, but ill-advised, to believe that we can specify the actions and behaviors required of a strategic leader for success in periods up to 20 or even fewer years in the future. We expect to see significant complexity and accelerating change as times move forward. We therefore believe that our best alternative for development is to provide emerging strategic leaders with multiple frameworks that help them foster mental agility. We develop this more sophisticated understanding by challenging the applicability of their current frames of reference and introducing alternative frames and models.

Some aspects of list-based approaches exemplified by leader competency mapping are superficially appealing, and there are strong cultural drivers and favored paradigms that help explain their dominant role as a tool for curriculum development. However, such an approach contains fundamental flaws to the extent that it should not be relied upon as the foundational means of leadership education. Education of strategic leaders is an endeavor ill-suited to an assembly line approach. We recommend an organizational learning-based process enabled by vastly expanded assessment and educational network components. Our recommended framework uses context-relevant study to justify continuous curriculum adjustment facilitated by a network of the various elements of the professional military education system. We further advocate using the network to improve leadership and curriculum development as well as teaching. A networked approach to joint leadership development can lead to multiple perspectives of leadership more appropriate to a rapidly changing environment and thus more beneficial to military professions.

Notes

1. We use the term leadership development to mean "the expansion of the organization's capacity to enact basic leadership tasks needed for collective work" as defined by Ellen Van Velsor and Cynthia D. McCauley, "Our view of leadership development," in *The Center for Creative Leadership Handbook of Leadership Development,* 2nd edition, eds. Ellen Van Velsor and Cynthia D. McCauley (San Francisco, CA: Jossey Bass, 2003), 1-22. Leader development is a subset of leadership development focusing on efforts to increase a person's capacity to lead.

2. U.S. Army HR System Project Plan (draft), USACGSC, Fort Leavenworth, KS, 21 January 2004.

3. Joe F. Donaldson and Paul Jay Edelson, "From Functionalism to Postmodernism in Adult Education Leadership," in *Handbook of Adult and Continuing Education,* eds. Arthur L. Wilson and Elisabeth R. Hayes (San Francisco, CA: Jossey-Bass, 2000), 193.

4. Gary Yukl, *Leadership in Organization.* 5th edition (Upper Saddle River, NJ: Prentice Hall, 2002).

5. Peter G. Northouse, *Leadership Theory and Practice* (Thousand Oaks, CA: Sage, 2004), 35-52.

6. Ibid., 50.

7. Ibid., 51.

8. Don M. Snider, "Officership: The Professional Practice," *Military Review* 83 (January–February 2003): 3-8.

9. T.O. Jacobs and Elliot Jaques, "Leadership in Complex Systems," in *Human Productivity Enhancement,* ed. J.A. Zeidner (New York: Praeger, 1986), 7-65.

10. For example, see R. Marion and M. Uhl-Bien, "Leadership in Complex Organizations," *Leadership Quarterly* 12 (2001): 393-418.

11. Joe L. Kincheloe, *Teachers as Researchers: Qualitative Inquiry as a Path to Empowerment* (New York: Falmer Press, 1991), 77.

12. Leonard Wong, Paul Bliese, and Dennis McGurk, "Military Leadership: A Context Specific Review," *Leadership Quarterly* 14 (December 2003): 21 (emphasis in original).

13. Robert L. Katz, "Skills of an effective administrator," *Harvard Business Review* 33 (September-October 1955): 90-102.

14. Northouse, 40.

15. Ibid.

16. Herbert Simon, "The Proverbs of Administration" (originally published in 1947), reprinted in *Classics of Public Administration,* 4th edition, eds. Jay M. Shafritz and Albert C. Hyde (Ft. Worth, TX: Harcourt Brace, 1997), 127-141.

17. Quoted from R. L. Shaw and Dennis N. T. Perkins, by Tara J. Fenwick, "Putting Meaning into Workplace Learning," in *Handbook of Adult and Continuing Education,* 296.

18. James G. March, *A Primer on Decision Making: How Decisions Happen* (New York: Free Press, 1994), 96-97.

19. Institutional theorists call it "sedimentation," portraying it as the most imbedded form of institutionalization. Sedimentation is based on "the historical continuity" of rules and structure "and especially on its survival across generations of organizational members." From Paul S. Tolbert, P. S. Zucker, and Lynn G. Zucker, "The Institutionalization of Institutional Theory," in *Studying Organization Theory and Method,* eds. Stewart R. Clegg and Cynthia Hardy (1996; London: Sage 1999), 178.

20. Chris Argyris, *Strategy, Change, and Defensive Routine* (Marshfield, MA: Pitman, 1985).

21. Paul A. Sabatier, *Theories of the Policy Process: Theoretical Lenses on Public Policy* (Boulder, CO: Westview, 1999) 6.

22. For example, see Christopher R. Paparone and James A. Crupi, "Insights for the Emerging Strategic Leader," unpublished manuscript, February 2004. The authors present leadership from three epistemological perspectives: modern, symbolic, and postmodern.

23. Guy B. Adams and Danny L. Balfour, *Unmasking Administrative Evil* (Armonk, NY: M.E. Sharpe, 2004), 31-36.

24. Ronald A. Heifetz. *Leadership without Easy Answers* (Cambridge, MA: Harvard University Press, 1994) 21-22.

25. Ibid.

26. The study results were briefed by Dr. Anna Simons of the Naval Postgraduate School to a group that included two of this chapter's authors at the Pentagon on 6 October 2003. Although the study has not been released to the public, the authors verified this interpretation of the study findings through personal communication with Dr. Simons.

27. Andrew Abbott, *The System of Professions: An Essay on the Division of Expert Labor* (Chicago, IL: University of Chicago Press, 1988), 8-9, 52-58.

28. For additional information see Otto Kroeger and Janet M. Thuesen, *Type Talk: The 16 Personality Types that Determine How We Live, Love, and Work* (New York: Dell 1988); and Kroeger and Thuesen, *Type Talk at Work: How the 16 Personality Types Determine Your Success on the Job* (New York: Dell, 2002).

29. The differences we refer to are differences in personality preferences as measured by the Myers-Briggs Type Indicator (MBTI). See Isabel B. Myers et al., *MBTI Manual: A Guide to the Development and Use of the Myers-Briggs Type Indicator,* 3rd edition (Palo Alto, CA: Consulting Psychologists Press, 1998). Introverts and extroverts differ in where they derive their personal energy. Simply stated, introverts get their energy internally; therefore, they prefer to be less public in their expressions and can be drained by social interaction. Extroverts, on the other hand, get their energy from others; consequently, they tend to think out loud and derive energy from social settings. We are not convinced that this distinction is as germane to the argument of this chapter as the other three preferences. ISTJ (introversion, sensing, thinking, judging) is the predominant personality type in the USAWC Class of 2004. Seventy percent of the Class of 2004 are sensors (versus relying on intuition)—they prefer facts and practical data and they focus on the present. Implications of an organization with lots of S's: they want practical application, like to get into the details, may have discomfort with uncertainty and ambiguity, and are most comfortable at the tactical level. Some 93 percent are thinkers (versus feelers)—they are objective, analytical, nonpersonal, and seek clarity. Organizations with lots of Ts want logical rationale for statements, can be overly critical and blunt, may want to discuss more than dialogue, and learn by arguing. Some 86 percent are judgers (versus perceivers)—they are decisive, structured, prefer a planned, orderly existence, and seek closure. They make lists and use them. Organizations with lots of Js may be prone to premature decisions, become impatient with theoretical discussions, and tend to see things as black and white instead of shades of gray.

30. Ibid., 44.

31. George B. Forsythe, Scott Snook, Philip Lewis, and Paul T. Bartone, "Making Sense of Officership: Developing a Professional Identify for 21st Century Army Officers," in *The Future of the Army Profession*, project directors Don M. Snider and Gayle L. Watkins, ed. Lloyd J. Matthews (New York: McGraw Hill, 2002), 357-78.

32. Raymond A. Noe, *Employee Training and Development* (Boston, MA: McGraw-Hill, 2002) 115-116.

33. Ibid., 116.

34. Barnard M. Bass, *Bass & Stogdill's Handbook of Leadership: Theory, Research, & Managerial Applications*, 3rd edition (New York: Free Press, 1990), 887.

35. In other words, competency maps will devolve to red tape, that is, "rules, regulations and procedures that remain in force and entail a compliance burden but do not advance the legitimate purposes the rules were intended to serve." From Barry Bozeman, *Bureaucracy and Red Tape* (Upper Saddle River, NJ: Prentice Hall, 2000), 12.

36. Personal communication with Chaplain (Col.) Winfield Buzby, 26 December 2004, Carlisle, Barracks, PA.

37. Christopher R. Paparone, Ruth A. Anderson, and Reuben R. McDaniel, Jr., "The United States Military: Where Professionalism Meets Complexity Science," *Military Review*, forthcoming.

38. Don M. Snider, "Jointness, Defense Transformation and the Need for New Joint Warfare Profession," *Parameters* 33 (Autumn, 2003): 17-30.

39. The Military Education Coordination Council (MECC) develops assessment standards, learning areas, and objectives in support of the Joint Chief of Staff's statutory responsibility for oversight of the joint education system.

40. The Teaching Grand Strategy Conference is an annual cooperative event between a number of institutions including professional military schools and civilian universities. It is oriented to those involved in strategic studies and provides a venue for interested students and faculty members to gather and discuss teaching methods and developments in the field.

28 | Strategic Leadership of the Army Profession[1]

Leonard Wong and Don M. Snider

In their introduction to the first edition of the *The Future of the Army Profession*, Don Snider and Gayle Watkins noted repeatedly that vocational professions—i.e., those regarded as a "calling" of trust and dedication—are all about people as opposed to technologies or organizational structures. They are quintessentially human institutions that are also categorized as "producing" organizations. In the Army's case, what is produced is the human expertise for fighting land campaigns within America's joint command structures.[2] Equally important, they also noted what type of producing organization the Army is not; it is not a pure bureaucracy manned by bureaucrats, nor is it a business with hired employees.

This critical distinction—the U.S. Army as profession, not bureaucracy or business—is of signal importance to the strategic leaders of the Army, *those for whom this chapter has been prepared.* For if they do not understand clearly the nature of the entity they are to lead, how can they possibly lead it wisely? This distinction is also of critical importance because those same strategic leaders are also responsible for the systems of professional development which produce the Army's future strategic leaders. Unfortunately, as of 2000 when Snider and Watkins wrote the research conclusions for the first edition of this anthology, the Army's leadership doctrines and its developmental systems were not sufficiently focused on strategic leaders.[3] Many leaders did not generally think in terms of the Army as a profession, and thus were not preparing Army juniors for such a leadership task. In fact, the 1999 version of FM 22-100, *Army Leadership,* seldom used the noun "profession" at all, simply describing the Army generically as an "organization."

We make this introductory point to raise the following question: "Can a strategic leader lead a profession as he or she would lead a bureaucracy or a business?" In other words, if the Army is to be a profession, and to be led as one, must the Army's strategic leaders adopt a different identity, develop different competencies, and employ different skills and techniques than if they viewed the Army as a bureaucracy? Our answer to that question is a resounding, "Yes!" It is the purpose of this chapter to make that case to the strategic leaders of the Army, both present and future, and to those who are in the process of developing them.

Before discussing strategic leadership in the Army, however, let us define what we mean by a strategic leader. Ironically, "strategic" is often used at both ends of the rank hierarchy. It is not uncommon to hear within the Army today of the "strategic captain" or "strategic corporal" guarding, say, the Brcko Bridge. This use of "strategic" broadens the definition to such a degree that *all* soldiers could conceivably take on action of strategic import. On the other end of the hierarchy, "strategic" is often used in the narrow sense that strategic leadership resides solely in the general officer ranks. An even more narrow interpretation views strategic leaders only at the 3-star level and above, those positions to which individuals are appointed rather than promoted. To clarify briefly, then, we assume in this chapter that, because of their increased responsibilities in this new era of global war with jihadist radical Islam, the capabilities of a strategic leader are now required at the level of brigade commander and at the colonel-level staff position. Further, to us, "strategic" refers to unique ways of thinking and leading—not just a level of war above tactical and operational. Such a manner of thinking is necessary for issues of more cognitive complexity, those with longer time horizons and important third and fourth order effects, all with higher levels of ambiguity and risk.

We will examine strategic leadership by first explaining briefly what we mean by "leadership of a profession" and then presenting three examples of recent decisions by the Army's strategic leaders that, when viewed from the perspective of a profession, were clearly of strategic import. We do this to provide a common understanding as we discuss "strategic" leadership and "strategic" decisions. Second, we briefly review the literature from the field of leadership, contrast it to current Army doctrine, pointing out strengths and weaknesses in that doctrine, and then draw conclusions as to how the Army might better develop its strategic leaders by imparting six preeminent metacompetencies. We conclude by drawing some implications from the analysis for the profession's strategic leaders.

Leadership of a Profession

Leaders of a vocational profession must have many of the same capabilities as leaders of other producing organizations such as bureaucracies or businesses. But professions do have some unique aspects that require different capabilities. As is discussed in more detail in the introductory chapter to this anthology, professions produce a unique product—human expertise and its ethical practice by members of the profession. Further, not only is the product different, but the internal structure, relationships, and means of social control necessary to provide that product are quite different from those in a business or bureaucracy. For example, professionals are more motivated intrinsically by their expert knowledge and dedicated to its application than they are by the extrinsic motivators offered by the institution in which they serve. They are more inclined to seek autonomy, self-development, altruistic satisfaction in service, and the opportunity to practice their art than to seek the extrinsic motivators offered bureaucratically. Thus it is the unique aspects of a particular type of strategic leadership, those belonging solely to a vocational profession, which we seek to explore.

In the abstract, then, strategic leaders of professions operate at the institution's boundary, focusing their efforts both outside and inside their profession.[4] As they work externally, their efforts are to analyze, to anticipate, and to some degree shape the external environment of the profession, particularly in those jurisdictions in which they do their expert work.[5] That external world includes both clients (in the Army's case, the American people) and competitors—those other organizations, whether professions or not, that seek to infringe or share the Army's claim on a particular jurisdiction of work. Of course, for the Army profession these "competitors" are, in the main, contractors and the other services. Such competition is, in fact, negotiated by the Army's strategic leaders within the formal and informal structures of DoD and Congressional policy-making.

As the strategic leaders of a profession look outside their profession, they seek at higher levels of analysis to understand competitive trends, those macro influences of technology, politics, organization (e.g., joint interdependence), and even enemy adaptations, etc. which potentially could cause jurisdictional changes for the Army. Their key focus is at the nexus of the profession's expert work and its work venues. Foreseeing these changes and developing and implementing the profession's action plan to adapt to them are the key strategic tasks, and they are continuous. For example, the 16 areas on which newly appointed Army Chief of Staff Gen. Peter Schoomaker decided to focus in 2002 can be understood as just such an action plan. During this iterative process, strategic leaders are also responsible for gaining/maintaining the Army's legitimacy for its expert work. The most straightforward manner to do this is to ensure that the work done by Army professionals is effective when assessed by mission standards and delivered ethically so as to maintain the trust of the client. As the Army's ongoing counterinsurgency operations in Afghanistan and Iraq so vividly demonstrate, these are daunting tasks indeed.

As external influences become better appreciated, the internal challenge for the Army's strategic leaders is to align the Army's management systems—e.g., research and development, force design and assessment, materiel acquisition, professional and ethical development, human resource management, etc.—with the leaders' external analysis. This will often mean breaking cultures and bureaucratic tendencies in behalf of the status quo and conforming such to the changing needs of the profession. More specifically, the internal focus is primarily on (1) the profession's expert knowledge,[6] and (2) those developmental systems that impart the requisite expertise to Army professionals and the units they lead. Expert knowledge is essential to the profession's continued existence, since expert knowledge is the essence of a profession. The evolution of this knowledge and its application provide the means for maintaining effectiveness and legitimacy in present jurisdictions and adapting to new ones. With regard to the second internal focus, strategic leaders must develop the Army' soldiers as professionals and communicate the profession's goals, values, and vision to this membership. This is how the profession's evolving identity meshes with and supports that of individual professionals, sustaining their motivation to continue to develop their own expertise.

In sum, maintaining congruence between the profession's external and internal jurisdictions is the key responsibility of strategic leaders of a profession. Change more often occurs externally, and the Army then adapts to it within its internal jurisdictions. This is the case today, as fighting insurgencies effectively is the newly demanded expertise, with the Army adapting, however belatedly, both its expert knowledge and how it develops its professionals and its combat units.

See p. 604

Summing up, we can break down the four critical tasks for leaders of a profession, particularly those at the strategic level, as follows:

- (External) Analyze macro influences from the evolving environment that will affect the nature of the profession's expert knowledge or the situations in which it is to be applied (jurisdictions);
- (External) Negotiate the Army's current and future jurisdictions of professional practice, i.e., those situations in which it does, or does not, practice its expert work;
- (Internal) Maintain the profession's expert knowledge and adapt it to changing demands of the external environment and the client, usually 6-10 years forward; and
- (Internal) Conform and align the Army's professional development systems with its evolving expert knowledge so as to produce professionals and units with the right expertise at the right time.

We turn now to a discussion of three recent cases that express these abstract concerns more concretely.

Strategic Decision-Making

Occasionally, Army strategic leaders will make far-reaching, culture-changing decisions that—because they do not address major weapon systems, create new doctrinal approaches to warfare, or suggest drastic changes to the personnel system—do not appear to be strategic decisions at all. Such was the case when Chief of Staff Gen. Eric Shinseki announced in October 2000 that the black beret would become the Army's standard headgear. Considering all the protests, emails, articles, and public ridicule that accompanied its introduction, it was hard to believe that the raucous debate originated from a decision concerning a hat. The hullabaloo over the beret was not about fashion, however. It was about change and the resistance to change. It was a foreshadowing of the difficult process of transforming an Army that had with such spectacular success spent the last half-century equipping, training, and preparing itself to fight World War III. That very success posed an obstacle to future change. Negotiating the Army's future jurisdictions, however, hinged on the ability to introduce change within the Army.

The need for change became obvious in 1990 when the only forces that could be deployed quickly against the armored columns of Saddam Hussein were the outgunned paratroopers of the 82nd Airborne Division. A decade later, the difficulties in deploying Task Force Hawk to Kosovo reinforced the growing concern that the Army was still working with a Cold War mindset in a post-Cold War world. General Shinseki well understood that B. H. Liddell Hart had it right when he said, "The only thing harder than getting a new idea into the military mind is to get an old one out."[7]

Accordingly, General Shinseki set in motion a dizzying whirl of transformation initiatives that introduced radical changes to the doctrine, training, technology, and thinking of the institution. In the lexicon of biology, the Army was undergoing

acclimatization, the process by which an organism adapts to an environment different from the one to which it was indigenous. Just as some animals shed their winter
coats to acclimatize to the onset of spring, the Army needed to keep its high-intensity conflict capability, yet shed some of the institution's assumptions and habits of
the Cold War to enable itself to deploy quickly against an asymmetrical foe.

But where did the black beret fit into all this? It was part of the process of
acclimatization, although at the individual level rather than the organizational.
Humans, individual professionals, also need to acclimatize as the profession's environment changes. For example, we become short of breath and tire easily when
moving to higher altitudes unless we acclimatize by ascending in piecemeal stages
that prepare us for the final assault. And that's how the beret entered the picture; it
evoked a small change in *attitude* that had to be confronted by every single member
of the profession as they put on their headgear, thus preparing the Army for the
larger paradigm shifts of the future. Yes, there were gasps when the beret policy was
announced—it isn't the most functional headgear and it does tread on tradition—
but viewing the beret retrospectively as a step in acclimatization confirms that the
Army did eventually catch its breath over this small change and later embraced
many more radical changes of Army transformation. By introducing the beret,
General Shinseki prepared the Army for even more change and adaptation.

A second example of a modest decision having strategic implications can be
found in the current overhaul of the officer personnel management system, to
include movement away from the "check the block" requirements delineated in DA
Pamphlet 600-3, *Commissioned Officer Development and Career Management
(1998)*—especially concerning the development of colonels. Assigning, evaluating,
utilizing, and promoting colonels with an approach resembling that used with general officers acknowledges that as officers move into strategic positions, fine-tuned
development is preferred over mass production techniques. With such an approach,
brigade command is no longer the only path to general officer; command tour
lengths can be extended or shortened according to the needs of the Army, not the
dictates of a regulation; and a larger, more diverse bench of strategically-oriented
colonels is developed.[8] By reaching deeper into the officer corps below the general
officer ranks to identify and develop strategic leaders, the Army will also engender
a deeper commitment from colonels as they are developed and utilized differently
from their experience in previous ranks.

This decision is strategic for several reasons. First, it is based on an analysis of the
future environment suggesting that "business as usual" is not adequate. The changing
nature of warfare and the subsequent additions to the profession's expert work call
for strategic leaders to be much more than just excellent tacticians of conventional
war. Strategic leaders will not be able to rely on technical competence alone to lead
the future Army. They will also need deep expertise across the other three fields of
expert knowledge of the profession, particularly the political-cultural, as they deal
increasingly with organizations and entities not traditionally affiliated with the Army.[9]
Therefore, a more diverse, well-balanced pool of strategic leaders will be required.

Second, this shift in the development and utilization of colonels reflects a deliberate effort to align the Army's professional development system with evolving

expert knowledge. Such a move to produce professionals with the right expertise at the right time institutionalizes the process that was largely left in the past to the serendipity of large numbers. Recognizing that the David Petraeus's and John Abizaid's of tomorrow might never emerge given the current formulaic officer management system based on bureaucratic principles, the decision substitutes an approach based on professional principles, which aim instead to develop and utilize colonels as strategic human resources.

Finally, this decision is a strategic decision because the intentional emphasis upon developing colonels will actually produce few immediate results. Instead, the fruits of this decision will become apparent years later as the Army gains not only a better prepared cohort of colonels to lead in diverse and challenging assignments, but also a larger pool of high-potential officers from which to select the next generation of flag officers. Revitalizing the developmental processes for colonels aligns the Army's expert knowledge with the recognition that the future environment will require a much broader base of strategic leaders.

A third example of what we mean by strategic decision-making is the course chosen by the profession's current leaders to "seek joint interdependence." The content of the decision has been succinctly publicized by former Acting Army Secretary Les Brownlee and Army Chief of Staff Gen. Peter Schoomaker:

> The touchstone of America's way of war is combined arms warfare. Each of our armed services excels in combining a wide variety of technologies and tools in each dimension—land, air, sea, and space—to generate a synergy of effects that creates overwhelming dilemmas for our opponents. Today, that same emphasis on combinations extends beyond each service to joint operations. No longer satisfied merely to de-conflict the activities of the several services, we now seek joint interdependence.
>
> Interdependence is more than just interoperability, the assurance that service capabilities can work together smoothly. It is even more than integration to improve their collective efficiency and effectiveness. Joint interdependence purposefully combines service capabilities to maximize their total complementary and reinforcing effects, while minimizing their relative vulnerabilities. . . . The air-, sea-, or land-power debates are over. Our collective future is irrefutably joint. To meet the challenges of expeditionary operations, the Army can and must embrace the capabilities of its sister services right down to the tactical level. In turn, that will require us to develop operational concepts, capabilities, and training programs that are joint from the outset, not merely as an after-thought.[10]

So why is this decision "strategic" in the sense of leading a profession? In our judgment at least three factors combine to make it so. First are the implications for the profession's internal jurisdictions. This decision requires the Army profession to develop new expert knowledge and to rapidly develop its professionals in the use of that knowledge. For example, combat arms leaders within Army tactical formations must now be adept in using sister-service sources of fire support instead of relying on organic mortars, artillery, or armed helicopters, which may not be a part of the armaments suite of a rapid deployment-employment expeditionary force. In turn, this requires the institutional side of the profession to adapt and conform, hopefully concurrently rather than sequentially, its developmental capacities (joint doctrine, Army doctrine, equipment adaptations, new training, etc.) to produce Army professionals with this new expertise. Quintessentially, conforming a profession's internal jurisdictions to new demands for either expert knowledge or expertise is the responsibility of its strategic leaders, and no one else. This can be done in a number of ways, one of which is creating an internal culture conducive to such innovation.[11] If professions do not adapt, it is usually because their strategic leaders have failed to lead.

Second, the decision to seek joint interdependencies is strategic because it is taken at the boundary of the profession and its external jurisdictions; much of the implementation must first be accomplished outside the profession, e.g., in the creation of joint doctrine, tasks, techniques, and procedures and the professional organizations that will produce them. One of the significant cultural implications of this decision is that it elevates the creation of expert knowledge in the joint arena to a position of primacy over that within the Army. This is quite in contrast to the pattern and priorities of the past four or five decades, a move clearly demanding cultural innovation in a number of forms on the part of the profession. The creation of the Army's Futures Center, which has implanted a large doctrine cell within Joint Forces Command, and the new assignment patterns and priorities for key Army war-fighters, are examples of the profession's innovative responses.

And third, the interdependence decision is strategic because it obviously is one with considerable risks. It simply is not known how effective such joint interdependence will be, nor how long it will take to create it. As Brownlee and Schoomaker note, "The ultimate test of interdependence is at the very tip of the spear, where the rifleman carries the greatest burden of risk with the least intrinsic technological advantage."[12] What is known is that for a nation at war the new nature of expeditionary operations has created the need to leverage every potential tool of speed, operational reach, awareness, and precision. But in doing so, major risks remain. Most often, it rests with strategic leaders to assess them amidst significant uncertainty and decide how much risk to accept on behalf of the profession, its practicing experts, and its clients.

The Search for Strategic Leader Competencies[13]

The search for strategic leader competencies (or knowledge, skills, attributes, or abilities) is a natural progression of the research in the field of leadership.[14] In the late 1980s, some social science researchers began to question whether leadership actually made a difference in organizations, while others suggested that perhaps the study of leadership had reached a dead end. Rather than disappearing, however, the study of leadership took on new energy with the emergence of study on leadership of organizations, in contrast with the traditional leadership approaches that focused on face-to-face interaction at lower levels. Studies of transformational leadership, organizational culture, visionary leadership, organizational change, and charismatic leaders re-invigorated the field of leadership. Thus, the notion of *strategic* leadership was introduced.

While lists of leadership competencies were very popular in the 1980s, the more recent literature distills strategic leadership to a few key skills, competencies, or steps in a process. For example, Stephen Covey states that strategic leaders have three basic functions: pathfinding, aligning, and empowering.[15] *Pathfinding* deals with tying the organization's value system and vision to the mission and environment through a strategic plan. *Aligning* consists of ensuring that the organizational structure, systems, and operational processes all contribute to achieving the mission and vision. *Empowering* is igniting the latent talent, ingenuity, and creativity in the people to accomplish the mission.

Other leadership theorists broach aspects of strategic leadership not included in Covey's schema. In his research on strategic leadership, James Bolt argues that there are three dimensions of a leader: business, leadership, and personal effectiveness.[16] The *business* dimension has traditionally been the focus in executive development. This dimension includes the creation of new kinds of organizations, leading change, and establishing how the organization works. The *leadership* dimension has typically been overlooked because many people do not believe it can be taught. According to Bolt, this dimension is developed by the study of a broad range of classical and contemporary leadership theories and skills. The *personal effectiveness* dimension, according to Bolt, has been neglected because of the widespread view that work and personal matters must be separated. The personal dimension concentrates on helping to clarify and develop an individual's purpose, vision, values, and talents. The emphasis on self-reflection is found in the "self-leadership" literature. This approach, actually as old as Thales's "Know thyself" (6th century, B.C.) or Shakespeare's "To thine own self be true" (17th century), is enjoying a renaissance.

A related aspect emerging in the strategic leadership literature is *self-efficacy.*[17] Self-efficacy refers to individuals' judgments about their perceived capabilities for performing specific tasks. Self-efficacy is the result of life experiences teaching one that he or she can, in fact, take actions with an effective impact on one's environment. This concept parallels the findings of the Army Training and Leader Development Panel (ATLDP). In the ATLDP report, one of the two leadership competencies commended for the 21st century is *self-awareness.* Self-awareness is the ability to assess abilities, determine strengths in the environment, and learn how to sustain strengths and correct weaknesses. The ATLDP report also argues that a second key leader competency is *adaptability.* According to the panel, adaptability is the ability to recognize changes to the environment, to determine what is new, and to ascertain what must be learned to remain effective. It also describes the learning process that follows those determinations.

Karl Weick states that in a world of uncertainty and doubt, leaders must focus on a particular set of properties. Two of those properties are *improvisation* and *lightness.*[18] Improvisation involves the flexible treatment of preplanned material. It is not about making something out of nothing. Instead, it is about making something out of previous experience, practice, and knowledge. Improvisation is a quality almost intuitive to good leaders at the tactical level, but seldom addressed at the strategic level.[19]

Weick's novel concept of "lightness" refers to the ability to drop heavy tools that are no longer useful. Weick's analogy is the foreman who yells "Drop your tools" to wildland firefighters who are trying to outrun an exploding fire.

Firefighters who refuse to drop heavy tools such as chainsaws are prone to be over-taken by the fire and perish (as has happened at least 23 times since 1990). For strategic leaders, the analogues to these now-unwieldy tools are dated presumptions that the world is stable, knowable, and predictable. Future strategic leaders must be able to drop no longer applicable perspectives, methods, or assumptions in a world of uncertainty.

In their review of strategic leadership, Kimberly Boal and Robert Hooijberg distill the essence of strategic leadership to three factors—effective strategic leaders must create and maintain *absorptive* and *adaptive capacity* in addition to obtaining *managerial wisdom*.[20] Absorptive capacity involves the ability to learn by recognizing new information, assimilating it, and applying it. Adaptive capacity involves the ability to change in response to variations in conditions. Managerial wisdom consists of discernment and intuition. Boal and Hooijberg's assertion that absorptive and adaptive capacities are required at the strategic level of leadership is very similar to the ATLDP report's emphasis on self-awareness and adaptability. Although these broad competencies are intended to apply to all levels of leadership, not just the strategic, it is interesting to see the parallel distillation of requisite leader capabilities to ever smaller numbers in both the military and academic literature.

In 1991, the U.S. Army War College hosted a conference on the fledgling field of strategic leadership. At that conference, certain aspects of strategic leadership based on Elliot Jaques's Stratified Systems Theory (SST) were discussed.[21] SST essentially argues for the existence of certain critical tasks that must be performed by leaders in effective organizations. At each ascending level in an organization, these tasks become increasingly complex and qualitatively different. Consequently, strategic leaders must function at higher levels of *cognitive complexity*—the ability to deal with abstract concepts applied within longer time frames. The influence of SST on the Army War College (and Army) is evident in the emphasis on cognitive complexity that now permeates much of the College's strategic leadership instruction.

In its *Strategic Leadership Primer*,[22] the Army War College provides a listing of strategic leader competencies under the three rubrics Be, Know, Do. The list is extremely comprehensive, apparently capturing every possible aspect of leadership, including disposition, actions, values, and skills. Consider:

BE

- The Values Champion—the standard-bearer, beyond reproach.
- Master of the Strategic Art—including ends, ways, means.
- Quintessential Student of History.
- Comfortable with Complexity.
- High in Personal Stamina—physical, mental, stress management.
- Skilled Diplomat.
- Possessed of Intellectual Sophistication, employing alternative frames of reference, displaying pattern recognition, and able to anticipate 2d, 3rd, and 4th-order effects.

KNOW

Conceptual

- Envisioning—anticipating the future, proactive thinking.
- Frame of Reference Development—including systems understanding, scanning, pattern recognition.
- Problem Management—competing issues, no right answers, ability to recognize and ignore irrelevant issues.
- Critical Self-Examination.
- Critical, Reflective Thinking.
- Effectiveness within Environment of Complexity.
- Skillful Formulation of Ends, Ways, Means.

Interpersonal

- Communication—to a much broader audience, negotiations, consensus-building across a variety of stakeholders; systems knowledge, sophisticated persuasion skills.
- Inspires Others to Act.
- Organizational Representation—to internal and external audiences/stakeholders.
- Skillful Coordination of Ends, Ways, Means.
- Master of Command and Peer Leadership.

Technical

- Understands Systems—political, economic, cultural, logistical, force management, and joint/combined interrelationships, etc.
- Recognizes and Understands Interdependencies—systems, decisions, organizations, etc.
- Information Age Technological Awareness—next generation awareness, sophisticated time/space selection.
- Skillful Application of Ends, Ways, Means.

DO

- Provides for the Future—visioning (long-term focus, time span, perspective).
- Initiates Policy and Organizational Direction.
- Shapes the Culture—values-based organization leverage diversity, understanding and accepting differences, multiple perspectives.
- Teaches and Mentors the Strategic Art.
- Manages Joint/Combined and Interagency Relationships.
- Manages National-Level Relationships.
- Represents the Organization.
- Leverages Technology.
- Leads and Manages Change—creating and building "learning organizations."
- Builds Teams and Consensus at Strategic Level (can't dictate action at this level)—co-opting, coalition-building, negotiating, etc.
- Practices the Strategic Art—allocates resources, develops and executes strategic plans derived from the interagency process.

Similarly, in FM 22-100, *Army Leadership*, the Army's doctrinal leadership manual, the skills and actions required of strategic leaders are set forth in a cumulative list of 41 competencies addressing the direct, organizational, and strategic levels.[23] Twenty-one competencies are provided for the strategic level alone:

- Communicating
- Negotiating
- Building staffs
- Developing frames of reference
- Motivating
- Executing
- Developing
- Leading change
- Learning
- Translating political goals into military objectives
- Dealing with uncertainty and ambiguity

- Using dialogue
- Achieving consensus
- Envisioning
- Employing strategic art
- Leveraging technology
- Communicating a vision
- Decision-making
- Strategic planning
- Strategic assessing
- Building

Strategic Leader Competencies: The Irreducible Minimum

In concept work for the latest revision of FM 22-100 (to be renamed FM 6-22), doctrine writers succeeded in reducing the competency list to eight, yet those competencies were linked to 55 "components" and over 200 "sample actions."[24] The draft revision did not specify any unique aspects of strategic leadership; it merely implied that strategic leaders somehow just did everything better!

In one sense, the Army War College and FM 22-100 lists of strategic leader competencies are *too* comprehensive. At the individual level, it is difficult to assess one's leadership ability when the lists suggest that a strategic leader must be omni-competent—he or she must be, know, and do it all. At the institutional level, the lack of discrimination makes it difficult to focus an institution's attention and resources. Hence, the task of identifying the competencies of future strategic leaders becomes one of reducing the massive lists to a few *metacompetencies* that will prove useful in directing leader development efforts toward producing leaders with strategic leader capability, and facilitating self-assessment by officers of their own strategic leader capability. [25]

From the existing literature on strategic leadership, the current lists of Army strategic leader competencies, and the dictates of current and future operating environments, we have derived six metacompetencies: *identity, mental agility, cross-cultural savvy, interpersonal maturity, world-class warrior*, and *professional astuteness*. Before addressing each of them, we should note that concentrating on just six metacompetencies does provide focus, but there are some associated disadvantages. First, some skills and abilities are not explicitly described by a metacompetency label. Rather they are subsumed within them. For example, strategic leaders need to be politically savvy—knowing when to compromise, understanding that many strategic decisions are not black and white, and knowing what is best in the long run for the nation and the Army. This ability is captured under the rubric *professional astuteness*, but is not obvious in the words *professional astuteness*. Thus, understanding the meaning and intent behind each metacompetency is much more important than creating a catchy mnemonic containing the first letter of each of the six labels. Similarly, the metacompetency labels may be misinterpreted if separated from their descriptions. For example, *cross-cultural savvy* includes the ability to work across organizational boundaries, but the metacompetency could be too narrowly interpreted to refer solely to working across national boundaries. In other words, the six metacompetency labels were not developed as a stand-alone list. The concepts behind the labels, not the labels themselves, are the focal points for leader development and assessment.

The following section describes each of the six metacompetencies. After a brief discussion of each, the means for developing each metacompetency in future officers is examined using the three domains of leader development—institutional, operational, and self-development. This chapter is not intended to provide an exhaustive treatment of strategic leadership—the civilian literature does that adequately. Nor is it intended as a blueprint to overhaul the Army's entire leader development system. Instead, this chapter contrasts the leadership needs of the future strategic environment with the current focus of strategic leader development, and discusses some indicated adjustment.

Identity

This metacompetency is derived from the work of Douglas Hall, who strongly influenced the conclusions of the ATLDP report. According to Hall, identity is "the ability to gather self-feedback, to form accurate self-perceptions, and to change one's self-concept as appropriate."[26] The ATLDP report uses the term, *self-awareness*, describing it as "the ability to understand how to assess [one's] abilities, know strengths and weaknesses in the operational environment, and learn how to correct those weaknesses."[27] The metacompetency of *identity* moves beyond simply knowing one's strengths and weaknesses as connoted by self-awareness. It includes the understanding of one's self-concept as an officer in the Army. Identity also includes an understanding of one's values and how they match up to the values of the Army. Identity implies maturation beyond self-awareness, as officers come to an understanding of who they are, not just how well they do things.

Identity, as opposed to self-awareness, also involves aspects of development over a career. In the corporate world, as an executive moves up to higher levels of responsibility, "he or she must learn to change the basis of his or her self-identity away from individual contributions as the basis for self-esteem and toward defining personal value and esteem through the accomplishments of subordinates."[28] In an officer's development of strategic leadership capability, the metacompetency of identity acknowledges that the role of a strategic leader goes beyond personal contributions and shifts to serving as a catalyst for success by subordinates and the organization as a whole.

Development of the identity metacompetency in officers can begin as early as pre-commissioning. In the early stages of an officer's career, identity focuses more on the recognition of one's strengths and weaknesses, but it also includes the establishment of a foundation of continual self-assessment and the desire to adjust one's self-concept when needed. In the institutional realm of leader development, identity can be developed through self-assessment tools, simulations, peer evaluations, and coaching. In the operational arena of leader development, identity can be developed through after-action reports, 360° feedback, job ratings, rewarding personal development, and the counsel of a mentor. Finally, identity can be developed through officer self-development based on reading lists and the use of a lifelong development plan.

Mental Agility

In addition to self-awareness, the ATLDP report recommends that the Army focus on developing the competency of adaptability, defined as "the ability to recognize changes in the environment; to determine what is new, what must be learned to be effective, and includes the learning process that follows that determination, all performed to standard and with feedback."[29] *Mental agility* builds on the ability to scan and adjust learning based on the environment, and entails aspects of cognitive complexity, improvisation, and lightness as found in the strategic leadership literature.

Strategic leaders operate in an environment of ambiguity and uncertainty. Typical strategic situations lack structure, are open to varying interpretations, and are characterized by information that is often far-flung, elusive, cryptic, or even contradictory.[30] Mentally agile strategic leaders possess the requisite cognitive skills to navigate in this milieu and alter their actions and those of their organizations in a manner necessary to function in this complex environment.

From a cognitive perspective, strategic leaders must learn how to scan the environment, understand their world from a systems perspective, and eventually envision different futures and directions for their organization. Scanning involves a constant search for information that affects current assumptions. Officers with mental agility search for more information and spend more time interpreting it.[31] They also analyze large amounts of sometimes conflicting information, trying to understand why things happen and identifying possible courses of action to change events. Mentally agile leaders know which factors really matter in the big picture; they identify root causes quickly, display a keen sense of priority, relevance, and significance, and integrate information from a variety of sources while detecting trends, associations, and cause-effect relationships. Just as important, mentally agile leaders explain complex situations with simple, meaningful explanations that others can grasp.

Mentally agile leaders efficiently gather and process relevant information from a systems perspective and then envision feasible futures within increasingly longer time horizons.[32] From a systems perspective, they challenge assumptions, facilitate constructive dissent, and analyze second- and third-order consequences of their decisions.[33] Mentally agile leaders are comfortable making important decisions with less than total information. More importantly, they know when to act decisively and when to act provisionally by experimenting to validate beliefs or assumptions. Once mentally agile strategic leaders have scanned the environment, assimilated the relevant subsystems, and envisioned the future effect of that information on the organization, they then adapt and implement learning mechanisms to alter the processes, structure, and behaviors of their organization to accommodate their envisioned future.

Because it is the level of the organization rather than the officer's rank that determines the nature of problems that will be encountered and the skills required, efforts to develop mental agility must begin early in an officer's career and not be delayed until an officer is about to be placed in charge of an organization at the strategic level.[34] From a school perspective, officers can be introduced to quantitative decision-making, critical thinking, and systems thinking during pre-commissioning and the officers' basic course. Throughout the officer's time at branch schools, simulations allow the officer to adapt and anticipate changing parameters and assumptions. Mental agility can best be developed with a program of instruction that encourages students to develop multiple points of view, consider alternative explanations and argue the merits of competing solutions to complex problems, synthesize as well as analyze, challenge existing frames of reference, and engage in collaborative tasks. In today's deployed Army, the uncertain and complex operating environment is producing leaders accustomed to adapting and thinking unconventionally.[35] In the garrison Army, the Army culture determines the degree of discretion extended to commanders to encourage innovation and improvisation. Ambiguous scenarios at the combat training centers and job variety in the assignment process also help to develop mental agility. Self-development of mental agility can be accomplished throughout a career by activities that stretch the cognitive horizons of the officer. Reading futures studies, publishing, or even reading business journals can also help to develop mental agility. Of course, there are demanding periods of an officer's career (e.g., S-3 or executive officer duty) when there is very little time for reading or self-development. Nevertheless, it is possible to develop mental agility through self-development when the opportunity arises.

Cross-Cultural Savvy

With the growing frequency of coalition warfare and the increasingly expeditionary nature of the Army, the necessity for *cross-cultural savvy* becomes obvious. The Army's future leaders clearly need to be well versed in interacting with cultures lying outside American borders. Cross-cultural savvy, however, refers to more than just the ability to work with non-U.S. militaries. This metacompetency includes the ability to understand cultures beyond one's organizational, economic, religious, societal, geographical, and political boundaries. A strategic leader with cross-cultural savvy is comfortable interacting with and leading joint, international, interagency, or inter-organizational entities. Future strategic leaders must be able to work with diverse groups of people and organizations ranging from 24-year-old congressional staffers, to Northern Alliance warlords, to representatives from nongovernmental organizations.

While cross-cultural skills have been desirable in the past, they will be even more critical for future strategic leaders due to several factors. First, globalization has vastly increased interaction with other nations. Second, the global war on terrorism is illustrating that the Army must coordinate closely with other services, agencies, and organizations in the new national security environment. Third, the Army has traditionally been accused of being somewhat inept in its dealings with Congress and the news media. In the competition for service work jurisdictions and legitimacy, it becomes increasingly important for Army officers to present the Army story effectively to those outside the Army culture. Finally, despite American military power, unilateral military action is becoming less common. Coalitions will continue to be vital to the security strategy.

Cross-cultural savvy implies that an officer can see perspectives outside his or her own boundaries. It does not imply, however, that the officer abandons the Army or American culture in pursuit of a relativistic worldview. Instead, the future strategic leader is grounded in national and Army values, but is also able to anticipate, understand, and empathize with the values, assumptions, and norms of other groups, organizations, and nations.

Cross-cultural savvy can be developed in future strategic leaders as early as pre-commissioning with courses in foreign languages, international relations, and regional studies. Time spent abroad or interning with various organizations can also help broaden the horizons of officers. In the institutional school setting, joint and interagency issues can be taught as well as electives focused on specific regions. Developing cross-cultural savvy in the institutional arena should move the officer from a general understanding and appreciation of other cultures as acquired early in the career to a gradual focus later in the career on particular cultures, organizations, or regions.

The operational domain also plays a key role in developing cross-culturally savvy leaders, especially during the four-to-fifteen year mark of military service. During this period, developing officers should have multiple tours outside the Army's mainstream units. Tours overseas or with foreign militaries, or in higher headquarters staff (joint staff, major commands), graduate school, fellowships or internships with Congress, or industry will contribute significantly to developing cross-culturally savvy officers. Deployments offer a particularly good opportunity to understand and work with different cultures and different organizations outside the military.

While self-development can certainly play a role in developing the cross-cultural savvy metacompetency, it is not the predominant tool because self-development cannot substitute for experience in working with non-Army organizations and cultures. Nevertheless, officers can gain insights through regional and language studies as well as foreign travel and vacations. Additionally, officers can pursue diverse readings on non-military organizations. As with all self-development strategies, care must be taken not to assume that self-development will make up for the lack of formal institutional or operational development. Too often, leader development is relegated to self-development despite the fact that self-development is often the first type of development to be shunted aside by the press of daily events.

Interpersonal Maturity

Many of the interpersonal skills required of strategic leaders are basically the same attributes needed at the organizational level. For example, much like a junior leader, strategic leaders are expected to display compassion when dealing with subordinates on sensitive issues. However, there are several interpersonal skills that, although based on direct and organizational leadership characteristics, are qualitatively different at the strategic level. Strategic leaders must possess an *interpersonal maturity* that goes beyond face-to-face leadership. Strategic leaders devote far more of their time dealing with outside organizations and leaders of other services, agencies, and nations. The power relationship between the strategic leader and individuals from these entities is markedly different from the power relationship typically experienced at the direct and organizational level.

Several interpersonal skills become very important at this level. Most important among these is empowerment. Strategic leaders need to share power with their subordinates, peers, and constituents. They must have the willingness and ability to involve others and elicit their participation based on the subordinate's knowledge and skills because tasks will be too complex or technical and information too widely distributed for leaders to solve problems on their own.[36] An interpersonally mature strategic leader needs to be persuasive and rely less on fiat, consulting with others rather than telling them.[37] Empowerment implies that the leader is a good listener; leadership at the strategic level is as much collaboration as it is authoritarian leadership. Interpersonal maturity implies that strategic leaders do not feel compelled to do all the talking and resist imposing a solution on others.[38]

Because of the unique power relationships, the skills of consensus-building and negotiation rise to the top of a strategic leader's interpersonal maturity. Consensus-building is a complicated process based on effective reasoning and logic which may take place over an extended period.[39] Peers, outside agencies, foreign governments, and other services will not necessarily respond to orders. In essence, the process of consensus-building is insurance that effective reasoning has taken place and that contentious issues have been resolved.[40] As part of this process, or even separate from it, strategic leaders will find that they need to understand the art of negotiation. Again, because many relationships at the strategic level are outside the chain of command and thus without clear subordination, leaders will find themselves in situations difficult or impossible to resolve without the ability to negotiate an agreeable solution through persuasion, compromise, and nonconfrontational anaylsis.

Interpersonal maturity also includes the ability to analyze, challenge, and change an organization's culture so as to align it with the ever-changing outside environment. Strategic leaders must therefore have skills in analyzing cultural assumptions, identifying functional and dysfunctional assumptions, and evolving processes that adjust the culture by building on its strengths and functional elements.[41] Strategic leaders then need to proactively manage change through the processes associated with embedding their vision within the organization and shaping organizational culture to support the vision. Noel Tichy describes the situation as follows: "As long as a culture fits the external environment, it succeeds, but when the external realities change, the culture has to change as well. . . . At certain critical stages, radical cultural shifts are needed, and without leadership, they just don't happen."[42]

Lastly, strategic leaders must have the interpersonal maturity to take responsibility for the development of the Army's future strategic leaders. Therefore, strategic leaders need to teach, coach, mentor, and create an environment where other leaders may do the same. Interpersonal maturity includes a determination to ensure that leader development is not neglected or forgotten in the pursuit of everyday mission accomplishment.

We believe that interpersonal maturity is best developed in the operational and self-development arenas. Thus, the institutional setting can provide a background in leadership theory or study of specific topics such as negotiation, creating a vision, or managing a culture, but interpersonal leadership must be modeled and coached, not taught in a classroom. Role models, mentors, and coaches become critical to developing strategic leaders with interpersonal maturity. Self-development of interpersonal maturity can include constant self-assessment as well as leadership studies. It should be noted that, unlike previously discussed metacompetencies, development of interpersonal maturity can be introduced later in an officer's career. Early stages of an officer's career should focus on direct and organizational leadership skills.

World-Class Warrior

This is the simplest and most understandable of the six strategic leadership metacompetencies. As a *world-class warrior*, strategic leaders move beyond tactical and operational competence. They understand the entire spectrum of operations at the strategic level to include theater strategy; campaign strategy; joint, interagency, and multinational operations; and the use of all the elements of national power and technology in the execution of national security strategy.

The ability to be a world-class warrior rests upon the foundation of technical and tactical competence formed early in an officer's career. The seeds of this metacompetency are planted in the study of military history and military art in the pre-commissioning period. As the officer moves into the field grade ranks, strategic insights along the full spectrum of operations may come from operational assignments in key staffs, particularly during deployments, and from simulations or interagency assignments. Additionally, mentoring and coaching can help develop strategic leaders in becoming world-class warriors. From the institutional perspective, the officer develops this metacompetency by establishing a foundation at the basic and career courses and adding a broader perspective with intermediate level education and the School of Advanced Military Studies. The strategic aspects of full-spectrum operations, however, are mostly introduced at the senior service college level. Self-development can consist of reading professional journals and military history, or taking advantage of online courses and simulations as they become available.

Professional Astuteness

In their initial study of the Army profession, Don Snider and Gayle Watkins arrive at one main conclusion concerning the state of the profession in 2000:

The Army's bureaucratic nature outweighs and compromises its professional nature. This is true in practice, but, of greater importance, it is regarded as true in the minds of the officer corps. Officers do not share a common understanding of the Army profession, and many of them accept the pervasiveness of bureaucratic norms and behaviors as natural and appropriate.[43]

Strategic leaders who are *professionally astute* understand that they are no longer merely members of a profession, but leaders of a profession, specifically of the Army profession as it serves the nation. They see the need to develop the future leaders of the profession, work with stakeholders, and communicate this responsibility to future leaders of the profession. In his book, *Good to Great* (2001), Jim Collins talks about "Level 5" leaders—leaders who can transform a company. He writes, "Level 5 leaders channel their ego needs away from themselves and into the larger goal of building a great company. It's not that Level 5 leaders have no ego or self-interest. Indeed, they are incredibly ambitious—but their ambition is first and foremost for the institution, not themselves."[44] In contrast, Level 4 leaders are often effective and charismatic, yet the company falls apart after they leave since Level 4 leaders put their personal success and egos ahead of building permanent institutional features that would perpetuate success.

The Army needs Level 5 strategic leaders—leaders who take responsibility for the Army as a profession. Leaders with professional astuteness get the mission accomplished, but they also have the insight and drive to do what is best for the profession and nation. This may include having political savvy, knowing when to compromise, or understanding the many constituencies that the Army serves. Additionally, strategic leaders with professional astuteness seek to ensure that the officer corps maintains its expertise across all four fields of expert knowledge—military-technical, moral-ethical, human development, political-cultural—with particular emphasis on the profession's ethic. Professional astuteness is a strategic leadership competency insuring that the Army takes deliberate steps to insure continuance of the Army as a profession, not merely a job, organization, bureaucracy, or occupation.

We believe a two-phased approach can be used to develop professional astuteness in the Army officer corps. The first phase is from pre-commissioning to the end of their four or five years of mandatory active service. During this period the need is for the pre-commissioning education and other developmental instruction to create at least three identifiable outcomes which will then be matured during the initial period of mandatory service. Those outcomes are:

- Understanding of Army officership (i.e., the identities of the officer) sufficiently broad to allow each individual to find intrinsic satisfaction in his or her own self-concept as an officer (initially seen as within an individual branch or specialty);[45]
- Acceptance of the Army profession's ethic; in other words, aligning one's personal concept of duty with the professional ethic such that the future "walk" of the officer will match the moral "talk" of the profession;[46] and
- Understanding of, and mutual relationship with, the Army profession and its unique role within American society that will motivate the officer toward sustained development and service as a member of that profession.[47]

The second stage of development for professional astuteness consists of the time after an officer's initial obligation up to selection for battalion command. During that time, development occurs in a professional culture that encourages:

- Deepening one's expertise across all four fields of the profession's expert knowledge with the freedom occasionally to fail without fatal career consequences;
- "Careers" in which individual officers find that professional satisfactions (developing and applying their expertise) far outweigh the irritation produced by the Army's bureaucratic fetishism;
- Pervasiveness of "candor" as the cultural norm, with all Army leaders at all levels at all times being absolutely frank in interpersonal relations and in official reports and communications; and
- Senior Army officers (as seen from each rank) daily leading by the example of their own moral character, following and policing the profession's ethic across all of its domains, particularly on issues requiring the moral courage for self-abnegation and seeing what's best for the profession from the larger perspective.[48]

Implications for Professional Development

The metacompetencies discussed above serve the purpose of focusing strategic leadership developmental efforts in six specific areas. Critics may correctly claim that other aspects of leadership have been omitted. But these six metacompetencies were derived from an analysis of the current and future operating environments and shaped specifically to produce optimum strategic leadership in those environments. As observed earlier in this chapter, including every conceivable facet of leadership in a more comprehensive competency list would dilute the ability to focus the development of leaders in anticipation of the actual challenges they are most likely to face.

In order for these metacompetencies to be useful, however, a new approach to the profession's development of strategic leaders must be taken. In the past, the Army's method has been to mass-produce leaders competent at the tactical and operational levels. The best officers that emerged from those ranks were automatically designated the Army's strategic leaders. This practice worked for the Cold War when the intersection of large cohorts of officers and a relatively predictable future environment produced a good fit between officers and this industrial-age leader development system. In effect, this was a *sequential* process of leader development wherein the developmental tasks of a later phase were not approached until the outcomes of the previous stage were largely at hand. For example, in this dated process, imparting strategic leadership in the Army (marked by world-class warriorship) was not really addressed until Army officers approached the Army War College. Such development was by and large the responsibility of that single institution. As another example, imparting facility in a foreign language (cross-cultural savvy) was generally not addressed until just prior to the assignment requiring its use.

In contrast to the sequential process of the Cold War model, we believe that in the new era of information-based warfare against asymmetric as well as conventional threats, the profession must adapt its processes of professional preparation so that most of the metacompetencies are developed concurrently. Our reasoning is little different from that of those who advocate concurrent or spiral development of military ideation (viz., joint and service doctrines) and military hardware/software.[49] The six metacompetencies of a strategic leader are now required earlier in a professional's career (at least as early as colonel), and some of them, e.g., cross-cultural savvy to include language training, are needed urgently at the tactical level very early in a career.

Thus, we believe the six metacompetencies should be aiming points for the leader development system from pre-commissioning through general officer. The emphasis in the early stages of an officer's career will continue to be on developing expert knowledge in a particular branch or specialty, but assignment officers, curriculum developers, and unit commanders should take deliberate actions to initiate development of the six metacompetencies. Thus, assignment officers should realize that by the time officers become senior captains, they should have an assignment away from the Army (e.g., graduate schooling or working with a nongovernmental organization) to encourage cross-cultural savvy. Likewise, ROTC instructors should begin the development of professional awareness by introducing cadets to the implications of joining the Army profession. By using the six metacompetencies as aiming points keyed to particular developmental assignments and experiences instead of mere descriptors, the Army can adapt the profession's human development processes from a sequential to a much more parallel mode, one better able to produce professionals at each level with increasing competence to think and act strategically.

Another implication of the foregoing analysis is the necessity for robust professional certifications at key places in a professional's career. It is well understood that vocational professions can maintain the trust of their clients and the motivation of their members only to the extent that each professional's expertise is certified by the profession. No heart patient would consider surgery by a surgeon who is not board-certified and who has not earned the professional degree of a medical doctor. But for the Army, it is fair to say, there is now no effective and recognized system of professional certifications. Solving this challenge to the profession is well beyond the scope of this chapter, except to note that the responsibility to do so rests squarely on the profession's strategic leaders. Their challenge is framed by the fact that no single aspect of officer management currently acts as the profession's certification of individual officer competence—neither the promotion system, nor the systems ascribing military education level (MEL 1-4) and joint education level (JPME 1-2). Over the past decade or more, their inter-relationships have changed so frequently as to render none capable of being *the* certifying system. Either the Army promotion system must be restored to its earlier role as a robust certification system, or such a certification system, likely applied to no more than three levels during a career (e.g., entry, mid-career, strategic leader) needs to be designed and implemented. No profession can long expect the client to view and treat it as a bona fide profession if an effective process of certification is lacking.

This chapter has addressed two key points. First, it takes deliberate effort to develop strategic leaders. They do not emerge by serendipity. They may have emerged through happenstance in the past, but the changing security environment demands a carefully crafted approach for the future. Second, strategic leaders must understand the difference between managing a bureaucracy and leading a profession. Bureaucracies can always hire largely fungible workers, required merely to be efficient in their non-expert work. Professions, however, must grow their own leaders. That takes time, forethought, and the direction and personal involvement of current strategic leaders. Such is the challenge for the Army profession today.

Notes

1. The views expressed herein are not necessarily those of the U.S. Military Academy, the U.S. Army War College, the Department of the Army, or the Department of Defense.

2. Les Brownlee and Peter J. Schoomaker, "Serving a Nation at War: A Campaign Quality Army with Joint and Expeditionary Capabilities," *Parameters* 34 (Summer 2004): 5-23.

3. See conclusions 1, 2, 3 and 8 of Section II titled "The State of the Army Profession, 2000 and 2004" in chap. 1 of the present anthology.

4. The discussion here will follow the framework adopted in chap. 1 of this anthology, that is, the theory of Prof. Andrew Abbott regarding competitive professions operating within a system of professions.

5. For the Army's currently negotiated jurisdictions, see Figure 1-2 in chap. 1 of the present anthology.

6. For a mapping of the Army profession's current expert knowledge, see chap. 9 of the present anthology.

7. As quoted in Robert Debs Heinl, *Dictionary of Military and Naval Quotations* (Annapolis, MD: U.S. Naval Institute, 1966), 190.

8. Based on discussions with Brig. Gen. Rhett Hernandez, Director, Officer Personnel Management Division, Human Resources Command, on 16 December 2004. See also "Q&A: Your officer career" (Interview with Brig. Gen. Rhett Hernandez), *Army Times*, 17 January 2005, 18.

9. See chaps. 11, 15 and 30 in this anthology for extended discussions of these new demands on the Army profession.

10. Brownlee and Schoomaker, 11.

11. See David A. Fastabend and Robert H Simpson, "The Imperative for a Culture of Innovation in the U.S. Army: Adapt or Die," *Army* Magazine, February, 2004, accessed at: http://www.ausa.org/www/armymag.nsf. For a discussion of the advantages inherent in professions for such innovation, see Eliot Freidson, *Professionalism Reborn: Theory, Prophesy and Policy* (Chicago, IL: University of Chicago Press, 1994), 175-178.

12. Brownlee and Schoomaker, 11.

13. This section is derived from Leonard Wong et al., *Strategic Leadership Competencies* (Carlisle Barracks PA: Strategic Studies Institute, U.S. Army War College, 2003).

14. A competency is an underlying characteristic of an individual that leads to effective or superior performance. It subsumes knowledge, skills, attributes, and abilities. Therefore, this chapter focuses on competencies, not the four elements.

15. Stephen R. Covey, "Three Roles of the Leader in the New Paradigm," in *The Leader of the Future: New Visions, Strategies, and Practices for the Next Era*, eds. Frances Hesselbein, Marshall Goldsmith, and Richard Beckhard (San Francisco, CA: Jossey-Bass, 1996), 149–159.

16. James F. Bolt, "Developing Three-Dimensional Leaders," in *The Leader of the Future: New Visions, Strategies, and Practices for the Next Era*, 161-173.

17. See Marshall Sashkin, "Strategic Leader Competencies," in *Strategic Leadership: A Multi-Organizational-Level Perspective*, eds. Robert Phillips and James G. Hunt (Westport, CT: Quorum Books, 1992), 139-160; and Robert Hooijberg, Richard C. Bullis, and James G. Hunt, "Behavioral Complexity and the Development of Military Leadership for the Twenty First Century," in *Out-of-the-box leadership: Transforming the Twenty-First-Century Army and Other Top-Performing Organizations,* eds. James G. Hunt, George E. Dodge, and Leonard Wong, (Stamford, CT: JAI, 1999), 111-130.

18. Karl Weick, "Leadership as the Legitimation of Doubt," in *The Future of Leadership: Today's Top Leadership Thinkers Speak to Tomorrow's Leaders,* eds. Warren Bennis, Gretchen Spreitzer, and Thomas Cummings (San Francisco, CA: Jossey-Bass, 2001), 91-102.

19. An interesting foray into this subject is that of Malcolm Gladwell, *The Power of Thinking without Thinking* (Boston, MA: Little, Brown, 2005).

20. Kimberly B. Boal and Robert Hooijberg, "Strategic Leadership Research: Moving On," *Leadership Quarterly* 11 (2001): 516-17.

21. The conference proceedings are described in *Strategic Leadership: A Multi-Organizational-Level Perspective,* eds. Robert Phillips and James G. Hunt (Westport, CT: Quorum Books, 1992).

22. Roderick R. Magee II, ed., *Strategic Leadership Primer* (Carlisle Barracks, PA: U.S. Army War College, 1998).

23. Headquarters, Department of the Army, Field Manual 22-100, *Army Leadership* (Washington, DC: U.S. Government Printing Office, 1999).

24. *Leader Competencies*, concept paper published by the Center for Army Leadership, Command and General Staff College, Fort Leavenworth, KS, https://cgsc2.leavenworth.army.mil/cal/calreviewdocs/FM22_100.asp accessed 1 December 2004.

25. The argument against long lists of competencies can be found in Jon P. Briscoe and Douglas T. Hall, "Grooming and Picking Leaders Using Competency Frameworks: Do They Work? An Alternative Approach and New Guidelines for Practice," *Organizational Dynamics* 28, no. 2 (Autumn 1999): 37-52.

26. Briscoe and Hall, 48-49.

27. Headquarters, Department of the Army, *The Army Training and Leader Development Panel Officer Study Report to the Army*, http://www.army.mil/atld accessed 1 December 2004.

28. Briscoe and Hall,49.

29. Lt. Gen. William M. Steele and Lt. Col. Robert P. Walters, Jr., "21st Century Leadership Competencies: Three Yards in a Cloud of Dust or the Forward Pass?" *Army* Magazine, August 2001, 31.

30. Sydney Finkelstein and Donald C. Hambrick, *Strategic Leadership* (New York: West Publishing Company, 1996), 39.

31. Boal and Hooijberg, 531.

32. Emil Kluever et al., "Striking a Balance in Leader Development: A Case for Conceptual Competence," *National Security Program Discussion Paper,* Series 92-02, 5.

33. Gregory Dess and Joseph Picken, "Changing Roles: Leadership in the 21st Century," *Organizational Dynamics* 29 (Winter 2000): 30.

34. Kluever, 7.

35. See Leonard Wong, *Developing Adaptive Leaders: The Crucible Experience of Operation Iraqi Freedom* (Carlisle Barracks, PA: Strategic Studies Institute, U.S. Army War College, 2004).

36. Edgar H. Schein, "Leadership and Organizational Culture," in *The Leader of the Future: New Visions, Strategies, and Practices for the Next Era,* 68.

37. Lawrence A. Bossidy and Marcia J. Avedon, "Getting an Executive View: An Interview with a Chief Executive Officer," in *The 21st Century Executive*, ed. Rob Silzer (San Francisco, CA: Jossey-Bass, 2002), 337.

38. Anthony J. Rucci, "What the Best Business Leaders Do Best," in *The 21st Century Executive*, 35.

39. Magee, 42.

40. Ibid.

41. Schein, 68.

42. Noel M. Tichy, *The Leadership Engine* (New York: Harper, 1997), 26.

43. Gayle L. Watkins and Don M. Snider, "Project Conclusions," in *The Future of the Army Profession*, proj. directors Don M. Snider and Gayle L. Watkins, ed. Lloyd J. Matthews (Boston, MA: McGraw-Hill, 2002), 537.

44. Jim Collins, *Good to Great: Why Some Companies Make the Leap . . . and Others Don't* (New York: Harper, 2001).

45. See chaps. 6, 7, 8, and 17 of this anthology for extended discussions on the subject of Army officership.

46. See chaps. 18 and 19 of this anthology for discussions of new demands on the Army's professional ethic.

47. Don M. Snider, "The [Missing] Ethical Development of the Strategic Leaders of the Army Profession for the 21st Century," conference paper, XIII Annual Strategy Conference, Carlisle Barracks, PA, 10 April 2002, 2.

48. Ibid., 3.

49. See A.K. Cebrowski, *Military Transformation: A Strategic Approach* (Washington DC: Office of the Secretary of Defense, 2003), 25-27; and Emily O. Goldman and Leslie C. Eliason, eds., *The Diffusion of Military Technology and Ideas* (Stanford, CA: Stanford University Press, 2003), particularly chap. 13 by the editors.

VII

The Army Profession and Its Political-Cultural Expertise

The Army profession serves its collective client, the American people, through a set of relationships with the citizenry's elected and appointed leaders and the nation's other government agencies. Known as "civil-military relations," such interactions with the clients' surrogates include competing for vital resources, fiscal and human, and advising civilian leaders and then receiving directives regarding where and when to apply the Army's expertise. Traditionally, Army leaders have viewed quite narrowly these political, social, and cultural interactions at the boundaries of the profession, fearing the politicization and thus tainting of the military institution. While those concerns remain, the events since 11 September 2001, particularly the Army's participation in the wars in Afghanistan and Iraq, have repeatedly placed Army leaders, both civilian and military, in the public's eye far more than in the past.

For a number of reasons there is little chance that this situation regarding the Army's public visibility will change in the future. America's preeminent global role, the necessity for American forces to work closely with those of coalition partners, the increased role of joint military commands and agencies, as well as that of the press and the staffs and agencies of the Executive and the Congress, all argue that greater external involvement on the part of the Army and its leaders will occur. Thus there can be no doubt that Army professionals of all ranks must develop more extensive political and cultural expertise if they are to represent effectively the profession in these proliferating interactions. However, these vitally important representations, particularly those shouldered by the profession's strategic leaders, require areas of expert knowledge that remain under-appreciated within the Army profession. This must change if the Army is to compete successfully within its jurisdictions in the 21st century.

Thus the five chapters in this concluding Part VII of the book hold unique importance in their examination of the effects of politics on the Army profession and the vital role of professional norms in the political and cultural interactions inherent in civil-military relations. Lt. Col. Suzanne Nielsen (Chapter 29) and Col. Matthew Moten (Chapter 33) look to the past for insights to the future and their findings are rich indeed. Also, central to this Part is the specific nature of professional norms for militaries serving democratic states, as addressed by Prof. Marybeth Ulrich in Chapter 30. These are norms for political participation, for rendering advice in the policy processes (amplified in Chapter 31), for dealing with the press, for a more constructive role for retired officers, and for balancing the social and military imperatives as democratic societies become more diverse and pluralistic (amplified in Chapter 32). These are difficult issues and doubtless not all readers will agree with the professional norms espoused here. They will, however, serve quite well to start the needed professional discussion.

These chapters focus us on the subtle but critical distinctions between appropriate and inappropriate behavior as the profession's strategic leaders work within these milieus—for example, the difference between rendering professional advice and advocating for a particular policy. Said another way, the profession's leaders must render military advice as a servant profession, and not as a political interest group. Thus, while it will certainly be difficult, the Army profession must nonetheless clarify appropriate norms for its members' actions at the military-political interface, and develop a deeper bench of strategic leaders with real political expertise. Since the profession's jurisdictional competitions are usually negotiated with civilian officials as the ultimate arbiters, Army practice and culture must be adapted to value that expert knowledge so that the profession may be fully represented in deliberations vital to its ability to serve the American people.

29 | Rules of the Game? The Weinberger Doctrine and the American Use of Force[1]

Suzanne C. Nielsen

The early 1990s saw a resurgence of concern about the condition of civil-military relations in the United States. Perhaps first strongly articulated in Richard Kohn's 1994 article, "Out of Control: The Crisis in Civil-Military Relations," a significant issue was whether senior military leaders were playing an inappropriate role in the policy-making process.[2] Kohn focused especially on Chairman of the Joint Chiefs of Staff Colin Powell's public positions against the integration of homosexuals into the armed services and against U.S. military intervention in Bosnia.[3] Although Kohn himself later acknowledged that the term "out of control" overstated his case with regard to the military as a whole, he was concerned about senior military leaders' influence and military politicization.[4]

In the view of some observers, after Gen. John Shalikashvili took over as Chairman in 1993 he initiated significant progress toward restoring "a functional balance" to civil-military relations.[5] He served less as a policy advocate, and seemed to focus more on giving purely military advice. However, a look at the complete record suggests that General Shalikashvili also at times publicly took positions about the proper ends of policy. When he was selected to be Chairman, General Shalikashvili had a reputation as critic of the Clinton administration's inaction in the Balkans.[6] General Shalikashvili also made some fairly broad policy statements as Chairman. For example, in remarks at George Washington University in 1995, he said the following:

> When we respond to a humanitarian tragedy and our hearts are most affected, we must be wary of the impulse to do more than provide relief. . . . No matter what we think we agree on, it should not be to rebuild or restructure other nations—that takes generations of sustained effort.[7]

Is this statement, which is intrinsically about policy goals, an appropriate comment from a professional military officer? In other words, is it based on professional military expertise? If not, what are the implications of military leaders acting in an extra-professional capacity?

The most recent conflict to serve as a test case for the interaction of civilian and military officials over use of force issues has been the conflict in Iraq. At first, active duty military officers seemed to take a lower public profile, with the spotlight falling instead on senior military leaders who had recently retired. Several of these officers, to include former four-star generals, were a regular presence on 24-hour news channels providing commentary and critique on the war—and periodically raising the ire of the Bush administration.[8] However, recent press reports have focused on the

627

views of serving military officials about the conduct of the war, to include a senior officer who voiced his dissatisfaction in these words:

> I do not believe we had a clearly defined war strategy [or] end state and exit strategy before we commenced our invasion. Had someone like Colin Powell been the chairman [of the Joint Chiefs of Staff], he would not have agreed to send troops without a clear exit strategy. The current OSD [Office of the Secretary of Defense] refused to listen or adhere to military advice.[9]

While the actions of active-duty military officers during the second Iraq War have not raised the same scholarly concern about an "out of control" military that surfaced in the 1990s, neither a civilian nor a military consensus yet exists as to the appropriate role of military officers in the foreign policy-making process in the United States.

In this chapter, I shall suggest a framework for thinking through the appropriate role for a professional military officer in the context of use-of-force decision-making. In this discussion, the term "professional" will be used in a significant and highly particular sense. The view of professions taken here is fundamentally informed by Andrew Abbott's seminal study *The System of Professions* (1988). Abbott defines professions as "exclusive occupational groups applying somewhat abstract knowledge to particular cases," with the tasks they perform being "human problems amenable to expert service."[10] In this light, then, professional military officers provide expert service in meeting society's needs in the realm of military security. This view of officers as the expert providers of a service is a starting point for establishing norms for their role in state decision-making concerning the use of force.

Based upon Abbott's definition of a profession, the argument below will proceed in four steps. I first suggest the relevance of Abbott's discussion of professional practice in thinking through the role of the professional military officer in decision-making on the use of force.[11] Second, I draw on works dealing with strategy and civil-military relations to fill in the content of the military officer's expertise. Once this groundwork has been laid, I use the insights from these two sections to analyze a particularly noteworthy attempt—the Weinberger doctrine—to establish guidelines for decision-making on the use of force in the United States. Focusing on that doctrine, I use it as a vehicle to discuss the professional officer's special expertise and role in the decision-making process. Finally, I note the implications for the future of the military profession flowing from the manner in which senior military leaders conduct themselves in rendering advice and making decisions on the use of force. Although many have examined the role of military officers in this process, their analyses have usually surfaced implications relevant to the health of civil-military relations or civilian control.[12] Here, instead, the focus will be on implications for the future of the military profession itself.

It is important to note at the beginning that my conclusions about the Weinberger doctrine do not necessarily reflect a consensus view among today's military officers. My assessment that the Weinberger doctrine constitutes a problematic guide for a professional military officer to adopt on use-of-force questions is in tension with some currently prevalent military attitudes as depicted by the recent survey findings of the

Triangle Institute for Security Studies Project on the Gap Between the Military and Civilian Society. For example, that study found that a majority of elite officers believe it is appropriate for the military to "insist" on use-of-force measures such as the development of an exit strategy.[13] The study then goes on to suggest that the choice of "insist" over the other alternatives of "be neutral," "advise," "advocate," or "no opinion," may reflect lingering distrust from the Vietnam period. While this may be true, the perspective developed here will challenge the appropriateness of its adoption as a requirement by military leaders.[14]

Professional Practice

When senior military officers participate in use-of-force decision-making, they are engaging in professional practice. Abbott's discussion of the three tasks of professional practice—diagnosis, inference, and treatment—provides a useful set of concepts for analyzing the manner in which military leaders provide advice and carry out decisions once they are made.[15]

The first task, that of diagnosis, involves taking information into the professional knowledge system. The professional sorts available facts according to professional rules of relevance, and evaluates them in accordance with rules of evidence. In so doing, the professional is attempting to structure the situation. In describing this process, called "colligation," Abbott gives the example of generals who "must ask leading questions of civilian politicians who 'don't know what they want.'"[16] Rules of relevance may be strict:

> If the client is an individual, such extraneous qualities often include his or her emotional or financial relation to the "problem." If the client is a group, they include irrelevant internal politics, financial difficulties, and so on. (A diagnosed problem may still be ambiguous, but the ambiguity will be profession-relevant ambiguity—ambiguity within the professional knowledge system.)[17]

An additional step in the diagnostic process is to classify a problem, which involves referring it "to the dictionary of professionally legitimate problems."[18] Classification is often related to expected successful treatments.

The second professional task is inference, which consists of reasoning about the connection between diagnosis and treatment. According to Abbott, "Inference is undertaken when the connection between diagnosis and treatment is obscure."[19] This would seem to be the case with many problems of matching military means to political ends. The costs and reversibility of treatment also affect the type of inference needed: "Where costs are prohibitive or there is no second chance, a professional must set a strategy from the outset."[20] Abbott argues that this is the case in military tactics: "Classic military tactics . . . work by construction. The tactician hypothesizes enemy responses to gambits and considers their impact on his further plans."[21]

The third and final task is treatment. Abbott describes treatment in this way: "Like diagnosis, treatment is organized around a classification system and a brokering process. In this case brokering gives results to the client, rather than takes information from the client."[22] In the military context, treatment consists of executing the use-of-force decision that has been made. Performed in combination, the three tasks discussed above—diagnosis, inference, and treatment—constitute professional practice and provide a useful way to think about the role of military leaders in use-of-force decision-making.

However, Abbott's discussion of professional practice is useful for an additional reason as well. It suggests mechanisms for future change:

> The central phenomenon of professional life is thus the link between a profession and its work, a link I shall call jurisdiction. To analyze professional development is to analyze how this link is created in work, how it is anchored by formal and informal social structure, and how the interplay of jurisdictional links between professions determines the history of the individual professions themselves.[23]

In the last sentence above, Abbott's emphasis is on interprofessional competition as a source for change, but a profession can affect the strength or shape of its jurisdiction in the course of its own work. Associated with each of Abbott's professional tasks are characteristics that may affect the strength of a given profession's jurisdiction. It will be useful to review these jurisdiction-related characteristics briefly here.

Beginning with diagnosis, Abbott argues that there are several aspects of this task that can affect jurisdictional vulnerability. First, there is the restriction of information: "To the extent that a profession restricts the relevant information or specifies the admissible types of evidence it risks competition with groups whose standards are less restrictive."[24] This could act as an incentive to meet the client on the client's own terms and not according to professional expertise.[25] Second, jurisdictional strength may be affected by both the clarity and encompassing nature of classification. Professions are more vulnerable to losing functions that they do not clearly identify as central to their work. "Since they are not claimed explicitly . . . on the main list of professional tasks, but rather implicitly by the dimensions of professional jurisdiction, they are held only weakly. Redefinition under a new system of abstractions can easily remove them."[26] One can easily imagine the relevance of such redefinition to the U.S. Army with reference to tasks such as foreign military training, antinarcotics operations, and perhaps even small-scale contingency operations more generally. If these tasks are not viewed as core functions, the Army is more likely to lose control over them to other state institutions or even to private corporations.

The nature of inference, the second task of professional practice, can also affect jurisdictional strength. Perhaps most relevant here, Abbott argues that the strength of a profession's hold on its jurisdiction is enhanced by logical inferential chains that are neither too short (in which case the matching of diagnosis to treatment becomes routine, thus obviating professionals), nor too long and too abstract (in which case professionals' claims to special expertise in fulfilling a task are weakened). Perhaps an example of this latter case is the tendency described by Peter Feaver for civilians to exercise assertive control over nuclear weapons policy and operations.[27] One explanation for such assertive control is undoubtedly the high levels of cost and risk associated with the use of nuclear weapons. However, Abbott's insight concerning long and abstract inferential chains points to a second factor. Reasoning about nuclear deterrence and escalation can be highly abstract and has (fortunately) never been tested. An extended and tenuous inferential chain could be one reason that military attempts to achieve autonomy in nuclear operational matters based on claims of expertise have not been more successful.

The third and final professional task, treatment, also has properties that affect jurisdictional strength. Abbott lists the following: measurability of results, specificity of treatment (generally the more specific, the stronger the hold of the profession), acceptability of the treatment to clients, and, perhaps most important, efficacy. Abbott argues that the prestige of professionals is enhanced when they conduct treatment on their own terms, but that in doing so they risk competition from those more willing to compromise professional practice:

> So it is that many professions meet clients on their own grounds—phrasing their treatments in common language, offering advice on professionally irrelevant issues, indeed promising results well beyond those predicted by the treatment structure itself. If they didn't do it, clients would take their problems to someone who would. A similar process forces professionals to keep a weather eye to treatment costs.[28]

If this dynamic holds in the civil-military relationship, it implies that both parties must prefer that the military officer play the role of professional advice-giver. If political leaders do not hold such a preference, the professional officer's incentive to abandon strictly professional grounds to maintain influence or relevance in the policy process becomes clear.

In sum, Abbott's discussion of professional practice is useful both because it provides a way to think through the role of military officers in use-of-force decision-making, and also because it suggests ways in which the conduct of professional work could affect the profession itself. According to Abbott:

> Every profession aims for a heartland of work over which it has complete, legally established control. . . . Every profession aims not only to possess such a heartland, but to defend and expand it. The few who are content with limited jurisdictions— actuaries, veterinarians—are quite atypical.[29]

Perhaps U.S. military services are "atypical" professions that are content with limited jurisdictions; perhaps not. If Abbott is right that professions shape their jurisdictions in the course of their work, it would be valuable for strategic military leaders to be conscious of this process and consider the implications of their professional choices in this light.

The Military's Professional Expertise

To this point, I have argued that Abbott's discussion of professional practice provides a useful way to think through the work of professional military officers as they participate in the state's decision-making about the use of force. Abbott's discussion of this concept also provides useful insights concerning the manner in which that role is played for the military itself. However, what has not yet been specified is the nature of the special expertise that the professional officer brings to bear. In other words, what is the content of expert military knowledge? In order to answer that question, it is useful to refer to Carl von Clausewitz's magisterial treatise *On War* (1832). In addition, since according to Abbott the work that societies consign only to experts can vary from society to society and from time to time, it is essential to refer to the acknowledged classics of American civil-military relations. The two texts that I will use for this purpose are Samuel Huntington's *The Soldier and the State* (1957) and Morris Janowitz's *The Professional Soldier* (1960).[30]

Clausewitz: Knowledge and Experience

One of the reasons Clausewitz's work has been so enduring is the timelessness of his insights into the nature of war as both a military and political phenomenon. His fundamental argument is that war is always political in nature, "merely the continuation of policy by other means."[31] That being so, politics provides the source of war, governs (at least to some extent) the means to be used, and also establishes the ends to be sought. War is a subordinate phenomenon, whose logic is deducible from the always-ascendant politics. However, within its subordinate realm, war is also unique; or, as Clausewitz says, war has its own grammar.[32] War has its own tools and, because its means include violence, takes place in a unique environment of danger, fear, physical exertion, and uncertainty. The uniqueness of war also stems from the fact that it is a form of human interaction—it takes place between living forces that react to each other's actions. These properties create the complexity of warfare, ensuring that "absolute, so-called mathematical, factors never find a firm basis in military calculations."[33] Mere abstract calculations cannot be relied upon to predict outcomes.

Because of these characteristics, Clausewitz argues that the most proficient experts in the grammar of war must have a combination of knowledge, experience, and even certain character traits. With regard to knowledge, Clausewitz focuses on what he calls the only means of war, combat: "However many forms combat takes . . . it is inherent in the very concept of war that everything that occurs *must originally derive from combat*."[34] The following excerpt elaborates on this point:

> Warfare comprises everything related to the fighting forces—everything to do with their creation, maintenance, and use. Creation and maintenance are obviously only means; their use constitutes the end. . . . If the idea of fighting underlies every use of the fighting forces, then their employment means simply the planning and organizing of a series of engagements. The whole of military activity must therefore relate directly or indirectly to the engagement.[35]

For Clausewitz, the military leader must be especially expert in the conduct of war (Clausewitz seems to classify the creating, maintaining, and training of military forces as subordinate activities).[36] This involves expertise in both tactics, "*the use of armed forces in the engagement*," and strategy, "*the use of engagements for the purpose of the war*."[37] To get an even more complete picture of the specific knowledge Clausewitz would require of the competent commander, one need only examine the level of detail that Clausewitz devotes to the topics of Books Four though Seven of his work, which are the engagement, military forces, the attack, and defense. A critical study of military history is necessary for the full development of this expertise.[38]

When discussing the highest level of command, Clausewitz adds new requirements without dropping any of those that have previously been levied. The supreme military commander must have a grasp of national policy, while remaining aware of what he can achieve with the military means at his disposal:

> He must be familiar with the higher affairs of state and its innate policies; he must know current issues, questions under consideration, the leading personalities, and be able to form sound judgments. . . . He must know the character, the habits of thought and action, and the special virtues and defects of the men whom he is to command. . . . He must be able to gauge how long a column will take to march a given distance under various conditions.[39]

In order to use military means to achieve the political purposes being sought, the military commander at the highest level must have both the skills of a military leader and a sound grasp of national policy.

When Clausewitz discusses the expertise of the military leader in the grammar of war, we can properly conclude that it is a transformational grammar he is discussing.[40] In the context of language, transformational grammar allows for the identification of underlying structure or a deeper relation between sets of concepts so that even if words are ordered differently or appear differently in different sentences, in their "deep structure" one can find similar meanings.[41] Clausewitz's conception of war as *"an act of force to compel the enemy to do our will"* is broad enough to allow many different combinations of military means and political ends to share in the same underlying meaning.[42] Clausewitz acknowledges this when he argues that in war many roads lead to success, shaped by both the ends being sought and the means chosen. Since even the personality of statesmen and commanders matters, "these questions of personality and personal relations raise the number of possible ways of achieving the goal of policy to infinity."[43] As long as there is decision by combat, whether or not fighting actually takes place, the military commander's expertise in the grammar of war is relevant.[44] A great advantage of this is that Clausewitz's concept is then open to being updated. For example, there is nothing inconsistent with Clausewitz's thought in the idea that knowledge of joint military operations (a topic that Clausewitz, who discusses only ground forces, does not touch on) is part of the expertise of today's grammar of war.

Returning to Abbott for a moment, we can usefully recall that he defines professionals to be those who apply abstract knowledge to particular cases. In this sense, is the knowledge Clausewitz describes professional? Clausewitz does see benefit, though limited, in the military leader's use of theory as long as it is closely related to (derived from and tested against) the historical record. At a minimum, it is valuable from an educational perspective:

> Theory exists so that one need not start afresh each time sorting out the material and plowing through it, but will find it ready to hand and in good order. It is meant to educate the mind of the future commander, or, more accurately, to guide him in his self-education, not to accompany him to the battlefield.[45]

Clausewitz clearly believes that those in senior levels of command must have strong intellectual abilities which theory can help develop but should not constrain when it comes to practice. This seems very much in line with Abbott, who recognizes the instructional value of what he calls "academic knowledge," but also recognizes that mastery of "prestigious academic knowledge" does not necessarily indicate an ability to excel in professional work.[46]

This point leads to what Clausewitz sees as an additional component of the special expertise of the military leader—experience. It is consistent for Clausewitz to emphasize experience given what he describes to be the special environment of warfare. The following passage is revealing:

> If one has never experienced war, one cannot understand in what the difficulties mentioned really consist, nor why a commander should need any brilliance and exceptional ability. Everything looks simple; the knowledge required does not look remarkable, the strategic options are so obvious that by comparison the simplest problem of higher mathematics has an impressive scientific dignity.[47]

Clausewitz argues that what uninitiated analysts tend to miss are all the aspects of war, to include physical danger, fear, physical exertion, uncertainty, and even the vagaries of weather, that together create "friction." Friction is what distinguishes "real war from war on paper," and makes true the claim that "everything in war is very simple, but the simplest thing is difficult."[48] For Clausewitz, the only lubricant for friction is experience—ideally in combat, but at a minimum in demanding peacetime exercises. Clausewitz argues:

> Action in war is like movement in a resistant element. . . . The good general must know friction in order to overcome it whenever possible, and in order not to expect a standard of achievement in his operations which this very friction makes impossible. . . . Practice and experience dictate the answer: "This is possible, that is not."[49]

A significant component of the professional expertise military leaders bring to bear is the experience they have gained through years of professional practice during peace and war.

A final requirement that Clausewitz requires of those at the top of their profession, or those with "military genius," has to do with character. For Clausewitz, genius in any complex activity requires *"a harmonious combination of elements"* which includes "appropriate gifts of intellect and temperament."[50] Because war is a dangerous realm, courage and self-confidence are essential traits in a military leader. For Clausewitz, the highest kind of courage is a combination of courage in the face of personal danger and courage to accept responsibility. This special temperament also includes an urge to act rationally, regardless of circumstances.

> Strength of character does not consist solely in having powerful feelings, but in maintaining one's balance in spite of them. Even with the violence of emotion, judgment and principle must still function like a ship's compass, which records the slightest variations however rough the sea.[51]

Although it is hard to deny the significance of this insight, it is also difficult to generalize from it. Perhaps we can never be confident in our measurement of a military leader until we observe him in extremis.

To sum up the argument to this point, Clausewitz concludes that the special expertise of the military officer is derived from a combination of experience and specialized knowledge in the grammar of war. To clarify this further, it is useful to look at what Clausewitz excludes as well as includes when discussing military expertise. He excludes at least three types of matters that are relevant to this chapter: domestic politics, the ends of policy, and interpretation of the international political environment. To see this in reference to domestic politics, it is useful to examine the manner in which Clausewitz bounds his conception of strategy. He argues:

> Strategy . . . does not inquire how a country should be organized and a people trained and ruled in order to produce the best military results. It takes these matters as it finds them in the European community of nations, and calls attention only to unusual circumstances that exert a marked influence on war.[52]

In other words, domestic political organization is beyond a theory of war. A second way Clausewitz makes this point is through his insight that one key to Napoleon's great success was that he transformed war itself by engaging the population in a fundamentally new way. This was a political change, which Napoleon made as an emperor who united the roles of politician and soldier in one person. As Clausewitz observed, "The tremendous effects of the French Revolution abroad were caused not so much by new military methods and concepts as by radical changes in policies and administration, by the new character of the French people, and the like."[53] The failure to grasp and adapt to these changes was primarily political because even if a purely military figure had recognized them, he could at most advise his government based on this recognition. An adequate response required the mobilization of society itself.

A second issue that is beyond military expertise, according to Clausewitz, is the ends of policy. Clausewitz makes this clear when discussing his conception of war as a trinity made up of the people, the commander and his army, and the government. The people are identified with the passions of war, and the commander and his army represent the creative element because they operate in "the realm of probability and chance." However, his strongest statement is about the government. He opines that "the political aims are the business of the government alone."[54] In the following comment, Clausewitz reveals both his views on the irrelevance of domestic political matters to the military officer, and the proper location of authority over policy goals:

> It can be taken as agreed that the aim of policy is to unify and reconcile all aspects of internal administration as well as of spiritual values, and whatever else the moral philosopher may care to add. Policy, of course, is nothing in itself; it is simply the trustee for all these interests against other states. That it can err, subserve the ambitions, private interests, and vanity of those in power, is neither here nor there. In no sense can the art of war ever be regarded as the preceptor of policy, and here we can only treat policy as representative of all interests of the community.[55]

In other words, even if policy is based on the selfish interests of the ruler alone, or even if it is mistaken, from the military commander's perspective it must be assumed to be in the interests of the entire community. The need to adjust political purposes based on available military means may on occasion slightly modify these purposes, but will not change them fundamentally.[56]

Finally, Clausewitz seems to place the primary responsibility for interpreting the international political environment on political rather than military leaders. Governments can contribute to their states' success in war by accurately interpreting the character of international relations. For example, Clausewitz notes that changes in international alignments can drastically affect the success of an offensive operation: "All depends on the existing political affiliations, interests, traditions, lines of policy, and the personalities of princes, ministers, favorites, mistresses, and so forth."[57] The ability to analyze these factors is the special expertise of political leaders, not military commanders.

Given this discussion of the special nature of military expertise, what does it imply for the role of military leaders in use-of-force decision-making? First, Clausewitz does expect military commanders to bring to bear a special expertise, since he recognizes that political leaders may lack detailed knowledge of military matters. Clausewitz does not believe that this is necessarily a problem because above all the policy-maker needs "distinguished intellect and strength of character," and "can always get the necessary military information somehow or another."[58] A second clear expectation is that commanders will remain aware, from the initiation of hostilities to their completion, of the subordination of military means to the political ends being sought. In Clausewitz's words, "If we keep in mind that war springs from some political purpose, it is natural that the prime cause of its existence will remain the supreme consideration in conducting it."[59] Finally, Clausewitz seems to expect close and continuous cooperation between political leaders and their senior military commander. In fact, he argues that if events allow it the supreme military commander should sit in on cabinet meetings so that the cabinet can be involved in the commander's activities. This is necessary because "no major policy can be worked out independently of political factors."[60] In sum, the military commander's role is to be the expert advisor and executor of policy whose function is always subordinate to the political purposes of the government.[61]

Do Clausewitz's Insights Hold in a Liberal, Democratic Context?

Despite the universality many attach to Clausewitz's work, it is nevertheless necessary to ask whether his insights remain valid in the context of a liberal democratic society such as the United States. To address this question, it is helpful to turn to the signature works of Samuel Huntington and Morris Janowitz—two authors who have written authoritatively about the military profession in the United States. Relying primarily on Huntington's *The Soldier and the State* and Janowitz's *The Professional Soldier*, I will address the question raised by this section in three parts. First, is Clausewitz's affirmation of the special expertise of the military professional valid in the American context? Second, do these authors agree with Clausewitz that the matters of politics, policy, and international relations should be excluded from the military officer's realm of special expertise? Third, do they agree with Clausewitz on the nature of the role that military officers should play in use-of-force decision-making?

So far as the military officer's special expertise is concerned, Huntington's and Janowitz's conceptions seem very close to those of Clausewitz. Huntington accepts the importance of both knowledge and experience; his summary of the central skill of the officer is captured in the idea that officers are experts in the "management of violence." This includes organizing, equipping, and training the force, planning for its use, and directing the force in and out of combat. He also agrees with Clausewitz that these tasks require a special expertise that can be acquired only through considerable training and experience. It is neither purely an art nor a craft, but "an extraordinarily complex intellectual skill requiring comprehensive study and training."[62]

Janowitz seems basically to agree. This is interesting given that one of the hypotheses of *The Professional Soldier* is that there was a convergence underway between the skills of soldiers and civilians. However, he points out that "the military professional is unique because he is an expert in war-making and in the organized use of violence."[63] Later, he resumes this train of thought: "Despite the rational and technological aspects of the military establishment, the need for heroic fighters persists. The pervasive requirements of combat set the limits to civilizing tendencies."[64] In the 1974 prologue to a new edition, Janowitz notes the continued preeminence of combat in the military's view of its work, adding that another distinguishing aspect of military professional work is the normality of risk: "Even when the military are engaged in essentially defensive, protective, and constabulary types of activities, the element of risk and uncertainty is viewed as part of the standard operating procedure."[65] In contrast to most civilian occupations, where risk arises only from uncharacteristic occupational failure, it is viewed by the military as an intrinsic aspect of its activities. In sum, with perhaps a few minor additions such as the idea of normality of risk, Clausewitz's conception of military expertise is reinforced by authoritative experts in American military sociology.

Regarding the second question, do Huntington and Janowitz agree with Clausewitz that domestic political affairs, the ends of foreign policy, and interpretation of the international political environment are areas outside the military officer's special expertise? Huntington strongly agrees on the first two, arguing:

> Politics deals with the goals of state policy. Competence in this field consists in having a broad awareness of the elements and interests entering into a decision and in possessing the legitimate authority to make such a decision. Politics is beyond the scope of military competence, and the participation of military officers in politics undermines their professionalism, curtailing their professional competence, dividing the profession against itself, and substituting extraneous values for professional values.[66]

Janowitz seems to agree that both of these activities are beyond the military's special competence, but suggests that members of the military might be tempted to try their hand anyway. Janowitz argues that because some military leaders are suspicious of the efforts of politicians to formulate national goals, "military literature is replete with self-generated efforts to ascertain the consensus of American society, as a basis for long-range planning."[67] Janowitz also notes the tensions between what he sees as two conflicting ideologies in the military over the use of force. One group, which he calls the absolutists, holds that only total victory is an acceptable military outcome. Members of the other group, which he labels the pragmatists, display greater flexibility with regard to acceptable military outcomes. Janowitz's preference for the pragmatists places him directly in Clausewitz's camp.[68]

The two authors together also raise a point about policy ends that Clausewitz does not discuss. Huntington argues that the professional "is judged not by the policies he implements, but rather by the promptness and efficiency with which he carries them out."[69] If so, this would make it easier for military leaders to be neutral about the ends of policy and act in a strictly professional manner. However, Janowitz points out in a discussion of the use of force in both Korea and Vietnam that "opposition to the expansion of the President's war-making powers has 'spilled over' in political criticism of the armed forces."[70] As Janowitz as well as many Vietnam veterans could attest, public judgments of the military will at times be political rather than based solely on military "promptness and efficiency." The fact that military officers may be held responsible in the public eye for policy failures does not mean that the ends of policy are within their professional purview, but it does explain why refraining from addressing policy goals could be difficult.

In sum, Huntington and Janowitz seem to agree with Clausewitz that domestic political affairs and the ends of policy fall outside the domain covered by professional military expertise. However, on the question of responsibility for interpreting the international political environment, things are not quite as clear. Huntington argues that one of the functions of the military officer is to "represent" security needs within the state's machinery based on "what he considers necessary for the minimum military security of the state in the light of the capabilities of the other powers."[71] However, this seems problematic given Huntington's logic elsewhere. First, though Huntington does specify that this function must be fulfilled within the government, it is difficult to draw the line between professional and political behavior for a military officer playing this advocacy role. Second, this representative function would appear to involve recommending trade-offs between uses of resources that only political leaders are really positioned to make. Finally, it is dangerous to attempt to separate an analysis of enemy capabilities from an analysis of political factors such as one's own national interests, as well as the likely alignments of the "other powers" affected in times of hostility. Once factors such as these are taken into account, it is doubtful that an assessment of military security needs could be founded on purely military expertise.

Janowitz also argues, although with a different emphasis, that part of the military officer's special expertise should be awareness of the political and social impact of the military's actions on international affairs. With an argument that seems more affected by the impact of the Cold War than the nature of the political system, Janowitz urges that "a 'political warfare' dimension has come to permeate almost every type of military operation in a 'no-war-no-peace' period."[72] In this environment, officers must be sensitive to and able to manage the political consequences of their actions. Janowitz believes that this has put a new strain on civil-military relations because "the more technical-minded officers are a hazard to the conduct of foreign policy; the more political-minded require more elaborate direction than is supplied by traditional forms of civilian supremacy."[73] Given that Janowitz's insight also seems to hold in the post-Cold War period, this addition to the content of military expertise originally laid out by Clausewitz seems useful when thinking about the special expertise of professional officers in the globally-engaged military of the United States.

The final question asked at the beginning of this section relates to the role military officers of a liberal, democratic society play in use-of-force decision-making. It is important to note that Clausewitz's arguments about political control over the use of force are based purely on the logic of strategic success. However, in a democratic context, civilian supremacy is based not just on strategic requirements, but also on political ideology. Peter Feaver lays out this logic very clearly: in a society that embraces democratic values, "the prerogatives of the protectee are thought to trump the protectors at every turn."[74] The citizens of a democracy temporarily delegate authority to a political leader, and wish to maintain control over both this individual and the military, the military being the political leader's agent. Feaver argues that "although the [uniformed] expert may understand the issue better, the expert is not in a position to determine the value the people will attach to different issue outcomes . . . only the civilian can set the level of acceptable risk for society."[75] Political leaders are then accountable for these choices to the citizens they represent.

Beyond recognizing the fundamental requirement for civilian supremacy in a democratic society, do Huntington and Janowitz agree with Clausewitz's views on the role of military officers in use-of-force decision-making? Basically, the answer is yes, although both Huntington and Janowitz go further in discussing potential problems. For example, Huntington discusses a list of potential grounds on which the military officer might disobey a political leader, including political ineptitude, illegality, immorality, and lack of professional competence. On the first of these grounds, political ineptitude, Huntington disclaims the legitimacy of military disobedience. On the second two, illegality and immorality, he argues that the political leader's interpretations deserve great weight. It is only on the last issue, lack of professional competence, that Huntington provides clear guidelines as to when disobedience can be justified. However, even here it is only in cases where a president orders an officer to "take a measure which is militarily absurd when judged by professional standards and which is strictly within the military realm without any political implications."[76] Given that significant actions will rarely be free from any political implications, the window opened here is either small or nonexistent. In any event, Huntington does go further than Clausewitz in addressing possible civil-military tensions.[77]

Janowitz's concerns run in a different direction, stemming in part from his disagreement with Huntington's assertion that a professional military is by its very nature apolitical. Instead, Janowitz argues that "the military is a unique pressure group because of the immense resources under its control and the gravity of its functions."[78] He sees this as relatively inevitable:

> Their activities as a pressure group, if responsible, circumscribed, and responsive to civilian authority, are a part of the decision-making process of a political democracy. Yet, at a point, knowingly or unknowingly, efforts to act as a leadership group can transcend the limits of civilian supremacy.[79]

In other words, some political activity by the military in a democracy is not shocking, and up to a point not abnormal or even a cause for concern. However, his idea that the military may become a political pressure group does more to explain the challenges facing senior military officers than it does to suggest a different conception of expert knowledge or a different appropriate role in use-of-force decision-making.

In sum, it would appear that Clausewitz's conceptions of the special expertise of military leaders and their role in use-of-force decision-making carry over into a democratic context relatively unscathed. In the grammar of war, the special expertise of a professional military officer is broadly defined. The expertise is developed through both education and experience. Having a particular competence also implies that some arguably relevant matters are excluded. Some of the most important of those excluded are domestic political matters and the derivation of policy goals. Finally, the professional military officer brings this special expertise to bear in the state's use-of-force decision-making, serving both as an adviser and executor of policy. At the same time, the professional officer never forgets that the ultimate objectives are political, and the use of military means must always be in support of those ends.

The Weinberger Doctrine—Rules of the Game?

To this point, I have argued that it is useful to think of the participation by military officers in use-of-force decision-making as part of their professional practice. Abbott's discussion of the tasks of diagnosis, inference, and treatment provides a way of thinking about strategic military leaders' work, and about how the performance of that work affects the future of the profession. Beyond that, I have drawn insights from works of strategy and civil-military relations to lend substance to the idea of professional expertise in a military context, and also to gather propositions about the role of military officers in use-of-force decision-making. This section will use this groundwork to examine the Weinberger doctrine, which is one policymaker's attempt to establish guidelines for use-of-force decision-making in the United States. The main question that this section seeks to address is whether, based on their professional military expertise and role in the process, military as well as civilian leaders will find the Weinberger doctrine a suitable set of guidelines for adoption. In the concluding section of this chapter, I will set forth the implications that military adoption of use-of-force guidelines not clearly based on professional criteria could have for the military profession itself.

The Weinberger Doctrine

On 28 November 1984, then Secretary of Defense Caspar Weinberger gave a speech to the National Press Club titled "The Uses of Military Power." This speech was part of a debate among key players within the Reagan administration over the appropriate uses of military power. It was not the first public address by one of

President Reagan's cabinet officials on the topic. On 3 April 1984, Secretary of State George Shultz had given a speech titled "Power and Diplomacy in the 1980s," whose main message was that effective diplomacy must be backed by military power. Reacting to the Long Commission's report on the bombing of the Marine barracks in Beirut the previous year and its assertion that more options based on diplomacy should have been pursued, Shultz argued that this not only was an unfair depiction of U.S. efforts in that case, but also reflected an erroneous American tendency to believe that diplomacy and military options are "distinct alternatives." In fact, he said, "The lesson is that power and diplomacy are not alternatives. They must go together, or we will accomplish very little in this world."[80] He also argued that the position and responsibilities of the United States in the 1980s demanded a robust form of American engagement:

> Whether it is crisis management or power projection or a show of force or peace-keeping or a localized military action, there will always be instances that fall short of an all-out national commitment on the scale of World War II. . . . It is highly unlikely that we can respond to gray-area challenges without adapting power to political circumstances or on a psychologically satisfying, all-or-nothing basis.[81]

Turning to Central America, Shultz also acknowledged the complex moral, social, and economic issues associated with American engagement there, but argued against those who would turn these issues into "formulas for abdication, formulas that would allow the enemies of freedom to determine the outcome."[82]

Some six months later, Shultz gave another address in which he laid out his position on the necessity to respond to the problem of terrorism with an "active strategy."[83] This strategy relied on recognition that terrorism had become an instrument of warfare used by enemies of the United States, and, to combat it, "we must be willing to use military force."[84] Shultz argued that it was important to try to build consensus for U.S. action in this area, but in the event of specific incidents "the decisions cannot be tied to the opinion polls."[85] In his memoirs, he explained that part of his motivation for this speech was what he perceived as the unwillingness by Weinberger and the Joint Chiefs to seriously consider a military response to terrorist incidents even in the face of credible intelligence.[86]

In was in this context that Secretary Weinberger gave his speech in November 1984 that laid out "six major tests to be applied when we are weighing the use of U.S. combat forces abroad."[87] These six tests are as follows:

1. The United States should not commit forces to combat overseas unless the particular engagement or occasion is deemed vital to our national interest or that of our allies.
2. If we decide it is necessary to put combat troops into a given situation, we should do so wholeheartedly, and with the clear intention of winning. If we are unwilling to commit the forces or resources necessary to achieve our objectives, we should not commit them at all.
3. If we do decide to commit forces to combat overseas, we should have clearly defined political and military objectives. And we should know precisely how our forces can accomplish those clearly defined objectives.

4. The relationship between our objectives and the forces we have committed—their size, composition and disposition—must be continually reassessed and adjusted if necessary.

5. Before the United States commits combat forces abroad, there must be some reasonable assurance we will have the support of the American people and their elected representatives in Congress.

6. The commitment of U.S. forces to combat should be a last resort.[88]

In his memoirs, Weinberger explains that he found it necessary to address a State Department view that "an American troop presence would add a desirable bit of pressure and leverage to diplomatic efforts, and that we should be willing to do that freely and virtually without hesitation." He goes on to note that "the NSC staff were even more militant . . . spend[ing] most of their time thinking up ever more wild adventures for our troops."[89] In Weinberger's view, the option of using force should be turned to only under much more restrictive circumstances.

Weinberger's speech was not met by universal accolades, nor was it the last public round in the Shultz-Weinberger debate. One of the most scathing popular responses to the speech was a *New York Times* article by William Safire titled "Only the 'Fun' Wars." In that piece, Safire argues that "the military mind has been brought to this surly, don't-call-us-until-you're-ready-to-abdicate-to-us philosophy by a serious of failures."[90] Safire critiques Weinberger's doctrine for its "popularity requirement," rejection of the utility of limited military action, vital interest criterion, and "moral blindness." He approvingly cites Edward Luttwak's comment that Weinberger's Defense Department is "like a hospital that does not want to admit patients."

Shultz's own public response came in a speech entitled "The Ethics of Power" delivered the following month.[91] His logic again runs counter to Weinberger's in several ways. First, the requirements that a "vital interest" be at stake and that force should be used only as a "last resort" sit uneasily with Shultz's repeated view that "power and diplomacy must always go together." One difficulty with the concept of vital interests is that, "for the world's leading democracy, the task is not only immediate self-preservation but our responsibility as a protector of international peace."[92] On the question of last resort, Shultz does acknowledge the value of resorting to force only when other means of influence are not adequate. However, he also points out that "a great power cannot free itself so easily from the burden of choice. It must bear responsibility for the consequences of its inaction as well as of its action."[93] In his memoirs, Shultz also argues that "the idea that force should be used 'only as a last resort' means that by the time of use, force is the *only* resort and likely a much more costly one than if used earlier."[94]

The third of Weinberger's tests that Shultz criticizes is the requirement for public support. In Shultz's view,

> There is no such thing as guaranteed public support in advance. Grenada shows that a president who has the courage to lead will *win* public support if he acts wisely and effectively. And Vietnam shows that public support can be frittered away if we do not act wisely and effectively.[95]

Again, Shultz supplements this comment in his memoirs, arguing that the requirement for public support "was the Vietnam syndrome in spades, carried to an absurd level, and a complete abdication of the duties of leadership."[96] Shultz continues with a bit of philosophy about the American political system:

> My view is that democratically elected and accountable individuals have been placed in positions where they can and must make decisions to defend our national security. . . . The democratic process will deal with leaders who fail to measure up to the standards imposed by the American people and the established principles of a country guided by the rule of law.[97]

Shultz goes on to acknowledge that, while he had supporters, there were many others who disagreed with his views on the necessity for tying together power and diplomacy. It seems likely that a lack of consensus on issues such as these is not unusual in American politics.[98]

Towards A Professional Military Perspective on the Weinberger Doctrine

With the Weinberger-Shultz debate in mind, as well as the earlier discussion of professional practice, military expertise, and the professional military officer's role in use-of-force decision-making, is it feasible to arrive at the content of a purely professional military perspective on the Weinberger doctrine? Here I will make the attempt, looking at each of Weinberger's six tests in turn. The central question is whether a uniformed officer, judging from a purely professional military perspective, could apply each of these tests.[99]

1. The United States should not commit forces to combat overseas unless the particular engagement or occasion is deemed vital to our national interest or that of our allies.

Given the arguments above, an officer using purely professional criteria cannot apply Test 1 for several reasons. First, there is the highly subjective task of prioritizing national interests. This is a task involving trade-offs among values that only political leaders are positioned to make. When it comes to the vital interests of allies, the task seems to become even more distant from the professional military officer's expertise. Second, this is inherently a question about which policy ends or goals are worth pursuing. Again, this task does not fall within the military leader's special expertise.

Given that it would be inappropriate for the military officer to employ Test 1 himself, should a military officer counsel a political leader to apply this test? Even here, I would argue that Test 1 is problematic. The president may judge it useful to commit forces to combat to protect an interest that is merely important if it is judged that such an action may avoid putting a vital interest at risk. Perhaps the most important role of the military professional is to provide an estimate of costs which may cause a political leader to moderate policy goals. Although a military officer may prefer that forces be committed to combat only when vital interests are at stake, this is less a product of military expertise than an expression of a particular value judgment.

2. If we decide it is necessary to put combat troops into a given situation, we should do so wholeheartedly, and with the clear intention of winning. If we are unwilling to commit the forces or resources necessary to achieve our objectives, we should not commit them at all.

Although Test 2 seems to be mere common sense, there are some concepts in the first sentence that are very subjective and need careful interpretation. First, there is the idea of committing forces "wholeheartedly." What does this mean? If it means relating military means to political ends in such a way as to achieve objectives at the lowest possible cost, it makes sense. Otherwise, its meaning and implications are unclear.

Second, and more problematic, is the idea of "winning." Is winning the same thing as achieving one's political objectives, even if the mission is peace enforcement or deterrence? The important point is that a professional who accepts the subordination of military means to political ends would also have to recognize that the political end is not always victory. Clausewitz is very clear on this point, noting that because war may have purposes that vary infinitely in scale, the only way to generalize about their purposes is to recognize that they all constitute a politically desired peace.[100] In other words, paraphrasing and at the same time disagreeing with Gen. Douglas MacArthur, there is a substitute for victory—the politically desired peace.

One reason this is worth highlighting is that in his memoir Weinberger seems to associate success with the departure of troops.[101] This hearkens to contemporary debates about exit strategies and timetables. Although these may be political requirements, there does not seem to be a basis within the special professional expertise of military officers to argue that they are a valid test to be passed when considering the use of force.

A second problematic association with the word "win" is that it could be taken to mean the military undertakes only operations like Desert Storm in which clear military victory is possible. General Shalikashvili notes that this could be a temptation for some, but rejects the idea of putting "a sign outside the Pentagon that says 'We only do the big ones.'"[102] It would be difficult to find a basis within the military's professional expertise for an argument that the military should be given only missions in which there will be a decisive outcome followed by a rapid troop withdrawal.

In sum, as an expert in war the officer must give the political decision-maker a professional opinion as to the military means necessary to achieve a political end. The officer may also appropriately counsel that the political leader apply the latter half of Test 2. Given his assessment of the military means needed to meet a particular goal, the military professional could appropriately suggest to the political leader that "if we are unwilling to commit the forces or resources necessary to achieve our objectives, we should not commit them at all." Once this counsel has been given, however, the political leader must be the final authority for the decision and bears the political and moral responsibility for its results.

3. If we do decide to commit forces to combat overseas, we should have clearly defined political and military objectives. And we should know precisely how our forces can accomplish those clearly defined objectives.

4. The relationship between our objectives and the forces we have committed—their size, composition and disposition—must be continually reassessed and adjusted if necessary.

Tests 3 and 4 are appropriately discussed together because they are closely related, and also because they are very consistent with the special expertise and professional practice of military officers. Regarding Test 3, as strategists, professional military officers could reasonably be expected to assist in the refinement of political purposes and the development of military objectives to support those purposes. Weinberger himself cites Clausewitz on this point: "No one starts a war—or rather, no one in his senses ought to do so—without first being clear in his mind what he intends to achieve by that war and who he intends to conduct it."[103] Military leaders should also provide estimates of military costs and risks so that political leaders can decide whether their goals are worth pursuing with military means. Even though the responsibility for developing the ends of policy belongs to political leaders, these political aims may need to be modified based on the ability of military means to meet them.

Military requests for a clear statement of goals—or military help in developing them—are not the same thing as military leaders embracing only certain goals. The first two are appropriate; the third is not. A clear political objective, for example, could be something like "give the peace process a chance to work." The greatest challenge to military professionalism here may not be in the test itself, but rather in avoiding the temptation to label as "unclear" political objectives that are merely disliked.

Test 4 seems even more unexceptionable. During an ongoing use of force, the situation will continue to develop and even political objectives may change. The tasks of diagnosis, inference, and treatment may take place in a continuous cycle. In fact, this test serves as a necessary supplement to the preceding provision about clarity of political and military objectives before committing forces.[104]

5. Before the United States commits combat forces abroad, there must be some reasonable assurance we will have the support of the American people and their elected representatives in Congress.

As Clausewitz recognized in *On War*, military leaders at the highest levels must be broadly familiar with the country's political affairs. To serve effectively, these senior leaders must have sensitivity to their civilian masters' political needs.[105] Such sensitivity may be extremely valuable in fostering the type of civil-military communication most likely to produce a coherent relationship between military means and political ends. However, that does not mean that it is appropriate for military professionals to set forth requirements for public support prior to operational deployments. As outlined above, the special expertise of the military professional does not include public opinion and political mobilization. While it is appropriate for military leaders to appreciate the potentially important role of popular support in gaining strategic success, it is not their particular area of expertise and therefore should not be the basis of their arguments.

If public support is in fact essential, it seems far more likely that political leaders have some familiarity with what is necessary to gain or sustain it. Also, still granting for the moment the idea that public support is essential, it is not entirely clear that public support is necessary prior to, as opposed to being attained and sustained during, actual hostilities. While Test 5 has some appeal, it is more of a political matter than a purely military one.

6. *The commitment of U.S. forces to combat should be a last resort.*
Again, this tenet goes beyond the appropriate ground on which military professionals should be standing when participating in use-of-force decision-making. In any particular situation, senior military leaders may be the most familiar with the death and destruction that are part of the environment of warfare. They also have the responsibility to take care of their troops as well as fulfill national purposes. This combination of knowledge and responsibility gives military leaders a special obligation to state potential costs and risks in any military operation. Nevertheless, the requirement that force be used only as a last resort pushes this obligation too far. Though senior military leaders should have familiarity with all the instruments of national power, including the diplomatic, informational, and economic as well as military, it is up to the political leadership to decide what mixture of instruments best serves national policy goals in any given case. There are risks, costs, and values at stake in such choices that only political leaders have the authority to make.

In sum, it would seem unexceptionable for the professional military officer to personally employ only two of the six tests, specifically Test 3 which relates to establishing clear objectives, and Test 4 which argues for the maintenance of a coherent relationship between military means and political ends. In other words, if military leaders were to seek a professional code governing the participation of the military officer in use-of-force decision-making, the Weinberger doctrine would be a problematic set of criteria to adopt. Military leaders who adopt all of Weinberger's tests are taking positions that distort proper conceptions of military professionalism—actions that could have implications for the military profession itself. The next and final section will suggest what some of those implications might be.

Why Clarity about the Role of Professional Military Officers Matters

There are two ways in which military participation in use-of-force decision-making could affect the future of the military profession. First, it could adversely impact on future interactions between political leaders and military officers. In other words, it could degrade the military professional's role as advisor. Second and more speculatively, it could bring into question the military's jurisdiction itself by shaping the scope of what is thought to be legitimate professional work. I will discuss each of these in turn.

The Professional Officer as Advisor

If a military officer expresses preferences among policy goals while acting in an official capacity, that officer may come to be seen as more of a political figure than a military expert. To some extent, the danger here is the same as could arise from politicization. Huntington argues that politicization can happen either when military leaders espouse policies that have nonprofessional sources (i.e., the substance is political), or when military leaders are used to publicly advocate policy ends regardless of content (the manner of presentation is political). As an example, he asserts that the Joint Chiefs played political roles in the Truman administration. They became policy advocates at the behest of President Truman, who found that they could play a useful role in justifying his foreign policies before Congress and the public. Eventually, Huntington argues, the influence of the Chiefs was substantially attenuated. He cites Senator Robert A. Taft, speaking of the Joint Chiefs in the spring of 1951: "I have come to the point where I do not accept them as experts, particularly when General Bradley makes a foreign policy speech. I suggest that the Joint Chiefs of Staff are absolutely under the control of the Administration."[106] This perception is particularly interesting because it shows that the benefits of behaving according to professional criteria go beyond enhancing civilian control. When military leaders confine their public utterances to positions based on professional expertise, they are also safeguarding their expert status and perhaps preventing the discounting of military advice.[107]

A second possibility, with potentially even more negative consequences, is that the public stances of military officers could lead these officers to be disregarded in use-of-force decision-making. This could happen if officers were known to embrace certain policy ends, and political leaders came to believe they could not trust those officers' opinions or behavior. It could also happen if military leaders publicly advocated preconditions for the use of force such as tests for vital interests, exit strategies, public support, and last resort. In Abbott's language, these factors relate to diagnosis in the sense that they could be seen as constraints on what the military decides to include in its "dictionary of professionally legitimate tasks." If this "dictionary" has been formulated in an overly restrictive way, political leaders may not seek military advice because they know in advance it would not be useful or acceptable. Political leaders seeking to conduct coercive diplomacy might not consult the leaders of an Army that does only "the big ones."

In the U.S. political system, with its rule of law and civilian supremacy, the fact that military leaders are not consulted for advice may not mean that forces are allowed to lie fallow—it may just mean that military leaders end up having less input as to how forces are used. Again with regard to Abbott's conception of professional practice, the military may be called upon only to provide a treatment conceived without benefit of military input. In this unfavorable scenario, military leaders are prevented from performing the tasks of diagnosis and inference because their conception of professional work was overly inflexible and formulaic.

Positions based on either an overly narrow or an overly broad conception of the military's professional expertise could ultimately have negative consequences. The input of military officers could come to be seen either as irrelevant to the needs of the policy-maker, or as having dubious professional credibility. Thus, for the professional to be standing on ground that is as firm as possible, his positions and arguments should be solidly based on professional expertise. Moreover, establishing a solid understanding within the profession of what that professional expertise includes would be of immense value.

A second implication of the discussion above is that both the substance of professional military advice and the manner of its presentation are important. The officer whose argument is based on professional knowledge or experience is perhaps on firm ground, but that same officer's position would be all the more solid if the argument were expressed in a professional way. Since views on what constitutes professional behavior may vary, again a validated understanding of standards among the strategic leaders of the profession would be useful.

Impact on the Military Institution Itself

Although in the short run it seems likely that the biggest impact of the manner in which military leaders do their professional work will be on their role as military advisors, over the long run it may impact more directly on the armed forces themselves. In considering this possibility, it is useful to return to Abbott's concept of jurisdiction and the idea of jurisdictional claims. Abbott argues that a profession claims monopoly over a certain set of tasks—its jurisdiction. In the case of the U.S. military, it seems most reasonable to assume that the audience to whom it is making jurisdictional claims is the nation and its people. Settlements of these claims as well as jurisdictional boundaries may change over time. It is thus clear that both restrictive and expansive claims of jurisdiction could have an adverse effect.

The first possibility, then, is that military leaders take an overly restrictive view of their jurisdiction and seek to limit the scope of what are seen to be professionally legitimate tasks. According to Abbott, one possible effect is that new actors will appear and claim those disclaimed tasks. Abbott suggests the following dynamic: "A powerful profession ignores a potential clientele, and paraprofessionals appear to provide the same services to this forgotten group."[108] While the idea of multiple clients does not carry over into the military context, the idea of new groups entering the scene to claim neglected tasks seems quite plausible. In the case of the U.S. Army on the issue of use of force, those new groups could be either other armed services or private military corporations. This is not to say that change along these lines is necessarily good or bad, but it does suggest that the conception of professional work implicit in the arguments made by military leaders in use-of-force decision-making could have this sort of effect, and that these leaders had best be aware of it.

A second possibility is that military leaders could develop an overly expansive conception of military jurisdiction. However, Abbott sounds an interesting note of caution:

> No profession can stretch its jurisdiction infinitely. For the more diverse a set of jurisdictions, the more abstract must be the cognitive structure binding them

together. But the more abstract the binding ideas, the more vulnerable they are to specialization within and to diffusion into the common culture without.[109]

Moreover, given the difficulty of being effective at a very large number of tasks at once, the danger of laying claim to an overly extended range of tasks is clear. As Abbott points out, the strength of a profession's jurisdictional claims rests on efficacy.

In sounding these cautionary notes, I am not making a case for any particular position between overly restrictive and overly expansive jurisdictions. My purpose rather is to suggest that the dynamics Abbott points to provide a helpful way of thinking through the implications of particular choices. It is important for service leaders to be aware that they are making choices which impact on their professional status as advisors and the professional work of their institutions as they participate in decision-making about the use of force.

Conclusion

The great sociologist Max Weber once stated, "Politics is a strong and slow boring of hard boards. It takes both passion and perspective."[110] Perhaps the same can also be said about how challenging it would be to achieve a consensus among the strategic leaders of the military profession about the issues raised here—the content of military professional expertise and the norms that should govern the professional military officer's participation in decision-making about the use of force. However, boring these hard boards would be worth the effort. Failure to be clear on these points could have seriously adverse consequences for the profession itself, however unintended.

Notes

1. The views expressed herein are those of the author and do not purport to reflect the position of the U.S. Military Academy, Department of the Army, or Department of Defense.
2. See Richard H. Kohn, "Out of Control: The Crisis in Civil-Military Relations," *The National Interest* 35 (Spring 1994): 3-17. See also Russell F. Weigley, "The American Military and the Principle of Civilian Control from McClellan to Powell," *The Journal of Military History* 57, no. 5 (October 1993): 27-58.
3. Kohn, "Out of Control," 13.
4. Richard Kohn in Colin Powell et al., "An Exchange on Civil-Military Relations," *The National Interest* 36 (Summer 1994): 29. For another view suggesting that the Joint Chiefs of Staff under President Clinton played an improper role in "circumscribing or preemptively vetoing policy options," see A.J. Bacevich, "Tradition Abandoned: America's Military in a New Era," *The National Interest* 48 (Summer 1997): 16-25.
5. See Lyle J. Goldstein, "General John Shalikashvili and the Civil-Military Relations of Peacekeeping," *Armed Forces and Society* 26, no. 3 (Spring 2000): 403.
6. Goldstein, "General John Shalikashvili," 393.
7. John M. Shalikashvili, "Employing Forces Short of War," *Defense* 3 (May/June 1995): 4.
8. Perry Smith, "Armchair Generals," *Wall Street Journal*, 17 April 2003, A12; and Thom Shanker and John Tierney, "Top-Ranked Officer Denounces Critics of Iraq Campaign," *New York Times*, 2 April 2003, A1.

9. Thomas E. Ricks, "Dissension Grows in Senior Ranks on War Strategy," *Washington Post*, 9 May 2004, A1. In this portion of the article, Ricks is quoting "a senior general at the Pentagon," who "spoke only on the condition that his name not be used."

10. Andrew Abbott, *The System of Professions: An Essay on the Division of Expert Labor* (Chicago, IL: University of Chicago Press, 1988), 8, 35.

11. Abbott, *The System of Professions*, 58.

12. Two recent examples are Deborah D. Avant, "Are the Reluctant Warriors Out of Control? Why the U.S. Military is Averse to Responding to Post-Cold War Low-Level Threats," *Security Studies* 6, no. 2 (Winter 1996/1997): 51-90; and Michael C. Desch, *Civilian Control of the Military: The Changing Security Environment* (Baltimore, MD: The Johns Hopkins University Press, 1999).

13. See *Project on the Gap Between the Military and Civilian Society: Digest of Findings and Studies*, First Revision (Durham, NC: Triangle Institute for Security Studies, 2000), 9-10. Accessed at http://www.poli.duke.edu/civmil/summary_digest.pdf on 12 August 2001. The study termed as "elite" those "officers at various ranks who have been identified for the education to prepare them for promotion and advancement."

14. An interesting novel that examines these tensions in the modern American military is Thomas E. Ricks, *A Soldier's Duty* (New York: Random House, 2001).

15. The following discussion of professional practice is drawn from chap. 2, "Professional Work," in Abbott, *The System of Professions*, 35-58.

16. Ibid., 41.

17. Ibid.

18. Ibid.

19. Ibid., 49.

20. Ibid., 48.

21. Ibid., 49.

22. Ibid., 44.

23. Ibid., 20.

24. Ibid., 44.

25. A book suggesting that military leaders have done this in the past, and that this constituted a military failure, is H.R. McMaster's *Dereliction of Duty*. My interpretation of McMaster's argument is that the Chiefs did not abide by professional rules of relevance in their dealings with President Johnson. They altered their opinions based on factors that, though important to Johnson, were irrelevant to the military situation in Vietnam. See H.R. McMaster, *Dereliction of Duty* (New York: HarperCollins Publishers, Inc., 1997), especially 323-34.

26. Abbott, *The System of Professions*, 44.

27. See Peter D. Feaver, *Guarding the Guardians* (Ithaca, NY: Cornell University Press, 1992), 9.

28. Abbott, *The System of Professions*, 48.

29. Ibid., 71.

30. These two works have the advantage of discussing the military profession in an American context, and in the 20th century. However, a disadvantage of using them is that they, at least in their original editions, are over 40 years old. Despite this limitation, I would argue that they are still useful for both their comprehensiveness and their provision of a useful baseline from which one can measure change.

31. Carl von Clausewitz, *On War*, trans. and eds. Michael Howard and Peter Paret (Princeton, NJ: Princeton University Press, 1976), 87. All citations from *On War* will be from this edition. Clausewitz used italics frequently; when quoting him, I will keep to his usage.

32. Ibid., 606.

33. Ibid., 86.

34. Ibid., 95.
35. Ibid.
36. Ibid., 128.
37. Ibid.
38. Ibid., 164. Clausewitz writes: "In the study of means, the critic must naturally frequently refer to military history, for in the art of war experience counts more than any amount of abstract truths."
39. Ibid., 146.
40. I am indebted to Prof. James Burk for bringing this concept to my attention.
41. *Encyclopedia Britannica*, britannica.com 1999-2000, s.v. "transformational grammar."
42. Clausewitz, *On War*, 75.
43. Ibid., 94.
44. Clausewitz argues that the only means of war is combat, but acknowledges that combat takes many different forms. In all military actions, the outcome rests on the assumption that if it came to fighting, the outcome would be favorable: "The decision by arms is for all major and minor operations in war what cash payment is for commerce. Regardless how complex the relationship between the two parties, regardless how rarely settlements actually occur, they can never be entirely absent." Ibid., 97.
45. Ibid., 141.
46. Abbott, *System of Professions*, 54.
47. Clausewitz, *On War*, 105.
48. Ibid., 119.
49. Ibid., 120.
50. Ibid., 100.
51. Ibid., 107.
52. Ibid., 144.
53. Ibid., 609.
54. Ibid., 89.
55. Ibid., 607.
56. Ibid., 87.
57. Ibid., 569.
58. Ibid., 608.
59. Ibid., 87.
60. Ibid., 608.
61. These arguments are further developed in Suzanne C. Nielsen, *Political Control Over the Use of Force: A Clausewitzian Perspective*, The Letort Papers (Carlisle Barracks, PA: U.S. Army War College, Strategic Studies Institute, 2001).
62. Samuel P. Huntington, *The Soldier and the State* (Cambridge, MA: The Belknap Press of Harvard University Press, 1957), 13.
63. Morris Janowitz, *The Professional Soldier* (London: Collier-Macmillan Limited, 1960; reprint, New York: The Free Press, 1964), 15.
64. Ibid., 33.
65. Morris Janowitz, "Prologue: The Decline of the Mass Armed Force," *The Professional Soldier* (London: Collier-Macmillan Limited, 1960; reprint, New York: The Free Press, 1964, 1974), xv.
66. Huntington, *Soldier and the State*, 71.
67. Janowitz, *The Professional Soldier*, 272. This military skepticism about the values of political elites and their military expertise still exists today. See *Project on the Gap Between the Military*

and Civilian Society: Digest of Findings and Studies, First Revision (Durham, NC: Triangle Institute for Security Studies, 2000), accessed at http://www.poli.duke.edu/civmil/summary_digest.pdf on 1 February 2001. Interestingly, even Caspar Weinberger expressed some skepticism about the role of political leaders. In justifying his "political support" test for the use of force, he argues: "Our government is founded on the proposition that the informed judgment of the people will be a wiser guide than the view of the president alone, or of the president and his advisers, or of any self-appointed elite." Caspar Weinberger, "U.S. Defense Strategy," *Foreign Affairs* 64 (Spring 1986): 689.

68. Janowitz, *The Professional Soldier*, 257-77.

69. Huntington, *Soldier and the State*, 73.

70. Janowitz, "Prologue," xlix.

71. Huntington, *Soldier and the State*, 72.

72. Janowitz, *The Professional Soldier*, 342.

73. Ibid.

74. Peter Feaver, "The Civil-Military Problematique: Huntington, Janowitz and the Question of Civilian Control," *Armed Forces and Society* 23, no. 2 (Winter 1996): 153.

75. Feaver, "Civil-Military Problematique," 154.

76. Huntington, *Soldier and the State*, 77.

77. A more useful and frequent example, not discussed by Huntington, arises when the president involves himself in tactical situations while ignorant of the actual situation on the ground. Such involvement could have potentially disastrous consequences. See Lloyd J. Matthews, "Political-Military Rivalry for Operational Control in U.S. Military Actions" (Carlisle Barracks, PA: U.S. Army War College, Strategic Studies Institute, 1998), 11-14.

78. Janowitz, "Prologue," xlviii.

79. Janowitz, *The Professional Soldier*, 343.

80. George Shultz, address before the Trilateral Commission on 3 April 1984, *Department of State Bulletin* 84, no. 2086 (May 1984): 13.

81. Shultz, Trilateral Commission address, 13.

82. Ibid., 14.

83. George Shultz, address before the Park Avenue Synagogue in New York on 15 October 1984, *Department of State Bulletin* 84, no. 2093 (December 1984): 16.

84. Ibid., 16.

85. Ibid.

86. George Shultz, *Turmoil and Triumph* (New York: Charles Scribner's Sons, 1993), 648.

87. Caspar Weinberger, remarks to the National Press Club on 28 November 1984, *Defense* 85 (January 1985): 9.

88. These are verbatim excerpts (though I changed his bullets to numbers for notational clarity) from Weinberger, National Press Club remarks, 10.

89. Caspar Weinberger, *Fighting for Peace: Seven Critical Years in the Pentagon* (New York: Warner Books, Inc., 1990), 159.

90. William Safire, "Only the 'Fun' Wars," *New York Times*, 3 December 1984, sec. A, 23. Among the failures, Safire mentions Vietnam, Desert One, and Lebanon. For another interesting press critique of the Weinberger doctrine, see George J. Church, "Lessons from a Lost War: What Has Viet Nam Taught about When to Use Power—and When Not To?" *Time*, 15 April 1985, 40.

91. George Shultz, address at the convocation of Yeshiva University in New York on 9 December 1984, *Department of State Bulletin* 85, no. 2095 (February 1985): 1-3.

92. Ibid., 2.

93. Ibid., 3.

94. Shultz, *Turmoil and Triumph*, 650.

95. Shultz, Yeshiva University address, 3.

96. Shultz, *Turmoil and Triumph*, 650.

97. Ibid.

98. Weinberger again responded publicly with regard to the justification for risking soldiers in combat: "The hope that a limited U.S. presence might provide diplomatic leverage is not sufficient." Caspar Weinberger, "U.S. Defense Strategy," 689.

99. Two interesting point-by-point discussions of the Weinberger doctrine can be found in Christopher M. Gacek, *The Logic of Force* (New York: Columbia University Press, 1994), 265-69; and Michael I. Handel, *Masters of War*, 2nd ed. (London: Frank Cass, 1992; reprint, 1996), 185-203. The analysis here has been informed by their insights, but has a different focus.

100. Ibid., 143.

101. See Weinberger, *Fighting for Peace*, 137, 150.

102. Shalikashvili, "Employing Forces Short of War," 5.

103. Cited in Weinberger, National Press Club remarks, 10.

104. I would like to thank Prof. Peter Feaver for helping me clarify my thinking on this point. Part of the expertise officers bring to bear is an awareness of the history of conflict leading them to recognize that objectives often shift as operations progress. Therefore, while it is very helpful to start out with a clear set of political and military objectives because they foster an integration of political ends and military means, it is likely that these objectives will shift during the course of military operations.

105. On this point, see Lloyd J. Matthews, "The Politician as Operational Commander," *Army*, March 1996, 29.

106. Huntington, *Soldier and the State*, 386.

107. As Lloyd J. Matthews points out, the American political system requires senior military officers to manage a constant tension "between the internal demands of conforming one's speech to service on the Commander in Chief's national defense team, and the external obligation for honesty and candor before the nation, Congress, and the citizenry." Matthews gives valuable guidelines for managing this tension in "The Army Officer and the First Amendment," *Army*, January 1998, especially 31, 34.

108. Abbott, *System of Professions*, 91.

109. Ibid., 84.

110. Max Weber, "Politics as a Vocation," *From Max Weber: Essays in Sociology*, eds. and trans. H.H. Gerth and C. Wright Mills (New York: Oxford University Press, 1953), 128.

30 Infusing Normative Civil-Military Relations Principles in the Officer Corps[1]

Marybeth Peterson Ulrich

Introduction

The backdrop of American military professionalism is the American political system. The heart of the American political system is embodied in the democratic institutions established in the Constitution. The Constitution's division of powers and authority, along with its system of checks and balances, "has succeeded not only in defending the nation against all enemies foreign and domestic, but in upholding the liberty it was meant to preserve."[2]

The American founders chose to establish a republic as the best way to uphold liberty and ensure the security of its citizens. In James Madison's words, "A Republic, by which I mean a Government in which the scheme of representation takes place, opens a different prospect, and promises the cure for which we are seeking."[3] Representative democracy entrusts the management of governmental affairs to those elected by virtue of their demonstrated aptitude or desire to take on the burden of responsibility for the "people's business."

Most of democratic theory is focused on ensuring that these political agents remain accountable to the polity. The founders' preference for republican democracy was rooted not in the belief that a system based on a "scheme of representation" and shared powers would produce the most efficient outcomes, but in a confidence that the democratic processes established embodied the best chance for the preservation of liberty.[4]

Civil-military relations in a democracy are a special application of representative democracy with the unique concern that designated political agents control designated military agents.[5] Acceptance of civilian supremacy and control by an obedient military has been the core principle of the American tradition of civil-military relations.[6] U.S. military officers take an oath to uphold the democratic institutions that form the very fabric of the American way of life. Their client is American society, which has entrusted the officer corps with the mission of preserving the nation's values and national purpose. Ultimately, every act of the American military professional is connected to these realities he or she is in service to the citizens of a democratic state who bestow their trust and treasure with the primary expectation that their state and its democratic nature will be preserved.

This chapter seeks to spark a dialogue on the current state of civil-military norms within the U.S. military profession. A framework is presented laying out key principles to consider when exercising professional judgment is this area. The development of a brand of professionalism within the officer corps that is consistent with these underlying principles is a crucial component of officership.

Democratic Military Professionalism

The military profession is unique because of the distinct function that society has entrusted to it, that is, to direct, operate, and control an organization whose primary function is the threat or use of deadly military might against enemy forces or targets which the political leadership designates. Military professionals in all political systems share a mandate to be as competent as possible in their functional areas of responsibility in order to defend the political ends of their respective states.[7] However, military professionals in service to democratic states face the added burden of maximizing functional competency without undermining the state's democratic character. These military professionals must practice a unique brand of professionalism which takes this into account.

Samuel Huntington in his classic work, *The Soldier and the State* (1957), posited that there is an inherent tension between the state exercising its responsibility to provide for the security of its democratic polity and the militaries established to fulfill this function. Indeed, the requirement to balance the functional imperative (providing for the national defense) with the societal imperative (preserving and protecting democratic values),[8] calls for the development of democratic military professionals.[9] Officers comfortable with their roles as democratic military professionals will be better equipped to navigate the complex terrain of American civil-military relations.

The Nature of National Security Communities in Democratic States

Democratic military professionals do not pursue their responsibilities to the state in isolation. They are part of a broader national security community comprised of national security professionals[10] from both the civilian and military spheres, other actors such as journalists and academics who contribute intellectual capital and foster debate, legislative bodies with constitutional responsibilities to oversee and provide resources for national security policy, and, finally, the public at large to whom all of the above are ultimately responsible. National security policy is the product of the overlapping participation of all members of a state's national security community.

National security professionals, however, have a unique role because they are charged with the responsibility to formulate and execute national security policy within the prescribed bounds of a democratic policy-making process. These officials, who may come from both the civilian and military spheres, have diverse functions requiring mutual cooperation in order to make and carry out policy.[11] Each national security professional's "home sphere" emphasizes different areas of competence. The civilian national security professional's career will be characterized by greater experience at the strategic and political levels while the military national security professional may be more rooted in technical expertise and operational knowledge related to the use of force. In order to craft effective national security policy, civilian and military national security professionals must develop overlapping areas of competence.

Scholars and practitioners alike recognize that the lines separating the competencies of military professionals and political leaders have become increasingly blurred. The existence of a core group of national security professionals, comprised of capable and respected colleagues with overlapping competencies in political and military affairs, is instrumental in achieving balanced civil-military relations and effective national security policy outcomes.

Implications for Democratic Military Professionals

Democratic military professionals must understand the breadth and depth of their participation in the national security process. They must recognize that, while participation within a national security community is often a collaborative process requiring the expertise and inputs of various actors, there are distinct differences in responsibilities stemming from one's constitutional role in the process. These differences may dictate certain limits upon the various legitimate actors in the process. While national security in democracies is conducted within the context of civil-military relationships, these civil-military relations necessarily have a specific structure that channels participants' competencies and responsibilities in order to maximize security at the least cost to democratic principles.

The scope of this chapter is limited to the development of a set of comprehensive norms for military professionals in their civil-military relations. Implications for other members of the national security community will develop throughout this chapter, but the emphasis here is to improve the quality of participation of democratic military professionals in the national security policy-making process. My focus is on officers' political-cultural expertise, which includes behaviors related to their participation in the process as policy collaborators and in their participation in the political process in general.

A starting assumption is that professional development programs in the civilian and military spheres, as well as the conventional wisdom extant in society at large, inadequately address officers' political-cultural expertise. Studies reviewing the curricula at the pre-commissioning and senior service college levels of professional military education reveal that fundamental principles related to civil-military norms are poorly understood at the undergraduate level.[12] Furthermore, 20+ intervening years of professional socialization to include attendance at a senior service college do not equip future senior military leaders with a thorough understanding of civil-military norms sufficient to navigate the ambiguities of "advice," "advocacy," "insistence," and "political participation."[13]

Even in the most advanced democracies such as the United States, participants in the national security process are continuously engaged in improving the competencies required to adequately exercise their national security responsibilities. When an area of competence is under-developed or the competency levels are not sufficiently balanced across the civilian and military spheres, the achievement of both the functional and societal imperatives is threatened.

First Principles for Military Professionals in Service to Democratic States

My professional experience as a cadet, officer, and civilian scholar with 24 years of socialization to the military profession, informs me that there is no commonly accepted theoretical framework upon which to evaluate various civil-military behaviors. Cadets' and officers' understandings vary widely regarding what they take to be professional civil-military relations norms. Meanwhile, military professionals at various stages of development observe a confusing range of behaviors illustrating the profession's failure to espouse a particular set of norms for civil-military relations.

The recommendations that follow in this chapter as each specific issue area is explored are rooted in a conceptual framework founded on two fundamental theoretical concepts that govern civil-military relations in democratic states. The first part of the framework examines the relationship between the competencies and responsibilities of actors from the civilian and military spheres who participate in the national security process. The second key piece of the framework stems from Samuel Huntington's contention that "military institutions of any society are shaped by two forces: a functional imperative stemming from the threats to the society's security and a societal imperative arising from the social forces, ideologies, and institutions dominant within the society."[14] This competition for preeminence between societal and functional imperatives is a primary source of tension in civil-military relations. The relationship between competency and responsibility along with the balance between the societal and functional imperatives will underpin the recommendations that follow.

Issue Area One: The Role of Military Professionals in the Policy-Making Process

A fundamental concept guiding national security professionals as they carry out their respective duties is that each position requires of the incumbent unique competencies and responsibilities. Distinctions between competencies and responsibilities are related to the nature of the position and the constitutional authority upon which it is based. The development of national security policy is optimized when civil-military relations are in balance, that is, when participants on both sides of the relationship maximize their respective competencies, and appropriately channel these competencies through their respective responsibilities. Conversely, sub-optimal policy outcomes are often the result of an imbalance between participants' competencies and their decision-making responsibilities. Such conditions also often result in strained civil-military relationships.

It may occasionally, or even frequently, be the case that military professionals perceive that their competence or expertise in a given issue area is superior to that of civilian authorities having the responsibility to make policy decisions in that same area. Military professionals may perceive that civilian decision-makers have set aside or discounted the military's expert advice in favor of counsel from national security professionals within the civilian sphere. Military professionals may perceive that the resultant policy outcome is poor. And, indeed, the policy outcome may be poor as a result of such an imbalance between competencies and responsibilities within the national security community.

However, democratic civil-military relations are characterized by military professionals who tolerate such poor policy-making outcomes in order to preserve the more fundamental, long-term interest of upholding the democratic character of the state. *Military institutions in service to democratic societies should espouse as a fundamental norm of civil-military relations that the profession's first obligation is to do no harm to the state's democratic institutions.* Usurping or undermining the decision-making authority of civilian decision-makers is a clear violation of the responsibilities inherent in each actor's constitutional role.

Professional judgment in this area depends on having in place a system for officer professional development that encourages the incorporation of democratic values into an officer's overall personal and professional values. This set of internal values and the cultivation of a sense of duty, honor, and professional obligation link the special requirements of service to a democratic state to the officer's overall professionalism.[15]

Table 30-1 highlights, from the military professional's point of view, the variations possible when civilian national security professionals exercise their competence and responsibility in the policy-making process.

The ideal match-up occurs when civilian leaders have high competence *and* responsibility. This results in effective policy exercised in compliance with norms of national security decision-making in a democracy. This option is found in Box 2 of Table 30-1. In these scenarios, civilian and military professionals pool their respective expertise in a collaborative process that culminates with the appropriate national security professional in the civilian sphere making the final decision. In this instance civilians with the highest level of responsibility in the policy-making process had the proper level of expertise and exercised it appropriately. The level of expertise was either inherent within the civilian policy-makers themselves or enhanced through effective collaboration with military experts. Democratic institutions were not diminished by officers intent on undermining the civilian policy-maker or pressing their policy preferences beyond the bounds of the policy-making process.

George C. Marshall's service at the highest levels of government from 1939 to 1950 epitomized the civil-military norms discussed above. As Chief of Staff of the

Table 30-1. *Relationship between Civilian Competency and Responsibility in the Inter-Agency Process.*

Army, Secretary of State, and Secretary of Defense, Marshall was the standard-bearer for a generation of officers that unwaveringly accepted the concept of civilian control. Indeed, professional judgment in this respect was so firm that American military leaders accommodated themselves to a not inconsiderable number of policy decisions incompatible with their professional strategic judgment. These instances ranged from the decision to support a strategy to hold the Philippines in 1941 despite the perceived lack of military means to do so, to acquiescence in the decision to invade North Africa in 1942 despite their concerns that such a diversion of military resources would dangerously prolong the initiation of a decisive cross-channel invasion.[16]

Marshall maintained professional norms across the scenarios depicted in the various boxes in Table 30-1. He resisted opportunities to go beyond the role of expert adviser to insist or dissent publicly when conditions of low civilian competence may have tempted him to do so. His example was also a good model for his staff in dealing with civilians at lower levels of responsibility, but with constitutional authority to make policy. Resisting opportunities to leverage military expertise and power to prevail in the bureaucratic disputes is also important to ensure that civilians continue to set political objectives at all levels.

Perceived deficiencies in competency on the civilian side were not, however, completely ignored. At times when Marshall or his staff perceived strategic competence to be lacking within the political leadership, he encouraged his staff to see such instances as opportunities as opposed to liabilities. For instance, he viewed President Franklin Roosevelt's shortfalls as a strategic thinker as an opportunity to educate the President on how he could best support the war effort.[17] Box 4 of Table 30-1 captures such a scenario. Policy outcomes are more or less effective depending on whether or not competent military advice was available to enhance the civilian policy-maker's decision. The military need not accept low levels of civilian military competence as a permanent condition. Such instances may represent opportunities to educate the civilian policy-maker through staff collaboration or trips to military installations, which, in turn, raise civilian expertise levels. Military professionals must also keep in mind that civilian policy-makers take into account the broader political context when deciding matters of military strategy, a context for which the military adviser has no responsibility. For instance, maintaining domestic and international support is critical to the sustainability of the overall strategy, and this is clearly the responsibility of the civilian leadership.

Marshall's frankness coupled with his unquestioning acceptance of civilian authority gained him the full confidence of Roosevelt. Roosevelt repeatedly offered Marshall command roles in the war, which were never realized due to each man's understanding that Marshall's contribution as expert adviser and honest broker in Washington was irreplaceable.[18] Marshall refrained both from capitalizing on his popularity in order to prevail in the policy-making process and from spending his enormous political capital to further his ambition or to advance his personal judgments. Marshall was never viewed as a competitor, but as a trusted source of counsel.

The policy scenarios in which democratic military professionals may find the most difficulty in maintaining professional norms occur when civilian competency is low (Boxes 1 and 3 of Table 30-1). Such scenarios require the military to refrain from the inappropriate leveraging of military expertise or using whatever political capital they may have to prevail in the policy-making process. Examples of such civil-military relations can often be found in states in the process of democratic transition from authoritarian rule. Democratic institutions are not yet fully developed, and competencies across the civilian and military national security spheres are uneven. Often the military possesses the lion's share of strategic expertise. Though dominant in military expertise, the military may be lacking in its appreciation of the broader political issues at play in the emerging democracy's strategy formulation.

The post-communist states of Central and Eastern Europe one decade into their transitions from authoritarian rule had largely mastered the task of subordinating their military institutions to civilian rule. However, in many respects national security strategies were at risk or failing due to the dearth of national security professionals with expertise in both political and military strategic competencies. Defense ministries and general staffs were unable to develop national security planning processes that effectively set priorities, coordinated resources to focus on the achievement of the stated objectives, and ensured the optimization of means allocated to defense. The political leadership, in many cases, lacked the interest, expertise, or both that are necessary to direct the overall formulation of national security policy.

As a result, the development of actual capabilities of post-communist armed forces has been slow, to be sure, but democratic institutions have not suffered from the intervention or overreach of military leaders in search of short-term gains for their institutions. Over time, competency in both spheres has grown. The political leaderships have assumed a heightened role in the national security planning process and national security institutions have begun to respond to the demands for more rational defense planning. Real collaboration in the national security policy-making process is beginning to take place with the potential to effect positive change in defense capabilities.

The post-Cold War era in U.S. civil-military relations has featured a series of incidents that one scholar of civil-military relations, Peter Feaver, has called "shirking" on the part of the military—that is, various degrees of military noncompliance with the political leadership's desired policy preferences.[19] These incidents include the military's reluctance to embrace the Somalia, Bosnia, and Haiti missions, the resistance to President Clinton's initiative to allow homosexuals to serve openly in the military, and efforts to resist dramatic changes in the military services' roles, missions, and force structure after the strategic reviews of the Clinton and George W. Bush administrations.[20]

Noncompliance may take various forms. One technique in the post-Cold War era has been to present only a limited range of options for the use of the military instrument of power, with each known to be unacceptable to the political leadership. When advising the administration of the elder George Bush on courses of action available for a potential Balkan intervention to achieve the political objective of reining in the violence in 1991, JCS Chairman Colin Powell put the price tag at 250,000 troops.[21] This calculation, however, was based on the assumptions interjected by Powell, himself, into the policy-making process, namely, that victory must be decisive and that overwhelming force must be used (the so-called Powell Doctrine). This preference for decisive force was incompatible with the political leadership's search for a course of action that could employ limited force to achieve limited political objectives. The military's actions, in this case, delayed action on a top-priority U.S. foreign policy initiative until conditions were acceptable to the military.[22] Other methods of military shirking include manipulating the defense bureaucracy[23] to shape outcomes more in line with preferred policy ends and expending political capital in a way that undermines the responsibility of the political leadership to implement their preferred policy end.

Such behavior may also negatively affect the role of the military profession in the affairs of state. The role of the military profession as a trusted policy collaborator possessing unique expertise may be compromised. Civilian policy-makers may come to view the military actors in the national security community as competitors in the decision-making process, more concerned with promoting their own institutional agendas than the national interest as discerned by civilian decision-makers.

Furthermore, a collaborative policy-making environment is impossible to achieve when either side works to intimidate the other. Fear on the part of the political leadership and lack of respect on the part of the military as an institution characterized civil-military relations in the Clinton administration. It was reported that President Clinton was more intimidated by the military than any other political force. For example, a former senior National Security Council official stated, "I don't think there was any doubt that he was out-and-out afraid of them."[24]

Finally, military professionals serving democratic states must also respond to legislative bodies empowered with oversight and budgeting authority and which may play a policy collaboration role with the executive. A unique problem within U.S. civil-military relations is the fact that the Constitution established dual control over the military. While the President enjoys the power of Commander-in-Chief, significant war-related powers also reside in Congress along with the authority to raise, support, and regulate armed forces. A single military agent serves two co-equal principals. American military professionals must accept their responsibility to provide expert advice to both Congress and the White House without exploiting either master or playing one off against the other in order to prevail in the policy process.

Recommended Civil-Military Norm: *The military profession's first obligation is to do no harm to the state's democratic institutions and the democratic policy-making processes that they establish. The civilian political leadership sets political objectives that the military supports in good faith. The military leadership should apply its expertise without "shirking" or taking actions that, in effect, have a self-interested effect on policy outcomes. Civil-military relations in a democracy require military professionals to fulfill constitutional obligations to both the executive and the legislature. A clear sense of the distinction between national security competency and the responsibility to exercise such competency through distinct roles in the national security policy-making process must be developed as the officer's career advances.*

Issue Area Two: Civil-Military Norms Vis-à-vis Dissent

An issue area closely related to civil-military norms in the policy-making process is the problem of dealing with dissent. Dissent is normally considered to issue only from the military sphere, since the ultimate power over decision-making in a democracy lies with the civilian leadership. However, legitimate disagreement is a regular visitor to any collaborative decision-making process. Norms should exist in both spheres to encourage healthy debate while recognizing that disparate responsibilities mandate ultimate deference to the civilian decision-maker.

History is rife with examples of military professionals whose professional expertise was not advanced with sufficient candor and vigor within the bounds of collaborative decision-making to influence civilian leaders' national security decisions. H.R. McMaster's *Dereliction of Duty* (1997), a widely read book among the current generation of American military officers, makes the argument that although the Joint Chiefs recognized that the graduated pressure strategy in Vietnam was fundamentally flawed, they did not vigorously express their professional judgment in the policy-making process. As a result, McMaster contends, that strategy was set without the best advice of the President's principal military advisers.[25] More recently, during the second Clinton administration, congressional leaders chastised the Joint Chiefs for continuing to support the fiscal 1999 defense budget, instead of forthrightly advocating a budget that adequately ensured the readiness of the armed forces.[26]

In the lead-up to the 2003 Iraq War, the Army's then Chief of Staff, Gen. Eric Shinseki, told Congress that in his professional judgment, based on his experience as commander of U.S. forces in postwar Bosnia-Herzegovina, "several hundred thousand troops" would be required to enforce order in postwar Iraq. Deputy Secretary of Defense Paul Wolfowitz gave Shinseki a sharp public rebuke, calling his estimate "wildly off the mark."[27] Subsequent events in Iraq, however, proved that Shinseki's professional judgment was closer to the mark than that of either Secretary Rumsfeld or his Deputy.

Thus, the expertise of military professionals, as manifested in their advice to civilian decision-makers, is a critical contribution to national security policy. In a system of dual control, military professionals must keep in mind that they remain accountable to both legislative and executive authority. Since his estimate was requested in an open Congressional hearing, General Shinseki's expertise was offered within the accepted bounds of dissent. Civilian policy-makers in both branches should encourage military professionals to offer their best advice and not punish military participants who work within the established bounds of dissent in democratic national security decision-making processes.

Military professionals in service to democratic states should then muster all of their expertise relevant to the achievement of a particular political objective that the civilian leadership sets forth. This is especially true when more strictly military competencies are at stake, such as judgments related to evaluating risks to soldiers and the tactical conduct of ongoing operations.[28] Civilian decision-makers rightfully expect that military professionals under their command be forthright and thorough, yet ultimately compliant to civilians with regard to the execution of national political objectives and the ways to achieve them.

Policy advocacy has its place within the bounded limits of a collaborative policy-making process, but advocacy actions counter to the civilian leadership's known preferences begin to usurp the civilian leader's distinct responsibilities. For instance, efforts to influence the terms of debate in public forums while national security professionals are still at odds in intra-governmental discussions may shift the military professional's status from objective expert to suspect competitor. Such actions both poison a collaborative decision-making environment that is critical to the achievement of optimal national security outcomes and demonstrate a willingness to overlook distinctions in responsibility across the civilian and military spheres to achieve short-term political gain. Professor Huntington wrote almost a half century ago that officers should stay focused on three responsibilities: (1) to represent the profession in both executive and legislative settings, public and private, (2) to advise political leaders on state policy, but only from the perspective of a military professional, and (3) to execute, implementing the policy of the state. Note that these responsibilities do not allow military leaders excessive advocacy or insistence on their views outside the policy of the state they serve.[29]

Resignation in protest is often discussed as an acceptable means of dissent that permits policy advocacy to spill beyond the normal channels of discourse between military and civilian actors in the national security policy-making process. Resignation, however, may not be the panacea sometimes suggested by those in favor of a more assertive role for military leaders. Military leaders should consider both the positive and negative consequences of resignation before resorting to this action. First, resignation is the extreme method of dissent. The intent is to publicly express disagreement with the responsible political leaders, thus pitting the resigning actor's political capital against that of the civilian policy-maker's. A resignation followed by news media outbursts, particularly those perceived as advancing institutional interests over national interests, may harm the objective status of the military profession in the democratic political process.

On the positive side, resignation represents a clear withdrawal from future participation in the policy-making process and consequently removes the threat that the resigning actor may continue to undermine the role of the political leadership within the official system.[30] The possibility of playing the role of "competitor" vis-à-vis the elected political leadership within the policy-making process is diminished, although a competitor role could be assumed once outside government.

Recommended Civil-Military Norm: *Military participants in the national security policy-making process should expect a decision-making climate that encourages a full exchange of expertise across the military and civilian spheres. Military professionals, furthermore, should have the expectation that their professional judgment will be heard in policy deliberations. However, military participants must develop the professional judgment to recognize when the bounds of the policy-making process might be breached. When acts of dissent take them beyond representation and advice to outright advocacy or public dissent, military leaders must acknowledge that they have gone beyond the limits of their roles and have begun behaviors that directly challenge the role of political leaders with the responsibility to make policy.*

Issue Area Three: Civil-Military Norms and Partisan Politics

Much attention has been paid in recent years to the increasing willingness of U.S. officers to identify themselves as members of a particular political party, in this case

Republican. While Morris Janowitz's research in the 1950s documented military officers' self-identification as political conservatives,[31] partisan identification as Republicans is a development of more recent decades. Despite Janowitz's finding that most officers of the pre-1960s were moderately conservative,[32] the ideological gradations within the two parties were such that these officers could have found a home in either the Democratic or Republican party at the time. Most officers of that era, however, chose not to profess a particular party affiliation.

Professor Ole Holsti's research has contributed hard data to the ongoing professional and scholarly dialogue concerning the growing gap between U.S. society and its military with regard to party identification. Using survey data resident in the Foreign Policy Leadership Project data base, Holsti showed that between 1976 and 1996 the proportion of officers who identified themselves as Republicans doubled from one-third to two-thirds.[33] Such scholarly research jibes with the observations of journalists who cover the military. For example, Tom Ricks's interviews with junior officers led him to conclude, "Today's junior officer seems to assume that to be an officer is to be a Republican."[34]

Ideological self-identification also points to a rise in professed conservatism in the officer corps. Holsti's data show that the ratio of conservatives to liberals in the officer corps went from four to one in 1976 to 23 to one in 1996.[35] The shift is due to the decline in self-identification of officers as liberals of any varietyeven moderate liberals. In 1996 only 3 percent of the officers surveyed reported an ideological self-identification as somewhat liberal or very liberal, while 73 percent reported that they were somewhat conservative or very conservative.[36]

While it may be reasonable to expect the ratio of conservatives to liberals in a culturally conservative, hierarchical institution such as the U.S. military to be something less than a mirror of American society, a 23 to one conservative to liberal ratio as evident in Holsti's data may begin to raise questions about whether or not the military sufficiently reflects the society it serves. By way of contrast, the data gathered in the 1999 Triangle Institute for Security Studies (TISS) survey (Table 30-2) revealed that civilian elites self-identified more evenly between conservatives and liberals, with 32 percent reporting that they were either somewhat conservative or very conservative and 37.5 percent weighing in as either very liberal or somewhat

	Very Liberal	Somewhat Liberal	Moderate	Somewhat Conservative	Very Conservative
Civilian Non-Veteran Leaders	12.6 %	24.9%	28.4%	23.3%	8.2%
Military Leaders	.3%	4.1%	28.4%	53.8%	12.8%
General Public (non-veterans)	7.8%	13.2%	24.4%	31.7%	18.5%

Table 30-2. *Ideological Self-Identification in the 1998-99 TISS Survey.*[37]

liberal (in contrast, only 4.4 percent of the officers in the 1999 survey reported an ideological self-identification as somewhat liberal or very liberal).

To fulfill its primary obligation to its client, the military must be granted by society the legitimacy to carry out its solemn function. Legitimacy is enhanced when the military institution is perceived to be "of society" in terms of being comprised of a representative cross-section of the population. The alternative outcome is to increasingly become a distinct group representing only limited characteristics and attitudes of the society at large. As the perception grows that the military's political ideology is dramatically divergent from the civilian elites entrusted as security policy-makers, the parallel assumption will grow that the military is an institution apart from the society it serves. Moreover, it may be seen as a self-serving, rather than a nation-serving institution. How an officer votes should remain an officer's prerogative in a democracy, but as the ideological gap between the larger officer corps and society at large grows, even mild forms of disagreement with civilian decision-makers may be seen as politically motivated.

Military sociologists who study organizational culture break military socialization into two dimensions—anticipatory and secondary. Anticipatory military socialization encompasses individuals who self-select to belong to the military, thus implying a fit between organizational and personal worldviews. Secondary military socialization accounts for the organization's role in instilling a worldview in its members.[38]

Accession policies should be examined to ensure that measures are in place to recruit more diverse elements of the citizenry to serve society as military professionals. Such moves as enhancing Reserve Officer Training Corps (ROTC) programs in Ivy League schools or in traditionally African American colleges may help to balance anticipatory socialization trends. Within the secondary socialization process, over which the military has more direct control, there should be a return to the premium placed on serving in a "servant-profession" vs. participation in a "self-serving" profession. Incorporating the principle of nonpartisanship as part of an officer's professional code (rather than relying on a mere tradition, which is always subject to erosion) could help maintain balance in U.S. civil-military relations.

The American military's tradition of political neutrality had its roots in the advent of the professionalization of the American military led by Gens. William Tecumseh Sherman and Emory Upton as well as Rear Adm. Stephen Luce in the decades following the Civil War.[39] The profession must take note that the long-term erosion of this tradition of political neutrality may have profound implications for the profession and its ability to faithfully serve society.

The American military at present needs to reinforce the professional norm that it can serve any political party in a principled fashion. Principled professionalism is not determined by congruity with a particular party's agenda. Soldiers, and their leaders, must be equally comfortable serving either party that society chooses to be governed by.

A collaborative vision of national security policy-making rejects the notion that military professionals simply and obediently execute the demands of the civilian government as apolitical beings somehow immune from pressures that "divided government" has brought to American political processes.[40] National security professionals from both the civilian and military spheres must be participants in the national security decision-making process if competencies from both spheres are to be sufficiently utilized.

Indeed, the very concept espoused here of a military officer as a national security professional schooled in the political-cultural expert knowledge[41]of security policy requires the participation of military professionals in civilian graduate programs in order to master many of the competencies shared by civilian national security professionals.[42] There are, however, important distinctions to be made between possessing a certain degree of political expertise in order to serve in a policy collaboration role, on one hand, and using it as the basis for abusing the limited responsibility of officers within the military sphere in the decision-making process, on the other.

Perhaps the most contentious area of this debate concerns norms governing policy advocacy that may stem from individual political preferences. The terms of this debate often revolve around whether military members' identities are thought to be rooted in their rights as citizens or in membership in a profession with circumscribed rights stemming from the unique obligation of the profession to society. "The mythic tradition of the citizen-soldier is dead," declared defense specialists Elliott Abrams and Andrew Bacevich.[43] The nature of modern war has spurred the gradual evolution of military forces comprised of volunteers whose military service is not a compulsory, transitory departure from civilian life, but rather a compensated choice to make military service their lives' callings.[44] Today soldiers consciously decide to depart civilian life to serve society within the military profession. In doing so, these all-volunteer force members are more beholden to professional norms than their conscripted forbears.

Those more approving of partisan behavior argue that "soldiers in uniform are, after all, citizens, and so long as they obey orders they retain the rights of expression of their counterparts in the civilian worldand most certainly so the moment they doff the uniform."[45] Though this position is possibly valid from a purely legal perspective, it ignores the impact that such political behavior can have on the profession's ability to perform its primary function in society. Society cannot be adequately served by a military profession that refuses to subordinate its individual and institutional interests to the greater national interest, or that is perceived to take sides in the political process.[46]

There was a general perception in the 2000 presidential campaign that "the military" supported Republican candidate George W. Bush. There is no hard evidence to support such a perception since exit polls of military voters do not occur, but conservative self-identification among military personnel as reported widely in the news media seemed to confirm that the Republican party and its presidential candidate were considered to be the "best fit" for the military culture.[47]

It is clear that military absentee ballots played a decisive role in the 2000 election when, in the Florida recounts, a 202 majority for the Democratic candidate Al Gore turned into a 537 vote edge for George W. Bush once the absentee votes were counted. The lawyering that ensued in the "long count" assumed that the military ballots, which comprised the majority of the overseas ballots, would be cast disproportionately for Bush. The Gore camp consequently pursued a strategy of throwing out all overseas ballots that did not meet the basic requirements of Florida state law. The Bush campaign, in return, berated the Democrats for denying members of the armed forces the right to vote.[48]

The 2000 election thus reinforced the perception of the Republicanization of the military that had been evolving over the previous two decades and brought to the fore two relevant political ramifications: the role of the military in facilitating the voting of its people and the courting of the military as an interest group. The military must be careful that it is not perceived as a tool for use by either party to harvest votes. The Federal Voting Assistance Program, although charged with facilitating the voting of all eligible voters overseas, is administered through the Department of Defense. It came under fire in the 2004 presidential campaign for administering voting procedures allowing soldiers to e-mail their votes to a private contractor, which in turn was charged with faxing the presidential ballots reflecting those votes to counties throughout the country. The press took issue with the lack of election observers at the contractors' offices and the Pentagon's handling of the ballots through the contractor instead of facilitating a process by which the ballots are sent directly to local election officials.[49]

The role of the absentee military ballots in the 2000 Florida recount also led to an intense battle for the overseas vote in the tight 2004 presidential race. The realization that overseas service members cast their ballots at a rate of 70 percent (compared to the 30 percent mark of U.S. civilians overseas in the 2000 election[50]) galvanized efforts to get the expatriate vote. Americans abroad were uniquely targeted as key "swing voters." They outnumber potential military absentee voters and their dependents by 3.7 million to 2.7 million.[51] While requests for absentee ballots surpassed the 2000 level among military voters in 2004, the Democrats, especially, hoped to benefit from aggressive "get out the vote" campaigns overseas to help counter the military vote.

There still seems to be a consensus within the U.S. military profession that the "tradition of an apolitical military is critical to our democratic system."[52] According to a Marine brigadier general survey response, "The military is held in high esteem by the American public because we remain neutral and nonpartisan. Once the institution is seen as 'looking out for itself,' instead of looking out for the country, we risk losing the trust of the American people."[53]

The problem is defining and clarifying professional norms regarding what acts are unacceptably "political." Involvement in a collaborative policy-making process in accordance with the norms laid out in Issue Area One constitutes engagement in politics, but in a manner that is consistent with the military professional's advisory and expert role. However, public expressions of partisan preferences that could be perceived as speaking for the profession itself fall outside professional norms. In this era of divided government, both budding professionals and seasoned veterans will have difficulty distinguishing between legitimate participation and behaviors that might steer the profession away from its apolitical roots toward self-serving partisanship.

Recommended Civil-Military Norm: *Principled officership requires adherence to an ethic of nonpartisanship. Military professionals must feel capable of serving* *objectively any political party that prevails in the democratic political process. The demands of principled officership must carry the day, even if they entail voluntary limitations on officers' liberties as citizens. Officers should consider the impact that their public profession of political beliefs has on their subordinates and on the servant relationship of the profession to society at large. Association by the military profession or by an unrepresentative number of its members with any single political party undercuts the legitimacy upon which the military depends to relate to the society it serves.*

Issue Area Four: Civil-Military Norms and Retired Officers

The development of professional norms governing the political activities of retired officers, especially retired general officers, is intrinsically linked to the goal of limiting the politicization of the profession. As one active duty two-star Marine general officer noted, "My concern is the effect of a retired general officer's commitment to a political party immediately after retirement on junior officers. Rather than the junior officer taking time to be fully informed on the current issues, there may be a tendency to blindly follow a senior that they admire for his/her service accomplishments."[54]

Another important consideration is the effect that retired officers' actions have on public perceptions of the military as an institutional actor in the political process. As one active duty four-star general officer put it, "Constitutional rights are not the issue. Judgment is. The public doesn't distinguish between active duty general [officers] and retired general [officers]. As a result, the entire military is politicized. If a retired general officer elects to run for office and enter the process that is fine but not otherwise."[55]

In a domestic political environment where the civil-military gap may be a growing phenomenon, such distinctions will be increasingly difficult to make. The practice of courting the endorsements of retired generals began in 1992 with the Clinton campaign's successful recruitment of former JCS Chairman Adm. William Crowe, who helped to deflect some of the controversy over whether or not Clinton had avoided the draft.[56] In 2000, the Bush campaign collected 27 flag-rank endorsements, several of whom enjoyed "celebrity" status.[57] Observers complained that the direct participation of these retired generals during the Republican convention and on the campaign trail itself was an attempt to manipulate public opinion to create the impression that "the military" was behind candidate Bush. If asked to identity general officers of the U.S. military, few Americans at the time could have named an Army four-star general officer on active duty, but many could likely recall the names Colin Powell and Norman Schwarzkopf as military heroes of the Gulf War experience.

Subsequently, in the 2004 wartime election, in which the Vietnam service records of the presidential candidates were an ongoing subplot, the race for retired general officer endorsements took on greater intensity. The Kerry campaign had 11 generals on stage at its convention, led by former USAF Chief of Staff Gen. Merrill McPeak, former JCS Chairman Gen. John Shalikashvili, and former Supreme Allied Commander in Europe, Gen. Wesley Clark.[58] The Bush campaign countered with an endorsement list exceeding 100 retired flag-rank officers.[59] In addition, it gave the commander of both the war in Afghanistan and the invasion of Iraq, Gen. Tommy Franks, a prominent speaking role at the Republican convention. Franks, who had retired in the summer of 2003 and declared himself a political independent, praised his former Commander-in-Chief: "I choose George W. Bush because he stands up for the American fighting man and woman and because he remembers our veterans."[60]

While these individual retired officers may justify their involvement in the last two presidential campaigns as merely exercising their rights as private citizens,[61] these individual decisions may by themselvesor certainly in the aggregatelook like an institutional preference. Retired Marine Corps Gen. Richard Neal, commenting on the endorsements in the 2000 campaign, said, "I didn't find fault with anyone that came forward and individually endorsed. I think what bothers me . . . is this idea of a coalition, of a group of generals and admirals coming together."[62]

This author believes the military profession would be well served if retired officers paid a greater price for the impact their individual actions have in politicizing the military and continuing to erode its needed stance of nonpartisanship. Professional self-policing rather than strict legal restrictions on retired officers' free speech rights is the only feasible course of action in this issue area. But it is also the case that retired professionals are no longer "practicing" professionals, even if the public so perceives them. Thus, the preferred method is to turn to the profession's internal capacity to educate officers of their responsibility in this area, fostering appropriate standards of professional behavior even after being placed on the retired rolls.

Andrew Abbott offers a framework to settle jurisdictional conflict across and within professions.[63] One potential application of this framework to the conflict between the professional obligations of active and retired officers is to recast the role of retirees as mentors within the profession. As the current stewards of national security accountable and subordinate to the political leadership, active duty senior leaders set the professional norms. These current strategic leaders can establish a constructive requirement for retired officers to reflect upon the adverse impact the unrestrained exercise of their political rights will have on the profession and its ability to participate neutrally in the political process.

Such professional self-regulation would, in effect, subordinate the retiree sphere of military professionals under the active strategic leadership in professional areas that have a continuing impact on the military profession. This will require a renegotiation of the boundaries of the internal jurisdictions within the profession. The new boundaries would both recognize retirees as mentors to the profession and obligate them to adhere to a set of professional norms aimed at preserving the military profession's ability to perform its exclusive function within society. A self-regulating profession develops norms in the formative developmental experiences of its new members and continuously reinforces such standards as new members progress to greater positions of responsibility in the profession.

Recommended Civil-Military Norm: *Retired officers have a continuing responsibility to act in ways that are not detrimental to the effectiveness of the military* *profession. While such professional obligations are more limited than those of the currently serving senior leadership, some degree of legal and moral professional obligation remains. Active duty strategic leaders, as the stewards of the profession's norms, should set the expectation that retirees consider carefully the impact of their individual and collective actions on the profession. Useful guidelines in this area include considering the impact particular activities could have on the active serving force, contemplating whether individual choices could be perceived as institutional positions, and finally exercising judgment regarding the degree to which the expression of partisan preferences impairs the military institution's capacity to be perceived as nonpartisan in the policy-making process.*

Issue Area Five: The Military and News Media Relations

The military and the press both play essential roles in the life of a democracy, yet these two institutions are often at odds with one another. America's founding fathers understood that a Constitutional amendment guaranteeing a free press was a critical tool for ensuring accountability of all government institutions. The democratic system is dependent on the Fourth Estate playing its role to inform the public. This is particularly true in time of war, when citizens deserve to know as much as possible about the conduct of such a significant national event.[65] Military professionals in service to democracies should strive for military-media relations based on the premise that America can win wars while still fully informing the American people through a free press.[66]

> You can find few, if any, career military people who can conceive that talking to a reporter not only is in the normal line of accountability and normal line of responsibility to taxpayers, but that it could possibly ever be of any benefit to them. They can only see the possibility that it could hurt their career. It's a deeply, deeply inbred attitude.
>
> —MELISSA HEALY, FORMER PENTAGON CORRESPONDENT, *LOS ANGELES TIMES*[64]

Military culture, understandably, places a premium on information security and may seek to cast a veil over ongoing operations to protect operational security and the lives of troops. The press, meanwhile, has an interest in getting as close to the action as possible to report the action in all its dimensions, favorable and unfavorable. A military commander may want to limit access to his troops for fear that their morale may be negatively affected and for fear that he himself may become victim of negative press reports. However, he should see the value of shaping coverage of the war in a positive light and understand that the press will play a critical role in this effort.[67]

Military-press relations were at a zenith in World War II when reporters wore uniforms and were subject to Pentagon accreditation (and, at times, capricious censorship). By the time of the Vietnam War the military had dropped its censorship restrictions, and journalists were free to roam the theater of war. However, military-media relations suffered due to the perception of many in the military that press coverage of the war contributed to the U.S. defeat.[68] While this view is still a contentious topic within the ranks, there is a broad consensus that the Vietnam experience soured the military on the news media and played a key role in limiting press access in later conflicts.[69]

The 1991 Gulf War saw the advent of the short-lived pool system whereby a limited number of reporters was selected to cover events of the Pentagon's choosing. Those members of the press not selected for the pool were tightly controlled and forced to rely on official briefings for their coverage. The press was universally dissatisfied with the pool system, issuing numerous scathing critiques including one from *Harper's* magazine publisher John MacArthur, who dubbed pool reporting a crushing defeat for freedom of the press.[70] The military, in hindsight, had regrets about restricting media access: "Army commanders who refused to allow reporters to join with them in the 1991 Gulf War were chagrined to learn that they received hardly any credit for their efforts, while the Marines, who welcomed reporters, may have received more than their share."[71]

On the eve of the 2003 Iraq War, Secretary of Defense Donald Rumsfeld issued a directive to all commanders informing them that the U.S. military would be taking the press to war. The concept of embedding was not entirely new. Some embedding occurred in the Balkans conflict in the 1990s, and "embeds" participated in Operation Anaconda in Afghanistan a year earlier. What was new was the magnitude of the effort. A total of 777 embedded journalists went to war with U.S. troops in Iraq—20 percent of these were from foreign news outlets.[72] The Pentagon conducted an unprecedented training program to acclimate the journalists to military life in wartime and to raise the comfort level of the media and the military.[73]

The use of embeds in the Iraq War has been both lauded and criticized. On the whole it did much to restore media-military relations and to educate a new generation of war correspondents, many of whom undertook their assignments with a limited understanding of military affairs. Unit commanders had megaphones in the form of their embed with which to communicate their message back home to the American people.[74] Access was unprecedented, and technology permitted the first live broadcasts in the midst of battle. Critics contend that the "soda straw" view did not serve the American people well because it neglected "big picture" coverage of the war and did not fully report the Iraqi side of the war. Complaints were also registered that the war coverage was sanitized for American viewers, who preferred scenes of victorious American soldiers over scenes of dead American or Iraqi soldiers and civilians.

Covering wars in the era following the 11 September 2001 terrorist attacks on U.S. soil introduces a new dynamic in that the press as an institution seemed conflicted between a desire to support patriotic causes and a desire to facilitate debate over national policy. George Wilson, the eldest embed at 70 and a distinguished defense correspondent, remarked, "My plea to the media is to ask, as often as you can: "Where are we going and why and what are the consequences?"[75] News organizations evaluating their prewar coverage in the still violent "Phase 4" stability operations have engaged in self-criticism for not questioning more strongly the rationale for the war and its potential consequences.[76]

Press coverage in the stabilization phase in Iraq has suffered owing to the end of the embeds program and to the risky security situation, which precludes press mobility throughout the theater of operations. Media-military relations also suffered as the military struggled to get out the "good news" stories of the reconstruction effort in the face of the concerted coverage of the latest insurgent attack. Getting the military's story out is a crucial component to the overall success of the strategy, dependent as it is on sustaining support at home while building trust among the Iraqi people.

Advances in technology allowing for real time transmittal of news makes it virtually impossible for the military to control press coverage in any theater of operations. Indeed, with the arrival of new forms of media on the scene, such as bloggers who independently file reports on internet sites, editorial vetting processes are bypassed. Military professionals must assume that in 21st century journalism the truth will always come out. The armed forces' professional military education system has a key role to play in the formation of service members' attitudes toward the press, their understanding of the press's role in a democratic society, and the mutual interests served through the fostering of positive military-media relations.

Recommended Civil-Military Norm: *The effectiveness and legitimacy of military professions serving democratic societies depends on their healthy interaction with the news media. The military institution must focus on winning the nation's wars and employing military power to achieve national interests. But the press has a responsibility to inform the American people so that they may hold all government institutions and the political leadership accountable for their actions. Within reasonable parameters of operational security, military professionals must seize the opportunities that occur to facilitate the press's function in a democratic society. At a minimum, military professionals should not engage in actions that undermine or harm the Fourth Estate's role in the American political system. The military as an institution, furthermore, should seek opportunities to educate the press in military affairs and educate its professional soldiers in media-military relations.*

Issue Area Six: Balancing the Functional and Societal Imperatives

In the civil-military relations literature, the functional imperative to provide for the national defense, and the societal imperative to preserve and protect the democratic processes of the republic, are often presented as competing and implicitly incompatible obligations.[77] The discussion on military-media relations highlighted the importance of viewing these imperatives as mutually reinforcing rather than opposing principles.[78]

Military professionals in service to democratic states, as noted in the beginning of this chapter, must be as functionally competent as possible to secure the national security interests of the state. Additionally, they are simultaneously charged with performing this function within the societal context of liberal democracy. Their responsibility is to defend the state while concurrently understanding that the pursuit of national security is conditioned by national values, national character, and the ideology of the state.

Developing norms in this issue area is inextricably linked to the desired professional judgment associated with the first two issue areas identified in this chapter, the military professional's role in the policy-making process and his approach to dissent in the context of civil-military relations. Mastering these first principles inherent in the responsibilities-competencies match-up is key to grasping the mandate to balance the functional and societal imperatives.

The history of American civil-military relations is replete with examples of the military institution battling with its civilian masters over the incorporation of societal values in the military. The integration of blacks and women both came amidst protests from within the military profession that such changes would harm the institution's ability to perform its function. In the case of President Harry Truman's initiative to integrate the armed forces through Executive Order 8981, Truman used his executive powers to make a first move toward enacting the broader civil rights agenda that he campaigned on in 1948. The desegregation order came the same day that he issued an executive order calling for fair employment within the federal government.[79] Both moves were aimed at correcting what Truman considered to be glaring injustices incompatible with national values.[80] Army Chief of Staff Gen. Omar Bradley opposed the President's desire for instant integration of the armed forces, arguing it "would be hazardous for [the United States] to employ the Army deliberately as an instrument of social reform."[81] Resistance was also rooted in postwar political realities that made the Army reluctant to alienate powerful Southern legislators and the large portion of its own officer corps that hailed from Southern states.[82] In the end, integration under Bradley was slow and gradual. Ironically, the functional imperative demanding that sufficient manpower be available to effectively man the units being sent to the Korean War spurred Bradley's successor, Gen. J. Lawton Collins, to fully comply with the integration order.[83]

A crucial barrier to giving women the same opportunities to advance through the officer ranks as men was removed in 1975 with President Gerald Ford's signing of Public Law 94-106, which called for the admittance of women to the service academies the following year. Clinging to tradition and citing an inevitable dilution of the nation's ability to produce combat leaders, the Army, Navy, and Air Force stood united in their opposition to Congressional pressure to open the academies' doors to women.[84] Such a stance was out of sync with various compelling forces at work within the societal imperative. First, indications of society's readiness to embrace the concept of equal opportunities for women was evident in Congress' passage of the Equal Rights Amendment (ERA) in March 1972.[85] Second, Congressional sentiment to admit women to the academies had been brewing for several years due to the frustrations felt by individual congressmen from both parties over not having their female nominees admitted. Additionally, lawsuits were crawling through the legal system on behalf of women applicants.[86] The Congressional hearings pitted the military's understanding of the functional imperative against the societal imperative. The services' arguments against encroachment on its professional autonomy clashed with the Congressional will to integrate. Ultimately women were admitted with the passage of amendments to DoD legislation pending in both the House and the Senate without much Congressional opposition.[87]

Democratic military professionals must develop the judgment required to distinguish between "social engineering" detrimental to the effectiveness of the profession, and legitimate evolutions of professional practices reflective of the democratic values of the state. Professional autonomy in a democracy does not mean that the profession can regulate itself in ways that are incompatible with democratic values. Many armies in service to authoritarian societies, such as those that characterized the former Soviet bloc, may have had long traditions of abusing conscripts, keeping its internal operations secret from the public, and excluding elements of the society from its ranks. But when democratic institutions began to take root, the newly empowered democratic civilian leaders—increasingly accountable to the newly empowered democratic citizenry—demanded change. The shift in the political system sparked inevitable changes in the form of military professionalism practiced in the state.[88]

Ideally, military institutions that are attuned to the discrepancies between professional norms and democratic norms will anticipate the inevitability of externally driven change. Such proactive behavior affords the military profession the opportunity to autonomously incorporate changes more on its own terms. In this regard, the next such adaptation is likely to be the open integration of gays into the military. Recent surveys show that societal attitudes are well ahead of the military on this issue. The 1999 TISS study reported that while 75 percent of military leaders are opposed to integrating gays, 57 percent of the public and 54 percent of civilian leaders are in favor of doing so.[89] The right configuration of societal forces and the political support of Congress may ultimately compel the change. Arguments that such a change will erode the functional imperative will likely be advanced again, but just as with the previous instances of integrating blacks and women the institution will likely adapt without significantly impairing its functional effectiveness. Such a result, however, depends on the military institution setting the appropriate standards within the profession and then providing the leadership to see that the professional standards are met.

Recommended Civil-Military Norm: *Tension between the functional and societal imperatives is a constant feature of civil-military relations in a democracy. Military professionals in service to democratic states must recognize that jurisdiction over their profession is limited in that it is inherently connected to societal values and the realities of civilian control, leaving ultimate control over their profession in the hands of their constitutional overseers. It is in the best interest of the military to foster the development of professionals who are engaged with their societies. Officers must stay abreast of societal forces and their reflection in the policy preferences of those empowered with civilian control—the President and Congress. Such engagement will allow the profession to better manage civilian-driven change and improve the prospects for retaining professional standards of good order and discipline essential to the functional imperative. Military institutions that fail to anticipate societal-driven change will inevitably succumb to the realities of the system of democratic political control, which allows civilians vested with the appropriate authority to demand that democratic values prevail. Military professionals must carefully dis-*

tinguish between their responsibilities to objectively advise on the potential adverse impact of societal-driven change and their professional inclination to thwart initiatives that threaten to alter the status quo of military culture.

Conclusion

This chapter has argued that, at present, the military profession in the United States does not subscribe to a single set of civil-military norms that regulate its participation in the policy-making process, in the general political process, and even in its relationship with the society it is charged to serve. Maintaining balanced civil-military relations that will best serve a democratic state's national security needs is a high-maintenance proposition, but it is essential to the achievement of high-quality national security policy outcomes. Infusing enlightened professional norms in this area would be a major contribution toward keeping U.S. civil-military relations on the track toward correcting some troubling trends.

Specific recommendations for each issue area have been discussed in this chapter. Common principles link the specific recommendations. The adoption of a coherent set of civil-military norms depends on the profession's acceptance of two key principles. The first is that while there may be overlapping competencies regarding the political leadership's and military participants' expert knowledge relevant to national security, there are distinct differences in the responsibility and authority of each within the political system. The second principle evident across the issue areas is the military professional's obligation to balance the functional and societal imperatives. Principled officership must include the realization that the profession's service takes place within the context of a society with a particular set of political and social values and within a specific democratic political system with unique processes of civilian control.

All levels of professional military education must focus on equipping officers at every stage of their professional development with a set of guiding principles that will ultimately result in the establishment of a shared set of civil-military norms within the American military profession. Such measures will enable officers to sort out the ambiguities inherent in collaborating in the national security-making process, participating in a democratic polity, and remaining an entity that is "of" and not "separate from" the society it serves.

Notes

1. The views and opinions expressed in this chapter are those of the author and are not necessarily those of the Department of the Army or any other U.S. government entity.
2. Richard H. Kohn, "The Constitution and National Security: The Intent of the Framers," in *The United States Military Under the Constitution of the United States*, ed. Richard H. Kohn (New York: New York University Press, 1991), 87.
3. James Madison, "The Federalist No. 10," in *The Federalist,* ed. Jacobe E. Cooke (Hanover, NH: Wesleyan University Press, 1961), 62.

4. Joseph A. Schumpeter, *Capitalism, Socialism, and Democracy* (New York: Harper & Brothers, 1950), 253.

5. Peter D. Feaver, "The Civil-Military Problematique: Huntington, Janowitz, and the Question of Civilian Control," *Armed Forces and Society* 23, no. 2 (Winter 1996): 155.

6. Russell F. Weigley, "The American Military and the Principle of Civilian Control from McClellan to Powell," *Journal of Military History,* Special Issue no. 57 (October 1993): 27.

7. Marybeth Peterson Ulrich, *Democratizing Communist Militaries: The Cases of the Czech and Russian Armed Forces* (Ann Arbor: University of Michigan Press, 2000), 10.

8. Samuel P. Huntington, *The Soldier and the State* (Cambridge, MA: Harvard University Press, 1957), 2.

9. Ulrich, 10-11, 116-153.

10. I attribute the idea that a distinct form of professionalism exists in "national security professionalism" to Peter J. Roman and David W. Tarr. These scholars created this concept as a distinct form of military professionalism related to the military professional's expertise in foreign and security policy as it is carried out across the government. I have adapted the concept to apply to both civilian and military participants in the national security process. See Peter J. Roman and David W. Tarr, "Military Professionalism and Policymaking: Is There a Civil-Military Gap at the Top? If So, Does it Matter?" in *Soldiers and Civilians: The Civil-Military Gap and American National Security,* ed. Peter D. Feaver and Richard H. Kohn (Cambridge, MA: Belfer Center for Science and International Affairs, 2001), 409-11.

11. Recognition that civilian and military officials often have overlapping roles in the policy-making process is found in Christopher P. Gibson and Don M. Snider, "Civil-Military Relations and the Potential to Influence: A Look at the National Security Decision-Making Process," *Armed Forces and Society* 25, no. 2 (Winter 1999): 193-218.

12. See Don M. Snider, Robert A. Priest, and Felisa Lewis, "Civilian-Military Gap and Professional Military Education at the Pre-commissioning Level," *Armed Forces and Society* 27, no. 2 (Winter 2001).

13. See Judith Hicks Stiehm, "Civil-Military Relations in War College Curricula," *Armed Forces and Society* 27, no. 2 (Winter 2001): 284-92. TISS survey data discussed in this article indicate that professional military education curricula need to clarify the distinctions between behavior that is advisory or advocative in nature—that is, merely offering counsel versus recommending in a pleading fashion. Officers' views on the appropriateness of "insisting" were also probed in the study. "Insisting" characterizes behaviors beyond counseling or forcefully recommending to include actions that demand vehemently and persistently. A significant number of officers surveyed replied that insistent behaviors were at times appropriate in civil-military relations. Finally, the term "political" is often unclear to officers. To many officers "political" tends to have a pejorative quality and is applied to anything pertaining to conflict among participants in democratic policy-making processes. A better understanding of the American political process and the legitimate role that officers play as participant-citizens and as contributors in policy-making could improve officers' comfort with processes that form the fabric of American political life.

14. Huntington, 2.

15. I attribute this insight to Lt. Col. John "Paul" Gardner, USA, U.S. Army War College Class of 2001.

16. Russell F. Weigley, "The American Military and the Principle of Civilian Control from McClellan to Powell," 42-46.

17. Forrest C. Pogue, "Marshall on Civil-Military Relationships," in *The United States Military under the Constitution of the United States, 1789-1989,* ed. Richard H. Kohn (New York: New York University Press, 1991), 205-206.

18. Pogue, 206.

19. Peter D. Feaver, "Crisis as Shirking: An Agency Theory Explanation of the Souring of American Civil-Military Relations," *Armed Forces and Society* 24, no. 3 (Spring 1998).

20. On resistance to force structure changes, see "Revolt of the Generals," *Inside the Ring,* 10 August 2001.

21. David Halberstam, "Clinton and the Generals," *Vanity Fair,* September 2001, 230-46.

22. Michael C. Desch, *Civilian Control of the Military: The Changing Security Environment* (Baltimore, MD: Johns Hopkins University Press), 32.

23. Ibid.

24. A former Clinton administration National Security Council official quoted in Halberstam, 230.

25. H.R. McMaster, *Dereliction of Duty* (New York: Harper, 1997), 327-28.

26. George C. Wilson, *This War Really Matters: Inside the Fight for Defense Dollars* (Washington, DC: Congressional Quarterly Press, 2000), chap. 6.

27. Peter Grier and Faye Bowers, "Rumsfeld: Mainly a Style Thing," *Christian Science Monitor,* 24 October 2003, 1.

28. Lt. Col. John W. Peabody, *The "Crisis" in American Civil-Military Relations: A Search for Balance Between Military Professionals and Civilian Leaders,* Strategy Research Project (Carlisle Barracks, PA: U.S. Army War College, 2001), 23.

29. Huntington, 72.

30. See Richard H. Kohn, "The Early Retirement of Gen. Ronald R. Fogleman, Chief of Staff, United States Air Force," *Aerospace Power Journal* 15, no. 1 (Spring 2001): 6. In this interview General Fogleman was careful to distinguish between a request for early retirement and resignation in protest. General Fogleman thought that resignation in protest violated the norms of civilian control by setting a precedent that military leaders might resign instead of accepting a decision they opposed.

31. Morris Janowitz, *The Professional Soldier* (New York: The Free Press, 1971), 236-41. Janowitz's data stem from a 1954 survey of Pentagon staff officers. He readily admits that the survey question asked only for a response based on general political orientation—neither party identification nor the specific content of the conservatism was provided.

32. Ibid. Of those surveyed, 45.3 percent reported that they were a little on the conservative side. An almost equal number of respondents, 21.6 percent and 23.1 percent, reported that they were conservative or a little on the liberal side, respectively (p. 238).

33. Ole Holsti, "A Widening Gap between the U.S. Military and Civilian Society?" *International Security* 23, no. 2 (Winter 1998/99): 11.

34. Thomas E. Ricks, "Is American Military Professionalism Declining?" *Proceedings* (July 1998); available from http://proquest.umi.com; Internet accessed 29 September 2004.

35. Ole R. Holsti, "A Widening Gap between the U.S. Military and Civilian Society?" 11.

36. Ibid., 13.

37. Ole R. Holsti, "Of Chasms and Convergences," in *Soldiers and Civilians: The Civil-Military Gap and American National Security,* 33.

38. Donna Winslow, *Army Culture,* Report published in fulfillment of U.S. Army Research Institute Contract No. DASW01-98-M-1868 (2000), 13.

39. Huntington, 230-31.

40. "Divided government" occurs when the president's party does not control Congress. See James Q. Wilson, *American Government: The Essentials,* 8th edition (Boston, MA: Houghton Mifflin, 2004), chap. 12.

41. See chap. 1 of this anthology.

42. For an extensive treatment of civilian and military competencies as factors influencing the contrasting power of military professionals and civilian policy-makers in the policy-making process, see Christopher P. Gibson and Don M. Snider, 193-218.

43. Elliott Abrams and Andrew J. Bacevich, "A Symposium on Citizenship and Military Service," *Parameters* 31, no. 2 (Summer 2001): 19.

44. Eliot A. Cohen, "Twilight of the Citizen-Soldier," *Parameters* 31, no. 2 (Summer 2001); this argument runs throughout the article.

45. Ibid. 28. Cohen presents but vehemently disagrees with this perspective.

46. Note again the principles of officership required for service in the 21st century in *United States Military Academy Strategic Vision—2010.*

47. See Steven Lee Myers, "The 2000 Campaign: The Convention; Pentagon Taking Opportunity for Show," *New York Times,* 28 July 2000; Richard H. Kohn, "General Elections; The Brass Shouldn't Do Endorsements," *Washington Post,* 19 September 2000, A23; Steven Lee Myers, "The 2000 Campaign: Support of the Military; Military Backs Ex-Guard Pilot Over Pvt. Gore," *New York Times,* 21 September 2000, A1; "Nonpartisan Military Best," *Omaha World Herald,* 16 October 2000, 6; David Wood, *Newhouse News Service,* "E-day Attack; Military Set to Invade the Polls; Observers Worry about Surge in Partisan Politics," *Times Picayune,* 20 October 2000, 5; David Wood, *Newhouse News Service,* "Military Breaks Ranks with Nonpartisan Tradition; Many in Service Turn to Bush, Reject Political Correctness," *Plain Dealer,* 22 October 2000, 16A. See also Ole R. Holsti, "Of Chasms and Convergences: Attitudes and Beliefs of Civilians and Military Elites at the Start of a New Millennium," 31-32.

48. E.J. Dionne, "Dirty Pool in Florida," *Washington Post,* 17 July 2001, A17.

49. "The Pentagon's Troubling Role," *New York Times,* 31 August 2004, 18.

50. "Focus on Voting Plan for Troops," *Associated Press,* 7 August 2004; www.military.com; accessed 26 September 2004.

51. Ibid.

52. Comment of an active duty Army general officer in response to the *U.S. Army War College Survey: Retired Generals and Partisan Politics* (October 2000). Survey was conducted by U.S. Army War College student, Lt. Col. William R. Becker as part of his Strategy Research Project, *Retired Generals and Partisan Politics: Is a Time Out Required?* (Carlisle Barracks, PA: USAWC, April 2000), 30.

53. Comment of Marine one-star general in response to the *U.S. Army War College Survey: Retired Generals and Partisan Politics* (October 2000). See Becker, 37.

54. Comments of Marine two-star general officer in response to the *U.S. Army War College Survey: Retired Generals and Partisan Politics* (October 2000). See Becker, 41.

55. Comments of active duty four-star general officer in response to the *U.S. Army War College Survey: Retired Generals and Partisan Politics* (October 2000). See Becker, 47.

56. Lawrence F. Kaplan, "Officer Politics," *The New Republic,* 13 September 2004, 23.

57. The Gore campaign did not report any high profile endorsements from retired generals. Gwen Ifill, "Military Endorsements," *Online NewsHour,* 25 September 2000; Accessed 26 September 2004.

58. A total of 11 general officers appeared on stage at the Democratic national convention. Two had speaking roles—a first for a major party political convention. General McPeak appeared in numerous campaign ads.

59. Kaplan, 23.

60. *FDCH,* "Text: Remarks by Retired General Tommy Franks to the Republican National Convention," 2 September 2004.

61. See Gen. John Shaliskashvili's argument in "Old Soldiers Don't Have to Fade Away," *Wall Street Journal,* 17 August 2004.

62. Ifill, "Military Endorsements."

63. See Abbott, *The System of Professions: An Essay on the Division of Expert Labor* (Chicago, IL: University of Chicago Press, 1988), 69-89. Abbott offers five "settlements" that can be applied to jurisdictional disputes: (1) The claim to full and final jurisdiction; (2) The subordination of one profession to another; (3) Division of labor that splits jurisdictional areas into

two interdependent parts; (4) Allow one profession an advisory role over another; (5) Divide jurisdictions not according to content of work, but according to the nature of the client.

64. Frank Aukofer and William P. Lawrence, *America's Team: The Odd Couple* (Nashville, TN: The Freedom Forum First Amendment Center, 1995), 83.

65. Aukofer and Lawrence, 79.

66. Frank A. Aukofer, "Embedded Journalists in the War Serve Truth," *Milwaukee Journal Sentinel,* 23 March 2003, 01J.

67. John Hughes, "War within a War, Two Major Campaigns Will Be Under Way," *Christian Science Monitor,* 18 December 2002, 9.

68. A 1995 survey indicated that a majority of military officers still believe that "news media coverage of the events in Vietnam harmed the war effort." However, the survey also showed that this view is not shared by the majority of the top brass. Aukofer and Lawrence, 31,40.

69. Alicia C. Shepard, *Narrowing the Gap: Military, Media, and the Iraq War* (Chicago, IL: McCormick Tribune Foundation, 2004), 19.

70. Shepard, 20.

71. Aukofer, "Embedded Journalists in the War Serve Truth."

72. Rick Atkinson, Lecture at the Army War College, 22 September 2004.

73. Barry Shlachter, "Military Helps Press Get in Shape for Iraq War," *Pittsburgh Post-Gazette,* 1 December 2002, A4.

74. Atkinson.

75. Shepard, 67.

76. Both the *New York Times* and the *Washington Post* engaged in high profile re-examinations of their pre-war coverage.

77. For a discussion of this conflict and its impact on military culture in greater depth, see John Hillen, "Must U.S. Military Culture Reform?" *Orbis* 43, 1 (Winter 1999), 43-57.

78. James Burk, "The Military's Presence in American Society, 1950-2000," in *Soldiers and Civilians,* ed. Peter D. Feaver and Richard H. Kohn (Cambridge, MA: Belfer Center for Science and International Affairs, 2001).

79. Robert H. Ferrell, *Harry S. Truman: A Life* (Columbia, MO: University of Missouri Press, 1994), 298.

80. McCullough, 588-89.

81. Omar N. Bradley, *A General's Life* (New York: Simon and Schuster, 1983), 485.

82. Leo Bogart, *Project Clear: Social Research and the Desegregation of the United States Army* (New Brunswick, NJ: Transaction Publishers, 1992), xxi-xxii.

83. Ferrell, 588-89.

84. Jeanne Holm, *Women in the Military* (Novato, CA: Presidio Press, 1993), 307.

85. Holm, 264.

86. Holm, 305-12.

87. The House amendment passed 303-96 and the Senate amendment was accepted without a roll call vote. Holm, 310.

88. Ulrich, 11.

89. Peter D. Feaver and Richard H. Kohn, "Project on the Gap between the Military and Civilian Society: Digest of Findings and Studies" (Chapel Hill, NC: Triangle Institute of Security Studies, October 1999). These findings are also reported in Feaver and Kohn, *Soldiers and Civilians.*

31 Army Professionalism: Service to What Ends?

Martin L. Cook

This chapter explores the concept of professionalism itself as a normative term. From an ethical perspective, the question is how to understand professionalism so that two equal values, somewhat in tension with one another, are preserved. On the one hand, the unquestioned subordination of military officers to Constitutionally legitimate civilian leadership is at the core of military professionalism in a democracy. Balancing that, however, is the equally important role of the professional expertise of the officer corps in providing professional military advice, unalloyed with extraneous political or cultural considerations. The possession of a body of professional knowledge is at the core of the concept of professionalism, and only clarity about the value and integrity of that professional knowledge distinguishes a professional military from a mere bureaucratic tool. One of the most critical jobs of the senior leadership of the Army profession is, indeed, to understand and exercise leadership for the profession as a whole in striking the appropriate balance among these imperatives.

A good deal of the contemporary confusion in the profession results from two equally distorted understandings of these issues: some emphasize subordination, to the virtual neglect of legitimate professional expertise; others emphasize professional expertise, to the point of undermining the military's subordination to political leadership. Proper conceptual clarification of the terms will substantially reduce those misunderstandings.

"Professionalism" as a Normative Term

Typical Army officers have a fairly limited moral vocabulary. The central terms are "integrity" and "professionalism," and those terms are rarely examined critically. One praises an officer by saying he or she has "integrity," and one criticizes by saying he or she lacks it. One criticizes a wide range of behaviors, from how an individual dresses to the orderliness of an office or even to the individual's ethical character by saying they show a lack of professionalism, and one praises an equally wide range of conduct by saying the individual "is a real professional."

A professional group can successfully manage to maintain a widely shared standard of conduct and professional self-understanding, even with such unexamined vocabulary, during times of relative stability in the profession and its environment. When members of the profession are engaged in common activities, when the environment and culture in which they do their professional work are stable, and when the assumptions about the nature and purpose of their work are widely shared, critical examination of that vocabulary is perhaps unnecessary.

But during times of great change in the nature, function, and well-being of the profession, such unexamined unanimity will be found inadequate to articulate the nature of the challenge. If, for example, a profession has become accustomed to acting in a given sphere with complete autonomy, great tensions will arise when societal or legal changes challenge or limit that autonomy. Consider, for example, the tensions managed health care has precipitated in the medical profession. Increasingly, medical professionals question whether physicians can be "true professionals" as their autonomy in medical practice is increasingly circumscribed by case managers and preferred-provider limitations. Was the way physicians experienced the conditions of their work before managed care a necessary condition of their professionalism? Or are the stresses now being experienced simply the kind of stress any change inevitably brings with it?[1]

By any measure, the officer corps of the Army is moving through a period of enormous change in the nature, purpose, and meaning of the profession.[2] In recent years, it has been deprived of its central defining threats that have shaped the nature and practices of the military culture for several generations. It has experienced a wrenching reduction in the size of the force, which in turn has had enormous effects on the normal officer career progression and prospects for professional advancement. Its equipment is aging and, it increasingly appears, in some cases not highly relevant to the kinds of military engagements it is being asked to perform. Among the military services, the Army in particular is undergoing a process of very rapid transformation in force structure, equipment, and doctrine that many do not fully understand or, in some cases, endorse.[3]

Not surprisingly, with so many shifts occurring Army officers in their professional role are somewhat unsure of themselves, a typical sign of a profession in transition and change. Before the current engagement in Operation Iraqi Freedom, its junior members (captains) were leaving the profession at higher rates than expected. Significant numbers of the most successful colonels were declining brigade command, thus effectively refusing professional advancement. Distrust between levels of the profession was extremely high, and morale was low.[4] Obviously, active military engagement, at least temporarily, necessarily blows away many of the constraints of micromanagement and gives officers at all levels opportunities for meaningful leadership and innovation that peacetime training does not. It will be important to monitor whether, when large-scale operational deployments abate, some of the lessons learned from that environment will help build a healthier future force or whether the weight of bureaucratic inertia will re-exert itself.

As is to be expected, the moral vocabulary of the profession is often invoked to "explain" what is occurring among Army officers. When officers don't behave in ways associated with earlier, more settled times, they are seen as "lacking integrity" and manifesting a diminished sense of "professionalism." When they rank force protection as their primary mission in far-flung peacekeeping operations, they manifest declining "professionalism."[5] When they fail to embrace the profession as essential to their personal sense of identity and leave military service after short careers, those who remain are inclined to blame the departing individuals for their failure to share the "professional" ethos.[6] In fact, however, the departing individuals may be barometers indicating that the shifts in the role and mission of the profession have been so great as to change their relation to the profession dramatically. Further, they may reflect shifts in broader societal attitudes toward work, family, and career loyalty that merely play out in military culture in distinctive ways, but which have significant parallels throughout the society.[7]

Before too quickly deploying the standard vocabulary of professionalism, one should pause and inquire whether the vocabulary is indeed adequate to the task. Unless the central terms are conceptually precise, one runs the risk of invoking the military's standard limited moral vocabulary in criticism of individuals and classes of officers without accurately grasping the phenomenon one wishes to describe.

Eliot Friedson shrewdly raises a caution about too uncritical an embrace of the language of "professionalism" to exhort and criticize. He notes the ideological sense of "profession" which allows the term to be used manipulatively:

> The ideology may be used by political, managerial, and professional authorities to distract workers from their objective lack of control over their work, to lead them to do the work assigned to them as well as possible, and to commit them to means and ends others have chosen for them.[8]

Friedson is suggesting that in circumstances in which workers have lost control over their work or become disillusioned with the resources and support available to them, one would expect their superiors to employ the language of professionalism. The function of that language is to motivate workers to labor on, oblivious to the objective shifts in the character and meaning of their work. In such a circumstance, professional workers are no longer able to define the scope and nature of their core professional competencies, and are being tasked to accomplish missions for which they feel ill prepared by their professional competence and experience.

Before embracing the conclusion that the root problem with the contemporary officer corps is a declining sense of professionalism, one should step back and determine the nature and purposes of the military officer corps as professionals. What is the fundamental nature and purpose of the profession? What are the timeless attributes of the profession that must be maintained in all circumstances, and what elements are contingent on particular historical and political circumstances? Are there elements that have historically been foundations of the self-understanding of the profession that are in flux?

Necessarily, one cannot address the issue of Army professionalism ahistorically. Besides the obvious changes in the size and mission of the Army and the generational shifts in attitudes among younger officers, there are still larger shifts in the society from which and within which the military recruits and functions. Is the "postmodern" military a reality?[9] Certainly the internal and external environments within which the military functions are changing dramatically. Charles Moskos suggests eleven critical dimensions in which the military of the future will be fundamentally different than the military of the Cold War. These dimensions are as diverse as the military's news media relations, force structure, perceived threat, and the roles of women and spouses in military culture.

If such fundamental changes are, indeed, in progress, it seems unlikely that the professional ethos of the profession will remain constant. Clearly in a time of enormous change in the nature, scope, purpose, and size of the military, some confusion and reconsideration of purpose are inescapable and appropriate. In this chapter, we will examine the question of the nature of the military as a profession in the contemporary context. The chapter will offer some reflections on continuity and change of the professional military ethic as it emerges from this period of transition and uncertainty. Finally, it will offer some normative suggestions regarding the shape military professionalism should take as the dust settles and it begins a period of renewed stability.

The Military Profession in a System of Professions

The conceptual framework of the larger Army professionalism study to which this chapter is a contribution is derived from Andrew Abbott's book, *The System of Professions: An Essay on the Division of Expert Labor*.[10] Fundamental to Abbott's conception of professions is the idea that professions apply bodies of abstract knowledge to a sphere of professional tasks. Societal recognition of the appropriateness of a profession's sphere constitutes its professional "legitimacy." Perhaps most important to Abbott's view is the idea that legitimacy is not a fixed, immutable fact. Rather, professions jockey for position within a given society as different professions and nonprofessional groups attempt to gain jurisdiction over spheres of human labor that have previously belonged to other professional groups, or alternatively as professions attempt to protect their historical jurisdiction from encroachments by competitor professions.

Within this framework, one may ask whether the current uncertainty in the Army officer corps is a manifestation of precisely this kind of jurisdictional conflict in progress. If the answer is affirmative, then the changed character of the nation's geopolitical situation (an "external system change" in Abbott's vocabulary) has required the Army (and the other military services) to engage in a wide range of activities that differ from the classic Cold War war-fighting mission. Those new demands and tasks differ considerably from the activities, behaviors, and expectations that defined the profession for 50 years.[11]

The jurisdiction of the Army, for example, has been large-scale armored and combined arms land warfare throughout the Cold War. While it could be assigned many other tasks, the core jurisdiction remained fixed, and the culture, values, and professional standards of the Army remained linked to that core jurisdictional function. Continuing this line of analysis, one sees that individuals raised in that professional culture may well experience professional confusion and uncertainty in the face of new and different tasks. So much of their professional self-understanding was bound to those tasks. So much of their body of professional knowledge, expertise, and agreed-upon ways of functioning were tied to that context.

It is to be expected that, in the face of quite different expectations, they question whether the new demands are consistent with their understanding of the profession. It should not be a surprise that professionals reared and rewarded within a relatively fixed set of assumptions about the nature and purpose of the profession experience discomfort and professional unsettlement as the verities of that context begin to dissolve.

If this view of what's occurring is correct,[12] then the question before the profession (in terms of Abbott's framework) is whether to participate in a jurisdictional competition for new roles and missions, or to cede some of the territory to other professional contenders.[13] In other words, given that the political leadership and American society generally are choosing to engage in peacekeeping and peace-enforcing missions around the globe—not to mention the open-ended constabulary and nation-building mission Iraqi Freedom now requires—the Army must either adapt to them or prepare for considerable professional stress.

In this evolutionary way of viewing the matter, the Army is analogous to a species that may or may not successfully adapt to a changing environment. In Abbott's view, professions live and die in the face of the evolutionary pressure of adaptation. Those that cling to forms superseded by external change face the prospect of joining astrologers and phrenologists in the dustbin of cultural history.

One common view—perhaps the majority view within the profession—takes for granted that the Army should and must embrace all tasks assigned by "society," and views the reluctance to do so on the part of some officers as evidence per se of a declining sense of professionalism in the officer corps. As Don Snider, John Nagl, and Tony Pfaff state the matter:

> In a democracy, an Army does not get to choose the missions it accepts—at least, no professional army does. The hesitancy of the U.S. Army to accept wholeheartedly the missions it is currently being given strikes the authors of this paper as cause for concern in the context of military professionalism. *We believe that means defining the Army's organizational purpose, its essence, simply as serving the American society, and fighting the conflicts they approve, when they approve them.* Any other essence or purpose statement places the institution in the illegitimate and unprofessional position of declaring its intellectual independence from the society it was formed to serve.[14]

A number of points are striking about this analysis. First, it asserts that "intellectual independence from the society" is unprofessional on its face. But in fact the question of intellectual independence is considerably more complex than this formulation suggests. Second, it presupposes that the "hesitancy" of the Army to accept current missions is itself "cause for concern" regarding the Army's professionalism. Third, it offers a definition of the core professional function "simply as serving the American society." On each of these points the correct analysis is considerably more complex, and complex in ways that bear directly on a proper understanding of professionalism for the future U.S. military.

What Are Professional Obligations?

A few preliminary remarks are in order to avoid misunderstanding. There is no question that military members are obligated to follow legal orders of their superiors and to serve American society as the society's civilian leaders see fit. Self-evidently, civilian control over the military means that the military does not pick and choose its own missions. The essence of the soldier's commitment to service entails the unlimited liability clause that he or she may be required to sacrifice life and limb in following those orders and striving to complete legally assigned missions.

In all those ways, the commitment (especially the voluntary commitment) of the soldier to selfless service of the society and dutiful obedience to Constitutionally valid authority is the root of the nobility of the profession, and the source of American society's trust in and respect for its profession of arms. Indeed, it is for these very reasons that any overt affiliation of the vast majority of the military with a single political party is cause for concern. It is why endorsement of political candidates and causes by prominent retired officers using their military reputations for political purposes is potentially damaging to the public's perception of the professionalism of its officer corps.[15]

Nevertheless, the view that the military is *merely* obedient is incompatible with retention of any meaningful sense in which military officership truly is a *profession*. Obedient service is a crucial element of military professionalism, granted. Further, there can be no question that at the end of the day the soldier's obligation comes down to that: to follow legal orders, even if he or she believes the orders to be misguided, foolish, and likely to cause his or her death. But leaping directly to this "bottom line" reality of the military life fails to articulate what is important about the intellectual component and expertise of the military as a profession, and threatens to eliminate the very conceptual space in which the exercise of professionalism can and does occur.

Intellectual independence from the society is the essence of professionalism, not at all evidence of a lack of it. As Eliot Friedson puts it in a chapter titled, "The Soul of Professionalism,"

> By virtue of that independence members of the profession claim the right to judge the demands of employers or patrons and the laws of the state, and to criticize or refuse to obey them. That refusal is based not on personal grounds of individual conscience or desire but on the *professional* grounds that the basic value or purpose of a discipline is being perverted. . . . Professional ethics must claim an independence from patron, state, and public that is analogous to what is claimed by a religious congregation.[16]

Friedson's vision is of the ideal type of a profession, necessarily to be qualified by parameters applied in the real world. This is perhaps especially true in the case of the military profession or any other profession embedded deeply in the bureaucracy of government and in an ethic of subordination to civilian control. Nevertheless, the ideal type has a useful heuristic purpose in stressing that professionals in essence possess unique knowledge and the skill to apply that knowledge in a given sphere of service. A formulation such as that of Snider and his co-authors, with its exclusive emphasis on obedient service, undercuts the centrality of the exclusive "abstract knowledge" aspect of Abbott's (or any other) model of professionalism. As Friedson expresses the point, "Professionalism entails commitment to a particular body of knowledge and skill both for its own sake and for the use to which it is put."[17]

Such discussion captures one of the central issues before us. How does one properly capture the inherent intellectual component of professionalism and professional expert judgment in such a way that they remain independent and critical? Clearly, in the case of the military profession in particular, there is a serious risk of overstating the professional mandate for intellectual independence and suggesting insubordinate or disobedient behavior based on that level of expert knowledge, which is presumably superior to that of the military's civilian masters.

On the other hand, if military officers are not actually in possession of a body of knowledge that constitutes the intellectual component of their profession, the idea of "professional military advice" becomes meaningless. In that view, skill and wisdom about how to employ military forces reside not among military officers at all, but among those who use the military as obedient tools, employed in ways and for ends beyond the purview of military officers themselves.[18]

But clearly this is not the case. Military personnel, especially officers, undergo extensive periodic education and training designed to impart professional knowledge and expertise, and they practice the application of that knowledge at all levels of their work—from field training exercises, through National Training Center rotations, to strategic exercises and war games. That extensive professional development indeed results in a degree of intellectual independence from the society they serve, grounded in their unique professional focus. The question of Army professionalism is wrongly framed by the suggestion that intellectual independence is somehow inherently unprofessional or even at odds with civilian control in a democracy. The proper question is not whether there is professional intellectual independence, but rather how the intellectual independence inherent in the very concept of professionalism is properly exercised. But this is just to pose the issue, not to resolve it.

Consider a circumstance in which professional military advice has been rendered but not accepted by the professional's civilian superiors. Here the officer must decide whether this is the occasion for obedient service and deference to civilian leadership (the normal case) or whether the course of action chosen by political leadership is so at variance with sound professional judgment that conscientious resignation should be entertained as a possibility. A related and important question is the degree to which retired officers remain members of the profession in the sense of articulating, applying, and extending the body of professional knowledge. For retired officers, freed from the legal constraints preventing serving officers from speaking freely, when (if ever) is it their right, or even their professional obligation, to criticize publicly the military-strategic decisions being made by civilian leadership in the name of professional military judgment. One thinks, for example, of the fairly scathing criticism of Iraqi Freedom currently being offered by Gen. Anthony Zinni, former head of U.S. Central Command, as a fruitful case for reflection on this point.

Unwillingness to render obedient service to policies an officer considers deeply flawed and utterly at variance with sound professional judgment is not necessarily evidence of a *lack* of professionalism but may on occasion be a high manifestation of it. Indeed, the very essence of a profession (as distinct from other occupations) is that the professional does possess and exercise independent judgment. To cite Friedson once again:

> [A]nother critical element of work that nourishes professionalism lies in the nature
> of the relationship between client and professional. . . . In the case of employment

in large-scale organizations we can put it crudely as whether or not policy is that customers are always right and that the organization and its members exist solely to serve, even cater to, their desires as long as they are willing to pay. Is the policy to provide whatever customers or clients desire, even if their capacity to evaluate the service or product is seriously limited and what they desire contradicts the better judgment of the professional?[19]

One of the most widely read and valued cautionary tales in contemporary U.S. military literature is H. R. McMaster's *Dereliction of Duty* (1997), a historical analysis of the relation of the Joint Chiefs of Staff with the Johnson administration during the Vietnam War.[20] The main point of McMaster's treatment is to demonstrate how the Joint Chiefs failed to deliver professional military advice to President Johnson regarding the conduct of the war in Vietnam. The book is widely read among the officer corps not primarily because of its historical value, but rather as a morality tale on the lack of military professionalism on the part of the Joint Chiefs. According to McMaster's account, the primary moral failure of the senior officers is that they did not effectively exercise their intellectual independence and insist, to the point of resignation if necessary, that their professional military judgment be heard and accorded due weight by political leadership.

Of course it goes without saying that it would be unprofessional in the extreme to appear to accept the guidance of political superiors and then to subvert it through less than enthusiastic implementation or downright evasion of the spirit and letter of the order. But of more practical concern, it is the attempt to "have it both ways"— maintaining one's status as a serving military officer while simultaneously being insubordinate to duly constituted leadership—that makes conduct unprofessional for our purposes here. It is not, I repeat, the intellectual independence of the professional.

It is this aspect of the issue that the Snider-Nagl-Pfaff quotation above correctly captures, that is, the observation that "hesitancy" to accept missions assigned by civilian authorities is a cause for concern regarding Army professionalism. But in order for the analysis to portray the problem accurately, we must assess the causes of the hesitancy. Insofar as hesitancy derives from application of the profession's body of knowledge, the root problem may not be solely the willing obedience to authority that is part of the essence of the military profession. In addition, it may derive from the changing character of the missions being demanded and, arguably, from the profession's legitimate concern that it is being tasked beyond existing resources and professional competency.

When professionals are asked to perform tasks that lie beyond their scope of training and competency, they may hesitate for good and professional reasons as well. A medical analogy would be the demand that a general practitioner of medicine perform coronary bypass surgery; a legal analogy, that a personal injury attorney is pressured to take a bank fraud case. Thus, before we draw the simple deduction that hesitancy implies lack of professionalism, we should explore the possibility that prudent disinclination, like intellectual independence, is a manifestation of high professional seriousness, not a lack of it. We would not think well of the professionalism of the general practitioner who attempted the heart bypass; perhaps we should at least pause to reflect before we assume that the combat arms officer reluctant to take on police missions is culpably resistant to authority.

The point is that there is both a social service dimension and an intellectual independence dimension to all genuine professions, and it is critical to strike the appropriate balance between them. If one stresses only the social dimension of professional obligation without giving equal weight to the profession's body of knowledge, one runs the risk of thinking of professions only as obedient servants.

To illustrate the point, consider the following. To say that physicians, lawyers, or ministers exist to serve society is, of course, correct. But to infer that they have an obligation *as professionals* to collect trash or serve as school crossing guards, should society ask that of them, is ludicrous.[21] The point of these examples is that simply serving society's requests can never be an adequate definition of the obligation of any profession (although one might imagine a nonprofessional defined as a universal factotum of the society).

The reason it cannot be adequate is that it neglects the profession's own internal dynamic in assessing its body of knowledge, determining its relevance to a given identified social need, and negotiating jurisdictional questions with the larger society. The essential point here is that it is a multilateral negotiation, not a unilateral one. In an occupation, at least one lacking union organization, the hiring party can define every detail of the nature, scope, and method of the work, and then hire individuals willing to perform that work on those terms. Garbage collectors do not arrive on the job with a body of professional knowledge about the manner and scope of their work. In a profession, however, the case is different. The profession brings its own superior sense of the scope and limits of its expertise to the negotiation. If professionals do not possess that sense, then they "are no longer able to exercise the authoritative discretion, guided by their independent perspective on what work is appropriate to their craft, that is supposed to distinguish them."[22]

Of course the society may confer legitimacy on a profession or withdraw it. It may, for example, decide that chiropractors or Christian Science practitioners or acupuncturists are, or are not, "health care providers" for the purpose of insurance coverage. It may decide that ancient and well-established bodies of "professional knowledge" confer no legitimacy on the supposed professionals (e.g., astrologers) even though some individuals and groups may continue to treat them as if they were professionals.

These considerations frame the central ethical dimension of the question of military professionalism: What is the essential nature of professionalism in the U.S. Army? How, in the present, ought that profession be reconceived to adapt to the new social, cultural, and geopolitical context within which the contemporary Army functions?

Toward a Normative Account of Army Professionalism

A normative account of professional officership will necessarily consider the following major elements: professional knowledge, professional cohesion, and professional motivation and identity.

Professional Knowledge

Entry into any profession entails initiation into a body of knowledge primarily, if not exclusively, generated, transmitted, and built upon by fellow members of the profession. New members become familiar with that body of knowledge, learn where the major energy of the field is currently going, and ideally aspire to contribute to it as they join the ranks. Individuals come to think of themselves as members of the profession, increasingly acquire a familiarity with its technical vocabulary and knowledge, and acquire the ability to speak its technical language with facility. They learn the identity of a pantheon of archetypal members of the profession and stories of their contributions to the profession. They become familiar with a set of institutions, awards, honors, and so forth that members of the profession know and value (and that generally individuals outside the profession do not). They pick up, almost unconsciously, the small cues in dress, attitude, speech, etc. that members use to signal to each other that they are members of the same professional group.

It is also important to note that in most professions there is a core of the "real" members of the profession who have fully imbibed this knowledge. But there is also a large penumbra of paraprofessionals, knowledgeable in some areas essential to the profession's jurisdiction, but weakly if at all encompassed in the profession as profession. To use medicine as an example once again, phlebotomists and x-ray technicians are essential to the core functions of medical care, but clearly are not members of the medical profession.

It is true that the kinds of missions being assigned to the post-Cold War Army may seem to many in the profession as not calling upon and exercising core professional competencies. For example, the units that are especially required for effective operations in Bosnia and Kosovo are civil affairs and military police units, which are in short supply and largely in the reserves. The logic of "task effectiveness" would have suggested long ago that the active-duty Army ought either to have converted a significant number of is combat units to civil affairs and military police functions or to explicitly renegotiate jurisdiction issues regarding those functions with the society the Army serves.[23] Precisely such transformation is now being undertaken, of course, but long after the logic of task effectiveness had obviously called for it.

Resistance to such force restructuring has been considerable, and it is important to understand the nature and source of such resistance correctly. To return to the health care analogy, consider the following. In a particular health crisis one might find that the demonstrated priority need is for low-technology public health workers and perhaps family practitioners. No matter how true and strong that objective demand, however, one could foresee that surgeons (for example) would resist being tasked to fulfill those roles.

The root issue is this. The nature of professional commitment is complex. True, surgeons have a shared commitment to patient care and welfare. But they have invested years of training, study, and practice in acquiring extremely technical knowledge and in learning its application. While from a certain level of generality all this is in the service of patient health and welfare, one simply cannot leap from that level of description to generate the professional obligation for surgeons to retool their professional work. To understand the group and individual psychology of the profession, one must come to grips with the tremendous personal and societal investment in their identity and expertise, not merely as health care worker or even as generic physicians, but *as surgeons*.

It is not adequate in describing this phenomenon to focus only on the grand organizing purpose of the activity in patient welfare. One must also see the degree to which mastery of complex skills, equipment, and abstract knowledge has become embedded in the very sense of self of the surgeon. One can predict with certainty that surgeons asked to care for patients in ways that do not draw on those skills (no matter how effectively they treat the patients) will experience professional disillusionment, lowered morale, and a diminished sense of commitment to the profession. The point would be equally valid for the "strategic leaders" of surgery as a profession in the face of a societal demand that their profession make such an adaptation.

One might be tempted to call such a reaction "unprofessional." After all, is not the essence of the medical profession a willingness to attend to the health and the welfare of patients? At some level, that is correct—and in the circumstance described, if the objective need is for the kinds of professional adaptation outlined, the result is indeed what Abbott would call a jurisdictional dispute. Further, should surgeons persist for a long period in their own internally defined sense of professional identity, their skills would become less and less relevant to the health needs of their society, and their profession would wither and perhaps even die for failure to adapt.

But clearly it is reasonable for at least a period of adjustment to occur. During that period, the profession collectively and surgeons individually would have to engage in some serious self-reflection and examination of their motives. Is their commitment to patients and health indeed their fundamental motivation? Or is retaining their attachment to a specific set of skills and knowledge as surgeons in fact their main motive?

Before their profession was undergoing challenge, of course, that was not a forced choice: they could have both, in the confidence that the skills they took professional pride and identity in mastering did indeed serve the well-being of patients. But now, in changed circumstances, what had been a happy convergence becomes a hard choice. Moreover, the profession may be so conservative, so wedded to its earlier self-understanding, that the client comes to lose faith and patience, and simply withdraws jurisdiction from the profession, awarding it instead to more flexible or newly minted groups willing to meet the demands of the changed situation.

Something analogous to this scenario may be what is occurring in the contemporary Army officer corps. Officers who have invested their lives and careers in mastering complex combat arms skills in particular branches of the Army (infantry, armor, etc.) experience an analogous professional disorientation when they are consistently tasked to execute missions which draw little if at all on their body of knowledge and its application. Yes, of course, they understand their function is to serve the nation selflessly. But in addition their entire professional careers have been guided by the mandate to acquire ever more sophisticated skills and abilities. Their entire sense of professional identity has been formed by storied exemplars of the profession: great combat leaders or heroic figures who sacrificed themselves in battle for the good of country and comrades.

Other communities and professions have different symbols, different archetypal stories, of course. But for professional soldiers, newly tasked with peacekeeping missions and humanitarian aid, it is understandable if they react by thinking, "This is not what I signed up for." It is understandable (even if not finally defensible) if their traditional symbol system and narrative of heroic self-sacrifice cannot justify death and injury on such missions—and that force protection thus emerges as a high value.

Of course, like the surgeons in the example above, it may turn out that the objective need of U.S. society is for continual capability to engage in operations other than war (and clearly, for the foreseeable future, that is precisely the case in Afghanistan and Iraq) and only rarely for the skills associated with more traditional combat arms. If that is the case, and if the Army is unwilling to embrace the missions and come to reverence the professional knowledge required to execute them as it does for combat skills, the profession will see its jurisdiction curtailed.

It is far from self-evident what should happen at this historical juncture. Just as surgeons, individually and collectively, would face some hard choices in the scenario suggested above, so would the officer corps. Assuming that some effective combat arms capability is a perpetual societal need, the Army may choose to make the case that the preservation of such capability is the essence of its understanding of military professionalism. Part of this problem is conceptual. For many years, the Army leadership has asserted that peacekeeping and nation-building skills were simply "lesser included" skills within the range of training for the "high end" of combat. It is becoming clear as the Iraq occupation proceeds that this is not always the case. On the other hand, in all but the most benign environments, peacekeeping forces will need to possess the training and equipment to use force, even lethal force, when their efforts are violently resisted. Hence, rethinking training so as to bring the right mix of skills and attitudes to each engagement will be a major challenge for the senior leadership of the profession.

If it takes that position and upholds it successfully, the Army should be prepared for radically downsizing, unless and until it is necessary to build up a significant combat force when large-scale combat looms again on the horizon. This pattern is traditional in American military matters—the period of the Cold War being quite anomalous viewed through the lens of American history and our customary suspicion of standing armies. Those civil affairs, policing, and other functions necessary to operations other than war could be transferred to another group or profession ("peacekeepers") who would enthusiastically embrace the culture, symbols, knowledge, and skills necessary to carry out those missions with professional effectiveness.

One should be leery of dismissing this possibility out of hand. Surgeons might well decide it was ultimately more important for them to maintain the purity of surgery as a profession than to maintain "market share." Some surgical skills will remain necessary, they might argue, and leave it to others to provide public health and general practice medicine (or, in Abbott's terms, cede the jurisdiction). So too, Army officers might conclude that they are willing to pay the price of reduced force structure and funding in the name of preserving the knowledge and skills central to the core functions of the combat arms (recognizing that they may, nevertheless, be order to fulfill those roles anyway, albeit without fully embracing them in their body of expert knowledge).

In that circumstance, if the society remains committed to conducting other-than-war operations, it will necessarily constitute a force for that purpose. Inevitably, some subset of military skills (organization, logistics, etc.) will be necessary to carry them out efficiently. But the agents who conduct them may wear different uniforms, share different symbols, venerate different heroes, and understand their professional motivations in fundamentally different ways than combat professionals do.

In other words, the issue is wrongly framed as "professionalism" (which would counsel universal obedience to "the client's" demands) versus "unprofessionalism" (which resists some demands as beyond the sphere of professional expectations). Or perhaps better, the issue actually includes elements of each. The real issue is an intellectual and leadership challenge *within* the profession. Is the profession of arms, having gained, transmitted, built, and capitalized upon a specific body of knowledge and its application in a particular form of expertise, flexible enough to choose to remake itself and compete for a new jurisdiction that requires different skills and bodies of expert knowledge?[24] This is the fundamental question before the profession, I would argue, at this historical juncture.

Professional Cohesion

Another central feature of a profession as distinct from a mere occupation is the manner in which individuals identify with the profession and with fellow members of the profession. As Friedson expresses the point:

> [T]he social organization of professions constitutes circumstances that encourage the development in its members of several kinds of commitment. First, since an organized occupation provides its members with the prospect of a relatively secure and life-long career, it is reasonable to expect them to develop a commitment to and identification with the occupation and its fortunes. . . . Second, since an organized occupation by definition controls recruitment, training and job characteristics, its members will have many more common occupational experiences in training, job career, and work than is the case for members of a general skill class. . . . Such shared experience . . . may be seen to encourage commitment to colleagues, or collegiality.[25]

There is considerable evidence that the contemporary Army officer corps is experiencing difficulty in this dimension of the evolving profession. Study after study has shown a deep distrust between levels of rank and status in the profession. Mentoring of junior officers by their superiors, even the most minimal sort such as discussion of Officer Evaluation Reports, has been lacking. Any suggestion that colonels and captains are in any sense of the word "colleagues" would be met with derision in the contemporary officer corps.

One might say that formal aloofness between ranks is inevitable in a rigidly hierarchical profession such as the military. But this would be false. The relation between senior attending physicians in teaching hospitals and their interns is every bit as hierarchical as the military; senior partners of major law firms are without doubt as superior to their junior associates as senior military officers are to their subordinates. In both cases, the professional fates of junior members of the profession are very much dependent on the assessment and evaluation they receive from their seniors.

Yet clearly law and medicine are more effective at instilling a sense of shared membership in a single profession than the contemporary military is. It seems equally clear that most junior physicians and lawyers identify senior members of the profession whom they admire and strive to emulate, and in some cases look to for mentoring. These professions and others as well find mechanisms (e.g., Medical Society committee work, formal dinners, and law firm social events) that allow and encourage engagement between junior and senior members on grounds of collegiality in addition to hierarchy.

At their best, professions instill and express the sense that all members of the profession are part of a continuous professional chain, linking the developing body of knowledge, expertise, and institutions through time. Army officers, too, bonded by a revered common oath to defend the Constitution, have felt the cohesion of a profession providing an emotional and psychological sense of continuity and connection between the generations of officers. While many contemporary officers do feel that continuity, it seems clear that something has diminished it in the contemporary state of the profession.[26]

There is much anxiety and not a little confusion in the contemporary Army about the professional connection between senior and junior officers. Sometimes it is expressed in terms of generational differences, sometimes in terms of respect and trust between age cohorts, sometimes in terms of how mentoring can be improved within the profession.[27] Each of these perspectives is relevant and important to understanding the challenges to professional cohesion and retention of officers. But I suspect the root problem lies in something more fundamental and attitudinal. There is no substitute for the fundamental mind-set that members of the profession, regardless of rank, are colleagues, engaged in a common enterprise that matters deeply to them. If that mind-set is present, then each member feels a loyalty to the other, grounded in his or her common professional identity. If each thinks of professional identity in this way, each takes pride and responsibility in preserving, developing, and transmitting the body of knowledge that resides at the core of the profession.

A powerful example of exactly this sort of engagement in a junior's professional development is apparent in Dwight Eisenhower's early career. During a posting as brigade adjutant in Panama, Eisenhower engaged in regular and extensive reading and discussion of professional literature with his commander, Fox Conner. One biographer, Geoffrey Perret, remarks, "Ike had always been exceptionally intelligent. What had been lacking until now was the time to read and the chance to talk over ideas with someone who was both a true intellectual and an accomplished soldier."[28] Perret attributes Eisenhower's intellectual awakening and deepened sense of the intellectual component of the profession to the fact that a senior officer and intellectual was willing and able to make it part of his responsibility to engage in professional development and dialogue with his subordinate.

Eisenhower's experience leads us to inquire about the presence of Fox Conner types in today's Army. To what degree do senior officers in today's officer corps both model the profession as soldier-scholar and aggressively seek out promising younger officers to assist in the junior's professional development? Only the soldier-*scholar* preserves both aspects of truly professional officership: excellence in performance of military skills as currently understood by the profession *and* contributor to the evolving body of professional knowledge and ideas that advances the profession through time. The United States Military Academy's strategic vision document well captures this essential dual requirement of the military professional. It states:

> While change is expected in any era of strategic transition, it nevertheless will severely test Army leaders. In order to serve the nation properly, the Army is pursuing an ambitious transformation agenda that will enable it to be strategically responsive and dominant at every point on the spectrum of operations—from actual combat to peacekeeping missions to humanitarian assistance. Forces will be more mobile, lethal, and agile, and better able to address the needs of our national security strategy. Leadership will also need to become more creative, able to cope with ambiguity, more knowledgeable about the intricacies of other world-views and cultures, more aware of emerging technologies, and capable of adapting rapidly to the changing contextual realities of evolving missions. In preparing its graduates for this service, West Point will continue to assess and update its developmental programs, as it has done in the past.[29]

Anecdotal evidence suggests that professional mentoring such as Ike received from Conner is a rarity in today's Army. Were it less rare, both the intellectual component of the professional and the bonds of trust between superiors and subordinates would in all likelihood be less problematic.

Professional Motivation and Identity

The fundamental issues of Army professionalism turn on the questions of the precise nature of professional motivation within the officer corps and the flexibility of the body of professional knowledge in adjusting to the new kinds of missions now being assigned to the military.

The author has argued elsewhere that the relation between the contemporary volunteer military and American society can usefully be construed as an implicit contract.[30] Military personnel volunteer to serve society in the application of coercive and lethal force. They serve on terms of unlimited liability, in which they follow lawful orders in full recognition that they may die or be severely injured in fulfillment of those orders. The terms of the contract may appear somewhat different, depending on whether it is viewed legally or morally. From the legal perspective, military personnel are obligated to follow all legally valid orders of their superiors. Morally, however, political leaders have implicit reciprocal contractual obligations to their volunteer military personnel. The terms of the "contract" are that the military officer agrees to serve the government and people of the United States. He or she accepts the reality that military service may, under some circumstances, entail risk or loss of life in that service. This contract is justified in the mind of the officer because of his or her moral commitment to the welfare of the United States and its citizens.

Such considerations are critical in our assessment of professionalism because they go to the heart of professional motivation and self-understanding. It is because of the ends to which their expertise and commitment will be devoted that officers are able to justify to themselves the grounds of their service. It is because they see themselves as engaged in defense of the values, security, and prosperity of their family and nation that their service has moral meaning. It is not surprising, therefore, that in a time of greatly diminished threat following the demise of the Soviet Union, some of that moral self-understanding is undergoing challenge. Further, deployments in Kosovo, Bosnia, and elsewhere have raised additional challenges to professional self-understanding and motivation.

On the one hand, soldiers engaged in those operations generally report that they enjoy the opportunity to exercise their professional skills and abilities. On the other hand, precisely because the reasons for those deployments do not clearly link up to the moral core of professional self-understanding, that is, defense of the vital interests and survival of the American people and state, many officers worry that they are eroding their core war-fighting competencies and wonder whether such operations are "what they signed up for."

It is unclear at this writing what the long-term effect of Operation Iraqi Freedom will be regarding these questions. Initially, the majority of American citizens and certainly of our military forces seem to have accepted the claim that regime change in Iraq was in the vital interest of the United States—that Iraq was a central front in the global war on terrorism and that its presumed possession of weapons of mass destruction posed an unacceptable risk to the United States and her allies. As the reality of the situation in Iraq and the basis on which the intervention was indeed justified becomes more clear, it is less certain to what degree those broadly shared beliefs will be sustainable in the minds of both the public and the military.

As other chapters in this book demonstrate, the particular "fight and win the nation's wars" understanding of the nature and purpose of the profession is not timeless. Rather, it has been forged in the remarkable and historically unique furnace of the Cold War, especially in the latter stages of the Cold War when the military transitioned to an all-recruited force. For those who chose to make the military their profession during this period, the threat was clearly identifiable and palpable, and the connection between their professional expertise and the defense of vital national interests was clearly visible. The Persian Gulf War in 1990-1991 provided a manifest demonstration of the professionalism and competence of that Cold War Army and to a large degree reinforced the professional values and assumptions that had shaped the reform of the Army after Vietnam.[31] Having "grown up" in an Army that took quite justifiable pride in that far-reaching reform and enhanced sense of professionalism, unsurprisingly many officers experience hesitation and reluctance to refocus their professional activities and self-understanding on activities ancillary to the war-fighting prowess that enabled that reform.

Perhaps the clearest expression of the connection between the war-fighting focus and the self-understanding of the profession is to be found in the Weinberger doctrine, which, to many officers, seems to state immutable truth. But the reality is more complex. As Suzanne Nielsen's Chapter 29 in the present book demonstrates, the doctrine is in some respects an attempt by the military to stipulate the contractual terms under which it is willing to be used by society, all in the guise of rendering objective professional military advice. In any event, Iraqi Freedom has rendered the Weinberger doctrine moot. While one might properly point out that the major combat phase of Iraqi Freedom saw an overwhelming defeat of the Iraqi military, the operation as a whole has lacked a clear exit strategy and an attainable strategic goal (depending on one's view of the specificity and likelihood of liberal democracy eventually prevailing in Iraq).

At root, however, the military does not set the terms of its social contract—certainly not unilaterally—and essentially not at all (although it is a negotiation to some degree between the profession and the society). As the times change and as the strategic needs of the nation change, the contract changes as well. As is made clear in the historical review of the profession by Leonard Wong and Douglas Johnson in the present book (Chapter 4), the only real constant in serving the nation is that the military provides a "disciplined, trained, manpower capable of deploying to a possibly dangerous environment to accomplish a mission."

The contemporary challenge of Army professionalism is for the profession itself to engage intellectually with the changing nature of the environment and to embrace fully the need to lead in its own adaptation to that environment. The strategic reality appears to be that further large-scale land warfare is not on the immediate horizon of probability but that many other uses of disciplined forces the Army can provide are. Given this reality, it makes little sense to cling desperately to a self-understanding of the profession that was functional in the Cold War. Neither can the Army afford to accept other types of missions only grudgingly, while funneling as much energy and as many resources as possible into maintaining the capability for the preferred professional activity of large-scale combat. What is required is for the Army's officer corps to enthusiastically embrace the reality that the nation requires a different and more complex set of skills of its Army today than defined it following the reforms of the 1970s. As with any profession in a time of change, it is psychologically understandable that a period of transition is necessary as the profession mentally assimilates the changed circumstances.

But finally the profession must come to recognize that the wider and more complex range of missions the contemporary strategic context necessitates falls within the profession's jurisdiction. In practical terms, that means the profession itself must apply its own body of abstract professional knowledge to that range of problems and, when necessary, devote the intellectual work required to expand and enhance that knowledge. If new kinds of units, equipment, and training are necessary for the effective prosecution of such missions, the profession itself should spend the political and intellectual capital to develop and acquire them.[32]

The contemporary Army transformation plan, in crafting a lighter and more deployable force, is a step in the right direction. But even that plan, still focused on large-scale land combat, will not be sufficient to address the widening range of missions the contemporary environment makes likely. Admittedly, the contemporary scene is confusing, and it is difficult to foresee with accuracy every kind of new mission the Army may be tasked to perform. But some are clear: peacekeeping and peace-enforcement missions will require larger numbers of civil affairs, military police, and psychological operations units. The assumption that units trained for high-end combat are really the most effective units to perform those missions is certainly debatable. Urban warfare and Special Forces operations against non-state actors in urban environments are likely missions. Countering an enemy's use of various kinds of weapons of mass destruction looms on the horizon. It is an essential obligation of the profession itself to engage intellectually to determine how best to structure, train, and equip itself to perform those missions with the greatest degree of effectiveness. Clearly, the Army is aware of such likely missions and is preparing, to some degree, to perform them. But equally clearly, until recently they were viewed as secondary to the core function, which is large-scale combat (even with the future Objective Force which will be lighter, more deployable, and more lethal).

The benefit of viewing professions through Abbott's lens is that it avoids examining them statically and ahistorically. We thus see the profession as evolving through time in interaction with its environment and with other claimants to the profession's jurisdiction. At the root of the challenge to Army professionalism is the necessity to generate and sustain the intellectual creativity to get ahead of environmental changes, to embrace them, and to demonstrate the intellectual flexibility to inspire the nation's confidence that the profession can meet the demands of the changing security environment with enthusiasm. It appears from the professional literature and reflections on the continuing actions in Iraq and Afghanistan that the profession is indeed beginning to come to grips with its changed professional environment and requirements. It is the essence of true professionalism to recognize its emergent professional challenges and issues, to apply and extend its body of professional knowledge creatively and innovatively so as to meet those challenges, and to provide to its client—the American society—the best possible professional service.

Notes

1. An insightful analysis of the changing status of medicine from a virtually autonomous profession to a more complex status as various bureaucratic constraints have been applied through managed care is to be found in Eliot Friedson, *Professionalism: The Third Logic* (Chicago, IL: University of Chicago Press, 2001), 179-196. The comparison of medicine and the military is instructive because, as a government entity, the military profession is and always has been embedded in a bureaucracy, whereas in the case of medicine in the 20th century, one can witness the gradual imposition of bureaucratic and market forces upon a more traditionally independent profession.

2. For a recent articulation of the sweep and scope of the changes envisioned, see Les Brownlee (Acting Secretary of the Army) and Peter J. Schoomaker (Army Chief of Staff), "Serving a Nation at War: A Campaign Quality Army with Joint and Expeditionary Capabilities," *Parameters* 34 (Summer 2004): 4-23. See also the astute analysis of the changed role of landpower itself in modern conflict in John Gordon IV and Jerry Sollinger, "The Army's Dilemma," *Parameters* 34 (Summer 2004): 33-45. This article notes that, for the foreseeable future, airpower is going to take the lead—if not to be the sole instrument of choice—in many

conflicts. To what degree, the authors ask, has the Army really absorbed the changing nature of its roles and missions in future joint fights? Implicitly, it asks whether the regnant conceptual models of the role of landpower itself may not be shifting as the capabilities of the other services offer options to joint commanders that were not available until the last decade or so.

3. A fascinating insight into the culture of Army officers in regard to their attitudes about those changes is to be found in Thomas G. Mahnken and James R. FitzSimonds' article, "Tread-Heads or Technophiles? Army Officer Attitudes toward Transformation," *Parameters* 34 (Summer, 2004): 57-72.

4. For representative samples among the sea of articles making these points, see Justin Brown, "Low Morale Saps U.S. Military Might," *Christian Science Monitor*, 8 September 2000, 3; and Fred Reed, "Military Service Warning Labels," *Washington Times*, 10 September 2000. For a deeper analysis of the causes of dissatisfaction in the lower ranks of the officer corps, see Leonard Wong, *Stifled Innovation? Developing Tomorrow's Leaders Today* (Carlisle Barracks: U. S. Army War College, Strategic Studies Institute, 2002).

5. Don M. Snider, John A. Nagl, and Tony Pfaff, *Army Professionalism, the Military Ethic, and Officership in the 21st Century* (Carlisle Barracks, PA: Army War College, Strategic Studies Institute, 2000).

6. Leonard Wong's study *Stifled Innovation?* cited above, is a helpful corrective to a too-easy and simplistic embrace of the comprehensive adequacy of a merely individual moral analysis of this problem. Indeed, to some degree, one can interpret Wong's study as showing that junior officers are failing to incorporate Army officership deeply into their personal identity precisely *because* they'd hoped for a more professional opportunity for development, growth, and application of professional knowledge than their experience of micromanaged life as company commanders affords them.

7. See Leonard Wong, *Generations Apart: Xers and Boomers in the Officer Corps* (Carlisle Barracks, PA: Army War College, Strategic Studies Institute, October, 2000).

8. Eliot Friedson, *Professionalism Reborn: Theory, Policy and Prophecy* (Chicago, IL: University of Chicago Press, 1994), 124. It is interesting to note that exactly the sort of institutional context Friedson's analysis offers is also part of Snider and Watkin's analysis of the Army's present situation. They write, "[T]here is a gross mismatch between institutional capabilities and national needs." See "The Future of Army Professionalism: A Need for Renewal and Redefinition," *Parameters* 30 (Autumn 2000): 8. Here again, Wong's *Stifled Innovation?* would suggest that to a large degree, Friedson's diagnosis may have a ring of truth.

9. Charles C. Moskos, "Toward a Postmodern Military: The United States as a Paradigm," *The Postmodern Military: Armed Forces after the Cold War,* eds. Charles C. Moskos, John Allen Williams, and David R. Segal (New York: Oxford University Press, 2000), 14-31.

10. Andrew Abbott, *The System of Professions: An Essay on the Division of Expert Labor* (Chicago, IL: University of Chicago Press, 1988).

11. On this point, see Gordon and Sollinger, passim, for a thoughtful review of major elements of those changes.

12. This is, of course, the basic thrust of the analysis offered in Snider, Nagl and Pfaff.

13. As an example, consider the discussion of the degree to which and whether the rapidly increasing precision and all-weather capability of airpower, combined with the virtually assured air supremacy of U.S. airpower in any future conflict, are rendering cherished assumptions about the Army's need for organic artillery unnecessary and replaceable by close air support provided by aviation assets.

14. Ibid., 21. Emphasis in original.

15. For a bracing and troubling analysis of the state of civil-military relations in the contemporary United States, and of the politicization of the U.S. military officer corps, see Richard H. Kohn, "The Erosion of Civilian Control of the Military in the United States Today," *Naval War College Review* 55 (Summer 2002): 9-59.

16. Friedson, *Professionalism: The Third Logic*, 221.

17. Friedson, *Professionalism Reborn*, 210.

18. To further illustrate this misunderstanding, suppose one were to say that because physicians serve patients and the health of the society more generally, it would be unprofessional of them to assert intellectual independence and superior knowledge of medicine. Clearly, it is only insofar as physicians do possess intellectual independence and superior knowledge that they are of any use to the society. To say that, however, is not to say that society lacks the right to limit the discretion of physicians to use that expertise as they see fit. Society may well (for example) rule out medical procedures that are medically indicated if they are too expensive from the perspective of public policy. In that case, the physician would have to decide whether to provide a less expensive alternative procedure, even though it was less desirable from a narrowly medical perspective. Presumably, there might be some point where resources are constrained such that the physician would feel so limited that it would be "unprofessional" to continue to practice medicine in such an environment.

19. Friedson, *Professionalism Reborn*, 211.

20. H. R. McMaster, *Dereliction of Duty: Johnson, McNamara, the Joint Chiefs of Staff and the Lies That Led to Vietnam* (New York: HarperCollins, 1997).

21. Needless to say, one can imagine some scenario in which trash collection or guarding school crossings becomes a critical social need. In that situation, one might well appeal to physicians to assist in those activities. But one would be appealing to them as citizens, or as benevolent individuals, not because of any obligation inherent in their professional status. If they are employees of an organization, one might even require such service of them in the exigency of the moment. But even in that case, they would not be rendering service *as professionals*, but rather merely as able-bodied employees.

22. Friedson, *Professionalism Reborn*, 211.

23. The term "task-effectiveness" was coined by Snider and Wadkins. To some degree, of course, this conversion is now—if somewhat belatedly—in progress: "[R]outine Army analysis demonstrated the need to increase its numbers of special forces, military police, and civil affairs capabilities within the active force shortly following the terrorist attacks of Sept. 11, 2001. . . . Hardest hit will be the Army's field artillery community, which recently lost a brigade's worth of National Guard artillerymen who are currently being trained to serve as military policy officers. The Army plans to disband a significant number of artillery battalions in the active force and the National Guard." Joe Barlas, Army News Service, 17 February 2004. One sees the strategic cost of viewing such activities as ancillary rather than critically important as one sees the effects of placing poorly trained National Guard MP units in critical prison control function in Iraq. Furthermore, as more and more such activities are placed in the hands of civilian contractors in Iraq, the unclarity of their legal and command and control status becomes ever more apparent and critical. But these emergent issues are themselves the effects of early force structure decisions which reflected an ethos that these were secondary functions, and that the active force needed to husband its resources for other purposes.

24. An interesting historical question arises which I am not competent to address. To what extent did experienced combat leaders following the Civil War experience a similar professional disorientation when they were tasked with garrisoning the West and with national development missions in the late 19th century?

25. Friedson, *Professionalism Reborn*, 122-123.

26. Edwin Dorn et al., *American Military Culture in the Twenty-First Century: A Report of the CSIS International Security Program* (Washington, DC: Center for Strategic and International Studies, February 2000).

27. See Wong, *Generations Apart*, for a full discussion of these issues.

28. Geoffrey Perrett, *Eisenhower* (New York: Random House, 1999), 88.

29. U.S. Military Academy, *United States Military Academy Strategic Vision—2020* (West Point: U.S. Military Academy, 1 July 2000), 4.

30. Martin L. Cook, "'Immaculate War': Constraints on Humanitarian Intervention," *Ethics and International Affairs* 14 (2000): 55-65.

31. See James Kitfield, *Prodigal Soldiers* (New York: Simon and Schuster, 1995) for a detailed account of the much eroded state of military professionalism in the aftermath of the Vietnam War and of the reforms then instituted to increase the effectiveness and professionalism of the Army. This is significant, I would argue, because it is precisely the culture and institutions created by those reforms that are now threatened with the challenges of the current situation.

32. It is heartening to note that the Army professional literature is beginning to show exactly the kinds of professional debate and reassessment one would expect as a profession begins to "step up to the plate" and rethink fundamental assumptions. The debate of only a few years ago ("transformation vs. no transformation") has now become a vigorous "of course, transformation, but exactly what form?" debate. The questions now are, "Can we really have an all-medium-weight force, or is some heavy armor still necessary?" "Are the rapid and universally air-deployable requirements for the future force necessary and realistic, or does only a part of the force need to meet those requirements?" etc.

32 | Professional Leadership and Diversity in the Army[1]

Mady Wechsler Segal and Chris Bourg

Introduction

In their article calling for a renewal and redefinition of Army professionalism, Don Snider and Gayle Watkins highlight three indicators of the Army's deteriorating relations with its client, the American society.[2] They assert that recruiting shortfalls, a widening "gap" between the attitudes and perspectives of the military and American society (something that is subject to debate), and the adverse public reaction to various well-publicized scandals involving the unethical behavior of some Army leaders reflect increasing societal dissatisfaction with the Army. These indicators make it clear that leadership and personnel issues shape the public's perception of the Army and its members. For the Army profession, organizational effectiveness and public support for, and satisfaction with, the profession are interrelated. An effective military can expect to receive a high level of support from a satisfied client. By the same token, a military with a positive, mutually supportive relationship with society will be more effective. A volunteer military divergent from its own populace in a democratic society will face continued problems of recruitment, retention, and legitimacy. Military effectiveness is well served by an Army supported by its wider society.

While many factors influence public perceptions of and support for the Army, we concentrate here on issues of personnel diversity. Diversity refers to the degree to which members of a group or organization differ in terms of both social identities and individual characteristics. We argue that the military's relationship with society and its effectiveness are enhanced by a commitment to the successful leveraging of diversity among Army leaders at all levels. "Leveraging of diversity," or capitalizing on diversity, means turning diversity into an advantage by using it to enhance performance and social legitimacy (which we discuss further below). We provide a general assessment of the current state of diversity in the Army, followed by recommendations designed to improve the manner in which the Army capitalizes on diversity. We then describe some important aspects of diversity beyond personnel composition that need to be considered for current and future missions.

Diversity and Professional Effectiveness

As a profession, the Army competes within a system of professions for members, resources, and jurisdiction.[3] An important element of this competition involves professional claims within the court of public opinion to the social and cultural right to perform the work it desires as well as the right to decide how the work is performed and by whom.[4] Snider and Watkins note that the Army must adapt to massive changes in the nature of its work and "is missing (and thereby losing) competitions with other professions and organizations at the boundaries of its expertise."[5] In addition, the Army must adapt to significant changes in the composition and attitudes of American society.

As recent U.S. census figures show, the American population is now more diverse than ever. This is especially true in the labor force, where the influx of women and racial minorities represents one of the most profound changes in the American workforce in recent years.[6] These less traditional sources of labor will soon come to constitute the majority of workers. By 2025, the labor force is expected to be 48% women and 36% minority.[7] In addition, there is increasing diversity among the college and college-bound population. Recent research indicates that the military increasingly competes with colleges, in addition to the labor force, in recruiting enlisted personnel.[8] The military also draws its officer corps from college graduates. The increasing diversity of both the labor force and the college-bound population means that for the Army to meet its recruitment needs, it must appeal to members of this new majority. In other words, in order to compete successfully within the system of professions, the Army must follow the lead of other professions and adapt its personnel policies to an increasingly diverse population.

Adapting its personnel policies and organizational culture to embrace and leverage diversity more fully will also help to close part of the supposed civil-military attitude "gap." As one of the few organizations in the United States with explicit legal restrictions on the employment of women and openly gay men and lesbians, the military's culture and policies are increasingly at odds with dominant public attitudes favoring equality. A December 2003 Gallup poll showed that 79% of Americans believe that gay men and lesbians should be allowed to serve openly in the military. Over 90% of respondents aged 18 to 29 agreed that people who are openly gay or lesbian should be allowed to serve in the armed forces.[9] Research also indicates that American high school students have become increasingly more egalitarian in their attitudes towards women's roles, with significant majorities of both males and females expressing support for gender equality in the workplace.[10] These attitudes extend to military roles as well, as the December 2003 Gallup poll reveals that only 16% of Americans think women should be ineligible for combat assignments. More than 80% of those polled think women should either be required to serve the same combat assignments as men, or should at least have the opportunity to do so. Respondents who were 18 to 29 years old were most supportive of allowing women to serve in combat roles.[11] The attitudes of younger Americans in general and high school students in particular are especially relevant to the future military, because today's high school students represent the Army's major recruiting pool and its source of future officers, and represent as well the nation's future civilian leaders, policy-makers, and voters. The disconnect between military policy and prevailing public attitudes contributes to a civil-military "gap," hindering the Army's ability to compete successfully with other professions both for members and for public support. As part of a commitment to a new professionalism, the Army should adapt its culture and policies to reflect more closely the egalitarian attitudes of its client. In other words, the Army must adopt and enforce policies and practices that reduce bias and discrimination and contribute to the successful management of a diverse workforce.

Diversity is directly related to professional effectiveness as well. Arguments of degradation of military effectiveness have been used in the past to exclude members of some groups, but such arguments derive from preconceived attitudes (i.e., prejudice) and are not supported by the accumulated scientific evidence. For example, while some argue that homogeneous groups are more cohesive and therefore more effective, there is little scientific support for that assertion. The scientific evidence linking cohesion with performance is mixed and inconclusive, as is the evidence that cohesion is lower in groups composed of diverse individuals.[12]

Traditional definitions of cohesion are not specific. The general definition is that group cohesion is the social glue that results from all the forces that keep group members attached to the group.[13] It is a group property. Traditional concepts of cohesion emphasized peer relationships. Relationships with those in authority were considered part of leadership, not cohesion. Attempts to measure cohesion have produced multiple definitions and have led to distinctions among different components or types of cohesion. For example, the term "horizontal cohesion" has been used to refer to the peer bonding of early conceptualizations, while "vertical cohesion" is used to refer to bonds between leaders and followers.[14]

The latest theoretical and methodological advances make a distinction between "task cohesion" and "social cohesion."[15] Task cohesion is the extent to which group members are able to work together to accomplish shared goals. This interdependence is the sort that Emile Durkheim conceptualized as organic solidarity based on a division of labor.[16] (He saw mechanical solidarity, based on similarity, as less functional.) Task cohesion includes the members' respect for the abilities of their fellow group members. For combat situations, it translates into the trust that group members have in each other, including faith that the group can do its job and thereby protect its members from harm. Task cohesion can be horizontal or vertical. The latter is the unit members' respect for and confidence in their leaders' competence. Social cohesion is a more affective dimension and includes the degree to which members like each other as individuals and want to spend time with them off duty. Vertical social cohesion would include the extent to which unit members believe that their leaders care about them.

Why is unit cohesion important for the military? The common wisdom is that units with higher cohesion are more effective, especially in combat. The accumulated evidence shows that there is sometimes a relationship between cohesion and group effectiveness, but there are three very important qualifiers to this relationship. First, the direction of causality is not established. Some evidence indicates that causality works in the direction opposite to what is usually assumed, i.e., that it is group success that produces cohesion.[17] Second, the evidence for a relationship between cohesion and group performance shows that it is task cohesion, not social cohesion, that is related to success.[18] Indeed, high social cohesion sometimes negatively affects performance.[19]

Third, there is evidence that vertical cohesion, or what we prefer to call effective leadership, affects both horizontal cohesion and performance.[20] Groups in which members have confidence that their leaders are competent and care about what happens to them are more likely to be successful in various ways. Good leaders by definition organize task activities within the unit in ways that foster task effectiveness, respect, and caring among group members.

Thus, even if performance is enhanced by cohesion (and the evidence is not clear on this), it is likely to be task cohesion, not social cohesion, that provides the positve effects. There is no evidence showing that diversity of race, gender, or sexual orientation interferes with task cohesion.

With the increasing variety of missions and tasks within the Army, the organization and units within it are most effective when they are composed of people with different strengths. Task cohesion and performance are based on a division of labor and the diverse capabilities of individuals within the group. Readiness and mission accomplishment are enhanced when there are people with diverse characteristics, including abilities, skills, and problem-solving styles. Diversity in these attributes is more likely when the group is composed of people from diverse social identity groups.

Retention of qualified and trained personnel has been an important problem for all the services. To retain people, the armed forces must treat them in such a way that they are satisfied with their lives in the service. If individuals perceive that the Army is not a place where they are treated well, then they "vote with their feet." On the positive side, when people are treated with respect within an organization, they tend to develop loyalty and commitment to the organization.

We argue that by adopting policies and leader practices designed to manage and leverage diversity successfully, the Army will improve not only the effectiveness of the organization, but also its relations with American society. This, in turn, will enhance the Army's ability to compete successfully within the system of professions. As the Army engages in the process of renegotiating its status and position as a profession, it must attend to an increasingly diverse and egalitarian-minded public. The effectiveness of the future Army will be enhanced by policies and practices that contribute to a public perception of the Army as a profession which successfully adapts to and turns to advantage the talents, skills, perspectives, and abilities of a diverse workforce and a diverse public client.

In applying the concepts of "managing" and "leveraging" diversity to the Navy, George Thomas provides the following definitions (which are equally applicable to the Army):

> To manage diversity is to *lead* in a manner that maximizes the ability of personnel to contribute to the Navy's missions. . . . *Leveraging diversity* is the linkage between diversity characteristics and force readiness. People feel that their differences make up an essential part of their worth and they feel most valued when they believe they are seen in their fullest dimensions, both as individuals and as members of their own group(s). To reach its fullest potential the Navy must capitalize on socially relevant differences and tap into the strength of all personnel, including those regarded as different.[21]

Managing diversity should not to be viewed as Equal Opportunity programs or Affirmative Action. It is *"not* a set of programs that are intended to improve the positions of women and minorities. . . . It is concerned with "organization culture and leadership" rather than compliance.[22] We view the successful leveraging of diversity as being composed of two interrelated elements: (1) the representation of diverse groups throughout an organization, and (2) the treatment of members of diverse groups by the organization and its leaders. In the next section, we provide a brief appraisal of the Army's progress in diversity issues.

Assessment of the Army's Leveraging of Diversity

In our assessment of the Army's treatment of diversity we concentrate on issues of the social identities of race, gender, and sexuality. This is part of a broader context where diversity includes differences among individuals in such characteristics as mental abilities, socio-economic status, region of origin, and parental status. We cover both representation and treatment.

In many ways, the Army is widely considered to have achieved enviable results when it has diversified by integrating previously excluded groups. In particular, the Army was ahead of other social institutions in racial integration. As of 2003, 23.9% of Army officers and 43.8% of enlisted personnel are members of racial/ethnic minorities; 12.8% of officers and 26.2% of enlisted personnel are black.[23] Some analysts hold the Army up as an example in race relations for the rest of the society to follow.[24]

While the Army's success in representation of diverse racial and ethnic groups is to be applauded, there remain areas of concern regarding racial diversity with the profession, both in representation and treatment. In the area of representation, people of color have higher concentrations among enlisted personnel than among officers. However, representation among officers has been rising over the past two decades. Analysis by rank shows that the representation of black officers (both men and women) is higher at the major and captain levels than at the more senior ranks. For enlisted personnel, the representation of blacks (both men and women) rises within grade cohorts going from E-1 to E-6, then declines going from E-7 to E-9. For Hispanic enlisted men, representation declines within grade cohorts going from E-1 to E-5, rises going from E-6 to E-7, and then declines going from E-8 to E-9. Representation of Hispanic enlisted women declines within grade cohorts going from E-1 to E-6, rises going to E-7, declines going to E-8, and then rises going to E-9.[25]

Of greater concern are issues of treatment. For example, results of personnel surveys indicate that many African-American soldiers are dissatisfied with the racial climate.[26] Even high-ranking black officers report experiences with racial discrimination.[27] Despite these shortcomings, the Army still appears to have a more positive race relations climate than most civilian institutions.

The Army has also made considerable progress in gender integration in the last several decades. Women's representation in the armed forces has increased substantially over the past 30 years, from approximately 2% in the early 1970s to about

15% of active duty personnel today.[28] Among enlisted personnel in the Army, women constitute 15.5 % of active duty personnel, 11.6% of the Army National Guard, and 24.9% of the Army Reserve.[29] Women's representation in the Army's commissioned officer corps is similar to that of the enlisted forces. As of December 2000, women were 15.4% of active duty officers, 10.2% of Army National Guard officers, and 25.7% of Reserve officers.[30] As of September 2002, active duty women officers' representation was down to 14.7%. Women continue to be significantly underrepresented in the Army relative to their representation in the civilian workforce. While we would not expect this representation to be equal, it could be higher than it is, even with current exclusions. Moreover, women are still excluded from 9% of the military occupational specialties in the Army, which constitute 30% of all active duty positions.[31]

Analysis of women's representation by rank shows generally that, among both enlisted personnel and officers, the higher the rank, the smaller the percentage of women. Women constitute 16.4% of grades E-1 to E-3, 17.5% of E-4, 15.0% of E-5, 12.2% of E-6, 11.7% of E-7, 10.4% of E-8, and 6.6% of E-9.[32] For officers, women's representation is 19.6% of second lieutenants, 19.4% of first lieutenants, 15.5% of captains, 13.4% of majors, 12.2% of lieutenant colonels, 8.6% of colonels, 4.7% of brigadier generals, 2.1% of major generals, and 2.3% of lieutenant generals.[33] While it takes time for women to reach the higher ranks—and women's representation at the lower ranks has been increasing over the past 20 years—women are still underrepresented at the higher ranks compared to their percentages of the earlier entry cohorts.

However, statistics show that women's representation at the higher ranks has been increasing over the years. For example, women's representation among colonels (O-6) has increased from 2.4% in 1988, to 4.0% in 1992, to 6.2% in 1996, to 8.1% in 2000.[34] Similarly, in grades E-7 to E-9, women's representation has grown from 3.9% in 1988, to 7.1% in 1992, to 10.1% in 1996, to 11.0% in 2000.[35] Furthermore, percentages of female lieutenant colonels in command assignments have increased over the past few years.[36] In 1995, 10% of female lieutenant colonels (and 13% of male lieutenant colonels) were in command assignments. The figures for 1996, 1997, and 1998 were similar: 11% of women (14% of men), 13% of women (14% of men), 14% of women (14% of men), respectively. For 1999, the situation changed dramatically for both male and female lieutenant colonels, with 23% of women and 22% of men in command assignments. These figures bode well for women's eligibility for promotion to colonel (O-6).

There is greater representation of African-Americans among military women than their percentage of the population and even greater than the percentage of military men who are African-American. In the Army, 45% of enlisted women and 24% of women officers are black. An extraordinary 63% of enlisted women are members of racial/ethnic minorities.[37] This shows the Army's attraction for women of color, who face the greatest obstacles to economic advancement in the civilian sector.[38] For example, the national median income of black women is only 85% of white women's—and that percentage has *decreased* since 1975.[39] Nationally, Hispanic women's median income is only 76% of white women's. Black women's median income is 83% of black men's, while Hispanic women's income is 90% of Hispanic men's.[40]

Evidence shows that there is much room for improvement in the treatment of women in the Army (as well as the other services). Sexual harassment is a common occurrence, especially crude and offensive behavior and unwanted sexual attention.[41] While the percentages of women experiencing such harassment decreased from 1995 to 2002, they are still high, with 48% of Army women reporting crude and offensive behavior. Lower-ranking women are most likely to be victims of harassment.

Even more troubling is the high frequency of gender harassment, including statements by men to women and other behavior indicating continued resistance to accepting women into the organization as legitimate participants worthy of respect as soldiers.[42] Gender harassment takes various forms, including resistance to women's authority, constant scrutiny of women, passing untrue rumors and gossip about women, sabotaging women's work, and making indirect threats.[43] Research on harassment shows that women are more likely to view sexist behavior (such as treating women differently, making offensive sexist remarks, and putting women down because of their sex) as having a more negative effect on them than other forms of sexual harassment. When asked in a sexual harassment survey in 1995 about the situation involving certain behaviors in the previous 12 months that had the most effect on them, 35% of respondents cited an instance of sexist behavior; in 2002 that figure was up to 64% for all DoD women and for Army women.[44] That figure was higher than that for any other category of undesirable behaviors. However, women were less likely to label this category of behavior as "sexual harassment." This distinction shows that the Army needs to pay as much or more attention to gender harassment as to sexual harassment. Gender harassment may negatively affect morale, which in turn may interfere with effectiveness.

The rates on surveys of women reporting having experienced sexual assault are low, but surveys are less likely to uncover such victimization because women who experience assault are unlikely to stay in the military. Incidences of rapes reported by women soldiers in Iraq and Afghanistan demonstrate that much more action is needed to prevent such assaults.

Resistance to accepting military women is sometimes voiced as accusations of inequitable treatment of male soldiers or lowering of military standards. Military men cite violations of principles of justice and of readiness goals to justify their opposition to women. This is especially apparent in complaints about the use of gender norms for physical fitness tests and the perception that the scoring is unfair.[45] But the evidence shows that the purpose of these tests is widely misunderstood by military personnel. Experts, both in and out of the military, say that these are intended as measures of physical fitness and health, not job performance. Gender norming is required for a valid measure of physical health. Interestingly, there are few complaints about the age norming of the tests. Even the politically diverse Congressional Commission on Military Training and Gender Related Issues (1999) unanimously recommended that military personnel be educated about the real purpose of the tests.

Carol Cohn's analysis shows that protests against the gender norms on the fitness test standards show "strong feelings of loss and anger about changes in the way the organization is gendered" and demonstrate men's antipathy toward women in the military.[46] Cohn maintains that even if the test requirements were exactly the same, men would find some other "focal point" for their dissatisfaction.

Changes in civilian society in the social construction of gender have been affecting the armed forces. There has been a transformation of values, norms, and beliefs about gender that has affected every institution of society (educational, political, legal, family, economic, etc.). As one of the most predominantly male institutions—and a gender-defining one—the military has been one of the last social organizations to gender integrate and adapt to this changing construction of gender.[47] Forces of resistance to change are evident in sexual harassment and gender harassment in the military. Resistance to gender integration in the armed forces can also be seen in conservative stances with regard to military gender integration by some members of Congress and by political pressure groups, despite considerable evidence of public support for greater gender integration in the military.[48]

With regard to sexuality, the military has officially excluded homosexuals from service since World War II. Gay men and lesbians have, of course, served in the military throughout its history. Enforcement of bans on the service of homosexuals has generally been lax during times of heightened manpower needs, such as wartime.[49] In 1993 the U.S. Congress codified a revised gay policy. This policy moved the military in the direction of seemingly greater tolerance for the presence of gay and lesbian service members by dropping the statement that homosexuality, per se, is incompatible with military service and by prohibiting asking recruits and others about their sexual orientation. However, the "Policy Concerning Homosexuality in the Armed Forces,"[50] colloquially known as "Don't Ask, Don't Tell, Don't Pursue," still requires gay and lesbian service members to maintain a level of secrecy about their sexuality and personal relationships not required of heterosexual service members.[51]

The secrecy requirement of current military policy makes estimating the percentage of service members who are gay or lesbian even more difficult than the already contested and difficult task of estimating the proportion of homosexuals in the larger population. We do know, however, that in 1998, 1,149 service members were discharged from the military for violating the "Don't Ask, Don't Tell" policy. This figure translates to a rate of three to four discharges per day, representing a significant increase in the number of service members discharged for homosexuality since the new policy was instituted in 1993. In 2003, the number of discharges had fallen to 787. Many more thousands of gay men and lesbians are currently serving.[52] With American military forces engaged in fighting in Afghanistan and Iraq, military discharges of gay and lesbian service members were lower in 2003 than at any other time since 1995. This change reflects the overall historical trend by which gay discharge numbers drop whenever American troops are engaged in major combat operations.[53]

The military's "Don't Ask, Don't Tell" policy has been criticized on grounds of both its failure to be justifiable on the basis of evidence and its lack of proper implementation. While Army leaders are not responsible for establishing policies regarding the service of openly gay men and lesbians, they are responsible for ensuring adherence and proper implementation of the current policy at all levels. A March 2000 Inspector General's survey of 75,000 service members found that 80% of service members had heard anti-gay remarks during the past year, and that 37% had witnessed or experienced targeted incidents of anti-gay harassment.[54] Discipline, morale, and cohesion are compromised when harassment and derogatory remarks directed at any group of people are tolerated. Moreover, harassment and maltreatment of any group, including homosexuals, violates the trust placed in military leaders both by the American public and by those who serve.

In response to the 1999 murder of Pvt. Barry Winchell for his perceived sexual orientation, the Department of Defense adopted the Anti-Harassment Action Plan (AHAP). The AHAP contains mandates for annual anti-harassment education and training, accountability for those who harass or condone harassment, and assessment of each service's compliance with the AHAP.[55] The Army "continues to lead the other services in AHAP implementation, though the bar remains low given that the other services have virtually ignored AHAP for the past three years." While the Army continues to make improvements in the provision of anti-harassment training, little progress has been made in implementing the accountability mandates of AHAP, and the Army is not measuring the effectiveness of its AHAP training programs.[56] Continued leadership emphasis on training and accountability is necessary for the Army to ensure that all soldiers are treated with respect, dignity, and honor. When soldiers are assured of treatment that is consistent with the Army's core values, effectiveness and readiness are enhanced, as is the Army's public image and relationship with society.

What policies and leader practices will build on and improve the Army's status with regard to acceptance and leveraging of diverse personnel? We deal with this in the next section.

How Does Leadership Relate to Diversity? Promoting Effective Leadership

The degree to which the organization accomplishes successful integration of previously excluded groups is a function of leadership commitment to that integration at all levels. Considerable social science research indicates the kinds of policies and practices that are likely to minimize bias and discrimination, and to promote the successful leveraging of a diverse workforce. Recent scholarly work on employment discrimination suggests that accountability in decision-making, equal resource policies, open information about pay, and the construction of heterogeneous, cooperative, and interdependent work-groups are key factors which appear to minimize discrimination and bias.[57] The fact that the Army currently employs many of these practices and policies accounts for much of the Army's success in the arena of racial integration.[58] In addition, there is social science research to guide successful policy and individual leader behavior.

What policies and practices (including the behavior of individual leaders) will improve the Army's ability to recruit, retain, manage, and leverage a diverse workforce successfully? Social science evidence points to at least three areas for improvement:

(1) decision-making accountability, (2) recognition of effects of discriminatory policies, and (3) leader behaviors and conditions that foster respect for diversity.

Decision-Making Accountability

Social psychological research has consistently and conclusively shown that stereotypes and biases influence our perceptions and evaluations of others.[59] It shows that it is extremely difficult to get people to attend to individuating information rather than stereotypes in assessing others. For example, even when given information that men and women in the target population were distributed equally across college majors, survey subjects continued to rely more on gender stereotypes than on information about individual interests in predicting whether a target individual was an engineering or a nursing major.[60]

However, the biasing effects of stereotypes on evaluative judgments have been shown to be greatly reduced when decision-makers know that they will be held accountable for the criteria they use for decision-making.[61] While current Army policies and practices emphasize accountability in many career-relevant decisions such as officer promotions and senior school selections, many career-relevant decisions are made by decision-makers who are not currently held accountable for their decisions. For example, junior officers are usually assigned to career-enhancing jobs such as company command by battalion commanders who are not currently held formally accountable for those decisions. Given white male predominance among key Army decision-makers, unconscious in-group preferences and reliance on gender and racial biases and stereotypes are likely to lead to systematic discrimination in selection for key jobs at the junior officer level. This may be one cause of the lower representation noted earlier of women and racial and ethnic minorities in the higher ranks, including among officers.

Research shows, however, that the effects of these tendencies are reduced when decision-makers know they will be held accountable for their decisions. We recommend that the Army develop programs that hold decision-makers at *all* levels responsible for ensuring that their decisions are not tainted by in-group preferences. Decision-makers should also be held accountable for the outcomes of their decisions in terms of representation of women and minorities selected for career-enhancing jobs, training, and school assignments. This accountability need not be implemented through rigid, restrictive, and bureaucratic policies. For example, decision-making accountability can be accomplished through educating leaders on the effects of unconscious stereotyping and bias, and through the establishment of decision-making procedures such as selection boards for all levels of career-relevant decisions. Including others in decisions such as company command selection will not only provide accountability but will also increase the effectiveness of the decision-making process by allowing input from other informed leaders. Leveraging diversity would be enhanced if leaders were rated on their ability and actions to create a climate that fosters mutual respect among unit members, including respect for diversity. These leader ratings should be not only by their supervisors, but also by their peers and subordinates.

Recognition of Effects of Discriminatory Policies

Research shows that when valued rewards are distributed among people working together in a goal-oriented context, individuals will implicitly assume that those with greater rewards are more competent than those with less.[62] The exclusion of women from units and military occupational specialties most closely associated with the Army's core combat mission systematically denies women access to organizationally valued positions. One expected consequence of this is that members of the Army come to believe that women are less valued and less competent members of the organization. In this way, the Army's combat exclusion policies not only contribute to the growing civil-military values "gap," but also contribute to gender integration difficulties within the Army.

In a similar way, military policy regarding homosexuality systematically denies gay and lesbian service members access to organizationally valued resources. For example, under current policy gay and lesbian service members are denied support for their personal and family relationships. Research has consistently shown that policies and practices that are perceived as supportive of military members' personal and family relationships have positive effects on job satisfaction and retention.[63]

The military's combat exclusion policy and anti-gay policy both systematically discriminate against specific groups of service members by denying them access to valued resources. Moreover, an expected consequence of these policies is that they encourage or reinforce expectations of lower competence and worth for members of the excluded groups. When policies treat certain groups in a discriminatory manner, organizational participants are likely to treat members of those groups in a discriminatory manner as well. For these reasons, the successful leveraging of diversity is hindered by the military's exclusionary policies regarding the full participation of gay men and all women.

What can Army leaders do to counter the effects of policies that require differential treatment of some service members? First, Army leaders need to be educated on the potential negative effects of discriminatory policies on the attitudes and perceptions of all service members. In order to mitigate the effects of such policies, Army leaders must aggressively seek to eliminate formal statements and informal banter within their units that reflect a devaluing of the contributions of any group of soldiers. Army leaders should consistently emphasize the value of all soldiers, regardless of social characteristics such as race, gender, and sexuality. In addition, Army leaders must communicate to their subordinates that the Army needs and values the contributions of all military specialties and units, not just those with combat designations. This will reduce the negative effects of the military's discriminatory policies on both Army morale and readiness and on public perceptions of the Army.

Individual Leader Behaviors

At the interpersonal level, leaders' behavior has been demonstrated to have strong effects on the treatment of diversity characteristics within military units. Leaders serve as role models for personnel in their units: military personnel often model their behavior toward others on the basis of the behavior of their leaders. Further, the degree to which leaders enforce nondiscriminatory behavioral guidelines affects the likelihood of such behavior occurring and recurring.

We know a great deal about the conditions that affect the success of managing diversity in groups. Much of the early theory and research was based on the "contact hypothesis," originally developed with regard to racial relations and adapted to integration of other previously excluded groups.[64] Research demonstrates that the process of integrating members of previously excluded groups into organizations and groups within organizations generally does not proceed smoothly. Problems are encountered when integrating the military and other social institutions. Integration problems tend to occur with various social characteristics, including race, ethnicity, and gender.

Early phases of integration are often characterized by negative attitudes toward the members of the newly admitted group. Such negative attitudes are usually accompanied by negative behaviors involving discrimination against the new group. Among such negative behaviors are social isolation and harassment of the new members. Breaking with tradition is hard and there are always sources of resistance to change in any institution. Resistance to change is strongest when there is long experience with, and/or identification with, the old ways of doing things. Part of men's resistance to women in previously all-male roles, especially those that have served as rites of passage to manhood, is the difficulty in proving masculinity if the challenge can also be met by a woman. Military men may also retain definitions of their roles as masculine by accepting individual women as exceptions—by disconnecting perceptions of an individual woman's success from their conceptions of "women" in general.

But research also shows us the conditions that tend to foster more effective integration.[65] More positive attitudes tend to develop when:

- interaction is sufficiently close and sustained that the members of the majority group have the opportunity to get to know the individual members of the minority group well;
- the minority group members are of at least equal social status to the majority group members;
- the minority group members constitute more than a small (token) minority of the work group;
- there are commonly shared goals;
- the situation is one that fosters cooperation rather than competition among members of the group;
- the social norms support equality and integration;
- those in positions of authority support the integration.

This last condition is very important. It is also amenable to control in the military services: integration of diverse members proceeds most smoothly and with the fewest problems if leaders are committed to making integration work and if they communicate that commitment. The greater the degree of public commitment expressed by leaders at each organizational level, the more successful will be the leveraging of diversity and the more effective the military units will be.

In addition to being committed voices in behalf of diversity, leaders can be models worthy of emulation by their subordinates. Soldiers observe their leaders' behaviors, and those actions often speak louder than their words. When leaders show in their behaviors on a day-to-day basis that they respect soldiers with diverse characteristics, this value is transmitted to their troops (both officers and enlisted personnel). These behaviors include the quality of their interactions with service members with diverse characteristics as well as what they say about members of identifiable groups. For example, the positive effects of anti-sexual harassment workshops or leaders' statements about commitment to diversity are negated if the same leaders treat women or members of other diverse groups with disrespect or tell sexist or racist jokes (the effects are negative whether or not members of the derogated groups are present).

Another area in which the Army has room for improvement involves creating situations which foster cooperation among diverse members of groups rather than competition. Current Army policy and culture encourage individual competition in many settings, despite official endorsement of cooperation. Emphasis on individual rankings at Officer Basic and Advanced Courses and at the United States Military Academy provide examples of settings in which diverse individuals are placed in direct competition with one another. Social psychological research shows that competition highlights differences and encourages stereotyping.[66] We recommend that the Army eliminate unnecessary competition in its professional training environments, and develop training programs that truly require cooperation among diverse individuals.

We further recommend that leaders at all levels be educated about the way their behaviors affect respect for diversity among their subordinates (and their peers). Of course, we expect that they will want to act in ways that have positive effects on leveraging and managing diversity. We also recommend that leaders be held accountable for the degree to which their behavior contributes to respect for diversity.

Additional Diversity Considerations

There are additional aspects of diversity beyond personnel composition and acceptance by race, gender, and sexual orientation that merit attention by the Army. Representation in the military of Americans by social class has been an issue in the past that has recently surfaced again. Recent wars have highlighted the class backgrounds of our enlisted soldiers. It is clear that many join to earn money for college because their families cannot afford to send them. The much-publicized story of Jessica Lynch exemplifies this motivation to enlist. Concerns about the inequity of this "economic conscription" may be one of the reasons for calls to re-institute conscription. However, another major reason behind calls for a draft is concern that the volunteer force does not provide enough personnel for the military operations to which the United States is committed. Such issues of equity and the public debates that are likely to ensue presage the need for attention by the armed forces.

Perhaps even more important for mission effectiveness is attention to cultural perspectives of Army personnel. Many current missions require knowledge about and sensitivity to cultural diversity. Successful military strategy depends on an ability to understand other cultures, both those we are fighting and those we intervene to help. Such a cultural diversity perspective is necessary for policy-makers in all branches of the government, as well as for those who have to carry out the missions that the policy-makers determine are appropriate for military personnel. To the extent that the Army is required to participate in missions requiring occupation and nation-building in other countries, understanding of other cultures is essential.

The increasing participation of soldiers in multinational missions also necessitates attention to differences among the cultures of those nations. Included in the differences is the treatment of diversity by the different nations and their armed forces. American soldiers are likely to be involved in joint operations with allies whose policies and practices with regard to race, gender, and sexual orientation of their troops differ from ours. These include, for example, nations whose militaries exclude women as well as those in which women are allowed in all positions, including those from which American women are excluded.

Many of our NATO allies permit female soldiers to serve in combat positions, and allow homosexuals to serve openly. NATO's respect for national sovereignty essentially requires that American military leaders support gays and lesbians serving in multinational NATO forces, as well as women serving in combat roles with our NATO allies. Recent research indicates that "the presence of openly gay and lesbian personnel in multinational units in which Americans serve has not had a negative impact upon cohesion or military performance."[67] Our policy-makers, military leaders, and all personnel serving in multinational operations need to remain aware and respectful not only of cultural differences among our allies, but also of differences in personnel policies, particularly with regard to the service of women and homosexuals.

Conclusions

We have analyzed the ways in which diversity contributes to the Army's core value of respect, to military professionalism, and to military effectiveness. Our assessment of Army diversity shows increasing representation in the recent past of members of racial and ethnic minorities—both men and women. Women's representation has increased, especially among women of color. Women are more concentrated in the lower ranks, but their representation in the higher ranks has been increasing. While people of color perceive a need for improvement in their treatment, the Army's racial climate appears better than that of many civilian institutions. Treatment of women has been improving, but still requires attention to eliminating sexual harassment and gender harassment. Gay men and lesbians are precluded from serving openly, but private sexual orientation is by policy not to be the basis of attention or harassment; appropriate education about policy is needed at all levels, as is enforcement of anti-harassment policy. Much existing social science knowledge can be applied to assisting Army leaders in improving the leveraging of diversity to enhance personnel retention, mission readiness, and military effectiveness. Improvement will come from accountability in decision-making, recognizing effects of differential treatment, promoting equitable treatment, educating leaders in the effects of their behaviors, providing positive models for leaders, and holding leaders accountable for their behaviors with regard to diverse personnel. Attention is also needed to other dimensions of diversity, including social class issues, cultures of other countries, and differential policies with regard to personnel diversity in other countries in multinational operations. Implementation of these recommendations will enhance the Army's core values and its mission effectiveness.

Notes

1. Support for writing this chapter was provided by the U.S. Military Academy and by the U.S. Army Research Institute for the Behavioral and Social Sciences under Contract No. DASW 0100K0016 and Contract No. W74V8H-05-K-0007. The views expressed in this chapter, however, are the authors' and not necessarily those of the contracting agencies or any other government entity. We appreciate the very able research assistance and advice provided by Darlene M. Iskra, and we thank Don M. Snider and Gayle L. Watkins for helpful comments on drafts of this chapter.

2. Don M. Snider and Gayle L. Watkins, "The Future of Army Professionalism: A Need for Renewal and Redefinition," *Parameters* 30 (Autumn 2000): 5-20.

3. Andrew Abbott, *The System of Professions: An Essay on the Division of Expert Labor* (Chicago, IL: University of Chicago Press, 1988); Snider and Watkins.

4. Abbott.

5. Snider and Watkins, 6

6. Howard N. Fullerton, Jr., "Labor Force Projections to 2008: Steady Growth and Changing Composition" *Monthly Labor Review* (November 1999): 19-32.

7. Howard N. Fullerton, Jr., "Labor Force Participation: 75 Years of Change, 1950-98 and 1998-2025," *Monthly Labor Review* (December 1999): 3-12.

8. Chris Bourg, "Trends in Intentions to Enlist and Attend College," in *Recruiting College-Bound Youth into the Military: Current Practices and Future Policy Options*, MR-1093, eds. M. Rebecca Kilburn and Beth J. Asch (Santa Monica, CA: RAND, 2003).

9. Gallup Poll, "Public OK with Gays, Women in Military" (23 December 2003).

10. Shelley J. Correll and Chris Bourg, "Trends in Gender Role Attitudes, 1976-1997: The Continued Myth of Separate Worlds" (paper presented at the annual meeting of the American Sociological Association, 1999).

11. Gallup Poll, "Public OK with Gays, Women in Military."

12. Elizabeth Kier, "Homosexuals in the U.S. Military: Open Integration and Combat Effectiveness," *International Security* 23 (Fall 1998): 5-39; David R. Segal and Meyer Kestnbaum, "Closure in the Military Labor Market: A Critique of Pure Cohesion,"in *The Future of the Army Profession*, project directors Don M. Snider and Gayle L. Watkins, ed. Lloyd J. Matthews (Boston, MA: McGraw-Hill, 2002), chap. 21. For a contrary view, see chap. 22 of the present anthology.

13. Dorwin Cartwright, "The Nature of Group Cohesiveness," 91-109; Leon Festinger, Stanley Schachter, and Kurt Back, "Operation of Group Standards," 152-64; and Stanley Schachter, "Deviation, Rejection, and Communication," 165-81; all in Dorwin Cartwright and Alvin Zander, eds., *Group Dynamics: Research and Theory*, 3d edition (New York: Harper & Row, 1968).

14. Robert MacCoun, "What Is Known about Unit Cohesion and Military Performance," in *Sexual Orientation and U.S. Military Personnel Policy: Options and Assessment* (Santa Monica, CA: RAND, 1993), 283-331.

15. Albert V. Carron and Lawrence R. Brawley, "Cohesion: Conceptual and Measurement Issues," *Small Group Research* 31, no. 1 (February 2000): 89-106.

16. Emile Durkheim, *The Division of Labor in Society* (New York: Free Press, 1893; reprint 1964, 1997).

17. Brian Mullen and Carolyn Copper, "The Relation Between Group Cohesiveness and Performance: An Integration," *Psychological Bulletin* 115 (March 1994): 210-27.

18. Ibid.

19. Carol Burke, "Pernicious Cohesion," in *It's Our Military, Too! Women and the U.S. Military*, ed. Judith H. Stiehm (Philadelphia, PA: Temple University Press, 1996), 205-91; Robert MacCoun and Donna Winslow, *The Canadian Airborne Regiment in Somalia: A Socio-Cultural Inquiry* (Ottawa: Canadian Government Publishing, 1997); Donna Winslow, "Rites of Passage and Group Bonding in the Canadian Airborne," *Armed Forces and Society* 25, no. 3 (Spring 1999): 429-57.

20. Margaret Harrell and Laura Miller, *Opportunities for Military Women: Effects Upon Readiness, Cohesion and Morale* (Santa Monica, CA: RAND, 1997); Nora Kinzer Stewart, *Mates & Muchachos: Unit Cohesion in the Falklands/Malvinas War* (Washington, DC: Brassey's, 1991).

21. George W. Thomas, *Managing Diversity in the 21st Century Navy*, vol. 1, *Introduction* (Monterey, CA: Naval Postgraduate School, Center for Diversity Analysis, 2000), 8.

22. Ibid, 10.

23. Department of the Army, *Army Demographics: FY03 Army Profile* (Department of the Army: Deputy Chief of Staff for Personnel, G-1), 2003. (available at http://www.armyg1.army.mil/hr/demographics/FY03ArmyProfileWebVs.pdf).

24. Charles C. Moskos and John Sibley Butler, *All That We Can Be* (New York: Basic Books, 1996).

25. ODCSPER, *DCSPER 441*. [instruction on-line] (Washington, DC: Office of the Deputy Chief of Staff for Personnel, U.S. Army, 1997); available from http:www.odcsper.army.mil/Directorates/hr/demographics/DCSPER-441.txt; Internet.

26. Brenda L. Moore and Schuyler C. Webb, "Perceptions of Equal Opportunity Among Women and Minority Army Personnel," *Sociological Inquiry* 70 (Spring 2000): 215-39; Jacquelyn Scarville et al., *Armed Forces Equal Opportunity Survey*, DMDC Report No. 97-027 (Arlington, VA: Defense Manpower Data Center, 1997).

27. Craig Thomas Johnson, *United States Army Officer Professional Development: Black Officers' Perspectives* (Carlisle Barracks, PA: U.S. Army War College, 1997).

28. Lory Manning, and Vanessa R. Wight, *Women in the Military: Where They Stand*, 4th ed. (Washington, DC: Women's Research and Education Institute, 2003). These figures are as of September 2003.

29. Margaret C. Flott, *Women in the U.S. Army* (Washington, DC: Department of the Army, Office of the Deputy Chief of Staff for Personnel, 2001). These figures are for 4 December 2000.

30. Ibid.

31. Ibid.

32. Ibid.

33. Ibid.

34. Lory Manning and Vanessa R. Wight,17.

35. Ibid.

36. Margaret C. Flott, *Lieutenant Colonel Command* [data presented to DACOWITS spring conference, 18-22 April, 2001] (Washington, DC: Department of the Army, 2001).

37. Manning and Wight, 14.

38. Francine D. Blau, Marianne A. Ferber, and Anne E. Winkler, *The Economics of Women, Men and Work,* 3d ed. (Upper Saddle River, NJ: Prentice Hall, 1998); Barbara Reskin and Irene Padavic, *Women and Men at Work* (Thousand Oaks, CA: Pine Forge Press, 1994); Paula S. Rothenberg, ed., *Race, Gender & Class in the United States: An Integrated Study,* 3d ed. (New York: St. Martin's Press, 1995); Daphne Spain and Suzanne M. Bianchi, *Balancing Act: Motherhood, Marriage and Employment Among American Women* (New York: Russell Sage Foundation, 1996).

39. Blau, Ferber, and Winkler, 139. The 85% figure is for 1995.

40. Ibid. These figures are for 1995.

41. Rachel N. Lipari and Anita R. Lancaster, *Armed Forces 2002 Sexual Harassment Survey,* DMDC Report No. 2004-01 (Arlington, VA: Defense Manpower Data Center, 2004; Lisa D. Bastian, Anita R. Lancaster, and Heidi E. Reyst, *Department of Defense 1995 Sexual Harassment Survey,* DMDC Report No. 96-014 (Arlington, VA: Defense Manpower Data Center, 1996); Department of the Army, *The Secretary of the Army's Senior Review Panel Report on Sexual Harassment,* 2 vols. (Washington, DC: Department of the Army, 1997); Juanita M. Firestone and Richard J. Harris, "Sexual Harassment in the U.S. Military: Individualized and Environmental Contexts," *Armed Forces and Society* 21 (Fall 1994): 25-43; David E. Rohall, Maria Bina Palmisano, and Mady Wechsler Segal, *Gender and Power Issues Affecting Perceptions of Sexually Harassing Behaviors among Military Personnel* (College Park: University of Maryland, 2001).

42. Rohall, Palmisano, and Segal; Lipari and Lancaster.

43. Laura L. Miller, "Not Just Weapons of the Weak: Gender Harassment as a Form of Protest for Army Men," *Social Psychology Quarterly* 60 (March 1997): 32-51.

44. Rohall, Palmisano, and Segal.

45. Carol Cohn, "How Can She Claim Equal Rights When She Doesn't Have to Do as Many Push-Ups as I Do? The Framing of Men's Opposition to Women's Equality in the Military," *Men and Masculinities* 3 (October 2000): 131-51; *Congressional Commission on Military Training and Gender-Related Issues, Final Report, July 1999,* vol. II, *Transcripts and Legal Consultants & Reports* [book on-line]; available from http://www.house.gov/hasc/reports/miscmaterials.html; Internet.

46. Cohn, 131.

47. Chris Bourg and Mady W. Segal, "Gender, Sexuality, and the Military," in *Gender Mosaics: Social Perspectives: (Original Readings),* ed. Dana Vannoy (Los Angeles, CA: Roxbury Publishing Company, 2001).

48. See James A. Davis, Jennifer Lauby, and Paul B. Sheatsley, *Americans View the Military: Public Opinion in 1982,* NORC Report 131 (Chicago, IL: National Opinion Research Center, University of Chicago, 1983.); Roper Organization, *Attitudes Regarding the Assignment of Women in the Armed Forces: The Public Perspective* (survey conducted for The Presidential Commission on the Assignment of Women in the Armed Forces, 1992).

49. Bourg and Segal, "Gender, Sexuality, and the Military."

50. *U. S. Code,* vol. 4, sec. 654.

51. Bourg and Segal, "Gender, Sexuality, and the Military."

52. Ibid.

53. Randy Shilts, *Conduct Unbecoming: Gays and Lesbians in the U.S. Military* (New York: St. Martin's Press, 1993).

54. Sharon E. Debbage Alexander et al., *Conduct Unbecoming: The Tenth Annual Report on "Don't Ask, Don't Tell, Don't Pursue, Don't Harass"* (Servicemembers Legal Defense Network, 2004).

55. Ibid.

56. Ibid.

57. William T. Bielby, "Minimizing Workplace Gender and Racial Bias," *Contemporary Sociology* 29, no. 2 (March 2000): 120-129; Barbara Reskin, "The Proximate Causes of Employment Discrimination," *Contemporary Sociology* 29, no. 1 (January 2000): 319-28; Cecilia Ridgeway and Shelley J. Correll, "The End(s) of Gender: Limiting Inequality through Interaction," *Contemporary Sociology* 29 (2000): 110-120.

58. Charles C. Moskos and John Sibley Butler, *All That We Can Be.*

59. Galen V. Bodenhausen, C. Neil Macrae, and Jennifer Garst, "Stereotypes in Thought and Deed: Social Cognition Origins of Intergroup Discrimination," in *Intergroup Cognition and Intergroup Behavior,* eds. Constantine Sedikides, John Schopler, and Chester A Insko (Mahwah, NJ: Lawrence Erlbaum Associates, 1998), 311-35.

60. Thomas E. Nelson, Michelle Acker, and Melvin Manis, "Irrepressible Stereotypes," *Journal of Experimental Social Psychology* 32 (January 1996): 13-38.

61. Barbara Reskin, Gerald R. Salanick, and Jeffrey Pfeffer, "Uncertainty, Secrecy, and the Choice of Similar Others," *Social Psychology* 41, no.3 (September 1978): 246-55; Phillip E. Tetlock, "The Impact of Accountability on Judgement and Choice: Toward a Social Contingency Model," *Advances in Experimental Social Psychology* 25 (1992): 331-76; Phillip E. Tetlock and Jennifer S. Lerner, "The Social Contingency Model: Identifying Empirical and Normative Boundary Conditions on the Error-and-Bias Portrait of Human Nature," in *Dual Process Theories in Social Psychology,* eds. Shelly Chaiken and Yaacov Trope (New York: Guilford Press, 1999), 571-85.

62. Wendy J. Harrod, "Expectations from Unequal Rewards," *Social Psychology Quarterly* 43, no. 1 (March 1980): 126-130; Ridgeway and Correll; Penni Stewart and James Moore, "Wage Disparities and Performance Expectation," *Social Psychology Quarterly* 55, no. 1 (March 1992): 78-85.

63. Mary C. Bourg and Mady W. Segal, "The Impact of Family Supportive Policies and Practices on Organizational Commitment to the Army," *Armed Forces & Society* 25 (Summer 1999): 633-52; Rose M. Etheridge, *Family Factors Affecting Retention: A Review of the Literature,* Research Report 1511 (Alexandria, VA: U.S. Army Research Institute for the Behavioral and Social Sciences, 1989); Dennis K. Orthner, *Family Impacts on the Retention of Military Personnel,* Research Report 1556 (Alexandria, VA: U.S. Army Research Institute for the Behavioral and Social Sciences, 1990); Mady Wechsler Segal and Jessie J. Harris, *What We Know About Army Families,* Special Report 21 (Alexandria, VA: Army Research Institute for the Behavioral and Social Sciences, 1993).

64. Gordon W. Allport, *The Nature of Prejudice* (Cambridge, MA: Addison-Wesley, 1954); Morton Deutsch and Mary Evans Collins, *Interracial Housing: A Psychological Evaluation of a Social Experiment* (Minneapolis: Univ. of Minnesota Press, 1951); Theodore M. Newcomb, "Autistic Hostility and Social Reality," *Human Relations* 1 (1947): 69-86; Samuel A. Stouffer et al., *The American Soldier: Adjustment During Army Life,* vol. I (Princeton: NJ: Princeton University Press, 1949); Robin M. Williams, *The Reduction of Intergroup Tension* (New York: Social Science Research Council, 1947).

65. Allport; Deutsch and Collins; Norman Miller and Marilynn B. Brewer, *Groups in Contact: The Psychology of Desegregation* (Orlando, FL: Academic Press, 1984); W. T. Moxley, "Leadership Considerations and Lessons Learned in a Mixed Gender Environment," *Minerva* 17, no. 3 and 4, (Fall/Winter 1999): 58-67; Newcomb; Thomas F. Pettigrew, "Intergroup Contact Theory," *Annual Review of Psychology* 49 (1998): 65-85; Stouffer et al.; Williams.

66. Susan T. Fiske, "Stereotyping, Prejudice, and Discrimination," in *Handbook of Social Psychology,* eds. D. F. Gilbert, S. T. Fiske, and G. Lindzey (New York: McGraw Hill, 1998), 357-411.

67. Geoffrey Bateman and Sameera Dalvi, *Multinational Military Units and Homosexual Personnel* (A report commissioned by the Center for the Study of Sexual Minorities in the Military, University of California, Santa Barbara, February 2004), 24.

33

Root, Miles, and Carter: Political-Cultural Expertise and an Earlier Army Transformation

Matthew Moten

In 1915, at the end of a distinguished public career including service as secretary of war, secretary of state, and U.S. senator, Elihu Root reflected back on the day his journey in federal service began:

> Sixteen years ago, in the month of July, having just finished the labors of a year and gone to my country home, I was called to the telephone and told by one speaking for President McKinley, "The President directs me to say to you that he wishes you to take the position of Secretary of War." I answered, "Thank the President for me, but say that it is quite absurd, I know nothing about war. I know nothing about the army." I was told to hold the wire, and in a moment came back the reply, "President McKinley directs me to say that he is not looking for anyone who knows anything about the army; he has got to have a lawyer to direct the government of these Spanish islands and you are the lawyer he wants." Of course I had then, on the instant, to determine what kind of a lawyer I wished to be and there was but one answer to make, and so I went to perform a lawyer's duty upon the call of the greatest of all our clients, the Government of our country. And I have never felt for a moment that I have stepped outside of the noble profession to which I had intended to devote my life.[1]

Thus commenced the tenure of one of our most effective secretaries of war, who in 1899 took on the formidable challenge of transforming the Army from a sleepy constabulary force that had just come within a whisker of failure during its first expeditionary mission in a half-century—the Spanish-American War—into a robust military instrument capable of meeting the needs of a budding world power. In Root's story, he portrays himself as a military novice. There was no artifice in that; he was as inexperienced as he said he was. Yet, just as tellingly, he takes on the mantle of a professional, an attorney. In that identity lay the key to his success in leading the military profession to transform itself. Elihu Root had grown up as a lawyer while the legal profession was growing and professionalizing in the late 19th century. Called upon to lead an American army that needed to change in order to meet new and unfamiliar global challenges in the 20th century, he naturally gravitated toward officers of the same reformist, progressive bent that had marked his own career in the law.

The historical setting of this chapter is the United States at the turn of the 19th century, a time of significant geopolitical change for the nation and its foreign policy, coupled with a recent strategic shock that pointed up the need for institutional reform and a general reassessment of the roles and missions of our armed forces. We will examine the central reforms of that era, including the initiative to found a war college, to create an Army general staff, and to replace the Army's commanding general with an Army chief of staff. This is a story of conflict and cooperation—the cooperation of reform-minded professional men fighting against entrenched power and tradition. The story involves a public clash between the senior military and civilian leaders of the defense establishment that makes current disagreements pale in comparison. It is also a case study of a daily working partnership between an Army officer and a secretary of war that provides an object lesson in effective civil-military relations. It argues that reforming the framework of the civil-military relationship was crucial to transforming the Army of a century ago.

Today, America is in another time of geopolitical change. Cold War stability gave way to more than a decade of uncertainty until terrorists administered a profound strategic shock to our nation on 11 September 2001. We have been involved in a "global war on terrorism" for almost three years, and we broadly recognize the need to transform our military forces to meet the threats and possibilities of a new era. Institutional reforms will almost certainly be part of that change.

Concurrent with this period of strategic instability, a vigorous debate has raged over the nature and health of American civil-military relations. For a decade the most vocal critics argued that the military had gained too much power vis-á-vis civilian leaders with unfortunate prospects for the future of national security. In the past three years, the pendulum seems to have swung in the opposite direction, a widely held perception being that senior military voices were all but muted in the strategic dialogue. Both concerns are overwrought, but the fact that perceptions could change so quickly indicates an unhealthy instability at the politico-military nexus. To be sure, part of the problem—and it is only a problem, not a crisis or a danger—lies in the vitriolic nature of modern American politics and the role that defense issues play in political debate. Those concerns are well beyond the scope of this study. Instead, I shall focus in this chapter on the role of officers in civil-military relations and attempts to define the kinds of professional skills—political-cultural expertise—that officers should develop to serve effectively at the intersection of political and military affairs.

The Army and Society: Late 19th-Century Reform and Professionalization

Elihu Root grew up the son of an upstate New York academic. Ambition, hard work, and brilliance carried him from these modest beginnings to the pinnacle of power and prestige in Manhattan financial, corporate, and legal circles. He called himself a Hamiltonian nationalist, trusting in the efficacy of activist government to order society and to build national power. But he was also a creature of his class who believed instinctively that only educated, professional men such as himself possessed the competence to govern. He worked most of his life to build systems and institutions that would provide such order while guarding against man's natural venality. He was a man of contradictions, one part corporate lawyer, one part progressive reformer. As an attorney, he spent much of his career on retainer to some of the most powerful and infamous corporations of the Gilded Age, the post-Civil War boom times of unbridled acquisitiveness. As a reformer, he often promoted causes inimical to the interests of those clients. He despised the status quo of New York party boss politics and championed electoral and voting rights reform. Root's "three Rs" were reform, restraint, and responsibility. In short, he was a quintessential, conflicted exemplar of the Progressive Era.[2]

Root was part of what Robert Wiebe has called the "new middle class" of the late 19th century. Isolated communities of the younger America gave way to an integrated nation growing more prosperous, more urban, and more specialized. Several civilian vocations began to professionalize, especially medicine, social work, education, and the law. For example, at mid-19th century the law had almost no standards of entry and little interest in professional education. When Root became an attorney in 1867, one of his colleagues ranked their vocation "next below patent-medicine mongering." Slowly, small clusters of elite attorneys began organizing to control standards of entry and to codify professional practices. One such group formed the Bar Association of New York City in 1870. Many other cities and states followed suit, and these efforts culminated in creation of the American Bar Association in 1878. Root was an active member of both the New York City Bar Association and the ABA. These professional groups worked to clean up the practice of law by enforcing codes of discipline and fostering professional education in colleges and universities. Many other civilian occupations followed similar late-19th century paths.[3]

Samuel Huntington argued in *The Soldier and the State* (1957) that the Army professionalized in the latter half of the 19th century because it remained in isolation from the rest of society. He failed to explain why, if it were divorced from the rest of America, the Army was becoming more professional at the same time and in the same ways as other American vocations. Subsequent historical research has shown that in this interpretation, as in so many others, Huntington was wrong. Army professionalization proceeded along a trajectory parallel to that of other professions and in response to many of the same stimuli. The bulk of officers were not isolated from society and were firmly connected with the progressive reforms of the era. Indeed, one historian has referred to officers of this period as "armed progressives" for the many ways in which their attempts to reform the Army mirrored those of their civilian counterparts in other prestigious occupations.[4]

A case in point: as various vocations professionalized, antagonisms predictably arose between older, more senior practitioners and young reformers.[5] The "old bulls" naturally resented assertions of the "young Turks'" that their time-honored practices were obsolescent. That conflict was also in evidence in the Army. A post-Civil War drawdown mustered out hundreds of thousands of soldiers, shrinking the Army to a fraction of its wartime size. In the small officer corps that remained, where promotion came only with seniority, a knot of war-era West Point graduates, "the '61 to '64 men," effectively blocked chances for advancement for a generation of their juniors. By 1891, the average first lieutenant was 45 years old.[6]

In the late-1870s a rival institution mounted a challenge to the Regular Army's professional jurisdiction. In response to railroad strikes in 1877, leaders of state volunteer units and urban businessmen found common cause in the need for a locally controlled "organized militia" that would stand ready to put down "communistic" strikers. In short order they formed a new National Guard Association, which soon garnered enough state and Federal support to muster militia forces totaling 100,000, or about four times as many soldiers as the Regular Army. Thus, junior Army officers found themselves buffeted on two sides. Not only were their seniors blocking their paths to advancement, but the National Guard was bidding to make them altogether superfluous. The approaching end of the Indian Wars only accentuated the situation.[7]

Younger regular officers began to fight back. Col. Emory Upton, who had earned lasting fame for his brilliant tactical innovation at the battle of Spotsylvania, became the young Turks' Isaiah. His book, *The Armies of Europe and Asia* (1878), a compelling report of his observer missions around the world, and "The Military Policy of the United States," an unpublished but widely circulated prescription for the American Army to emulate recent Prussian successes, provided young officers with elitist, professionalist answers to their National Guard rivals.[8] Disdainful of the combat records of Guard formations, Upton argued instead for a return to the "expansible army" concept, first proposed in the wake of the War of 1812, entailing the addition of a corps of federally controlled reserves to be trained by regulars for mobilization in time of war. Disciples of Upton took up the banner and began to lobby for a national army reserve that would remain reliably under federal control, in contrast to the state-run militias. That stimulus spurred them to commence a flurry of professional activity. Professional journals began to flourish as officers wrote articles on military history, European military innovations, weapon technology, tactics, and strategy. Young professionals began to lobby for a renaissance of military training and education. Proponents of various branches worked to resurrect "schools of application" to improve training and develop tactical doctrine. Arthur Wagner and Eben Swift successfully reformed the Infantry and Cavalry School at Fort Leavenworth into a first-rate school for staff officers. Several officers, including Army commanding generals William T. Sherman and John M. Schofield, championed still higher-level military education and the need to replace the antiquated Army bureau system. They advocated establishment of a modern general staff and an Army war college to provide the general staff officers to man it.[9]

Foremost among the officers pushing for this last, strategic-level reform was an assistant adjutant general in the War Department, William H. Carter. An 1873 graduate of West Point, Carter was by all accounts a gifted officer, both war hero and military intellectual. He had served two decades on the western frontier in the infantry and cavalry, earning a Medal of Honor in combat against the Apaches in 1881. Carter had drunk deeply of Upton's work and had become a staunch advocate of professionalization. He was also a leader in the battle for a federal reserve force and against the National Guard. Still, he was "behind the hump" of Civil War veterans and keenly felt the pressures of professional stagnation. In 1898, at the age of 47 and after a quarter-century of commissioned service, he was still a major.[10] Despite his progressive ideas, Carter and his dreams of establishing a war college were to languish while the Army tried to shake off 35 years of constabulary atrophy as it mobilized for an expeditionary war in Cuba.

The Strategic Situation: The Spanish-American War and a New Foreign Policy

Teddy Roosevelt pronounced the campaign to take Santiago in 1898 to have been "within measurable distance of a military disaster." That description aptly described the public perception of the entire Spanish-American War. The Army's shortcomings included a cumbersome high command, poor strategic planning capability, and severe difficulties mobilizing and transporting troops. A special presidential commission later found the Army's performance spotty, if not as bad as many believed. Still, the war had exposed severe institutional and organizational problems, and for a short time there was public impetus for military reform.[11]

Moreover, the war made it clear that reform was in order for other reasons. The conditions that had caused reform heralded a long-term change in American foreign policy and military strategy. America had expansionist, even imperialist designs. Since 1865 the small constabulary Army had remained in the United States, employed in pacifying the conquered South and in strike-breaking, but mostly guarding the frontier and the continental coastline—missions that we would today call homeland defense. The expeditionary Spanish-American War had found the Army wanting in large-unit operational and strategic skills, for which it had no formal preparation. The United States, bidding to become a great power, now had colonies to protect in the Philippines and the Caribbean. Plans to complete an interocean canal at the Isthmus of Panama only added to America's growing ambitions.[12]

The nation's strategic considerations changed as its interests expanded. Still, threats to the United States and its possessions were few and predictable. Trouble from the unstable Mexican republic was unlikely, but the long southern border bore watching, and guarding it was clearly an Army responsibility. Germany, Great Britain, and Japan all boasted strong naval power, and while the United States had good relations with all three, especially the British, they nevertheless presented possible threats to the American coast and ports. Preparing for that unlikely eventuality fell on the Navy and the Army's coastal defense establishment. More likely were threats to U.S. interests abroad, including violations of the Monroe Doctrine in the Caribbean islands or in Panama, or raids on new American possessions in the Pacific. Each of these concerns pointed up the need for ready military and especially naval forces.[13]

Two new aspects of expansionist American policy demanded robust offensive forces as well: the need to defend the newly-won Philippines and maintaining the "Open Door"—preserving the political integrity of and American commercial access to China. Solving the problem of reinforcing the Philippines in the event of Japanese attack—requiring a swift Pacific crossing by a robust Army-Navy force—would continue to vex military planners for decades, until it finally proved impossible in 1941. While there was considerable political debate about whether either of these foreign policy goals was worth the myriad costs, each demanded a blue-water navy and ready land forces.[14] Thus, in the final days of the 19th century, both postwar reassessment of military capability and a change in national strategy indicated the need for military reform, or, as we are wont to say today, transformation.

Secretary Root, General Miles, and Major Carter

Elihu Root arrived in Washington in July 1899, succeeding the incompetent Russell Alger, at whose feet rightly lay the blame for many of the organizational and operational calamities of the Spanish-American War. Although he had ostensibly been hired to administer America's new colonies, Root found that he was responsible for prosecuting an ongoing war in the Philippines. Just as quickly, he discovered that the Army's disorganization demanded his immediate attention.[15]

Among the first people he met at his new War Department offices was Nelson A. Miles, a Civil War veteran and legendary Indian fighter who had become Army commanding general in 1895. The youngest son of a comfortable Massachusetts family, Miles had gone to seek his fortune in Boston when the Civil War broke out. Despite his lack of formal schooling and military training, he employed his family's resources to land a lieutenancy in a volunteer infantry regiment. Combat suited him. Time and again he demonstrated bravery, a cool head under fire, and a knack for being in the right place at the right time. Miles ended the war with a brevet commission as a major general and command of the First Division in the Army of the Potomac. During the Indian Wars, Miles earned plaudits for his imaginative and relentless campaigns against the Sioux, which ended in the surrender of that proud tribe. A newspaper reporter who accompanied his regiment found him "a splendid field soldier, prompt, bold, and magnetic. He was always in high spirits, which is a good thing in a commanding officer."

In later campaigns, unfortunately, he combined those qualities of leadership with vaulting ambition, self-promotion, and a reputation for duplicity whether dealing with Army rivals or Indian enemies. Though exceptionally successful in the Indian wars, he emerged from them roundly distrusted. When he became the Army commanding general, the warrior continued to divide the world starkly into friends and enemies. Poorly educated and captive of his own experience, he was slow to develop the new skills necessary to serve effectively in Washington. Nevertheless, his frontier exploits and high rank gained him frequent mention as a presidential candidate, speculation he did nothing to discourage in his frequent interviews with reporters. Unsurprisingly, Miles developed a poisonous relationship with Secretary Alger, engaging in public recriminations with him over the Army's shortcomings in Cuba. With good reason, Root approached his principal subordinate warily.[16]

Next door to Root's office were the Adjutant General, Maj. Gen. Henry C. Corbin, and his assistant, Maj. William H. Carter. Corbin had bridged the gap between Miles and Secretary Alger, acting in effect as Army chief of staff for President McKinley during the war. Corbin and Root hit it off well and the adjutant general began at once to help the secretary learn the ropes.[17]

Major Carter was to play an even more important role. Root's biographer, Philip C. Jessup, here describes the 46-year-old major:

> A tall, thin, brilliant young officer . . . who had not sunk into the depths of a government armchair but who had been doing a lot of thinking about Army reorganization. He had a good record of active service but was essentially the scholar and student of military science. He was invaluable to the new Secretary."[18]

Carter began immediately helping Root to understand the problems behind the Army's disorganization. He introduced the secretary to Emory Upton's thought and discussed his ideas about creating an Army general staff. Root also read Spenser Wilkinson's encomium to the German general staff, *The Brain of an Army* (1890). He reviewed the Dodge Commission report on the Army's shortcomings in the recent war and interviewed the chairman, Grenville Dodge. Seemingly tireless, Root shook up the sleepy War Department with his long hours, disciplined work habits, and hunger for detail. He devoted every moment he could spare from colonial administrative issues to learning about the Army. Carter briefed the secretary often, helping him to understand both the necessity for organizational change and the likely opposition to it. Reflecting a classic conflict of the Progressive Era, Carter warned Root that there "was not much enthusiasm [for reform] among older officers in the War Department, and the inertia there reacted unfavorably in Congress."[19]

Defining the Problem: The Army's Need to Transform

The problems in the War Department were threefold: command, strategic planning, and mobilization. The problem in command dated back 80 years to the creation of the position of Army commanding general. That office had hovered in constitutional limbo, somewhere below the president, but not reliably subordinate to the secretary of war. Statutes kept the commanding general from controlling the Army bureau system and sometimes from issuing orders to the line Army. Secretaries of war and commanding generals suffered habitually bad relations, including some of the most vicious feuds in American public administration. Gen. John Schofield, who served as secretary of war and later as commanding general, developed the only effective peacetime solution: as commanding general he willingly subordinated himself to the secretary and acted as chief of staff. His example was much in the mind of Army reformers, especially Major Carter.[20]

The Army's inability to plan for strategic contingencies stemmed from the fact that no one was trained for strategic planning and no one was assigned the responsibility. The Army's staff, such as it was, comprised a collection of fiercely independent bureau chiefs overseeing distinct portfolios—adjutant general, inspector general, quartermaster general, etc. The bureau system had been a major leap forward in military administration when Secretary John C. Calhoun had shaped it in the wake of the near-disaster of the War of 1812. The idea had been to develop staff expertise in areas of high-level administration and to empower bureau chiefs with authority and long tenure. These chiefs became expert in their responsibilities, but they tended to become jealous of their prerogatives and increasingly out of touch with the line army they were supposed to support. To complicate matters of command, they reported directly to the secretary of war, not the commanding general. The system worked well enough in peacetime, but showed its impotence in the Mexican War, the Civil War, and most recently in the Spanish-American War. The most damaging wartime shortcoming was that no single bureau was responsible for operational or strategic planning, and no one had authority to coordinate them all, except the secretary himself.[21]

The third major problem was the lack of an efficient method of mobilizing for war. The constabulary army was pitifully small, both absolutely and in comparison to its European counterparts. Yet it had probably been large enough for its frontier and coastal defense missions. Then, the Spanish-American War had demonstrated the need for ready reserves and the ability to muster, equip, train, and deploy them quickly. The addition of overseas possessions not only increased the need for a larger army, but also implicitly demanded a strategy to mobilize and defend those territories.

A Civil-Military Partnership: Root, Carter, and Political-Cultural Expertise

In his first several months on the job, Root worked with Carter to shore up his own limited knowledge of military matters generally and the U.S. Army particularly. At the same time, the two men were forming a civil-military partnership that was essential to their ability to address the Army's problems. They quickly developed a mutual respect and interdependence. They shared a facility for interpersonal relations—candor, patience, clarity of communication, political skill—that enabled them to trust one another and to deal with others effectively. Carter's professional expertise, especially his political-cultural skills, proved invaluable to Root, who relied on him heavily. They both demonstrated exceptional capacity for reaching across cultural boundaries—an ability to work with people from other backgrounds, Root with the military, Carter with civilians, both of them with Congress. Their partnership, based on that cross-cultural ability, their professional maturity, their mutual trust, and their belief in the importance of effective civil-military relations, enabled them to work interdependently to formulate plans for reforming the Army and to pursue them together over several years.[22]

By December 1899 Root was ready to act. In his first Annual Report as secretary of war, he laid out his plan to reform the Army. Echoing the words of his most distinguished predecessor, John C. Calhoun, Root drew two fundamental conclusions from his months of study:

> First. That the real object of having an Army is to provide for war.
>
> Second. That the regular establishment in the United States will probably never be by itself the whole machine with which any war will be fought.[23]

Root recognized that the first statement would seem little more than a truism, but he explained that 33 years of relative peace had left the Army more efficient than effective—"an elaborate system admirably adapted to secure pecuniary accountability and economy of expenditure" but which precluded "the effective organization and training of the Army as a whole for the purposes of war." He listed four necessary steps to prepare the Army for war: systematic study of plans for action in all possible contingencies; adequately providing for modern war materiel; merit selection of officers for promotion, rather than the simple rule of seniority; and finally large-scale field maneuvers. Toward these ends he made several specific proposals, the first of which was to establish an Army war college, which would provide instruction in "the larger problems of military science" and also act as a de facto general staff. He also made arrangements to begin rotating as many officers as possible through such a war college. He intended to have line officers begin rotating for fixed periods to the Army bureaus and then back to their regiments, so as to begin reconnecting staff and line.[24]

To meet the implicit requirements of his second general conclusion, Root called for legislation to codify the relations between regulars and volunteers and to establish standards for mobilization and training of the reserve force so that all might know how to prepare for mobilization long before it occurred. He also supported a joint Army-Navy board to study strategic plans and render an annual report. The faculties of the two war colleges (the Naval War College had been established in 1881) could contribute to that endeavor.[25]

This annual report was and still is an exceptionally readable document that carefully lays out the nation's military problems and establishes a vision for addressing them. Root meant for the report to be read. He mailed it to congressmen, newspaper editors, and Wall Street colleagues, sending a strong signal that a time for reform was at hand. Root received praise for his vision from all corners. Senator Redfield Proctor, chairman of the Military Affairs Committee, was effusive: "The country and Army for all time will bless you for that report. Carried into effect it creates an Army."[26]

Yet Root was careful not to overreach. He did not yet call for replacing the commanding general or for abolishing the bureau system. What he could do by his own authority, he did. He convened a board to consider establishing a war college. When he discovered that he already had authority under existing legislation, he asked for and received a small appropriation toward that end. A year later, in 1901 Root founded the Army War College in Washington. True to his intent, it acted as both school and general staff for its first few years.[27] Root was gently fitting a wedge into the cracks of the old system. He would later drive it home.

Carter's role in the reform process steadily expanded. Having gained Root's confidence early with his erudition, he maintained it by being an exceptionally proficient staff officer. When Root needed a memo concerning the war college, Carter drafted it. When he needed orders to create the war college, Carter produced them. Carter advised Root on where internal opposition to Army reform would originate, and how to counter it. With Carter's assistance, Root sent letters to all generals and colonels soliciting their views on the need for reform and legislation to effect it. As Root began to deal with Congress on these issues, Carter became an all-purpose legislative liaison, writing letters to senators, drafting testimony, preparing witnesses for and accompanying them to congressional hearings, even drafting legislation. When senators questioned how the Army could possibly receive orders without a commanding general, Carter drafted mock orders as the new General Staff would do in order to demonstrate the form. In the words of Root's biographer, Carter fulfilled "the roles of all the staff departments but Root planned the strategy and directed the operations."[28]

In early 1900 they drafted an Army reorganization bill that included a number of the measures Root had been advocating in his annual reports. Root testified twice to promote the legislation and initial indications were favorable, but as the months wore on a series of amendments weakened the bill almost beyond recognition. Carter wanted to press the committees to reverse themselves, but Root was patient and determined to get what he could for the moment. The 1901 authorization's only significant accomplishment was an increase in the size of Army, which was badly needed, especially in the Philippines. Moreover, the increase was a matter that many officers had said was important to them when Root had asked their views.[29] Demonstrating that he was paying attention to their concerns would help to garner their support for the rest of the reforms he sought.

Root's Annual Report of 1901 pressed further for reform, expounding on the need for a general staff "for the study of great questions, the consideration and formation of plans, forethought against future contingencies, and coordination of the various branches." Newly promoted Lieutenant Colonel Carter worked as liaison with Congress to draft a bill to create a general staff corps with a chief of staff rather than an army commanding general. Carter's draft bill went before both military affairs committees in early 1902.[30]

The Miles Reaction

Key to educating Congress was blunting the opposition of the "old bulls" in the Army. Foremost among these was the commanding general, Nelson Miles. Miles failed his first personal test with the new secretary. Asked for his confidential advice on the selection of officers to command new volunteer regiments, Miles betrayed Root's trust by leaking his proposed names to the press. Matters never improved between the two. From that point forward, Miles mocked the concept of civilian control in word and deed. He opposed Root at every turn, often publicly, and attempted to block reform, especially as it applied to his own office and to the Army bureaus. He had unsuccessfully worked to insert an amendment to the 1901 bill to reduce some of the flexibility that Root had requested. Root and Roosevelt, the latter having soured on Miles before Root arrived in Washington, determined to crush the old general. When Miles improperly commented publicly on a Navy disciplinary matter, Root officially reprimanded him. Miles appealed the matter to President Roosevelt, who granted him an interview and then used the opportunity to upbraid him in person. At this point, the commanding general's opposition to Army reform became public and bitter.[31]

On 2 March 1902, General Miles testified before the Senate committee and condemned his secretary's legislation in severe and emotional terms. Appealing to the sentiments of his fellow Civil War veterans on the committee, he defended the current system: "The fruit of the best thought of the most eminent patriots and ablest military men that this country has produced should not be destroyed by substituting one that is more adapted to the monarchies of the Old World." He charged that a general staff would tend to "Germanize or Russianize the small army of the United States." His main concern was the loss of the commanding general's authority to an "all-powerful General Staff" which would be "only subject to the control of the Secretary of War, whose knowledge of affairs military may be meager or nil." As he warmed to his task "he asserted that the bill was calculated to accomplish no purpose except to allow the Secretary of War and the Adjutant General to promote the interests of their personal favorites."[32] The secretary of war and the commanding general were in open, public conflict over a matter of policy.

The Root Reforms

After the hearing, Carter talked to the committee chairman, Senator Joseph Hawley of Connecticut, who warned him that, as a result of Miles's testimony, "favorable action on the bill could not be expected that session." Carter returned immediately to the War Department to report to Root. Together they plotted "a campaign of education on the subject of a General Staff before the next session of Congress should convene."[33]

They put that plan into action the next day and continued until a General Staff bill passed a year later. Carter drafted and Root signed a letter to the committee correcting Miles's earlier testimony. They arranged for another hearing the next month with two retired officers, Lt. Gen. John M. Schofield and Maj. Gen. Wesley Merritt, as witnesses. Three circumstances helped make Schofield's testimony especially illuminating and persuasive. First, as we noted earlier, he had been secretary of war and later commanding general of the Army during his long career. That unique perspective had allowed him, as commanding general, to see the wisdom of acting as a chief of staff to coordinate and implement the policies of the secretary of war. He had long advocated just such a legislative change. The second was Carter's assistance to the general in preparing for testimony, including accompanying him to the hearing, in case he might "wish to refresh his memory." Third was the list of questions that Root had provided the committee, probably drafted by Carter, to draw the Civil War veteran out. Afterward, members of the committee pronounced themselves persuaded and ready to approve the general staff bill.[34]

Root and Carter pressed on. They solicited letters from active Army field generals in support of the reorganization. In his Annual Report for 1902, Root made a lucid, seven-page argument for a general staff, bolstered by support from senior Army leaders active and retired to demonstrate that General Miles's views were in the minority. He sent the report to more than two dozen newspaper editors and garnered wide public support.[35]

The month of December 1902 proved decisive. With increasing public and congressional support, Root appeared before both authorizing committees to argue forcefully for his plan. Carter accompanied him as legislative advisor. After Root's persuasive performance, their head count showed that solid majorities of both committees now supported the bill to create a general staff. The Army inspector general later testified, as did the chief of the Record and Pension Office, and succeeded in gaining an exemption for their two bureaus from the reorganization, meaning they would not be subject to the supervision of the new chief of staff. Root and Carter decided to accept those changes in order to get a bill that would establish the reality of a general staff in legislation. The bill passed on 14 February 1903, and President Roosevelt signed it into law at the White House. He presented the ceremonial pen to William Carter.[36]

The law was written to take effect in August, which coincided quite intentionally with the mandatory retirement of Nelson Miles, who left office on the 8th, with little recognition and no ceremony from the War Department. The post of commanding general retired with him. Lt. Gen. Samuel B.M. Young became the Army's first chief of staff a week later.[37]

The new general staff would take several years to prove itself. Implementing orders had to be drafted, new general staff officers selected and assigned, and procedures worked out. To be sure, tension between the old bureaus and the chief of staff did not die quickly—the final battle in that war did not take place for another decade. William Carter, one of the first general officers on the new general staff, continued to play an important role in its evolution for years to come.[38]

Developing Political-Cultural Expertise

In the 1903 Annual Report, Root explained why the general staff law was so important:

> It will be perceived that we are here providing for civilian control over the military arm, but for civilian control to be exercised through a single military expert of high rank, who is provided with an adequate corps of professional assistants to aid him in the performance of his duties, and who is bound to use all his professional skill and knowledge in giving effect to the purposes and general directions of his civilian superior, or make way for another expert who will do so.[39]

It is hard to imagine a better description of effective civil-military relations. Root also expressed the hope that they had resolved "the problem of reconciling civilian control with military efficiency" that had vexed the War Department and the Army for over a century. One can quarrel with the idea of exercising civilian control "through a single military expert," and adjustments to the system over the past century have more than tinkered with that concept. But ensuring the existence of an effective military arm reliably subordinate and responsive to civilian authority was an issue of paramount importance. Just more than a century later, we struggle with it still.

In fact, over the past decade a school of thought has posited a "crisis" in American civil-military relations. Adherents have argued that the American military was "out of control," citing evidence ranging from the 1993 contretemps over gays in the military to a calculated snub of President Clinton when he landed on the Navy carrier USS *Theodore Roosevelt*. The general trend was deemed to be "disturbing" or "dangerous," although the precise nature of the dangers to the national security seemed to fade into imprecision as these arguments neared their conclusions. However, what ailed the civil-military relationship in this view could be remedied only by a more compliant officer corps. The problem in this partnership was all on the military side, and it was up to the professional military to fix it.[40]

What a difference a new administration makes! Few observers advance the "out of control" thesis today. Secretary Rumsfeld and his team in the Pentagon seem to have mastered civilian control of the military in short order. Indeed, the concern over the past few years has been that senior officers have been too cowed by senior administration officials to offer straightforward, if unwelcome, professional advice.

The truth, of course, is that neither of these conflicting caricatures is entirely true. Neither is entirely false. The military was not out of control under the Clinton Administration and it is not intimidated now. But the fact that perceptions of civil-military relations could change so quickly is evidence that something is not healthy about the relationship. To the degree that problems in civil-military relations exist, they exist, almost by definition, on both sides. However, addressing the issues on the political side of the ledger is not our chief concern here. Instead, the balance of this chapter will address the professional military's responsibilities in civil-military relations. Specifically, it will focus on the development of political-cultural expertise, the professional military skills associated with civil-military relations.

What are those skills? The literature on the subject is rather thin. In the 2002 edition of the present anthology, *The Future of the Army Profession*, Marybeth Peterson Ulrich began the work of codifying political-cultural skills in her article, "Infusing Civil-Military Relations Norms in the Officer Corps." In a recent study on strategic leadership development, Leonard Wong and a team of Army War College researchers distilled six metacompetencies that characterize effective senior military leaders, all of which are more or less relevant to the practice of civil-military relations. Those works, along with a critical analysis of some of Huntington's theoretical constructs in *The Soldier and the State*, will provide the basis for the following attempt to codify political-cultural skills, using the episodes surrounding the Root reforms as a case in point.[41]

These skills, as we shall see, are more subtle and complex than the tactical and technical skills that junior officers must master. They are intellectual, attitudinal, and interpersonal in nature, encompassing the following attributes: (1) capacity for career-long, professional growth; (2) ability to view the military service broadly as a professional institution; (3) understanding and appreciation of the realities of civilian control of the military; (4) ability to cross cultural boundaries; and (5) capacity for developing interdependent professional relationships.

Continuing Professional Growth

Officers at the politico-military nexus are generally not in the flower of youth. Carter was 52 when the General Staff bill became law. Miles was 63. At that time the natural order of a military career dictated that those who interacted with civilian policy-makers would typically have long careers of service behind them. A century later, a formulaic personnel management system standardizes officers' careers so that they are even more likely to be rather senior by the time they engage in civil-military relations at the highest levels. Thus, they will have to master unfamiliar skills later in life, a task that challenges us all. When the call comes, to paraphrase Root, they will have to determine what kind of officers they wish to be.

Young officers develop a sense of professional identity through acculturation, training, education, and experience. They tend to identify with their units, their soldiers, their branches, and the kinds of tactical and technical skills they develop. Yet as officers mature, especially as they reach levels of strategic leadership, professional identity must continue to grow. Officers must broaden their intellectual and cultural horizons. This process involves rising above the comfortable confines of one's professional parameters—growing beyond the tactical and into the operational, strategic, and even political realms. This growth is not a leave-taking: officers should not neglect their tactical roots, but should use that training and experience as a base upon which to build further professional expertise. Professional growth requires developing new skills without losing others.[42]

Professional maturity is marked by a critical and searching intellect. It encompasses critical thinking, a tolerance for ambiguity, a healthy skepticism for facile explanations and simplistic arguments. It requires constant struggle against habit, mental lethargy, and prejudice. It is difficult to acquire and easy to lose. It takes work. The surest path to this capacity is through formal, advanced education followed by a lifetime of continuous self-guided study and stimulating reading. If the path of formal schooling is not open, professional growth and maturation still demand dedication to an ethos of lifelong learning. Regardless of how much schooling one receives, mature professionals must become and remain autodidacts at heart.

Both Miles and Carter had well established professional identities as courageous soldiers and Indian fighters long before they arrived at the War Department. They were both highly decorated and respected warriors. The difference between them was a capacity for continued professional growth. Conservative, hypersensitive, vainglorious, egocentric, and poorly educated, Miles divided his world neatly into opposing camps of friends and enemies—there were no shades of gray. As commanding general, he remained stuck in his self-concept as an Indian fighter. Regardless of the Army's obvious shortcomings in the Spanish-American War, Miles stubbornly resisted any type of institutional change. Carter, on the other hand, had made himself expert in institutional military history and organization through a long program of independent study. He was ready, when the moment arrived, to assist Root in learning about the Army as an organization and in guiding it along a much needed path of reform.[43]

As seasoned soldiers serving in the War Department, Carter and Miles were both thrust into responsibilities ideally requiring political-cultural skills. They approached the new challenges of civil-military relations, and especially their respective relations with Secretary Root, in radically different ways. Granted, these approaches reflected differences in their respective positions and responsibilities, but more important were differences in their personalities, values, attitudes, and skills. Despite many disadvantages vis-à-vis Miles, Carter was far more successful in accomplishing his reformist aims than Miles was in thwarting them, largely because his political-cultural skills were more highly developed. That development began with a capacity for continuing professional growth.

A Broad Perspective of The Military as a Professional Institution

There are many ways to look at an army. The U.S. Army today is an instrument of national military power. It is a large, corporate body with over a million employees. It is a hierarchical bureaucracy with thousands of headquarters, regulations, and procedures. It is a vast agency of the federal government with worldwide responsibilities and annual expenditures in excess of $100 billion. It is an interest group competing with other governmental entities to protect its turf, its resources, and its membership.

Those charged with responsibilities in the civil-military arena must be astute enough to view the Army first and foremost as a profession. They should not be so naïve as to neglect the Army's other roles, but they should emphasize its professional nature. Strategic leaders must see themselves as leaders of a profession and take responsibility for the maintenance of the profession's institutions. They must manifest an ability to evaluate institutional culture and have the courage to challenge it to respond to new environmental demands. A related and equally important skill is taking responsibility for developing the strategic leaders of the future.[44]

In the milieu of civil-military relations, strategic leaders should act as counselors to their clients—purveyors of professional expertise—and as spokesmen for the profession to their civilian superiors. These roles help elucidate what Samuel Huntington defined as a natural tension in civil-military relations between what he called the functional and the societal imperatives. For the military profession, the functional imperative is the necessity to be manned, equipped, trained, and ready to accomplish assigned missions. The societal imperative is the need for the military to remain reliably subordinate to duly established civilian authority in accordance with the Constitution and federal law. Huntington asserted that the "interaction between these two forces is the nub of the problem of civil-military relations."[45] Military professionals, and especially strategic leaders of the profession, have an equal and often conflicting responsibility for seeing that the profession adheres to both of these imperatives, or, as Root would have it, for "reconciling civilian control with military efficiency."

Nelson Miles, the uniformed head of the Army, could not view his service as a profession. He assiduously protected his prerogatives and the Army's organization as it had existed since the Civil War. He discounted the inadequacies exposed in the Spanish-American War and took no responsibility for addressing them. He defended the status quo and the authority of his office. He neglected both the functional imperative, seeing to the future readiness of the Army, while spurning the societal imperative. His relations with two secretaries of war and two presidents were embarrassingly quarrelsome. He subordinated himself to civilian authority only under threat of punishment.

Carter, on the other hand, took a broad view of the Army as a professional institution. He saw the need for an Army war college and a hierarchical system of schools, for a more rational system of officer promotions, for reform of the bureau system, for a strategic planning capability in the War Department. In short, he saw the need to reform a profession. Fortunately for him, he found a professional client in Secretary Root who was as keen to shake up the institution as he was, so that he faced no conflict between his functional and societal responsibilities.

The Realities of Civilian Control of The Military

Carter and Miles had radically different views of civilian authority. Miles hardly recognized his responsibilities to it. Carter interacted effectively with both Secretary Root and members of Congress.

Today's officer corps labors under a handicap unknown to Carter and Miles: the pervasive influence on the professional culture of Samuel Huntington's ideal form of civil-military relations, "objective civilian control."[46] Objective civilian control maximizes military professionalism, and hence national security, by divorcing the military from political life. It erects a wall between policy and strategy that neither the general nor the politician should breach. This is the preferred archetype of von Moltke the Elder: the Kaiser and Bismarck would define the political aim and then stand aside while the Prussian army prosecuted the war toward accomplishment of a well-defined military objective.

Seen as an ideal theoretical type, much as Clausewitz developed his notion of "absolute war" as a dialectical prerequisite for understanding "real war," objective civilian control has much to recommend it.[47] In an ideal world, military professionals would remain unequivocally subordinate to their political masters, who would, in turn, develop clear, unambiguous, and unchanging policy goals prior to a forthright declaration of war. Already well-equipped and well-trained for any contingency, soldiers would then develop military objectives to achieve the political aims of government free of constraint or interference and prosecute war to assured victory. There is no societal and functional tension, because the two imperatives inhabit separate but compatible worlds.

Yet reality intrudes. The brick wall that Huntington would erect between the Soldier and the State is thinner than a membrane. It is the boundary between air and water. On a quiet day, the surface is easy to observe. But on a stormy and turbulent sea, the most experienced sailor would be hard-pressed to say where the sky ended and the water began. The physical properties of liquid and gas are fundamentally different. Indeed, describing these qualitative differences is among the most elementary tasks of chemistry. Yet, when conditions are right, passing from one medium to the other is effortless. Likewise, in the real world of civil-military relations, soldiers sometimes stray into the realm of policy-making, while civilian leaders involve themselves in professional military matters, such as operational planning and even battlefield decisions. These activities, warfare and politics, are fundamentally different, but passing from one medium to the other can be effortless. No Huntingtonian wall separates political and military matters in practice.[48]

Yet Huntington's theory has influenced two generations of military professionals to think of objective control not as a theoretical ideal, but as a practical goal to be achieved. Mature professionals should reject that notion. They must work in the real world where subjective civilian control is the norm and is accepted as the norm. Soldiers and politicians alike should understand that the daily negotiation of civil-military relations means that each will cross the thin politico-military boundary regularly. As Clausewitz put it, at the highest level the art of war turns into policy. . . . [T]he assertion that a major military development, or the plan for one, should be a matter for *purely military* opinion is unacceptable and can be damaging. Nor indeed is it sensible to summon soldiers, as many governments do when they are planning a war, and ask them for *purely military advice*. But it makes even less sense for theoreticians to assert that all available military resources should be put at the disposal of the commander so that on their basis he can draw up purely military plans for a war. . . . No major proposal for war can be worked out in ignorance of political factors; and when people talk, as they often do, about harmful political influence on the management of war, they are not really saying what they mean. Their quarrel should be with the policy itself, not with its influence.[49]

What Clausewitz has to say about war and planning for war applies to periods of peace and, indeed, of military reform and transformation as well. American military professionals today readily accept the concept of civilian supremacy. They must further learn to accept the discomfiting idea that in subjective control civilian and military leaders share overlapping areas of competence and jurisdiction. Military leaders make operational decisions with political ramifications just as civilians make policy that affects operational matters.[50]

Eliot Cohen has developed an understanding of subjective control that he terms "the unequal dialogue," a continuous conversation between military and civilian leaders, a vigorous and candid give-and-take, in which civilians will always emerge preeminent.[51] That last phrase may be difficult for some officers to swallow, for it demands a high level of professional maturity—a sense of self-abnegation, a tolerance for ambiguity, a willingness to accept compromise between important but competing values.

Yet military professionals would serve the nation and the profession well to replace Huntington's wall with Cohen's unequal dialogue. For the essential flaw in Huntington's theoretical wall of objective civilian control is that he establishes a split responsibility for the functional and societal imperatives: officers protect the functional and civilians protect the societal. This bifurcation of responsibility demands too little of military professionals and their civilian superiors alike. Indeed, such a boundary is unnatural and infeasible in human interaction. Instead, both can and should maintain a joint responsibility for the functional and the societal imperatives as our Constitution requires and daily reality demands. Officers swear an oath to defend the Constitution. So do civilian officials, and the Constitution makes them accountable to the electorate to provide for the common defense. Moreover, "at the highest level the art of war turns into policy," where officers and civilian leaders alike can and often do demonstrate competencies in each others' jurisdictions. Thus, both civilians and officers have the ability and the responsibility to uphold the functional and the societal imperatives of civil-military relations.

Crossing Cultural Boundaries

Joint responsibility shared between military professional and civilian client creates an obligation on both sides to cross cultural boundaries and to engage with one another. Yet the inherently political world of Washington is one that many soldiers disdain and hope never to enter because it is so foreign to their socialization and other military experiences. Thus, the capacity for professional growth is especially important as officers begin to cross cultural boundaries into the civilian world.

The first and fundamental requirement is to see the profession as part of society. The military profession comes from society. It serves society. It protects society. It is and should be open to everyone in American society who can meet its exacting standards of entry and performance. There is an unfortunate tendency on the part of some in the military and some who presume to speak for it to disdain American civilian society as decadent, immoral, or corrupt, and to set the military profession above and apart from it in a moral sense.[52] That tendency is both illogical and dangerous. It is illogical because it imputes to the military profession values that it does not profess for itself, and dangerous because military-cultural elitism can undermine the fundamental definition of a professional as a servant of society. As Sir John Hackett noted in his Lee Knowles lectures on military professionalism:

> What a society gets in its armed forces is exactly what it asks for, no more and no less. What it asks for tends to be a reflection of what it is. When a country looks at its fighting forces it is looking in a mirror; if the mirror is a true one the face that it sees there will be its own.[53]

The military profession should look often into that mirror to ensure that the reflection is a true one.[54]

With that perspective in mind, military officers should recognize the necessity for working with civilians as part of one's duty as a steward of the profession. In Washington, officers will routinely interact with civilians from a number of agencies, including the Army Secretariat, other services, the Office of the Secretary of Defense, the State Department, the Homeland Security Department, the National Security Council, and the White House, as well as the House and the Senate and their authorizing and appropriations committees and their staffs. Strategic leaders and their staffs must represent the profession in a wide variety of venues with members of these organizations. In these settings, military professionals must present themselves as experts and as honest brokers. To do so they must be in, but not of, the political arena.

Political-cultural expertise requires officers to understand political processes. Just as tactical and operational success demands both a doctrinal and a situational understanding of one's enemy, political-cultural engagements require officers to study political leaders, policy issues, and governmental procedures. Obviously, this is not to say that officers should view civilians as the enemy, but that the skills involved in intelligence preparation of the battlefield are transferable. It is important to study other agencies and their cultures, including their missions, motivations, bureaucratic procedures, and jargon. Military professionals will compete with these agencies for roles, missions, and resources. Understanding how one's competitors see the world is crucial in these jurisdictional contests.

Operating effectively in the political-cultural world also means being engaged with society. Officers must understand the interplay of political issues—domestic and international, social and economic, state and federal. They must be eclectic consumers of news—newspapers, magazines, television, radio, and the internet. News comes in various forms, and many outlets have a partisan ax to grind. Officers should avoid selective information-gathering, preferring instead to get as broad and representative a spectrum of opinion as possible. A steady diet of propaganda dulls the mind and imagination.

An ethos of nonpartisanship in a partisan world protects the profession. The officer corps must be scrupulously nonpartisan in word and deed. Professional military education should promote nonpartisanship as a bedrock value of an officer corps serving a democratic republic. This is not to say that officers should have no political opinions or, as some have suggested, that they should not vote. Service to country does not entail the loss of citizenship through disenfranchisement. But no hint of political partisanship should ever impinge on an officer's performance of duty. Equating professionalism with any ideology or party is dangerous, both to the military and to society, as the history of Nazi Germany or any number of totalitarian regimes and failed states will attest. Professional credibility both inside and outside the institution derives from the oath of office, professional expertise, and a steadfast adherence to institutional values. This is especially true in the political world, where the temptations toward partisanship are strongest. Politics in Washington is tough, partisan business, and officers at the political-military boundary should recognize and appreciate that. Most civilians respect the professional military, partly because of its nonpartisanship, and professionals should protect and nurture that standing.[55]

Developing Interdependent Professional Relationships

The daily working reality of civil-military relations does not reside solely or even largely in the high-profile interplay between the Chairman of the Joint Chiefs and his colleagues on the National Security Council. Instead, the heavy lifting is done in the hundreds of interactions among generals and colonels, assistant secretaries and their deputies, and members of Congress and their staffs. The crux of political-cultural expertise, which builds on all the skills discussed thus far, is a capacity for developing interdependence—professional relationships of mutual trust and respect. It is the ability to work across the conference table with men and women in other professional and political cultures to accomplish goals that are important both to the national defense and to the future of the Army profession.

A presumption of good faith on the part of all actors as they serve the nation goes a long way in developing smooth relationships. An assistant secretary in another agency will likely not see his duty in the same way as an Army officer in the Pentagon sees his. That does not mean that either of them is wrong or unpatriotic. An iron law of politics is that where one stands depends upon where one sits. One should try to see issues from the other point of view, both in good faith and as a means to better understand how to negotiate.

The skills of persuasion, negotiation, and consensus-building have obvious applications in the political-cultural realm. Thorough preparation to gain mastery of the issues at stake is fundamental. Knowing what is important, unimportant, and non-negotiable for one's interlocutors is crucial to negotiation. An air of calm reasonableness in a tense meeting can help one lead a fractious group toward consensus. The abilities to reason effectively, to write quickly, briefly, and well, and to employ effective rhetoric can afford a negotiator key advantages. The skills of negotiation and consensus-building are well codified, but little understood. Study and practice in this field will, like most education, put one far ahead of those lacking such preparation.[56]

Two types of civil-military relationships bear specific mention. The first is the relation between an officer and a direct civilian superior. Here the theoretical abstraction of objective civilian control begins to crumble under the weight of practical experience—the professional relationship between boss and subordinate in daily contact. Both parties should accept the practical utility of Eliot Cohen's "unequal dialogue"—a continuing discussion of policy and implementation involving a candid and vigorous sharing of ideas and information wherein each party contributes. The special contribution of the military professional is military expertise developed over a long career of service, now abetted by political-cultural skills. There may be divisions of labor, and those divisions may fall neatly into political and military categories. But they may not, depending on the preferences of the civilian superior.

This relationship should have agreed-upon rules about confidentiality and disclosure. Another way of saying this is that both parties should recognize bounds between advice and dissent. The first step is to define those parameters. For public figures, this definition will involve discussing when and what the officer may say in open forums or to news media. It may also delimit the officer's negotiating authority in venues where the civilian is not present. Most importantly, these parameters define when, where, and how the two will disagree, and when manifestations of disagreement will stop. For the sole purpose of this relationship is to carry out administration policy within a context where using military means is a possibility. At the end of the day, the civilian policy-maker will have the final word, just as in any relationship between a boss and a subordinate. The soldier must accept that requirement or be gone.

Another special kind of civil-military relationship is that between soldiers and members of Congress and their staffs. The Constitution divides responsibility for the common defense between the Executive and the Legislature. The military services are equally accountable to both branches, although not directly subordinate to Congress. Many officers find themselves dealing with Congress frequently in the exercise of its enumerated powers, especially those of authorization, appropriation, regulation, and oversight. These engagements can be tricky even for the most experienced Washington hand. Understanding the tensions between the Executive branch and Congress, between the House and Senate, between the majority and the minority, between authorizers and appropriators, and between personal staffers and committee staffers only begins to scratch the surface. Navigating those shoals requires exceptional skill, political acumen, and integrity. The uninitiated should seek training in congressional relations, which is available on both a formal and an informal basis. There are myriad rules of the trade, but the most fundamental gets back to the need to build relationships based upon trust. Of course, no one can do that with all 535 members and their staffs. But officers with specific portfolios carrying responsibilities for congressional relations can and should seek out those members and staffers who have interests and authority over their issues. A good rule of thumb, frequently broken by Army officers, is to get well acquainted with a member before you have to go and ask for his help. Another is to be unfailingly honest. Although not everyone on Capitol Hill may adhere to Army values, those values are admired and respected there.

In all the swirling tensions listed above, it is easy for officers to find themselves caught between competing interests. Indeed, for those who spend any appreciable time in Washington, finding oneself in such a storm is almost inevitable. The only sure reliance at such a moment is in the anchor of one's values. If one has been assiduous in preparation, careful to know the right answers to expected questions, scrupulous in not saying more than one knows or promising more than one can deliver, and if one has been consistently honest, then that officer is standing on solid ground. Even so, all that may not be enough to protect one from the storm of political controversy. Such qualities as a sense of humor, a philosophical attitude, and a clear conscience will provide limited shelter.[57]

As we have seen, William Carter demonstrated an exceptional ability to develop lasting and productive relationships during the four years he worked with Root to reform the Army. For Root he was teacher, staff officer, counselor, legislative liaison, and alter ego. He knew where the boundaries were—Carter was carrying out Root's policy. But he quickly developed a relationship of trust that enabled him to influence that policy in its formulation, legislation, and implementation. Carter likewise gained the trust of many on Capitol Hill, becoming a conduit of information between the committees and the Secretary, assisting other officers with testimony, demonstrating how the General Staff would work in practice, and even drafting legislation.

Miles, too, demonstrated an ability to persuade a Senate committee when his testimony almost single-handedly killed the general staff bill in March 1902. Yet his professional cretinism, his disdain for civilian control, and his inability to foster lasting professional relationships eventually led to his disgrace.

Trust and Civil-Military Relations

In his Annual Report for 1903, Root generously gave credit to his assistant, by this time Brigadier General Carter,

> for the exceptional ability and untiring industry which he has contributed to the work of devising, bringing about, and putting into operation the General Staff law. He brought thorough and patient historical research and wide experience, both in the line and the staff, to the aid of long-continued, anxious, and concentrated thought upon the problem of improving military administration, and if the new system shall prove to be an improvement the gain to the country will have been largely due to him.[58]

It was a fitting and public tribute to a military professional. Carter returned the compliment in his own narrative, written years later:

I want to record my deep appreciation of the opportunity afforded me by the Secretary of War to present to him briefs for the Army during four years as I saw its needs. Elihu Root was known to me and the Army generally as one of the leading lawyers of the Nation, but when after four years we regretfully parted with him we knew the Army had been served by one of the really great statesmen of the century. He sacrificed the opportunity to be Vice President and President in order to carry to completion the work he had undertaken as Secretary of War.[59] Without his kindly, but firm, insistence upon a reform of our military system, the Army would have carried on in the World War under the same disadvantages and discouragements that confronted it in 1898.

It was a source of genuine satisfaction to me to make researches and prepare the technical details of bills for the reorganization of our Army, and its system of administration and command under Secretary Root's supervision. I never lost sight for a moment of the fact that whatever of success should be attained would be due to the courageous and aggressive backing which the Secretary gave always when once the course had been charted. It is certain that no Army officer, or group of officers, could have overcome the opposition to any change in the War Department system had not the Secretary safeguarded the bill for a General Staff Corps at every step of its progress through Congress.[60]

Two professionals were paying tribute to one another. Two progressives were lauding each other's devotion to the cause of government efficiency and reform. Especially noteworthy was Carter's recognition that neither he nor all the "young Turks" in the Army could have overcome the conservative power of Miles and the "old bulls" without the power, courage, and persistence of their civilian chief. Transformation of the Army had required a reformation of civil-military relations in the service. Ironically, that change in civil-military relations had demanded a strong civil-military partnership. At the right moment in history, Root and Carter both determined what kind of professional they each wished to be, and went on to perform their duties "upon the call of the greatest of all our clients, the Government of our country." They produced a professional partnership of the first order.

There are problems with civil-military relations today, but the problems are not insoluble. Professional soldiers hold a sacred trust in behalf of the nation, ensuring its security and the liberties of its people within the framework of the Constitution. A fundamental aspect of that responsibility is helping to manage the civil-military relationship. But soldiers cannot discharge that duty without active and informed assistance from their clients. Unlike other professions—medicine, law, the clergy— the military does not minister to individuals. Instead, the professional military's client is society in the aggregate. Thus civilian leaders stand for society as a whole in the civil-military relationship, acting as both clients and superiors to the professional military. They are jointly responsible with the professional military for the health and maintenance of the civil-military relationship, for upholding the societal and functional imperatives. Society demands of its military readiness, obedience, and professional excellence. The electorate should insist as well that its representatives, that is, the civilian leadership of the military, be knowledgeable, objective, and nonpartisan in providing for the common defense. Indeed, it ought to demand the sort of professional maturity and atmosphere of trust that Elihu Root brought to office over a century ago.

Years after Root and Carter had both departed the War Department, General Carter said in a note of appreciation to his old chief: "It was only because you trusted me that I was able to do my best work."[61] Americans must demand of civilian and military leaders alike the professional maturity and judgment that leads to such mutual trust, and the strategic leaders of the Army profession must develop the political-cultural expertise necessary to provide it.

Notes

1. Secretary of War Henry Stimson later recounted this conversation, told in Root's own words: "Address by Col. Henry L. Stimson," in *Elihu Root: Addresses Made in His Honor* (New York: The Century Club, 1937), 24-25. See also Philip C. Jessup, *Elihu Root* (New York: Dodd, Mead, & Co., 1938), 215; Walter Millis, *Arms and Men: A Study of American Military History* (New York: G.P. Putnam's Sons, 1956), 173.

2. Warren Zimmerman, *First Great Triumph: How Five Americans Made Their Country a World Power* (New York: Farrar, Straus and Giroux, 2002), 124-147. The period of the Progressive Era is a topic of debate, but it began roughly with the turn of the 19th century and failed to survive the First World War.

3. Robert H. Wiebe, *The Search for Order, 1877-1920* (New York: Hill and Wang, 1967), 111-117; Zimmerman, 128.

4. Samuel P. Huntington, *The Soldier and the State: The Theory and Politics of Civil-Military Relations* (Cambridge, MA: The Belknap Press of the Harvard University Press, 1957), 222-69; John M. Gates, "The Alleged Isolation of US Army Officers in the Late 19th Century," *Parameters* 10, no. 3 (September 1980): 32-45; Peter Karsten, "Armed Progressives: The Military Organizes for the American Century," in *Building the Organizational Society: Essays on Associational Activities in Modern America,* ed. Jerry Israel (New York: The Free Press, 1972), 197-232.

5. Wiebe, 131-132.

6. Karsten, 216-18. The best treatment of this period in the history of the officer corps is a chapter entitled "Promotion's Very Slow" in Edward M. Coffman, *The Old Army: A Portrait of the American Army in Peacetime, 1784-1898* (New York: Oxford University Press, 1986), 215-86.

7. Karsten, 217-18.

8. Upton was driven to suicide in 1881 by the effects of what was likely a brain tumor—excruciating headaches, seizures, and depression. His manuscript was finally published, largely at the behest of our protagonists, Root and Carter, in 1904. Russell F. Weigley, *History of the United States Army* (New York: Macmillan, 1967), 277. Among the recommendations contained in his *The Armies of Asia and Europe* was one advocating creation of "a war academy to educate officers in the art of war, and to prepare them for the staff and to hold high command." See George S. Pappas, *Prudens Futuri: The US Army War College, 1901-1967* (Carlisle Barracks, PA: Alumni Association of the US Army War College, 1967), 8.

9. Karsten, 219-21; Weigley, 275-81.

10. *Register of Graduates and Former Cadets of the United States Military Academy* (West Point, NY: Association of Graduates, 2000), 4-50; Jerry K. Sweeney, ed., *A Handbook of American Military History: From the Revolutionary War to the Present* (Boulder, CO: Westview Press, 1996), 118; Jessup, 225-26.

11. Allan R. Millett and Peter Maslowski, *For the Common Defense: A Military History of the United States of America,* Revised and Expanded (New York: The Free Press, 1994), 326; Clayton E. Kahan "Dodge Commission or Political Dodge?: The Dodge Commission and

Military Reform" (unpublished M.A. thesis, University of Houston, July 2003), concludes that the commission was a political whitewash that had no impact on the reforms that followed.

12. Millett and Maslowski, 316-17.

13. Ibid., 317-18.

14. Ibid., 318-19.

15. Jessup, 220-22.

16. Robert M. Utley, *Frontier Regulars: The United States Army and the Indian, 1866-1891* (Lincoln: University of Nebraska Press, 1973), 288-90, 369-96; Robert Wooster, *Nelson A. Miles and the Twilight of the Frontier Army* (Lincoln: University of Nebraska Press, 1993), passim, 1-37, 265-74.

17. Jessup, 222. Teddy Roosevelt predicted trouble between Miles and Root: "I very much fear that he will find difficulty in getting on with Miles. As you know, Miles unfortunately has the Presidential bee in his bonnet." Jessup, 226; Millett and Maslowski, 280, 286.

18. Jessup, 225-26.

19. William Harding Carter, "Creation of the American General Staff," 68th Congress, 1st Session, Senate Docs. II (serial 8254), no. 119, 1924, 1-2; Weigley, 314-15; Jessup, 223-24, 242-43.

20. Carter, 16-21; Weigley, 192-194; Jessup, 241-42; William H. Carter, *The American Army* (Indianapolis, IN: Bobbs-Merrill, 1915), 170-204.

21. Carter, *The American Army*, 170-183.

22. Carter, "Creation of the American General Staff," 2-5.

23. Report of the Secretary of War, *Annual Reports of the War Department* (Washington, DC: GPO, 1899), 1: 45-56.

24. Elihu Root, "Extract from the Report of the Secretary of War for 1899" in *The Military and Colonial Policy of the United States*, eds. Robert Bacon and James B. Scott (Cambridge, MA: Harvard University Press, 1916), 350-59; Jessup, 253.

25. Root, 359-63.

26. Jessup, 252-53.

27. Carter, "Creation of the American General Staff," 3-14. The order creating the War College also redesignated the Infantry and Cavalry School at Fort Leavenworth as the General Service and Staff College.

28. Carter, "Creation of the American General Staff," 3-49: Jessup, 260.

29. Jessup, 254-56.

30. Carter, "Creation of the American General Staff," 15-29.

31. Jessup, 243-51; Carter, "Creation of the American General Staff," 31-43.

32. Carter, "Creation of the American General Staff," 31; Wooster, 243.

33. Carter, "Creation of the American General Staff," 35; Jessup, 259-60.

34. Carter, "Creation of the American General Staff," 35-36; Jessup, 261.

35. Jessup, 261; Carter, "Creation of the American General Staff," 35-43.

36. Jessup, 261; Carter, "Creation of the American General Staff," 43-50.

37. Jessup, 261-62; Carter, "Creation of the American General Staff," 50.

38. Carter, "Creation of the American General Staff," 50-65.

39. Elihu Root, "Extract from the Report of the Secretary of War for 1903" in *The Military and Colonial Policy of the United States,* 429.

40. Richard Kohn is the dean of this school. His two most often cited works on the subject are "Out of Control: The Crisis in Civil Military Relations," *National Interest* 35 (Spring 1994), and "The Erosion of Civilian Control of the Military in the United States Today," *Naval War College Review* 55 (Summer 2002). Others include Michael Desch, *Civilian Control of the Military: The Changing Security Environment* (Baltimore, MD: Johns Hopkins University

Press, 1999); Peter D. Feaver and Richard Kohn, eds., *Soldiers and Civilians: The Civil-Military Gap and American National Security* (Cambridge, MA: MIT Press, 2001); Russell F. Weigley, "The American Military and the Principle of Civilian Control from McClellan to Powell," *Journal of Military History* 57 (1993): 27-59; Weigley, "The American Civil-Military Cultural Gap: A Historical Perspective, Colonial Times to the Present" in *Soldiers and Civilians*; Gregory D. Foster, "Failed Expectations: The Crisis of Civil-Military Relations in America," *The Brookings Review* (Fall 1997), 46-48; Andrew J. Bacevich, "Discord Still: Clinton and the Military," Washington *Post*, 3 January 1999, C 1. For other views of the argument, see Richard K. Betts, *Soldiers, Statesmen, and the Cold War Crises*, Morningside Edition (New York, NY: Columbia Univ. Press, 1991), passim; and Lloyd J. Matthews, *The Political-Military Rivalry for Operational Control in U.S. Military Actions: A Soldier's Perspective* (Carlisle Barracks, PA: U.S. Army War College, SSI, 1998), 26-34.

41. Marybeth Peterson Ulrich, "Infusing Civil-Military Relations Norms in the Officer Corps," in *The Future of the Army Profession*, project directors Don M. Snider and Gayle L. Watkins, ed. Lloyd J. Matthews (Boston, MA: McGraw-Hill Primis Custom Publishing, 2002), 245-70; See also chap. 30 of the present book for an updated version of this chapter. With a charter from the Army Chief of Staff, Wong and his team reviewed the extant literature on strategic leadership with an eye toward helping the Army to develop future strategic leaders and to assist aspiring strategic leaders in their own self-assessment. These metacompetencies include identity, mental agility, world-class warrior, cross-cultural savvy, interpersonal maturity, and professional astuteness. Leonard Wong, Stephen Gerras, William Kidd, Robert Pricone, and Richard Swengos, "Strategic Leadership Competencies," unpublished study, Strategic Studies Institute, Carlisle Barracks, PA, September 2003.

42. This paragraph draws upon the "identity" metacompetency, which involves professional maturation beyond identifying one's strengths and weaknesses, to an "ability to gather self-feedback, to form accurate self-perceptions, and to change one's self-concept as appropriate." At the strategic level, identity "goes beyond personal contributions and shifts to serving as a catalyst for success by subordinates" and others in one's organization. Wong, et al., 5-6.

43. Wooster, 269-71. To be sure, Emory Upton's writings, elitist and militarist as they were, were not the perfect primers for military reorganization, but at the time they were probably the best extant stimuli for reform.

44. Wong et al., 8-10. These thoughts derive from the concepts of interpersonal maturity and professional astuteness.

45. Huntington, 2.

46. For a discussion of the influence of this idea on the military profession, see Eliot Cohen, *Supreme Command: Soldiers, Statesmen, and Leadership in Wartime* (New York: The Free Press, 2002), 225-48.

47. Carl von Clausewitz, *On War*, edited and translated by Michael Howard and Peter Paret. Introductory essays by Peter Paret, Michael Howard, and Bernard Brodie; with a commentary by Bernard Brodie. (Princeton, NJ: Princeton University Press, 1976), 75-89 and passim.

48. Clausewitz used a water metaphor to describe friction in war: "Action in war is like movement in a resistant element. Just as the simplest and most natural of movements, walking, cannot easily be performed in water, so in war it is difficult for normal efforts to achieve even moderate results. A genuine theorist is like a swimming teacher. . . ." Clausewitz, 120. For a treatment of the politico-military intersection in operational decision-making, see Matthews, passim.

49. Clausewitz, 607-08. Emphasis in the original.

50. Ulrich, 249-54.

51. Cohen, 208-24.

52. For a typical example of the genre, see John Hillen, "Must US Military Culture Reform?" *Parameters* 29, no. 3 (Autumn 1999): 9-23. Hillen describes American culture in the 1990s as "narcissistic, morally relativist, self-indulgent, hedonistic, consumerist, individualistic, victim-centered, nihilistic, and soft." Hillen, 18.

53. Sir John Hackett, *The Profession of Arms* (Washington, DC, 1986), 34. Originally delivered as the 1962 Lee Knowles Lectures at Trinity College, Cambridge.

54. An impediment to societal engagement seems to originate once again in the pervasiveness of another flaw in Samuel Huntington's thought. Huntington asserted that professional officers tend by ideology to divorce themselves from society. He argued that this separation is especially true in American society, which, he posited, is intrinsically liberal while the officer corps' worldview is naturally conservative. Huntington argued that officers' isolation from society was a necessary precondition for professionalism. That argument stemmed from a highly selective reading of history. In fact, contra Huntington, officers through American history have belonged to all political parties, have subscribed to various ideologies, and have hailed from all regions of the country. Officers fought on both sides of the Civil War. As noted above, the professionalization of which the Root reforms were a part resulted from the progressivism that young officers such as William Carter shared with civilian reformers across the country. Thus, American military officers have not been consistently conservative.

    Since the Vietnam War, and long after Huntington wrote, a confluence of trends has tended to make the modern officer corps more ideologically conservative than in the past. The end of the military draft, the beginning of the all-volunteer Army, a politicization of defense issues, the eviction of ROTC detachments from many college campuses, and indeed the influence of Huntington's thought itself, have abetted the self-selection of conservatives into the military. Many military conservatives have found Huntington's professional isolation argument congenial to their own views of society. Huntington, 59-79,143-62. See Kohn, "The Erosion of Civilian Control," 25-27, for a discussion of the politicization of the military.

55. Marybeth Peterson Ulrich discusses nonpartisanship and societal engagement in "Infusing Civil-Military Relations Norms in the Officer Corps," 256-66. Richard Kohn has suggested that officers should choose not to exercise their franchise in the effort to project nonpartisanship. Kohn, "The Erosion of Civilian Control," 27-29.

56. Wong et al., 8-9.

57. A special issue of *Military Review*, March-April 1999, entitled "The Army and Congress" provides several valuable perspectives on these relations. It is an excellent primer for anyone beginning to develop the political-cultural skills necessary for Army-congressional relations. See also Robert R. Ivany, "Soldiers and Legislators: A Common Mission," *Parameters* 21 (Spring 1991): 47-61.

58. Elihu Root, "Extract from the Report of the Secretary of War for 1903," in *The Military and Colonial Policy of the United States*, 431.

59. Largely because of Root's performance as secretary of war, McKinley was actively considering him for the ticket in 1900. Had he been elected vice president, then he, not Roosevelt, would have succeeded to the presidency upon McKinley's assassination and death the next year. Jessup, 230-39.

60. Carter, "Creation of the American General Staff," 62-63.

61. Jessup, 259.

About The Contributors

Deborah Avant is Associate Professor of Political Science and International Affairs at George Washington University, where she teaches courses on international security and civil-military relations. Her research has focused on civil-military relations, military change, and the relationship between politics and violence. She is the author of *Political Institutions and Military Change: Lessons From Peripheral Wars* (Cornell University Press, 1994) and many articles, the most recent of which include "From Mercenaries to Citizen Armies: Explaining Change in the Practice of War" in *International Organization* (2000), and "U.S. Military Attitudes Toward Post-Cold War Missions" in *Armed Forces and Society* (2000). Dr. Avant's book titled *The Market for Force*, which looks at the impact of privatizing security on democratic accountability, was published by Cambridge University Press in 2005.

Peter A. Baktis is a Chaplain (Major) presently serving as the Officer Task Analyst at the U.S. Army Chaplain Center and School. He holds a B.A. degree from Concordia College, a Master of Divinity degree from St. Vladimir's Orthodox Theological Seminary, and a Master of (Sacred) Theology degree from the General Theological Seminary in New York City. Chaplain Baktis is also a graduate of the Command and General Staff College. He has served in a series of chaplaincy assignments in the United States and Germany, as well as deployments to Iraq, Kuwait, Bosnia, and Kosovo. He also represents the Chaplain Corps as a member of the Operation Iraqi Freedom Study Group. Chaplain Baktis has published some 17 articles and reviews in theological journals and *The Chaplaincy*.

Charles Barry is a consultant on defense policy and management information systems in Washington, DC. He heads his own consulting firm and is also affiliated with the Center for Technology and National Security Policy at the National Defense University. Mr. Barry has been a military strategist for more than 20 years and is considered an authority on strategy relating to transatlantic relations. His books include *The Search for Peace in Europe (1993)*, *Security Architecture for Europe (1995)*, and *Reforging the Trans-Atlantic Relationship (1996)*.

Paul T. Bartone received his Ph.D. from the University of Chicago in 1984 in psychology and human development. Following graduate studies, he was commissioned in the Army as a research psychologist, and has served on active duty since. He has conducted numerous field studies on psychosocial stress, health, and adaptation among military personnel and their families during deployments ranging from the Gulf War through Bosnia, as well as a number of peacetime disaster situations. He is now at the U.S. Military Academy where he teaches in the Department of Behavioral Sciences and Leadership and serves as Director of the Leader Development Research Center. He is currently coordinator of the European Research Group on Military and Society (ERGOMAS) Working Group on Morale, Cohesion, and Leadership. Recent publications include the chapter "Hardiness as a Resiliency Resource under High Stress Conditions" in *Post-Traumatic Psychological Stress: Individual, Group, and Organizational Perspectives on Resilience and Growth*; and "Factors Influencing Small Unit Cohesion in Norwegian Navy Officer Cadets" in *Military Psychology*.

James A. Blackwell, a graduate of the U.S. Military Academy (1974), is Corporate Vice President of Science Applications International Corporation, where he is the Director of the Strategic Assessment Center. The Center conducts studies and analyses on the long-range future of warfare. He was the principal investigator for the Director, Net Assessment, Office of the Secretary of Defense, in producing the study titled "The Strategic Meeting Engagement: Experimentation and Transforming the U.S. Military." He is also the author of *On Brave Old Army Team: The Cheating Scandal That Rocked the Nation, West Point 1951* (Presidio Press, 1996). Dr. Blackwell's research interests are the operational level of war, doctrine, technology, and the defense industrial base. Most recently, Dr. Blackwell served as Executive Director of the Independent Panel (the "Schlesinger Panel") that investigated DoD Detention Operations in Iraq at Abu Ghraib.

Chris Bourg is Associate Director for Communications for the Stanford University Libraries and Academic Information Resources. She has a Ph.D. in sociology from Stanford University and served ten years as an active duty Army officer. Her research interests include issues of gender and sexuality in the military.

Kevin Brancato is currently writing his Ph.D. dissertation in economics at George Mason University. He has a B.A. in mathematics and statistics from Columbia University. He has worked as an associate cost analyst with the RAND Corporation and before that as a research associate at the Federal Reserve Bank of New York. He specializes in cost-benefit analysis, regression analysis, data visualization, macro-econometric modeling, and system dynamics. A list of publications is available at http://www.rand.org/Abstracts/ under Brancato, K.

John W. Brinsfield is a retired Chaplain (Colonel) serving as the U.S. Army Chaplain Corps Historian at the Army Chaplain School, Ft. Jackson, SC. He has a Master of Divinity degree from Yale Divinity School, a Ph.D. in church history from Emory University, and a D.Min. in ethics from Drew University.

He has been an instructor at the Army Chaplain School, in the Department of History of the U.S. Military Academy, and at the Army War College. During Operations Desert Shield and Desert Storm he served in the Army Central Command Headquarters in Riyadh, Saudi Arabia. Chaplain Brinsfield served two tours at Forces Command, the last as Deputy FORSCOM Chaplain from 1999 to 2002. After the attacks on the Pentagon and World Trade Center on 11 September 2001, Chaplain Brinsfield interviewed more than 60 chaplains at both sites who assisted in the rescue/recovery operations. These interviews became the basis for two chapters in the most recent Chaplain Corps history, *The Gunhus Years, 1999-2003*. He is the author or co-author of three books, including *Religion and Politics in Colonial South Carolina; Encouraging Faith, Supporting Soldiers: A History of the Army Chaplain Corps, 1975-1995;* and *Faith in the Fight: Civil War Chaplains.*

Craig Bullis is currently Professor of Behavioral Sciences at the Army War College. He recently retired as a lieutenant colonel in the field artillery. He earlier served as a professor in the Department of Behavioral Sciences and Leadership at USMA. Recent publications include "Mapping the Route of Leadership Education: Caution Ahead," *Parameters* (Autumn 2004) (co-author); "Essentials of Culture Change: Lessons Learned the Hard Way," *Consulting Psychologist Journal* (2003) (co-author); and "Developing the Professional Army Officer: Implications for Organizational Leaders," *Military Review* (May/June 2003). He has a Ph.D. in management from Texas Tech University.

James Burk is a Professor of Sociology at Texas A&M University. He previously taught at McGill University and the University of Chicago, where he earned his master's and Ph.D. degrees. He has served as editor of *Armed Forces and Society*, and presently is Chair-Elect of the Peace, War, and Social Conflict Section of the American Sociological Association. He also sits on the executive council of the Inter-University Seminar on Armed Forces and Society, and is a member of the board of editors of *Armed Forces and Society*. A student of political sociology, he has published numerous articles on problems of democratic renewal with an emphasis on civil-military relations and political culture. His latest work is "The Military's Presence in American Society, 1950-2000," in *The Military Profession and American Society in Transition to the 21st Century*, eds. Peter D. Feaver, Richard H. Kohn, and Lindsay Cohn (MIT Press).

Randi C. Cohen, Ph.D., is the founder of Beetrix LLC, a research and consulting firm in Boston. She works with diverse clients, from Fortune 500 companies to nonprofit organizations, helping them gain fuller insights into their constituents. Employing advanced qualitative methodologies and sociological frameworks, her studies have ranged from evaluations of financial services to assessments of military actions. Dr. Cohen has been a visiting scholar at the School of Management of Boston College, and has taught marketing in Boston University's MBA program.

Ruth Collins, Colonel, U.S. Army Retired, has served for nearly 30 years in a variety of personnel management, leadership, and educational assignments. She is currently a faculty instructor in the Department of Distance Education of the Army War College, and for the previous four years was a faculty instructor in the Department of Command, Leadership, and Management, occupying the George C. Marshall Chair of Military Studies. Recent publications include "Personnel Transformation: The Dynamics of Change," *Army AL&T Magazine* (July-August 2002); and "The Road to Mentoring: Paved with Good Intentions," *Parameters* (Autumn 2002) (co-author). Colonel Collins is pursuing her doctoral degree in adult education from Pennsylvania State University.

Martin L. Cook, Ph.D., is Professor of Philosophy and Deputy Department Head at the U.S. Air Force Academy. Prior to his arrival in Colorado Springs, he was the Elihu Root Professor of Military Studies and Professor of Ethics, Department of Command, Leadership, and Management, Army War College. He previously was a tenured member of the faculty at Santa Clara University, and has taught at the College of William and Mary, among other institutions. His most recent publications include "Immaculate War: Constraints on Humanitarian Intervention" in *Ethics and International Affairs* (2000); "Why Serve the State? Moral Foundations of Military Officership" in *The Leader's Imperative: Ethics, Integrity, and Responsibility*, ed. J. Carl Ficarrotta (Purdue University Press, 2001); and "Two Roads Diverged, and We Took the One Less Traveled: Just Recourse to War and the Kosovo Intervention" in *Kosovo: Contending Voices on the Balkan Intervention*, ed. William Buckley (Eerdmans, 2000).

G. F. Deimel is an armor officer currently serving as a career manager and assignments officer for Armor Branch in the U.S. Army's Human Resources Command. His previous assignments include multiple division-level staff positions and commander of armored cavalry and headquarters troops. Captain Deimel earned a B. S. degree with a major in international and strategic history from the U.S. Military Academy and is currently pursuing a master's degree in international security studies from Georgetown University. He is a past recipient of the Department of the Army MacArthur Leadership Award.

Antulio J. Echevarria II is the Director of Research in the Strategic Studies Institute at the Army War College, having retired at the rank of lieutenant colonel in May 2004. He holds M.A. and Ph.D. degrees in history from Princeton University. He is the author of *After Clausewitz: German Military Thinkers before the Great War* (University Press of Kansas, 2001). Dr. Echevarria has also published articles in *The Journal of Strategic Studies, Journal of Military History, War in History, War & Society, Naval War College Review, Parameters, Joint Force Quarterly, Royal United Services Institute, Military Review, Airpower Journal, Marine Corps Gazette,* and *Military History Quarterly*.

Morten G. Ender earned his M.A. and Ph.D. from the University of Maryland. He is currently the Sociology Program Director and Associate Professor of

Sociology in the Department of Behavioral Sciences and Leadership at the U.S. Military Academy where he teaches Sociological Theory, Cinematic Images of War and the Military, and Armed Forces and Society. Professor Ender is the author of *Military Brats and Other Global Nomads: Growing Up in Organization Families* (Greenwood, 2002). His co-authored book, *Inequalities: Readings in Diversity and Social Life*, is forthcoming. Most recently, he co-authored the chapter titled "Evolution of Sociology at West Point, 1963-2001" appearing in *West Point: Two Centuries and Beyond*, ed. Lance Betros (McWhiney Foundation, 2004).

George B. Forsythe is a colonel in the U.S. Army and Professor and Vice Dean for Education at the U.S. Military Academy. A 1970 graduate of the Academy, he holds an M.A.C.T. (social psychology) and Ph.D. (higher education) from the University of North Carolina at Chapel Hill. Colonel Forsythe has served in command and staff positions in Europe and Korea, and recently returned from Afghanistan and Iraq where he assisted with the establishment of national military academies in both countries. His current research interests are in leader development, officer education, and program assessment; he has published numerous books, book chapters, and journal articles on these topics. Most recently, he co-authored the chapter titled "The Evolving USMA Academic Curriculum, 1952-2002" appearing in *West Point: Two Centuries and Beyond*, ed. Lance Betros (McWhiney Foundation, 2004).

Frederick M. Franks, Jr., General, U.S. Army Retired, is a Visiting Scholar in the William E. Simon Center for the Study of the Professional Military Ethic at West Point, and works with the Army as a senior observer in the Battle Command Training Program for senior commanders and staffs. He also teaches senior level battle command in seminars at military schools in the United States and United Kingdom. He is a graduate of the Military Academy, holds two master's degrees from Columbia University, and is a graduate of the National War College. He served in the Vietnam War in 1969-70, where he was twice wounded, and later commanded VII Corps during Operations Desert Shield/Desert Storm in the Gulf War. He completed 35-plus years of military service in 1995 as commander of the U.S. Army Training and Doctrine Command. General Franks has published in magazines and journals on battle command and most recently collaborated with Tom Clancy on the book, *Into the Storm: A Study in Command*, published in 1997.

Remi Hajjar is the Deputy Sociology Program Leader, Department of Behavioral Sciences and Leadership, U.S. Military Academy. He holds an M.A. degree in sociology from Northwestern University, and has served on active duty for 11 years. He is the author of "McDonaldization of Leadership" in *Special Readings, PL300: Military Leadership* (course text). Major Hajjar presented a provisional study titled, "Is Iraq a Class War?" at the IUS Conference in October 2004. He is a 1993 graduate of the Military Academy.

Margaret C. Harrell (Ph.D., Cultural Anthropology, University of Virginia) is a senior social scientist at the RAND Corporation and the associate director of the Forces and Resources Policy Center in the RAND National Defense Research Institute. Her expertise is in military manpower and personnel systems; military families; military quality of life; system dynamics simulation modeling; and qualitative research methods. Dr. Harrell also has an M.S. in systems analysis from George Washington University; her research reflects a mixture of qualitative and quantitative expertise. She has recently led or co-led projects addressing future officer career management, the management of general and flag officers, joint officer management, the management of Special Operations Forces, military spouse employment, and the feasibility and advisability of sabbatical leaves for officers. She also teaches a course on qualitative research methods for RAND researchers. A list of publications is available at http://www.rand.org/Abstracts/ under Harrell, M.

Richard D. Hooker is Commander, XVIII Airborne Corps Combat Support Brigade, having deployed to Iraq in January 2005. Colonel Hooker's previous assignment was as Joint Planner in the Office of the Chief of Staff at the Department of the Army. He earlier commanded 2nd Battalion, 505th Infantry, 82nd Airborne Division. Among other assignments, he served as Special Assistant to the Chairman, Joint Chiefs of Staff. Colonel Hooker earned a Ph.D. in international relations from the University of Virginia, and has written numerous articles for professional military journals. He edited and was co-author of *Maneuver Warfare: An Anthology* (Presidio Press, 1994). His second book, *By Their Deeds Alone: Battle Studies for the 21st Century*, was published in 2004.

David H. Huntoon, Jr., is a U.S. Army major general, serving as Commandant of the Army War College. His previous assignment was as Director of Strategy, Plans, and Policy, Army G3, the Pentagon. He is a 1973 graduate of the Military Academy and subsequently earned an M.A. degree in international relations from Georgetown. He is a graduate of the U.S. Army Command and General Staff College, from whose Advanced Military Studies program he received a master's degree in military arts and sciences. General Huntoon later served as Deputy Commandant at the College. He was an Army War College Fellow at the Hoover Institute, Stanford University, in 1994-95. An infantryman, he has served in command and staff assignments in Germany and Korea, and commanded the 3rd Infantry Regiment (The Old Guard) at Ft. Myer, VA. While serving in the Plans Directorate of XVIII Airborne Corps at Ft. Bragg, NC, he was the Senior War Plans Officer (Operation Just Cause) and Deputy Director of Plans (Operations Desert Shield and Desert Storm).

T. Owen Jacobs presently occupies the Leo Cherne Distinguished Visiting Professor of Behavioral Science Chair at the Industrial College of the Armed Forces, National Defense University. Previously he was Chief of the Strategic Leadership Technical Area of the Army Research Institute. He received B.A. and M.A. degrees from Vanderbilt University and a Ph.D. from the University of Pittsburgh. His latest publication was "Trust in the Military Profession" in *The Future of the Army Profession* (McGraw-Hill, 2002) (co-author).

Douglas V. Johnson II is a research professor at the U.S. Army War College's Strategic Studies Institute, where he has served since 1985. A 1963 graduate of the Military Academy, he served two tours each in Germany and Vietnam, and took his master's degree in history at the University of Michigan and Ph.D. in history at Temple University. He has taught history of the military art at West Point and was one of the founding faculty of the School of Advanced Military Studies at Ft. Leavenworth. He has taught the USAWC Army After Next (now Transforming the Army) Special Program seminar for the past six years. During his 16 years at the War College, he supervised the revision of Field Manual 100-1 (now FM 1), *The Army*, in 1986, 1991, 1994, and 2001. His chapter in the present book, co-authored with Leonard Wong, stems from his long association with that field manual and his history background. His fields of study are military history (specializing in the AEF in WW I), future studies, civil-military relations, national security strategy, and technology.

Thomas A. Kolditz is a colonel in the Army and currently Professor and Head of the Department of Behavioral Sciences and Leadership at the Military Academy. He holds a B.A. degree with double major in psychology and sociology from Vanderbilt University; M.A. and Ph.D. degrees in social psychology from the University of Missouri; M.M.A.S from the School of Advanced Military Studies; and M.A. in strategic studies from the Army War College. Colonel Kolditz's research and teaching activities span applied social psychology and leadership development, to include ethnographic field research examining cohesion during the recent hostilities in Iraq. Publications include *Why They Fight: Combat Motivation in the Iraq War* (Strategic Studies Institute Monograph, 2003) (co-author); and "Evolution of Sociology at West Point, 1963-2001" in *West Point: Two Centuries and Beyond*, ed. Lance Betros (McWhiney Foundation, 2004) (co-author).

Richard Lacquement, a lieutenant colonel in the Army, is a professor of strategy and policy at the U.S. Naval War College. He is a field artillery officer with combat experience during Operation Desert Storm and Operation Iraqi Freedom. He is also a strategic plans and policy specialist and was an assistant professor in the U.S. Military Academy's Department of Social Sciences, where he taught American Politics, International Relations, and International Organizations. He is the author of *Shaping American Military Capabilities after the Cold War* (Praeger, 2003). Lieutenant Colonel Lacquement earned a Ph.D. in public policy from Princeton University.

Philip Lewis is a professor of psychology at Auburn University where he directs the graduate program in Industrial and Organizational Psychology and teaches undergraduate and graduate courses on personality, adolescent and adult development, and managerial development. His research on the conceptual development of leaders has been supported by the U.S. Army Research Institute for the Behavioral and Social Sciences and the National Research Council. In 1993-94 he was the Distinguished Visiting Professor at West Point in the Department of Behavioral Sciences and Leadership. While at West Point he helped initiate a longitudinal study of the conceptual development of cadets in the class of 1998.

James Marshall is a U.S. Congressman from Georgia, serving on the House Armed Services Committee. In 1968, he interrupted his education at Princeton to enlist in the Army and volunteer for service in Vietnam, where he was an Airborne-Ranger-qualified reconnaissance platoon sergeant. He was wounded and decorated for heroism in ground combat. After his tour, he returned to Princeton and completed his baccalaureate degree, following which he earned a law degree from Boston University. He later joined the faculty of the Mercer University Law School. Prior to entering Congress, he was the mayor of Macon, Georgia, in which position he became well known for his successful efforts to advance the cause of race relations.

Lloyd J. Matthews is a retired Army colonel. He received the B.S. degree from the U.S. Military Academy, M.A. from Harvard University, and Ph.D. from the University of Virginia, and is a graduate of the Army War College and Armed Forces Staff College. His military assignments included command at platoon, company, and battalion levels; advisory duty in the Vietnam War; editorship of *Parameters*, the Army War College quarterly; and an English professorship and the associate deanship at the U.S. Military Academy. Following retirement from the Army, he served as a project manager in Saudi Arabia and later Turkey. Colonel Matthews has published well over 100 articles, features, reviews, monographs, and editions on professional topics, including the article "Is the Military Profession Legitimate?" in the January 1994 issue of *ARMY*. He was editor of the 1st edition of *The Future of the Army Profession* (McGraw-Hill, 2002). Most recently, Colonel Matthews served on the editorial staff for the August 2004 *Final Report of the Independent Panel to Review DoD Detention Operations* [at Abu Ghraib] ("Schlesinger Panel Report").

John Mark Mattox is the Chief of the Nuclear Policy and Surety Branch of the U.S. European Command Headquarters. He holds a B.A. degree from Brigham Young University, a Master of Military Arts and Science degree from the Army Command and General Staff College, and M.A. and Ph.D. degrees from Indiana University. Lieutenant Colonel Mattox earlier served in such positions as nuclear policy planner at Supreme Headquarters Allied Powers Europe; acting operations officer (S-3) of an air assault field artillery battalion of the 101st Airborne Division during the 1991 Gulf War; commander of an air assault field artillery battery; and assistant professor of English at the Military Academy. He is also an adjunct associate professor of philosophy with the University of Maryland and has been a regular lecturer at the NATO School in Oberammergau, Germany. He has published articles on theoretical linguistics, military tactics, nuclear policy, just war theory, and ethics.

Michael J. Meese, a colonel in the Army, is currently assigned as Professor and Deputy Head of the Department of Social Sciences at West Point. Previous to that he was the U.S. Military Academy Fellow at the National War College where he taught courses in national strategy, military policy, and bureaucratic politics. In 2003, he deployed as special adviser on political, economic, and military issues to Maj. Gen. David Petraeus, Commander, 101st Airborne Division (Air Assault), in Mosul, Iraq. He has also served as Executive Officer to the Assistant Chief of Staff (Operations) in Bosnia-Herzegovina during the conduct of peacekeeping and counterterrorism operations. He is a 1981 graduate of West Point and holds Ph.D., M.P.A., and M.A. degrees from the Woodrow Wilson School of Public and International Affairs at Princeton University.

Sean Morgan, a major in the Army, is an assistant professor of economics in the Department of Social Sciences at the U.S. Military Academy. He was recently Special Staff Officer to Maj. Gen. Raymond Odierno, Commanding General, 4th Infantry Division, in Kirkuk, Iraq. There he planned and executed economic development projects for postwar reconstruction efforts, drawing largely on his earlier research into the feasibility of creating an accredited private organization to perform peacekeeping and nation-building activities on behalf of the United Nations and other international political organizations. Major Morgan is a 1992 graduate of West Point and earned an MBA from Harvard.

Matthew Moten is an associate professor and Chief of the Military History Division, Department of History, U.S. Military Academy. Colonel Moten holds a Ph.D. from Rice University and is author of *The Delafield Commission and the American Military Profession* (Texas A&M Press, 2000). He was commissioned in armor from USMA in 1982. Prior to his West Point assignment, he served on the Army Staff as a speechwriter and then legislative advisor to the Chief of Staff, U.S. Army. He deployed to Iraq on temporary duty in January 2005.

John Nagl is Operations Officer, 1st Battalion, 34th Armor, Fort Riley, Kansas. He received a B.S. degree from the U.S. Military Academy plus M.Phil. and D.Phil. degrees from Oxford University and an MMAS from the Army Command and General Staff College. Lieutenant Colonel Nagl has served in various command and staff positions in the continental United States, Southwest Asia, and Germany. He taught international relations and national security studies at USMA. He is the author of *Learning to Eat Soup with a Knife: Counterinsurgency Lessons from Malaya and Vietnam* (Praeger, 2002).

Suzanne C. Nielsen, a major in the Army, is currently serving in the 501st Military Intelligence Brigade in the Republic of Korea. She received her Ph.D. from Harvard University. Her dissertation, "Preparing for War: The Dynamics of Peacetime Military Reform," won the American Political Science Association's Lasswell Award for the best dissertation completed in the field of public policy in 2002 and 2003. Prior to her assignment to Korea in 2002, she taught international relations as a faculty member in the Social

Sciences Department at West Point. Her most recent publication was a co-authored article titled "Teaching Strategy and Security in Cyberspace: An Interdisciplinary Approach," which appeared in *International Studies Perspectives* in May 2003.

Dallas Owens joined the Strategic Studies Institute in July 2003 after a 27-year Army career. His recent military assignment venues include the Army War College, Army Headquarters Operations Center, and Logistics Directorate (J-4), Joint Staff. He served as a Port Operator during Operations Desert Shield/Desert Storm and as an infantryman in Vietnam. He is the author of *AC/RC Integration: Today's Success and Transformation's Challenge* (2001). He holds degrees in sociology from the University of North Carolina, Charlotte (B.A.), Utah State University (M.S.), and the University of Tennessee (Ph.D.), and has served on the faculty of Clemson University, North Carolina State University, University of Virginia, and University of Colorado.

Christopher R. Paparone, an Army colonel, is assigned to the J3/4 Directorate of U.S. Joint Forces Command as the Deputy Director for Logistics and Engineering. Previous to that assignment he was Director of Public Administration Studies in the Department of Command, Leadership, and Management of the Army War College. During his 27 years of service, he has served in various command and staff positions in the continental United States, Panama, Saudi Arabia, Bosnia, and Germany. Colonel Paparone has published frequently in *Army Logistician* and *Military Review*, his latest being an article titled "Deconstructing Army Leadership" in *Military Review*. He has a Ph.D. in public administration from the Pennsylvania State University.

Jeffrey Peterson is a Doctoral Fellow at the RAND Graduate School in preparation for service as an Academy Professor in the Department of Social Sciences of the Military Academy. An armor officer, he has served in a variety of operational assignments, the most recent as Squadron Executive Officer for 2/3 ACR at Ft. Carson, Colorado. Upon completion of his doctoral studies at RAND, Lieutenant Colonel Peterson will command an armor battalion before returning to USMA. He served in Iraq during Operation Desert Storm, in Korea as the S-3 for 1-72 AR, and at Guantanamo Bay for humanitarian operations. He has contributed to various RAND publications concerning military leader development for the contemporary operating environment, the applications of networked capabilities in low-intensity contingency operations, and the effects of personnel stabilization on unit performance.

Tony Pfaff is a Middle East/North Africa Foreign Area Officer whose assignments include service with the Joint Intelligence Directorate (J2), the United Nations Iraq-Kuwait Observer Mission, and the faculty of the Military Academy, where he taught philosophy. Lieutenant Colonel Pfaff holds a bachelor's degree in economics and philosophy from Washington and Lee University and a master's degree in philosophy from Stanford University, where he was a graduate fellow at the Stanford Center for Conflict and Negotiation. He has written numerous articles on ethics and most recently served as the military ethics consultant for the Schlesinger Panel reviewing Department of Defense detention procedures. He deployed for Operations Desert Shield/Storm with the 82nd Airborne Division and for Operation Able Sentry with the 1st Armored Division.

George Reed has served for over 24 years in a wide variety of Army assignments including law enforcement, combat support, corrections, and investigations. In 2001 he joined the faculty of the Army War College, Department of Command, Leadership, and Management, where he currently serves as the Director of Command and Leadership Studies. Colonel Reed has presented academic papers on such topics as "Strategic Leader Development: Training for Certainty, Educating for Uncertainty" and "Developing Strategic Leaders and Organizational Transformation." He holds a Ph.D. in public policy analysis from St. Louis University.

Mike Sanders earned his Ph.D. in experimental psychology (human factors) from Texas Tech University in 1973. He has held the position of Ft. Bragg Office Chief, U.S. Army Research Institute, since 1993. He has over 30 years of experience in recruiting, assessing, selecting, training, and developing military aviators and Special Operations Forces personnel. As adjunct professor in the Psychology Department of North Carolina State University, Dr. Sanders works with professors and graduate students on research and development in support of the U.S. Special Operations Command.

Nadia Schadlow is a senior program officer at the Smith Richardson Foundation, where she focuses on the development of projects on security and foreign policy issues central to the strategic interests of the United States. Ms. Schadlow is currently a Ph.D. candidate at the Johns Hopkins University's Nitze School of Advanced International Studies. Her dissertation deals with the U.S. Army's experiences in the conduct of military government. Previously, Ms. Schadlow served as a career civil servant in the Office of the Secretary of Defense.

Peter Schirmer is a management systems analyst for RAND whose research activities are in the areas of military officer career management, military personnel systems, and Army transformation. Before joining RAND, he spent five years working on state-level public policy issues and later conducted industry research for investment banking. He has an MBA from Georgetown University and a master's degree in public policy from the University of Michigan. A list of publications is available at http://www.rand.org/Abstracts/ under Schirmer, P.

Mady Wechsler Segal, Ph.D., is Professor of Sociology, Distinguished Scholar, teacher, and Associate Director of the Research Center on Military Organization at the University of Maryland. A prolific writer, she has focused on women in the military and military families in her recent research.

Don M. Snider, Ph.D., was appointed to the civilian faculty of the U.S. Military Academy in 1998. This followed a 28-year military career in the Army, five years in Washington, DC, as analyst and director of political-military research at the Center for Strategic and International Studies, and three years as the Olin Professor of National Security Studies at West Point. He was co-project director of a privately funded, two-year research effort, published under the title, *The Future of the Army Profession* (McGraw-Hill, 2002). Among his most important early publications was a two-part series appearing in the September and December 1987 issues of *Parameters,* constituting at that time the definitive public explication of the 1986 Goldwater-Nichols legislation. Other publications include "The Civil-Military Gap and Professional Military Education at the Pre-commissioning Level" in *Armed Forces and Society*, Winter 2001 (co-author); and "The Future of Army Professionalism: The Need for Renewal and Redefinition" in *Parameters*, August 2000 (co-author). Most recently he was co-author of the article "Christian Citizenship and American Empire" in the fall 2003 issue of *Faith and International Affairs.*

Scott A. Snook is a retired Army colonel, serving as Academy Professor in the Department of Behavioral Sciences and Leadership at the Military Academy, where he teaches courses in systems leadership and leading organizations through change. He also teaches on leadership of complex organizations in the Harvard Business School's executive education programs and works with Prof. John Kotter as a member of Harvard's emerging Global Leadership Initiative. He is currently on sabbatical, serving as the USMA Superintendent's strategic planner in the Academy's Office of Policy, Planning, and Analysis. He has served in various military command and staff positions, including participation in operations in Grenada in 1983. A Military Academy graduate (1980), he also has an MBA from the Harvard Business School and earned his Ph.D. from Harvard University in organizational behavior. His book *Friendly Fire* was published by Princeton University Press in 2000. He has also co-authored a book that explores the role of "common sense" in leadership titled *Practical Intelligence in Everyday Life* (Cambridge University Press, 2000).

Elizabeth A. Stanley is Associate Director of the Center for Peace and Security Studies and Associate Director of the Security Studies Program in the Edmund A. Walsh School of Foreign Service at Georgetown University. Until 1996, Ms. Stanley served as a U.S. Army captain in military intelligence, with postings in Korea, Germany, Italy, Macedonia, and Bosnia. Her most recent publication is "Technology's Double-Edged Sword: The Case of U.S. Army Digitization" in *Defense Analysis* (Winter 2001). She holds a B.A. in Soviet and East European studies from Yale, an MBA from MIT's Sloan School of Management, and a Ph.D. in government from Harvard. Ms. Stanley has taught at MIT, Harvard, and Georgetown.

Richard Swain, a retired Army colonel, is the Professor of Officership, William E. Simon Center for the Study of the Professional Military Ethic, U.S. Military Academy. He is currently coordinating a project involving all service academies in rewriting the DoD pamphlet, *The Armed Forces Officer*, conceived to "provide a foundation of thought, conduct, standards, and duty for officers." His latest work is *Neither War Nor Not War: Army Command in Europe during the Time of Peace Operations; Tasks Confronting USAREUR Commanders, 1994-2000* (SSI, 2003). He is a graduate of the Military Academy (1966) and holds an M.A. and Ph.D. in history from Duke University. Colonel Swain served in the Vietnam War in 1967-68 and 1969-70.

Harry J. Thie (D.B.A., George Washington University) is a senior management scientist at the RAND Corporation whose research activities are in the areas of defense manpower, personnel, and training; resource management; and organization and management. Before joining RAND in 1991, Dr. Thie served in a variety of positions in the Department of the Army and the Office of the Secretary of Defense. He is a Fellow and former director and officer of the Military Operations Research Society; is a member of the Institute for Operations Research and the Management Sciences, and of the Inter-University Seminar on Armed Forces and Society; and has served as a consultant to the Army Science Board and to the Defense Science Board and and as a committee member within the National Research Council. He teaches policy analysis as part of the RAND Graduate School program on defense analysis. A list of publications is available at http://www.rand.org/Abstracts/ under Thie, H.

Marybeth Peterson Ulrich is Associate Professor of Government in the Department of National Security and Strategy at the Army War College. She is a graduate of the U.S. Air Force Academy and earned her Ph.D. in political science from the University of Illinois. She served 15 years on active duty as an Air Force officer, which included tours as a navigator on KC-135Q refueling tankers and as an instructor in the Department of Political Science at the Air Force Academy. She is currently serving in the USAF Reserve. Dr. Ulrich has written extensively in the field of strategic studies with special emphasis on national security democratization issues in post-communist Europe, European security, and civil-military relations. Her book, *Democratizing Communist Militaries: The Cases of the Czech and Russian Armed Forces*, was published by the University of Michigan Press in February 2000. Most recently, her paper titled "Promoting Professionalism through Security Cooperation" was published by the Association of the U.S. Army (2003).

Gayle L. Watkins, Ph.D., is the founder of Clove Brook Enterprises, a research-consulting firm in Cold Spring, New York. During her 23-year Army career, Lieutenant Colonel (Retired) Watkins served in logistics positions in the United States and Europe before joining the faculty of the Military Academy. While at West Point, she directed the Leadership and General Management programs and conducted studies in personnel issues for the Army. Her research has ranged from studies of social identity to qualitative assessments of military actions. She co-authored "The Future of Army Professionalism: A Need for Renewal and Redefinition" in *Parameters* (Autumn 2000), and was co-project director of the first edition of the present book.

Leonard Wong is Associate Research Professor of Military Strategy (Human and Organizational Dimensions) in the Army War College's Strategic Studies Institute. He served in the Army for over 20 years, including service as a leadership instructor at the U.S. Military Academy. During assignments on the Army Staff in the Pentagon, he was an analyst in the Program Analysis and Evaluation Directorate and later in the Office of the Deputy Chief of Staff for Personnel, and Director of the Office of Economic and Manpower Analysis. He has authored several articles, chapters, and papers on organizational issues in the Army such as downsizing, leadership, and junior officer retention. His monograph *Generations Apart: Xers and Boomers in the Officers Corps* was published by the Strategic Studies Institute in 2000. He is a registered Professional Engineer and holds a B.S. from the Military Academy plus M.S.B.A. and Ph.D. degrees from Texas Tech University.

Todd Woodruff is an Army major, serving as an instructor of sociology and leadership in the Department of Behavioral Sciences and Leadership at the Military Academy. He holds a B.S. and MBA. from Southern Illinois University and an M.A. in sociology from the University of Maryland. Major Woodruff's research and teaching activities range from leadership theory to military sociology, with a focus on the intersection of military families, soldier identity, and leadership.

Paul Yingling is an Army lieutenant colonel, serving as Executive Officer, 212th Field Artillery Brigade, Fort Sill, Oklahoma. He received a B.A. from Duquesne University and an M.A. from the University of Chicago, and is a graduate of the Command and General Staff College and the School of Advanced Military Studies. He has served in a variety of command and staff positions in the continental United States, Southwest Asia, Germany, Bosnia-Herzegovina, and Korea.